Handbook of Behavioral Assessment *edited by Anthony R. Ciminero, Karen S. Calhoun, and Henry E. Adams*

Counseling and Psychotherapy: A Behavioral Approach *by E. Lakin Phillips*

Dimensions of Personality *edited by Harvey London and John E. Exner, Jr.*

The Mental Health Industry: A Cultural Phenomenon *by Peter A. Magaro, Robert Gripp, David McDowell, and Ivan W. Miller III*

Nonverbal Communication: The State of the Art *by Robert G. Harper, Arthur N. Wiens, and Joseph D. Matarazzo*

Alcoholism and Treatment *by David J. Armor, J. Michael Polich, and Harriet B. Stambul*

A Biodevelopmental Approach to Clinical Child Psychology: Cognitive Controls and Cognitive Control Theory *by Sebastiano Santostefano*

Handbook of Infant Development *edited by Joy D. Osofsky*

Understanding the Rape Victim: A Synthesis of Research Findings *by Sedelle Katz and Mary Ann Mazur*

Childhood Pathology and Later Adjustment: The Question of Prediction *by Loretta K. Cass and Carolyn B. Thomas*

Intelligent Testing with the WISC-R *by Alan S. Kaufman*

Adaptation in Schizophrenia: The Theory of Segmental Set *by David Shakow*

Psychotherapy: An Eclectic Approach *by Sol L. Garfield*

Handbook of Minimal Brain Dysfunctions *edited by Herbert E. Rie and Ellen D. Rie*

Handbook of Behavioral Interventions: A Clinical Guide *edited by Alan Goldstein and Edna B. Foa*

Art Psychotherapy *by Harriet Wadeson*

Handbook of Adolescent Psychology *edited by Joseph Adelson*

Psychotherapy Supervision: Theory, Research and Practice *edited by Allen K. Hess*

Psychology and Psychiatry in Courts and Corrections: Controversy and Change *by Ellsworth A. Fersch, Jr.*

Restricted Environmental Stimulation: Research and Clinical Applications *by Peter Suedfeld*

Personal Construct Psychology: Psychotherapy and Personality *edited by Alvin W. Landfield and Larry M. Leitner*

Mothers, Grandmothers, and Daughters: Personality and Child Care in Three-Generation Families *by Bertram J. Cohler and Henry U. Grunebaum*

Further Explorations in Personality *edited by A.I. Rabin, Joel Aronoff, Andrew M. Barclay, and Robert A. Zucker*

Hypnosis and Relaxation: Modern Verification of an Old Equation *by William E. Edmonston, Jr.*

Handbook of Clinical Behavior Therapy *edited by Samuel M. Turner, Karen S. Calhoun, and Henry E. Adams*

Handbook of Clinical Neuropsychology *edited by Susan B. Filskov and Thomas J. Boll*

The Course of Alcoholism: Four Years After Treatment *by J. Michael Polich, David J. Armor, and Harriet B. Braiker*

Handbook of Innovative Psychotherapies *edited by Raymond J. Corsini*

The Role of the Father in Child Development (Second Edition) *edited by Michael E. Lamb*

Behavioral Medicine: Clinical Applications *by Susan S. Pinkerton, Howard Hughes, and W.W. Wenrich*

Handbook for the Practice of Pediatric Psychology *edited by June M. Tuma*

Change Through Interaction: Social Psychological Processes of Counseling and Psychotherapy *by Stanley R. Strong and Charles D. Claiborn*

Drugs and Behavior (Second Edition) *by Fred Leavitt*

(*continued on back*)

D1710875

HANDBOOK OF
CLINICAL
NEUROPSYCHOLOGY

Volume 2

HANDBOOK OF CLINICAL NEUROPSYCHOLOGY

Volume 2

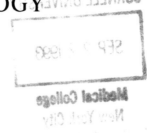

Edited by

SUSAN B. FILSKOV

THOMAS J. BOLL

A WILEY-INTERSCIENCE PUBLICATION

JOHN WILEY & SONS,

New York • Chichester • Brisbane • Toronto • Singapore

Library of Congress Cataloging in Publication Data:

(Revised for vol. 2)

Main entry under title:

Handbook of clinical neuropsychology.

    (Wiley series on personality processes 0195-4008)
    "A Wiley-Interscience publication."
    Includes bibliographies and indexes.
    1. Neuropsychiatry.   2. Neuropsychology.
I. Filskov, Susan B.   II. Boll, Thomas J.   III. Series.

RC341.H25   616.8   80-15392
ISBN 0-471-88411-1

Printed in the United States of America

10 9 8 7 6 5 4 3 2 1

To our parents and children,

    Harold and June Filskov
    Steven and Laura Rifkin

    Robert and Agnes Pittelkow
    Jennifer, Alisa, and Jeffrey Boll

Contributors

KENNETH M. ADAMS, Ph.D.
Division Head
Division of Neuropsychology
Department of Psychiatry
Henry Ford Hospital
Detroit, Michigan

RONA ARIEL, M.A.
Graduate Student
University of Nebraska Medical Center
Department of Psychiatry
Omaha, Nebraska

JEFFREY T. BARTH, Ph.D.
Director
Neuropsychology Assessment
   Laboratory
Department of Behavioral Medicine
   and Psychiatry
University of Virginia School of
   Medicine
Charlottesville, Virginia

STANLEY BERENT, Ph.D.
Associate Professor of Psychiatry
The University of Michigan
Ann Arbor, Michigan

JOSEPH BLEIBERG, Ph.D.
Director
Psychology Department
Rehabilitation Institute of Chicago
Assistant Professor
Northwestern University
Department of Rehabilitation
Medicine and Psychiatry
Chicago, Illinois

THOMAS J. BOLL, Ph.D.
Medical Psychology Program
University of Alabama at Birmingham
Birmingham, Alabama

ROBERT A. BORNSTEIN, Ph.D.
Chief
Neuropsychology Laboratory
Assistant Professor of Psychiatry,
   Neurology and Neurosurgery
Department of Psychiatry
Ohio State University
College of Medicine
Columbus, Ohio

GREGORY G. BROWN, Ph.D.
Staff Psychologist
Neuropsychology Division
Psychiatry Department
Henry Ford Hospital
Detroit, Michigan

ROBERT A. CATANESE, Ph.D.
Department of Psychology
University of South Florida
Tampa, Florida

CAMPBELL M. CLARK, Ph.D.
Department of Nuclear Medicine
National Institutes of Health
Bethesda, Maryland

BRYAN E. CONNELL, M.A.
Doctoral Candidate
Medical Psychology Program
Department of Psychology
University of Alabama
Birmingham, Alabama

LOUIS D. COSTA, Ph.D.
Professor of Psychology and
    Dean of Social Sciences
University of Victoria
Victoria, British Columbia
Canada

LEONARD DILLER, Ph.D.
Chief
Behavioral Sciences/Clinical
    Psychological Services
Institute of Rehabilitation Medicine
New York University Medical Center
New York, New York

CARL B. DODRILL, Ph.D.
Associate Professor
Epilepsy Center
University of Washington
Harborview Medical Center
Seattle, Washington

STEPHEN P. FARR, Ph.D.
Assistant Professor
Department of Psychiatry
Texas Tech University Health
    Sciences Center
School of Medicine
Lubbock, Texas

SUSAN FILSKOV, Ph.D.
Associate Professor of Psychology,
    Psychiatry and Behavioral Medicine
Director, Psychological Services
University of South Florida
College of Medicine
Tampa, Florida

STEPHANIE P. FISHER-WHITE, M.A.
Graduate Student
Department of Psychology
Texas Tech University
Lubbock, Texas

JAMES GNADT, Ph.D.
Postdoctoral Fellow
Department of Developmental
    Neurobiology
Salk Institute
San Diego, California

CHARLES J. GOLDEN, Ph.D.
Professor of Medical Psychology
Department of Psychiatry
University of Nebraska Medical Center
Omaha, Nebraska

ELLEN E. GOLDEN, M.D.
Staff Pediatrician
Boys Town Institute
Clinical Assistant Professor of
    Pediatrics
Creighton University Medical School
Omaha, Nebraska

HAROLD GOODGLASS, Ph.D.
Director
Psychology Research
Boston Veterans Administration
    Medical Center
Professor of Neurology
Boston University School of Medicine
Boston, Massachusetts

WAYNE A. GORDON, Ph.D.
Assistant Clinical Professor of
    Rehabilitation Medicine
Supervisor of Research
Behavioral Sciences Program
Institute of Rehabilitation Medicine
New York University Medical Center
New York, New York

ROGER L. GREENE, Ph.D.
Associate Professor of Psychology
Texas Tech University
Lubbock, Texas

BILL H. GRIMM, Ph.D.
Senior Clinical Psychologist
Rehabilitation Institute of Chicago
Associate Professor
Northwestern University
Department of Psychiatry
Chicago, Illinois

JAMES A. LEWIS, M.D.
West Florida Neurological Associates
New Port Richey, Florida

STEPHEN N. MACCIOCCHI, Ph.D.
Clinical Neuropsychologist
Neurological Rehabilitation Associates
Waynesboro, Virginia

JOSEPH D. MATARAZZO, Ph.D.
Chairman
Department of Medical Psychology
Oregon Health Sciences University
Portland, Oregon

G. VERNON PEGRAM, Ph.D.
Director
Sleep Disorders Center of Alabama
Montclair Baptist Hospital
Birmingham, Alabama

JANIS M. PEYSER, Ph.D.
Director
Medical Psychology
Medical Center of Vermont
Clinical Assistant Professor
Department of Psychology and
    Psychiatry
University of Vermont and
The College of Medicine
Burlington, Vermont

CHARLES M. POSER, M.D.
Department of Neurology
Harvard Medical School
Multiple Sclerosis Unit
Beth Israel Hospital
Boston, Massachusetts

KARL H. PRIBRAM, M.D., Ph.D.
Professor of Neuroscience
Departments of Psychology and of
    Psychiatry and Behavioral Sciences
Stanford University
Stanford, California

BYRON P. ROURKE, Ph.D.
Professor
Department of Psychology
Head, Neuropsychology Unit
University of Windsor
Windsor, Ontario
Canada

MARY RUCKDESCHEL-HIBBARD, M.Ed.
Psychologist
Behavioral Science Department
Institute of Rehabilitation Medicine
New York University Medical Center
New York, New York

ELBERT W. RUSSELL, Ph.D.
Director
Neuropsychology Laboratory
Veterans Administration Medical
    Center
Miami, Florida

MARY ANN STRIDER, Ph.D.
Assistant Professor of Medical
    Psychology
Department of Psychiatry
University of Nebraska Medical Center
Omaha, Nebraska

DEBRA WEILER, Ph.D.
Department of Psychology
University of Georgia
Athens, Georgia

BARBARA C. WILSON, Ph.D.
Chief
Neuropsychology Section
Department of Neurology
North Shore University Hospital
Cornell University Medical College
Manhasset, New York

Series Preface

This series of books is addressed to behavioral scientists interested in the nature of human personality. Its scope should prove pertinent to personality theorists and researchers as well as to clinicians concerned with applying an understanding of personality processes to the amelioration of emotional difficulties in living. To this end, the series provides a scholarly integration of theoretical formulations, empirical data, and practical recommendations.

Six major aspects of studying and learning about human personality can be designated: personality theory, personality structure and dynamics, personality development, personality assessment, personality change, and personality adjustment. In exploring these aspects of personality, the books in the series discuss a number of distinct but related subject areas: the nature and implications of various theories of personality; personality characteristics that account for consistencies and variations in human behavior; the emergence of personality processes in children and adolescents; the use of interviewing and testing procedures to evaluate individual differences in personality; efforts to modify personality styles through psychotherapy, counseling, behavior therapy, and other methods of influence; and patterns of abnormal personality functioning that impair individual competence.

Irving B. Weiner

University of Denver
Denver, Colorado

Preface

Since the first volume of the *Handbook of Clinical Neuropsychology* was published in 1981, the field of neuropsychological literature has changed significantly. Until that time, the field was notable for the dearth of hardcover books of almost any description. Since then, there has been a burgeoning of texts on broad as well as specific topics that has reflected not so much the growth of the field of neuropsychology as the significant increase in professional and popular awareness of this field that has occurred in the 1980s. The number of persons seeking training at all levels, the recognition of the need to provide neuropsychological training in doctoral-level programs and in internship programs, and the number of institutions capable of providing this training have risen startlingly since 1980. The use of neuropsychological knowledge, procedures, and techniques, not only by professionals formally trained in neuropsychology, but also by those providing general health services who have had some exposure to neuropsychological activities, has grown apace.

The present *Handbook* is not a recapitulation of the first, but, rather, an entirely new and independent volume that covers a broad range of topics, focusing on new areas of interest and issues likely to be important in the next five to ten years.

Like the earlier *Handbook,* this one is designed to serve a reference purpose. In Part One, professional scientific contact, conflict, and overlap in training, investigation, and patient care among professionals in neuropsychology, behavioral neurology, and health psychology are discussed. Part Two deals primarily with assessment-oriented issues. Assessment of language, children's abilities, general neurological functions, and nontraditional neuropsychological disorders is covered, as well as information about traditional approaches. Part Three encompasses conditions of medical and physical concern that also have neuropsychological implications. Careful evaluation of memory functions and two types of deteriorating neurological disorders are discussed in detail. Part Three also covers the role of personality and affective processes in conjunction with neurocognitive deficits. A general overview and conceptualization of neuroaffective processes is followed by a discussion of affective disruption and psychosocial consequences in specific neuropsychological disorders. The discussion of sleep disorders is the first formal coverage of this important topic in the neuropsychological literature. Part Four focuses on several issues of current and future significance for neuropsychology. Discussion of rehabilitation, unfortunately, continues to fall within the realm of needed future research. Research design, statistics, and computer technology are of current and future concern to those attempting to advance knowledge. The complexities of brain focalization and localization are covered in the penultimate chapter. As in the earlier volume, the last chapter of this volume discusses the training and preparation of neuropsychologists and ties in with the issues raised in Part One. We are fortunate to have chapters of such breadth and depth, as well as chapters that complement the initial coverage provided in the first volume.

Much of the resolution of conflict predicted in the first *Handbook* appears to have come to pass. Largely, the battle of the batteries is losing whatever preeminence it once had, and instead, energies are being directed toward collaborative struggle for understanding of the broadest possible role for neuropsychology within a health care delivery and research system.

Professional progress in the field of neuropsychology has been almost as impressive as scientific progress. As already mentioned, the identification of neuropsychology as an area of psychological content and process that must be grasped, at least to a certain degree, by all practitioners appears safely established. The recognition, as well, that clinical neuropsychology is a specialty that can be understood completely and practiced fully only by persons having had extensive and time-consuming training represents a growth mark for all of psychology, which has struggled to distinguish generalist and specialist issues. The recognition of clinical neuropsychology by the American Board of Professional Psychology as a specialty area for the diplomate process is just such a landmark step. There is no question that neuropsychology has arrived as a mainstream area of knowledge and practice within the field of clinical health service provision. During the next two decades, the breadth and depth of the service provided by clinical neuropsychologists will expand, and the sophistication with which our current state of knowledge is applied will increase.

We want to express our thanks for the exceptionally diligent work of each of our authors, who have labored long and hard to provide the best possible type of scientific clinical coverage in their respective areas. Our thanks to the editors at John Wiley & Sons for their understanding, support, and technical aid in all aspects of this project.

SUSAN B. FILSKOV
THOMAS J. BOLL

Tampa, Florida
Birmingham, Alabama
January 1986

Contents

PART FOUR   CURRENT ISSUES AND FUTURE PERSPECTIVES

HANDBOOK OF
CLINICAL
NEUROPSYCHOLOGY

Volume 2

PART ONE

Interfaces of Neuropsychology with Medicine and Psychology

CHAPTER 1

Clinical Neuropsychology
and Behavioral Neurology:
Similarities and Differences

Byron P. Rourke and Gregory G. Brown

The purpose of this chapter is to compare and contrast the two modes of approach to the clinical aspects of the study of brain-behavior relationships that characterize clinical neuropsychology and behavioral neurology. In light of the purposes of this book, emphasis is given to the similarities and differences of these two approaches to brain-behavior relationships in their impact on the diagnosis, assessment, and treatment of the brain-damaged individual.

Both clinical neuropsychology and behavioral neurology are relatively new disciplines that have their historical foundations rooted primarily in the latter half of the nineteenth century. At that time, the study of human psychology from an empirical or quasi-empirical viewpoint was undertaken primarily by persons with extensive training in human anatomy and physiology (Boring, 1950). These investigators came from a variety of philosophical traditions, but their common aim was essentially the elucidation of those conditions and parameters that affect human beings' psychophysical relationships with themselves and their world.

There were clearly differences in emphasis among these investigators: Some accentuated the physiological side of the psychophysical relationship, whereas others were more inclined to emphasize what we would refer to today as the "behavioral" aspects of the relationship. At that time, there was no hard and fast distinction between psychology and medicine, and hence there were no hard and fast distinctions between the harbingers of clinical neuropsychology (a specialty eventually to emerge within psychology) and behavioral neurology (a specialty that would emerge within medicine). Those who were interested in studying the relationships between physiology (including cerebral structures and functions) and behavior were inclined to view themselves as bound together by a common goal rather than individualized as a function of their various backgrounds in physiology and physics (e.g., Helmholtz), medicine (e.g., Broca), philosophy and psychology (e.g., Wundt), and so on.

For reasons too numerous and complex to elucidate here, psychology and medicine began to emerge as distinct specialties by the end of the nineteenth and the beginning of the twentieth centuries. In addition, within medicine there began to be a distinction evident between those who specialized in physiological-behavioral interactions (psychiatrists) and those who studied diseases of the nervous system (neurologists). Although connected in name through their common fellowships in neurology and psychiatry, these two branches of medicine diverged rather dramatically in focus and methodology until well into the second half of the twentieth century. Thus, it was not until the 1960s that the term *behavioral neurology* as a specialty within neurology became at all well known. Indeed, it would seem appropriate to characterize the emergence of this specialty as a reemergence of an emphasis on behavior as a crucial element of the brain-behavior relationship.

Meanwhile, in psychology, the trend during the early part of the twentieth century was to relegate the study of psychophysiological relationships to physiological psychology and to emphasize purely behavioral considerations in virtually all other branches of "pure" psychology. Even within the applied areas of psychology, the trend was to emphasize behavior-behavior relationships rather than the interaction between human physiology (including brain structure and function) and behavior. As was the case for behavioral neurology, it was not until the latter half of the twentieth century that human neuropsychology began to emerge with an identifiable presence within psychology. Such scientists and practitioners as Donald Hebb, Ward Halstead, Brenda Milner, Ralph Reitan, Hans-Lukas Teuber, and Arthur Benton were primarily responsible for the emergence of human neuropsychology as an area of scientific endeavor and applied interest. Behavioral neurology during the same period would appear to owe much of its beginnings to the seminal contributions of Aleksandr Luria and Norman Geschwind.

GENERAL ISSUES

Definitions

Behavioral Neurology

No particular definition of *behavioral neurology* has gained wide acceptance, perhaps because no one has felt the need to define it more explicitly than as a subspecialty within neurology. As such, it would probably be characterized by most as that branch of medicine that focuses on the pathology of the nervous systems with special reference to the behavioral correlates of such pathology. In addition, it would appear that behavioral neurologists are concerned principally with the extent to which behavior can elucidate normal and disordered brain structure and function. In this sense, the diagnostic potential of behavior is the main focus. Continued study of the behavior of the well-diagnosed brain-lesioned patient by the behavioral neurologist would also seem to emphasize the role such behavior can play in the refinement of knowledge regarding structure-function interactions within the nervous system (e.g., Heilman & Valenstein, 1979).

Clinical Neuropsychology

Two widely acknowledged definitions of clinical neuropsychology are those of Manfred Meier and Les Davison. Meier defined *clinical neuropsychology* as "that component of the human neuropsychological enterprise which emphasizes the use of objective psychological methods in the assessment of higher cortical functions" (Meier, 1974, p. 289). Davison saw the various types of clinical neuropsychology as having in common the fact that they constituted "*comprehensive* approaches to *applied* problems concerning the *psychological* effects of brain damage in *humans*" (Davison, 1974, p. 3). It should be clear that the definition offered by Meier differs from that of Davison in that Meier focuses on the assessment of "higher" cortical functions and their elucidation through the application of objective psychological methods. Davison's definition allows for the application of techniques other than objective psychological methods in order to elucidate the psychological ramifications of disordered brain function. Meier's definition veers closer to what many would view as behavioral neurology in that it seems to suggest that the aim of clinical neuropsychological inquiry is the explanation of normal and disturbed brain structure and function. However, it is important to note that the explanation Meier offers for the role of the clinical neuropsychologist in this same publication (Meier, 1974) places a great deal of emphasis on the role of the clinical neuropsychologist in rehabilitation. This emphasis is certainly apparent in the definition offered by Davison, who goes somewhat further than Meier in describing the manner in which neuropsychological assessment can be used for purposes of intervention and remediation.

General Similarities and Differences

According to Davison (1974), clinical neuropsychology and behavioral neurology are similar insofar as they are both disciplines that focus on human problems of brain-behavior relationships that have clinical significance. However, he goes on to point out that, whereas clinical neuropsychologists are inclined to follow the tradition of empirical psychology in attempting to operationalize their definitions of behavior, behavioral neurologists are more inclined to emphasize the conceptual or notional dimensions of behavior. Thus, the behavioral neurologist is, according to Davison, open to "varying the operations used to elicit conceptually similar behavior as he examines different subjects" (Davison, 1974, p. 6). Certainly, the examination method developed by Luria (1973b) is of this sort. In addition, the criticisms levelled by Luria and Majovski (1977) at Reitan and other North American neuropsychologists were based largely on the perceived reluctance of the North American clinical neuropsychologist to vary the operations (tests and measures) to suit the individual characteristics of patients.

At this juncture, we should be quick to add that this characterization of North American clinical neuropsychology by Luria and Majovski is not one with which all North American clinical neuropsychologists would agree. For example, the particular process approach of the "Boston group" (Milberg, Hebben, & Kaplan, 1985) would embrace Luria's suggestions regarding variations in modes of approach for the elicitation of "conceptually similar behaviors."

Be that as it may, the mainstream of clinical neuropsychology in North America emphasizes the measurement of continuously distributed variables within a psychometric tradition that attempts to achieve at least equal interval scaling of the operations in question. This emphasis stands in marked contrast to the tradition within medicine generally and behavioral neurology in particular that emphasizes dichotomous classification through the use of the pathological sign approach. This is not to say that behavioral neurologists confine themselves to the search for signs and symptoms of brain dysfunction in their patients. Indeed, there are many who attempt to use measures that are more firmly grounded in the North American psychometric tradition. However, a clear tendency in the behavioral neurology approach to the study of brain-behavior relationships emphasizes the individual case study and the elucidation of syndromes within the individual case that are defined principally in terms of the presence or absence of the signs and symptoms thought to be associated with the syndrome in question.

The benefits of this approach are manifold. Certainly, the insights and concepts that have emerged from the exhaustive individual case studies carried out by Luria, Geschwind, and other behavioral neurologists have been immensely heuristic in the study of brain-behavior relationships. And it is also the case that the dogged determination of clinical neuropsychologists in the North American tradition to employ comprehensive and consensually validatable operational definitions of such concepts have often been fragmentary and perhaps even inappropriate (e.g., the work of Golden and his associates in attempts to operationalize Luria's methodology).

In the remainder of this chapter, we will compare behavioral neurology and neuropsychology as complementary approaches to assessment and rehabilitation and will consider research where appropriate. Some of the contrasts between the two methods are logically implied by differences of technique; others are a matter of tradition.

DIAGNOSIS AND ASSESSMENT

In their daily work, both behavioral neurologists and neuropsychologists gather behavioral information to help make diagnoses. With both approaches, inferences are made about the existence, course, and focus of brain disease. Additionally, clinicians in both camps may infer which adaptive capacities remain in a patient with brain disease and what the prospects are for successful rehabilitation or naturally occurring recovery of function. The many differences between the two diagnostic assessment approaches have increasingly prompted debate about their relative advantages and disadvantages. We will discuss four topics about which the two camps differ: flexibility, brevity, test construction, and qualitative versus quantitative analysis.

Flexibility

The collection of clinical data in neurology is highly sequential; decisions made early in the assessment focus the line of investigation and limit the domain of behavior assessed. Kleinmuntz (1968) has shown that clinically experienced neurologists engage in fewer sequential steps and arrive at an accurate decision more often than do less experienced house officers. This decision tree (Markov process) approach requires the examiner to select from a large pool of items those that are relevant to the decision point under investigation. Combining the decision tree technique with items tailored to specific questions about the subject at hand makes the development of elegant theories about individual patients a plausible goal. Despite its elegance, this type of analysis of brain-behavior relationships has important limitations that are less troublesome for a fixed battery approach.

The focusing produced by the decision tree approach is a form of selective attention. Early decisions must be accurate; otherwise, examiners may painstakingly assess irrelevant details while missing more important general points. The clinician who concludes incorrectly that a dyspraxic patient's inability to follow commands is a comprehension deficit may obsessively ponder the apparent subtle phonemic, semantic, or syntactic dimensions of the patient's comprehension deficit without gaining any information about the patient's dyspraxia. Although the frequency with which errors occur early in the clinical decision making process is, in part, a function of the skill of the clinician, it is also a function of the population frequency distribution of the clinical state being assessed (Meehl & Rosen, 1955). Some effects of base rates on the accuracy of clinical decision making are considered next.

The accuracy of a decision at any node of a decision tree, including the early nodes, is determined not merely by the inherent sensitivity of a test or sign but also by the base rate of the condition in the clinical population from which the patient comes. Table 1.1A shows the hit rate of a clinical sign that accurately identifies 90% of the cases with the actual disease (hits) and misidentifies as diseased only 30% of those cases without the disease (false positives). The hit rate for this sign is 80% when its base rate in the population is 50%. If the base rate for the condition drops to 10%, then only 72% of 100 cases are correctly identified, despite identical true positive and false positive rates (see Table 1.1B). Notice that the use of the clinical sign in the first case increased diagnostic accuracy from 50%, based on assigning all cases to one diagnostic state, to 80%. But in the second example, an assignment strategy that placed every case in the most common state would have produced a 90% correct classification, while the use of the clinical sign would have actually reduced the hit rate to 72%. In some instances, clinical judges would be more accurate if they were to assume that a particular patient is typical of cases sent to them (i.e., ignore a node in the decision tree) than use a clinical sign that, although valid, is not very powerful. Willis (1984) has recently shown how the appropriate consideration of base rates alters the interpretation of the efficacy of actuarial rules for neuropsychological diagnosis.

One assessment strategy often practiced is to use a quick screening test, with modest effectiveness, to select cases for more thorough and effective evaluation. This successive hurdles approach need not improve the accuracy of a clinician's predictions even when the second test is highly effective at detecting false positives. Table 1.2 shows one hypothetical result of applying a clinical sign to decide whether some disease state is

Table 1.1. Effects of Base Rates on Neurobehavioral Judgments

	Disease Present		
	Yes	*No*	*Total Predicted*
A. 50–50 Base Rate			
Disease predicted			
Yes	45	15	60
No	5	35	40
Total actual	50	50	100
B. 10–90 Base Rate			
Disease predicted			
Yes	9	27	36
No	1	63	64
Total actual	10	90	100

Table 1.2.   Predictive Accuracy of a Highly Effective Test Following a Less Effective Screening Test

	Actual Condition		
	Present	*Not Present*	*Total Predicted*
A. Screening Test with 30–70 Base Rate			
Predicted condition			
Present	10	5	15
Not present	20	65	85
Total actual	30	70	100
B. High-Efficacy Test Applied to Cases with Predicted Condition Present by Screening Test			
Predicted condition			
Present	9	.5	9.5
Not present	21	69.5	90.5
Total actual	30	70.0	100.0

present or not. The base rate of occurrence of the trait in the population is 30%, yielding a hit rate of 70% if a clinician simply decided to classify each patient as normal. The use of the particular sign represented in Table 1.2A produces a hit rate of 75%. Suppose that the clinical judge tries to confirm the presence of the condition among the 15 people whom the screening labeled positive with a test that has a 90% accuracy in classifying cases. When the base rate is 30%–70% and the second test has an equal propensity toward making false positive and false negative errors, then the second test will reclassify as negative one patient who actually had the condition and 4.5 patients who did not. The use of the highly effective test improves the overall hit rate to 78.5%, a 3.5% change from the hit rate of the screening test alone. The successive hurdles approach may yield only modest improvement over classification based solely on base rates.

The failure to properly consider base rates is one important source of diagnostic error for both behavioral neurologists and clinical neuropsychologists, but its effects are particularly pernicious when wrong decisions about what tests to give are made early in the evaluation. In such instances, information critical to understanding the case may never be gathered. The use of a fixed battery of tests is one simple and obvious way to avoid the powerful effects of base rates on test selection. Such battery approaches are in wide use among clinical neuropsychologists (Reitan & Davison, 1974); fixed batteries may also be used by physicians to protect against errors caused by unfavorable base rates (Lusted, 1968) although, as discussed below, more comprehensive data gathering may be a sign of a more skilled clinician.

Base rates not only dictate an a priori probability that combines with diagnostic information to produce a clinical decision, but they also form the basis for the primary strategy that guides the production of hypotheses about disease in individual cases. For example, Elstein, Shulman, and Sprafka (1978) found that physicians identified incidence or probability (i.e., base rates) as the major strategy for generating hypotheses about a cause of a patient's presenting complaints. Tversky and Kahneman (1974) show that expert decision makers estimate the frequency of an event by the ease with which instances of a class can be remembered; they call this judgmental heuristic availability. But the use of availability of retrieved instances of a class to estimate a base rate leads to bias when variables other than the base rate affect successful retrieval. Tversky and Kahneman found that, in addition to base rates, familiarity, salience, variation in the selection of retrieval cues, and illusory correlations (commonly held false beliefs about the frequency of occurrence of two events that are resistant to contradictory data) can all affect the retrieval of instances of a class. Although clinicians do incorporate base rate information in their decisions, a reliance on the availability heuristic to estimate base rates leads to biased judgments.

When decisions about which tests to administer are made in a strictly sequential manner, errors made early lead to an evaluation of the patient in a way that is unrelated to the fundamental features of a case. Even these rather early and potentially devastating errors in judgment could be compensated for if clinical judges were biased against overestimating the validity of their techniques, an attitude that would lead clinicians to question their initial conclusions about a case. However, as Einhorn and Hogarth (1978) have shown, judges are often biased in the direction of overestimating the validity of their techniques and, therefore, tend to avoid searching for information that would disconfirm their hypotheses.

The flexible approach to the assessment of a patient's behavior, characterized by sequential decisions about which domains of behavior to investigate, can bring needed focus to an evaluation, especially when one is confronted with the necessity of choosing among a large array of diagnostic possibilities. The flexible approach is used most often as a screening technique in those instances in which giving a patient all the possible tests available to the clinician is impossible. However, in its most radical form, this approach can result in major diagnostic errors due to inaccurate decisions arrived at early in the decision-making process. The alternative to the flexible approach is to use a fixed battery, or routine, composed of items that are well studied and are of known and acceptable reliability and validity. Standard textbooks in neurology (e.g., Gilroy & Meyer, 1979) often stress the need for combining a fixed and routine examination of essential neurological functions with the more flexible approach mentioned above; an analogous approach has been recommended for the neuropsychological assessment of children (Rourke, Bakker, Fisk, & Strang, 1983). Once the assessment proceeds past the screening stage, it is very important for evaluation techniques to avoid the difficulties caused by lack of attention to base rates, insufficient data collection, and the misinterpretation of the relevance of the data collected for the hypotheses being considered. Otherwise, the errors made by screening methods are compounded by techniques meant to confirm or disconfirm hypotheses generated by screening data. The use of a routine and comprehensive assessment is one technique that consultants can use to help attenuate errors made by screening techniques.

Brevity

Brevity is a virtue offered by Luria and Majovski (1977) in support of Luria's technique. With the growing emphasis on cost containment and cost reduction policies, the pressure to perform brief assessments will become more difficult to resist.

Brief assessment techniques generally have poor reliability. The relationship between test length and reliability is expressed by the Spearman-Brown formula:

$$r_{nn} = \frac{nr_{ll}}{1 + (n-1)r_{ll}} \qquad (1)$$

where r_{nn} is the reliability of the test after its length has been increased n times from the initial test length that yielded a reliability of r_{ll}. Thorndike (1967) presents the formula and discusses its use in practical test construction.

One can see the effects of list length on reliability by applying the Spearman-Brown formula to a 3-item abbreviation of the 14-item Similarities subtest from the Wechsler Adult Intelligence Scale—Revised (WAIS-R). Wechsler (1981) reports a test-retest correlation of .86 for the Similarities subtest for a group of 48 persons between the ages of 45 and 54 years who were tested between two and seven weeks apart. The Spearman-Brown formula indicates that this reliability will fall to .57 if the number of items drops from 14 to 3.

The lower reliability of techniques using fewer items is accentuated when using difference scores to infer the presence of a syndrome or profile. For example, clinicians often are willing to infer that a patient may have difficulty with verbal associative reasoning that cannot be explained by his knowledge of word meanings on the basis of an examination of the difference between the Vocabulary and Similarities subtests from the Wechsler scales. We adopted the formula given by Magnusson (1967, p. 93) to calculate the reliability of difference scores from two tests, G and H:

$$r = \frac{\bar{r} - r_i}{1 - r_i} \tag{2}$$

where r is the reliability of the difference score, $\bar{r}$ is the average of the reliabilities of the two tests $[\bar{r} = (r_g + r_h)/2]$, and r_i is the intercorrelation of the two tests. We take the pertinent data from the WAIS-R manual and use formula 2 to estimate the difference score for the Similarities and Vocabulary subtests at their standard lengths. From Table 11 in the WAIS-R manual (Wechsler, 1981), one sees that the reliability of Similarities is .86 and Vocabulary is .91; long $\bar{r} = (.86 + .91)/2 = .885$, from Table 15, $r_{i\text{-long}} = .73$. Using formula 2:

$$r_{long} = \frac{.885 - .73}{1 - .73} = .57$$

Compare this result with that obtained using a 3-item Similarities test and a 5-item Vocabulary test. The reliability of the 3-item Similarities test was calculated above: $r_{s\text{-short}} = .57$. The reliability of the 35-item Vocabulary test is .91; the Spearman-Brown formula estimates that the reliability a 5-item version of Vocabulary is .59. The average reliability is $\bar{r} = .58$. Since the intercorrelation of the two tests is constrained by their individual reliabilities, we adjusted the intercorrelation by a factor expressing the proportion that the average reliability of the two short forms represents of the average reliability of the long forms: Using formula 2:

$$r_{short} = \frac{.58 - .478}{1 - .478} = .195$$

Reducing the 14-item Similarities test to 3 items and the 35-item Vocabulary test to 5 items reduces the reliability of the difference score from a modest .57 to an unacceptable .192.

Luria has argued that the reliability of his evaluation can be increased by a "careful analysis of disturbances of different functions, which are of the same type and which are due to derangement of the same factors" (Luria, 1973a, p. 960). Luria advances syndrome analysis as a method of increasing the reliability of his technique. For example, finding worse performance on a Similarities test than one would expect from the patient's Vocabulary score would help corroborate a hypothesis of poor verbal reasoning elicited by a patient's poor performance on a proverb interpretation test. Such syndromes are usually composed of normal and abnormal signs, many of which are difference scores. To the degree that the difference scores involved in the syndrome analysis are unreliable, the convergence or divergence of clinical signs will be quixotic. The valid characterization of syndromes composed of patterns of normal and abnormal difference scores presupposes highly reliable measures. Attempts to achieve brevity entail unavoidable sacrifices in reliability, typically reducing confidence in the difference score and attenuating validity. The reader should consult Sutcliffe (1980) for a discussion of the conditions under which poor reliability of difference scores is most likely to influence the power of common statistical tests used in hypothesis-testing studies of validity.

Test Construction

Behavioral neurologists select neurobehavioral tasks primarily in terms of their face validity. Clinical experience could provide a basis for selecting specific items that are in fact sensitive to the neurobehavioral impairment that the items are intended to detect. But behavioral neurologists generally do not systematically discuss item selection or test construction beyond the level of face validity (Benson & Geschwind, 1984; Luria, 1973b), leaving unanswered questions about generalizability, convergent validity, divergent validity, and differential sensitivity of items.

Considerably greater attention has been focused on test construction by psychologists. Benton, Hamsher, Varney, and Spreen's (1983) discussion of the development of their Line Orientation Test demonstrates the critical contribution that difficulty level makes to the sensitivity of a task. They report data on an early version in which lines at different orientations were presented tachistoscopically to the center of vision for 300 milliseconds. This technique correctly classifies 13 of 22 patients with right hemisphere lesions while misclassifying none of the 21 patients with left hemisphere lesions. When the study was repeated under conditions of unlimited time exposure to a subject, the majority of patients made perfect or near-perfect scores: The change in the difficulty level of the task greatly reduced its ability to discriminate left-hemisphere from right-hemisphere lesioned patients. It was only when the task was again made more difficult that its sensitivity to right hemisphere dysfunction returned. In addition to difficulty level, reliability, variance, and the skew of test scores can affect a test's sensitivity to deficit (Chapman & Chapman, 1973). Failure to attend to such issues would be expected to have adverse affects on concurrent and predictive validity (Rourke & Adams, 1984).

Qualitative versus Quantitative Analyses

Luria has made the qualitative description of the patient the primary, immediate goal of his neuropsychological analysis (Luria, 1973a). He argues that there are usually several functionally equivalent ways to complete a behavioral task and that a focal brain lesion may destroy one approach while leaving others intact. Hempel (1965) has shown that the existence of functionally equivalent mechanisms is a characteristic of any functional analysis of a complex system. Consequently, Luria's principle of variable mechanisms producing a constant result (Luria, 1973b, p. 28) is implied by his attempt to study the brain as a functional system. The qualitative analysis of the patient's deficits may reveal which of several functionally equivalent mechanisms generated the response. Simply determining the accuracy of a patient's performance may obscure the neurobehavioral mechanism that produced the response. This line of argument concludes that the analysis of brain function must be qualitative rather than quantitative.

Our analysis of this argument begins with a discussion of the two concepts involved, quality and quantity. A qualitative analysis is an act of classification. One uses features that are relevant to a group of objects to divide the group into classes; such critical features are criteria of group membership (Hempel, 1952). Deciding that a patient cannot speak correctly because he cannot analyze speech sounds correctly places that patient into a class of patients with defects in phonemic analysis. If qualitative analysis is an act of classification, then qualities, properties, and features can be represented by those classes of objects possessing the qualities, properties, or features that serve as criteria for group membership (Russell, 1919/1971; Quine, 1951). While qualities may be properties of a single object, quantity is a property of collections of objects: The wise men are three; the apostles, 12. Since number is a property, it is also a class, but a class with classes as elements. Three is the class of trios; 12 the class of dozens (Russell, 1919/1971; Quine, 1962).

Quality and quantity are clearly related. Since numbers are classes, numbering requires classification; a quantitative analysis presupposes a qualitative one. Further, classification may depend on quantitative information, as in numerical taxonomy or discriminant function analysis.

Critics of quantitative methods often object to simply noting whether a response is accurate or inaccurate; they urge a classification of the type of error or a description of the kinds of intermediate steps that produced the response. Despite the intent, these objections are not with the metrical aspects of quantitative data but with the qualitative analysis upon which the metric is built. Those who urge an error analysis are objecting to the classification of a response as simply right or wrong; they are not objecting to the assumptions (e.g., transitivity or additivity) that determine the level of measurement. These criticisms of quantitative methods should cause quantitatively oriented clinicians to consider more carefully the initial classification upon which their numerical analysis is built; useful data can be lost when an analysis of error types or intervening steps is omitted. But these arguments are not sufficient reasons to avoid quantitative analysis.

The several advantages of quantitative measures over simple classification are reviewed by Hempel (1952). Ordinal, interval, and ratio measures often make possible distinctions among objects that are lumped together into classes. For example, patients classified as Wernicke's aphasics show considerable variability in their capacity to discriminate phonemes (Blumstein, Baker, & Goodglass, 1977), despite the critical role that aural comprehension deficits play in defining this syndrome. By making possible more detailed distinctions, quantitative measures are more likely than are classificatory (qualitative) variables to detect individual differences.

Ordinal, interval, and ratio measures can characterize the relative positions of objects, making possible measures of association between two variables that reflect individual differences on both variables in a more general fashion. Studies by Blumstein, Baker, and Goodglass (1977) and Varney and Benton (1979) have found that errors in phonemic hearing significantly correlate with aural comprehension deficits in aphasia, although the correlations are far from unity. These modest correlations show that, while auditory comprehension deficits are associated with deficits in phonemic hearing, much of the reliable variance on aural comprehension tasks cannot be explained by variance on the phonemic hearing measures. Such conclusions could not possibly be reached unless the measures chosen reflected the individual differences in both phonemic hearing and aural comprehension.

Greater descriptive precision makes for greater subtlety in formulating general laws. Blumstein's (1981) analysis of the distributional differences of voice onset time between voiced and voiceless stop consonants is an example of the subtlety of a quantitative neurolinguistic technique. Blumstein has used voice onset time to define precisely the distinction between phonetic and phonemic errors. She uses this analysis to show that the speech output of anterior aphasics is characterized by both phonemic and phonetic errors, while the speech of posterior aphasics reveals phonemic but not phonetic errors, indicating that the speech deficit of anterior aphasias is partly a disorder of articulation. Blumstein's study is an example of how quantitative data (voice onset time) can increase the clarity of a qualitative distinction (phonetic versus phonemic errors). An analysis of the distributions of a quantitative variable for different classes of events, coupled with cutting scores, is an effective method for reducing the arbitrary nature of defining a boundary between two classes that overlap. At times, a quantitative analysis can provide the most important evidence for a qualitative distinction.

The use of numerical variables makes possible the application of mathematical concepts and techniques to the tasks of prediction, hypothesis testing, and explanation. Factor analysis (Halstead, 1947), regression analysis (Ben-Yishay, Diller, Gerstman, & Gordon, 1970), discriminant function analysis (Wheeler, Burke, & Reitan, 1963; Adams, 1979), and Markov models (Kraemer, Peabody, Tinklenberg, & Yesavage, 1983), among other techniques, have proved useful for predicting responses to rehabilitation, validating tests, and providing a theoretical analysis of task performance.

REHABILITATION

If one accepts Davison's broad conceptualization of clinical neuropsychology as the discipline that constitutes comprehensive approaches to the psychological effects of brain damage in humans, then the activities of a neuropsychologist extend well beyond diagnostic efforts. Much of the work of a neuropsychologist begins after the nature of the patient's brain lesion is clarified; some work, such as studies of high-risk individuals, precedes diagnosis.

Clinical neuropsychologists often develop rehabilitation programs. With the prominent exception of Aleksandr Luria, behavioral neurologists have not been actively involved in measuring therapeutic outcome or in developing intervention strategies for rehabilitation. Although the qualitative information provided by Luria's techniques holds considerable promise for focusing rehabilitation on neurobehavioral processes that underlie a patient's symptoms, the paucity of work in rehabilitation done by behavioral neurologists would make it premature to compare a behavioral neurological approach to rehabilitation with a clinical neuropsychological one. Instead, we will discuss briefly some aspects of rehabilitation that seem particularly suited to the training and skills of psychologists.

Reviews of interventions and rehabilitation of patients with brain lesions (Diller & Gordon, 1981a, b) have identified several problems that any rehabilitation system must address. Naturally, one set of problems concerns the immediate neuropsychological effects of the patient's brain lesion. However, patients with cerebral disease often have medical problems involving other organs, such as cardiac disease, urinary incontinence, peripheral vascular disease, pulmonary disease, and so on. Such problems must be prevented or ameliorated by rehabilitation management in order to keep them from interfering with the rehabilitation of neuropsychological impairments. In addition to poor performance on formal neuropsychological measures, patients seeking rehabilitation have difficulties with skills that directly involve activities of daily living. The patient's typical living environment also plays a major role in rehabilitation outcomes and therefore needs to be assessed when a program of rehabilitation is developed. Part of this assessment involves analyzing activity patterns of individual patients.

Psychologists can play important roles in solving the problems presented by each of the considerations mentioned above, but Diller and Gordon (1981a) see a particular need for neuropsychologists to become more interested in assessing and studying functional competency, patterns of activities in natural settings, and environmental supports. For example, techniques developed in organizational psychology could be brought to bear on assessing the functioning of patients in job settings. Research from the environmental psychology literature is developing formal measures of psychological properties of environments. Moos (1979) has described a Work Environment Scale and a Family Environment Scale to assess the social climate of a person's job and family environments. The precise description of real world correlates of neuropsychological measures, coupled with valid measures of environmental demands and supports, creates the possibility that neuropsychologists can develop a clinical service unique among the various clinical neuroscience disciplines.

A provisional neuropsychological model for intervention along these lines has recently been developed (Rourke, Bakker, Fisk, & Strang, 1983). In this model, an attempt is made to link considerations arising from the neuropsychological assessment of children to the short-term and long-term developmental tasks with which they must deal. The importance of generating prognostic statements that take into consideration the quality and availability of therapeutic resources as these relate to the child's remedial needs and remedial capacities are emphasized. In all of this, the presence, type, location, age of onset, and chronicity of the child's brain lesion are viewed as potentially crucial determinants of response to treatment. This sort of ecological approach to the habilitation and rehabilitation of the brain-impaired child is particularly desirable, useful, and suited to the background of preparation in psychology and the neurosciences that should characterize the clinical neuropsychologist (Meier, 1981). Of special import in the current context is the focus on the forging of specific links between neuropsychological assessment and individualized remedial programming within a context that allows for the rigorous testing of the concurrent and predictive validity of all aspects of this enterprise within the actual environments that a brain-damaged person confronts now and those that he or she can be expected to face in the future (Strang & Rourke, 1985).

AT-RISK POPULATIONS

As the role of genetic and familial factors in the development of neurobehavioral syndromes becomes clearer, the opportunity to study patients before a clinical syndrome is manifest will become more commonplace. An excellent early example of such research is Lyle and Gottesman's (1979) research on Huntington's disease. They studied 88 offspring of patients with Huntington's disease, all of whom were without symptoms at the time of assessment. Those who developed Huntington's disease 15–20 years later had lower WAIS IQs at the original assessment than those who were free of symptoms after this extended follow-up period. If replicated, these results provide evidence for a clinical state that antedates the diagnosis of Huntington's disease.

In clinical research of this sort, it is easy to see the importance of standardized, reliable sampling of a wide range of adaptive abilities. Controlled, systematic neuropsychological assessment of sensory-perceptual, motor and psychomotor, linguistic, mnestic, and higher-order concept-formation and problem-solving abilities are crucial if predictive validity is to be established for such diseases as Huntington's disease. Indeed, the careful selection of reliable tests, standardized testing conditions, and appropriate statistical psychometric methods are the tasks that colleagues in behavioral neurology should expect of the "compleat" clinical neuropsychologist. In these and myriad other research and clinical enterprises, it should be—and often is—the case that the special skills of these disciplines complement each other.

SUMMARY

In this brief presentation, we have attempted to compare and contrast the modes of approach to the clinical study of brain-behavior relationships that characterize clinical neuropsychology and behavioral neurology. We have focused on aspects of decision making under conditions of uncertainty that are germane to much of the diagnostic and assessment enterprise. Our emphasis in this connection has been on the psychological parameters that must be considered when questions of flexibility, brevity, test construction, and the interaction of qualitative and quantitative approaches to diagnosis and assessment are considered.

It is clear that we view behavioral neurology as having a somewhat restricted interest in the appreciation of neurological disease from a behavioral standpoint. This poses no particular problem, since we see the task of the clinical neuropsychologist to involve, among other things, a particular focus upon the development of at least interval-level scales of behavior that meet commonly accepted criteria for reliability and validity. In addition, we view the relevance of these measures as a question that can be answered only with respect to the ecological validity of such observations, a task for which the clinical neuropsychologist should be particularly suited.

The problems with a strictly individualized approach to diagnostic and assessment were also emphasized. At the same time, it is clear that failure to appreciate the appropriate role of qualitative dimensions in the measurement of brain-behavior relationships can lead to a vapid and meaningless generation of irrelevant data. Indeed, the potential of neuropsychological measurement can be spent fruitlessly when issues of nominal classification and other qualitative dimensions of behavior are given short shrift.

In the last analysis, we view the roles of the clinical neuropsychologist and the behavioral neurologist as essentially complementary. These two specialties, having emerged from psychology on the one hand and neurology on the other, should focus attention on issues that occupied their parent disciplines during the nineteenth century, when they too were only nascent trends within the scientific and clinical realms. One would hope that the sorts of analyses attempted in this chapter will serve to alert both clinical neuropsychologists and behavioral neurologists to their current and future potential for cooperation as well as to the pitfalls and culs de sac they are likely to encounter if such cooperation is not practiced.

REFERENCES

Adams, K. M. (1979). Linear discriminant analysis in clinical neuropsychological research. *Journal of Clinical Neuropsychology, 1,* 253–272.

Benson, D. F., & Geschwind, N. (1984). Aphasia and related disturbances. In A. B. Baker (Ed.), *Clinical neurology* (Vol. 1, rev. ed., Ch. 10, pp. 1–28). New York: Harper & Row.

Benton, A. L., Hamsher, deS. K., Varney, N. R., & Spreen, O. (1983). *Contributions to neuropsychological assessment: A clinical manual.* New York: Oxford University Press.

Ben-Yishay, Y., Diller, L., Gerstman, L., & Gordon, W. (1970). Relationship between initial competence and ability to profit from cues in brain-damaged individuals. *Journal of Abnormal Psychology, 75,* 248–259.

Blumstein, S. E., Baker, E., & Goodglass, H. (1977). Phonological factors in auditory comprehension in aphasia. *Neuropsychologia, 15,* 19–30.

Blumstein, S. E. (1981). Neurolinguistic disorders: Language-brain relationships. In S. B. Filskov & T. J. Boll (Eds.), *Handbook of clinical neuropsychology* (Vol. 1, pp. 227–256). New York: John Wiley & Sons.

Boring, E. G. (1950). *A history of experimental psychology* (2nd ed.). Englewood Cliffs, NJ: Prentice-Hall.

Chapman, L. J., & Chapman, J. P. (1973). Problems in the measurement of cognitive deficits. *Psychological Bulletin, 79,* 380–385.

Davison, L. A. (1974). Introduction. In R. M. Reitan & L. A. Davison (Eds.), *Clinical neuropsychology: Current status and applications.* New York: John Wiley & Sons.

Diller, L., & Gordon, W. A. (1981a). Interventions for cognitive deficits in brain-injured adults. *Journal of Consulting and Clinical Psychology, 49,* 822–834.

Diller, L., & Gordon, W. A. (1981b). Rehabilitation and clinical neuropsychology. In S. B. Filskov & T. J. Boll (Eds.), *Handbook of clinical neuropsychology* (Vol. 1, pp. 702–733). New York: John Wiley & Sons.

Einhorn, H. J., & Hogarth, R. M. (1978). Confidence in judgment: Persistence of the illusion of validity. *Psychological Review 85,* 395–416.

Elstein, A. S., Shulman, L. S., & Sprafka, S. A. (1978). *Medical problem solving: An analysis of clinical reasoning.* Cambridge, MA: Harvard University Press.

Gilroy, J., & Meyer, J. S. (1979). *Medical neurology* (3rd ed.). New York: Macmillan.

Halstead, W. C. (1947). *Brain and intelligence: A quantitative study of the frontal lobes.* Chicago: University of Chicago Press.

Heilman, K. M., & Valenstein, E. (1979). Introduction. In K. M. Heilman & E. Valenstein (Eds.), *Clinical neuropsychology* (pp. 3–21). New York: Oxford University Press.

Hempel, C. G. (1952). Fundamentals of concept formation in empirical science. In O. Neurath, R. Carnap, & C. Morris (Eds.), *International encyclopedia of unified science* (Vol. II, No. 7). Chicago: University of Chicago Press.

Hempel, C. G. (1965). *Aspects of scientific explanation.* New York: Free Press.

Kleinmuntz, B. (1968). Processing of clinical information by man and machine. In B. Kleinmuntz (Ed.), *Formal representation of human judgement.* New York: John Wiley & Sons.

Kraemer, H. C., Peabody, C. A., Tinklenberg, J. R., & Yesavage, J. A. (1983). Mathematical and empirical development of a test of memory for clinical and research use. *Psychological Bulletin, 94*, 367–380.

Luria, A. R. (1973a). Neuropsychological studies in the USSR: A review (Pt. 1). *Proceedings of the National Academy of Science, USA, 70*, 959–964.

Luria, A. R. (1973b). *The working brain*. New York: Basic Books.

Luria, A. R., & Majovski, L. V. (1977). Basic approaches used in American and Soviet clinical neuropsychology. *American Psychologist, 32*, 959–968.

Lusted, L. B. (1968). *An introduction to medical decision making*. Springfield, IL: Charles C. Thomas.

Lyle, D. E., & Gottesman, I. I. (1979). Subtle cognitive deficits as 15 to 20-year precursors of Huntington's Disease. In T. N. Chase, N. S. Wexler, & A. Barbeau (Eds.), *Advances in neurology* (pp. 227–238). New York: Raven Press.

Magnusson, D. (1967). *Test theory*. Reading, MA: Addison-Wesley.

Meehl, P., & Rosen, R. (1955). Antecedent probability and the efficiency of psychometric signs, patterns or cutting scores. *Psychological Bulletin, 52*, 194–216.

Meier, M. (1974). Some challenges for clinical neuropsychology. In R. M. Reitan & L. A. Davison (Eds.), *Clinical neuropsychology: Current status and applications*. New York: John Wiley & Sons.

Meier, M. J. (1981). Education for competency assurance in human neuropsychology: Antecedents, models, and directions. In S. B. Filskov & T. J. Boll (Eds.), *Handbook of clinical neuropsychology* (Vol. 1, pp. 754–781). New York: John Wiley & Sons.

Milberg, W. P., Hebben, N., & Kaplan, E. (1985). The Boston process approach to neuropsychological assessment. In I. Grant & K. M. Adams (Eds.), *Neuropsychological assessment in neuropsychiatric disorders: Clinical methods and empirical findings*. New York: Oxford University Press.

Moos, R. H. (1979). Evaluating family and work settings. In P. I. Ahmed & G. V. Coelho (Eds.), *Toward a new definition of health* (pp. 337–360). New York: Plenum.

Quine, W. V. O. (1962). *Mathematical logic* (rev. ed.). New York: Harper & Row.

Reitan, R. M., & Davison, L. A. (Eds.). (1974). *Clinical neuropsychology: Current status and applications*. New York: John Wiley & Sons.

Rourke, B. P., & Adams, K. M. (1984). Quantitative approaches to the neuropsychological assessment of children. In R. E. Tarter & G. Goldstein (Eds.), *Advances in clinical neuropsychology* (Vol. 2, pp. 79–108). New York: Plenum.

Rourke, B. P., Bakker, D. J., Fisk, J. L., & Strang, J. D. (1983). *Child neuropsychology: An introduction to theory, research, and clinical practice*. New York: Guilford.

Russel, B. (1971). *Introduction to mathematical philosophy*. New York: Simon & Schuster. (Original work published 1919).

Strang, J. D., & Rourke, B. P. (1985). Adaptive behavior of children with specific arithmetic disabilities and associated neuropsychological abilities and deficits. In B. P. Rourke (Ed.), *Neuropsychology of learning disabilities: Essentials of subtype analysis* (pp. 302–328). New York: Guilford.

Sutcliffe, J. P. (1980). On the relationship of reliability to statistical power. *Psychological Bulletin, 88*, 509–515.

Thorndike, R. L. (1967). Reliability. In D. N. Jackson & S. Messick (Eds.), *Problems in human assessment* (pp. 217–240). New York: McGraw-Hill.

Tversky, A., & Kahneman, D. (1974). Judgment under uncertainty: Heuristics and biases. *Science, 185*, 1124–1131.

Varney, N. R., & Benton, A. L. (1979). Phonemic discrimination and aural comprehension among aphasic patients. *Journal of Clinical Neuropsychology*, *1*, 65–73.

Wechsler, D. (1981). *WAIS-R manual*. New York: Psychological Corporation.

Wheeler, L., Burke, C. J., & Reitan, R. M. (1963). An application of discriminant functions to the problem of predicting brain damage using behavioral variables. *Perceptual and Motor Skills*, *16*, 417–440.

Willis, W. G. (1984). Reanalysis of an actuarial approach to neuropsychological diagnosis in consideration of base rates. *Journal of Consulting and Clinical Psychology*, *52*, 567–569.

CHAPTER 2

Interfaces between Neuropsychology and Health Psychology

**Robert A. Bornstein, Louis D. Costa,
and Joseph D. Matarazzo**

Psychology is a dynamic profession that continuously adapts to the development and acquisition of knowledge from within the field itself as well as from external influences. Within the context of psychology, two areas that have experienced dramatic growth in the 1980s are health psychology and neuropsychology. This growth is reflected in the recent creation of the divisions of Health Psychology (Division 38) and Clinical Neuropsychology (Division 40) within the American Psychological Association (APA). The emergence of these two fields is further reflected by the proliferation of research and the establishment of numerous specialty scientific journals in these areas. As indicated by the title of this chapter, these two areas overlap to a considerable extent. In this chapter, we offer our personal observations on the interrelationships of these fields. Toward that end, we trace some relevant aspects of developments in these areas, describe some work already accomplished that demonstrates their interaction, and suggest a few possible areas for future collaborative efforts that could incorporate neuropsychological expertise.

THE SEARCH FOR DEFINITIONS IN NEUROPSYCHOLOGY AND HEALTH PSYCHOLOGY

Our discussion of the interaction of health psychology and clinical neuropsychology is based not only on how these terms are defined but also on the aggregate, over the coming years, of the contributions of the individual professionals who identify with each of these areas. To a large extent, the definitions of these fields are also influenced by their different as well as common interrelationships with other professional disciplines. For example, clinical neuropsychology evolved in relationship to the medical disciplines of neurology and neurosurgery. In that context, clinical neuropsychology began to appear as an emerging distinct specialty when many neuropsychologists "earned their spurs" with their professional colleagues by demonstrating the ability to localize lesions (Costa, 1983). From the outset, clinical neuropsychology was—and it continues to be—seen as one of several disciplines primarily concerned with the study of brain-behavior relationships. Davison (1974) has used the term *clinical neuropsychology* to refer to "comprehensive approaches to applied problems concerning the psychological effects of brain damage in humans" (p. 3). Within this field are a wide variety of theoretical orientations and assessment procedures with the common goal of objectively measuring the behavioral effects of cerebral dysfunction. In some hospital settings, the questions asked of the clinical neuropsychologist remain: Where is the dysfunction and how severe is it? Costa has suggested that if this type of diagnostic service is all that is offered by clinical neuropsychology, then this is all that will be requested. However, forces from both inside and outside the discipline have contributed to changing the role of the neuropsychologist. The advent and current widespread availability of computerized axial tomography (CAT) scans has to a large degree eliminated the need for neuropsychologists to be primarily concerned with identification of probable lesion location or etiology, although the ability to do so continues to be of some academic interest and personal gratification. The development of other neurodiagnostic and imaging technologies (e.g., nuclear magnetic resonance and positron emission tomography) will further influence the role of the neuropsychologist in such endeavors. In spite of these developments, rich clinical neuropsychological assessment data will continue to represent a unique and complementary contribution by psychology to the clinical investigation and treatment of patients with cerebral dysfunction. This is not to suggest, however, that the role of the neuropsychologist will remain unifocal or stagnant. The developments in our parallel medical disciplines, combined with technological advances within our discipline (e.g., computerized cognitive remediation) have resulted in an expansion of neuropsychological activity into the areas of intervention as well as an increase in the variety of patients referred for neuropsychological assessment. To be explicit, present-day clinical neuropsychology is perhaps most simply defined as a branch of human neuropsychology concerned with (1) assessment of the cognitive, behavioral, and emotional effects of disorders with neurological manifestations; (2) the amelioration through intervention and rehabilitation of the behavioral consequences of such disorders; and (3) research dedicated to the improvement of the assessment and intervention process. Costa, in his conceptualization of clinical neuropsychology as a discipline in evolution, has discussed some other internal and external forces that will contribute to the future growth and diversification of clinical neuropsychological activity. For example, the present acceleration in the growth of knowledge in the fundamental bases of cognition, including new insights into attentional processes and memory, quite likely will open up new areas of practice and inquiry for clinical neuropsychologists whose interest is the neurologically normal individual.

One of the forces likely to have an impact in neuropsychological practice is the field of health psychology. Many psychologists both within and outside this field have been concerned about its nature, scope, and definition. In addition to the term *health psychology,* a number of other terms have appeared that seem to embrace similar areas of professional interest and activity. Among these are *medical psychology, behavioral medicine,* and *psychological medicine.* Numerous authors have proposed schematic organizations of the composition of this variously defined field. Descriptions of the nature of this field deal explicitly or implicitly with several significant issues:

1. Is the field embraced by these various terms at this time a single field with an interest area definable in terms of a target patient population or locus of

employment? Alternatively, is it a discipline or subdiscipline in its own right, like neuropsychology or industrial psychology? That is, does it have a core of unique principles, methodologies, and practices that differentiate it from other subdisciplines of psychology?

2. Does health psychology represent the extension of the methodology of a single subdiscipline (e.g., behavioral analysis, clinical intervention via biofeedback, epidemiology) to the health service delivery area?

3. Is the field best construed as a branch of medicine, in the broadest sense, or as a branch of psychology?

Asken (1979) defines medical psychology as the "study of psychological factors related to any and all types of physical health, illness and its treatment at the individual, group and systems level" (p. 67). Asken's scheme subsumes several subdisciplines (including clinical neuropsychology) under the umbrella of medical psychology. From the viewpoint of neuropsychology as a distinct professional subdiscipline, there may be some objection to its being incorporated in a field not necessarily endorsed by the majority of neuropsychologists. Also incorporated in Asken's framework of medical psychology are the areas of rehabilitation medicine and behavioral medicine (and, one may infer by extension, health psychology). The common ground of the various divisions in his conceptualization is that they can be differentiated from traditional psychological activity in that the disorders they address are likely to have a nonpsychiatric physician as the principle care agent.

Using a pragmatic and functional approach, Matarazzo, Carmody, and Gentry (1981) described medical psychology as "the practice of psychology by psychologists within (and for other medical psychologists, outside) the medical school establishment (as well as in hospitals and other related medical settings). This includes not only clinical services, but also the important roles of medical educator and researcher. Furthermore, it includes all subspecialties of psychology, e.g., clinical, social, developmental, and physiological. It is an inclusive rather than exclusive definition of psychological activities" (p. 308). Other, more circumscribed definitions (Pomerleau & Brady, 1979) define medical psychology as "a broad field of activity, one in which psychometric assessment, projective testing and personality theory have played major roles. The emphasis in medical psychology has been on the understanding of medical illness in its psychological and social context rather than on therapy" (p. xi). Matarazzo, Carmody, and Gentry also offered a more formal definition of medical psychology that is essentially identical to their definition of health psychology. They suggest that the term *medical psychology* is merely descriptive and that the adjective is placed before *psychology* merely to distinguish the wide range of activities carried out by psychologists in medical settings from those carried out in other settings. Thus, such terms as *medical psychology, military psychology, industrial psychology, pediatric psychology, rehabilitation psychology,* and *consumer psychology* are equally useful because they explicitly denote the primary setting in which the craft of psychology is practiced and by implication connote the probable forms in which the subject matter, including course content and professional and scientific pools of knowledge and skills in psychology, is applied.

Gentry, Street, Masur, and Asken (1981), in a survey of training opportunities in medical psychology, defined the term as follows: "Medical psychology is the application of the concepts and methods of normal and abnormal psychology to medical problems.

It refers to the cooperative effort between behavioral scientists and medical practitioners in the diagnosis, treatment, and prevention of physical illness and reflects an acceptance of the importance of psychosocial factors in part or in whole to aspects of physical illness" (p. 226). This definition has the advantage of conceptualizing a general sphere of academic and professional interest without defining the field in the context of other established disciplines.

Masur (1979) has offered a conceptualization of medical psychology and behavioral medicine that incorporates the discussions held at the Yale Conference on Behavioral Medicine (Schwartz & Weiss, 1978). According to Masur, medical psychology is a subdiscipline of behavioral medicine, rather than the reverse, as suggested by Asken. In the context of the Yale conference, behavioral medicine is defined as an interdisciplinary field concerned with the development and integration of behavioral and biomedical science knowledge and techniques relevant to health and illness and the application of this knowledge and these techniques to prevention, diagnosis, treatment, and rehabilitation (Schwartz & Weiss, 1978). Masur noted that the word *behavioral* contributed to the misperception by the psychological community that behavioral medicine reflected a particular orientation toward behavior therapy. Although some of the more well-known behavioral medicine interventions (e.g., biofeedback and relaxation training) were derived from behavior therapy, both Masur and Asken stress that the field does not embrace a particular theoretical orientation. Rather, Masur suggests that the word *behavioral* be construed in the generic sense, as referring to behavioral science in general. In Masur's definition, neuropsychology is one of a number of psychological and nonpsychological disciplines that contribute to the general field of behavioral medicine. While demonstrating the interaction of various disciplines, this definition does not require the subjugation of individual disciplines. Rather, as defined in the Yale conference, behavioral medicine is an interdisciplinary field that does not fall under the specific domain of a single profession (e.g., medicine). The possibility that the term *behavioral medicine* might imply such a relationship has led some authors to suggest alternative terms (Adler, Cohen, & Stone, 1979). However, the alternative terms do not necessarily reflect the interdisciplinary component espoused by the Yale conference.

The avoidance of a specific theoretical orientation is not shared by all authors who have attempted to structure the field of behavioral medicine. Swan, Piccione, and Anderson (1980) describe their behavioral medicine (clinical internship) training program as reflecting a "primary emphasis on data-based behavioral approaches to physical disorders and health maintenance" (p. 343). This approach agrees with Pomerleau's position, which incorporates an emphasis on the application of behavioral principles to the treatment and prevention of medical problems. Pomerleau and Brady suggest that "behavioral medicine can be defined as (a) the clinical use of techniques derived from the experimental analysis of behavior—behavior therapy and behavior modification—for the evaluation, prevention, management, or treatment of physical disease or physiological dysfunction; and (b) the conduct of research contributory to the functional analysis and understanding of behavior associated with medical disorders and problems of health care" (p. xii).

The increasing activity in the field of behavioral medicine is further reflected by a recent special issue of the *Journal of Consulting and Clinical Psychology,* which demonstrates the wide variety of activities included in this area. In fact, in one of the articles, Agras (1982) suggests that the growth of research and clinical endeavor in behavioral medicine has been so rapid that a precise view of the form of its ultimate emergence is not yet possible. Furthermore, Agras suggests that the field is currently in a transitional and formative stage, which creates uncertainty about future developments. He suggests that one way of viewing the development of behavioral medicine is to regard it as an emerging network of communication between an array of behavioral, social, biomedical, and medical disciplines previously not well connected. Because of the ongoing active development of the field, the network of disciplines is not yet well defined. With the great promise of interdisciplinary research and clinical activity, it is possible that a large number of psychological and medical specialties may have input into the general field of behavioral medicine. Agras also argues that a comprehensive behavioral medicine program should include aspects of disease prevention and health promotion.

With this addition by Agras, the concept of behavioral medicine becomes similar to the concept of behavioral health espoused by Matarazzo (1980), discussed below. The added emphasis on health, in contrast to exclusive emphasis on illness, is also reflected in the term *health psychology,* which is used by several authors to describe the same field and is in fact the formal name of Division 38 within the American Psychological Association. Adler, Cohen, and Stone provided a description of some themes and prospects for development in the field of health psychology. In their view, the term *health psychology* is preferable to other terms (*medical psychology, psychosomatic medicine,* and *behavioral medicine*) for describing the newly emerging developments because it reflects a broader perspective and provides a better framework for the development of the discipline. In particular, they suggest that the use of the term *psychology* is desirable because it implies a firm grounding in psychological perspectives and methods. In addition, they suggest that the term *health* is preferable to *medicine* because of the connotations associated with the latter.

Related to these searches for an appropriate definition of the field, several authors (Adler, Cohen, & Stone, 1979; Belar, Wilson, & Hughes, 1982; Matarazzo, 1983; Sladen, 1979) have discussed the issues of obtaining training in the discipline of health psychology. Belar, Wilson, and Hughes view health psychology as a broad, generic field and imply that neuropsychology is one of a number of areas subsumed within the discipline of health psychology. In the early stages of development of these various fields, one may assume that these authors were writing in the hope of stimulating continuing dialogue inasmuch as they no doubt are aware that their APA colleagues in Division 40 (Neuropsychology) would not take too lightly the suggestion from colleagues in Division 38 (Health Psychology) that neuropsychology is encompassed by health psychology.

As the charter president (1978–1979) of the Division of Health Psychology, Matarazzo has written extensively on the development of health psychology and its relationship to behavioral medicine and behavioral health (Matarazzo 1980, 1982, 1983, 1986; Matarazzo, Carmody, & Gentry, 1981; Matarazzo and Carmody, 1983). One of the purposes of these reports was to attempt to provide a historical frame of reference in which to view contemporary developments in health psychology. Matarazzo reminds us that the relationship between psychology and medicine is not a recent development. In addition to the history of psychological study of the role of the mind in the expression of physical disease, which dates back to the time of Socrates, modern psychologists have, since the beginning of this century, participated in medical education. Psychological interest and participation in medical training is currently reflected in the growing number of psychologists employed in hospitals and on the faculties of medical schools (Matarazzo, Carmody, & Gentry, 1981; Matarazzo, Lubin, & Nathan, 1978; Nathan, Lubin, Matarazzo, & Perseley, 1979). The diversity of psychological input to medical research and training is demonstrated by the fact that, unlike the situation in the past, employment of psychologists today is no longer restricted to departments of psychiatry. Rather, psychologists are now found in departments of neurology, neuro-surgery, pediatrics, rehabilitation, and medicine, to name just a few. In addition, psychologists in increasing numbers are also found in schools of dentistry (Sachs, Eigenbroade, & Kruper, 1979) and public health (Matthews & Avis, 1982). The interested reader will find a more extensive discussion of these issues elsewhere (Matarazzo, 1983; Matarazzo, Carmody, & Gentry, 1981; Matarazzo & Carmody, 1983). This brief discussion is presented here primarily to illustrate the point that the recent surge of psychological interest in issues related to physical health represents a reemergence, rather than an initial emergence, of the relationship between psychology and medicine.

In the attempt to stimulate further thought and discussion regarding definitions of the field of health psychology, Matarazzo offered his elaboration on the definition of previous terms (e.g., *behavioral medicine*) and coined new terms to describe other aspects of the relationship between psychology and physical health. Regarding behav-ioral medicine, Matarazzo and Carmody draw attention to the interdisciplinary nature of the field inherent in the definition of the Yale conference (Schwartz & Weiss, 1978). As Matarazzo and Carmody point out, behavioral medicine is not limited to the contributions of any single discipline or theoretical mode. Rather, psychology is included in the interdisciplinary field emerging as behavioral medicine alongside the disciplines of medicine, sociology, epidemiology, nutrition, anthropology, biochemistry, dentistry, and others, each of which appears to offer important potential contributions to that interdisciplinary field.

To give the necessary added emphasis to the element of prevention in the definition of behavioral medicine, Matarazzo (1980, 1982) also coined the term *behavioral health* and defined it as an "interdisciplinary field dedicated to promoting a philosophy of health that stresses individual responsibility in the application of behavioral science knowledge and techniques to the maintenance of health and the prevention of illness and dysfunction by a variety of self-initiated individual or shared activities" (p. 813). He noted that, although such disciplines as sociology and epidemiology and private organizations that lobby for new protective health legislation have much to offer the field of behavioral health (e.g., primary prevention), psychology is ideally suited to help individuals develop more healthful life-styles because it has the longest history of formal research on individual human behavior, a well-established scientific knowledge base, practical applied experience, and the educational and institutional supports to make substantial early contributions in the parallel fields of behavioral health and behavioral medicine.

EMERGING SUBDISCIPLINES IN BEHAVIORAL MEDICINE AND BEHAVIORAL HEALTH

In the general context of psychology's contribution to behavioral health, a wide range of opportunities for collaboration with other disciplines in the health field are becoming available to psychologists. One example of this partnership among the disciplines of psychology, epidemiology, nutrition, biochemistry, and cardiology is the subspecialty of behavioral medicine that focuses on cardiology and behavior, which has recently been named *behavioral cardiology*.

A potential, emerging subdiscipline of behavioral medicine and behavioral health, behavioral cardiology is an interdisciplinary field concerned with the development and integration of behavioral and biomedical science, knowledge and techniques relevant to cardiovascular health and illness and related conditions, and the application of this knowledge and these techniques to prevention, diagnosis, treatment, and rehabilitation (Matarazzo, Conner, et al., 1982). Behavioral cardiology, only one of the potential multitude of outgrowths or future subspecialties within the scope of behavioral medicine and behavioral health, focuses on the study of processes by which people develop certain behavior patterns, attitudes, and life-styles that either prevent or are associated with coronary heart disease and other cardiovascular dysfunctions. Psychologists involved in behavioral cardiology today are working in, among other areas, weight maintenance and loss, smoking prevention and cessation, nutrition, attitude change, and stress prevention and reduction programs, in which they collaborate with cardiologists, nutritionists, biochemists, physical fitness specialists, epidemiologists, and others. This type of collaboration by psychology will most certainly not be limited to cardiology but, rather, may serve as a prototype for the development of other subdisciplines that will emerge as more and more psychologists pursue their careers in medical settings (e.g., behavioral endocrinology) or with other populations of individuals interested in health (e.g., in school and work-site prevention programs).

HEALTH PSYCHOLOGY AS A DISCIPLINE-SPECIFIC FIELD

As noted above, behavioral medicine and behavioral health (as well as potential subdisciplines, such as behavioral cardiology) are by definition and action interdisciplinary activities attracting individual scientists, teachers, and practitioners from diverse medical, behavioral, and related professional backgrounds. In addition to these interdisciplinary areas, individuals in each of the separate disciplines with common interests and views have begun to form discipline-specific interest groups within each of their own specialties. Thus, discipline-specific associations of such practitioners as holistic physicians, health economists, liaison psychiatrists, psychologists interested in family practice, behavioral neuropsychologists, and medical sociologists have been formed. Within the zeitgeist of these latter developments, APA's own discipline-specific divisions of Health Psychology and Clinical Neuropsychology were established. The former is a scientific, educational, and professional organization for psychologists interested in or at present working in areas at the various interfaces of medicine (primarily internal medicine) and psychology. The latter is a sister organization of psychologists working primarily at the interfaces of psychology and the fields of medicine involved with the neurosciences.

Acknowledging the potential contributions to behavioral health and behavioral medicine by psychologists with a variety of professional, academic, and scientific orientations, Matarazzo (1980) offered an early, and deliberately interim, definition of the emerging field of health psychology intended to provide a structure to encompass the collective efforts of psychologists in each of these areas. He defined health psychology as "the aggregate of the specific educational, scientific, and professional contributions of the discipline of psychology to the promotion and maintenance of health, the prevention and treatment of illness, and the identification of etiologic and diagnostic correlates of health, illness and related dysfunction (and to the analysis and improvement of the health care system and health policy formation)" (p. 815). The phrase in parenthesis at the end of this definition was added as a result of a poll of the members of the Division of Health Psychology (Matarazzo, 1982). Experience since 1980 indicates that this functional definition is broad enough as a rubric with which many psychologists may identify that it will serve its intended interim role. According to this definition, health psychology encompasses the ever-changing boundaries of accumulating new knowledge contributed to the fields of health and illness by psychologists. As such, health psychology encompasses not only clinical practice but also teaching, research, and administration. Furthermore, it is an umbrella term meant to include contributions to our knowledge of health and illness from all the fields of psychology: clinical, social, industrial, developmental, experimental, physiological, neuropsychology as well as others.

In fact, Matarazzo's definition of health psychology is little more than the generic field of psychology modified by the adjective *health* to designate the particular focus of some of the applications of the discipline, much like industrial psychology, generic psychology, clinical psychology, and consumer psychology. Matarazzo (1983, 1986) has developed this view in more detail in his discussion of issues to be considered by faculties interested in offering new graduate training programs in health psychology.

THE RELATIONSHIP OF NEUROPSYCHOLOGY AND HEALTH PSYCHOLOGY

Within the context of that definition of health psychology as the broad area of professional interest and activity whose contributions are related to health, illness, and related matters, the field of neuropsychology would appear to have great potential for contribution. In contrast to some definitions of medical psychology (Asken, 1979) and health psychology (Belar, Wilson, & Hughes, 1982) that conceive of neuropsychology as a subdiscipline of those specific disciplines, the broad definition of health psychology does not attempt to establish the validity of a discipline of health psychology by incorporating previously established subspecialties. Rather, the definition of the charter president of Division 38 (accepted by vote of the members of that division) recognized that a number of different subsets of individuals within psychology will apply the accumulated generic knowledge of theory, methodology, and individual elements of knowledge, tools, and technology of psychology in a variety of forums (industrial, health, the nervous system, etc.). Some of these subsets of individuals, of which neuropsychologists are one example, will be likely to have a high percentage of members interested in health psychology (instead of only the neurosciences) by virtue of the history and nature of the subdiscipline itself. Other specialties, such as social and industrial psychology, may have relatively few individuals whose professional interests and activities are related to psychology as it interfaces with health. Nevertheless, the key issue in Matarazzo's definition is that health psychology is not yet a specialty of psychology with unique methods and measures but, rather, a wide umbrella of professional interest and activity that attracts psychologists from diverse backgrounds who

Table 2.1.   Patterns of Divisional Affiliation among Members and Fellows of APA Division 40

Members Holding Membership in Other Divisions		Members Holding Membership in Only One Other Division	
Division Number	Number of Members	Division Number	Number of Members
12	275	12	48
42	195	42	28
38	181	38	25
40 (exclusively)	179	1	25
29	114	22	21
1	106		
22	104		

contribute the unique approaches of their particular subareas to the development and advancement of our understanding of health, illness, and related matters. In Chapter 21, we present a fuller discussion of the complexities of whether health psychology or neuropsychology is an area with unique *proficiencies,* and we consider as well the distinction between a de facto and de jure specialty.

Certain indexes indicate the close association of health psychology and neuropsychology. For example, a review of the divisional affiliation of members of Division 40 as of June 1983 revealed that of its 904 members and fellows, 181 (20%) also held memberships in Division 38. As may be seen in Table 2.1, membership in Division 38 was the third most commonly held supplemental division affiliation, followed closely by those Division 40 members who held memberships only in Division 40. Among the subset of Division 40 members affiliated with only two divisions, Division 38 was again the third most commonly held joint affiliation. This indicates that, although divisions 38 and 40 are both relatively new (established since 1978), there appears to be a substantial number of individuals who feel sufficiently aligned to seek membership in both divisions. Of course, there is no indication which, if either, of these represents the individuals' primary affiliation. Nevertheless, these patterns do suggest a close association between these two emerging fields of psychological interest and endeavor.

INTERFACE BETWEEN CLINICAL NEUROPSYCHOLOGY AND HEALTH PSYCHOLOGY

As suggested above, the subdiscipline of clinical neuropsychology has developed in close association with the medical subdisciplines of neurology and neurosurgery. For many years, the primary, if not sole, focus of clinical neuropsychology has been the assessment of the psychological effects of cerebral dysfunction. Our experience in the field suggests that the majority of individuals employed as clinical neuropsychologists were associated with medical school or hospital departments of neurology, neurosurgery, and, to a somewhat lesser extent, psychiatry. Although today the role of neuropsychological evaluation in lesion diagnosis and localization has been obviated to a great extent by recent developments in neurodiagnostic imaging techniques, there continues to be an expanding role for the neuropsychologist in the hospital setting. This is reflected to some extent by the increasing collaboration in clinical and research activities with physicians from departments other than those with which neuropsychologists have typically been associated. Those and other new frontiers and horizons being explored by neuropsychologists exemplify the interface between health psychology and clinical psychology.

Although relevant in a discussion of the contributions of neuropsychology to a generic health psychology, an extensive review of the neuropsychological literature in the investigation of neurological and neurosurgical conditions is far beyond the scope of this chapter. However, to give some examples, neuropsychologists have made numerous contributions toward the development of greater understanding of such conditions as Huntington's disease (Boll, Heaton, & Reitan, 1974; Norton, 1975; Smith, 1981); multiple sclerosis (Ivnik, 1978; Matthews, Cleeland, & Hopper, 1970; Goldstein & Shelly, 1974; Reitan, Reed, & Dyken, 1971); Parkinson's disease (Reitan & Boll, 1971; Boller, 1980; Tweedy, Langer, & McDowell, 1982); and such acquired neurological dysfunctions as head injuries (Levin, Benton, & Grossman, 1982; Brooks, 1972, 1974, 1976; Mandleberg & Brooks, 1975; Brooks, Aughton, Bond, Jones, & Rizvi, 1980; McKinlay, Brooks, Bond, Martinage, & Marshall, 1981) and alcohol and drug abuse (Grant, Adams, & Reed, 1979; Grant et al., 1978; Adams, Grant, & Reed, 1980; Grant, Reed, & Adams, 1980). Although the characterizations and documentation of the psychological and behavioral effects of cerebral dysfunction occurring in these conditions has been a prominent focus in clinical neuropsychology, there have been increasingly frequent attempts to broaden the perspective of neuropsychological activity. Much of the growth in neuropsychological clinical and research activity has been parallel to the major themes of activity expressed in the umbrella definition of health psychology. To reiterate, the primary themes of that definition are (1) promotion of health and prevention of illness, (2) identification of etiologic factors and diagnostic correlates of health and illness, and (3) treatment of illness. The remainder of this chapter is devoted to describing some ways clinical neuropsychologists apply their specific part of the generic psychological knowledge base to these three principal themes.

Promotion of Health and Prevention of Illness

If one considers that, historically, the prominent activity of clinical neuropsychology has been the documentation of the behavioral-psychological consequences of brain dysfunction, it may be difficult to imagine how such a discipline might play a role in health promotion or illness prevention. However, some examples may illustrate this point. The first example is of particular importance because it demonstrates that present-day neuropsychologists have been interested in such matters for many years, long before the recent reemergence of interest in the concepts of behavioral health and health psychology. Specifically, Reitan and Shipley (1963) investigated the relationship between serum cholesterol levels and performance on the Halstead-Reitan battery in a sample of 156 clinically healthy men between 25 and 65 years of age. The goal of the study was to examine the effects of lowering serum cholesterol levels on neuropsychological performance. The mean cholesterol level was 243 mg%, which is just beyond the upper limit of normal. Approximately one-third of the sample elected active treatment and were prescribed sitosterols; the other two-thirds of the sample elected to attempt reduction of their cholesterol levels via dietary control. Reitan and Shipley reported that among subjects 40 years or older, the subjects who achieved at least 10% reduction of cholesterol levels (after six months) achieved greater overall improvement in neuropsychological performance than comparably aged patients who did not achieve a reduction in cholesterol levels. The results thus suggested that in healthy men, reduction of cholesterol levels by 10% or more (even when baseline levels were not excessively high) may have beneficial effects on measures of mental alertness and ability. This study demonstrates one way in which neuropsychological measures may be employed in studies to demonstrate the beneficial effects on neurocognitive functioning of factors related to the promotion of health in currently healthy individuals.

Neuropsychologists have also been involved in activities related to the prevention of illness. One important role involves encouraging patient compliance with prescribed medical regimens. That is, once a suspected precursor of a disease process (such as obesity, mild hypertension, or elevated serum cholesterol) that has not yet reached the level of significant disease is identified or diagnosed, it is vital that the potential patient adhere to the treatment prescribed by his or her physician to alleviate this symptom and prevent the disease outright. However, in spite of this seemingly obvious point, it has been estimated that between 33% and 50% of such potential or actual patients do not comply with prescribed medical treatments (Stone, 1979). While many neuropsychologists may not be directly interested or involved in the areas of improving patient adherence, others might be concerned, for example, with stroke prevention via compliance with antihypertensive medication in otherwise symptom-free individuals.

These new areas within which neuropsychologists will apply their particular elements of the fund of psychological knowledge to health are likely to increase in number and scope. Specifically, as some older approaches to prevention or medical treatment of diseases are improved or new treatments are discovered, there is in some cases an increased burden of responsibility on the individual patient to take a more active role in the prevention or treatment process. This greater participation is associated with increased concern that the individual be capable of performing the prerequisite components of the regimen. It is in this expanding field of interest in compliance that neuropsychologists and neuropsychological measures quite likely will have an expanded role. One basic tenet of neuropsychology is that our measures reflect the patterns of a given patient's relative strengths and weaknesses, and it is not difficult to conceive of how our comprehensive test batteries can be viewed in the context of the question: Can this patient perform the tasks required by a home treatment program? (As pointed out earlier, our methodological approaches may not substantially change, but the questions asked of neuropsychologists may.) As the complexity of the interventions or treatments increases, it will become increasingly necessary to evaluate a number of cognitive, attitudinal, and behavioral areas in order to evaluate the individual's ability to comply with the prescribed regimen. In addition to the neuropsychologist's assessment of the ability to comply, it may be necessary in some instances to combine the input of other health psychologists to assess and enhance a patient's or potential patient's willingness to comply. This type of collaboration by psychologists from different backgrounds of experience addressing different aspects of the same problem in a given individual patient or group is a good example of health psychology in action.

Such a model of cooperation is already in practice in the multicenter National Institutes of Health (NIH) Multiple Risk Factor Prevention Program, aimed at prevention of cardiovascular pathology, and in the NIH Diabetes Complication and

Control Trial. In regard to the latter, long-term care of patients with diabetes has the objective of maintainence of good health by medication in already ill individuals and in prevention and control of adverse complications, which affect both the peripheral and the central nervous system. Some of the newer therapies in diabetes attempt to reduce the potential frequency of hypoglycemic episodes by achieving a more precise control of glucose in the belief that this will reduce the probability of complications. Patients included in the NIH study were required to maintain a very strict dietary regimen. As part of the evaluation of the overall level of success of this project, patients underwent a pretreatment neuropsychological examination to ensure (1) that they did not already have neuropsychological deficits and (2) that they had the ability (in terms of memory, judgment, etc.) to comply with the treatment. In conjunction with the neuropsychological input, psychologists with expertise in behavioral medicine consulted with each patient to facilitate and enhance compliance with the study protocol. Similar clinical and research protocols involving neuropsychologists and other psychologists working in the health fields are likely to become increasingly common.

Another example of the expanding role of neuropsychological measures in the maintenance of higher levels of health in individuals already identified as ill is in the area of patients with renal dysfunction. One of the newest developments in the treatment of these patients involves the use of a new form of dialysis referred to as continuous ambulatory peritoneal dialysis (CAPD), in which the patient learns to perform the procedure without assistance. This method requires much more direct patient participation in treatment and considerably less constricting contact with the hospital environment. Because of the greater demand on the patient, it is important to carefully screen and select those patients who will be capable of meeting those demands. In the series of patients reported by Tutty and Oreopoulos (1980), the neuropsychological test battery used in their study of the effects of CAPD was also used to determine a patient's suitability for CAPD as opposed to more traditional forms of dialysis. In addition, patients who experienced difficulties with the technique after training or who had repeated episodes of peritonitis were reexamined to determine whether the problems were due to cognitive deterioration or emotional factors.

Although the primary role of neuropsychological measures is in the assessment of individual strengths and weaknesses related to the integrity of cerebral dysfunction, the two studies cited above are examples of how the data can be applied to the promotion and maintenance of health.

Neuropsychological Correlates in Health and Illness

A second major theme of health psychology is the identification of etiologic and diagnostic correlates of health and illness. In spite of the potential for neuropsychologists to be interested and involved in health-related clinical and research practices, it is most likely that many neuropsychologists in the foreseeable future will follow the historical precedent of being primarily involved with the effects of disease processes. This is not to say, however, that the activities of most hospital-based neuropsychologists will remain static. In fact, there is considerable evidence that the opposite will increasingly be the case.

The principal change likely to occur is in regard to the type of patient referred for neuropsychological evaluation. In the past, the primary clinical and research concern has been in the evaluation of patients with known or suspected primary neurological disease, such as stroke, tumors, epilepsy, degenerative or demyelinating disease, and so on. Hence most referrals historically have tended to come from departments of neurology, neurosurgery, and, in some centers, psychiatry. However, a review of the recent literature and of the programs of recent scientific meetings of the International Neuropsychological Society and Division 40 of the American Psychological Association reveals considerable growth and diversity in the type of patients being examined by neuropsychologists.

In addition to studies of the effects of primary neurological conditions, initial steps have been made in the investigation of neuropsychological sequelae in a wide variety of nonneurological diseases that in some cases have potential neurological complications. The complexity of these issues is demonstrated by the fact that nearly all the body organ systems, as well as some specific diseases, have been investigated in this way. Just a few of the more recent examples are studies of patients with Cushing's syndrome (Whelan, Schteingart, Starkman, & Smith, 1980); folic acid deficiencies (Botez, Fontaine, Botez, & Bachevalier, 1977); hypercalcemia (Torpa, Blumetti, & Numann, 1983); systemic lupus erythematosus (Fordyce, Blaschke, & Prigatano, 1983); increased lead absorption (Baloh, Sturm, Green, & Gleser, 1975); asthma (Dunleavy & Baade, 1980); chronic obstructive pulmonary disease (Adams, Sawyer, & Kvale, 1980; Grant, Heaton, McSweeny, Adams, & Timms, 1982); uremia and chronic renal failure (Ryan, Souheaver, & DeWolfe, 1980; Souheaver, Ryan, & DeWolfe, 1982); and acute lymphocytic leukemia (Berg, Ch'ien, Lancaster, Bowman, & Ochs, 1983). Although the studies cited here suggest a relatively recent interest in the neuropsychological features associated with a large number of systemic diseases, it should be noted that almost from the outset there has been a concurrent interest in the scientific investigation of such phenomena (Reitan, 1953a, b; Apter, Halstead, Eisele, & McCullough, 1948).

As suggested earlier, one precursor of disease worthy of note because of its long history of neuropsychological interest is hypertension. This physiologic imbalance has both neurological and nonneurological sequelae and is sometimes considered in the context of studies of actual diagnosable pathology, such as cerebrovascular disease (e.g., Kelly, Garron, & Javid, 1980). However, hypertension in the absence of related pathologic states has also been a topic of specific interest in series of studies (Apter, Halstead, & Heimburger, 1951; Reitan, 1954; Spieth, 1965; Goldman, Kleinman, Snow, Bidus, & Korol, 1974; Boller, Vrtunski, Mack, & Kim, 1977). These studies, as well as some of those previously cited, serve to demonstrate the fact that neuropsychological interest in concerns arising from traditionally nonneurological areas is not a recent development but rather has existed almost from the inception of the field of clinical neuropsychology. Therefore, the contemporary surge of interest in such questions in reality represents a contemporary expression of this interface between clinical neuropsychology and health psychology.

Obviously, the studies cited above do not exhaust the realm of possibilities but rather exemplify new horizons in the clinical and scientific study of brain behavior relationships in health and disease. These initial tentative steps barely scratch the surface in relationship to developments that certainly will follow. As noninvasive neurodiagnostic techniques are further developed and perfected (e.g., positron emission tomography, nuclear magnetic resonance, cerebral blood flow, etc.) and applied in conjunction with neuropsychological assessment techniques, one may expect the opening of new dimensions in our studies of physiological parameters of cerebral function and dysfunction. Recent volumes of *Advances in Neurology* (Schoenberg, 1979) and *Handbook of Clinical Neurology* (Vinken & Bruyn, 1979) devoted to neurological aspects of systemic disease suggest this will be an inviting and clinically scientifically challenging area for years to come.

In addition to the studies of neuropsychological correlates of disease of various systems, there is another aspect of the identification of etiologic correlates of health and illness in which neuropsychologists have been involved. This is the area of epidemiology. Psychologists have long had a heritage of conducting standardization studies to establish the normal range of performance on a particular test or battery of tests. These large-scale normative studies of a particular test (such as the Wechsler IQ tests) incorporate some epidemiologic principles, but in general neuropsychologists have not been involved in studies of the epidemiology of diseases with which they deal on a clinical basis. Certain exceptions to this generalization, although rare, are worthy of mention.

For example, Klonoff and colleagues (Klonoff & Robinson, 1967; Klonoff & Thompson, 1969) reported a large-scale study of the epidemiology of head injuries in children and adults. In addition, Klonoff (1971) presented further data from his study with children that focused on predisposing factors, accident conditions, accident proneness, and sequelae. In conjunction with this project, Klonoff also gathered an extensive normative data base on a large sample of normal children (Klonoff & Low, 1974; Klonoff & Paris, 1974). Such a combined epidemiologic and normative study is a rarity in the neuropsychological literature. Also of note is the study of the prevalence of hyperactivity carried out by Trites and coworkers (Trites, Dugas, Lynch, & Ferguson, 1979). In that study, using epidemiological sampling procedures, a large stratified random sample of elementary school children ($n = 14,083$) was obtained to gather teachers' ratings on the prevalence of hyperactivity. The study is noteworthy because of the exceptionally large sample and the sophisticated sampling procedures employed and as an example of the collaboration between neuropsychology and epidemiology. In addition to these two large studies, neuropsychologists also participated in the Framingham Heart Study (Kaplan et al., 1979).

Neuropsychological Aspects of Treatment

The third main theme of the working definition of health psychology characterizes it as a discipline that is making a contribution to the treatment of illness; and neuropsychologists have been active in a number of aspects of this area. Some lines of neuropsychological activity have been in the development of remediation techniques and the assessment of the effects of such treatment.

Remediation Techniques

Although evidence suggests that neuropsychological test batteries are sensitive to a wide variety of behavioral deficits, there has not been within clinical neuropsychology, in contrast to rehabilitation psychology, a widespread interest in active remediation of those deficits. Among the many deficits that occur, most of the interest by neuropsychologists in rehabilitation of cognitive deficits appears to have been in the areas of memory and spatial neglect. Diller and Gordon (1981) have discussed in some detail the relationship of clinical neuropsychology and rehabilitation. They note that the diagnosis or documentation of cognitive deficit is the end of the process for some health practitioners, whereas for the rehabilitation team, such documentation represents the beginning.

Although the major contributions have come from rehabilitation psychologists, some neuropsychologists have found employment in rehabilitation settings and have developed extensive programs for the remediation of cognitive deficits associated with brain injury (e.g., Diller and others at the Institute of Rehabilitation Medicine). Other neuropsychologists have focused their efforts on the development of techniques for remediation of specific cognitive deficits, such as memory deficits (Lewinsohn, Danaher, & Kikel, 1977; Lewinsohn et al., 1977). Neuropsychologists working in more acute care general medical settings have often not been involved in the rehabilitation process but, instead, contribute their professional skills in the area of diagnosis and evaluation. This is not for lack of interest or desire but rather because of the paucity of readily available neuropsychological treatments or the physical plant to house the necessary personnel and equipment. The unavailability of treatment capacity is compounded by certain logistic realities in the medical management of patients with neurological disease or injury. That is, frequently the rehabilitation of these patients does not take place in the acute care hospital; rather, the patient is transferred to a long-term rehabilitation hospital in which no neuropsychologist with the needed neuroscience background or, in fact, any psychologist is in residence. In spite of this somewhat underutilization of the neuropsychologist in rehabilitation, there are a number of ways in which all neuropsychologists may have an impact on the rehabilitation process.

To a considerable extent at present, the neuropsychologist's greatest asset in making suggestions for rehabilitation lies in the strength of our assessment batteries. By means of a thorough neuropsychological examination, we are able to identify critically important elements of a patient's relative strengths and weaknesses and to use these data to form reasoned clinical opinions as to potentially effective ways of reeducating particular patients (e.g., tactual, visual, auditory). Our assessments of some of the behavioral and/or conceptual deficits that exist may also be of value to the other members of the rehabilitation team (e.g., physiatrists, psychiatrists, nurses, occupational therapists, and physical therapists), who may modify their approach to a patient on the basis of individual neuropsychological strengths and weaknesses.

In some instances, a neuropsychologist's or rehabilitative psychologist's suggestions for rehabilitation may revolve around how best to circumvent a particular deficit or the identification of the sensory processing modality that appears to be most intact. In other cases, the neuropsychologist may be able to make practical suggestions regarding the use of various aids for use in daily living to compensate for deficits (e.g., the use of tape recorders for patients with auditory attention span or memory deficits). Occasionally one learns of commercially available products that may be adapted for such remediation. For example, two popular toys (Simon and Merlin) require the user to tap out a sequence on sensors that emit tones and/or different-colored lights. The toys are programmed to be able to increase the length of the sequence to be copied by the user. These toys seemingly have potential value in the rehabilitation of patients with visual attention or sequencing deficits. The adaptation of similar products is limited only by the neuropsychologist's or rehabilitation psychologist's knowledge of their availability and by his or her imagination.

One other aspect of treatment or other intervention that deserves mention as an important use of neuropsychological assessment is the prediction of how the deficits we identify in our assessments will influence a patient's daily life. It is probably not an uncommon experience among neuropsychologists to be asked questions such as. How will my ability to put blocks in a board when I'm blindfolded help you decide if I can go back to work? In a very real sense, from the patient's point of view, the question of how the injury will affect the patient's life is the crucial question. While we must try to predict future performance on the basis of the results of our present examination, almost no empirical data directly addresses the question of which deficits in which tasks affect which daily activities. Some preliminary work in this area merits mention because of the contribution it has made in the day-to-day practice of clinical neuropsychology. Heaton and colleagues in Colorado have published a series of papers on the use of neuropsychological test data in the prediction of everyday functioning (Heaton, Chelune, & Lehman, 1978; Newnan, Heaton, & Lehman, 1978; Heaton & Pendleton, 1981). While other similar reports have appeared periodically (Dennerll, Rodin, Gonzalez, Schwartz, & Lin, 1966; Schwartz, Dennerll, & Lin, 1968; Dikmen & Morgan, 1980; McSweeny, Grant, Adams, & Prigatano, 1983), the reports by Heaton and colleagues have been particularly useful in addressing such commonly raised and critically important questions as: Should this patient be allowed to drive?

While neuropsychologists will continue to contribute this form of useful and pragmatic input into treatment and rehabilitation planning, considerable change is already occurring. In this day of newly introduced technologies to improve the quality of living, it is no surprise that the rapidly expanding field of microcomputer technology provides one impetus for such change. Since 1975, there has been a dramatic increase in the application and availability of computer technology in almost all facets of contemporary life. As a part of these developments, some neuropsychologists are turning their professional interest and creativity to the adaptation and development of software for use in rehabilitation. In some instances, existing programs developed originally for entertainment have been recognized for their potential rehabilitation value. For example, many of the game cartridges available for home computer systems (e.g., Atari, Intellevision, Apple, etc.) require visuomotor coordination, while others require linguistic or mathematical skills. Many of the available programs have been described in terms of their potential uses for rehabilitation by Lynch (1981, 1983). In addition to adapting existing software, some neuropsychologists with expertise in computer programming are developing programs to meet the unique needs of each of their patients (Bracy, 1983; Gianutsos, 1982). Individualized computer programs for the specific needs of particular patients represent a quantum leap in the sophistication of rehabilitation programs. Extensive computer diagnostic and remediation programs have also been developed by Doehring for use with learning-disabled children. This combination of computer-based diagnosis and patient-specific treatment represents another horizon for the application of computers to neuropsychology and rehabilitation. Given the explosion in the developments in computer technology, it is impossible to predict the long-term future. However, one glimpse into the future that triggers many aspects of one's imagination in its implication for neuropsychology is the application of computer technology to the treatment of patients with spinal cord injuries. It is now possible for some paraplegic patients to walk with the aid of a computer. One may only wonder if similar developments for patients with cerebral deficits might not also be a possibility.

Effects of Treatment

Another important activity in the area of treatment has been the use of neuropsychological assessment techniques to measure the effects of treatment of both neurologic and systemic disease. As noted above in regard to the diagnostic correlates of disease, neuropsychologists have examined the subspecialty-relevant effects of treatment for a variety of systemic diseases, including chronic obstructive pulmonary disease (Bornstein, Menon, York, Sproule, & Zak, 1980); acute lymphocytic leukemia (Soni, Marten, Pitner, Duenas, & Powazek, 1975; Baron, Gluck, Braillier, & Leikin, 1981; Ivnik, Colligan, Obetz, & Smithson, 1981; Berg, Ch'ien, Lancaster, Bowman, & Ochs, 1983); open heart and cardiac bypass surgery (Sotaniemi, 1980 a, b; Juolasmaa et al., 1981; Sy & Novelly, 1980; Sotaniemi, Juolasmaa, & Hokkanen, 1981); and diabetes (NIH Diabetes Complication and Control Trial).

One area that has been examined by a growing number of investigators is the effects of cerebral revascularization in patients who have undergone carotid endarterectomy or extracranial-intracranial anastomosis. This complex of disorders has been the subject of investigation by neuropsychologists since shortly after the introduction of the techniques. Although numerous studies have been performed, there is still no clear consensus as to whether these revascularization procedures effect an improvement in cognitive function that can be related to physiological changes in cerebral perfusion. A recent, well-designed and -controlled study by Parker, Granberg, Nichols, Jones, and Hewett (1983) found no beneficial effect on neuropsychological functioning from carotid endarterectomy at six months' follow-up. On the other hand, a study by Kelly, Garron, and Javid (1980) is of interest because these authors considered the possible effects of systemic biomedical variables in the expression of improved performance. Specifically, they reported that patients with lower admitting systolic blood pressure achieved a greater improvement than did patients with higher blood pressures.

The potential for future clinical and research activity in this area is bright. Investigation of the neuropsychological correlates of systemic disease with possible secondary neurological sequelae will undoubtedly be paralleled by similar studies of the changes in performance that occur with the treatment and alleviation of those conditions. As new treatments are developed for various diseases and conditions, there will be other new avenues for neuropsychologists to explore. In still other areas, neuropsychologists will be involved in the assessment of various other clinically based treatment issues. For example, are there differences in the quality of survival (as measured by our assessment procedures) between brain tumor patients treated with surgery alone and those who receive surgery combined with radiation? In addition, do aneurysm patients treated early have better neuropsychological outcome than patients treated later in the course of their condition? Besides these potential studies of increasingly challenging questions, the assessment of such treatments in the future will be combined with evaluation of other indexes of cerebral function. Thus it will not be uncommon to see reports of the effect of some treatment both on neuropsychological measures and, for example, on cerebral blood flow. The burgeoning developments in neurodiagnosis utilizing brain imaging techniques suggests that such methods will enhance the present understanding of the physiological correlates of neuropsychological performance.

SUMMARY

Health psychology is a discipline-specific term that describes the various clinical, research, and administrative activities of psychologists with diverse areas of professional skill and interest in the general arena of health and illness. This inclusive definition underscores the fact that psychologists with a wide variety of specific skills (e.g., clinical, experimental, social, physiological, neuropsychological) may all contribute to the development and understanding of the psychological factors in promotion and maintainence of health, the diagnosis and documentation of the effects of illness, and the development and application of treatments to alleviate the behavioral effects of such illnesses. Clinical neuropsychologists have a long history of interest in such matters dating almost to the inception of the field of clinical neuropsychology. In the general health setting, neuropsychological activity has broadened and will continue to broaden its perspective and activity with respect to the type of patient being referred, the nature of the referring questions, and the diversity of the professional relationships, both intradisciplinary and extradisciplinary. It will become increasingly common for neuropsychologists to collaborate with psychologists with other areas of expertise (e.g., behavioral medicine) in both clinical and research activities. This increasing collaboration between psychologist-specialists emphasizes the importance of training new generations of psychologists who recognize and appreciate the particular skills of the various subdisciplines of psychology. The issue of how and when subdiscipline-specific training is implemented is the subject of Chapter 21.

REFERENCES

Adams, K.M., Grant, I., & Reed, R.J. (1980). Neuropsychology in alcoholic men in their late thirties: One year follow-up. *American Journal of Psychiatry, 137,* 928–931.

Adams, K.M., Sawyer, J.D., & Kvale, P.A. (1980). Cerebral oxygenation and neuropsychological adaptation. *Journal of Clinical Neuropsychology, 2,* 189–208.

Adler, N.E., Cohen, F., & Stone, G.C. (1979). Themes and professional prospects in health psychology. In C.G. Stone, F. Cohen, & N.E. Adler (Eds.), *Health psychology* (pp. 573–590). San Francisco: Jossey-Bass.

Agras, W.S. (1982). Behavioral medicine in the 1980's: Nonrandom connections. *Journal of Consulting and Clinical Psychology, 50,* 797–803.

Apter, N.S., Halstead, W.C., Eisele, C.W., & McCullough, N.B. (1948). Impaired cerebral function in chronic brucellosis. *American Journal of Psychiatry, 105,* 361–366.

Apter, N.S., Halstead, W.C., & Heimburger, R.F. (1951). Impaired cerebral functions in essential hypertension. *American Journal of Psychiatry, 107,* 808–813.

Asken, M.J. (1979). Medical psychology: Toward definition, clarification and organization. *Professional Psychology, 10,* 66–73.

Baloh, R., Sturm, R., Green, B., & Gleser, G. (1975). Neuropsychological effects of chronic asymptomatic increased lead absorption. *Archives of Neurology, 32,* 326–330.

Baron, I., Gluck, R., Braillier, D., & Leikin, S. (1981). *Long-term neuropsychological effects of central nervous system prophylaxis in acute lymphocytic leukemia.* Paper presented at International Neuropsychological Society, Atlanta.

Belar, C.D., Wilson, E., & Hughes, H. (1982). Health psychology training in doctoral psychology programs. *Health Psychology, 1,* 289–299.

Berg, R.A., Ch'ien, L.T., Lancaster, W., Bowman, W.P., & Ochs, J. (1983). *Neuropsychological effects of acute lymphocytic leukemia and its treatment.* Paper presented at International Neuropsychological Society, Mexico City.

Boll, T.J., Heaton, R., & Reitan, R.M. (1974). Neuropsychological and emotional correlates of Huntington's chorea. *Journal of Nervous and Mental Disease, 158,* 61–69.

Boller, F. (1980). Mental status of patients with Parkinson disease. *Journal of Clinical Neuropsychology, 2,* 157–172.

Boller, F., Vrtunski, B., Mack, J.L., & Kim, Y. (1977). Neuropsychological correlates of hypertension. *Archives of Neurology, 34,* 701–705.

Bornstein, R., Menon, D., York, E., Sproule, B., & Zak, C. (1980). Effects of venesection on cerebral function in chronic lung disease. *Canadian Journal of Neurological Sciences, 7,* 293–296.

Botez, M.I., Fontaine, F., Botez, T., & Bachevalier, J. (1977). Folate responsive neurological and mental disorders: Report of 16 cases. *European Neurology, 16,* 230–246.

Bracy, O.L. (1983). *Developing software for modifying impaired attentional skills: Suggestions and observations.* Paper presented at International Neuropsychological Society, Mexico City.

Brooks, D.N. (1972). Memory and head injury. *Journal of Nervous and Mental Disease, 155,* 350–355.

Brooks, D.N. (1974). Recognition memory, and head injury. *Journal of Neurology, Neurosurgery and Psychiatry, 37,* 794–801.

Brooks, D.N. (1976). Wechsler Memory Scale performance and its relationship to brain damage after severe closed head injury. *Journal of Neurology, Neurosurgery and Psychiatry, 39,* 593–601.

Brooks, D.N., Aughton, M.E., Bond, M.R., Jones, P., & Rizvi, S. (1980). Cognitive sequelae in relationship to early indices of severity of brain damage after severe blunt head injury. *Journal of Neurology, Neurosurgery and Psychiatry, 43,* 529–534.

Costa, L. (1983). Clinical neuropsychology: A discipline in evolution. *Journal of Clinical Neuropsychology, 5,* 1–11.

Davison, L.A. (1974). Introduction. In R.M. Reitan & L.A. Davison (Eds.), *Clinical neuropsychology: Current status and applications* (pp. 1–18). Washington, DC: Winston.

Dennerll, R.D., Rodin, E.A., Gonzalez, S., Schwartz, M.L., & Lin, Y. (1966). Neurological and psychological factors related to employability of persons with epilepsy. *Epilepsia, 7,* 318–329.

Dikmen, S., & Morgan, S.F. (1980). Neuropsychological factors related to employability and occupational status in persons with epilepsy. *Journal of Nervous and Mental Disease, 168,* 236–240.

Diller, L., & Gordon, W.A. (1981). Rehabilitation and clinical neuropsychology. In S.B. Filskov & T.J. Boll (Eds.), *Handbook of clinical neuropsychology* (Vol. 1, pp. 702–733). New York: John Wiley & Sons.

Dunleavy, R.A., & Baade, L.E. (1980). Neuropsychological correlates of severe asthma in children 9–14 years old. *Journal of Consulting and Clinical Psychology, 48,* 214–219.

Fordyce, D.J., Blaschke, J., & Prigatano, G.P. (1983). *Neuropsychological examination of patients with systemic lupus erythematosus.* Paper presented at International Neuropsychological Society, Mexico City.

Gentry, W.D., Street, W.J., Masur, F.T., & Asken, M.J. (1981). Training in medical psychology: A survey of graduate and internship training programs. *Professional Psychology, 12,* 224–228.

Gianutsos, R. (1982). *Personal computing and the transformation of an injured brain into an active mind.* Paper presented at American Congress of Rehabilitation Medicine, Houston.

Goldman, H., Kleinman, K.M., Snow, M.Y., Bidus, D.R., & Korol, B. (1974). Correlation of diastolic blood pressure and signs of cognitive dysfunction in essential hypertension. *Diseases of the Nervous System, 35,* 571–572.

Goldstein, G., & Shelly, C.H. (1974). Neuropsychological diagnosis of multiple sclerosis in a neuropsychiatric setting. *Journal of Nervous and Mental Disease, 158,* 280–290.

Grant, I., Adams, K.M., Carlin, A.S., Rennick, P.M., Judd, L.L., & Schooff, K. (1978). The collaborative neuropsychological study of polydrug users. *Archives of General Psychiatry, 35,* 1063–1074.

Grant, I., Adams, K.M., & Reed, R.J. (1979). Normal neuropsychological abilities of alcoholic men in their late thirties. *American Journal of Psychiatry, 136,* 1263–1269.

Grant, I., Heaton, R.K., McSweeny, A.J., Adams, K.M., & Timms, R.M. (1982). Neuropsychological findings in hypoxemic chronic obstructive pulmonary disease. *Archives of Internal Medicine, 142,* 1470–1476.

Grant, I., Reed, R.J., & Adams, K.M. (1980). Natural history of alcohol and drug related brain disorder: Implications for neuropsychological research. *Journal of Clinical Neuropsychology, 2,* 321–331.

Heaton, R.K., Chelune, G.J., & Lehman, R.A. (1978). Using neuropsychological and personality tests to assess the likelihood of patient employment. *Journal of Nervous and Mental Diseases, 166,* 408–416.

Heaton, R.K., & Pendleton, M.G. (1981). Use of neuropsychological tests to predict adult patient's everyday functioning. *Journal of Consulting and Clinical Psychology, 49,* 807–821.

Ivnik, R.J. (1978). Neuropsychological stability in multiple sclerosis. *Journal of Consulting and Clinical Psychology, 46,* 913–923.

Ivnik, R.J., Colligan, R., Obetz, W., & Smithson, W. (1981). *The effect of prophylactic cranial radiation on neuropsychological functioning among children in remission from acute lymphocytic leukemia.* Paper presented at International Neuropsychological Society, Atlanta.

Juolasmaa, A., Outakoski, J., Hirvenoja, R., Tienari, P., Sotaniemi, K., & Takkunen, J. (1981). Effect of open heart surgery on intellectual performance. *Journal of Clinical Neuropsychology, 3,* 181–197.

Kaplan, E., Albert, M., Wolf, P., Veroff, A.E., Rosen, W., Dawber, T., Macnamara, P., & Kannel, W. (1979). *Neuropsychological testing of the Framingham heart study population.* Paper presented at American Psychological Association, New York.

Kelly, M.P., Garron, D.C., & Javid, H. (1980). Carotid artery disease, carotid endarterectomy and behavior. *Archives of Neurology, 37,* 743–748.

Klonoff, H. (1971). Head injuries in children: Predisposing factors, accident conditions, accident proneness and sequelae. *American Journal of Public Health, 61,* 2405–2417.

Klonoff, H., & Low, M. (1974). Disordered brain function in young children and early adolescents: Neuropsychological and electroencephalographic correlates. In R.M. Reitan & L.A. Davison (Eds.), *Clinical neuropsychology: Current status and applications* (pp. 121–178). Washington, DC: Winston.

Klonoff, H., & Paris, R. (1974). Immediate, short-term and residual effects of acute head injuries in children: Neuropsychological and neurological correlates. In R.M. Reitan & L.A. Davison (Eds.), *Clinical neuropsychology: Current status and applications* (pp. 179–210). Washington, DC: Winston.

Klonoff, H., & Robinson, G.C. (1967). Epidemiology of head injuries in children. *Canadian Medical Association Journal, 96,* 1308–1311.

Klonoff, H., & Thompson, G.B. (1969). Epidemiology of head injuries in adults. *Canadian Medical Association Journal, 100,* 235–241.

Levin, H.S., Benton, A.L., & Grossman, R.D. (1982). *Neurobehavioral consequences of closed head injuries.* New York: Oxford University Press.

Lewinsohn, P.M., Danaher, B.G., & Kikel, S. (1977). Visual imagery as a mnemonic aid for brain-injured persons. *Journal of Consulting and Clinical Psychology, 45,* 717–723.

Lewinsohn, P.M., Glasgow, R.E., Barrera, M., Danaher, B.G. Alperson, J., McCarty, D.L., Sullivan, J.M., Zeiss, R.A., Nyland, J., & Rodrigues, M.R. (1977). Assessment and treatment of patients with memory deficits: Initial studies. *JSAS Catalog of Selected Documents in Psychology, 7,* 79 (Ms. No. 1538).

Lynch, W.J. (1981). *TV games as therapeutic interventions.* Paper presented at American Psychological Association, Los Angeles.

Lynch, W.J. (1983). *Cognitive retraining using microcomputer games and other commercially available software.* Paper presented at International Neuropsychological Society, Mexico City.

Mandleberg, J.A., & Brooks, N. (1975). Cognitive recovery after severe head injury. *Journal of Neurology, Neurosurgery and Psychiatry, 38,* 1121–1126.

Masur, F.T. (1979). An update on medical psychology and behavioral medicine. *Professional Psychology, 10,* 259–264.

Matarazzo, J.D. (1980). Behavioral medicine and behavioral health: Frontiers for a new health psychology. *American Psychologist, 35,* 807–817.

Matarazzo, J.D. (1982). Behavioral health's challenge to academic, scientific, and professional psychology. *American Psychologist, 37,* 1–14.

Matarazzo, J.D. (1983). Education and training in health psychology: Boulder or bolder. *Health Psychology, 2,* 73–113.

Matarazzo, J.D. (1986). Relationships of health psychology to other segments of psychology. In G.C. Stone, S.M. Weiss, J.D. Matarazzo, N.E. Miller, J. Rodin, C.D. Belar, M.J. Follick, & J.E. Singer (Eds.), *Health psychology: A discipline and profession.* Chicago: University of Chicago Press.

Matarazzo, J.D., & Carmody, T.P. (1983). Health psychology. In M. Hersen, A.E. Kazdin, & A.S. Bellack (Eds.), *The clinical psychology handbook* (pp. 657–682). New York: Pergamon.

Matarazzo, J.D., Carmody, T.P., & Gentry, W.D. (1981). Psychologists on the faculties of United States schools of medicine: Past, present, and possible future. *Clinical Psychology Review, 1,* 293–317.

Matarazzo, J.D., Connor, W.E., Fey, S.G., Carmody, T.P., Pierce, D.K., Brischetto, C.S., Baker, L.H., Connor, S.J., & Sexton, G. (1982). Behavioral cardiology with an emphasis on the Family Heart Study: fertile ground for psychological and biomedical research. In T. Millon, C.G. Green, & R.B. Meagher (Eds.), *Handbook of health care psychology* (pp. 301–336). New York: Plenum Press.

Matarazzo, J.D., Lubin, B., & Nathan, R.G. (1978). Psychologists' membership on the medical staffs of university teaching hospitals. *American Psychologist, 33,* 23–29.

Matthews, C.G., Cleeland, C.S., & Hopper, C.L. (1970). Neuropsychological patterns in multiple sclerosis. *Diseases of the Nervous System, 31,* 161–170.

Matthews, K.A., & Avis, N.E. (1982). Psychologists in schools of public health: Current status, future prospects and implications for other health settings. *American Psychologist, 37,* 949–954.

McKinlay, W.W., Brooks, D.N., Bond, M.R., Martinage, D.P., & Marshall, M.M. (1981). The short-term outcome of severe blunt head injury as reported by relatives of the injured persons. *Journal of Neurology, Neurosurgery and Psychiatry, 44,* 527–533.

McSweeny, A.J., Grant, I., Adams, K., & Prigatano, G. (1983). *The relationship of neuropsychological status to quality of "everyday" life functioning in health and chronically ill persons.* Paper presented at International Neuropsychological Society, Mexico City.

Nathan, R.G., Lubin, B., Matarazzo, J.D., & Persely, G.W. (1979). Psychologists in schools of medicine, 1955, 1964, and 1977. *American Psychologist, 34,* 622-627.

Newnan, O.S., Heaton, R.K., & Lehman, R.A. (1978). Neuropsychological and MMPI correlates of patient's future employment characteristics. *Perceptual and Motor Skills, 46,* 635-642.

Norton, J.C. (1975). Patterns of neuropsychological test performance in Huntington's disease. *Journal of Nervous and Mental Diseases, 161,* 276-279.

Parker, J.C., Granberg, B.W., Nichols, W.K., Jones, J.G., & Hewett, J.E. (1983). Mental status outcomes following carotid endarterectomy: A six-month analysis. *Journal of Clinical Neuropsychology,* pp. 345-353.

Pomerleau, O., & Brady, J.P. (Eds.). (1979). *Behavioral medicine: Theory and practice* (pp. xi-xii). Baltimore: Williams & Wilkins.

Reitan, R.M. (1953a). Intellectual functions in myxedema. *AMA Archives of Neurology and Psychiatry, 69,* 436-449.

Reitan, R.M. (1953b). Intellectual and affective changes in chronic brucellosis. *American Journal of Psychiatry, 110,* 19-28.

Reitan, R.M. (1954). Intellectual and affective changes in essential hypertension. *American Journal of Psychiatry, 110,* 817-824.

Reitan, R.M., & Boll, T.J. (1971). Intellectual and cognitive functions in Parkinson's disease. *Journal of Consulting and Clinical Psychology, 37,* 364-369.

Reitan, R.M., Reed, J.C., & Dyken, M.L. (1971). Cognitive, psychomotor and motor correlates of multiple sclerosis. *Journal of Nervous and Mental Disease, 153,* 218-224.

Reitan, R.M., & Shipley, R.E. (1963). The relationship of serum cholesterol changes to psychological abilities. *Journal of Gerontology, 18,* 350-356.

Ryan, J.J., Souheaver, G.T., & DeWolfe, A.S. (1980). Intellectual deficit in chronic renal failure: A comparison with neurological and medical-psychiatric patients. *Journal of Nervous and Mental Disease, 168,* 763-767.

Sachs, R.H., Eigenbrode, C.R., & Kruper, D.C. (1979). Psychology and dentistry. *Professional Psychology, 10,* 521-528.

Schoenberg, B.C. (Ed.). (1979). *Neurological epidemiology: Principles and clinical applications. Advances in neurology* (Vol. 19). New York: Raven.

Schwartz, G.F., & Weiss, S.M. (1978). Yale Conference on Behavioral Medicine: A proposed definition and statement of goals. *Journal of Behavioral Medicine, 1,* 3-12.

Schwartz, M.L., Dennerll, R.D., & Lin, Y. (1968). Neuropsychological and psychosocial predictors of employability in epilepsy. *Journal of Clinical Psychology, 24,* 174-177.

Sladen, B.C. (1979). Health care psychology and graduate education. *Professional Psychology, 10,* 841-851.

Smith, A. (1981). Principles underlying human brain functions in neuropsychological sequelae of different neuropathological processes. In S.B. Filskov & T.J. Boll (Eds.), *Handbook of clinical neuropsychology* (Vol. 1, pp. 175-226). New York: John Wiley & Sons.

Soni, S.S., Marten, G.W., Pitner, S.E., Duenas, D.A., & Powazek, M. (1975). Effects of central-nervous-system irradiation on neuropsychological functioning of children with acute lymphocytic leukemia. *New England Journal of Medicine, 293,* 113-118.

Sotaniemi, K.A. (1980a). Brain damage and neurological outcome after open-heart surgery. *Journal of Neurology, Neurosurgery and Psychiatry, 43,* 127-135.

Sotaniemi, K.A. (1980b). Clinical and prognostic correlates of EEG in open-heart surgery patients. *Journal of Neurology, Neurosurgery and Psychiatry, 43,* 941-947.

Sotaniemi, K.A., Juolasmaa, A., & Hokkanen, E.T. (1981). Neuropsychologic outcome after open-heart surgery. *Archives of Neurology, 38,* 2-8.

Souheaver, G.T., Ryan, J.J., & DeWolfe, A.S. (1982). Neuropsychological patterns in uremia. *Journal of Clinical Psychology, 38,* 490–496.

Spieth, W. (1965). Slowness of task performance and cardiovascular disease. In T.A. Welford & J.E. Birren (Eds.), *Behavior, aging and the nervous system.* Springfield, IL: Charles C Thomas.

Stone, G.C. (1979). Patient compliance and the role of the expert. *Journal of Social Issues, 35,* 34–59.

Swan, G.E., Piccione, A., & Anderson, D.C. (1980). Internship training in behavioral medicine: Program description, issues, and guidelines. *Professional Psychology, 11,* 339–346.

Sy, M.J., & Novelly, R.A. (1980). *Neuropsychological changes following open heart surgery.* Paper presented at International Neuropsychological Society, San Francisco.

Torpa, A.J., Blumetti, A.E., & Numann, P. *Neuropsychological deficits associated with hypercalcemia.* Paper presented at International Neuropsychological Society, Mexico City.

Trites, R.L., Dugas, E., Lynch, G., & Ferguson, H.B. (1979). Prevalence of hyperactivity. *Journal of Pediatric Psychology, 2,* 179–188.

Tutty, L.M., & Oreopoulos, D.G. (1980). *Metabolic correlates of neuropsychological measures in patients with renal dysfunction.* Paper presented at Canadian Psychological Association, Calgary.

Tweedy, J.R., Langer, K.G., & McDowell, F.H. (1982). Effect of semantic relations on the memory deficit associated with Parkinson's disease. *Journal of Clinical Neuropsychology, 4,* 235–247.

Vinken, P.J., & Bruyn, B.W. (Eds.). (1979). *Handbook of clinical neurology* (Vol. 38). *Neurological manifestations of systemic diseases.* Amsterdam: North Holland.

Whelan, T.B., Schteingart, D.E., Starkman, M.N., & Smith, A. (1980). Neuropsychological deficits in Cushing's syndrome. *Journal of Nervous and Mental Disease, 168,* 753–757.

PART TWO

Assessment

CHAPTER 3

The Psychometric Foundation of Clinical Neuropsychology

Elbert W. Russell

Clinical neuropsychology rests on two foundations: neurology and psychometrics. More specifically, clinical neuropsychology uses psychological testing procedures, or psychometrics, to evaluate pathologic brain processes. This is a more exact formulation of the usual definition of clinical neuropsychology, which is the study of brain-behavior relationships for clinical purposes.

While the advances in experimental neuropsychology have generally been derived from the development of psychometric tests (e.g., almost all the studies cited by Hecaen & Albert [1978] used psychometric tests), the clinical application of neuropsychology is even more dependent on such testing procedures. Since a person's entire mental functioning is studied, psychometrically designed groups of tests are required. Such groups, or batteries, of tests are not as necessary for hypothesis testing in experimental neuropsychology.

There appear to be two major approaches to neuropsychology: the neurological and the psychological (see Chapter 1). These approaches are related to the two foundations of neuropsychology. In the neurological approach, procedures tend to be modeled on the type of examination that has been developed by neurology as a branch of medicine. The psychological approach, by contrast, emphasizes the type of examination that has been developed in psychological clinical assessment procedures. Since the early 1900s, the field of intelligence has developed its own psychometric methods of examination and abilities measurement. That is, the psychological approach consists of the use of psychometric methods to study mental processes.

In regard to theory, the neurological approach derives its basis from neurology. Its theoretical basis has been well established by such people as Luria (Luria & Majovski, 1977), Hecaen (Hecaen & Albert, 1978), Milner (1971), and Walsh (1978). By contrast, the psychological foundation of neuropsychology has never been fully formulated or explicated in any public or published manner, though it was described to some extent in various chapters in the first volume of Filskov and Boll's *Handbook of Clinical Neuropsychology* (1981). Consequently, the psychological approach to neuropsychology, particularly as exemplified in the Halstead-Reitan Battery (HRB) method, has been roundly criticized by people grounded in the neurological approach as having no theoretical basis. Luria (Luria & Majovski, 1977) has written that the Halstead-Reitan neuropsychological battery—and by implication the psychological approach in general—has no theoretical foundation. He states, "the battery lacks grounding in a theoretical formulation of the brain's function organization governing psychological processes affecting behavior" (p. 961). This critique is echoed in an otherwise excellent neuropsychology textbook by Kolb and Whishaw (1980).

In spite of this criticism, there is in fact an extensive theoretical basis for the psychological approach to neuropsychology. It should be noted that this basis applies to all clinical neuropsychological methods that make extensive use of psychometric measurement and not just to the Halstead-Reitan Battery. This theoretical basis is derived from at least three sources. First, the neuropsychologists who utilize psychometric methods are generally quite familiar with basic neurological theory, as exemplified in the works of Luria (1973, 1980) and Hecaen and Albert (1978). For instance, Reitan himself has an extensive knowledge of neurology, equivalent to that of many neurologists (personal knowledge). This is also true of many of the other major neuropsychologists who make extensive use of psychometric methods. Thus the findings of neuroscience and experimental neuropsychology are part of the theoretical basis for the psychological approach to neuropsychology as well as for the neurological approach to neuropsychology.

In addition, adherents of the psychometric approach have a second source for their theory: clinical lore. There are very few published accounts of this lore (Klove, 1963; Smith, 1981). Each of the "schools" of clinical neuropsychological testing developed over a period of time a large body of unpublished clinical lore. This is particularly true of the Halstead-Reitan Battery approach. Many of the most skilled practitioners using the HRB have published relatively little of their understanding of relationships found in the battery. Unfortunately, some of those who have published works related to the HRB, as well as most of those who criticize it, have had relatively little familiarity with this large body of lore and are unaware of the power and intricacies of this battery in practice (Reitan, 1964).

The third source of theory for the psychological approach to neuropsychology is the entire field of psychometrics. This field is probably the most scientifically developed and most sophisticated branch of psychology (Cattell, 1971; Guilford, 1967; Horn, 1976; Kline, 1979; Nunnally, 1978). The psychological approach to clinical neuropsychology utilizes knowledge and procedures that have been developed in the psychometric branch of psychology over a period of at least 70 years (DuBois, 1970; Guilford, 1967).

In fact, the unique contribution of psychology to neuropsychology, a contribution that cannot be duplicated by neurology or behavioral neurology, can be summarized in one word: psychometrics. It should be noted at this point that the term *psychometrics* is often held in some disrespect by many neuropsychologists. There is some feeling that psychometrics does not represent a high level of psychology. Possibly this is because a person may be trained to give psychometric tests with only a bachelor's degree or, in some cases, a high school degree. (In fact, psychologists should make more use of such technicians, since they may do an excellent job of testing.)

However, the major aspects of psychometrics, such as test construction theory and methods, are more highly developed and more sophisticated than the methods used in any other area of psychology. The statistical experimental methods, and often even the tests used in other areas of psychology, have generally been derived from the field of psychometrics. It is rather strange that psychologists who supposedly value the scientific method often feel that techniques such as psychotherapy or the clinical usage of unstandardized tests are more advanced than psychometric methods derived from the stringent use of scientific and statistical methods. Nevertheless, it is exactly the use of scientific and statistical methods that accounts for the unique contribution of psychometrics, and in turn of the psychological approach, to neuropsychology. This is the one contribution of psychology to neuropsychology that is not duplicated by any branch of the medical field.

In this regard, the newest advances in psychometrics have not been applied to any extent in neuropsychology. At least two of the recent major texts in psychometrics, those by Kline (1979) and Nunnally (1978), hardly mention neuropsychology, although they do cover almost all other areas of psychology in some detail. In 1978, Nunnally wrote, "In spite of the truism that important individual differences manifested on psychological tests ... must be represented somehow or other in the human brain, it is surprising that physiological psychology has contributed so little about possibly important forms of human abilities that could be turned into practicable tests" (p. 527). Thus, unfortunately, specialists in neither psychometrics nor neuropsychology are particularly aware of what people in the other field are doing. This has resulted in the situation that the psychometrics used in neuropsychology today are largely equivalent to methods developed during the late 1940s and early 1950s. Thus the psychometric aspect of neuropsychology appears to be about 40 years out of date. Very few tests or batteries of tests used in neuropsychology can meet the criteria set by the APA manual *Standards for Educational and Psychological Tests* (1974).

RELATIONSHIP OF PSYCHOLOGICAL TESTS TO THE BRAIN

The basic question concerning the relationship of psychological tests to the brain is, of course, how functions (abilities), as measured by psychological tests, are related to the brain. That is, what are the theoretical bridges between abilities testing and brain functioning? At this point, neuropsychology has developed a number of testing procedures either by trial and error or by applying general psychometric tests, such as the WAIS and ability tests, to neuropathological processes. While the theoretical basis for that application has never been delineated, several theoretical bridges appear to exist.

Necessity for Testing

The most basic principle related to neuropsychological testing procedures is the apparent fact that a function cannot be known to exist unless there is a testing procedure for that function. If one does not have some form of testing procedure, even though informal, such as asking questions or listening to the particular way in which a patient says things, then there is no way of determining that a function exists. And if a function is not known to exist, then, of course, one cannot know either how much it is impaired or where in the brain it exists.

This principle seems so obvious that it is rather surprising to note that, historically, neurologists have repeatedly proposed that a particular area of the brain has no function when performance on none of the existing tests has been impaired by damage to that area. One illustration of this is that, for a considerable amount of time, some neurologists suggested that the giant structure, the corpus callosum, did not have any function, since patients who lacked the corpus callosum or had it destroyed did not appear to show any symptoms (Walsh, 1978). Obviously, what was needed was a more refined testing procedure. When this was developed, the function of the corpus callosum became apparent. Thus history demonstrates that the "silent areas" of the brain are silent only when we do not have tests for the functions that reside in those areas. For instance, the gradual determination of frontal lobe functions has been due to slow development of tests for those functions. Only recently have several such tests, such as fluency tests, been developed (Lezak, 1983).

A study of a function requires some measurement of that function. This is as true for the neurological approach as it is for the psychological approach to neuropsychology. The type of testing for each approach is simply different. The neurology approach uses brief, all-or-none types of tests, while the psychometric approach uses graded scales of homogeneous items.

Measurement of Cortical Functioning

A second part of the theoretical bridge between psychological test and cortical functioning lies in the understanding that abilities tests (such as intelligence tests) are actually measuring cortical functioning. These tests were not originally developed with any reference to brain functioning, and few psychologists, even today, think of them as measures of brain functioning. However, it is rather obvious from a neuropsychological point of view that abilities tests are tests of association area functioning in the brain. Although not developed as neuropsychological tests, abilities tests are in fact, and always have been, neuropsychological tests. The difference between these tests and the more specifically designed neuropsychological tests are that they were by and large developed on normal populations.

This understanding may explain, in part, why the Wechsler tests are the most completely accepted tests in American neuropsychology (Lezak, 1983), although they were not originally designed to be neuropsychological tests. Apparently they are the only tests that are almost universally used by neuropsychologists in the United States and England (Filskov & Leli, 1981; Lezak, 1983; McFie, 1975).

The users of the Luria Nebraska Battery (LNB) feel that, since their measure of cognitive functioning is sufficient to measure intellectual ability (Golden, 1981), they do not need to supplement the LNB with the WAIS. However, a recent study by Shelly and Goldstein (1982) indicates that the WAIS generally loads on factors that are quite separate from those loading on the LNB items. Consequently, a full examination of patients with brain damage would require the WAIS in addition to the LNB. (It should be noted that by adding the WAIS to the LNB, the time for testing using the LNB will begin to be comparable with the time necessary for the HRB and other neuropsychological batteries.)

This understanding that intellectual and cognitive abilities tests are in fact tests of cortical functions means that psychometric theory and its sophisticated methods can be directly applied to testing cortical abilities in neuropsychology. From a theoretical bridge point of view, it is important to realize that the particular form adopted for psychometric tests during the 80 or more years of their development was not arbitrary. The particular form of intellectual abilities tests and the principles involved in their structure were discovered or worked out through many years of studying how to measure human intellectual functioning. This functioning, of course, was cortical functioning. Consequently, the principles and procedures used in psychometrics were developed because of the way that the brain or cortex works. Thus the principles and methods of ability and intelligence testing can be applied to neuropsychological testing. They were derived from actual brain functioning and are thus isomorphic with brain functioning.

Sensory and Motor Tests

The first major finding of psychometrics (Guilford, 1967) was that there was almost no relationship between intelligence and the accuracy or keenness of sensory abilities (Boring, 1950). These early studies demonstrated this lack of relationship as an empirical fact without understanding the reason for this lack of correlation. The finding was actually contrary to the theory of that time. This theory was that since intelligence consisted in associations between sensations, it should be highly correlated with them. The finding that they were not correlated was thus not understandable.

It is only with our present understanding of cortical functions that we can understand why sensory and motor abilities are not strongly related to intelligence. These types of functions are simply related to different parts of the brain. The sensory and motor tests are related to the subcortical nervous system tracts and/or projection areas of the brain, whereas intelligence and cognitive abilities tests are measuring the functioning of the association areas of the cortex. From contemporary neuropsychological theory, there is no particular reason why these types of functions should be related. Parenthetically, it should be noted that some neuropsychological testing, such as the LNB, still mix sensory and motor test items with items of higher cortical functions in the same scale (Golden, 1981). Consequently, it appears that a lesson that was established over 80 years ago in psychology is still not recognized in some areas of neuropsychology.

Definition of Intelligence

While psychometrics contributes to neuropsychology, neuropsychology can make a contribution to psychometrics, which it has not done so far (Nunnally, 1978). The neurological understanding of mental functions provides some foundation for psychometrics where no such foundation previously existed. For instance, the ancient problem in psychometrics of determining what intelligence tests are measuring is in part resolved by the understanding that intelligence is measuring the adequacy of association area cortical functioning. A definition of intelligence that is not redundant is that intelligence is the adequacy of association area functioning. On a gross level, this is not redundant, since damage to limited areas of the cortex impairs some intellectual functions much more than others. This establishes a direct relationship between areas of the brain and intellectual functions, both of which can be defined without reference to the other. Thus the problems in psychometrics can be resolved to some extent by reference to neuropsychological findings.

There are four major areas related to a theoretical bridge between psychometrics and neuropsychology: (1) the neurological basis for the scaling techniques used in neuropsychology, (2) the relationship between general types of intellectual functions and areas of the brain, (3) the differential sensitivity of intellectual abilities tests to brain damage in general, and (4) the theoretical basis for a pattern analysis of brain damage and for designing batteries of tests so as to reflect different types of brain functioning and organic damage.

SCALING

One of the major problems in neuropsychological testing is determining what types of scales are appropriate. This determination is based on an understanding of how different types of scales are related to brain conditions. The major types of scales are nominal, ordinal, interval, and ratio (Nunnally, 1978). Nominal scales classify an object, person, or function into one of two classes. As such, a nominal scale may simply indicate the existence or nonexistence of a function or type of behavior. These scales constitute the brief plus-minus type of testing. Ordinal scales have several classes that are assumed to stand in a quantitative relationship to each other such that a series is formed in which one class is greater than the next regarding some attribute. The amount of difference is not specified; only the ranking, or order, of difference between the classes is assumed. In interval scales, the assumption is that the differences between classes of items are equal from one item to another. The interval scale is characterized by a constant unit of measurement that can assign a real number to any pair of objects in a set. As such, many arithmetic procedures can be applied to these scales. In the ratio scale, a true zero point can be assigned to the scale as its origin. Thus, the numbers associated with the ratio scale represent true values with a true zero point such that one score can be said to have twice the amount of the measured function as another score. All numerical methods can be applied to such scales.

Most psychometric measures use interval scales. While a constant difference in amount can be assumed, a true, or meaningful, zero can seldom be established for psychological attributes. This is obviously true for such personality variables as creativity. In regard to intellectual abilities, a meaningful zero point usually cannot be established because subjects begin to fail to perform a particular test or type of test (e.g., a proverbs test) at a point far above zero, which would represent a complete lack of intelligence. The problem is that such tests have too high a bottom. There are, however, certain areas in which a meaningful zero can be established. Memory is one of these areas. On a memory test, a person who can remember no items in a specified period of time can meaningfully be said to have zero memory. In this case, a meaningful ratio can be established such that a person who remembers 12 items can be said to have half the memory of a normal person if the mean for a normal control is 24 items.

There would seem to be no problem concerning the theoretical basis for determining which type of scale to use in neuropsychology, except that a proportion of neuropsychologists do not use interval scales but rather use nominal scales. That is, the neurological approach, as exemplified by Luria (1973; Luria & Majovski, 1977), primarily uses tests that are nominal in nature. Luria determines whether a patient can or cannot perform a particular test without attempting to determine how well that person can perform that test. This approach is in accord with the methods used in medical neurology. By and large, the type of testing used in neurology, even in the mental status examination, is to determine whether a patient can or cannot pass certain one item tests.

This raises the question as to what the basis is for using interval scales in psychological neuropsychology, since these are not used in neurology. There appear to be at least two bases for use of interval, and occasionally ratio, scales in neuropsychology: (1) increased accuracy and (2) isomorphism with the nature of cortical association area functions. Since accuracy of measurement is derived from the nature of cortical association area functioning, the nature of that functioning will be discussed first.

Measurement of Association Area Functions

The history of psychometric development of cognitive and intellectual measures shows that, in general, interval scales provide the best measurement of intellectual functions. This finding is in contradistinction to neurological usage, which generally entails brief plus-minus nominal scales. The reason for this difference appears to lie in the way the association areas of the central nervous system function. Intellectual functions are measures of abilities found in the association areas of the cortex, whereas the functions generally measured by neurology, with the exception of mental status, are functions either in the projection areas of the brain or in the tracts and subcortical nuclei of the nervous system. The theory proposed here is that the functions in the association areas of the brain exist in a graded form.

Thus, impairment of various cortical functions follows a graded scale, in that damage, unless very severe, does not cause the function to disappear but, rather, to be impaired to a certain degree. This effect is in contrast to that of damage to functions or behaviors related to subcortical areas and projection areas of the nervous system, which tends to have an all-or-none form. Damage to these areas of the nervous system generally either does not effect these functions at all or impairs them relatively completely. This relative all-or-none effect is well known for the visual projection area and visual pathways. Damage to these pathways and the visual projection area generally produces a relatively complete hole, or scotomata, in the visual field. Areas that are not directly damaged function at near the normal level. It is quite common for patients with large scotomata in their visual fields just outside the macular area to have normal central vision.

This all-or-none theory was recently tested for tactual sensation. Russell (1980b) compared the distribution of impairment derived from pure tactual sensation, a projection area function, to that of three tests of association area functions. The test of tactual sensation was the Von Frey Hairs Test, which provides a graded scale for pure fine touch. Hairs of varying calibrated thickness are pressed against the skin to determine whether they can be felt. The number 1 hair is finest, being only a little heavier than a human hair, while the number 9 hair is almost as heavy as a broom straw. This scale was compared to the results from the WAIS Block Design Test, the Speech Perception Test, and the Trail-making Test B using the same subjects. The results of these tests are given in Figures 3.1 and 3.2. The pure tactile data (Figure 3.1) fell into what might be called a relative all-or-none distribution. That is, the tactile scores of most of the patients with brain damage were within normal limits (numbers 1 to 3). however, a few of the brain-damaged subjects had severe impairment of touch. There were only a few cases that fell between these extremes. The normal subjects had no scores outside the normal range.

This type of profile is quite different from that found with the cognitive functions (Figure 3.2), which had long, graded distributions. While the distributions were not that of a normal curve, they nevertheless had a graded form. In fact, the variation was considerably greater than found in normal functioning.

From this study, it is evident that the association area functions are impaired in a graded manner. Consequently, the way to accurately measure association area functions is through use of graded scales. On the other hand, brief all-or-none tests are adequate for the projection areas and tracts of the central nervous system. Although the brief neurological all-or-none tests are well adapted for tracts and projection areas of the

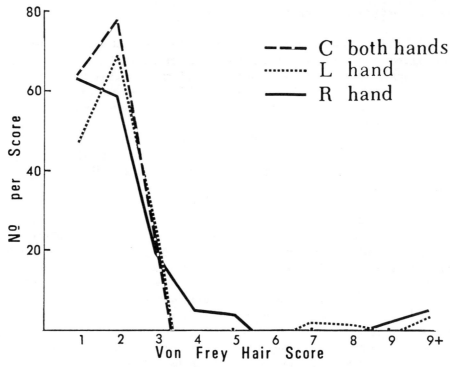

Figure 3.1.   The number of subjects for each Von Frey Hair Score (C, control subjects, both hands; L, left hand of brain-damaged subjects; R, right hand of brain-damaged subjects).

brain, they are not isomorphic with the way the association areas of the brain function. Homogeneous, graded scales are necessary to reflect the way association areas function.

This finding provides one of the explanations for the popularity of the WAIS. The WAIS provides not only an IQ measure but also individual scales that directly reflect the type of impairment produced by lesions in the association areas of the cortex.

It should be noted that the mental status portion of the medical neurological examination, which examines association area functions, does not use graded scales but, rather, employs brief tests such as are used for other parts of the neurological examination. The question arises as to how neurology is able to use these brief tests for functions that are in fact impaired in a graded manner. On examination, the method is seen to be relatively simple (Russell, 1980b). The mental status tests are in fact made up of items that could be derived from a graded scale for cognitive functions, such as information (e.g., the names of the recent presidents of the United States). However, the few questions (items) that are used are set at a level roughly equivalent of that of the low average ability (IQ of approximately 80). Consequently, if by history it is known that a person had at least average intelligence in the past and that person is now unable to answer these questions, one can be fairly certain of a deterioration of functions. This method is adequate when one is dealing with rather severe impairments or gross changes in mental abilities. However, it is inadequate in dealing with the subtler changes.

In summary, the advantage of nominal tests in examining cortical association area functions is that they are quick to administer while being sufficiently adequate if there is a gross disturbance of intellectual functions. The disadvantage is that they are not

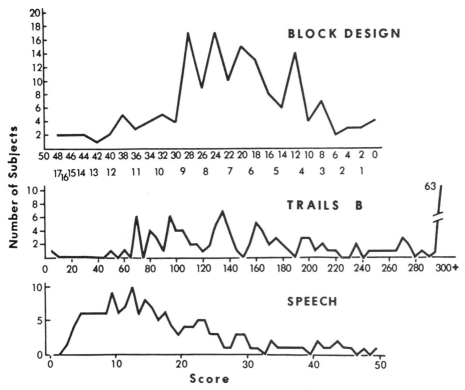

Figure 3.2. The number of brain-damaged and control subjects per score for Block Design, Trail-making Test B, and Speech Perception.

able to provide the fine differentiation that is equivalent to the type of impairment found with many kinds of brain damage. Consequently, they cannot indicate the amount of impairment that has occurred. This means that they have a greatly reduced sensitivity for borderline conditions.

Accuracy

From a practical point of view, the major contribution of psychometric measurement to neuropsychology is accuracy. The advantage of scaled tests over the brief tests used in the neurological approach is the same advantage that using a thermometer has over feeling a person's forehead in order to tell whether there is a fever. Feeling the forehead is faster and in many cases will suffice. The advantage derived from measuring the degree of fever is far more than just knowing that there is a fever. It tells how much fever there is. Consequently, at least in a medical setting, the thermometer has largely replaced touching the patient's forehead to determine temperature.

The advantage of measurement may be illustrated by an incident that recently occurred in a pediatric hospital. The pediatric neurologist at that hospital stated that he could estimate the IQ of a child within a few points of the child's measured IQ. In the experience of the psychologist who worked on the unit, the neurologist could do this in most cases. Consequently, the psychologist herself questioned the need for psychological testing.

However, the statement by the neurologist actually pointed out the advantage of measurement. First, if there was any difference in a patient's verbal and nonverbal intelligence, the nonverbal ability of the patient could not be determined from talking to the patient. Specific types of nonverbal measures are required to determine nonverbal ability. Second, even within the verbal area, the neurologist was actually saying that he, with his many years of medical training, was able to determine the patient's verbal intellectual level almost as well as a high school or college graduate trained in testing could do using a standardized intelligence test. In other words, the test enabled a person untrained in neurology to determine the amount of intelligence in a patient more accurately than all the training and experience that the pediatric neurologist had received. The pediatric neurologist was in fact using the psychometric test that could be given by a high school graduate as the standard for determining his competence.

At some level, every form of examination is quantitative. Luria criticizes the quantitative method (Luria & Majovski, 1977), yet, if one examines his method, it is obvious that he is covertly using a crude normative quantitative method. He states that "the symptoms [tasks or tests] we observed are simple and do not present any difficulties in the *intact* persons" (p. 965, italics added). This statement implies two things. First, since the intact (i.e. normal) person can do these tasks, Luria is actually using a norm, the normal or average person, against which he compares the ability of the patient being tested. Second, he is using a pass-fail criterion, which constitutes a nominal quantitative method. By creating graded scales and applying methods of standardization, more-developed psychometric methods merely refine the type of crude covert comparison used by Luria and all neurologists during examination. Such refinements greatly increase the accuracy of a given examination method.

Neuropsychological Measurement

The major difference between the usual psychometric approach in psychology and the use of testing in neuropsychology is that traditional psychological testing was developed on normal individuals, whereas neuropsychological testing has been designed to accommodate people with severe impairment of their intellectual functions. There are several differences between measurement in brain-damaged people and in normal people. The three examples of cognitive impairment given in Figure 3.2 illustrate some of these differences.

First, the distribution of ability does not follow a normal curve. The actual distribution, of course, is related somewhat to the type of brain-injured patients selected for the sample. That is, in a facility where most of the brain damage is mild, the curve will approach a normal curve. However, if the facility requesting testing deals with severe damage, then the curve will be quite different from the normal distribution. The distributions shown in Figure 3.2 are probably fairly typical of those found in a general hospital with a neurological unit. The type of distribution is strongly skewed. The normal end of the curve approaches that of normal distribution, whereas the tail of the skewed curve stretches far down toward the completely impaired range. One can also see that the distribution is strongly affected by the type of test used. The Block Design Test shows a fairly unskewed, almost plateaulike distribution, whereas the Trail-making Test B and the Speech Perception Test show very strongly skewed distributions with extremely long tails. This skew means that some statistics, such as t-tests, which assume normality, are often not applicable to studies of patients with brain damage. In designing scale scores, great care must be taken that the scale approximates the distribution of the actual impairment. Plotting a distribution to examine the form of the test distribution is important in designing a test.

Another characteristic of neuropsychological tests that is to some extent apparent in the Figures 3.1 and 3.2 is the extreme range required for testing neuropsychological impairment. Since brain damage may produce impairment varying from normality to zero, the range must be quite extended. Brain damage impairment itself stretches from what would be equivalent to a high normal IQ that is probably around a 120 down literally to zero, that is, unconsciousness or death. Thus the scales designed for adequate measuring of brain-damaged functions must be quite extended. One of the advantages of the Wechsler Intelligence Scale is that the scales are fairly long. However, it is common for a fairly severely brain-damaged patient to run off the bottom of the scales on the WAIS. Experience indicates that a range of at least five standard deviations from the mean of the normal group is probably generally required for most tests of brain damage (personal knowledge).

As an example of this range problem, the Tactual Performance Test (TPT) 10 does not have a sufficient bottom. Patients with even moderate impairment reach the bottom of the scale (Russell, 1982a). Consequently, the actual amount of impairment cannot be determined by this test if the impairment is at all severe. This problem was handled by setting up a single-scale that uses the TPT 6 in place of the TPT 10 for severely impaired patients (Russell, 1982a).

The more standard problems in developing neuropsychological scales, such as the problem of validity and reliability, have been taken up in many thorough papers and need not be repeated here (Russell, Neuringer, & Goldstein, 1970; Parsons & Prigatano, 1978). However, one element in the development of the scales is rather important though often overlooked: the need for scales to use homogeneous items (Anastasi, 1983; Nunnally, 1978). It is perhaps so axiomatic that homogeneous items are needed in test development that it is often overlooked in dealing with the requirements for neuropsychological testing. Homogeneity of items simply means that the items vary in difficulty but are all measuring the same thing. A scale that mixes sensory and motor items is obviously not a homogeneous scale. The difficulty, of course, with a hetero-geneous scale is that one does not know by looking at the final score which types of items are impaired. To use an extreme example, if a scale is made up of half sensory items and half motor items, with a cutting point of only one-quarter of the items to separate brain damage from no brain damage, a person could be in the brain-damaged range while having absolutely no motor defects at all, since the defects would all be sensory. As long as the only question was whether there was brain damage or not such a scale could be valid. However, if one wanted to know whether the damage produced sensory or motor impairment, the scale would be useless. The general principle of homogeneity of scales is that unless the scale items are homogeneous, one does not know what the scale is measuring.

RELATIONSHIP OF FUNCTION TO AREA

At present, most of the work in neuropsychology is devoted to determining what functions are related to what areas of the brain. However, the general theory bridging test, function, and the area is somewhat vague.

The relationship of a particular function to a particular area of the brain has been a major point of contention in neurology for a century and a half. A strict localizationist concept of brain functioning would make the theory behind the relationship of a test to an area of the brain quite simple. That is, an area of the brain would simply be related to a test. The only question or problem would be to discover the particular test. However, as has been well discussed by Luria (1973) and others (Walsh, 1978), this strict localizationist theory is inadequate and has been replaced for most people in neuropsychology by Luria's concept of a system. In his theory, every function involves an interactive system of many areas of the brain. The system itself constitutes the function, and the different areas make separate contributions to the overall system. When brain damage involves part of the system, the entire system is affected. This means that individual parts of the system cannot be isolated for study. Rather, brain damage changes the entire system. A neuropsychologist examining a person with brain damage would notice change in the system rather than a reduction of scores on a particular test. This, of course, is the basis for the qualitative approach in which the examiner looks for changes in the way a patient performs a task rather than whether the patient can or cannot perform the task.

However, logically Luria's theory implies that a test of individual functions is not possible. That is, he thinks that at most a test simply brings out a particular way in which an entire system is qualitatively changed. As such, the test demonstrates how a damaged person would change the way he or she handles the required task. If true, this would mean that the type of testing of separate functions performed by adherents of the psychological approach is impossible or at best completely inadequate.

Thus, from Luria's theoretical point of view, only the qualitative approach to neuropsychological testing is adequate. In light of Luria's concept of a system, whether individual functions can be measured and how tests can be applied to individual functions are questionable. This then brings into question the entire concept of neuropsychological testing using psychometric methods in which the amount of impairment of a specific function is measured. Taken to its extreme, the ultimate paradox in Luria's concept of a system is that it is impossible to use his own tests to determine the area of brain damage, since any brain damage anywhere will affect the entire system.

However, Luria does use individual tests that can be passed or failed. He employs hundreds of individual tests which when impaired by brain damage are scored as having been failed (Luria & Majovski, 1977). His tests have been the basis for Christensen's (1975, 1984) battery of individual tests and indirectly for the LNB (Golden, 1981). The individual items in both of these tests seem to work. Also, because the psychological approach has been used successfully in testing for a good many years, it appears to be a legitimate form of testing. Thus, on a practical level, it would seem that it is possible to test individual functions using specific tests of those functions.

Some modification or further application of Luria's theory needs to be developed in order to apply his theory to testing and the quantitative approach. Luria admits that damage in one area of the brain affects the system differently from damage in another area, since different components are impaired. This difference can be detected and measured on tests. More specifically, this theoretical basis for the psychological, or quantitative, approach has at least two parts. The first is derived from an examination of the difference between the qualitative and quantitative approaches, and the second is derived from the concept of components in Luria's functional system.

Quality versus Quantity

From a psychometric perspective, the difference between a qualitative and a quantitative approach to measurement appears to be spurious. An old axiom in measurement theory is that "everything that exists, exists in some quantity." A corollary of this is that any qualitative aspect of brain damage that can be specified or described clearly enough to enable another person to observe it as distinct from other phenomena can be counted and measured. That is, if one can describe something clearly enough to enable another person to observe it, that other person can count it whenever it occurs. Measurement is essentially counting either the instances of something's occurring or the degree of change from one occurrence to another. As such, the essence of quantitative measurement is not different from that of qualitative observation. Another way of putting it is that, from the psychometric point of view, the difference between qualitative and quantitative examination of a subject is simply whether a nominal or another type of scale is used. A qualitative approach simply makes use of nominal scales rather than interval or ratio scales.

Since, from a psychometric point of view, qualitative scales are simply nominal scales, any specifiable qualitative change can be transformed into a quantitative measure. This has been done repeatedly in the history of psychology and neuropsychology. In reference to the HRB, the scoring system for the aphasia cross developed by Russell, Neuringer, and Goldstein (1970) transformed a qualitative method. Previously, the cross had simply been examined visually to determine any qualitative change (Boll, 1981). It became apparent that these qualitative changes ranged in degree of severity and that a scale of severity of impairment could thus be established. The Boston Aphasia Examination (Goodglass & Kaplan, 1983) also illustrates how qualitative effects can be measured by scales, which were incorporated in the construction of the examination for many types of aphasia symptoms.

Qualitative differences among subjects may be quantified in several ways. First, when the qualitative behavior occurs in low frequency, a number of the behaviors related to the same type of damage can be placed in one set. Then the instances can be counted. In high-frequency behaviors, the scale may be constructed to represent the strength of the occurrence of the behavior, for example, by measuring the degree of rotation for block rotation (Satz, 1966a). There are probably many other ways in which to quantify qualitative differences that a neuropsychologist interested in test development can use once the general approach and possibility of quantification is recognized.

System Components

Since Luria's concept of a system appears to be the most adequate theoretical concept of general brain functioning, the problem for psychometric theory is to determine how individual tests can be used to measure parts of such a system. This determination can be made through an examination of the implications of Luria's concept (Luria, 1973). As Luria conceived it, the system itself is composed of many components. Each component is related to a particular area of the brain. A function or piece of behavior is produced when the components are related to each other in a certain manner. Thus, to fully understand a system, one must (1) analyze the system, that is, break it down into its components; and (2) examine the synthesis of the components that constitutes the various relationships in the system.

From a theoretical point of view, the problem Luria has in dealing with a system that cannot be broken into parts is the same problem that holism has in general: there is a tendency in holistic theory for everything to be equivalent to everything else. When one must deal with the whole system and not its components, it is difficult or impossible to analyze the system in order to determine the relationship among components. As a result, in practice when Luria (1973, 1980; Luria & Majovski, 1977) deals with this system, he sets up many individual tests for the different components of this system. Consequently, in practice his system can be analyzed into components.

This analysis, then, becomes a basis for neuropsychological measurement. Luria consistently refers to "elements" (1973, p. 31) of a system, "working zones" (p. 31), "components" (p. 34), and in some cases "elementary functions" (p. 30). The basis for neuropsychological testing is measurement of a component of the entire system. The component of a system involves one working zone; as such, it is an elementary function. Thus an elementary function may be defined as that function which is related to a specific limited area (working zone) of the brain. According to this definition, an elementary function is one that is impaired when a specific, rather limited area of the brain is damaged.

The theory of elementary functions is critical in both experimental and clinical neuropsychology. Until an elementary function has been isolated, adequate studies of the localization of that function cannot be performed. That is, if a test can measure only a compound function, its location in the brain cannot be adequately determined, since compound functions are related to many areas of the brain.

The isolation of an elementary function requires the development of a specific measure for that function. In other words, the further development of neuropsychology depends on test development. Neuropsychology will not advance until there has been further development of tests and testing theory such as is being accomplished in the area of psychometrics and to some extent in experimental neuropsychology.

From a theoretical point of view, the question is: How can an elementary function be isolated from the rest of the system so that it can be studied? There are several methods of isolating parts of a system. First, a particular system does not use the entire brain but selects only parts of the brain as components to that function. For instance, when a person answers a request to define a particular word, that person may not use the right hemisphere at all. Any specific activity selects a certain group of elementary functions as parts of that system, and consequently an examination test may be designed for only part of the functions in the brain. The form of the required examination tasks may reduce the system to relatively few components.

In addition, a particular task required by a test places different stress on different elements in a functional system. That is, through changing the type of task, the stress on the different components in a system may be varied. For example, vision is a component in many functional systems. The visual element in that system may be stressed by giving the person very fine print to read in a graded scale, such as in a visual acuity examination. On the other hand, the amount of stress on the visual components of the system can be reduced by using print large enough so that all but persons with severe visual acuity problems will have no trouble seeing it. In addition, that particular component of the system can be tested individually using an eye examination. If a subject's visual acuity is normal and the print is large, the examination places no stress on visual acuity, and one can disregard the visual component in the system as the cause of any impairment found in testing the individual. Thus a measure constructed to be a specific test of an elementary function should be designed to place stress on the crucial component of the total system and on no other component.

In summary, there are at least three methods of separating an elementary function from a system: (1) isolating a number of elements in the brain, (2) placing stress on a particular elementary or component function of a system, and (3) testing to determine that the other components of the system are functioning normally. This list is probably not exhaustive. Using such methods, a component or elementary function can be individually tested even though it is a part of a total system.

Classification of Neuropsychological Functions

Luria's concept of a system provides a means of classifying functions into three major types. The first type of function has just been discussed: the elementary function, which is related to only one area of the brain. However, most tests require tasks that involve or stress several areas of the brain. Such tests measure complex or compound functions, which involve or stress two or more elementary functions. In practice, a function is defined by the tests used to measure it. How this is done is a problem for test theory and component analysis.

The concept of compound functions has several implications. One of these is that part of test construction and theory consists of breaking down compound functions into their elementary components. Various tests and procedures can be designed to separate the different elementary functions in a compound function. Thus one part of neuropsychology should be devoted to isolating elementary functions, that is, to component analysis.

A second implication is that measures of compound functions are necessary as a part of a general neuropsychological battery. Since compound functions involve several different elementary functions, tests of compound functions cover larger areas of the brain than do tests of elementary functions. Thus a test of a compound function is generally more sensitive to brain damage anywhere in the brain than is a test of an elementary function. A full neuropsychological test battery will require some measures of compound functions as well as elementary functions. The problem with using exclusively tests of elementary functions to measure brain damage is that such tests are sensitive only to damage to particular areas of the brain in chronic brain damage. If the areas of the brain covered by the measures of elementary functions are not damaged, then such tests would not indicate the existence of brain damage.

The third type of function related to Luria's system might be called a general function. A general function is one that is impaired regardless of where the damage occurs in the brain. There is some possibility that general functions may be due to damage to areas of the brain that have general input to all other areas, such as the reticular formation (Luria 1973). The two major functions now commonly recognized to be general in brain damage are mental speed and attention.

The major discussion in the area of neuropsychology theory during the 1950s was whether there was a general effect, as well as specific effects, of brain damage. The consensus of most studies of that time was that both types of effects existed (Satz 1966b; Tueber, 1975; Teuber & Weinstein, 1955, 1958). Subsequently, however, the general effects were not studied to any extent, and neuropsychological theory became almost an exclusive examination of specific effects.

At this point, the distinction needs to be made between a general function and a general effect of brain damage. A general function is a brain function related to all areas of the cerebral cortex such that damage to any area of the brain will affect that function. While *general function* refers to brain functioning, *general effect* of brain damage applies to tests. A general effect is one in which a lesion produces nonspecific impairment on tests related to many areas of the cortex. An impairment to a general function produces a general effect, but a general effect may involve aspects of testing other than impairment of a general function.

It is now clear that there is not one general effect of brain damage but that there are several kinds of general effects. Thus part of the theoretical requirement for understanding brain damage is to separate the different types of general effects and develop measures for each. General effects include impairment of a general function; impairment of a compound function; diaschisis, or distant effects (Smith, 1981); fluidity of functions (Russell, 1980a); and diffuse, or multifocal, brain damage (Smith, 1981). These fairly well-known effects account for the fact that a lesion may produce a general effect or nonspecific impairment of intellectual abilities. There are also some other possibilities that might be mentioned for completeness. One of these is the concept of plasticity (Kolb & Whishaw, 1980). This type of general effect is common with damage that occurs early in the development of the brain. Finally, one might consider the qualitative concept that a person with brain damage shifts from a more abstract way of thinking to a more concrete one (Walsh, 1978). However, abstract thinking may be a form of fluidity. The more common causes of a general effect of brain damage are examined more thoroughly later in this chapter.

Component Analysis

The theoretical understanding that elementary functions are components of a total functional system implies that one concern of neuropsychology should be component analysis. Component analysis (Sternberg, 1977) may be achieved on two different levels. On the purely psychometric level, it is a process through which a particular mental function is analyzed in order to isolate the components of that function. This can be achieved without any direct reference to the brain (Anastasi, 1983; Sternberg, 1979). The second type of component analysis is the direct attempt to show that a particular function is related to only one part of the brain.

In the psychometric, or experimental, approaches to understanding intellectual abilities, there are at present two general schools of thought: the trait school (Anastasi, 1983; Guilford, 1967; Carroll, 1976) and the process school. The rapprochement of trait and process theories occurs with the understanding that each requires the other. That is, to test the elements of a process, the tests of the individual components must be used. These components are traits. On the other hand, measures of traits themselves do not tell how the elements interact with each other. This requires the study of process. Trait theory does not by itself explain the interaction of the elements. Thus, trait theory is needed to isolate the particular elements in the process, and process theory is needed to explain how the traits interact with each other. Carroll (1976) and Guilford (1967) made some attempt to unite these two approaches.

An example of such unification is the concept of memory as being composed of short-term memory, long-term consolidation, long-term storage, and retrieval (Russell, 1981b). Each of these is a separate element in memory and requires separate tests in order to show how it is related to the others. For instance, trait theory has long shown that short-term memory, as indicated by Digit Span, is almost completely uncorrelated with long-term memory, as tested by the Wechsler Memory Scale, figural and logical memory half hour test (Russell, 1981b; 1982b). However, the fact of their separation might mean that they are entirely different kinds of functions and have no relationship. Process theory shows that one is a basic component of the other and that they are parts of the same general process of memory, although as traits they are almost completely unrelated (Russell, 1981b, 1982b).

It should be noted that brain damage is a natural manipulation of mental functions and enables investigators to study both traits and processes. Brain damage, when studied correctly, can be used to isolate elementary functions and can thus clarify the elementary components of a total process and demonstrate a relationship among elements in a process. When brain damage shows clearly that a certain process occurs, theory must account for that process.

DIFFERENTIAL SENSITIVITY OF TESTS

The most common criterion for the validity of a neuropsychological test has been the ability of the test to differentiate patients with brain damage from control patients. This criterion has been used in almost every study designed to validate a test of brain damage. While this criterion seems almost ridiculously obvious, no theoretical basis for this requirement has been given. This criterion assumes that brain damage has a general effect on tests, which is in opposition to the underlying unspoken assumption in the neurological approach to neuropsychology today that there is a one-to-one relationship between specific tissue damage and specific impairment of functions, not a general effect. While almost every neuropsychologist denies this one-to-one relationship assumption in theory, in practice it is the basis of much neuropsychological research. Logically, if brain damage does not produce a generalized effect, the only effect comes from a particular area of the brain that is damaged. If this concept that there is no general effect is correct, the demonstration that brain damage in general impairs a test is meaningless as a criterion. The only valid criterion is the location of a specifically damaged area when a particular test is impaired.

However, almost everyone with actual clinical experience in neuropsychological testing is aware that there are general effects and that some tests tend to be more impaired by brain damage in general than others (Teuber, 1975). This means that the criterion of separating brain-damaged from control patients as a first validity requirement for a test is reasonable.

At present, the theoretical basis for general brain-damaged effects is quite weak. During the early years of psychological neuropsychology—that is, during the 1940s and 1950s—the primary concern of neuropsychologists was with the general effect of brain damage. This was a period of holism in which it was felt that because the brain as a whole is affected by brain damage, one would expect a general effect. Beginning in the 1950s, the concepts concerning brain damage changed so that neuropsychologists expected each type of brain damage to produce a different kind of effect. It became popular to state that there is "no such thing as brain damage." Consequently, at the present time, there appears to be a general psychological rejection of any theory concerned with the general effects of brain damage. Yet various kinds of general effects are partly responsible for the different effects of different types of lesions.

Luria's work provided an example of such rejection. Luria himself was not particularly interested in any kind of damage except focal damage. He stated that "neuropsychology has become an investigative tool in the diagnosis of local brain lesions" (Luria & Majovski, 1977, p. 962). Examination of Luria's writing shows that he did not study diffuse brain damage to any extent, nor did he study diagnostic patterns with coordinated groups of tests. According to the principle of testing given earlier that the correct testing procedure is needed in order to observe a particular effect of a brain lesion, his testing method was simply not adapted to deal with generalized effects of brain damage. This kind of testing requires graded scales used in coordinated groups. Luria's methods were adapted to studying the effects of rather severe focal lesions. However, for most practicing clinical neuropsychologists, the bulk of the patients they see are neither severely damaged, nor is the damage focal. Probably the type of patient Luria describes in his books would account for less than one-fourth of the total patients tested in usual neuropsychological practice in the United States.

One of the theoretical contributions of psychometric testing not recognized in the neurological approach is the realization that brain damage *does* produce generalized effects as well as focal effects (Satz, 1966; Teuber, 1975; Teuber & Weinstein, 1955). A well-known effect that is recognized by those using a coordinated battery of graded scales is that *in acute focal lesions, the areas of severe impairment are almost always embedded in a background of general impairment of brain functioning*. Luria and people who follow the neurological approach appear to be unaware of this background impairment. Luria and Majovski (1977) have stated, in regard to focal lesions, that "other forms of activities in which this factor is not included remain intact" (p. 965). Much the same thing has been said by other people using neurological approaches, for instance, Christensen (1979). It is inconceivable that Luria and other such neuropsychologists were unaware of these generalized effects. However, evidently the general effects did not form a part of their theory and consequently were not used.

One of the results of the general lack of interest in the general effects of brain damage has been the failure of neuropsychologists to differentiate among types of general effects. Several of these general effects will now be presented, along with their implications and different relationships to testing.

General Functions

One type of general effect is produced by impairment of a general function. Probably the most accepted general function is that of mental or psychomotor speed. Speed is an element in many psychological tests that measure brain damage. Tests such as the Digit Symbol and Trail-making tests both require high levels of mental speed. Since mental speed is generally impaired in brain damage, any test with speed as a requirement will usually be impaired. This is one component that makes the Digit Symbol Test (Lezak, 1983; Russell, 1979) and Trail-making Test B (Lezak, 1983; Spreen & Benton, 1965) among the most sensitive to brain damage.

Some neuropsychologists have felt that all general effects are produced by impairment of mental speed. The effects of aging have been considered to be due to a reduction in mental speed as one ages (Botwinick, 1977). However, using the WAIS, it has been demonstrated that even without the speed element, older patients still have more trouble with many of the performance tests than they did with the verbal tests (Botwinick, 1977). The effect of mental speed on tests can be eliminated to a certain extent by using power tests rather than speed tests. Most memory tests are power tests in that there are no time limits for recall of material once the recall has started. Nevertheless, memory tests are quite vulnerable to the effects of aging (Haaland, Linn, Hunt, & Goodwin, 1983; McCarthy, Logue, Power, Ziesat, & Rosensteil, 1980).

Fluidity

A second type of general effect is related more to the type of test material presented than to a general function. This effect is related to the concept of fluidity. In the early 1930s, it was discovered that some tests were more sensitive to brain damage in general than others (Babcock, 1930). This finding became the central concept of neuropsychology during the 1940s and early 1950s. In the 1940s, four different psychologists proposed theories derived from this differential sensitivity. Hebb (1941, 1949) proposed the theory that there were two kinds of intelligence, A and B. Cattell (1943) discussed fluid and crystallized intelligence. Halstead (1947) described the difference between the psychometric and biological intelligence, and, finally, Wechsler (1945) developed his deterioration scale. Since Cattell (1943) and later Horn (1966, 1976) developed this concept most completely in their theory of fluid and crystallized intelligence, recent work has generally accepted their terms. While not widely used in neuropsychology at present, the concept of fluidity, or of fluid and crystallized intelligence, has recently gained wide acceptance in the geriatric study of brain functioning (Botwinick, 1977; Hayslip & Sterns, 1979).

The basis of this theory is that functions requiring active processing by the brain (fluid intelligence) are more affected by brain damage in general than are well-learned functions (crystallized intelligence) (Reed & Reitan, 1963a, 1963b). The less a function requires "thinking out" a solution to a problem and the more it relies on previously learned material, the more crystallized that ability becomes and the more resistant it is to the effects of brain damage and aging (Finlayson, 1977). Reed and Reitan (1963a, 1963b) used the term *adaptive ability* rather than *fluid ability*. It should be noted that factor analysis by Horn (1976) has differentiated other general factors besides fluid and crystallized abilities, such as mental speed and visualization. However, from the point of view of examining brain impairment, the crystallized versus fluid intelligence distinction is particularly important.

Historically, almost all of the psychological or psychometric clinical neuropsychological tests have utilized this concept of fluidity, that is, differential sensitivity to brain damage. The primary criterion of whether a measure is related to brain damage has been to determine whether the particular measure strongly separates patients who have brain damage from those who do not. This criterion utilized the theory that some functions are more impaired by brain damage than others, which is essentially the theory of fluidity.

However, this criterion is often overused in selection of tests for a neuropsychological battery. In a full battery tests that are not sensitive to brain damage are needed as a comparison to those with high sensitivity. One of the earliest tests of brain damage, the Shipley Institute of Living Scale (Shipley, 1940), was based on this comparison. The Hunt-Minnesota Test for Organic Brain Damage (Hunt, 1943) was also based on this concept.

In order to understand the pattern produced by different forms of brain damage, one needs to understand not only the effects of focality but also the effects of fluidity. A

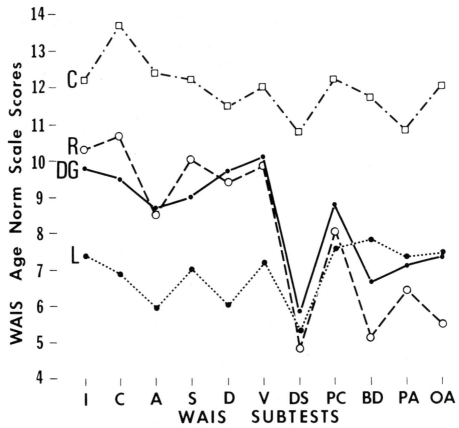

Figure 3.3. WAIS subtest mean profiles using age norms for control subjects and three types of brain damage (C, controls; DG, degenerative diffuse damage; R, right hemisphere damage; L, left hemisphere damage).

study of Russell (1979) of the patterns on the WAIS demonstrates that both these principles interact to produce several different patterns. The results of this study are provided in Figure 3.3. This study found that the pattern of diffuse damage looks very much like the pattern produced by right hemisphere damage. Left hemisphere damage produced a pattern in which there is not much difference between impairment to verbal abilities and impairment to performance abilities.

In this study, four groups of 40 patients each, representing control, right-hemisphere–damaged, left-hemisphere–damaged, and diffusely damaged patients were matched and compared. They showed three different patterns on the WAIS. These patterns were evidently produced by the interaction between the lateralization effect and the fluidity effect. Since most of the performance tests are both right hemisphere and fluid abilities tests, right hemisphere damage looks like diffuse degenerative damage, which affects fluid abilities more than crystallized abilities. On the other hand, verbal tests of the WAIS are both crystallized and left hemisphere tests. Consequently, left hemisphere damage tends to cancel out these effects, resulting in only a mild reduction in the verbal abilities for left hemisphere lesions compared to the effect of right hemisphere lesions.

The ideal neuropsychology battery would contain tests of both fluid and crystallized functions as well as tests of elementary functions related to each area of the cortex. In fact, focal damage is more accurately measured by tests that are crystallized, since these are generally less sensitive to distant effects than are fluid tests.

Today, a full brain damage battery must do much more than simply determine whether a person has brain damage. Consequently it should contain many tests of relatively crystallized functions, which are rather insensitive to brain damage. For instance, the tapping test in the HRB is not highly sensitive to brain damage in general (Lazek, 1983), but it is highly sensitive to the effects of lateralization (Reitan, 1964). Consequently, its contribution to a full battery of tests is this sensitivity to lateralization, not an ability to separate brain damage from normal subjects.

Distant Effects

Probably the most accepted general effect of brain damage is what has been called a distant effect. This may be due to diaschisis (Kolb & Whishaw, 1980; Teuber, 1975). Diaschisis is one of the major effects that Smith (1975, 1981) has called to the attention of neuropsychologists. The principle of distant effects is that an acute or progressive focal lesion impairs functions in undamaged tissue at a distance from the area of actual tissue damage. Teuber (1975) called such an effect override. There is some question as to the cause of this distant effect. While in some cases it is probably produced by edema or compression, diaschisis is evidently a major contributor (Smith, 1975; Teuber, 1975). The concept of diaschisis holds that there is an effect of damaged tissue on other distant nondamaged tissue beyond that produced by compression and edema. Diaschisis may be related to what has been called the shock effect in spinal shock or to spreading cortical depression in the brain (Kolb & Whishaw, 1980; Teuber, 1975).

It is part of clinical lore that a battery with graded scales almost always finds that functions at a distance from the actual area of tissue damage are impaired in acute and progressive cases. The impairment appears to be greater close to the area of tissue damage and gradually becomes less as one proceeds away from the area of damage. There is also the question of whether diaschisis crosses white matter and, if so, whether the effect is not greatly attenuated (Smith, 1975). In any case, this effect has hardly been recognized and obviously has not been well studied. The effect is well illustrated in Luria's *The Working Brain* (1973) in a diagram (p. 136) showing the effects on the speech area of lesions in various distant parts of the brain. Interestingly, Luria discusses this concept in his book at only one point (p. 104).

Distant effects apparently impair fluid functions to a considerably greater extent than crystallized functions. Usually, the more sensitive a test is to brain damage in general, the more easily it is impaired by distant lesions. This, of course, is one aspect of fluidity that makes fluid functions better indicators of brain damage in general but worse indicators of focality. The opposite is true for crystallized functions, which are poor indicators of brain damage in general but better indicators of the locus of a lesion.

Chronicity Effect

A related type of effect is what may be called the chronicity effect (Russell, 1981a). In the chronicity effect, as a resolving lesion becomes chronic, the distant effects gradually recede so that there is a return of functions in areas that do not have tissue damage. This means that in an acute lesion, the distant effects are quite strong, especially for fluid functions, whereas in a lesion that is a year or more old, the distant effects may have all but disappeared. In the chronic lesion, there may be a sharp separation in impairment between the functions related to the area of tissue damage and those functions for areas outside the area of damage. For elementary functions, this produces a "punch card" effect, in which functions related to damaged areas are impaired, while functions related to undamaged areas are normal. However, while the elementary functions outside the area damaged generally return to a normal level, the compound functions that have components related to the area of damage will be impaired by a chronic lesion.

While only a moderate amount of research has been done on the chronicity effect, it is fairly well known to people using the psychological approach. Several studies have generally substantiated the chronicity effect, including studies of the WAIS by Bond (1975); aphasia by Kertesz (1979); dyslexia by Newcombe, Hiorns, Marshall, and Adams (1975); and long-term effects on many measures by Teuber (1975). In the chronicity effect, there is overall a rapid improvement at first that lasts about three months, which is followed by a longer period of slower recovery from three months to a year. Some recovery may continue for several years for some conditions. These studies also demonstrated that rates and even patterns of recovery may vary greatly for different conditions or different types of abilities. There was also some support for the punch card effect in chronic damage (Teuber, 1975). Functions in the area directly damaged by a lesion seldom completely recovered, whereas distant functions tended to recover more fully. Kertesz (1979) also reviewed the literature in this area, which appeared to be generally in agreement with the chronicity effect.

In regard to general intelligence, Bond (1975) found exactly what is predicted by the chronicity effect. Recovery of WAIS functions occurred at a decelerating speed, but the performance items (fluid intelligence) took longer to recover than the verbal (crystallized intelligence) skills. In fact the performance IQ may continue to improve for several years (Mandleberg & Brooks, 1975).

A study by Russell (1981a) also illustrates the chronicity effect. In this study, a patient with a focal lesion due to herpesencephalitis was tested five times over a period of six years. The results are given in Figure 3.4. The area of major damage was in the left occipitoparietal region and so produced an impairment of reading ability. In agreement with the findings of Kertesz (1979) and of Newcombe and colleagues (1975), Figure 3.4 demonstrates that within about 16 months all functions not related to reading ability had returned to normal; however, the patient's reading ability remained permanently impaired.

It has long been known that the pattern of impairment on such tests as the WAIS is different for acute lesions than for chronic lesions (Fitzhugh, Fitzhugh, & Reitan, 1962). Acute lesions produce a strong lateralized effect on the Wechsler tests, whereas chronic lesions do not show such an effect. This difference between the verbal and performance abilities on the Wechsler tests for recently and chronically brain-damaged patients can be explained if one assumes that the lateralized impairments are primarily due to distant effects. That is, relatively few patients in most studies have severe lesions directly in the area that would badly impair particular tests on the WAIS. Rather, most of the impairment in recent or acute brain damage is due to distant effects. As the distant effects disappear, there would be a return to a normal balance between verbal

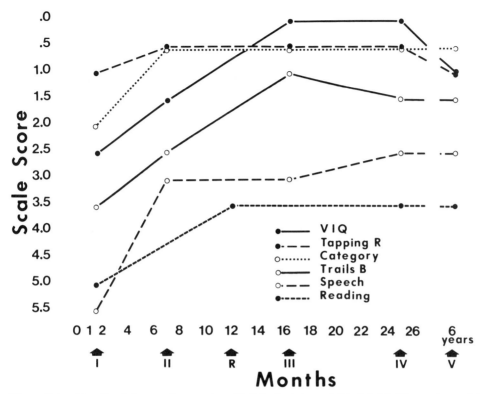

Figure 3.4. Results of six tests for a patient (F. B.) administered 1½, 7½, 16, 25 months, and 6 years after illness. One WRAT Reading Test was given at 12 months. The Verbal IQ (VIQ) was arbitrarily assigned scale score values. VIQs extended from 88 to 110. Other tests described are Halstead Tapping Test, Halstead Category Test, Trail-making Test B, and Speech Perception Test.

and nonverbal abilities. This change was found with the case reported above (Russell, 1981a).

Diffuse Brain Damage

A fairly large proportion of the types of brain damage that neuropsychologists see in practice are not those with focal lesions but those with either multifocal or diffuse forms of brain damage. Such brain damage includes head trauma, cerebral arteriosclerosis, and the degenerative diseases, such as Alzheimer's disease and normal-pressure hydrocephalus.

In such cases, the general effect of brain damage is produced by the diffuse form of the brain damage itself. Nevertheless, the patterns of diffuse damage appear to vary from one form of damage to another and are not due to either fluidity or impairment of a general function, though both may contribute. This variation appears to be due to the interaction of the agent causing the damage with the other factors that produce generalized effects of damage. An example is that Alzheimer's disease, a diffuse degenerative disease, tends to affect fluid abilities much more than crystallized abilities.

On the other hand, apparently neither head trauma nor cerebral arteriosclerosis affects brain functions purely on the basis of how fluid the function being tested is.

At this point, the relationship between tests of memory and these different types of generalized effects is largely uninvestigated. Apparently, many types of damage that affect fluidity strongly, such as Alzheimer's disease (Barbizet, 1970) and chronic alcoholism (Russell, 1981b), produce rather severe impairment of recent memory (the consolidation of long-term memory), while leaving immediate memory and long-term storage only mildly affected. On the Revised Wechsler Memory Scale, the figural memory test appears to be somewhat more influenced by diffuse degenerative types of damage than does the test containing verbal, logical memory stories (Haaland, Linn, Hunt, & Goodwin, 1983). What sometimes appears to be lateralization to the right hemisphere is evidently merely a greater sensitivity of the figural memory test to diffuse damage. This observation appears to be in line with the fluidity effect, although it is difficult to say that one type of memory is more fluid than another. The effects of head trauma on memory have been well studied and are fairly well known (Russell, 1981b). By contrast, the effects of cerebral arteriosclerosis, although recognized as impairing memory, are not well known.

PATTERN ANALYSIS OR SYNTHESIS

Since Halstead's (1947) pioneering work, neuropsychologists of all persuasions tend to use groups, or batteries, of tests (Boll, 1981) in their examination processes. The controversy does not concern whether to use batteries of tests but, rather, whether to use a set battery or a flexible battery (Lezak, 1984; Russell, 1984). In spite of this widespread use of batteries, the theory behind the use of a battery is only vaguely formulated. Halstead (1947) and Reitan (1955) felt that the accuracy of diagnosing brain damage was increased when a number of tests were used. Apparently, since various tests have different sensitivities to different kinds of organic conditions, the ability to pick up all types of brain damage is increased when a variety of tests is utilized. The overall score from a battery of tests acts as a compound function and so is sensitive to damage in all areas of the brain as well as to various types of general effects.

While these reasons for using a battery are both necessary and rather obvious when the problem is merely assessing the existence of an organic condition, the full assessment of brain damage effects requires a more complex theoretical basis. In a full assessment, various tests are compared to each other in order to isolate a pattern of results indicating the type and location of the condition. The basis for such a comparison is Teuber's double dissociation of symptoms (Christensen, 1984; Kolb & Whishaw, 1980; Luria, 1973; Teuber, 1955). The concept of a double dissociation of symptoms—or, in psychometric terms, double dissociation of test results—is fairly well accepted in experimental neuropsychology. However, a well-designed test battery should also be structured according to the concept of double dissociation of measures (Luria, 1973) or multiple dissociation of measures. Since Teuber's concept is so crucial for both experimental and clinical neuropsychology, it will be explained in some length here.

In neuropsychology, there are two forms of single dissociation of test results: by area and by test (see Table 3.1). In a dissociation by area, a test, A, is thought to be related to a particular area if that test is impaired by damage to that area and not by damage to other areas. For instance, in Table 3.1, if test A is impaired with patients who have right hemisphere damage and not impaired with patients who have left hemisphere damage, test A is thought to be a test of the right hemisphere. The major problem with this single dissociation is that the amount of damage may simply be greater in the right hemisphere sample than in the left. Thus the test reflects the severity of the lesion and not the locality of damage.

The second form of single dissociation is a dissociation by test. If test A is more impaired than test B by right hemisphere damage, then it can be said that test A is more of a right hemisphere test than is test B. This combination eliminates the problem of a greater amount of damage in one area, since both tests are given to people with damage in the same area. However, the difficulty with this type of dissociation is that test A may simply be more sensitive to brain damage in general than test B. Thus, if you gave these two tests to patients with diffuse damage, test A would be more impaired than test B. This, of course, is the problem with the difference between fluid and crystallized abilities. Apparently the difference between impairment of various tests on the WAIS with brain-damaged patients may often be due to fluidity rather than to lateralization (Russell, 1979, 1980a).

Double dissociation occurs when two tests are found to be differentially impaired by damage in two areas of the brain. For instance, in Table 3.1, test A and test B are related to the right and left hemispheres of the brain. Double dissociation occurs when test A and not test B is impaired by lesions on the right hemisphere while test B but not A is impaired by lesions in the left hemisphere. Thus, in such a case, it is clear that test A is measuring a function in the right hemisphere while test B is measuring a function in the left hemisphere. This may be clearly seen in Table 3.1.

In clinical usage, this dissociation is reversed (Christensen, 1984). Thus, two tests that have been related by experimentation to different areas of the brain become the means of assessing the location of damage. For instance, with the two tests A and B above, once their relationship to lateralization in the brain is known, the laterality of a

Table 3.1.   Double and Multiple Dissociation Used in Research and Clinical Practice

| Type of Dissociation | Research Area | | | |
	R		L	
By area		A↓	B↑	
By test	A↓	B↑		
Double	A↓	B↑	A↑	B↓

| Type of Damage | Clinical Practice, Multiple Dissociation | | | |
	RF	RP	LF	LP
R lateralized	A↓	B↓	C↑	D↑
RF focal	A↓	B↑	C↑	D↑
Diffuse	A↓	B↓	C↓	D↓
Normal	A↑	B↑	C↑	D↑

NOTE: A, B, C, D = tests. For clinical practice, it has been established that test A is related to the right frontal area (RF), test B to the right posterior area (RP), test C to the left frontal area (LF), and test D to the left posterior area (LP). ↓ = impaired, ↑ = not impaired.

lesion can be diagnosed. In Table 3.1, using more tests (A, B, C, D) in which A is related to the right frontal area, B to the right posterior, C to the left frontal, and D to the left posterior, the focality of the lesion can be refined to the right frontal area, if A is impaired and B, C, and D are not. If A and B are impaired and C and D are not, then the lesion is right hemisphere. By contrast, if C and D are impaired and A and B are not, the lesion is in the left hemisphere. If neither A, B, C, nor D are impaired, there is no brain damage, and if A, B, C, and D are all impaired, there is diffuse brain damage. While these examples are simplified, they do demonstrate how a battery of tests can be used.

A whole battery of tests can be used to assess the multiple dissociations of functions only after the tests have been matched to particular areas of the brain or to particular types of functions, such as fluid or crystallized. With such knowledge, a neuropsychologist may be able to determine not only the location of damage but the type of damage (Reitan, 1964). For example, in the previously discussed (Russell, 1979) analysis of the Wechsler Intelligence Scale using different groups of patients, three patterns of impairment found were related to four kinds of brain damage or lack of brain damage. See Figure 3.2.

The inferential use of test batteries that have not been formally coordinated so as to provide scale scores, such as the traditional method of analyzing the HRB (Boll, 1981), applies the same principles. In fact, Luria (1973), using the neurological approach, also employs this method. However, in this case, the coordination is based on the neuropsychologist's long aquaintance with the subtests. The examiner knows what amount of impairment on one test is equivalent to a particular amount on another test. In this way, experienced examiners can compare two or more tests "in their heads." The problem with this method is that it requires long experience to build the mental norms, and it is often difficult to communicate the thinking involved to students or researchers who want to learn or verify inferential patterns.

A formally coordinated battery of tests must meet several requirements, which can be derived from the theory just presented. The first requirement is the utilization of scale scores with a rather wide range. As explained earlier, this is necessary because the amount of impairment of abilities tests in the area of neuropsychology is greater than that expected for the normal population. The use of scale scores provides a way of comparing various tests, thus increasing the sensitivity of the tests to varying impairments and increasing their ability to assess subtle patterns.

Second, the scales must be homogenous. If a scale is heterogeneous, one does not know which of the component functions being measured is in fact impaired. Such scales cannot be meaningful when compared to each other.

The third requirement is coordination of tests, or simultaneous norming; that is, all of the scales need to be normed together on one population to ensure that the scale scores are equivalent to each other. Norming that is done for different tests on different populations leaves open the question as to whether these scales scores are in fact equivalent.

Comparison of the recent norms derived for the revised Wechsler Memory Scale (Haaland, Linn, Hunt, & Goodwin, 1983; McCarthy, Logue, Power, Ziesat, & Rosenteil, 1980) demonstrates this difference. The various studies have found somewhat different norms for this test, which has six subtests. If each subtest had been normed in a different study, there would be no way to determine whether the differences between scales were due to differences in the scales or to different norming populations. As it is, the differences found in the study of Haaland and colleagues (1983) between subtests clearly represent differences between tests, since the norming used one population and the same standards for scoring. Overall, Haaland's norms may be somewhat lower than those found in other settings, since she apparently used very strict criteria for determining errors. Nevertheless, the differences between subtests are not due to differences in norming procedures.

The last requirement for a battery of neuropsychological tests that is derived from the concept of simultaneous norming is that of a set battery. If the battery changes with each patient tested, no simultaneous norming can be done. Thus, at least for the norming procedure, a set battery is required. Also, the patterns used in various indexes (Russell, 1984) or keys (Russell, 1975; Russell, Neuringer, & Goldstein, 1970; Selz & Reitan, 1979) are based on a certain set of tests. As such, they cannot be used except with a set battery. This is often true for inferential assessment of patients. For a clinician who is familiar with a set battery of tests, missing tests often produce considerable uncertainty in the inferential process due to a lack of crucial tests or a lack of confirming redundancy (Russell, 1984).

Methods of Pattern Analysis

The methods of pattern analysis are just beginning to be developed in neuropsychology. Many of these are like the methods that have been used with the Minnesota Multiphasic Personality Inventory (MMPI) (Dalstrom & Welsh, 1960; Kleinmutz, 1968). A number of types of indexes have been developed. They represent a way of abstracting information from complex data. The earliest forms of indexes were additive or averaging indexes. The Halstead index (1947) and the Rennick index (Russell, 1984; Russell, Neuringer, & Goldstein, 1970) are examples of this.

Another form of index is the comparison index, which is based on the concept of double dissociation. The indexes compare several tests and develop a score that states a relationship between tests. A complex comparison index has recently been developed by Russell (1984). It places the lateralization key (Russell, Neuringer, & Goldstein, 1970) into an index form so that the amount of lateralized damage is indicated by a single index number. Lateralization indexes, about five of which have been devised (Russell, 1984), are generally ratios.

The most developed form of index that has been created up to this point is probably the key method devised by Russell (Russell, Neuringer, & Goldstein, 1970). This index is basically an algorithm that subdivides a group of patients on the basis of specific test results until a patient can be assigned to a single category. The original key would separate normal from brain-damaged subjects and then separate brain damage into right, left, and diffuse types. There was also a key that separates damage into acute and static types. The lateralization key has held up well, whereas the process key has been somewhat less successful (Anthony, Heaton, & Lehman, 1980; Goldstein & Shelly, 1982). This key method has been placed into a sophisticated computer program by Goldstein and Shelly (Matthews, 1981).

Despite the existence of these indexes, the primary method of recognizing a pattern is still inferential. Different types of damage, as well as damage in different areas, produce varying patterns in complex batteries of tests. People who are familiar with the batteries have learned to recognize such patterns. Reitan and his followers have been particularly well known for their ability to recognize such patterns (Reitan, 1964). However, few of these methods of recognizing patterns have been published, and consequently they have not been verified. Reitan recognized early that the patterns are often rather subtle and that gross summaries of test results tend to "wash out" the subtle patterns (Reitan, 1964). Due to this subtlety and a lack of publications, few of these inferential patterns have been verified, and most remain part of neuropsychological lore.

Computer Programs

The most recent development in neuropsychological testing is the computerization of various elements of testing. The computer programs vary from Goldstein and Shelly's program, which is quite sophisticated, utilizing the entire HRB (Matthews, 1981), to several relatively simple analyses of the Wechsler Intelligence Scales. Without examining this area in depth, a warning should be given at this point. Computer analysis is to an extent a fad, but one that will undoubtedly give rise to good lasting programs and a new way of analyzing data. The warning is one that is already standard for computer work in other areas, but it applies particularly strongly to neuropsychology. It is the GIGO admonition: "garbage in, garbage out." What this means is that the results one obtains from the most sophisticated computer program are no better than the information fed into the machine. In regard to neuropsychology, this means that computer programs cannot take the place of good test development. This development is the basis for all neuropsychological analysis. Poor tests, even put together in the most sophisticated computer program, produce poor results. The difficulty is that the very sophisticated-looking computer printout can give the appearance of validity when in fact there is none.

Battery Construction

In constructing a battery of neuropsychological tests, one faces several problems, including those of efficiency, coverage, and validity. The problems related to validity are so extensive and so often discussed that they will not be examined here. The problem of efficiency is compounded by the problems of coverage and test length. The problems of efficiency and coverage can be discussed separately, although they are related. In order to illustrate how a battery can be composed on theoretical grounds, two batteries are also discussed. These batteries apply to two areas of neuropsychology in which the theoretical basis is relatively well known: aphasia and memory.

Paradox of Efficiency

The longer the individual tests are in a battery, the fewer are the tests that can be given but the more reliable are the results. For this reason, the problem of efficiency catches the designer of a neuropsychological battery in a three-way conflict among accuracy, coverage, and brevity of administration. A battery may have any two of these characteristics but not all three. For instance, Christensen's battery (1975) covers a large number of functions and areas of the brain but lacks accuracy in the measurement of the individual functions, since it uses brief all-or-none tests. Brief batteries, such as that of Erickson, Calsyn, and Scheupbach (1978), which is composed of four tests selected from the HRB and WAIS, lack coverage while retaining accuracy.

Most traditional neuropsychological batteries, whether the HRB or those proposed by Lezak (1983) or Smith (1975), require many hours to administer a fairly large number of relatively long scales. They provide an accurate measure of many different functions. However, the sacrifice is made in brevity.

There appears to be almost no way around the fact that good coverage and accuracy in measurement requires time. The Luria Nebraska Battery (Golden, 1981) attempts to overcome this problem by containing many items scored according to brief, nominal or plus-minus scales. The items are then placed into 14 scales. As in Christensen's original version (1975), the individual items cover a large area and a large number of functions in the brain but in an inaccurate manner. In the NLB, the individual scales are heterogeneous, and their meaning is at best only roughly related to a general area or function. The battery as a whole appears to be a fairly good measure of the existence of brain damage (Shelly & Goldstein, 1982) due to its wide coverage; however, its ability to accurately measure specific functions in various areas is questionable. For this reason, at best it should be considered a screening test rather than full-scale battery for neuropsychological testing (Lezak, 1983).

Coverage

Adequate coverage in a neuropsychological test battery requires sampling of functions so as to include measures from all areas of the cerebral cortex as well as all major mental functions. Sampling of areas is based on the neurological concepts of which functions are related to which areas. Since elementary functions have a relatively direct relationship to a single area of the cortex, the test battery should have tests for known elementary functions in each area or lobe. The areas of the brain whose functions are more completely known can be more completely covered. For instance, there should be tests to cover speech areas in finer detail than right hemisphere functions. The Boston Aphasia Test (Goodglass & Kaplan, 1983) and the Western Aphasia Test (Kertesz, 1979) are models for coverage of these areas. The textbooks in neuropsychology (Filskov & Boll, 1981; Kolb & Whishaw, 1980; Walsh, 1978) and chapters in these books (Filskov, Grimm & Lewis, 1981) provide the general theory necessary for selecting tests.

The problem of covering functions is less direct than that of covering areas. According to the theory presented here, at least three further considerations shape the selection of tests: (1) functions that have not been related to an area of the brain, (2) compound functions, and (3) the fluidity of functions. Many identified functions have no known correspondence to areas. In memory, for instance, the areas related to long-term storage are not known. Since immediate memory and long-term memory consolidation are evidently separate types of memory (Milner, Corkin & Teuber, 1968), there should be separate tests for each of them. Also, although both verbal, immediate memory, as measured by the Digit Span, and calculations ability are thought to be in approximately the same area of the brain (Warrington, Logue, & Pratt, 1971; Walsh, 1978), they should be measured separately because the two are quite distinct types of functions.

Some tests of compound functions need to be included in a battery as indicators of the existence and severity of brain damage in general. Since many functions are covered by tests of compound functions, this information can be obtained more efficiently using a compound function than through the use of many tests of elementary functions. Also, for practical purposes, at the present time there may be no known tests of elementary functions for some areas covered by a compound function. Finally, the concept of fluidity needs to be taken into consideration in selecting tests. Fluid ability tests are more sensitive to organic impairment than are crystallized abilities tests, and they measure the type of functions that involve judgment and thinking. These functions may be badly impaired by slowly progressive diffuse types of damage before the impairment is recognized in everyday activities, since crystallized functions are not yet impaired to any great extent. In such cases, a person's business or professional judgment may slip before his or her knowledge of an area is effected. On the other hand, crystallized functions are less impaired by distant effects and so provide a better measure of focality. They also provide an indication of how a person is functioning in well-learned activities. Finally, the comparison of fluid to crystallized abilities provides the most accurate measure of brain damage. There may be a large difference between performance on Vocabulary (crystallized ability) and Block Design (fluid ability) Tests, indicating an early stage in a progressive degenerative disease, when the person's verbal and full-scale IQ are still well over 100. Thus both fluid and crystallized abilities tests should be included in the battery.

Aphasia

A number of batteries for aphasia are in use. The advantage of the Boston Aphasia Test (Goodglass & Kaplan, 1983) and the Western Aphasia Test (Kertesz, 1979) for neuropsychology is that they are designed on the basis of the neuropsychological concepts of aphasia. More exactly, the theory supporting these tests is the theory proposed by Wernicke and Geschwind (Kolb & Whishaw, 1980). The tests on the Boston Aphasia examination were selected in order to cover all types of aphasia according to that theory. The Wernicke-Geschwind theory relates different types of aphasia to different areas of the brain. For instance, expressive aphasia is related to the Broca's area, in the left frontal lobe, whereas receptive aphasia is related to Wernicke's area. The tests were then designed to cover all of the areas of the brain that are related to aphasia. In addition, tests of different types of aphasia, even though related to the same area, were also selected. Thus, a thorough coverage was obtained for all major types of aphasia. Scale scores were derived for each subtest and profiled on a percentile-score profile so that the impairment in one area could be directly compared to another area. This enables the examiner to determine which type of aphasia and/or areas are most impaired. Thus, an area related to a focal lesion, as well as the type of aphasia, may be determined for such purposes as localization of damage or rehabilitative speech training.

Memory Battery

The selection of tests to be placed in the memory battery should be designed to follow existing theory of memory. One form of this theory was summarized recently (Russell, 1981b). The attempt is to obtain as complete a coverage as possible of all the general types of memory that have been identified and the areas of brain related to memory.

Since some types of memory have been related to different areas of the brain, these two aims can often be accomplished without duplication of tests. The left hemisphere is generally related to verbal memory, whereas the right hemisphere is concerned with nonverbal or figural memory. Thus a test battery should be designed so that, for every type of memory process, there will be a pair of similar tests, one verbal and one figural.

The tests should be selected to represent the different types of memory processes that are known, both verbal and figural. For short-term memory in the verbal area, the Digit Span Test is the traditional test (Russell, 1981b; Kolb & Whishaw, 1980). The test related to figural short-term memory that has become widely accepted is the Corsi Block Board Test (Russell, 1981b; Kolb & Whishaw, 1980). Long-term memory has at least three aspects (Russell, 1981b): (1) a consolidation process, which neurologists call recent memory; (2) long-term storage, which involves material that has been in memory for a number of years (remote memory); and (3) interference with learning by other tasks, especially if these are similar in nature. In regard to long-term memory consolidation, several aspects are involved. Recall of both verbal and figural material can be measured by the revised Wechsler Memory Scale (Russell, 1979, 1982b, 1985).

Recognition can be tested in several ways. One way is through the Recurring Words and Figures Tests (Kimura, 1963; Milner, 1971). In this test, subjects look at a long series of words or figures and simply state which ones they have seen previously. The test also examines the ability to determine sequence of words and figures by having the person state how far back in the list the person saw the word or figure. The ability to recognize that a word or figure that has been previously presented is a posterior function, whereas the ability to tell how far back in the list the word or figure was presented is a frontal function. A test of verbal categorized learning is the Auditory Verbal Learning Test (Buschke & Fuld, 1974). In this test, a list of 15 words is read, and then the subject recalls as many of the words as possible. Four trials of reading and recall are done to determine the amount of learning with each trial. This procedure could be used for figural as well as verbal material, although a figural form of this test has not yet been developed. Another aspect of memory that needs to be examined is the effect of interference from other learned material. This is also tested by the Auditory-Verbal Learning Test by interposing another list of words to learn between the fifth and sixth trial.

Finally, long-term memory storage needs to be measured. Several tests for long-term memory have been developed. Some are based on knowledge of events seen on television shows (Harvey & Crovitz, 1979; Squire & Slater, 1975). The person is asked to identify names of major TV shows of the last several decades. A figural form of this test is the Facial Recognition Test, or the famous faces test (Albert, Butters, & Levin, 1972). In this test, pictures of famous people from the past are presented. This group of tests is certainly not definitive, and other batteries have been developed (Matthews, 1981); however, it provides an example of how a battery could be developed.

SUMMARY

This chapter has attempted to develop and explicate several theoretical bridges that connect psychometric theory with neuropsychology. These bridges provide the theoretical basis for the psychological approach to neuropsychology. The first principle for these bridge theories was that, in order to know that a function exists, an appropriate testing procedure is needed. Second, graded scales are required for neuropsychological testing of the association areas of the cortex, since graded scales are isomorphic with the way in which the cerebral cortex association areas process information. Third, Luria's concept of a functional system can be the basis for understanding the relationship between brain functioning and specific neuropsychological measures. The "components" of his system are in fact elementary functions of the brain that can be tested. Fourth, the differential sensitivity of various tests to brain damage in general is due to the general effects of brain damage. Several of these types of general effects were explicated, along with some of the interactions among such general effects and elementary functions. Fifth, the basis for a neuropsychological test battery was shown to be compound function testing and Teuber's double dissociation of symptoms or functions used with elementary functions.

The development of a coordinated test battery requires adequate coverage of the areas of the brain and of cognitive functions, homogeneous scales, and simultaneous norming. Such a battery would be both thorough and accurate. The paradox of efficiency was also discussed. There is an opposition between three requirements of battery construction: brevity, accuracy, and coverage. The paradox is that a battery may be designed to fulfill any two of these, but not all three.

From this discussion, it is clear that there is a theoretical foundation for clinical neuropsychology. This foundation is now adequate, though obviously incomplete. As such, it becomes the basis for test interpretation, improving existing batteries, and developing new batteries of neuropsychological tests. The theory itself enables the construction of criteria for determining the adequacy of a neuropsychological test battery. This theory at best represents only the beginning of theory development in psychological neuropsychology. However, it demonstrates that such theory does exist and that the psychological approach to neuropsychology has progressed considerably beyond its empirical beginnings.

REFERENCES

Albert, M. S., Butters, N. & Levin J. (1972). Memory for remote events in chronic alcoholics and alcoholic Korsakoff patients. In H. Begleiter & M. Kissen (Eds.), *Alcoholic intoxication and withdrawal* (pp. 201–209). New York: Plenum.

American Psychological Association, American Educational Research Association, National Council on Measurement in Education (1974). *Standards for educational and psychological tests*. Washington, DC: Author.

Anastasi, A. (1983). Evolving trait concepts. *American Psychologist, 38*, 175–184.

Anthony, W. Z., Heaton, R. K., & Lehman, R. A. (1980). An attempt to cross-validate two actuarial systems for neuropsychological test interpretation. *Journal of Consulting and Clinical Psychology, 48*, 317–326.

Babcock, H. (1930). An experiment in the measurement of mental deterioration. *Archives of Psychology, 18*, No. 117, 68.

Barbizet, J. (1970). *Human memory and its pathology*. San Francisco: W. H. Freeman.

Boll, T. J. (1981). The Halstead-Reitan neuropsychology battery. In S. B. Filskov & T. J. Boll (Eds.), *Handbook of Clinical Neuropsychology* (Vol. 1, pp. 577–608). New York: John Wiley & Sons.

Bond, M. R. (1975). Assessment of psychosocial outcome after severe head injury. In Ciba Foundation Symposium 34, *Outcome of severe damage of the central nervous system* (pp. 141–157). Amsterdam: Elsevier.

Boring, E. G. (1950). *A history of experimental psychology* (2nd ed.). New York: Appleton-Century-Crofts.

Botwinick, J. (1977). Intellectual abilities. In J. E. Birren & J. W. Shaie (Eds.), *Handbook of the Psychology of Aging* (pp. 580–605). New York: Van Nostrand Reinhold.

Buschke, H., & Fuld, P. A. (1974). Evaluating storage retention and retrieval in disordered memory and learning. *Neurology, 24*, 1019–1025.

Carroll, J. B. (1976). Psychometric tests as cognitive tasks: A new "structure of intellect." In L. Resnick (Ed.), *The nature of intelligence* (pp. 27–56). New York: Lea & Febiger.

Cattell, R. B. (1943). The measurement of adult intelligence. *Psychological Bulletin, 40*, 153–193.

Cattell, R. B. (1971). *Abilities: Their structure, growth and action*. Boston: Houghton Mifflin.

Christensen, A. (1975). *Luria's neuropsychological investigation*. New York: Halstead.

Christensen, A. (1979). A practical approach to the Luria methodology. *Journal of Clinical Neuropsychology, 1*, 241–248.

Christensen, A. (1984). The Luria method of examination of the brain-impaired patient. In P.E. Logue & J.M. Schear (Eds.), *Clinical neuropsychology: A multidisciplinary approach* (pp. 5–28). Springfield, IL.: Charles C Thomas.

Dahlstrom, W. G., & Welsh, G. S. (1960) *An MMPI handbook*. Minneapolis: University of Minnesota Press.

DuBois, P. H. (1970). *A history of psychological testing*. Boston: Allyn & Bacon.

Erickson, R. C., Calsyn, D. A., & Scheupbach, D. S. (1978). Abbreviating the Halstead-Reitan neuropsychological test battery. *Journal of Clinical Psychology, 34*, 922–926.

Eson, M. E., Yen, J. K., & Bourke, R. S. (1978). Assessment of recovery from serious head injury. *Journal of Neurology, Neurosurgery and Psychiatry, 41*, 1036–1042.

Filskov, S. B., & Boll, T. J. (Eds.). (1981). *Handbook of clinical neuropsychology* (Vol. 1). New York: John Wiley & Sons.

Filskov, S. B., Grimm, B. H., & Lewis, J. A. (1981). Brain-behavior relationships. In S. B. Filskov & T. J. Boll (Eds.), *Handbook of clinical neuropsychology* (Vol. 1, pp. 34–73). New York: John Wiley & Sons.

Filskov, S. B., & Leli, D. A. (1981). Assessment of the individual in neuropsychological practice. In S. B. Filskov & T. J. Boll (Eds.), *Handbook of clinical neuropsychology* (Vol. 1, pp. 545–576). New York: John Wiley & Sons.

Finlayson, M. A. J. (1977). Test complexity and brain damage at different educational levels. *Journal of Clinical Psychology, 33*, 221–223.

Fitzhugh, K. B., Fitzhugh, L. C., & Reitan, R. M. (1962). Wechsler-Bellevue comparisons in groups with "chronic" and "current" lateralized and diffuse brain lesions. *Journal of Consulting Psychology, 26*, 306–310.

Golden, C. J. (1981). A standardized version of Luria's neuropsychological tests: A quantitative and qualitative approach to neuropsychological evaluation. In S. B. Filskov & T. J. Boll (Eds.), *Handbook of clinical neuropsychology* (Vol. 1, pp. 608–644). New York: John Wiley & Sons.

Goldstein, G., & Shelly, C. (1982). A further attempt to cross-validate the Russell, Neuringer, and Goldstein neuropsychological keys. *Journal of Consulting and Clinical Psychology, 50*, 721–726.

Goodglass, H., & Kaplan, E. (1983). *The assessment of aphasia and related disorders* (2nd ed.). Philadelphia: Lea & Febiger.

Guilford, J. P. (1967). *Nature of human intelligence*. New York: McGraw-Hill.

Haaland, K. Y., Linn, R. T., Hunt, W. C., & Goodwin, J. S. (1983). A normative study of Russell's variant of the Wechsler Memory Scale in a healthy elderly population. *Journal of Consulting and Clinical Psychology, 51*, 878–881.

Halstead, W. C. (1947). *Brain and intelligence*. Chicago: University of Chicago Press.

Harvey, M. T., & Crovitz, H. F. (1979). Television questionnaire techniques in assessing targeting in long-term memory. *Cortex, 15*, 609–618.

Hayslip, B., & Sterns, H. L. (1979). Age differences in relationships between crystallized and fluid intelligences and problem solving. *Journal of Gerentology, 34*, 404–414.

Hebb, D. O. (1941). Clinical evidence concerning the nature of normal adult test performance. *Psychological Bulletin, 38*, 593 (Abstract).

Hebb, D. O. (1949). *Organization of behavior: A neuropsychological theory*. New York: John Wiley & Sons.

Hécaen, H., & Albert, M. L. (1978). *Human neuropsychology*. New York: John Wiley & Sons.

Horn, J. L. (1966). Integration of structural and developmental concepts in the theory of fluid and crystallized intelligence. In R. B. Cattell (Ed.), *Handbook of multivariate experimental psychology* (pp. 553–561). Chicago: Rand McNally.

Horn, J. L. (1976). Human abilities: A review of research and theory in the early 1970s. *Annual Review of Psychology, 27*, 437–485.

Hunt, H. F. (1943). A practical clinical test for organic brain damage. *Journal of Applied Psychology, 27*, 375–386.

Kertesz, A. (1979). *Aphasia and associated disorders: Taxonomy, localization and recovery*. New York: Grune & Stratton.

Kimura, D. (1963). Right temporal lobe damage: Perception of unfamiliar stimuli after damage. *Archives of Neurology, 8*, 264–271.

Kleinmutz, G. (1968). The processing of clinical information by man and machine. In B. Kleinmutz (Ed.), *Formal representation of human judgment* (pp. 149–186). New York: John Wiley & Sons.

Kline, P. (1979). *Psychometrics and psychology*. New York: Academic Press.

Klove, H. (1963). Clinical neuropsychology. *Medical Clinics of North America, 47*, 1647–1658.

Kolb, B., & Whishaw, I. Q. (1980). *Fundamentals of human neuropsychology*. San Francisco: W. H. Freeman.

Lezak, M.D. (1983). *Neuropsychological assessment* (2nd ed.). New York: Oxford.

Lezak, M.D. (1984). An individualized approach to neurological assessment. In P.E. Logue & J.M. Schear (Eds.), *Clinical neuropsychology* (pp. 29–98). Springfield, 1L.: Charles C Thomas.

Luria, A. R. (1973). *The working brain*. New York: Basic Books.

Luria, A. R. (1980). *Higher cortical functions in man* (2nd ed.). New York: Basic Books.

Luria, A. R., & Majovski, L. V. (1977). Basic approaches used in American and Soviet clinical neuropsychology. *American Psychologist, 32*, 959–968.

Mandleberg, I. A., & Brooks, D. M. (1975). Cognitive recovery after severe head injury. *Journal of Neurology, Neurosurgery and Psychiatry, 38*, 1121–1126.

Matthews, C. G. (1981). Neuropsychology practice in a hospital setting. In S. B. Filskov & T. J. Boll (Eds.), *Handbook of clinical neuropsychology* (Vol. 1, pp. 645–685). New York: John Wiley & Sons.

McCarty, S. M., Logue, P. E., Power, D. G., Ziesat, H. A., & Rosensteil, A. K. (1980). Alternate-form reliability and age-related scores for Russell's Revised Wechsler Memory Scale. *Journal of Consulting and Clinical Psychology, 48*, 296–298.

McFie, J. (1975). *Assessment of organic intellectual impairment*. London: Academic Press.

Milner, B. (1971). Interhemispheric differences in localization of psychological processes in man. *British Medical Bulletin, 27*, 272–277.

Milner, B., Corkin, S., & Teuber, H. L. (1968). Further analysis of the hippocampal amnesic syndrome: 14-year follow-up of H. M. *Neuropsychologia, 6*, 215–234.

Newcombe, F., Hiorns, R. W., Marshall, J. C., & Adams, C. B. T. (1975). Acquired dyslexia: Patterns of deficit and recovery. In Ciba Foundation Symposium 34, *Outcome of severe damage to the central nervous system* (pp. 227–244). Amsterdam: Elsevier.

Nunnally, J. C. (1978). *Psychometric theory* (2nd ed.). New York: McGraw-Hill.

Parsons, O. A., & Prigatano, G. P. (1978). Methodological considerations in clinical neuropsychological research. *Journal of Consulting and Clinical Psychology, 46*, 608–614.

Reed, H. B. C., & Reitan, R. M. (1963a). Changes in psychological test performances associated with normal aging process. *Journal of Gerontology, 18*, 271–274.

Reed, H. B. C., & Reitan, R. M. (1963b). A comparison of the effects of the normal aging process with effects of organic brain damage on adaptive abilities. *Journal of Gerontology, 18*, 177–179.

Reitan, R. M. (1955). Investigation of the validity of Halstead's measures of biological intelligence. *Archives of Neurology and Psychiatry, 73*, 28–35.

Reitan, R. (1964). Psychological deficits resulting from cerebral lesions in men. In J. M. Warren & K. Akert (Eds.), *The frontal granular cortex and behavior* (pp. 295–312). New York: McGraw-Hill.

Russell, E. W. (1975). Validation of a brain-damaged versus schizophrenia MMPI key. *Journal of Clinical Psychology, 31*, 659–661.

Russell, E. W. (1979). Three patterns of brain damage on the WAIS. *Journal of Clinical Psychology, 35*, 611–620.

Russell, E. W. (1980a). Fluid and crystallized intelligence: Effects of diffuse brain damage on the WAIS. *Perceptual and Motor Skills, 51*, 121–122.

Russell, E. W. (1980b). Tactile sensation: An all-or-none effect of cerebral damage. *Journal of Clinical Psychology, 36*, 858–864.

Russell, E. W. (1981a). The chronicity effect. *Journal of Clinical Psychology, 37*, 246–253.

Russell, E. W. (1981b). The pathology and clinical examination of memory. In S. B. Filskov, & T. J. Boll (Eds.), *Handbook of clinical neuropsychology* (Vol. 1, pp. 287–319). New York: John Wiley & Sons.

Russell, E. W. (1982a). *Comparison of the TPT 10 and 6 hole form boards*. Paper presented at the 90th Annual Convention of the American Psychological Association, Washington, DC.

Russell, E. W. (1982b). Factor analysis of the revised Wechsler Memory scale tests in a neuropsychological battery. *Perceptual and Motor skills, 54*, 971–974.

Russell, E. W. (1984). Developments in neuropsychological indices and keys. In P. E. Logue & J. M. Schear (Eds.), *Clinical neuropsychology: A multidisciplinary approach* (pp. 50–98). Springfield, IL: Charles C Thomas.

Russell, E. W. (1985, August). *Renorming the Revised Wechsler Memory Scale*. Paper presented at the 93 Annual Convention of the American Psychological Association, Los Angeles, CA.

Russell, E. W., Neuringer, C., & Goldstein, G. (1970). *Assessment of brain damage: A neuropsychological key approach*. New York: John Wiley & Sons.

Satz, P. (1966a). A block rotation task: The application of multivariate and decision theory analysis for the prediction of organic brain disorders. *Psychological Monographs, 80*, (2l, Whole No. 629).

Satz, P. (1966b). Specific and nonspecific effects of brain lesions in man. *Journal of Abnormal Psychology, 71*, 65–70.

Selz, M., & Reitan, R. M. (1979). Rules for neuropsychological diagnosis: Classification of brain function in children. *Journal of Consulting and Clinical Psychology, 47*, 258–264.

Shelly, C., & Goldstein, G. (1982). Intelligence, achievement, and the Luria Nebraska Battery in a neuropsychiatric population: A factor analytic study. *Clinical Neuropsychology, 4*, 164–169.

Shipley, W. C. (1940). A self-administering scale for measuring intellectual impairment and deterioration. *Journal of Psychology, 9*, 371–377.

Smith, A. (1975). Neuropsychological testing in neurological disorders. In W. J. Friedlander (Ed.), *Advances in neurology*, (Vol. 7, pp. 49–110). New York: Raven.

Smith, A. (1981). Principles underlying human brain functions in neuropsychological sequelae of different neuropathological processes. In S. B. Filskov & T. J. Boll (Eds.), *Handbook of clinical neuropsychology* (Vol. 1, pp. 175–226). New York: John Wiley & Sons.

Spreen, O., & Benton, A. L. (1965). Comparative studies of some psychological tests for cerebral damage. *Journal of Nervous and Mental Disease, 140*, 323–333.

Squire, L. R., & Slater, P. C. (1975). Forgetting in very long-term memory as assessed by an improved questionnaire technique. *Journal of Experimental Psychology: Human Learning and Memory, 1*, 50–54.

Sternberg, R. J. (1977). *Intelligence information processing and analogical reasoning: the componential analysis of human abilities*. Hillsdale, NJ: Erlbaum.

Sternberg, R. J. (1979). The nature of mental abilities. *American Psychologist, 34*, 214–230.

Teuber, H. L. (1955). Physiological psychology. *Annual Review of Psychology, 6*, 267–296.

Teuber, H. L. (1975). Recovery of function after brain injury. In Ciba Foundation Symposium 34, *Outcome of severe damage to the central nervous system* (pp. 159–190). Amsterdam: Elsevier.

Teuber, H. L. & Weinstein, S. (1955). General and specific effects of cerebral lesions. *American Psychologist, 10*, 408–409.

Teuber, H. L., & Weinstein, S. (1958). Equipotentiality versus cortical localization. *Science, 127*, 241–242.

Walsh, K. W. (1978). *Neuropsychology: A clinical approach*. New York: Churchill Livingstone.

Warrington, E. K., Logue, V., & Pratt, R. T. C. (1971). The anatomical localization of selective impairment of auditory verbal short-term memory. *Neuropsychologia, 9*, 377–387.

Wechsler, D. (1945). A standardized memory scale for clinical use. *Journal of Psychology, 19*, 87–95.

CHAPTER 4

Neurological Diagnostic Tests

James A. Lewis

From the perspective of the neurologist, neuropsychological evaluation is simply part of an array of laboratory tests available to help diagnose and manage patients. In the interest of increasing the ability of the psychologist and the physician to communicate with each other, this chapter describes the other laboratory procedures the neurologist might turn to in evaluating a patient, attempts to show when they might be used, and describes some of the idiosyncrasies of the jargon used by the clinician.

In the broadest possible sense, the patient-physician interaction may be thought of as a process of transduction. The input to the process is the patient's complaint; the output, some prescribed course of action aimed at relieving the complaint. Throughout most of medical history, the value of the physicians' treatment was almost entirely psychological, although a few classic pharmaceuticals did have some symptomatic action, and the hygienic advice offered was not always totally destructive. In the nineteenth century, the nature of the process began to change. Physicians came to recognize a logical connection between the patient's complaints and definable derangements in the structure and function of body organs and systems. Instead of treating symptoms, the physician began to attempt to reveal the nature of some specific pathophysiological entity that was causing the symptoms in hopes of ultimately being able to treat the cause itself. Techniques of physical examination developed based on physiological and anatomical principles unknown to the ancients. History taking from the patient became a process of subtle education, one of shaping the patient's complaints, an attempt to translate them into terms that would have physiological significance. As the complexities of the structure and function of the body became increasingly clear, the history and physical examination was recognized as being inadequate for the full elucidation of the diverse pathological entities lurking behind the presenting complaints. Physicians turned to the laboratory for help.

The nature of laboratory tests is generally misperceived by the public and probably by many physicians. The popular view is vividly exposed in a scene from a 1960 movie, *Ocean's 11*. One of the characters is in a physician's office; he says: "Give it to me straight. Is it Big Casino?" The doctor places a chest x-ray film (upside down, incidentally) on a view box, glances at it for an instant, then nods grimly. Among the many assumptions illustrated by this scene are that diseases have clear signatures that laboratory tests can elicit, physicians can read laboratory tests in a rapid and unambiguous fashion, and laboratory tests are always right.

In fact, there are no diseases that can be invariably diagnosed by any laboratory test. The process of making a diagnosis appears to be similar to fitting a key into a lock: there are many points of possible congruence between the expected attributes of any disease and the things that can be defined by examining and testing the patient. The closer the two patterns fit together, the more likely it is that the patient has the disease. The fit is not established by any single feature.

At the core of the encounter between a neurologist and a patient, the neurologist is interested in learning whether the patient's complaints appear to stem from disordered hardware or software. If the nervous system appears to be intact in structure and function, the patient is relegated to the care of psychiatrists or psychologists; in a somewhat peculiar twist of jargon, the complaints are dismissed as "functional" if all systems are found to be functioning normally. The patient's complaints are ones of hardware if a structural lesion can be demonstrated or if gross dysfunction on the basis of chemical derangement is present.

When the decision has been made that the patient has a hardware problem, the neurologist faces the question of the location and nature of the lesion, which leads in turn to a program of treatment.

The techniques of the neurological examination have been described briefly in the first volume of *The Handbook of Clinical Neuropsychology* (Filskov, Grimm, & Lewis, 1981). At the end of the history and the examination, the physician almost always has a strong sense of the probability that a lesion exists and of its location. The physician turns to tests of the structure and function of the nervous system to confirm the hypothesis. Neuroradiological tests (and related ultrasound imaging procedures) are used to detect structural changes in the brain. Until the advent of the standardized neuropsychological examination, the only test of function available, besides the neurological exam itself, was electroencephalography (EEG). Electroencephalographic tests will be discussed in sufficient detail for the concerned psychologist to be able to read the reports, relate them to the patient's diagnoses, and appreciate their shortcomings, which at times may be considerable.

ELECTROENCEPHALOGRAPHY

The living brain is surrounded by a shell of electrical energy. Electroencephalography is the collection of techniques used in the detection, recording, and interpretation of this electrical appendage for the purpose of diagnosis and study of the brain.

The first human EEG was reported by Berger in 1929 (Gloor, 1969). In 1936, Grey Walter showed that the EEG could be used in diagnosing brain tumors (Walter, 1936). In 1937, Gibbs and colleagues published a paper attempting to establish epilepsy as a "cerebral dysrhythmia" defined by the appearance of paroxysmal activity in the EEG (Gibbs, Gibbs, & Lennox, 1937). These examples of clinical utility of the EEG led to an immense proliferation of EEG laboratories throughout the world, a development open to some criticism (Matthews, 1964). The number of EEG laboratories in the United States today is unknown but can be estimated in excess of 10,000.

The brain's electrical field is reflected as a pattern of voltage contours on the scalp. The EEG consists of a record of voltage differences between electrodes placed on the scalp. A major component of the electrical activity of the brain is a positive potential of considerable magnitude, around 1500 microvolts, which changes only very slowly over time. Superimposed on this standing potential, like ripples on the surface of a pond, are much smaller fluctuations, generally in the range of 50–100 microvolts. The EEG detects these relatively fast, small electrical waves; the steady, or standing, component is ignored by the equipment available in clinical laboratories. Although some research suggests that studying the steady potential can be valuable (Adey, 1969), it cannot be "seen" by the usual techniques of EEG and thus has been ignored in the major literature of electroencephalography.

To obtain an EEG, a technologist places 21 electrodes in carefully measured positions on the head, adds a ground electrode, and then records for 10–20 minutes while the patient is in relaxed wakefulness. This procedure is followed by some minor physiological activation techniques: the patient is asked to voluntarily hyperventilate for 3–5 minutes and is also given a series of repetitive flash stimulations from a strobe light positioned just in front of the eyes. Finally, when possible, the patient is allowed to go to sleep for another 10–20 minutes of recording.

A single channel of recording represents the voltage measured between any two electrodes on the head and is typically written as an ink line on graph paper running through the machine at 30 millimeters per second. Modern EEG instruments usually record 16–20 channels at a time. A montage is a collection of electrode pairs needed to drive the 16–20 recording pens arranged to map the electrical field of the scalp in some anatomically meaningful fashion. The usual record consists of three or more montages chosen to measure the electrical envelope in different perspectives. The entire procedure is noninvasive, totally safe, and costs in the range of $100–$200 in most laboratories at the present time.

When the electroencephalographer "reads" a record, he or she estimates (or occasionally measures) the frequency and voltage of waves in any channel, estimates their variability, and notes how they change with varying physiological states. The symmetry of homologous left and right scalp channels is noted. A record is normal when the expected frequencies for age are present in an acceptably symmetrical fashion. An abnormal record may be too slow, too fast, or too asymmetrical or even lack evidence of cerebral rhythms. The electroencephalographer's report consists of a technical description of the recording, a classification of the record as normal or abnormal, and an explanation of the significance of the EEG findings as applied to the patient's individual history.

The rhythms recorded by the EEG fall into a few fairly discrete categories. It is as if the brain contains generators, neural machines, that can produce only a limited range of activities. The output of a given generator can be described by its frequency range in Hertz (Hz), or cycles per second; its variability; its typical location on the scalp; its average size (amplitude of waves in microvolts); and its response to change in physiological state. Almost all people appear to have an alpha generator. This produces rhythmic activity of 8–13 Hz located over the posterior scalp, particularly the occipital area; waves are generally around 50–100 microvolts in amplitude but show a regular pattern of waxing and waning ("spindling") in size. The dominant hemisphere is usually slightly lower in alpha amplitude. Alpha generally becomes much smaller in voltage, or disappears altogether, when the eyes are open, a phenomenon called alpha blocking. Since almost everybody shows more alpha rhythm (with eyes closed) than anything else, it is called the dominant rhythm. A large literature exists on the alpha

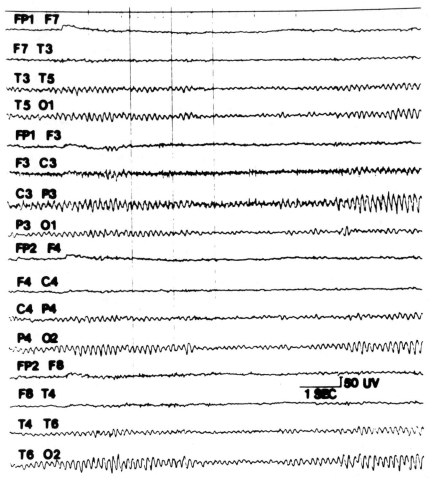

Figure 4.1. This is a 16-channel EEG on for normal person. It is most easily viewed as four blocks of four channels each. Adjacent pairs of electrodes are connected in a front-to-back fashion to sequentially map the left temporal, left parasagittal, right parasagittal, and right temporal areas; this is called a differential montage. The letters on the left margin indicate which electrode pairs drive a given channel; F is frontal, T is temporal, and so on, with odd-numbered placements on the left scalp, even-numbered on the right. The key in the lower right indicates the horizontal distance that the paper moves in one second and the vertical displacement of the pens by a 50-microvolt signal. When the electrode designations are omitted on subsequent figures, the montage is the same as in this figure; all the tracings are at the same speed and sensitivity as this one. The record shows alpha rhythm of 10 Hz and around a 75-microvolt amplitude over the posterior scalp, with very low voltage beta rhythm anteriorly.

rhythm, which is somewhat surprising because variations in alpha only rarely have any diagnostic value, the origin of alpha is unknown, and the significance of variations in alpha between individuals is completely obscure (see Figure 4.1). One suspects that alpha rhythm may be one of the most thoroughly studied, irrelevant phenomenon known to biology.

Any rhythmic activity faster than 13 Hz is called beta. Most people appear to have two or more beta generators, producing different rhythms identifiable by changes in amplitude, frequency, and distribution. The usual clinical EEG shows some beta activity around 20 Hz in the frontal and central scalp.

Activity of 4–7 Hz is called theta. In the normal waking adult, theta tends to be much less readily identifiable than alpha, taking up one-third or less of the record (a measure called "percent time" in the older literature) as opposed to 85%–95% for alpha. In young children, theta activity is present in a much greater amount and often forms the dominant rhythm.

Activity below the theta frequency range is only present as brief, isolated waves in the normal waking adult. This is delta activity. It is the dominant rhythm in normal adult sleep, in normal waking infants around term, and in many pathological states.

The generators discussed so far produce background activity, rhythms that are more or less continuously present. In addition to background rhythms, transient events are present in the EEG. These are uncommon in the normal waking adult in the eyes-closed states. With the eyes open, about 15% of people show well-defined, sharp transients of 150–200 milliseconds in duration over the posterior scalp when they are actively looking at things; these are lambda waves. In sleep, all normal subjects show large waves of delta activity around the vertex of the head, called K-complexes (the name has historical significance only). These are usually intermixed with brief bursts of 12–14 Hz rhythm that wax and wane in amplitude and are thus called sleep spindles. In newborn children, even in wakefulness, transient waves are very common.

The strength of the EEG as a clinical test is its great sensitivity to pathologic states: if the brain is sick, the EEG is likely to be abnormal. Its weakness is the lack of specificity. Except for broad categories, it is unlikely that the EEG will help identify the nature of the patient's disease.

If the brain as a whole becomes sick because of endogenous or exogenous poisoning or a degenerative condition, the EEG tends to become slow. There is a general correlation between the degree of involvement of the brain by the pathological process and the degree of slowing of the EEG. With an early or mild encephalopathy there may be intermittent bursts of theta-range activity interrupting a normal background. This may be hard to distinguish from simple drowsiness. In children, theta is abundant in normal individuals; subtle changes in encephalopathy may be overlooked, or normal amounts of theta may be overinterpreted.

As the brain becomes more encephalopathic, more continuous theta activity appears, intermixed with delta activity. As the patient sinks into an unarousable coma, delta activity becomes predominant. With progressive brain failure, episodes of suppression of voltage appear; finally, more prolonged episodes of intense suppression or absence of electrical activity occur, alternating with bursts of delta-range slowing. This burst-suppression pattern is usually a grim sign of a brain on the edge of death. However, an identical pattern can be seen in drug coma without the presence of any persistent brain damage (see Figure 4.2, for example); and a very similar pattern is considered normal for premature infants.

The changes described so far deal with encephalopathy, or generalized impairment of brain function. Such a condition is usually due to some metabolic disorder; a poisoning from an endogenous source, as in liver failure; or an exogenous source, such as a prescription drug or alcohol. Focal diseases of the hemispheres present with a similar evolution of slowing but, as might be expected, the slowing is confined to one hemisphere or lobe in the typical case. When the electroencephalographer sees a localized region of delta activity, he or she can be reasonably certain that some underlying structural disease is present. Without historical information, the elec-

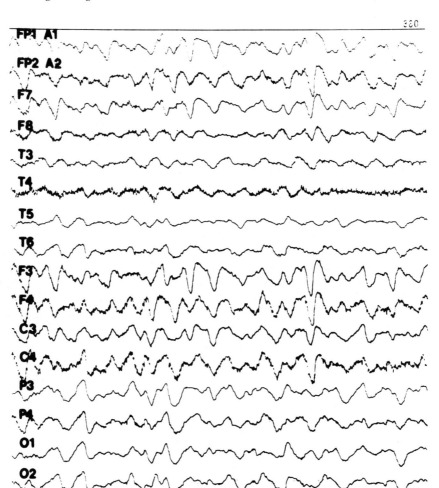

Figure 4.2. This 47-year-old woman was toxic from several cardiac drugs used at excessive doses. Electrodes alternate from left to right, each scalp placement being compared to the relative inactive ipsilateral ear electrode (a referential montage). The first eight channels are frontal through temporal, the next eight parasagittal. The record is dominated by delta slowing, with some intermixed theta. The patient recovered promptly, and the EEG returned to normal when the drugs were stopped.

troencephalographer is unable to guess whether the lesion is an acute infarction, an old infarct, a tumor, an abscess, or an area of contused cortex from recent trauma (see Figure 4.3).

When focal disease kills brain cells, electrical activity stops, so in fact the EEG sign of a destructive lesion is an area of electrical silence. It is rare to see focal electrical silence in clinical practice. Most lesions either do not totally destroy all cells in the area, or they are small enough that the surrounding brain, often compressed, inflamed, or edematous, produces slowing that masks the small zone of inert tissue. At times, the slowing produced by a focal lesion may appear at a considerable distance from the lesion itself; this is called projected slowing and implies that the theta and delta

238

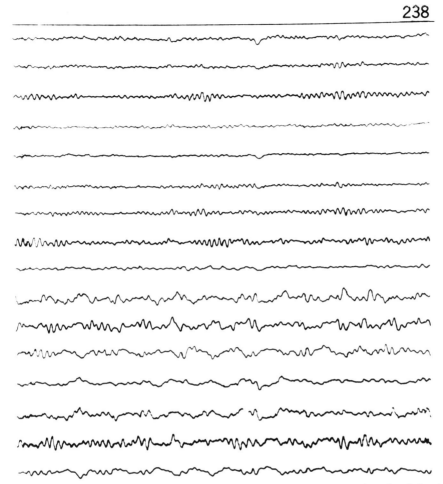

Figure 4.3.   The patient is a 78-year-old with progressive intellectual deterioration following a stroke three years earlier. He has a left hemiparesis and is moderately demented. The activity from the left hemisphere looks normal here, although mild slowing is apparent on other pages of the record. The right hemisphere is producing mixed theta and delta slowing. CT scan showed diffuse atrophy and a right brain cyst.

generators associated with the lesion are pumping their abnormal activity along white-matter pathways to some distant site. Projected slowing is more metaphor than established fact, but the empirical observation remains that focal slowing may give misleading information about the localization of a lesion. Another sign of focal disease is the spike, or fast, sharply configured transient event, discussed in detail below. Lesions that are irritating to the brain because of their acuteness, such as metastatic tumors, are often accompanied by spikes (see Figure 4.4). On the other hand, very chronic focal lesions associated with the production of gliotic scars can also be a source of EEG spikes and clinical seizures.

When the brain dies, the production of electrical activity stops. The record from a dead brain is often described as flat or isoelectric. Actually, when brain death is suspected, the technologist institutes a variety of techniques to detect any existing

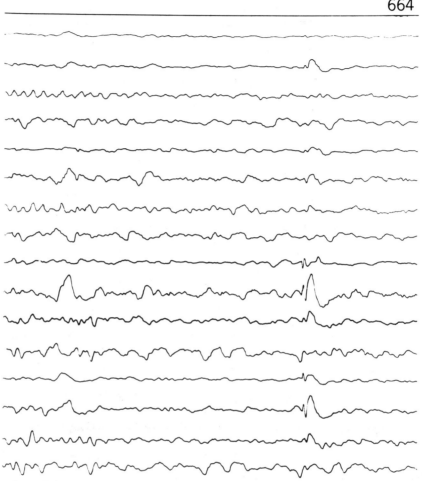

Figure 4.4. This 71-year-old smoker was known to have a lung tumor with metastasis to his lymph nodes. He presented at the hospital with a series of generalized convulsions; examination showed a mild left hemiparesis. This is a referential montage; the first three channels are left temporal, the next five left parasagittal, the next five right parasagittal, and the last three right temporal. There is diffuse slowing, but careful perusal shows it to be worse on the right. There are spikes over both hemispheres, but the ones on the right are larger, show more complex configuration, and actually lead the left spikes slightly in time, clearly identifying them as originating from the right brain. This patient's CT scan is seen in Figure 4.8.

cerebral activity; the use of these special techniques invariably results in a record that is anything but flat, containing large amounts of biological artifact, such as heartbeat and muscle activity, and electrical noise. The failure to detect any cerebral activity with a properly run record, in the absence of factors that might suppress activity (e.g., toxic levels of barbiturates or severe hypothermia) is strong confirmatory evidence that the brain has died. However, the diagnosis of brain death is always a clinical one, and the presence of electrocerebral silence in the EEG is not sufficient to establish the diagnosis. Indeed, it is a misconception that the EEG is a necessary tool in diagnosing brain death: no published criteria *require* an EEG for the diagnosis of brain death.

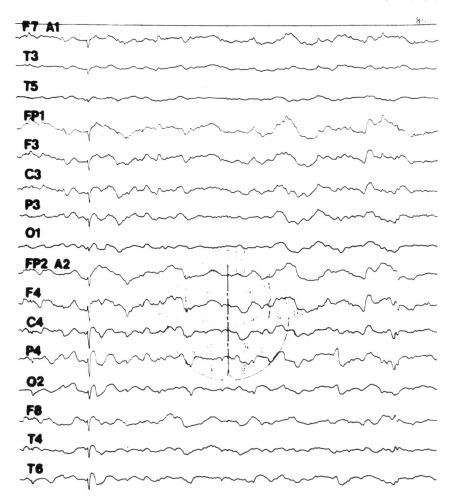

Figure 4.5. The patient is a 5-year-old, recorded a few hours after his first two generalized convulsions. Although he is awake, the record is diffusely slow because of his postictal state (compare to Figure 4.4). Spikes are seen over the right hemisphere; they are longer in duration than in Figure 4.4 and have a more pronounced slow wave. The child's exam and CT scan were entirely normal.

The one area in which the EEG can be said to have specificity for diagnosis is epilepsy. During an epileptic seizure, the EEG is very likely to show repetitive electrical discharges occurring at a fast rate; these usually have a sharp configuration and are thus called spikes. They are called spike waves when regularly alternating with slow elements. Unfortunately for the neurologist trying to be sure about the diagnosis of epilepsy, even in patients with active epilepsy, it is uncommon to obtain an EEG during a seizure, since seizures occur more or less randomly and infrequently in most patients. The value of spikes in the EEG of the epileptic patient recorded between seizures (the interictal record, in EEG jargon) is less certain. However, the ictal record is so singular and striking that the presence of spikes in the interictal EEG has by association become almost synonymous with the diagnosis of epilepsy (see Figure 4.5). It is difficult to extract information from the literature to determine the specificity of EEG spikes for epilepsy, since the sign itself has become so strongly associated in the neurologist's mind with the disease. In the best study in the literature (Ajmone-Marsan & Zivin, 1970), a large group of patients who unequivocally had epilepsy on clinical grounds were found to have nondiagnostic EEGs in 17% of the cases, despite numerous repeated recordings for all subjects.

It is equally difficult to be sure how often a patient without clinical seizures might have spikes in the EEG. Not all waves with a sharp appearance would be called spike by every electroencephalographer. Spikelike transients are much more common in children than in adults. Patients with significant brain disease are more likely to produce EEG spikes than platonically ideal normal subjects. Also, noncerebral waves (artifacts to the electroencephalographer) can look exactly like spikes. For all these reasons, the reported incidence of spikes in a nonepileptic population ranges from 1% to 10%. It is likely that unequivocal spikes occur in less than 1% of otherwise healthy adults.

Given these figures, the positive predictive value of EEG spikes (even with interictal recording) is very good when testing is done in a laboratory where many epileptic patients are recorded; when used in a population in which epileptics are only occasionally encountered, it is much weaker (Lewis, 1982). The value of a normal EEG in ruling out epilepsy, its negative predictive value, is substantially less.

As with slow activity, spikes can show two broad patterns of occurrence: focal and generalized. Intuitively, it is appealing to try to correlate the patterns of spikes with the clinical type of seizure, since seizures fall into two broad classes: partial or generalized. In partial seizures, the clinical attack begins in a restricted region of one hemisphere; in generalized attacks, both hemispheres are involved in the seizure activity from the onset. In a general way, the association of focal spikes with partial seizures and generalized spikes with generalized seizures is true, particularly when considering the ictal record. In any given patient, however, significant deviations may be found. These deviations usually take the form of focal electrical signs in patients whose seizures are always generalized clinically. The presence of such signs may reflect a rapid spread of seizure activity from an initiating region of a localized pathologic state, giving the appearance of a generalized seizure to what is actually a focal disease. This process is called secondary generalization.

Thus the neurologist can use the EEG to detect the presence of abnormally functioning brain tissue and even quantitate the degree of dysfunction. In the particular set of clinical disorders called the epilepsies, the EEG has strong diagnostic value. Newer uses of the EEG are less universal but at present are becoming increasingly popular and may ultimately prove to be of considerable value. One of these is the use of EEG plus other physiological monitoring devices in the sleep laboratory in a technique called polysomnography. By using measures of EEG activity, eye movement, muscle tension, and sometimes other variables, normal sleep can be divided into a series of stages. During the night, normal individuals cycle through a series of relatively quiet sleep states characterized by K-complexes, sleep spindles, and mixtures of theta and delta activity, and then periodically enter a state characterized by low voltage, theta-beta EEG and the presence of rapid, conjugate eye movements (REM sleep). Most dreaming occurs during REM sleep. A variety of disorders have been recognized in the last two decades in which the normal sleep cycles are grossly distorted or in which pathological events can occur in various stages of sleep. In patients with narcolepsy, for example, the first REM period may occur at the onset of sleep; in normal individuals, the first

REM period never appears before 90 minutes of non-REM sleep. Narcoleptics typically have more frequent and prolonged arousals at night and when recorded in the daytime show a consistently greater tendency to fall asleep early in an EEG, often falling directly into REM sleep. Depressed patients typically show a REM period within the first hour of sleep, although not at sleep onset, and have far fewer of the slowest EEG stages of non-REM sleep than do normal individuals.

Another new EEG technique attracting considerable attention is the study of evoked potentials (Da Silva, 1982). These are transient waves in the EEG produced by sensory stimulation. They are normally of such low amplitude that they are lost in the background EEG rhythms, but they can be extracted by computer techniques of summation (adding together segments of EEG that are time-locked to repetitive sensory stimuli) and averaging. These techniques produce waves of characteristic configuration and distribution for each modality of stimulation that can be used diagnostically (Celesia, 1982). The early components of these evoked potentials are strongly linked to the hardware function of the brain. A plaque of demyelination in the optic nerve of a patient with multiple sclerosis may be too small to be detected by careful tests of vision, but it will often slow the responses conducted to the brain when the patient views a pattern of reversing dark and light squares, resulting in an evoked response with a delayed major positive wave. The late components of the evoked potential are much more sensitive to software changes in the brain. When an individual listens to a series of repetitive identical clicks, the occurrence of an occasional stimulus that is different in pitch or intensity or even omitted altogether will produce evoked responses with larger positive waves occurring around 300 milliseconds after delivery (or failure to deliver) the stimulus. This P300 component can be manipulated in size and latency solely by instructing the patient to either attend to, ignore, or otherwise process the rare stimuli. Thus, the standard EEG waves and the early components of the evoked potentials are brain waves; the later components could be called mind waves. Since many forms of electrical activity exist that are more or less independent of sensory stimulation, such as the P300 wave produced in response to an omitted click, these can be considered event related, rather than evoked, responses. The classic sensory evoked response is thus only one of a broader category of brain events correlated to behavioral states. The longer-latency mind waves have tremendous promise as tools for studying the human psyche (Knight, 1984; Pfefferbaum, Wenegrat, Ford, Roth, & Kopell, 1984).

NEURORADIOLOGY

The rise of medicine as a science is synonymous with the development of anatomical and, later, biochemical pathology. Neurology has recapitulated this evolutionary history in its quest for a concrete image of brain lesions (Oldendorf, 1980). This quest has included the study of skull films, pneumoencephalography, arteriography, and, finally, computed tomography. Minor side roads along the way have been isotope brain scan and echoencephalography.

Early in the history of radiology, neurologists attempted to learn about the structure of the brain by looking at the skull, which is all that can be seen on a routine radiograph of the head. A kind of roentgenological phrenology developed, in which subtle changes in the appearance of the skull were imputed with great value in detecting changes in the brain. At the annual American Academy of Neurology postgraduate course in neuro-radiology, it was common for an entire day to be devoted to discussion of skull x-ray films, the session beginning at 9 A.M. and ending after midnight. This was mostly ritual, since the skull reflects very little about the brain, and with the advent of computed tomography, the numbers of skull roentgenograms done at major centers have dropped to a point near zero.

The pneumoencephalogram (PEG) is a roentgenogram of a head into which air has been introduced. The procedure was invented after the observation of air surrounding the brain and outlining its structure in a patient with head trauma; the air had been forced into the head through a skull fracture by the traumatic event. In the diagnostic version, air is introduced into the subarachnoid space through a needle in the lumbar spine. It is allowed to bubble upward and outline the structures at the base of the brain; the patient is then literally flipped in a somersault to percolate air into the upper ventricular system and subarachnoid space. Structural lesions, such as tumors and areas of atrophy, show up as distortions in the envelope of air surrounding the brain and filling its ventricular cavity.

The pneumoencephalogram detects large structural lesions almost anywhere in the brain. Small lesions are detected if they are suitably located in relation to the structures that fill with air; but many lesions are located elsewhere in the brain. The cost of obtaining a PEG is relatively small in terms of serious reactions, if by serious one means life-threatening. But obtaining a PEG is a brutal procedure in terms of patient discomfort. One patient described the injection of air into the ventricles as "a sledge-hammer inside the head." Days of headache and fever are expected afterward. The test is virtually never performed today.

Arteriography was the next method attempting to image the brain. In this technique, an iodinated organic compound is injected into the arterial system and a rapid sequence of roentgenograms obtained. The pictures show filling of large cerebral arteries, small arteries, capillaries, and veins in turn. Arteriography is most valuable when information about the blood vessels themselves is desired. Vessels that are narrowed by arteriosclerotic plaques can be easily seen, as can ulcerated craters within an arteriosclerotic lesion. Often, a vessel completely obstructed by a blood clot or plaque can be identified by its absence on the arteriogram. Surgeons also use arterio-grams to identify vascular lesions that may require surgery, such as aneurysmal dilations of blood vessels and arteriovenous malformations.

Arteriograms are often helpful in detecting other kinds of lesions. Many brain tumors elicit a florid proliferation of blood vessels in surrounding brain. An arteriogram may show abnormal arteries feeding the tumor; an abnormal quantity of capillaries in the tumor (producing a cloudlike mass on the film called a tumor blush); or veins that fill earlier than normally due to the rapid circulation through the tumor. If none of these changes is present, tumors and other masses in the brain (subdural or intracerebral hematomas and abscesses) may distort the normal vascular anatomy enough to reveal their presence.

Digital subtraction angiography (DSA) is a modern variant of the arteriogram. It used to be necessary to inject contrast material directly into an artery in order for it to be concentrated enough to be detected on the x-ray film. This initially meant a direct carotid artery puncture by the neurologist; later, catheter techniques were developed, using a long plastic tube threaded proximally from a larger vessel in the arm or groin. Now, by using computerized enhancement, it is possible to visualize the arterial circulation following an intravenous injection of contrast medium. This is a significant improvement, since arterial catherization carried some risks, including pain, arterial clotting, bleeding at the puncture site, and potential dislodgement of fragments of atherosclerotic plaque that could embolize to the brain. At the time of this writing, DSA is not adequate for visualizing the circulation within the brain, and it gives somewhat poorer visualization of the major vessels in the neck than does a standard arteriogram. It is excellent for screening the neck vessels for major disease, and its technical shortcomings will probably be overcome in the near future. One hazard of any angiographic procedure is the potential for allergic reactions to the iodinated substance. Although usually minor, such reactions are occasionally lethal.

The isotope brain scan utilizes the intravenous injection of an organic chemical labeled with a radioactive atom, often technetium. Radiation-sensitive cameras can then record the flow of isotope through the brain. The abnormal blood vessels often present in areas of tumor or stroke may show up as hot spots where isotope collects; dynamic studies can detect areas of reduced flow where major occlusions have occurred. Thus the technique gives similar data to that provided by the angiogram without as high a risk of allergic reaction. However, the information obtained from the isotope scan is much less specific than that from the angiogram and the spatial resolution very much poorer. The isotope brain scan is following the skull film into near extinction.

For a brief period in the 1960s, attempts were made to utilize beams of high-frequency vibrations (ultrasound) passed through the head to locate intracranial structures. The walls of the skull and the ventricles would send back echoes that could be used to detect shifts of the midline caused by tumors or swelling. The procedure was technically difficult, it detected only gross pathologic states, and it has now disappeared from use in adults. In newborn infants, ultrasound scans give much more detailed images of the brain because of the thinness of the skull and the presence of normal openings in the skull; echoencephalograms are widely used in newborn nurseries. Ultrasound imaging of carotid arteries is also used as a screening test for arteriosclerosis. Complete occlusion of blood vessels and high-grade stenosis are easily detected on ultrasound images of the vessels, whereas a completely normal-appearing vessel makes it reasonably unlikely that further information will be found by angiographic roentgenograms. The use of ultrasound imaging of the blood vessels in combination with other noninvasive tests of vascular function, such as ophthalmoplethysmography (OPG, the recording of blood pressure from the intraocular retinal artery), constitutes a vascular laboratory workup that many authorities regard as nearly as informative as angiography.

During the 1970s, a technique of x-ray visualization of the brain was developed that revolutionized clinical neurology and neurosurgery. This was computerized tomography. With this technique, a series of slices are made through the brain by a beam of x-rays. Images are not printed directly onto film. The beam is measured by a series of radiation detectors whose output is analyzed by a computer, processed according to a complex algorithm, and then displayed on a cathode screen as a reconstituted image of the brain slices. A series of images is generated that presents the brain in anatomical sections, as would be produced by a pathologist at a brain cutting. With modern scanners, slices in horizontal, coronal, and parasagittal planes can be obtained; but the horizontal (or near horizontal) section remains the most commonly used.

In the first computed tomograph, the beam rotated around the central axis of the body, and the technique was euphoniously known as a CAT scan (for computerized axial tomography). Since the beam does not actually have to rotate around the

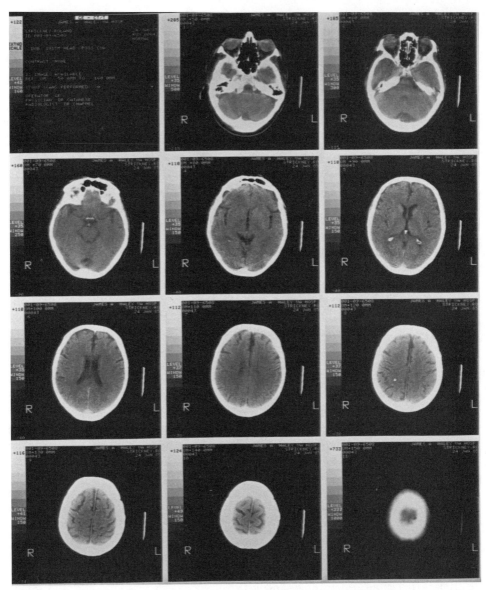

Figure 4.6. This is a normal sequence of unenhanced CT images. The pictures are read from upper left to lower right, reading left to right. Individual pictures are numbered or can be described by the anatomical level, such as "the level of the heads of the caudate nuclei." The accepted tradition is to display the left side of the head on the viewer's right (opposite to the way brains are displayed by pathologists and neurologists).

midline, the name now formally agreed upon for the technique is simply *CT scan*; and since CT images can now be made of all parts of the body, it is most appropriately described as a brain or head CT scan (see Figure 4.6). The term *CAT scan* rolls off the tongue so easily, however, that the approved but more pedestrian usage, *CT*, will probably never be universal. It should also be noted that the term *brain scan* historically refers to the method of imaging with radioisotopes. Since this technique (at least in its current incarnation) is so vastly inferior to CT scanning, neurologists recently trained may never have seen an isotope scan, and *brain scan* is often used when *head CT scan* is meant.

The normal brain is faithfully imaged by CT scanning. Any pathological brain condition that produces structural changes is accurately represented by CT scanning if the lesion is big enough and if its density is sufficiently different from brain to be detected. The image reconstituted by the computer consists of an array of three-dimensional cells called voxels. Each cell represents a volume of brain and is displayed according to its photon-absorbing properties, or density. Denser structures are seen as light areas, and less dense areas as dark ones. The usual image is thus a black and white picture, with the skull white, the fluid-filled ventricular system dark, and the gray and white tissues of the brain in intermediate shades of gray. A lesion has to be at least several voxels wide to be seen and sufficiently different in density from adjacent brain to stand out. The absolute size of a lesion required for it to be seen on CT varies with the particular machine (newer instruments have smaller voxels) and its location, but as a rough rule of thumb, it is approximately 0.5 centimeter.

Obviously, not all pathological conditions of the brain produce structural lesions. If a patient were to die after being positioned in the CT instrument, the subsequent series of routine images would be exactly the same as if the patient were alive, even though the brain was clearly very pathological.

After the routine CT scan, a series of contrast-enhanced images is now almost always obtained. The patient is given a bolus of iodinated contrast material intravenously after the baseline pictures are obtained, and the series is then repeated. Blood vessels stand out as dense structures, and the more vascular gray matter is clearly differentiated from white matter. Frequently, a significant lesion is not detected on the baseline series but is obvious on the contrast-enhanced images.

CT technology has been evolving rapidly. Each new generation of scanners produces pictures of higher resolution, may use less radiation, or may process pictures more rapidly. Even with the newest instruments, the test requires that the patient remain still for some seconds; minutes are needed on older instruments, requiring sedation for some patients, with the subsequent risk of drug reaction. Patients can also have allergic reactions to the contrast material. Perhaps the most painful part of the procedure is the cost, which is currently in the $500–$600 range.

Lesions on CT scans can be seen only as areas of increased or decreased density. In a strict sense, little more can be said about a lesion than that it is an area of increased or decreased absorption of x-rays. However, experience has shown that various lesions have typical absorption characteristics, and it is possible for the neurologist or radiologist to make highly accurate interpretations as to the nature of the pathologic condition from looking at the CT scan. When the clinical findings are taken into consideration, the CT scan interpretation can approach certainty.

The iron in hemoglobin makes blood a strong photon-absorbing substance. There is not enough blood within a voxel containing a blood vessel for this to be evident on the routine CT scan, but when an abnormal collection of blood occurs in the brain, a high-density lesion results. If the ventricular system is seen as a dense, white structure, a subarachnoid hemorrhage would be strongly suspected. The diagnosis would be confirmed by knowing that the patient was hypertensive, had the explosive onset of excruciating headache a few hours earlier, and was now comatose. Hypertensive or traumatic hematomas can also appear within the substance of the brain itself (see Figure 4.7).

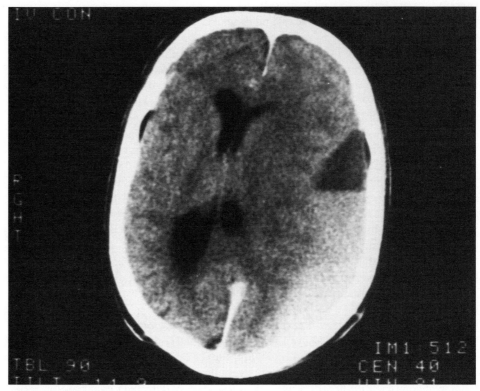

Figure 4.7. This single CT image shows a huge subdural hematoma overlying the left hemisphere. There have been two episodes of bleeding, giving a layer of dense new blood beneath an older layer of degenerated fluid. There is a shift of the brain to the left due to swelling.

Neoplastic tissue is usually denser than normal brain tissue. In addition, tumors often have a rich blood supply, they may accumulate excessive amounts of calcium, and they can contain hemorrhages. For these reasons, the CT image of a tumor is one of a high-density lesion often surrounded by a considerable area of tissue edema, represented as region of decreased tissue absorption (see Figure 4.8a). Tumors that are metastatic often appear as one or more discrete densities, while primary tumors are often more diffuse or poorly delineated or appear as a multicentric mass.

It is not always possible to differentiate a tumor from an abscess. Abscesses destroy tissue and appear as spots of decreased density; but a typical abscess is surrounded by a rim of very vascular tissue, the abscess capsule, which appears as a dense ring, particularly on the contrast phase. Unfortunately, the dense and hypervascular tissue of a tumor can surround a core of necrotic tissue, giving an identical picture of a ring lesion that enhances just like an abscess (see Figure 4.8b).

The typical occlusive stroke is seen as an area of decreased density on the CT scan, often with a distribution that is characteristic for the occluded vessel. In the first 12–24 hours of the stroke, the CT scan may appear entirely normal. Over the next several days, an area of low density develops that may extend considerably beyond the zone of infarcted brain due to the development of edema. The edema then gradually resolves, leaving a well-defined region of infarction (see Figures 4.9a and 4.9b). During the

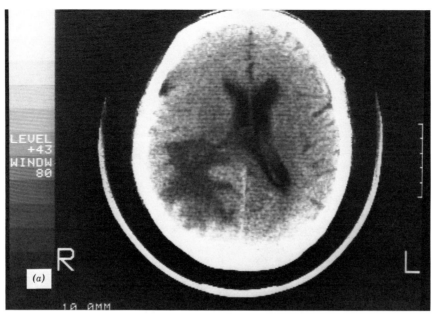

Figure 4.8a. This CT scan shows an area of edema in the right hemisphere, with a barely perceptible area of increased density posteriorly.

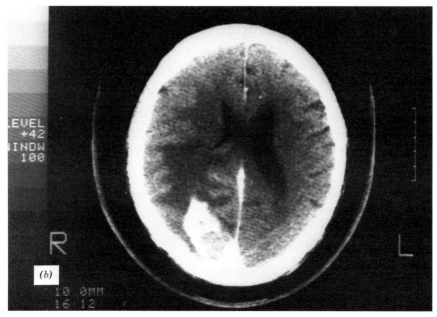

Figure 4.8b. With contrast infusion, an irregular ring of enhancement can be seen at the same level as in Figure 4.8a. The patient had a metastatic tumor.

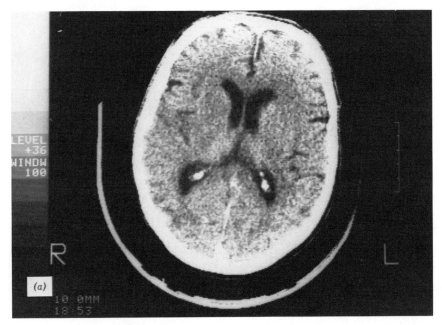

Figure 4.9a.   The patient suffered the abrupt onset of left-sided weakness. A CT scan within 24 hours of onset was normal.

phase of resolution, contrast enhancement may show increased vascularity in the cortex, a phenomenon known as "luxury perfusion." This seems to be a part of the brain's attempt to cope with the stroke by increasing regional blood flow.

It has long been thought that many occlusive strokes have some bleeding at the site of the infarction. It is actually uncommon to see free blood in the region of an occlusive stroke on the CT scan; sometimes some speckling of blood is present. Patients with primary hemorrhage often present as a stroke, but the hemorrhage seen on the CT scan fills the whole area of the stroke in such cases. Many patients with clinically unequivocal strokes have normal CT scans. In some, it may be simply that a single CT scan is done too early in the course of the evolution of the stroke. In others, the lesion may be too small to be visualized; this is certainly the case in many strokes of the brainstem and in the very common small lacunar stroke, located in the internal capsule or other deep white matter.

Dementia is an area of great interest in contemporary neurology. As patients age, some decline in the ability to think and remember appears inevitable. When these cognitive skills are impaired out of proportion to the changes expected with age, the patient is said to have dementia. In any population of demented patients, the majority have Alzheimer's disease. All the dementias are characterized by atrophic changes in the brain; the sulci become wider, the gyri flatten, and the ventricular system enlarges. In Alzheimer's disease, these changes are accompanied by characteristic histopathological lesions, including senile plaques and neurofibrillary tangles. The senile plaque is an island of amyloid in the cortex, surrounded by distorted cellular processes; neurons are lost throughout the cortex and replaced by these plaques. Many of the remaining neurons are distorted by masses of coiled helical filaments called tangles, which have characteristic staining properties with metallic dyes. Pick's disease is a

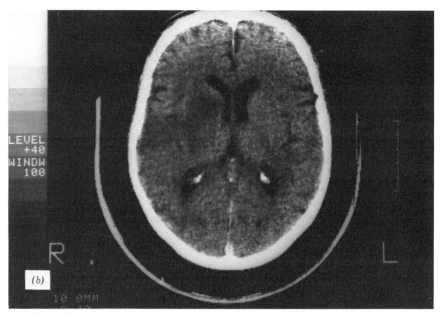

Figure 4.9b.   CT scan done a week after onset shows a low-density lesion in the right hemisphere consistent with a cerebrovascular accident.

much rarer form of dementia. The atrophy in this condition is more likely to be confined to the frontal and temporal lobes, and the cellular inclusions have a different morphology.

In a population of healthy elderly patients, variable degrees of atrophy may be seen on the CT scan (Hughes & Grado, 1981), while the EEG often shows slowing. In a population of demented patients, these changes are more prominent. However, there is a large degree of overlap, and individual patients who are unequivocally demented may show less "abnormality" than some of the elderly patients who are clearly not demented. While strong correlations can be shown among atrophy, EEG slowing, and loss of cognitive skills, the relationship remains statistical (Coben, Danziger, & Berg, 1983; Damasio, et al., 1983; Eslinger, Damasio, Graff-Radford, & Damasio, 1984; Kemper, 1984).

There has been ongoing debate about the relationship between Alzheimer's disease and the dementia of the very elderly. Patients with senile dementia exhibit histopathological changes essentially identical to Alzheimer's disease, although the latter is typically diagnosed in patients in the presenium. Traditionally, Alzheimer's disease has been viewed as a premature aging. Recent biochemical research suggests that this is not true; Alzheimer's disease appears to represent a distinct entity (Rosser, Iverson, Reynold, Mountjoy, & Roth, 1984).

Other dementing illnesses also exist. Creutzfeldt-Jakob disease is a severe and rapidly progressive form of dementia associated with myoclonic jerks, atrophy, and fasciculations. The EEG shows a characteristic pattern of suppression of normal rhythms with interspersed bursts of sharp and slow activity. The brain shows a diffuse loss of neurons with a spongy vacuolation of the neuropil. Formerly, the disease was classified as a degenerative disorder, along with Alzheimer's disease, but it is now recognized to be caused by a chronic infection with an atypical agent called a prion (Bockman, Kingsbury, McKinley, Bendheim, & Pruisner, 1985). It seems highly likely that Alzheimer's disease is also caused by prions.

Huntington's disease is a dominantly inherited disorder that usually appears in early middle age. Clinically it is characterized by psychiatric symptoms; dementia; and chorea, a movement disorder. Both cortical and subcortical neurons are lost, but the basal ganglia are particularly involved, and the CT scan in fully developed cases shows a fairly characteristic butterfly pattern of ventricular involvement due to the loss of the heads of the caudate nuclei. The chromosome carrying the Huntington's gene has recently been identified, and intensive efforts are now under way to identify the gene itself.

In normal-pressure hydrocephalus, a relatively mild and slowly progressive dementia is seen, accompanied by urinary incontinence and spastic gait. The CT shows large ventricles but relatively preserved cortex; lumbar puncture reveals normal or only minimally elevated cerebrospinal fluid (CSF) pressure despite the ventricular enlargement, thus the name. Radioisotopes injected into the lumbar subarachnoid space demonstrate an abnormal CSF circulation, with tracer accumulating in the ventricles without the usual rapid flow laterally and upward over the hemispheres. If the ventricular system is surgically shunted, some of these patients show arrest or even reversal of their dementia.

Several techniques currently being studied may produce even more valuable images of the brain than those obtained with CT scanning. In nuclear magnetic resonance (NMR), the brain is placed in a complex magnetic field and then stimulated with a burst of radio waves; it responds by producing a series of electromagnetic signals that can be used to create a computer-reconstructed image similar to the CT scan. The technique is now being called MRI (magnetic resonance imaging). The first advantage of this system is that it does not require the use of x-rays. As far as can be told at this time, the technique is without risk. Another interesting feature is that the image can be varied according to a number of technical parameters, giving the potential for a variety of different images from the same brain (Buonanno, Kistler, DeWitt, Pykett, & Brady, 1983). The MRI is much more sensitive in detecting the presence of white matter plaques in multiple sclerosis than is traditional CT (Lukes, Crooks, & Aminoff, 1983). Presumably, as the technique is developed, other highly specific imaging methods will evolve for other diseases. Positron emission tomography (PET) scanning combines features of isotope scanning and computer image reconstruction. A unique feature of the PET scan is the use of metabolically active carrier molecules for the radioactive label. For example, deoxyglucose is taken up initially by the brain as if it were glucose, but the molecule does not continue to be metabolized. Thus, active areas of the brain, when exposed to a transient pulse of blood carrying deoxyglucose labeled with a radioactive atom, accumulate radioactivity. These active areas then radiate positrons for a brief period of time. The positrons decay into pairs of photons, which are used to make a tomographic image. The image shows regions of the brain active at the time of administering the pulse of labeled drug. This technique is a bridge between the static, structural images of the brain produced by other radiological methods and the image of functional activity obtained with electroencephalograms. Using labeled oxygen atoms, PET scanning has been able to contribute new insight into the evolution of ischemic stroke (Frackowiak & Wise, 1983). Labeled neurotransmitters can be used to demonstrate the distribution of receptor sites in the living brain. The research potential for this technique is enormous.

SUMMARY

Unfortunately for the patient who wants a straight answer to the question: "Is it Big Casino?," the physician is usually limited to a reply in the form of: "Probably." A major component of this probability estimate comes from the history, the neurological examination, and the subliminal information gathered as the physician interacts with the patient. By the time the physician resorts to laboratory studies, he or she either has a pretty good idea of what will be found or at least has a limited number of hypotheses that will be tested by a deeper look into the structure and function of the brain. The information from the laboratory further elevates the physician's hunches toward incarnation as a diagnosis, but at the point the diagnosis is made, it still is a statement of probability much more often than one of absolute certainty. In this context, the experienced neuropsychologist will limit the information supplied to the clinician to statements of function. It is reasonable to add supporting information in the form of: "Such performance deficits are often seen in patients with frontal lobe disease." The report that reads: "This patient has frontal lobe damage, as shown by . . . " will rightly be met with skepticism, if not frank hostility.

It is also well to remember the clinical aphorism *Absence of proof is not proof of absence*. A disease can be said to be present with a high level of confidence if the history, examination, and laboratory studies all show a high degree of congruence with the expected profile of the disease; but its presence can never be ruled out by negative results of a test or examination.

REFERENCES

Adey, W. R. (1969). Slow electrical phenomena in the nervous system. *Neurosciences Research Progress Bulletin, 7.*

Ajmone-Marsan, C., & Zivin, L. (1970). Factors related to the occurrence of typical paroxysmal abnormalities in the EEG of epileptic patients. *Epilepsia, 11,* 361–381.

Bockman, J., Kingsbury, D., McKinley, M., Bendheim, P., & Pruisner, S. (1985). Creutzfeldt-Jakob disease prion proteins in human brain. *New England Journal of Medicine, 312,* 73–78.

Buonanno, F. S., Kistler, J., DeWitt, L., Pykett, I., & Brady, T. (1983). Proton (^{1}H) nuclear magnetic resonance (NMR) imaging in stroke syndromes. *Neurological Clinics, 1,* 243–262.

Celesia, G. C. (1982). Clinical evaluation of evoked potentials. In E. Niedermeyer & F. Lopes de Silva (Eds.), *Electroencephalography* (pp. 665–683). Baltimore: Urban and Schwarzenberg.

Coben, L., Danziger, W., & Berg, L. (1983). Frequency analysis of the awake resting EEG in mild senile dementia of Alzheimer type. *Electroencephalography and Clinical Neurophysiology, 55,* 372–380.

Damasio, H., Eslinger, P., Domasio, A., Rizzo, M., Huang, H., & Demeter, S. (1983). Quantitative computed tomographic analysis in the diagnosis of dementia. *Archives of Neurology, 40,* 715–719.

Da Silva, F. (1982). Event-related potentials: Methodology and quantification. In E. Niedermeyer & F. Da Silva (Eds.), *Electroencephalography* (pp. 655–664). Baltimore: Urban and Schwartzenberger.

Eslinger, P., Damasio, H., Graff-Radford, N., Damasio, A. (1984). Examining the relationship between computed tomography and neuropsychological measures in normal and demented elderly. *Journal of Neurology, Neurosurgery, and Psychiatry, 47,* 1319–1325.

Filskov, S. B., Grimm, B. H., & Lewis, J. A. (1981). Brain-behavior relationships. In S. B. Filskov & T. J. Boll (Eds.), *Handbook of clinical neuropsychology* (pp. 39–73). New York: John Wiley & Sons.

Frackowiak, R. S., & Wise, R. (1983). Positron tomography in ischemic cerebrovascular disease. *Neurologic Clinics, 1*, 183–200.

Gibbs, F., Gibbs, E., & Lennox, W. (1937). Epilepsy: A paroxysmal cerebral dysrhythmia. *Brain, 60*, 377–388.

Gloor, P. (1969). Hans Berger, on the electroencephalogram of man. *Electroencephalography and Clinical Neurophysiology*, (Suppl. 28).

Hughes, C., & Grado, M. (1981). Computed tomography and the aging brain. *Neuroradiology, 139*, 391–396.

Kemper, T. (1984). Neuroanatomical and neuropathological changes in normal aging and dementia. In M. Albert (Ed.), *Clinical neurology in aging*, (pp. 9–52). New York: Oxford University Press.

Knight, R. (1984). Decreased response to novel stimuli after prefrontal lesions in man. *Electroencephalography and Clinical Neurophysiology, 59*, 9–20.

Lewis, J. A. (1982). The value of the EEG as a laboratory test. *American Journal of EEG Technology, 22*, 113–124.

Lukes, S., Crooks, L., & Aminoff, M. Nuclear magnetic resonance imaging in multiple sclerosis. *Annals of Neurology, 13*, 592–601.

Matthews, W. B. (1964). The use and abuse of electroencephalography. *Lancet, 2*, 577–579.

Oldendorf, W. H. (1980). *The quest for an image of brain*. New York: Raven Press.

Pfefferbaum, A., Wenegrat, B., Ford, J., Roth, W., & Kopell, B. (1984). Clinical application of the P3 component of event-related potentials. 2. Dementia, depression, schizophrenia. *Electroencephalography and Clinical Neurophysiology, 59*, 104–124.

Rosser, M., Iverson, L., Reynold, G., Mountjoy, C., & Roth, M. (1984). Neurochemical characteristics of early and late onset types of Alzheimer's disease. *British Medical Journal, 288*, 961–964.

Walter, W. G. (1936). Location of cerebral tumors by EEG. *Lancet, 2*, 305–308.

CHAPTER 5

Nontraditional and Threshold Considerations in Neuropsychological Assessment

Thomas J. Boll

Human clinical neuropsychology has made progress across a continuum of responsibility, recognition, and scientific accomplishment. The earliest forms of neuropsychological investigations were accomplished in what would now be recognized as a behavioral neurological format, rather than a primarily or formally psychological one. These investigations, dating from earliest medical writings, recognized the effects of blows to and diseases of the head upon human behavior. Within the last century, more focused and formalized investigations, still primarily within the behavioral neurological format, attended to the effects of intracranial disorders upon specific types of mental capacities. The discovery, initially by Dax in the 1830s but given widest recognition through Broca's presentation in the 1860s (Broca, 1865), that damage to the left cerebral hemisphere produced decrements in language capacity is probably the most notable milestone in this type of development. Other investigations examined effects of damage to the frontal part of the brain upon basic psychological functions, such as appetite, sexuality, and aggressiveness as well as more complex issues of social adjustment. These studies were followed rather quickly by investigations of specific disease processes, such as cerebral neoplasms; the major degenerative and demyelinating diseases, such as Parkinson's disease and multiple sclerosis; and the disorders of greatest prevalence, especially cerebrovascular disorders that could be characterized as having specific effects. While these investigations were certainly ground breaking, and in some instances even professionally earthshaking, they seem relatively obvious and pedestrian in light of the degree of sophistication to which we have become accustomed recently. Nevertheless, as recently as the 1950s and early 1960s, issues of the role of the right cerebral hemisphere were barely discussed, and issues of whether behavioral measurements could accurately reflect the integrity of brain functions represented the frontier of human clinical neuropsychology. While this is not intended to be an historical review, nevertheless these few statements serve to place the remainder of the discussion in a broader context, thereby underlining the very real and amazing changes in focus that neuropsychological activities have undergone, even in the last 10 years.

Current neuropsychological developments can be characterized in a number of ways. One type of characterization is by specific psychological context, such as attention, memory, language processes, and affective functions. The developments can also be characterized neuroanatomically by considering investigations of the frontal lobes or subcortical structures as they may relate to various psychological capacities, as well as the more traditional cortical investigations, particularly as they continue to need additional attention in childhood disorders. This chapter will take yet another approach. Threshold areas will be identified and used to indicate the degree of sophistication that now characterizes neuropsychological investigation and the breadth and generality of neuropsychological approaches within the overall field of human measurement and diagnosis. No longer can neuropsychological investigation be viewed as solely oriented toward the diagnosis of brain damage. Nor can neuropsychological examination be seen as appropriate only for those patients with clear and obvious neurological diseases and disorders.

PSYCHOLOGICAL EMPHASIS

The first development, or threshold, is the movement within neuropsychology toward a more psychological, rather than a neurodiagnostic, emphasis. In a psychological sphere, in addition to the use of behaviors for exquisite neuroanatomical appreciation, which represents a continuing and legitimate investigational area, neuropsychologists provide, with increasing sophistication, psychological descriptions designed primarily to help in understanding the person, rather than the person's neuroanatomy. This represents a major role, function, and purpose of neuropsychological undertakings in a sizable percentage of currently functioning neuropsychology laboratories.

What we are probably describing here is a genuine maturing of the field of neuropsychology. The first step was to establish the basic validity of neuropsychological activities. The place for this was in centers where neuropsychological disorders were most prominent and where documentation could be most clear: the neurological and neurosurgical centers in patients with well-known neurological disorders. Having done that, the field had the opportunity to take more than a single course. The first course that was taken—and one that will continue to be pursued—was the development of increasingly sophisticated methods of documenting and detailing the neurocognitive consequences of increasingly subtle varieties of neurological disorder. This is a valid pursuit and one which continues to provide the scientific underpinning for advances in other areas.

The threshold of awareness of human psychological difficulties produced by brain-based or brain-altering disorders is lowering almost yearly. Our realization has increased that many generalized, initially mild, and in some instances slowly progressive and not obviously disabling conditions may reduce mental acuity, produce changes in personality, and alter coping patterns effecting complex human interrelationships, not to mention occupational task performance. Within the past decade or so, it has been possible to document that conditions known to produce significant eventual physical disability produce, at least in a reasonable portion of patients, significant mental disability well before this disability is superficially or clinically obvious and well before the disorder produces significant concomitant physical disruption. Examples of this type of development include our broadened awareness of the neuropsychological concomitants of Parkinson's disease, Huntington's chorea, and multiple sclerosis (Reitan & Boll, 1971; Boll, Heaton, & Reitan, 1974; Chapter 14). Investigations of these three conditions, commonly seen as the most significant primary neurological degenerative diseases just a decade ago, have been dwarfed by the emergence of concern about and investigation of a primary neurological degenerative disease once thought of as relatively rare and even esoteric: Alzheimer's disease (see Chapter 15).

From an historical point of view, it is worth noting that as recently as the 1950s, patients who experienced significant deterioration of mental functions were routinely given psychiatric diagnoses and housed, on a chronic basis, in psychiatric facilities. Subsequent understanding developed in the 1960s led most commonly to a diagnosis for such patients of arteriosclerotic cerebral vascular disease (ASCVD). It was not until the middle 1970s that a sizable percentage of these patients could expect to receive a diagnosis consistent with their actual neuropathology. At that time, one of the more trivial but frequently heated debates in neuropsychology—the debate as to why certain measurement procedures could not make an accurate distinction between degenerative cerebrovascular disease and primary neuronal degenerative disease—simply disappeared when it was recognized that the neuropsychological data had probably been right all along. The failure to find difference was in fact a reflection of the absence of such a difference, rather than a reflection of the inadequacy of the data gathered. The recency of this issue speaks to the rapidity of the progress we are enjoying. The nature of the debate reflects that our preconceived ideas often cause us to fail to see the information before us. It also points out the accuracy of the neuropsychological data that has been available in assessing human functions, even though in some instances we were unable to appreciate its accuracy for a considerable period of time.

HEAD INJURY

A condition that may represent a prototype for current and future medical-neurological-neuropsychological (with an emphasis on the *psychological*) investigation and clinical understanding is head injury. For more than a few decades, the head-injured patient was, almost without exception, one who had received an injury sufficient to result in significant physical or mental disability requiring some period of time spent undergoing one or a number of varieties of formal rehabilitation. Such patients, without exception, went through a period of acute and dramatic, often life-threatening illness and prolonged hospitalization. They experienced, at least initially, obvious mental incapacity followed by gradual and significant, if imperfect, improvement over a course of months, rather than days or weeks. During this time, many neuropsychological syndromes could be appreciated and carefully documented. While much was learned from attention to such patients, much was also ignored. The dramatic nature of neurocognitive symptoms and the significant degree of neurological disruption produced by the injury tended to focus attention on a more limited aspect of brain-behavior relationships: the development of complex language, personality, and memory disorder syndromes.

The parallel or, in most instances, subsequent development of significant disruptions across the broad range of human life activities, however, was largely ignored by neuropsychological investigators. Return to work was of some interest. The ability to return to family life; the ability to function adequately as a member of the family; the degree of environmental, social, and inter- and intrapersonal stress produced by such a patient in the entire family complex; and the significant misunderstandings that such a patient's later behaviors produced, not only in family members, but in employers and fellow citizens, while possibly of some concern to individual neuropsychological clinicians, were not commonly encountered in the neuropsychology literature. These questions were given little attention until the very recent and significant interest in minor head injury. With the development of interest in this neurological phenomena, awareness developed, not only of the human effects produced by such minor injuries, but also of similar effects in patients with much more severe brain damage. Therefore, the study of minor head injuries has not only produced significant information about the brain-behavior relationships affected by subtle changes in brain integrity but has also expanded neuropsychological interests to the full range of effects and individuals affected by both mild and severe neurological disruption.

Data indicating the occurrence of as many as 9 million head injuries in any single year in the United states have been published (Caveness, 1977). When one considers the fact that most relatively minor injuries go unreported and, in most instances, totally untreated and even unrecognized, the relationship of this phenomena to temporary primary psychological disruptions and longer-term secondary psychological disruptions is just being uncovered (for additional information on incidence rates, see Chapter 17).

EXTERNAL FACTORS IN NEUROPSYCHOLOGICAL ADJUSTMENT

An area of obvious threshold significance for current development is the complex interrelationship between head injury and interpersonal adjustment, which may well begin before the injury itself. Premorbid adjustment, both medically and psychologically, must be considered, along with myriad socioeconomic variables, if one is to adequately predict the effect, not only of the neurological trauma, but of the neuropsychological deficit on an individual's final coping capacity and level of posttraumatic functioning (Rutter, Chadwick, Schaffer, & Brown, 1980; Chadwick, Rutter, Brown Schaffer, & Traub, 1981; Brown, Chadwick, Schaffer, Rutter, & Traub, 1981; Chadwick, Rutter, Schaffer, & Shrout, 1981). In fact, a continuing thread in the new social and neuropsychological investigations is the importance of those factors supporting and characterizing the individual—independent of the medical neurological event (whether they precede it or coexist with it)—that may influence the nature of the event or its likelihood of occurrence. More important, such factors may, and clearly do in many instances, influence the characteristics that the individual brings to the event and are then of subsequent importance with regard to the nature of the outcome that is likely or possible. Obviously, an individual with compromised intellectual functions, severe psychological disruption, and extensive limitations of socioenvironmental resources is likely to appear less adequately recovered following any sort of an event than is an individual who brings to that event a significantly more advantaged set of premorbid circumstances. This is not to say that every individual who has a head injury is a compromised host or that every individual who has a less than adequate outcome was in some way disabled before the injury. It does, however, raise the issue, discussed thoughtfully by Rutter (1977), of the interactional, transactional, and additive effects of any sort of medical disruption on overall life functioning.

These considerations further tend to lower the threshold of necessary awareness of possible susceptibility to negative behavioral consequences of medical-neurological events. If, as the data continue to suggest, individuals with a poor socioeconomic background, compromised psychological adjustment, and disruptive home environment are more likely to have negative outcomes following any sort of acute medical event or in the face of chronic medical illness, then several steps must be taken. First, individuals from such environments must be seen as at greater risk for long-term consequences of illnesses and accidents. Rather than being encouraged to become involved in situations that are high risk in themselves for these kinds of diseases, disorders, and traumas, such persons should be most insulated from them. Second, the health care must be adjusted to take into account the fact that, while secondary psychological characteristics have a particular prevalence among upper middle class individuals, the prevalence is significantly higher among persons from more disrupted and less advantageous circumstances. Therefore, the overall conceptualization of the normal treatment process, the normal recovery phase, and the normal morbidity from any disease or disorder will have to take into account all relevant variables rather than attempting to deal with the disease as though it exists in some sort of vacuum, which is manifestly not the case. Reconstitution of an environment able to support an individual and reintegration of that individual into the environment may become a construction and habilitation, rather than a reconstruction and rehabilitation, project. Likewise, an individual already marginal with regard to a variety of coping capacities may well suffer significantly greater deficits from an injury than may a person whose supporting environment, both internal and external, appears to provide significant reserves not enjoyed by that person's less socially and biologically robust counterpart. For that reason, notions that suggest that an individual who is already compromised is in some fashion less worthy of attention and compensation following a significant injury because the person brought less to the injury may be the reverse of the most practical position. While any individual injured deserves every possible consideration, one could make the argument that individuals who are compromised hosts to begin with represent that population for whom the greatest expenditure of energy and resources should be directed, as they are the ones who are likely to suffer disproportionately from any reduction in their already meager capacity to make their way adequately.

Recent research reports and reviews focusing on the consequences of minor craniocerebral trauma have been unanimous in their reporting of mental sequelae immediately and even for some extended period following relatively minor head injury. These reports also have documented an increasing sensitivity of neuropsychological measurements, or at least an increasing awareness on the part of neuropsychologists looking at their measurements, to the consequences of injuries that, in an earlier day, may not have been deemed worthy of attention (Rimel, Giordani, Barth, Boll, & Jane, 1981; Barth, et al., 1983; Boll, 1983; Boll & Barth, 1983). Klonoff, Low, and Clark (1977), in prospective study utilizing a relatively extensive battery of neurocognitive measurements, found that children with very minor medical neurological damage to the head were, in an alarmingly high percentage of instances, documented to be experiencing continued recovery four and even five years postinjury. In fact, these investigators reported that over 27 percent of the children who premorbidly had no evidence of need for special educational attention found themselves in other than regular classroom placements for at least a year. Given the very minor nature of the injuries to the majority of children in the Klonoff study, this by itself is a powerful indicant that children, far from being invulnerable to the consequences of injury to the brain, may well be significantly disrupted beyond the point that might be identified if careful neuropsychological evaluations are not provided. Levin and Eisenberg (1979) documented in a similar fashion that, while children with much greater degrees of cerebral damage were obviously more impaired and for a longer period of time, children with very minor injuries, including those in whom unconsciousness could not be documented, were, at least for a period of time, demonstrably less able than normal peers according to several neurocognitive measures.

Impairment of higher cognitive functions on even an *apparently* temporary basis, and even when relatively short-term, can be seen to be significantly disruptive in an individual for whom day-to-day mental performance is the requirement, such as a child in school. That there may be long-term consequences of such "temporary" injury requires only the further recognition that a period of failure, disruption, disorganization, and incapacity can result relatively directly in anxiety, task avoidance, and uncertainty, not to mention failed background-task development, upon which future skills must be built. If, even for a relatively short period of time, a child is unable to benefit from class lessons for which no make-up work is provided and of which no recognition is even present, then the child is in a significantly more precarious position than that child who is taken out of school due to prolonged illness or even due to such happy circumstances as a winter vacation. The latter children are given take-home assignments, are recognized as having missed a period of time in class, and are, on occasion, dealt with specially in anticipation of or following their period of absence. Following a head injury, a child may miss only a day or two of school, if that. While in school, the child may appear to be attending even though mental processes are clearly subnormal. Such children typically receive no special consideration, attention, or preparation. On the contrary, a child who suddenly and inconsistently fails to perform at expected levels may receive considerable negative comment, pressure, and disapproval, while at the same time struggling with altered mental acuity of which neither the child, the child's parents, nor teacher are aware.

The importance of recognizing these seemingly temporary deficits and knowing that they may be longer lasting than current clinical capacity allows us to identify is underlined by a careful study by Gronwall and Wrightson (1975). They found that college students who returned to apparently normal functioning after a relatively brief period of recovery from head trauma and functioned in an entirely acceptable fashion were, nevertheless, documented to have less mental stamina than a perfectly normally functioning group of college mates. These students, although having finished a college curriculum and, therefore, presumably reasonably normal, were unable to withstand the relatively minor stresses of reduced oxygen at high altitudes as well as were matched controls fully three years after their head injury. That these students might dysfunction in similar situations of adversity—whether induced by additional sessions of reduced oxygen or by more normally occurring situations, such as high emotional stress, loss of sleep, illness, or medication—suggests that heightened awareness of the future as well as current risks sustained by patients who have experienced cerebrocranial trauma must be developed. Gronwall and Wrightson also documented that, among other ways such individuals may be at risk, they were at risk for increasingly negative consequences of subsequent head injuries. While such individuals may appear to be going into a second head injury in a fashion entirely equal to that of a nonpreviously injured colleague, such is not the case. An individual who has sustained a second head injury is documentably (Symonds, 1962) less able to withstand the negative effects of that injury and emerge sequelae free than is a nonpreviously injured individual.

The neurocognitive consequences of head injury and the attendant broader psychological consequences with regard to reactions to stress, resilience, emotional capacity, and ability to perform in a wide variety of environmental circumstances is only beginning to receive the breadth of appreciation that appears appropriate on the basis of data long available.

A series of studies by Rutter and colleagues (Rutter, Chadwick, Shaffer & Brown, 1980; Chadwick, Rutter, Brown, Shaffer & Traub, 1981; Brown, Chadwick, Shaffer, Rutter & Traub, 1981; Chadwick, Rutter, Shaffer & Shrout, 1981), while excellent in many respects, draws a conclusion that any head injury in children producing post-traumatic amnesia of less than one week is unlikely to produce significant neurocognitive consequences. While the unreliability of posttraumatic amnesia even in adults has recently been discussed and its limitations as a marker for head injury more fully realized recently (Gronwall & Wrightson, 1975), additional comments about the Rutter studies are warranted. It appears that something of a straw man has been created with regard to expectancies about what these studies refer to as dose-response relationships. Failing to find this expected relationship leads Rutter and colleagues to question the likelihood that relatively minor injuries will produce significant deficits by themselves. Unfortunately, no rationale for such expectation is provided. There is no documentation that *dosage* as applied to head injury variables is comparable to the measurability of pharmacologic dosage. They point out that, except in very severe head injury, no medical dose-response relationship has been established. However, even in severe injury, the presence of skull fracture is known to be without prognostic significance. The complexity of measuring the severity of the head injury cannot be gainsaid, nor can it simply be dismissed by reference to one marker, such as posttraumatic amnesia. It is well known that many persons with penetrating head injuries have no unconsciousness and no posttraumatic amnesia, and yet they experience significant destruction of brain tissues and mental faculties. On the other hand, persons who have sustained significant impairment of frontal lobe functions may reveal essentially no measurable neurocognitive deficits in the traditional areas of problem solving, learning, memory, attention, and IQ. Yet such patients may be so severely dysfunctional as to be totally incapacitated on the basis of loss of initiative and self-monitoring functions known to be relatable to frontal lobe disorders. Furthermore, the complexity of the neuropathological process involved in minor head injury as this process is distributed throughout the brain is just being subjected to fairly careful scrutiny. Therefore, expectations extrapolated from experiences with severe head injury with regard to posttraumatic amnesia as a marker may or may not stand the test of time as a predictor of severity in mild head injury. It is even possible that posttraumatic amnesia, like length of unconsciousness, except at the extreme, may turn out to be an irrelevant variable. In addition, psychosocial background factors, well appreciated by the Rutter group, may add yet unappreciated variability to an individual child's experience of neurocognitive sequelae following head injury without diminishing the significance of the head injury itself.

Head injury is far from the only condition in which severity or dosage is poorly determined. This is also the case for conditions of obvious neuropathological significance with well-documented neurocognitive deficits, such as encephalitis and viral hepatitis. Not only is the pathophysiology of the neuropsychological alterations of viral hepatitis not well understood, but there is an absence of clear correlation between severity and clinical histologic disease and neuropsychological symptoms (Apstein, Koff, & Koff, 1979).

While adding complexity to research undertaking, such difficulties do not in any way demonstrate that, although some children may show the effect more than others, the effect is not there simply because as an overall group, average results can be obtained. Average results can in no way be confused with normal results according to IQ or other measurements. In fact, by restricting oneself to measures of central tendency as it relates to variability, our own research has been used to show that individuals with marked learning disabilities, as well as individuals with well-documented epilepsy, cannot be demonstrated to have neurocognitive problems (Reitan & Boll, 1973). When more sophisticated measures involving individual comparisons were used, however, these same individuals were found not only to follow a pattern that is very characteristic of that seen in individuals with known neurological deficits from other causes, but to follow a pattern that is clearly deficient in comparison with normal groups. This, however, required ratings of the presence of numbers of individual disorders rather than simply looking at average performance, particularly on measures routinely used in clinical procedures, such as IQ tests.

Failure to find, with any population, increased incidence of special education placement—cited as further evidence of lack of sequelae by Rutter—also represents a negative finding of little persuasive capacity. While the presence of a child in a special education class probably reflects the fact that something has gone wrong, there are many reasons (other than normal performance) to explain why a child may not be in a special class. The most obvious is that many school systems simply do not have the financial capacity to provide special education experiences for every educationally deserving child. Therefore, only the most severely impaired or only children of a specific type or category may qualify. In a school system where the competitive level of the overall group is relatively low or where the financial resources are extremely limited, many individuals who would be found, on individual investigation, to be in significant need of special resources, may be, in the context of their school environment, unable to obtain those resources or, even worse, may not be identified as needing them. Therefore, while positive findings, as is so often the case, carry significant weight, negative findings must be viewed somewhat more cautiously.

It should also be pointed out that Rutter's studies provided fairly complete neurocognitive measurements of only severely injured children. Those with the mildest injuries—and thus the most likely to have sustained injuries requiring the most careful kind of mental measurement and for whom overall and generalized deficits may not be the characteristic pattern—were given the most restricted number of psychological tests. Even though the Rutter group is to be congratulated for the careful work with the more severe group, and even though they have entered a note of important caution, the data from multiple centers suggesting negative consequences from minor injuries must be taken seriously.

Two lessons can be learned about the consequences of minor head injury. One is that, in the entire history of medicine, never have new, sophisticated investigational procedures designed to provide additional understanding of the anatomical, physiological, or behavioral condition of the human being served to dismiss as absent conditions previously thought to be present. In fact, just the opposite has been the case. New procedures designed to assess the anatomical, physiological, and behavioral capacity of individuals have, without exception, been able to document the presence, rather than the absence, of conditions previously thought to be spiritual, psychological, or in some other fashion basically unreal—that is, not actually present. Stress fractures and subtle anatomical anomalies not visualizable on plain x-ray films can now be identified through nuclear scans and computerized tomographic procedures. Therefore, it is extremely unlikely that our neurocognitive measures, which have been able to demonstrate over the last half century increasing degrees of validity and sensitivity to the presence of psychological consequences of many disorders previously thought to be mentally uninvolving, have now gone too far.

The second lesson is that neuropsychologists must become more aware of their psychological foundations. They must recognize the fact that multiple factors enter into any incapacity in human functioning. All that produces cognitive dysfunction is not necessarily, primarily, or even secondarily neurological in nature. Antecedent factors, such as disruptive environment, poor opportunity, and primary emotional pathology not tied to neurological dysfunction can all result in compromised mental performance. The effects of these factors may, in some circumstances, appear strikingly similar to the effects likely to be produced by neurological events themselves. Obviously, in attempting to appreciate the neurocognitive sequelae of any event, one must understand that which the patient has brought to that event and that which the patient is likely to have left once the event has occurred. Clearly, a person cannot be expected to recover to a position that he or she had not attained initially. Therefore, Rutter's warning, in the broadest sense, that all aspects of a patient's psychological situation must be understood in order to properly appreciate the neurocognitive sequelae of a craniocerebral trauma is both an appropriate warning and a specific challenge to further research.

In undertaking such research, however, one must be careful not to expect a linear relationship between findings attributable to severe injury and those found in minor injury. Second, one must be extremely cautious in extrapolating models—for instance, applying models from pharmacologic research to research concerning minor neurocognitive deficits—lest one be disappointed on the basis of expectations inappropriate to the conditions being investigated (Casson et al., 1984; Prigatano, Stahl, Orr & Zeiner, 1982; Lezak, 1978).

THE RELATIONSHIP BETWEEN NONNEUROLOGICAL DISORDERS AND NEUROCOGNITIVE PROCESSES

A further development, or threshold, is the growth of neuropsychological sophistication in the investigation of the relationship between nonneurological disorders and neurocognitive processes. The quality of the survival of many medical disorders may be compromised by changes in higher mental process capacity. This is now grist for the neuropsychologists' mill (see Chapter 10). The very existence of a chronic disorder in almost any human system may signal risk for compromised neurocognitive capacity. Investigations of patients with extremes of endocrinologic dysfunctions, such as myxedema (Reitan, 1955) and Cushing's syndrome (Whelan, Schteingart, Starkman, & Smith, 1980) have demonstrated the presence of concomitant neurocognitive deficits. While not all patients suffering these types of disorders are necessarily psychologically impaired, the risk of such impairment is sufficiently high in a reasonable number of such patients that routine care should include attention to this possible aspect of a general system disorder. In the careful study of Cushing's syndrome referred to above, 37% of the total population studied did not show neurocognitive deficits; one-third showed mild difficulties; 23% showed at least moderate difficulties in the areas of language and nonlanguage higher cognitive functions; and 11% showed not only higher cognitive deficits but also difficulties in lower-level psychological functions, such as those related to the motor and sensory systems. Overall, over 60% of the total population showed difficulties in "nonverbal visuo-ideational, and visuo-memory functions" in a pattern identified as similar to those seen in other patients with neuropathological processes, such as toxicity, infectious cerebral disorders, and anoxia.

The most prevalent endocrinologic disorder is diabetes. Diabetes has been associated with peripheral neurological complaints in up to 90% of patients who live into adult years. While intellectual deficits of at least a mild nature have been found in certain populations of patients with diabetes (Ack, Miller, & Weil, 1961), it is particularly noteworthy that the psychological consequences of diabetes appear to be closely tied to its psychological management. In other words, patients who have frequent bouts of ketoacidosis and who, in many other respects, exhibit poor diabetic control experience a significant increase in a broad range of negative psychological consequences. This range extends from areas most central to cognitive academic performance, such as reading skills, to the presence of primary emotional disturbance. Gath, Smith, and Baum (1980) not only demonstrated that management and diabetic control have an impact on a broad range of neurocognitive functions but also indicated that psychological-behavioral factors, which may be utilized to implement compliance (with medication regimens and diet, for example), must figure in any neurocognitive evaluation procedure. Such a procedure represents a significant preventive habilitational exercise for neuropsychologists interested in exerting an influence on the outcome of a chronic disease process.

Patients with metachromatic leucodystrophy have been found, even in the early stages, to demonstrate significant abnormalities in tasks demanding spatial capabilities and in broad-ranging verbal functions, such as those measured by the Wechsler scale (Manowitz, Kohn, & Miller, 1977; Thalhammer, Havelec, Knoll, & Wehle, 1977). Even more subtle types of neurocognitive data have been obtained by Christomanou, Martinius, Jaffe, Betke, and Forster (1980), who showed that *carriers* of various lipodoses show symptoms of impaired neurological and neurocognitive functioning in a manner not necessarily identical with but similar to that seen in patients symptomatic with those conditions. Christomanou and colleagues were able to demonstrate that neuropsychological data provided support for the hypothesis that low enzyme levels are associated with certain neurocognitive deficiencies, and that metachromatic leukodystrophy (MLD) carriers are impaired compared with normal controls in both visuospatial and verbal cognitive tasks. Similar findings by Christomanou, Jaffe, Martinius, Cap, and Betke (1981) again demonstrated sensitivity of neurocognitive measurements to impairments in functioning of *carriers* of globoid cell leucodystrophy (Krabbe's disease). While it is still premature to assume that neurocognitive measures can serve as a marker for biochemical genetic carriers of certain diseases and disorders, it is clear that neurocognitive measures can demonstrate a continuum of pathologic behavioral states well beyond those indicated by the clinical symptoms. Furthermore, this kind of subtle investigation documents the fact that neurocognitive consequences of disease states may be far more prevalent and demand greater consideration in overall treatment and management than has previously been thought. This is so even in conditions that, on the surface, appear to have little relationship to intellectual capacity.

Neuropsychological investigations are generally viewed as being much more likely to produce evidence of impairment than evidence of normality in conditions at risk. Even though the definition of *at risk* has been considerably expanded, as physicians and investigators become more sophisticated about the potential for risk in a broad range of medical conditions, investigations demonstrate that certain conditions entail no neurocognitive risk. Such findings may eliminate the necessity for individual neuropsychological examination in every case as part of routine clinical care. Such was the finding by Hallert and Astrom (1983) in the study of a group of adults with lifelong intestinal malabsorption due to celiac disease. Despite the fact that they carried out a reasonably complete neurocognitive examination, they were not able to demonstrate that patients who had had this condition for up to 50 years were consistently impaired, nor did such patients' performances suggest organic brain disease or dysfunction. These findings were made despite the fact that 10% of adult celiac patients experience neurological complaints, mostly of a peripheral nature, and as many as 5% report seizures at some time during their lives. Negative findings can never carry the same degree of confidence as do positive findings; for example, infantile malnutrition and later severe malnourishing syndromes, such as that associated with alcoholic dementia, represent areas of continuing human risk. Nevertheless, it appears that with adequate dietary management and early medical diagnosis, individuals with a lifelong malabsorption syndrome can look forward to adequate intellectual development and functioning. The health care industry should be at least as interested in reassuring patients of the benign aspects of their condition as they are in counseling them about the more malignant ones. Furthermore, in children with such conditions, when disruptions in intellectual development do occur, accurate information allows the clinician to pursue other etiologies, such as genetically induced learning disabilities, the consequences of head injury, or other such disruptive forces, instead of leaping to the automatic conclusion that the condition of most prominence is necessarily responsible for all the patient's difficulties.

Medical treatments and diagnostic procedures affecting a far broader range of patients than those admitted for or attended to because of neurologically related conditions are increasingly seen affecting a patient's mental status and, specifically, his or her neurocognitive competence. The neuropsychological examination is, in turn, becoming a more standard and traditional part of a number of diagnostic workups and part of ongoing treatment regimens as well. Examples of this include the excellent studies by Hammock, Milhorat, and Baron (1976) demonstrating that ongoing management of patients with longstanding hydrocephalus is significantly advanced by routine neurocognitive examinations. Hammock, Milhorat, and Baron (1976) found that subtle changes in mental status according to measures of extreme cognitive sensitivity were the first changes to show in a deteriorating condition due to shunt failure or other difficulties related to the hydrocephalus. At the other end of the age spectrum, elderly patients were investigated by Seymour, Henschke, Cape, and Campbell (1980). These investigators found that a significant percentage of patients 70 years of age and older admitted for nonneurological and nonpsychiatric complaints were experiencing disruptions in neuropsychological functions. Of that group of patients, 25% were classified initially as demented and another 16% as experiencing an acute confusional state. The patients in this study were admitted to a general hospital because of acute physical illness, yet almost 40% of them showed abnormalities on their admission mental status examination. It is important to note that those patients with the poorest mental status also proved to have the worst overall physical prognosis. Furthermore, a specific relationship was found of an inverse nature between mental alertness and degree of dehydration and volume depletion. This suggests that awareness of patients' mental status ought to be required in admissions units dealing with elderly patients. Specific information, rather than a general impressionistic approach, may well yield information relevant not only to long-term prognostic understanding but also to particular aspects of the patient's need for treatment in the acute phase.

Yet another area in which routine evaluation of a patient's neurocognitive status appears to offer useful information about the effectiveness of treatment is that of childhood brain tumors. A careful review by Mulhern, Crisco, and Kun (1983) indicates that at least 40% of children with brain tumors exhibit clinically significant behavioral and/or emotional disturbance. While idiopathic and primary hydrocephalus has been well documented to be associated with declines in mental functions, children with brain tumors, presenting initially with hydrocephalus, were not in a worse prognostic group than those for whom hydrocephalus was not part of the initial presenting complaint. Treatment variables did, however, have a significant effect on long-term outcome. Mulhern and colleagues indicate that children undergoing a combination of chemotherapy and irradiation display a greater number of neuropsychological disabilities than do children treated with chemotherapy alone. Furthermore, children treated for tumors with surgery and cranial radiation exhibited greater neuropsychological compromise than children treated with surgery alone. Within groups of children suffering brain tumors, it appears that those who acquire brain tumors early and those for whom cranial irradiation and chemotherapy is initiated early (obviously, overlapping groups) show greater incidences of neuropsychological deficits than do children experiencing this disorder and its attendant treatment at a somewhat later age. Neuropsychological examination is being established not only as a tool to investigate the efficacy of various kinds of treatment but also as a routine part of the ongoing evaluation of a patient's overall clinical situation during treatment. Recognition of special needs for schooling; appreciation of changes affecting a child's day-to-day functioning as these are produced by the progression and remission of the disease and by the institution of various therapeutic regimens; and the ability to predict long-term quality of outcome, not simply medically but for the child as a whole person, all are entirely dependent on adequate neurocognitive investigation for their completeness. Neuropsychological evaluation cannot be omitted from modern therapy for children with brain disorders of this type.

Dupuytran recognized that cerebral changes occurred not uncommonly in burn victims and published this recognition over 150 years ago. Mohnot, Snead, and Benton (1982) have reported that even cursory investigation of mental status revealed a 5% incidence of significant behavioral dissruption due to encephalopathy despite absence of any history of neurological disease or disorder. Progress over the last 150 years appears to have been made, in the sense that fewer children suffering significant burns now experience the negative consequences of encephalopathy than once was the case. One could quite easily make the case, however, that there has yet to be anything remotely resembling a very probing study of the actual mental status of these patients. In every instance, severe alteration in mental state, easily recognizable even upon clinical examination and without the benefit of any sensitive neuropsychological procedures, was required for the child to qualify as impaired. Unless the underlying mechanisms of burn encephalopathy are qualitatively different from the underlying mechanisms of every other kind of neurocognitive disrupter, the likelihood is exceedingly high that had more careful and quantified types of investigations been applied, a significantly higher yield would have been produced. The treatment of severe burns is a long-term proposition at best. It is one in which cooperation, especially from young children, can be difficult under ideal circumstances. Knowledge of a child's mental status and ability to understand and be communicated with appears to be central to maximizing the child's potential to benefit from, participate in, and not obstruct the most effective use of the therapeutic tools available. Simply to assume that the patient is in the same mental state at all times or, even worse, that the mental state of the patient is essentially something that can be disregarded in the long-term management of severe burn injuries hardly represents the most forward-looking approach to the management of a complex, chronic, painful, and involving medical injury.

The recognition that accidents and illnesses of a wide variety, not simply those obviously involving craniocerebral trauma, can have neurocognitive effects is expanding into the area of occupational concern as well. Recent investigation by Vaernes and Eidsvik (1982) demonstrated that evidence of neurocognitive dysfunction can occur in individuals whose IQs appear entirely normal. These investigators found that among professional deep-sea divers, eight out of nine who had experienced "near miss accidents in diving" demonstrated a "syndrome of subcortical/limbic dysfunction, specific memory deficits, low autonomic reactivity, sustained attention problems, and emotional lability." It has been previously and repeatedly found that decompression illness produces a high incidence of central nervous system impairment and neurocognitive deficits (Rozsahgyi, 1959; Peters, Levin, & Kelly, 1977). When these observations are coupled with previous findings that divers and diver trainees had a significantly higher proportion of pathological EEG records and this proportion was related to the number of years spent diving (Kwaitkowski, 1979), it suggests that this occupational group is at high risk. Part of their ongoing care must extend beyond standard physical examinations for fitness to dive. It must be expanded to neurocognitive appreciation of the consequences of diving. While divers may choose to take the risk, it is only reasonable that they should be apprised of what that risk actually is, rather than being led to believe that if their physical examination is normal, all other systems of the body can be assumed normal as well. As the central nervous system is minimally attended to in physical examination procedures, this assumption could not be further from the truth.

Perhaps the occupation in which failure of adequate routine attention as part of the generalized assessment for fitness is most flagrant is professional boxing. As powerfully demonstrated by Casson and colleagues (1984), the evidence is present for all to see that a career in boxing is far less likely to terminate with an intact central nervous system than is a career in most other occupations and professions. In fact, in this recent study, "every subject had more than one abnormal neuropsychological test score, and all who were administered the Wechsler Memory Scale scored in the abnormal range." These findings were made despite the fact that most of the subjects had had quite successful boxing careers. These results were found in individuals who were not abnormal according to standard physical neurological examination. The role of occupational medicine cannot achieve full recognition, nor can preventive medicine be seen as fully exercising its appropriate role, until attention is routinely paid to all systems of the body at risk in various occupational groups. The singular omission of careful central nervous system investigation, even in circumstances in which known central nervous system disrupters are inherent in the occupational situation, is only recently receiving redress.

Similarly, central nervous system toxins, irritants, teratogens, and disrupters broadly considered are now beginning to receive careful attention within the environment as a whole. While many of these areas represent frontier investigations and while some are still subject to considerable controversy, the recognition that congenital factors, environmental factors, and product-induced factors can produce compromise in neurocognitive functions is the first step toward treatment and, one would hope, eventual prevention of these largely synthetic environmental risk factors.

Congenital infections pre-, peri-, or postnatally passed from mother to child, such as cytomegalo virus and toxoplasma virus, produce among patients with symptomatic forms of these infections significant disruptions in capacities related to the central nervous system. High instance of severe intellectual loss, hearing impairment, and even, in some subjects, severe motor impairment have been reported (Saigal, Lunyk, Larke, & Chernesky, 1982). While these disorders are severe and obvious, a significantly large percentage—as high as 2.5% (Stagno, Pass, & Dworsky, 1982)—of all live births have the same virus in asymptomatic form. A serious question has been raised as to whether these children, already identified as having a 14% incidence of hearing impairment, may also have additional difficulties with higher cognitive functions. Subjective reports of children with learning disabilities and poor academic progress have not been subject to adequate evaluation with appropriate controls to determine whether an unexpectedly high percentage of these individuals are, in fact, experiencing additional neurocognitive deficits. Several less than adequately controlled and somewhat less than ideally quantified reports have suggested that this is the situation. Our laboratory, among others, is pursuing more carefully constructed investigations to determine whether this can be substantiated. These children may be experiencing these difficulties on the basis of other factors more related to the environment than to their congenital viral infection. Certainly, if it should be discovered that a high percentage of such victims experience learning disabilities, for example, the public health implications of an infection of this frequency would be quite serious. It is only through such investigations that appropriate public health policy can be established. It is unlikely that a sufficient treatment or prevention effort will be mounted for any condition unless its consequences are well understood and of sufficient magnitude to warrant the cost involved. Obviously, no informed decision can be made until adequate data are provided. It is quite likely, in this and other basically subtle conditions, that neurocognitive data will define the negative consequences of the condition, rather than data reflecting somewhat more obvious physical or medical handicaps.

Inflicted, as opposed to *acquired*, may well become a category to describe the condition of children and adults who have sustained impairments due to environmental toxins. The carefully pursued investigations of Needleman and colleagues (Needleman et al., 1979) to determine the neuropsychological consequences of even a subtly elevated body burden of lead reflects the kind of effort that is required in order to have significant impact upon public policy. Lead-based paints, car emissions, food and drink containers made from lead, and toys containing a lead base were part of our routine environmental scene for many years, with little thought given to the possible risks incurred. This is true despite the fact that the impression has existed for a long time that lead in our environment has produced mental mischief. An excellent review of lead and lead poisoning in antiquity has recently been published (Nriagu, 1983). As with all similar conditions, the ease with which one can establish a connection between a particular poison and higher mental impairment is greatest when the impairment is most severe. Here too, however, issues of lack of linearity in dose-response relationships, due to the complex relationships of other toxicologic factors, such as rate of deposit, site of greatest deposit, rapidity of absorption and dissipation, and length of exposure, all work to complicate any lead-behavior relationship ratio. At the mildest levels, it might be expected that the most subtle effects are often those associated with the highest and most complex mental processes. As individuals most at risk for the largest portion of environmental impairments are those with relatively less overall life advantage, the complexity is further increased. Nevertheless, the burden of an extensive body of literature reviewed by Nriagu, by Needleman and colleagues (1979), and by Rutter (1980) strongly indicates that lead is a source of disruption of subtle mental processes and ongoing inadequacy of development in children with even relatively mild exposure histories. In fact, in a now classic piece of research that predicts much of more recent findings, Byers and Lord (1943) reported that they found "poor scholastic attainment, motor deficits, despite the fact of reasonably adequate psychometric levels. For a few children, successive psychological examinations showed significant drop in the intelligence quotient. These drops are felt to be the result of failure of mental development, rather than of mental deterioration. As a result, though the chronological age advanced, mental growth did not keep up with it." Therefore, the expectation is not that individuals exposed to such negative influences will be rendered significantly disabled or incapacitated in a relatively short period of time. Rather, the consequences continue over a period of years or even decades. Disabilities due to truncation in development or to failure of development in areas actually not part of the behavioral repertoire of the child at the time the disorder was initiated may play a greater role than those disabilities most obvious upon identification of the disorder.

Persons who have sustained prolonged exposure to very low-level carbon monoxide poisoning may experience a plethora of inconsistent, medically undocumentable, emotionally disrupting symptoms. In such cases, inappropriate treatment and delay of treatment may be more the rule than the exception. Furthermore, many individuals' capacity to adapt even to very negative circumstances is sufficiently broad that undoubtedly many live for a considerable period of time or perhaps their entire lives experiencing difficulties they assume have no particular etiology but are simply a burden of life that must be borne. To date, no adequate neurocognitive investigation of the effect of slow onset, low-dose carbon monoxide poisoning has been carried out. In fact, the multiple sources of carbon monoxide exposure (passive smoking, for example) rarely figure in routine physical examinations or even more thorough ones, and thus the likely connection between patients' complaints and the ingestion of this poison goes uninvestigated. Furthermore, because routine neurocognitive investigation of patients has not yet become totally enmeshed in the medical system, many patients with complaints that could be documented as a decline in mental acuity, as opposed to a simple tendency to complain, pass through the system without the opportunity to have their symptoms properly documented. As with justice, treatment delayed may well effectively turn out to be treatment denied. The long-range consequences of significant symptom development may be appreciably more difficult to undo than are the specific symptoms themselves.

The excellent reviews by Weiss (1983) and by Fein, Schwartz, Jacobson, and Jacobson (1983) represent the best sources documenting the breadth of subtle behavioral disruptions produced by the broad range of chemicals in our environment, which until recently were either ignored, taken for granted, or overtly characterized as having no behavioral impact before any adequate data had even been gathered, much less analyzed and disseminated.

SUMMARY

The science of psychology has exquisite ability to gather data adequately and to gather adequate data. We are not tied to impressionistic findings taken from biased sources. This ability affords us an outstanding opportunity and entails a serious responsibility to develop health care knowledge and provide health care services to patients whose disorders and complaints are dismissed or misunderstood because the disorder driving them has not enjoyed sufficient recognition. All disorders will not prove to produce neuropsychological mischief. Some will. Discovering the nature of the disorders, the type of mischief, and the effective remedies represents the frontier of neuropsychological health care at least for the rest of this century.

ACKNOWLEDGMENT

A portion of this chapter was developed for presentation as a presidential address for the Division of Clinical Neuropsychology, American Psychological Association Meeting, Toronto, 1984, and is published in the *Journal of Clinical and Experimental Neuropsychology*.

REFERENCES

Ack, M., Miller, I., & Weil, W.B. (1961). Intelligence of children with diabetes mellitus. *Pediatrics, 28*, 764–770.

Apstein, M.D., Koff, E., & Koff, R.S. (1979). Neuropsychological dysfunctions in acute viral hepatitis. *Digestion, 19*, 349–358.

Barth, J.T., Macciocchi, S., Giordani. B., Rimel, R., Jane, J., & Boll, T.J. (1983). Neuropsychological sequelae of minor head injury. *Neurosurgery, 13*, 529–532.

Boll, T.J. (1983). Minor head injury in children: out of sight but not out of mind. *Journal of Clinical Child Psychology, 12*, 74–80.

Boll, T.J., & Barth, J. (1983). Mild head injury. *Psychiatric Developments, 3*, 263–275.

Boll, T.J., Heaton, R., & Reitan, R.M. (1974). Neuropsychological and emotional correlates of Huntington's chorea. *Journal of Nervous and Mental Disease, 158*, 61–69.

Broca, T. (1865). Sur la faculté du langage articulé. *Bulletin de la Société d'Anthropologie, 6*, 493.

Brown, G., Chadwick, O., Shaffer, D., Rutter, M., & Traub, M. (1981). A prospective study of children with head injuries. 3. Psychiatric sequelae. *Psychological Medicine, 11*, 63–78.

Byers, R.K., & Lord, E.E. (1943). Late effects of lead poisoning on mental development. *American Journal of Diseases of Children, 66*, 471–494.

Casson, I.R., Siegel, O., Sham., R., Campbell, E.A., Tarlau, M., & Di Domenenico, A. (1984). Brain damage in modern boxers. *Journal of the American Medical Association, 251*, 2263–2667.

Caveness, W. (1977). Incidences of cranial-cerebral trauma in the United States. *Transactions of the American Neurological Association, 102*, 136–138.

Chadwick, O.,Rutter, M., Brown, G., Shaffer, D., & Traub, M. (1981). A prospective study of children with head injuries. 2. Cognitive sequelae. *Psychological Medicine, 11*, 49–61.

Chadwick, O., Rutter, M., Shaffer, D., & Shrout, P.E. (1981). A prospective study of children with head injuries. 4. Specific cognitive deficits. *Journal of Clinical Neuropsychology, 3*, 101–120.

Christomanou, H., Jaffe, S., Martinius, J., Cap, C., & Betke, K. (1981). Biochemical, genetic, psychometric, and neuropsychological studies in heterozygotes of a family with globoid cell leucodystrophy (Krabbe's disease). *Human Genetics, 58*, 179–183.

Christomanou, H., Martinius, J., Jaffe, S., Betke, K., Forster, C. (1980). Biochemical, psychometric, and neuropsychological studies in heterozygotes for various lipidoses. *Human Genetics, 55*, 103–110.

Fein, G.G., Schwartz, P.J., Jacobson, S.W., & Jacobson, J.L. (1983). Environmental toxins and behavioral development: A new role for psychological research. *American Psychologist, 39*, 1188–1197.

Gronwall, D., & Wrightson, P. (1975). Cumulative effect of concussion. *Lancet*, 995–997.

Hallert, C., & Astrom, J. (1983). Intellectual ability of adults after life-long intestinal malabsorption due to celiac disease. *Journal of Neurology, Neurosurgery and Psychiatry, 46*, 87–89.

Hammock, M.K., Milhorat, T.H., & Baron, I.S. (1976). Normal-pressure hydrocephalus in patients with myleomeningocele. *Developmental Medicine and Child Neurology, 18*(Suppl. 37), 55–68.

Klonoff, H., Low, M.D., & Clark, C. (1977). Head injuries in children: A prospective five-year follow-up. *Journal of Neurology, Neurosurgery and Psychiatry, 40*, 1211–1219.

Kwaitkowski, S.R. (1979). Analysis of the EEG records among divers. *Bulletin of Industrial Medicine, 2*, 131–135.

Levin, H.S., & Eisenberg, H.M. (1979). Neuropsychological outcome of closed head injury in children and adolescents. *Child's Brain, 5*, 281–292.

Lezak, N.T. (1978). Living with the characterologically altered brain-injured patient. *Journal of Clinical Psychiatry, 6*, 592–598.

Manowitz, P., Kohn, H., & Miller, M. (1977). Neuropsychological findings in siblings and parents of patients in metachromatic leukodystrophy. *Abstracts of the Congress of the International Neuropsychology Society*. Oxford, England.

Mohnot, D., Snead, O.C., & Benton, J.W. (1982). Burn encephalophy in children. *Annals of Neurology, 12*, 42–47.

Mulhern, R.K., Crisco, J.J., & Kun, L.E. (1983). Neuropsychological sequelae of childhood brain tumors: A review. *Journal of Clinical Child Psychology, 12*, 66–73.

Needleman, H.L., Gunnoe, C., Leviton, A., Reed, R., Peresie, H., Maher, C., & Barrett, P. (1979). Deficits in psychologic and classroom performance of children with elevated dentine lead levels. *New England Journal of Medicine, 300*, 689–695.

Nriagu, J.O. (1983). *Lead and lead poisoning in antiquity*. New York: John Wiley & Sons.

Peters, B.H., Levin, H.S., & Kelly, P.J. (1977). Neurologic and psychologic manifestations of decompression illness in divers. *Neurology, 27*, 125–127.

Prigatano, G.P., Stahl, N.L., Orr, W.C., & Zeiner, H.K. (1982). Sleep and dreaming disturbances in closed head injury patients. *Journal of Neurology, Neurosurgery and Psychiatry, 45*, 78–80.

Reitan, R.M. (1955). Intellectual functions in myxedema. *AMA Archives of Neurology and Psychiatry, 73*, 436–449.

Reitan, R.M., & Boll, T.J. (1971). Intellectual and cognitive functions in Parkinson's disease. *Journal of Consulting and Clinical Psychology, 37*, 364–369.

Reitan, R.M., & Boll, T.J. (1973). Neuropsychological correlates of minimal brain dysfunction. *Annals of the New York Academy of Science, 205*, 65–88.

Rimel, R.W., Giordani, D., Barth, J.T., Boll, T.J., & Jane, J. (1981). Disability caused by minor head injury. *Journal of Neurosurgery, 9*, 221–228.

Rozsahgyi, I. (1959). Late consequences of the neurological forms of decompression sickness. *British Journal of Industrial Medicine, 16*, 311–317.

Rutter, M. (1977). Brain damage syndromes in childhood: Concepts and findings. *Journal of Child Psychology and Psychiatry, 18*, 1–21.

Rutter, M. (1980). Raised lead levels and impaired cognitive-behavioural functioning: A review of the evidence. *Developmental Medicine and Child Neurology, 22* (Suppl. 1), 1–25.

Rutter, M., Chadwick, O., Shaffer, D., & Brown, G. (1980). A prospective study of children with head injuries. 1. Design and methods. *Psychological Medicine, 10*, 633–645.

Saigal, S., Lunyk, O., Larke, R.P.B., & Chernesky, N.A. (1982). The outcome in children with cytomegalo virus infection. *American Journal of Diseases of Childhood, 136*, 896–905.

Seymour, D.G., Henschke, P.J., Cape, R.D.T., & Campbell, A.J. (1980). Acute confusional states and dementia in the elderly: The role of dehydration/volume depletion, physical illness and age. *Age and Aging, 9*, 137–146.

Stagno, S., Pass, R.F., Dworsky, M.E. (1982). The relative importance of primary and recurrent maternal CMV infections in the outcome of congenital infection. *New England Journal of Medicine, 306*, 945–949.

Symonds, C. (1962). Concussion and its sequelae. *Lancet, 1*, 1–5.

Thalhammer, O., Havelec, L., Knoll, E., & Wehle, E. (1977). Intellectual level (IQ) in heterozygotes for phenylketonuria (PKU). *Human Genetics, 38*, 285–288.

Vaernes, R.J., & Eidsvik, S. (1982). Central nervous system dysfunctions after near-miss accidents in diving. *Aviation, Space, and Environmental Medicine*, 803–807.

Weiss, B. (1983). Behavioral toxicology and environmental health science: Opportunity and challenge for psychology. *American Psychologist, 39*, 1174–1187.

Whelan, T.B., Schteingart, D.E., Starkman, M.N., & Smith, A. (1980). Neuropsychological deficits in Cushing's syndrome. *Journal of Nervous and Mental Disease, 168*, 753–757.

CHAPTER 6

An Approach to the Neuropsychological Assessment of the Preschool Child with Developmental Deficits

Barbara C. Wilson

This chapter examines an approach to the clinical assessment of the preschool child with suspected or identified developmental deficits. Methods and procedures for the integration and interpretation of assessment data are offered, illustrative case material is provided, and implications of using assessment data for remediation and prediction are addressed. This approach has been developed within the Neuropsychology Division, Department of Neurology, at North Shore University Hospital, Manhasset, New York, a teaching center of Cornell University Medical College. The neuropsychology staff has found the approach applicable across the age range from infants to adults and for the assessment of acquired as well as developmental deficits.

CURRENT STATUS

There has been increasing interest in the development of clinical assessment methods for application to the handicapped or high-risk infant and preschool population. The interest became an expressed need with the passage of Public Law 94-142 by the Congress of the United States. This law, the Education for all Handicapped Children Act, mandates that a free and appropriate education be provided to all handicapped persons from birth to 21 years of age and that an individualized program of instruction be developed and recorded for each child identified as having a handicapping condition. Both identification and formulation of the individualized educational program (IEP) require some delineation of the child's patterns of function and dysfunction, and it is here that the child neuropsychologist has a role to play.

The current status of clinical assessment methods and procedures in child neuropsychology is at the level at which adult neuropsychology found itself perhaps 25 years ago. The range of standardized assessment instruments is limited, particularly for the child under six years of age. The development of the data base necessary for the interpretation of assessment data in brain-behavior terms is in the beginning stages; so,

121

therefore, is the status of prediction. Issues of normal neurological development and the interactions among development, central nervous system function, and environment are poorly understood. Is the brain a "dependent variable" (Bakker, 1984)? There remain a good deal of controversy and as yet unasked questions surrounding the issue of central nervous system plasticity. This chapter is not designed to pursue these issues but merely to indicate the state of our knowledge at the present time.

For the preschool child, some standardized tests, which are described later, assess cognitive level, language function, and motor and sensory-motor integration skills. There is not, however, an articulated framework for the clinical interpretation of data. Moreover, the nature of the concerns brought to clinical assessment require the integration of developmental concepts and knowledge within a clinical neuropsychological assessment schema. It is fair to say that all preschool and infant assessments require an appreciation of the multivariate nature of the problem the children bring to assessment and frequently require a multivariate assessment approach.

Outcome and prediction studies are legion in the infant domain (e.g., Hagbard, Olow, & Reinand, 1969; Gaiter, 1982; Drillien, 1972; Broman, Nichols, & Kennedy, 1975; Drillien, Thomson, & Burgoyne, 1980; Lipper, Lee, Gartner, & Grellong, 1981) but limited for the preschool population (e.g., Wolpaw, Nation, & Aram, 1977; Evans & Bangs, 1972). The studies are too frequently founded on a medical model. That is, cognitive development is studied as a function of diagnosis, etiology, or pathogenesis rather than in terms of discernible behavioral commonalities or developmental patterns. A diagnostic label supports the inference that one is dealing with a unitary syndrome and, therefore, with a unitary cognitive profile. No wonder that results of such studies are so often inconclusive, not unlike the studies in the adult literature that group heterogeneous patients under a given rubric (e.g., *right parietal group*) and look in vain for homogeneity of results (Smith, 1981).

The rationale for the early identification of developmental disabilities and the implementation of early intervention programs is based on the assumption that benefits will accrue in terms of enhanced development and performance of children involved in such programs. The literature on efficacy of early intervention and on prediction of outcome in such instances is limited (Wilson & Metlay, 1980; Aram & Nation, 1980; Evans & Bangs, 1972; Silva, 1980; Weiss, 1981–1982). At a minimum, such studies require a rational basis for the selection and measurement of neuropsychological functions and an appropriate design for the evaluation of outcome. Again, this chapter is not designed to pursue these issues in any detail but to point out the relationship between adequate assessment strategies and studies dealing with outcome and prediction.

AN ASSESSMENT MODEL

In defining an assessment strategy, our practice has been first to determine the behaviors we wish to evaluate and then to select methods and procedures appropriate to the assessment of these behaviors. The model we find most useful may be described as a branching hypothesis-testing model. We do not subscribe to a fixed battery approach, since this may serve to limit the range of assessment.

Certain points of view or, less kindly, professional biases have been among the determinants in the formulation of the model to be described. The first concerns itself with the issues of localization of function in the young child. Scant data exist to support inferences about brain-behavior relationships in the normally developing child and even less for making such inferences about developmentally atypical children or children with acquired encephalopathies, for whom inconclusive data are available.

Over the years, studies involving brain-behavior relationships in adults have yielded results that still do not enjoy unanimous acceptance among investigators. In the early childhood area, with the terra incognita of interactions between development and damage or dysfunction, imputing mediation of the Peabody Picture Vocabulary Test to the left parietal lobe is as gratuitous as any inferential localization of function in the young child (e.g., Hartlage, Telzrow, DeFillippes, Shaw, & Noonan, 1983). Such an approach moves child neuropsychology too far, too fast, and in a questionable direction. The brain-behavior relationships demonstrated in adults may not hold when applied to the developing system, let alone to a system developing atypically. In the absence of data, the rule of parsimony should apply.

As most clinicians are aware, the IQ is, in general, not an illuminating datum. The more atypical the child, the less useful the number. Too frequently, the IQ is used as a major determinant in program placement. The use of the IQ as a predictor is questionable at best among handicapped populations and irrelevant with reference to handicapped preschool children.

One of the concerns about the IQ or any summary score, such as the Illinois Test of Psycholinguistic Abilities (ITPA) Psycholinguistic Age (PLA) (Kirk, McCarthy, & Kirk, 1968) and the Bayley Mental Development Index (MDI) (Bayley, 1969), when applied to a handicapped population arises from the fact that the score results from combining scores reflecting areas of function and dysfunction and often results in: (1) a loss of information and (2) spurious representation of the child's level of function. Take, for example, the child with developmental language delay (developmental dysphasia, primary language disorder) characterized by significant auditory semantic comprehension deficits who is given an auditory-verbal, language-loaded test such as the Stanford-Binet (Terman & Merrill, 1973) or the McCarthy Scales of Children's Abilities (McCarthy, 1970). The resultant summary score, the IQ, or its equivalent is reflective of the disorder, not necessarily of the child's cognitive abilities. Such a child may do very well with visually mediated cognitive and visual-constructional tasks, but a measure such as the Stanford-Binet IQ score cannot reflect this. Wilson and Wilson (1977) compared IQs and equivalent scores obtained from 59 preschool language-disordered children based on the Stanford-Binet (L–M), the McCarthy Scales of Children's Abilities, the Hiskey-Nebraska Test of Learning Aptitude (Hiskey, 1966), and the Pictorial Test of Intelligence (French, 1964). All tests were administered within a three-month period for the group and within six weeks for any given child. The mean IQ scores increased systematically across the four tests as language loading decreased and ranged from a mean IQ of 62.2 (standard deviation [SD] 16) on the Stanford-Binet to 92.2 (SD 13.5) on the PTI.

Early childhood assessment must be viewed as indicating the child's level of function in various areas at the time of assessment and the rate of change in the performance level over time, the datum of major significance. Except in cases of significant central nervous system abnormality, such as anencephaly, hydranencephaly, and progressive neurologic disease, predictions of ultimate cognitive development are difficult to make in a very young impaired child. A high-risk neonate may show excellent motor development and "look good," only to demonstrate a significant language deficit later.

An infant with significant dysfunction of the motor system may turn out to have good cognitive skills. One cannot assess functions that are not ready to appear in terms of developmental sequences, nor can one readily predict the level of integration of emerging cognitive functions until such integration is called upon.

Caveats regarding clinical assessment cut across age ranges and are most relevant in the younger age groups; reliability of measures is less certain in the zero to five years group. The influence of state increases as age decreases. Infant scales frequently require that state be scored in relationship to each item. Attending behavior in young children is generally brief and variable and exerts an indeterminate influence on reliability. The use of a single subtest score to define a deficit performance of a given function is, therefore, problematic in this age range. In such an instance, using more than one measure of the behavior in question makes sense.

Reporting the results, both written and verbal, should be responsive to the referral issue, functional, and subject to ready interpretation by a multidisciplinary group. Typically, a handicapped child, multivariate by definition, has working in his or her behalf a multivariate team often consisting of parents, a physician, a language pathologist, an occupational and/or physical therapist with or without special training in neurodevelopmental and/or sensory-motor integration therapy, a special education or early childhood teacher, a social worker, a behavioral psychologist, and, at some point, a school psychologist. The child clinical neuropsychologist must be able to communicate the results of the evaluation to this interdisciplinary group so that the information is useful in the planning and implementation of intervention programs and in the evaluation of progress over time. Informing parents of evaluation results makes clarity and studied understatement a necessity. As with most clinician-patient relationships of this kind, statements made to the parent or the care giver are often scrutinized for hidden meaning. When the clinician is talking with the anxious parents of a handicapped child, if the words are heard at all, they will be reviewed and re-reviewed, interpreted and reinterpreted. While responsible reporting is an ethical concern, it takes on added dimensions in such situations.

APPROACH TO ASSESSMENT

The approach that we have found most useful in the assessment of cognitive function in all children starts with a review of the referral issues and the history. The more clearly focused the referral question, the easier it is to focus the evaluation. A referral that reads "CBC, urinalysis, and psychometrics" from an admitting house officer sheds no light on the nature of the concerns. Issues of preoperative baseline measures, differential diagnosis, and the effects of surgical or pharmacological interventions may suggest the need for the selection of specific measures. The question of developmental delay may lead in other directions. The child is often referred for assessment by an agency or school. It is informative to note the degree of consonance between the agency's reason for referral and the parents' concerns about the child. Sometimes there are two agendas. Both may need to be addressed.

We find that a review of the history is always very useful. Except in cases of some genetic syndromes and problems, such as congenital hypothyroidism, we do not believe that knowledge of etiology or pathogenesis of developmental problems contributes to the prediction of either cognitive development or patterns of cognitive function. We do believe that historical information provides a general matrix within which to view the child and provides cues for the generation of hypotheses. For example, a 2-1/2-year-old child is referred to us for evaluation, with retardation a possible concern. The behavior that has fostered concern is the child's inadequate language development. The history does not suggest any encephalopathic insult. Motor milestones were achieved at age-appropriate levels. History does reveal the frequent occurrence of serous otitis media; myringotomies are being considered. An increasing number of studies suggest a strong relationship between a history of frequent ear infections, concomitant fluctuating conductive hearing losses in young children, and developmental language disorders (Needleman, 1977; News Note, 1985). Given this information, otological, audiological, and language evaluations would be requested as part of a multivariate assessment. If the history indicates that such a child has been treated for neonatal meningitis, the high probability of intake of ototoxic drugs would need to be considered, and, again, hearing and language evaluations would be required. If the family history indicates the presence of learning disabilities, the index of suspicion would be raised relative to the presence of a developmental language disorder (Owen, 1978). A history of prolonged febrile seizures beginning in the first year of life would indicate a higher risk for mental retardation (Nelson & Ellenberg, 1978). A history of significant feeding problems during infancy and drooling at age 3 in a child with expressive language deficits would lead to the notion of neuromotor dysfunction as a possible contributing factor. An appropriate oromotor evaluation would be high on the list of priorities (Sheppard & Mysak, 1984; Blakeley, 1980). Not all children identified as failure-to-thrive patients have endocrine, metabolic, or psychiatric problems. We have seen several who, on oromotor evaluation, were demonstrated to have tongue thrust, retention of primitive oromotor reflexes, and/or oral dyspraxia, among other oromotor deficits, which inhibited the development of adequate feeding patterns and contributed to a significant dysphagia. The careful taking of a history can frequently point the way to appropriate assessment strategies. For additional information regarding the possible relationships between early historical variables and developmental sequelae, see, for example, Berenberg (1977) and Shaffer and Dunn (1979).

There are as many history forms as there are settings in which children are evaluated. The one we use for our preschool population is provided in the chapter appendix. The form was generated in collaboration with Pediatric Neurology and the Speech and Hearing Center at North Shore University Hospital and is used by these services. When a child is to be seen by more than one of these services, the completed history form is duplicated and supplied to the service, saving the parents the job of having to complete the forms at each stop along the way.

Basis for Selection of Measures

Our initial selection of measures id designed to sample complex cognitive functions. Based on the results of that initial sampling, additional measures of specified functions are selected. If specified complex behaviors appear less efficient than others (e.g., auditory semantic comprehension), then functions presumed to underlie or to relate to these behaviors will be studied (e.g., aspects of auditory discrimination). This represents an if-then hypothesis testing approach to which we subscribe.

For example, if a preschool child is consistently age-appropriate in visual cognitive and visual spatial abilities, and functions less efficiently in auditory-verbal areas, requiring repetition of verbally presented materials, or demonstrates apparent difficulty in the formulation of expressive language, one would need to question whether the child's less adequate auditory-verbal skills reflect auditory semantic comprehension problems or problems with the building blocks of auditory semantic comprehension by the application of (1) additional measures of auditory semantic comprehension and measures of, (2) retrieval skills, (3) short-term auditory memory, (4) auditory discrimination, (5) auditory acuity, (6) formulation skills, and (7) oromotor function, in whatever combination seems appropriate based on continued appraisal of if-then hypotheses.

Clinical Observations as Data

Clinical observations provide data critical to the assessment endeavor and should not be undervalued. The child who asks "What?" too frequently, who provides apparently tangential responses, who circumlocutes, or who appears to have a puzzle solved at the conceptual level but cannot organize his or her movements adequately to complete the puzzle satisfactorily may obtain the same score on a given test as another child who behaves very differently. The levels of performance are the same; the contents of the performances are not. A score tells you what a child "got"; it does not tell you how the child got it. For purposes of diagnosis, for research insights into brain-behavior relationships, and for the development of intervention and evaluation strategies, both classes of data, quantitative and qualitative, are necessary.

It is important to remember that the test instruments we use have been standardized on normal populations, to which we compare the performance of atypically developing children. This is one reason that consideration of patterns of function, rather than magnitude of scores, is typically more useful. It would be simple but misleading to state that an atypically developing child 5 years of age is performing like a normal 3-year-old. There are significant differences in performance between the 3- and 5-year-olds in question, different outcomes to be considered, and different teaching strategies to be devised. A handicapped 5-year-old is not a tall, normally developing 3-year-old. In the absence of clinical norms that reflect the current level of cognitive function and, more appropriately, the developmental implications of given rates of change over time, we use what data are available. But we should use it with some caution.

NEUROPSYCHOLOGICAL CONSTRUCTS

Various schemata are available to describe the content of an evaluation, including constructs that describe aspects of higher cognitive function. Our constructs are defined by their measures and have proved helpful in the organization of assessment data (e.g., Wilson & Wilson, 1978; Wilson & Risucci, 1983, 1986). This schema of our assessment model involves working with these neuropsychological constructs, examining complex cognitive functions in terms of the constructs, attempting to tease out areas of presumed function at lower levels of complexity, and using historical and observational data as hypothesis generators for both diagnostic and intervention purposes. We believe that this approach leads to early identification of children with developmental problems and some degree of specificity as to the nature of those problems. It has been our experience that it provides a basis for functional discrimination among children who have been grouped together on the basis of level of performance rather than content of performance. Not all children whose IQs place them in the retarded range are retarded, and not all children with average ITPA scores have average language abilities.

Language Constructs

We begin with an examination of clinically derived language-related constructs. Our selection of measures that define the constructs is constrained by what is available for the age range in question and by what we, idiosyncratically perhaps, have found most useful. If the constructs do reflect a recognizable aspect of behavior, tests other than those noted here should be able to serve as well. We work with these constructs across age groups and do, of necessity, substitute tests as we move out of the Wechsler Preschool and Primary Scale of Intelligence (WPPSI) (Wechsler, 1963) and into the WISC age range, for example. These constructs need to be validated, and we are in the process of such validation studies now.

Administration of the kinds of subtests described below within an hypothesis-testing model of assessment provides quantitative data that may be helpful in demonstrating the presence of deficient language-related function. Because of the nature of the task demands, it is not uncommon for young children to score well on such standardized tests as the Verbal scale of the WPPSI but to have significant language-processing problems nonetheless. Some of the subtests require single-word responses or overlearned associations. Others provide full credit for answers that contain significant syntactic or morphologic errors or suggest real problems with language formulation. Wilson and Risucci (1983) identified a subtype of language-disordered children all of whom had Verbal subtest scores within the average range. Their difficulties were in the expressive domain, which was not quantitatively demonstrable. It is here that clinical observations make the difference. If a child asks "What?" very frequently, is the problem memory, discrimination, or hearing ability? Or is the child stalling for time while language is being organized? These are among the hypotheses to be generated on the spot. Is the child who gives a well-organized but tangential response showing evidence of receptive difficulties, and if so, at what level? Then there is the child who receives high scores on verbal measures but who responds with one or two word utterances, demonstrates faulty syntax, has retrieval problems, and gestures very frequently. All such clinical observations are necessary for the interpretation of quantitative data that do not really describe the child (Allen & Rapin, 1982; Aram & Nation, 1980; Rapin & Wilson, 1978; Wilson and Wilson, 1978). The emphasis on language-disordered children stems from the fact that they are frequently misidentified; their numbers are not insignificant, with estimates ranging from 3% (Allen & Bliss, 1978) to 8.5% of all children (Wolpaw, Nation, & Aram, 1977).

Auditory Integration

The tasks of auditory integration constitute a child's ability to receive and process auditory stimuli when performance is not dependent on semantic comprehension or the formulation of complex vocal responses. Auditory, or phonemic, discrimination from the Goldman-Fristoe-Woodcock (G-F-W) Auditory Skills Battery (1974–1976) and sound blending from the ITPA are among such tasks.

Auditory Cognition

The ability to respond to questions in an auditory-input–vocal-output paradigm is known as auditory cognition. The examiner asks a question or makes a statement, and the child is asked to respond vocally. The examiner makes inferences about the child's ability to hear, process, decode, remember, retrieve, and program the phonological motor speech and cognitive content of the oral responses. Only the response can be observed. The auditory cognitive demand may vary in difficulty, as reflected in three clinical factors which follow.

AUDITORY COGNITIVE 1.   Auditory Cognitive 1 is tapped by questions posed by the examiner. The questions are simple in construction, and the responses may be a single word or overlearned associative responses, such as required by the ITPA Auditory Reception subtest.

AUDITORY COGNITIVE 2.   To test Auditory Cognitive 2 functions, the examiner poses questions whose forms are relatively simple and require the production of a simple vocal response that taps acquired information. The WPPSI Information subtest is an example.

AUDITORY COGNITIVE 3.   Tests of Auditory Cognitive 3 functions involve a more complex question form, such as in the WPPSI Comprehension subtest, and require formulation of a unique and more complex vocal response. This is one of the few subtests for this age range that require the formulation of any significant amount of language. Qualitative analysis of these data can provide cues as to the presence of an expressive language disorder in a child whose spontaneous language may appear appropriate.

Auditory Memory (Short Term)

Tasks involved in the assessment of short-term auditory memory can be defined in terms of the content and structure of the stimuli. Auditory memory may require repetition of stimuli or the recall of material just heard.

AUDITORY MEMORY 1.   Auditory Memory 1 is assessed by the repetition of linguistically meaningful stimuli such as sentences, as in the WPPSI Sentences subtest.

AUDITORY MEMORY 2.   Assessment of Auditory Memory 2 involves the recall of contextual material just heard. Verbal Memory 2 of the McCarthy Scales is an example of such a subtest. Such subtests provide the examiner with another opportunity to evaluate language formulation as well as recall.

AUDITORY MEMORY 3.   Functions related to Auditory Memory 3 are assessed by the repetition of nonredundant, nonlinguistically organized stimuli, such as unrelated words or digits, as exemplified by the McCarthy Verbal Memory 1 subtest or the ITPA digit repetition tasks.

Retrieval

A subtle and not infrequent problem among children with language disorders is retrieval. Retrieval (Ret.) measures are available for visually, phonemically, and semantically cued retrieval, but norms are available only for the latter type for the preschool child.

RETRIEVAL-SEMANTIC.   Assessment of semantic retrieval skills requires a vocal, within category response, for example, names of animals in response to "Tell me all the animals you know." The Verbal Fluency subtest of the McCarthy Scales is an example of such a task.

Visual Constructs

Visual-Spatial

Visual-spatial constructs refer to functions which require the analysis and synthesis of visually presented material. Whether the stimuli are representational or nonrepresentational in content, the response requires integration of visual, perceptual, cognitive, and motor functions. Poor performance may be related to the interaction among a combination of variables.

VISUAL-SPATIAL 1.   The analysis and synthesis of nonrepresentational stimuli are required. The WPPSI Block Designs subtest is an example.

VISUAL-SPATIAL 2.   The analysis and synthesis of representational stimuli are required. The Puzzles subtest of the McCarthy Scales is an example.

Visual Cognition

Classes of behavior that require verbal or motor responses to visual stimuli are subsumed under the visual cognition construct. The complexity of the task demands range from simple discrimination to higher-order problem solving.

VISUAL COGNITIVE 1.   The functions in Visual Cognitive 1 are defined by match-to-sample tasks, such as those in the Form Discrimination subtest of the PTI.

VISUAL COGNITIVE 2.   The functions in Visual Cognitive 2 are defined by tasks that tap higher cognitive-linguistic abilities, such as grouping, categorization, and analogic concepts. Applicable measures include Picture Association, Hiskey-Nebraska (H-N), Similarities, Pictorial Test of Intelligence (PTI), Visual Association, and ITPA.

Visual Memory (Short Term)

Tasks that involve the brief exposure of a visual array and the immediate reconstruction of that array constitute the functions of visual memory.

VISUAL MEMORY 1.   Tasks involving representational stimuli are used to tap the functions represented by Visual Memory 1. The Visual Attention Span subtest of the Hiskey-Nebraska is an example.

VISUAL MEMORY 2.   Tasks involving nonrepresentational stimuli (Visual Sequential Memory of the ITPA, Knox Cubes on the Arthur Point Scale, 1974) are used in the assessment of Visual Memory 2.

VISUAL MEMORY 3.   Assessment of Visual Memory 3 requires only a single stimulus to be held in short term store, as exemplified by the Immediate Recall subtest of the PTI.

Motor Constructs

Fine Motor Function

Fine motor function may be assessed by use of the Purdue Pegboard, with norms now available down to 3 years of age (Wilson, Iacoviello, Wilson, & Risucci, 1982) and by dominant-hand-only bead stringing tasks (Beads, H-N).

Graphomotor Function

The graphomotor function construct is defined by tests that measure the child's ability to copy line drawings. Geometric Designs from the WPPSI and Draw-a-Design from the McCarthy Scales are two such tasks. Each requires the child to copy straight lines and a circle and then requires complex integration of lines and figures. Although the stimuli are not identical, both subtests clearly tap the same function. It is of uneasy interest to note that the correlation between the WPPSI and McCarthy graphomotor scores obtained from 59 language-disordered children between 3 years and 8 months and 4 years and 3 months of age was only .08 (Wilson & Wilson).

PSYCHOLOGICAL TESTS

Table 6.1 presents a list of standardized tests that might be included in a child neuropsychologist's armamentarium, the relevant age ranges, and the publisher of each. The list is not exhaustive but represents the measures we use most frequently. Following is a brief description of what a variety of tests or subtests appears to assess. Not all the tests listed in Table 6.1 are so treated, although most are. Examiners choose among subtests that appear to tap similar or related functions and work toward the construction of operational definitions of neuropsychological constructs. There are tests listed in Table 6.1 that many clinicians report as inadequate, while others find them useful. Task analyses and reasonable technical data leave room for the selection of "clinician-friendly" tests. The Kaufman ABC is a new test battery (Kaufman & Kaufman, 1983) that appears to be promising but has not yet been used broadly enough, so its utility with handicapped children is unknown.

Wechsler Preschool and Primary Scales of Intelligence: 3 Years, 10 Months, and 16 Days to 6 Years

Verbal Scale

INFORMATION.   Questions are presented by the examiner that tap the child's store of acquired information (e.g., "What color is grass?"). The range of correct answers to

Table 6.1. Standardized Tests Available for Use with Preschool Children

Name of Test	Age Range	Publisher or Vendor
Cognitive Measures		
Bayley Scales of Infant Development	0.1 mo to 30+ mo	Psychological Corporation New York, NY
Hiskey-Nebraska Test of Learning Aptitude (H-N)	3 yr 0 mo to 16 yr 11 mo	Marshall S. Hiskey 5640 Baldwin Lincoln, NB
Kaufman Assessment Battery for Children (K-ABC)	2 yr 6 mo to 12 yr 5 mo	American Guidance Service Circle Pines, MN
Leiter International Performance Scale	2 yr 0 mo to adult	Western Psychological Service Los Angeles, CA
Merrill-Palmer Scale of Mental Tests	1 yr 6 mo to 5 yr 11 mo	Western Psychological Service Los Angeles, CA
McCarthy Scales of Children's Abilities (McC)	2 yr 6 mo to 8 yr 6 mo	Psychological Corporation New York, NY
Pictorial Test of Intellegence (PTI)	2 yr 10 mo to 8 yr 0 mo	Houghton-Mifflin Boston, MA
Stanford-Binet Intelligence Scale	2 yr 0 mo to adult	Houghton-Mifflin Boston, MA
Wechsler Preschool and Primary Scale of Intelligence (WPPSI)	4 yr 0 mo to 6 yr 6 mo	Psychological Corporation New York, NY
Language Measures		
Goldman-Fristoe-Woodcock Auditory Skills Battery (G-F-W) G-F-W Auditory Selective Attention Tests G-F-W Diagnostic Auditory Discrimination Test Part I G-F-W Diagnostic Auditory Discrimination Test Parts II and III G-F-W Auditory Memory Tests G-F-W Sound-Symbol Tests	3yr 0 mo to 86 yr 0 mo	American Guidance Service Circle Pines, MN
Goldman-Fristoe-Woodcock Test of Articulation	2 yr 0 mo to 16 yr 0 mo	American Guidance Service Circle Pines, MN
Goldman-Fristoe-Woodcock Test of Auditory Discrimination	3 yr 8 mo to 70+ yr 0 mo	American Guidance Service Circle Pines, MN
Illinois Test of Psycho-linguistic Abilities (ITPA)	2 yr 0 mo to 10 yr 4 mo	Western Psychological Services Los Angeles, CA
Peabody Picture Vocabulary Test—Revised (PPVT-R)	2 yr 3 mo to 18 yr 5 mo	American Guidance Service Circle Pines, MN
Preschool Language Assessment Instrument	3 yr 0 mo to 6 yr 0 mo	Grune & Stratton Orlando, FL
Test of Auditory Comprehension of Language (TACL)	3 yr 0 mo to 6 yr 11 mo	Learning Concepts Austin, TX
Test of Early Language Development (TELD)	2 yr 0 mo to 7 yr 11 mo	Pro-Ed Austin, TX
Test of Language Development (TOLD)	4 yr 0 mo to 8 yr 11 mo	Pro-Ed Austin, TX
Token Test for Children	3 yr 0 mo to 12 yr 5 mo	Teaching Resources Hingham, MA
Motor Measures		
Bruinks-Oseretesky	4 yr 6 mo to 14 yr 6 mo	American Guidance Service Circle Pines, MN
Test of Motor Proficiency	4 yr 6 mo to 14 yr 6 mo	American Guidance Service Circle Pines, MN
Purdue Pegboard	2 yr 6 mo to 5 yr 11 mo	Lafayette Instrument Co. Lafayette, IN

any given question is very limited. The questions are brief, and a correct response may involve a single word. The child needs to be able to hear, process, decode, remember, retrieve, program for production, and produce the vocal response. A breakdown in any of these related functions can contribute to deficient performance before the store of information ever becomes an issue. These same comments apply to many of the auditory vocal subtests described below.

COMPREHENSION.   The child is required to produce a unique response to a complex question. Content is scored and may receive full credit in spite of semantic, syntactic, or organizational difficulties. This is one of the few instances that provides an opportunity to assess quality of expressive language in response to structured questions. It sometimes provides the initial clue to the presence of deficits in formulation or organizational abilities in the child who appears to be fluent in spontaneous discourse.

ARITHMETIC.   The first four items involve visual stimuli that are presented while the examiner is asking questions. The issue of apprehension of the visual stimulus arises; the issue of bimodal sensory input becomes a concern for some distractable children, who often perform more adequately if the visual and auditory stimuli are presented sequentially rather than simultaneously. The remainder of the items are presented vocally and require mental arithmetic. If these kinds of items are translated into visual terms or supported by visual cues, some children who could not otherwise do so can indicate their knowledge of quantitative concepts.

VOCABULARY.   Word knowledge is assessed by presenting a word and asking the child to define it. Children may produce syntactically inadequate but semantically acceptable answers and score reasonably well. Some language-disordered children fail on these items because of retrieval and organizational deficits, and are able to demonstrate knowledge of word meaning if stimuli are presented visually.

SIMILARITIES.   The first items require the appreciation of semantic categories and the ability to retrieve from within those categories (e.g., "You ride on a train, and you can also ride on a ———.") The later items require a more complex concept of similarity, with items such as "How are beer and wine alike?" The stimulus-response paradigm is auditory-vocal.

SENTENCES.   The Sentences subtest is optional and is frequently omitted. It provides one of a few opportunities to assess repetition skills, short-term memory, or however one wishes to characterize the function. All the caveats about input-output auditory-vocal processing pertain. Two general classes of errors include repetition of some words in the sentence, losing both word sequence and meaning, and a response in which meaning is maintained but word order is lost or other words are substituted. Analysis of the errors is often more useful than the score if one is still hypothesis testing.

   Given that the verbal IQ is calculated without regard to the quality of the language production, it is no wonder that some language-disordered preschool children can score as well as they do. The scale does not purport to be a language measure; the point is that one should not make the assumption that language or linguistic processes are necessarily intact because the verbal IQ is adequate.

Performance Scale

PICTURE COMPLETION.   The child is presented with small black and white line drawings of common objects and asked to identify the missing part of each pictured item. The nature of the stimuli may present problems before the cognitive content is addressed. If the child has problems with materials such as this, then visual and visual discrimination need to be considered before visual cognitive abilities may be questioned. Naming problems will sometimes surface here.

BLOCK DESIGN.   Visual constructional skills are assessed, taking into account vision, discrimination, and motor functions. The child is asked to reproduce a two-dimensional block design, first from a model and then from a pictorial representation. The role of verbal cognitive strategies cannot be ignored and sometimes helps to explain discrepant scores. Verbal strategies are easier to apply to some stimulus situations than to others.

ANIMAL HOUSE.   The Animal House subtest is probably the most complex task on the WPPSI, as Coding may be on the other Wechsler scales. Good performance is facilitated by rapid paired associative learning of color names and animal names, good visual-motor sequential function, fine motor and practice function, adequate attending behavior, and low level of distractability. Performance is further facilitated by comprehension of rather wordy directions that some receptively disordered children never get past. The child is asked to place a peg of a given color into a hole under the picture of a given animal. The givens are presented in a key at the top of a five-by-five matrix. The factors contributing to adequate performance are relatively easy to specify; those that may contribute to deficient performance in a given child are less apparent because of the multiple factors involved and the interactions among deficits that may occur.

GEOMETRIC DESIGN.   The child is asked to copy a series of geometric figures, starting with a circle. Graphomotor skills can appear to be compromised due to problems anywhere from the visual-input to the motor-programming end of the task. The more adequate the discrimination as to the basis for the performance deficits, the more helpful are the results in planning remedial or compensatory strategies.

MAZES.   The Mazes subtest assesses visual-motor skills, motor planning, and spatial analysis. It is a complex perceptual task; comprehension of directions is sometimes an issue.

Hiskey-Nebraska Test of Learning Aptitude: 3 Years and 0 Months to 16 Years and 11 Months

Separate norms are available for hearing-impaired and normal children. Directions for nonverbal, mimed instructions are provided in the manual and may be used for the hearing-impaired, bilingual, or language-impaired child. None of the subtests requires verbal responses. All require the ability to apprehend visual stimuli; some involve complex motor acts. Each subtest yields an MA equivalent. A deviation IQ score may be obtained from tabled values for the hearing children. Four of eight subtests are dropped after age 10, and four are added. Although the H-N is a very useful clinical tool, particularly with special populations and because of the age range, there is a troublesome lack of technical data concerning the test. Distributions of scores for individual subtests are not available. Although a minimal problem at the preschool level, the level of item difficulty is too discontinuous for older children. For example, an increase in raw score from 7 to 8 on Paper Folding yields an increase in MA from 9 years and 0 months to 11 years and 6 months, a gain of 2 years and 6 months on the basis of a single item.

BEAD PATTERNS: 3 YEARS AND 0 MONTHS TO 10 YEARS AND 11 MONTHS.   The Bead Patterns subtest involves three diverse tasks but yields one score. The first segment requires the stringing of one-half inch beads, a dominant-hand-only measure of fine motor skill. The score is based on the number strung in one minute. The second segment, involving three items, requires the child to copy bead patterns from a model strung by the examiner. The third segment, consisting of three items, requires the child to reproduce a bead sequence from memory after a brief exposure. One score reflects the three segments.

PICTURE IDENTIFICATION: 3 YEARS TO 10 YEARS.   The Picture Identification subtest is a match-to-sample task. The stimuli are small black and white drawings of common objects. Visual acuity, visual-perceptual, and cognitive demands are involved. With the progression of items, the task demands change, requiring attention to differences in inner detail among otherwise visually identical objects, rather than attention to a match among visually diverse but semantically related items (e.g., butterflies). As with so many visual tasks, verbal mediation is a facilitative strategy for many.

MEMORY FOR COLOR: 3 YEARS AND 0 MONTHS TO 10 YEARS AND 11 MONTHS.   Strips of colored plastic are the stimuli in the Memory for Color subtest, a visual memory task. The number of stimuli increases from one to six over trials. A pointing response is required, and sequencing is irrelevant. The ability to name and remember color names clearly facilitates performance.

PICTURE ASSOCIATION: 3 YEARS AND 0 MONTHS TO 10 YEARS AND 11 MONTHS.   The task, involving small black and white drawings, requires the linguistic concept of category. The child is asked to select one of four items that "belongs with" three pictured items that are categorically related. Although this is a nonvocal task, it is certainly a verbal one.

PAPER FOLDING: 3 YEARS AND 0 MONTHS TO 10 YEARS AND 11 MONTHS.   The child is asked to reproduce a paper pattern modeled by the examiner. The items progress from single folds to patterns that require six folds. This complex task requires motor planning and coordination, memory for visual sequences, and an appreciation of spatial relationships. Although the task embodies visual-spatial elements, post hoc visual-spatial analysis is not a primary task demand in this instance, since the final product must follow the step-by-step procedure demonstrated by the examiner. That is, if the resulting triangle, which appears identical to the sample, is not arrived at using the same sequence of folds, the item is scored as incorrect.

VISUAL ATTENTION SPAN: 3 YEARS AND 0 MONTHS TO 16 YEARS AND 11 MONTHS.   The Visual Attention Span subtest involves black and white representational pictures of common objects. In this visual memory subtest, the child is asked to duplicate from memory a briefly viewed stimulus sequence from an array that increases from 6 to 18 pictures over trials. The sequences to be remembered increase from one to seven items. Correct sequencing is not required, although it earns a bonus point. Whether the sequencing skill is present or absent cannot be deduced from the score. Many children use a naming strategy to assist in recall. Some come up with inadequate labels, and some forget the labels they come up with. The error analysis is in the eye of the beholder and can yield helpful information.

BLOCK PATTERNS: 3 YEARS AND 0 MONTHS TO 16 YEARS AND 11 MONTHS.   The Block Patterns subtest requires the child to construct a three-dimensional block pattern from a two-dimensional, printed sample. The patterns start simply, with the stacking of three one-inch cubes, and progress to complex constructions requiring the appreciation of cues to three-dimensional relationships. Visual spatial analysis and synthesis, motor planning, and coordination appear to be the major components.

COMPLETION OF DRAWINGS: 3 YEARS AND 0 MONTHS TO 16 YEARS AND 11 MONTHS.   The Completion of Drawings subtest is a nonvocal analog of the Picture Completion subtest on the Wechsler Scales. The child is asked to draw in the part of the picture that is missing. Elegance of execution is irrelevant as long as the graphomotor response is interpretable. Visual-perceptual and recognition skills are involved; graphomotor ability must meet minimal standards. The contribution of language is not quantitatively demonstrable, but with many children, labeling, naming parts while scanning, and so on are explicit. Some children have difficulty with vocal naming but understand the concepts nonetheless. Such children frequently fare better on this measure than on the Picture Completion subtest, in which naming is necessary for most items. If a child does poorly on one of these subtests, it can be instructive to administer the other.

Kaufman Assessment Battery for Children: 2 Years and 6 Months to 12 Years and 5 Months

The Kaufman Assessment Battery for Children (K-ABC) is a new assessment instrument (1983) that includes 16 subtests, 11 with norms available for children below 5 years of age. Building on a theoretical base, the Kaufmans developed subtests grouped into three scales: Sequential Processing, Simultaneous Processing, and an Achievement Scale. The intent is to assess cognitive strategies as well as cognitive level, and to provide an estimate of academic and preacademic skills.

EXPRESSIVE VOCABULARY: 2 YEARS AND 6 MONTHS TO 4 YEARS AND 11 MONTHS.   The name Expressive Vocabulary suggests that the child is asked to provide oral definitions for words; in fact, the youngster is asked to *name* pictures of representational items. Although the child's lexicon is tapped, word retrieval, and not vocabulary alone, influences performance. Visual processing is obviously involved.

FACES AND PLACES: 2 YEARS AND 6 MONTHS TO 12 YEARS AND 5 MONTHS.   The Faces and Places test examines the child's general fund of knowledge. Pictures of well-known places, people, and characters are presented, and the child must identify them.

ARITHMETIC: 3 YEARS AND 0 MONTHS TO 12 YEARS AND 5 MONTHS. Orally presented word problems and relevant pictorial cues are presented simultaneously in the Arithmetic test. While this test is designed primarily to assess conceptual arithmetic skills, the word problems require complex linguistic processing and memory skills.

WORD ORDER: 4 YEARS AND 0 MONTHS TO 12 YEARS AND 5 MONTHS. The Word Order test is an auditory-visual sequential memory task. The examiner says series of words, and the child must point to the pictures of these words in the identical sequence. This task involves simultaneous bimodal processing, auditory memory, visual scanning, and sequencing skills.

NUMBER RECALL: 2 YEARS AND 6 MONTHS TO 12 YEARS AND 5 MONTHS. The Number Recall test involves a digit repetition task requiring good attending skills and focused repetition.

TRIANGLES: 4 YEARS AND 0 MONTHS TO 12 YEARS AND 5 MONTHS. In the Triangles test, a two-dimensional constructional task, the child is asked to assemble triangular pieces to form patterns identical to the target item. Skills in visual spatial analysis and synthesis are tapped; deficient motor planning can affect performance.

HAND MOVEMENTS: 2 YEARS AND 6 MONTHS TO 12 YEARS AND 5 MONTHS. The examiner demonstrates a sequence of hand movements that the child is asked to repeat. This task is primarily a measure of imitative praxis. A verbal mediation strategy may be employed but is probably less important than in the visually mediated tasks.

GESTALT CLOSURE: 2 YEARS AND 6 MONTHS TO 12 YEARS AND 5 MONTHS. Visual stimuli consisting of incomplete black and white pictures are presented and must be named. This is a complex task involving functioning in visual processing, recognition involving visual synthesis, and word retrieval skills.

RIDDLES: 3 YEARS AND 0 MONTHS TO 12 YEARS AND 5 MONTHS. The child is given attributes of items and is asked to name the object that the attributes describe. This task involves receptive language, conceptual linguistic skills, and word retrieval.

FACE RECOGNITION: 2 YEARS AND 6 MONTHS TO 4 YEARS AND 11 MONTHS. One or two photographs of faces are briefly exposed, and the child must then identify them in an array of faces. This task involves no auditory-vocal processing. Verbal mediation may facilitate performance.

MAGIC WINDOW: 2 YEARS AND 6 MONTHS TO 4 YEARS AND 11 MONTHS. The child is asked to identify pictures of common objects; pictures are exposed so that the entire object is never seen at one time. Instead, parts of the object are sequentially presented through an opening in a rotating disc. This is a complex perceptual cognitive measure. Visual processing, aspects of visual memory, synthesis, and word retrieval are among the processes tapped.

McCarthy Scales of Children's Abilities: 2 Years and 6 Months to 8 Years and 6 Months

The McCarthy (McC) Scales include 18 subtests that are grouped into six scales. Some subtests appear on more than one scale. The author recommends that the scale scores be used in preference to the individual subtest scores. However, in spite of the less adequate reliability of the individual subtest scores, a good deal of essential clinical information is discarded if subtest scores are not evaluated.

BLOCK BUILDING.   The Block Building task examines visual constructional skills. The examiner builds three-dimensional block patterns while the child watches. The child is then asked to reproduce the design while the model remains in view. Visual perception, visual spatial abilities, and praxis are involved.

PUZZLE SOLVING.   The child is asked to assemble puzzles of representational items. Unlike other puzzle tasks, the child is given the name of the object the puzzle will form before construction. This task involves visual-perceptual, spatial, and motor skills. In addition, verbal mediation strategies may be used to facilitate performance.

VERBAL MEMORY 1.   On the Verbal Memory 1 test, a repetition task, the child is asked to repeat two different types of stimuli: series of unrelated word sequences and sentences. Although only one summary score results, differential performance on word series and sentences is common. Some children seem to have difficulty with sequencing and perform poorly when asked to repeat the unrelated words. However, when presented with the added contextual information found in sentences, performance seems to be facilitated. Functioning on this task may be disrupted by difficulties in auditory processing, auditory memory, sequencing, and expressive language. Useful information about the child's syntactic abilities may be derived from the child's errors on sentence repetition.

VERBAL MEMORY 2.   On the Verbal Memory 2 test, the child is asked to retell a short story immediately after having heard it. The score is the sum of the number of salient bits of information recalled. Syntax and sequential organization are not formally assessed and therefore are not reflected in the score, but review of the responses, which should be noted verbatim, may provide the examiner with essential information about the child's expressive language skills. The child may have difficulty telling the story for a variety of reasons only one of which is auditory memory. Frequently, formulation and retrieval problems appear to contribute to poor performance. Although not a part of the standardized procedure, difficulties can be probed by asking structured questions. Children with formulation problems are usually able to answer correctly, but those with memory problems are not. As is true for all tasks presented in the auditory modality, difficulties with auditory processing and/or attention impede performance.

OPPOSITE ANALOGIES.   In the Opposite Analogies test, an auditory cognitive task, the child is asked to give one-word vocal responses that complete verbal analogies. Though the items range in difficulty, they tend to involve overlearned associations.

Because the child can provide the correct response on the basis of a single-word association, higher-order conceptual-linguistic skills are generally not invoked.

PICTORIAL MEMORY.   The examiner labels pictures of representational items that are briefly exposed. After the display has been removed, the child is asked to recall the names of the pictures. Even though the information is presented to the visual and auditory modalities, the auditory input appears to be the salient feature to which most children attend. Auditory memory appears to be the most important skill involved.

NUMBER QUESTIONS.   In the Number Questions test, an auditory-verbal task, the child must give a vocal response to orally presented questions. Various content areas are tapped by the items. Some are questions regarding general information (e.g., "How many ears do you have?"). Other items are word problems that involve mental computation. As the items become longer and linguistically complex, greater demands are made on auditory memory, auditory processing, and receptive language skills.

TAPPING SEQUENCE.   The Tapping Sequence test is a complex and multimodal task that purports to examine memory and perceptual motor skills. The child must recreate sequences he or she has just seen and heard the examiner execute on a toy xylophone. Due to the task demands, a breakdown in performance may be due to any number of contributing factors, such as sequencing, motor skills, or visual-motor integration difficulties. Because children often respond to the xylophone as a toy, the examiner should differentiate between playful behavior and an inability to perform the task for other reasons. Qualitative observations frequently can provide more information than can the summary score. If information about visual sequential memory involving a motor output is required, small blocks may be substituted for the xylophone, minimizing the play response. This changes the task so that norms do not really apply, but the target behavior can be assessed, albeit clinically.

WORD KNOWLEDGE.   Part I of the two-part Word Knowledge test involves vocal presentation of words and requires the child to point to the corresponding pictures. On Part II, the child must define words. While only a single summary score is derived, the task measures both receptive and expressive language skills. As is evident, a single score can mask differential performance.

LEG COORDINATION.   The purpose of the Leg Coordination task is to examine gross motor skills involving the lower extremities. The integrity of the overall motor system should be taken into account in interpreting the results.

ARM COORDINATION.   The Arm Coordination task purports to measures gross motor skills, when in fact complex visual-motor skills are very much involved, as in catching a ball.

RIGHT-LEFT ORIENTATION.   The Right-Left Orientation test is designed to examine personal and extrapersonal right-left orientation; pointing responses to verbal commands are required. Auditory memory and receptive language skills may influence performance, since the commands are vocally presented.

IMITATIVE ACTION.   The examiner performs actions that the child is asked to duplicate. Praxis is examined with this task.

NUMERICAL MEMORY.   The Numerical Memory test is a sequential digit repetition measure. Separate scores are available for backward digit repetition and forward digit repetition.

VERBAL FLUENCY.   The Verbal Fluency test is a semantically cued word retrieval task in which the cues are category labels. Within a brief time period, the child is asked to name as many items as possible, falling within each of four categories.

COUNTING AND SORTING.   The child is asked to follow lengthy and linguistically complex directions and is then asked to demonstrate knowledge of quantitative and spatial concepts. Both vocal and nonvocal responses are necessary.

CONCEPTUAL GROUPING.   The Conceptual Grouping test examines the child's ability to categorize by shape, color, size, or a combination of these attributes. Auditory processing, receptive language, and linguistic skills are involved in performance.

DRAW-A-DESIGN.   The child is asked to copy geometric forms. Performance on this measure involves visual perceptual, spatial planning, and graphomotor skills.

DRAW-A-CHILD.   The child is asked to draw a human figure. The score reflects the number of elements drawn as well as the quality of drawing. Although the cognitive aspects of the task are clearly more relevant for scoring purposes, a child with poor graphomotor skills may score poorly on Draw-a-Design yet receive an adequate score on this measure.

Pictorial Test of Intelligence: 2 Years and 10 Months to 8 Years and 0 Months

Verbal directions are limited and a pointing response is required for each subtest. Responses are selected from a display containing four black and white drawings, one in each quadrant of an 11-by-11-inch card. This is a relatively easy test for which to develop alternative response modes and is therefore very useful with motorically impaired children.

FORM DISCRIMINATION.   The target stimulus is presented on a three-by-three-inch card. The response card is then presented and the child is asked to point to the item that looks identical to the target stimulus. In order to comply with the task demands, the child must understand the concept of *same*. The task primarily involves visual perceptual skills, but verbal mediation can be a useful strategy.

SIMILARITIES.   A four-item visual display is presented, and the child is asked to identify the picture that is *different* from the other three. For some items, the discrimination is based on differences in detail (e.g., different number of apples on a tree). With other items, the difference is at the conceptual level (e.g., which of four food items is not a dessert). Two different cognitive skills are involved. An error analysis is necessary in order to determine where the problems lie.

IMMEDIATE RECALL.   Pictures of representational and nonrepresentational objects are singly and briefly presented and subsequently must be recognized on the four-item visual display card. The memory load on this task is restricted to a single item. Labeling clearly facilitates performance.

PICTURE VOCABULARY.   The child is asked to point to the picture on the multiple-item display card that represents the meaning of a word presented vocally. The task involves word knowledge and efficient visual perceptual skills.

SIZE AND NUMBER.   The child is asked to point to the picture on the display card that is the best pictorial representation of the answer to a vocally presented question. The Size and Number test taps knowledge of quantitative, cognitive-linguistic concepts, such as *most* and *longest*, and computational skills. Since the verbal input is complex and often lengthy, auditory processing and memory and receptive language contribute to performance.

INFORMATION AND COMPREHENSION.   The examiner asks the child questions concerning general knowledge. The child must point to the picture on the multi-item display card that answers the question. The verbal input on this test tends to be more complex and lengthy than that on other subtests, so there are greater demands on auditory processing and receptive language skills.

Bayley Scales of Infant Development: 0.1 Months to 30+ Months

The Bayley Scales provide the examiner with two separate scales with which to assess infant and toddler behavior. Gross motor coordination, fine motor skills, and visual motor functioning are examined with the motor scale. The mental scale covers a wider range of behavior. Information may be derived regarding auditory, visual, sensory, and motor functioning as well as cognitive, expressive, and receptive language skills.

A summary score is derived for each of these scales, yielding a Psychomotor Development Index and a Mental Development Index. However, because of the diversity of behaviors described by a summary score, it yields no information about areas of relative strengths and weaknesses. The age range and mean age of acquisition are listed individually for each test item and may be used to gain more specific information about the levels of functioning in each area. For example, the examiner may group all of the items that tap receptive language skills in order to estimate level of performance. This can be done for each of the behavioral areas assessed, and a profile of relative efficiencies can be developed.

It is important to point out that many items on the mental scale require proficiency in more than one skill area, as is true with most measures. A child with a motor impairment, for example, may have the cognitive skills necessary for the completion of a form board but may be unable to perform the task due to her or his motor difficulties. Consequently, the child's physical abilities should be evaluated before the more complex tasks are administered, so that the testing situation may be set up to facilitate maximal performance.

Peabody Picture Vocabulary Test: 2 Years and 3 Months to 18 Years and 5 Months

A word is presented vocally to the child, who must point to its pictorial referent on a visual display containing four items. The Peabody Picture Vocabulary Test is a measure of receptive vocabulary that makes demands on auditory and visual processing and on retrieval skills. A single-norm–referenced score may be obtained.

Goldman-Fristoe-Woodcock Auditory Diagnostic Battery

Auditory discrimination skills are examined by the Auditory Diagnostic Battery. There are three sections, each of which requires the child to point to the one of two pictures that represents a word presented vocally by the examiner. "Lure" items are pictures that are phonemically similar to the target. Parts II and III are administered only if Part I is completed adequately. Although summary scores are derived for each section, items are clustered into categories of specific sound contrasts through an item analysis. It is thus possible to obtain information regarding the specific speech-sound contrasts that are difficult for the child to perceive. A training period precedes the test in order to familiarize the child with the vocabulary. This is a crucial consideration in interpretation, especially with preschoolers.

Goldman-Fristoe-Woodcock Selective Attention Tests

The Selective Attention battery consists of a variety of measures that examine auditory processing under varying conditions of background interference. Performance is assessed under background conditions including a fanlike noise, a voice reading a story, and an ambient level of cafeteria noise. The response paradigm is identical to that described above for the G-F-W Auditory Diagnostic Battery. Separate scores are available for each of the three listening conditions.

Goldman-Fristoe-Woodcock Sound-Symbol Tests

Sound Mimicry

The child is asked to repeat nonsense words of increasing length. Word recognition skills cannot, therefore, facilitate performance. Instead, the child must rely on auditory perceptual abilities and repetition skills alone.

Sound Recognition

The Sound Recognition test is a sound-blending task that requires a pointing, not a vocal, response. As in similar tasks, words are broken down into individual phonemes, and the child must blend them to form words. A training period precedes the test to verify that the child is familiar with all of the vocabulary words used.

Sound Blending

For the Sound Blending task, the child is asked to blend isolated phonemes to form words. A vocal response is required. Auditory synthesis and vocal production are required.

For each of the Goldman-Fristoe-Woodcock tests described above, a tape recorder is used for stimulus presentation to provide for a standard stimulus and to preclude lip reading. The use of headphones is recommended. The norms for all the G-F-W tests range from 3 years and 4 months to 86 years and 0 months.

Illinois Test of Psycholinguistic Abilities: 2 Years and 6 Months to 10 Years and 4 Months

AUDITORY RECEPTION.   The child is asked to give a yes-no response when posed with brief, syntactically uncomplicated questions. Each item requires the decoding of two key vocabulary words. Auditory processing and receptive language skills are essential determinants of performance. The yes-no response paradigm ensures that there is a 50% chance of guessing correctly.

VISUAL RECEPTION.   A photograph of a real object is briefly exposed and then removed from view. The child is presented with a four-item multiple choice display from which to select the item falling into the same semantic category as the target stimulus. This visual cognitive task requires a pointing, not a vocal, response. Cognitive linguistic skills, word retrieval, and visual perceptual skills are implicated.

AUDITORY ASSOCIATION.   One-word responses are required in order to complete verbal analogies. While cognitive-linguistic skills are involved, many of the items consist of overlearned associations. As a result, the child may give the correct answer because the response word is highly associated with the key word preceding it and not because he or she has understood or conceptualized the analogy.

VISUAL ASSOCIATION.   The Visual Association subtest is composed of two conceptually distinct sets of task demands, although only one summary score is derived. For the first part, the child is presented with a visual display composed of a stimulus picture and four possible response items. The child is asked to point to the item most closely associated with the target stimulus. For the second part, the child must complete visual analogies. The exemplar item consists of two pictures that present an analogic relationship. On the same page, the child is presented with a target stimulus and asked to find the item among four that is related to it as the exemplar items are related. Conceptual-linguistic skills are involved in both parts of this test; however, different levels of processing are required for each section. A child may perform well on the first part but may have difficulty on the second, more complex set of items. This will not be apparent in the score.

AUDITORY SEQUENTIAL MEMORY.   The Auditory Sequential Memory test requires sequential repetition of series of digits. Poor performance may be related to difficulties in auditory processing, auditory memory, sequencing skills, speech production, or attention.

VISUAL SEQUENTIAL MEMORY.   Sequences of nonrepresentational shapes are presented for a brief period. The child is then asked to recreate the sequences from memory. Some children who perform poorly on visual memory tasks with an inherent "language pull," such as the H-N Visual Attention span subtest, perform more efficiently on this measure. Although any visual stimulus potentially can be named, nonrepresentational stimuli are more difficult to label. Some children do better under these conditions. Sequencing, visual perception, and memory are involved.

VERBAL EXPRESSION.   On the Verbal Expression subtest, an expressive language measure, the child is asked to respond to an open-ended request to describe several common objects. The score reflects the number of salient bits of information mentioned. This is more a naming task of sorts, since maximum credit can be obtained by merely listing attributes. Scoring does not reflect any assessment of syntax, semantic usage, morphology, or any of the other areas usually thought of in connection with expressive language.

MANUAL EXPRESSION.   Pictures of common objects are presented, and the child is asked to demonstrate their use gesturally rather than vocally. Before executing the gesture, the visual stimulus must be apprehended and recognized, and there must be a conceptual understanding of the object's function. A breakdown in performance may also occur at the level of motor planning, since ideomotor practic skills are heavily involved.

GRAMMATIC CLOSURE.   The initial stimulus consists of a picture and a descriptive sentence presented simultaneously, followed by a second picture and an incomplete sentence related to the initial stimulus. The child is asked to supply the one-word response that best completes the second sentence. For example, the child might see a picture appropriately coupled with the sentence, "This man is a painter." Then the child would see a second picture, showing a man painting, paired with the statement, "Here he is———." This task primarily assesses grammatic competence without making heavy demands on conceptual linguistic skills.

SOUND BLENDING.   For the Sound Blending test, an auditory perceptual task, the child is asked to blend isolated sounds into words. While only one summary score can be derived, the task demands are not uniform. Differential performance may be obtained when the child is given real words, in which recognition provides important cues, or nonsense words or is required to point to pictures to demonstrate recognition. Cognitive-linguistic demands are minimal.

AUDITORY CLOSURE.   Single words with phonemes deleted are presented, and the child is asked to give the completed word forms. Auditory perceptual skills are tapped, with real words used as stimuli. Word recognition skills facilitate performance; that is, the child may recognize the word even though only one salient "piece" has been perceived. The child's difficulty with perceptual processing of this kind may be masked and become evident only in other contexts in which unfamiliar, nonsense words or word strings are used.

VISUAL CLOSURE.   The child must find the hidden figures embedded in a complex picture. The Visual Closure subtest is a timed task. It requires many component skills, including visual perception, visual scanning, and figure-ground analysis.

The Token Test for Children: 3 Years and 0 Months to 12 Years and 5 Months

The Token Test for Children is one of the modified versions of the Token Test, which was originally used to detect aphasic disorders in adults with neurologic dysfunction (DeRenzi & Vignolo, 1962). On each of the five sections, the child must respond to verbal commands by a motor response. Parts I–IV are composed of directions of increasing length requiring retention of two to six bits of nonredundant information. For example, "Touch the *red circle*" is typical of a Part I command, and "Touch the *small yellow circle* and the *large green square*" is typical of a Part IV command. The task demands are altered on Part V so that the child is required to decode syntactically and semantically complex sentences. The memory load is similar to that in Part III. "Instead of the white square, touch the yellow circle" is a typical Part V item. This task involves auditory processing and decoding, auditory memory, and motor planning. The relative contributions of the skills necessary for adequate performance on each section may vary. Part IV seems to more heavily tap sequential memory, while Part V more heavily taps syntactic and semantic processing. Certain subtypes of language-disordered children may perform adequately on Part V, in which the redundancy provided by syntax is useful, and increasingly less proficiently on Parts I–IV, in which auditory sequential memory is more critical. The opposite pattern—proficiency on Part IV and poor performance on Part V—is common among children with auditory semantic comprehension problems.

Purdue Pegboard: 2 Years and 6 Months to 5 Years and 11 Months

The Purdue Pegboard is a sensory-motor test that has been used as a screening device for the detection of neurologic dysfunction in adults and school-aged children (Costa, Vaughan, Levita, & Farber, 1963; Rapin, Tourk, & Costa, 1966). Normative data recently have become available for preschool children (Wilson, Iacoviello, Wilson, & Risucci, 1982). This is a timed fine motor task requiring the child to place pegs in a board. The pegs measure 2.54 centimeters in length and 2 millimeters in width. The pegboard has been cut down to accommodate the shorter reach of the younger children. Separate scores are available for preferred and nonpreferred hands individually and for both hands working simultaneously.

INTEGRATION OF DATA AND PROFILE DEVELOPMENT

Assuming an appraisal of the referral question, the history, the collection of quantitative data based on a branching model, and the inclusion of observational data, what should be done next? There needs to be an integration, a pulling together, of all the available information, a formulation of the neuropsychological status of the child, and the development of at least first-line suggestions as to intervention strategies. Starting with our model of neuropsychological constructs, we have been working with a method of profiling and profile analysis that demonstrates the systematic nature of the data and appears to have clinical utility. The profiles are part of the case material presented below. A brief description of the way in which they are developed may be helpful in their interpretation and, perhaps, in their clinical application (Culbertson, 1981).

Scores on subtests thought to reflect a given construct are aggregated. The mean score of each aggregate is plotted, and it is these scores that represent the constructs plotted in the profile. When scores that are to be aggregated are clearly discrepant, the most reliable of the measures are selected. The determination of reliability is made on the basis of the information presented in the technical manuals.

There are few, if any, pure measures of any neuropsychological function; subtests are selected to represent a construct based on clinical decisions as to which tests measure most of what functions. When possible, two or more measures of a given construct are administered. Only standardized tests are used, and each is expressed in terms of its own metric. The Wechsler subtests have a mean score of 10 and a standard deviation of 3; the ITPA has a mean score of 36 and a standard deviation of 6; the McCarthy Scales of Children's Abilities present means and standard deviations for each subtest as a function of age; and so on.

To facilitate the evaluation of these data, simplify profile construction, and provide a readily understandable metric to an interdisciplinary audience, we convert our scores into z scores ($x - M/\sigma$) and then into percentiles. Although some information may be lost at the extremes, the loss makes little difference at the clinical level and can be retrieved for research purposes if necessary.

Table 6.2 provides a listing of the subtests we have selected as descriptive of the given constructs, and those preferentially included are so indicated. Since the pool of subtests from which to select is much more limited for the preschool age range than for the school-age range, some constructs are represented by only one or two subtests.

Case Studies

As a way of integrating the information discussed above, case studies are presented below. They have been selected to demonstrate the usefulness of the referral question and the frequent utility of the history as well as to demonstrate the profiles themselves. We have attempted to select cases that provide a range of developmental problems that can be systematically studied and that indicate the nature of the recommendations that flow from the clinical and quantitative assessment data.

John: Chronological Age, 3 Years and 6 Months

John was referred for neuropsychological evaluation because of severe delay in the development of expressive language. The question revolved around the level of cognitive function and recommendations for appropriate intervention.

Pregnancy, birth, and delivery were without incident. History revealed that John had difficulty feeding and was thought to be a failure-to-thrive child. Motor milestones were uniformly delayed. John had frequent episodes of serous otitis media and, inferentially, a fluctuating conductive hearing loss. Family history was noncontributory.

John was very anxious during the initial testing session. Cursory oromotor examination revealed profuse drooling and significant oromotor dysfunction. John handled table foods by mashing them with his tongue against the roof of his mouth; lateral tongue movements were very limited. He was referred for a neurological examination, which revealed bilateral corticospinal and corticobulbar tract impairment with pseudobulbar palsy.

John was unable to produce running speech; utterances were intelligible in a shared context only and if the utterance contained no more than two words. Although

Table 6.2   Examples of Subtest Composition of Clinically Derived Factors and Constructs

Constructs	Factors	Subtests
Auditory perception (AP)	AP1	ITPA Auditory Closure
	AP2	ITPA Auditory Closure
Auditory discrimination (AD)	AD-Q	G-F-W Quiet
	AD-N	G-F-W Noise
Auditory cognitive (AC)	AC1	WPPSI Similarities
		ITPA Auditory Association
	AC2	WPPSI Information
		WPPSI Vocabulary
	AC3	WPPSI Comprehension
Auditory memory (AM)	AM1	WPPSI Sentence
		McC Verbal Memory I
	AM2	McC Verbal Memory II
	AM3	McC Numerical Memory I
		McC Numerical Memory II
Retrieval (Ret.)	RS	McC Verbal Fluency
Visual spatial (VSp)	VSp1	WPPSI Block Designs
		H-N Block Patterns
	VSp2	McC Puzzles
Visual cognitive (VC)	VC1	WPPSI Picture Completion
		ITPA Visual Reception
	VC2	ITPA Visual Association
		H-N Picture Association
		PTI Similarities
	VC3	ITPA Manual Expression
Visual memory (VM)	VM1	H-N Visual Attention Span
		H-N Memory for Color
	VM2	ITPA Visual Sequential Memory
	VM3	PTI Immediate Recall

somewhat dyspraxic, John communicated mainly by gesturing and facial expression. He was well related, demonstrated communicative intent, and, although less fearful as the sessions progressed, remained a very anxious child.

Results of the formal assessment are presented in Figure 6.1. John was able to demonstrate his auditory discrimination skills only when a pointing response was necessary. He was unable to demonstrate ability on any of the aural-oral measures; although largely a function of his unintelligible speech, it was hard to know how adequate his auditory receptive skills were and whether they contributed to his deficient performances across the board. Tasks involving visual input were handled within the low average to average range, with a single exception; VC3, requiring gestural interpretation of pictures, yielded a below average score. In a number of instances, John seemed unable to organize the motor response. He attempted each item, but as with his speech, there were times when his "one-word gestures" were unintelligible, with dyspraxia contributing to the problem in each instance.

Hand functions, fine and graphomotor, further reflected John's neurological impairment. He appeared to have a right-hand preference.

John was finally identified as a neurologically impaired child with significant expressive deficits secondary to oromotor dysfunction. He was thought to have potentially adequate cognitive skills in those areas that did not require oral communi-

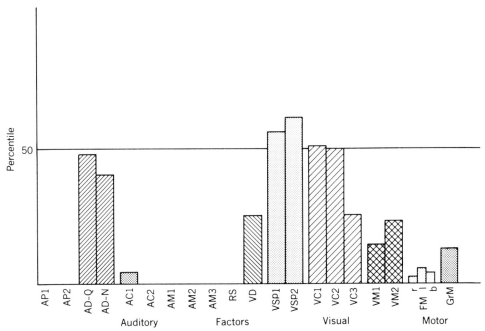

Figure 6.1.   The neuropsychological profile of John at 3 years and 6 months of age. John's severe delay in expressive language proved to be related to frank neurological impairment that precluded the possibility of intelligible speech. A total communication program, involving sign language, among other strategies, was provided to supply John with a method of communication.

cation. The level of auditory receptive skills remained an open question. There was a suggestion of some difficulty in following directions during the evaluation, but longer-term observations would have been necessary to clarify this. There are factors that could have contributed to an auditory receptive deficit, including the lack of autofeedback and the history of early and frequent bouts of serous otitis media.

John was referred to a nursery school that provides services to children with language disorders. He was placed in a class that emphasized total communication, including sign language and cued speech in conjunction with spoken language. Prognosis for expressive language was deemed poor, and emphasis on alternative methods of communication was given a priority.

Danny: Chronological Age, 4 Years and 3 Months

Danny was referred for neuropsychological evaluation because of "mildly delayed development" in all areas. There were questions about his general level of cognitive development and appropriate educational placement.

Danny was the product of a full-term, uncomplicated pregnancy, birth, and delivery. The neonatal course was without incident. Sitting and walking were mildly delayed, appearing at 8 and 17 months, respectively. Although Danny was described as a good communicator, speech and language development were clearly delayed. Danny experienced six febrile seizures between 2 and 3 years of age. Results of neurological examination at 3 years of age were negative except for the notation of excessive

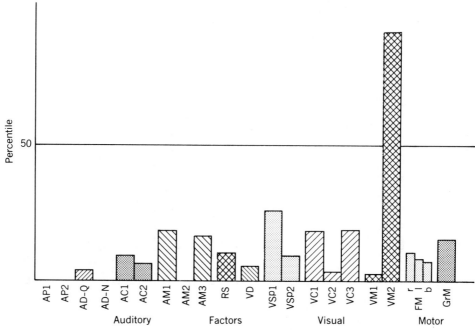

Figure 6.2.   The neuropsychological profile of Danny at 4 years and 3 months of age. Danny demonstrated below-average functioning in most conceptual areas. He appeared to be a diffusely impaired child, secondary to a static encephalopathy of unknown origin.

drooling and limited language production. Family and later medical histories were noncontributory.

Danny presented as a friendly, cooperative child who communicated by means of gestures and poorly articulated one- and two-word utterances. The results of the evaluation, profiled in Figure 6.2, revealed a range of functioning from deficient to low average. He showed significant difficulty with all auditory-verbal tasks other than sequential memory, and low average abilities in visual-spatial skills and in aspects of simple visual cognitive functions. His performances were uniformly deficient in the more complex conceptual areas, based on either visual or auditory input. His single superior score was achieved on VM2, which involves visual memory for representational items, which constitute a "splinter skill." Fine motor skills were deficient; graphomotor performance fell within the limits of other skill areas. Right-hand preference was apparent. Gross motor coordination was poor. Evidence of primitive oromotor reflexes was noted.

On the basis of the evaluation, Danny was identified as a diffusely impaired youngster whose behavior probably reflected a static encephalopathy of unknown origin. A special education program was recommended that would address the totality of his developmental disabilities.

In most areas, Danny seemed to be functioning at a presymbolic level. His general deficits in coordination, sensory-motor integration, and elemental linguistic concepts defined the content of an appropriate intervention program. An evaluation by a neurodevelopmentally trained therapist was recommended to address Danny's sensory-motor deficits. Speech and language therapy were recommended. These services

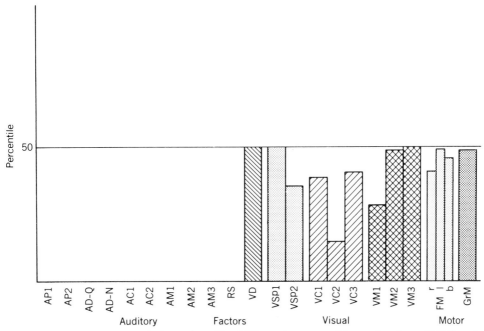

Figure 6.3.   The neuropsychological profile of Gina at 3 years and 3 months of age. Childhood psychoses and mental retardation were diagnoses under consideration at the time of the referral. The evaluation led to an inferential diagnosis of auditory-verbal agnosia. A total communication program was initiated in an attempt to provide Gina with a working receptive modality.

were to be provided within a special preschool program within which appropriate content areas could serve as vehicles for motor and sensory motor development.

Gina: Chronological Age, 3 Years and 3 Months

Gina was referred for neuropsychological evaluation by Child Psychiatry because of "mutism" and a behavioral disturbance. Gina was described as essentially nonverbal. She demonstrated communicative intent, relying on grunts, body language, and pointing. Temper tantrums and destructive behavior were daily occurrences. Results of a pediatric neurology examination at 2 years and 10 months were negative. EEG and CT studies were read as normal. An audiological evaluation documented normal hearing bilaterally. The primary question concerned differential diagnosis; childhood psychosis and mental retardation were the diagnoses under consideration.

History indicated that Gina was postmature, delivered by caesarean section at 43 weeks of gestation. There had been no onset of labor; induction was attempted without success. Meconium-stained amniotic fluid suggested fetal distress. In spite of this history, Apgar scores were 9 and 9 after one and five minutes. All developmental milestones were delayed. Gina sat at 11 months and did not ambulate independently until 21 months. Family history was noncontributory. Results of the evaluation, presented in Figure 6.3, indicated severe receptive and expressive language deficits. Although Gina was able to perform within the average range on visual match-to-sample, within-semantic-category grouping, visual-spatial, and visual memory tasks, she was unsuccessful on all measures of auditory input, regardless of response mode, and had significant difficulty with conceptually complex visually mediated tasks. Right-hand preference seemed in evidence.

A diagnosis of auditory-verbal agnosia was suggested by the results of the evaluation and by Gina's interactive behavior. She concentrated on visual cues, knew how to "follow the leader" in situations with other children, and responded to affective cues. She was referred to a program for language-disordered children and was placed in a total communication program. Acquisition of signs was initially slow. Once she began to understand the association between object, word, and sign, she began to acquire sign vocabulary and began to use signs for words other than nouns, apparently incorporating signs for syntactic as well as semantic context. Acquisition of signs appeared to act as a stimulus to the production of spoken language. Her vocal output was minimal and, after one year, limited to two-word phrases. Prognosis for fluent expression was guarded and acquisition of linguistic concepts was slow, but steady. The ultimate level of language acquisition and overall cognitive development was open for conjecture, although her use of total communication, receptively and expressively, clearly helped.

The behavioral disturbance was believed to be reactive to Gina's severe language disorder. A behavior management program was initiated in school and at home. As language demands became more appropriate and as language concepts developed, along with a mode for their communication, the behavior disorder abated, although Gina remained at high risk for emotional problems.

Sharon: Chronological Age, 4 Years and 4 Months

Sharon was referred for neuropsychological evaluation at the request of her parents relative to planning for her entrance into kindergarten. The parents were aware that Sharon had diffuse central nervous system damage, although she appeared to them to be a bright child. They were concerned about the possible need for special educational services.

Sharon was born prematurely, at 32 weeks gestation, with a birth weight of 3 pounds and 8 ounces. Hyperbilirubinemia was treated with a four-day course of phototherapy. Although language development proceeded normally, significant delays in motor development were noted. At 1 year and 11 months, a diagnosis of cerebral palsy with spastic quadriplegia was confirmed by a pediatric neurologist. Sharon's ambulation was limited; she used a wheelchair most of the time. Hand function was adequate for most self-care tasks, but graphomotor and fine motor skills were noted as deficient.

Sharon presented as a well-related, cooperative, spontaneous, and verbal youngster. She was playful and at the same time highly motivated to succeed. Results of the evaluation are presented in Figure 6.4 and indicate excellent skills in all auditory-verbal domains, with scores in the low average to deficit range for tasks in the visually mediated areas. It is of interest that, although she scored within the deficit range on a visual memory task employing nonrepresentational stimuli, Sharon did extremely well on the visual memory task that depended on pictures of common objects. Sharon quickly and accurately named the pictures, converting the task from a visual to a verbal one. She was significantly less able to generate labels for the abstract shapes in the initial memory task. Although she did reasonably well on most of the visually mediated measures, the relative efficiencies between modalities was striking.

Given her general level of performance socially and cognitively, placement recommendation was made for an in-district regular kindergarten. It was also recommended

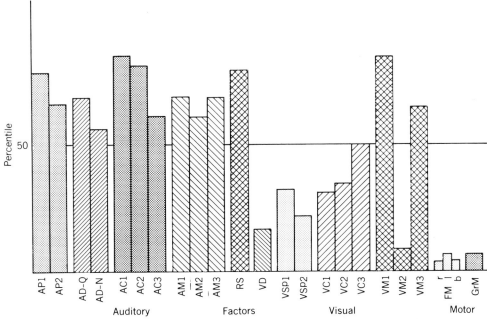

Figure 6.4. The neuropsychological profile of Sharon at 4 years and 4 months of age. Sharon was a cerebral palsied child with spastic quadriplegia. The profile indicates good cognitive skills in most areas, with difficulties noted in visually mediated tasks.

that services be provided to help Sharon develop verbal strategies to assist her in managing visually mediated tasks. One might predict that map reading, learning to tell time, and perhaps the spatial aspects of calculations might be difficult for her without explicit strategies for "talking her way through them."

Kenny: Chronological Age, 3 Years and 9 Months

Kenny was referred for neuropsychological evaluation by a pediatric neurologist requesting information as to cognitive status and further delineation of his developmental disorder. At 3 years of age, Kenny was seen by a child psychologist and identified as autistic. He was then seen by the referring neurologist, who believed Kenny to be a neurologically impaired child with a massive communication disorder. Results of EEG and CT studies were negative. Kenny had been receiving speech and language therapy since the age of 3 years and 8 months, with minimal progress noted.

Kenny was the product of an uneventful full-term pregnancy. The neonatal course was without incident. Kenny was subject to recurrent bouts of serous otitis media from 1 year of age; at 1 year and 10 months, he had bilateral myringotomies, repeated one year later. There was a high probability that he had been experiencing intermittent, fluctuating hearing losses until that time. The audiological evaluation at 3 years and 9 months indicated normal hearing bilaterally.

Motor milestones were within normal limits, although Kenny was described as "very clumsy." Language development was thought to be normal until his third birthday, when his parents realized that he was not putting sentences together. A speech and language evaluation documented pronomial confusion, echolalia, problems with language formulation, and intermittent problems with auditory semantic comprehension and/or an attentional deficit. The pragmatic use of language was noted to be significantly below expectations.

Kenny entered the testing situation with great anxiety and found it difficult to separate from his mother. He cried at the outset of each session and was restless and easily distracted. He occasionally appeared out of contact with the examiner, demonstrating autisticlike behavior at those times.

The evaluation confirmed Kenny's expressive language problems and also documented fine and gross motor deficits. Kenny proved to be more than clumsy; he had significant oromotor dyspraxia, as typified by his inability to imitate oral postures or to produce verbal strings on command. Body dyspraxia was evident, typified by his inability to imitate body postures and to perform "make-believe" motor acts on command, although he was able to produce the behaviors spontaneously. This deficit appeared to interact with many of his behaviors, including such things as organizing the scanning of a visual array. Although a mild receptive language disorder might have been present, it was clear that much of Kenny's problem was related to his great difficulty in organizing a vocal response. This difficulty might have been occurring at the cognitive-linguistic level; it was certainly occurring at the production level.

Kenny's neuropsychological profile is presented in Figure 6.5a. He achieved higher scores on all auditory-verbal measures than on those that required any kind of a motor response, particularly a motor sequencing response. Reference to the subtests and the required responses helped to explain the scores. Most of the items required one- or two-word responses, which Kenny could generate. When more language was required, on the comprehension items, for example, Kenny fared less well in terms of language output. The available measures are typically scored on the basis of semantic content, not on syntax or organization. Telegraphic speech, syntactic deficits, or significant wordfinding difficulties are not reflected in the scores. The diagnosis for Kenny could never be made on the basis of test scores alone.

It is noteworthy that Kenny appeared to be hyperlexic; he was able to decode words at the second-grade level with no difficulty, although he did not understand most of the words.

Recommendations were made for motor speech therapy to address the dyspraxia and for therapy with an occupational therapist trained in sensory-motor integration techniques to work with the other manifestations of Kenny's motor planning and motor integration problems within the context of a special education preschool program.

The impact of development, assisted by special programming, is well demonstrated in Kenny's case. He was reevaluated at 4 years and 8 months of age. He had been enrolled in a special nursery school program for approximately 10 months previously and had been receiving the recommended therapies. For this evaluation, Kenny was outgoing and available. No autistic features were noted. He was spontaneous and conversational. Language skills, receptive and expressive, had improved, but problems were still in evidence. Atypical prosodic elements became apparent with Kenny's increased length of utterance. Major gains were noted in Kenny's pragmatic use of language. Fine and gross motor skills continued to be markedly deficient. The increasing demands for more sophisticated graphomotor production and other hand activities once Kenny entered kindergarten was a cause for concern; emphasis on basic activities was recommended. For example, Kenny continued to use a palmar grasp rather than a

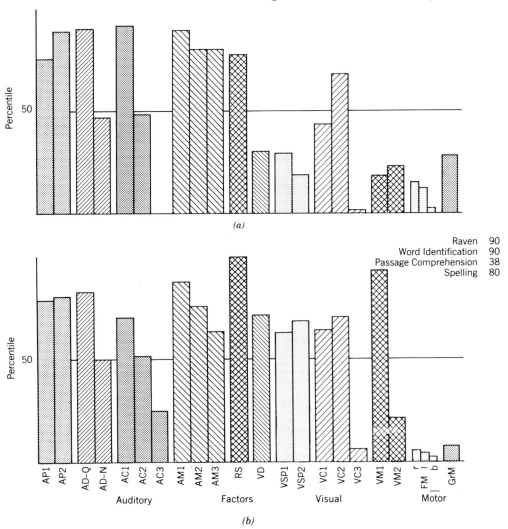

Figure 6.5. (*a*) The neuropsychological profile of Kenny at 3 years and 9 months of age. This child was finally identified as dyspraxic, with an associated expressive language disorder. (*b*) Kenny's profile at 6 years and 10 months of age. The pattern is essentially unchanged, although his behavior and language production skills has improved markedly. The observational data were necessary for an adequate interpretation of the profile, since the relevant behaviors were not captured in the test scores.

three-point pinch; he was unable to ground his arm while using a pencil or crayon. Appropriate function in such areas was deemed necessary before more sophisticated cutting, pasting, and coloring activities could be mastered. Speech therapy was to continue, with some emphasis on the prosodic aspects.

The most recent evaluation, at 6 years and 10 months of age, found Kenny to have improved in all areas. His profile, given in Figure 6.5*b*, indicates high-level cognitive skills in all areas, although residual deficits are still in evidence. Some are subtle, as indicated in AC3, in which his language formulation problem was still in evidence.

Kenny's spontaneous language was excellent, but he still had relative difficulty in formulating on demand. The tasks involved here required Kenny to use gestures to convey the meaning of pictures. His difficulty in the organization of these motor acts was striking. The motor disability showed itself even on memory tasks. VM1 requires a pointing response; VM2 requires the ordering of small chips in a tray to reproduce the stimulus array. He had great difficulties with the VM2 task. As the materials were being put away, Kenny said that he knew which ones went where, that he could not "do" it but he could "tell" it. He had generated labels for the figures. The test was readministered, and Kenny "named" the chips in proper sequences. His fine and graphomotor skills continued to be deficient and will probably be among his less adequate performance areas. Given his manual dyspraxia, typing as a substitute might be difficult for him, although he may be able to use the letter names as verbal mediation organizational cues. It was recommended that he be given some instruction on a large-key typewriter to see if he might become proficient. If not, he may have to rely on tape recorders as he goes on in school.

Kenny's outlook is good, by and large. The discrepancy between his word identification skills (90%) and passage comprehension (38%) suggests an incipient language-based learning disability. Kenny's progress was to be carefully monitored, and language and occupational therapy were to be continued.

Sara: Chronological Age, 2 Years and 10 Months

Sara was referred for neuropsychological assessment as part of an inpatient workup. Sara had been admitted to the hospital with a tentative diagnosis of seizure disorder based on a maternal report of two brief episodes of eye rolling and clonic movements of the upper extremities. On admission, it was apparent that the child was suffering from more than a possible seizure disorder. She was nonverbal, made fleeting eye contact, and was essentially unresponsive to verbal stimuli. She appeared to relate more appropriately to her mother but was essentially isolated.

History indicated that Sara was the product of a full-term pregnancy. Threatened miscarriage was treated by hormone therapy during the first trimester. Birth was induced at term "for convenience." Sara weighed 7 pounds and 4 ounces at birth. Motor milestones were normally acquired. Reportedly, speech had begun at 10 months, with Sara saying her sister's name and "mama." Speech ceased, behavior regressed, and contact with others became minimal. She was described as more easily frustrated, screeching and hitting her head with her hands, and rubbing her eyes constantly. Results of previous pediatric examination was negative; a psychiatric evaluation rendered a diagnosis of childhood schizophrenia, which the parents did not accept.

Results of inpatient neurological, EEG, and CT studies were negative. A formal neurological evaluation was impossible because of Sara's lack of response to others. A child psychiatrist made a diagnosis of infantile autism. In our evaluation, during a play session in which doll house furniture and flexible dolls were provided, Sara engaged in constructive, symbolic play for 10–15 minutes. She appropriately organized the furniture within the house and placed the dolls, seated, around the table. It was high level play for a child nearly 3 years old, let alone one who behaved as Sara did. This behavior indicated that linguistic concepts had been incorporated and were available to her. An alternative diagnosis of severe primary communication disorder was considered, allowing for a more favorable prognosis, and Sara was referred for an extended

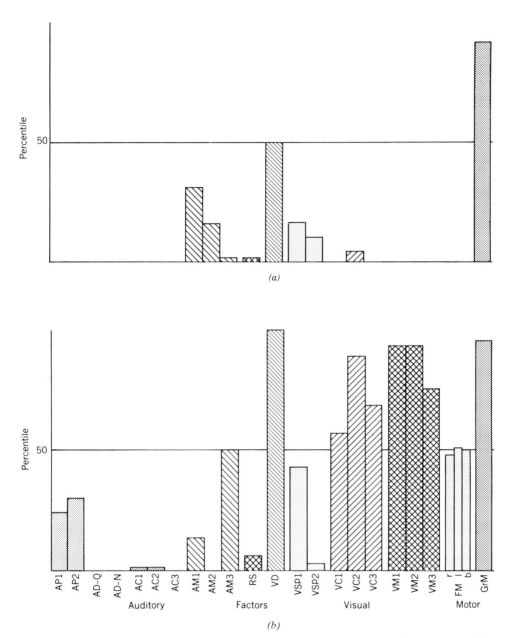

Figure 6.6. (*a*) Neuropsychological profile of Sara at 3 years 11 months of age. Sara carried various diagnoses, including childhood schizophrenia, infantile autism, and primary language disorder. This evaluation suggests that she could do little more than echo what she heard. (*b*) Sara's evaluation at 5 years and 0 months of age suggests progress in visually mediated areas. (*c*) Sara's evaluation at 11 years and 3 months of age demonstrates average to superior performances in most areas, with suggestions of subtle residual auditory receptive deficits.

155

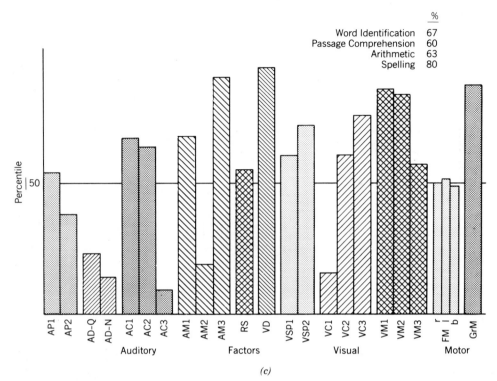

Figure 6.6.* (*Continued*).

diagnostic evaluation. She became a part-time student in a special program for language-disordered children. The goals were to shape attending behavior and to encourage appropriate, rather than her inappropriate, vocal behavior. Sara entered the program on a full-time basis at 3 years and 10 months of age. Figure 6.6*a* represents her neuropsychological profile at 3 years and 11 months. She was able to do very little beyond echo in response to auditory-verbal demands, although she performed visual match-to-sample tasks adequately. Graphomotor skills were superior; timed motor skills could not be assessed because Sara did not appear to understand the directions or to benefit from repeated demonstrations.

At 4 years and 2 months of age, average scores were obtained on most visually mediated measures. Fine motor skills were intact, and left-hand preference was noted. Auditory receptive skills were still extremely deficient, while auditory memory scores continued to fall within the average range. Sara was using vocal language; utterances were brief but acceptable when spontaneously generated. They tended to be tangential or associative when responding to others.

Figure 6.6*b* presents Sara's neuropsychological profile at 5 years and 0 months of age. She was beginning to respond more appropriately to verbal directions but could not yet respond to auditory cognitive demands. Most visually guided tasks yielded scores in the average to superior range. Her behavior was more appropriate, and she was able to engage in cooperative play.

Sara became involved in a longitudinal study and is being seen annually for neuropsychological evaluation. Her most recent, at 11 years and 3 months of age, is presented in Figure 6.6c. Most functions fall within the average to superior range, including several measures of academic achievement. Aspects of auditory receptive skills suggest subtle residual difficulties.

Sara has been in a regular class for the last year, receiving language therapy twice a week. Her teachers comment that she requires more explanation of directions and of new material than do most of her classmates, but once she understands, she is able to move on independently. Although she is accepted by her peers, she is not "groupy" and tends to have one or two friends at a time.

Sara became involved in psychotherapy this year. The need was probably overdetermined. It is possible that modifying her "label" from *schizophrenia* or *autism* to *language disorder* made a difference in outcome. Self-fulfilling prophecies are powerful!

FURTHER COMMENTS ON ASSESSMENT

It is evident that, for us, clinical observations are sources of data. In addition to observations made during the normal course of events, it is possible, and from our point of view desirable, to "fool around" during an evaluation. This translates into hypothesis testing by creating immediate situations extraneous to formal assessment procedures by modifying those procedures, by modifying response modes, and by modifying the physical situation. The aim is to acquire additional information as to how the child solves problems, which variables facilitate performance, and which disrupt performance. For example, a child is unable to relate the salient features of a story included as a subtest in VM2. Did the child remember the information? Did he or she not adequately comprehend it? Could he or she not formulate the necessary language? After administering the subtest according to standardized procedures, it is possible, for example, to provide structured questions, such as "What was the boy's name?," "Where was he going?," and so on. For children with organizational problems, the provision of such structure permits them to demonstrate that they have remembered the information. Providing a verbal mediation model to a child who has been unable to deal with a verbal memory task, such as the Pictorial Memory subtest on the McCarthy Scales, using other but similar stimulus materials may provide information relevant to remedial strategies. Clinical "fooling around" is hypothesis testing in the absence of appropriate, standardized measures and helps to fill in the gaps between the numbers.

Adaptation of the Test Situation

There are situations in which the test administration procedures must be modified in order to obtain meaningful information. When test administration procedures are modified, test norms no longer strictly apply. The whole issue of goals of an assessment enters here. For some, adherence to standardized procedures is important and a "cannot do" score is felt to be sufficient information. For others—and we generally find ourselves in this group—the goal of the assessment is to obtain all information possible about the functioning capacities of the child and to facilitate the production of

maximum performance. This can occur after standard procedures have proved inadequate or inappropriate and "cannot do" or "minimal estimate" are appropriately
recorded. For example, for the child who has difficulty with visual tracking, assisting
the child in scanning an array by pointing to the items one at a time helps to give a
measure of visual sequential memory rather than visual dyspraxia. Extending block
design time limits for the child with a neuromuscular disorder involving the upper
extremities in order to estimate the child's visual constructional abilities rather than his
or her motor disability seems to make sense. As to modifying the child's physical
status, it helps all children, but particularly children with truncal instability, to be
seated on a chair that allows the feet to be flat on the floor, thus providing stability. The
match in height between chairs and tables is important as well; a discrepancy can alter
significantly the child's hand activity patterns (Holt & Reynell, 1967). One can inhibit
the occurrence of an asymmetrical tonic neck reflex in a neuromuscularly disordered
child and provide the opportunity to work with materials in the midline by allowing the
child to lie on the floor, stomach over a bolster. Provision of alternative response
modes, such as foot tapping or eye blinking to the nonverbal motorically dysfunctional
child permits the estimate of cognitive development in many areas. We have had such
experience with a group of school-aged youngsters with cerebral palsy, all nonverbal
and severely motorically involved. They had been grouped together on the basis of
"performance level" and assumed to be retarded because they could not "perform."
After some months of "fooling around," selecting measures that lent themselves to a
range of nonverbal responses, and the behavior shaping of a diversity of such response
modes on this group (including eye blink Morse Code for a child, who, via "fooling
around," we discovered could read and spell), assessments were undertaken. Results of
the assessments of these children indicated that the range of cognitive level extended
from global retardation to above average performance on such nonverbal measures as
the Raven-Coloured Progressive Matrices. The results were not definitive in terms of
firm normative support, since administration procedures were modified. However,
information was derived that was adequate and useful in the development of more
appropriate and individualized educational programs.

Implementation for Remediation

Neuropsychologists have been called upon for a long time to become involved in the
development of intervention, remedial, or rehabilitation strategies for the adult patient.
More recently, this has been extended to child neuropsychology as well. Diagnosis
need not and should not be an end in itself. However, the translation of diagnostic data
to remedial strategies is not simple and is complicated by the lack of isomorphism
between our professional language and concepts and those of the clinicians who treat.
Physicians, educators, occupational and physical therapists, and parents frequently
become members of the treatment team. The need to communicate across disciplines is
critical, particularly when therapeutic intervention is the focus. The program of an
effective diagnostic-treatment team needs to include joint conferencing among those
who assess, rather than just the sharing of written reports. There needs to be joint
planning in terms of content, methods, and goals of the treatment program so that the
various aspects can be coordinated and well integrated for presentation to the child. It
is also necessary to build in methods for the evaluation of program efficacy. If the

program is data based and remedial strategies flow from diagnostic data, the evaluation of the program is more feasible than the evaluation of a program in which the rationale is based on someone's "bag of tricks."

TOWARD THE DEVELOPMENT OF SYNDROME-SPECIFIC REMEDIATION

Starting from the individual child's neuropsychological profile, we have been involved in the development of remedial programs for preschool children that address a broad range of cognitive deficits. The notion of "syndrome-specific" remediation paradigms becomes more and more likely as one continues to hear from other clinicians and to experience the "That's a Johnny Smith" phenomenon. Clinicians are aware of commonalities among patterns of disorders and talk shorthand to each other in describing a given child as "another Johnny Smith." They, we, are talking about the identification of subtype members. Typologies in the neuropsychology literature identify subtypes in both school-aged (Mattis, French, & Rapin, 1975; Petrauskas & Rourke, 1979; Satz & Morris, 1981) and preschool children (Aram & Nation, 1975). With the single exception of the Mattis, French, and Rapin study (1975) of reading-disabled children, which was an early attempt to bridge the clinical-inferential and quantitative realms in the development of typologies, all are based on quantitative approaches such as Q-factor analysis. Working toward the goal of syndrome-specific remediation paradigms, we are developing an approach to classification that is based on the assessment and profiling methods described earlier in this chapter and on the clinical "sorting" of these profiles into subtypes using data-based inclusion rules for subtype membership (Wilson & Risucci, 1983, 1986). We consider this effort to be Generation 1. Generation 2, now in progress, will include quantified (scaled) expressions of clinical observations to be added to the existing psychometric data base. The purpose of adding the observational data is to enhance discrimination among subtypes and subtype members. Psychometric data alone leave something to be desired in this regard, as demonstrated by several of the case studies presented earlier.

An empirical validation model of the typology is being developed in parallel and has already been applied with gratifying results to the Generation 1 data (Risucci, 1983). Observations thus far support the view that the medical diagnosis is generally not useful in the prediction of patterns of cognitive function. In pilot studies conducted in our laboratory, the subtypes we have identified thus far in the preschool population emerge across a variety of other diagnostic groups, including learning-disabled students, children with cerebral palsy, and children with hydrocephalus. The differences appear to lie in the frequency of occurrence of given subtypes within any diagnostic group. For example, there are more children in subtypes characterized by visual-spatial deficits among cerebral palsied children than among learning-disabled children. The latter group tends to be heavily represented among the language-related subtypes. Representation of subtypes across diagnostic categories makes intuitive sense: since one central nervous system mediates behavior and, one hopes typically functions systematically, it should be systematic in its dysfunction as well. Systematic functioning has been demonstrated for adults and school-aged children and is suggested by a sizable body of clinical data and careful research. It is our contention that the same systematic functioning is true of preschool children, albeit complicated by developmental issues.

SUMMARY

It is indeed possible to obtain a systematic, reliable, and clinically meaningful assessment of a preschool child. The use of observational data is essential in the interpretation of quantitative data and in the development of remedial strategies.

If the purpose of an assessment is to provide maximal information about a child's cognitive development and best guesses as to methods of intervention, a systematic evaluation is essential, but within a sufficiently flexible framework to provide for ongoing hypothesis testing. An evaluation is like an expanding balloon: it cannot be contained in a box.

ACKNOWLEDGMENT

With many thanks. I acknowledge the assistance of former and current interns in clinical neuropsychology who worked with us in our unit. To Ellen Goldberger and Denise Karen Zeidler, thanks for your help with the task analysis of subtests and with the preparation of figures, both tedious tasks, elegantly done. To Susan Leslie and Peter Pinto, thanks for your help with the references, another tedious job well done. To Mona McAllister, thanks for your pointing out to me the important notion of the multivariate child.

REFERENCES

Allen, D. V., & Bliss, L. S. (1978). *Evaluation of procedures for screening preschool children for signs of impaired language development* (Report No. 1-NS-2355). Bethesda, MD: National Institutes of Health, Department of Health, Education and Welfare.

Allen, D. A., Rapin, I. (1982). Language disorders in preschool children: Predictors of outcome—A preliminary report. *Brain and Development, 2*, 73–80.

Aram, D. M., & Nation, J. E. (1975). Patterns of language behavior in children with developmental language disorders. *Journal of Speech and Hearing Research, 18*, 229–241.

Aram, D. M. & Nation, J. E. (1980). Preschool language disorders and subsequent language and academic difficulties. *Journal of Communication Disorders, 13*, 159–170.

Arthur, G. (1974). *A point scale of performance tests: Revised form II.* New York: Psychological Corporation.

Bakker, D.J. (1984). The brain as a dependent variable. *Journal of Clinical Neuropsychology, 6*, 1–16.

Bayley, N. (1969). *Bayley scales of infant development.* New York: Psychological Corporation.

Berenberg, S. R. (Ed.). (1977). *Brain: Fetal and infant.* The Hague, Netherlands: Martinus Nijhoff.

Blakeley, R. W. (1980). *Screening test for developmental apraxia of speech.* Tigard, OR: C.C. Publications.

Broman, S. A., Nichols, P. L. & Kennedy, W. A. (1975). *Preschool IQ: Prenatal and early developmental correlates.* Hillsdale, NJ: Lawrence Erlbaum Associates.

Costa, L. D., Vaughan, H. G., Levita, E., & Farber, N. (1963). The Purdue Pegboard as a predictor of the presence and laterality of cerebral lesions. *Journal of Consulting Psychology, 27*, 133–137.

Culbertson, J. (1981). Psychological evaluation and educational planning for children with central auditory dysfunction. In R. W. Keith (Ed.), *Central auditory and language disorders in children* (pp. 13–29). Houston: College Hill Press.

DeRenzi, E., & Vignolo, L. (1962). The token test: A sensitive test to detect receptive disturbances in aphasics. *Brain, 85,* 665–678.

Drillien, C. M. (1972). Abnormal neurologic signs in the first year of life in low birthweight infants: possible prognostic significance. *Developmental Medicine and Child Neurology, 14,* 575–584.

Drillien, C. M., Thomson, A. J. M., & Burgoyne, N. (1980). Low birthweight children at early school-age: A longitudinal study. *Developmental Medicine and Child Neurology, 22,* 26–47.

Evans, J. S., & Bangs, T. (1972). Effects of preschool language training on later academic achievement of children with language and learning disabilities. *Journal of Learning Disabilities, 5,* 585–592.

French, J. L. (1964). *The pictorial test of intelligence.* New York: Houghton Mifflin.

Gaiter, J. L. (1982). The effects of intraventricular hemorrhage on Bayley developmental performance in preterm infants. *Seminars in Perinatology, 6,* 305–315.

Goldman, R., Fristoe, M., & Woodcock, R. W. (1974–1976). *Auditory skills test battery.* Circle Pines, MN: American Guidance Service.

Hagbard, L., Olow, I., & Reinand, T. (1969). A follow-up study of 514 children of diabetic mothers. *Acta Pediatrica, 48,* 184.

Hartlage, L. C., Telzrow, C. F., DeFellipes, N. A., Shaw, J. B., & Noonan, M. (1983). Personality correlates of functional asymmetry in preschool children. *Clinical Neuropsychology,* 14–15.

Hiskey, M. S. (1966). *The Hiskey-Nebraska test of learning aptitude.* Lincoln, NB: Union College Press.

Holt, K. S., & Reynell, J. K. (1967). *Assessment of cerebral palsy* (Vol. 2). London: Lloyd-Luke.

Kaufman, A. S., & Kaufman, N. L. (1983). *Kaufman assessment battery for children.* Circle Pines, MN: American Guidance Service.

Kirk, S. A., McCarthy, J. J., & Kirk, W. D. (1968). *Illinois test of psycholinguistic abilities.* Urbana: University of Illinois Press.

Lipper, E., Lee N., Gartner, L. M., & Grellong, B. (1981). Determinants of neurobehavioral outcome in low birthweight infants. *Pediatrics, 67,* 502–505.

Mattis, S., French, J. H., & Rapin, I. (1975). Dyslexia in children and adults: Three independent neuropsychological syndromes. *Developmental Medicine and Child Neurology, 17,* 150–163.

McCarthy, D. (1970). *McCarthy scales of children's abilities.* New York: Psychological Corporation.

Needleman, H. (1977). Effects of hearing loss from early recurrent otitis media on speech and language development. In B. F. Jaffee (Ed.), *Hearing loss in children: A comprehensive test* (pp. 640–649). Baltimore: University Park Press.

Nelson, K. B., & Ellenberg, J. H. (1978). Prognosis in children with febrile seizures. *Pediatrics, 61,* 720–727.

News Note (1985). Pediatrics Academy address on language-otitis media link. *ASHA, 27,* 12.

Owen, F. W. (1978). Dyslexia: Genetic aspects. In A. L. Benton & D. Pearl (Eds.), *Dyslexia: An appraisal of current knowledge* (pp. 265–284). New York: Oxford University Press.

Petrauskas, R. J., & Rourke, B. P. (1979). Identification of subtypes of retarded readers: A neuropsychological, multivariate approach. *Journal of Clinical Neuropsychology, 1,* 17–37.

Rapin, I., Tourk, L. M., & Costa, L. D. (1966). Evaluation of the Purdue Pegboard as a screening test for brain damage. *Developmental Medicine and Child Neurology, 8,* 45–54.

Rapin, I., & Wilson, B. C. (1978). Children with developmental language disorders: Neurologic aspects and assessment. In M. Wyke (Ed.), *The dysphasic child* (pp. 13–41). New York: Academic Press.

Risucci, D. A. (1983). *Empirical validation of a typology of language-impaired preschool children.* Unpublished, Hofstra University, Hempstead New York.

Satz, P., & Morris, R. (1981). Learning disability subtypes: A review. In F. J. Pirozzolo & M. C. Wittrock (Eds.), *Neuropsychological and cognitive processes in reading.* New York: Academic Press.

Shaffer, D., & Dunn, J. (Eds.). (1979). *The first year of life: Psychological and medical implications of early experience.* New York: John Wiley & Sons.

Sheppard, J. J., & Mysak, E. D. (1984). Ontogeny of infantile oral reflexes and emerging chewing. *Child Development, 55,* 841–843.

Silva, P. A. (1980). The prevalence, stability and significance of developmental language delay in preschool children. *Developmental Medicine and Child Neurology, 22,* 768–777.

Smith, A. (1981). Principles underlying human functions in neuropsychological sequelae of different neuropathological processes. In S. B. Filskov & T. J. Boll (Eds.), *Handbook of clinical neuropsychology* (Vol. 1, pp. 175–226). New York: John Wiley & Sons.

Terman, L. M., & Merrill, M. A. (1973). *Stanford-Binet intelligence scale.* (3rd ed.). Boston: Houghton Mifflin.

Wechsler, D. (1963). *Wechsler preschool and primary scale of intelligence.* New York: Psychological Corporation.

Weiss, R. S. (1981–1982). INREAL intervention for language handicapped and bilingual children. *Journal of Development for Early Childhood, 4,* 40–51.

Wilson, B. C., Iacoviello, J. M., Wilson, J. J., & Risucci, D. (1982). Purdue Pegboard performance in normal preschool children. *Journal of Clinical Neuropsychology, 4,* 19–26.

Wilson, B. C., & Metlay, W. (1980). *Program evaluation and evaluation research in neuropsychology.* Paper presented at the International Neuropsychological Society, San Francisco.

Wilson, B. C., & Risucci, D. (1983, February). *Studies in child neuropsychology: Subtypes of preschool language disordered children.* Paper presented at the International Neuropsychological Society, Mexico City.

Wilson, B.C., & Risucci, D. (1986). A model for clinical-quantitative classification—Generation I: Application to language disordered preschool children. *Brain and Language* (in press).

Wilson, B. C., & Wilson, J. J. (1977, Oct.). *Early identification, assessment and implications for intervention.* Paper presented at the American Academy for Cerebral Palsy and Developmental Medicine, Atlanta.

Wilson, B. C., & Wilson, J. J. (1978). Language disordered children: A neuropsychologic view. In B. Feingold & C. Banks (Eds.), *Developmental disabilities of early childhood* (pp. 148–171). Springfield, IL: Charles C Thomas.

Wilson, J. J., & Wilson, B. C. (1980). [The relationship between two tests of graphomotor function in preschool children]. Unpublished raw data.

Wolpaw, T., Nation, J. E., & Aram, D. M. (1977). Developmental language disorders: A follow-up study. In M.S. Burns, & J.R. Anderson (Eds.), *Selected papers in language and phonology: Vol. 1. Identification and diagnosis of language disorders.* Evanston, IL. Institute for Continuing Professional Education.

APPENDIX

NEUROPSYCHOLOGY
NORTH SHORE UNIVERSITY HOSPITAL
400 Community Drive
Manhasset, New York 11030
Telephone: (516) 562-3054

CHILDREN'S HISTORY FORM

Today's Date _____

I.   GENERAL INFORMATION

Child's name (include nickname, if any) _____

Birth date _____ CA _____

Home address _____

Phone # _____ Business phone # _____

School district _____

Referred by _____

    Address _____ Phone # _____

Parent's Names   Father _____ Mother _____

Sisters and brothers (names and ages) _____

_____

_____

Pediatrician _____

    Address _____ Phone # _____

Informants _____

II.   PRESENTING PROBLEM

_____

_____

_____

_____

_____

_____

_____

_____

_____

III.   PREGNANCIES

Was this child adopted?   Yes _____ No _____

Did you have any of the following complications during this
pregnancy? If so, indicate which month. _____

Anemia _____   High blood pressure _____

Swollen ankles _____   Kidney disease _____

Heart disease _____   German measles _____

Toxemia _____   Staining _____ Bleeding _____

RH or other blood incompatibility _____ Vomiting _____

Virus _____ Threatened miscarriage or early
                              contractions _____

Chronic illness(s) such as diabetes, kidney infection,
    thyroid, etc. _____

Other illness(s) _____

_____

Hospitalization _____ When? _____ Why? _____

_____

Operation _____

Injury _____

Severe shock or emotional upset _____

Which medications, if any, did you take during this pregnancy? _____

How much weight did you gain during this pregnancy? _____

Did you have any other complications? _____ If so, what? _____

_____

_____

List all of your pregnancies in order, including the child to be seen. If a pregnancy ended in miscarriage, state at which month. If you have had more than six pregnancies, continue the list on the back of this page.

Year	Name	Length of Pregnancy (mos.)	Birth Weight	Birth Length	Sex	Complications

IV.   BIRTH HISTORY

Name of hospital _____

How many hours from first contraction to birth? _____

Were you given medication?   Yes _____ No _____ What kind? _____

    Why was it given? _____

Were you under anesthesia during childbirth?   Yes _____ No _____

    What kind? _____

Was labor induced?   Yes _____ No _____ Why? _____

How? _____

Was the baby born head first?   Yes _____ No _____ Don't know _____

Were forceps used? Yes _____ No _____ Why? _____
_____

Did you have a Cesarian section?   Yes _____ No _____ Why? _____
_____

Did the baby have any bruises?   Yes _____ No _____ Where? _____

Did the baby have any birthmarks?   Yes _____ No _____ Where? _____

Were twins delivered?   Yes _____ No _____ Which born first? _____

Were they identical?   Yes _____ No _____

Did the baby have breathing problems?   Yes _____ No _____ Don't know _____

Was the cord around the neck?   Yes _____ No _____ Don't know _____

Did the baby cry quickly?   Yes _____ No _____ Don't Know _____

Was the baby's color normal?   Yes _____ No _____ Don't Know _____

    Blue? _____   Yellow? _____

If the baby was yellow (jaundiced), did the baby receive:

    Oxygen   Yes _____ __ No _____ How long? _____

    Transfusion   Yes _____ No _____ How long? _____

    Phototherapy (lights)   Yes _____ No _____ How many days? _____

Were there any other complications before you took the baby home?

    Yes _____ No _____ What? _____

Was the baby placed in an incubator or special crib?

    Yes _____ No _____ How long? _____

How long after birth did you take the baby home? _____

V.   EARLY HISTORY

A. General

Did the baby have feeding problems?   Yes _____ No _____

    Describe them. _____

        Was the baby colicky?   Yes _____   No _____   How long? _____

        Was the baby breast fed?   Yes _____   No _____   Until what age? ____

Age stopped drinking from bottle? _____

Did the baby require formula changes?   Yes _____ No _____

    Describe them. _____

Difficulty sucking as an infant?   Yes _____   No _____

Difficulty chewing as an infant?   Yes _____   No _____

Difficulty swallowing as an infant?   Yes _____   No _____

Difficulties now? _____

Drooling past 2 1/2?   Yes _____ No _____

Did the baby have sleeping problems?   Yes _____ No _____

    Describe them. _____

Was the baby normally active?   Yes _____ No _____

    Describe. _____

Was the baby limp?   Yes _____ No _____

Was the baby stiff?   Yes _____ No _____

Did the baby show unusual trembling?   Yes _____ No

Did the baby fail to grow normally?   Yes _____ No _____

Did the baby fail to gain weight?   Yes _____ No _____

Was this baby different in any way from brothers or sisters?

    Yes _____ No _____ Describe how: _____

    _____

B. Motor

Was your child's development different in any ways from the
development of your other children?   Explain. _____

    _____

    _____

    _____

Crawl _____

Sit without support _____

Stand without support _____

Walk without support _____

Hand preference _____ Age when noticed _____

Toilet training (when begun, accomplished, problems, accidents):

Urine _____

Bowel _____

Bed wetting _____

C. Speech, Language, and Hearing

  1. Was child very quiet as a baby (did not babble and coo as much as most babies)? _____

      Did child cry excessively? _____

2. How old was child when child began to say meaningful words consistently? _____
   How old was child when child began putting two or three
   words together in a phrase? _____

3. Did parents ever think child had a hearing problem? _____ What made them
   think so? _____

4. Does child respond consistently to sounds and speech? _____
   Can child tell where a sound is coming from (turns head, etc.)? _____
   Does child play radio, TV, record player at "normal" volume? _____
   Very loud? _____ Very soft? _____

5. How much does this child talk now? _____
   How much of this speech can mother or father understand? All _____ _____
   Most _____ Some _____ Little _____
   Do other adults understand child?
   Do playmates tease child about child's speech?

6. How does child make need known to others? Gestures _____ Single words _____
   Sentences _____ Appropriate vocabulary _____

7. Does child seem to speak as well as others of same age? _____
   Does child seem to hear and respond as well as others of same age? _____

8. Does child understand what is said to him or her as well as other children
   the same age? _____ Can child follow simple directions? _____
   A series of directions? _____

9. Does child's voice sound like other children's voices? _____
   If not, describe. (You may check more than one.) Very soft _____
   Very loud _____ Hoarse _____ High or low pitch for age and sex _____
   Nasal _____ Congested _____

10. How do you think child feels about his or her speech or language?
    Unaware of any problem _____ Self-conscious _____ Other _____

11. Have parents done anything to help child with his or her speech or language? _____
    If so, explain _____
    What is child's reaction to this help? _____

12. Does child have problems with any of the following? Pronouncing words _____
    (Note specific sounds if possible.) Small vocabulary _____
    Not speaking _____ Stuttering or stammering _____
    Describe. _____

13. Has your child received speech or language therapy?
    When? _____
    Where? _____

VI. MEDICAL HISTORY

List previous evaluations (eg., audiological, medical, psychological, neurological, speech, ENT, EEG, etc.):

Where and Name of Person Who Saw Child	When Evaluation Was Done	Why Evaluation Performed	Results and Recommendations

_____

_____

_____

Does your child currently take any medicines on a regular basis?

If so, give name of medicine, dose, how often it is given, and the reason he or she takes it.

_____

_____

What major childhood illnesses has your child had (e.g., mumps, measles, chicken pox, etc.)?
Give dates. _____

_____

Does (did) your child suffer from frequent colds? _____

Does (did) your child suffer from frequent ear infections? _____

In past years, what medicines has your child taken for more than a week?

Please state kind, dates, reason, and how much taken. _____

_____

_____

Has your child had ear surgery? _____

Has your child ever had an injury to the head or spine? If so, give date and explain. _____

_____

Has your child ever had high fevers? Please write the degree and describe. _____

_____

_____

Has your child ever had convulsions? Describe type of convulsion (if known),

when it occurred, and how long it lasted. _____

_____

_____

Has your child ever had fainting spells? _____

_____

Does your child have any allergies? Describe. _____

_____

Vision problems? _____

Hearing problems? _____

Hospitalizations (reasons, dates, places, outcomes, child's reaction) _____

_____

_____

_____

Has child had emotional, adjustment, or behavioral problems? _____

_____

_____

VII.   DESCRIPTION OF CHILD

Child's personality (parents' description) _____

_____

Does the child separate easily? _____

_____

_____

Interaction with other children (siblings and peers) _____

_____

_____

Does child prefer to play alone?   Yes _____ No _____

Interaction with adults (parents and others) _____

_____

_____

Favorite activities and toys _____

_____

_____

_____

TV _____

_____

Self-care (initiative and capability) _____

_____

_____

_____

Sleeping (nightmares, hours of sleep, napping) _____

_____

_____

Habits (head banging, thumb sucking, nail biting, tics or twitches, toe walking,

staring into space) _____

_____

_____

_____

_____

_____

_____

VIII.   SOCIAL HISTORY

Who lives in the home? _____

What, if any, language other than English is spoken in home? _____

Are parents separated? _____ Divorced? _____ If so, how old was child when
this occurred? _____ Is either parent deceased? _____ Was either parent married
previously (which)? _____ Are there significant conflicts between
parent and child?   Yes _____ No _____

Are there significant conflicts between the children?   Yes _____ No _____

Who disciplines and how? _____

_____

How does child respond to discipline? _____

Have there been any incidents in the child's life that you believe caused noticeable
changes in his or her behavior? _____

_____

Peer group experience (dates, place, number of children, child's reaction):

_____

_____

_____

_____

_____

IX.   FAMILY HISTORY

Under parents, list names of children in order of birth:

	Name	Age	Education (grade)	Occupation	Health	School or Behavior Problem
Mother						
Father						
Children						

Did anyone in your immediate family or other relative have any of the following? If so, who?

Neurological disease   Yes _____ No _____

Seizures (epilepsy)   Yes _____ No _____

Hearing problems   Yes _____ No _____

Visual problems   Yes _____ No _____

Color weakness or blindness   Yes _____ No _____

Emotional problems   Yes _____ No _____

Mental retardation   Yes _____ No _____

Slowness in talking   Yes _____ No _____

Slowness in walking   Yes _____ No _____

Hyperactivity   Yes _____ No _____

Learning problems   Yes _____ No _____

Left-handedness   Yes _____ No _____

Problems similar to those of child   Yes _____ No _____

Does any disease run in the family?   Yes _____ No _____

   What? _____

_____

Give any other pertinent information that you feel would be helpful to us in the evaluation
of your child. _____

_____

_____

_____

_____

_____

_____

_____

_____

_____

_____

_____

_____

CHAPTER 7

The Assessment of Language after Brain Damage

Harold Goodglass

The neuropsychologist is frequently faced with the need to determine whether a patient has an abnormality of language use. If such an abnormality exists, it must be evaluated in terms of its type, severity, implications for organic etiology and localization, its impact on the patient's function, and its implications for rehabilitation. While one tends to associate organically based disorders of communication with aphasia, there are a number of phenomena, such as dysarthria, tangentiality of discourse, and mild impairments of word finding, that are not necessarily aphasic in origin. The emphasis of this chapter is on the assessment of aphasia. However, an effort is made to provide the reader with criteria for distinguishing some of the symptoms that border on aphasia from those that are indeed components of an aphasic syndrome.

WHAT LANGUAGE VARIABLES SHOULD BE OBSERVED?

It is possible to assemble a battery of tasks that tap various productive and receptive language skills using only common sense and drawing on the vast assortment of proficiency tests available to the educational specialist. Such a battery, devised without any familiarity with the clinical features of aphasia, could hardly fail to give a quantitative index of aphasic impairment and some indication of the relative impairment of certain functions compared to others. It is highly unlikely, however, that such a battery would prove useful in any finer analysis of the aphasic disorder in terms of identifying a recognized syndrome or in correlating the language deficit with the site of injury.

Systematic observation of aphasic patients over the past century has brought to the attention of clinical investigators a number of dimensions of language that are important in distinguishing among several distinctive types of aphasia as well as in distinguishing aphasia from other disorders. Some of these refer to a deficit, that is, reduced capacity in some component of language; others refer to an abnormality of performance that is characteristic of certain forms of aphasia. We begin with a review of these features of language.

Fluency

The term *fluency* as applied to typology of aphasia has a particular connotation that is not identical with the colloquial meaning of the word. Fluency is an important variable because it permits the first step in the classification of the disorder and is a function that can be judged reliably in 75%–80% of subjects. Goodglass, Quadfasel, and Timberlake (1964) and Kerschensteiner, Poeck, and Brunner (1972) showed that aphasics clustered bimodally along the dimension of fluency, and Benson (1967) demonstrated that the fluent versus nonfluent dichotomy corresponds to postrolandic versus prerolandic site of lesion, respectively.

Fluency in aphasia can be defined operationally in terms of the length of uninterrupted word runs that a patient can characteristically produce in his or her most successful efforts during free conversation. Specifically, patients who can produce uninterrupted runs of six or more words in at least one out of eight to ten starts are considered fluent aphasics. Obviously, this definition is much more liberal than the everyday usage of the term would imply. Fluent aphasics are often severely impaired in word retrieval and may have many aborted sentence starts. On the other hand, the utterances of nonfluent aphasics virtually never exceed four uninterrupted words, with the possible exception of such stereotyped comments as "I know what it is."

The variable of fluency is highly correlated with preservation of grammatical facility, ease of articulation, and preservation of normal rhythm and intonational pattern, each of which is discussed below.

The most important caution in applying the concept of fluency to the speech output of an aphasic patient is that its value for classification disappears in the case of mild or largely recovered disorders, when the patient is able to assume most of the burden of conversing with little prompting from the examiner. At this stage of recovery, patients who had a nonfluent aphasia in the early postonset period often regain considerable facility in producing sentence strings without interruption.

It was noted above that fluency is usually correlated with the preservation of grammar. It must be emphasized that this association is not invariable. In particular, the ability to produce long and grammatically accurate spoken sentences is *not* by itself an index of fluency, since such an ability is compatible with a disorder in which words are produced with painfully labored articulation and with a separate stress on almost every syllable. This is a nonfluent disorder, almost invariably involving the foot of the motor strip or underlying white matter.

Articulation

Articulatory disorders affect the patient's facility to produce voluntarily the sounds and sound sequences of language. In this connection, the term *voluntarily* is important, because aphasic patients who may be unable, on request, to form the sounds of a word, even to initiate individual speech sounds, may occasionally utter well-articulated remarks in the course of examination. The features that distinguish the articulatory component of aphasia are variability and the appearance of awkwardness and effort. Variability is manifested in the change in performance between conditions of reciting memorized sequences (e.g., counting), repeating words or phrases after the examiner, and naming objects or conversing. Patients who may be severely impaired in the motor aspects of conversational speech may recite familiar word series with little motor awkwardness or even perfectly normal facility. Repetition, too, may facilitate speech production. This variability distinguishes aphasia from other types of articulatory difficulty (e.g., dysarthria) in which the impairment of motor control for production of speech sounds is constant across all types of speech-eliciting situations.

The awkward and effortful quality of the aphasic's speech is to be distinguished from other, nonaphasic dysarthrias that may have a rapid and slurred quality.

An important feature to be noted is the quality of the articulatory errors. Typical of one class of aphasics are clumsy and inaccurate renditions of recognizable targets, sometimes involving simplification of consonant clusters (e.g., "pay" for "play"). Typical of another class of aphasics is the facile production of ill-chosen target sounds, sometimes with repeated attempts to self-correct (e.g., "sencil, no sentle...pentle..." for "pencil"). The former pattern is associated with anterior speech zone lesions and reduced, effortful speech output. The latter pattern occurs in a context of otherwise "fluent" speech. The inadvertent production of off-target sounds with facile articulation is termed *literal paraphasia* and is characteristic of patients with postrolandic lesions. Literal paraphasic errors are not considered a disorder of articulation per se.

Prosody

The rate, rhythm, and intonation pattern, or "speech melody," is termed *prosody*. Nonfluent aphasics invariably have disordered prosody, if only because their flow of words is interrupted by pauses. While the listener may detect intonational cues that indicate either that a sentence is still continuing or that it is complete, even this degree of speech melody may be lost. That is, each word may be produced with the intonation of a one-word sentence.

An aberration of prosody often observed with nonaphasic, right-brain–injured patients is a marked reduction in melodic intonation, sometimes to the point of a total, mechanical-sounding monotone. Since these patients are unable to imitate changes in voice pitch or to sing, even though they can still recognize melody, they are said to have *motor aprosody*.

Grammar and Syntax

Selective impairment in the expression of grammatical forms is a feature of many nonfluent aphasic patients. These patients characteristically delete "small grammatical words," such as articles, prepositions, and auxiliary verbs, as well as forms of the verb *to be*. Their output relies heavily on major nouns in order to convey information. In dramatic cases of this disorder, called *agrammatism,* a patient may give a narrative using only a string of disconnected nouns and verbs. In mild cases, the patient may produce some short complete sentences interspersed with others that are agrammatic. Similar difficulties appear in repetition and writing.

Another form of disordered syntax is heard in fluent aphasia, particularly in cases with lesions of the posterior temporal lobe, or *Wernicke's aphasia.* In these cases, however, syntax is not reduced by omission of small words and simplification of sentence forms. Instead, the patient may produce copious output, with confused syntax and inappropriately chosen words. Grammatical elements, such as pronouns, prepositions, and inflections, may be interchanged or occasionally omitted, but for the most part they fall into place correctly as required by the immediate context. This disorder, called *paragrammatism,* is highly indicative of left temporal lobe involvement.

Floridly paragrammatic speech may suggest to the inexperienced clinician the jargon of a schizophrenic. In fact, transcribed paragrammatic speech may be difficult to distinguish from some schizophrenic productions on purely structural linguistic grounds. However, paragrammatic aphasic speech is free of bizarre delusional or highly personalized references, nor does it display the play with permutations of a word sometimes heard in schizophrenic speech. The easiest differentiation, however, is on the basis of history and patient behavior. Schizophrenic jargon is a relatively rare feature with modern treatment methods and is associated with the indifference to personal interaction of the severe schizophrenic. Wernicke's aphasics, on the other hand, usually show normal interpersonal warmth and effort to communicate, although they may not recognize the incomprehensibility of their speech. Further, the onset of this speech pattern in Wernicke's aphasics is usually associated with a stroke or other relatively acute neurological event in a person without psychiatric history. Severely paragrammatic output, indistinguishable from Wernicke's aphasia, may also be heard in many patients with advanced Alzheimer's disease. Since these patients may be confused and unreachable, differential diagnosis may be difficult without recourse to the medical history, which usually refers to an earlier stage of the illness, in which memory defect and word-finding difficulties were the chief problems.

Paraphasia

Aphasic patients not only have reduced access to intended utterances but, as noted, are prone to inadvertent output errors, which are grouped under the term *paraphasia.* In verbal paraphasia, errors affect primarily the selection of a lexical item (e.g., "I spoke to my mother" instead of "I spoke to my wife"); in literal paraphasia, they affect the selection and ordering of sounds within a word (e.g., "taxcis" for "cactus"); in paragrammatism, they affect the coherence of a total sentence (e.g., "She's working her work out of there" used to refer to a woman washing dishes at the sink).

The examiner must note whether paraphasias occur at all and which of the three forms of paraphasia predominates, since this observation bears strongly on the type of aphasia and the probable site of the brain lesion producing it. The specific association between aphasic types and paraphasic type is elaborated in the review of the syndromes of aphasia later in this chapter.

Word Finding

Virtually all aphasic patients suffer from reduced access to their vocabulary of lexical items for production, whether in the context of continuous speech or in picture naming. This difficulty may range from total failure to retrieve words to occasional blocking of the name of an object or a person. As with the term *fluency,* the term *word-finding difficulty* has a special meaning in relation to aphasia. It refers specifically to problems of accessing the principal nouns, verbs, and adjectives in speech—that is, the lexical elements—and not a generalized inarticulateness that encompasses both lexical and grammatical words. The word *anomia* (i.e., loss of word names) is often used to describe this deficit.

Since contrasting forms of aphasia may produce opposite effects on the lexical versus the grammatical elements of speech, one index of the severity of anomia is the relative dearth of information-carrying terms in the message. The patient who is severely anomic sometimes produces grammatically well-organized and fluent but "empty" speech.

Word-finding difficulty appears in subtly differing clinical forms that have clear implications for distinguishing between subtypes of aphasia. The clinician must observe, for example, whether the patient characteristically substitutes paraphasic errors for intended targets, whether such paraphasias are usually word substitutions or usually literal paraphasias. In literal paraphasias, it appears that the phonological structure of the word has been partly or wholly recovered at a subarticulatory level and that the patient is making a stab at completing it. Another variable to be noted is how the patient responds to being primed with the first sound of the word: whether such priming almost invariably helps, never helps, or often leads to completion with an irrelevant word. The differential diagnostic implications of these variations are elaborated in the discussion of syndromes of aphasia. Their theoretical bearing on the nature of the word retrieval process is currently a topic for research.

Repetition

While the ability to repeat from a spoken model may seem to have little to do with everyday communication, the status of this capacity is an important aspect of the integrity of the language apparatus. In various forms of aphasia, repetition may be disproportionately impaired or, in contrast, remarkably well preserved. Impaired repetition is marked by particular types of errors, which themselves are clinical markers for specific aphasia types and lesion sites.

Auditory Comprehension

The notion that aphasia could be classified into "expressive" and "receptive" types was based not only on an inadequate characterization of expressive language but on a primitive view of auditory comprehension as a unitary process. As examples of the seeming paradoxes in auditory comprehension, we may cite the following:

1. Some patients may deal infallibly with lexically complex sentences, such as "What is the apparatus you would use to communicate with another person at a great distance," but cannot follow instructions to "Touch the fork with the pencil."

2. Some patients can carry out errands involving the use of objects (e.g., "Take the cup from your table and put some water in it from the sink") but cannot respond to the name of the object out of context (e.g., "Show me the cup")

3. Some patients can respond appropriately to conversation dealing with their immediate life situations but not with the simplest items relating to general factual knowledge.

This is only a partial list of the problems in auditory comprehension that make its assessment a challenge to the examiner. Variations in pattern of performance within the modality of auditory comprehension are, to some degree, related to type of aphasia. For the most part, however, the hierarchy of difficulty illustrated in the foregoing examples remains fairly stable across patients of various types, but the overall level of auditory comprehension varies enormously among subtypes of aphasia, compared to other language input and output channels.

Reading

More than any other language modality, reading has been the area in which selective deficits produced by brain injury have been applied to the understanding of the normal process. Because of the complexity of the cognitive skills entailed in the use of an alphabetic reading system, there are many points at which reading may be vulnerable. Some of these are apparent on considering what is entailed in the reading of various types of words. For example, the fact that such abbreviations as *lbs.* and *Mrs.* and such irregularly spelled words as *colonel* are read with just as clear a subjective sense of their sound as are regularly spelled words shows that letter-string–to–sound associations need not be mediated by grapheme-to-phoneme recoding. On the other hand, the fact that an unfamiliar word, for example, *Mr. Zakzonk,* can also be sounded shows that the grapheme-to-phoneme pathway is also a part of normal reading. The notion that a written word is understood only after its sound has been recaptured is also contradicted by observations from aphasia (as well as by the reading of deaf mutes).

What soon becomes clear from clinical observation is that oral reading entails different operations than does silent reading and that these tasks must be clearly distinguished from each other in the examination. For example, the task of oral reading reveals that, in some aphasics, retrieval of the sound of free or bound grammatical morphemes is lost. The result is that oral reading sounds like the speech of a patient with agrammatism. This defect need not imply a corresponding loss of the meaning of the grammatical morphemes. It is usually, but need not be, accompanied by agrammatic speech in conversation. Thus, oral reading is a performance in which the profound psychological difference between the lexical and grammatical elements of speech is expressed in symptoms that dissociate one type of word from the other. Another feature related to the autonomous nature of oral reading is the occasional preservation of fluent oral reading with virtually no comprehension, which is somewhat similar to the symptom of hyperlexia in children with developmental disorders. Oral reading without comprehension is found in some patients with the syndrome of transcortical sensory aphasia.

The study of organic reading disorders also reveals major differences in symptoms between alexias produced by interruption of visual input to the left hemisphere language zone and those produced by injury within the language zone itself, that is, between pure alexia and aphasic alexia. In pure alexia, there is little if any language disorder. That is, words spelled aloud to the patient with pure alexia are understood instantly and precisely, and these patients may write normally. On the other hand, for the aphasic alexic, access to word meaning may be only approximate and may be limited to very common words; their writing is usually impaired as much or more than their speech.

Thus, the examination of reading is structured in terms of our current understanding of how the reading process may be affected. This is a far cry from assessing reading by means of scholastic achievement tests. Yet even scholastic achievement tests have their place in the assessment of aphasia, when it is appropriate to quantify reading capacity in a patient who has recovered well beyond the level at which specific processing defects, other than slowness, are detectable.

Writing

After injury to the language zone, writing usually suffers more than any other modality of communication and is more often reduced to a totally nonfunctional level, regardless of type of aphasia. Because writing is so sensitive to the effects of aphasia, a sample of free narrative writing or writing sentences from dictation should be a part of any screening examination for brain damage, no matter how brief. By the same token, because writing does not always discriminate between different forms of aphasia, it has not been studied as analytically as have speech, reading, and auditory comprehension.

Like reading, writing is subject to varied forms of symptoms arising from the complexity of our alphabetic system, but as a motor skill, it also is subject to defects that are very closely analogous to the disorders of spoken language. It is sometimes assumed that writing is simply spoken language recoded into alphabetic form. In some aphasic patients, this appears to be the case, as their written output seems to be very similar to their speech. However, in some instances the linguistic content of writing is impaired in a different way from that of speech.

Like speech, the motor aspect of writing may be impaired at the level of basic motor control, which is consistent across all stimulus situations, or at a "higher level," in which overlearned operations, such as signing one's name, are retained and dissociated from the production of other writing. Motor control may be impaired simply because the patient's hemiplegia forces the patient to use the nonpreferred left hand. In some instances, a generalized apraxia affecting all paper and pencil work with either hand makes writing impossible, just as it does simple drawing. Most patients can be taught, through practice, to develop legible writing with their left hand, provided their impairment is at the level of motor skill.

Beyond the level of motor control, however, writing involves the recall of particular visual-motor sequences in association with concepts of words, of phonological patterns, or of letters. Consider the analogy with the ability to read irregularly spelled words and abbreviations or novel, phonetically regular names or nonsense syllables. In the case of writing, we also include the ability to transcribe from one form of writing to another, for example, from print to longhand.

Thus, at the level of elementary writing skill, we confront the interaction of many complementary routes to performance, all predicated on some degree of motor control of the writing hand. Beyond the level of elementary skills, the process of writing may also be injured in ways that are quite analogous to those of oral expression and of reading: in word finding, access to grammatical forms, and the organization of connected discourse. However, the examiner must be prepared to find that disorders of word finding or syntax that appear in writing are not present in the speech or reading of the same patient.

THE ASSESSMENT PROCESS

The assessment of aphasia begins with engaging the patient in conversation. This quickly orients the examiner as to the level of responsibility that he or she must assume in order to have some exchange of information. It also provides an opportunity to assess whether the patient is sufficiently alert and behaviorally responsive for the examiner to judge whether the patient is aphasic. A diagnosis of aphasia is not possible unless a patient is able to attend and shows, by behavior, that he or she is attempting to interact with the examiner. In particular, one cannot diagnose aphasia in patients with akinetic mutism, which is usually produced by a midline lesion of the brain affecting the third ventricle. Patients with akinetic mutism are awake and follow others with their eyes but rarely give a clear sign of interacting with an examiner. A patient in this state may or may not have aphasia in addition to akinetic unresponsiveness. It is not possible to assess the presence of aphasia under these conditions.

The role of aphasia may also be undeterminable in confusional states. The confused patient may speak freely, sometimes appropriately, sometimes tangentially, and sometimes totally irrelevantly, with respect to the examiner's questions, and may fade in and out of contact. While one may detect what appears to be anomia and impaired auditory comprehension, it is often hazardous to label a patient aphasic while the patient remains in a confusional state.

Given that the patient is responsive and interactive, the examiner may evaluate from free conversation both the severity of the aphasia as an impediment to communication and the major characteristics that determine whether it falls into a particular syndrome and, if so, which one. This portion of the examination should always be tape recorded for analysis at the examiner's leisure.

If it becomes evident that the patient is incapable of voluntary speech, the opening interview, of course, is very short and consists of exploring the patient's ability to nod yes and no or to point appropriately in response to personally relevant questions. Can the patient show where his or her major trouble is, for example, by pointing to the mouth to indicate inability to talk or to the hemiplegic side. Can the patient agree or disagree appropriately to true or false questions about the patient's current location, name, home town, occupation, and so on? On this basis, it is possible to determine whether any exchange of information is possible. From the speed and accuracy of the patient's nonverbal responses, one can also obtain a preliminary estimate of the status of auditory comprehension.

The technique of interviewing a patient with limited verbal output is aimed at providing maximum opportunity for spontaneous speech by the patient. Yes-no questions should be kept to a minimum, and persistent probing for one-word factual responses it not a very productive approach. Topics that commonly lead to production of free conversation are telling how the illness began, especially the details of who assisted the patient and arranged for hospitalization, an account of the patient's occupational history and what the work consisted of, and conversation about the patient's family and children.

In addition to free conversation, it is useful to have a sample of narrative speech elicited by the description of a pictorial situation or by the recital of a well-known fable. The amount of speech produced and its quality may change considerably in response to a picture to be described. Compared with relatively open-ended free conversation, a visual stimulus immediately at hand sometimes serves to enhance both

·word retrieval and the correct use of grammatical forms. The technique for eliciting a speech sample is of little concern in the case of patients with fluent aphasia, as it is very easy to get them talking freely on almost any topic. It is, however, valuable to provide a structured task, (e.g., picture or story narration) for fluent aphasics as well.

The elicitation of a free-conversational sample has been emphasized because this part of the examination provides more information per unit of time than any other single procedure. The severity of the aphasia may be characterized in terms of restrictions on the amount of information that can be exchanged and in terms of the degree of the responsibility that the patient can assume vis-à-vis the examiner in this exchange.

Once an estimate of severity has been made, the examiner should note whether the patient's output can be characterized as fluent or nonfluent, using the criteria described earlier (see "Fluency"). While the great majority of patients can be assigned easily to one side or other of the dichotomy, this is not always true. A particular subgroup of patients responds with severe blocking and output limited to short expressions, such as "Well I...it's a...I can't..." to open-ended questions. In contrast, they often name pictured objects easily and, with the stimulus of a pictorial situation, may produce well-formed sentences of moderate length.

This pattern of fluctuation between grossly nonfluent speech and runs of fluent speech production characterizes transcortical motor aphasics: patients with deep-going anterior lesions that usually spare the cortical Broca's area but extend anterior or superior to it. In some instances of mixed aphasia or of partially recovered aphasia, a fluent-nonfluent assignment cannot be made.

The examiner can further obtain from the free speech sample an assessment of articulatory difficulty, prosody, and grammatical usage, all of which are closely associated with the fluency-nonfluency dimension. Since these features have been described earlier in the chapter, they will not be elaborated here. All of these represent variables of central importance for characterizing the status of a patient's language system and for arriving at a diagnosis within the general sphere of aphasia. Important as these variables are, they do not lend themselves to scoring by objective methods. An approach to quantifying them through rating scales is described by Goodglass and Kaplan (1972).

Disorders of voice volume, particularly *hypophonia,* are characteristic of deep white-matter lesions of the anterior speech zone. Hypophonia is not, per se, an aphasic symptom, but it is frequently a part of the total picture of a subcortical aphasia.

Continuing with the evaluation of free conversation, the examiner also needs to specify the occurrence of paraphasia and the adequacy of lexical information in comparison to the fluency of the output. Paraphasia is of primary significance in distinguishing among subtypes of fluent aphasia. In particular, misnaming of isolated nouns, or verbal paraphasia, is a common feature in almost all forms of aphasia, although its absolute frequency is usually greater in Wernicke's than in Broca's aphasia. The three patterns that are most distinctive among fluent aphasics are (1) copious paragrammatic speech, including both literal and verbal paraphasia, the hallmark of Wernicke's aphasia; (2) a predominance of phonemic paraphasia with repeated attempts at self-correction, characteristic of conduction aphasia; and (3) fluent, anomic speech with many circumlocutory expressions and relatively few paraphasic errors, a pattern that marks anomic aphasia.

Misjudgments in classifying patients are common in certain forms of verbigeration commonly termed *fluent and paraphasic.* The following forms of output are occasionally found in severe aphasics and do not qualify as either fluent or paraphasic:

1. A running, ill-defined mumble in which it is difficult to ascertain individual words or sounds, most often seen in patients with bilateral lesions.

2. Extended runs of repetition of a single nonsense form (e.g., "taka, taka, taka"), sometimes produced with a sentencelike intonation.

3. Runs of a more varied sequence of syllables that involve only a narrow range of consonant-vowel combinations. Although they may be uttered in a conversational setting with sentencelike intonation, they cannot be segmented into words and do not contain recognizable grammatical morphemes, which are heard in the speech of the most severely paragrammatic fluent aphasics. This is very similar to the glossolalia of individuals who take part in religious ecstasies, referred to as "speaking in tongues," but it may have a quite different mechanism.

These forms of output may be found in aphasics with either good or poor comprehension. In spite of such pseudofluency, patients who can overcome this stage of disability and produce meaningful words may prove to have laborious and distorted articulation.

From our present knowledge, these adaptations to aphasia represent sporadic phenomena that cannot yet be linked to a particular lesion locus.

Examination of Auditory Comprehension

One of the values of the free-conversation situation is that it gives the examiner the opportunity to observe the patients' comprehension in a naturalistic framework involving personally relevant material. This condition commonly demonstrates a level of comprehension that would not be expected from formal testing. Aside from this condition, most aspects of auditory comprehension can be assessed in depth and objectively with structured tasks. These tasks should examine lexical comprehension, the ability to decode syntactical relationships, the size of the information load that can be managed by the patient, and the patient's ability to make the inferences needed to understand a paragraph.

Lexical Comprehension

The ability to extract meaning from individual words and to draw inferences from the simple contiguity of words is usually tested through a multiple-choice pointing response. The examiner names an object (or a color or a letter, etc.), and the patient demonstrates comprehension by pointing to it. Performances may differ between identifying objects in a small array on the table and identifying objects in their accustomed location in the room. Most important, the examiner should be aware that dramatic dissociations between the auditory comprehension of different classes of words are common and should be explicitly examined. The categories most regularly observed to differ are objects, colors, letters, numbers, body parts, and map locations. Goodglass, Klein, Carey, and Jones (1966) reported that the comprehension of letter names was most frequently the most difficult.

These authors also found that severe failure to comprehend the names of body parts is most commonly observed in Wernicke's aphasics. Our unpublished data reveal that both Wernicke's and global aphasics often show remarkably well-preserved ability to point to named locations on an outline map of the United States along with paradoxically severe impairment in comprehending the names of their own body parts. We also observe that patients who fail to identify body parts by name may point correctly to the location of articles of clothing. For example, such patients may point to collar but not neck, to shoe but not foot, to sleeve but not arm, and so on, an observation that emphasizes the special nature of the category of body-part names.

A further characteristic of lexical comprehension that should be noted by the examiner is that the meaning of words is not lost entirely but that some semantic elements may be responded to. One technique for exploring such partial auditory comprehension is incorporated in Goodglass and Kaplan's (1972) approach. Stimuli of three different categories (e.g., colors, numbers, and actions) appear grouped by category on a single card, so that the patient may demonstrate comprehension of the category by looking in the right place and possibly selecting the wrong member of the category. Similarly, in testing the comprehension of body parts, the most common form of failure is that the patient looks toward or moves his or her hand to the correct general area but fails to locate the precise part named; for example, the patient may point to the lip or cheek when asked for chin. Another common form of failure is confusion, on the basis of their common functions, among various joints, for example, elbow for knee, wrist for ankle, and the like.

A characteristic of reduced lexical comprehension is that it is most severe for the word spoken out of context and improves when the object name is embedded in an action. For example, patients who do not understand "Show me your eyes" almost invariably respond appropriately to "Shut your eyes." Patients frequently comprehend action terms better than object names, so it is useful to ask patients to show how they sleep, yawn, pray, or swim if they do not perform correctly in response to objects.

Another approach to exploring lexical comprehension is by giving a functional definition of an object to be identified. For example, the patient may be asked to show a "device you wear to improve your vision" or a "place you would go to see your own reflection." Many patients with well-preserved lexical comprehension demonstrate their ability to extract the meaning of a concept from such a concatenation of words of low frequency.

Syntactic Comprehension

The ability to derive meaning from individual lexical items or from sentences in which the lexical information in several words converges to identify a single concept may be perfectly preserved in patients who fail to understand relationships that are signaled by grammatical terms or by word order. Such failures are commonly demonstrated when the relationships between the terms can plausibly be reversed, as in "my sister's husband" versus "my husband's sister" or "The lion was killed by the tiger" versus "The tiger was killed by the lion." Problems with construction of this type, which Luria (1970) referred to as *logico-grammatical* relationships, may be found in aphasics of all types. They may be just as severe in patients with well-preserved lexical comprehension as in patients who fail to grasp some word meanings.

In addition to possessive and to subject-object comprehension in the passive voice, other constructions falling in this category are before-after ("The truck arrived before the bus"), comparative ("The girl is bigger than the boy"), and agent-object constructions ("Touch the pencil with the fork"). Most of these sentence types can be tested by means of a verbal framework or pictorial multiple choice. For example, comprehension of the possessive can be examined by means of the following: "A mother cat and her baby kitten were playing on the floor, and I picked up the kitten's mother [alternatively, "the mother's kitten"]. Which one did I pick up—the big one or the little one?"

The agent-object relationship is best tested by having the patient carry out a series of commands involving such objects as a spoon, a pencil, and a fork. Begin with "Pick up the spoon and now with the spoon point to the pencil." This is followed by "Now point to the fork with the pencil," and so on. In spite of coaching, many patients never learn to understand the meaning signalled by the words *with* and *to*. They will consistently pick up the first of the objects named and use it as the pointing implement. That is, they will perform correctly with sentences in the form "With the fork, point to the pencil" but but incorrectly with sentences in the form "Point to the pencil with the fork."

Syntactic complexity created by the embedding of subordinate modifying clauses places a severe processing load on aphasics of all types (Blumstein, Goodglass, Statlender, & Biber, 1983). Such sentences are particularly difficult when alternative interpretations are plausible (e.g., "The dog who bit the cat ran away" versus "The cat who bit the dog ran away"). The sentences can be quite easy when the lexical restrictions are so strong that syntactic word-order cues can be overlooked (e.g., "The car that ran over the nail got a flat tire"). The examiner who creates test sentences for auditory comprehension must therefore be aware of the type of relational information encoded in the syntax and the degree to which lexical meaning, as opposed to syntactic elements, determine the interpretation of the sentence.

Informational Load

A traditional method of quantifying auditory comprehension is to give the patient commands of varying numbers of elements to carry out, ranging from single commands ("Put the pencil in your pocket") to three or four-fold commands ("Put the pencil in your pocket, fold the paper in half, and open my desk drawer"). At bedside examinations, it is often necessary to improvise such items using whatever is at hand. It appears intuitively obvious that an aspect of a patient's comprehension is the amount of information the patient can process in a single message. While this assumption has not been challenged, neither is it clear that the quantity of information that can be managed is a dimension independent from the capacity to deal with syntactic complexity, except insofar as it depends on short-term auditory memory. In constructing such items, the examiner must be sensitive not only to the length of the commands but also to the arbitrariness ("Put the watch on the floor") versus the predictability ("Take off your glasses") of the relationships between words. In commands involving a series of adjective-noun combinations (e.g., "Pick up the red triangle and the blue circle"), retaining the word order also poses a special memory load. Experience with the Token Test (DeRenzi & Vignolo, 1962), which involves items of this type, shows that it is sensitive to the effects of aphasia of all types but not selectively sensitive to Wernicke's aphasia, in which comprehension of individual word meanings is most impaired (Orgass & Poeck, 1966; Poeck, Kerschensteiner, & Hartje, 1972).

Examination of Naming Ability

Access to the names that denote concepts (abstract and concrete nouns, actions, etc.) is impaired in aphasics of all types, and, for most aphasics, a score in a test of naming in response to visual confrontation is primarily an index of severity of aphasia rather than a differential indicator of the type of aphasia. In order to extract diagnostic information from a naming task, it must be considered in relation to the patients' fluency of speech output, as described above under "Word Finding."

The formal assessment of word finding is basically the straightforward task of picture or object naming. However, there are a number of variables involving the stimuli used and the sensory modality of presentation that enter into the testing procedures. In addition, the type of error made and the patient's response to cuing can be of primary importance in identifying the pattern of the patient's disorder.

As with lexical comprehension, the ability to name may vary dramatically from one class of terms to another. Specifically, the naming of letters, numbers, and colors may be affected totally differently from the naming of objects. The most common observation is that numbers and letters are accessible for naming, while anomia for objects may be virtually complete.

This pattern is common in patients with fluent aphasias of the posterior speech zone. Selective problems with colors are not uncommon, but their association with type of aphasia is not yet documented, with a rare exception. An isolated *color name aphasia* is frequently observed with pure alexia, or word blindness, described below.

Thus, the minimally adequate examination of naming ability requires the patient to name, on visual confrontation, objects, colors, letters, numbers, and actions. Most standard aphasia examinations do not include a sufficient sampling of uncommon objects to document milder naming disorders, and it is often valuable to add a more extensive picture-naming test, such as the Boston Naming Test (Kaplan, Goodglass, & Weintraub, 1983). If naming is tested only via visual confrontation, it is possible that some important, though relatively infrequent, specific problems may be missed, and it is therefore useful to include an examination of naming in relationship to tactile stimulation and naming in response to verbally given definitions. Modality-specific dissociations may be discovered in cases of agnosia or in cases of interruption of callosal transmission from the other hemisphere.

Thus, the first clue to the fact that a patient has a visual agnosia for objects may be that the patient fails to name correctly on visual presentation but does name correctly when actual objects are placed in the patient's hand or when asked to respond to a functional definition (e.g., "What do you shave with?"). On the other hand, response to orally presented definitions assumes adequate auditory comprehension. A rarely used, yet valuable procedure is the naming of objects in response to hearing their characteristic sound, either live or tape recorded. In those cases occasionally encountered in which a naming deficit is exclusively related to visual presentation of objects, both tactile and auditory stimulation may demonstrate the integrity of naming through another channel. It should be emphasized, however, that in the vast majority of cases, impaired naming is a central disorder that shows parallel deficiencies in all channels of stimulation (Goodglass, Barton, & Kaplan, 1968; Spreen, Benton, & Van Allen, 1966).

Finally, the examiner should observe *how* the patient fails. The qualitative features of the failed response may be difficult to express in numbers, but they carry a great deal of information. Does the patient make a recognizable attempt at articulating the target word but fail to implement the motor articulatory act? Is this failure in the context of awkward and difficult articulation in all the patient's utterances? Does the patient promptly recognize the word when it is offered by the examiner? Can the patient then repeat it with somewhat improved articulation? Given the initial sound as a priming stimulus, is the patient likely to complete the word correctly? The foregoing pattern is most characteristic of patients with anterior speech zone lesions, that is, Broca's aphasics.

Another pattern of failure involves a partially accurate production in which some phonemes or syllables are transposed, omitted, or substituted (i.e., literal paraphasia) and in which the patient is keenly aware of the inaccuracy and makes repeated attempts at self-correction. While, in a sense, this can also be called a failure of articulation, it differs from the previously described pattern in that the incorrectly chosen phonemes are uttered with facility and the general context of the patient's production is one of fluent and facile articulation. This pattern is the mark of *conduction aphasia.*

Does the patient produce a variety of paraphasic responses: incorrectly chosen words, literal paraphasia, verging on total neologisms? Does the patient fail to respond to phonemic priming most of the time? This is the pattern seen regularly, in association with impaired comprehension, in Wernicke's aphasia, the aphasia of posterior temporal lobe lesions.

Finally, does the patient typically comment on the function of the object (circumlocution), making few semantic word substitutions and rarely any literal paraphasias? This is the most typical pattern of the anomic aphasic.

Patients who impulsively provide inappropriate completions when primed with the opening sound are likely to have frontal lobe impairment with impaired naming, good repetition, and good comprehension.

Serial Speech

The recitation of memorized sequences, such as counting and reciting the days and months, is typically superior to other speech performance in aphasia. It represents *nonpropositional,* or automatized, speech output, which may be partially or wholly preserved when no other communication remains available. The examination of these performances is not particularly revealing in mild aphasics. It is extremely revealing, however, in severe aphasics. When automatized series are remarkably well preserved, one should look for the other characteristics of transcortical aphasia, described below.

Repetition

The examination of repetition is approached with two questions. Is the level of performance on repetition notably worse or notably better than performance on other tasks? If repetition is worse, does the quality of errors and the type of material that elicits errors match the pattern observed in conduction aphasia? In the majority (i.e., 75%–80%) of aphasic patients, performance under repetition is commensurate in level and quality of performance with performance in other forms of expressive speech.

In order to determine whether the grossly impaired patient has any capacity to repeat, the examiner presents easy, single words and expressions (e.g., *house, table, hello, thank you*). The items are then increased in difficulty in terms of articulatory considerations, length of span required, grammatical structure, and lexical composition, as explained below.

Articulatory Considerations

Patients with repetition disorders are particularly sensitive to easy "tongue twisters" of the type that involve alliterative repetitions of stop consonants, as in such words as *hippopotamus* and *basketball player*. These difficulties are of no special significance in patients with obviously disordered articulation; they are of significance in patients whose general level of output is fluent.

Length of Repetition Span

Repetition span is governed in part by the patient's status in the fluency dimension and in part by immediate auditory memory. Patients who are extremely nonfluent in conversation are usually limited in the number of successive syllables for which they can provide a motor plan, and their solution when that length is exceeded is to delete words and unstressed syllables, especially unstressed grammatical morphemes. Thus, "He closed the door" may be abridged to "Closed the door" or "Close door." Easy repetition of strings far longer than those produced in spontaneous speech suggests transcortical motor aphasia.

When repetition span is very limited, it is important to probe for auditory memory constraints. Can the patient detect differences in two repetitions of a digit string in which one digit is changed in the second series? Such difficulties may appear in patients whose comprehension and productive fluency are surprisingly spared. They help the examiner understand why repetition may be faulty.

Grammatical Considerations

Accuracy in sentence repetition varies with the grammatical form of test sentences in Broca's aphasics but not in fluent aphasics. Sentences in the form of simple subject-verb-object declaratives may be repeated correctly, but yes-no interrogatives are often converted to subject-verb-object order. For example, "John closed the door" may be repeated correctly, while "Is John coming home?" may be reproduced as "John is coming home." Sometimes the rising question intonation on the last word is maintained, but the word order reverts to the more common declarative order. Problems related to grammatical form, particularly as it affects word order, are usually related to similar limitations in the form of conversational speech. Such problems are observed particularly in nonfluent patients by means of short test sentences three to five words in length. While short sentences place constraints on repetition, the fact that these constraints are not notably different in type or degree from those in free conversation means that one is not dealing with a selective repetition disorder.

Next we consider problems related, not to grammatical form per se, but to the use of lexical versus grammatical morphemes.

Lexical Make-up of the Material to Be Repeated

Most patients who have a selective disorder for repetition are particularly baffled by sentences composed primarily of pronouns, copulas, or other "empty" verbs and grammatical morphemes. They perform relatively well in reproducing sentences using nouns and picturable actions. For example, contrast "John is the boy who painted the house" with a sentence in virtually the same grammatical form: "He is the one who did it." The string of grammatical morphemes represented by the second sentence presents particular difficulty to patients with conduction aphasia. A test item that has acquired the status of a shibboleth for conduction aphasia is repetition of "No ifs, ands, or buts!" suggested by Geschwind.

The reason for the selective problem in the repetition of strings of grammatical morphemes is not clear. We conjecture that their semantic emptiness reduces their codability in immediate auditory memory.

Forms of Errors in Repetition Tasks

As we have noted, the task of repetition may produce failures that simply reflect problems apparent in other aspects of the patient's language: impairment of the motor articulatory act, sharply reduced auditory span, reduced span for planning utterances, and impaired access to grammatical structures. Similarly, patients whose free speech is fluent but extremely paraphasic commonly show similar paraphasic substitutions in repetition, with obliviousness to their own errors.

However, in patients whose repetition is disproportionately impaired, there are also some observations to be made concerning errors specific to naming. One is the propensity to make literal paraphasias both in single-word and sentence repetition and another is the tendency to paraphrase by substituting either grammatical morphemes or lexical terms. Of particular interest is the observation that the production of literal paraphasias, so common with polysyllabic nouns, disappears with numbers. Instead, errors in multiplace numbers take the form of verbal paraphasia, for example, "five seventy-two" repeated as "five sixty-four."

Examining Reading

The evaluation of reading skills can be logically subdivided into the levels of letter recognition, word reading, and sentence and paragraph comprehension. Tests designed around these three levels, in fact, make an excellent framework for reading assessment. However, recent research on selective processing defects in reading (and their bearing on models of normal reading) have opened the door to more sophisticated approaches within the same basic framework. We will begin this section with a discussion of the three levels of organization.

Letter Recognition

It has become obvious from clinical study that loss of familiarity with letters as individual symbols is a mark of certain forms of severe alexia. But letter recognition is not adequately tested by having the patient point to letters in response to their names. Such a task entails a step of auditory comprehension, which may be impaired without affecting letter recognition. A multiple-choice presentation requiring the patient to match letters across writing styles is suggested (e.g., matching a block-printed stimulus with a lower-case version of the same letter placed among several distractor items).

Word Recognition

Spoken words should be matched against a multiple-choice presentation in which the written target word appears among distractors that resemble it either in form or in meaning. This procedure, however, may be completed on the basis of phonetic matching without comprehension of the written word. As a test of word comprehension, the examiner should present names of objects on a card for the patient to select from a multiple choice of actual objects. Body parts, colors, and objects situated around the room may be included in this sampling.

Sentence Comprehension

Many patients can demonstrate their ability to read for meaning by carrying out written commands of various levels of complexity. However, this method fails with some individuals who do nothing because they do not seem to realize that the written instruction requires some action on their part. Consequently, we recommend presenting sentences in which the final word is left blank for the subject to select an appropriate word from a multiple-choice set. Items across a wide range of difficulty can be devised, and, empirically, this format has proven easy for patients to grasp.

Oral Reading

The status of the patient's oral reading ability should always be examined, both through the oral reading of single words and of sentence or paragraph material. The list of words to be read aloud should include regularly spelled words (*time, zoo*), irregularly spelled words (*sugar, cough*), grammatical morphemes (*with, for, am*), and words with inflectional or derivational endings (*playing, quickly*). Sentences for oral reading should provide an opportunity to see how the patient deals with both nouns and grammatical morphemes (e.g., "The cheese was eaten by the mouse").

Selective Processing Deficits in Reading

Attention to highly selective forms of reading disorder has made aphasiologists aware of features that deserve special attention in the evaluation, both for diagnosis and for planning treatment. These features include graphophonemic processing deficit, deep dyslexia, surface dyslexia, and oral reading without comprehension.

GRAPHOPHONEMIC PROCESSING DEFICIT.   A subgroup of reading-impaired patients have lost the ability to use the phonic value of letters to arrive at the sound of a word. The first clue to this problem is that they misread many words by substituting a semantically related one in oral reading, for example, reading *sick* as *medicine.* Closer examination shows that even when they read a word correctly, it is on a whole word-to-sound associative basis. When asked to select nonwords, such as unusual names (*Mr. Grice, Mr. Tash*) or nonsense syllables, from a list, they are unable to perform.

DEEP DYSLEXIA.   Loss of grapheme-to-phoneme processing usually appears along with loss of ability to read aloud the grammatical morphemes of English whether spelled phonetically (*as, if, am*) or irregularly (*were, who*). The combination of deficits expressed by the dropping out of grammatical morphemes and the appearance of semantic paralexias is called *deep dyslexia.*

SURFACE DYSLEXIA.   A considerably less common disorder is one in which the patient fails to segment written words appropriately into letter groups for the application of phoneme-to-grapheme rules but applies these rules inappropriately to part of a letter sequence. The patient may then misinterpret the word on the basis of the misreading. For example, *chair* may be called *c-hair, home* may be read as *homm-ee,* and irregularly spelled words may be regularized (e.g., *break* as *breek*).

ORAL READING WITHOUT COMPREHENSION.   A pattern seen in some patients with transcortical sensory aphasia involves the remarkable preservation of all aspects of oral reading, without comprehension of the words either individually or as connected text.

Examining Writing

The status of the mechanics of writing, that is, the recall and coordination of the movements for forming letters, represents a consideration unique to the modality of writing. In other respects, however, the examination of writing is analogous to the examination of speech.

Mechanics of Writing

The examiner compares the patient's ability to form letters in block printing and in cursive writing under automatized conditions (writing name and address, copying, writing letters and easy words from dictation). The examiner notes whether the patient copies from a model slavishly or uses his or her own writing style.

Recall of Individual Words

Can the patient write words from dictation and in response to pictorial presentation of objects to be named in writing? Do errors take the form of phonetically based misspelling or the substitution of semantic associations? With respect to writing of single words from dictation, it is important to sample words from different grammatical categories, particularly prepositions, pronouns, and auxiliary verbs, in addition to abstract and concrete nouns. As in reading, there are patients who can write nouns but not grammatical morphemes.

Sentence and Paragraph Writing

If the patient shows some writing at the one-word level, the next step is to explore writing of connected material from dictation and in free composition.

APHASIA BATTERIES

The foregoing section, "The Assessment Process," was intended to provide a broad rationale for the examination of language, that the clinician can apply to informal bedside testing or to a formal quantified procedure. A number of published aphasia examinations on the market meet some of the examination objectives pointed out in the foregoing discussion. It is impractical to design a formal examination that provides for all contingencies. When they wish to have quantified and repeatable measures, most examiners choose one of the commercially available tests. Below, we describe the features of four of the better-known aphasia examinations, each of which has advantages in certain applications.

Eisenson's Test

Eisenson's *Examining for Aphasia* (1946, revised 1954), is the earliest of the published aphasia examinations. Its major advantage is that it provides a roughly quantified survey of most of the language performance skills, with stimulus plates conveniently incorporated into the examination manual. This makes it particularly useful as an aid in bedside testing or in screening for aphasia. It is not sensitive to mild impairments of function.

A criticism of this test is the labeling of various test tasks under inappropriate headings. For example, the sampling of word repetition ability is labeled *apraxia,* and auditory and written word comprehension tasks both appear under the heading *agnosia.*

Thus, examiners who have their own framework of aphasia as a guide can use this examination as a conveniently packaged inventory of tasks whose significance they can interpret themselves. Examiners who lack such a framework will find the Eisenson test useful primarily as a screening device. Impairments should be noted in terms of the actual operations involved rather than by the label assigned to them.

Minnesota Differential Diagnostic Test for Aphasia

The Minnesota Differential Diagnostic Test for Aphasia (MDDTA) (Schnell, 1965) is a comprehensive, well-organized test suitable over a wide range of impairments. Some subtests of the MDDTA are designed to probe particular language functions (e.g., phoneme discrimination) analytically. Other subtests involve complex communicative tasks (e.g., "Name three things a good citizen should do") or cognitively difficult items.

The strong points of MDDTA are its thoroughness, applicability over a wide range of impairments, and rational organization in terms of categories that have a face correspondence to the performances sampled.

The shortcomings of the test are its length, the confounding of measures of intellectual ability with aphasia, and the neglect of fluency, paraphasia, and agrammatism as quantifiable features applicable to diagnosis.

Porch Index of Communicative Abilities

The Porch Index of Communicative Abilities (PICA) (1967) is the most thoroughly standardized of current tests in terms of rigor of test procedures and of scoring rules, and yields scores that have well-established interscorer reliability and can be expressed in terms of an overall impairment in each of the input and output modalities of language. However, since it has a relatively low ceiling, it is insensitive to milder cases.

The advantage of the PICA is the stable quantitative score, which makes it attractive in tracing recovery and for certain research applications in which a global measure of degree of aphasia is desirable. The drawback of the PICA is the difficulty of training scorers to follow the complex multidimensional scheme. The PICA also has the fault of labeling tasks in a way that creates problems in interpreting their significance. For example, since many auditory comprehension tasks require response via pointing or other movement, they are labeled *gestural,* as though measurement of the adequacy of gesture per se were the goal of the test. The information on auditory comprehension is available in the scores, but the clinician must override the unfortunate terminology to extract it. Like the Eisenson's test and the MDDTA, the PICA does not require the examiner to listen for or quantify the dimensions of fluency, grammatical adequacy, or paraphasia, so it is of limited use in conjunction with modern views on aphasic syndromes and their lesion loci.

Boston Diagnostic Aphasia Examination

The Boston Diagnostic Aphasia Examination (BDAE) (Goodglass & Kaplan, 1972, revised 1983) is comprehensive in terms of its analytic approach to language skills and includes subtests with discriminating power over a wide range of severity of impairment. It is the first to introduce a sampling of free conversation and narrative for the explicit purpose of rating fluency, articulation, grammatical competence, and paraphasia.

While the authors deny that score profiles can be assigned in cookbook fashion to standard syndromes of aphasia, they emphasize the value of recognizing the named syndromes and claim that their procedure provides the information the examiner needs for diagnosis. Like the PICA, the revised BDAE allows raw scores to be plotted as percentiles of a normative sample to yield a profile.

The disadvantages of the BDAE are its length and the fact that some of the rating scales require a judgment based on clinical experience. In allowing the examiner some leeway in dealing with the patient, the authors sacrifice the rigor associated with the PICA.

Neurosensory Center Comprehensive Examination

The Neurosensory Center Comprehensive Examination for Aphasia (NCCEA) (Spreen & Benton, 1969) provides comprehensive coverage of all of the input and output channels of language through 20 quantified scales for which conversion to percentile values is provided. It is suitable for severe to moderate levels of aphasia, and some of the subtests discriminate at mild levels. Norms for nonaphasics are provided. This is the only battery that explicitly tests object naming with tactile as well as visual presentation. Examination of other language skills, such as auditory comprehension, however, is less analytic than in the BDAE.

The NCCEA does not include an evaluation of free conversation and therefore neglects some of the variables cited here as important in classification of aphasia.

Other Batteries

The foregoing review of currently used aphasia tests is not meant to be exhaustive. It could be extended to include Kertesz's Western Aphasia Battery (WAB) (1979), which is similar in principle to, but briefer than, the BDAE, and Holland's Communicative Activities of Daily Living (CADL) (1980). The latter, as its name suggests, is geared to the functional status of communication in real life.

THE SYNDROMES OF APHASIA

This chapter began with a review of the dimensions of language in which aberrations appear after brain injury. From clinical observation, we have learned that these deficits do not appear in free variation with each other and that there are a number of commonly recurring patterns associated with particular lesion sites within the language zone of the left hemisphere. In this section, these syndromes will be reviewed.

The fact that such selective impairments of components of language are associated with particular lesions and lesion combinations is the basis of whatever understanding we have of the anatomy of language. To a considerable extent, this knowledge derives from the fact that the vascular supply of the brain is vulnerable to stroke at certain points, so that roughly similarly located focal lesions are encountered in a sizable proportion of stroke patients.

There is also, however, considerable variability in the location and extent of lesions due to stroke, and, correspondingly, a significant proportion of cases of aphasia that do not fit a recognized recurring pattern. Many older patients have suffered multiple strokes; the effects of most multiple-lesion sites are simply not known—they are not merely the sum of the deficits found with each of the injuries alone. The same can be said of large lesions involving a number of adjacent areas. Other reasons for variability in the symptomatology of aphasia are differences in brain organization produced by early injury or congenital brain anomalies, or by slowly growing tumors. Deviations from the most common pattern of brain organization are often signaled by left-handedness or by a history of learning disability in the patient or close blood relatives (Geschwind & Behan, 1982). As is well known, a significant percentage of left-handers may develop aphasia from a right cerebral injury, a result rarely found in right-handers.

In spite of these factors leading to variability in the symptoms of aphasia, as many as half of aphasics seen after a first stroke show a pattern of deficits that can be identified with one of the named syndromes. For those who do not fit clearly into one of the categories, the syndromes can serve as anchor points for the description of the observed pattern.

Nonfluent Disorders

When, on the basis of speech output, a patient is considered to be nonfluent, the patient may fall into the category of Broca's aphasia, mixed nonfluent aphasia, transcortical motor aphasia, aphemia, or global aphasia. With the exception of global aphasics, who commonly have large lesions encompassing most of the speech zone, nonfluent aphasics usually have a predominantly prerolandic lesion.

Broca's Aphasia

The diagnostic term *Broca's aphasia* is applied to patients who demonstrate good to excellent lexical comprehension (see "Lexical Comprehension") and whose nonfluent speech is almost invariably awkward or distorted in articulation. Articulation may even be impaired to the point where the patient can produce no intelligible speech, even on imitation. However, Broca's aphasics *usually* improve in articulation when given a model for repetition. A frequent concomitant of Broca's aphasia is reduced syntax in speech production, which may be so severe as to result in one-word holophrastic sentences; milder disturbances meet the description of *agrammatism* given earlier in this article. Broca's aphasics usually read better than they write.

Mixed Nonfluent Aphasia

Although not one in general use, the term *mixed nonfluent aphasia* has been introduced by Goodglass and Kaplan (1983) to distinguish a group of patients who differ from Broca's aphasics only in the greater severity of their impairment in auditory compre-hension. Corresponding to their increased severity is the greater extent of their lesions, which involve the anterior parietal region as well as the posterior frontal lobe.

Transcortical Motor Aphasia

The distinctive feature of the transcortical syndromes is the remarkably spared ability to repeat sentences after the examiner. Transcortical motor aphasics have great difficulty in formulating speech on their own and are usually called *nonfluent* because their attempts to converse result in short utterances chiefly of stereotyped phrases. Nevertheless, since many of these patients occasionally produce a well-articulated, grammatically complete sentence, the variability in their production may make it impossible to term them either *fluent* or *nonfluent*. Unlike Broca's aphasics, these patients have normal articulation. Many can perform well in naming with visual confrontation or in giving one-word factual responses to questions, contrasting dramatically with their helplessness in more open-ended conversation.

Transcortical motor aphasia is usually associated with a lesion deep to but sparing the classical Broca's area and often extending to the cortex anterior or superior to Broca's area.

Aphemia

The term *aphemia* has come into use for a disorder that affects articulation only, with little or no impact on other aspects of language. The aphemic patient is initially totally anarthric and gradually recovers slow, laborious articulation characterized by syllable-by-syllable prosody but accurate word choice and syntax. The articulatory deficit is not improved by repetition or automatic speech. The lesion producing aphemia is small, located at the foot of the motor strip or in the underlying white matter. This disorder, though related to aphasia, is probably best regarded as a nonlinguistic and nonaphasic disorder.

Global Aphasia

The term *global aphasia* denotes not only a degree of severity of aphasia that precludes any significant communication but also involvement of all levels of language, oral and written. Global aphasics may be capable of uttering a few interjections or stereotyped syllables or phrases, and their comprehension may be adequate for agreeing or disagreeing appropriately to questions of immediate personal relevance. Some patients with a global aphasia produce a fluent output of syllables in which no segmentation into words is discernable and that is usually limited to a small range of consonant-vowel combinations. This output should not be confused with *paraphasia*, produced by Wernicke's aphasics.

Global aphasia is usually the product of a large lesion involving both pre- and postrolandic speech zones. It sometimes results from a second stroke when neither lesion alone would have been expected to produce a severe aphasia.

The Fluent Aphasias

The fluent aphasias are all marked by preservation of articulatory facility and relatively good preservation of the rate and prosody of speech. The subtypes of fluent aphasia vary in the propensity for paraphasic output and the type (semantic, literal, or paragrammatic) of paraphasia. They vary as well with respect to the involvement of auditory comprehension and of the capacity for repetition. As in the case of the nonfluent aphasias, patterns that cannot be clearly assigned to one subtype may often be well described in terms of the features by which they resemble or differ from one of the named syndromes.

Wernicke's Aphasia

The most common form of fluent aphasia, Wernicke's aphasia is manifested by fluent, sometimes copious paragrammatic speech and markedly impaired comprehension of single words. The lesion producing Wernicke's aphasia usually includes the cortex of the superior temporal gyrus and may extend to the adjacent supramarginal and angular gyri.

Wernicke's aphasics produce semantically ill-chosen words and phonologically disordered renditions in which a fragment of an English word may be detected but that may be neologistic. Their speech, however, retains the elements of grammar, in that grammatical words and inflectional endings appear where they are expected. In the early stages of the illness, these patients are usually totally anomic and may produce grossly paraphasic responses in the effort to name objects or pictures. Similarly, their efforts to repeat words or sentences retain few elements of the stimulus, embroidered with paraphasic intrusions. With recovery, the paraphasia diminishes and comprehension improves. While many patients with initially severe Wernicke's aphasia regain fairly good functional communication, the pattern of impaired lexical comprehension, some degree of anomia, and occasional paraphasia persist.

A common feature of Wernicke's aphasia is unexpected cheerfulness and the patient's unawareness of his or her erroneous speech.

Anomic Aphasia

The term *anomic aphasia* refers to a disorder in which speech is fluent and grammatically intact but lacking in the nouns and verbs that carry the informational load of the message. Auditory comprehension is not noticeably impaired in anomic aphasia.

While the prototypical pattern of anomic aphasia accompanies a lesion of the posterior parietal lobe (angular gyrus), anomic aphasics may have lesions elsewhere. The term has come to include disorders of word finding having somewhat differing clinical features and diverse causative lesions. In fact, isolated impairment of word finding is the most common language problem to appear after closed head injury or with a brain tumor remote from the language zone.

Patients who are anomic following a parietal or temporoparietal lesion have a number of distinctive characteristics, both in the quality of their output and in associated deficits, which do not emerge from a simple consideration of their performance profile. They often have some degree of press of speech and spontaneously use "empty" circumlocution as they encounter lexical terms that do not come to mind. Because of their lesion site, the course of their aphasia may show that the current picture evolved from a full Wernicke's aphasia. Similarly, involvement of the angular gyrus region may result in a severe reading and writing disorder.

Anomia with little other impairment of language is also seen in patients who have suffered a subcortical left frontal lobe lesion. These patients may have a tendency toward the pattern of transcortical motor aphasia, in that they have little to say on their own but repeat extremely well. Even in those frontal cases where there is no impairment in spontaneity of conversational speech, however, we do not see the press of circumlocutory speech shown by patients with posterior speech zone lesions. Another feature occasionally encountered in patients with "frontal anomia" is the impulsive production of a totally unrelated word or the completion of a phonemic cue with an inappropriate word. For example, when primed with "ca" for the picture of a cactus, the patient may say "cabbage" but unconcernedly acknowledge that it is not right.

Conduction Aphasia

In the form of fluent aphasia known as *conduction aphasia,* the ability to repeat after the examiner is selectively impaired, while auditory comprehension is typically mildly or minimally affected. Free conversation is marked by fairly frequent literal paraphasia, which the patient tries to self-correct, for example, "I dropped the paker... caker...

cape ... P.A.P.E.R. ... paper on the floor." The combination of good comprehension and literal paraphasia in a basically fluent delivery is usually enough to identify this syndrome, and repetition problems are almost invariably associated with this pattern. As we have already described the factors affecting repetition and the approach to examining it, this need not be repeated here. It is to be noted that conduction aphasics are almost unique in making many repeated attempted self-corrections during naming tests without appearing to lose track of the target for which they are aiming (Kohn, 1984).

Transcortical Sensory Aphasia

Associated with extensive deep-going lesions of the parietotemporal region, transcortical sensory aphasia is similar to Wernicke's aphasia, in that patients are paraphasic, impaired in comprehension, and anomic. The distinctive difference is their remarkably accurate repetition. Like transcortical motor aphasics, they also tend to reuse the words of the examiner in beginning to answer a question. A striking feature in some of these patients is their ability to read aloud fluently but without comprehension.

Pure Aphasias

While aphasias affecting a single language modality are relatively uncommon, they are extremely interesting for case study and for the investigation of relationships between lesion site and behavioral deficit. Their evaluation is improved by the examiner's alertness to a number of special features.

PURE ALEXIA.   Also known as *word blindness* and *alexia without agraphia,* pure alexia is a selective impairment of reading invariably due to interruption of visual input to the left posterior language area. Such an interruption may be due to a lesion lying deep in the left occipitoparietal area or, more commonly, a lesion destroying both the left visual cortex and the posterior portion (splenium) of the corpus callosum. The clinical features are a marked loss of ability to recognize words at sight, while the ability to write and the ability to understand orally spelled words is unaffected or nearly so. Short words and individual letters may be recognized, and the examiner should be alert to the patient's reading some words by spelling them to him- or herself.

PURE WORD DEAFNESS.   In the rare disorder known as *pure word deafness,* speech can no longer be understood, although there are few or no aphasic elements in speech production, reading, or writing. Auditory acuity may be intact or, if affected, not sufficiently impaired to account for the comprehension deficit. Some patients with pure word deafness are considerably aided by lip reading.

The speech of these patients may be quite normal. In cases that are less "pure," some features of Wernicke's aphasia, in the form of paraphasic errors, may be present. The intactness of reading comprehension and of writing distinguish this condition from Wernicke's aphasia.

Pure word deafness is usually produced by bilateral lesions in the temporal lobe, but it is also known to occur with a unilateral left temporal lesion small enough to affect the primary auditory center and underlying white matter without destroying Wernicke's area.

Patients with pure word deafness should always be examined for their ability to recognize environmental nonspeech sounds (auditory agnosia), for their ability to sing and to recognize familiar melodies, and for their ability to count taps. Auditory agnosia of some degree is often present, but complete loss of expressive and receptive melodic ability and of ability to count taps is almost always found in cases with bilateral injury.

SUMMARY

The neuropsychologist is frequently called on to distinguish aphasia from other speech and language impediments and to make inferences concerning the lesion which produces the deficit. In this chapter the major factors to be attended to are first reviewed and described. These include fluency of output, articulation, word finding, paraphasic errors, auditory comprehension, reading, and writing. It is emphasized that an informative evaluation takes into account the known qualitative features of aphasic symptoms, and not merely the level of success on achievement tests.

The principles of an aphasia examination are reviewed, beginning with an assessment of free conversation and proceeding to the examination of specific modalities of input and output. The objective is to provide the examiner with the basic knowledge needed to conduct either a bedside examination or a more elaborate test. Some of the better known published examinations are reviewed.

The chapter concludes with a review of the syndromes of aphasia and their associated anatomical bases.

ACKNOWLEDGMENTS

The preparation of this chapter was supported in part by the Medical Research Service of the Veterans Administration and in part by USPHS Grants NS 07615 and NS 06209.

REFERENCES

Benson, D.F. (1967). Fluency in aphasia: Correlation with radioactive scan localization. *Cortex, 3,* 373–394.

Blumstein, S., Goodglass, H., Statlender, S., & Biber, C. (1983). Comprehension strategies determining reference in aphasia: A study of reflexivization. *Brain and Language, 18,* 115–127.

DeRenzi, E., & Vignolo, L.A. (1962). The token test: A sensitive test to detect receptive disturbances in aphasics. *Brain, 85,* 665–678.

Eisenson, J. (1954). *Examining for aphasia* (rev. ed.). New York: Psychological Corporation.

Geschwind, N., & Behan, P. (1982). Left-handedness: Association with immune disease, migraine, and developmental learning disorder. *Transactions of the National Academy of Science, 79,* 5097–5100.

Goodglass, H., Barton, M.I., & Kaplan, E. (1968). Sensory modality and object naming in aphasia. *Journal of Speech and Hearing Research, 11,* 488–491.

Goodglass, H., & Kaplan, E. (1972). *The assessment of aphasia and related disorders* (rev. ed. 1983). Philadelphia: Lea & Febiger.

Goodglass, H., Klein, B., Carey, P., & Jones, K.J. (1966). Specific semantic word categories in aphasia. *Cortex, 2,* 74–89.

Goodglass, H., Quadfasel, F.A., & Timberlake, W.H. (1964). Phrase length and the type and severity of aphasia. *Cortex, 1,* 133–153.

Holland, A.L. (1980). *Communicative activities in daily living: A test of functional communication for aphasic adults.* Baltimore: University Park Press.

Kaplan, E., Goodglass, H., & Weintraub, S. (1983). *The Boston Naming Test.* Philadelphia: Lea & Febiger.

Kerschensteiner, M., Poeck, K., & Brunner, E. (1972). The fluency-nonfluency dimension in the classification of aphasic speech. *Cortex, 8,* 233–247.

Kertesz, A. (1979). *Aphasia and associated disorders: Taxonomy, localization, and recovery.* New York: Grune & Stratton.

Kohn, S. (1984). The nature of the phonological disorder in conduction aphasia. *Brain and Language, 23,* 97–115.

Luria, A.R. (1970). *Traumatic aphasia.* The Hague: Mouton.

Orgass, B., & Poeck, K. (1966). Clinical validation of a new test for aphasia: An experimental study of the token test. *Cortex, 2,* 222–243.

Poeck, K., Kerschensteiner, M., & Hartje, N. (1972). A quantitative study of language understanding in fluent and non-fluent aphasia. *Cortex, 8,* 299–303.

Porch, B. (1967). *The Porch index of communicative ability.* Palo Alto, CA: Consulting Psychologists Press.

Schuell, H. (1965). *The Minnesota test for differential diagnosis of aphasia.* Minneapolis: University of Minnesota Press.

Spreen, O., & Benton, A.L. (1969). *Neurosensory center comprehensive examination for aphasia.* Victoria, Canada: University of Victoria.

Spreen, O., Benton, A.L., & Van Allen, N.W. (1966). Dissociation of visual and tactile naming in amnesic aphasia. *Neurology, 16,* 807–814.

CHAPTER 8

Effects of Sex and Handedness on Neuropsychological Testing

Susan B. Filskov and Robert A. Catanese

The importance of demographic variables in the interpretation of neuropsychological test data has been acknowledged for many years (Parsons & Prigatano, 1978). The continuing paucity of normative data contained in the manuals of major neuropsychological test batteries is truly appalling (Golden, Hammeke, & Purisch, 1980; Reitan, 1979). Numerous studies have indicated the strong effects of age and educational-intellectual factors on individual performance (Fromm-Auch & Yeudall, 1983; Heaton, Grant, & Matthews, in press; Paucker, 1980; Seidenberg et al., 1984). Less well reviewed but certainly with experimental significance are the effects of sex and handedness on clinical neuropsychological instruments. The objectives of this chapter are to review the experimental and clinical literature and provide some perspective on how these variables may affect performance on neuropsychological tests.

SEX DIFFERENCES IN ABILITIES

It has now almost been taken as a given that males excel in spatial abilities relative to their female counterparts, while the reverse is true for a variety of verbal skills (Maccoby & Jacklin, 1974; McGee, 1979, 1982; Harris, 1980, 1981; Wittig & Peterson, 1979; Nyborg, 1983). McGee's (1979, 1982) review of the experimental literature suggests that males perform better on spatial tasks, such as Thurstone's Primary Mental Abilities Space Test (Thurstone & Thurstone, 1941), the Mental Rotations Test (Vandenberg & Kuse, 1979), the Differential Aptitude Space Relations Test (Bennett, Seashore & Wasman, 1974), and the Embedded Figures Test (Maccoby & Jacklin, 1974). In turn, females excel in language tasks, such as verbal fluency (Benton & Hamsher, 1977; Bennett, Seashore, & Wasman, 1974), spelling (Bennett, Seashore, & Wasman, 1974), and verbal learning (Ivison, 1977). Most evidence suggests that these differences emerge during puberty (McGee, 1979, 1982; Nyborg, 1983) and continue into old age (Cohen & Wilkie, 1979).

Explanations of these findings have come from a variety of sources. One widely held theory suggests that fundamental sex differences in cerebral organization of the brain account for the observed variations in spatial and verbal skills. Consistent findings indicate that right-handed males show more distinct hemisphere lateralization for spatial and verbal abilities, with spatial skills being represented by the right hemisphere of the brain and verbal skills being represented by the left hemisphere. In comparison, females show greater bilateral representation of these abilities (e.g., McGee, 1982).

Evidence for these lateralization differences come from numerous sources, including the clinical literature, which has shown that males with left hemisphere lesions exhibit more profound deficits in verbal abilities than do females with similar lesions (McGlone, 1976, 1978). In addition, it has been found that males with right hemisphere damage exhibit more impaired spatial functioning than do females with similar damage (McGlone & Kertesz, 1973) and that females with left hemispherectomies exhibit significantly more spatial deficits than do their male counterparts (Kohn & Dennis, 1974).

The experimental literature also supports the notion of greater lateralization of spatial and verbal abilities in men. Using dichotic listening procedures, it was found that males exhibit greater right ear (left hemisphere) dominance for verbal stimuli and greater left ear (right hemisphere) dominance for nonverbal stimuli relative to their female counterparts (Lake & Bryden, 1976; Knox & Kimura, 1970). Similar patterns of greater lateralization of functions in men have been found in the visceral and tactile modalities (Witelson, 1976) as well.

The exact mechanism by which greater lateralization of function translates to higher scores on measures of that function remains elusive. If greater lateralization suggests increased specialization (with the implication that this is better or more effective), it would explain the superior performance of males on spatial tasks. However, the same reasoning would predict males to be superior on verbal tasks, since males also apparently have more lateralized verbal abilities. Clearly, there is little if any empirical support for this (Maccoby & Jacklin, 1974; Wittig & Peterson, 1979). Conversely, it is also inconsistent to argue that greater overlap of verbal and spatial functions in women hinders efficient spatial processing in the right hemisphere (presumably through some "interference" mechanism) but facilitates verbal processing in the left hemisphere. Bryden (1979) suggests that apparent spatial abilities differences may be due to variations in subjects' *strategies* for completing the task rather than differences in spatial skills per se. For instance, McGlone and Kertesz (1973) found a high correlation between Block Design scores and an aphasia battery in females with left hemisphere lesions, suggesting that females may rely on their verbal abilities to solve spatial tasks more than men do (Filskov & Locklear, 1982). Newcombe (1982) suggests that greater lateralization in males may be correlated but causally unrelated to superior spatial ability. Clearly, the cerebral organization theory of spatial and verbal sex differences needs further refinement.

Hormonal variations have also been causally linked to apparent sex differences in spatial abilities, with contributory evidence arising from three different areas of research (Nyborg, 1983; McGee, 1979, 1982). First, the developmental literature indicates that before puberty there are few difference in spatial abilities between the sexes (e.g., Maccoby & Jacklin, 1974) but that during and after puberty, which coincides with the body's rapid hormonal changes, observed gender-related cognitive differences start to emerge (McGee, 1979, 1982; Tanner, 1969).

The second area of research implicating hormonal factors is the study of chromosomally abnormal individuals, particularly those with Turner's syndrome. Interest in these phenotypic females with only one sex chromosome (XO) rather than the normal pair (XX) stems from the finding that their intelligence level is normally distributed throughout the intellectual range (McGee, 1982; Garron, 1977) but that they concurrently exhibit impaired spatial abilities and hormonal abnormalities (Nyborg, 1983; Nielson, Nyborg, & Dahl, 1977; Alexander, Ehrhardt, & Money, 1966). Furthermore, short-term treatment with the sex hormone estrogen increases spatial ability in a group of Turner's syndrome females to a level equivalent to that of unafflicted, matched sisters (Nyborg & Nielson, 1981).

The third area of research implicating hormonal factors is the relationship of physical androgeny in both males and females to spatial skills. Peterson (1976), for example, found that less-androgenized (less-masculine) males, as measured by physical secondary sex characteristics (hip size, shoulder width, body strength, distribution of body hair) scored higher on Thurstone's Primary Mental Abilities Space Test (Thurstone & Thurstone, 1941) than did males with more masculine body types, duplicating the earlier findings of others (Broverman, Klaiber, Kobayashi, & Vogel, 1968). The reverse was true for females, in that more masculine females performed better on spatial tasks relative to their more feminine female counterparts (Broverman, Klaiber, Kobayashi, & Vogel, 1968). The evidence for hormonal contributions to gender differences in spatial abilities is intriguing, but, as with the case of cerebral lateralization theories, more refinement is needed, especially regarding mechanisms by which hormone variations affect changes in ability.

While cerebral lateralization and hormonal variation theories are receiving increasing attention, other theories attempting to explain the etiology and basic mechanisms of the expression of spatial skills have been put forth, including genetic models (Vandenberg, 1967; Harris, 1980; McGee, 1979, 1982); socialization–social learning models, in which sex differences are attributed to differential reinforcement of "sex-appropriate" behavior (Harris, 1979; Nash, 1979); and multifactorial models that argue that numerous socialization, genetic, hormonal, and neuropsychological factors combine to determine the level of spatial functioning (DeFries et al., 1974). The reader is referred to the reviews of Nyborg (1983) and McGee (1979) for more information on these theories as well as a more complete analysis of the hormonal and cerebral organization theories of sex differences in spatial abilities briefly discussed here.

SEX DIFFERENCES ON NEUROPSYCHOLOGICAL TESTS

While sex differences in spatial orientation are of great academic and clinical interest, the results of this literature review pose two major problems for the practicing clinical neuropsychologist, both of which stem from the fact that most of the cited studies come from the experimental, rather than the clinical, literature. First, while many of the cited tests may be effective as dependent variables in research investigations, their clinical utility for the type of evaluations conducted by the neuropsychologist have yet to be demonstrated. As such, these measures are typically not used by neuropsychologists today. Second, the sex differences in spatial scores rarely amount to more than one-half of a standard deviation, indicating significant overlap of scores between male and female populations, and thus limiting the practical utility of these measures, as they currently stand, for the individual clinical case (Lezak, 1983).

We now turn our attention to sex differences on the more popular neuropsychological assessment devices. It should be noted that both the major test batteries, the Halstead-Reitan and Luria–Nebraska Neuropsychological Test Batteries, do not report data on sex differences and do not even discuss possible confounding effects. The vast majority of studies found in the literature focus on sex effects of single tests from the Halstead-Reitan Neuropsychological Test Battery (HRNB) using small sample sizes. A large standardization of the HRNB is currently being conducted (Heaton, Grant, & Matthews, in press).

The Halstead-Reitan Neuropsychological Test Battery and Allied Procedures

Possibly because of its ease of administration, the Finger Oscillation (Finger Tapping) Test has been one of the more widely investigated neuropsychological test instruments, especially with unimpaired essentially normal populations. It is also on this measure that one of the most consistent and reliable sex difference appears (Fromm-Auch & Yeudall, 1983; Seidenberg et al., 1984; Gordon & O"Dell, 1983; Gordon, O'Dell, & Bozeman, 1981; Chavez, Trautt, Brandon, & Steyaert, 1983; Dodrill, 1979; Morrison, Gregory, & Paul, 1979; King, Hannay, Masek, & Burns, 1978). On this measure of motor speed (see Boll, 1981, for a complete description of this and other measures of the HRNB) males consistently outperformed females with both the dominant and nondominant hands. No studies utilizing unimpaired populations found contradictory results, but it should be kept in mind that most of the reports used a young adult population. Of the two studies reporting data on sex differences in older normative samples, Pauker (1980) found male superiority on this measure in an age-stratified sample. Additionally, Fromm-Auch and Yeudall (1983) sampled across the age spectrum and reported that males outperformed females from adolescence into old age.

It is also of interest to note that several of the studies found that group mean scores, especially for females, fell in the impaired range (e.g., Chavez, Trautt, Brandon, & Steyaert, 1983; King, Hannay, Masek, & Burns, 1978; Pauker, 1980) with respect to the cutoff score originally established by Halstead (1947) and maintained by Reitan (1955). This would indicate an unacceptably high false positive rate (incorrect labeling of the performance as impaired), especially for females, and attests to the need not only for new cutoff scores but also for differential cutoffs for males and females to account for sex differences. Despite the frequent observation of gender differences, few have bothered to publish separate normative data (Russell, Neuringer, & Goldstein, 1970, and Fromm-Auch & Yeudall, 1983, being notable exceptions). Morrison, Gregory, and Paul (1979) note that the observed sex difference on Finger Tapping may not reflect any neurological differences or cultural influences in dexterity training, but may actually reflect the larger hand size of the male, which may accommodate the apparatus more readily. Evidence for this hypothesis increased indirectly when Gordon, O'Dell, and Bozeman (1981) documented that males had significantly longer index fingers than did females. More direct supportive evidence of this hypothesis came from Dodrill's (1979) findings that when hand size was controlled for, sex differences in finger tapping speed disappeared.

Although the Grip Strength Test is generally considered part of the HRNB Allied Procedures (scores from this measure do not contribute to the Halstead Impairment Index), it is discussed next because it, too, is strongly influenced by the sex of the subject. Although not investigated as frequently as is Finger Tapping, the magnitude of the sex difference in favor of males is large enough to dismiss the notion that the difference could occur by chance (Gordon & O'Dell, 1983; Gordon, O'Dell, & Bozeman

1981; Fromm-Auch & Yeudall, 1983; Seidenberg et al., 1984; Dodrill, 1979). Gordon, O'Dell and Bozeman (1981) found that young college males could exert over twice the pressure on a hand dynamometer than could college females, for both the dominant and nondominant hands. Fromm-Auch & Yeudall (1983) found that the male superiority was maintained throughout adulthood among a mixed general population sample, although the magnitude of the sex difference was not quite as strong as that mentioned earlier. Again, the need for separate norms for males and females is apparent.

One of the more surprising findings was the sex difference that *failed* to emerge. Numerous studies and normative samples failed to elicit any gender differences on the Tactual Performance Test (TPT) (Fromm-Auch & Yeudall, 1983; Kupke, 1983; Chavez, Schwartz, & Brandon, 1982; Anter-Ozer, 1982; Fabian, Jenkins, & Parsons, 1981; Gordon, O'Dell, & Bozeman, 1981; Dodrill, 1979; King, Hannay, Masek, & Burns, 1978), and this was true for the Total Time, Memory, and Localization components, three scores that contribute to the Halstead Impairment Index. These results were surprising, given the strong spatial components of the tasks and the supposed male superiority on such tasks. Reitan (1955) believes that successful completion of the test requires an ability for visualization of the spatial configuration of the shapes in terms of the spatial interrelationships. Reitan (1955) also reports correlational data that suggest that the TPT relies on spatial abilities; he found that the Total Time measure on the TPT correlated highly and negatively with the Block Design subtest of the Wechsler-Bellevue Scale, a task that basically taps spatial abilities. In light of the previous discussion of male superiority on spatial tasks, it was surprising that sex differences so consistently failed to emerge. In fact, two reports (Fabian, Jenkins, & Parsons, 1981; Gordon & O'Dell, 1983) found that females were actually superior on the Memory component of the TPT, and two reports (Chavez, Schwartz, & Brandon, 1982; Gordon & O'Dell, 1983) also found females to be superior on the Localization component. Male superiority failed to emerge despite the method of presentation of the blocks (random versus standardized) (Chavez, Schwartz, & Brandon, 1982), the level of anxiety in subjects (King, Hannay, Masek, & Burns, 1978), or the type of TPT apparatus used (standard versus portable model) (Kupke, 1983). However, a sex of subject to sex of examiner interaction was found (Kupke, 1983), indicating that both males and females performed better when tested by an examiner of the opposite sex compared to subjects tested by an examiner of the same sex. These subtle interpersonal variables that may influence test performance might call into question whether true sex differences actually exist or whether psychometrists (traditionally a female job in many clinical settings) get better performances from male patients.

As with Finger Tapping, several authors have noted that the existing cutoff scores used by Reitan (1955) for the TPT may be too high. King and colleagues (1978), Anter-Ozer (1982), and Cauthen (1978) have all reported unacceptably high rates of incorrect labeling performance of subjects as impaired and suggest that Reitan's cutoff scores may be applicable only to subjects with a relatively high IQ. They suggest a readjustment of cutoff scores for use with individuals of average and less than average intelligence. Thus, while it does not appear that separate norms for males and females are needed for the TPT, the possibility of changing existing cutoff scores should be examined.

For the remaining tests associated with the HRNB, only limited research is available on sex differences using essentially unimpaired subjects, and most of these report that few if any gender differences confound test scores. Thus, based on two studies, no differences referable to gender emerged on the Category Test, Speech Sounds Perception Test, the Seashore Rhythm Test, and such allied procedures as the Trail-Making Test (Fromm-Auch & Yeudall, 1983; Dodrill, 1979). Additionally, Kupke (1983) failed to find sex-related differences on either the standard apparatus or a portable version of the Category Test.

Other scattered findings revealed no significant gender difference on Aphasia Screening errors or Sensory Perceptual Examination errors, although Dodrill (1979) found that males make slightly, but significantly, fewer errors on the constructional apraxia items of the Aphasia Screening Test using a modified five-point scoring system (Dodrill & Troupin, 1977). Clearly, no reliable statements concerning sex differences on these neuropsychological instruments can be made on such a limited research basis.

The Reitan-Indiana Neuropsychological Test Battery for Children

Although sex differences in children have received wide attention in the experimental literature, much less is known about gender differences in commonly used neuropsychological procedures for children. Using the lower age extension of the HRNB—the Reitan-Indiana Neuropsychological Test Battery for Children—Townes, Trupin, Martin, and Goldstein (1980) found sex differences independent of age effects for a group of 456 unimpaired kindergarten and second-grade children. These authors found boys to be superior in a combined score of grip strength and finger-tapping speed relative to the girls, a finding that extends across the age spectrum (Fromm-Auch & Yeudall, 1983). Boys also excelled in the Target Test, a measure of spatial memory. In contrast, significant differences in favor of the girls were found in Matching Pictures (verbal reasoning), the aphasia items of the Aphasia Screening Test (language skills), and a combined score on the Matching Figures and Matching Vs tests (serial perceptual matching). The authors conclude that primary school–aged boys appear to have an edge in the acquisition of spatial and motor skills but a relative disadvantage in the early acquisition of language-related abilities and pattern-matching skills. The latter abilities were found by the authors to be most highly related to academic achievement, suggesting that boys are at a developmental disadvantage during the primary school years, which may account for the overrepresentation of males with learning disabilities (Witelson, 1976). Because the sample used by Townes and colleagues (1980) for these analyses consisted of bright (mean WISC-R Full Scale IQ in the High Average Range), middle-class, Caucasian children, these sex differences may not generalize to all elementary school–aged children. It is interesting to note that the motor and spatial skills superiority of boys appeared before puberty, which is inconsistent with the experimental literature reported earlier that claims that differences generally emerge at the time of puberty (Nyborg, 1983; McGee, 1979).

Klesges (1983) found that the sex variable accounted for 20%–23% of the variance associated with test scores on the Tactual Performance Test time for the nondominant hand and the Memory Score, the Marching Test, and the Color Form Test in a group of young children aged 5 to 8 years. However, these scattered findings disappeared when older children (aged 9–14) were assessed with the intermediate-level test battery, the Halstead Neuropsychological Test Battery for Children. It is unclear whether the disappearance of these gender differences in older children reflects maturational factors (since, for instance, there do not appear to be any sex differences on TPT scores in adults) or whether the initial findings were an artifact of the low sample size (14 boys and 8 girls). In compiling norms for normal children on neuropsychological assessment instruments, other authors (e.g., Hughes, 1976; Knights & Watson, 1968) have not published separate norms for boys and girls, implying no sex differences.

HANDEDNESS DIFFERENCES IN ABILITIES

Although left-handers as a group make up approximately 10% of the general population and appear to be overrepresented in several unique neuropsychological samples, for example, mental retardates (Hicks & Barton, 1975), epileptics (Bolin, 1953), reading-disabled (Zurif & Carson, 1970), and alcoholics (Bakan, 1953), systematic normative data have not been collected. Indeed, most stringently controlled experimental and clinical studies exclude left-handers from their subject pool as a source of error variance. No mention of handedness effects is made in the manuals for the Halstead-Reitan Battery (Reitan, 1979) or the Luria-Nebraska Neuropsychological Battery (Golden, Hammeke, & Purisch, 1980).

A number of studies have found that left-handed persons display relatively more spatial deficits than do right-handed persons (Johnson & Harley, 1980; Levy, 1969; Miller, 1971). In a manner parallel to sex differences, it has been argued (Levy, 1969, 1972; Levy & Gur, 1980) that left-handers perform less well on spatial tasks relative to their dextral peers and that these variations occur because of less distinct hemispheric lateralization (and, presumably, less specialization of function) in sinistrals.

Before continuing, it should be noted that left-handers have historically been studied in a context of being inferior, unskilled, pathologic, and even morally degenerate (Herron, 1980). Over the centuries, they appear to have inspired fear, suspicion, and emnity in others. However, one does not have to travel so far back to find evidence of strong prejudice. In 1937, the noted psychologist Cyril Burt described left-handers as "fumblers and bunglers at whatever they do" (Burt, 1937, p. 287). In providing historical background, Herron (1980) notes that proportionately more sinistrals have been described as neurotic, stutterers, criminals, moral degenerates, and a variety of other unflattering labels impugning their character and ability. Most are aware of how prejudice against sinistrals has made its way into the vernacular of different cultures. The very word *sinister* is of Latin origin and translates as both "left-handed" and "evil," while in France, the word for left-handed (*gauche*) also means "clumsy." Hardyck and colleagues (Hardyck, Petrinovich, & Goldman, 1976; Hardyck & Petrinovich, 1977) have argued that deficits associated with left-handedness are a function of lingering prejudices that lead to selective inattention to those numerous empirical studies reporting *no* differences referable to handedness. Furthermore, they note that in those studies reporting differences associated with handedness, the degree of reduced functioning in left-handers is clinically negligible despite the statistical significance of the difference. In evaluating the literature on handedness, care needs to be taken in separating empirically based fact from prejudice-based rhetorical fiction.

As previously alluded to, spatial abilities remain the most controversial area in which deficits are still ascribed to sinistrals. Much of the controversy has been fueled by the work of Levy (1969, 1972; Levy & Gur, 1980), who found in her original study of bright graduate students that left-handers had a Wechsler Adult Intelligence Scale

(WAIS) Performance IQ on the average of 25 points lower than their Verbal IQ. Based on these findings, Levy (1969) hypothesized that left-handers have less complete cerebral lateralization of verbal functions than do right-handers and that the bilateral representation of language skills interferes with right hemispheric spatial functioning, thus leading to lower scores on tests designed to measure this ability.

The first part of the hypothesis has received support from a number of experimental and clinical studies. From the experimental research literature, Bryden (1973) used a tachistoscopic procedure in which he briefly flashed verbal material to each visual field of right- and left-handers. Results indicated that right-handers perceive visually presented verbal material better when it is presented to the right visual field than to the left, indicating stronger representation of verbal functions in the left hemisphere of the brain. In contrast, left-handers exhibited no differences in perception regardless of which visual field received the stimuli. Studies using dichotic listening tasks have yielded similar results in the auditory modality (Bryden, 1975; Satz, Achenbach, Patishall, & Fennell, 1965). When verbal material is presented to each ear, right-handers exhibit a clear right ear superiority, while left-handers show less difference between ears (Bryden, 1975).

A task-interference experimental procedure has also supported the notion that sinistrals exhibit less distinct lateralization of language functions (Berry, Hughes, & Jackson, 1980; Lomas & Kimura, 1976). For example, Berry and colleagues compared right-and left-handers' performance on two tasks (a right-hemisphere–mediated spatial task similar to the WAIS Block Design subtest and a left-hemisphere–mediated sequential task in which subjects had to subtract 7 from a typed list of four-digit numbers) performed separately and jointly. No handedness effect was found when the two tasks were performed independently. However, when the tasks were performed jointly, a significant advantage was found for dextrals, who presumably experienced no interference effects because of their more complete hemispheric separation of functions. In contrast, the poorer performance of left-handers was attributed to the hemispheric interference they experienced because of less distinct hemispheric specialization.

Finally, a body of anecdotal and clinical evidence has arisen supporting the hypothesis of differential cerebral organization in left-handers compared to right-handers. For example, Levy (1972) has reported that the recovery of language functions after cerebral insult is more frequent and rapid in left-handers than in right-handers, which is consistent with the notion that language is bilaterally represented in left-handers. Furthermore, for right hemisphere lesions, sinistrals are found to be twice as likely to exhibit language disorders as dextrals. Because of the methodological flaws associated with these clinical findings, this evidence must be considered weak. However, although some might argue that the cumulative data from the clinical and experimental literature indicate a preponderance of evidence in favor of less cerebral lateralization of verbal functions in left-handers, others would argue that the validity of such "supportive" data is questionable. Satz (1977), for example, has questioned the utility of using dichotic listening and tachistoscopic tasks to determine hemispheric dominance, arguing that factors other than cerebral dominance influence performance on these tasks.

The second part of Levy's hypothesis, that the bilateral representation of language skills interferes with right-hemisphere–mediated spatial functioning, has proved to be equally controversial. It appears that for virtually every study reporting handedness effects on spatial abilities (e.g., Levy, 1969; Nebes, 1971; Miller, 1971; Johnson & Harley, 1980), there is another study failing to duplicate the finding (e.g., Hardyck, Petrinovich, & Goldman, 1976; Newcombe & Ratcliffe, 1973; Anter-Ozer, 1982; Gregory & Paul, 1980). The inconsistent results are probably a function of failure to control for one or more of the important variables accounting for variance in the dependent variable, thus leading to erroneous or spurious results.

To the credit of the experimental literature, the sources of error variance in studying sinistrals are becoming increasingly recognized, if not always successfully controlled. Too often, left-handers have been treated as a homogeneous group, when in fact important differences within the sinistral population exist. For example, it was presumed early on that left-handedness was an all-or-nothing phenomenon, when in fact there can be degrees of left-handedness ranging from strong to weak or mixed handedness. It is those individuals with mixed handedness that are now hypothesized to have less distinct lateralization of brain functioning (e.g., Herron, 1980). The incidence of family sinistrality has also been associated with degree of lateralization. Hardyck and Petrinovich (1977) concluded that less distinct cerebral lateralization occurred only in those left-handers with a family history of sinistrality. Nonfamilial left-handers appeared to be equivalent to right-handers in that language functions were more distinctly lateralized to the left hemisphere and spatial abilities to the right hemisphere (see also Levy & Gur, 1980). Hand posture employed by the individual while writing was a third within-group factor that characterized left-handers. Thus, Levy and Reid (1976) found that left-handers who wrote in the inverted style (with pencil pointing toward the bottom of the page) were language dominant in the left hemisphere, while left-handers who wrote in the noninverted, "normal" style (with pencil pointing toward the top of the page) were language dominant in the right hemisphere. While these are some of the major hypotheses used to explain differences among left-handers, it should be noted that they are not universally supported (McKeever, 1979; McKeever & Van Deventer, 1980; Eme, Stone, & Izral, 1978).

Other sources of error variance confounding the study of spatial ability in sinistrals are related to issues of measuring and sampling. Any study purporting to measure left-right differences must be able to reliably assess handedness. Yet it has been found (Satz, Achenbach, & Fennell, 1967) that, on the basis of self-report, left-handers are more likely to be misclassified than are right-handers. These authors found that among those who reported left-handedness, only 61% were strongly left-handed, while 22% actually exhibited mixed handedness, and 17% were right-handed. While the use of handedness questionnaires reduces misclassification, such questionnaires are still essentially self-reports subject to the same error. Behaviorally anchored ratings scales show more promise in reducing misclassification.

The manner in which subjects are sampled in a study also critically affects results. Annett and Turner (1974) have argued that when unselected groups of right and left-handers are compared, there are no differences in groups in a variety of abilities. However, when analysis is done only on those performing at the low end of the distribution, there tends to be an overrepresentation of left-handers (see also Herron, 1980, Hardyck, Petrinovich, & Goldman, 1976). Thus there appears to be an important difference between sinistrals in the general population and those found in extreme groups. It would be convenient if the differences fell along one of the dimensions of left-handedness described earlier, but it appears that current models are still too simplistic to explain the complexities of brain-behavior relationships. Perinatal birth stress has been one hypothesis (Bakan, Dibbs, & Reed, 1973) offered to explain this difference, in that left-handedness and representation in extreme groups may both be the product of some pathologic prenatal or perinatal event.

EFFECTS OF HANDEDNESS ON CLINICAL NEUROPSYCHOLOGICAL TESTS

As with sex differences, the effects of handedness on neuropsychological functioning are of great academic and experimental interest, but once again it becomes difficult to make inferences on an individual clinical case based on group experimental differences that are small to begin with (if found at all) and that are found through assessment techniques not typically used by clinical neuropsychologists. However, unlike the larger available literature on gender differences, few studies have been reported on more popular clinical neuropsychological measures using unimpaired, normative populations. One obvious reason for this is the relative paucity of available sinistrals.

Gregory and Paul (1980) compared three groups of unimpaired college males (right-handers, left-handers with an inverted writing style, and left-handers with a noninverted writing style) on the Halstead-Reitan Neuropsychological Test Battery. For approximately 40 dependent variables, the inverted-style left-handers had scattered deficits on four measures when compared to the other two groups, who did not differ on any measure. The four deficient scores were on the Vocabulary and Picture Completion subtests of the WAIS, Trails B, and Trails Total Time. Of note was the lack of any differences among groups on the Tactual Performance Test and the Block Design subtest of the WAIS, both of which have strong spatial components. Anter-Ozer (1982) also failed to find significant handedness differences on the TPT, regardless of the sex of the subject, the degree or familial history of left-handedness, and the writing style of her subjects. These reports fail to support the experimental literature suggesting right-handed spatial superiority and, pending further research, provide initial data that suggest that no special considerations need be given to sinistrals on the basis of their handedness.

SUMMARY

While the sex of the individual needs to be considered within the context of other important demographic variables (e.g., age, education, and handedness), certain conclusions based on this literature review can be drawn regarding the effects of sex per se on traditional neuropsychological test instruments.

Gender effects play their most significant role on Finger Tapping and Grip Strength, with males consistently and reliably outperforming their female counterparts. Clearly, use of a single set of norms for males and females is inappropriate and will lead to a high percentage of false positive judgments, especially among females.

Despite a large experimental literature claiming a male superiority in spatial abilities, no special gender considerations need be made on the Tactual Performance Test. This was perhaps the most surprising finding of the review, and future research will have to address this seeming discrepancy. Perhaps our notion of spatial abilities is too gross and undifferentiated, and in time different subtypes of spatial skills will be identified, with a differential pattern of gender effects emerging. An alternative hypothesis may be that, despite the face-valid notion that the TPT has significant spatial components, empirical observations will determine that other factors outweigh and suppress any spatial ability factor intrinsic to the test.

If the Halstead Impairment Index as originally developed is to receive continued use (a question worth debating), cutoff scores that maximally separate normal from brain-damaged individuals and that take into account preexisting legitimate differences need to be reassessed. This is particularly true in the Finger Tapping Test, in which separate cutoff scores are needed for males and females. There is enough evidence to suggest that, on the TPT also, although only a single set of norms are needed, the cutoff points separating normal from impaired performance need reevaluation.

At least based on the gender variable alone, initial findings indicate that no special considerations are needed on the Category Test, the Speech Sounds Perception Test, the Seashore Rhythm Test, and the Trail-Making Test. Conclusions about sex effects on other allied procedures await further study.

In the assessment of left-handers, care should be taken to establish the presence or absence of familial sinistrality and indications of perinatal or postnatal trauma. Observations should be made of the writing style. Detailed questions regarding the strength of the handedness (e.g., the Annett questionnaire) should be asked. Individual instances of mixed lateral dominance may require further testing.

At this point, the sparse evidence suggests that special evaluation of test results of left-handers need not be considered, except to assume that higher scores will be obtained by the preferred hand on psychomotor tasks. However, in the event that inconsistent neuropsychological test findings are found for a left-handed individual, the possibility of bilateral or right-hemisphere representation of language should be explored.

REFERENCES

Alexander, D., Ehrhardt, A.A., & Money, J. (1966). Defective figure drawing, geometric and human, in Turner's syndrome. *Journal of Nervous and Mental Disorders, 142,* 161–167.

Annett, M., & Turner, A. (1974). Laterality and the growth of intellectual abilities. *British Journal of Educational Psychology, 44,* 37–46.

Anter-Ozer, N.S. (1982). Gender and handedness effects on tactile-spatial abilities. Unpublished doctoral dissertation, University of South Florida.

Bakan, P. (1953). Left-handedness and alcoholism. *Perceptual and Motor Skills, 36,* 514.

Bakan, P., Dibbs, G., & Reed, P. (1973). Handedness and birth stress. *Neuropsychologia, 11,* 363–366.

Bennett, G.K., Seashore, H.G., & Wasman, A.G. (1974). *Manual for the Differential Aptitude Tests: Forms S and T.* (5th ed.). New York: Psychological Corporation.

Benton, A.L., & Hamsher, K. (1977). *Multilingual aphasia examination.* Iowa City: University of Iowa.

Berry, G.A., Hughes, R.L., & Jackson, L.D. (1980). Sex and handedness in simple and integrated task performance. *Perceptual and Motor Skills, 51,* 807–812.

Bolin, B.J. (1953). Left-handedness and stuttering as signs diagnostic of epileptics. *Journal of Mental Sciences, 99*, 483–488.

Boll, T.J. (1981). The Halstead-Reitan neuropsychology battery. In S.B. Filskov & T.J. Boll (Eds.), *Handbook of clinical neuropsychology* (Vol. 1, pp. 577–607). New York: John Wiley & Sons.

Broverman, D.M., Klaiber, E.L., Kobayashi, Y., & Vogel, W. (1968). Roles of activation and inhibition in sex differences in cognitive abilities. *Psychological Review, 75*, 23–50.

Bryden, M.P. (1973). Receptual asymmetry in vision: Relation to handedness, eyedness and speech lateralization. *Cortex, 9*, 418–432.

Bryden, M.P. (1973). Perceptual asymmetry in vision: Relation to handedness, eyedness and speech lateralization. *Cortex, 9*, 418–432.

Bryden, M.P. (1979). Evidence for sex-related differences in cerebral organization. In M.A. Wittig & A.C. Petersen (Eds.), *Sex-related differences in cognitive functioning: Developmental issues*. New York: Academic Press.

Burt, C. (1937). *The backward child*. New York: Appleton-Century-Crofts.

Cauthen, N. (1978). Normative data for the Tactual Performance Test. *Journal of Clinical Psychology, 34*, 456–460.

Chavez, E.L., Schwartz, M.M. & Brandon, A. (1982). Effects of sex of subject and method of block presentation on the Tactual Performance Test. *Journal of Clinical and Consulting Psychology, 50*, 600–601.

Chavez, E.L., Trautt, G.M., Brandon, A., & Steyaert, J. (1983). Effects of test anxiety and sex of subject on neuropsychological test performance: Finger tapping, trail making, digit span and digit symbol tests. *Perceptual and Motor Skills, 56*, 923–929.

Cohen, D., & Wilkie, F. (1979). Sex-related differences in cognition among the elderly. In M.A. Wittig & A.C. Petersen (Eds.), *Sex-related differences in cognitive functioning*. New York: Academic Press.

DeFries, J.D., Vandenberg, S.G., McClearn, G.E., Kuse, A.R., Wilson, J.R., Ashton, G.C., & Johnson, R.C. (1974). Near identity of cognitive structure in two ethnic groups. *Science, 183*, 338–339.

Dodrill, C.B. (1979). Sex differences on the Halstead-Reitan neuropsychological battery and other neuropsychological measures. *Journal of Clinical Psychology, 35*, 236–241.

Dodrill, C.B., & Troupin, A.S. (1977). Psychotropic effects of carbamazepine in epilepsy: A double-blind comparison with phenytoin. *Neurology, 27*, 1023–1028.

Eme, R., Stone, S., & Izral, R. (1978). Spatial deficit in familial left-handed children. *Perceptual and Motor Skills, 47*, 919–922.

Fabian, M.S., Jenkins, R.L., & Parsons. O.A. (1981). Gender, alcoholism, and neuropsychological functioning. *Journal of Consulting and Clinical Psychology, 49*, 138–140.

Filskov, S.B., & Locklear, E. (1982). A multidimensional perspective on clinical neuropsychology research. In P.C. Kendall and J.N. Butcher (Eds.), *Handbook of research methods in clinical psychology*. New York: John Wiley & Sons.

Fromm-Auch, D., & Yeudall, L.T. (1983). Normative data for the Halstead-Reitan Neuropsychological Tests. *Journal of Clinical Neuropsychology, 5*, 221–238.

Garron, D.C. (1977). Intelligence among persons with Turner's syndrome. *Behavior Genetur, 7*, 105–127.

Golden, C.J., Hammeke, T.A., & Purisch, A.D. (1980). *The Luria-Nebraska Neuropsychological Battery*. Los Angeles: Western Psychological Services.

Gordon, N.G., O'Dell, J.W. (1983). Sex differences in neuropsychological performance. *Perceptual and Motor Skills, 56*, 126.

Gordon, N.G., O'Dell, J.W., & Bozeman, N. (1981). Variation in neuropsychological performance as a function of sex. *Journal of Psychology, 109*, 127–131.

Gregory, R., & Paul, J. (1980). The effects of handedness and writing posture on neuropsychological test results. *Neuropsychologia, 18*, 231–235.

Halstead, W.C. (1947). *Brain and intelligence*. Chicago: University of Chicago Press.

Hardyck, C., & Petrinovich, L. (1977). Left-handedness. *Psychological Bulletin, 84*, 385–404.

Hardyck, C., & Petrinovich, L.F., & Goldman, R.D. (1976). Left-handedness and cognitive deficit. *Cortex, 12*, 226–279.

Harris, L.J. (1980). Sex differences in spatial ability: Possible environmental, genetic, and neurological factors. In M. Kinsbourne (Ed.), *Asymmetrical function of the brain*. Cambridge, England: Cambridge University Press.

Harris, L.J. (1981). Sex-related variations in spatial ability. In L.S. Liben, A.H. Patterson, & N. Newcombe (Eds.), *Spatial representation and behavior across the life span*. New York: Academic Press.

Heaton, R.K. (1985). *Importance of demographic variables in interpreting scores on the Halstead-Reitan Battery*. Symposium conducted at the meeting of the International Neuropsychological Society, San Diego.

Heaton, R.K., Grant, I., & Matthews, C.G. (In press). Differences in neuropsychological test performances associated with age, education and sex. In I. Grant & K.M. Adams (Eds.), *Neuropsychological assessment in neuropsychiatric disorders: Clinical methods and empirical findings*. New York: Oxford University Press.

Heaton, R.K., Grant, I., Matthews, C.G. (In press). *Manual for demographic corrections of neuropsychological test scores*. Lutz, FL: Psychological Assessment Resources.

Herron, J. (1980). *Neuropsychology of left-handedness*. New York: Academic Press.

Hicks, R.E., & Barton, A.K. (1975). A note on left-handedness and severity of mental retardation. *Journal of Genetic Psychology, 127*, 323–324.

Hughes, H.E. (1976). Norms developed. *Journal of Pediatric Psychology, 1*, 11–15.

Ivison, D.J. (1977). The Wechsler Memory Scale: Preliminary findings toward an Australian standardization. *Australian Psychologist, 12*, 303–312.

Johnson, O., & Harley, C. (1980). Handedness and sex differences in cognitive tests of brain laterality. *Cortex, 16*, 73–82.

King, G.D., Hannay, J., Masek, B.J., & Burns, J.D. (1978). Effects of anxiety and sex on neuropsychological tests. *Journal of Consulting and Clinical Psychology, 46*, 375–376.

Klesges, R.C. (1983). The relationship between neuropsychological, cognitive, and behavioral assessments of brain functioning in children. *Clinical Neuropsychology, 5*, 28–32.

Knights, R.M., & Watson, P. (1968). The use of computerized test profiles in neurological assessment. *Journal of Learning Disabilities, 1*, 696–709.

Knox, C., & Kimura, D. (1970). Cerebral processing of nonverbal sounds in boys and girls. *Neuropsychologia, 8*, 227–238.

Kohn, P., & Dennis, M. (1974). Selected impairments of visual spatial abilities in infantile hemiplegics after right cerebral hemidecortication. *Neuropsychologia, 12*, 505–512.

Kupke, T. (1983). Effects of subject sex, examiner sex and test apparatus on the Halstead Category and Tactual Performance Tests. *Journal of Clinical and Consulting Psychology, 51*, 624–626.

Lake, D.A., & Bryden, M.P. (1976). Handedness and sex differences in hemispheric asymmetry. *Brain and Language, 8*, 266–282.

Levy, J. (1969). Possible basis for the evolution of lateral specialization of the human brain. *Nature, 224*, 614–615.

Levy, J. (1972). Lateral specialization of the human brain: Behavioral manifestations and possible evolutionary basis. In J.A. Kiger (Ed.), *The biology of behavior*. Corvallis: Oregon State University Press.

Levy, J., & Gur, R. (1980). Individual differences in psychoneurological organization. In J. Herron (Ed.), *Neuropsychology of left-handedness*. New York: Academic Press.

Levy, J., & Reid, M. (1976). Variations in writing posture and cerebral organization. *Science, 194*, 337–339.

Lezak, M.D. (1983). *Neuropsychological assessment* (2nd ed.). New York: Oxford University Press.

Lomas, J., & Kimura, D. (1976). Intrahemispheric interaction between speaking and sequential manual activity. *Neuropsychologia, 14*, 23–33.

Maccoby, E.E., & Jacklin, C.N. (1974). *The psychology of sex differences*. Stanford, CA: Stanford University Press.

McGee, M.G. (1979). Human spatial abilities: Psychometric studies and environmental, genetic, hormonal and neurological influences. *Psychological Bulletin, 86*, 889–918.

McGee, M.G. (1982). In M. Potegal (Ed.), *Spatial orientation: Developments and Physiological Bases*. New York: Academic Press.

McGlone, J. (1976). *Sex differences in functional brain asymmetry* (Research Bulletin 378). London: University of Western Ontario.

McGlone, J. (1978). Sex differences in functional brain asymmetry. *Cortex, 14*, 122–128.

McGlone, J., & Kertesz, A. (1973). Sex differences in cerebral processing of visual spatial tasks. *Cortex, 9*, 313–320.

McKeever, W.F., & Van Deventer, A.D. (1980). Inverted handwriting position, language laterality and the Levy-Nagylaki genetic model of handedness and cerebral organization. *Neuropsychologia, 18*, 99–102.

McKeever, W.F. (1979). Handwriting posture in left-handers: Sex, familial sinistrality and language laterality correlates. *Neuropsychologia, 17*, 429–444.

Miller, E. (1971). Handedness and pattern of human ability. *British Journal of Psychology, 62*, 111–112.

Morrison, M.W., Gregory, R.J., & Paul, J.J. (1979). Reliability of the finger tapping test and a note on sex differences. *Perceptual and Motor Skills, 48*, 139–142.

Nash, S.C. (1979). Sex role as a mediator of intellectual functioning. In M.A. Wittig & A.C. Peterson (Eds.), *Sex-related differences in cognitive functioning*. New York: Academic Press.

Nebes, R.D. (1971). Handedness and the perception of part-whole relationships. *Cortex, 7*, 350–356.

Newcombe, N. (1982). Sex-related differences in spatial ability: Problems and gaps in current approaches. In M. Potegal (Ed.), *Spatial orientation: Developmental and physiological bases*. New York: Academic Press.

Newcombe, F., & Ratcliffe, G. (1973). Handedness, speech lateralization and ability. *Neuropsychologia, 11*, 399–407.

Nielsen, J., Nyborg, H., & Dahl, G. (1977). *Turner's syndrome*. Aarhus, Denmark: Acta Jutlandica (University of Aarhus).

Nyborg, H. (1983). Spatial ability in men and women: Review and new theory. *Advances in Behavior Research and Therapy, 5*, 89–140.

Nyborg, H., & Nielsen, J. (1981). Sex hormone treatment and spatial ability in women with Turner's syndrome. In W. Schmid & J. Nielsen (Eds.), *Human behavior and genetics*. Amsterdam: Elsevier/North Holland Biomedical Press.

Parsons, D.A., & Prigatano, G.P. (1978). Methodological considerations in clinical neuropsychological research. *Journal of Clinical and Consulting Psychology, 46*, 608–619.

Pauker, J.D. (1980). *Standards for the Halstead-Reitan Neuropsychological Test Battery based on a non-clinical, adult sample.* Paper presented at the Annual Convention of the Canadian Psychological Association, Calgary, Canada.

Petersen, A.C. (1976). Physical androgyny and cognitive functioning in adolescence. *Developmental Psychology, 12*, 533–542.

Reitan, R. (1955). Investigation of the validity of Halstead's measures of biological intelligence. *American Medical Association Archives of Neurology and Psychiatry, 73*, 28–35.

Reitan, R.M. (1979). *Manual for administration of neuropsychological test batteries for adults and children.* Tucson, AR: Author.

Russell, E.W., Neuringer, C., & Goldstein, G. (1970). *Assessment of brain damage: A neuropsychological key approach.* New York: John Wiley & Sons.

Satz, P. (1977). Laterality tests: An inferential problem. *Cortex, 13*, 208–212.

Satz, P. Achenbach, K., & Fennell, E. (1967). Correlations between assessed manual laterality and predicted speech laterality in a normal population. *Neuropsychologia, 5*, 295–310.

Satz, P., Achenbach, K., Patishall, E., & Fennell, E. (1965). Ear asymmetry and handedness in dichotic listening. *Cortex, 1*, 377–396.

Seidenberg, M. Gamache, M.P., Beck, N.C., Smith, M., Giordani, B., Berent, S., Sackellares, J.C., & Boll, T.J. (1984). Subject variables and performance on the Halstead Neuropsychological Test Battery: A multivariate analysis. *Journal of Clinical and Consulting Psychology, 52*, 658–662.

Tanner, J.M. (1969). Growth and endocrinology of the adolescent. In L.I. Gardner (Ed.), *Endocrine and genetic diseases of childhood*, Philadelphia: W.B. Saunders.

Thurstone, L.L., & Thurstone, T.G. (1941). *The Primary Mental Abilities Tests.* Chicago: Science Research Associates.

Townes, B.D., Trupin, E.W., Martin, D.C., & Goldstein, D. (1980). Neuropsychological correlates of academic success among elementary school children. *Journal of Clinical and Consulting Psychology, 48*, 675–684.

Vandenberg, S.G. (1967). Hereditary factors in psychological variables in man, with a special emphasis on cognition. In J.N. Spuhler (Ed.), *Genetic diversity and human behavior.* Chicago: Aldine.

Vandenberg, S.G., & Kuse, A.R. (1979). Spatial ability: A critical review of the sex-linked major gene hypothesis. In M.A. Wittig & A.C. Petersen (Eds.), *Sex-related differences in cognitive functioning: Developmental issues.* New York: Academic Press.

Witelson, S.F. (1976). Sex and the single hemisphere: Specialization of the right hemisphere for spatial processing. *Science, 193*, 425–427.

Wittig, M.A., & Petersen, A.C. (1979). *Sex-related differences in cognitive functioning: Developmental issues.* New York: Academic Press.

Zurif, E.B., & Carson, G. (1970). Dyslexia in relation to cerebral dominance and temporal analysis. *Neuropsychologia, 8*, 351–361.

CHAPTER 9

Disease Process, Onset, and Course and Their Relationship to Neuropsychological Performance

Stephen P. Farr, Roger L. Greene, and Stephanie P. Fisher-White

In some contexts, brain damage is discussed as a basic, unitary dysfunction, that has a singular clinical picture regardless of underlying physiologic causes and etiology. In other sources, brain damage is discussed as a multifaceted entity with a unique clinical picture that depends on the specific etiologic factors and disease processes represented. The latter position is accepted as a basic premise by most neuropsychologists, yet the former position still has its advocates. Even in recent texts, it is not uncommon to find a statement such as "all organic brain syndromes, regardless of their cause and severity, are associated with disturbances of orientation, memory, intellect, judgment, and affect" (Sandok, 1975, p. 1060).

This chapter discusses briefly the basic premises regarding brain damage found in the standard psychiatric and psychologic literature and reviews the empirical data on the Wechsler Adult Intelligence Scale (WAIS) and Halstead-Reitan Neuropsychologic Test Battery (HRB) that can be used to support or refute such statements. Among the issues addressed are the following:

1. Does the tempo of the physiologic process affect the clinical presentation? That is, do slow, progressive processes cause fewer impairments and symptoms than do acute processes? Are the former more likely to produce permanent, irreversible changes in physiologic functioning while the latter produce temporary, reversible changes?
2. Are differential patterns of neuropsychologic functioning manifested by different physiologic processes?
3. Among commonly used neuropsychologic techniques, are some tests more sensitive to brain damage than others?

Although most neuropsychologists might assume that these issues have been resolved, there is no body of literature that addresses them simultaneously and empirically.

Each major disease grouping selected for inclusion in this chapter will be reviewed with an identical format. First, an overview is provided that describes the expected neuropsychologic deficits in each specific disease process. Because of space limitations, this overview summarizes only the general nature of the expected pattern of deficits, and no attempt is made to document each aspect of the clinical picture. The description of each type of disease process is integrated from a number of general references in order to develop a composite clinical picture (Bigler, 1984; Freemon, 1981; Golden, Moses, Coffman, Miller, & Strider, 1983; Lezak, 1983; Strub & Black, 1981). When appropriate, references to more substantive reviews of each type of disease process are provided at the end of the section for the interested reader. Second, the pattern of expected deficits within each disease process is translated into hypothesized performance on the WAIS and HRB. Third, the existent literature on WAIS and HRB data in each disease process is tabulated and summarized so that direct comparisons can be made with the hypothesized patterns of expected deficits.

After each type of disease process has been examined on the basis of the existent literature, comparisons among the various groupings of disease processes are made. These comparisons address the question of whether a specific disease process is more likely to affect adversely some neuropsychologic functions more than others. Next, the disease process is classified as slow or rapid to determine whether the nature of the onset of the disease process has a differential effect on WAIS and HRB performance. Finally, the disease are reclassified as progressive, static, or remitting to assess whether the course of the disease process has a differential effect on WAIS and HRB performance.

LIMITATIONS OF THE EXISTENT LITERATURE

The reader may be surprised that more samples of brain-damaged patients are not represented in Tables 9.1–9.7. There are several contributing factors. First, a large number of the early studies on WAIS and HRB performance used a generic category of brain-damaged patients composed of whatever disease processes were available. These early studies were important in demonstrating how brain-damaged patients performed on the WAIS and HRB as contrasted with normal or other reference groups identified as appropriate controls; however, they provide no aid in identifying the effects of specific disease processes and are not included in the tables. Second, a number of studies report on the performance of specific disease processes within brain-damaged patients but do not provide any raw data or other means of identifying how the patients actually performed on the WAIS or HRB. For example, a study that reports that epileptic patients performed more poorly on the HRB than did psychiatric patients cannot be used if the actual level of performance is not presented in some manner. Thus studies that do not provide raw data or some means of estimating the level of performance on the WAIS and HRB are excluded. Third, there is a tendency for many neuropsychologists to employ idiosyncratic tests in clinical practice and in research that preclude a basis for comparing their data with other samples. A study that reports that a specific category of brain-damaged patients performed poorly on a 10-item word list recalled after a 3-minute delay provides little information that is helpful to an effort such as the present one. Consequently, it is necessary to exclude a number of sound studies that rely primarily on tests other than the WAIS and HRB. Also, studies using either the Wechsler-Bellevue I or the Wechsler-Bellevue II are excluded, since most neuropsychologists use the WAIS or the more current Wechsler Adult Intelligence Scale—Revised (WAIS-R).

Thus, a limited number of studies can be used to contrast systematically the effects of different disease processes on standard measures; they consist of efforts that identify specific diagnostic categories of brain-damaged patients and present raw data on either the WAIS or the HRB. Even though both techniques frequently are employed in neuropsychologic evaluations, few studies have reported data on *both* the WAIS subtests and the HRB. Consequently, comparisons between WAIS and HRB performance for a specific disease process are in many cases quite difficult to make solely from the existing literature. While the review of the literature discussed is comprehensive, it is not exhaustive, and it is possible that an appropriate study may have been overlooked.

DEFICIT AND DISEASE CLASSIFICATION

Seven separate diagnostic categories of brain-damaged patients are contrasted in terms of performance on the WAIS and the HRB. Then, in order to examine the issue of onset and course, two onset and three disease course groups are formed from the diagnostic classifications. Group composition takes the following form:

   I. Diagnostic groups
     A. Head trauma
     B. Neoplasm
     C. Cerebrovascular (stroke)
     D. Degenerative
     E. Epilepsy
     F. Alcoholic
     G. Learning disability
  II. Onset groups
     A. Slow (neoplasm, degenerative, epilepsy, alcoholic, learning disability)
     B. Rapid (head trauma, cerebrovascular)
 III. Course groups
     A. Static (epilepsy, learning disability)
     B. Progressive (neoplasm, degenerative, alcoholic)
     C. Remitting (head trauma, cerebrovascular)

Each of these disease process, onset, and course groups is discussed in turn. First the WAIS and then the HRB performance for each diagnostic group are reviewed. Each section concludes by listing those WAIS and HRB tests most and least affected by the particular disease under consideration. After the basic data have been provided for each disease process, comparisons among these groups are made to illuminate the various issues presented.

For convenience, the HRB tests are identified by the following short forms: Categories (Category Test); TPT Total Time (Tactual Performance Test); TPT Mem. (TPT Memory); TPT Loc. (TPT Localization); TPT Time Right (Right Hand); TPT Time Left (Left Hand); TPT Time Both (Both Hands); Rhythm (Seashore Rhythm Test); Speech (Speech Sounds Perception Test); Tapping Right (Finger Tapping Test, Right

Hand); Tapping Left (Finger Tapping Test, Left Hand); Trails A (Trail-making Test, Part A); and Trails B (Trail-making Test, Part B).

HEAD TRAUMA

The specific neuropsychologic deficits seen in closed head injuries are a direct function of the severity of the injury and the patient's age. In general, the more severe the injury and the older the patient, the more serious are the observed deficits. The severity of the injury is usually assessed by the duration of coma and the length of the posttraumatic amnesia. When the coma persists for more than 6–24 hours and/or the posttraumatic amnesia is greater than 1–7 days, the injury is defined as severe. Levin, Benton, and Grossman (1982) and Brooks (1984) have provided an excellent overview of the research on closed head trauma that should be consulted by any serious student of this form of neuropsychologic insult.

Since a closed head injury is not focalized, the neuropsychologic deficits are assumed to be bilateral without clear localization. The classic symptoms of a closed head injury are attention and concentration difficulties, memory problems, and emotional changes. Insomnia, headaches, and dizziness frequently are reported in milder closed head injuries but less frequently in more severe injuries. After the acute recovery phase, limited deficits are seen in old and overlearned verbal abilities. In addition, in more severe head injuries, significant deficits in problem-solving and higher conceptual processes are expected.

When this pattern of neuropsychologic deficits is integrated into a clinical picture, the following WAIS and HRB results are expected. First, Verbal IQ should be higher than Performance IQ, and scores on Information and Vocabulary should be higher than the other subtests on the WAIS, since they assess old and overlearned, verbal abilities. Second, performance on Arithmetic, Digit Symbol, and Rhythm should be affected adversely, since they require sustained attention and concentration. Finally, performance on Categories and Trails B should be relatively poorer than on the other HRB tests, since they require higher conceptual processes and problem-solving abilities.

Table 9.1 provides a summary of the quantitative data available on the WAIS and HRB in head trauma samples. Weighted totals based on the sample sizes for each study are provided in Table 9.1 to summarize the data. Russell, Neuringer, and Goldstein (1970) rating equivalents also are provided as a separate row for the HRB data so that comparisons can be made directly among the various HRB tests.

The head trauma patients showed a mild, general deficit on the WAIS. Performance IQ and most Performance subtests were more adversely affected than were Verbal IQ and subtests; and while scores on Verbal subtests seemed to be affected to approximately the same degree (with the exception of Comprehension), those on Performance subtests displayed more variation. Performance on Picture Completion was affected only minimally and was in the same general range as that on most of the Verbal subtests. Digit Symbol was the most adversely affected of all the Performance subtests, as had been expected. But the relative rankings on Object Assembly and Block Design would not have been predicted, since Block Design is usually seen as being very sensitive to neuropsychologic deficits.

Most of the HRB tests also demonstrated a mild deficit, which would be expected with head trauma. However, a surprising finding was that performance on Trails A,

Table 9.1. Summary of Relevant Variables in Studies of Head Trauma Patients

Study	Patient Type	N M	N F	Age M	Age SD	Education M	Education SD	Patient Status	Time Post	Charted Measure
Becker (1975)	Closed head injury	10	0	20	(1.7)	—		Inpatient naval hospital	<2 wks	WAIS
Drudge et al. (1984)	Closed head injury	13	2	24.8	(6.3)	12.6	(2.4)	Inpatient university hospital	3 mo	WAIS, HRB
Dye et al. (1981)	Closed head injury	48		23.8		—		Outpatient university hospital	<3 yr	HRB
Farr & Greene (1983)	Generalized trauma	42		31.7	(12.9)	—		Outpatient university hospital	18 mo	WAIS, HRB
Mandleberg (1975) (A)	In PTA closed head injury	14		29.3	(13.8)	10.31	(1.4)	Inpatient university hospital	2–16 wk	WAIS
Mandleberg (1975) (B)	Out of PTA closed head injury	14		29.5	(14.3)	10.25	(1.6)	Inpatient university hospital	2–16 wk	WAIS
Mandleberg & Brooks (1975)	In PTA closed head injury	10		28.3	(13.4)	10.42	(1.9)	Inpatient university hospital	0–3 mo	WAIS
O'Donnell et al. (1983)	Generalized trauma	5	15	25.0	(3.5)	12.7	(1.5)	—	39 mo	WAIS, HRB

WAIS Study	VIQ	PIQ	FSIQ	Info.	Comp.	Arith.	Sim.	Digit Span	Vocab.	Digit Symbol	Pict. Comp.	Block Design	Pict. Arrang.	Object Assem.
Becker (1975)	93.7	80.3	87.1	9.1	8.6	8.2	8.7	8.2	9.6	6.4	8.5	6.6	7.3	6.1
Drudge et al. (1984)	85.9	74.7	79.3	8.0	6.7	6.3	7.8	7.3	7.5	5.7	6.2	6.5	5.7	5.7
Farr & Greene (1983)	93.1	91.1	91.5	9.0	10.2	9.2	8.9	7.4	9.3	6.4	9.2	8.8	8.6	8.0
Mandleberg (1975) (A)	97.5	87.4	92.9	9.1	11.1	8.4	9.2	8.8	9.9	5.6	8.8	9.3	7.3	7.5
Mandleberg (1975) (B)	105.9	92.0	100.1	10.3	12.1	11.0	10.4	9.8	11.3	7.0	9.5	8.8	8.2	9.1
Mandleberg & Brooks (1975)	91.6	73.2	82.4	7.5	8.1	8.6	8.5	8.0	8.4	4.2	7.3	6.3	6.2	5.6
O'Donnell et al. (1983)	96.3	89.5	93.0	—	—	—	—	—	—	—	—	—	—	—
Weighted totals	94.8	86.4	90.5	8.9	9.8	8.8	8.9	8.1	9.4	6.1	8.5	8.1	7.6	7.3
Number	129	129	129	109	109	109	109	109	109	109	109	109	109	109

HRB Study	Category	TPT Total Time	TPT Mem.	TPT Loc.	TPT Time Right	TPT Time Left	TPT Time Both	Rhythm (errors)	Speech Perception (errors)	Tapping Right	Tapping Left	Trail A	Trail B	Impair. Index (Halstead)
Drudge et al. (1984)	89.3	23.5	4.9	1.3	—	—	—	7.6	10.1	32.8	29.4	95.6	192.3	.8
Dye et al. (1981)	74.4	1.37[a,b]	6.0	2.9	—	—	—	7.3	12.5	43.7	—	54.8	140.3	.7
Farr & Greene (1983)	73.7	17.8	6.2	3.0	7.4	5.9	4.6	10.0	10.7	38.5	34.8	62.4	164.0	—
O'Donnell (1983)	60.4	25.5	6.4	2.2	—	—	—	6.6	10.1	29.7	—	71.8	139.5	—
Weighted totals	73.7	18.1	6.0	2.6	7.4	5.9	4.6	8.1	11.2	38.4	33.4	65.0	154.4	.7
Rating equivalents	2	2	1	2	1	2	3	2	3	3	3	4	3	
Number	125	125	125	125	42	42	42	125	125	125	57	125	125	63

[a] Calculated weighted mean.
[b] Min./block.

which was in the severe range of impairment (Russell, Neuringer, & Goldstein, 1970), was the most adversely affected of all the HRB tests. Scores on Trails B were also adversely affected, as were both Tapping scores; all of these measures were in the moderate range of impairment.

These data support a general pattern of neuropsychologic deficit in head trauma patients. First, as expected, there is a mild, general deficit in all areas, which is consistent with a generalized trauma. Second, verbal abilities are affected less than are performance abilities. Third, motor speed may play a major role in the decline in scores. Finally, Trails A and B seem to be particularly sensitive to the deficits seen in head trauma patients.

NEOPLASTIC PROCESSES

Neoplastic processes, or brain tumors, can be divided into two primary categories: extrinsic and intrinsic. Extrinsic tumors are space occupying masses that lie outside the cerebral hemispheres themselves. Intrinsic tumors, on the other hand, are infiltrating or penetrating masses that actually grow into the cerebral matter. Although there are many types of brain tumors, meningiomas are the best examples of extrinsic tumors, while glioblastomas and astrocytomas are examples of intrinsic tumors.

The effects of brain tumors on neuropsychologic abilities tend to be a function of tumor size, location, and rate of growth. Larger tumors produce more widespread deficits, both because of the direct effects of the tumor and the more widespread effects that result from the increased intracranial pressure. There is a gradual increase in impairment as tumors increase in size, and confusion and demented states may be seen in more advanced cases. The focal symptoms of a tumor are a direct effect of its specific location. Thus, virtually any neuropsychologic deficit can result from a tumor, depending on its location within the cerebral hemispheres. Finally, the faster the tumor grows, the greater the disruption that can be expected in neuropsychologic abilities.

It should be noted that tumors tend to be progressive. Intrinsic tumors may be rapidly growing. Their onset, however, remains less rapid than that of cerebrovascular (stroke) processes and head trauma. Extrinsic tumors (e.g., meningiomas) grow very slowly, and their effects may not be seen until late in life, despite the involvement of a rather large mass. Yet it seems that the increase in the mass of the tumor, no matter how rapid, still allows for some adjustment in functioning.

Certain apparent differences between the performances of patients with extrinsic tumors and that of patients with intrinsic tumors would be expected on both the WAIS and the HRB. Extrinsic tumors would be expected to produce less severe or less focused deficits, and they should involve a greater area of the brain and hence involve more neuropsychologic abilities. Intrinsic tumors, on the other hand, should produce more severe decrements in specific neuropsychologic abilities, while other abilities are left virtually unaffected.

Table 9.2 provides a summary of the quantitative data available on the WAIS and HRB in patients with neoplasms, but several general comments are necessary before interpreting these data. First, there is little published quantitative data on this disease process. Second, although it would make sense conceptually to separate neoplastic processes into subgroups depending on the hemisphere involved, small sample sizes and apparently limited differences by hemisphere led to our decision to combine the

Table 9.2. Summary of Relevant Variables in Studies of Neoplasm Patients

Study	Patient Type	N		Age		Education		Patient Status	Time Post	Charted Measure
		M	F	M	SD	M	SD			
Boll (1974)	Mixed	40	—	42.7	(11.5)	10.5	(3.5)	—	—	WAIS, HRB
Farr & Greene (1983)	Postsurgical (mixed)	8	—	28.6	(7.62)	—	—	Outpatient university hospital	44 mo	WAIS, HRB
Right										
Haaland & Delaney (1981) (A)	Presurgical (right)	15	—	47	(13)	11	(3)	—	—	WAIS, HRB
Hochberg & Slotnick (1980) (A)	Postsurgical (right)	6	—	43.2	—	—	—	Outpatient	12–30 mo	HRB
McGlone (1977) (A)		9	0	44.8	—	≈11.6	—	Inpatients	3.0 mo	WAIS
McGlone (1977) (B)		0	3	46.0	—	≈10.9	—	Inpatients	2.5 mo	WAIS
Left										
Haaland & Delaney (1981) (B)	Presurgical (left)	14	—	45	(18)	12	(4)	—	—	WAIS, HRB
Hochberg & Slotnick (1980) (B)	Postsurgical (left)	2	—	33	—	—	—	Outpatient	12–30 mo	HRB
McGlone (1977) (C)		5	0	58.3	—	≈10.1	—	Inpatient	1.0 mo	WAIS
McGlone (1977) (D)		0	6	42.5	—	≈11.6	—	Inpatient	1.4 mo	WAIS

219

Table 9.2. *(Continued)*

WAIS Study	VIQ	PIQ	FSIQ	Info.	Comp.	Arith.	Sim.	Digit Span	Vocab.	Digit Symbol	Pict. Comp.	Block Design	Pict. Arrang.	Object Assem.
Boll (1974)	92.0	92.4	90.5	—	—	—	—	—	—	—	—	—	—	—
Farr & Greene (1983)	94.3	83.8	89.4	9.0	9.8	7.8	11.0	6.8	10.3	6.1	9.0	7.3	8.2	6.7
Right														
Haaland & Delaney (1981) (A)	100.0	97.0	99.0	—	—	—	—	—	—	—	—	—	—	—
McGlone (1977) (A)	106.7	92.0[a]	—	—	—	—	—	—	—	—	—	—	—	—
McGlone (1977) (B)	96.3	92.0[a]	—	—	—	—	—	—	—	—	—	—	—	—
Left														
Haaland & Delaney (1981) (B)	94.0	94.0	94.0	—	—	—	—	—	—	—	—	—	—	—
McGlone (1977) (C)	84.2	92.0[a]	—	—	—	—	—	—	—	—	—	—	—	—
McGlone (1977) (D)	106.0	109.0[a]	—	—	—	—	—	—	—	—	—	—	—	—
Weighted totals	95.6	93.6	92.7	9.0	9.8	7.8	11.0	6.8	10.3	6.1	9.0	7.3	8.3	6.7
Number	100	100	77	8	8	8	8	8	8	8	8	8	8	8

HRB Study	Category	TPT Total Time	TPT Mem.	TPT Loc.	TPT Time Right	TPT Time Left	TPT Time Both	Rhythm (errors)	Speech Perception (errors)	Tapping Right	Tapping Left	Trail A	Trail B	Impair. Index (Halstead)
Boll (1974)	85.0	26.2	5.0	.3	9.9	8.3	8.1	7.9	6.1	45.3	35.0	122.2	207.7	—
Farr & Greene (1983)	—	21.2	7.0	1.8	8.6	7.8	5.0	—	—	47.2	39.7	83.6	229.6	—
Right														
Haaland & Delaney (1981) (A)	—	—	—	—	—	—	—	—	—	46.0	43.0	—	—	.6
Hochberg & Slotnick (1980) (A)	85.3	22.0	8.0	3.0	9.2	7.6	5.3	—	—	—	—	—	106.8	—
Left														
Haaland & Delaney (1981) (B)	—	—	—	—	—	—	—	—	—	42.0	48.0	—	—	.7
Hochberg & Slotnick (1980) (B)	89.0	22.0	—	—	—	—	—	—	—	26.5	33.5	—	96.5	—
Weighted totals	85.6	23.8	6.1	1.2	9.3	8.0	6.6	7.9	6.1	43.9	42.3	115.8	196.1	.6
Rating equivalents	3	3	1	3	2	3	4	2	1	2	2	5	4	—
Number	31	16	16	16	16	16	16	8	8	45	45	48	56	29

[a] Calculated estimate.

available data. Third, it also would seem that whether the neuropsychologic evaluation was carried out pre-or postsurgery should have direct implications for the results found. Again, the limited data suggest no differences between evaluations conducted pre- or postsurgery, so these groups were not created. Thus, the samples have been summarized in Table 9.2 as a generic neoplasm group, regardless of the time of evaluation. Finally, it would be interesting to be able to contrast the performance of patients with different forms of neoplastic processes, but these data have not been published. Clearly research is needed that evaluates the neuropsychologic deficits found in neoplastic processes as a function of the hemisphere of involvement, nature of the process (intrinsic, extrinsic, or metastatic), and the course of the process.

There are only limited data on WAIS performance in neoplastic processes, which makes any conclusions very tentative. There is little variation among the three IQ scores, despite rather marked variation among the subtests. Verbal IQ is only slightly higher than Performance IQ, and scores on the Verbal subtests tend to be higher than those on the Performance subtests. Digit Span and Arithmetic are the most adversely affected Verbal subtests, which could suggest deficits in attention or concentration, since these subtests are found on the Freedom from Distractibility factor of the WAIS (Matarazzo, 1972). The Performance subtests are much more variable and consequently are harder to summarize on such limited data. Scores on Digit Symbol, Object Assembly, and Block Design (in that order) are the most adversely affected among the subtests. Again, the finding that performance on Object Assembly is more adversely affected than that on Block Design was not expected.

The HRB data tend to more variable, and performance on these tasks was more adversely affected than performance on the WAIS. The various tests are in the mild to moderate range of impairment, according to the ratings of Russell and colleagues (1970). Performance on Trails A is in the very severe range of impairment, while results on Trails B are in the severe range. Categories, TPT Total Time, and TPT Localization are in the moderate range.

In summary, due to limited data, it is difficult to discern a reliable pattern of neuropsychologic deficit in neoplastic processes. However, it does appear that the larger deficits are seen in the areas of complex problem solving (Categories, TPT Total Time) and new learning (TPT Localization, Trails B). Still, the severe impairment indicated on Trails A does not easily fit into any pattern, since motor speed and verbal abilities tend to be relatively intact in this group.

CEREBROVASCULAR DISORDERS

Among the most frequent forms of brain damage are cerebrovascular disorders, or strokes. The essential characteristic of a stroke is disruption of the blood supply to a specific part of the brain. Strokes may be classified as occlusive or hemorrhagic. Occlusive, or obstructive, strokes result when a foreign object disrupts the blood supply; in a hemorrhagic stroke, there is an actual bleed into the surrounding brain tissue. In the latter condition, the brain deficits tend to be more widespread and are less likely to follow the arterial distribution. Strokes cause a variety of neuropsychologic deficits, since they may result from occlusion or hemorrhage in any of the cerebral arteries. However, because they tend to occur in only one cerebral hemisphere, they can potentially provide information on the lateralization of functions. Strokes have an acute onset, and frequently there is little indication of any impending problems, although transient ischemic attacks (TIAs) may precede a stroke in some cases. TIAs are characterized by temporary aphasic symptoms, confusion, and mild hemiparesis, which last for less than 24 hours and result in total recovery.

Since strokes are more likely to affect the left middle cerebral artery than the other arteries or the right hemisphere, the neuropsychologic deficits seen in a stroke of that artery will be described to illustrate the disease process. The classic signs of a stroke of the left middle cerebral artery are aphasia, right hemiparesis, and a right visual field deficit. The aphasia may be either receptive or expressive, depending on the exact location of the stroke. In any case, significant language and/or speech deficits are common. The right hemiparesis may vary from a total loss of motor function of the right side of the body to mild levels of dysfunction in only an arm or leg. The right visual field deficit has limited impact on the patient's neuropsychologic functioning and may be overlooked as long as the neuropsychologist is careful to keep test materials within the left visual field. Patients with such strokes would be expected to have lower Verbal IQs than Performance IQs. They should perform reasonably well on TPT and Tapping with the nondominant hand and demonstrate fewer deficits on these tasks than on those that require more language skills, such as Speech Sounds Perception. Categories might also be within the normal range, since the patient needs limited expressive language and speech skills for task completion.

The degenerative arteriosclerotic disorders might also be considered a type of cerebrovascular condition. These disorders have a very slow onset over a number of years and frequently result in dementia. Since the role of cerebrovascular factors are unclear in this category, and since the disease process is similar to that of a number of other degenerative disorders and in marked contrast to the acute onset and specific deficits seen in strokes, studies of the degenerative arteriosclerotic disorders will be examined in the next section, "Degenerative Diseases."

Table 9.3 provides the limited amount of quantitative data on the WAIS and HRB that are available on cerebrovascular processes. As noted above for neoplastic disease processes, there are no systematic data on neuropsychologic deficits in stroke patients, and studies tend to report only partial information on a limited number of WAIS subtests and/or HRB tests.

Right hemisphere strokes tend to produce consistently a lower Performance IQ than Verbal IQ. However, four of the seven studies of left hemisphere strokes also found that Performance IQ was slightly lower than Verbal IQ. The differences between Performance and Verbal IQs are clearly much larger in patients with right hemisphere strokes. It also appears that scores on the Performance subtests tend to be extremely variable in both right and left hemisphere strokes, while results on Verbal subtests tend to be less variable and less adversely affected in both stroke groups. Patients with visual neglect or who were seen as more severely impaired always performed more poorly than patients who did not have visual neglect or were only mildly impaired.

As with the WAIS, data from the HRB are sparse. The only consistent findings are that Tapping is slower in the hand contralateral to the stroke, but none of the Tapping speeds is particularly slow. Also, performance on Trails A and B is in the very severe range of impairment in both stroke groups.

In view of the limited data, it seems premature to describe a pattern of neuropsychologic deficits in stroke patients. It may be that the aphasic and motoric deficits are paramount in stroke patients to a degree that consistently precludes complete standard

Table 9.3. Summary of Relevant Variables in Studies of Cerebrovascular Patients

Study	Patient Type	N M	N F	Age M	Age SD	Education M	Education SD	Patient Status	Time Post	Charted Measure
Right										
Ben-Yishay et al. (1968)	Right	24		61.5	—	12.1	—	Inpatient rehabilitation hospital	4.7 mo	WAIS
Campbell & Oxbury (1976) (A)	Right with visual neglect	6		58.7	—			—	3-4 wk	WAIS
Campbell & Oxbury (1976) (B)	Right without visual neglect	8		58.8	—			—	—	WAIS
Costa et al. (1969) (A)	Right	19	31	—				—	WAIS	WAIS
Gruen (1962) (A)	Right	13		≈60		≈7		—	WAIS	
Haaland & Delaney (1981) (A)	Right	17		56.0	(13)	12.0	(3)	—	23 mo	WAIS, HRB
Inglis et al. (1982) (A)	Right	20	0	65.5	(8.3)	9.7	(2.2)	Inpatients	25.5 mo	WAIS
Inglis et al. (1982) (B)	Right	0	20	68.3	(11.2)	9.7	(2.9)	Inpatients	25.5 mo	WAIS
Karlin & Hirschenfang (1960) (A)	Right	16		58.0	—			Institutionalized patients		WAIS
McGlone (1977) (A)	Right	12	0	53.9	—	11.6	—	Inpatients	3.0 mo	WAIS
McGlone (1977) (B)	Right	0	9	53.5	—	10.9	—	Inpatients	2.5 mo	WAIS
Meyer (1970) (A)	Right (mild)	12		≈60	—	≈9	—	—	—	WAIS, HRB
Meyer (1970) (B)	Right (severe)	42		≈60	—	≈9	—	—	—	WAIS, HRB
Oxbury et al. (1974) (A)	Right with visual neglect	7		59.0	—			Inpatient	3-4 wk	WAIS
Oxbury et al. (1974) (B)	Right without visual neglect	10		58.8	—			Inpatient	3-4 wk	WAIS
Weinberg et al. (1977) (A)	Right (severe)	25		61.5	(9.8)	12.9	(4.2)	—	9.9 wk	WAIS
Weinberg et al. (1977) (B)	Right (mild)	34		65.7	(10.9)	11.4	(3.4)	—	10.5 wk	WAIS
Weinberg et al. (1979) (A)	Right (severe)	24		65.4	(10.6)[a]	12.5	(4.0)[a]	—	7 wk[a]	WAIS
Weinberg et al. (1979) (B)	Right (mild)	29		65.4	(10.6)[a]	12.5	(4.0)[a]	—	7 wk[a]	WAIS
Left										
Costa et al. (1969)	Left	17	29	≈60	—	—		—	—	WAIS
Gruen (1962) (B)	Left	15				≈7	(5)	—	—	WAIS
Haaland & Delaney (1981) (B)	Left	26		56.0	(7)	12		—	28 mo	WAIS, HRB
Inglis et al. (1982) (C)	Left	20	0	66.5	(9.0)	9.9	(4.3)	Inpatient	25.5 mo	WAIS
Inglis et al. (1982) (D)	Left	0	20	70.6	(10.3)	10.5	(2.3)	Inpatient	25.5 mo	WAIS
Karlin & Hirschenfang (1960) (B)	Left	12		64.5	—	—		Institutionalized patients	—	WAIS
McGlone (1977) (C)	Left	11	0	53.9	—	10.1	—	Inpatient	1.0 mo	WAIS
McGlone (1977) (D)	Left	0	8	53.5	—	11.6	—	Inpatient	1.4 mo	WAIS
Meyer (1970) (C)	Left (mild)	15		≈60	—	≈9	—	—	—	WAIS, HRB
Meyer (1970) (D)	Left (severe)	26		≈60	—	≈9	—	—	—	WAIS, HRB
Oxbury et al. (1974) (C)	Left	15		56.3	—	—		Inpatient	3-4 wk	WAIS

Table 9.3. (Continued)

WAIS Study	VIQ	PIQ	FSIQ	Info.	Comp.	Arith.	Sim.	Digit Span	Vocab.	Digit Symbol	Pict. Comp.	Block Design	Pict. Arrang.	Object Assem.
Right														
Ben-Yishay et al. (1968)	—	—	—	—	—	10.7	10.3	8.8	—	2.8	—	4.5	5.0	3.6
Campbell & Oxbury (1976) (A)	—	—	—	—	—	9.6	—	8.8	—	—	—	5.0	—	—
Campbell & Oxbury (1976) (B)	—	—	—	—	—	10.0	—	10.8	—	—	—	11.0	—	—
Costa et al. (1969) (A)	—	—	—	9	8.0	—	6	—	—	—	—	3	—	—
Gruen (1962) (A)	—	—	105.0	6.7	—	—	—	—	—	—	—	7.7	—	—
Haaland & Delaney (1981) (A)	111.0	99.0	—	11.4	10.8	11.0	11.0	11.4	11.8	—	9.8	7.3	8.1	7.0
Inglis et al. (1982) (A)	107.4	87.8	—	10.3	10.3	9.1	9.8	10.4	11.0	—	10.8	9.4	8.7	9.0
Inglis et al. (1982) (B)	100.9	96.4	—	—	—	—	—	—	—	—	3.5	4.0	3.0	3.5
Karlin & Hirschenfang (1960) (A)	—	—	—	—	—	—	—	—	—	1.0	—	—	—	—
McGlone (1977) (A)	113.2	97.0[b]	—	—	—	—	—	—	—	—	—	—	—	—
McGlone (1977) (B)	98.3	94.0[b]	—	—	—	—	—	—	—	—	—	—	—	—
Meyer (1970) (A)	92.8	89.4	90.9	—	—	—	—	—	—	—	—	—	—	—
Meyer (1970) (B)	89.0	76.2	82.6	—	—	—	—	—	—	—	—	—	—	—
Oxbury et al. (1974) (A)	—	—	—	—	—	—	—	9.0[c]	—	—	—	4.3[c]	—	—
Oxbury et al. (1974) (B)	—	—	—	—	—	—	—	10.6[c]	—	—	—	10.3[c]	—	—
Weinberg et al. (1977) (A)	—	—	—	—	—	—	—	9.5	—	—	5.5	—	—	4.3
Weinberg et al. (1977) (B)	—	—	—	—	—	—	—	10.7	—	—	10.1	—	—	12.6
Weinberg et al. (1979) (A)	—	—	—	—	—	—	—	10.4	—	—	5.0	—	—	4.5
Weinberg et al. (1979) (B)	—	—	—	—	—	—	—	11.0	—	—	8.1	—	—	13.9
Weighted totals	99.7	88.2	89.3	9.4	10.0	10.3	8.5	10.2	11.4	2.1	7.8	4.8	6.3	7.8
Number	132	132	71	103	53	78	114	207	40	40	168	174	80	192
Left														
Costa et al. (1969) (B)	—	—	—	9	9.3	—	—	—	—	—	—	6	—	—
Gruen (1962) (B)	—	—	—	6.8	—	—	7	—	—	—	—	7.8	—	—
Haaland & Delaney (1981) (B)	87.0	94.0	90.0	8.0	6.8	7.8	7.4	7.2	7.5	—	10.8	9.7	10.3	9.0
Inglis et al. (1982) (C)	84.1	99.4	—	8.2	7.6	8.2	9.5	8.4	8.2	—	9.2	7.4	8.7	8.2
Inglis et al. (1982) (D)	89.9	89.6	—	—	—	—	—	—	—	—	2.0	3.0	0.0	2.0
Karlin & Hirschenfang (1960) (B)	—	—	—	—	—	—	—	—	—	0.0	—	—	—	—
McGlone (1977) (C)	88.4	104.4[b]	95.6	—	—	—	—	—	—	—	—	—	—	—
McGlone (1977) (D)	98.3	95.3[b]	83.3	—	—	—	—	—	—	—	—	—	—	—
Meyer (1970) (C)	95.7	95.3	—	—	—	—	—	—	—	—	—	—	—	—
Meyer (1970) (D)	86.0	81.7	—	—	—	—	—	—	—	—	—	—	—	—
Oxbury et al. (1974) (C)	—	—	—	—	—	—	—	8.3[c]	—	—	—	7.4[c]	—	—
Weighted totals	88.7	92.8	88.7	8.3	7.8	8.0	7.7	7.9	7.9	0.0	8.2	6.9	7.3	7.1
Number	126	126	67	101	55	40	86	55	40	12	52	128	52	52

HRB Study	Category	TPT Total Time	TPT Mem.	TPT Loc.	TPT Time Right	TPT Time Left	TPT Time Both	Rhythm (errors)	Speech Perception (errors)	Tapping Right	Tapping Left	Trail A	Trail B	Impair. Index (Halstead)
Right														
Haaland & Delaney (1981) (A)	—	—	—	—	—	—	—	—	—	50.0	44.0	—	—	.6
Meyer (1970) (A)	—	—	—	—	—	—	—	—	—	—	—	135.2	238.9	—
Meyer (1970) (B)	—	—	—	—	—	—	—	—	—	—	—	185.2	371.8	—
Weighted totals	—	—	—	—	—	—	—	—	—	50.0	44.0	174.1	342.3	.6
Rating equivalents	—	—	—	—	—	—	—	—	—	1	1	5	5	—
Number	—	—	—	—	—	—	—	—	—	17	17	71	71	17
Left														
Haaland & Delaney (1981) (B)	—	—	—	—	—	—	—	—	—	41.0	49.0	—	—	.8
Meyer (1970) (C)	—	—	—	—	—	—	—	—	—	—	—	105.6	209.7	—
Meyer (1970) (D)	—	—	—	—	—	—	—	—	—	—	—	202.3	370.8	—
Weighted totals	—	—	—	—	—	—	—	—	—	41.0	49.0	166.9	311.9	.8
Rating equivalents	—	—	—	—	—	—	—	—	—	3	0	5	5	—
Number	—	—	—	—	—	—	—	—	—	26	26	41	41	26

[a] Combined from figure.
[b] Estimated from figure.
[c] Age scale score.

assessment and construction of a standardized sample group. Nonetheless, it would seem that the neuropsychologist could provide valuable information on other skills and functions within a solely clinical framework.

DEGENERATIVE DISEASES

Degenerative disease processes have attracted a significant amount of neuropsychologic research. The stage of the disease course is particularly important in degenerative disease processes, since the neuropsychologic differences are manifested primarily in the early stages. However, the onset of most of these degenerative disease processes also is so insidious that it frequently is difficult to establish precisely the course of the disease from its earliest stages. Thus, it is hard to be sure at what point in the disease course different samples of degenerative patients are being evaluated. In the final stages of most degenerative processes, the deficits are so widespread and the patient is so debilitated that few functions remain to be evaluated.

Three different forms of degenerative disease processes will be examined in turn: (1) Huntington's chorea, (2) a generic category of dementias, and (3) multiple sclerosis (MS). In the second category, no attempt is made to delineate Alzheimer's disease from Pick's disease, since this differential diagnosis is made most reliably at autopsy; nor are presenile dementias differentiated from senile dementias, since the patient's age is the only criterion for distinguishing between the two diagnoses. However, different patterns of neuropsychologic deficit that would be expected in primary degenerative dementia and cerebrovascular-related dementia are outlined.

Some preliminary comments apply to all of these degenerative disease processes. Labeling a disease process degenerative is sometimes assumed to imply a consistent and constant decrement in performance across all neuropsychologic functions. This is not characteristic of any degenerative disease process, for some functions (such as old and overlearned verbal skills) are particularly resistant to any form of disease process, while other cognitive functions may show disproportionate sensitivity to the existence of a widespread disease process. Also, many of these degenerative processes are characterized by fluctuations in the level of performance (e.g., short-term variations in multi-infarct dementia and periods of actual remission in multiple sclerosis).

Huntington's Chorea

Despite the relative rarity of Huntington's chorea, the disease has been researched rather extensively. Huntington's chorea is characterized by two main features: choreiform movements and dementia. During the early stages (usually defined as the first year after the onset of distinct choreiform movements), minimal intellectual deterioration is seen. The patient is distractible, there is a slowing of the speed of mental processes, and new learning skills and problem-solving abilities become the primary areas of deficit. Immediate and remote memory, however, are within normal limits. During this stage of the disease course, the patient is expected to have difficulty with Block Design, Digit Symbol, Object Assembly, and Trails.

As the disease process continues its course, there is a continual decline in performance until ultimately there are no focal symptoms. Speech becomes dysarthric, rather than aphasic, as is seen in the other forms of dementia, and there is a generalized impairment in memory, with even remote memory being adversely affected. Old and overlearned verbal skills are the best preserved and the last skills to be affected. Thus, performance on WAIS subtests such as Information and Vocabulary are expected to remain relatively constant until the final stages of the disease process.

Table 9.4 provides the quantitative data on the WAIS and HRB in patients with Huntington's chorea. Verbal IQ is consistently approximately about 10 points higher than Performance IQ. Performance on Information, Similarities, and Vocabulary appear to be virtually unaffected by this disease process. Scores on Arithmetic and Digit Span are affected adversely, which may reflect problems in attention and concentration. Results on all the Performance subtests appear to be affected adversely, with those on Digit Symbol, Picture Arrangement, and Object Assembly being most affected, in that order. It is unexpected that performance on Block Design is not among those most affected by Huntington's chorea.

Performance across all the HRB tests appears to be in the mild to moderate range of impairment, and those tests with large motor components (TPT Total Time, Tapping, and Trail B) are in the severe range of impairment. Thus, it appears that both the WAIS and HRB are sensitive to the motor components of Huntington's chorea.

Primary Degenerative Dementia

The primary degenerative dementias are characterized by a gradual and continual decline in the level of performance that cannot be attributed to any other organic causes. There is a progressive loss of neuropsychologic functions, including memory, learning, attention, and judgment. In the early stages of the dementing process, the patient demonstrates new learning difficulties, is distractible, displays constructional deficits, and shows decreased performance in complex problem solving and on abstraction tasks. The patient is expected to have problems with Trails, Categories, Block Design, Arithmetic, Object Assembly, and Similarities. Performance IQ is lower than Verbal IQ, since old, overlearned verbal skills (Information and Vocabulary) are retained.

In the intermediate stages of the dementing process, the patient begins to display a wider variety of intellectual, memory, and neuropsychologic deficits. Language skills begin to deteriorate, and the patient's speech becomes concrete and tangential with perseverative qualities. In the final stages, the patient becomes aphasic, apraxic, and essentially totally incapacitated.

Table 9.4 provides the quantitative data available on the WAIS and HRB in patients with primary degenerative dementia. All three IQs tend to be in the same range in this disease process and are about 15 points below average. Vocabulary appears to be the Verbal subtest on which performance is most resistant to this disease process, with scores on Information and Comprehension also relatively unaffected. Performance on Similarities is lower in this sample than with other degenerative disease processes. Results of all the Performance subtests are affected adversely and even more than would be expected based simply on the age of the patients. If the weighted totals for the WAIS subtests are converted into age scale scores, a notable decrease across all Performance subtests remains. Performance on Digit Symbol, again, is the most

Table 9.4. Summary of Relevant Variables in Studies of Degenerative Patients

Study	Patient Type	N M	N F	Age M	Age SD	Education M	Education SD	Patient Status	Time Post	Charted Measure
Huntington's Chorea										
Aminoff et al. (1975)	Huntington's	11	—	50.9		—			6.3 yr	WAIS
Boll et al. (1974)	Huntington's	8	3	46.9	(10.8)	12.2	(2.7)	Inpatients	>12 mo–10 yr	HRB
Butters et al. (1978) (A)	Huntington's (mod.–severe)	12	10	46.5		13.1		Inpatients	3–15 yr	WAIS
Butters et al. (1978) (B)	Huntington's (very mild)	5	1	36.2		14.2		Inpatients	>12 mo	WAIS
Caine et al. (1978)	Huntington's	12	6	48.1		—		Inpatients	1–8 yr	WAIS
Fedio et al. (1979)	Huntington's	5	5	40.8		13.0		Patients and patients at risk		WAIS
Josiassen et al. (1982)	Huntington's	8	5	45.5		12.7		Research patients	1 mo–8 yr	WAIS
Norton (1975)	Huntington's	5	1	46.8	(2.3)	11.8	(2.9)	—	3.9 yr	WAIS, HRB
Sax et al. (1983)	Huntington's	16	13	45.6	(11.4)	—		—	1–9 yr	WAIS
Taylor & Hansotia (1983)	Huntington's	5	11	39.5		11.5		—	6.4 yr	WAIS, HRB
Primary Degenerative Dementia										
Bigler et al. (1981a)	Alzheimers	13	6	63.8	(6.6)	13.5	(3.2)	Inpatient & outpatient	—	WAIS
Farr & Greene (1983)	Degenerative (mixed)	5		49.7	(9.9)	10.9		Outpatient university hospital	56 mo	WAIS, HRB
Perez et al. (1975) (B)	Alzheimers	10		62.2	(11.4)	13.7	(3.5)	—		WAIS
Russell (1980)	Degenerative (mixed)	35		—		—		—		WAIS
Storrie & Doerr (1980)	Alzheimers	9		72.		—		Outpatient	1.8 yr	WAIS, HRB
Cerebrovascular										
Boll (1974)	Cerebrovascular disease	40		43.7	(10.6)	11.3	(3.0)	—		WAIS, HRB
Delaney et al. (1980)	Transient ischemic attack	15		58.2		10.9		—	48 hr	HRB
Goldstein et al. (1970)	Caroid endarterectomy	6		66.0	(5.6)	9.7	(1.9)	Inpatient university hospital	—	WAIS, HRB
Matarazzo et al. (1976) (A)	Caroid endarterectomy	15	0	62.0		9.0		Inpatient university hospital	—	HRB
Matarazzo et al. (1976) (B)	Diffuse cerebral vas.	16		60.0		11.0		Inpatient university hospital	—	HRB
Perez et al. (1975) (A)	Multi-infarct	16		69.3	(11.4)	10.5	(4.0)	—		WAIS
Multiple Sclerosis										
Beatty & Gange (1977)	Multiple sclerosis	5	21	43.1		12.8		Outpatient	—	HRB
Goldstein & Shelly (1974)	Multiple sclerosis	20		42.7	(7.8)	13.1	(3.2)	VA	—	WAIS, HRB
Ivnik (1978)	Multiple sclerosis	14		38.0	(9.3)	12.5	(2.7)	Outpatient	—	WAIS, HRB
Marsh (1980)	Multiple sclerosis	17	31	35.6	(10.5)	13.8	(1.9)	Research patient	9.50 (7.43) yr	WAIS
Matthews et al. (1970)	Multiple sclerosis	11	19	33.9	(9.6)	12.4	(3.1)	Outpatient	<2 yr	WAIS, HRB
Reitan et al. (1971)	Multiple sclerosis	25	5	36.4	(9.6)	14.0	(2.3)	Research patient	10.43 yr	WAIS, HRB

WAIS Study	VIQ	PIQ	FSIQ	Info.	Comp.	Arith.	Sim.	Digit Span	Vocab.	Digit Symbol	Pict. Comp.	Block Design	Pict. Arrang.	Object Assem.
Huntington's Chorea														
Aminoff et al. (1975)	—	—	74.4	—	—	5.6	7.4	5.8	8.6	3.7	5.3	5.4	4.4	—
Butters et al. (1978) (A)	91.0	81.0	86.0	9.7	7.8	9.4	9.3	8.2	9.5	5.8	8.4	7.5	7.3	6.3
Butters et al. (1978) (B)	102.0	97.0	100.0	11.5	10.7	9.3	10.7	9.2	11.0	9.5	10.8	10.5	7.7	9.3
Caine et al. (1978)	93.6	91.0	92.1	9.1	9.1	7.6	10.0	7.1	9.7	4.3	8.3	7.7	6.7	7.3
Fedio et al. (1974)[a]	101	91	97	10.3	11.0	9.2	10.9	8.0	11.6	6.0	9.2	8.0	7.5	7.5
Josiassen et al. (1982)	101.2	91.8	91.8	11.3	9.4	9.2	11.3	8.9	11.2	8.2	10.1	8.5	7.9	8.1
Norton (1975)	84.2	68.3	76.3	7.3	7.0	4.8	8.8	6.3	8.3	2.3	4.8	2.8	3.8	2.8
Sax et al. (1983)	96.0	87.0	91.0	—	—	—	—	—	—	—	—	—	—	—
Taylor & Hansotia (1983)	84.8	79.1	83.3	8.8	7.4	6.6	9.2	7.2	8.6	5.9	7.0	7.1	6.8	6.1
Weighted totals	94.8	85.9	88.3	9.7	8.7	7.9	9.7	7.6	9.7	5.7	8.0	7.3	6.7	6.8
Number	120	120	131	91	91	102	102	102	102	102	102	102	102	102
Primary Degenerative Dementia														
Bigler et al. (1981a)	90.6	79.8	85.1	8.7	7.8	6.1	6.9	6.2	8.7	2.4	4.8	3.9	3.8	4.1
Farr & Greene (1983)	94.0	81.6	88.4	9.8	10.0	5.8	8.4	7.2	11.2	4.8	7.0	4.6	6.2	6.0
Perez et al. (1975) (B)[b]	65.9	67.0	64.6	4.9	—	2.8	1.4	—	—	—	2.2	3.2	3.3	—
Russell (1980)	—	—	—	10.2	9.7	8.5	9.3	9.3	10.3	6.0	8.9	6.7	7.1	7.3
Storrie & Doerr (1980)	96.	87.	92.	9.7	9.9	7.2	8.1	6.1	9.9	6.1	8.6	6.3	6.6	5.6
Weighted totals	86.4	78.5	82.2	9.1	9.2	6.9	7.5	7.8	9.9	4.9	6.9	5.4	5.7	6.1
Number	43	43	43	78	68	78	78	68	68	68	78	78	78	68
Cerebrovascular														
Boll (1974)	97.0	97.9	96.4	—	—	—	—	—	—	—	—	—	—	—
Goldstein et al. (1970)	107.2	103.2	107.7	10.5	11.5	8.0	10.5	8.5	10.8	8.0	10.2	6.8	5.8	8.7
Perez et al. (1975) (A)[b]	89.2	86.7	87.7	11.6	—	6.9	7.2	—	—	—	5.9	14.3	9.5	—
Weighted totals	96.0	95.5	95.2	11.3	11.5	7.2	8.1	8.5	10.8	8.0	7.0	12.2	8.5	8.7
Number	62	62	62	22	6	22	22	6	6	6	22	22	22	6
Multiple Sclerosis														
Goldstein & Shelly (1974)	110.7	96.3	104.2	11.9	12.9	12.3	11.6	9.8	11.5	6.1	10.6	8.8	8.4	8.2
Ivnik (1978)	107.7	97.7	103.4	11.5	12.0	11.4	11.1	10.5	11.0	7.5	10.0	9.7	8.8	7.6
Marsh (1980)	108.8	99.4	105.2	12.0	12.1	10.1	11.8	10.9	12.4	9.6	10.8	9.7	9.9	9.2
Matthews et al. (1970)	103.4	94.7	99.6	10.7	11.3	10.3	10.6	9.3	11.1	7.5	9.4	9.8	8.1	8.4
Reitan et al. (1971)	113.4	104.5	109.9	11.5	12.7	10.9	12.2	9.7	12.1	7.1	10.7	10.6	8.5	9.3
Weighted totals	108.8	98.9	104.7	11.6	12.2	10.7	11.5	10.1	11.8	7.9	10.4	9.8	8.9	8.7
Number	142	142	142	142	142	142	142	142	142	142	142	142	142	142

Table 9.4. (Continued)

HRB Study	Category	TPT Total Time	TPT Mem.	TPT Loc.	TPT Time Right	TPT Time Left	TPT Time Both	Rhythm (errors)	Speech Perception (errors)	Tapping Right	Tapping Left	Trail A	Trail B	Impair. Index (Halstead)
Huntington's Chorea														
Boll et al. (1974)	96.1	19.3[c]	4.4	1.5	6.3[c]	8.4[c]	4.6[c]	9.3	14.4	26.3	23.2	61.8	203.5	.9
Norton (1975)	114.5	—	—	—	—	—	—	10.0	23.1	21.8	17.0	—	—	—
Taylor & Hansotia (1983)	—	—	—	—	3.2[c]	4.1[c]	—	—	—	30.0	27.1	62.4	182.3	1.0
Weighted totals	102.6	—	4.4	1.5	—	—	—	9.5	17.5	27.3	24.0	62.2	191.0	.9
Rating equivalents	3	—	2	3	—	—	—	2	3	4	4	3	4	—
Number	17	—	11	11	—	—	—	17	17	33	33	27	27	27
Primary Degenerative Dementia														
Farr & Greene (1983)	87.0	25.3	5.0	.5	9.7	9.4	6.2	6.4	11.0	43.2	34.0	76.2	389.4	—
Storrie & Doerr (1980)	91.0	28.0	4.0	1.0	9.7	9.9	8.4	—	—	44.0	41.0	127.0	199.0	.8
Weighted totals	89.6	27.0	4.4	.8	9.7	9.7	7.6	6.4	11.0	43.7	38.5	108.9	267.0	.8
Rating equivalents	3	3	2	3	2	4	4	2	2	2	2	5	4	—
Number	14	14	14	14	14	14	14	5	5	14	14	14	14	9
Cerebrovascular														
Delaney et al. (1980)	86.5	57.8[a]	5.6	2.2	—	—	—	4.3	6.8	—	—	46.7	144.9	—
Goldstein et al. (1970)	79.2	29.7	3.2	.7	12.9	9.8	7.0	5.8	10.5	26.2	33.5	50.8	145.2	.7
Matarazzo et al. (1976) (A)	76.3	22.8	5.8	2.2	—	—	—	6.3	12.9	42.7	—	57.8	174.3	.7
Matarazzo et al. (1976) (B)	82.4	32.5	5.4	1.1	—	—	—	6.5	6.4	34.1	—	36.4	146.4	.9
Weighted totals	81.4	36.7	5.3	1.7	12.9	9.8	7.0	5.7	8.9	36.3	33.5	61.9	163.5	.8
Rating equivalents	3	4	2	3	3	4	3	2	2	3	3	3	3	—
Number	52	52	52	52	6	6	6	52	52	37	6	52	52	37
Multiple Sclerosis														
Beatty & Gange (1977)	—	—	—	—	—	—	—	—	—	39.9	36.6	42.9	130.3	—
Goldstein & Shelly (1974)	75.3	2.1[c]	5.1	2.3	2.3[c]	1.9[c]	2.1[c]	6.6	8.7	33.2[e]	33.2[e]	56.5	127.1	—
Ivnik (1978)	52.3	39.1	5.6	2.8	—	—	—	5.9	5.8	43.4	36.2	40.1	94.9	.6
Matthews et al. (1970)	44.1	1.0[d]	6.8	3.8	2.3[c]	3.8[c]	2.9[c]	5.9	7.4	31.5[f]	31.5[f]	50.3	123.4	.5
Reitan et al. (1971)	50.7	—	6.2	2.4	3.2[c]	3.8[c]	2.9[c]	4.7	7.9	37.7	32.4	64.4	137.1	.6
Weighted totals	54.1	—	6.2	2.9	—	—	—	5.7	7.6	36.5	33.7	52.1	125.6	.6
Rating equivalents	2	—	1	2	—	—	—	1	1	3	3	3	3	—
Number	94	—	94	94	—	—	—	94	94	120	120	120	120	74

[a] Estimated from figure.
[b] Mean adjusted for covariates of age and education.
[c] min/block.
[d] block/sec.
[e] Calculated.
[f] Calculated weighted mean.

adversely affected among the subtests, followed by that on Block Design and Picture Arrangement.

Although there is very little data on the HRB in patients with primary degenerative dementia and any conclusions therefore must be tentative, it does appear that this disease process is characterized by a rather consistent pattern of mild to moderate impairment across all the HRB tests. It is remarkable that Trails A and B, respectively, are the most sensitive indexes of this disease process within the HRB. The motor impairment evidenced on the HRB in primary degenerative dementia appears to be slightly less than that seen in other degenerative groups and much less than that noted in Huntington's chorea.

Cerebrovascular Dementias

Multi-infarct dementia, in contrast to primary degenerative dementia, has a more acute onset, and its course is more irregular, presumably reflecting its cerebrovascular basis. There also are a number of expected differences in the pattern of neuropsychologic functions in multi-infarct dementia that delineate it from a primary degenerative dementia. First, there is an inconsistent pattern of neuropsychologic deficit, which is thought to be the byproduct of multiple "minor" strokes. Second, the level of impairment tends to fluctuate on a short-term basis, and the patient reports that he or she can function better on some days than others. Third, memory functions tend to be less impaired than other neuropsychologic functions. Finally, other degenerative cerebro-vascular disease processes should not show the stepwise course characteristic of multi-infarct dementia and should be, in this way, similar to other degenerative processes.

Table 9.4 provides the quantitative data on WAIS and HRB performance in patients with degenerative cerebrovascular processes. This disease process is unusual in that it is one of the few in which there is considerably more HRB than WAIS data. Thus, the conclusions based on the WAIS data for this disease process must be viewed cautiously. All three IQs appear to be in the same range and only slightly below average. Scores on most of the Verbal subtests appear to be unaffected by this disease process, with results on Information, Comprehension, and Vocabulary actually being above average. Performance on Similarities, again, is lower than might be expected in this group, much as was seen in patients with primary degenerative dementia. Scores on the Performance subtests are so variable within and between the two studies that no conclusions seem tenable.

Results on all the HRB tests appear to be affected adversely, with most scores in the moderate range of impairment. The pattern of impairment on the HRB in patients with cerebrovascular degenerative diseases appears to be very similar to that seen in patients with primary degenerative dementia. The relationship between these two groups is different on the WAIS, however, with patients with primary degenerative dementia consistently performing slightly worse on all the Verbal subtests.

Multiple Sclerosis

Multiple sclerosis is an unusual degenerative disease in that it can go into stages of remission for as long as several years before relapse. The remissions tend to become shorter as the disease progresses. MS is characterized by a demyelinating process in the long motor and sensory tracts. As a consequence, the early signs of MS are likely to involve motor or sensory features, with little effect on neuropsychologic functions. Thus, the patient has problems with timed motor tasks, including most of the Performance subtests of the WAIS, TPT, and Tapping. In the later stages of MS, more neuropsychologic deficits are seen. The patient begins to demonstrate deficits in new learning, abstracting ability, nonverbal reasoning, and memory functions. In the final stages of the disease process, the patient evidences a global dementia.

Table 9.4 provides a summary of the quantitative data available on the WAIS and HRB in patients with MS. This patient group is one of the first in which the expected pattern of test results is actually seen. Verbal IQ is consistently 10 points higher than Performance IQ, with the Verbal IQs at the upper end of the normal range of intelligence. However, scores on the Performance subtests are affected less in this disease process than in the other forms of degenerative diseases. Results on Picture Completion and Block Design are almost exactly scale scores of 10, which is not typical of any other degenerative disease process. Performance on Digit Symbol again is the most adversely affected among the subtests, followed closely by performance on Object Assembly and Picture Arrangement.

The HRB data also are indicative of relatively few deficits, other than on those tests with substantial motor components. Performance on Categories, TPT Memory and Localization, Rhythm, and Speech is within the normal range, and patients with no other degenerative disease process have such a large number of unaffected HRB tests. In contrast, scores on tests with motor components (TPT Total Time, Tapping, and Trails) are all in the moderate range of impairment. Thus, there is a clear pattern of test results in MS that shows deficits in areas with substantial motor components, while other functions are within or above the average range.

EPILEPSY

Despite the fact that epilepsy is probably one of the most prevalent disorders in which neuropsychologists could play a role, epilepsy has received little systematic attention outside of the work of Matthews, Dodrill, and their colleagues. Dodrill (1981) has provided an excellent review of the work on this disease process, and the interested reader is referred to that source for additional information.

It is important, when considering the neuropsychologic sequelae of epilepsy, to determine whether the process is focalized and of a known etiology or whether it has a diffuse nature and an unknown etiology. The pattern of neuropsychologic deficits varies as a function of these two general parameters as well as a number of other variables. Clinicians need to be aware of these potential differences, since studies frequently use samples composed of different varieties of epilepsy. The types of seizure patients that are sampled and their relative proportions within the sample directly affect the expected pattern of neuropsychologic functioning. In general, a more severe and a wider range of intellectual and neuropsychologic deficits are seen in patients whose seizures are of long duration, are high in frequency, have an early onset, and are of unknown etiology. In such cases, the epileptic process tends to be more diffuse in nature. As a result, the neuropsychologic deficits are diffuse or nonlocalized; no characteristic pattern of deficits is expected. When the epileptic seizures are focal and localized to one cerebral hemisphere and are of known etiology, specific neuropsychologic deficits tend to reflect the hemisphere involved. It also is important to recognize that some forms of epilepsy do not have any neuropsychologic sequelae; this may be due to the relative mildness of the epilepsy or to the fact that deficits are apparent only during seizures and do not manifest themselves during seizure-free intervals.

Regardless of the type of epilepsy, disruption or interference with attention and concentration skills are a common problems, and distractibility is seen frequently. Patients with epilepsy are slower on speeded motor tasks and tasks requiring sustained attention and concentration. However, numerous studies (Matthews & Harley, 1975) have demonstrated that decreased motor speed performance on neuropsychologic tests is a function of the level of anticonvulsant medication rather than a result of epilepsy per se.

Based on the attention and motoric deficits common to most epilepsies, the following pattern of test performance is predicted. First, epileptic patients will perform more poorly on those Wechsler subtests that require sustained attention and concentration, such as Arithmetic, Digit Span, and Digit Symbol. These three subtests load on the Freedom from Distractibility factor of the WAIS (Matarazzo, 1972). Second, all three WAIS IQs should be lower in samples of epileptic patients than in patients with other disease processes. Third, performance on the HRB should be characterized by a general decrement in the level of functioning. Performance on tests that have a strong motor component, such as TPT, Tapping, and Trails, should be affected adversely. Performance on the Rhythm test should also be relatively poor because of the required attention and concentration.

Table 9.5 provides the quantitative data on the WAIS and HRB for patients with epilepsy. This disease process has the largest sample of any reported in this chapter, a reflection of the fact that it has been studied extensively. All three WAIS IQs appear to be nearly equivalent and about 5 IQ points below average. Only performance on Arithmetic and Digit Span is adversely affected among the Verbal subtests (likely reflecting attention and concentration difficulties), and results of all other Verbal subtests are nearly at scale scores of 10. The general pattern on the Performance subtests is a common one. That is, scores on Digit Symbol are the most adversely affected in patients with epilepsy, followed by scores on Object Assembly and Picture Arrangement. Also, results of Block Design are the best among the Performance subtests and only slightly lower than those of most of the Verbal subtests.

The HRB appears to be characterized by a very mild level of decrement across all the tests. According to the rating equivalents of Russell and colleagues (1970), results of the only two tests on which performance is in the moderate range of impairment barely exceed the criterion for that ranking. Thus, the HRB data are consistent with a mild, generalized decrement in all neuropsychologic functions.

ALCOHOLIC PROCESSES

In contrast to the dearth of research that seems to characterize some of the disease processes mentioned above, the neuropsychologic deficits associated with alcohol usage have received relatively extensive research attention. The issues of whether the effects of alcohol usage are reversible and whether the deficits produced by alcohol are diffuse or more characterized by right cerebral hemisphere dysfunction are beyond the scope of this chapter. However, a number of recent reviews of the work in this field (Miller & Saucedo, 1983; Parsons & Farr, 1981) may prove useful to the interested reader.

Table 9.5. Summary of Relevant Variables in Studies of Epilepsy Patients

Study	Patient Type	N M	N F	Age M	Age SD	Education M	Education SD	Patient Status	Time Post	Charted Measure
Batzel et al. (1980) (A)	Epilepsy (unemployed)	30	—	≃30.29	—	11.45	(2.21)	—	≃16.18 yrs.	HRB
Batzel et al. (1980) (B)	Epilepsy (underemployed)	8	—	≃30.29	—	12.75	(1.49)	—	≃16.18 yrs.	HRB
Batzel et al. (1980) (C)	Epilepsy (employed)	20	—	≃30.29	—	13.40	(1.90)	—	≃16.18 yrs.	HRB
Dikmen & Morgan (1980) (A)	Epilepsy (employed)	43	—	32.39	(9.63)	13.21	(2.63)	Outpatient	11.94 yrs.	WAIS, HRB
Dikmen & Morgan (1980) (B)	Epilepsy (unemployed)	67	—	31.40	(10.69)	10.77	(3.28)	Outpatient	14.12 yrs.	WAIS, HRB
Dodrill (1978)	Epilepsy	30	20	27.34	(8.98)	11.96	(1.93)	Outpatient seizure	14.90 (9.68) yrs.	HRB
Dodrill & Troupin (1975)	Epilepsy (mixed)	17		27.41	(6.04)	12.88	(2.0)	Outpatient seizure	13.64 (4.57) yrs.	HRB
Dodrill & Wilkus (1978) (A)	Epilepsy (mild)	35		≃27.3	(8.4)	≃11.9	(2.1)	Outpatient seizure	≃14.3 yrs.	HRB
Dodrill & Wilkus (1978) (B)	Epilepsy (moderate)	63		≃27.3	(8.4)	≃11.9	(2.1)	Outpatient seizure	≃14.3 yrs.	HRB
Dodrill & Wilkus (1978) (C)	Epilepsy (marked)	13		≃27.3	(8.4)	≃11.9	(2.1)	Outpatient seizure	≃14.3 yrs.	HRB
Farr & Greene (1983)	Epilepsy (mixed)	12		32.22	(14.99)	—		Outpatient university hospital	10.37 yrs.	WAIS, HRB
Matthews & Harley (1975)	Epilepsy (non-toxic)	28		28.3	(13.0)	12.4	(3.9)	Outpatient	—[a]	WAIS, HRB
Seidenberg et al. (1981a) (A)	Epilepsy	12	13	21.8	(6.3)	10.5	(2.1)	Outpatient (unimproved)	11.8 yrs.[a]	WAIS
Seidenberg et al. (1981a) (B)	Epilepsy	12	10	22.3	(6.1)	10.9	(4.8)	Outpatient (improved)	13.7 yrs.[a]	WAIS
Seidenberg et al. (1981b)	Epilepsy	18		20.3	(5.4)	9.9	(1.9)	Outpatient (unimproved)	12.1 yrs.[a]	HRB
Tureen et al. (1968)	Epilepsy	117	60	21.9		11.5		Outpatient		HRB

WAIS Study	VIQ	PIQ	FSIQ	Info.	Comp.	Arith.	Sim.	Digit Span	Vocab.	Digit Symbol	Pict. Comp.	Block Design	Pict. Arrang.	Object Assem.
Dikmen & Morgan (1980) (A)	104.8	101.7	103.3	10.7	11.1	10.5	11.1	10.2	11.1	8.8	9.8	11.0	9.2	10.0
Dikmen & Morgan (1980) (B)	93.8	90.6	92.0	9.1	9.5	8.0	9.3	8.3	9.3	6.8	8.2	8.4	8.3	8.3
Farr & Greene (1983)	87.5	88.3	87.9	7.2	7.7	6.8	9.3	6.4	8.1	6.3	8.1	8.4	7.7	7.8
Matthews & Harley (1975)	102.9	96.3	100.2	10.4	9.8	10.9	10.3	10.0	10.0	8.9	9.4	9.6	8.5	8.4
Seidenberg et al. (1981a) (A)	90.4	84.0	86.8	7.2	8.6	7.7	8.7	8.1	7.6	7.0	8.0	7.7	8.0	6.8
Seidenberg et al. (1981a) (B)	92.0	86.1	88.8	8.2	8.6	7.9	9.5	7.9	8.0	7.7	8.0	7.6	7.9	7.1
Weighted totals	96.5	92.4	94.0	9.2	9.6	8.8	9.8	8.4	9.4	7.6	8.7	9.0	8.4	8.3
Number	197	197	197	197	197	197	197	197	197	197	197	197	197	197

HRB Study	Category	TPT Total Time	TPT Mem.	TPT Loc.	TPT Time Right	TPT Time Left	TPT Time Both	Rhythm (errors)	Speech Perception (errors)	Tapping Right	Tapping Left	Trail A	Trail B	Impair. Index (Halstead)
Batzel et al. (1980) (A)	59.7	25.5	7.0	3.1	—	—	—	7.5	—	—	—	—	142.2	—
Batzel et al. (1980) (B)	64.8	23.6	7.1	4.3	—	—	—	7.1	—	—	—	—	108.4	—
Batzel et al. (1980) (C)	44.5	12.0	7.7	4.8	—	—	—	5.1	—	—	—	—	61.7	—
Dikmen & Morgan (1980) (A)	49.4	.7[b]	7.4	4.1	—	—	—	4.7	7.3	48.9	44.2	29.1	84.7	.4
Dikmen & Morgan (1980) (B)	67.8	1.9[b]	6.4	2.1	—	—	—	7.9	11.8	41.9	36.2	56.6	137.9	.6
Dodrill (1978)	59.6	26.4	6.9	3.4	10.6	9.5	6.3	6.1	8.1	43.6[c]	38.8[c]	44.2	123.2	.6
Dodrill & Troupin (1975)	61.7	.7[b]	7.6	2.8	—	—	—	6.5	8.7	44.9	—	37.3	111.7	.6
Dodrill & Wilkus (1978) (A)	51.1	18.3	7.9	4.4	—	—	—	5.3	7.6	47.6	—	33.2	102.8	.5
Dodrill & Wilkus (1978) (B)	65.5	25.5	6.8	2.8	—	—	—	7.2	8.5	44.5	—	46.2	124.5	.6
Dodrill & Wilkus (1978) (C)	82.5	38.0	6.1	1.9	—	—	—	11.9	14.2	36.7	—	72.8	192.9	.8
Farr & Greene (1983)	84.4	18.4	6.1	3.2	7.3	7.0	4.1	13.2	15.1	36.3	31.7	51.3	146.1	—
Matthews & Harley (1975)	45.2	—	—	—	—	—	—	6.4	6.6	—	—	34.8	100.6	—
Seidenberg et al. (1981b)	73.2	1.2[b]	5.6	2.9	—	—	—	8.7	11.1	38.2	—	45.6	121.4	.8
Tureen et al. (1968)	55.9	18.1	6.9	3.3	—	—	—	6.6	10.0	42.1	—	—	138.0	.6
Weighted totals	59.2	21.3	6.9	3.2	10.0	9.0	5.9	6.9	9.5	43.2	39.6	43.3	124.7	.6
Rating equivalents	2	3	1	2	2	4	4	2	2	2	2	2	3	—
Number	581	408	553	553	62	62	62	581	523	495	172	346	581	521

[a]Calculated value.
[b]Calculated weighted mean.
[c]min., block.

Table 9.6. Summary of Relevant Variables in Studies of Alcoholic Patients

Study	Patient Type	N M	N F	Age M	Age SD	Education M	Education SD	Patient Status	Time Post	Charted Measure
Claiborn & Greene (1981)	Alcoholic	25	0	44.84	(9.69)	11.96	(2.73)	VA inpatient	<10 yrs.	HRB
Eckardt & Matarazzo (1981)	Alcoholic	91	0	42.2	(10.0)	13	—	Inpatient	15.9 (10.9) yrs.	HRB
Farr & Greene (1983)	Alcohol & substance abuse	12	—	42.69	(16.63)	—	—	Outpatient	10.71 mo.	WAIS, HRB
Grant et al. (1979) (A)	Alcoholic (acute)	43	—	36.8	(6.4)	12.6	(2.4)	VA inpatient	< 3 wks. abst.	HRB
Grant et al. (1979) (B)	Alcoholic (abstinent)	39	—	37.4	(5.8)	13.3	(2.7)	Outpatient	>18 mo. abst.	HRB
Gudeman et al. (1977)	Alcoholic	27	14	45.2	(10.8)	13.6	(2.3)	Inpatient state hospital	9.5 yrs.	WAIS, HRB
Long & McLachlan (1974)	Alcoholic	22	—	44.64	—	13.9	—	Inpatient	8.9 yrs.	HRB
Miller & Orr (1980)	Alcoholic	36	0	46.6	—	12.1	—	VA inpatient	12.7 yrs.	WAIS, HRB
O'Leary et al. (1979)	Alcoholic	38	—	49.8	(6.8)	12.6	(2.3)	VA inpatient	—	WAIS, HRB
Prigatano (1977)	Alcoholic	22	—	47.0	(11.0)	12.5	(2.9)	VA inpatient	15.2 (10.0) yrs.	HRB
Silberstein & Parsons (1980)	Alcoholic	0	25	42.0	—	12.3	—	Inpatient	< 1 yr.	WAIS, HRB
Smith et al. (1973)	Alcoholic	26	—	45.3	—	13.8	—	Private inpatient	24.4 yrs.	HRB
Tarter et al. (1983) (A)	Alcoholic (seizure withdrawal)	22	—	47	—	11	—	VA inpatient	15.22 yrs.	WAIS, HRB
Tarter et al. (1983) (B)	Alcoholic (without seizure)	12	—	48	—	12	—	VA inpatient	16.17 yrs.	WAIS, HRB

WAIS Study	VIQ	PIQ	FSIQ	Info.	Comp.	Arith.	Sim.	Digit Span	Vocab.	Digit Symbol	Pict. Comp.	Block Design	Pict. Arrang.	Object Assem.
Farr & Greene (1983)	95.8	91.6	94.3	9.3	9.8	9.4	8.8	6.1	9.9	5.6	8.6	6.8	8.3	7.8
Gudeman et al. (1977)	114.6	112.4	114.4	12.1	11.9	12.1	12.4	11.6	13.1	9.7	11.8	10.0	10.9	10.5
Miller & Orr (1980)	102.4	95.3	99.3	10.8	10.0	9.2	10.2	9.2	13.4	6.5	9.3	8.0	7.3	7.8
O'Leary et al. (1979)	—	—	—	11.8	12.5	10.2	12.6	9.5	12.0	8.3	11.2	9.0	9.2	10.9
Gilberstein & Parsons (1980)	—	—	—	—	12.5	—	12.1	10.2	—	10.6	10.5	9.8	—	—
Tarter et al. (1983) (A)	98.3	96.2	97.2	10.0	10.4	8.9	10.0	8.4	9.0	7.1	8.8	8.2	7.0	8.4
Tarter et al. (1983) (B)	103.7	97.7	101.4	11.0	10.3	10.4	9.7	9.3	11.1	6.2	9.3	8.7	8.0	8.3
Weighted totals	105.2	101.0	103.7	11.0	11.3	10.2	11.3	9.6	12.0	8.1	10.3	8.9	8.8	9.3
Number	123	123	123	161	186	161	186	186	161	186	186	186	161	161

HRB Study	Category	TPT Total Time	TPT Mem.	TPT Loc.	TPT Time Right	TPT Time Left	TPT Time Both	Rhythm (errors)	Speech Perception (errors)	Tapping Right	Tapping Left	Trail A	Trail B	Impair. Index (Halstead)
Claiborn & Greene	—	—	8.4	1.8	9.6	7.8	4.8	5.2	11.0	49.9	44.9	55.6	131.0	—
Eckardt & Matarazzo (1981)	75.2	19.7	7.1	2.9	—	—	—	5.9	10.0	44.3	—	39.9	97.3	—
Farr & Greene (1983)	65.3	24.0	5.8	1.8	9.2	8.2	6.7	8.4	21.4	46.6	39.4	51.3	175.6	—
Long & McLachlan (1974)	57.3	15.0	7.6	4.2	6.9	5.2	3.1	4.0	4.9	38.3	35.0	—	—	—
Miller & Orr (1980)	90.0	22.9	6.8	2.4	9.0	7.6	6.3	6.5	9.4	38.1	36.7	61.3	150.0	.7
O'Leary et al. (1979)	62.0	21.1	6.5	3.9	5.2	7.3	5.2	—	—	—	—	41.0	105.6	—
Grant et al. (1979) (A)	35.7	12.8	8.3	4.5	—	—	—	4.2	5.6	51.6	—	—	66.2	.3
Grant et al. (1979) (B)	37.2	13.1	8.1	4.5	—	—	—	3.6	4.5	51.7	—	—	64.8	.2
Gudeman et al. (1977)	47.8	12.2	7.2	3.2	—	—	—	3.1	9.1	50.2	44.4	39.5	95.4	—
Prigatano (1977)	65.0	21.7	6.4	3.0	—	—	—	4.3	8.7	46.5	—	—	—	.5
Smith et al. (1973)	56.8	16.4	6.8	3.3	—	—	—	4.4	6.5	55.5	—	29.0	66.5	.4
Silberstein & Parsons (1980)	48.8	16.9	7.4	3.4	—	—	—	—	—	—	—	34.6	74.1	—
Tarter et al. (1983) (A)	72.6	23.3	6.3	2.3	—	—	—	7.9	13.5	50.2	41.8	45.1	125.4	—
Tarter et al. (1983) (B)	82.8	23.0	5.8	2.4	—	—	—	6.4	13.1	44.0	39.0	59.1	159.2	—
Weighted totals	60.9	18.0	7.2	3.2	7.7	7.2	5.2	5.1	8.9	47.2	40.5	43.7	86.8	.5
Rating equivalents	2	2	1	2	1	3	3	1	2	2	2	2	1	
Number	429	429	454	454	133	133	133	391	391	391	170	328	432	140

It is clear that prolonged alcohol abuse produces cognitive deficits. However, the type and severity of deficits are particularly sensitive to the stage of the disease process, the age of the patient, the nutritional status of the patient, and a number of other moderator variables identified by extensive research. Memory deficits—the hallmark of alcoholism—may range from relatively minor to the more extreme and classic type seen in Korsakoff's psychosis. Intermediate memory is impaired significantly, and the storage and retrieval of new information is poor in the more advanced stages of alcoholism and virtually nonexistent in the patient with Korsakoff's psychosis. Deficits in the following areas also are reported in this population: complex problem solving and abstract reasoning processes, spatial and visuospatial processes, ability to organize perceptual-motor tasks, speed-dependent visual scanning tasks, and synthesis of spatial elements. In general, as task difficulty or complexity increases, more impairment is seen in all these areas. In the face of these cognitive deficits, it should be noted that verbal abilities remain intact and Vocabulary measures in particular tend to remain unaffected. That is, well-established or overlearned verbal abilities, if affected at all, tend to demonstrate minimal deficits.

It is not necessary to hypothesize the expected pattern of scores on the WAIS and HRB, since they have been summarized previously. Parsons and Farr (1981) note that "lowered scores on WAIS Digit Symbol and Block Design and HRB Category test, TPT Total Time, TPT Localization, and Trails B are interpretable as stemming from deficits in problem-solving skills, while the normal to above normal Verbal IQs suggest relatively intact language function" (pp. 340–341). Their data also indicate that performance on Object Assembly is impaired as frequently as on the other tests they listed.

Table 9.6 provides the quantitative data on the WAIS and HRB in alcoholic patients. Verbal IQ is consistently a few points higher than Performance IQ in all studies reviewed, with the Full-Scale IQs very near the average of the population. Scores on the Verbal subtests also are consistently above average, except for those on Digit Span, which are slightly below average. In contrast, results of the Performance subtests are consistently slightly below average, with those of Digit Symbol being the most adversely affected.

There is a general pattern of mild impairment across all the tests within the HRB. However, while there was a consistent pattern of performance on the WAIS, the alcoholics were extremely variable on the HRB. For example, scores on Categories ranged from normal to the moderate level of impairment. Similar ranges of scores were seen on TPT Total Time and Trails A and B. It is well known that age is an important moderator variable in determining the level of neuropsychologic impairment seen in alcoholics (Grant, Adams, & Reed, 1979), which may be one of the factors producing the extreme variability in scores on the HRB. It is surprising that the alcoholics did not show greater impairment on those measures assumed to assess complex problem solving (Categories, TPT, Trails B), since these are notorious deficits in alcoholics.

The pattern of mild impairment found in studies of alcoholics reviewed for this effort appears to be a function of the age of the patients. Grant and colleagues (Grant, Adams, & Reed, 1979) have demonstrated that patients younger than 40 years of age tend to have minimal, if any, neuropsychologic deficits, in marked contrast to patients over that age. These findings may be related to some function of both the length of time that the patient has been drinking as well as the level of consumption over that drinking period. There also are notable sex differences in the effects of alcohol on neuropsychologic functions; these are currently being investigated by Parsons and colleagues (Silberstein & Parsons, 1980).

LEARNING DISABILITIES

Learning disability is a generic term used to describe a problem in learning that is not the result of trauma, social or cultural deprivation, or lack of educational opportunity. Such problems in learning are characterized by a level of achievement below age expectancy, a determination based on an assessment of the discrepancy between the level of intellectual and academic functioning in individuals with an IQ of 85 or higher. A plethora of research has debated the exact nature of learning disabilities and how they should be defined. Argument over these issues is beyond the scope of this chapter. Instead, the focus of this section is on the neuropsychologic deficits that would be anticipated in persons with learning disabilities and that could be assessed by the WAIS and HRB. Of course, the focus of these tests restricts the age range to adults. Although learning disabilities most often are seen as problems faced by children in educational environments, adults also have or retain the learning disabilities they had as children. It is only since approximately 1975 that adults with learning disabilities have begun to be recognized and examined.

Learning disabilities sometimes are described as functional deficits, since there is no evidence of any impairment in the neurological substrata. In fact, if there is any evidence of neurological dysfunction, a diagnosis of a learning disability is not likely to be made. These functional deficits in learning disabilities are opposed to the structural deficits, which are seen as underlying the other disease processes described in this chapter.

Table 9.7 provides the quantitative data on the WAIS and HRB in adults with learning disabilities. Although there have been many studies of children with learning disabilities, adults with this dysfunction have received little systematic attention. Verbal IQ is consistently a few points lower than Performance IQ in these studies, with all three WAIS IQs near an average of 100. Again, a familiar pattern is seen on the Verbal subtests, of which performance on Arithmetic and Digit Span is the most adversely affected. Scores on both Information and Vocabulary also are affected adversely, and it is unusual to see what are usually characterized as old, overlearned verbal skills being affected. Only the results of Digit Symbol are below average among the Performance subtests.

The HRB tests are characterized by either normal performance or only very mild levels of deficit. The relatively mild deficits on Tapping and Trails B might suggest that a motor component is being affected adversely, which would also account for the lower performance on Digit Symbol. It does appear that learning disabilities in adults have only very mild effects on neuropsychologic functions.

ONSET AND COURSE OF DISEASE PROCESS

Now that the performance on the WAIS subtests and the HRB tests has been described for each of the diagnostic groups, it is possible to begin the task of forming onset and process groups for the purpose of making intergroup WAIS and HRB performance comparisons. The first comparison will be between the group with slow onset of symptoms and that with rapid onset. Then three composite groups will be considered on the basis of the expected course of the disease process—static, progressive, and remitting—for a similar analysis.

Table 9.7. Summary of Relevant Variables in Studies of Learning Disability

Study	Patient Type	N M	N F	Age M	Age SD	Education M	Education SD	Patient Status	Time Post	Charted Measure
Blalock (1982)	Learning disability	57	23	25	—	<12	—	Adults	—	WAIS
Cordoni et al. (1981)	Learning disability	48	9	19.3	(2.1)	<12	—	College students	—	WAIS
Frauenheim & Heckerl (1983)	Learning disability	11		27.0	—	11.6	—	Adults	—	WAIS
Farr & Greene (1983)	Learning disability (mixed)	19		26.0	(12.0)	—		Outpatient	—	WAIS, HRB
O'Donnell et al. (1983)	Learning disability	52	8	19.2	(2.0)	12.1	(1.1)	College students	—	HRB
Whitworth (1984)	Learning disability	40		≈20	—	<12	—	College students	—	WAIS

WAIS Study	VIQ	PIQ	FSIQ	Info.	Comp.	Arith.	Sim.	Digit Span	Vocab.	Digit Symbol	Pict. Comp.	Block Design	Pict. Arrang.	Object Assem.
Blalock (1982)	104.5	105.1	103.2	—	—	9.5	12.3	9.2	10.7	10.0	11.5	12.2	10.9	12.0
Cordoni et al. (1981)	—	—	108.0	9.6	12.5	6.7	8.3	5.3	8.0	6.6	11.5	12.5	10.8	12.0
Frauenheim & Heckerl (1983)	85	104	92	6.8	10.8	6.5	9.3	7.4	7.8	6.6	8.8	9.2	8.5	8.9
Farr & Greene (1983)	91.1	92.6	91.1	7.4	9.5	6.5	9.3							
Whitworth (1984)	97.3	106.5	101.2	7.6	10.4	7.1	10.9	9.4	8.6	9.1	11.1	11.5	11.0	11.7
Weighted totals	99.5	103.8	102.4	8.4	11.2	8.1	11.1	8.7	9.3	8.9	11.0	11.6	10.6	11.4
Number	150	150	207	127	127	127	127	127	127	127	127	127	127	127

HRB Study	Category	TPT Total Time	TPT Mem.	TPT Loc.	TPT Time Right	TPT Time Left	TPT Time Both	Rhythm (errors)	Speech Perception (errors)	Tapping Right	Tapping Left	Trail A	Trail B	Impair. Index (Halstead)
Farr & Greene (1983)	68.1	17.6	6.0	3.3	7.4	6.2	4.4	7.0	9.9	40.6	39.3	45.1	126.7	—
O'Donnell et al. (1983)	43.4	12.9	8.1	5.0	—	—	—	5.1	5.3	50.8	—	28.5	81.2	—
Weighted totals	49.3	14.0	7.6	4.6	7.4	6.2	4.4	5.6	6.4	48.3	39.3	32.5	92.1	—
Rating equivalents	1	1	1	2	1	3	3	2	1	2	2	1	2	—
Number	79	79	79	79	19	19	19	79	79	79	19	79	79	—

Slow and Rapid Onset

Degenerative, epileptic, neoplastic, alcoholic, and learning disabled patients are classified as having a slow onset of disease. Head trauma and cerebrovascular patients are classified as having suffered a rapid onset.

Table 9.8 provides a summary of the WAIS data for the disease process groups, reclassified into slow and rapid onset groups, and Table 9.9 provides similar data on the HRB. It is apparent that more research has been conducted on slow- than on rapid-onset diseases, with almost three times as many patients studied on the WAIS and ten times as many on the HRB. Slow-onset disease processes appear to have minimal impact on performance on Verbal IQ and its contributing subtests. Results of Digit Span and Arithmetic are the most adversely affected of the Verbal subtests, and they are only slightly below average. In contrast, scores on Performance IQ and the Performance subtests are all below average, with Digit Symbol, Picture Arrangement, and Object Assembly being the most adversely affected. In what by now has become a familiar outcome, Block Design is only slightly affected by slow-onset disease processes.

Rapid-onset disease processes have a significant adverse affect on all of the WAIS variables. Verbal IQ is 5 points below average, and Performance IQ is 10 points below average. Scores on all the Verbal subtests are in the same range, slightly below average, except for the Similarities score, which is the most adversely affected of all the Verbal subtests. Results on the Performance subtests are substantially below average, with those on Digit Symbol and Block Design being the most adversely affected.

When slow- and rapid-onset disease processes are contrasted in terms of WAIS performance, there is a consistent pattern in which the rapid-onset group scores more poorly across all the subtests except Arithmetic and Digit Span. The differences between these two onset groups are most extreme on the Performance subtests, for which they exceed one standard deviation on some subtests and are almost one-half a standard deviation on all remaining subtests. The differences between these two groups on the Verbal subtests generally are less than one-half a standard deviation. Thus, it appears that scores on the Performance subtests are more adversely affected by rapid-onset disease processes, although there are consistent differences across the entire WAIS.

The slow-onset group tends to demonstrate a mild level of impairment on nearly all the HRB tests. Only performance on Trails A, TPT Time Left, and TPT Time Both is more adversely affected in this group. Thus, it appears that slow-onset disease processes are characterized by only mild levels of impairment, as assessed by the HRB. The weighted total for each test in the HRB generally is slightly above the criterion used to classify performance on that test as in the brain-damaged range.

The rapid-onset disease group also demonstrates a pattern of general impairment across all the HRB tests. It is somewhat surprising that performance on the HRB is not more adversely affected across all the tests. Clearly, results on Trails A and B are the most adversely affected of all the HRB tests in the rapid-onset group, with scores on Trails A being slightly poorer than those on Trails B. Scores on the other HRB tests are generally in the range of mild impairment.

When slow- and rapid-onset disease process groups are contrasted on the HRB, there is a consistent pattern for the rapid-onset group to perform more poorly on the

Table 9.8. Summary of WAIS Variables in Disease Onset and Disease Course Groups

WAIS	VIQ	PIQ	FSIQ	Info.	Comp.	Arith.	Sim.	Digit Span	Vocab.	Digit Symbol	Pict. Comp.	Block Design	Pict. Arrang.	Object Assem.
Onset														
Slow														
Weighted totals	99.2	95.2	97.2	9.9	10.6	8.9	10.3	8.8	10.4	7.5	9.4	9.0	8.4	8.7
Number	937	937	982	826	825	837	862	836	811	836	862	862	837	811
Rapid														
Weighted totals	94.5	89.1	89.7	8.9	9.3	9.2	8.4	9.2	9.5	4.7	8.1	6.3	7.1	7.5
Number	387	387	267	313	217	227	309	371	189	161	329	411	241	353
Course														
Static														
Weighted totals	97.8	97.3	98.3	8.9	10.2	8.5	10.3	8.5	9.4	8.1	9.6	10.0	9.3	9.5
Number	384	347	404	324	324	324	324	324	324	324	324	324	324	324
Progressive														
Weighted totals	100.0	94.0	96.5	10.6	10.8	9.2	10.4	9.0	11.1	7.1	9.2	8.4	7.9	8.1
Number	590	590	578	502	501	513	538	512	487	512	538	538	513	487
Remitting														
Weighted totals	94.5	89.1	89.7	8.9	9.3	9.2	8.4	9.2	9.5	4.7	8.1	6.3	7.1	7.5
Number	387	387	267	313	217	227	309	371	189	161	329	411	241	353

Table 9.9. Summary of HRB Variables in Disease Onset and Disease Course Groups

HRB	Category	TPT Total Time	TPT Mem.	TPT Loc.	TPT Time Right	TPT Time Left	TPT Time Both	Rhythm (errors)	Speech Percepion (errors)	Tapping Right	Tapping Left	Trail A	Trail B	Impair. Index (Halstead)
Onset														
Slow														
Weighted totals	61.2	20.2	6.9	3.1	8.6	7.8	5.6	6.1	9.0	43.5	37.9	49.4	118.1	.6
Rating equivalents	2	2	1	2	2	3	4	2	2	2	2	3	2	
Number	1297	998	1273	1273	250	250	250	1227	1169	1214	579	1014	1361	837
Rapid														
Weighted totals	73.7	18.1	6.0	2.6	7.4	5.9	4.6	8.1	11.2	40.0	39.3	115.3	237.9	.7
Rating equivalents	2	2	1	2	1	2	3	2	2	3	2	5	4	
Number	125	125	125	125	42	42	42	125	125	168	100	237	237	106
Course														
Static														
Weighted totals	58.0	20.1	7.0	3.4	9.4	8.3	5.5	6.7	9.1	43.9	39.6	41.3	120.8	.6
Rating equivalents	2	2	1	2	2	3	4	2	2	2	2	2	2	
Number	660	487	632	632	81	81	81	660	602	574	191	425	660	521
Progressive														
Weighted totals	64.5	20.3	6.8	2.9	8.2	7.6	5.6	5.4	8.9	43.2	37.0	55.3	115.5	.6
Rating equivalents	2	2	1	2	1	3	4	1	2	2	2	3	2	
Number	637	511	641	641	169	169	169	567	567	640	388	589	701	316
Remitting														
Weighted totals	73.7	18.1	6.0	2.6	7.4	5.9	4.6	8.1	11.2	40.0	39.3	115.3	237.9	.7
Rating equivalents	2	2	1	2	1	2	3	2	2	3	2	5	4	
Number	125	125	125	125	42	42	42	125	125	168	100	237	237	106

entire HRB, with the exception of the timed TPT measures. The differences between the two onset groups are the largest on Trails A and B, and generally quite small on the other HRB tests. The finding that the rapid-onset group performs slightly faster than the slow-onset group on all the TPT timed measures is very surprising. Since the TPT measures in the rapid-onset group are available only on the head trauma patients, who tend to be in their twenties, it is possible that these small differences in TPT time measures are an artifact of age. However, when the head trauma patients (rapid onset) are contrasted with the epileptic patients (slow onset), who tend to be in the same age range, the same pattern of performance is seen on the timed TPT measures.

There were actually fewer tests within the HRB than the WAIS that discriminated between the two onset process groups. Several alternative hypotheses might explain this pattern of findings. First, the HRB tests generally may be more sensitive to all forms of brain damage and therefore less able to distinguish between the nature of the onset process. This assumption is certainly compatible with the empirical manner in which specific tests were developed for the HRB. These tests were originally chosen as techniques that successfully discriminated between brain-damaged and non-brain–damaged groups. Brain-damaged populations originally chosen for this purpose were mixed and quite heterogeneous without regard to rapidity of disease onset. A second possibility is that the nature of the onset rate may not be as important as has been conjectured in the literature. That is, although it has been a viable hypothesis that the patient should be able to adapt in a more effective fashion to a slowly developing lesion than to a rapid one, this assumption may not be tenable. It may be that once the most immediate and acute effects of brain damage have resolved, brain damage is just brain damage, at least as rate of onset relates to any specific pattern of performance on the HRB. We have little doubt that this issue is complex beyond our original assumptions. Validating the clinical lore regarding the relationship between onset rate and pattern of dysfunction promises to be a formidable task.

Static, Progressive, and Remitting Courses

The data set was also partitioned on the basis of the course of the disease process: static, progressive, or remitting. The static disease group consisted of patients with epileptic or learning disability disorders; the progressive disease group consisted of patients with neoplastic, degenerative, and alcoholic diagnoses; and the remitting disease group consisted of patients who had suffered head trauma or had cerebrovascular disease. Since the course of the disease process is confounded with the nature of onset (slow or rapid), comparisons between these two levels of analysis should be made cautiously. The distinction between the static and progressive disease processes is a subclassification of the slow-onset category; all groups within the rapid-onset category also are within the remitting disease process category. For some conceivable groups, such overlap does not exist (e.g., a rapid-onset process which is progressive, such as viral infections), but special cases such as these simply did not occur in sufficient numbers to warrant inclusion in the present analysis.

Tables 9.8 and 9.9 provide a summary of the WAIS and HRB for the disease process groups. As noted above, the remitting group is identical to the rapid-onset group; therefore, the description provided previously for the WAIS and HRB performance of the rapid-onset group also serves to describe the remitting course group.

The static disease course group tends to score very consistently and only slightly below average across the entire WAIS. All three IQs are only two points below average. It is interesting to note that scores on Information and Vocabulary, which are presumed to test old, overlearned verbal skills, are not the highest among the Verbal subtests; instead, results on Comprehension and Similarities are the best among the Verbal subtests, and both are slightly above average. It could be conjectured that static disease processes have an adverse effect on the acquisition of information or the speed of learning, and, as a consequence, scores on Information and Vocabulary are lower in such disease course groups. Results on all the Performance subtests are in the same range and only slightly below average except for those on Digit Symbol. Again, it could be argued that the lower score on Digit Symbol reflects a speed of learning variable. Also, scores on Block Design are the highest among the Performance subtests and are exactly average. It appears that diseases with a static course have only a minimal and generalized impact on WAIS scores.

The progressive disease course group is much more variable on the WAIS. Verbal IQ is exactly 100, while Performance IQ is six points below average. Scores on all the Verbal subtests are average or above with performance on Arithmetic and Digit span being the lowest. Again, a common pattern is seen, in which Arithmetic and Digit Span are the two verbal subtests on which scores are most adversely affected by a progressive disease course. Results on the Performance subtests are well below average except for those on Picture Completion. Performance on Digit Symbol is the most adversely affected among all the Performance subtests and is almost one standard deviation below the mean. Scores on the other Performance subtests are over one-half a standard deviation below the mean. It seems that progressive disease courses can be characterized by limited impact on verbal abilities and rather significant effect on the Performance subtests.

There are clear differences when the three disease course groups are contrasted on the WAIS. The static disease course group consistently performs more poorly on every Verbal subtest and better on every Performance subtest than does the progressive course group. The remitting course group consistently performs more poorly on every Performance subtest than does either the static or the progressive course group. That is, the three disease course groups can be ranked in terms of scores on the Performance subtests of the WAIS, with the static group scoring highest, followed by the progressive course group, and then the remitting course group. There are fewer differences among the three disease course groups on the Verbal subtests, although the remitting group does more poorly overall on all the Verbal subtests than does either of the other two groups.

The static disease course group performs consistently in the mild range of impairment across all the HRB tests. All the weighted totals are above the criterion for brain damage, with the exception of those for TPT Memory. The TPT times for right, left, and both hands are progressively more impaired, according to the rating equivalents of Russell and colleagues (1970), in this disease course group as well as in the other two groups. It is possible that one of the characteristics of the performance of brain-damaged patients on the TPT is a slower learning curve than in reference populations, which would tend to indicate that their performance was becoming more impaired across the three trials. In any case, the pattern of poorer performance across the three TPT trials is not limited to any one disease course group, although the static group's times are slightly poorer than those of the other two groups.

The progressive course group also performs in the mild range of impairment across most of the major HRB measures. Scores on all these tests except TPT Memory and Rhythm are above the criterion for performance in the brain-damaged range. The Halstead Impairment Index of 0.6 seems to summarize aptly the performance of the progressive course group (i.e., the group demonstrates mild impairment across most of the HRB tests).

When the three disease course groups are contrasted on the HRB tests, a number of interesting relationships emerge. The remitting group generally performs more poorly on all the HRB tests except for the TPT timed measures. On these measures, the remitting group performs better than both the other groups, yet the TPT Memory and Localization scores are poorest in the remitting course group. It is not clear what factor contributes to the relatively good scores on the TPT timed measures in the remitting course group, when results on Trails A and B are in the severe range of impairment and the other HRB tests are performed poorly. There is generally little difference between the performance of the static and progressive disease course groups on the HRB. It seems that the HRB does not differentiate well among these three disease course groups. Only Trails A would come close to separating the three groups on any reliable basis, with the static, progressive, and remitting course groups being ranked from best to worst, in that order.

SUMMARY

As expected, the Wechsler IQs as composite measures were not as sensitive to the presence of brain damage as were the individual subtests. In general, the WAIS IQs tended to be 5–10 IQ points below average in most of the disease process groups; however, in the alcoholic and learning-disabled samples, the IQs were above average. Only in the degenerative disease processes (excluding MS) did the IQs approach nearly 15 points (one standard deviation) below average.

As a general pattern, Digit Symbol was the WAIS subtest on which performance was most affected by brain damage in all disease process groups. Thus, the conventional wisdom that Digit Symbol is one of the WAIS subtests most sensitive to brain damage appears to be well substantiated, although Digit Symbol is not differentially sensitive to the various types of disease processes, onset, or course. That is, performance on Digit Symbol appears to be affected adversely by any type of brain damage regardless of type, mode of onset, or course. Block Design, which also is thought traditionally to be sensitive to brain damage, was characteristically not as sensitive as Object Assembly or Picture Arrangement. In fact, only in the cerebrovascular and primary degenerative dementia samples and in the rapid-onset disease group was Block Design among the two subtests most sensitive to brain damage. Arithmetic and Digit Span tended to be the Verbal subtests most sensitive to any type of disease process, onset, or course. Again, like Digit Symbol, these two subtests were not differentially sensitive to the type of disease process, onset, or course. Performance on the other four Verbal subtests (Information, Comprehension, Similarities, and Vocabulary) tended to be relatively unaffected by most of the disease processes, which is consistent with the clinical lore that old and overlearned verbal abilities are generally not affected by brain damage.

Supporting the contention that the HRB tests are generally more sensitive to the presence of brain damage than is the WAIS, there was a consistent trend for performance on the HRB tests to be more adversely affected than that on the WAIS subtests in all the disease processes. Halstead's Impairment Index, which is a composite measure based on a number of the HRB tests, classified virtually all the disease process, onset, and course groups in the same range of brain damage. Thus, the Impairment Index, a composite measure like the WAIS IQs, was not as differentially sensitive to the presence of brain damage as were individual tests within the HRB. Only in alcoholic patients did the Impairment Index classify some of the patients in the non–brain-damaged range, and these patients were characteristically younger than the other alcoholic patients. The importance of age as a moderator variable in neuropsychologic performance in alcoholic patients has been noted.

Both Trails A and B were among the HRB tests on which performance was most affected by brain damage in all the disease process groups. Occasionally, this outcome was the result of the patients in a specific disease process (e.g., Huntington's chorea, MS) being unable to complete other HRB tests. The ability of patients to complete Trails A and B even when severely impaired by brain damage may be a real asset in obtaining quantitative data on some of these disease processes. The finding that Trails A frequently was more sensitive to disease process than was Trails B was not expected. In some senses, it may be very simple tasks, such as those measured by Trails A or reaction time, that are most sensitive to the presence of any form of disease process. In addition to Trails A and B, TPT Total Time was differentially sensitive to disease process. There was a trend for TPT Time measures for Right, Left, and Both hands to be classified as reflecting progressively more severe impairment according to the rating equivalents of Russell and colleagues (1970). This pattern is most obvious in Table 9.9. The issue of whether practice effects are differentially sensitive to disease process has not been investigated in any systematic manner, and it is an issue worthy of further research. Performance on both Rhythm and Speech was virtually unaffected by any type of disease process, and Categories appeared not to be differentially sensitive to disease process. Results on Categories, much as on the Impairment Index, appeared to be affected by any form of brain damage.

A number of general conclusions can be made. The most striking finding is the lack of raw data reported in the literature. The fact that raw group data on WAIS and HRB performance are virtually nonexistent in some populations (patients with neoplasms, cerebrovascular disorders, and learning disabilities) is quite surprising.

The frequency with which the various disease processes are seen in clinical practice and the amount of research on these disease processes deserves some comment. Cerebrovascular disorders, for example, are among the leading causes of brain impairment and virtually have not been reported in any systematic manner by neuropsychologists. Huntington's chorea is relatively rare by any standard, and yet it represents a significant portion of the research effort. In contrast, the limited amount of research on neoplastic processes is consistent with the frequency with which such disease processes occur. Clearly, there is a need for systematic additional research by the neuropsychological community on a number of the disease processes that are encountered frequently. Such attention should not preclude the examination of less frequently encountered disease processes, but attention should be addressed to those conditions that most neuropsychologists are likely to see in practice.

There are also a number of topical issues in neuropsychology that can be addressed as part of a study of disease process. For example, the issue of whether there are sex differences in degree of lateralization of neuropsychologic functions could be examined within a larger study of cerebrovascular or neoplastic disease processes, since these processes produce lateralized deficits. Similarly, the stage of the disease process could be examined as a larger study of the course of any of the more common disease groups, such as stroke. Without basic information on the level of performance in these populations, it is not possible to begin to integrate the issues raised in this chapter with an exploration of the full effect of many moderator variables, such as age, education, and socioeconomic status, which have been more thoroughly explored elsewhere in the literature.

On the basis of the limited data available, several tentative conclusions appear warranted. First, the HRB is more sensitive to brain damage than is the WAIS. Although this statement is not profound, it does substantiate the role of the HRB in the evaluation of neuropsychologic deficits.

Second, the list of tests commonly assumed to be most sensitive to brain damage within the WAIS and HRB warrant more focused reevaluation. While Digit Symbol and Trails B seem particularly sensitive to brain damage, in specific disease processes Trails A may be more sensitive than Trails B. In general, the sensitivity of Trails A to brain damage needs to be investigated further. Block Design and Categories may be less sensitive than previously thought.

Third, it appears that differential patterns of WAIS and HRB performance and test sensitivity may be related to disease process, and these patterns warrant further investigation. The WAIS and HRB seem to be less sensitive to disease course than to disease process, although enough differences exist to warrant further study. There are few reliable differences on the HRB between slow- and rapid-onset disease processes. The clinical lore that the rate of onset of the disease process has an appreciable effect on neuropsychologic performance may need to be reconsidered if further research also cannot detect any substantial differences between slow- and rapid-onset groups.

Fourth, there is a need to begin to identify distinct subgroups within the broader diagnostic groups that have been used in research and in clinical practice to date. The need for neuropsychologic research on discrete subgroups of neoplastic and cerebrovascular processes seems clear.

Fifth, some of the HRB tests, specifically Rhythm and Speech, either appear in most groups to provide little information on the presence or absence of brain damage or are quite insensitive to differential disease and process states of higher cortical impairment.

Three questions opening the chapter concerned (1) the tempo of the disease process and its effect on the clinical presentation, (2) possible differential patterns of neuropsychologic functioning in different disease states, and (3) the possible differential sensitivity of standard evaluative techniques such as the WAIS and HRB within these disease processes. To the extent that relevant literature was available, an attempt was made to address these issues. In spite of the long-standing popularity of the WAIS and HRB, usable data in several key areas were limited. Nonetheless, this initial effort indicates that more attention to onset- and course-related issues is warranted. The value of improved quantitative understanding of these issues should be clear, since they are directly related to the longitudinal nature of the rehabilitative effort, in which the discipline of neuropsychology is becoming ever more active.

ACKNOWLEDGMENTS

We wish to acknowledge the contribution of Ms. Kathy Seamster for her patience and effort in providing clerical support.

REFERENCES

Aminoff, M.J., Marshall, J., Smith, E.M., & Wyke, M.A. (1975). Pattern of intellectual impairment in Huntington's chorea. *Psychological Medicine, 5,* 169–172.

Batzel, L.W., Dodrill, C.B., & Fraser, R.T. (1980). Further validation of the WPSI Vocational Scale: Comparisons with other correlates of employment in epilepsy. *Epilepsia, 21,* 235–242.

Beatty, P.A., & Gange, J.J. (1977). Neuropsychological aspects of multiple sclerosis. *Journal of Nervous and Mental Disease, 164,* 42–50.

Becker, B. (1975). Intellectual changes after closed head injury. *Journal of Clinical Psychology, 31,* 307–309.

Ben-Yishay, Y., Diller, L., Gertsman, L., & Haas, A. (1968). The relationship between impersistence, intellectual function and outcome of rehabilitation in patients with left hemiplegia. *Neurology, 18,* 852–861.

Bigler, E.D. (1984). *Diagnostic clinical neuropsychology.* Austin: University of Texas Press.

Bigler, E.D., Steinman, D.R., & Newton, J.S. (1981). Clinical assessment of cognitive deficit in neurologic disorder: 1. Effects of age and degenerative disease. *Clinical Neuropsychology, 3,* 5–13.

Blalock, J.W. (1982). Persistent auditory language deficits in adults with learning disabilities. *Journal of Learning Disabilities, 15,* 604–609.

Boll, T.J. (1974). Psychological differentiation of patients with schizophrenia versus lateralized cerebrovascular, neoplastic, or traumatic brain damage. *Journal of Abnormal Psychology, 83,* 456–458.

Boll, T.J., Heaton, R., & Reitan, R.M. (1974). Neuropsychological and emotional correlates of Huntington's chorea. *Journal of Nervous and Mental Disease, 158,* 61–69.

Brooks, N. (Ed.). (1984). *Closed head injury: Psychological, social, and family consequences.* New York: Oxford University Press.

Butters, N., Sax, D., Montgomery, K., & Tarlow, S. (1978). Comparison of the neuropsychological deficits associated with early and advanced Huntington's disease. *Archives of Neurology, 35,* 585–589.

Caine, E.D., Hunt, R.D., Weingartner, H., & Ebert, M.H. (1978). Huntington's dementia: Clinical and neuropsychological features. *Archives of General Psychiatry, 35,* 377–384.

Campbell, D.C., & Oxbury, J.M. (1976). Recovery from unilateral visuo-spatial neglect. *Cortex, 12,* 303–312.

Claiborn, J.M., & Greene, R.L. (1981). Neuropsychological changes in recovering men alcoholics. *Journal of Studies on Alcohol, 42,* 757–765.

Cordoni, B.K., O'Donnell, J.P., Ramaniah, N.V., Kurtz, J., & Rosenshein, K. (1981). Weschler Adult Intelligence score patterns for learning-disabled young adults. *Journal of Learning Disabilities, 14,* 404–407.

Costa, L.D., Vaughan, H.G., Jr., Horwitz, M., & Ritter, W. (1969). Patterns of behavioral deficit associated with visual spatial neglect. *Cortex, 5,* 242–263.

Delaney, R.C., Wallace, J.D., & Egelko, S. (1980). Transient cerebral ischemic attacks and neuropsychological deficit. *Journal of Clinical Neuropsychology, 2,* 107–114.

Dikmen, S., & Morgan, S.F. (1980). Neuropsychological factors related to employability and occupational status in persons with epilepsy. *Journal of Nervous and Mental Disease, 168*, 236–240.

Dodrill, C.B. (1978). A neuropsychological battery for epilepsy. *Epilepsia, 19*, 611–623.

Dodrill, C.B. (1981). Neuropsychology of epilepsy. In S.B. Filskov & T.J. Boll (Eds.), *Handbook of clinical neuropsychology* (Vol. 1, pp. 366–395). New York: John Wiley & Sons.

Dodrill, C.B., & Troupin, A.S. (1975). Effects of repeated administrations of a comprehensive neuropsychological battery among chronic epileptics. *Journal of Nervous and Mental Disease, 161*, 185–190.

Dodrill, C.B., & Wilkus, R.J. (1978). Neuropsychological correlates of the electroencephalogram in epileptics: 3. Generalized nonepileptiform abnormalities. *Epilepsia, 19*, 453–462.

Drudge, O.W., Williams, J.M., & Kessler, M. (1984). Recovery from severe closed head injuries: Repeat testings with the Halstead-Reitan Neuropsychological Battery. *Journal of Clinical Psychology, 40*, 259–265.

Dye, O.A., Saxon, S.A., & Milby, J.R. (1981). Long-term neuropsychological deficits after traumatic head injury with comatosis. *Journal of Clinical Psychology, 37*, 472–477.

Eckardt, M.J., & Matarazzo, J.D. (1981). Test-retest reliability of the Halstead Impairment Index in hospitalized alcoholic and nonalcoholic males with mild to moderate neuropsychological impairment. *Journal of Clinical Neuropsychology, 3*, 257–269.

Farr, S.P., & Greene, R.L. (1983). *Disease type, onset, and process and its relationship to neuropsychological performance.* Unpublished manuscript.

Fedio, P., Cox, C.S., Neophytides, A., Canal-Frederick, G., & Chase, T.N. (1979). Neuropsychological profile of Huntington's disease: Patients and those at risk. *Advances in Neurology, 23*, 239–255.

Frauenheim, J.G., & Heckerl, J.R. (1983). A longitudinal study of psychological and achievement test performance in severe dyslexic adults. *Journal of Learning Disabilities, 16*, 339–347.

Freemon, F.R. (1981). *Organic mental disease.* Jamaica, NY: Spectrum.

Golden, C.J., Moses, J.A., Jr., Coffman, J.A., Miller, W.R., & Strider, F.D. (1983). *Clinical neuropsychology: Interface with neurologic and psychiatric disorders.* New York: Grune & Stratton.

Goldstein, S.G., Kleinknecht, R.A., & Gallo, A.E., Jr. (1970). Neuropsychological changes associated with carotid endarterectomy. *Cortex, 6*, 308–322.

Goldstein, G., & Shelly, C.H. (1974). Neuropsychological diagnosis of multiple sclerosis in a neuropsychiatric setting. *Journal of Nervous and Mental Disease, 158*, 280–290.

Grant, I., Adams, K., & Reed, R. (1979). Normal neuropsychological abilities of alcoholic men in their late thirties. *American Journal of Psychiatry, 136*, 1263–1269.

Gruen, A. (1962). Psychologic aging as a pre-existing factor in strokes. *Journal of Nervous and Mental Disease, 134*, 109–116.

Gudeman, H.E., Craine, J.F., Golden, C.J., & McLaughlin, D. (1977). Higher cortical dysfunction associated with long term alcoholism. *International Journal of Neuroscience, 8*, 33–40.

Haaland, K.Y., & Delaney, H.D. (1981). Motor deficits after left or right hemisphere damage due to stroke or tumor. *Neuropsychologia, 19*, 17–27.

Hochberg, F.H., & Slotnick, B. (1980). Neuropsychologic impairment in astrocytoma survivors. *Neurology, 30*, 172–177.

Inglis, J., Ruckman, M., Lawson, J.S., MacLean, A.W., & Monga, T.N. (1982). Sex differences in the cognitive effects of unilateral brain damage. *Cortex, 18*, 257–276.

Ivnik, R.J. (1978). Neuropsychological stability in multiple sclerosis. *Journal of Consulting and Clinical Psychology, 46*, 913–923.

Josiassen, R.C., Curry, L., Roemer, R.A., DeBease, C., & Mancall, E.L. (1982). Patterns of intellectual deficit in Huntington's disease. *Journal of Clinical Neuropsychology, 4,* 173–183.

Karlin, D.B., & Hirschenfang, S. (1960). A comparison of visuosensory and visuomotor disturbances in right and left hemiplegics. *American Journal of Opthalmology, 50,* 627–631.

Levin, H.S., Benton, A.L., & Grossman, R.G. (1982). *Neurobehavioral consequences of closed head injury.* New York: Oxford University Press.

Lezak, M.D. (1983). *Neuropsychological assessment* (2nd ed.). New York: Oxford University Press.

Long, J.A., & McLachlan, J.F.C. (1974). Abstract reasoning and perceptual-motor efficiency in alcoholics: Impairment and reversibility. *Quarterly Journal of Studies on Alcohol, 35,* 1220–1229.

Mandelberg, I.A. (1975). Cognitive recovery after severe head injury: 2. Wechsler Adult Intelligence Scale during post-traumatic amnesia. *Journal of Neurology, Neurosurgery, and Psychiatry, 38,* 1127–1132.

Mandelberg, I.A., & Brooks, D.N. (1975). Cognitive recovery after severe head injury: 1. Serial testing on the Wechsler Adult Intelligence Scale. *Journal of Neurology, Neurosurgery, and Psychiatry, 38,* 1121–1126.

Marsh, G.G. (1980). Disability and intellectual function in multiple sclerosis patients. *Journal of Nervous and Mental Disease, 168,* 758–762.

Matarazzo, J.D. (1972). *Wechsler's measurement and appraisal of adult intelligence.* Baltimore: Williams & Wilkins.

Matarazzo, J.D., Matarazzo, R.G., Weins, A.N., Gallo, A.E., Jr., & Klonoff, H. (1976). Retest reliability of the Halstead Impairment Index in a normal, a schizophrenic, and two samples of organic patients. *Journal of Clinical Psychology, 32,* 338–349.

Matthews, C.G., Cleeland, C.S., & Hopper, C.L. (1970). Neuropsychological patterns in multiple sclerosis. *Diseases of the Nervous System, 31,* 161–170.

Matthews, C.G., & Harley, J.P. (1975). Cognitive and motor-sensory performances in toxic and nontoxic epileptic subjects. *Neurology, 25,* 184–188.

McGlone, J. (1977). Sex differences in the cerebral organization of verbal functions in patients with unilateral brain lesions. *Brain, 100,* 775–793.

Meier, M.J. (1970). Objective behavioral assessment in diagnosis and prediction. In A.L. Benton (Ed.), *Behavioral change in cerebrovascular disease* (pp. 119–154). New York: Harper & Row.

Miller, W.R., & Orr, J. (1980). Nature and sequence of neuropsychological deficits in alcoholics. *Journal of Studies on Alcohol, 41,* 325–337.

Miller, W.R., & Saucedo, C.F. (1983). In C.J. Golden, J.A., Moses, J.A. Coffman, Jr., W.R. Miller, & F.D. Strider (Eds.), *Clinical neuropsychology: Interface with neurologic and psychiatric disorders* (pp. 141–195). New York: Grune & Stratton.

Norton, J.C. (1975). Patterns of neuropsychological test performance in Huntington's disease. *Journal of Nervous and Mental Disease, 161,* 276–279.

O'Donnell, J.P., Kurtz, J., & Ramanaiah, N.V. (1983). Neuropsychological test findings for normal, learning-disabled, and brain-damaged young adults. *Journal of Consulting and Clinical Psychology, 51,* 726–729.

O'Leary, M.R., Donovan, D.M., Chaney, E.F., Walker, R.D., & Schau, E.J. (1979). Application of discriminant analysis to level of performance of alcoholics and nonalcoholics on Wechsler-Bellevue and Halstead-Reitan subtests. *Journal of Clinical Psychology, 35,* 204–208.

Oxbury, J.M., Campbell, D.C., & Oxbury, S.M. (1974). Unilateral spatial neglect and impairments of spatial analysis and visual perception. *Brain, 97,* 551–564.

Parsons, O.A., & Farr, S.P. (1981). The neuropsychology of alcohol and drug use. In S.B. Filskov & T.J. Boll (Eds.), *Handbook of clinical neuropsychology* (Vol. 1, pp. 320–365). New York: John Wiley & Sons.

Perez, F.I., Rivera, V.M., Meyer, J.S., Gay, J.R.A., Taylor, R.L., & Mathew, N.T. (1975). Analysis of intellectual and cognitive performance in patients with multi-infarct dementia, vertebrobasilar insufficiency with dementia, and Alzheimer's disease. *Journal of Neurology, Neurosurgery, and Psychiatry, 38*, 533–540.

Prigatano, G.P. (1977). Neuropsychological functioning in recidivist alcoholics treated with disulfiram. *Alcoholism: Clinical and Experimental Research, 1*, 81–86.

Reitan, R.M., Reed, J.C., & Dyken, M.L. (1971). Cognitive, psychomotor, and motor correlates of multiple sclerosis. *Journal of Nervous and Mental Disease, 153*, 218–224.

Russell, E.W. (1980). Fluid and crystallized intelligence: Effects of diffuse brain-damage on the WAIS. *Perceptual and Motor Skills, 51*, 121–122.

Russell, E.W., Neuringer, C., & Goldstein, G. (1970). *Assessment of brain damage: A neuropsychological key approach.* New York: John Wiley & Sons.

Sandok, B.A. (1975). Organic brain syndromes: Introduction. In A.M. Freedman, H.J. Kaplan, & B.J. Sadock (Eds.), *Comprehensive handbook of psychiatry* (Vol. 1, pp. 1060–1064). Baltimore: Williams & Wilkins.

Sax, D.S., O'Donnell, B., Butters, N., Menzer, L., Montgomery. K., & Kayne, H.L. (1983). Computed tomographic, neurologic, and neuropsychological correlates of Huntington's disease. *International Journal of Neuroscience, 18*, 21–36.

Seidenberg, M., O'Leary, D.S., Berent, S., & Boll, T. (1981). Changes in seizure frequency and test-retest scores on the Wechsler Adult Intelligence Scale. *Epilepsia, 22*, 75–83.

Seidenberg, M., O'Leary, D.S., Giordani, B., Berent, S., & Boll, T.J. (1981). Test-retest IQ changes of epilepsy patients: Assessing the influence of practice effects. *Journal of Clinical Neuropsychology, 3*, 237–255.

Silberstein, J.A., & Parsons, O.A. (1980). Neuropsychological impairment in female alcoholics. In M. Galanter (Ed.), *Currents in alcoholism* (Vol. 7, pp. 481–495). New York: Grune & Stratton.

Smith, J.W., Burt, D.W., & Chapman, R.F. (1973). Intelligence and brain damage in alcoholics: A study in patients of middle and upper social class. *Quarterly Journal of Studies on Alcohol, 34*, 414–422.

Storrie, M.C., & Doerr, H.O. (1980). Characterization of Alzheimer type dementia utilizing an abbreviated Halstead-Reitan Battery. *Journal of Clinical Neuropsychology, 2*, 78–82.

Strub, R.L., & Black, F.W. (1981). *Organic brain syndromes: An introduction to neurobehavioral disorders.* Philadelphia: F.A. Davis.

Tarter, R.E., Goldstein, G., Alterman, A., Petrarulo, E.W., & Elmore, S. (1983). Alcoholic seizures: Intellectual and neuropsychological sequelae. *Journal of Nervous and Mental Disease, 171*, 123–125.

Taylor, H.G., & Hansotia, P. (1983). Neuropsychological testing of Huntington's patients: Clues to progression. *Journal of Nervous and Mental Disease, 171*, 492–496.

Tureen, R.G., Schwartz, M.L., & Dennerll, R.D. (1968). The Halstead-Reitan neuropsychological battery in brain-damaged, normal, and epileptic subjects. *Perceptual and Motor Skills, 27*, 439–442.

Weinberg, J., Diller, L., Gordon, W.A., Gertsman, L.J., Lieberman, A., Lakin, P., Hodges, G., & Ezrachi, O. (1979). Training sensory awareness and spatial organization in people with right brain damage. *Archives of Physical Medicine and Rehabilitation, 60*, 491–496.

Weinberg, J., Diller, L., Gordon, W.A., Gertsman, L.J., Lieberman, A., Lakin, P., Hodges, G., & Ezrachi, O. (1977). Visual scanning training effect on reading-related tasks in acquired right brain damage. *Archives of Physical Medicine and Rehabilitation, 58,* 479–486.

Whitworth, R. (1984, April). *Differences between anglo and Mexican-American students classified as learning disabled.* Paper presented at the annual meeting of the Southwestern Psychological Association, New Orleans.

PART THREE

Disorders

CHAPTER 10

Neuropsychology and Medical Disorders

Charles J. Golden, Mary Ann Strider, Rona Ariel, and Ellen E. Golden

Traditionally, neuropsychologists have concentrated on diseases that directly affect the central nervous system (CNS), such as tumors, CNS strokes, Alzheimer's disease, and the other disorders most often discussed in neuropsychological papers and texts. There has been relatively little emphasis on medical disorders whose primary effect is on other parts of the body but whose secondary effects may impair brain function. Indeed, in many cases, these secondary effects on brain function are seen as psychiatric functional disorders or regarded as stress reactions to the disease, causing the physician and psychologist not to recognize the neuropsychological consequences of the disorders.

In recent years, there has been increasing recognition of the possible roles of these diseases. Given the frequency of many of the problems we discuss in this chapter, it may well be possible that more brain disorders arise from nonneurological diseases than from the diseases normally associated with neuropsychology. Such a finding would not be surprising since the brain is heavily dependent on the functioning of the body and vice versa. Although it constitutes only 2% of the body weight, the brain demands 15% of the body's cardiac output and 20% of its available oxygen. As a consequence of its high metabolic level, even mild interruptions of available oxygen or other metabolites can interfere with brain function, as can changes in the balance of available metabolites. Similarly, the brain is quite sensitive to the presence of toxins generated or retained by the dysfunction of other bodily systems.

For the purpose of the present chapter, we will restrict our discussion to those conditions whose primary effect is on other systems of the body and in which the brain dysfunction is simply a secondary result of the more primary problem. Thus, we will generally ignore all those medical disorders that are most frequently discussed within the neuropsychological literature. The chapter also assumes a basic familiarity with the functions of the human body. It ignores many of the complications arising from the interactions of multiple systems in favor of discussing the relative effects on the brain of disorders of particular body systems. These restrictions are largely in the interest of keeping the chapter within a reasonable number of pages. Similarly, the discussion focuses on the brain itself, rather than on the peripheral parts of the central nervous system.

Many of the areas to be discussed here have been inadequately investigated at present, offering a fertile field for careful investigators. There are a number of reasons for this state of affairs. First, neuropsychologists have largely found themselves working with referrals and in institutional departments concerned with neurologic diseases rather than in departments of internal medicine and similar settings. Psychologists working in these alternative settings have generally been concerned more with therapy (e.g., behavioral approaches to medical management, biofeedback, and other related techniques) and generally have had little training in neuropsychology. Thus, when there have been studies, they have most often used instruments more common in general clinical psychology as tests of organicity (e.g., Bender-Gestalt and the Wechsler Adult Intelligence Scale [WAIS]), which have little value in specifying the effects of conditions that are often subtle except under extreme conditions. This practice has limited greatly the value of the research that is available.

Another related problem is the dependence of neuropsychologists on physicians to identify these disorders. Further research challenges occur because many conditions are difficult to diagnose in their early stages. If they are caught, they are promptly treated, resulting in little time for study. In more advanced cases, in which symptoms are obvious and gross, study reveals little information that allows these conditions to be individually identified.

Because of such lack of data, this chapter uses the experience of the authors with a limited sample of cases in each of these areas, along with what can be gained from the literature, to pose hypothesis and research directions for this fledgling area. The literature review is not intended to be exhaustive but, rather, selective, illustrating the kinds of studies that are available. The discussions are presented according to specific bodily systems.

HEMOLYTIC SYSTEM

The primary function of the hemolytic (blood) system is the delivery of metabolites, oxygen, glucose, and other essential material to the body and brain and to return waste products of body metabolism from these organs. The blood consists of several constituents. Red blood cells carry oxygen to the body. Thus, an abnormal decrease in these cells can result in a deprivation of oxygen. These deficits can occur in a wide variety of ways. Absence of required nutrients; abnormalities in the bone marrow, which produces these cells; and toxic agents can cause deficient manufacture of red blood cells, a condition known as anemia. When the problem is so severe as to deprive the brain of oxygen, the patient shows a variety of symptoms, including lethargy, depression, problems in concentration and attention, diffuse organic brain syndromes, convulsions, and impairment of judgment and other higher-level (prefrontal) skills. These symptoms can progress, with eventual hemorrhaging in cerebral arteries, causing focal deficits characteristic of the location.

It should be noted that these symptoms are not unique to these problems, but, rather, describe a syndrome common to many diseases that results in a general state of cerebral hypoxia. This commonality of symptoms is caused by the relatively greater demands of the prefrontal and some subcortical areas for oxygen. This occurs because these areas coordinate widely disparate cell aggregates and thereby have a higher metabolic rate. Deficits of a more focal nature generally await the appearance of focal hemorrhages or the progression of the disease. Thus, it is rare in early stages to see classic aphasic or specific disorders of such skills as reading and naming. This state of affairs renders many neuropsychological tests insensitive to these disorders and inappropriate for this population.

Such disorders also create other medical problems that interfere with neuropsychological assessment. The individual has less endurance and ability to withstand long psychological tests, causing declines in function that can be a result of physical fatigue or the natural depression that accompanies severe physical illness. In such cases, it can be quite difficult to separate depressions caused by brain dysfunction from those that are reactions to the disease itself. This condition requires close and sensitive evaluation in the assessment of such persons.

Other problems can result from an excess of red blood cells or an excess of the platelets in the blood, making it more viscous. Polycythemia is not usually associated with hypoxia until quite late, when clotting becomes a problem. It is hypothesized that viscous blood becomes more sluggish, resulting in decreased oxygen carrying capacity. These symptoms include headaches, dizziness, visual and hearing problems, and parasthesias, in addition to the symptoms discussed above. Deficits in platelets can cause small bleeds in the brain and elsewhere due to coagulation defects, resulting in major destruction of brain tissue. This can occur secondary to such diseases as leukemia or as a result of infection, irradiation, or massive blood transfusions. These problems, as well as red blood cell dysfunction, may also arise from primary blood diseases. For example, Matoth, Zaizov, and Frankel (1971) examined 20 children with chronic thrombocytopenia (decreased number of platelets) and found that over 50% showed mildly abnormal electroencephalograms (EEGs), compared to 15% in a control group. Unfortunately, few studies in this area have looked at many diseases with an adequate neuropsychological battery, so most conclusions are based on anecdotal evidence rather than on good research data.

The plasma portion of blood contains water, electrolytes, and organic substances such as proteins, fats, sugars, and hormones. Defects in fluid electrolyte balance can result in edema (swelling) of the brain, with consequent impairment of brain function. Disorders that interrupt the electrolyte balance of the brain can result in poor transmission of nerve impulses.

White blood cells are responsible for attacking and ingesting foreign particles, such as bacteria; cleansing the blood of potentially dangerous material; and removing clots or other dead tissue. A lack of white cells can result in rampant infections that attack the brain. When white blood cells are found in excess, as in leukemia, they function poorly and also cause vulnerability to infection. Other immune function defects may lead to attacks on healthy tissue.

Abnormally high levels of clotting factors and certain plasma proteins can result in the creation of clots that may partially or fully close off vessels in the body either suddenly or more slowly over a long period of time. When the vessels involved directly serve the brain, this can result in infarction, ischemia, or occlusion. When other parts of the body are involved, this can cause specific organ system dysfunctions that in turn affect the brain.

DIGESTIVE SYSTEM

The primary function of the digestive system is to ingest food and to extract from that food those constituents necessary for the survival of the body. The system also acts to allow the absorption of these necessary constituents. Disorders generally result in a loss of one or more important materials necessary for the functioning of the brain and other organs of the body.

Important functions (for our purposes) can be broken down by specific organ. The stomach produces the intrinsic factor necessary for the absorption of vitamin B_{12}.

Vitamin B_{12} is necessary as a coenzyme involved in the production of nerve impulses. Absence of vitamin B_{12} may result in abnormal EEGs in 60% of all cases (Walton, 1954). Shulman (1967) found memory deficits in 75% of such patients, and forms of dementia have been identified that appear to respond to treatment with B_{12} (Hunter, Jones, & Matthews, 1967) if the disease is acute. However, long-term deficiency may result in permanent brain damage (Roos, 1974; Roos & Willanger, 1977). Vitamin B_{12} and folic acid are essential for the manufacture of red blood cells. Therefore, deficits in B_{12} result in pernicious anemia with symptoms previously discussed.

From the stomach, food passes into the small intestine, where most absorption takes place. The small intestine itself is dependent on substances from the liver, gallbladder, and pancreas to perform its functions correctly. The liver serves as the main chemical factory of the body and detoxifies chemicals that cannot be metabolized for nutrition so that they can be excreted.

Alcohol has a toxic effect on the liver, as do many other ingested drugs, which may result in cirrhosis of the liver and reduce its functions. The liver is responsible for storing vitamin B_{12}, along with vitamins A and D. It helps maintain blood glucose levels and manufactures clotting proteins. Liver insufficiency can result in low blood glucose levels, which starve the brain of the glucose necessary to maintain cell metabolism. Severe brain damage, coma, or death can result. Acute liver damage can give rise to poorly understood toxins as well. Acker, Aps, Majumdar, Shaw, and Thompson (1982) found a strong relationship between computed tomography (CT) scan changes in the brains of alcoholics and the greater severity of liver disease. Similar results have been reported by us after examining brain density data from a previous study (Golden et al., 1981), as well as in clinical studies of alcoholics with and without brain dysfunction.

Because of these varied functions, damage to the liver is of serious consequence to brain function. Hepatic encephalopathy involves impaired intellectual functioning, reduced consciousness, slowed reaction time, and labile emotionality. For example, Elsass, Lund, and Ranek (1978) gave select tests to 30 cirrhotic patients, comparing their performance to 30 patients with diffuse brain damage. They found that the two groups were quite similar except for increased attentional deficits in the liver-impaired patients. Rehnstrom and colleagues (1977) assessed 41 liver disease patients and found impaired intellectual performance regardless of the cause of the liver disease. They reported rapid changes in patients' conditions depending on liver functions at the time of assessment.

The liver also produces bile, which is in turn stored in the gallbladder. Further important materials that also aid digestion are generated by the pancreas. Food is mixed with all these substances at the top of the small intestine (the duodenum) and then proceeds through the small intestine for absorption. Blockage of bile results in a failure to absorb fatty acids, while impairment of the pancreas interferes with the absorption of fat, protein, and starches. Further activity takes place in the colon, which aids in the absorption of water and electrolytes. Since water is necessary for the operation of the entire body and electrolytes are essential for nerve function, disorders in the digestive system can also affect the functioning of the brain. Water dehydration can result in personality changes, including increased irritability in early stages, and later progress to delirium, coma, and eventually death. Acute losses may lead to symptoms similar to these seen in Guillain-Barré syndrome (Krause, Winter, Scheglmann, & Reuther, 1982). Water excess can result in electrolyte imbalance, also resulting in impaired nerve functioning, causing a generalized impairment of brain function, with overlearned skills being relatively impaired. Water excess can also lead to brain edema, as noted earlier, and acutely may cause convulsions.

Much interest in the literature has centered around deficits in the absorption of the water-soluble B vitamins: thiamine (B_1), niacin, riboflavin (B_2), B_{12}, and folic acid. These vitamins serve as coenzymes and are involved in the process of nerve impulse transmission. Severe thiamine deficiency from any cause produces Wernicke's encephalopathy and is suspected in some cases of senile dementia. The symptoms of Wernicke's encephalopathy are difficulty in concentration, disturbances in sleep, confusion, staggering gait, vision problems, and eventually stupor and coma. The disorder is seen most commonly in cases of chronic alcoholism and severe malnutrition.

Victor, Adams, and Collins (1971) reported on a two-month follow-up of patients who survived acute Wernicke's encephalopathy. Gait problems had reversed in only half the patients, while memory problems remained in most patients, although confusion generally cleared. Eighty-four percent of the patients developed Korsakoff's psychosis. Pathological changes include hemorrhages in the thalamus, hypothalamus, and gray matter of the upper brain stem.

In general, almost all studies of vitamin deficiency have concentrated on persons with severe deficits. Little attention has been devoted to persons with minor deficiencies or those who vary across the normal range of vitamin availability. One interesting attempt to address these issues, however, was recently published by Goodwin, Goodwin, and Garry (1983).

In this study, the authors examined whether subclinical deficiencies in vitamins in the elderly might affect the cognitive functioning of 260 healthy men and women who were at least 60 years of age. Nutritional status of the patients was evaluated by three-day food records and biochemical analysis for specific nutrients. The neuropsychological tests included the Halstead-Reitan Category Test and the Wechsler Memory Scale (WMS).

Intake levels of nutrients were not correlated with the neuropsychological tests. However, blood levels were correlated significantly in two instances: riboflavin with WMS at .14 ($p < .05$) and vitamin C with WMS at .15 ($p < .05$). In order to look at nonlinear relationships, the authors compared the performance of the bottom 5%, bottom 10%, and top 90% of the population, on the assumption that these lower groups might represent those with subclinical nutritional deficiencies. Mild relationships were found between the Category Test and vitamin C and folate. WMS relationships were found for protein, thiamine, riboflavin, pyridoxine, niacin, and folate. In all cases, these relationships were based on t-tests, and all relationships were mild, with considerable overlap in group scores.

Clearly, this study could be criticized for running a large number of correlations and t-tests and possibly capitalizing on chance variance, as well as giving significance to very small differences in group means due to the use of very large sample sizes. Results were also inconsistent: in some cases, the bottom 10% showed a significant difference, while the bottom 5% did not. As suggested by the low correlations, even when there was a linear relationship, the amount of variance accounted for was quite minimal (under 3%).

Despite these legitimate caveats, the study still stands as an excellent first attempt in an area where we can only expect very small relationships. The study certainly suggests that increased research is mandatory in this area with improved designs, including the use of a more comprehensive neuropsychological battery or batteries of tests. Since memory correlates appeared the strongest, it would be quite useful to examine whether more complex forms of memory delay and memory interference not measured on the WMS might show even stronger relationships with these types of subtle dysfunctions, or whether long-term memory or intermediate memory might also show relationships. Research into other aspects of cognition is also necessary. Finally, given the statistical limitations of this study, replication is absolutely necessary.

Mineral deficiencies, primarily in potassium and sodium, can lead to numerous symptoms. Aita (1964) reported that excess potassium can produce listlessness and muscle paralysis, while depletion may cause weakness, confusion, and eventually coma. Calcium deficit may result in tetany and convulsions as well as delirium. Sodium depletion leads to cerebral edema, whereas sodium excess may be asymmptomatic until acute collapse, convulsions, coma, and death. In elderly patients, diuretic medication (used to alter water retention caused by cardiac problems) may produce electrolyte imbalances that cause similar problems, including both depression and paranoia (e.g., Taylor, 1979).

Little is known in many cases about the isolated loss of specific nutrients, and there is a lack of studies on specific disease states with homogeneous etiologies. There is also a dearth of work that might identify whether some symptoms may act as precursors to others on a neuropsychological level. However, our experience suggests that many of the same functions that are most sensitive to hypoxia are also sensitive to these imbalances, although overlearned verbal skills and long-term memory are less affected in early stages. It appears clear that neuropsychological symptoms probably exist long before the more dramatic symptoms appear. Early cases of these disorders have not been well studied, since such populations are difficult to identify and are usually promptly treated when they are identified. It is quite likely that some unknown percentage of serious psychiatric problems may be due to some of these problems.

CARDIOVASCULAR SYSTEM

The cardiovascular system plays a clear and important role in the support of brain functions. The system is primarily responsible for the delivery of blood, and the nutrients and other substances within blood, to all of the organs of the body as well as for picking up waste products and returning them to the appropriate organs for disposal. The system must maintain blood flow at levels necessary to the activity level of a patient, while maintaining pressure within the system as a whole within certain predefined limits. Since the brain is heavily dependent on a large percentage of cardiac output, it is very sensitive to changes outside normal variations and may react with either acute or temporary shut down, or suffer long-term irreversible damage.

The cardiac system is set so that perfusion of the brain is usually preserved even at the cost of other organs. As a result, minor disorders may not affect the brain immediately. However, prolonged deficiencies eventually affect brain function, as can massive short-term disruption. Prolonged dysfunction results in the pattern of long-term hypoxia, already discussed, in which deficits are seen primarily in attention, concentration, and more complex cortical functions, with less impairment in overlearned skills, such as speech and reading. Memory deficits are usually seen in these disorders as well. In this hypoxic state, the brain is also more sensitive to acute variations or to short-term worsening of chronic problems. Thus, several episodes of short-term loss of oxygenation superimposed on general hypoxia may create much greater losses than predicted by the overall length of time in which the brain is deprived of oxygen. After a serious cardiac arrest, the deficits may be missed because of the more serious threats to the patient's continued existence, only to be noticed after the patient returns home or to work. Early testing of such patients can be useful in identifying areas of function that may interfere with the patient's return to normal life.

Extreme drops in blood pressure caused by heart failure can result in dizziness or confusion, which may progress to delirium in the acute stages and dementia in more chronic cases. Deficits can occasionally be focal, as some areas react to the stress of anoxia differentially. These reactions include such focal signs as the aphasias. These deficits may be permanent or temporary and may vary considerably among individuals.

Increased blood pressure (hypertension) may cause the rupturing of the weaker vessels within the brain (stroke), producing the symptoms characteristic of injury to the area affected. Hypertension can result from several sources. It can be caused by restriction of the size of the vessels within the body. This is most often caused by changes in the elasticity of the vessels themselves or by a buildup of material on the vessel walls (such as cholesterol plaques), which restricts the size of the vessels. Increases in blood viscosity may cause a need for higher cardiac pressures, which in turn overloads the elasticity of the vessels. Also, elasticity of blood vessels decreases with age. The brain itself plays a role in blood pressure control, and this function too is impaired by hypoxia.

In general, hypotension has only mild or generally unnoticeable effects on brain functioning but can produce diffuse damage either acutely or chronically, depending on the vulnerability of the brain. It has been our experience that brains that have been previously damaged are more sensitive to the effects of this and other conditions, with apparent deficits being far greater than might be effected by the nadere of the specific condition alone. In more severe hypotensive cases, there may be fainting (with the possibility of additional damage caused by head trauma), convulsions (rare), or loss of cognitive skills.

A restriction of blood flow to the kidneys (from any cause) can cause the release of a substance that facilitates constriction of the vessels, which in turn leads to hypertension. Genetic factors promote hypertension. For example, some individuals develop hypertension after large (or even small) intakes of caffeine or caffeinlike substances. The effects of hypertension are generally similar regardless of actual cause.

Cardiac disease may be caused by the development of bacterial endocarditis, an infection of heart tissue caused by the collection of bacteria in damaged valves or endocardium. This infection weakens the heart and impairs delivery of nutrients and oxygen to the brain. In addition, clots laden with bacteria may form and be transmitted by the bloodstream to the brain itself, causing stroke-impaired blood flow and secondary infection. An abscess must be strongly considered in cases in which focal neuropsychological signs develop in a patient with recent heart problems. These conditions can cause a wide variety of symptoms, depending on the brain areas involved and how widespread the disorder becomes. Cognitive impairment from subtle worsening of cardiac vascular disease may initially be labeled psychiatric because the patients exhibit depression or confusion as their initial symptoms.

Other treatment for cardiac problems, especially surgery, may cause problems as well. Brain perfusion may be reduced while the patient is connected to an artificial heart during surgery. Thrombosis, embolism, anoxia, or toxic-allergic reactions to anesthesia (rare) or other medications may occur. Infections can spread to the brain from the sites or surgery, or the heart may fail to normally regulate blood flow after surgery, causing periods of hypoxia. General stress can result in the hemorrhaging of small or large vessels that were initially weak.

Studies using EEG tracings have indicated that heart surgery patients show more abnormalities after heart surgery than they do before (Brobeck, 1979). In general, if these abnormalities do not return to normal within a month, permanent brain damage has likely occurred. Patients with pre-existing neuropsychological deficits are more at risk for the development of complications from surgery (Kilpatrick, Miller, Allan, & Lee, 1975).

A popular area of research has been the study of patients undergoing surgery for the relief of narrowing or blockage of the internal carotid arteries (endarterectomies). Such patients often have a history of transient ischemic attacks characterized by a variety of often mild, short-lived neuropsychological symptoms. Studies have focused on whether such operations cause a lessening of risk for future strokes and allow improvements in neuropsychological functioning. Most commonly, these studies have used the WAIS or Halstead-Reitan test batteries, although individually designed research batteries have been employed as well.

Some studies have reported definite improvement as a result of such operations, although the degree and type of improvement has been inconsistent (Borstein, Benoit, & Trites, 1981; Owens et al., 1980; Jacques, Garner, Tager, Rosenstock, & Fields, 1978; King, Gideon, Haynes, Dempsey, & Jenkins, 1977; Haynes, Gideon, King, & Dempsey, 1976; Perry, Drindwater, & Taylor, 1975; Horne & Royle, 1974; Goldstein, Kleinknecht, & Gallo, 1970). Other studies have failed to report any improvement or even reported functional decline (Matarazzo, Matarazzo, Gallo, & Weins, 1979; Drake, Baker, Blumenkrantz, & Dahlgren, 1968; Murphy & Maccubbin, 1966; Williams & McGee, 1964). Matarazzo and colleagues concluded that most of the improvement reported in other studies represented test-retest improvement rather than actual skill improvement. Objections can also be raised regarding the idea that patients should improve. In some cases of carotid artery blockage or partial blockage, there is no actual decline in the total blood flow available to the brain, since flow speeds simply increase to make up for less available width in the artery or collateral circulation develops through the other carotid if the disorder develops slowly. No study has clearly demonstrated the degree of actual blood flow impairment to the brain from these conditions through the use of regional cerebral blood flow or other similar techniques. As a consequence, although this area represents one of the most heavily researched areas within this subfield, we still are unable to reach definitive conclusions on the effects of these operations.

Lishman (1978) has noted that many patients with mild impairment of the cardio-vascular system show personality changes, including depression, paranoia, irritability, anxiety, and psychosis. Such changes have not been well studied and may be the result of brain dysfunction, reactions to the disease, or, more likely, a combination of both. Nielsen and colleagues (1983) reported subtle signs of dementia in 7 of 13 cardiac patients 1 to 3 years after a cardiac arrest. Of importance is their report that the signs of dementia were not obvious on clinical interview and thus may be missed if more extensive examination is not completed.

Another possible use for neuropsychological testing in cardiac patients is in predicting outcome from serious cardiac surgery. Although most such attempts have met with failure, Sotaniemi (1982) found that if a battery of tests was used (including neuropsychological as well as neurological tests), one could identify which patients were likely to have cerebral complications following open heart surgery. In this study, 24 of 28 cases predicted to be high-risk cases had cerebral complications associated with the surgery. More work needs to be done in this area, but it does suggest a promising use of neuropsychological testing.

Cardiovascular disorders also create other medical problems throughout the body that further interfere with neuropsychological assessment. Cardiovascular patients lack endurance, and observed declines in function on psychological tests can be a result of physical fatigue or the natural depressions that accompany severe physical illness. As noted, it can be quite difficult to separate depressions induced from brain dysfunction from those that are reactions to the disease itself.

RESPIRATORY SYSTEM

The lung takes in oxygen, releases carbon dioxide, and assists in the regulation of the acidity (pH) of the blood. Air is drawn into intimate contact with a thin membrane that is richly supplied with blood vessels. This semipermeable membrane allows gas diffusion. The lung functions to dispose of carbon dioxide (CO_2), a waste product formed from food digestion, and to take in oxygen (O_2), which is essential to energy processes in the body.

Respiratory movements are under the control of the respiratory center in the medulla. Damage to the brain's respiratory center can lead to aberrant breathing patterns or the requirement of artificial ventilation (breathing machine) to maintain life.

A loss of lung elasticity causes poor expiration. This rigidity most frequently occurs from chronic bronchitis, but aging alone results in some tissue stiffness. Asthma, lung edema, and membrane thickening also impair elasticity. Emphysema occurs when there is dilation of microscopic air sacs, loss of elasticity, and decreased surface area for gas exchange. Fluid or air between the lung and chest wall impairs respiration. Anything that causes narrowing of airways, such as asthma or bronchitis, reduces respiration. The lung can become inflamed, as in pneumonia, and then fluid forms within the lung, reducing oxygen exchange.

Our main interest in lung function stems from the high metabolic need of the brain for oxygen carried in blood. Fresh oxygen is continually added to the blood flowing from the heart through the lungs and is delivered to tissues in the body and organs. Carbon dioxide is picked up by the blood and brought to the lungs where it is expired.

Blood pH must remain within a limited range to maintain a viable medium for body protein and enzyme activity. The respiratory center has the main role in controlling blood pH, in association with the kidneys. The carbon dioxide blood level cues the healthy respiratory center to increase breathing if carbon dioxide is high or to reduce respiration if the level is low. A low carbon dioxide level induces increased excitability in nerves and muscles, and can bring about spontaneous spasms. This state is known as tetany. Carbon dioxide is a vasodilator; therefore, a low CO_2 level reduces cerebral blood flow, and the person feels dizzy and has trouble thinking, as happens with neurotic hyperventilation.

Asphyxia occurs when there is an oxygen lack and CO_2 buildup in the body. Anoxia is a state of complete oxygen deprivation; when less severe, it is called hypoxia. In anoxia, the person becomes disoriented and passes quickly into coma. There are several types of anoxia (Barcroft, 1920; Lishman, 1978).

Anoxic anoxia is due to lack of oxygen in the inspired air or is the result of lung diseases that prevent available oxygen from entering the blood. A second type is called *anemic anoxia* and is due to a deficiency of hemoglobin. This is most frequently caused by a state of anemia, but it may also be the result of carbon monoxide poisoning or abrupt blood loss as in gastrointestinal hemorrhage. Smith and Brandon (1973) assessed carbon monoxide victims and found that almost half had memory impairment at follow-up, and irritability and impulsiveness occurred commonly in one-third of patients. Symptoms may remain for up to a year.

A third type of anoxia, *stagnant anoxia*, results from blood difficulties; despite adequate oxygen content, oxygen tension, and hemoglobin carrying capacity, blood flows at such a slow rate that it does not supply tissues with enough oxygen to meet their needs. Another type is *histotoxic anoxia* (metabolic). In this condition, there is a failure in the tissue cells to extract oxygen from the blood. This occurs in cyanide or carbon disulfide poisoning and with hypoglycemia. *Overutilization anoxia* occurs locally in the brain during epileptic seizures, due to the high metabolic demands.

The brain can only survive complete anoxia for six minutes. The cerebral cortex and the myocardium are most vulnerable to anoxia. It appears that with less than total oxygen deficit, brain cells may continue to survive but will cease neuronal firing. With improved nutrition and restored oxygen, some cells may recover, although they will remain weakened and vulnerable. Not all cells will necessarily recover, however, and there are wide individual differences in reactions to such conditions.

Neuropsychological research in the area of brain damage in lung disorders is quite limited. Chronic obstructive pulmonary disease (COPD) has been studied mainly by physiological and biochemical means. Studies by Krop, Block, and Cohen (1973) and Block, Castle, and Keitt (1974) have used some neuropsychological measures in assessing COPD patients; they report that depressed neuropsychological functioning was prevalent, although comparisons to normal control groups were not used.

Fix, Golden, Naughton, Cass, and Bell (1982) examined the neuropsychological performance of 66 patients with COPD on a large battery of tests, including several WAIS subtests, the Stroop Color and Word Test, the Benton Visual Retention Test, and subtests from the Halstead-Reitan Battery. The independent measures in the study included forced expiratory volume during the first second, the most sensitive of pulmonary measures to patient deterioration and demise (Boushy & Thompson, 1973). In addition, data were collected on arterial blood gases, including the partial pressure of oxygen and carbon dioxide, as well as arterial oxygen saturation.

Overall, the patients scored at the seventy-fifth percentile on the intellectual tasks but generally showed borderline normal or borderline impaired performance on the neuropsychological tests. Since the group was chosen for chronic COPD, the physiological measures were generally clearly in the impaired range. Correlations between individual neuropsychological tests and the physiological measures ranged from essentially zero to .48 with highest correlations found for Digit Symbol and the color-word interference card of the Stoop Color and Word Test. Multiple correlations were highest for the partial pressure of oxygen in arterial blood $(.63, p < .05)$ and for forced expiratory volume in the first second $(.59, p < .05)$. The authors concluded that there was a relationship generally between complex integrative functions and the physiological indicators of COPD similar to the types of deficits seen in chronic alcoholism and metabolic disorders. The deficits were consistent with impairment in the frontal and subcortical areas, consistent with the higher oxygen demand of these areas.

In general, it was found that the severity of the cognitive deficits was generally much milder than the degree of COPD. This suggests that there may be compensatory mechanisms available that protect the brain partially. Compensation may be represented by increased blood flow to improve oxygen delivery. The finding by Buchweitz, Sinha, and Weiss (1980) that the brain receives over twice as much oxygen as is actually necessary for functioning may also be related (although one cannot expect 100% efficiency in such functions).

Studies related to this area have attempted to see if increasing oxygen input can be successful in improving test scores. Several studies using either hyperbaric oxygen or low-flow oxygen therapy have shown improvement in cognitive skills in seriously deteriorated patients with generally more severe initial deficits than in the above study (e.g., see Edwards, 1974; Fowler, 1975; Jacobs et al., 1969; Krop, Block, and Cohen, 1973; Kass et al., 1975).

In a study of a less severely impaired population than represented by these studies or by Fix, Golden, Daughton, Kass, and Bell (1982), investigators Schraa, Dirks, Jones, and Kinsman (1981) reported a high incidence (65%) of Bender-Gestalt abnormalities in a chronic asthmatic population. The limitations of the test battery do not allow for speculation as to the nature of the deficit, but the study does suggest that this is an area open to further investigation.

Persons with impaired lung functions are likely to be more cerebrally vulnerable to another event that can alter brain metabolism. They may react with severely acute symptoms to even mild brain trauma, drug influence, or alcohol use.

URINARY SYSTEM

The kidneys assist in the maintenance of water balance, blood pH, and electrolyte balance. The functional unit of the kidney is a nephron, which consists of filter tubes. There are estimated to be about 1 million nephron units in each kidney (Green, 1978).

Blood goes to the kidneys directly from the aorta by way of the renal arteries. The renal arteries divide into a net of intertwined capillaries shaped into a tiny ball. This coil ball of capillaries is called the glomerulus. The blood returns from the kidney via the renal vein. Blood flow is slowed as it goes through the glomerulus, giving time for water ions and small molecules such as urea to diffuse outward. These substances are filtered, and unwanted material is passed on to the bladder. Some substances, such as glucose, are returned to the blood stream for further use.

Kidney damage can result in protein wastage and edema, a condition called nephrosis. Inflammation (nephritis) may also impair the functioning of the kidneys. When kidney function is impaired and urine production is reduced, the waste products that are usually excreted are retained in the body, leading to potentially fatal disorders. Diet may be used to control such problems up to a point, but eventually dialysis may be required. In dialysis, the patients's blood is filtered through an artificial kidney. Dialysis treatments may take up to six hours three times a week.

Severe psychological, as well as neuropsychological, complications are known to arise from dialysis. Depression is common, both as a result of the body's dysfunction as well as stress on the patient. The patient may then be unable to follow the necessary medical regimen, further exacerbating the disease. Other phenomena, however, show that some symptoms and behavior can be related to interference with nervous system functioning (Marshall, 1979).

It is well known that cognitive functioning is severely impaired in uremia. Characteristic symptoms such as sluggish mentation, lethargy, anorexia, nausea and vomiting, tremors, sleepiness, and convulsions have been widely recognized (Ginn, 1975; Raskin & Fishman, 1976). These symptoms are relieved by dialysis. It is important to note that there is a time lag between treatment on dialysis and subsequent improvement or deterioration of the patient's behavior or mental status changes. Lewis, Neil, Dustman, and Beck (1980) found performance on a test of visual-motor speed and accuracy was best 24 hours after dialysis. The reason for this lag is not known, although it is hypothesized to represent a delay in cellular recovery or in distribution of toxic agents.

It is now well recognized that an encephalopathy called *dialysis disequilibrium syndrome* may be a consequence of the dialysis procedure itself (Marshall, 1979). This syndrome has characteristic course. Over two to three months, the patient develops intermittent slowing speech, with stuttering and word-finding problems. Symptoms usually are more predominant during or right after dialysis. This progresses to difficulty in producing sentences, and myoclonus and dyspraxic movements occur. Severe memory loss, concentration problems, and at times overt psychosis develops. Other symptoms appear toward the end of the dialysis run and may subside over several hours, but the delirium, when it appears, may persist for several days. Evidence suggests that shifts of sodium and potassium, with movement of water into the brain (edema), may cause the disequilibrium syndrome (Raskin & Fishman, 1976). It is still unclear which toxic metabolites or end products are responsible for the documented changes.

There is also a *dialysis dementia*, an ultimately fatal encephalopathy seen in long-term dialysis (Alfrey et al., 1972; Manhurkar, Dhar, & Salta, 1973). It is first characterized by a disturbance in speech, with facial grimacing, convulsions, and eventually dementia. The symptoms initially occur during the dialysis and clear after a period of time, but eventually these remissions no longer occur and the syndrome progresses. The pathogenesis of this disorder remains unknown and no successful treatment has been found.

There are reports of subdural hematomas in dialysis patients (Talalla, Halbrook, Barbour, & Kurze, 1970). Their occurrence appears to be related to two possibilities. Many of these patients are given anticoagulant drugs so that they can maintain their shunts against thrombosis. In addition, patients with kidney failure can have abnormal bleeding. The symptoms may look similar to the dialysis disequilibrium syndrome and sometimes are very difficult to clinically differentiate from it. However, the persistence or worsening of symptoms between dialysis runs alerts one to consider a subdural hematoma as opposed to the disequilibrium syndrome, and neuropsychological assessment can aid in documenting the patient's functional level.

Assessment of mental status and neuropsychological functioning in uremic patients can provide useful treatment recommendations. Obtaining good baseline measures early in the diagnosis of renal disease allows more valid assessment of any later deterioration and response to dialysis when initiated. The timing of neuropsychological assessment of dialysis patients must be considered. Patients fluctuate greatly during the dialysis regimen. It appears that metabolic effects, which modulate brain functioning, vary widely and produce different performance patterns.

Ryan, Souheaver, and DeWolff (1981) reported comparative neuropsychological assessments on chronic hemodialysis patients, undialyzed uremic patients, and medically-psychiatrically ill patients. On the Halstead-Reitan Battery, significant differences were found between the kidney patient group and the comparison group of medical-psychiatric patients. Dialysis patients did perform better than uremic patients on some tasks but were impaired relative to the medical-psychiatric group. A valuable aspect of this study was the clear indication that chronic hemodialysis patients cannot be considered essentially normal in their neuropsychological functioning.

ENDOCRINE SYSTEM

The endocrine system includes the following glands: pituitary, thyroid, four parathyroids, two adrenals, the pancreas, two gonads, the placenta in pregnancy, and the thymus. Hormones are chemical substances produced by the endocrine glands and are secreted directly into the blood. The hormones circulate in the blood and influence the activity of distant organs.

The *pituitary gland* lies in a bony cavity at the base of the skull, suspended from the hypothalamus. Its two sections have quite different functions. The posterior pituitary is directly behind the chiasma of the optic nerve. A tumor of the pituitary can, from pressure, cause some visual field defects or complete blindness. The posterior pituitary produces two hormones: antidiuretic hormone (ADH) and oxytocin. ADH has as its function the regulation of reabsorption of water by the kidney tubules. It also causes vasoconstriction of blood vessels and, if present in large amounts, hypertension. Oxytocin is important in pregnant women because it produces contractions of the uterus and facilitates lactation.

The anterior pituitary gland, which is thought to be controlled by inhibiting and releasing factors from the hypothalamus, releases at least six hormones: human growth hormone, thyrotropic hormone, ACTH (adrenocorticotrophic hormone), prolactin, and two gonadotrophic hormones. The human growth hormone (somatotropin) reacts on body tissue generally. During childhood it stimulates the growth of bone and muscle tissue, and an overactivity may lead to giantism, while underactivity produces dwarfism. It does not appear essential to nervous system development, and therefore low production produces undersized but not retarded individuals.

The *thyroid gland* has two pear-shaped lobes molded to the sides of the trachea. Thyroid hormones stimulate metabolism. They act in all cells of the body, increasing the rate at which food is converted into heat and energy. The functioning of the thyroid gland requires iodine in the diet, and people who are deficient in iodine may develop an iodine deficiency goiter, or swelling of the thyroid gland. This results in underactivity of the gland. A goiter, however, may also be due to a tumor that may result from overactivity of the gland.

Underactivity of the thyroid gland (called hypothyroidism) results in the lowering of the body's metabolism. This condition in adulthood is called myxoedema. When such a condition occurs in children, it may produce cretinism (dwarfism and mental retardation). In underactivity of the thyroid, the patient develops lowered body temperature, lowered heart rate, sluggish activity, and generalized edema. The patient appears lethargic and has slow cognitive functioning. Appetite is reduced, and hearing, taste, and smell may be impaired as mucoid material is deposited (Lishman, 1978). Depression is a frequently entertained diagnosis because myxoedema has an insidious onset; it may exist for several months before striking symptoms demand attention. Psychosis with mental confusion, paranoia, auditory hallucinations, and delirium features can develop. In some cases, a dementia picture is seen. Coma, when it occurs, carries a high mortality rate. When hypothyroidism had been undiagnosed for long periods, intellectual and memory deficits may remain (Jellinek, 1962). In such suspected cases, repeated assessment of functioning is necessary.

Overactivity of the thyroid is called hyperthyroidism. Metabolic rate increases, temperature may rise, faster heartbeat is maintained, and the patient may complain of difficulties staying asleep. Patients with overactive thyroids may present as very nervous and irritable, overactive, and possibly paranoid. They may lose weight and have an anxious, staring expression with possible protrusion of the eyeballs. The hyperarousal can produce concentration problems due to distractibility and persons may be diagnosed as manic. An acute reaction of delirium and organic psychoses occasionally accompany hyperthyroidism. Accurate diagnosis and treatment of thyroid disorders usually yields good results.

The two *adrenal glands* are situated on each side of the kidneys. The central part of the adrenal gland releases mainly adrenalin and noradrenalin, substances called catecholamines, and is triggered by sympathetic nervous stimulation. Excessive production of catecholamines can result in high blood pressure. When present in excess, aldosterone causes sodium and water retention and a loss of potassium. The adrenal cortex also produces several corticosteroids.

The hormonal functions of the adrenal cortex are complex. They have antiallergic and anti-inflammatory properties and are also involved in protein metabolism. The excess of cortisol with resulting edema, increased blood pressure, and blood glucose gives rise to a condition called Cushing's disease. Cushing's disease may present with personality changes, complaints of fatigue and wakefulness, and menstrual irregularities. Psychiatric difficulties, usually depression, have been reported in about half of the diagnosed cases; 15% or more show psychosis (Michael & Gibbons, 1963). Treatment of the endocrine disorder is highly effective in reversing the symptoms. Whelan, Schteingart, Starkman, and Smith (1980) found varying degrees of diffuse cerebral dysfunction in two-thirds of the group they studied. Impairment was more frequent and severe on nonverbal, visual-ideational, and visual-memory measures.

Underactivity of the adrenal gland is called Addison's disease. It can occur because of atrophy, or the gland may be destroyed by tuberculosis. The patient has increased vulnerability to infections and a low blood sugar. The patient may comment on a salt craving, and personality changes may be observed. The patient becomes more quiet and seclusive, unexpressive, and apathetic; exhibits psychomotor retardation; and may show depressive and paranoid aspects. Psychotic behavior may occur, with paranoid delusions, agitation, and even hallucinations. Memory deficits are quite common (Michael & Gibbons, 1963). Psychological abnormalities common to chronic exhaustion are seen, fostering a diagnosis of depression or dementia. Clinical reports hold that recovery is highly successful, but neuropsychological studies are not available.

There are four *parathyroid glands*, which are situated close to the thyroid gland. They produce parathormone, which helps maintain the plasma calcium level. Reduction of the parathyroid gland leads to a low plasma calcium. The result of this is excitability of nerves and neuromuscular junctions, ultimately leading to tetany. Similar increased excitability of nerve cells in the brain may lead to convulsions. Decreased activity of these glands also may produce kidney stones, bony problems, and frank psychosis.

The *pancreas*, the digestive role of which has already been mentioned, also has an endocrine function. It produces insulin in the beta cells of the islets of Langerhans; insulin regulates carbohydrate metabolism and facilitates the entry of glucose into cells, thus lowering blood sugar. The level of blood sugar itself stimulates the secretion of insulin.

If damage to the beta cells occurs, inadequate amounts of insulin are secreted, and the condition called diabetes mellitus results. Carbohydrate metabolism is abnormal, and glucose accumulates in the blood (hyperglycemia). When glucose cannot enter the cells and be oxidized for energy, fat and protein are metabolized. This gives rise to ketone bodies, which are toxic to brain cells. If ketone bodies reach a high blood level, coma may result. The symptoms of ketosis appear more slowly than hypoglycemic symptoms seen in hyperinsulinism.

In cases of hyperinsulinism, in which there is an overproduction of the hormone or when a diabetic patient has been given too much insulin and eaten too little, the result is hypoglycemia, when the blood sugar falls precipitously and brain cells suffer a glucose deficit. Stages of hypoglycemia are similar to stages of anesthesia. A person initially shows emotional instability and personality changes before more definite mental confusion occurs. The patient feels weak and sweaty, with tachycardia, feelings of anxiety, and tremors. These persons may appear manic or intoxicated and show temper outbursts or extreme lethargy and apathy. This progresses to mental confusion and later loss of consciousness and deep coma.

There is wide nervous system involvement in diabetes mellitus. Thirty percent of the patients with diabetes are at risk for functional brain impairment from repeated comas and hypoglycemic episodes. Neuropsychological functioning can vary greatly in diabetes mellitus patients, depending on their state of diabetic control. The examiner must be sensitive to the patient's endocrine status in interpreting the acuteness or chronicity of any found deficits. Repeated evaluations are required to assess residual damage.

Strider (1982), using the Luria-Nebraska Neuropsychological Battery, compared 40 insulin-dependent diabetes mellitus patients and 40 nondiabetic patients hospitalized for nonneurological problems. A significantly higher incidence of brain impairment in the diabetic group was observed, with 32% of the diabetics showing evidence of brain damage. This finding is particularly meaningful because the diabetic subjects were screened for possible confounding causes of brain damage. No person with a history of stroke, heart attack, head trauma, alcoholism, kidney failure, or serious small vessel disease was included. No diabetic was tested at a point in time close to any acute metabolic difficulty. The severity of the impairment found was characterized as mild to moderate in most cases, being subtle and not suspected by the clinicians or others dealing with these patients. Looking at the subgroups of early-onset versus later-onset diabetics in the sample, there was a higher incidence of brain impairment in the later-onset persons (47%), and the dysfunction was of a mild degree. Early-onset subjects had a much lower incidence (19%) but a more severe level of damage. Clinically, all of these brain-impaired, early-onset subjects had a history of poor control and noncompliance with their treatment regimen. There was a significant correlation in this early onset group between brain damage and history of low blood sugar, lending support to the body of evidence that frequent hypoglycemia (Marks & Rose, 1965; Greenblat, Murray, & Root, 1946) may be a causal factor of irreversible brain damage.

Pulsinelli, Levy, Sigsbee, Scherer, and Plum (1983) have suggested that diabetics may also be prone to greater response to defects in other systems. They reported that elevated blood glucose levels were associated with worse outcome after an ischemic stroke. It could be argued that this is due to a presence of more preexisting deficits in such patients, or it may reflect the inability of the brain to adequately recover in the absence of adequate levels of insulin. This, again, is an area of interaction important to neuropsychology.

IMMUNE SYSTEM

The immune system includes the lymphatic system, which has vessels similar to blood vessels and is integrated with the cardiovascular system. Its primary purposes are to defend against invasion by outside agents, to gather up and destroy worn-out cells, and to make antibodies that protect against foreign substances. It also stores white blood cells and produces hormonal substances that help regulate development of new red cells. The lymphatic system is composed of the spleen, lymph vessels and nodes, lymph fluid, and defensive cells.

The spleen serves as a storage center for red cells and filters and destroys old red blood cells. It also makes some types of white cells (lymphocytes).

The lymph system has its own tiny vessels, which drain fluid from the tissue spaces. These vessels merge into larger ducts, which eventually feed into the bloodstream. Lymph nodes act as barriers, preventing large particles or foreign cells from entering the bloodstream. Lymph vessels are dumping streams for the body, removing the large proteins and particulate matter that, if not removed, would disrupt water and electrolyte balance, increase pressure on the capillaries, shut down blood flow, and eventually result in death. Lymph fluid is similar to blood but contains mostly white lymphocytes and has only a few red cells, amino acids, and electrolytes. Lymph fluid is formed in the liver, intestine, and lymph system. Without body motion, lymph flow is not maintained effectively, and this is one of the reasons why patients need to keep as active as possible when they are confined to bed.

White cells of the immune system that eat invading organisms are called *phagocytes*. Other immune cells, the *lymphocytes*, carry substances that react directly with invading cells or toxins. Some of these cells attack only specific organisms. Natural immunity patterns arise from the thymus early in life and later are continued by white blood cells alone. Immunity can also be developed against unfamiliar organisms, but only after a first exposure. These sensitized lymphocytes produce *antibodies*, and the agents they are taught to recognize and attack are termed *antigens*. The major disadvantage of this process is that it takes a period of time for the body to develop antibodies after first assimilating the antigen code, allowing some infections to do a great deal of damage. However, subsequent attacks are usually repelled because the body then has the antibodies present. Slowly developing infections usually give the immune system sufficient time to make specific antibodies, so they are not as destructive.

IMMUNE-NEUROENDOCRINE INTERACTIONS

The CNS and endocrine system both play important roles in the regulation of the immune response. This is particularly true under conditions of stress. Stress has its greatest effect in terms of the individual's cognitive interpretation of events and their meaning. This then influences the action of the endocrine system, which produces hormones triggering reactive effects throughout the body. Cells respond in an attempt to adapt to the imbalances caused by the stress. The hypothalamus and pituitary secrete hormones that influence the adrenal gland. This in turn releases other hormones that modulate various immune responses, stimulating or suppressing particular immune cell production or activity level.

Glucocorticoids appear to have a suppressing effect on inflammation and provide resistance to infection and the symptoms of autoimmune diseases. Various biogenic amines and other neurotransmitters also influence immune responses, although their effects are less well understood and are only implicated because of their association with various immune disorders. The secretions of the various endocrine glands appear to be released in rather complex combinations to modulate immune responses, and these interactions are currently an active area of research (Ader, 1981).

Although the immune cells are highly directed to eliminate foreign substances, they generally respect and avoid the body's own cells. In some diseases, however, this recognition ability fails and the person's own cells are attacked by the immune system, causing inflammation and widespread destruction to healthy tissues. Such a condition is known as *autoimmunity*. Although not yet well understood, it appears to result from different types of processes: defects in the manufacture of some of the cell recognition codes (like misprints on manuscripts) or errors in duplication of the body's own proteins such that they are incorrectly identified as foreign. Invading agents may also mimic the body's own proteins so closely that these proteins are then attacked by the immune cells along with the unwelcome guest. Many types of nonspecific diseases are now believed to be related to autoimmune processes. Examples of some of these are the connective tissue diseases of middle and later life, such as rheumatoid arthritis, systemic lupus erythematosus (SLE), and rheumatic fever, as well as such disorders as AIDS (Autoimmune Deficiency Syndrome).

CONNECTIVE TISSUE SYSTEM

Connective tissue is the fibrous tissue that provides the support to hold cells together and forms a protective covering around the body and in all internal organs. Large amounts of connective tissue are found in bones and joint tissues. The connective tissue system is composed of ligaments, tendons, cartilage, skin, blood vessels, internal membrane linings, and sheath coverings of organs and muscles. These cells also constitute a large portion of organs, such as the eyeballs, lungs, heart, kidneys, and liver (American Rheumatism Association Committee, 1973).

There are three basic types of connective tissue fibers, all made of long chains of proteins and different amounts of other materials such as carbohydrates and acids. *Collagen* is the dominant structural material, and its cells make up about 25% of total body protein. It is found mostly in the skin, tendons, ligaments, and sheath coverings. *Reticulin* is made up of fine, branching filaments, and is mostly found around blood vessels and muscle fibers and in solid organs such as the liver, kidney, and spleen. *Elastin* fibers are very stretchable and are found abundantly in blood vessels, ligaments, and eyes and in lesser amounts throughout the body.

All connective fibers are imbedded in *ground substance*, a gelatinous mixture of proteins and large sugar molecules. These sugars, or glycosaminoglycans, can bind large amounts of water and help to regulate fluid balance. The connective cells and ground substance also perform essential repair functions for healing wounds.

Bones provide a rigid framework for organ attachments and leverage for body movements, and also contain the marrow needed to produce blood cells. The joints are the connections between bones and are composed of different tissues that allow various degrees of separation and movement. The thick fluid in the joints is a liquid ground substance that acts as a lubricant and source of nutrient for the joint linings.

Disorders of connective tissue can either be inherited or acquired. The genetic maladies are uncommon and are not discussed here. The acquired conditions generally include rheumatoid arthritis, systemic lupus erythematosus, progressive systemic sclerosis (PSS), polymyositis and dermatomyositis, Sjogren's syndrome, amyloidosis, various forms of vasculitis, and rheumatic fever. Although different in terms of severity and the age groups affected, these diseases all display features associated with inflammation and destruction or alteration of connective tissues. Because so many structures in the body can be affected, the diseases are considered systemic. Common symptoms include fatigue, fever, muscular weakness, joint swelling and pain, skin lesions, gastrointestinal erosions with hemorrhages, peripheral vascular dysfunctions, neuropathologies, and blood cell disorders such as anemia and thrombocytopenia. The course of the illness may vary greatly from patient to patient, with periods of remission and exacerbation, a chronic mild illness, severe and rapidly progressing deterioration, or fluctuations between mild and severe episodes. Some patients with these diseases may become severely disabled due to crippling joint deformities or loss of function in major organs such as the kidneys. The initial symptoms can mimic those of many other diseases because they are so variable, and thus they are difficult to diagnose and treat.

Comprehensive neuropsychological research has been meagerly reported in connective tissue disease patients. Medical literature indicates that the effects on the brain and central nervous system of these diseases are variable and generally unpredictable. The small vessel inflammation and destruction can produce focal ischemic lesions in many organs, causing them to malfunction and reduce their support to the brain. Vessels in the brain may also be affected, although pathological studies have been inconsistent in confirming this with most of the disease types except giant cell arteritis (American Rheumatism Association Committee, 1973). Hypertension is a frequent outcome of these diseases. Compression effects or ischemia may produce peripheral neuropathy, with sensory or motor losses in digits and limbs. Diffuse or focal cerebral infections may occur due to the suppression of immune responses from the drugs taken for treatment.

Although evidence of the disease process itself occurring within the brain has not been confirmed, studies have indicated the presence of immune complexes associated with connective disease processes in the choroid plexus of the brain (Atkins, Kondon, Quismorio, & Friou, 1972; Bresnihan, et al., 1979); Bresnihan, Oliver, Grigor, & Hughes, 1977; Winfield, Lobo, & Singer, 1978). Psychoses, severe depression, and mental confusion have been reported frequently in patients. Reactions to corticosteroids, antihypertensives, antidiuretics, anti-inflammatory agents, and other treatment drugs may produce changes in emotional or mental state, although it is often difficult to separate these from the effects of the disease itself.

CNS effects have most frequently been reported with SLE, including emotional disorders, convulsions, chorea, and cerebrovascular accidents with focal neurological deficits. These effects usually occur in patients with highly active and severe disease, and they account for up to 25% of the fatalities because of cerebral hemorrhage or seizures. In early stages of the disease, CNS effects may be mild and transient or may so resemble a psychiatric disorder that the patient is given a diagnosis such as psychosis or depression (Bennett, Bong, & Spargo, 1978; Hughes, 1979).

SUMMARY

In this overview, we have attempted to describe some of the ways various physical dysfunctions and/or diseases may produce brain impairment. Often data are not available on the effects of physical disorders on brain function. In evaluating medical patients, neuropsychologists must be knowledgeable about the physiological functioning of the individual. Acquiring such knowledge is a challenge, since few if any psychology training programs provide such courses, leaving professionals to their own resources in this lengthy studious process. It was our dual intent to make clinicians more aware of the complexity of such cases and to emphasize the possible multiple factors influencing neuropsychological assessment of medical patients to encourage future research focusing on these questions.

REFERENCES

Acker, W., Aps, E. J., Majumdar, S. K., Shaw, G. K., & Thomson, A. D. (1982). The relationship between brain and liver damage in chronic alcoholic patients. *Journal of Neurology, Neurosurgery and Psychiatry, 45*, 984–987.

Ader, R. (Ed.). (1981). *Psychoneuroimmunology.* New York: Academic Press.

Aita, J. A. (1964). *Neurologic manifestations of general diseases.* Springfield, IL: Charles C Thomas.

Alfrey, A. C., Mishell, J. M., Burks, J., Conttgaglia, R. H., Lewin, E., & Holmes, J. H. (1972). Syndrome of dyspraxia and multifocal seizures associated with chronic hemodialysis. *Transactions of the American Society for Artificial Internal Organs, 18*, 257–261.

American Rheumatism Association Committee. (G. P. Rodnan, Ed.). (1973). *Primer on the rheumatic diseases* (7th ed.). Atlanta: Arthritis Foundation.

Atkins, C. J., Kondon, J. J., Quismorio, F. P., & Friou, G. J. (1972). The choroid plexus in systemic lupus erythematosus. *Annals of Internal Medicine, 76*, 65–72.

Barcroft, J. (1920). Anoxemia. *Lancet, 2*, 485–489.

Bennett, R. M., Bong, D. M., & Spargo, B. H. (1978). Neuropsychiatric problems in mixed connective tissue disease. *American Journal of Medicine, 65*, 955–962.

Block, A. J., Castle, J. R., & Keitt, A. S. (1974). Chronic oxygen therapy treatment of chronic obstructive pulmonary disease at sea level. *Chest, 65*, 279–288.

Borstein, R. A., Benoit, B. G., & Trites, R. L. (1981). Neuropsychological changes following carotid endarterectomy. *Canadian Journal of Neurological Science, 8*, 127–132.

Bresnihan, B., Hohmeister, R., Cutting, J., Travers, R. L., Waldburger, M., Blacj, C., Jones, T., & Hughes, G. R. (1979). The neuropsychiatric disorder in systemic lupus erythematosus: Evidence for both vascular and immune mechanisms. *Annals of the Rheumatic Diseases, 38*, 301–306.

Bresnihan, B., Oliver, M., Grigor, R., & Hughes, G. R. V. (1977). Brain reactivity of lymphocytotoxic antibodies in systemic lupus erythematosus with and without cerebral involvement. *Clinical and Experimental Immunology, 30*, 333.

Brobeck, J. R. (Ed.). (1979). *Best & Taylor's physiological basis of medical practice* (10th ed.). Baltimore: Williams & Wilkins.

Drake, W., Baker, M., Blumenkrantz, J., & Dahlgren, H. (1968). The quality and duration of survival in bilateral carotid occlusive disease: A preliminary survey of the effects of thromboendarterectomy. In J. Toole, R. Siekert, & J. Whisnant (Eds.), *Cerebral vascular disease.* New York: Grune & Stratton.

Elsass, P., Lund, V., & Ranek, L. (1978). Encephalopathy in patients with cirrhosis of the liver: A neuropsychological study. *Scandianavian Journal of Gastroenterology, 13*, 241–247.

Fix, J. A., Golden, C. J., Daughton, D., Kass I., & Bell C. W. (1982). Neuropsychological deficits among patients with chronic obstructive pulmonary disease. *International Journal of Neuroscience, 16*, 9–105.

Ginn, H. E. (1975). Neurobehavioral dysfunction in uremia. *Kidney International, 7* (Suppl. 2), 217–221.

Golden, C. J., Graber, B., Blose, I., Berg, R., Coffman, J., & Bloch, S. (1981). Differences in brain densities between chronic alcoholics and normal control patients. *Science, 211*, 508–510.

Goldstein, S. G., Kleinknecht, R. A., & Gallo, A. E., Jr. (1970). Neuropsychological changes associated with carotid endarterectomy. *Cortex, 6*, 308–322.

Goodwin, J. S., Goodwin, J. M., & Garry, P. J. (1983). Association between nutritional status and cognitive functioning in a healthy elderly population. *Journal of the American Medical Association, 249*, 2917–2921.

Green, J. H. (1978). *Basic clinical physiology*. Oxford, England: Oxford University Press.

Greenblat, M., Murray, J., & Root, H. F. (1946). Electroencephalographic studies in diabetes mellitus. *New England Journal of Medicine, 234*, 119–121.

Haynes, C. D., Gideon, D. A., King, C. D., & Dempsey, R. L. (1976). The improvement of cognition and personality after carotid endarterectomy. *Surgery, 80*, 699–704.

Horne, D. J., & Royle, J. P. (1974). Cognitive changes after carotid endarterectomy. *Medical Journal of Australia, 1*, 316–317.

Hughes, G. V. R. (1979). *Connective tissue diseases* (2nd ed.). Oxford, England: Blackwell Scientific.

Hunter, R., Jones, M., & Matthews, D. M. (1967). Post-gastrectomy vitamin-B12 deficiency in psychiatric practice. *Lancet, 1*, 47.

Jacques, S., Garner, J. T., Tager, R., Rosenstock, J., & Fields, T. (1978). Improved cognition after external carotid endarterectomy. *Surgery and Neurology, 10*, 223–225.

Jellinek, E. H. (1962). Fits, faints, coma and dementia in myxoedema. *Lancet, 2*, 1010–1012.

Kilpatrick, D. G., Miller, W. C., Allan, A. N., & Lee, W. H. (1975). The use of psychological test data to predict open-heart surgery outcome: A prospective study. *Psychosomatic Medicine, 37*, 62–73.

King, G. D., Gideon, D. A., Haynes, C. D., Dempsey, R. L., & Jenkins, C. W. (1977). Intellectual and personality changes associated with carotid endarterectomy. *Journal of Clinical Psychology, 33*, 215–220.

Krause, K. H., Winter, R., Scheglmann, K., & Reuther, R. (1982). Electromyographic signs of neurogenic involvement in hypokalemic paralysis as a result of diuretic abuse. *Electroencephalography and Electromyography, 13*, 113–116.

Krop, H. D., Block, A. J., & Cohen, E. (1973). Neuropsychological effects of continuous oxygen therapy in chronic obstructive pulmonary disease. *Chest, 64*, 317–322.

Lewis, E. G., O'Neill, W. M., Dustman, R. E., & Beck, E. C. (1980). Temporal effects of hemodialysis on measures of neural efficiency. *Kidney International, 17*, 357–363.

Lishman, W. A. (1978). *Organic psychiatry: The psychological consequences of cerebral disorder*. Oxford, England: Blackwell Scientific.

Manhurkar, S. D., Dhar, S. K., & Salta, R. (1973). Dialysis dementia. *Lancet, 1*, 1412–1415.

Marks, V., & Rose, F. C. (1965). *Hypoglycaemia*. London: Blackwell Scientific.

Marshall, J. (1979). Neuropsychiatric aspects of renal failure. *Journal of Clinical Psychiatry, 40*, 81–85.

Matarazzo, R. G., Matarazzo, J. D., Gallo, A. E., Jr., & Weins, A. N. (1979). IQ and neuropsychological changes following carotid endarterectomy. *Journal of Clinical Neuropsychology, 1*, 97–116.

Matoth, Y., Zaizov, R., & Frankel, J. J. (1971). Minimal cerebral dysfunction in children with chronic thrombocytopenia. *Pediatrics, 47*, 698–706.

Michael, R. P., & Gibbons, J. L. (1963). Interrelationships between the endocrine system and neuropsychiatry. *International Review of Neurobiology, 5*, 243–302.

Murphy, F., & Maccubbin, D. A. (1966). Carotid endarterectomy: A long-term follow-up study. In J. Shillito (Ed.), *Clinical neurosurgery* (Vol. 13). Baltimore: Williams & Wilkins.

Nielsen, J. R., Gram, L., Rasmussen, L. P., Damsgaard, E. M., Dalsgaard, M., Richard, T. C., & Beckmann, J. (1983). Intellectual and social function of patients surviving cardiac arrest outside the hospital. *Acta Medica Scandinavica, 213*, 37–39.

Owens, M., Pressman, M., Edwards, A. E., Tourtellotte, W., Rose, J. G., Stern, D., Peters, G., Stabile, B. E., & Wilson, S. E. (1980). The effect of small infarcts and carotid endarterectomy on postoperative psychological test performance. *Journal of Surgical Research, 28*, 209–216.

Perry, P. M., Drindwater, J. E., & Taylor, G. W. (1975). Cerebral dysfunction before and after carotid endarterectomy. *British Medical Journal, 4*, 215–216.

Pulsinelli, W. A., Levy, D. E. Sigsbee, B., Scherer, P., & Plum, F. (1983). Increased damage after ischemic stroke in patients with hyperglycemia with or without established diabetes mellitus. *American Journal of Medicine, 74*, 540–544.

Raskin, N. H., & Fishman, R. A. (1976). Neurologic disorders in renal failure. *New England Journal of Medicine, 294*, 204–210.

Raskind, M. (1983). Nutrition and cognitive function in the elderly. *Journal of the American Medical Association, 249*, 2939–2940.

Rehnstrom, S., Simert, G., Hansson, J. A., Johnson, G., & Vang, J. (1977). Chronic hepatic encephalopathy: A osychometrical study. *Scandinavian Journal of Gastroenterology, 12*, 395–311.

Roos, D. (1974). Neurological complications in a selected group of partially gastrectomized patients with particular reference of B12 deficiency. *Acta Neurologica Scandinavica, 50*, 719–752.

Roos, D., & Willanger, R. (1977). Various degrees of dementia in a selected group of gastrectomized patients with low serum B12. *Acta Neurologia Scandinavica, 55*, 363–376.

Ryan J. J., Souheaver, G. T., & DeWolff, A. S. (1981). Halstead-Reitan test results in chronic hemodialysis. *Journal of Nervous and Mental Disease, 169*, 311–314.

Schraa, J. C., Dirks, J. F., Jones, N. F., Kinsman, R. A. (1981). Bender Gestalt performance and recall in an asthmatic sample. *Journal of Asthma, 18*, 7–9.

Shulman, R. (1967). Psychiatric aspects of pernicious anaemia: A prospective controlled investigation. *British Medical Journal, 3*, 266–270.

Smith, J. S., & Brandon, S. (1973). Morbidity from acute carbon monoxide poisoning at three-year follow-up. *British Medical Journal, 1*, 318–321.

Sotnaiemi, K. (1982). Prediction of cerebral outcome after extracorporeal circulation. *Acta Neurological Scandinavica, 66*, 697–704.

Strider, M. A. (1982). Neuropsychological concomitants of diabetes mellitus. *Dissertation Abstracts*.

Talalla, A., Halbrook, H., Barbour, B. H., & Kurze, T. (1970). Subdural hematoma associated with long-term hemodialysis for chronic renal disease. *Journal of the American Medical Association, 212*, 1847–1849.

Taylor, J. W. (1979). Mental symptoms and electrolyte imbalance. *Australian and New Zeland Journal of Psychiatry, 13*, 159–160.

Victor, M., Adams, R. D., and Collins, G. H. (1971). *The Wernicke-Korsakoff Syndrome*, Oxford, England: Blackwell Scientific.

Walton, J. N., Kiloh, L. G., Osselton, J. W., & Farrall, J. (1954). The electroencephalogram in pernicious anaemia and subacute combined degeneration of the cord. *Electroencephalography and Clinical Neurophysiology, 6*, 45–64.

Wehlan, T. B., Schteingart, D. E., Starkman, M. N., & Smith, A. (1980). Neuropsychological deficits in Cushing's syndrome. *Journal of Nervous and Mental Disease, 168*, 753–757.

Wilimas, J., Goff, J. R., Anderson, H. R., Jr., Langston, J. W., & Thompson, E. (1980). Efficacy of transfusion therapy for one to two years in patients with sickle cell disease and cerebrovascular accidents. *Journal of Pediatrics, 96*, 205–208.

Williams, M., & McGee, T. (1964). Psychological study of carotid artery occlusion and endarterectomy. *Archives of Neurology, 10*, 293–297.

Winfield, J. B., Lobo, P. I., & Singer, A. (1978). Significance of anti-lymphocyte antibodies in systemic lupus erythematosus. *Arthritis and Rheumatism, 21*, 215.

CHAPTER 11

Psychopathology and Other Behavioral Considerations for the Clinical Neuropsychologist

Stanley Berent

The first report of the task force on education, accreditation, and credentialing in clinical neuropsychology was completed in 1981. The work represented a joint effort by members of the International Neuropsychological Society (INS) and the Division of Clinical Neuropsychology (Division 40) of the American Psychological Association. According to this task force report, "A major function of the clinical neuropsychologist is to assess current behavioral disturbances that are associated with central nervous system dysfunction." Further on, this document states, "a definitive competency in neuropsychological assessment requires the ability to integrate medical, neurological, and behavioral interview data with the neuropsychological findings for the purpose of relating behavior to neurologic status." This chapter concerns the "behavioral" side of this integration.

The neuropsychologist receives referrals from a variety of sources. Referrals from psychiatrists may seek help in documenting central nervous system involvement in a behavioral syndrome, while referrals from neurologists may request help in differentiating functional from organic components in a clinical picture so that the most appropriate disposition can be made. The intimate relationship that exists between mind and body has been recognized for centuries. Neurotic and other behavioral disturbances are known to be regular sequelae of neurologic insult (Geschwind, 1975; Levin & Grossman, 1978). According to Geschwind (1975), many disorders that might benefit from psychiatric intervention are misdiagnosed as untreatable neurologic conditions, while progressive and even life-threatening neurologic manifestations may go unnoticed because of a belief that the patient is suffering from a psychiatric condition. One past study (Maltzburg, 1959) found that neurologic disorders may account for 30% or more of all first admissions to mental hospitals.

In light of Geschwind's disconcerting observation and in order to manifest the "ideal competence" called for in the INS task force report, the clinical neuropsychologist should have a practical grasp of psychopathology. In the routine practice of neuropsychology, behavior serves as the primary vehicle by which clinicians approach their task. There is the immediate need to understand this behavior in order to render accurate diagnoses, contribute to effective treatment planning, and to compose realistic prognostic statements. Even when the clinical neuropsychologist is not the professional who directly treats the behavioral aspects of a given case, it is the neuropsychologist who is often looked to for recommendations concerning such intervention.

It is not intended that this chapter serve as an exhaustive treatment of the topic of psychopathology. Such a task would literally require volumes to complete. Nor will this work focus on neuropsychological explanations of observed behavioral phenomena as exemplified in work on the biochemistry of depression. Psychometric approaches to behavioral analyses, techniques of treatment intervention for behavioral disorders, and the other considerations just mentioned will be included only to the extent that such information contributes to the purposes stated below.

In this chapter, I hope to convince the reader of the necessity of understanding psychopathology, and, in addition, I discuss some historical, philosophical, and practical factors that together help to explain the state of affairs in the area of understanding both normal and abnormal behavior. A general theoretical orientation to neuropsychological practice is suggested. Finally, some principles of behavior are described that might aid clinical neuropsychologists in their work.

These stated purposes are important for a basic handbook such as the present volume because psychopathological considerations are too often neglected in the routine practice of clinical neuropsychology. The practice of clinical neuropsychology can be seen as representing one of the many facets of health psychology. To date, this entire area of psychological endeavor has suffered from a lack of emphasis on considerations of behavior. As Millon, Green, and Meagher (1982) point out, clinical psychology has not contributed as much as one might hope to the area of health psychology. While most of the neuropsychology profession would likely agree with this observation, the reasons for such neglect may be unclear or even misunderstood by many in the field. A few reasons are (1) present models of psychopathology lack utility when applied to patients in the health setting; (2) training programs in clinical neuropsychology have yet to be standardized, and many currently available routes employed by students who seek a career in neuropsychology do not contain the study of psychopathology in their curricula; and (3) guidelines for a specialty (or subspecialty) of clinical neuropsychology are not yet finalized. Both as an outcome and as a contribution to the continuation of this state of affairs, the potential relevance and helpfulness of these areas of understanding are often not reflected in the clinical questions asked in referrals to neuropsychologists. It is my hope that the material contained in this chapter will add to the recognition of the need to change this situation.

DEFINITIONS OF NORMAL AND ABNORMAL BEHAVIOR

Buss (1966) lists three approaches that have been used to define normality: (1) statistical approaches, (2) ideal mental health, and (3) presence or absence of certain behaviors as definitions of normal and abnormal.

A statistical approach seeks to define normality on the basis of what is most frequent in a given population. Within such a scheme, abnormality is treated by exclusion or statistical deviation from the mean. Some obvious difficulties are evident in such an approach to normality. Statistically, one might assume that what most people do is likely to represent an adaptive style of living. On the other hand, there is abundant evidence to suggest the contrary. Instances of violence, smoking, alcohol abuse, and other drug abuse are but several examples of high-frequency but maladaptive behaviors.

The second approach to normality—normality as ideal mental health—has been reflected in a variety of proposals. Johoda (1958), for example, listed a set of criteria for deciding that a person is mentally healthy. These criteria included the following: (1) self-insight, (2) balance of psychic forces, (3) self-actualization, (4) resistance to stress, (5) autonomy, (6) competence, and (7) correct perception of reality.

A model such as Johoda's is subject to many criticisms. The terms employed in such models are often vague. These terms are usually defined on the basis of a theory whose assumptions may remain unproven or even untestable. From a neuropsychological point of view, the terms used in such a model may lack utility in some specialized setting, such as a medical hospital. Buss (1966) presents two additional criticisms of this approach to normality. First, the ideal nature of the criteria employed may exclude too many people. Since most people never reach these ideal states, such a model holds that the majority of the population is abnormal. While some might argue that such a situation prevails from time to time, one need not employ a model that ensures such negative comment in the majority of instances. Second, common sense would suggest that there are many ways of adjusting to the world and achieving some personal happiness in so doing. Any attempt to list all possible alternatives would be cumbersome at best and more likely impossible. In addition, it could be that the process of adjusting itself, as opposed to the outcome of this process, is an important variable to consider in determining normality and abnormality. As suggested by Horowitz (1982), these adjustment strivings might lead an individual through stages that to the outside observer appear to be bizarre or otherwise abnormal. In reality, such strivings might represent effective strategies for coping with unusual or even traumatic experiences such as often encountered in medical illness.

The alternative to the first two approaches is to define normality by specifying criteria that determine abnormality. Such an approach has the benefit of allowing for operational definitions of specified behaviors and thus is suited to sorely needed research on this topic. Employing such a model, Scott (1958) advanced five criteria of abnormality: (1) presence of psychiatric diagnosis, (2) history of psychiatric hospitalization, (3) evidence of social maladjustment, (4) presence of subjective discomfort, and (5) results of objective psychological inventories and tests that are positive for abnormality.

In a similar approach, Buss (1966) offered what he termed three practical criteria of abnormality. These criteria consisted of: (1) discomfort (manifested in somatic pain, anxiety or worry, or depression); (2) bizarreness (deviations in behavior from accepted standards or from consensually validated reality such as might occur in hallucinations or delusions); and (3) inefficiency (inability to meet the responsibilities of assigned roles).

The fact that systems such as those proposed by Scott and Buss lend themselves to operational definition might be met with some enthusiasm by neuropsychologists. It renders the criteria employed in these models meaningful for psychometric evaluation. The criteria of inefficiency in Buss' scheme, for example, can be defined on the basis of psychological measurement. Inability to meet the responsibilities of assigned roles can potentially be measured in two ways: by comparing actual performance with potential performance or by comparing performance with the requirements of a given role. In fact, information of potential usefulness to the clinical neuropsychologist may be found using all three of Buss' approaches to normality. On the other hand, all are susceptible to serious criticisms related to their utility in the mental health field and, even more important, in the medical setting.

The majority of models concerned with psychopathology are derived from the area of traditional mental health. Before advancing to other criticisms of such models, it is worthwhile to mention that it has been difficult to apply existing models of psychopathology to the problems encountered in neuropsychological and general health psychology settings. The fact that for many decades the mental health professions developed in isolation from general medicine served to enhance the concept of mind and body as separate entities. Many of these models seem to implicitly assume that psychological dysfunction occurs in an otherwise healthy person. Such theories often provide their own reference, which may have little relation to the world beyond the limits of the model. A behavioral entity that may be commonplace in the medical setting may be impossible to deal with if the model employed fails to recognize its existence. Many traditional models from mental health, for example, are notably silent about the modifying effects on behavior of various medical disorders and illnesses, such as stroke, myocardial infarction, amputation, and other medical conditions.

Problems of Validity

The validity of many of the premises contained in traditional models of normal and abnormal behavior are often weakly substantiated. For example, the Midtown Manhattan Study (Srole, Langner, Michael, Opler, & Rennie, 1962) revealed that large numbers of disturbed persons have never received psychiatric attention. This means that the lack of recorded psychiatric history for a given patient may tell relatively little about the individual's behavioral stability. It is also true that history of such attention may be less than useful. As Szasz (1961) pointed out some years ago, community pressures and other extrapsychiatric considerations often play a determining role in psychiatric diagnosis.

The Concept of Organicity

Traditional mental health models have influenced the practice of clinical neuropsychology. The theories employed have often influenced the types of questions asked of the psychologist. These referral questions reflect concepts that may be generalized to other areas of clinical practice, and they have influenced conceptualization within neuropsychology. One concept that is insidiously present in current neuropsychological practice is that of organicity. Many models for understanding abnormal behavior within traditional mental health emphasize ideas derived from psychoanalysis. Often, these models seek to explain abnormal behavior as the consequence of intrapsychic conflicts. A lack of physical explanation for the observed behavior must either be taken for granted or substantiated by examination. In the employment of such models, the psychologist's role became one of applying psychometrics to discover the presence or absence of an organic etiology for the observed abnormal behaviors. I believe that psychodynamic and psychoanalytic considerations are important components of understanding human behavior, and I am not arguing against such formulations. It is when these ideas are viewed as explanatory in an either-or way that their usefulness in the medical setting is less than ideal. Interpreted in this narrow way, the model serves to perpetuate distinctions between mind and body that are contrary to the current state of our knowledge about human behavioral functioning. As pointed out by Small (1973), the patient should not be automatically placed in the general categories of organic or brain-damaged. Each person must be viewed in terms of his or her own unique limitations, and these limitations must be individually assessed.

Personality Models and Their Inadequacies

As with other models from traditional mental health, attempts have been made to apply models of personality to the problems dealt with in neuropsychology in particular and health psychology in general. Personality traits have been liberally applied to neurologic patient groups over the past 20–30 years. Propositions have been made concerning "right-hemisphere personality styles," the "epileptic personality," and the "Huntington's patient personality," to name but a few. Recently, however, such notions have come under attack (Herman, Dikmen, & Wilensky, 1982). As with some other systems from traditional mental health fields already discussed, personality theory is not a particularly good model to apply in neuropsychology. Even in the realm of mental health proper, the effectiveness of personality theory as a model has been questioned (as perhaps best reflected in the conscious attempt to be atheoretical in the third edition of the *Diagnostic and Statistical Manual of the American Psychiatric Association*). The personality model tremendously underemphasizes individual differences and at the same time overemphasizes common attributes among people. These models fail to allow the inclusion of many important contributions to observed behavior, and they encourage a view that sees the most obvious and potentially unifying event that might be shared by a designated group of individuals as causing the behavior. That is, because a particular person may have multiple sclerosis, that disorder would serve to explain the behavior manifested by the individual. Understanding of behavior has simply grown beyond the confines demanded by such a model. Early notions about epileptic patients, for instance, were based largely on observations of institutionalized patients. It is now commonly known that such individuals represent no more than 10% of the total population of epileptics. Further, as Goffman (1961) and others have shown, much of what is observed in inpatient settings is a product of institutionalization itself, rather than the disorder for which the person was hospitalized.

It is indeed true that individuals in a given situation may often appear to react or behave similarly. Situational variables themselves are known to greatly affect the behavior exhibited in given situations. Also, there are but a limited number of ways in which a person can or will react to a given situation. All organisms, for example, have the option of fight or flight in reacting to danger. Lewin (1935) has described a number of conflict situations that might be encountered by people. These conflict situations demonstrate that any individual's behavioral options are limited and somewhat predictable in such specified situations.

The conflict situations described by Lewin have been summarized by Morgan and King (1966). Lewin termed two common situations *approach-approach* and *avoidance-avoidance*. In the approach-approach situation, the person must choose between two equally attractive goals—for example, going to dinner and seeing a movie. Two alternative solutions to this mild dilemma would be to satisfy one goal and then the other or to give up one in favor of the other. Another typical conflict situation is avoidance-avoidance, represented by two negative goals. Such a situation usually results in vascillation and may lead to attempts to escape the situation. For example, in a clinical setting, a person may not want to take antiepileptic medications because of unpleasant side effects. This same person may also wish to avoid the seizures that could occur by not taking the medications. Put in such conflict, most people will likely react in similar ways. A personality approach to the avoidance-avoidance example just given might lead to the conclusion that epileptics are indecisive and to a view of indecisiveness as an attribute or part of an epileptic personality.

Employing such a model as personality limits one's view, and, at worst, it might lead the professional away from dealing with the real concerns being experienced by the patient. This might prevent the clinician from helping the patient to resolve issues and, continuing the above example, to take the necessary medication as indicated.

Case Example

An epileptic patient was failing to take her medication largely for reasons related to the type of conflict described above. A similar conflict in her thinking led her to insist to her physician that she was taking her medicine. She continued to experience seizures, and, in the face of subtherapeutic blood levels of the drug, the physician continued to raise the dosage. Finally, in desperation, the patient took the medications, but at the now elevated dosage. This resulted in drug toxicity, and the patient required hospitalization.

Theorizing about patient personality types has been wrong because of conceptual flaws in the model. Findings from any particular study may have been correct, but the attribution of those findings to the underlying medical disorder was destined to be wrong because the model could not take into account the myriad contributions to the observations. Some later study that yielded findings contradictory to the earlier one would not necessarily disprove it. Different results may simply reflect the inadequacies of the original model in explaining the findings. When populations were similar between studies, as with studies of the 10% of epileptics who were institutionalized, findings were very likely to be similar. This reinforced notions of the adequacy of the model. As the stigma of epilepsy has subsided, as changes in health care delivery systems have occurred, and as new medications and other technologies have become available, patients representing populations different from those originally studied have been entered into research. This has resulted in findings that are discrepant with earlier ones.

DIAGNOSTIC VALUE OF EXPERIENTIAL PHENOMENA

A recent study (Sowa, Giordani, Berent, & Sackellares, 1983) concerned patients' reports of certain experiences that many professionals believe are related to certain neurologic conditions. Certain experiential phenomena, such as déjà vu experiences, occur during temporal lobe seizures. Clinically, such experiential symptoms have been used to support the diagnosis of complex partial seizures. The prevalence of experiential symptoms such as the one just mentioned was evaluated in 150 patients seen at the outpatient neurology clinic of the University of Michigan. Independently of the investigators, 50 of these patients were diagnosed as having complex partial seizures; 50 were diagnosed as having generalized seizures; and 50 patients carried other, nonepileptic, neurologic diagnoses. While these "characteristic" experiential symptoms were found to be most prevalent in the epilepsy patients, they were not found to be unique to any one of the groups studied. The results of this study indicate that certain experiential symptoms in themselves may be of little diagnostic value.

Aside from problems of relevance to clinical neuropsychology, many traditional theories in mental health either are simply wrong or contain elements yet to be scientifically proven. In many cases, important premises in these models remain controversial either because of conflicting results of research efforts or because of differences of opinion between individuals identifying with such models. Kubie (1954), for instance, suggested that normal, healthy individuals show a predominance of conscious over unconscious urges. In criticizing this position and its implications for mental health, Redlich (1957) maintained that unconscious strivings are not necessarily irrational or counterproductive for the individual. Thus, even if one could objectively measure and differentiate conscious from unconscious urges in the patient, Redlich's contentions would raise questions about the usefulness of such information for determining the normality and mental health of the individual.

THE NEED FOR A LESS RESTRICTIVE MODEL

Models derived from traditional mental health theories are often too restrictive for optimal usefulness in neuropsychology. These theories often attempt to explain behavior in simple cause and effect relationships. Even when they are right, they are often only partially right because they fail to recognize the multiple contributions to any given behavioral occurrences. A broader view is needed than is contained in many of these models in order to make more complete our understanding of behavior. As already mentioned, a second limitation to many of the traditional mental health ideas in terms of their applicability to the medical setting results from their development in isolation from medical disorder. This has led to attempts to force models that simply do not fit the material at hand. For example, Barnes and Lucas (1974), tried with only minimal success to use the Halstead-Reitan procedure to differentiate between cerebral dysfunction and psychogenic disorder. Sillitti (1982) has reviewed more than a decade of research on the Minnesota Multiphasic Personality Inventory (MMPI) and concludes that attempts to develop a reliable and valid way of using results from this instrument to indicate organic brain dysfunction have failed. While the Sc scale of the MMPI showed the most promise, it ultimately could not be used to differentiate schizophrenia from organic brain syndrome. It may not be the failure of psychometric techniques or instruments that is evidenced in these studies. Rather, it may be that the problems lie with the questions being asked of these instruments. A fresh approach, perhaps an existential one, would consider multiple contributions to observed behavior. Rather than being applied to the determination of causes of behavior in an absolute fashion, observations from interviews and psychological testing would be considered in light of their meaningfulness to the patient and in terms of quantification and reliability. The neuropsychologist could then examine the consequences of such a measurement and the consequences of its interaction with other variables. A given individual might be seen as being influenced by a variety of circumstances whose bases derive from social, economic, behavioral, psychodynamic, physical, and other relevant origins. Each component might serve some contributory function to the total clinical picture, and each might have its own consequences in terms of diagnosis, treatment, and other aspects of patient management.

Bonhoeffer (1912) recognized that entirely different physical illnesses can lead to similar or apparently identical behavioral manifestations. The neuropsychologist need not be committed to a model that assumes that different behaviors necessarily reflect different and characteristic causes. As further pointed out by Bonhoeffer (1912), there is a relationship between physical illness and mental disturbance, but the behavioral manifestation needs to be determined by circumstances other than the nature of the physical disease itself. Bonhoeffer himself developed a conceptual model based on observations made in the medical setting. His notions of "acute exogenous reactions" came to greatly influence the development of psychiatric thought in America (Bleuler, 1975) and led to the use of terms, such as *reaction*, that persist to this day instead of other words, such as *disease* and *illness*, used earlier to describe behavioral disturbance.

Neuropsychologists do benefit from these influences, but there remains need for further changes in theoretical orientation if our understanding of psychopathology is to be increased in the future. Reiss, Levitan, and McNally (1982) recommended that the idea of multiple handicaps replace the concept of primary emotional disturbance. Instead of trying to determine whether a problem is primarily emotional or organic, both conditions are diagnosed so that appropriate interventions can be prescribed for each.

A failure to employ such thinking has served as the basis for continued difficulties in communication among disciplines concerned with the disorders encountered in brain-behavior relationships. As Geschwind (1975) points out, neurologists speak of psychiatry's failure to recognize the brain as the organ of the mind, while psychiatrists complain that neurology fails to deal with a patient as a whole person who is both biological and psychological at the same time. Neither discipline, Geschwind says, has dealt adequately with the area between these two alternatives. The point of view expressed here is that emphasized by Millon (1982) when he observes that a fresh concept is needed, one that synthesizes mind and body. These two traditional polarities are complementary and are but facets of a single, integrated human being. Continued failure to transcend this arbitrary distinction of mind and body will serve to stymie efforts to develop effective solutions to the clinical problems encountered in neuropsychological practice.

The research literature in neuropsychology is rampant with the influences of traditional models, such as those that reflect the mind-body distinction. For example, affective psychosis is a condition often observed in patients who have suffered a head injury (Levin, Benton, & Grossman, 1982). Studies of this topic reflect debates about whether the depression is the result of preinjury personality (Lishman, 1973) or of the direct consequences of brain damage that might manifest themselves in such conditions as changes in brain metabolism (Levin & Grossman, 1978). Such debates often neglect the idea of multiple contributions to observed psychopathologic states. Levin, Benton, and Grossman (1982) indicate awareness of the broader view by pointing out the importance of alterations in neurotransmitter function that occur in head injury but also by suggesting the important contribution of past experiences of the individual and other seemingly extrinsic factors, such as pending litigation. There are so many factors to consider, in fact, that it is no wonder that one would hope for a simple, even unitary model that might serve to adequately explain the phenomena under study. Psychodynamically speaking, for instance, people with any type of medical illness may suffer experiences of loss. They may lose the freedom to move about at will, their job, their past abilities, or important relationships. Anxieties and fears about continued disability are often present in such individuals. There is the lack of predictability about the future, and the individual may have concerns in the area of self-control. When the body has been injured, a patient may manifest fears associated with altered self-concept, body image, or even self-esteem. Some individually ascribed meaning to the injury, the circumstances surrounding the injury, or even the consequences of the injury might stimulate old fears or preoccupations that were dormant in the affected individual.

Case Example

A 60-year-old man suffered a stroke that left him partially paralyzed on the left side. He recuperated effectively from a medical point of view, but he experienced increasing anxiety that appeared to many to be paradoxical in the face of his progressing improvement. In interview, this man eventually verbalized that the incident had reminded him of a serious injury he had suffered during combat in World War II. He told the interviewer of a traumatic battle experience in which he had been bayoneted and left as dead on a pile of corpses. The experience of his stroke had revived his unresolved feelings surrounding that earlier experience.

To neglect the importance of such phenomena is to neglect influential factors that may serve to explain the patient's clinical picture. The science of neuropsychology has been reluctant to deal with such phenomena, perhaps because experimental methodology simply has not yet provided the technology to study so many relevant variables at once. The clinician who is sensitive to such considerations may, on the other hand, feel that scientific research has produced little of relevance to everyday clinical practice. This could lead clinicians to isolate themselves from the objective realities that might be discovered by continued scientific study. Since both these tendencies must be resisted, models are needed that both lead to scientific inquiry and serve the clinician. An optimistic view would be that revised clinical models, advances in statistical techniques and research design, and technological advances in computerization may all combine to effect this happy end.

THE NEED FOR AN ATHEORETICAL STANCE

Knowledge about explanatory principles of behavior grows daily. In the last few years alone, neuropsychology has increasingly come to appreciate the contributions to behavior from such areas as vocation, family, social interactions, culture, and even economics. Many of these areas were not considered in early theories of behavior.

Weiner (1982) blames what he terms the preoccupation with the field of intrapsychic conflict for the neglect of other important determinants of behavior: determinants from social and other behavioral origins. As Weiner (1977, 1978, 1981) has pointed out, major attention to the role of the social environment in physical illness is only fairly recent. For Weiner (1982), the shift from an exclusively intrapsychic view to an adaptational one allows for a conceptual framework for consideration of such extra-psychodynamic factors.

Avoiding Polemics

Too often in psychology, a shift in conceptual thinking has been accompanied by partisan thinking. The polemical arguments between behavior therapists and psychoanalysts over such topics as symptom substitution is but one example. The reader might be cautioned against such polemical thinking and be encouraged to adopt an open-minded view that explanatory principles derived from any theory are useful if they aid our understanding of behavior in a practical way. The neuropsychologist should incorporate each new explanatory principle and apply it in attempting to understand behavior in the clinical situation. At present, an atheoretical stance is necessary, even though it may prove distasteful to some. Behavioral technology may one day allow for some unifying theory, but at present it does not. It is an orientation to understanding behavior, as opposed to a single theory, that is required at present. The orientation needs to recognize individual differences as well as commonalities. It must account for the multiple contributions to observed behavior witnessed daily in clinical practice. The orientation should be to the immediacy of the patient's existence, coupled with recognition of the historical contribution of past experiences to present observations.

The Idea of Complaint and Complainable Behaviors

The information afforded by present models of psychopathology may be made more clinically useful when related to the idea of complaint. A complaint is a verbalization or other communication that something is wrong. A complaint may be made by an individual about him- or herself, or it may be given by another person about a particular individual. It is a complaint that brings a person to the doctor. The doctor, in turn, sees the complaint as a sign that something underlying the complaint may not be normal. When viewed through the complaint model, the previously presented notions of inefficiency, discomfort, bizarreness, and other like observations become indications that something may be wrong. the clinician can then consider the various possible contributions to these signs and then (1) seek to evaluate the presence and nature of these contributions and (2) plan corrective interventions when needed in order to remove the complaint. For some aspects of medical illness, the attention in response to a complaint is directed toward discovering the underlying cause as opposed to trying to decide whether the complaint itself is abnormal. Since cause may remain unknown or be multiple for many behavioral phenomena, the analogy to medicine is maintained by substituting the idea of contribution for cause. What are the factors contributing to the observed or reported complaint?

Case Example

An aging woman brought her 45-year-old mentally retarded son to her physician. She requested an evaluation, complaining that her son had recently evidenced a change in his behavior. Diagnosed as mildly mentally retarded at an early age, the son had always been docile, according to the mother, but had recently become destructive and hostile. He had broken several pieces of furniture in the house and, on one occasion, had struck the mother. Thinking that a further deterioration in the patient's intellectual picture could be present, the physician referred the son for a neuropsychological evaluation.

The neuropsychologist approached the case as a complaint that needed comprehensive understanding. As a part of the neuropsychological evaluation, an interview was conducted with the son, the mother, and both together. During these interviews, the mother confided that these episodes had frightened her and, upon further questioning, admitted that she had begun to consider institutionalizing her son. An extensive interview (which should probably be seen as a regular part of neuropsychological evaluation) revealed that the mother's husband had died approximately one year earlier. The mother was soon to be 65 years old and had begun planning to retire on social security benefits. She professed concerned about the management of her son without the husband's help and on the limited income that would be provided during her retirement. She also admitted that since the death of her husband, she had become increasingly aware of her son as a grown and physically large man who possessed limited intellectual resources and controls. She also professed concern about who would care for him if she should die.

What must be obvious in this case example is that a variety of factors subserve the complaint picture. These factors include social, economic, psychological, and other considerations. It should also be noted that who the patient is in this particular situation becomes somewhat unclear. The designated patient's behavioral change had served to communicate the mother's difficulties as well as those of the patient.

The husband's death had left this mother with extra responsibilities in caring for her son. His death had also served to remind her of her own mortality and had prompted her concern about a variety of things, not the least of which included her wish to provide continued security for her son in the event of her own death. These factors contributed to a situation of increased tension and stress that likely caused the "complainable" occurrences. As Reiss, Levitan, and McNally (1982) point out, individuals with limited intellectual resources respond to many of the same environmental stimuli that affect persons with normal intellectual function. Intellectual and cognitive limitations may hinder their ability to adjust to these demands.

When more than one person is involved in a complaint picture, such as the family presented here, it is the individual with intellectual limitations whose problems appear to be more obvious. This person is the one who is most likely to referred as the patient. Attention directed *only* to this named patient may fail to take into account other aspects of the situation that would lead to a comprehensive and helpful understanding of the complaint.

This practical approach, employing the idea of complaint, provided for a meaningful analysis of the behavioral picture presented in this case. Such an analysis indicated treatment strategies. In this case, brief counseling assisted in decision making, implementation of those decisions, and acceptance of them. The complaint was attended to.

THE NEED FOR RESEARCH

The orientation to clinical practice must also recognize the need for scientifically based research in the area of psychopathology. Research needs to expand beyond strict adherence to some specific model of psychopathology, no matter how time-honored that model might be (Bleuler, 1975). Researchers need to examine how past theory has influenced or even limited conceptualizing in the present. For example, a significant portion of present thinking about psychopathology has been greatly colored by ideas from bacteriology. This thinking has led to attempts to trace behavioral observations to some underlying factor in a fashion analogous to tracing a pathologic physical syndrome to a specific pathogenic organism. In Kraepelin's time, attempts were made to relate mental disturbance to underlying poisons and also to relate these behavioral observations to specific metabolic disturbances as well as to infectious disease (Bleuler, 1975). In some cases, such as pellagrous dementia and paresis, these efforts were substantially rewarded. Such successes could, however, lead the field into thinking that all behavior is so determined. To quote from Kety (1979), "most of our normal, everyday behavior is determined not by the biological machinery in our brains that simply mediates that behavior, but by the experiential information we have stored, by how we are taught and educated, and by the values that are instilled in us. The language we speak, the value system we uphold, the occupations we choose, and the goals we set are to a very large extent based on that information that simply cannot be reached through physical, chemical, biological, or neurophysiological techniques" (p. 12). Perhaps one day our knowledge may be greater than at present and allow basic physical explanations for a variety of complex behaviors. For now, Kety's statements appear worthy of attention.

In spite of such observations, however, many present-day efforts are strikingly similar to those of the late 1800s. At that time, effort was made to tie behavior to various poisonous substances, such as alcohol, tea, and morphine. Today, food additives, caffeine, and other noxious substances are hypothesized as substrates for various disorders (e.g., hyperactivity in children). In the 1800s, the attempt was to relate metabolic disturbance to specific behavioral syndromes. It is easy to understand the pessimism reflected by some writers who have observed the redundancy in our efforts. Eron (1979), for example, concluded that people have learned very little about the causes of abnormal behavior and, further, that what has become known has actually been known for centuries. Eron feels that what best characterizes the literature on psychopathology is an ebb and flow of recurring ideas. Progress that has been made, Eron believes, has been too little and too sporadic. The only real progress, according to that author, has been in social reforms, but even these reforms have usually been transient and reversed by economic adversity. He concludes that progress in the area of abnormal behavior is likely to continue to repeat this past record and that a real breakthrough in understanding is unlikely.

If one is to avert Eron's catastrophic predictions, it will be necessary not only to adopt a fresh view in conceiving of psychopathology but also to maintain what is useful from traditional models available to the neuropsychologist. Information is contained in these models that is of extreme relevance to our subject matter. Neurotic manifestations, for example, appear to be the most common psychopathological effect of head injury (Lishman, 1973; Miller, 1961). Such conditions are generally found in mild head injuries, in which there may be momentary or no loss of consciousness (Levin, Benton, & Grossman, 1982; Rimel, Giordani, Barth, Boll, & Jane, 1981). These neurotic behaviors usually require no hospitalization and, in fact, may go unnoticed by treating professionals (Rimel, Giordani, Barth, Boll, & Jane, 1981). These important behavioral phenomena, however, have received too little study are are, therefore, poorly understood, with no consensus regarding their classification (Levin, Benton, & Grossman, 1982).

CLASSIFYING ABNORMAL BEHAVIOR

The clinical neuropsychologist should have a working knowledge of psychopathology as reflected in formal psychiatric diagnostic schemes. It was early recognized that classification would be necessary in dealing with abnormal behavior if any progress was to be made toward understanding the principles underlying such behavior. Most present-day approaches to classification stem directly from early attempts at this process made by Kraepelin (1909). Four general categories of abnormal behavior have usually been included in most classification systems (Buss, 1966): (1) neuroses, (2) psychoses, (3) psychosomatic disorders, and (4) conduct disorders.

Traditionally, some other areas have been talked about, including disorders of childhood, subnormal intelligence, and brain damage.

Neuroses

While the neuroses are commonly divided into types, a unifying theme in neuroses is usually thought to be anxiety. In the third edition of *The Diagnostic and Statistical Manual of Mental Disorders* (DSM III) (Williams, 1980), for instance, many of the problems traditionally classified as neurotic have been subsumed under the topic of anxiety disorders. As an emotion, anxiety undoubtedly plays an important role in the individual's ability to survive. Borrowing concepts from the psychology of learning described in textbooks, such as the one by Hall (1966), anxiety behavior that is observed in clinical practice can be viewed as a combination of escape and avoidance learning strategies. Once learned, an anxiety response may be stimulated in a given individual by events that most would agree deserve such a reaction. In the medical setting, such a realistic basis for reactions to threat represent an all too often experience. Anxiety may, however, be stimulated by thoughts, or a person's approach to the world may be of such a nature that otherwise innocuous situations become anxiety provoking. Simply stated, when anxiety is due in substantial part to the individual experiencing it, it might be thought of as neurotic. Whether seeming more or less "realistic," anxiety is an emotion to be recognized and attended to by the neuropsychologist. Anxiety can be an important factor affecting doctor-patient interactions (Ezriel, 1950) and performance on neuropsychological test measures (King, Hannay, Masek, & Burns, 1978), or it may importantly subserve more directly the patient's complaint picture.

Eron and Peterson (1982) point out that abnormal behavior can best be regarded as the result of an interaction between what the person carries around inside and the specific situation in which the individual is embedded.

To digress a bit further from our main topic of classification, the ways in which normal individuals handle anxiety have important implications for human interaction in general and the doctor-patient relationship in particular. The clinical neuropsychologist should become expert in such principles of communication and interpersonal interaction so that he or she can recognize their consequences in interview and other patient interactions but also so that these factors can be taken into consideration in advising others in the consultation process. Such considerations take one beyond the individual and lead one to consider society, culture, and other institutions and their mores for dealing with basic emotions in an individual member of a particular group. As pointed out by Morgan and King (1966), the desire for social approval is so deeply engrained in most people that they would readily conform to the expectations of others rather than risk disapproval. An individual's need for acceptance by others may be so strong, in fact, that it generalizes to complete strangers. An experiment by Allport (1924) revealed that a given individual would give more restricted judgments in the presence of a group of strangers than they would when alone. The presence of others, then, appears to cue an individual to cautiousness and to leave the person less free than might otherwise be the case to state opinions in an open manner. Information such as this suggests that anxiety levels in individual patients can be expected to be somewhat higher in the doctor-patient setting than in situations in which the patient feels more comfortable and less threatened.

Continuing along this line, it is important for the clinical neuropsychologist to be sensitive to and aware of his or her own needs and limitations. Individuals may subtly or openly seek to intimidate other individuals into stating specified opinions or attending to certain tasks. Threat of social rejection or other punishment can serve as a powerful reinforcer for conforming behavior. Fear of such rejection, whether based on actual and immediate evidence, or in response to anticipations generalized from past experiences, can lead an individual to cooperate or, more accurately, to collude in identifying with another point of view. In the doctor-patient situation, the doctor usually has the upper hand. A busy schedule or a desire to find a quick and easy solution to the patient's complaints may lead the doctor inadvertently to take advantage of the patient's susceptibility to such influence and could actually lead to misinterpretation or misdiagnosis.

Ezriel (1950) presented a description of human communicative interactions that serves to elucidate mechanisms through which individuals put pressure on others and, in turn, are influenced by others. Ezriel described three basic ways in which individuals regularly relate to one another. He referred to these as the required relationship, the avoided relationship, and the catastrophic. In the required type of relating, individuals interact in ways that they believe meet the expectations of the other person. In return, a given individual may want the other to meet his or her own expectations. The person avoids behaving in ways that might fail to meet the expectations, often fantasized, of the other, and he or she pressures the other person to reciprocate. This required relationship exists, according to Ezriel, because of a belief that catastrophe might follow some direct expression of his or her true (avoided) thoughts or feelings. Such a person may maintain a cognitive statement that directs these interactions that could be verbalized as, "If I say directly and openly how I feel, it will not meet the expectations of what you want to hear. You will become unhappy with me and may reject me, and that will be terrible." This way of thinking, according to Ezriel, permeates human interactions. It fosters collusive, rather than cooperative, relationships and militates against honesty and sincerity in human interactions. Becoming aware of this human tendency allows the clinical neuropsychologist to not only avoid contributing to interactions of this sort with patients but also enables the psychologist to help the patient and other professionals to avoid such collusiveness.

Psychoses

Psychotic behaviors are those that people usually think of when they conceive of mental illness. These behaviors represent bizarre and often extreme breaks with reality. Traditionally, these behaviors have been divided into two groups based on whether the primary symptoms are affectual or in the person's thinking. The former have been termed *major affective disorders* and the latter *schizophrenias*.

Schizophrenia

DSM III attempts to be as specific as possible in diagnoses and to adhere to what is known about the disorder from research that has seemingly reached a point of consensus. According to this publication, a person in the active phases of schizophrenia shows symptoms involving multiple psychological processes. There is evidence of a deterioration from previous levels of functioning, and, in addition, the disorder must have persisted for at least six months.

It is important for the neuropsychologist to have a working grasp of disorders such as schizophrenia because bizarre and deviant behaviors are not uncommon in the medical setting and do not in themselves necessarily reflect enduring mental disturbance. Reactions to acute stress, transient drug reactions, and brief metabolic disturbances are but some conditions that might be accompanied by extreme behavioral disturbance. It would be of little use for the clinical neuropsychologist to label such patients schizophrenic.

The criterion in DSM III that onset be before age 45 is not well documented, and it is planned to exclude this in the next edition (Spitzer, 1982, personal communication). To diagnose schizophrenia, the observed disturbances must be judged to be not due to affective disorder. Nor should they be the direct result of organic brain syndrome. At some point, schizophrenia always involves delusions, hallucinations, or disturbances in the form of thought.

Delusions and Hallucinations

In general, a delusion is represented by a fixed idea that seems to bear little or no relationship to the world of knowledge beyond the individual's own thinking. For example, a patient may insist that he is the King of Denmark even though there appears to be no basis in reality for such a claim. At times, as in this example, the delusional nature of the patient's claim may be obvious. More often in clinical practice, delusions are manifested subtly. In fact, there exist some real problems that may hinder the clinician's attempts to label a patient's thinking as delusional because determination of a delusion rests largely on an analysis of the content of the patient's report, on its truth or falsity. In my experience, many seemingly highly fanciful stories told by patients have been shown to be true when extensively investigated. One patient, for example, told of having shot down 50 enemy planes during combat. Although his recounting of these episodes appeared at the time to be quite fanciful, a review of his military records revealed that he was truthful in his stories.

Even if it were possible to locate corroborating evidence for every seeming delusion, how many clinicians are likely to have the time available for such investigations? An alternative is to focus our attention on process rather than content. The clinician should be interested in why the patient is sharing such information. Does it relate to the topics under discussion at the time? Is it presented in clear and concise terms? Does the process of communicating reflect the formal attributes of effective speech? Answers to these and similar questions may serve to reveal more about the patient than would making a subjective estimate of the truthfulness of the content.

When it comes to determining their presence, hallucinations involve problems similar to those encountered with delusions. In general, when hallucinatory, the patient appears to be seeing, hearing, feeling, or otherwise perceiving something that is not present in terms of physical stimuli external to the person. Like delusions, hallucinations may seem obvious to the clinician, or they may be manifested in a subtler fashion. As with delusions, the process parameters of the hallucination may be more clinically useful than a simple determination of presence or absence. For example, the patient's emotional reaction to such an experience may serve to comment on the relative acuteness or chronicity of the clinical condition. Extreme fear or even panic may reflect the patient's unfamiliarity with such an experience, while seeming acceptance or indifference may suggest a long-term condition.

Thought Disorder

Disturbances in the form of thought are generally referred to as thought disorder or formal thought disorder. Thought disorder is to be distinguished from difficulties the patient might show in content of thinking. Peculiar thought content may be observed in many people and is usually of no formal diagnostic relevance. On the other hand, if an individual performs an action on the basis of peculiar thinking, this may be of diagnostic significance. In such a case, the individual may be demonstrating difficulties in self-control or sound judgment. In other words, to wish someone dead may or may not seem distasteful to the professional hearing about such thinking. To put this thought into action should be of immediate concern to everyone.

The most common example of thought disorder is usually referred to as loosening of associations. In loosening of associations, the patient appears to shift ideas from one subject to another without paying attention to the usual references employed in "normal" discourse. A person may make statements that show a lack of meaningful relationship and at the same time no awareness of their absurdity. In schizophrenia, the person may make statements that are often idiosyncratic or autistic in choice of reference. Analogies are sometimes chosen that show no concern for knowledge shared by the listener.

Other difficulties of formal thought may be reflected in poverty of speech, incoherence, extreme vagueness, overly abstract or overly concrete expression, or repetitive or stereotyped speech. There may also be instances of neologisms, perseverations, "clang" associations, or periods of blocking, during which the person seems to be unable to go on with what he or she was saying.

Current thinking about schizophrenia is that it is likely a collection of disorders rather than a single entity. It is important to recognize that the disorder is phasic. The patient may have periods of days, weeks, or months of lucid behavior. At times, the patient appears to digress into characteristic symptoms of the disorder only around certain topics. The latter point emphasizes again the importance of interview in the neuropsychological examination. Through probing in the interview situation, the psychotic tendencies may become manifest and be recognized as an important factor to consider in planning for a particular patient. In making such determinations, it is important for the clinical neuropsychologist to remember that the diagnostic categories are not exclusionary. Each discernible factor represents but one contribution to a total clinical picture. A diagnosis of schizophrenia in no way precludes further clinical exploration and possible additional diagnoses.

Affective Disorders

In the affective disorders, mood predominates. In DSM III, such disturbances are seen as reflecting either mania or depression that is not judged to be due to any other physical or mental disorder. Mood is seen as prolonged emotion that comes to pervade all aspects of the person's mental life. These disorders are generally subclassified according to whether the observed syndromes include predominantly mania, depression, or a combination of both.

Classification of The Diagnostic and Statistical Manual of the Mental Disorders (Third Edition)

DSM III reduces the mental disorders to primary categories that in many ways appear to be similar to the traditional categories of the past. Some of the major categories listed in DSM III include the following: (1) disorders usually first evident in infancy, childhood, or adolescence (including such clinical phenomena as mental retardation, attentional deficits, conduct disorders, and anxiety disorders of childhood or adolescence); (2) organic mental disorders (including such designations as dementia and substance-induced disorders, such as alcohol intoxication); (3) schizophrenic disorders; (4) affective disorders; (5) anxiety disorders (including such occurrences as anxiety neuroses, phobias, and posttraumatic stress disorders); and (6) dissociative disorders (also referred to as hysterical neuroses, dissociative type).

DSM III is the official standard of the American Psychiatric Association for the classification for psychopathology. As such, it represents the official reference in this area in the majority of institutions and agencies in the United States. The authors of DSM III have tried to be objective and open in recognizing the limitations of present knowledge and at the same time provide an organized basis for diagnosis that would be compatible with continued research.

An especially valuable component of DSM III is its multiaxial evaluation. This system allows information that might be useful in treatment planning and prognosis to be recorded on each of five axes. Axes I and II include all the mental disorders. Personality and specific developmental disorders are assigned to axis II, while all other mental disorders are assigned to axis I. Axis III is reserved for physical disorders and conditions. Axis IV allows for designation and thus recognition of severity of psychosocial stressors, while axis V records the highest level of adaptive functioning evidenced by the patient in the past year. This approach allows for inclusion of a variety of pertinent information not previously possible in official diagnostic systems. It also allows for assignment of several relevant conditions at one time.

DMS III has many weaknesses, but it is probably more in keeping with present understanding of behavior than any past attempts to classify the mental disorders. The work was overseen by a task force that represented a variety of disciplines, including psychiatry, psychology, and epidemiology. In its work, this task force developed and worked toward a number of laudable goals. Several of these goals include the following: (1) clinical usefulness of proposed categories, (2) reliability of diagnostic designations,

(3) educational usefulness of employed concepts, and (4) consistency with research findings.

The work attempted to reflect the demand for a biopsychosocial model of psychopathology. It has by necessity, however, become nomenclature without a model. It is atheoretical. Its lack of theory will be welcomed by many but frustrating to others.

Labeling

In closing this section on classification, it might be wise to comment on the caution that should be exercised in the labeling process. Labeling can have enormous power in influencing the professional's handling of a given case (Eron & Peterson, 1982; Ullman & Krasner, 1969). Once a person is labeled with a diagnosis—schizophrenia, for example—people often tend to automatically put the person in a category and to expect behavior usually ascribed to schizophrenics. Treatment of the person takes on the characteristics of how one is expected to treat schizophrenics, and communications may even be given to the person concerning the roles deemed appropriate for a schizophrenic individual (Eron & Peterson, 1982). The same caution holds for other labels as well.

Case Example

A 26-year-old female patient had spent the first 16 years of her life institutionalized because of a misdiagnosis of mental retardation. When finally tested, it was revealed that her actual intelligence quotient was in the 120 range. The misdiagnosis had resulted from her being deaf. This patient reported that her greatest frustrations in attempting to deal with the world outside the institution had to do with learning social roles that were new and different from those taught her in the institutionalized setting. Even though the patient was not retarded, she had been responded to as if she were and had been actively encouraged to respond in ways expected of a retarded person. She described, for instance, a game that was played in the institution, a game called Monster. In this play, one person acts as the monster and chases all the others, who in turn flee from the monster. The game left her unchallenged, and the patient would at times leave the play to linger near the staff so as to observe their interactions. When she was noticed in their proximity, these caretakers would send the patient back to the game, instructing her to "stay where you belong." Eventually, and fortunately, this individual's behavior led to her being seen as obstinate and unmanageable, and she was discharged from the institution.

ADDITIONAL PRINCIPLES OF BEHAVIOR IN THE HEALTH SETTING

This chapter has emphasized the lack of an adequate model of psychopathology to apply to the health arena. There are a number of principles of behavior that are known, and these principles can be constructively applied until an adequate model is developed. As pointed out by Cobb (1976), attention needs to be paid to the practical events that constitute life stress: existential considerations in the patient's life. A host of such considerations hold relevance for observed dysfunction. These include topics surrounding pregnancy, birth, transitions to adult roles, hospitalization, employment and loss of employment, bereavement, aging, retirement, threat of death, and other such practical occurrences of everyday life. Too little attention has sometimes been paid to such factors, and yet they often serve to explain clinical observations or at least to explain them in part. Attention to these often mundane considerations can sometimes lead to dramatic shifts in observed behavior.

Case Example

A severely schizophrenic woman was talking almost incoherently to a doctor. From the conversation, the doctor did glean that she was concerned about dragons and demons that had been attacking her at night in the hospital. Perhaps somewhat frustrated, the doctor mentioned that to hear her talk, one would think the hospital was a primitive jungle. At that point, the patient became coherent and extremely lucid. She asserted to the doctor that he would like living in this hospital no better than she. The fellow patients were all "crazy" and liked to play games by sneaking up on the patient and scaring her when she was asleep. At other times, personal items would be stolen. She continued with a long and lucid story, educating the doctor about the realities of inpatient hospitalization in that particular ward. There is probably little doubt that the doctor's perhaps inadvertent attention to an existential concern on the part of the patient allowed for the subsequent, if only temporary, lucidity.

Predictable Reactions to Illness

Stress is an important consideration in the health setting. Eron and Peterson (1982) conclude that there is a definite link between level of stress and abnormal behaviors of various kinds. There have been attempts to construct theories of psychological reactions to illness that considered stress an important component in such theorizing. Bonhoeffer, mentioned earlier in this chapter, is one theorist who has done so. Horowitz (1982) suggests two kind of reactions, or stages, to stress. He terms these reactions *intrusive* and *denial states*. For Horowitz, serious life events evoke many regular themes. The content of these themes depends on the individual but often contains similar and recurrent elements among individuals. Some representative themes include the following:

1. Fear of repetition (e.g., a person who suffers myocardial or cerebral infarction may fear having another one).
2. Shame over helplessness or emptiness (e.g., a person who has been accustomed to acting as bread winner in a family may feel guilty over no longer being able to fulfill that role).
3. Rage at the "source" (anger may often be expressed toward some symbolic figure that can, at times irrationally, be considered responsible for the disorder; such reactions may be toward others but can also be against oneself, and they may also be intimately involved in motivating litigation in many instances).
4. Guilt or shame over aggressive impulses (this type of reaction might also include guilt over other primitive impulses in addition to aggression; e.g., the

head-injured survivor of a car accident in which someone else died might feel guilty because of some negative feelings harbored about that individual).

5. Fear of aggression (the patient may complain that, with increased irritability, he or she has become concerned about striking out at someone).

6. Survivor guilt (the guilt of an injured survivor of an incident in which others were not so fortunate is widely reported as a component of posttraumatic stress syndrome).

7. Fear of identification or merger with victims (many seizure patients complain about the waiting room in the doctor's office because they do not want to think that they are like the other patients that they see there; in this context, it is important to remember that stereotyped and biased thinking may develop or persist even in the individual who suffers from the condition about which he or she holds some bias).

Weiner (1982) points out that illness itself constitutes a change in people's lives to which they must adapt. Additional demands for adaptation are imposed by the nature of the illness and its manifestations—whether it comes on gradually or abruptly, whether it is treatable, whether it carries stigma, and whether it requires hospitalization, special technical procedures, or surgery. Weiner also states that adaptation is not only a function of past ability to cope but also a function of the symptoms themselves, which may have unique meaning to the person. Such meaning may be physical as well as cognitive. Symptoms may alter metabolism, and treatment for those symptoms may also affect function (e.g., effects of medication). These effects may lead to altered perceptions, memories, and problem-solving abilities, in short, all special functions subserving ability to cope and adapt.

A lowered intelligence level in itself may interfere with adaptive function and has been related to increased risk of emotional disturbance in chronic situations (Menolascino, 1970; Phillips, 1967; Polter, 1965). Low IQ may also interfere with opportunity for adequate treatment of emotional problems (Reiss, Levitan, & McNally, 1982). Many people with low IQ become aware of their limitations and suffer from lowered self-esteem and depression as a result (Edgerton, 1967; Foale, 1956; Stephens, 1953). Even transient disorders of intellect can have repercussions that persist beyond the time of the acute effects of the disorder.

Case Example

A successful trial lawyer suffered a head injury in a motor vehicle accident. Despite the fact that neuropsychological test results suggested that his memory and intelligence had returned to normal premorbid levels, the patient was unable to reassume his previously assigned roles. Confidence in his own abilities had been severely eroded during the transient period of difficulties with memory and concentration. Some attention had to be paid to this area of difficulty before normal life roles could again be pursued by this individual.

Thus, in the seemingly simple area of level of intellectual functioning, one may observe the importance of multiple contributions to manifested behavior. Cattell (1971) further identified several behavioral considerations that interact with and affect the meaningfulness of IQ level for a particular individual. He called these ability factor stimulators and believed them to be correlated with performance on ability tests. For Cattell, such things as neurosis, alertness, objectivity, criticalness, flexibility in thinking, self-assurance, and self-control all served to influence intelligence and maximal employment of intelligence. Turner, Willerman, and Horn (1976) looked at Cattell's factors and found that they did influence Wechsler Adult Intelligence Scale (WAIS) scores.

Chameleons and Beavers

To understand behavior, the neuropsychologist must have a good grasp of normal coping and adaptation. Lazarus (1966) describes two broad types of adjustive processes that are exhibited by people. The person may direct attention toward inhibiting the internal demand or may seek to alter the environmental demand. Altering oneself to fit the environment or attempting to change the environment to fit one's needs are ideas represented in almost every theoretical approach to coping and adaptation. Piaget (1952), for example, referred to accommodation (pertaining to oneself) and assimilation (pertaining to the environment). A colorful description of these processes was provided by Lerner (1937), who referred to chameleons (those individuals who cope and adapt by changing to meet the environment's demands) and beavers (those who busy them-selves attempting to change the environment).

Horowitz (1982) makes the very useful observation that much of what we see in patients that appears to be abnormal may, in fact, represent attempts to cope with the stresses of illness. Such attempts may carry both positive and negative consequences for the individual. Significantly, these attempts may influence the attitudes of profes-sionals or detract their attention from other crucial considerations. The behavior of patients that reflects such efforts at coping and adaptation must be understood and put into perspective. They have consequences for the behavior observed, including behavior observed in psychological testing. Heightened profiles exhibited by medical patients on personality inventories such as the MMPI, for example, may be more parsimoniously explained in many instances as reflections of increased efforts to cope and adapt than as reflections of formal psychiatric disturbance. Further, the nature of the profile may reveal a great deal about the individual's characteristic style of coping and adaptation—that is, whether the individual tends to incorporate physical complaints as a means of expressing emotional concerns and whether coping strategies are primarily repressive in nature or more controlling in their manifestation. Patients who cope by attempting to be in control of a situation may appear in the hospital setting to be demanding or even unreasonable in their demands. Such patients may seek more information about their disorders than treating personnel are inclined to give. Such patients may seem obnoxious and unlikable as a result of these strivings.

Since normal coping strategies may become exaggerated at times of stress, a person may easily appear to be more disturbed than is actually the case. A person who routinely employs a repressive approach to coping and adaptation may appear to be hysterically neurotic. This could mislead the professional into thinking that symptoms are hysterically based and serve to obscure an otherwise sensible clinical diagnosis.

In the practice of clinical neuropsychology, attention may have to be paid to family and friends of patients as well as to patients. These individuals are affected by and do affect the patient. Parental reactions to having a retarded child, for example, can include guilt, overprotectiveness, and rejection (Foale, 1976; Hagaman, 1980). Reiss, Levitan, and McNally (1982) point out that such parental reactions may increase stress for the child and at the same time have direct consequences for the parents. One model in the practice of neuropsychology that I employ in my clinical setting regularly entails an interpretive interview with both patient and significant others in the patient's life. During such interviews, results of evaluations are shared and recommendations are given.

These considerations are relevant for both chronic and acute considerations. Increasingly, attention is paid to such factors even in the emergency room situation. Not only is attention directed to the acutely injured patient in such situations, but psychosocial intervention is offered to family and friends as well (de Vito, 1982; Epperson-SeBour, 1982).

The impact of environment and social considerations on medical disorder has, in fact, become indisputably documented (Bruhn, Chandler, Miller, Wolf, & Lynn, 1966; Harburg et al., 1973; Stout, Morrow, Brandt, & Wolf, 1964; Weiner, 1982). The difficulty has been in finding an effective vehicle to bring such information to manifestation in clinical practice.

The impact of illness produces, among other things, change in what otherwise may have been a stable social environment. Stability imposes a minimum of adaptive demands on a person (Weiner, 1982). Illness or injury brings an abrupt change and an increase in demands to adjust. In unstable social environments, the effects of adaptive demands may be manifested in injury or illness. For instance, such environments may be conducive to raised blood pressure (Harburg, et al., 1973). Epidemiologic studies also suggest that socioeconomic factors and behavior patterns may predispose toward head injury (Levin, Benton, & Grossman, 1982). Other factors that are positively related to head injury include history of previous injury, age between 15 and 30 years, being male, coming from a lower socioeconomic status, alcohol abuse, and divorce. Such associated factors in head injury and other disorders need to be understood in terms of their contribution to the total clinical picture and in how they affect treating personnel.

SUMMARY

Commenting on the current state of psychopathology, Ross and Pelham (1981) suggest that there are currently many more unanswered questions than there are answers. This observation characterizes psychopathology in general, perhaps more so in childhood than in adult problems, and certainly in regard to psychopathologic conditions as manifested in the medical setting. We need to know much more about normal behavior in order to more fully comprehend deviations from normality. We need further knowledge about the normal course of development, the normal development of information processing, normal peer relating, and normal occurrences in biochemical and neurological functioning. As knowledge of such normal courses of development increases, the field will be better able to formulate and treat useful hypotheses in the study of psychopathology (Ross & Pelham, 1981).

Even if research to date has failed to yield a comprehensive and effective unifying model of psychopathology, it has provided many principles that might be used toward understanding psychopathology. Abnormal behavior can best be regarded as a result of an interaction between what the individual carries around inside and the specific details of the situation in which the individual is embedded (Eron & Peterson, 1982). Weiner (1982) has called for concern with the social as well as psychobiological factors associated with disease. He stresses the impact and meaning of being ill on individuals, their families, and even others in the social group to which the individual belongs. For Weiner and others, social and psychological factors play some role in the predisposition to, initiation of, response to, and maintenance of every disease. There are multiple contributions (or causes) to every condition observed by the clinical neuropsychologist.

The clinical view of the neuropsychologist should be existential, phenomenological, and characterized by common sense. It should employ principles learned from research that serve to tell us some practical information about patients in terms of diagnosis, treatment, prognosis, and patient management. As opposed to being reductionistic, neuropsychologists should employ a Gestalt-oriented philosophy in their thinking about behavior. According to Murphy (1949), early Greek thinkers repeatedly stressed oranizational relationship over atomistic conceptualizations. They looked for laws of arrangement and principles of synthesis and order. Such mathematical approaches have, throughout history, proven more fruitful than have more atomistic approaches. It is in such platonistic thinking that a Gestalt psychology finds its roots. In spite of the tendency to search for simple elements to explain behavior—for example, the specific site of lesion in the brain or the germ of schizophrenia—the trend has fortunately been away from such analysis and toward a more Gestalt-oriented view. It is likely that effective models of psychopathology will ultimately develop from such an orientation. The neuropsychologists' interest in behavior and brain leaves them at the interface of mind and body considerations. Such a profession is in a unique position to contribute substantially to the development of these models.

ACKNOWLEDGMENTS

I wish to thank the following individuals for their advice and support in the completion of this chapter: V.J. Berent, E. Berker, T.J. Boll, H.G. Buchtel, B. Giordani, A. Smith, and C. Steiner.

REFERENCES

Allport, F.H. (1924). *Social psychology*. Boston: Houghton Mifflin.

Barnes, G.W., & Lucas, G.J. (1947). Cerebral dysfunction versus psychogenesis in Halstead-Reitan tests. *Journal of Nervous and Mental Disease, 158*, 50–60.

Bleuler, M. (1975). Acute mental concomitants of physical diseases. In D.F. Benson & D. Blumer (Eds.), *Psychiatric aspects of neurologic disease*. New York: Grune & Stratton.

Bonhoeffer, K. (1912). Die psychosen im gefolge von akuten infektionen: Allgemein erkrankungen und inneren erkrankungen. In G. Aschaffenburg (Ed.), *Handbuch der psychiatrie*. Leipzig, Germany: Deuticke.

Bruhn, J.G., Chandler, B., Miller, M.C., Wolf, J., & Lynn, R.N. (1966). Social aspects of coronary heart disease in two adjacent, ethically different communities. *American Journal of Public Health, 56*, 1493–1506.

Buss, A.H. (1966). *Psychopathology*. New York: John Wiley & Sons.

Cattell, R.B. (1971). *Abilities: Their structure, growth, and action.* Boston: Houghton Mifflin.

Cobb, S. (1976). Social support as a moderator of life stress [Presidential Address to American Psychosomatic Society]. *Psychosomatic Medicine, 38,* 300–314.

de Vito, R.A. (1982, October). New dimensions in the diagnosis and treatment of emergency psychiatric disorders. *Proceedings of the Third National Symposium on Psychosocial Factors in Emergency Medicine.* Psychosocial clinicians in emergency medicine, Chicago.

Edgerton, R.B. (1967). *The cloak of competence: Stigma in the lines of the mentally retarded.* Berkeley: University of California Press.

Epperson-SeBour, M. (1982, October). Family response to trauma. *Proceedings of the Third National Symposium on Psychosocial Factors in Emergency Medicine.* Psychosocial clinicians in emergency medicine, Chicago.

Eron, L.D. (1979). The role of the psychologist in the medical center in the year 2000. In T.A. Williams & J.H. Johnson (Eds.), *Mental health in the 21st century.* Lexington, MA: Lexington Books.

Eron. L.D., & Peterson, R.A. (1982). Abnormal behavior: Social approaches. *Annual Review of Psychology, 33,* 231–264.

Ezriel, H. (1950). A psychoanalytic approach to group treatment. *British Journal of Medical Psychology, 23,* 59–74.

Foale, M. (1956). The special difficulties of the high-grade mental defective adolescent. *American Journal of Mental Deficiency, 60,* 867–877.

Geschwind, N. (1975). The borderland of neurology and psychiatry: Some common misconceptions. In D.F. Benson & D. Blumer (Eds.), *Psyciatric aspects of neurologic disease.* New York: Grune & Stratton.

Goffman, E. (1961). *Asylums.* Garden City, NY: Doubleday.

Hagaman, M.B. (1980). Family adaptation to the diagnosis of mental retardation in a child and strategies of intervention. In L.S. Szymanski & P.E. Tanguay (Eds.), *Emotional disorders of mentally retarded persons.* Baltimore: University Park Press.

Hall, J.F. (1966). *The psychology of learning.* New York: J.B. Lippincott.

Harburg, E., Erfurt, J.C., Hauenstein, L.S., Chape, C., Schull, W.J., & Schork, M.A. (1973). Socio-ecological stress, suppressed hostility, skin color, and black-white male blood pressure. *Psychosomatic Medicine, 35,* 276–296.

Herman, B.P., Dikmen, S., & Wilensky, A. (1982). Sensitivity of the MMPI to psychopathology in epilepsy. *Proceedings of the American Epilepsy Society.* Phoenix.

Horowitz, M.J. (1982). Psychological processes induced by illness, injury, and loss. In T. Millon, C. Green, & R. Meagher (Eds.), *Handbook of clinical health psychology.* New York: Plenum.

INS Task Force on Education, Accreditation, and Credentialing (1981). *INS Bulletin* (Meier, Manfred, et al., Eds.), September, 5–10.

Johoda, M. (1958). *Current concepts of positive mental health.* New York: Basic Books.

Kety, S.S. (1979). Research. In T.A. Williams & J.H. Johnson (Eds.), *Mental health in the 21st century.* Lexington, MA: Lexington Books.

King, G.D., Hannay, H.J., Masek, B.J., & Burns, J.W. (1978). Effects of anxiety and sex on neuropsychological tests. *Journal of Consulting and Clinical Psychology, 46,* 375–376.

Kraepelin, E. (1909). *Psychiatry.* Leipzig, Germany: Barth.

Kubie, S. (1954). The fundamental nature of the distinction between normality and neurosis. *Psychoanalytic Quarterly, 23,* 167–204.

Lazarus, R. (1966). *Psychological stress and the coping process.* New York: McGraw-Hill.

Lerner, E. (1937). *Constraint areas and the moral judgment of children.* Menasha, WI: George Banta.

Levin, H.S., Benton, A.L., & Grossman, R.G. (1982). *Neurobehavioral consequences of closed head injury.* New York: Oxford University Press.

Levin, H.S., & Grossman, R.G. (1978). Behavioral sequelae of closed head injury: A quantitative study. *Archives of Neurology, 35,* 720–727.

Lewin, K. (1935). *A dynamic theory of personality.* New York: McGraw-Hill.

Lishman, W.A. (1973). The psychiatric sequelae of head injury: A review. *Psychological Medicine, 3,* 304–318.

Maltzburg, B. (1959). Important statistical data about mental illness. In S. Arieti (Ed.), *American handbook of psychiatry.* New York: Basic Books.

Menolascino, F.J. (1970). *Psychiatric approaches to mental retardation.* New York: Basic Books.

Miller, H. (1961). Accident neurosis. *British Medical Journal,* 919–925, 992–998.

Millon, T. (1982). On the nature of clinical health psychology. In T. Millon, C. Green, & R. Meagher (Eds.), *Handbook of clinical health psychology.* New York: Plenum.

Millon, T., Green, C., & Meagher, R. (Eds.) (1982). *Handbook of clinical health psychology.* New York: Plenum.

Morgan, C.T., & King, R.A. (1966). *Introduction to psychology.* New York: McGraw-Hill.

Murphy, G. (1949). *Historical introduction to modern psychology.* New York: Harcourt, Brace & World.

Phillips, I. (1967). Psychopathology and mental retardation. *American Journal of Psychiatry, 124,* 29–35.

Piaget, J. (1952). *The child's conception of number.* New York: Humanities Press.

Polter, H.W. (1965). Mental retardation: The Cinderella of psychiatry. *Psychiatric Quarterly, 39.* 537–549.

Redlich, F.D. (1957). The concept of health in psychiatry. In A.H. Leighton, J.A. Clausen, & R.N. Wilson (Eds.), *Exploration in social psychiatry.* New York: Basic Books.

Reiss, S., Levitan, G.W., & McNally, R.J. (1982). Emotionally disturbed mentally retarded people. *American Psychologist, 37,* 361–367.

Rimel, R.W., Giordani, B., Barth, J.T., Boll, T.J., & Jane, J.A. (1981). Disability caused by minor head injury. *Neurosurgery, 9,* 221–228.

Ross, A.O., & Pelham, W.E. (1981). Child psychopathology. *Annual Review of Psychology, 32,* 243–278.

Scott, W.A. (1958). Research definitions of mental health and mental illness. *Psychological Bulletin, 55,* 29–45.

Sillitti, J. (1982). MMPI: Derived indicators of organic brain dysfunction. *Journal of Clinical Psychology, 38,* 601–605.

Small, L. (1973). *Neuropsychodiagnosis in psychotherapy.* New York: Brunner/Mazel.

Sowa, A.M.V., Giordani, B., Berent, S., & Sackellares, J.C. (1983). Experiential phenomena in patients with complex partial seizures. *Proceedings of the Annual Meeting of the American Academy of Neurology.*

Srole, L., Langner, T.S., Michael, S.T., Opler, M.K., & Rennie, T.A.C. (1962). *Mental health in the metropolis: The midtown Manhattan study.* New York: McGraw-Hill.

Stephens, E. (1953). Defensive reactions of mentally retarded adults. *Social Casework, 34,* 119–124.

Stout, C., Morrow, J., Brandt, E.N., Jr., & Wolf, S. (1964). Unusually low incidence of death from myocardial infarction: Study of an Italian-American community in Pennsylvania. *Journal of the American Medical Association, 188,* 845–849.

Szasz, T.S. (1961). The uses of naming and the origin of the myth of mental illness. *American Psychologist, 16,* 59–65.

Turner, R.G., Willerman, L. & Horn, J.M. (1976). Personality correlates of WAIS performance. *Journal of Clinical Psychology, 32*, 349–354.

Ullman, L.P., Krasner, L. (1969). *A psychological approach to abnormal behavior*. Englewood Cliffs, NJ: Prentice-Hall.

Weiner, H. (1977). *Psychobiology and human disease*. New York: Elsevier.

Weiner, H. (1978). The illusion of simplicity: The medical model revisited. *American Journal of Psychiatry, 135*, 27–33.

Weiner, H. (1981). Social and psychological factors in disease. In W.R. Grove (Ed.), *The fundamental connection between nature and nurture: A review of the evidence*. Lexington, MA: Lexington Books.

Weiner, H. (1982). Psychobiological factors in bodily disease. In T. Millon, C. Green, & R. Meagher (Eds.), *Handbook of clinical health psychology*. New York: Plenum.

Williams, J.B.W., (Ed.). (1980). *Diagnostic and statistical manual of mental disorders* (3rd ed.). Washington, D.C.: American Psychiatric Association.

CHAPTER 12

Affective Disturbances Associated with Brain Damage

Mary Ruckdeschel-Hibbard, Wayne A. Gordon, and Leonard Diller

The cognitive and perceptual impairments secondary to unilateral brain damage have been well discussed in the neuropsychological, psychiatric, and neurological literature. Extensive test batteries have been developed to describe the linguistic disturbances following left brain damage (LBD) and the perceptual disorders that are the consequences of right brain damage (RBD). Studies have been undertaken to examine the effectiveness of speech therapy for LBD patients (Sarno & Levita, 1979; Sarno, Silverman, & Sands, 1970; Schuell, Jenkins, & Jiménéz-Pabón, 1964). The development of remediation programs for the visual information processing deficits in RBD patients has proven to be a fruitful research effort for many researchers (Diller & Gordon, 1981a, b; Gordon & Diller, 1983; Gordon et al., 1985; Sivak, Olson, Kewman, Won, & Henson, 1981; Weinberg et al., 1977, 1979; Weinberg, Piasetsky, Diller, & Gordon, 1982; Zihl, 1981). Unfortunately, far less attention has been devoted to describing, diagnosing, and treating the affective disorders that are the consequences of either right or left hemisphere damage (Tucker, 1981).

In this chapter, literature pertinent to the understanding of emotional behaviors following brain damage are reviewed, and the following areas of research are highlighted: (1) the different emotional behaviors that have been observed in patients following lateralized brain damage, (2) the measurement of emotional reactions of brain-damaged patients, (3) the anatomical and cognitive correlates of emotional responses in brain-damaged patients, and (4) the relationship between affect communication deficits and emotional state in brain-damaged patients.

EMOTIONAL REACTIONS FOLLOWING BRAIN DAMAGE: OBSERVATIONAL DIFFERENCES IN PATIENT BEHAVIOR

Emotional reactions following lateralized brain damage were initially noted in the literature as clinical observations embedded within neurological case descriptions. As early as 1914, Babinski noted that RBD patients frequently displayed symptoms of anosognosia, that is, denial or unawareness of their left hemiplegia coupled with euphoria and indifference. These emotional responses, termed the *indifference reaction* (IR), appear to be paradoxical, as they are seemingly inappropriate reactions to the realities of a patient's medical situation (Babinski, 1914). Goldstein (1939) coined the term *catastrophic reaction* (CR) to describe behaviors of individuals when faced with tasks they are unable to competently complete. Goldstein describes CR as a common phenomenon following brain damage. It is characterized by a patient's suddenly becoming dazed, agitated, unfriendly, evasive, and even aggressive (Goldstein, 1952). While Goldstein used the description of CR as a generalized response to brain damage, his work has commonly been cited as support for the observation that CR is a specific response of left brain-damaged patients to their loss of linguistic abilities (Heilman & Valenstein, 1979; Tucker, 1981). These divergent emotional responses following brain damage, that is, an indifference reaction following RBD and a catastrophic reaction following LBD, have remained largely unchallenged in the neurological and neuropsychological literature. Consequently, they have become accepted as the emotional sequelae of lateralized brain damage.

Several general interpretations have been postulated for these diverse emotional reactions. They include a grief reaction to physical loss (Fisher, 1961; Robinson & Benson, 1981; Shapiro & McMahan, 1966); a lack of effective and well-modulated defenses (Bordon, 1962); denial (Weinstein & Kahn, 1955); and a loss of the general ability to abstract (Goldstein, 1952). The influence of premorbid personality factors, intrahemispheric locus of brain lesion, and general motivational factors have also been considered pertinent to the understanding of the emotional behaviors in patients following cerebral damage (Horenstein, 1970; Ullman, 1962; Ullman & Gruen, 1960). These factors, while all plausible explanations of the observed affective responses, fail to adequately explain the divergent emotional responses of RBD and LBD patients.

The negative emotional reactions of LBD patients with aphasia have traditionally been considered more severe than those of RBD patients. This assertion is based on the deduction that, phenomenologically, basic communication deficits result in greater feelings of loss than do the perceptual deficits commonly associated with RBD. Indeed, the emotional responses of indifference and euphoria in RBD patients are more difficult to explain. Their presence has frequently been associated with severe perceptual deficits (Denny-Brown, Meyers, & Horenstein, 1952); orientation difficulties (Ullman & Gruen, 1960); and denial of illness, that is, anosognosia (Weinstein & Kahn, 1955). Few systematic evaluations of these explanations are to be found in the literature.

The empirical validation of CR and IR in brain-damaged patients is limited to three studies comparing the emotional behavior of LBD patients and that of RBD patients (Gainotti, 1969, 1972; Hécaen, 1962). Observer ratings of patient behavior were utilized in these studies in order to categorize emotional reactions. Unfortunately, it is unclear whether these two researchers were describing the same phenomena. In his 1972 study, Gainotti provided the specific criteria used to classify patients' behavior (See Table 12.1). However, it remains unclear whether these were the same criteria that he used to classify the patients in his earlier study (1969) or if they were similar to those initially applied by Hécaen (1962). Although both authors report that CR is more prevalent in LBD patients and that IR predominates in RBD patients, two points are of interest. First, Hécaen reports that in his sample of LBD patients, abnormal affective reactions were as likely to be catastrophic in nature (i.e., 28%) as they were to be indifferent in nature (i.e., 26%). Second, Gainotti, in his 1972 study, found no significant difference in the frequency with which depressive behaviors were observed in his RBD and LBD patients. Despite this finding, Gainotti suggests that "catastrophic or the anxious-*depressive* [italics mine] reactions" (p. 46) were found to be more frequent among LBD patients, while IR prevailed in RBD patients. Thus, Gainotti associated depressive symptomatology with left brain damage, although his data failed to support this assertion.

These three studies have served as important cornerstones for further research into the role of cerebral asymmetry in both the processing and communication of emotional information in a wide variety of neurological, psychiatric, and normal populations. However, these specific emotional responses following lateralized brain damage, per se, have not been well studied. Indeed, literature concerning several aberrant patient populations renders questionable the generalizability of CR and IR as manifestations of asymmetrical cerebral functioning. These findings are briefly highlighted below.

Emotional Behaviors of Neurological Patients

The emotional responses of diverse neurologically impaired populations provide erratic support for the notion that CR follows left brain involvement and IR follows right brain involvement. For example, studies of patients' behavior following unilateral intracarotid amobarbital injections have frequently been used to support the existence of different roles of the two cerebral hemispheres in the processing of emotions. Following inactivation of the left cerebral hemisphere, patients have been found to exhibit a dysphoric mood, while euphoric or maniacal reactions frequently accompanied right cerebral inactivation (Perria, Rosadini, & Ross, 1961; Terzian, 1964; Terzian & Cecotto, 1954). These findings have been far from uniform. Reverse reactions have been noted by Tsunoda and Oka (1976), and negative findings were observed by Milner (1967) using the same technique.

Based on an extensive case review of individuals with pathological brain disorders, Sackeim and colleagues (1982) suggest that the nature of the emotional responses in patients differs depending on the nature of brain lesion—that is, whether the lesion is permanent or irritative in nature—rather than the side of the brain that has been damaged. For example, pathological laughter was more frequently noted in patients with destructive right hemisphere lesions as well as in epileptic patients observed during left temporal lobe seizures (i.e., gelastic epilepsy). Pathological crying was more frequently noted in patients with destructive left hemisphere lesions and epileptic patients observed during right temporal lobe seizures (i.e., dacrystic epilepsy) (Sackeim et al., 1982). These seemingly contradictory findings between the emotional responses described above were interpreted to suggest that (1) in permanent (i.e., destructive) brain lesions, the predominant emotional response observed results from disinhibition of the *contralateral* cerebral hemisphere and (2) in irritative lesions, such as in epilepsy, the predominant emotional response observed results from excitation within the *ipsilateral* cerebral hemisphere. Thus, Sackeim suggests that the origin of negative, or depressive, mood states is the right hemisphere, while positive mood states originate from the left hemisphere. This theory has been both supported (Bear & Fedio, 1977) and criticized (Tucker, 1981) in the literature.

In a study of interictal (i.e., between seizures) emotional behavior, Bear and Fedio (1977) note differences between self-report and observer ratings of emotional state in epileptic patients. Left temporal lobe epileptics rated themselves as more depressed than did right temporal lobe epileptics on self-report questionnaires. In contrast, observers rated right temporal lobe patients as significantly more depressed than left temporal lobe epileptics. The authors interpret the discrepant ratings in self- and observer reports to suggest an exaggeration of depressive state in left temporal lobe patients and a minimization of these feelings in right temporal lobe epileptics. These findings support Sackeim's (Sackeim et al., 1982) interpretation that the right hemisphere plays a role in depression and further suggests that those patients with right hemisphere involvement may minimize their symptoms.

In traumatic brain damage (TBD) patients with a documented affective disorder, Lishman (1968) found symptoms of depression, irritability, and apathy to be more frequent in patients with right, rather than left, hemisphere involvement. This study, again, suggests that depression is a right hemisphere phenomenon.

In summary, the literature cited above on emotional responses in divergent neurologically impaired populations provides meager evidence of consistent lateralized affect responses following cerebral damage. The reader is left in a confused state as to whether the proposed CR and IR phenomenon truly exist.

Emotional Behaviors of Psychiatric Patients

The emotional responses of psychiatric populations provide further evidence to challenge the accepted belief in lateralized asymmetry with regard to emotional responses. For example, a left frontotemporal locus has been suggested for symptoms of paranoia, anger, mania, and euphoria in psychiatric populations (Flor-Henry & Koles, 1980). The latter two behaviors have traditionally been ascribed to the right hemisphere (Babinski, 1914; Hécaen, 1962; Hécaen, de Ajuriaquerra & Massonet, 1951). The diagnosis of schizophrenia has been more frequently associated with a left cerebral hemisphere dysfunction (Flor-Henry, 1969, 1974; Serafetinides, 1972). This dichotomy is challenged, however, by findings of Albert and Anderson (1977) in which schizophrenic patients with clinical symptoms of flattened affect were noted to have right cerebral hemisphere dysfunction. In addition to flattened affect, these schizophrenic patients exhibited impaired affect communication skills and impaired imagery abilities. These latter behaviors provide some interesting parallels to the emotional behaviors frequently observed in RBD patients and suggest a right hemisphere role in adequate affect expression.

In psychiatric patients with diagnosed affect disorders, a right frontotemporal lobe dysfunction has been suggested by two groups of investigators (Flor-Henry, 1974, 1976; Yozawitz et al., 1979). The greater the right hemisphere dysfunction, the more likely a patient is to minimize self-report of symptoms (Bruder & Yozawitz, 1979). These findings support those of Bear and Fedio (1977) and again suggest minimization to be a right hemispheric phenomenon.

Right hemisphere dysfunction in psychiatric patients has been strongly linked to symptoms of depression and anxiety (Flor-Henry & Koles, 1980; Goldstein, Filskov, Weaver, & Ives, 1977; Kronfol, Hamsher, Digre, & Waziri, 1978). Depression has also been associated with right hemisphere slowing on the electroencephalogram (EEG) (D'Elia & Perris, 1973; Perris, 1974). Tucker (1981) proposes that the right hemisphere slowing on EEG in depressed psychiatric patients may also be indicative of lowered levels of arousal. Interestingly, unilateral right hemisphere electroconvulsive shock therapy (ECT) has been shown to be more effective than either bilateral or left hemisphere ECT for relief of depressive symptoms (Cohen, Penick, & Tarter, 1974; Deglin & Nikolaenko, 1975).

In summary, the literature on emotional reactions in a variety of psychiatric populations provides minimal clinical support for the presence of asymmetrical emotional responses following lateralized brain damage. In contrast to the widely held notion, this body of literature suggests that depression, and perhaps minimization of severity of depressive symptoms, is more commonly a right hemisphere, rather than a left hemisphere, phenomenon. These descriptions, however, appear to be contradictory and suggest a need for a more precise examination of both the patients studied and the criteria used for classification.

EMOTIONAL REACTIONS FOLLOWING BRAIN DAMAGE: CLINICAL RATINGS AND SELF-REPORT OF AFFECT STATE

Lateralized emotional responses of brain-damaged patients were initially inferred from behaviors observed by clinicians during standard neurological or neuropsychological examinations. For example, the majority of criteria Gainotti (1972) used to label a patient's emotional responses (see Table 12.1) were based on an individual's behavioral response to a neutral, or perhaps threatening, test situation rather than on the exploration of intrapsychic feelings of the individual. The question could be asked whether the emotional behaviors of CR and IR observed in brain-damaged patients were congruent with the patients' own reports of their emotional states.

A review of the literature was undertaken to determine if reports of intrapsychic state in brain-damaged individuals were congruent with observer reports of CR and IR behaviors. In the process of this review, several historical points are of interest:

1. Research conducted before 1970 often studied heterogeneous groups of patients (i.e., groups containing mixed diagnoses, such as tumors, seizure disorders, trauma, etc.). More recent studies have begun to limit samples to more homogeneous groupings.

2. The relationship between affect response patterns and specific location of damage within a given hemisphere has been infrequently studied.

3. Relatively few studies have examined the association between cognitive and perceptual impairments and affect state.

4. Neurochemical abnormalities, normally associated with psychiatric depressive disorders, are now being evaluated in brain-damaged populations.

5. Recent studies of affect state in brain-damaged patients have utilized a wide variety of traditional psychiatric and psychological measurements to assess affect state.

The study of affect state in brain-damaged populations is of growing clinical interest, as evidenced by the rapid increase in publications on this topic since 1970. A summary of these recent studies is presented in Table 12.2. Before 1970, the Minnesota Multiphasic

Table 12.1. Patterns of Emotional Behavior Taken into Account and Criteria of Evaluation

Emotional Reactions	Criteria of Evaluation
Catastrophic Reactions	
Anxiety reaction	Restlessness, hyperemotionality, and vegetative signs of anxiety
Tears	Sudden bursts of tears, or tendency to weep after an increasing anxiety reaction
Aggressive behavior	Irritation and/or expressions of anger toward the examiner
Swearing	Vocative utterances (swears, curses, religious invocations, etc.)
Displacement	Displacement of anxiety or aggressiveness on extraneous events
Refusal	Sharp, cold refusal to go on with the examination
Renouncement	Depressed, desolate decision of renouncing the test
Compensatory boasting	Tendency to perform the test with bragging, anxious precipitancy
Depressive Mood	
Discouragement	Expressions of depressed, disheartened evaluation of illness and incapacity
Anticipations of incapacity	Declarations of incapacity advanced before beginning the test
Declarations of incapacity	Tendency to emphasize failures with declarations of incapacity during the test
Rationalizations	Excuses (scanty education, weariness, want of spectacles, etc.) in order to justify failures
Valorization of past abilities	Tendency to boast of past cleverness in order to compensate for present incapacity
Indifference Reactions	
Indifference	Apparent indifference toward failures, or lack of interest for events concerning the family
Jokes	Tendency to joke in a fatuous, euphoric, or ironical way
Anosognosia	Explicit denial of illness, or lack of consciousness of hemiplegia or of aphasia
Minimization	Acknowledgment of hemiplegia, but tendency to attribute it to weariness, injections, arthrosis, etc.

SOURCE: Gainotti, (1972). Cortex, 8, 44.

Personality Inventory (MMPI) was the sole empirical measure used to assess subjective emotional responses in brain-damaged populations. Using the MMPI, several authors have documented evidence of heightened emotionality, which, they suggest, is supportive of the CR in LBD populations (Black, 1975; Flor-Henry, 1969; Gasparrini, Satz, Heilman, & Coolidge, 1978; Hillbom, 1960). An equal number of investigators have failed to find different affect response patterns on the MMPI that are based on either caudality or laterality of cerebral lesions (Andersen & Hanvik, 1950; Dikman & Reitan, 1974; Freidman, 1950; Meier & French, 1965; Williams, 1952). Black (1975) and Gasparrini and colleagues (1978) compared the MMPI profiles of RBD patients and LBD patients and found the profiles of the RBD patients to be normal when contrasted with those of the LBD patients. Hence, the validation of CR and IR responses using the MMPI has been weak. The lack of consistent findings on the MMPI lead Dikman and Reitan (1974) to suggest that location of brain lesion, per se, does not appear to have a major influence on MMPI profiles when groups of patients with mixed lesion types are examined.

The relationship between the side of brain damage and the incidence of depression is an issue over which there is much conflict in the literature. Robinson and colleagues have consistently found LBD patients to be more depressed than either RBD patients (Robinson & Benson, 1981; Robinson & Price, 1982) or traumatic brain-damaged patients (Robinson & Szetela, 1981). In addition, the Dexamethasone Supression Test (DST), a neurochemical measure traditionally used to diagnose endogenous depression in psychiatric populations, has been used by Finklestein and colleagues (1982) in their study of LBD and RBD stroke patients. These investigators noted abnormal DST suppression, vegetative signs, and observer ratings of depression to be related in the majority of the LBD patients.

In contrast to the studies cited above, depression has been frequently associated with right brain damage. In studies employing self-report measures of affect, RBD patients and LBD patients showed equivalent depression (Kerns, 1980;Ruckdeschel-Hibbard, 1984). Significantly higher levels of depression were reported for RBD stroke patients when their data were compared with those of a sample of age-matched, nondisabled individuals or medical patient populations (Gordon & Diller, 1983). Two studies using clinical observer ratings of depression (Folstein, Maiberger, & McHugh, 1977; Robins, 1976) report RBD patients to be more depressed and anxious than LBD patients. Ruckdeschel-Hibbard (1984) found that RBD patients with severe perceptual impairments and hemianopsia rated themselves as less depressed than did the clinical observer. In contrast, self-report and observer ratings of depression were congruent for RBD patients without severe perceptual deficits. Finally, Finklestein and colleagues (1982) report that the frequency of vegetative signs of depression (i.e., sleep and appetite disturbances) and abnormal DST results were similar in both RBD and LBD populations.

Finklestein and colleagues (1982) interpret their findings as follows:

> The clinical expression of depressed mood appeared to be closely allied with vegetative and neuroendocrine disturbance in patients with left hemisphere stroke, but seemed separate from these disturbances in patients with right hemisphere strokes. From a different perspective, disturbed appetite and sleep with abnormal DST results in patients with right hemisphere stroke might identify a syndrome that is potentially treatable by anti-depressant therapy, even in the absence of overt behavioral signs of depressed mood. (p. 467)

The lack of overt behavioral signs of depressed mood in RBD patients may be indirectly interpreted as evidence of denial or minimization of feelings, or it may reflect a more basic inability of the RBD patients to effectively communicate affect information to the clinical observer. Unfortunately, since no self-report measures of affect were utilized by Finklestein and colleagues, the extent of subjective feelings of depression in these patients is unknown. Despite this limitation, the Finklestein study (1982) provides an important key to the understanding of emotional reactions in RBD patients, since it documents that there may be a subgroup of RBD patients with vegetative signs of depression who may be minimizing their dysphoric affect state.

Table 12.2. Recent Studies of Emotional Reactions in Brain Damaged Patients

Authors	Sample[a]	Etiology of Brain Damage	Affect Measures		Findings
			Observer Rating	Self-report	
Dikman & Reitan (1974)	27 LDB 32 RBD	Mixed[b]		MMPI[c]	All brain-damaged groups showed some evidence of emotional disturbance characterized by neurotic-like manifestations. No differences were associated with laterality of lesion
Black (1975)	15 LBD 20 RBD	Missle wounds		MMPI	Increased depression, paranoid ideation, and deviant thinking were more common in LBDs RBDs had normal profiles
Robins (1976)	4 LBD 12 RBD 2 Bilateral 18 Medical controls	Vascular	HRSD[d]		Brain-damaged subjects had higher depression scores than controls 3 of the LBDs had the lowest depression when compared to other brain-damaged subjects
Folstein, Maiberger, & McHugh (1977)	10 LBD 10 RBD 10 Orthopedic controls	Vascular	PSE[e] HRSD	Visual analogue scale	RBDs were more irritated and depressed than LBD or control groups
Gasparrini, Satz, Heilman, & Coolidge (1978)	16 LBD 8 RBD	Mixed		MMPI	LDBs were more anxious, agitated, and withdrawn When groups were equated for severity of cognitive deficits, LBDs were significantly more depressed; no evidence of depression in RBDs
Kerns (1980)	12 LBD 12 RBD	Vascular		Lubin[f] Self-Evaluation: extent of cognitive-physical deficits	LBDs and RBDs were equally depressed LBDs rated their cognitive-physical impairments as more severe, while RBDs minimized their functional deficits
Robinson & Benson (1981)	25 LBD	Vascular	HRSD	Visual analogue mood scale	Nonfluent aphasics were more depressed than either fluent or global aphasics
Robinson & Szetela (1981)	18 LBD 11 TBD	Vascular and trauma	HRSD	Visual analogue mood scale	The severity of depression in LBDs was correlated with closeness of lesion to anterior pole of cerebrum 60% of LBDs versus 20% of TBDs had significant depression

312

Study	Sample[a]	Diagnosis[b]	Measures	Findings
Finklestein et al. (1982)	13 LBD, 12 RBD, 13 Medical controls	Vascular	HRSD[d]; Interview regarding signs of vegetative depression	69% LBDs versus 25% RDBs had moderate to severe depression. 62% LBDs versus 42% RBDs had abnormal DST tests[g]. Vegetative signs and abnormal DST were better indexes of depression in RBDs. 4 RBDs were indifferent and not depressed
Robinson & Price (1982)	47 LBD, 37 RBD, 19 Brain stem	Vascular	PSE[e], HRSD; Zung[h]	LBDs were more depressed than RBD or brain stem subjects. The severity of depression was lowest in RBDs. Patients with left frontal damage were more likely to develop depression within the first 2 years after onset of brain damage
Gordon & Diller (1983)	30 RBD, 82 Nondisabled, 113 Cancer, 95 Spinal cord	Vascular	MAACL[i]	At 4 months postrehabilitation, RBD patients were more depressed than age-matched nondisabled control group, cancer patients, or spinal-injured adults
Hier, Mondlock, & Caplan (1983a,b)	41 RBD	Vascular	Ratings of anosognosia	36% of RBDs exhibited denial of illness during first week after onset. Anosognosia was associated with large lesions, particularly of the parietal lobe. Median duration for recovery from anosognosia was 11 weeks after onset
Ruckdeschel-Hibbard (1984)	35 RBD, 19 LBD	Vascular	HRSD; MAACL BDI[j]	LBDs and RBDs were equally depressed on self-report indices of depression. RBD patients with severe perceptual deficits were more depressed on clinical rating than on self-report. In RBDs, self-reported depression was independent of severity of perceptual deficit

---

[a]LBD, left brain-damaged patients; RBD, right brain-damaged patients; TBD, traumatic brain-damaged patients.

[b]Diagnoses include vascular, trauma, tumor, and seizure disorders.

[c]Minnesota Multiphasic Personality Inventory (Hathaway & McKinley, 1951).

[d]Hamilton Rating Scale for Depression (Hamilton, 1967).

[e]Present State Exam (Luria & McHugh, 1974).

[f]Lubin Depression Adjective Checklist (Lubin, 1965).

[g]Dexamethasone Suppression Test (Carroll, Martin, & Davies, 1968).

[h]Zung Self-Rating Scale for Depression (Zung, 1965).

[i]Multiple Affect Adjective Checklist (Zuckerman & Lubin, 1965).

[j]Beck Depression Inventory (Beck, Ward, Mendelson, Moch, & Erbargh, 1961).

Emotional behaviors traditionally associated with the IR (i.e., indifference, joking, anosognosia, and minimization) (Gainotti, 1972) have been less frequently examined in the literature. The presence of anosognosia—that is, implicit or explicit denial of paralysis—has been discussed by Weinstein and Kahn (1955) as being primarily a right brain damage phenomenon. However, their sample included bilateral and left hemisphere brain-damaged patients that also evidenced anosognosia. Two recent studies (Finklestein et al., 1982; Hier, Mondlock, & Caplan, 1983a,b) documented the presence of a cluster of behaviors that could be categorized as denial in a subgroup of RBD patients. In a study by Hier and colleagues (1983a), 36% of right hemisphere stroke patients had evidence of anosognosia during the acute phase of recovery from brain damage. In a longitudinal follow-up of these patients (Hier, Mondlock, & Caplan, 1983b), the median duration of recovery from anosognosia was reported to be 11 weeks. During the rehabilitation phase of recovery, Finklestein and colleagues (1982) found 33% of their RBD sample to be indifferent to their neurological deficits. These same patients exhibited neither behavioral signs of depression nor appetite disturbance and had minimal sleep difficulties and normal DST results.

Hier and colleagues (1983a) define anosognosia as failure to acknowledge the stroke or neurological disorder. While Finklestein and colleagues do not operationally define the term indifference, it seems that both groups of investigators are documenting the same phenomenon. The findings from these studies suggest that the presence of anosognosia, or denial, in RBD patients (1) appears only in a small subgroup of RBD individuals, (2) is time-limited to either the acute and/or early rehabilitation phase of recovery from brain insult, and (3) may preclude the existence of either behavioral or vegetative signs of depression in these individuals. Unfortunately, no longitudinal study has investigated both affect state and the presence of anosognosia in RBD patients; thus, the issue of whether RBD patients with initial evidence of anosognosia become depressed at a later stage of recovery is uncertain.

Several authors have documented minimization as an RBD phenomenon. While finding RBD patients to be as depressed as LBD patients, Kerns (1980) noted that RBD patients tended to minimize the severity of their cognitive and physical impairments. Ruckdeschel-Hibbard (1984) interprets the discrepancy found between self-report and observer ratings of depression in RBD patients with severe perceptual impairments as evidence for minimization of depressive symptoms in this RBD subgroup. Absence of vegetative or depressive symptoms in RBD patients in the Finklestein study (Finklestein et al., 1982) may also be interpreted as suggesting a minimization of the severity of affect disturbance in RBD individuals. These studies validate the presence of minimization initially associated with IR by Gainotti (1972) and further suggest that minimization may occur in response to both physical and emotional sequelae of right brain damage.

In summary, the literature exploring the affect state of patients following brain damage provides some validation for the initial observation of CR following LBD but minimal support for IR following RBD. In RBD, evidence exists of minimization of both neurological impairments and emotional distress. However, the most prevalent finding in the literature is one of depression, rather than indifference, in the majority of RBD patients. The classic term *indifference* appears to encompass only a portion of RBD patients. Thus, a discrepancy appears to exist for the majority of RBD patients between the behavioral label of IR and the subjective report of actual affect state.

ANATOMICAL AND COGNITIVE CORRELATES OF EMOTIONAL RESPONSES IN LATERALIZED BRAIN DAMAGE

Emotional reactions following lateralized brain damage need to take into account the influence of both lesion location within a given hemisphere and severity of coexisting cognitive-perceptual impairments resulting from brain insult. When these factors are considered, different patterns of affective response appear to emerge following both left- and right-sided brain damage.

Different patterns of affect behaviors have been observed in LBD patients, depending on both the severity and type of aphasic difficulties. Gainotti (1969, 1972) found that LBD aphasics were more likely to exhibit CR than were nonaphasic LBD patients. Patients with nonfluent, or expressive, aphasia were observed to have more frequent and dramatic emotional outbursts, and to be more depressed than patients with fluent aphasia. These findings were corroborated by Robinson and colleagues (Robinson & Benson, 1981; Robinson & Szetela, 1981; Robinson & Price, 1982), who consistently found nonfluent aphasic LBD patients to be more depressed than either fluent or global patients. Gainotti (1969, 1972) noted that fluent aphasics were more apt to express discouragement but were less depressed than were nonfluent aphasics. Of clinical interest, fluent aphasic LBD patients' behaviors are often described in terms quite similar to those behaviors associated with IR in RBD populations. More specifically, fluent aphasics have been reported often to appear unconcerned or unaware of their speech deficits and at times to appear inappropriate or euphoric (Benson 1973, 1980; Robinson & Benson, 1981; Sarno, 1981).

The severity of depression in LBD patients has been related to the presence of anterior cerebral damage and the closeness of the lesion to the frontal pole of the left cerebrum (Robinson & Benson, 1981; Robinson & Szetela, 1981; Robinson & Price, 1982). Overall cerebral lesion size has been inversely correlated with depression in fluent aphasics and positively correlated with depression in global aphasics (Robinson & Benson, 1981). More extensive lesion size and sensorimotor impairments have been associated with moderate to severe mood disturbance in LBD, but not RBD, patients (Finklestein et al., 1982; Gainotti, 1969).

Heightened levels of arousal, as measured by the galvanic skin response (GSR), have been documented in LBD patients when compared to RBD populations (Heilman & Valenstein, 1972). Heilman suggests that this is a manifestation of disinhibition in the left hemisphere, which, in turn, may explain the heightened emotionality associated with CR. The emotional lability of LBD patients has also been interpreted as reflecting a partial release of limbic system functions from inhibitory control of higher cortical centers (Lamendella, 1977).

In summary, the presence of expressive aphasic deficits, proximity of lesion to the anterior pole of the left cerebrum, and lesion size have been suggested as correlates of depressive symptomatology following LBD. Left brain-damaged patients with more posterior lesions and fluent aphasic deficits appear less depressed and less aware of their impairments.

In RBD patients, the specific influence of either lesion location or cognitive-perceptual impairments on emotional behavior has been frequently discussed but has received little empirical attention. In the early literature, indifference was commonly reported in patients with severe perceptual impairments, specifically in those patients with neglect of contralateral space (Denny-Brown, Meyers, & Horenstein, 1952) and with spatial disorientation (Ullman & Gruen, 1960; Weinstein & Kahn, 1955). Several authors suggest that the greater the perceptual deficits, the more severe the resulting emotional disorder (Horenstein, 1970; Ullman & Gruen, 1960; Weinstein & Freidland, 1977), but these authors have failed to specify the exact nature of these affect changes. In addition to mood changes, global disturbances of consciousness, denial, and confabulation have been attributed to RBD patients with severe neglect (Weinstein & Friedland, 1977). Gainotti (1969, 1972) found a positive relationship between the presence of the IR and perceptual neglect in RBD patients but clearly states that the presence of neglect was neither a necessary nor sufficient feature of the IR.

Right parietal damage has been associated with clinical manifestations of indifference (Finklestein et al., 1982) and anosognosia (Hier, Mondlock, & Caplan, 1983a). This association must be considered cautiously, since only a small percentage of RBD patients with parietal lobe damage was found to exhibit these IR characteristics in both studies.

An interesting explanation of the emotional responses of RBD patients has been suggested by Heilman and colleagues (Heilman, Schwartz, & Watson, 1977; Heilman & Valenstein, 1972; Watson, Heilman, Cauthen, & King, 1973). These investigators propose that RBD patients with indifference and neglect have a basic attention-arousal-activation deficit that is caused by a dysfunction in the corticolimbic-reticular loop. In support of this theory, bilateral arousal disturbances have been documented in both GSR (Heilman & Valenstein, 1979) and reaction time measures (DeRenzi & Faglioni, 1965). Lamendella (1977) suggests a similar theory of combined limbic–right hemisphere system dysfunction as the etiology of indifference behaviors in RBD patients. Lamendella further suggests that RBD patients, due to "impaired limbic functioning at the neopallial level, would tend to be less conscious of emotional implications of their disorder and for this reason to be relatively indifferent toward it" (p. 199).

Two recent studies suggest that the self-reported depression in RBD patients is independent of either severity of perceptual deficits (Gordon & Diller, 1983; Ruckdeschel-Hibbard, 1984) or the extent of cerebral damage, as measured by computed tomographic (CT) scans (Gordon & Diller, 1983). These findings challenge the earlier literature (Horenstein, 1970; Ullman & Gruen, 1960; Weinstein & Freidland, 1977) that had postulated a postive relationship between severity of perceptual impairments and mood changes in RBD patients, suggesting instead that there is a dissociation between severity of depression and perceptual impairments in RBD populations.

In summary, severe perceptual dificits, low levels of arousal, and parietal lobe damage have been suggested as correlates of IR behaviors in RBD patients. In contrast, self-reported depression in RBD individuals is independent of either extent of brain damage or severity of perceptual deficit.

AFFECT COMMUNICATION IMPAIRMENTS FOLLOWING BRAIN DAMAGE: THE APROSODIAS

There is a growing literature documenting lateralized differences in the ways in which brain-damaged patients express or understand affect information. More specifically, RBD patients, when compared to LBD patients or non–brain-damaged individuals, have documented impairments in both the comprehension and expression of affect information. Ross (1981) suggests that aspects of affect prosody and emotional gesturing are functions of the intact right hemisphere. Furthermore, Ross' (1981) data lend themselves to the interpretation that the functional anatomic organization of the right hemisphere for the processing and communication of affect information mirrors that of propositional language in the left hemisphere. This premise leads one to conclude that there are right hemisphere deficits in affect comprehension and expression that are analogs of the left hemisphere aphasias. Thus, since there are sensory, motor, global, and other aphasias (i.e., deficits in the expression and comprehension of propositional language), there are parallel deficits in the expression and comprehension of affect information. These right hemispheric deficits in the comprehension and expression of affect have been labeled *aprosodias* (Ross, 1981). A summary of the types of aprosodias found in RBD patients and their left hemisphere analogs (i.e., types of aphasias), is presented in Table 12.3. Support for the presence of these affect deficits in RBD patients is derived from a series of case descriptions by Ross and colleagues (Ross, 1982; Ross & Mesulam, 1979; Ross & Rush, 1981). Weintraub and Mesulam (1983) have made a similar observation in children. They suggest that while left hemisphere dysfunction may produce dyslexia, right hemisphere damage suffered early in life may produce chronic emotional difficulties and disturbances in expression of affective information.

The behavioral consequence of these aprosodic deficits is that RBD individuals may appear indifferent or inappropriate to those around them because their expression and understanding of affect may be impaired. Hence, the term *indifference* in RBD patients may well reflect these affect communication deficits, rather than the actual subjective affect state of the individual.

Affect Comprehension Impairments: The Sensory Aprosodias

A summary of the empirical studies of affect comprehension in brain-damaged populations is presented in Table 12.4. In normal speech, at least two messages are processed: the sematic (i.e., what is said) and the affect (i.e., how it is said). Mehrabian (1972) states that 93% of a message's affect is conveyed to the listener by nonverbal (nonsemantic) means. The comprehension of affect therefore is based primarily on proper discrimination of the prosodic elements in speech: pitch, tone, inflection, and stress. Right brain-damaged patients, when compared to LBD patients, display greater deficits in both the comprehension of humor and affect information. Wechsler (1973) initially found that RBD patients had greater difficulty recalling emotionally laden narrative than did LBD patients. In a series of studies conducted by Gardner and colleagues (Brownell, Michel, Powelson, & Gardner, 1981; Gardner, Ling, Flamm, & Silverman, 1975; Wapner, Hamby, & Gardner, 1981), RBD patients have demonstrated impaired comprehension of humor in both visual (i.e., cartoons) and auditory (i.e., verbal jokes) modalities.

Right brain-damaged patients' difficulty with affect comprehension has been demonstrated by their inability to identify the intended emotional tones of a given statement. The actual extent and severity of these affect comprehension deficits is disputed in the literature. Heilman and colleagues (Heilman, Scholes, & Watson, 1975; Tucker, Watson, & Heilman, 1977) have reported severe auditory affect comprehension deficits

Table 12.3. Aphasias and Aprosodias

	Aphasias				Aprosodias[a]			
	Fluency	Repetition	Comprehension	Reading Comprehension	Spontaneous Prosody and Gesturing	Prosodic Repetition	Prosodic Comprehension	Comprehension of Emotional Gesturing
Motor	Poor	Poor	Good	Good	Poor	Poor	Good	Good
Sensory	Good	Poor	Poor	Poor	Good	Poor	Poor	Poor
Global	Poor	Poor	Poor	Poor	Poor	Poor	Poor	Poor
Conduction	Good	Poor	Good	Good	Good	Poor	Good	Good
Transcortical motor	Poor	Good	Good	Good	Poor	Good	Good	Good
Transcortical sensory	Good	Good	Poor	Poor	Good	Good	Good	Good
Mixed transcortical	Poor	Good	Poor	Poor	Poor	Good	Poor	Poor
Anomic (alexia with agraphia)	Good	Good	Good	Poor	Good	Good	Good	Poor

SOURCE: Ross (1981). *Archives of General Psychiatry, 38,* 1345, Copyright 1981, American Medical Association.

[a]The existence of the conduction and anomic aprosodias has been hypothesized; the others have been described. Motor, sensory, global, and transcortical sensory aprosodias have good anatomical correlation with lesions in the left hemisphere known to cause homologous aphasias.

in RBD patients, while Schlanger (Schlanger, Schlanger, & Gertsman, 1976) found that RBD and LBD patients were equally proficient at affect comprehension tasks. These discrepant findings may possibly be explained by the different patient character- istics of the RBD patients in each of the studies; that is, Heilman and colleagues restricted their sample to RBD patients with neglect, while Schlanger and colleagues did not. In a replication of the study by Tucker and colleagues, Ruckdeschel-Hibbard (1984) found affect comprehension abilities to be selectively impaired in those RBD patients with hemianopsia and severe perceptual neglect. This study delimits the extent of affect comprehension impairments to a subgroup of RBD patients and suggests that the extent of these deficits, even in RBD patients with neglect, is less severe than was initially suggested by Heilman and colleagues.

Affect comprehension deficits in RBD patients have been documented in the visual, as well as the auditory, domain. In a normal interchange, the human face serves as a primary vehicle for the expression of emotions. Studies of facial perception have provided cues concerning emotional sensitivity in the intact brain (Cicone, Wapner, & Gardner, 1980). In RBD patients, impaired processing, recognition, and memory of neutral faces (i.e., prosopoagnosia) are well-documented perceptual impairments (Benton & Van Allen, 1968; DeRenzi & Spinnler, 1966; Hácaen, Ajuriaquerra, & Massonet, 1951; Warrington & James, 1967; Yin, 1970). Research specific to recognizing the intended affect of human face is less abundant. DeKosky, Heilman, Bowers, and Valenstein (1980) and Cicone, Wapner, and Gardner (1980) found that RBD patients perform consistently poorer than do LBD or non–brain-damaged control subjects on tests of facial affect comprehension. Ruckdeschel-Hibbard (1984) documented impaired visual affect comprehension only in RBD patients with hemianopsia and severe perceptual deficits. This could suggest a perceptual basis for faulty task performance. Studies by both Cicone, Wapner, and Gardner (1980) and Ruckdeschel-Hibbard (1984) failed to demonstrate a consistent relationship between performance on facial recognition tasks and performance on facial affect recognition tasks. This would indicate that prosopoagnosia and visual affect comprehension deficits may be inde- pendent in RBD patients.

To determine whether affect comprehension abilities in auditory and visual modalities were related, Ruckdeschel-Hibbard (1984) compared RBD and LBD patient perfor- mance on both auditory and visual affect comprehension tasks. Affect comprehension abilities were consistent across modalities for LBD patients but not for RBD patients. In RBD patients, affect comprehension performance in one modality bore no relation- ship to competence in the other modality.

Affect Expression Impairment: The Motor Aprosodias

Relatively few studies have empirically evaluated affect expression abilities in brain- damaged patients (see Table 12.4). In a study restricted to RBD patients with perceptual neglect, Tucker, Watson, and Heilman (1977) found that RBD patients had significantly more difficulty expressing affect statements than did members of a non–brain-damaged control group. Interestingly, RBD patients were most accurate at expressing the emotion of indifference. Danly, Shapiro, and Gardner (1982) and Shapiro and Danly (1985) in studies of acoustical analysis of speech patterns, document flattened affect,

Table 12.4. Studies of Affect Communication Impairments in Brain-Damaged Patients

Authors	Sample	Etiology of Brain Damage	Cognitive-Perceptual Evaluation	Affect Evaluation	Findings
Comprehension of Humor Studies					
Wechsler (1973)	19 RBD[a] 17 LBD[b] 44 Normal controls	Mixed (i.e., vascular, tumor and trauma)	None	None	Brain-damaged subjects had poorer recall of neutral and emotional narratives than did controls RBDs had greater difficulty recalling emotionally laden narrative and made more symbolic self-referential distortions than did LBDs
Gardner, Ling, Flamm, & Silverman (1975)	19 RBD 41 LBD 14 Normal controls	?	None	None	Brain-damaged subjects had poorer comprehension of intended humor in cartoon stimuli than did controls RBDs performed better when labeled captions to cartoons were provided as a linguistic aide; LBDs performed better on cartoons without captions Behaviorally, RBDs were either muted or overly expansive in test responses
Wapner, Hamby, & Gardner (1981)	16 RBD 10 LBD 25 Normal controls	?	None	None	RBDs had greater difficulty than LBDs with appreciation of humor in both verbal and visual modalities (i.e., in understanding jokes or cartoon stimuli) Anterior RBDs had a tendency to embellish affect stimuli, while posterior RBDs committed more errors
Brownell, Michel, Powelson, & Gardner (1981)	12 RBD 12 Normal controls	?	None	None	RBDs picked more nonsequitur endings for jokes than did normals RBDs had an abnormal appreciation of humor (i.e., treated nonhumorous items as more humorous than did normals)

320

Auditory Affect Comprehension Studies

Study	Subjects	Etiology	Notes	Mood measures	Findings
Schlanger (1973)	38 LBD 19 Normal controls	?	LBD group divided into high and low verbal on aphasia screenings	None	LBDs were more impaired than normals on recognition of meaningful affect comprehension test (97% accuracy normal versus 76% accuracy high verbal versus 35% accuracy low verbal) High verbal subjects did better than low verbal subjects on meaningful affect comprehension test
Heilman, Scholes, & Watson (1975)	6 RBD 6 LBD	?	All RBDs had severe neglect	None	RBDs and LBDs performed equally well on auditory comprehension of neutral stimuli RBDs had impaired auditory affect comprehension (25% RBD accuracy versus 62% LBD accuracy)
Schlanger, Schlanger, & Gerstman (1976)	20 RBD 40 LBD	?	LBD group divided into high and low verbal on aphasia screening	None	RBDs and LBDs performed equally well on comprehension of both meaningful and meaningless affect recognition tasks (70% RBD accuracy versus 77% LBD accuracy high verbal versus 66% LBD accuracy low verbal
Tucker, Watson, & Heilman (1977)	11 RBD 7 LBD	?	All RBDs had severe neglect	None	RBDs had both impaired affect comprehension (31% RBD accuracy versus 75% LBD accuracy) and impaired affect discrimination (54% RBD accuracy versus 84% LBD accuracy)
Ruckdeschel-Hibbard (1984)	35 RBD 19 LBD	Vascular	Perceptual-congnitive deficits evaluated	HRSD[c] MAACL[d] BDI[e]	Affect comprehension and discrimination abilities were selectively impaired in RBDs with concomitant hemianopsia and perceptual impairments (affect comprehension = 64% RBDs with hemianopsia versus 68% RBDs with normal vision versus 76% LBDs with normal vision; affect discrimination = 71% RBDs with hemianopsia versus 90% RBDs with normal vision versus 89% LBDs with normal vision) Affect comprehension deficits were independent of severity of depression in RBDs

Table 12.4. *(Continued)*

Visual Affect Comprehension Studies

Authors	Sample	Etiology of Brain Damage	Cognitive-Perceptual Evaluation	Affect Evaluation	Findings
Cicone, Wapner, & Gardner (1980)	21 RBD 18 LBD 10 Normal controls	?	Facial recognition abilities evaluated	None	RBDs had impaired facial recognition (77% RBD accuracy versus 100% LBD and control accuracy) as well as impaired facial affect recognition (70% RBD accuracy versus 86% LBD versus 95% control) RBDs were helped by verbal cues to interpret intended affect in visual stimuli Facial recognition and facial affect recognition abilities were independent ($r = .28$) for RBDs
DeKosky, Heilman, Bowers, & Valenstein (1980)	9 RBD 9 LBD 9 Normal controls	?	All RBDs had neglect. Facial recognition abilities evaluated	None	RBDs had impaired facial recognition (81% RBD accuracy versus 100% LBD control accuracy) and impaired facial affect recognition (55% RBD accuracy versus 70% LBD versus 94% controls) RBDs had impaired facial affect discrimination (71% RBD accuracy versus 91% LBD versus 99% control)
Ruckdeschel-Hibbard (1984)	35 RBD 19 LBD	Vascular	Perceptual-cognitive evaluations	HRSD MAACL BDI	Facial affect comprehension was selectively impaired in RBDs, with concomitant hemianopsia and perceptual deficits (60% accuracy for RBDs with hemianopsia versus 81% for LBDs with normal vision versus 79% for LBDs with normal vision) Facial affect recognition and facial recognition were independent abilities in RBDs ($r = .29$ for RBDs with hemianopsia; $r = .24$ for RBDs with normal vision) Affect comprehension abilities in visual and auditory modalities were unrelated in RBDs

Affect Expression Studies

Study	Subjects	Etiology		Depression	Findings
Tucker, Watson, & Heilman (1977)	8 RBD 8 Medical controls	?	All RBDs had neglect	None	RBDs had difficulty with affect expression (28% RBD accuracy versus 59% accuracy controls) RBDs were most accurate at evoking tones of indifference
Buck & Duffy (1980)	10 RBD 10 LBD 10 Normal controls 9 Parkinson's	?	Aphasia screening for LBDs	None	When compared to LBD or control subjects, RBDs had impaired nonverbal affect expression (on a 7-point scale of expressiveness, RBD = 3.4 versus LBD = 5.25 versus control = 4.10) LBDs may have heightened nonverbal expressive abilities
Danly, Shapiro, & Gardner (1982)	10 RBD 10 Normal controls	?	?	None	Right anterior lesion subjects had flattened prosody and less modulation, while right posterior lesion patients tended to exaggerate prosody Both RBD groups had normal syntactic structure
Shapiro & Danly (1985)	11 RBD 5 LBD 5 Normal controls	Vascular	None	None	Right anterior lesion subjects had less modulation and decreased ability to use declarative interrogative contrasts Right anterior and central lesion subjects had decreased ability to produce emotional modulations, while right posterior subjects exhibited exaggerated emotional pitch and modulation

[a]RBD, right brain-damaged patients.
[b]LBD, left brain-damaged patients.
[c]Hamilton Rating Scale for Depression (Hamilton, 1967).
[d]Multiple Affect Adjective Checklist (Zuckerman & Lubin, 1965).
[e]Beck Depression Inventory (Beck, Ward, Mendelson, Mock, & Erbargh, 1961).

less pitch variation, and restricted intonational range of speech in both right anterior (i.e., prerolandic) and right central (i.e., pre- and postrolandic) brain-damaged patients. Right brain-damaged patients with more posterior lesions (i.e., postrolandic) had exaggerated pitch variation and intonational range. In these studies, the patients were asked to assume an acting role, in which their expression of affect prosody was evaluated. No study has yet attempted analysis of the prosodic abilities of such patients during more affect-laden samples of behavior, such as analysis of portions of a patient's responses during a clinical interview regarding the patient's current mood state. This domain clearly requires further investigation.

Motor aprosodias involve deficits in both prosodic and gestural abilities (Ross, 1981). Studies of nonverbal gesturing abilities in brain-damaged patients are few. Buck and Duffy (1980) studied nonverbal expression of RBD, LBD, Parkinson's patients, and normal control subjects. Patients were rated by outside observers on their ability to convey a select mood nonverbally. Right brain-damaged patients were rated as showing more nonverbal expression than Parkinson's patients but significantly less nonverbal expression than either LBD or normal groups. Reduced spontaneous facial expression in frontal lobe epileptic patients has been documented by other authors (Kolb & Milner, 1981; Kolb & Taylor, 1981), but these findings were independent of side of hemispheric involvement.

Ross and Mesulam (1979) describe two clinical cases of RBD patients with supra-sylvian fissure infarcts who were aware of their motor aprosodias. Of clinical interest, both patients experienced a full range of affect but had been diagnosed as having flattened affect due to the presence of motor aprosodia. This finding highlights the potential discrepancy that may exist between an RBD patient's affect state and observer ratings of a patient's emotions due to the presence of an aprosodia.

The presence of affect communication deficits, or aprosodias, in RBD patients provides a logical explanation for the discrepancy between earlier observations of RBD patients' emotional behavior—namely, indifference—and more recent findings of depression in RBD populations. More specifically, the clinical description of indifference in RBD patients may reflect faulty affect communication abilities—that is, flattened affect expression or inability to comprehend affective stimuli appropriately—rather than the actual emotional state of the individual, which is depression. In order to adequately understand the RBD patient's actual emotional response, Ross (1981) suggests that the clinician pay strict attention to the *propositional description* of a patient's mood and feelings, disregarding the flattened affect that is frequently observed in a patient's behavior. Recent studies of affect responses that utilized observer ratings and/or self-report measures of affect (see Table 12.2) focus on the patient's propositional descriptions of mood rather than relying on the aberrant and aprosodic behaviors of the patient to evaluate affect state. When such measures are employed, RBD patients seem as depressed as LBD patients.

SUMMARY

The available literature describing emotional behaviors, emotional state, and affect communication impairments in brain-damaged patients has been reviewed. A brief summary of the major points appears to be in order.

First, two differing emotional reactions have been clinically noted in brain damaged patients: catastrophic reactions following LBD and indifference reactions following RBD. Some support for these lateralized emotional behaviors is gained from literature on brain-damaged and psychiatric patient populations. The adequacy of this dichotomy of emotional reactions (i.e., CR following LBD and IR following RBD) has been challenged by recent studies. The need to reexamine the appropriateness of these labels is suggested.

When the intrahemispheric locus of the lesion and cognitive-perceptual deficits are jointly considered, different patterns of emotional behaviors are observed in LBD and RBD groups that are contrary to the expected CR-IR dichotomy. For example, LBD patients with receptive aphasia associated with posterior lesions have been noted to be often unaware of their speech impairments, unconcerned, and at times, euphoric. These behaviors appear to be descriptive of IR, which has traditionally been attributed to RBD. In contrast, more severe depression has been found in LBD patients with anterior lesions and expressive aphasia. These examples of different patterns of emotional responses following unilateral brain damage suggest the need to control for both lesion location and cognitive-perceptual deficits when diagnosing and interpreting the emotional behaviors of brain-damaged patients.

Research using traditional psychiatric and psychological measurement of affect state is often in conflict with observations of brain-damaged patients' emotional behavior. The presence of depression following LBD has been documented in studies using both self-report and observer rating of depression. Yet the certainty that depressive reactions are exclusive to LBD has been challenged. The presence of IR following RBD has been supported only occasionally. Indeed, RBD patients' self-report indexes have suggested equal or greater depression, anxiety, and irritability compared with LBD patients or medical control patients. Hence, a lack of association appears to exist between clinical observation of RBD patients' emotional behaviors and the patients' report of subjective affect state.

A growing literature suggests that brain-damaged patients have increased difficulty in a variety of affect communication tasks: comprehending humor, comprehending affect in spoken communication, and expressing affect either verbally or nonverbally. These affect deficits are consistently greater for RBD patients than for LBD patients or non–brain-damaged persons. The clinical description of indifference in RBD patients may in fact reflect these faulty affect communication abilities rather than the patients' actual emotional state.

In conclusion, the terms *CR* and *IR* following lateralized brain damage appear more descriptive of patients' behaviors than of their affect state. Patterns of emotional reactions and behaviors vary depending on site of damage and type of cognitive deficit concomitant with the damage in a given cerebral hemisphere. Self-report and clinical ratings of patients' subjective affect state suggest that both RBD and LBD patients may be similarly depressed. The behavioral manifestations of depression may differ in both patient groupings: LBD patients may exaggerate their emotional distress, while RBD patients may minimize these symptoms. For RBD patients, a more accurate assessment of mood may be obtained from a verbal report of a patient's feelings or an evaluation of more vegetative signs of depression.

Further work is clearly indicated in both the diagnosis and the treatment of emotional reaction and affective deficits in brain-damaged persons.

CLINICAL IMPLICATIONS

The literature reviewed in this current chapter suggests that emotional reactions and affect state in patients following lateralized brain damage are far from uniform. Rather, patients' emotional state appears to vary depending on the combined influences of premorbid coping style, duration of time since onset of damage, intrahemispheric location of lesion, and severity of cognitive-perceptual deficits that exist. Furthermore, the presence of affect communication deficits, specifically following RBD, may artificially mask a patient's ability to express affect messages appropriately or, conversely, render a patient unable to respond appropriately to affective communication from others.

Given the complexity of this issue, how does the clinician adequately and accurately diagnose affect state in brain-damaged persons? Two clinical cases of RBD patients will be presented to help illustrate how the clinician can successfully integrate information obtained from both psychological and neuropsychological inquiry to accurately assess a brain-damaged patient's affect state. The first patient to be considered showed evidence of implicit denial, mild euphoria, and minimization, behaviors related to IR in RBD. This patient also displayed a mild to moderate depression and impaired affect comprehension abilities. The case of the second patient helps to illustrate how an expressive aprosodia and severe perceptual deficits can mask the actual severity of depression in an individual.

Case 1

Mrs. M. A. is a 67-year-old retired beautician who suffered a right cerebrovascular accident (CVA). A CT scan revealed a subcortical infarct of the right internal capsule. Mrs. M. A. was seen for a clinical interview 10 weeks postonset of the CVA while undergoing an active rehabilitation program. A brief neurological assessment at that time revealed that, on visual confrontation, she had normal vision and a moderate paralysis of her left face, arm, and leg.

Clinical Impression of Patient's Emotional Behaviors

Mrs. M. A. appeared unduly cheerful at times during the interview. Despite her laughter, she appeared agitated and mildly depressed. When discussing either her physical disability or her medical condition, Mrs. M. A.'s responses were suggestive of implicit denial. While she would not deny the presence of a stroke, she quickly evaded further discussion by using jokes or minimizing the extent of the disability. Her responses are presented on the following page.

Despite these somewhat inappropriate comments surrounding discussion of her medical condition, Mrs. M. A. was quite appropriate during the remainder of a clinical interview, which focused on her present affect state. During the interview, the patient completed the Beck Depression Inventory (BDI) and was concurrently rated on the Hamilton Rating Scale for Depression (HRSD). Her scores for both measures are summarized in Table 12.5. The patient admitted to having increased fatigue, lowered energy level, mild irritability, feelings of sadness, and altered body image since her CVA. She admitted to a marked change in appetite accompanied by a weight loss of over 20 pounds. Hence, vegetative signs of depression were present.

Clinical Question	Patient's Response
What physically happened to you that brought you to the hospital?	I had a stroke....I don't want to even remember the date it happened. I went to a local hospital. I had such a good time there. I put a sign on my bed which read, "Arm and Leg for Sale," but nobody bought them! [Laughter]
Are you having any difficulty moving your leg?	Yes—I just started walking, so it's difficult to evaluate.
Are you having any difficulty moving your arm?	I'm having trouble with swelling in it. [Does not mention paralysis.]
How about *moving* your arm?	Oh, I have some strength in it.
Are you worried about your medical condition?	I'm not.... What comes, comes. Sometimes I think about it for a while, and then I go and feed the birds. [Laughter]

As seen in Table 12.5, Mrs. M. A. reported more somatic than nonsomatic items on the BDI. Clinical ratings on the HRSD for somatic items were congruent with self-report. However, nonsomatic manifestations of depression were rated as more severe by the clinical observer. Hence, evidence of minimization of the severity of the patient's depression is suggested.

Further evaluation of perceptual and affect comprehension abilities revealed that Mrs. M. A. did not exhibit perceptual impairments but that she did have moderate

Table 12.5.   Depression Profile for Mrs. M. A.

Hamilton Rating Scale for Depression (HRSD)[a]	Rating	Beck Depression Inventory (BDI)[b]	Rating
Somatic Items			
Somatic complaints (i.e., fatigue, etc.)	1	Fatigability	1
Motor retardation or agitation	1	Work retardation	1
Appetite change	2	Anorexia	2
Weight loss	2	Weight loss	3
		Body image change	1
Subtotal	6	Subtotal	8
Nonsomatic Items			
Anxiety, psychic	1		
Agitation	2	Irritability	1
Work or interest changes	1		
Depressed mood	1	Sadness	1
Helplessness	1		
Lack of insight	1		
Subtotal	7	Subtotal	2
Total	13	Total	10

[a]HRSD scoring has been modified to a 3-point scale; 0, no evidence of a symptom; 2, severe symptoms.
[b]BDI scoring is based on a 4-point scale; 0, no difficulty; 3, maximum severity of symptom.

deficits in her ability to identify affect in the auditory domain (i.e., her score on Auditory Affect Comprehension [Tucker, Watson, & Heilman, 1977] was 9 out of 16 correct).

In summary, Mrs. M. A. presented some evidence for indifference, including inappropriate euphoria and minimization of both her disability and the severity of her depression. Despite these behaviors, the patient appeared to be mildly to moderately depressed, as evidenced by clinical ratings and vegetative markers of depression. Her impaired affect comprehension abilities may help to explain some of her inappropriate affect behaviors.

Case 2

Mrs. E. K. is a 64-year-old retired secretary who suffered two right cerebral infarctions. The initial CVA, which occurred in February, was relatively mild, resulting in only residual weakness of her left arm and leg. After multiple transient ischemic attacks (TIAs), the patient experienced a second, and more severe, right CVA in May of the same year. Residual deficits from the second stroke included marked paralysis of her face, arm, and leg as well as a visual field impairment. A CT scan revealed multiple right cerebral hemisphere infarctions. An EEG was found to be abnormal, again suggesting right hemisphere dysfunction. The patient had a past history of hypertension, obesity, and chronic myositis.

Mrs. E. K. was seen for a clinical interview four weeks after her second stroke while she was undergoing an active rehabilitation program. A brief neurological assessment at that time revealed marked paralysis of her left extremities as well as a partial visual field impairment.

Clinical Impression of Patient's Emotional Behaviors

Mrs. E. K. appeared depressed throughout the clinical interview. While she was extremely verbal and articulate regarding her present affect state, she spoke in a monotone voice devoid of any affect intonation. She was also agestural throughout the interview. Her physical appearance was unkempt. Her eye contact was poor.

Mrs. E. K. was realistically aware of both her medical condition and the extent of her disability, although discussion of these issues resulted in her expression of a need to escape from focusing on them. Her responses are presented on the following page.

During the remainder of the clinical interview, Mrs. E. K. completed the BDI and was concurrently rated by the clinician on the HRSD. The profile of her self-report and observer ratings of depressive symptoms are presented in Table 12.6. Her scores on both measures are in the severely depressed range. As seen in Table 12.6, she admitted to considerable somatic manifestations of depression: moderate sleep disturbance, extreme fatigue, and total lack of initiative. Her extreme weight loss, 57 pounds, was attributed to a weight reduction diet and not a loss of appetite. She admitted to having headaches, mild irritability, indecision, feelings of intense worthlessness, pessimism, and self-dislike. Mrs. E. K. minimized the severity of her depression (admitted to only feeling sad and blue) on the BDI but did admit that her depression was getting worse. She expressed some suicidal ideation ("If I had another stroke, I'd stop taking my heart medication so I'd die") but denied a present wish to act upon these thoughts. Further-

Clinical Question	Patient's Response
What physically happened to you that brought you to the hospital?	Fell down...had a stroke in February. Eight weeks later, I had a second stroke. A brain scan confirmed this. Now I have no movement in my arm or leg.
What are your biggest problems now?	Getting my son-in-law and daughter back together again. [The patient begins to cry over the recent divorce of her daughter. Note that the patient ignores her own physical difficulties.]
What are your biggest problems with *yourself*?	I don't care about myself....I use lots of escapes right now.
Are you worried about your medical condition?	Extremely...I had two strokes....I don't want another. [Cries] I want to be free of all this...run away from everything.

Table 12.6.   Depression Profile for Mrs. E. K.

Hamilton Rating Scale for Depression (HRSD)[a]	Rating	Beck Depression Inventory (BDI)[b]	Rating
Somatic Items			
Insomnia, initial	1	Insomnia	2
Insomnia, middle	2		
Somatic complaints (i.e., fatigue, etc.)	2	Fatigability	3
Motor retardation or agitation	2	Work retardation	3
Weight loss	2	Weight loss	3
Hypochrondiasis	2		
Subtotal	11	Subtotal	11
Nonsomatic Items			
Anxiety, psychic	1		
Agitation	2	Irritability	1
Anxiety, somatic	2		
Work or interest changes	1	Indecisiveness	1
Depressed mood	2	Sadness	1
		Crying	1
Hopelessness	2	Pessimism	3
Helplessness	2		
Suicide	1	Suicidal ideas	1
Worthlessness	2	Self-accusation	3
		Self-dislike	3
		Sense of failure	2
Guilt	2	Guilt	2
		Expectation of punishment	3
Subtotal	17	Subtotal	22
Total	28 (severe depression)	Total	33 (severe depression)

[a]HRSD scoring has been modified to a 3-point scale; 0, no evidence of a symptom; 2, severe symptoms.
[b]BDI scoring is on a 4-point scale; 0, no difficulty; 3, maximum severity of symptom.

more, she was quite verbal regarding her feelings of guilt and her wish to be punished for her past failures in life. She viewed the stroke as a just punishment.

On further evaluation, Mrs. E. K. was found to have severe perceptual neglect, as evidenced by extremely poor performance on a simple cancelation task (a score of 37/105 correct on the Cancelation "H" Test [Weinberg et al., 1977]) and the Raven's (1965) Coloured Progessive Matrices (a score of 8/36 correct, with virtually all answers selected from the right side of the page). She also demonstrated a mild deficit in affect comprehension (a score of 14/16 correct on the Affect Comprehension Test [Tucker, Watson, & Heilman, 1977]). Although her affect expression abilities had not been systemically evaluated, it was clear from her behavior and verbal responses elicited during an emotion-laden interview that Mrs. E. K. was both agestural and motor aprosodic.

In summary, Mrs. E. K. presented a pattern of severe agitated depression combined with affect expression deficits and severe perceptual impairments.

On completion of this assessment, Mrs. E. K.'s physician was contacted regarding the apparent severity of her depression. The physician was surprised at the level of her self-reported depression. A review of her medical chart indicated no mention of depression by the other members of the rehabilitation team, including the nursing staff, occupational therapists, physical therapists, and so on. At the time of initial evaluation, the clinical psychologist's report noted the patient to be "friendly alert, and cooperative. She has chronically felt inadequate, was a worrier, and felt frustrated at not achieving her potential." While this report represented a partial picture of the patient's affect state, it clearly minimized the severity of her depression. The presence of her motor aprosodia resulted in the perception by others that the patient was considerably less distressed than she actually felt.

Mrs. E. K. was subsequently placed on an antidepressant medication. One month after the initiation of this psychotherapeutic medication, the patient was reported to be considerably less depressed.

Suggested Protocol for Assessment of Affect Disturbances in Brain-Damaged Patients

Based on the body of literature reviewed in this chapter, the following cognitive and affect domains should be routinely evaluated to assure accurate assessment of the emotional state of brain-damaged persons.

Assessment of General Mentation and Severity of Cognitive-Perceptual Deficits

Measures such as the Mini Mental State Exam (Folstein, Folstein, & McHugh, 1975) are useful tools for quickly assessing a patient's general mentation. Assessment of cognitive-perceptual deficits is typically part of a standard clinical assessment of a brain-damaged patient. The relationship between cognitive deficits and observed behaviors of the brain-injured patient is an important key to understanding how brain-damaged patients may interact with their environment. For example, patients with severe perceptual deficits and hemianopsia may have difficulty maintaining eye contact, may misread facial expressions, or may ignore persons in their neglected visual fields. These behaviors may be misinterpreted by family and medical staff as indications of a lack of interest or an indifferent attitude rather than a manifestation of a perceptual impairment.

Assessment of Affect Expression and Comprehension Abilities

A patient's ability to convey affect prosody during emotionally charged situations—that is, while discussing affect-laden material during the clinical interview—as well as spontaneous gestural abilities should be assessed. The clinician should also evaluate affect comprehension and expression abilities outside the clinical interview. Ross and Rush (1981) have suggested that the clinician do a brief evaluation of these deficit domains. For example, using a neutral sentence, such as, "I am going to the other movie," the clinician may assess comprehension of affect prosody by alternately saying the sentence to the patient in a happy, sad, angry, and neutral fashion. The patient is asked to identify the emotional tone conveyed by the examiner. Affect expression abilities can then be assessed by having the patient say the same neutral sentence using each of these affect tones.

Assessment of a Patient's Self-Report of Cognitive-Physical Deficits

Open-ended questions regarding a patient's perception of his or her medical condition, extent of cognitive-perceptual deficits, and physical impairments should be interspersed within a clinical interview. The information obtained from the patient can then be compared to actual neurological and neuropsychological test data to further evaluate issues of denial and minimization. For example, a patient with complete paralysis of the upper extremity may report that he or she can perform all activities as independently as before or that there has been a great improvement in functioning.

Assessment of a Patient's Self-Report of Depression

Standard psychology measures, such as the Multiple Affect Adjective Checklist (MAACL) (Zuckerman & Lubin, 1965) and the Beck Depression Inventory (BDI) (Beck, Ward, Mendelson, Mock, & Erbargh, 1961), are suggested. The instrument should be read to the patient, rather than self-administered, to assure that all items are addressed and are cognitively understood by the patient.

Clinical Ratings of a Patient's Depression

Observer ratings, such as the Hamilton Rating Scale (Hamilton, 1967), are useful in measuring both the behavioral and the intrapsychic aspects of depression. If observer ratings are used concurrently with self-report indices, discrepancies between patient self-report and observer ratings of affect can be documented. Thus, such issues as denial, minimization, and exaggeration of affect state can be empirically examined.

Independent Evaluation of Vegetative Signs of Depression

Ratings of sleep, appetite, and weight disturbances should be obtained from sources independent of the patient—nursing staff, weight charts, medication records, family interview, and so on—to assure accurate documentation of symptom severity.

This systematic assessment has wide application in neuropsychology, and its use better enables the clinician to diagnose, treat, and understand persons with affect disturbances associated with brain damage.

ACKNOWLEDGMENTS

The authors would like to thank Susan Egelko, Karen Langer, Mary Sano and Pat Gwozdz for their assistance with the preparation of this manuscript. This work was supported by Grant No. G008300039 from the National Institute of Handicapped Research.

REFERENCES

Albert, M., & Anderson, L. (1977). Imagery mediation of vocal emphasis in flat affect. *Archives of General Psychiatry, 34*, 208–212.

Andersen, A. L., & Hanvik, L. (1950). The psychometric localization of brain lesions: The differential effect of frontal and parietal lesions on MMPI profiles. *Journal of Clinical Psychology, 6*, 177–180.

Babinski, J. (1914). Contribution a l'étude des troubles mentaux dans l'hémplegie organique cérébrale (anosognosie). *Review Neurologic* (Paris), *27*, 845–848.

Bear, D., & Fedio, P. (1977). Quantitative analysis of interictal behavior in temporal lobe epilepsy. *Archives of Neurology, 34*, 454–467.

Beck, A., Ward, C., Mendelson, M., Mock, J., & Erbargh, J. (1961). An inventory for measuring depression. *Archives of Psychiatry, 4*, 561–567.

Benson, D. F. (1973). Psychiatric aspects of aphasia. *British Journal of Psychiatry, 123*, 555–566.

Benson, D. F. (1980). Psychiatric problems in aphasia. In M. T. Sarno & O. Hook (Eds.), *Aphasia: Assessment and treatment*, (pp. 192–201). New York: Masson.

Benton, A., & Van Allen, M. W. (1968). Impairment of facial recognition in patients with cerebral disease. *Cortex, 4*, 344–358.

Black, F. W. (1975). Unilateral brain lesions and MMPI performance: A preliminary study. *Perceptual and Motor Skills, 40*, 87–93.

Bordon, W. (1962). Psychological aspects of stroke: Patients and family. *Annuals of Internal Medicine, 57*, 689–692.

Brownell, H., Michel, D., Powelson, J., & Gardner, H. (1981). *Verbal humor deficits in right brain-damaged patients*. Paper presented at the Academy of Aphasia, London, Ontario.

Bruder, G., & Yozawitz, A. (1979). Central auditory processing and laterality in psychiatric patients. In J. Gruzelier & P. Flor-Henry (Eds.), *Hemisphere asymmetries of function and psychopathology*. Amsterdam: Elsevier.

Buck, R., & Duffy, R. (1980). Nonverbal communication of affect in brain-damaged patients. *Cortex, 16*, 351–362.

Carroll, B. J., Martin, F., & Davies, B. (1968). Resistance to suppression by dexamethasone of plasma 11 O.H.C.S. levels in severe depressive illness. *British Medical Journal, 3*, 285–287.

Cicone, M., Wapner, W., & Gardner, H. (1980). Sensitivity to emotion expressions and situations in organic patients. *Cortex, 16*, 145–158.

Cohen, B. D., Penick, S. F., & Tarter, R. (1974). Antidepressant effects of unilateral electro-convulsive shock therapy. *Archives of General Psychiatry, 31*, 673–675.

Danly, M., Shapiro, B., & Gardner, H. (1982). *Dsyprosody in right brain-damaged patients: Linguistic and emotional components*. Paper presented at the Academy of Aphasia, New Paltz, New York.

Deglin, V. L., & Nikolaenko, N. (1975). Role of the dominant hemisphere in the regulation of emotional states. *Human Physiology, 1*, 394.

D'Elia, G., & Perris, C. (1973). Cerebral function dominance and depression: An analysis of EEG amplitude in depressed patients. *Acta Psychiatricia Scandinavica, 49*, 191–197.

DeKosky, S., Heilman, K., Bowers, D., & Valenstein, E. (1980). Recognition and discrimination of emotional faces and pictures. *Brain and Language, 9*, 206–214.

Denny-Brown, D., Meyers, J., & Horenstein, S. (1952). The significance of perceptual rivalry resulting from parietal lesions. *Brain, 75*, 433–471.

DeRenzi, E., & Faglioni, P. (1965). The comparative efficiency of intelligence and vigilance detecting hemisphere damage. *Cortex, 1*, 410–433.

DeRenzi, E., & Spinnler, H. (1966). Visual recognition in patients with unilateral cerebral disease. *Journal of Nervous and Mental Diseases, 142*, 515–525.

Dikmen, S., & Reitan, R. (1974). MMPI correlates of localization cerebral lesions. *Perceptual and Motor Skills, 39*, 831–840.

Diller, L., & Gordon, W. (1981a). Rehabilitation and clinical neuropsychology. In S. B. Filskov & T. J. Boll (Eds.), *Handbook of clinical neuropsychology* (Vol. 1, pp. 702–733). New York: John Wiley & Sons.

Diller, L., & Gordon, W. (1981b.) Intervention for cognitive deficits in brain-impaired adults. *Journal of Consulting and Clinical Psychology, 49*, 822–834.

Finklestein, S., Benowitz, L., Baldessarini, R., Arana, G., Levine, D., Woo, E., Bear, D., Moya, K., & Stroll, A. (1982). Mood, vegetative disturbance and dexamethasone suppression test after stroke. *Annals of Neurology, 12*, 463–468.

Fisher, S. (1961). Psychiatric considerations of cerebral vascular disease. *American Journal of Cardiology, 7*, 379–385.

Flor-Henry, P. (1969). Schizophrenic-like reactions and affective psychoses associated with temporal lobe epilepsy: Etiological factors. *American Journal of Psychiatry, 126*, 148–151.

Flor-Henry, P. (1974). Psychosis, neurosis and epilepsy: Developmental and gender-related effects and their aetiological contributions. *British Journal of Psychiatry, 124*, 144–150.

Flor-Henry, P. (1976). Lateralized temporal-limbic dysfunction and psychopathology. *Annals of the New York Academy of Science, 280*, 777–779.

Flor-Henry, P., & Koles, Z. J. (1980). EEG studies of depression, mania and normal: Evidence for partial shift of laterality in the affective psychoses. *Advances in Biological Psychiatry, 4*, 21–23.

Folstein, M. F., Folstein, S., & McHugh, P. R. (1975). A practical method for grading the cognitive state of patients for clinicians. *Journal of Psychiatric Research, 12*, 189–198.

Folstein, M., Maiberger, R., & McHugh, P. R. (1977). Mood disorders as a specific complication of stroke. *Journal of Neurosurgery and Psychiatry, 40*, 1018–1020.

Freidman, S. H., (1950). *Psychometric effects of frontal and parietal lobe brain damage.* Unpublished doctoral dissertation. University of Minnesota.

Gainotti, G. (1969). Réactions "catastrophiques" et manifestations d'indifférence au cours des atteintes cérébrales. *Neuropsychologia, 7*, 195–204.

Gainotti, G. (1972). Emotional behaviors and hemispheric side of lesion. *Cortex, 8*, 41–55.

Gardner, H., Ling, K., Flamm, L., & Silverman, J. (1975). Comprehension and appreciation of humor in brain-damaged patients. *Brain, 98*, 399–412.

Gasparrini, W., Satz, P., Heilman, M., & Coolidge, F. (1978). Hemispheric asymmetries of affective processing determined by Minnesota Multiphasic Personality Inventory. *Journal of Neurology, Neurosurgery, and Psychiatry, 41*, 470–473.

Goldstein, K. (1939). *The organism: A holistic approach to biology: Derived from pathological data in man*. New York: American Books.

Goldstein, K. (1952). The effect of brain damage on the personality. *Psychiatry, 15*, 245–260.

Goldstein, S., Filskov, S., Weaver, L., & Ives, J. (1977). Neuropsychological effects of electro-convulsive therapy. *Journal of Clinical Psychology, 33*, 798–806.

Gordon, W. A., & Diller, L. (1983). Stroke: Coping with a cognitive deficit. In T. G. Burish & L. A. Bradley (Eds)., *Coping with chronic disease: Research and applications* (pp. 113–135). New York: Academic Press.

Gordon, W., Ruckdeschel-Hibbard, M., Egelko, S., Diller, L., Shaver, M.S., Lieberman, A., & Ragnarrson, K. (1985). Perceptual remediation in patients with right brain damage: A comprehensive program. *Archives of Physical Medicine and Rehabilitation, 66*, 353–359.

Hamilton, M. (1967). Development of a rating scale for primary depressive illness. *British Journal of Social Clinical Psychology, 6*, 278–296.

Hathaway, S. R., & McKinley, J. C. (1951). *The Minnesota Multiphasic Personality Inventory Manual*. New York: Psychological Corporation.

Hécaen, H. (1962). Clinical symptomatology in right and left hemispheric lesions. In V. B. Mountcastle (Ed.), *Interhemispheric relations and cerebral dominance* (pp. 215–243). Baltimore: John Hopkins Press.

Hécaen, H., de Ajuriaquerra, J., & Massonet, J. (1951). Les troubles visuo-constructifs par lésion parieto-occiptal droite: Rôle des pertubation vistibularies. *Encephale, 1*, 122–179.

Heilman, K. M., Scholes, R., & Watson, R. T. (1975). Auditory affect agnosia: Disturbed comprehension of affective speech. *Journal of Neurology, Neurosurgery and Psychiatry, 38*, 69–72.

Heilman, K. M., Schwartz, H. D., & Watson, R. T. (1977). Hypoarousal in patients with neglect syndrome and emotional indifference. *Neurology, 28*, 229–232.

Heilman, K. M., & Valenstein, E. (1972). Frontal lobe neglect. *Neurology, 28*, 229–232.

Heilman, K. M., & Valenstein, E. (Eds.). (1979). *Clinical neuropsychology*. New York: Oxford University Press.

Hier, D. B., Mondlock, J., & Caplan, L. R. (1983a). Behavioral abnormalities after right hemisphere stroke. *Neurology, 33*, 337–344.

Hier, D. B., Mondlock, J., & Caplan, L. R. (1983b). Recovery of behavioral abnormalities after right hemisphere stroke. *Neurology, 33*, 345–350.

Hillbom, E. (1960). After-effects of brain injuries. *Acta Psychiatrica et Neurologica Scandinavica, 35*, 5–169.

Horenstein, S. (1970). Effects of cerebrovascular disease on personality and emotionality. In A. Benton (Ed.), *Behavioral change in cerebrovascular disease* (pp. 171–193). New York: Harper & Row.

Kerns, R. (1980). *Depression following stroke: Self-evaluations, neuropsychological evaluations and laterality of lesions as predictor variables*. Unpublished doctoral dissertation, Southern Illinois University, Carbondale, Ill.

Kolb, B., Milner, B. (1981). Observations on spontaneous facial expression after focal cerebral excisions and after intracaroted injections of amytal sodium. *Neuropsychologia, 19*, 505–514.

Kolb, B., & Taylor, L. (1981). Affective behavior in patients with localized cortical excisions: Role of lesion site and side. *Science, 214*, 89–90.

Kronfol, Z., Hamsher, K., Digre, K., & Waziri, R. (1978). Depression and hemisphere function: Changes associated with unilateral ECT. *British Journal of Psychiatry, 132*, 560–567.

Lamendella, J. T. (1977). The limbic system in human communication. In H. Whitaker & H. A. Whitaker (Eds.), *Studies in neurolinguistics* (Vol. 3, pp. 157–222). New York: Academic Press.

Lishman, W. A. (1968). Brain damage in relation to psychiatric disability after head injury. *British Journal of Psychiatry, 114*, 373–410.

Lubin, B. (1965). Adjective check list for measurement of depression. *Archives of General Psychiatry, 12*, 57–67.

Luria, R., & McHugh, P. R. (1974). The reliability and clinical ability of the present state examination. *Archives of General Psychiatry, 30*, 866–871

Mehrabian, A. (1971). *Non verbal communication.* Chicago: Aldine Atherton.

Meier, M. J., & French, L. A. (1965). Some personality correlates of unilateral and bilateral EEG abnormalities in psychomotor epileptics. *Journal of Clinical Psychology, 31*, 3–9.

Milner, B. (1967). Discussion of the subject: Experimental analysis of cerebral dominance in man. In C. H. Millikin & F. L. Darley (Eds.), *Brain mechanism underlying speech and language* (pp. 175–184). New York: Grune & Stratton.

Perria, L., Rosadini, G., & Ross, G. (1961). Determination of side of cerebral dominance with amobarbital. *Archives of Neurology, 4*, 173–181.

Perris, C. (1974). Averaged evoke responses (AER) in patients with affective disorders. *Acta Psychiatrica Scandinavica, 255*, 89–98.

Raven, J.G. (1965). *Guide to using the coloured progressive matrices.* London: H.K. Lewis and Co., Ltd.

Robins, A. M. (1976). Are stroke patients more depressed than other disabled subjects? *Journal of Chronic Disease, 29*, 479–482.

Robinson, R. G., & Benson, D. F. (1981). Depression in aphasic patients: Frequency, severity, and clinical-pathological correlations. *Brain and Language, 14*, 282–291.

Robinson, R. G., & Price, T. R. (1982). Poststroke depressive disorders: A follow-up study of 103 patients. *Stroke, 13*, 635–640.

Robinson, R. G., & Szetela, B. S. (1981). Mood change following left hemispheric brain injury. *Annals of Neurology, 9*, 447–453.

Ross, E. D. (1981). The aprosodias. *Archives of Neurology, 38*, 561–569.

Ross, E. D. (1982). The divided self. *The Sciences*, 8–10.

Ross, E. D., & Mesulam, M. (1979). Dominant language functions in the right hemisphere? *Archives of Neurology, 36*, 144–148.

Ross, E. D., & Rush, J. (1981). Diagnosis and neuroanatomical correlates of depression in brain-damaged patients. *Archives of General Psychiatry, 38*, 1344–1354.

Ruckdeschel-Hibbard, M. (1984). *Affect communication impairments in brain-damaged individuals.* Unpublished doctoral dissertation, New York University, New York.

Sackeim, H. A., Greenberg, M. S., Weiman, A. L., Gur, R. C., Hungerbuhler, J. P., & Geschwind, N. (1982). Hemispheric asymmetry in the expression of positive and negative emotions. *Archives of Neurology, 39*, 210–218.

Sands, E., Sarno, M. T., & Shankweiler, D. (1969). Long-term assessment of language function in aphasia due to stroke. *Archives of Physical Medicine and Rehabilitation, 50*, 202–206.

Sarno, M. (Ed.). (1981). *Acquired aphasia.* New York: Academic Press.

Sarno, M., & Levita, E. (1979). Recovery in treated aphasia in the first year post-stroke. *Stroke, 10*, 663–670.

Sarno, M., Silverman, M., & Sands, E. (1970). Speech therapy and language recovery in severe aphasia. *Journal of Speech and Hearing Research, 13*, 607–623.

Schlanger, B. B. (1973). Identification by normal and aphasic subjects of semantically meaningful and meaningless emotionally toned sentences. *Acta Symbolica, 4*, 30–38.

Schlanger, B. B., Schlanger, P., & Gerstman, L. (1976). The perception of emotionally toned sentences by right hemisphere-damaged and aphasic subjects. *Brain, 3*, 396–403.

Schuell, H., Jenkins, J., & Jiménéz-Pabón, E. (1964). *Aphasia in adults: Diagnosis, prognosis and treatment.* New York: Harper & Row.

Serafetinides, E. A. (1972). Laterality and voltage in the EEG of psychiatric patients. *Diseases of the Nervous System, 33*, 622–623.

Shapiro, B. E., & Danly, M. (1985). The role of the right hemisphere in the control of speech prosody in propositional and affective contexts. *Brain and Language, 25*, 19–36.

Shapiro, L. N., & McMahan, A. W. (1966). Rehabilitation statement: Problems in patient staff interaction. *Archives of General Psychiatry, 15*, 173–177.

Sivak, M., Olson, P., Kewman, D., Won, H., & Henson, D. (1981). Driving and perceptual/cognitive skills: Behavioral consequences of brain damage. *Archives of Physical Medicine and Rehabilitation, 62*, 476–483.

Terzian, H. (1964). Behavioral and EEG effects of intracarotid sodium amytal injections. *Acta Neurochirurgica, 12*, 230–239.

Terzian, H., & Cecotto, C. (1954). Su un nuovo methodo per la delerminazione e lo studio della dominanza emisferica. *Giornale di Psichiantria e di Neuropatologia, 87*, 889–924.

Tsunoda, T., & Oka, M. (1976). Lateralization for emotion in the human brain and auditory cerebral dominance. *Proceedings of the Japan Academy, 52*, 528–531.

Tucker, D. M. (1981). Lateral brain function, emotion and conceptualization. *Psychological Bulletin, 89*, 19–46.

Tucker, D., Watson, R. G., & Heilman, K. M. (1977). Affective discrimination and evocation in patients with right parietal disease. *Neurology, 27*, 947–950.

Ullman, M. (Ed.). (1962). *Behavioral change in patients following strokes.* Springfield, IL: Charles C Thomas.

Ullman, M., & Gruen, A. (1960). Behavioral changes in patients with strokes. *American Journal of Psychiatry, 117*, 1004–1009.

Wapner, W., Hamby, S., & Gardner, H. (1981). The role of the right hemisphere in the appreciation of complex linguistic materials. *Brain and Language, 14*, 15–33.

Warrington, E. K., & James, M. (1967). An experimental investigation of facial recognition in patients with unilateral cerebral lesions. *Cortex, 3*, 317–326.

Watson, R. T., Heilman, K. M., Cauthen, J. C., & King, F. A. (1973). Neglect after cingulectomy. *Neurology, 23*, 1003–1007.

Wechsler, A. F. (1973). The effects of organic brain disease on recall of emotionally charged vs. neutral narrative test. *Neurology, 23*, 130–135.

Weinberg, J., Diller, L., Gordon, W. Gerstman, L., Lieberman, A., Lakin, P., Hodges, G., & Ezrachi, O. (1977). Visual scanning training effect on reading-related tasks in acquired right brain damage. *Archives of Physical Medicine and Rehabilitation, 58*, 480–486.

Weinberg, J., Diller, L., Gordon, W. Gerstman, L., Lieberman, A., Lakin, P., Hodges, G., & Ezrachi, O. (1977). Visual scanning training effect on reading-related tasks in acquired right brain damage. *Archives of Physical Medicine and Rehabilitation, 58*, 480–486.

Weinberg, J., Piasetsky, E., Diller, L., & Gordon, W. (1982). Treating perceptual organization deficits in nonneglecting RBD stroke patients. *Journal of Clinical Neuropsychology: 4*, 59–75.

Weinstein, E., & Freidland, R. F. (1977). Behavioral disorders associated with hemi-inattention. In E. Valenstein & R. F. Friedlan (Eds.), *Advances in neurology: Vol. 18. Hemi-inattention and hemisphere specialization* (pp. 51–62). New York: Raven Press.

Weinstein, E. A., & Kahn, R. L. (Eds.). (1955). *Denial of illness: Symbolic and physiological aspects.* Springfield, IL: Charles C Thomas.

Weintraub, S., & Mesulam, M. (1983). Developmental learning disabilities of the right hemisphere. *Archives of Neurology, 40*, 463–468.

Williams, H. L. (1952). The development of a caudality scale for the MMPI. *Journal of Clinical Psychology, 8*, 293–297.

Yin, R. K. (1970). Face recognition by brain-injured patients: A dissociable ability? *Neuropsychologia, 8*, 395–402.

Yozawitz, A., Bruder, G., Sulton, S., Sharpe, L., Gurland, B., Fleiss, J., & Costa, L. (1979). Dichotic perception. Evidence for right hemisphere dysfunction in affective psychosis. *British Journal of Psychiatry, 135*, 224–237.

Zihl, J. (1981). Recovery of visual function in patients with cerebral blindness: Effects of special practice with saccadic localization. *Experimental Brain Research, 44*, 159–169.

Zuckerman, M., & Lubin, B. (1965). *Manual for the multiple affect adjective checklist.* San Diego, CA: Educational and Industrial Testing Services.

Zung, W. (1965). A self-rating depression scale. *Archives of General Psychiatry, 12*, 63–70.

CHAPTER 13

Psychosocial Consequences of Epilepsy

Carl B. Dodrill

This chapter presents an example of how brain disorders and psychosocial functioning are interrelated. Perhaps such relationships are no better illustrated than in cases of epilepsy, where there is definite evidence for brain dysfunction, where the seizures themselves may produce a wide variety of psychosocial consequences, and where treatment for the disorder may itself produce a range of difficulties. For these reasons, epilepsy is a disorder that lends itself to the study of the interrelationships between brain disorders and psychosocial problems, and it is therefore of particular interest to neuropsychologists.

This chapter first raises the question as to why we would expect to see psychosocial-emotional problems in epilepsy. Next, the various types of psychosocial problems often found in epilepsy are described, along with the constellations of difficulties most frequently seen. The presumed biological bases for psychiatric difficulties are also noted. Attention will then be turned to interrelationships between these types of problems and performance on neuropsychological tests and in particular on those measures of the Halstead-Reitan Neuropsychological Test Battery for Adults. Finally, the question of remediation of psychosocial problems in epilepsy is discussed, along with a literature review of what has been accomplished in this area thus far.

WHY PSYCHOSOCIAL PROBLEMS IN EPILEPSY?

Before discussing the various types of problems often noted in persons with seizure disorders, it would be worthwhile to address the question of why one would expect to find emotional and psychosocial difficulties in this group any more than would be found in the general population. Two types of reasons deserve consideration.

First, there are biological reasons why one might expect more difficulties in persons with epilepsy than in normal or control individuals not associated with any patient group. At the time of the seizure, the brain is clearly not functioning well because, of course, seizures come from the brain. Bona fide epileptic seizures represent one of the clearest forms of evidence that the brain is dysfunctional. It is also known, however, that even between seizures most persons with epilepsy continue to demonstrate brain dysfunction, as evaluated by interictal electroencephalogram (EEG) recordings. Such EEGs may show frank epileptiform abnormalities consistent with the diagnosis of epilepsy (Zivin & Ajmone Marsan, 1968), or they may demonstrate a variety of nonepileptiform EEG abnormalities (Dodrill & Wilkus, 1978). Since the brain is the biological basis for mental abilities, if its functioning is compromised, one might expect to find evidence of this if one looks closely enough. Indeed, Rodin, Shapiro, and Lennox (1977) completed comprehensive evaluations of 369 patients with epilepsy and found that only 23% had epilepsy with no evidence of other significant intellectual, behavioral, or neurological problems.

A second general type of hypothesis to account for psychosocial and emotional difficulties in epilepsy is primarily environmental. Persons with epilepsy often feel that they are somehow strange or different because of their seizures. The responses received from others upon hearing of the condition often confirm these subjective feelings. In general, people are often made uneasy even by the term *epilepsy* and may immediately envision someone flailing around on the ground and foaming at the mouth. Even among professionals (including neurologists and neuropsychologists), epilepsy is not a favorite topic of discussion or inquiry. Such professionals are often better trained in less common disorders and have limited understanding of the mechanisms of epilepsy. One result may be a feeling on the part of patients that professionals do not truly understand; thus, an important source of support may be missing. Persons with epilepsy may also withdraw from others because of their dread of possible attacks and consequent embarrassment. The net result of any or all of these factors can be significant social withdrawal and substantial emotional problems.

In any given case, it is of course possible that a combination of biological and social factors may result in the difficulties noted. Sorting out the causes of particular problems in any patient can be a difficult but also a rewarding experience. It can also provide insights into the importance of neuropsychological deficits with respect to the day-by-day functioning of these people. Before considering the role of impairment in brain functions, let us first take a close look at the types of psychosocial problems found in epilepsy.

TYPES OF PSYCHOSOCIAL PROBLEMS IN EPILEPSY

Any attempt to identify those difficulties in epilepsy that are appropriately labeled *psychosocial* is a truly staggering task. More than 5000 articles were listed under "Social Problems" and "Emotional (Psychiatric) Disturbance" in the *Epilepsy Indexes* by 1981 (Epilepsy Branch, National Institute of Neurological and Communicative Disorders and Stroke, 1981; Penry, 1978). An even cursory review of these entries reveals numerous papers on highly diverse topics with data obtained under varying guidelines and from different groups of people with seizure disorders. One might with some justification conclude that to discuss these difficulties in any meaningful way would be to discuss the psychosocial problems that humans in general face! At the same time, the concerns noted do tend to group themselves, and for the purposes of this chapter, four different clusters will be identified and discussed in the sections that follow, including problems of emotional adjustment, problems in interpersonal relationships, problems in vocational and financial adjustment, and problems in medical treatment.

Problems of Emotional Adjustment

Although this chapter is directed primarily toward psychosocial problems in epilepsy, emotional or psychiatric concerns are of direct relevance since they have a substantial bearing on how a person behaves in social situations. Furthermore, there has been a very strong tendency for professionals to focus on this general area, and, indeed, it appears that perhaps 80% or more of the literature dealing with emotional and various types of psychosocial aspects of epilepsy focuses on emotional concerns. A distillation of the findings from the literature follows.

Research Using the Minnesota Multiphasic Personality Inventory

Studies using the Minnesota Multiphasic Personality Inventory (MMPI) are among those of greatest interest to the neuropsychologist, no doubt because of the familiarity of this test and also because of the objectivity involved. Table 13.1 presents a summary of all the studies that have been published on the MMPI utilizing groups of persons with epilepsy and that have included scale-by-scale data. The groups assessed and the essential conclusions are noted for each study. In many cases, these studies had as their basic purpose the comparison of patients with different types of epilepsy, differences in age at onset of seizures, and differences with respect to etiology. A great deal has been postulated with respect to differences in seizure type, a topic that is discussed in a separate section. With respect to etiology, Matthews and Kløve (1968) found that individuals with seizure disorders of unknown etiology had slightly better adjustment than did those of known etiology. This is probably related to the fact that they also tend to have greater intelligence and less neuropsychological impairment (Kløve & Matthews, 1966). Many individuals have assumed that earlier age at onset of epilepsy is associated with greater psychological disturbance, but that assumption has not been supported in any consistent manner. Perhaps the most sophisticated approach to this particular problem was undertaken by Hermann, Schwartz, Karnes, and Vahdat (1980), who demonstrated that age at onset was related to emotional problems in a complex way when seizure type was simultaneously considered.

Apart from the specific purposes for which the studies reported in Table 13.1 were undertaken, some general comments about the profiles are in order. First, the majority of these studies produced profiles that are elevated to a greater or lesser degree. Where there are fewer elevations, there is usually also evidence that the sample is a selected one, for example, excluding persons with low intellectual levels or persons who could not read. A particular problem here appears to be the fact that on many occasions, the MMPI is given in conjunction with a full battery of neuropsychological tests, and it tends to be put at the end of that battery. If there is not time to administer the MMPI, then in effect that subject is excluded from all studies of emotional functioning in epilepsy. Individuals who demonstrate more impairment and greater psychiatric difficulties thus tend to be excluded, as do those who have difficulty in reading. Despite this, however, when subjects from all studies are simultaneously considered and a general MMPI rule is applied (Goldberg, 1972), the average profile overall is abnormal. In addition, it is observed that most frequently the peak points on the profiles are D and Sc. All other scales are much less often identified as peak point scales for individual groups.

Several of the studies summarized in Table 13.1 provided the opportunity to compare other medical groups (either neurologic or nonneurologic) with persons having seizure disorders (Kløve ' Doehring, 1962; Matthews, Dikmen, & Harley, 1977; Matthews & Kløve, 1968; Warren & Weiss, 1969). The findings of these studies are instructive in that they demonstrate no consistent difference between the groups with epilepsy and the groups with other medical conditions. This of course argues against any postulation of an "epileptic personality," a concept that should have been vanquished decades ago. It is certainly possible that individuals with epilepsy may be more depressed than are average persons and that worry, tension, and anxiety may appear more frequently, as well as unusual thought processes, but this would not necessarily lead us to believe that there is something unique about persons with seizure disorders with respect to their personalities. On the contrary, since epilepsy is really a series of disorders rather than a univocal medical problem, a simple personality pattern would seem most unlikely.

In the review of the MMPI studies done with persons having seizure disorders, it was of interest to note that comparison groups routinely were medical patients of one type or another and that in no instance did the normal control group consist of "off the street" persons who were not affiliated with any medical group. I identified such an unaffiliated group of 74 people who closely matched 74 persons with a variety of seizure disorders. The normal controls were obtained from the same general geographical area where the persons with epilepsy were found. Each control had a completely negative neurological history and was tightly matched with each epileptic on the variables of age, sex, education, and race. Details of this matching procedure have already been described (Dodrill, 1978), but the MMPI comparisons have not previously been reported. These are given in Figure 13.1. Highly statistically significant differences were found on the majority of the scales of the MMPI, and the group with epilepsy always demonstrated more difficulties. The profile obtained is generally characteristic of samples of people with seizure disorders, although it is somewhat more elevated than is found in many cases. In part, the reason for this is no doubt related to the fact that no one was eliminated from the sample because of an inability to read (a tape-recorded version of the MMPI was used when needed) or because of the lack of time (additional time was provided). In addition, it should be noted that these people were obtained from a hospital setting and that they may therefore demonstrate more difficulties than persons with easy-to-manage seizure disorders, who may tend to be treated by local general practitioners. Despite this, it would appear that, had normal control subjects been employed in most of the studies referred to in Table 13.1, significantly better adjustment would have been found among the control subjects than among persons with epilepsy.

Emotional Adjustment in Relation to Seizure Type

There has been a strong tendency to associate complex partial (temporal lobe, psychomotor) seizures with increased emotional problems in comparison with other seizure types. As was indicated in Volume 1 of this *Handbook,* however, there are a number of problems in drawing such a conclusion, and objective evidence for it is lacking (Dodrill, 1981). Unfortunately, there is also a tendency to confuse emotional maladjustment with behavioral characteristics sometimes seen in persons with complex partial seizures. Such characteristics may include deepened emotionality, hypergraphia, sense of personal destiny, and philosophical interest (Bear & Fedio, 1977; Sherwin, 1977; Waxman & Geschwind, 1975). It is of interest to note that these characteristics are most frequently found when evaluative procedures other than formal testing, such as by the MMPI, are used. Such characteristics should not be confused with emotional maladjustment in epilepsy, even though some of them are probably more adaptive

Table 13.1. Studies Reporting Complete MMPI Profiles on Patients with Epilepsy

Investigators (Year)	Groups of Patients with Epilepsy	Essential Findings
Richards (1952)	Military personnel	Profile (uncorrected for K) showed mild elevation of 2-3 type
Kløve & Doehring (1962)	Mixed seizure types, known etiology; mixed seizure types; unknown etiology	No differences were shown between the groups; profiles were somewhat elevated, with 2-8 pattern
Meier & French (1965)	Psychomotor group with unilateral epileptiform EEG discharges; psychomotor group with bilateral discharges	Bilateral group had poorer adjustment generally; profile for bilateral group was somewhat elevated, with 2-8 pattern; profile for unilateral group was not elevated significantly
Shaw (1966)	Mixed seizure group; "pseudoepileptic" group with or without concurrent epilepsy	Patients with pseudo-seizures had generally poorer adjustment; extent of profile elevation could not be determined
Matthews & Kløve (1968)	Major motor, psychomotor, and mixed seizure groups, all with known etiology; major motor, psychomotor, and mixed seizure groups, all with unknown etiology	Persons with mixed seizures and with known etiologies tended to have the worst adjustment; slight to significant profile elevations had a variety of high points
Warren & Weiss (1969)	Vocational rehabilitation clients with heterogeneous seizure disorders	Profile was elevated in 2-7-8 configuration
Mignone, Donnelley, & Sadowsky (1970)	Psychomotor group; non-psychomotor group	The nonpsychomotor group had slightly poorer adjustment; profiles were somewhat elevated, with 2-8 pattern
Glass & Mattson (1973)	Temporal lobe epilepsy; focal seizures of non-temporal lobe origin	The temporal lobe group had slightly (but not significantly) poorer adjustment; profiles were slightly to substantially elevated, with 2-8 pattern
Stevens (1975)	Psychomotor group; generalized seizure group	The psychomotor group had slightly (but not significantly) poorer adjustment; profiles were somewhat elevated, with 2-8 pattern
Dodrill & Troupin (1977)	Mixed seizure group but emphasizing complex partial seizure disorders	Profiles were somewhat elevated, with 2-8 pattern

342

Table 13.1.   (*Continued*)

Investigators (Year)	Groups of Patients with Epilepsy	Essential Findings
Matthews, Dikmen, & Harley (1977)	Groups with generalized convulsive epilepsy who had early age at onset of seizures	Later age at onset group was slightly worse, but many of early age at onset patients could not read; later group showed 2-4-8 pattern of profile elevation
Hermann, Schwartz, Karnes, & Vahdat (1980)	Groups with temporal lobe epilepsy having childhood, adolescent, and adult onset; parallel groups with patients having generalized epilepsy	Interaction found between seizure type and age at onset; variety of profile patterns were shown
Hermann, Dikmen, Schwartz, & Karnes (1982)	Groups with temporal lobe epilepsy who did and who did not demonstrate ictal fear; group with generalized epilepsy	Group with fear during seizures was worst, with significantly elevated 2-8 profile; temporal lobe group without fear had a somewhat elevated 2-3 pattern; generalized group was only slightly elevated
Hermann, Dikmen, & Wilensky (1982)	Groups with complex partial seizures, with and without secondarily generalized seizures	The group with secondarily generalized seizures had poorer adjustment and an elevated profile of the 2-8 pattern
Dikmen, Hermann, Wilensky, & Rainwater (1983)	The two groups reported by Hermann, Dikmen, and Wilensky (1982) plus a group with generalized convulsive seizures	No substantial differences were shown across the groups; complex partial group had best adjustment, and other groups had somewhat elevated profiles of the 2-8 type

than others, and it is particularly important that they not be grouped under a general term such as *psychopathology*. Such a practice has contributed greatly to confusion in the literature.

Before leaving the question of seizure type, it is worth noting that there is some suggestion that the number of seizure types is more related to the likelihood of problems in emotional adjustment than are the particular types involved. More seizure types are associated with more emotional problems. This hypothesis was initially formulated clearly by Rodin, Katz, and Lennox (1976) and has been most recently confirmed by Hermann, Dikmen, and Wilensky (1982). The reason for this may pertain to subtle differences in brain functioning, to increased likelihood of adverse effects of seizures themselves upon functioning, or both.

Psychosis and Epilepsy

A number of investigations have been conducted on possible relationships between psychosis and epilepsy. These investigations have focused on whether there is an

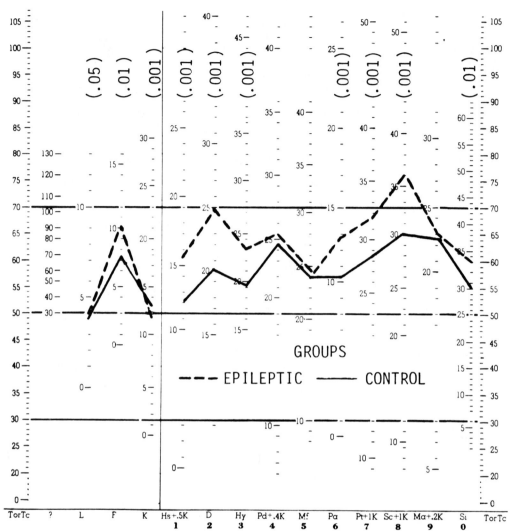

Figure 13.1. Average profiles of 74 patients with epilepsy and 74 control subjects on the Minnesota Multiphasic Personality Inventory (profile form copyright © 1966 by the Psychological Corporation; reproduced by permission).

increased (or decreased) incidence of psychosis in cases of epilepsy and on the question of laterality as related to type of psychosis. Studies in this area have suffered from several types of problems. First, it is by no means clear that *psychosis* means the same in Europe as it does in the United States. This is not a trivial point. The majority of these studies fail to identify how it was determined that a patient was "psychotic." It is naive to assume that the same populations are being dealt with in these various studies.

A second significant problem with studies on psychosis is that some of them began with psychiatric populations and identified those persons who also had epilepsy, while others began with groups of epileptics and identified those persons who were also psychotic. The former studies tend to be authored by psychiatrists and the latter by neurologists. The former tend to find an increased incidence of psychosis in epilepsy, and the latter do not. In addition, the former tend to produce results that relate laterality of focus with certain psychiatric symptom patterns. For example, schizophrenic-like disorders may be associated with epilepsy arising from the left cerebral hemisphere, and affective disorders may be associated with epilepsy arising from the right cerebral hemisphere (Flor-Henry, 1976). The studies authored primarily by neurologists tend not to report such findings (e.g., Stevens, 1966). In addition to these uncertainties, there is by no means unified agreement on predisposing conditions that might result in the appearance of a psychosis in a person with epilepsy. For example, Sherwin, Peron-Magnan, Bancaud, Bonis, and Talairach (1982) found that persons with epilepsy involving the language-related hemisphere at the inception of a seizure were at a significantly increased risk for the development of psychosis. However, Taylor (1975), using what might appear to be a fairly similar surgery group, found that handedness, sex, and presence or absence of "alien tissue" (i.e., small tumors, hamartomas, and focal dysplasia) in the resected temporal lobe were the variables related to the appearance of psychosis.

To effectively summarize these findings in the area of psychosis and epilepsy is difficult or impossible. It would appear that there may be at least a slightly increased incidence of psychosis among patients with epilepsy (Toone, Garralda, & Ron, 1982), but there is no unitary hypothesis that can account for all of the empirical findings (Parnas & Korsgaard, 1982). It would appear that the data supporting a relationship between a schizophrenic-like psychosis and lesions of the left cerebral hemisphere are stronger than data supporting a relationship between affective psychoses in the right cerebral hemisphere (Toone, Garralda, & Ron, 1982), but even this is probably best perceived as somewhat equivocal.

Epilepsy and Hysteria

The estimate has been offered that from 5% to 36% of patients thought to have epilepsy may have hysterical or pseudoepileptic attacks rather than or in addition to genuine seizures (Desai, Potter, & Penry, 1979; Pond, Bidwell, & Stein, 1960; Ramani, Quesney, Olson, & Gumnit, 1980). The episodes observed may include not only major convulsive episodes but also more minor attacks that so closely mimic genuine epilepsy that the difference cannot be definitely ascertained without long-term EEG monitoring accompanied by closed circuit television monitoring. This procedure is expensive and requires extended hospitalization as one waits for a seizure to appear. However, its value is clearly documented (Gulick, Spinks, & King, 1982; Mattson, 1980; Ramani & Gumnit, 1982). It frequently provides useful diagnostic information, and it is the preferred procedure when the nature of the attacks is in question.

The majority of patients demonstrating psychogenic or pseudoepileptic seizures demonstrate conversion symptomatology, but such symptoms are not restricted to hysteria (Chodoff, 1982; Ramani & Gumnit, 1982). It is of interest to note that the majority of patients in studies of pseudoepileptic seizures are females, as is true in hysteria (Flor-Henry, Fromm-Auch, Tapper, & Schopflocher, 1981). It is also true that sexual exploitation of females in childhood or adolescence may be associated with later appearance of pseudoepileptic seizures (Goodwin, Sims, & Bergman, 1979; Gross, 1970; LaBarbera & Dozier, 1980).

Formal psychological testing has occasionally been reported with patients having pseudoepileptic seizures. Hovey, Kooi, and Thomas (1959) developed a series of profile indicators to differentiate persons with genuine epilepsy from other groups, but this work could not be crossvalidated by Jordon (1963). Hovey, Kooi, & Thomas (1959) also attempted to develop on an empirical basis a scale to separate these groups, but this was not successful. Richards (1952) developed an MMPI scale to differentiate persons with epilepsy from other groups but did not apply it to persons having pseudoepileptic attacks. Finally, in a recent paper (Wilkus, Dodrill, & Thompson, 1984), a series of MMPI rules identifying hysterical types of personality patterns was shown to differentiate between epileptic and pseudoepileptic patients at high levels of statistical confidence.

At first, the application of neuropsychological tests to epileptic and pseudoepileptic groups would appear to have particular relevance, since it might be assumed that persons with genuine epilepsy would demonstrate impairment in brain functions and that the pseudoepileptic group would not. However, genuine neurological problems in patients with pseudoepileptic seizures have been suggested on a number of occasions (Ramani & Gumnit, 1982; Roy, 1977; Slater, 1965; Standage & Fenton, 1975). Furthermore, in one study (Wilkus et al., 1984), it was demonstrated that positive neurological histories were equally frequent in epileptic and pseudoepileptic cases and that there was no difference between these groups on any of a substantial series of intellectual and neuropsychological tests. It appears that persons with pseudoepileptic seizures do indeed suffer a compromise in brain functions and that this makes them less able to cope with problems in everyday life. The pseudoepileptic attacks appear to be manifestations of emotional problems that have developed. Exactly why they developed in some cases but not in others is not clear, however.

Using the Pseudo-Neurologic Scale of the MMPI, Shaw (1966) was able to differentiate between patients having genuine epilepsy and patients who, in addition to having genuine epilepsy, also had pseudoseizures. The study was quite successful in differentiating between these two groups of patients, but this could only be partially replicated by Wilkus et al. (1984). Thus, the complexity of the problem is once again evident.

Assessing Other Types of Psychosocial Problems

We will now leave the area of emotional functioning and turn to all other types of psychosocial problems in persons having seizures. It will become apparent, however, that all other types of difficulties, even taken together, have commanded less attention than those in the emotional area. This is true even though the other areas of concern may be equally important. This tendency either to ignore these other types of problems or to deal with them unsystematically led my colleagues and me at the Regional Epilepsy Center of the University of Washington to develop an objective method of assessing these other types of problems, an inventory known as the Washington Psychosocial Seizure Inventory (WPSI) (Dodrill, Batzel, Queisser, & Temkin, 1980). Basic information concerning this inventory was presented in Volume 1 of this *Handbook* (Dodrill, 1981) and will not be repeated here. Briefly, however, this inventory contains 132 items, to which patients respond yes or no. It was developed in a manner similar to that of the MMPI, with empirical keying of each item. Professionals intensively evaluated a large group of persons with epilepsy with respect to several areas of psychosocial difficulty: Family Background, Emotional Adjustment, Interpersonal Adjustment, Vocational Adjustment, Financial Status, Adjustment to Seizures, Medicine and Medical Management, and Overall Psychosocial Functioning. In addition, the inventory has three validity scales to detect improperly completed answer sheets. It has been demonstrated that, to a considerable degree, the inventory produces estimates of difficulties in adjustments for each area that mimic those obtained by professionals after intensive individual evaluations (Dodrill, et al., 1980). The inventory is mentioned here because results obtained with it form the basis for some of the findings discussed below.

Problems in Interpersonal Relationships

Interpersonal adjustment may be discussed in several different contexts, the first of which pertains to adjustment of the person with epilepsy to family members and adjustment of the family members to the person with epilepsy. There is no doubt that having a person with epilepsy in a family affects the functioning of that family and the interaction among the family members (Grove, Goocher, Wilcox, & Andrews, 1980). In families having a child with epilepsy, for example, it has been demonstrated that in comparison with control families, there is a tendency toward an autocratic matriarchal structure. In this setting, disagreements between family members are minimized, and a plan of action based on the opinion of the mother is more readily formed (Ritchie, 1981). Over short periods, such families appear to be more efficient in the solving of problems, but a persistence of this form of interaction may eventually lead to undesirable effects.

Epilepsy disrupts the sense of control and competence, with ultimate impact on self-image and perceived autonomy (Ziegler, 1981). Decreased social confidence and increased behavioral difficulties may result (Hermann, Black, & Chhabria, 1981). One index of possible social adjustment problems in the home is whether the child is currently placed in school at the expected grade level (Hodgman et al., 1979). In the latter study, it was also observed that better seizure control and less neurological disability were associated with *less* open communication in the family. In addition, it was noted that denial appears to be more frequently operative in those cases in which there is decreased intelligence and probably more neuropsychological impairment. Depression is common among family members of individuals with neurological disorders, but techniques for dealing with this have been identified (Lezak, 1978). With respect to adults seen in a specialized epilepsy center, as many as 30% may demonstrate definite difficulties in the area of family relationships on an inventory such as the WPSI (Dodrill, 1983).

Beyond the area of family relationships, various other interpersonal concerns have at times been reported with people having epilepsy. One of the most common of these pertains to aggressive behavior which has sometimes been reported, particularly in cases of complex partial or temporal lobe epilepsy (Blumer, 1977; Pincus, 1980; Serafetinides, 1965; Taylor, 1969). Occasional homicide during an epileptic attack has also been claimed (Gunn, 1978), and one such incident is also known to me. However, any general tendency toward aggressive behavior has been disputed (Ramani & Gumnit, 1981; Rodin, 1973; Stevens & Hermann, 1981). One of the difficulties here pertains to the various ways in which *aggression* is defined. For example, I was interviewing a patient with complex partial seizures when the patient had an attack and stood up. I also stood up and moved closer to the patient, whereupon the patient with both hands pushed me away with a vigorous and sudden shove. Was that an act of aggression? On another occasion, I was called into a room where a patient was having a psychomotor seizure, and the patient grabbed my necktie and would not let go until the seizure began to resolve. Was that an act of aggression? On both occasions, backing off from the patient (as far as the necktie would allow!) and not attempting to restrain or otherwise provoke the patient resulted in a resolution of the difficulty in a matter of seconds. It is likely, however, that had an active effort been undertaken to restrain the patient, some further acts of "aggression" would have been demonstrated, a point that has been stressed by Rodin (1973). In my experience, these patients are not truly aggressive or violent unless provoked or restrained, and their actions are not well organized even under those circumstances. When the actions are purposeful and show planning, the question should be raised as to whether a seizure is actually in progress.

Much more common than acts of aggression are interpersonal difficulties pertaining to a lack of general social fluency or ability to relate effectively to others. Anxiety in social situations, concerns in dealing with persons of the opposite sex, a distrust of others, and an inability to approach other people without appearing somewhat peculiar are commonly observed. In one large study (Dodrill, 1983), these tendencies were observed in about 55% of adults with epilepsy. This study was not done in exactly the same way as that of Rodin, Shapiro, and Lennox (1977), but it was noted in that study that epilepsy was associated with behavioral problems that included interpersonal difficulties in 54% of the cases. It would appear that many of these individuals had deficits in social skills. Impairment in brain functions may of course limit social perceptiveness and ability to respond effectively in interpersonal situations.

The final type of problem in interpersonal relationships worthy of at least brief discussion pertains to relationships between patients and physicians. In general, little can be pointed to in the way of difficulties in the literature with respect to this type of relationship, and it is likely that this is at least in part due to the fact that patients who do not like their doctors tend to go to others. There is a group of patients, however, who tend to respond negatively to their physicians, who conclude that their physicians are not knowledgeable, and so on. When this is the case, it is often observed that these persons demonstrate a sociopathic or psychopathic type of personality profile, with general difficulties in dealing with authority figures, problems in family relationships, and so on.

Problems in Vocational and Financial Adjustment

One major problem facing the adult with epilepsy is in securing employment. In one sizable study (Dodrill, 1983), about 60% of adults with epilepsy reported concerns in the vocational area. A large survey conducted of people with epilepsy (Perlman, 1977) resulted in the following conclusions: (1) 50% of adults with epilepsy report difficulties in securing a job because of seizures; (2) discrimination in the job market is perceived as the most serious problem facing adults with seizures; (3) job counseling is identified as the most needed direct service; and (4) access to transportation to get to work is a major problem.

Unemployment in epilepsy varies from approximately 20% to 50% (Fraser, 1980). Furthermore, there is evidence that state and federal rehabilitation programs have, if anything, served fewer people with seizure disorders in recent years than previously (Wright, 1975) and that when they have served these clients, they have not been particularly effective (Fraser, 1980). The reasons for this are unclear but probably include a lack of understanding of clients with epilepsy and a tendency to rely upon skills training as opposed to job development and placement strategies.

The question may be asked as to what variables are associated with unemployment in epilepsy. There is now fairly good evidence that seizure frequency and seizure type are essentially unrelated to employment (Batzel, Dodrill, & Fraser, 1980; Dennerll, Rodin, Gonzalez, Schwartz, & Lin, 1966). Neuropsychological variables, on the other hand, have consistently shown relevance to employment (Batzel, Dodrill, & Fraser, 1980; Dennerll, Rodin, Gonzalez, Schwartz, & Lin, 1966; Dikmen & Morgan, 1980; Schwartz, Dennerll, & Lin, 1968). In each of these studies, differences have been reported between employed and unemployed epileptic groups on a wide range of neuropsychological variables, particularly including those pertaining to memory, alertness, and flexibility in thinking. Tests of intelligence also differentiate employed and unemployed persons with epilepsy, and it is clear that the unemployed samples are inferior intellectually and have increased impairment in brain functions. Decreased adaptive abilities are associated with less effective performance in everyday life. Personality and social variables were also evaluated in the majority of these studies, but they tend to be less relevant to vocational status. One exception to this was the study by Batzel and colleagues (1980), in which the WPSI was used. In this study, the WPSI Vocational Scale demonstrated greater discriminability between various levels of employment-unemployment than all other intellectual, neuropsychological, and personality measures, including the MMPI.

One outgrowth of a lack of employment pertains to insufficient money to meet daily needs. The extent of this difficulty has not been identified with precision, but it is obviously great (Commission for the Control of Epilepsy and Its Consequences, 1977; Epilepsy Foundation of America, 1975). It is probably also true, in any population, that those individuals most needing services are least likely to be able to pay for them. Local, state, and federal subsidy programs are frequently used by persons having seizure disorders. In one large group of adults with epilepsy, the WPSI identified 60%–65% who reported not having sufficient money to meet daily needs (Dodrill, 1983). It is interesting that researchers using the WPSI found, in countries with better developed plans of socialized medicine than in the United States, fewer financial concerns are reported by persons with epilepsy (Dodrill, Beier, Tacke, Tacke, & Tan, 1983).

Problems in Medical Treatment

There are two areas of common concern with respect to medical treatment. The first pertains to finding a physician who is interested in epilepsy and who has the technical competence to provide adequate treatment. In many instances, travel to a specialized medical center is necessary to obtain updated and comprehensive treatment for difficult to manage seizure problems. For this reason, the National Institute of Neurological and Communicative Disorders and Stroke, in the mid 1970s, began to set up a series of comprehensive epilepsy programs across the United States to help disseminate information about epilepsy and to generate new data as well. It was for this reason also that the Epilepsy Foundation of America (EFA; 4351 Garden City Drive, Landover, MD, 20785) has a continually updated referral list that can be used as a resource for the person with epilepsy. Difficulties in this area nevertheless remain.

A second type of problem pertaining to medical treatment is compliance in taking medication prescribed for seizures. The problems here are not unlike those which have been described with many chronic diseases for which patients are asymptomatic most of the time. A tendency exists to stop taking the medication or to take it only in an irregular manner, and this may be true whether or not the medication is effective. If the medication is effective, nothing happens, and one may conclude that the medication is not doing any good because there are no seizures anymore. On the other hand, if there are seizures, there is a tendency to conclude that the medication is not doing any good because there are seizures. From a behavioral perspective, there is very little in the way of obvious reinforcement, other than possibly the absence of a negative condition. The only exceptions are those cases in which, when medication is discontinued, the rate of seizures immediately increases dramatically. There is also a tendency to blame the medication for any untoward effects felt and to conclude that one would be much better off if one did not have to take the drugs. In reality, however, this is not true, as was demonstrated many years ago by Somerfeld-Ziskind & Ziskind (1940), who showed that children with epilepsy who took phenobarbital improved more in mental abilities than did those children untreated with medication. The latter group had many more seizures. Thus, a person would be worse off in the vast majority of instances if medication was not taken, but convincing many patients of this is another matter. At any rate, investigators in the area of epilepsy have suggested that possibly as many as one-third to one-half of all patients with seizure disorders do not take their medication regularly and consistently (Desai, Riley, Porter, & Penry, 1978; Mucklow & Dollery, 1978; Peterson, Mclean, & Millingen, 1982). This is a leading reason why many patients continue to have seizures. An insightful study of the reasons for noncompliance from the patient's viewpoint has recently appeared (Trostle, Hauser, & Susser, 1983).

PATTERNS OF PSYCHOSOCIAL PROBLEMS IN EPILEPSY

A review of all those psychosocial difficulties identified above tends to lead one to the conclusion that there is a morass of problems that are hard to organize and understand, much less change. To help deal with this problem, a study was undertaken to determine which patterns or constellations of difficulties most commonly exist in persons with epilepsy (Dodrill, 1983). Three hundred adults with epilepsy were administered the WPSI, which was discussed earlier. By using this inventory, it was possible to address the question of which problems and combinations of problems are most and least frequent in their appearance. In a manner similar to that used with the MMPI, peak points on each profile were evaluated, and the two peak points for each profile were considered, regardless of the extent of their elevations. Ignoring which of the two was highest for any patient, the profiles may be classified into 21 groups. When this was done, it was noted that six two-scale high-point combinations occurred more frequently than expected by chance: Emotional, Financial 13.3%; Vocational, Financial 13.3%; Emotional, Adjustment to Seizures 12.0%; Emotional, Vocational 10.7%; Emotional, Interpersonal 9.3%; and Vocational, Adjustment to Seizures 6.3%. Thus, only a handful of different problem combinations account for the most prominent psychosocial problems seen in about two-thirds of this large group.

In the same way that several two-scale high-point combinations are seen more frequently than by chance, it is also noted that there are combinations of problems that very rarely appear. The six least frequent of these are: Family Background, Medicine and Medical Management (MMM) 0.3%; Financial, MMM 1.3%; Interpersonal, MMM 1.3%; Interpersonal, Adjustment to Seizures 1.3%; Interpersonal, Financial 1.7%; Family Background, Vocational 1.7%. Only rarely do these constellations of problems appear. More than any other method of analysis, this approach has helped us to realize that psychosocial problems in epilepsy can be organized and that they are not manifested randomly. Such an analysis would seem to be helpful in systematically developing treatment plans and in bringing order to this very difficult area.

PSYCHOSOCIAL-NEUROPSYCHOLOGICAL INTERRELATIONSHIPS

We now come to the topic of interrelating psychosocial problems in epilepsy with neuropsychological functioning. It has always appeared to me that persons with demonstrated impairment in brain functions, as revealed by neuropsychological tests, have fewer "adaptive abilities" with which to deal with problems in everyday life. Such a postulation is hardly remarkable and is consistent with the well-known studies of Halstead (1947) and Reitan (1955). If the adaptive abilities of individuals are decreased, the individuals are less able to cope with the strains and stresses of everyday life. If they are less able to cope with such stressors, they are more likely to show emotional and psychosocial problems. If this line of thinking is correct, greater impairment in brain functions would be associated with more emotional and psychosocial problems. In addition, a model could be set up that might be applicable to other types of neurological disorders resulting in neuropsychological impairment.

Despite the seeming reasonableness of this approach, for a number of years it was not believed that there was any definite relationship between intellectual-neuro-psychological variables and emotional-psychosocial adjustment in epilepsy. Using the MMPI, Matthews and Kløve (1968) and Stevens, Milstein, and Goldstein (1972) found no relationships between these general groups of variables, and a later investigation (Matthews, et al., 1977) resulted in only equivocal findings. However, two other papers (Batzel, Dodrill, & Fraser, 1980; Dikmen & Morgan, 1980) appeared that could be interpreted as supporting a positive relationship. In addition, Hermann (1981) demonstrated that differences across patient groups could be found using Goldberg's rules for the MMPI classification of groups of profiles (Goldberg, 1972). When profiles as a whole, rather than single scales, were considered, clearer differences were in evidence that would support a relationship between intellectual-neuropsychological and emotional-psychosocial functioning.

A more detailed examination of the interrelationships between the two basic areas in question is of both theoretical and practical interest to the neuropsychologist. The results of one comprehensive study (Dodrill, 1980) will therefore be presented in greater detail than in the original paper in an effort to illustrate salient points. In this study, 100 persons having a diversity of seizure types were each evaluated in four areas: (1) intelligence, using the Wechsler Adult Intelligence Scale; (2) neuropsychological functioning, using the Neuropsychological Battery for Epilepsy (a modified Halstead-Reitan Neuropsychological Test Battery for patients with seizure disorders; Dodrill, 1978); (3) emotional adjustment, using the MMPI; and (4) psychosocial adjustment, using the WPSI. Although more detailed analyses were completed, a single summary score was used to represent each of the four areas: the WAIS Full Scale IQ, the percentage of scores outside normal limits on 16 neuropsychological tests (approximates the Halstead Impairment Index), the average MMPI profile elevation (omitting Mf), and the score on the Overall Psychosocial Functioning Scale of the WPSI, respectively. In a similar manner, the patients were then divided into four groups according to WAIS Full Scale IQ (111 and above, 90–110, 80–89, 79 and below), and the percentage of scores outside normal limits on the neuropsychological tests (0%–25%, 26%–50%, 51%–75%, 76%–100%). One-way analyses of variance were then undertaken across the groups using the MMPI and the WPSI as outcome measures.

Figure 13.2 presents the average MMPI profiles when the patients were divided according to WAIS Full Scale IQ. There were no differences whatever between the three brightest groups of patients, and although the dullest group (IQ scores of 79 or less) had obviously elevated MMPI scales on several occasions, the variance in scores was such that statistical significance at the .05 level was never obtained. This analysis presents what one can expect to find if standard measures of abilities and personality are used: there are no substantial differences, but there are tendencies with extreme groups that could become significant if only those groups were used or if a procedure based on several aspects of each profile was employed.

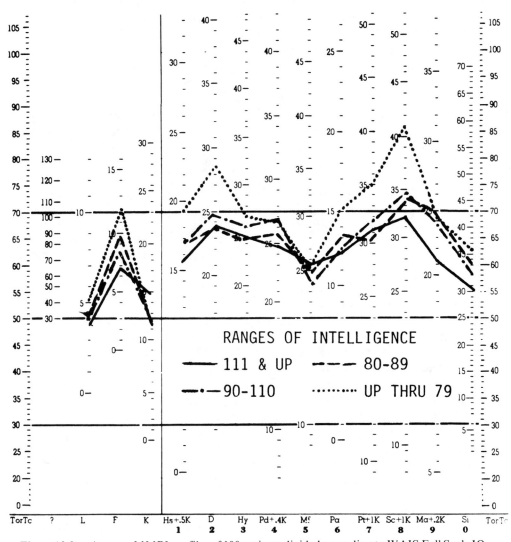

RANGES OF INTELLIGENCE

——— 111 & UP   ———— 80-89

——•— 90-110   ·········· UP THRU 79

Figure 13.2.   Average MMPI profiles of 100 patients divided according to WAIS Full Scale IQ.

If patients are once again divided up in exactly the same way according to WAIS Full Scale IQ but the outcome variables are those of the WPSI, statistical significance occasionally emerges as is demonstrated in Figure 13.3. This represents a situation in which one but only one of the test measures has been intended for and developed upon people with epilepsy. Poorer psychosocial adjustment is generally associated with decreased intelligence, but the relationship is imperfect.

Turning to the area of neuropsychological impairment, when individuals were divided according to percentage of scores outside normal limits on the Neuropsychological Battery for Epilepsy, several statistically significant findings emerged on the MMPI (Figure 13.4). The contrast between Figure 13.2 and Figure 13.4 may be interpreted as representing the difference between a test of intelligence and a battery of neuropsychological tests in terms of power to relate emotional problems to tests of abilities.

Finally, Figure 13.5 presents the results relating the neuropsychological tests to the WPSI. The findings here are perhaps just a little stronger and a little more consistent than with the MMPI. An examination of the average profiles in Figure 13.5 reveals that they do not overlap except in two instances, in which the most impaired group had better performance than did the adjacent group. Figures 13.2, 13.3, and 13.4 demonstrate less uniformity in the ordering of means.

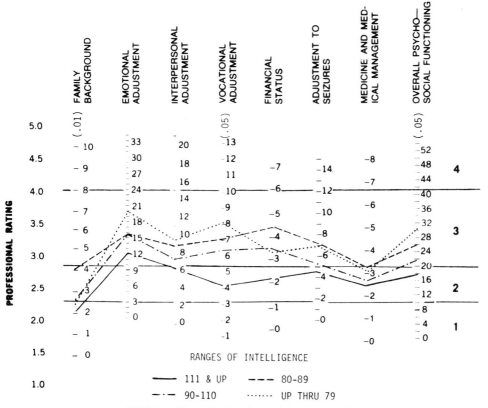

Figure 13.3.   Average WPSI profiles of 100 patients divided according to WAIS Full Scale IQ.

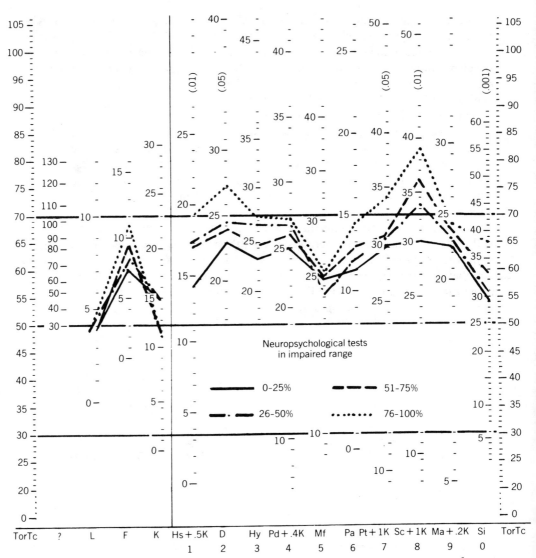

Figure 13.4. Average MMPI profiles of 100 patients divided according to percentage of scores outside normal limits on the Neuropsychological Battery for Epilepsy.

The findings discussed above have ramifications beyond the study of adults with epilepsy. One implication is that results of studies relating tests of abilities to adjustment are likely to produce results substantially depending on the tests used. Figures 13.2, 13.3, 13.4, and 13.5 could have represented four separate studies, the results of each of which would have been interpreted somewhat differently. Thus, it seems likely that future studies will produce a diversity of findings depending, at least in part, on the test used. Neuropsychological tests are more likely to produce positive results than are tests of general abilities. Similarly, tests designed to be sensitive to the emotional and psychosocial problems often noted with a particular disorder might be more sensitive than tests of general adjustment. When neuropsychological tests are combined with tests of adjustment designed for a particular disorder, maximal relationships are likely to be found.

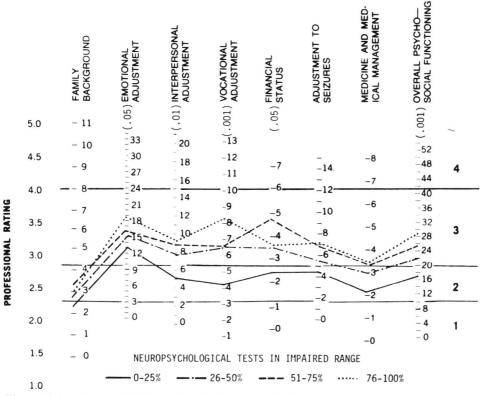

Figure 13.5.   Average WPSI profiles of 100 patients divided according to percentage of scores outside normal limits on the Neuropsychological Battery for Epilepsy.

REMEDIATION OF PSYCHOSOCIAL PROBLEMS IN EPILEPSY

We now turn to an area of great interest to us all and that pertains to helping to resolve the problems and conditions that have been described. One is chagrined to discover that although there are literally thousands of articles describing emotional and psychosocial problems in epilepsy, there are only a few giving solid techniques for dealing with these problems. This section focuses on these articles. It should be observed, however, that there is a series of papers in which needs are underscored and in which general programs (especially multidisciplinary programs) for remediation are described. The difficulty with this portion of the literature, however, is that in most cases specific techniques are not offered and in most cases no results are described. We need far more in the way of describing specific techniques and their effective results and far less in the way of general descriptions of programs.

Vocational Habilitation and Rehabilitation

Many persons with epilepsy are unemployed despite the fact that probably more specific steps have been taken in this area than in any other area of psychosocial concern. One well-developed program for remediation has been described by Fraser (1980). The program has three general phases. The first is the identification of deficient job-seeking skills and the taking of steps to remedy these deficiencies. Adults with epilepsy often lack work experience, have no network of work-related contacts, and demonstrate poor self-image so that they are unable to present themselves clearly and confidently to employers. Such persons begin by going through an eight-hour training program in identifying sources of job leads, calling employers for interviews, completing applications, identifying appropriate jobs through newspaper advertisements, learning how to go through a job interview, and learning how to disclose the fact of epilepsy. Instruction is given in small groups with respect to each of these points, and role-playing procedures are undertaken so that the counselor can see something of how each person would approach each situation. In addition, video-taping of role-playing procedures is also accomplished, so that clients can see how they approach each situation. Thus, this technique is very practical in terms of identifying deficient areas, in obtaining instruction and specific practice in those areas that are deficient, and in securing feedback about performance. If job-seeking skills are not found to be adequate at the end of this portion of the program, individual counseling is undertaken, or referral is made to a three-week job skill program in the community.

A second part of the program described by Fraser (1980) consists of a Job Club, which meets for two hours weekly and involves a small group of job-ready clients who need to make contacts with employers and to actually secure positions. In the first part of each Job Club session, the current status and efforts of each client are reviewed in turn, and the entire group is encouraged to help think of solutions to the problems of the other clients. In so doing, support is communicated to each person, the development of problem-solving skills is prompted, and a movement-oriented focus is maintained. In the second part of each session, an employer from the community appears and makes a presentation about the company represented, how hiring is done in that company, and what the company looks for in each job applicant. The clients are free to ask questions, and they are more able to ask them in this situation than in individual job interviews. Before each session ends, every client sets up goals for the next week with respect to job interviews and other job-related activities.

The third and final phase of the program described by Fraser (1980) is actually obtaining a job and maintaining the position. The amount of attention required during this time varies significantly from one person to the next. A counselor in frequent contact with various clients can often perceive when difficulties begin to arise and can assist the client in working out those problems before they become major or overwhelming.

The program described above is very practical and highly directed toward manifest needs. Specific skill development with supportive but directive feedback characterizes this approach, and the result is the placement of a large number of clients who have never been successfully employed and who have many limitations, including decreased intelligence and significant impairment in brain functions. Other programs might be mentioned as well. Perhaps the best developed of these, and the one having the broadest range of influence, is that of the Training and Placement Service of the Epilepsy Foundation of America (Anderson, 1981; Wells, 1981). This program has counselors in many parts of the United States and has resulted in the placement of a large number of clients with epilepsy.

Social Skills Training

As is well known, persons with epilepsy often lack many types of basic social skills. One approach to this problem is through systematic learning by which new and desirable methods of dealing with problems in life are learned and old and undesirable methods are done away with. The "learned helplessness" model often applies (Hermann, 1979).

Fraser and Smith (1982) give a completely developed rationale for a social learning approach to the development of a variety of skills in persons with epilepsy. The classes described focus on relaxation, assertiveness training, conversation skills, mood management, problem-solving skills, management of leisure time, and human relationships. Additional programs directed toward helping people develop independent living skills are also described. It appears that this type of program is on solid theoretical and practical grounds, and, as such, it deserves further attention and development. The difficulty has been, however, that significant and persisting changes in behavior have not been reported in the literature as a result of this general approach, at least to my knowledge. Similar approaches have been described on several occasions, but there is a lack of solid outcome data to demonstrate that they actually work. There may well be more than one reason for this, but undoubtedly one of the reasons is that many of these people have not learned certain skills in life because their neuropsychological deficits have made it difficult for them to do so. The same deficits would continue to make learning difficult, even under conditions of more directed training. In chronic conditions in which defective methods of coping are firmly established and there are biological reasons for these methods, change appears difficult. This represents one of the most important and yet vexing problems in the psychosocial aspects of epilepsy.

Self-Help Groups

There has risen up from people with epilepsy themselves a grass roots movement to band together into groups and to help themselves in solving the problems of daily life rather than looking to professionals. The groups vary from one time to the next and from one place to the next, and some seem to represent an attitude that people with epilepsy can help each other better than anyone else. At times, professionals may even be looked at askance because most do not have epilepsy, while in other instances services they offer may be utilized in limited ways. Because of the nature of these groups, it is difficult to find a detailed description of them in the literature, and only occasionally are relevant papers given at professional meetings (Droge, Arntson, & Norton, 1981; McGovern & Jones, 1980).

Because of the nature of self-help groups, their extent and influence is difficult to evaluate at this time. From a positive viewpoint, they represent an effort on the part of patients themselves to help deal with their problems and to assist one another in so doing. As such, this effort is to be applauded, and it can only be hoped that such groups avail themselves of knowledge and assistance from a variety of sources in order to enhance their own effectiveness.

Compliance in the Taking of Antiseizure Medications

Several investigators have reported efforts to improve compliance in the taking of medications for seizures. These efforts have included reducing the interval between clinic visits (Wannamaker, Morton, Gross, & Saunders, 1980), taking serum anticonvulsant levels and providing patients with feedback (Sherwin, Robb, & Lechter, 1973), simplifying the drug regimen so that medication is taken less frequently (Zaccara & Galli, 1979), and providing convenient dispensers of medication that allow a patient to see when a dose has not been taken (Lund, 1973). It is of interest to note that all of these methods have been successful in producing increased serum drug levels, and most have resulted in improved seizure control. With any given patient, one or more of these methods is likely to be more effective than the others. Furthermore, it is entirely possible that the types of patterns shown on neuropsychological tests may be of value not only in identifying those patients who are likely not to be compliant, but also in indicating which therapeutic approach might be most effective in solving the problem.

Miscellaneous Efforts at Remediation

In addition to those efforts at remediation described above, a variety of sources of assistance exists to help people with epilepsy. A number of these sources are described by Levinson (1982), including help in finding physicians with expertise in epilepsy, tax breaks that may be used by people with epilepsy, methods by which financial assistance may be obtained, lists of special educational and vocational opportunities for which many people with epilepsy qualify, and housing programs. A directory of various federal, state, and local resources is also included to meet needs in these areas.

The Epilepsy Foundation of America has also been very active in assisting persons with epilepsy to deal with a variety of medical and psychosocial concerns. The Public Information and Education Department responds to many requests and provides information from EFA's National Library. This library has substantial information of interest to both professionals and patients. For example, it includes microfiche copies of almost all scientific articles ever published on epilepsy. EFA also has a low-cost drug program to make antiseizure medications more readily available to persons who need them. In general, EFA provides substantial resources for dealing with a variety of problems commonly found in persons with epilepsy.

SUMMARY

In this chapter, a number of concerns with respect to psychosocial functioning in epilepsy have been described. It has been shown that these problems tend to be found in certain patterns, or clusters. The problems are of great significance in practical terms, and they have a substantial negative effect on functioning in everyday life. It has also been demonstrated that these concerns are related to indications of adequacy of brain functions and that the greater the brain impairment, the greater the psychosocial and emotional concerns. The extent to which such concerns are identified in any particular investigation depends, among other factors, on the tests or inventories used.

Efforts at remediation of these difficulties beyond the usual therapeutic techniques have also been described. In the area of remediation, limitations are obvious, and it is clear that much more work needs to be accomplished. This represents a challenge for the neuropsychologist. It may be that neuropsychologists are the best equipped of all professionals to help individuals with epilepsy in the psychosocial areas because neuropsychologists understand the nature of the brain dysfunction involved. Thus, they can assist by specifying the strengths and weaknesses that will be found with any individual patient. Using this understanding as a basis, they can formulate treatment programs that maximize the strengths and minimize the limitations found in any given person with epilepsy and that help that person make the best adjustment possible. Neuropsychologists have yet to become active in such endeavors in any substantial way, but it appears that, rather than merely identifying brain-related difficulties, such efforts would constitute one of the major ways in which they could contribute to the welfare of persons with epilepsy and other brain-related disorders.

ACKNOWLEDGMENTS

This study was supported by grants NS 17277, NS 17111, and NS 04053 awarded by the National Institute of Neurological and Communicative Disorders and Stroke, National Institutes of Health, Public Health Service, Department of Health and Human Services. The original development of the Washington Psychosocial Seizure Inventory was supported in part by a grant from the Epilepsy Foundation of America.

REFERENCES

Anderson, R.A. (1981). Training and placement services: An employment services model program for persons with epilepsy. In M. Dam, L. Gram, & J.K. Penry (Eds.), *Advances in epileptology: XIIth Epilepsy International Symposium* (pp. 245–251). New York: Raven Press.

Batzel, L.W., Dodrill, C.B., & Fraser, R.T. (1980). Further validation of the WPSI Vocational Scale: Comparisons with other correlates of employment in epilepsy. *Epilepsia, 21,* 235–242.

Bear, D.M., & Fedio, P. (1977). Quantitative analysis of interictal behavior in temporal lobe epilepsy. *Archives of Neurology, 34,* 454–467.

Blumer, D. (1977). Treatment of patients with seizure disorder referred because of psychiatric complications. *McLean Hospital Journal* [Special issue], 53–73.

Chodoff, P. (1982).. Hysteria in women. *American Journal of Psychiatry, 139,* 545–551.

Commission for the Control of Epilepsy and Its Consequences. (1977). *Plan for nationwide action on epilepsy* (4 vols.). Bethesda, MD: U.S. Department of Health, Education and Welfare.

Dennerll, R.D., Rodin, E.A., Gonzalez, S., Schwartz, M.L., & Lin, Y. (1966). Neurological and psychological factors related to employability of persons with epilepsy. *Epilepsia, 7,* 318–329.

Desai, B.T., Potter, R., & Penry, J.K. (1979). The psychogenic seizure by videotape analysis: A study of 42 attacks in 6 patients. *Neurology, 29,* 602.

Desai, B.T., Riley, T.L., Porter, R.J., & Penry, J.K. (1978). Active noncompliance as a cause of uncontrolled seizures. *Epilepsia, 19,* 447–452.

Dikmen, S., Hermann, B.P., Wilensky, A.J., & Rainwater, G. (1983). Validity of the Minnesota Multiphasic Personality Inventory (MMPI) to psychopathology in patients with epilepsy. *Journal of Nervous and Mental Disease, 171,* 114–122.

Dikmen, S., & Morgan, S.F. (1980). Neuropsychological factors related to employability and occupational status in persons with epilepsy. *Journal of Nervous and Mental Disease, 168,* 236–240.

Dodrill, C.B. (1978). A neuropsychological battery for epilepsy. *Epilepsia, 19,* 611–623.

Dodrill, C.B. (1980). Interrelationships between neuropsychological data and social problems in epilepsy. In R. Canger, F. Angeleri, & J.K. Penry (Eds.), *Advances in epileptology: XIth Epilepsy International Symposium* (pp. 191–197). New York: Raven Press.

Dodrill, C.B. (1981). Neuropsychology of epilepsy. In S.B. Filskov & T.J. Boll (Eds.), *Handbook of clinical neuropsychology* (Vol. 1, pp. 366–395). New York: John Wiley & Sons.

Dodrill, C.B. (1983). Psychosocial characteristics of epileptic patients. In A.A. Ward, Jr., J.K. Penry, & D. Purpura (Eds.), *Epilepsy*. New York: Raven Press.

Dodrill, C.B., Batzel, L.W., Queisser, H.R., & Temkin, N.R. (1980). An objective method for the assessment of psychological and social difficulties among epileptics. *Epilepsia, 21,* 123–135.

Dodrill, C.B., Beier, R., Tacke, I., Tacke, U., & Tan, S-Y. (1983). International comparison of psychosocial problems in adults with epilepsy. In M. Parsonage, R.H.E. Grant, A.G. Craig, & A.A. Ward, Jr. (Eds.), *Advances in epileptology: XIVth Epilepsy International Symposium* (pp. 71–77). New York: Raven Press.

Dodrill, C.B., & Troupin, A.S. (1977). Psychotropic effects of carbamazepine in epilepsy: A double-blind comparison with phenyton. *Neurology, 27,* 1023–1028.

Dodrill, C.B., & Wilkus, R.J. (1978). Neuropsychological correlates of the electroencephalogram in epileptics: III. Generalized nonepileptiform abnormalities. *Epilepsia, 19,* 453–462.

Droge, D., Arntson, P., & Norton, R. (1981, May). *The social support function and epilepsy self-help groups.* Paper presented at the meeting of the International Communication Association, Minneapolis.

Epilepsy Branch, National Institute of Neurological and Communicative Disorders and Stroke (1981). *Indexes to the accessions of the epilepsy information system* (Vol. 4). Bethesda, MD: U.S. Department of Health and Human Services.

Epilepsy Foundation of America (1975). *Basic statistics on the epilepsies.* Philadelphia: F.A. Davis.

Flor-Henry, P. (1976). Lateralized temporal-limbic dysfunction and psychopathology. *Annals of the New York Academy of Sciences, 280,* 777–795.

Flor-Henry, P., Fromm-Auch, D., Tapper, M., & Schopflocher, D. (1981). A neuropsychological study of the stable syndrome of hysteria. *Biological Psychiatry, 16,* 601–626.

Fraser, R.T. (1980). Vocational aspects of epilepsy. In B.P. Hermann (Ed.), *A multidisciplinary handbook of epilepsy* (pp. 74–105). Springfield, IL: Charles C Thomas.

Fraser, R.T., & Smith, W.R. (1982). Adjustment to daily living. In H. Sands (Ed.), *Epilepsy: A handbook for the mental health professional* (pp. 189–221). New York: Brunner/Mazel.

Glass, D.H., & Mattson, R.H. (1973). Psychopathology and emotional precipitation of seizures in temporal lobe and nontemporal lobe epileptics. *Proceedings of the 81st Annual Convention of the American Psychological Association, 8,* 425–426.

Goldberg, L.R. (1972). Man versus mean: The exploitation of group profiles in the construction of diagnostic classification system. *Journal of Abnormal Psychology, 79,* 121–131.

Goodwin, J., Sims, J., & Bergman, R. (1979). Hysterical seizures: A sequel to incest. *American Journal of Orthopsychiatry, 49,* 698–703.

Gross, M. (1970). Incestuous rape: A cause for hysterical seizures in four adolescent girls. *American Journal of Orthopsychiatry, 49,* 704–708.

Grove, D.N., Goocher, D.E., Wilcox, J.K., & Andrews, J. (1980). Impact of childhood epilepsy on the family system: A preliminary report. In R. Canger, F. Angeleri, & J.K. Penry (Eds.), *Advances in epileptology: XIth Epilepsy International Symposium* (pp. 247–252). New York: Raven Press.

Gulick, T.A., Spinks, I.P., & King, D.W. (1982). Pseudoseizures: Ictal phenomena. *Neurology, 32,* 24–30.

Gunn, J. (1978). Epileptic homicide: A case report. *British Journal of Psychiatry, 132,* 510–513.

Halstead, W.C. (1947). *Brain and intelligence: A quantitative study of the frontal lobes.* Chicago: University of Chicago Press.

Hermann, B.P. (1979). Psychopathology in epilepsy and learned helplessness. *Medical Hypotheses, 5,* 723–729.

Hermann, B.P. (1981). Deficits in neuropsychological functioning and psychopathology in persons with epilepsy: A rejected hypothesis revisited. *Epilepsia, 22,* 161–167.

Hermann, B.P., Black, R.B., & Chhabria, S. (1981). Behavioral problems and social confidence in children with epilepsy. *Epilepsia, 22,* 703–710.

Hermann, B.P., Dikmen, S., Schwartz, M.S., & Karnes, W.E. (1982). Interictal psychopathology in patients with ictal fear: A quantitative investigation. *Neurology, 32,* 7–11.

Hermann, B.P., Dikmen, S., & Wilensky, A.J. (1982). Increased psychopathology associated with multiple seizure types: Fact or artifact? *Epilepsia, 23,* 587–596.

Hermann, B.P., Schwartz, M.S., Karnes, W.E., & Vahdat, P. (1980). Psychopathology in epilepsy: Relationship of seizure type to age at onset. *Epilepsia, 21,* 15–23.

Hodgman, C.H., McAnarney, E.R., Myers, G.J., Iker, H., Parmelee, D., Schuster, B., & Tutihasi, M. (1979). Emotional complications of adolescent grand mal epilepsy. *Journal of Pediatrics, 95,* 309–312.

Hovey, H.B., Kooi, K.A., & Thomas, M.H. (1959). MMPI profiles of epileptics. *Journal of Consulting Psychology, 23,* 155–159.

Jordan, E.J. (1963). MMPI profiles of epileptics: A further evaluation. *Journal of Consulting Psychology, 27,* 267–269.

Kløve, H., & Doehring, D.G. (1962). MMPI in epileptic groups with differential etiology. *Journal of Clinical Psychology, 18,* 149–153.

Kløve, H., & Matthews, C.G. (1966). Psychometric and adaptive abilities in epilepsy with differential etiology. *Epilepsia, 7,* 330–338.

LaBarbera, J.D., & Dozier, J.E. (1980). Hysterical seizures: The role of sexual exploitation. *Psychosomatics, 21,* 897–903.

Levinson, R.W. (1982). Resources for epilepsy: Access and advocacy. In H. Sands (Eds.), *Epilepsy: A handbook for the mental professional* (pp. 225–263). New York: Brunner/Mazel.

Lezak, M.D. (1978). Living with the characterologically altered brain injured patient. *Journal of Clinical Psychiatry, 39,* 592–598.

Lund, M. (1973). Failure to observe dosage instructions in patients with epilepsy. *Acta Neurogica Scandinavica, 49,* 295–306.

Matthews, C.G., Dikmen, S., & Harley, J.P. (1977). Age at onset and psychometric correlates of MMPI profiles in major motor epilepsy. *Diseases of the Nervous System, 38,* 173–176.

Matthews, C.G., & Kløve, V.E. (1968). MMPI performances in major motor, psychomotor and mixed seizure classifications of known and unknown etiology. *Epilepsia, 9,* 43–53.

Mattson, R.H. (1980). Value of intensive monitoring. In J.A. Wada & J.K. Penry (Eds.), *Advances in Epileptology: Xth Epilepsy International Symposium* (pp. 43–51). New York: Raven Press.

McGovern, S., & Jones, O.M. (1980). The development of self-help groups. In J.A. Wada & J.K. Penry (Eds.), *Advances in epileptology: Xth Epilepsy International Symposium* (pp. 413–416). New York: Raven Press.

Meier, M.J., & French, L.A. (1965). Some personality correlates of unilateral and bilateral EEG abnormalities in psychomotor epileptics. *Journal of Clinical Psychology, 21,* 3–9.

Mignone, R.J., Donnelly, E.F., & Sadowsky, D. (1970). Psychological and neurological comparisons of psychomotor and nonpsychomotor epileptic patients. *Epilepsia, 11,* 345–359.

Mucklow, J.C., & Dollery, C.T. (1978). Compliance with anticonvulsant therapy in a hospital clinic and in the community. *British Journal of Clinical Pharmacology, 6,* 75–79.

Parnas, J., & Korsgaard, S. (1982). Epilepsy and psychosis. *Acta Psychiatrica Scandinavica, 66,* 89–99.

Penry, J.K. (Ed.). (1978). *Indexes to the epilepsy accessions of the epilepsy information system* (Vols. 1–3). Bethesda, MD: U.S. Department of Health, Education and Welfare.

Perlman, L.G. (1977). *The person with epilepsy: Lifestyle, needs, expectations.* Chicago: National Epilepsy League.

Peterson, G.M., McLean, S., & Millingen, K.S. (1982). Determinants of patient compliance with anticonvulsant therapy. *Epilepsia, 23,* 607–613.

Pincus, J.H. (1980). Can violence be a manifestation of epilepsy? *Neurology, 30,* 304–307.

Pond, D.A., Bidwell, B.H., & Stein, L. (1960). A survey of epilepsy in fourteen medical practices: I. Demographic and medical data. *Psychiatirca Neurologia and Neurochirigua, 63,* 217–236.

Ramani, V., & Gumnit, R.J. (1981). Intensive monitoring of epileptic patients with a history of episodic aggression. *Archives of Neurology, 38,* 570–571.

Ramani, V., & Gumnit, R.J. (1982). Management of hysterical seizures in epileptic patients. *Archives of Neurology, 39,* 78–81.

Ramani, V., Quesney, L.F., Olson, D., & Gumnit, R.J. (1980). Diagnosis of hysterical seizures in epileptic patients. *American Journal of Psychiatry, 137,* 705–709.

Reitan, R.M. (1955). An investigation of the validity of Halstead's measures of biological intelligence. *Archives of Neurology and Psychiatry, 53,* 28–35.

Richards, T.W. (1952). Personality of the convulsive patient in military service. *Psychological Monographs, 66* (14, Whole No. 346).

Ritchie, K. (1981). Research note: Interaction in the families of epileptic children. *Journal of Child Psychology and Psychiatry, 22,* 65–71.

Rodin. E.A. (1973). Psychomotor epilepsy and aggressive behavior. *Archives of General Psychiatry, 28,* 210–213.

Rodin, E.A., Katz, M., & Lennox, K. (1976). Differences between patients with temporal lobe seizures and those with other forms of epileptic attacks. *Epilepsia, 17,* 313–320.

Rodin, E.A., Shapiro, H.L., & Lennox, K. (1977). Epilepsy and life performance. *Rehabilitation Literature, 38,* 34–39.

Roy, A. (1977). Non-convulsive psychogenic attacks investigated for temporal lobe epilepsy. *Comprehensive Psychiatry, 18,* 591–593.

Schwartz, M.L., Dennerll, R.D., & Lin, Y. (1968). Neuropsychological and psychosocial predictors of employability in epilepsy. *Journal of Clinical Psychology, 24,* 174–177.

Serafetinides, E.A. (1965). Aggressiveness in temporal lobe epilepsy and its relation to cerebral dysfunction and environmental factors. *Epilepsia, 6,* 33–42.

Shaw, D.J. (1966). Differential MMPI performance in pseudo-seizure epileptic and pseudo-neurologic groups. *Journal of Clinical Psychology, 22,* 271–275.

Sherwin, A.L., Robb, J.P., & Lechter, M. (1973). Improved control of epilepsy by monitoring plasma ethosuximide. *Archives of Neurology, 28,* 178–181.

Sherwin, I. (1977). Clinical and EEG aspects of temporal lobe epilepsy with behavioral disorder: The role of cerebral dominance. *McLean Hospital Journal* [Special issue], 40–50.

Sherwin, I., Peron-Magnan, P., Bancaud, J., Bonis, A., & Talairach, J. (1982). Prevalence of psychosis in epilepsy as a function of the laterality of the epileptogenic lesion. *Archives of Neurology, 39,* 621–625.

Slater, E. (1965). Diagnosis of "hysteria." *British Medical Journal, 1,* 1395–1399.

Somerfeld-Ziskind, E., & Ziskind, E. (1940). Effect of phenobarbital on the mentality of epileptic patients. *Archives of Neurology and Psychiatry, 40,* 70–79.

Standage, K.F., & Fenton, G.W. (1975). Psychiatric symptom profiles of patients with epilepsy: A controlled investigation. *Psychological Medicine, 5,* 152–160.

Stevens, J.R. (1966). Psychiatric implications of psychomotor epilepsy. *Archives of General Psychiatry, 14,* 461–471.

Stevens, J.R. (1975). Interictal clinical manifestations of complex partial seizures. In J.K. Penry & D.D. Daly (Eds.), *Advances in neurology* (Vol. 11, pp. 85–112). New York: Raven Press.

Stevens, J.R., & Hermann, B.P. (1981). Temporal lobe epilepsy, psychopathology, and violence: The state of the evidence. *Neurology, 31,* 1127–1132.

Stevens, J.R., Milstein, V., & Goldstein, S. (1972). Psychometric test performance in relation to the psychopathology of epilepsy. *Archives of General Psychiatry, 26,* 532–538.

Taylor, D.C. (1969). Aggression and epilepsy. *Journal of Psychosomatic Research, 13,* 229–236.

Taylor, D.C. (1975). Factors influencing the occurrence of schizophrenia-like psychosis in patients with temporal lobe epilepsy. *Psychological medicine, 5,* 249–254.

Toone, B.K., Garralda, M.E., & Ron, M.A. (1982). The psychoses of epilepsy and the functional psychosis: A clinical and phenomenological comparison. *British Journal of Psychiatry, 141,* 256–261.

Trostle, J.A., Hauser, W.A., & Susser, I.S. (1983). The logic of noncompliance: Management of epilepsy from the patient's point of view. *Culture, Medicine, and Psychiatry, 7,* 35–56.

Wannamaker, B.B., Morton, W.A., Jr., Gross, A.J., & Saunders, S. (1980). Improvement in antiepileptic drug levels following reduction of intervals between clinic visits. *Epilepsia 21,* 155–162.

Warren, L.W., & Weiss, D.J. (1969). Relationship between disability type and measured personality characteristics. *Proceedings of the 77th Annual Convention of the American Psychological Association, 4,* 773–774.

Waxman, S.G., & Geschwind, N. (1975). The interictal behavior syndrome of temporal lobe epilepsy. *Archives of General Psychiatry, 32,* 1580–1586.

Wells, W.A. (1981). New directions in epilepsy rehabilitation: A vocational training program in innovative techniques for rehabilitation of people with epilepsy. In M. Dam, L. Gram, & J.K. Penry (Eds.), *Advances in epileptology: XIIth Epilepsy International Symposium* (pp. 235–244). New York: Raven Press.

Wilkus, R.J., & Thompson, P.M. (1984). Intensive EEG monitoring and psychological studies of patients with pseudoepileptic seizures. *Epilepsia, 25,* 168–175.

Wright, G.N. (Ed.). (1975). *Epilepsy Rehabilitation.* Boston: Little, Brown.

Zaccara, G., & Galli, A. (1979). Effectiveness of simplified dosage schedules on the management of ambulant epileptic patients. *European Neurology, 18,* 341–344.

Ziegler, R.G. (1981). Impairments of control and confidence in epileptic children and their families. *Epilepsia, 22,* 339–346.

Zivin, L., & Ajmone Marsan, C. (1968). Incidence and prognostic significance of "epileptiform" activity in the EEG of non-epileptic subjects. *Brain, 91,* 751–778.

CHAPTER 14

Neuropsychological Correlates of Multiple Sclerosis

Janis M. Peyser and Charles M. Poser

In 1969, Namerow and Thompson made the observation that multiple sclerosis (MS) is a disease characterized by enigmas. Not only are we ignorant of the cause or causes of the disease, but we cannot adequately explain many of the accumulated clinical and epidemiological facts pertaining to the illness. This statement is, unfortunately, as true today as it was then.

Multiple sclerosis is a disease that affects the white matter of the central nervous system (CNS) producing lesions known as plaques that appear to attack the myelin sheath exclusively, most often sparing the axons and neurons. Lesions do involve the gray matter occasionally. It is essentially a disease of young adults, causing neurological dysfunction at a time of life when careers have been launched, productivity is at its peak, and families have just become established.

Multiple sclerosis carries an aura of mystery and fear. It is often, unfortunately, referred to as the crippler of young adults, when in fact only a small proportion, perhaps 20%–25% of patients, eventually do become severely handicapped. In reality, the disease is more benign than is usually suspected, and not only are many persons with the disease able to carry out normal or nearly normal professional and personal lives, but in a small number of well-documented instances, the disease never makes itself known symptomatically (Mackay & Hirano, 1967; Gilbert & Sadler, 1983; Herndon & Rudick, 1983).

In addition to the motor and sensory disturbances that characterize the disease, lesions in the cerebral white and gray matter may be the source of cognitive deficits, mood disturbance, personality change, and, in a minority of cases, psychosis. Unfortunately, these neuropsychological correlates of MS have been among the most neglected and misunderstood aspects of the disease. It is our intention in this chapter to familiarize the reader with the basic disease process in MS, to review the neuropsychological aspects, and to suggest future lines of research into one of the most fascinating areas of this complex disease.

NEUROLOGIC ASPECTS

Etiology and Pathogenesis

Two major schools exist today regarding the cause of the illness (Poser, 1978). One group of investigators favors the idea that the disease is due to a so-called slow virus, one with a very long incubation period, lasting for several years, which persists in the body for an equally long period of time. It is believed that the disease is acquired at some time in childhood even though it may not become manifest until many years later. In actuality, numerous searches for such a virus since the mid-1960s have failed. Because it has been repeatedly demonstrated that patients with MS have considerably higher levels of antibodies against measles than does the rest of the population, the measles virus, possibly in an altered form, has been the favorite suspect for many years. However, it has also been demonstrated that the nonaffected siblings of MS patients have high levels of antibodies not only to measles but also, as do the patients themselves, against many other viruses (Brody, Sever, & Hanson, 1971). Some of the epidemiological data to be reviewed later do, however, support the concept of an environmental factor, quite possibly a virus.

The other major theory proposes that MS results from an alteration of the body's immune system triggered by a wide variety of virus infections, not necessarily a single one (Poser, 1978). There are two possibilities: that the immune system is too active or that it is deficient. It is regrettable that the truly immense number of studies of the alterations of the immune system in multiple sclerosis have failed to increase our understanding of the pathogenesis of the disease, with so many of these reports remaining unconfirmed and extremely controversial.

The lack of a true animal experimental model for MS continues to hamper research in this area. Claims have been made that such a model does in fact exist: in some animals, a chronic, relapsing, and remitting form of experimental encephalomyelitis (EAE) has been produced (Wisniewski & Keith, 1977), a condition induced by injecting the experimental animal with either complete myelin or the encephalitogenic portion of myelin, the myelin basic protein. While there are superficial clinical resemblances with multiple sclerosis, the mechanism for the actual destruction of the myelin sheath seen in these animals is quite different from what has been reported to occur in MS. It is quite possible that MS is a disease that affects only humans and for which no animal model can be devised.

One possible breakthrough in the pathogenesis has resulted from the demonstration, first by means of radionuclide brain scan (Poser, 1972) and more recently and even more convincingly by means of enhanced computer assisted tomography (Poser, 1980), of an alteration of the normally present impermeability of the blood-brain barrier, reflecting what is considered to be activity of the disease process. This rekindles a very old theory that the plaques of MS invariably arise around a small blood vessel and result from the destruction of the myelin by some substance that passes from these blood vessels into the substance of the brain.

Epidemiology and Genetics

A truly enormous amount of data has been accumulated that clearly demonstrates that MS is significantly more prevalent in the higher latitudes of the northern and southern hemispheres (Poser, 1979a; Kurtzke, 1977). Thus, it is more prevalent among both Caucasians and non-Caucasians in the northern, as opposed to the southern, United States; in Scandinavia, as opposed to Spain, Italy, and Greece; and in Tasmania, as opposed to northern Australia. Furthermore, studies conducted in Israel and in South Africa revealed that immigrants moving from an area of high incidence, such as northern Germany, to an area of low incidence, such as Israel, carry with them the high incidence of the country of origin unless immigration takes place before the age of 15

(Dean & Kurtzke, 1970). Even more impressive was the observation that, while adult Jewish immigrants from northern Europe to Israel still had a high incidence of MS, as opposed to immigrants from Asian and African countries, their children had all "acquired" the local incidence (Leibowitz, Kahana, & Alter, 1969). These data speak quite strongly in favor of an environmental factor; what this factor is remains unknown, although a great deal of attention has been paid to the level of development, particularly in the field of sanitation, of areas of high incidence (Alter, 1972).

The latitude-incidence correlation has some unexplained and intriguing exceptions, which include Japan, with a very low incidence, and the Shetland and Orkney islands, with an even higher incidence that expected on the basis of high latitude. Furthermore, what some have called an epidemic of MS seems to have occurred in the Faeroe Islands coincidentally with the presence of British troops during World War II (Kurtzke & Hyllested, 1979).

The epidemiologic data can also be interpreted as pointing to a higher incidence of MS in individuals of Germanic, including Anglo-Saxon and Scandinavian, origin (Poser, 1979a). The disease is extremely rare in Asians, is significantly less common among American blacks, and has never been found among African blacks. It has also been known that the disease is familial in approximately 10% of the cases. Thus, the importance of a genetic factor in the causation of MS has long been suspected.

Studies of hereditary histocompatibility antigen patterns have shown that several histocompatibility antigens located on the sixth chromosome appear to occur in statistically significantly higher numbers in MS patients than in control populations. Thus, in northern European and North American Caucasians, the HLA antigens A3, B7, and particularly Dw2 were found to be prevalent. Interestingly, these same antigens were not demonstrated in Israeli Jews and in Japanese patients with MS. Of equal import is the fact that certain of these antigens, such as B12, were found to be less common in MS patients than in control groups, suggesting the possibility of protective genetic factors as well (Poser, 1979a).

It must be emphasized that at this time the demonstration of the presence of the A3, B7, and Dw2 HLA antigens in an individual does *not* suggest a predisposition to the disease. Numerous studies of families with more than one blood-related member with MS have failed to demonstrate, in most instances, any kind of genetic concordance that would make these discoveries applicable to an individual (Ebers, et al., 1982). While it is clear that the antigens A3, B7, and Dw2 are not the genes responsible for MS. it is likely that such genes not only exist but are located very close by. Thus, the hope of identifying prone individuals and developing methods of prevention are certainly within the realm of possibilities at some time in the future.

One final epidemiologic point is that MS affects women more than men in a ratio of about 1.5 to 1. However, among patients with later onset, the sex ratio is closer to 1 or even reversed (Poser, Alter, Sibley, & Scheinberg, 1984).

Diagnosis

Because of the lack of a single specific diagnostic test for multiple sclerosis, the diagnosis is a clinical one based on the identification of more than one lesion involving the white matter of the nervous system by means of the history, the neurological examination, and ancillary procedures. A number of diagnostic schemes have been used for many years, but the best known and most widely used is that of Schumacher and colleagues (1965). The criteria are as follows: (1) there must be objective abnormalities on neurologic examination attributable to dysfunction of the central nervous system; (2) on neurologic examination or by history, there must be evidence of involvement of two or more separate parts of the central nervous system; (3) the objective neurologic evidence of central nervous system disease must reflect predominantly white matter involvement (i.e., fiber tract damage); (4) the involvement of the neuraxis must have occurred temporally in one of the following patterns: (a) in two or more episodes of worsening separated by a period of 1 month or more, each episode lasting at least 24 hours; or (b) in a slow or stepwise progression of signs and symptoms over a period of at least 6 months; (5) the age of the patient at the onset of the disease must fall within the range of 10–50 years, inclusive; and (6) the patient's signs and symptoms cannot be explained better by some other disease process, a decision that must be made by a physician competent in clinical neurology.

One of the major problems with the clinical diagnosis of MS is that the symptoms are not only transient, often lasting not more than hours or minutes, but are often of the type associated with hysterical conversion reactions. If symptom onset closely follows a stressful event or if there is psychological elaboration of a genuine sign or symptom, the diagnostic dilemma increases. The tendency to confuse early MS and hysteria has long been noted (see Buzzard, 1897) and neurologists continue to struggle with the problem. Unfortunately, failure or delay in diagnosing MS, with the overt or covert message that patients' symptoms are "all in their head," can be very distressing, as is illustrated by the actual relief many patients feel upon finally receiving a diagnosis of demyelinating disease. It would be difficult to improve on the advice of an early author (Gowers, 1898), who advocated ignoring any symptoms of hysteria until after a thorough search for those of an organic nature.

A number of ancillary tests and procedures have provided a great deal of help in the diagnostic process (Poser, Paty, Scheinberg, McDonald, & Ebers, 1984). One of the oldest and simplest is the hot bath test, an inexpensive and harmless method of producing abnormal neurologic signs by producing hyperthermia (Malhotra & Goren, 1981). Neurophysiological techniques for the measurement of evoked potentials arising from stimulation of visual, auditory, and somatosensory pathways have not only been extraordinarily useful in confirming the presence of lesions suspected on the basis of symptom report and signs demonstrated by the neurologic examination but, even more important, have revealed the presence of lesions that had remained completely asymptomatic (Deltenre, et al., 1979; Chiappa, 1980). Refinements in the measurement of protein components in the cerebrospinal fluid (CSF) have led to the demonstration of the presence of special types of immunoglubin G, termed *oligoclonal bands*, in well over 90% of patients with MS (Ebers & Paty, 1980). It must be cautioned, though, that abnormalities in these laboratory tests are not spsecific for MS, and the results must be used for confirmation of clinical suspicion rather than as the sole basis of diagnosis (Chiappa & Roper, 1982).

The computed tomography (CT) scan can be useful in demonstrating the presence of scattered lesions and, in particular, the very classical periventricular lesions. The yield, however, is relatively small but may be markedly increased by administering double the usual dose of iodine-containing contrast material and delaying the procedure by an hour to an hour and a half (Ebers & Paty, 1984). This permits the contrast material to penetrate the blood-brain barrier in areas where the permeability has been altered to only a minor degree. Again, it must be cautioned that certain types of vascular disease and metastic tumors can give a deceptive picture of MS, and such studies should not be used in isolation to make the diagnosis.

The newer technique of magnetic resonance imaging (MRI) may prove to be of additional value because of its greater resolution (Young, Pallis, Budder, Legg, & Steiner, 1981). It is also a safer procedure that does not require exposure of the patient to ionizing radiation and does not depend on the injection of potentially harmful iodine-containing contrast material to enhance its diagnostic yield. Unfortunately, its extremely high cost and complex installation requirements may limit its avilability. A very small study (Eber & Paty, 1984) comparing the number of MS lesions demonstrated by means of double-dose delayed CT scanning and those seen on MRI revelaed that in some instances plaques seen on one were not seen on the other. These techniques, which are based on quite different properties of the cerebral tissue, may eventually provide different information about the nature of the plaque and the alteration of the brain tissue that it causes.

Because of the development of these new ancillary clinical and laboratory procedures, a new set of diagnostic criteria was published by Poser, Paty, Scheinberg, and colleagues (1983). This classification incorporates the results of the previously described evoked response studies, tissue imaging techniques, measurements of cerebrospinal fluid IgG content and oligoclonal bands, and neuropsychological evaluation. While these new guidelines were designed primarily for use in research, the need for rigid diagnostic criteria in clinical practice is illustrated by the increasing frequency with which the diagnosis of MS is based on inadequate anamnestic and examination data and the erroneous interpretation of results of various laboratory tests.

Clinical Aspects

All parts of the CNS may be affected by plaques, but a number of areas are more commonly involved symptomatically than others. In terms of frequency of signs and symptoms, the following occur in more than 75% of patients at some time: ocular disturbances, muscle weakness, spasticity and hyperreflexia, Babinski's sign, absent abdominal reflexes, dysmetria or intention tremor, and bladder disturbance. Other combinations that occur in approximately 50%–75% of patients include nystagmus, gait ataxia, dysarthria or scanning speech, paresthesias, and objective alterations of vibratory and position senses (Poser, Presthus, & Horsdal, 1966). Mental disturbances, which will be the subject of more intensive review later, are also reported.

The chief characteristics of the symptoms of MS are multiplicity and the tendency to vary in nature and severity with the passage of time. The onset is usually acute or subacute, with subsequent disease course characterized by exacerbation and remission in about 70% of cases. Complete remission of the first symptoms occurs frequently, but with subsequent attacks, remissions may not occur or are incomplete. The clinical course extends for one or many decades in most cases but very rarely terminates in death within a few months of onset. Detailed clinical observations of many MS patients over periods of 10–20 years, as well as careful analysis of the exacerbations, separating new signs or symptoms from recurrences of previously experienced ones, indicates that in a significant number of patients the disease becomes static and therefore may be considered to be arrested.

It must be emphasized that the clinical manifesations of MS represent only the tip of the proverbial iceberg. Time and time again it has been demonstrated that the number of plaques found at autopsy is much greater than those suspected on the basis of clinical signs and symptoms. Namerow and Thompson (1969) have emphasized this problem and have pointed out that "one should be clear in differentiating the disease process *per se* from the cause of symptoms, since the two may at times be quite independent" (p. 774). This, of course, refers also to the often vexing problem of determining if any exacerbation represents the occurrence of new plaques or simply the manifestation of an old plaque resulting from a physiological alteration. Thygesen (1953), who studied in great detail 105 attacks of the disease in 60 MS patients, pointed out that new symptoms suggestive of a new plaque (although not necessarily so) occurred in ony 19% of these attacks. An attack often involves a previously damaged site of the central nervous system and is a true copy of previously remitted symptoms. It would seem, therefore, that clinical exacerbations can with equal probability (and probability as low as 1 in 5) represent either evidence of the production of new plaques or the symptomatic expression of existing plaques through physiologic alterations.

Of the various factors and events that can bring on symptoms of MS, either recurrences of previously experienced ones or new ones, heat is the best known. The ability of nerve fibers that have lost part or all of their myelin sheath to conduct an impulse is blocked with even small rises in body temperaure. Other factors include changes in calcium concentration, dehydration, and the very common intercurrent infection, in particular of the bladder. Less well appreciated is the fact that emotional stress and physical trauma can similarly bring on exacerbations of the disease (Poser, 1979b). While there is no evidence that can be interpreted as suggesting that such stressful events lead to the formation of new placque, many clinical observations clearly establish that already existing but aymptomatic plaques can be brought into clinical evidence with symptoms that may well remain permanent. Similarly, serious aggravation of already existing symptoms may also result. This knowledge underlines the great importance of maintaining patients with MS not only in optimum physical condition but also paying close attention to their psychological health as well.

Other studies contributing to the understanding of the clinical aspects of this disease are those of chronic MS plaques, which have demonstrated that a continued, very slow destruction of what is left of the myelin, coupled with scarring secondary to the disease process, may account for some of the slow progression that occurs in patients (Prineas & Connel, 1978).

The inability to accurately determine the activity of the multiple sclerosis process has been a major problem, particularly with regard to attempts to design therapeutic trial protocols and evaluating the efficacy of such treatment. The remitting and relapsing course of the disease has always suggested that the disease activity is also intermittent. This, however, may not be true. The appearance of signs and symptoms may represent, as we have just seen, the results of physiologic alterations rather than disease activity per se. Conversely, the appearance of enhancing lesions on CT scan without corresponding signs or symptoms suggests that active lesions may occur without any clinical manifesations (Ebers & Paty, 1984). Not enough prospective studies have been done to determine if, rather than being an intermittent disease process, MS is not in fact a continuous one that manifests itself at different times in different parts of the central nervous system. The CT scan enhancing lesions have been shown to disappear rather promptly with the administration of ACTH or other cortiocosteroids, which strongly supports the concepts that these drugs do affect the permeability of the blood-brain barrier and may also have a beneficial effect on the course of illness.

The demonstration of asymptomatic lesions through such techniques as evoked responses and NMR raises a number of extremely important points. One is that the disease may exist for a long time, perhaps even years, without manifesting itself, thus throwing into question a number of studies that have attempted to relate the onset of the disease to particular events. A second point is that the disease may be considerably more benign than is usually expected. Finally, it suggests that activity of the disease process cannot be judged simply by the recurrence or appearance of symptoms, that is, purely by clinical evaluation (Likowsky & Elmore, 1982).

In general, when one considers that many exacerbations, perhaps even 80%, are the result of preventable environmental changes and that a lesion of MS may remain asymptomatic for many years, even for a lifetime, the prognosis of the disease appears to be considerably better than has been believed in the past.

Treatment

In the absence of complete knowledge of etiology and pathogenesis, specific methods of treatment remained nonexistent.

Symptomatic treatment remains of great importance, but very few real advances have been made in recent years in that regard, with the exception of the introduction of the muscle relaxant drug baclofen, useful for the reduction of muscle spasm and clonus in the wheelchair and bedridden patient. Control of the extremely incapacitating bladder problems has improved with the use of a variety of parasympatholytic drugs, such as propantheline bromide, as well as new methods of urine collection. It is no longer necessary for the MS patient with urinary frequency, urgency, and stress incontinence to remain in close proximity to a bathroom at all times, thus preventing the patient from leaving the house for work, play, and social activities.

Despite great controversy, ACTH and corticosteroids remain in great use. Their antiedema, anti-inflamatory, and vascular membrane stabilizing effects are undeniably of value in *some* patients with MS. When one realizes that it is clinically or electrically impossible to differentiate between complete destruction of the myelin sheath and absent or reduced function secondary to inflammation and swelling, one can understand that ACTH and/or corticosteroids may be quite effective in the latter situation but totally ineffective in the former. A large enough number of neurologists have found these drugs to be of some benefit in a large enough number of patients to warrant their continued use, in particular during acute exacerbations, care being taken to determine that these exacerbations are *not* the result of physiological alterations, emotional stress, physical trauma, heat, infection, or other known precipitating factors (Poser, 1980).

A number of other treatments have been suggested based on rationales ranging from the intelligent to the totally ridiculous. Such fads come and go, some of them hanging on for periods of time, always fed by a steady stream of unfortunates seeking the magic bullet or the miraculous cure (Schumacher, 1971). Among those that seem to be based solely on a complete lack of understanding of MS are rocker shoes, megavitamins, hyperbaric oxygen, snake venom, colostrum, and the like. Treatments with a somewhat more scientific basis include plasmapheresis, immunosuppressants, linoleic acid, copolymer I, and, the latest entry, interferon.

The problems of designing reliable and convincing double-blind controlled therapeutic trials remain very serious (Brown, et al., 1979). Among the many difficulties are those of selection criteria (Poser, et al., 1983), matching patients and controls (which may well prove to be an insurmountable problem, in view of the inherent variability and dissemination of the disease), choice of therapeutic agents, and methods of evaluating results of treatment.

Because MS patients and their families must be the participants in therapeutic trials of promising agents, they, as well as the physicians conducting the trials, must be aware of the fact that the placebo effect of any kind of therapeutic regimen, of simple rest at home, or of hospitalization and removal from the stresses and strains of daily life is extremely powerful. It should also be pointed out that patients may be highly motivated by an enthusiastic investigator using a specific form of treatment, who thus provides the patient with considerable attention and who may unwillingly reinforce this placebo effect.

While new forms of treatment are being sought, patient care continues to focus on symptomatic management when possible; rehabilitation techniques, including mechanical aides and environmental design; and, above all, education and support for patients and their families.

NEUROPSYCHOLOGICAL ASPECTS

That cognitive and affective disturbance may occur in MS has long been known, and early case reports often included descriptions of such impairment. For example, Charcot, in his 1874 lecture series, attributed the following changes to most patients: "There is marked enfeeblement of memory; conceptualizations are formed slowly; the intellectual and emotional faculties are blunted in this totality. The dominant feeling appears to be a sort of almost stupid indifference in reference to all things. It is not rare to see the patient give way to foolish laughter or, on the contrary, melt into tears without reasons" (Charcot, 1877, p. 160).

Moxon, the first British author to write on MS since Carswell, included impairment of intellect and control of emotions as two of the critical diagnostic indicators. Of his case 1, he said: "The mental state throughout was characteristic. There was a singular instability of emotional equilibrium, so that laughing and crying were far too ready. Her intellect was narrowed, without unclearness, so that on the daily course of things before her eyes she replied tolerably well, but could not go much beyond this" (Moxon, 1875, pp. 452–453).

Case series soon followed reporting varying frequencies of intellectual, emotional, and psychotic disturbances in MS, often inextricably lumped under the term *psychic* manifestations. (Spiegel, 1891; Strumpell, 1891/1929; Ziehen, 1902/1929; Philippe & Cestan, 1903/1929; Müller, 1904/1906; Berger, 1905/1906; Bramwell, 1905; Seiffer, 1905/1929; Raecke, 1906; Duge, 1914/1929).

Two studies published in the 1920s are often cited together in support of the historical controversy over the precise prevalence of intellectual decline in particular

(Cottrell & Wilson, 1926; Ombredane, 1929). However, they are rarely reviewed in any detail, and thus crucial differences in focus and methodology are lost.

Cottrell and Wilson were interested primarily in the emotional or affective symptoms of MS, which they felt had never been adequately analyzed. Therefore, the psychiatric interview carried out in 100 unselected cases by Cottrell was structured around questions of emotional content, thought content, bodily feeling, and affective expression. Intellectual function was of only peripheral concern to these investigators and not examined in any detail; intellectual deterioration was reported in only two cases.

Ombredane, on the other hand, was concerned primarily with intellectual deficits, which his own experience and that of other continental authors placed among the characteristic symptoms of MS. Accordingly, he constructed a detailed examination of various cognitive functions, including attention, several aspects of memory, manipulation of spatial and temporal relationships, comprehension, imagination, calculation, and judgment. Based on this examination, Ombredane found that out of 50 random cases, 36 had definite intellectual difficulty, yielding a proportion of 72%. In 6 of these patients, the intellectual deficit took the form of a global dementia; the remaining 30 patients had selected deficits or a partial dementia, which he called the "dementing syndrome of MS." Of the latter group, Ombredane stated that the patients expressed opinions that made sense and that easily deceived the observer into considering their mental status normal, but as soon as one asked the patient to carry out intellectual exercises, the deficits became apparent.

Ombredane's testing techniques were forerunners of the neurobehavioral and neuropsychological evaluation methods currently in use, and his estimate of the frequency of cognitive deficit was much more in keeping with modern estimates than was Cottrell and Wilson's. It is unfortunate that Ombredane's thesis was not readily avilable in English and that no attempt was made to replicate it in the English-language literature.

Much of the impetus for mid-twentieth-century views of intellectual deficit came from Cottrell and Wilson's work and, perhaps more important, from the 1921 meeting of the Association for Research in Nervous and Mental Diseases (ARNMD) on MS. That commission concluded, on the basis of very inadequate data, that intellectual deterioration was not an important part of the symptomatology of MS. This view was perpetuated in the mainstream of neurologic literature and can be found even today in such standard texts as that of Adams and Victor (1977).

Meanwhile, in the neuropsychological literature, a different story was being told. Formal testing techniques were being applied, beginning with the Rorschach. Although this may accurately be considered a primitive neuropsychological tool, the protocols of MS patients were generally considered indicative of brain damage when analyzed for characteristics of this (Scheinberg, Blackburn, Kaim, & Stenger, 1953; Ross & Reitan, 1955). Harrower did not find Rorschach results suggestive of organicity in her sample of MS patients, but this group was biased by the exclusion of any subject with an IQ below the average range (Harrower, 1950; Harrower & Kraus, 1951).

Soon more sophisticated psychometric and neuropsychological techniques were applied to the question of cognitive disturbance in MS. In recent years, there has also been a resurgence of interest in, and a new conceptual approach to, affective disturbances and other psychopathologic conditions in MS. The balance of this chapter selectively reviews the neuropsychological literature; data on affective disturbance, psychosis, and personality adjustment is included so that the reader may understand just what is known about certain important neuropsychological aspects of MS and what directions future research might take.

Cognitive Disturbance

Samples of MS patients numbering up to 100 have been compared on a varietry of measures to normative data, to normative data factored by individual premorbid estimates, and to such diverse control groups as normal subjects, psychiatric populations, heterogenous brain-damaged groups, and patients with other degenerative neurologic diseases. Excluding from consideration those studies based on outdated measures or IQ tests alone, which are unreliable in documenting neuropsychological deficits, the general conclusion to be drawn on the basis of this literature is that cognitive impairment of some type is a frequent occurrence in patients with multiple sclerosis.

A study by Reitan, Reed, and Dyken (1971) exemplifies work finding significant differences between the performance of MS patients and that of normal control subjects on a standard neuropsychological battery. The Halstead-Reitan Battery was administered to 30 MS patients in whom the diagnosis was considered unequivocal. Disease length was quite variable, ranging from less than 1 year to 10.43 years. The same tests were administered to 30 normal control subjects matched for sex, age, and education. Statistically significant differences were observed on all tasks, with the exception of three Wechsler-Bellevue Verbal subtests and the Time Sense Test, which has since been dropped from the battery, with the largest differences seen on measures that depend at least in part on adequate motor functioning.

Research by Matthews, Cleeland, and Hopper (1970) illustrates work comparing the performance of MS patients to that of "brain-damaged" control subjects on the Halstead-Reitan Battery and additional motor measures. Thirty MS patients diagnosed by the Schumacher criteria were selected for study. Length of disease information was not provided for the sample. Each MS patient was individually matched for age, sex, education, and Wechsler Adult Intelligence Scale (WAIS) Full Scale IQ with a patient with CNS disease other than MS. This brain-damaged group was heterogenous, including cases of idiopathic epilepsy, closed head injury, cerebrovascular accident (CVA), CNS degenerative disease, toxic encephalopathy, Parkinson's disease, and neoplasm. Significant differences between the two groups occurred only on pure motor measures, Trails A, tactile form recognition, and minutes per block on the Tactual Performance Test (TPT). In each instance, the MS group performed more poorly. Point biserial correlations eliminated Trails A, tactile form recognition, and TPT as important variables, leaving grooved pegboard, static and kinetic tremor, and finger tapping rate as the major discriminating measures.

In both these studies, the poor motor performances of the MS patients stand out. In fact, it has been suggested that presumed cognitive deficits in MS patients are merely an artifact of motor deficits or vulnerability to motor fatigue (Diers & Brown, 1950; Fink & Houser, 1966; Beatty & Gange, 1977). Careful examination of this data reveals that such is not the case. MS patients exhibit significantly greater impairment than do normal subjects and impairment equal to that of subjects with other types of pathologic CNS conditions on abstract conceptualization tasks, such as the Category Test, which have no appreciable motor component and no time factor involved in scoring (Ross &

Reitan, 1955; Matthews, Cleeland, & Hopper, 1970; Reitan, Reed, & Dyken, 1971; Goldstein & Shelly, 1974; Ivnik, 1978b; Peyser, Edwards, Poser, & Filskov, 1980). Comparisons of MS patients and subjects with muscular dystrophy, other neurologic disease, or physical impairment confirm the presence of intellectual impairment or deterioration independent of motor impairment or fatigue (Surridge, 1969; Jambor, 1969; Staples & Lincoln, 1979).

Certainly, many MS patients have significant motor weakness or tremor, which could interfere in test performance. To just what extent lower scores on tasks such as the Wechsler Performance subtests reflect motor as opposed to problem-solving skills has been the subject of some debate (Marsh, 1980; Vowels & Gates, 1984). Parsons, Stewart, and Arenberg (1957) examined the source of the significantly poorer scores of MS patients relative to scores of normal control subjects on the Grassi Block Substitution Test, a task similar to Block Design. The group differences held even when the effects of visuomotor difficulty were controlled by matching Performance IQs, and it was determinmed that accuracy rather than time accounted for the group differences. While we are inclined to agree that motor problems do not provide the whole basis for impaired scores on tests such as the WAIS or the Tactual Performance test, we would nevertheless urge great caution in the use of heavily motor-dependent tests in group experimental designs. Greater reliance must be placed on the results of nonmotor tasks (Peyser & Becker, 1984).

It has also been suggested that the psychological distress associated with chronic disease or other psychopathologic conditions, particularly depression, has a detrimental effect on the intellectual performance of MS patients (Goldstein & Shelley, 1974). While the possibility of pseudodementia in MS is not an unreasonable proposition, it has not proven to exist in populations in which it has been directly studied. Ross and Reitan's (1955) MS group performed worse than did a control group, which, while technically labeled normal because they had no known pathologic cerebral conditions, actually consisted of depressed, anxious, and paraplegic persons. Jambor (1969) found that his population of MS patients who had been psychiatrically identified as depressed did no more poorly, and in fact did better on some measures, than did nondepressed MS patients. Similarly, Surridge found distinct differences in performance on mental status examination (MSE) between MS patients and patients with muscular dystrophy, a diagnosis that carries equal or graver implications in terms of physical disability and death. We found in our sample no correlation between depression, as measured by Scale 2 of the Minnesota Multiphasic Personality Inventory (MMPI), and number of errors on the Category Test (Peyser, Edwards, Poser, & Filskov, 1980). Schiffer and colleagues have demonstrated that patients with a history of major depressive episodes do not perform differently on neuropsychological screening than do those without such episodes (Schiffer, Caine, Bamford, & Levy, 1983). In a related vein, Rao and colleagues have concluded, through statistical analysis and comparison with pain patients, that neither psychosocial factors nor psychotropic medications prescribed for mood disturbances are major determinants of memory impairment in patients with chronic progressive MS (Rao, Hammeke, McQuillen, Khatri, & Lloyd, 1984). Heaton and colleagues also found no significant differences in neuropsychological test performance between medicated and unmedicated groups of MS patients (Heaton, Nelson, Thompson, Burks, & Franklin, 1985).

To reiterate, cognitive impairment does occur in MS patients. It does not appear to be secondary to extraneous or other disease-related factors. It seems eminently reasonable to assume, then, that it is the direct result of demyelinating plaques involving cortical and, primarily, subcortical structures.

Prevalence

Studies such as that of Reitan, Reed, & Dyken (1971) demonstrate that intellectual impairment occurs in a sufficient number of MS patients to render them statisticallay different, as a group, from normal subjects. It would be more useful, from a clinical point of view, to have answers to the questions of exactly how many MS patients exhibit cognitive deficits and in what degree of severity.

Parsons, Stewart, and Arenberg (1957) noted that 65% of their 17 subjects with a mean disease of 7.7 years were impaired in terms of abstracting ability, as tested by the Grassi. Desmedt and colleagues arrived at the same figure after examining 46 patients with a mean disease length of 15.7 years for deterioration from estimated premorbid levels in WAIS scores (Desmedt, Severts, Geutjens, & Medaer, 1984). In a group of 108 subjects with a mean length of illness of approximately 10 years, Surridge (1960) found evidence of intellectual deterioration in 61% on formal mental status examination. Staples and Lincoln (1979) found 60% of their 64 MS patients to have memory impairment. Disease length is not reported by Staples and Lincoln; instead, the patients are described as having "severe longstanding disability" for a mean of 15.9 years. Peyser, Edwards, Poser, and Filskov (1980), studying a random sample of 52 patients with a mean reported length of illness of 10.31 years and a mean diagnosed length of 6.81 years, found nearly 55% to be impaired on the Category Test. Bertrando, Maffei, and Ghezzi (1983) found the same percentage to be impaired on the Luria Nebraska Neuropsychological Battery in a study of 22 patients with a mean illness length of 7.7 years. It appears, then, that if one looks at a population of patients who are heterogenous in terms of disease length, somewhat more than half will show evidence of some form of cognitive impairment.

The first empirical evidence of differences in rate of impairment in the two subtypes of MS comes from a recently completed study by Heaton, Nelson, Thompson, Burks, & Franklin (1985) of 100 MS patients with a mean age of 37.4 years and mean disease length of 9.4 years. This population was drawn from consecutive admissions to a regional MS clinic, excluding those patients in acute exacerbation or too severely impaired to complete testing, and was further broken down into remitting-relapsing (N-57) and chronic-progressive (N-43) groups. Blind clinical ratings of an expanded Halstead-Reitan Neuropsychological Battery placed 68% of the remitting-relapsing group in the impaired range, while 98% of the chronic-progressive group fell in that range. Lower percentages of impairment were derived when only those measures with no motor component were analyzed, but the ratio of impairment between the two groups remained approximately the same. It is interesting to note that the average of the rates of pure cognitive impairment for the remitting-relapsing (46%) and chronic-progressive (72%) groups is in keeping with estimates from the more heterogenous groups studied previously.

Severity

There has been a trend in the neuropsychological literature to characterize cognitive deficit in MS as mild (Goldstein & Shelly, 1974; Beatty & Gange, 1977). The first group of authors to do so was Reitan, Reed, & Dyken (1971), who stated, "The patients with MS showed relatively mild impairment in tasks requiring abstract reasoning and logical analysis, an area that has been shown to be more seriously deficient in many studies of patients with other types of cerebral disease or damage" (p. 218).

Looking at the mean Category score of 50.07 obtained by the MS sample in their study, it is not difficult to see how Reitan, Reed, and Dyken drew this conclusion. However, as a point of comparison, we might note that the mean Category scores of heterogenous brain-damaged populations to whom MS patients have been compared have not been much higher than this (Ross & Reitan, 1955; Matthews, Cleeland, & Hopper, 1970; Ivnik, 1978b). In the one report in which the brain-damaged controls had much higher Category scores, the MS group also did (Goldstein & Shelly, 1974).

Rather than attempt to infer gradation of deficit from group means, it is more satisfactory to look at those studies that have examined this question directly. Surridge (1969) quantified intellectual deterioration by three grades based on whether patients could still function at something like the premorbid level and whether they could still take part in normal family conversation. Of the patients studied, 40.7% showed evidence of slight deterioration; 13.9% moderate deterioration; and 6.5%, severe deterioration. This is a particularly useful quantification strategy because, while it is not without problems in terms of subjectivity, it goes to the heart of the information that patients and families want to know. These data suggest that approximately 20% of patients would exhibit prominent problems in work or social situations. Depending on the particular job demand, a much higher percentage might have problems in that area while still being able to function in a satisfactory manner socially.

Other investigators have quantified impairment data from test performance, and some functional inferences might be made from their studies (Parsons, Stewart, & Arenberg, 1957; Rao, Hammeke, McQuillen, Khatri, & Lloyd, 1984; Desmedt, Severts, Geutjens, Madaer, 1984). Generally speaking, the percentages of patients in the moderate and severe groupings are higher than in the Surridge study, which may be related to differences in patient population or in sampling techniques. The group of Rao and colleagues, for example, was composed of chronic progressive MS patients, while the sample of Desmedt and colleagues was largely composed of hospitalized patients. However, Vowels and Gates (1984) have recently cited data on 100 MS patients tested through the Victorian MS Society in Australia. One-third were described as having marked deficits in frontal lobe functioning along with significant memory impairment and flattening of affect. Another one-half had moderate frontal impairment and of these functions, and one-half also had memory impairment and/or flattening of affect. These data would also suggest that the percentage of patients having severe and incapacitating neuropsychological deficits is even higher than in Surridge's study.

Course of Cognitive Impairment

The whole issue of the natural history of intellectual involvement in MS is of great importance, as it has implications not only for our understanding of the disease process but also for the counseling information that patients and their families receive.

Several studies have attempted, or purported, to address this issue, and their results, along with clinical observations, are often taken to indicate that intellectual deterioration is tied to disease severity of progression in general. This conclusion deserves close scrutiny.

Some investigators have related cognitive impairment to physical impairment. A typical method has been to divide patients into groups of mild, moderate, and severe disability and then to compare performances on tasks such as the Wechsler scales or the Grassi. Pratt (1951); Harrower (1951); Baldwin (1952); Parsons, Stewart, and Arenberg (1957); Fink and Houser (1960); and Staples and Lincoln (1979) have all found that severely disabled patients performed significantly more poorly than did the mildly disabled groups, or at least they found a trend in this direction.

In contrast to the works cited above, Peyser, Edwards, Poser, & Filskov (1980) found that Category scores did not correlate significantly with Kurtzke (1965) disability status ratings. Using a measure more difficult to interpret because of its resistance to decline, Marsh (1980) found no correlation between WAIS and Kurtzke scores. Kurtzke scores were found to be identical in groups of patients with and without brain-damage profiles on the Luria Nebraska Battery (Bertrando, Maffei, & Ghezzi, 1983). In chronic progressive MS patients, Rao and colleagues discovered no correlation between failure on a hypothesis-testing task and physical impairment, nor did they find differences in the Kurtzke ratings of those patients with memory impairment and those without (Rao & Hammeke, 1984; Rao, Hammeke, McQuillan, Khatri, & Lloyd, 1984). Desmedt, Severt, Geutjens, and Madaer (1984) failed to discover significant differences in physical impairment between intellectually deteriorated and undeteriorated subjects. Heaton, Nelson, Thompson, Burks, & Franklin (1985) have also concluded that cognitive dysfunction is largely independent of degree of physical disability.

We are generally of the opinion that physical disability is a red herring, at least in the way in which it has been studied to date. Physical disability is not necessarily proportionate to degree of neurologic involvement or extent of disease process. For example, a single lesion in the spinal cord rendering an individual paraparetic or paraplegic makes that patient an automatic four or five on the eight-point Kurtzke Disability Status Scale. Conversely, widespread CNS involvement has been demonstrated in patients who were close to symptom free at the time of death (Mackay & Hirano, 1967; Namerow & Thompson, 1969). A more apt question with regard to disability and intellectual deficits is to what extent cognitive deficits contribute to or impose functional limitations on the individual in his or her daily life.

The relationship of cognitive impairment and length of disease is a separate question, one that fewer investigators have examined. Peyser, Edwards, Poser, & Filskov (1980) noted a significant correlation coefficient between length of disease and impairment in abstract conceptualization, although the actual percent of variance accounted for was quite small. Similarly, Heaton, Nelson, Thompson, Burks, & Franklin (1985) described a modest correlation between disease length and neuropsychological functioning. Ivnik (1978a) studied the performances of three groups of MS patients, each of whom had been administered the Halstead-Reitan Battery for clinical reasons. Groupings were based on disease length: 1–5 years, 6–10, and greater than 10. The only area in which the "older" patients performed more poorly was in number of tactile extinctions. Ivnik went on to speculate that the failure to demonstrate any decline, which was deemed surprising in that even the motor performances failed to discriminate among the groups, was related to the neurologists' referral patterns and the patients' exacerbation-remission status at the time of testing. Ivnik felt that patients might be likely to be referred earlier in the disease course if their symptoms were particularly severe. However Rao and colleagues have also failed to find differences in disease length in MS patients with and without memory and abstracting impairment (Rao & Hammeke, 1984; Rao, Hammeke, McQuillan, Khatri, & Lloyd, 1984). While it may be inappropriate to generalize from their findings with the chronic progressive form of the disease, Knehr (1962); Beatty and Gange (1977); Bertrando, Maffei, and Ghezzi (1983); Desmedt, Severts, Geutjens, and Madaer (1984); and Vowels and Gates (1984), report similar results.

Other sources and types of information support these recent works, indicating that a cognitive impairment is not necessarily a late phenomenon in multiple sclerosis. Early cognitive loss and dementia as the presenting symptoms are documented in single and series presentations (Bergin, 1957; McLardy & Sinclair, 1964; O'Malley, 1966; Koenig, 1968; Young, Saunders & Ponsford, 1976; Goodstein & Ferrell, 1977). Borberg and Zahle (1946), studying euphoria and dementia in 330 patients, reported that in 41.6% of cases, the abnormalities were demonstrable within the first three years of disease onset and went on to say that most abnormalities were probably present long before they were diagnosed. Canter (1951a), who had a unique opportunity to compare Army General Classification Test (AGCT) scores before and after diagnosis in 23 MS patients, found significant losses after an average illness duration of four years.

It would not be surprising to find ultimately that there is some correlation between cognitive deficit and disease length, as, presumably, the chances of documenting almost any given sign or symptom increase with disease length. The available information, however, suggests that assumptions that cognitive decline is strictly tied to disease length or complacency regarding the late appearance of these symptoms are unwarranted.

Even more intriguing is the question of what happens to cognitive deficits once they are observed. We know that the pathologic lesions of MS vary in degree of symptomatic severity, giving the disease its characteristic picture of exacerbation and remission. Some of these lesions, despite apparently complete clinical remission, are still detectable with appropriate diagnostic tools, as seems to be the case with optic nerve lesions on evoked potential testing. One could speculate on the whole gamut of possibilities for expression of cerebral plaques through neuropsychological deficit in MS. Cerebral plaques could be asymptomatic or symptomatic; deficits could be observed on testing but perhaps not be apparent clinically, depending on the patient's situation; cognitive deficits could remit completely, remain stable, or increase in severity across time. Complicating the whole issue, of course, is the cumulative acquisition of plaques and the as yet unknown pathophysiologic factors influencing diseased expression or activity.

Earlier work by Canter (1951a), with the AGCT and Wechsler-Bellevue scales suggests a decline in performance even across the relatively short time span of six months. Text-retest studies are scarce in the recent literature. Ivnik (1978b) found that his group of 14 MS patients scored largely the same on the Halstead-Reitan Battery following an average interval of 37 months, with worsened performance on some motor measures, compared to a brain-damaged control group, which scored the same or improved on the various tests. While such results raise the possibility that cerebral plaques remain symptomatic at least on sophisticated testing, Ivnik's data are based on test-retest referrals made for clinical reasons. Thus, there is a possible bias in his sample if only those patients who were clinically in trouble of some sort were included.

The need for sound research on the natural history of cognitive impairment in MS remains critical. We need to evaluate patients neuropsychologically as they present with the first signs and symptoms that raise the possibility of a demyelinating process, with interval reevaluations thereafter. Patients must be compared in exacerbation and remission states as well. Correlations between neuropsychological laboratory findings and clinical mental status and complaints must also be made, and new imaging techniques, such as NMR, may at last make clinicopathologic correlations possible.

Characterization of Impairment

When MS patients are compared to heterogenous brain-damaged control subjects, the MS patients typically perform worse on motor tasks (Ross, Reitan, 1955; Matthews, Cleeland, & Hopper 1970; Goldstein & Shelley, 1974; Ivnik, 1978b). This is almost undoubtedly due to the additional cerebellar and spinal lesions of the MS patients. We have found in our sample, for example, high correlations between ratings of cerebellar disturbance and pegboard performance.

Rao and colleagues recently reported that chronic progressive MS patients with severe memory impairment had greater fine motor coordination deficits than did patients with lesser or no memory impairment. Since the memory task was not motor dependent, these investigators suggested that both memory and motor signs are the result of a similar distribution of plaques within the CNS, as has also been postulated to be the case with dementia in Parkinson's disease (Pirozzola, Hansch, Mortimer, Webster, & Kukowski, 1982; Rao, Hammeke, McQuillan, Khatri, & Lloyd, 1984). Autopsy work by Ikuta and Zimmerman (1976) may lend some support to this notion. In correlating locus of plaques in 70 patients, they found that 100% of patients who had extensive cerebellar involvement also had cerebral plaques. We would caution, however, that attempts to classify MS by anatomic subtypes have not been particularly successful in the past, and this whole area is at the moment purely speculative.

When MS patients are compared to normal control subjects and to neurologic control subjects without known cerebral involvement, abstract conceptualization and memory are most often identified as areas of impairment (Ross & Reitan, 1955; Parsons, Stewart, & Arenberg, 1957; Jambor, 1969; Surridge, 1969; Reitan, Reed, & Dyken 1971; Beatty & Gange, 1977; Staples & Lincoln, 1979; Peyser, Edwards, Poser, & Filskov, 1980; Lincoln, 1981; Rao, Hammeke, McQuillan, Khatri, & Lloyd, 1984; Rao & Hammeke, 1984; Vowels & Gates, 1984). There may be some element of experimenter bias here, as these have been the cognitive operations most frequently singled out for study in investigations in which a standard battery or survey approach is not used. Perhaps this is not only because memory and abstracting ability are considered important for daily function, but also because these skills are comparatively easy to study on tasks that are not subject to contamination by subtentorial motor involvement.

Recently, abstracting tasks have been combined with other tests assessing processes that are presumably frontal in origin, such as card sorting and word fluency. The results of such studies are assumed to indicate significant frontal lobe involvement in MS patients (Lincoln, 1981; Sevush & Sheremata, 1983; Vowels & Gates, 1984).

Spatial operations are perhaps the most difficult to assess cleanly in patients with MS, as motor function is typically required in the evaluation of these processes. Rao, Hammeke, McQuillen, Khatri, and Lloyd (1984) have noted that spatial recall on a low motor task was slightly worse than verbal recall in chronic progressive MS patients. Future research in this area will require considerable investigator creativity.

Old or overlearned verbal information or skills generally show fairly good preservation in MS, which is not surprising, since these are relatively impervious to many types of cerebral insult (Baldwin, 1952; Ross & Reitan, 1955; Matthews, Cleeland, & Hopper, 1970; Reitan, Reed, & Dyken, 1971; Goldstein & Shelley, 1974; Staples &

Lincoln, 1979; Peyser, Edwards, Poser, & Filskov, 1980; Lincoln, 1981; Vowels & Gates, 1984; Heaton, Nelson, Thompson, Burks, & Franklin, 1985).

Classic, focal aphasic disturbances are usually thought of as being uncommon in MS, although they have been reported (Bender, 1950; McLardy & Sinclair, 1964; Mackay & Hirano, 1967; Surridge, 1969; Kahana, Leibowitz, & Alter, 1971; Olmos-Lau, Ginsberg, & Geller, 1977) Language operations are only rarely included in the experimental arena in MS, with deficits being reported in naming and word fluency (Jambor, 1969; Lincoln, 1981; Sevush & Sheremata, 1983; Heaton, Nelson, Thompson, Burks, & Franklin, 1985). However, as with motor and other cognitive tasks, the potentially confusing presence of cerebellar speech disturbances must be considered in language evaluation.

We might point out that there is nothing unique about a pattern of impairment characterized by disturbance of memory and abstraction in the face of preservation of overlearned verbal skills. This pattern is, for example, quite typical of early Alzheimer's disease. But while the types of impairment thus far documented in MS patients may not have great differential diagnostic significance, the case management implications of this knowledge are quite clear.

Neuroanatomic and Neuropathologic Correlates

Autopsy data indicate that cerebral involvement in MS is almost universal and quite significant. In 70 unselected cases, Ikuta and Zimmerman (1976) found that 51% of cases had extensive plaque formation, another 26% had large plaques, and 20% had small plaques. Only 2 cases, or 3%, had no cerebral involvement. Data from Brownell and Hughes (1962) indicate that plaques can occur virtually anywhere in the cerebrum. They are of course predominantly located in the white matter, but 26% of 1,594 cerebral plaques (found in 22 consecutive cases, indicating what *extensive* can mean) were located at the junction of cortex and white matter, in the cortex itself, or in the central gray matter. The largest single percentage, 40%, were located periventricularly; 22% were located in the frontal lobes. Looking at autopsy data in 60 consecutive cases from a somewhat different perspective, Lumsden (1970) found that 90.3% of cases had periventricular demyelination, while 93.5% had plaques within the gyri, with the largest single percentage of these located within the superior frontal gyrus.

These data establish quite clearly the difficulties inherent in trying to make one-to-one correlations between neuropsychologic deficit and anatomic lesion in MS, given the sheer multiplicity of both lesion number and site.

However, the data also indicate the high prevalence of periventricular and frontal lobe plaques, potential causes of, among other things, limbic and frontal dysfunction. Some authors have made the case that many, if not all, of the various personality changes, mood disturbances, and cognitive deficits in MS can be accounted for by frontal lobe dysfunction (Sevush & Sheremata, 1983; Rao & Hammeke, 1984; Rao, Hammeke, McQuillen, Khatri, & Lloyd, 1984; Vowels & Gates, 1984). Most recently, limited preliminary data from positron emission tomography (PET) scanning research have suggested equal and bilateral deafferentation of both the temporal and the frontal cortex in patients with subcortical lesions in these lobes (Sheremata, 1985).

Ventricular enlargement, when present, has been correlated with degree of intellectual impairment (Barnard & Triggs, 1974; Rao, Glatt, Hammeke, Rhodes, & Pollard, 1984). Atrophy of the corpus callosum associated with gross ventricular enlargement has also been proposed as a mechanism of mental impairment (Barnard & Triggs, 1974).

Patients with other neurologic evidence of cerebral involvement, including hemi-paresis with ipsilateral sensory loss, convulsions, aphasia, homonymous hemianopsia, abnormal EEG, and abnormal CAT scan, do not exhibit greater neuropsychological impairment than do those with predominantly spinal cord or cerebellar disease mani-festation (Schiffer, Caine, Bamford, & Levy, 1983). This finding is particularly inter-esting, as it suggests that the presence or absence of other neurologic markers of cerebral involvement cannot be reliably used to predict cognitive disturbance or as an indication for neuropsychological consultation.

As yet, methods of visualizing plaques during life have been fairly gross and unsatisfactory, and psychometric correlations have also been problematic (Kalb & LaRocca, 1985). As newer methods for imaging the lesions of MS and dating their activity become available, serial neuropsychological evaluations will be important in establishing neurobehavioral correlations.

Psychopathology

As with other diseases and lesions of the central nervous system, affective, personality, and psychotic disturbances may occur in MS, and represent some of the most intriguing sequelae of this disease. In science, *intriguing* is a euphemism meaning that the unknown equals or exceeds the known. We will now explore the known and unknown issues in psychopathology associated with multiple sclerosis.

Euphoria

The affective disturbance that has had the longest, the most curious, and at times the most misunderstood association with multiple sclerosis is euphoria. Characterized as a marked inconsistency between the patient's mood and his or her physical disability, a sense of complacency if not outright optimism in the face of physical deficit, euphoria was frequently mentioned in early case reports and by the turn of the century had come to be considered a hallmark of the disease, at least insofar as mental changes were concerned (Ross, 1915; Brown & Davis, 1921; Birley & Dudgeon, 1921; Sacks & Friedman, 1922; Brown & Davis, 1922; Cottrell & Wilson, 1926.

In spite of its historical position as the hallmark emotional characteristic, there has been little consensus on the actual prevalence of euphoria in MS. Estimates range from as low as 5% to as high as 63% in surveyed samples (Brown & Davis, 1921; Cottrell & Wilson, 1926; Langworthy, Kolb, & Androp 1941; Sugar & Nadell, 1943; Borberg & Zahle, 1946; Braceland & Giffin, 1950; Sai-Halasz, 1956; Surridge, 1969; Kahana, Leibowitz, & Alter, 1971).

While differences in sampling and examination methods account for some of the variation in these estimates, at the heart of the matter is the subjectivity of the diagnosis, the degree of indifference versus frank elevation of mood accepted as evidence of euphoria, and the examiner's personal assumptions concerning mood disturbance. Baldwin (1952), for example, feels that cheerfulness exhibited by MS patients is mistakenly called euphoria based on the examiner's feeling that the patient should be depressed. She further hypothesizes that such cheerfulness is a culturally determined and reinforced behavior among the chronically ill that may indeed mask a depression. Arguing exactly the opposite point, Borberg and Zahle (1946) state that euphoria is often misjudged by lay observers as a voluntary effort to bear the burden of the disease heroically.

A particularly interesting but, we believe, unfortunate conceptualization of euphoria and its relationship to the disease process arose during the middle part of this century. We would like to digress for a moment into the convolutions of this position, in hopes of laying it to rest forever.

While early students of MS apparently considered a euphoric mood state the direct result of the disease process, having moria in general paresis as a model, and scattered reports continued to assert a connection between euphoria and dementia (Brown & Davis, 1921; Cottrell & Wilson, 1926; Borberg & Zahle, 1946; Braceland & Giffin, 1950; Sai-Halasz, 1956), a psychodynamic interpretation of euphoria was put forward with considerable vigor by several authors.

Sugar and Nadell (1948), in an observation study of dubious methodology, determined that euphoria was the prevailing mood in 15 of their series of 28 patients. (Dysphoria was the prevailing mood in five, and in the other eight, mood was labile.) The authors further stated that in 23 of the 28 subjects, the abnormal mood state was an exaggeration of the prevailing mood premorbidly, concluding that affective disturbance in MS patients followed from their previous personality makeup.

A series of reports then appeared linking euphoria to a premorbid personality style, most often characterized as immature or hysterical, which was purportedly typical of the MS patient (Langworthy, 1948, 1950; Adams, Sutherland, & Fletcher, 1950; Grinker, Ham, & Robbins, 1950; Langworthy & LeGrand, 1952; Geocaris, 1957; Philippopoulos, Wittkower, & Cousineau, 1958). Groups of patients, many of them quite small and almost uniformly drawn from psychoanalytic files or other psychiatric populations without regard to the sampling bias this introduced, were described as psychosexually immature and emotionally abnormal long before any signs of organic disease appeared. In some instances, the negative descriptions of MS patients knew no bounds. Grinker, Ham, and Robbins (1950), for example, said that with the progression of disease, the "patient may neurologically actually become the infant that he has always been psychologically" (p. 459).

Not surprisingly, causal relationships between personality style and subsequent disease development were proposed by these authors. The most popular was a psychosomatic vascular etiology in the formation of cerebral plaques, based on vascular spasm precipitated by inner rage reactions that had no outlet. The most outrageous was a disturbance of myelination during early childhood based on these psychologically disturbed individuals' greater constitutional need for, but failure to meet, external dietary sources. A wide variety of stresses and changes in life situation were considered the final precipitants of overt neurologic symptoms.

A key supposition in these writings is that euphoria is an extension of the premorbid, predisposing personality style of the MS patient. As Grinker and colleagues (1950) put it, "according to fundamental, premorbid character, the patients repressed all negative feelings and seemed satisfied and cheerful with what they received" (p. 548). Langworthy (1950) stated that "patients with multiple sclerosis are often foolishly euphoric, possibly because their anxiety is converted" (p. 603). In this formulation, then, euphoria is akin to *la belle indifférence*. This position was abetted by early MMPI studies that attempted to document a uniform response to the disease and generally characterized patients as neurotic, with elevations appearing on scales 1, 2, and 3 (Canter, 1951b; Shontz, 1955; Ross & Reitan, 1955; Gilberstadt & Farkas, 1961). The fact that women outnumber men in this disease and a long-held popular notion of an association between MS and hysteria (e.g., Brain, 1930) may have been subtle contributants as well.

The idea that euphoria is based on a hysterical or neurotic personality style in MS is untenable on a number of counts. Gross errors in sampling techniques of the type previously described, lack of objective data, and lack of controls render most of these "studies" invalid from a scientific point of view. In controlled research, no difference in premorbid personality styles has been found between MS patients and patients with other neurologic diseases, and hysteria was in fact less common in the MS patients (Pratt, 1951). It is also interesting to note that the previously cited investigators, who based descriptions of MS patients as neurotic on MMPI profiles, used male only or male predominant samples as the basis for their generalizations. There is actually evidence that men, not only in response to MS but to other chronic diseases and pain problems as well, demonstrate greater distress or psychopathologic disturbances on standard measures than do women (Bourestom & Howard, 1956; Peyser, Edwards, & Poser, 1980; Wilson, Olson, Gascon, & Brumback, 1982). That there may be a link between stress or trauma and onset or exacerbations in MS has been the subject of many commentaries but few well-designed studies (Keschner, 1950; Pratt, 1951; Grinker, Ham, & Robbins, 1950; Langworthy, 1950; Adams, Sutherland, & Fletcher, 1950; Paulley, 1977; Mei-tal, Meyerowitz, & Engel, 1950; Poser, 1980; Miller, 1964; Russell, 1964; Warren, Greenhill, & Warren, 1982). The existence of a contributory relationship, possibly through the immune system, is an entirely plausible notion, but such a formulation most certainly does not depend on a premorbid hysterical personality style.

A careful study by Surridge (1969) reasserted the connection between euphoria and CNS involvement. This investigator studied 108 MS patients under the age of 40, to counteract possible involutional effects on mood, along with 39 muscular dystrophy control subjects. He found that 26 MS patients, or roughly one-quarter of the sample, could be called euphoric on the basis of interview and psychiatric evaluation. All but two of the euphoric patients exhibited other evidence of intellectual deterioration, and there was a strong correlation between increasing euphoria and increasing intellectual deterioration.

Surridge also noted that 11% of the MS patients demonstrated anosognosia and that the majority of these were euphoric. While he was referring to frank denial of neurologic deficit, similar phenomena had been reported earlier at even higher levels. Cottrell and Wilson (1926) coined the term *eutonia sclerotica* for the sense of physical well-being, unwarranted by objective condition, found in 84% of their sample of 100 consecutive cases. Sugar and Nadell (1943) observed a genuine sense of physical well-being in half of their 28 patients, while Harrower (1950; Harrower & Kraus, 1951) found that "an overdose of excessive cordiality" (p. 465) along with a marked absence of concern, anxiety, and emotional preoccupation with bodily symptoms characterized the test protocols of MS patients. Sai-Halasz (1956) states that hyponosognosia was a comparatively frequent phenomenon in his sample of 200 MS patients (although he does not give a specific figure); it does not always run parallel to euphoria, but it is associated with a decrease in critical power and frequently with other symptoms of frontal character. Sai-Halasz attributes hyponosognosia to a parietal focus.

While the existing data makes a very good case for euphoria's being a pathologic mood state resulting from CNS involvement, a number of questions remain unanswered. Since it has been variously stated that euphoria is an early symptom (Borberg & Zahle, 1946), that it increases with length of disease (Brown & Davis, 1922), and that duration plays no role (Sai-Halasz, 1956), it seems safe to say that we know nothing reliable concerning the natural history of euphoria in MS. To some extent, this may be tied to questions concerning the natural history of cognitive disturbance, but we should point out that euphoria is not a necessary concomitant of intellectual deterioration, as it appears that substantially greater numbers of patients show evidence of intellectual deficit than of euphoria. The specifics of the relationship of euphoria to lesion site or disease process have not been determined. We might speculate that euphoria is in some cases the result of generalized deficits so severe that the patient simply fails to appreciate his or her limitations. Whether there is an increased association with anterior plaques, what role periventricular plaques interrupting corticothalamic projections might play, or whether there is an increased association with right hemisphere involvement, as with anosognosia and anosodiaphoria in right hemisphere CVA, all remain to be seen.

Depression

Despite the popularity of euphoria as *the* abnormal mood state in MS, several authors have asserted, on grounds ranging from "experience" to careful research, that depression is an equally or more prevalent finding (Braceland & Giffin, 1950; Baldwin, 1952; Gallineck & Kalinowsky, 1958; Surridge, 1969; Baretz & Stephenson, 1981).

What can be stated with certainty is that problems in terminology and definition are equally or more serious with depression than with euphoria. There is a significant difference between depression defined as a dysphoric mood state and depression as defined by Diagnostic and Statistical Manual (DSM) or Research Diagnostic Criteria (RDC) criteria for major depressive syndrome. That is, when investigators speak of depression, it is necessary to understand whether they are referring to a simple mood state or a full-blown syndrome with neurovegetative signs. There are also problems with, or at least noteworthy differences in, the varying identification of depression by self-report scale and by clinical interview. If the latter method is used, additional variation may be introduced into the data depending on whether the investigator considers masking of depression. Accordingly, there is great variation in incidence figures, based on what is actually being reported (Cottrell & Wilson, 1926; Sugar & Nadell, 1943; Braceland & Giffin, 1950; Sai-Halasz, 1956; Surridge, 1969; Baretz & Stephenson, 1981; Schiffer, Caine, Bamford, & Levy, 1983; Schiffer & Babigan, 1984).

As with euphoria, depression may be found in early case reports. In some instances, there was the apparently implicit assumption that depression was related to plaques, but Vulpian (1896) attributed sadness to the course of the disease and resulting dependency of the patient. At the 1921 ARNMD meeting on MS, Jelliffe (1921) expounded on psychological reactions to the disease process, and Brown and Davis (1921) classified depressions as secondary rather than primary correlates of the disease. Thus, the concept of depression evolved into a functional reaction to knowledge of diagnosis and to physical impairments. Relatively little was written about depression in the middle part of this century. In part, this may have been due to the fact that the psychiatric focus at that time was on premorbid personality characteristics. But in larger part, it may have been related to the face validity of depression as a reactive process. After all, it is understandable that someone who has an incapacitating or potentially incapacitating disease might be depressed. Bolstering this notion is the fact that consistent correlations between depression and cognitive deficit have not been demonstrated (Jambor, 1969; Peyser, Edwards, Poser, & Filskov, 1980; Schiffer, Caine, Bamford, & Levy, 1983).

However, work demonstrating greater depression in MS patients than in patients with other neurologic diseases or physical handicaps forces us to call this assumption into question.

Whitlock and Siskind (1980) retrospectively compared 30 MS patients to 30 neurologic control subjects with degenerative cerebellar, motor neuron, and muscular diseases. Eight of the MS patients had had depressive episodes before diagnosis of their neurologic illness, while none of the control subjects had. Since diagnosis, 16 of the MS patients had episodes meeting the criteria for endogenous depression, while only 5 of the control subjects had. These researchers also found a significantly higher level of depression in the MS group, as measured by the Beck Depression Inventory, at the time of study, This parallels the distinct trend in Surridge's work of finding multiple sclerosis patients to be more depressed than muscular dystrophy patients. Baldwin (1952) also reported significantly higher scores on the D scale of the MMPI in her MS group compared to a control group matched for level of neurologic disability. In an epidemiologic study of psychopathology in MS, Schiffer and Babigan (1984) identified all patients with diagnoses of MS (381), amyotrophic lateral sclerosis (ALS; 124), and temporal lobe epilepsy (TLE; 402) seen at the University of Rochester hospitals during the years 1965–1978. The ALS group was chosen as a control because of the grave prognosis of that illness; TLE was selected as another control neurologic disease by virtue of its chronic and intermittent nature. The MS and TLE groups had significantly greater match to the psychiatric register for the county than did the ALS group, of whom only 4.8% had had formal mental health contact. While the MS and TLE groups had similar rates of psychiatric contact, 19.3% and 22.9%, respectively, the MS patients were significantly more likely to have received a diagnosis of depressed affect than were the TLE patients.

Even more intriguing are a number of case reports of major depressive disorders or depressive psychoses as the presenting symptom in MS (Malone, 1937; Borberg & Zahle, 1946; Bergin, 1957; Mur, Kumpel, & Dostal, 1966; Young, Sounders, & Ponsford 1976; Goodstein & Ferrell, 1977; Matthews, 1979; Kellner, Davenport, Post, & Ross, 1984). Goodstein and Ferrell, for example, present a series of three cases in which depressive episodes meeting the DSM-III criteria for a major depressive disorder with melancholia or the criteria for a RDC major depressive disorder, endogenous subtype, preceded clinical evidence for the diagnosis of MS. Each case had been refractory to usual therapeutic measures, one of the diagnostic clues that Goodstein and Ferrell say should lead to a thorough neurologic workup for MS. Parenthetically, each patient had cognitive impairment on the Halstead-Reitan Battery at the time of diagnosis.

In considering the greater depression seen in MS patients compared to those with other conditions, one could still argue that the disease process in MS is so unique that reactive depressions preferentially occur in this illness. MS is, for example, unpredictably progressive, making comparisons to such stable deficits as spinal cord injury problematic. Another difficulty MS patients face is the fact that many of their important deficits are hidden from public view (Burnfield & Burnfield, 1978); this stands in opposition to a disease such as ALS, which, having an undeniably grave prognosis, is likely to spontaneously generate tremendous familial and professional support.

However, in cases in which depressive episodes precede major neurologic signs and symptoms, one cannot say that physical deficits or knowledge of the diagnosis caused a reactive depression. The question then becomes: Was the depression a separate and unrelated phenomenon, or was it related to demyelination within the central nervous system? Based on our knowledge of neurotransmitter abnormalities associated with major depressive disorders in general (Baldessarini, 1983) and analogous work by Robinson and Szetela (1981) on depressive disorders following left hemisphere CVA attributed to disruption of norepinephrine pathways, we find it most plausible to assume that organically based depression can be a presenting symptom in MS. An increasing number of investigators feel that depressive episodes, both pre- and post-diagnosis, are at least in part based on pathologic CNS conditions (Malone, 1937; Borberg & Zahle, 1946; Goodstein & Ferrell, 1977; Whitlock & Siskind, 1980; Dalos, Rabins, Brooks, & O'Donnell, 1983; Schiffer, Caine, Bamford, & Levy, 1983; Schiffer & Babigian, 1984).

It is appropriate to at least mention suicide in any discussion of depression, and the reader may be thinking of another chronic CNS disease with associated emotional disturbance, Huntington's disease, which has a relatively high suicide rate. The only widely available figure is in the survey study by Kahana and colleagues of Israeli MS patients, which puts the suicide rate at 3%, or 14 times that of the general population of that country. This finding is in contrast to general clinical lore and to a more obscure study by Schwartz and Pierron (1972). These investigators surveyed Michigan death certificates from the period 1955–1971, finding 408 instances in which MS was listed as the cause of death. Only four of these were reported as suicide, making the frequency of suicide the same percentage of deaths attributed to suicide in the United States. In Vermont, a state that has both a high rate of suicide and a high incidence of MS, not a single suicide in the past eight years had MS (E. McQuillen, personal communication). On closer reflection, a facile explanation for the difference in suicide rates between Huntington's disease and multiple sclerosis can be found in the fact that Huntington's disease is directly heritable, and anyone having this illness will have watched a relative deteriorate and eventually die in a particularly unpleasant fashion, while such is not the case in MS. The relatively low rate of suicide among MS patients may also be based on the fact that these patients have a tendency toward unusual optimism and denial regarding their disease.

There is still much to be learned about depression in MS in terms of both simple and general dysphoria and distinct major depressive illness, and future researchers must specify which type of affective disturbance they are considering. Beyond knowing that depressive disorders may be the initial presentation, we really know nothing of the natural history of depression in MS. The first clue to neurologic correlates is in Schiffer's 1983 study (Schiffer, Caine, Bamford, & Levy, 1983), in which he and his colleagues found a significantly greater number of patients with a history of major depressive disorder in that group of patients with other neurologic evidence of cerebral involvement. He has elsewhere proposed (Schiffer & Babigan, 1984) that potential explanations for the increased rate of depressive diagnoses in MS, and hence lines for future research, include structural involvement of limbic regions by demyelination, possible shared genetic vulnerabilities to both depression and MS, and selective alterations of monoamine metabolism within the CNS.

Other Mood and Personality Changes

Emotional lability has also been stressed as a symptom in patients with multiple sclerosis. This must, of course, be separated from the forced laughter and crying of pseudobulbar palsy, but most authors have observed the distinction, identifying modest percentages of patients with disorders of emotional expression characterized by overreactive mood, facility of emotional expression, and/or affective expression that is incongruent with underlying mood state (Birley & Dudgeon, 1921; Cottrell & Wilson, 1926; Sugar & Nadell, 1943; Braceland & Giffin, 1950; Sai-Halasz, 1956; Lemere, 1966; Kahana, Leibowitz, & Alter, 1971). When outward expression does not match emotional feeling, it is apparently most likely that the affect is euphoric while mood is depressed (Cottrell & Wilson, 1926; Sugar & Nadell, 1943; Surridge, 1969). Emotional lability is almost universally attributed to organic involvement.

Other personality changes, most notably irritability, have been described as well in MS (Braceland & Giffin, 1950; Sai-Halasz, 1956; Lemere, 1966; Surridge, 1969; Peyser, Edwards, & Poser, 1980; Rao, Hammeke, McQuillen, Khatri, & Lloyd, 1984; Vowels & Gates, 1984). Surridge found that personality changes characterized by irritability (at 20.4%), apathy (9.3%), and increased sexuality (3.7%) were significantly more common among MS than in a control group of muscular dystrophy patients and correlated highly with intellectual deterioration.

As a final note on this topic, we would point out that there is a substantial body of literature on emotional or psychological adjustment to multiple sclerosis. To be sure, there are a number of issues patients must deal with pertaining to chronic disease and potential or real physical disability in general and the unique problems of MS in particular. However, we hope that future research on this topic will take into account the limiting or extenuating role of intellectual deficit in psychological reaction to this disease.

Psychosis

Psychoses in MS are reported on a case-by-case basis in the literature, either singly (Bassoe, 1917; Howes, 1927; Arbuse, 1938; Schmalzbach, 1954; Parker, 1956; McLardy & Sinclair, 1964; Hollender & Steckler, 1972; Awad, 1983) or in series (Ross, 1915; Malone, 1937; Langworthy, Kolb & Androp, 1941; Geocaris, 1957; Gallineck & Kalinowsky, 1957; Mur, Kumpel, & Dostal, 1966; Matthews, 1979). Actual prevalence figures are few in number and poor in agreement.

The number of diagnosed cases of MS among psychiatric admissions is less than 1 in 1300 (Brown & Davis, 1921; Howes, 1927; Parker, 1956; Hollender & Steckler, 1972), although early on, Brown and Davis made the observation that estimates made on the basis of hospital data are likely to be inaccurate, as physical impairment may render the patient "psychiatrically nonpotential." In survey studies, Kahana, Leibowitz, and Alter (1971) recorded psychoses at 6% in a series of 295, while Langworthy, Kolb, and Androp (1941) found that 16, or 8%, of a series of 199 had behavioral disturbances requiring psychiatric hospitalization, although it is not clear that all of these were for psychotic disturbances. In research based on record review and individual psychiatric interview, Surridge (1969) found one case of schizophrenia in 108 MS patients.

Unlike some other CNS diseases, such as Huntington's disease, in which the psychopathologic condition assumes a similar form in most patients, MS does not exhibit a particular character or common tone of psychoses, according to authors reporting in the literature. To our reading, and of course with the benefit of more modern understanding of the role of the CNS in behavior, many of the reports sound more like general behavioral regression than schizophrenia, while others seem to have been acute confusional states. Some of the reports feature visual hallucinations, which lends support to the thought that they are organic. Hypersexuality in the absence of any other indication of mania has been reported. While this has been rather amusingly attributed to various causes in the past, including supposition of Langworthy, Kolb, and Androp (1941) that it represents psychological denial of impotence, today it is known that hypersexuality indicates limbic system dysfunction.

Psychoses in MS apparently tend to occur before diagnosis. In such cases, workup of the apparently psychotic patient leads to the diagnosis of MS, so in that sense they can be a presenting feature. There is also a tendency for these episodes to be of brief duration and nonrecurrent (Borberg & Zahle, 1946; Schmalzbach, 1954; Parker, 1956; Bergin, 1957; Geocaris, 1957; Philippopoulos, Wittkower, & Cousineau, 1958; Mur, Kumpel, & Dostal, 1966; Hollender & Steckler, 1974; Matthews, 1979).

In all, both the literature and clinical experience suggest that psychosis is not a common problem in MS, occurring in perhaps fewer than 1% of patients, but when it does occur, an organic substrate should be suspected.

NEUROPSYCHOLOGICAL EVALUATION

There are three important roles for neuropsychological evaluation in MS, the foremost being case planning and management. In the absence of definitive treatment or cure for MS, symptomatic management and psychological support are of the utmost importance. Job performance, family and peer interaction, and the acquisition of and compliance with such therapeutic measures as self-catherization are all dependent on the integrity of certain intellectual processes. Problems in any of these areas should be a signal for a neuropsychological evaluation, even if intellectual deficit is not immediately apparent to the examining physician.

The importance of formal evaluation, performed by a qualified neuropsychologist using validated measures, is underscored by research directly comparing neurologists' estimates of cognitive deficit and identification via neuropsychological testing. Peyser, Edwards, Poser, & Filskov (1980) found that almost one-half of patients judged to be cognitively intact on neurologic examinations were actually impaired on the Category Test. Heaton, Nelson, Thompson, Burks, & Franklin (1985) and Sevush and Sheremata (1983) have reported similar findings. This is to some extent a reflection of the relative preservation of old and overlearned verbal skills of the types readily observable in an examination setting. Time constraints and in some cases inadequate patient self-report may compound the problems neurologists have in making these assessments (Lincoln, 1981; Peyser, 1983; Schiffer, Rudick, & Herndon, 1983).

Proposing neuropsychological evaluation can be a difficult task for anyone responsible for the care of an MS patient. There are already a number of sensitive issues that the neurologist and patient must confront, including loss of basic physical capabilities, bowel and bladder incontinence, and sexual dysfunction. The fact that the course of these symptoms cannot be predicted with certainty in any given patient only adds insult to injury. As an eminent colleague of ours recently commented, "It's not that we haven't known about cognitive deficits in MS, but there has been a conspiracy of silence."

Demands by employers, family members, and care givers that the MS patient is unable to meet can be extremely threatening and frustrating, and in our experience patients are actually relieved to learn the source of their problem even if that cause is cerebral involvement. Two case examples are illustrative. A man in his thirties who had had MS for some years complained to his neurologist that he was not doing well at his job, although he could not say why this was the case. His physician, being unable to clarify the complaint by history or neurologic examination, referred him for neuropsychological evaluation. The patient proved to have a significant visuospatial disturbance and constructional dyspraxia, and it became immediately apparent why he could not do his job, since he was employed as a draftsman. Had appropriate evaluation not taken place, this man might have been fired from his job rather than being placed on disability. The second case concerns a woman in her twenties who had been unsuccessfully treated for depression by various psychiatrists for three years and who was finally referred to the inpatient psychiatric unit of our hospital. The ostensible reason for admission was rapid mood swings, which on examination proved to be pseudobulbar palsy. A subsequent neurologic workup led to the diagnosis of MS. This woman had also given a very clear history of increasing memory disturbance, which was interfering with her ability to do her job, but she and her family had been told that this was a symptom of her depression. Her family was as frustrated as she was, wondering why she did not simply "snap out of it." Neuropsychological evaluation in conjunction with the neurological workup documented and provided the basis for her cognitive complaint and affective disturbance and resulted in the modification of unrealistic job and family demands.

A second role of neuropsychological evaluation is in the initial diagnosis. While early diagnosis as yet has no treatment implications in terms of arrest of the underlying disease process, it does have major financial and psychological ramifications for the patient. In the interval between symptom onset and incontrovertible diagnosis, a period that has been years in length in many cases, an individual may go to great expense in obtaining numerous consultations and experience considerable emotional wear and tear. Beginning the adjustment process, obtaining appropriate symptomatic relief, and establishing a good relationship with health care systems are all dependent on or facilitated by timely diagnosis. Neuropsychological evaluation can be the means of identifying a second CNS lesion in a person who presents with the first signs and symptoms of a demyelinating process. Neuropsychological evaluation has recently been accepted as a diagnostic tool in the research diagnostic criteria for MS, and we have elsewhere outlined the rudiments of examination in these cases (Peyser & Becker, 1984).

Finally, we have noted several areas in which further applied and correlative neuropsychological investigations are needed. In fact, the need is so crucial that the International Federation of Multiple Sclerosis Societies (IFMSS) recently appointed a Cognitive Function Study Group to promote research in this area. However, in order to proceed with the acquisition of knowledge so sorely needed, future investigators must be aware of certain design problems inherent in working with MS populations.

Sampling techniques are of critical importance. There is very little room left for studies based on data available in neuropsychology service files from clinical referrals, as these populations are subject to incalcuable skewing. Random sampling of clinic and hospital records is one appropriate means of gathering patient names for research call-in. For questions related to the natural history of MS, selection of consecutive cases. presenting for diagnostic workup is the method of choice.

To properly compare studies from different centers, adequate characterization of the research population is necessary in terms of both patient demographics and disease characteristics. Some of these factors are obvious, but one worth mentioning is disease length, which may be calculated either from time since diagnosis or time since first symptom attributable to demyelinating disease. Because of the often lengthy gap between symptom onset and the sometimes indeterminant point of formal diagnosis, the latter method is probably preferable. Disease state of remission or exacerbation should also be specified insofar as it can be determined. Attention may be profitably paid to disease type: remitting-relapsing versus chronic progressive. The Kurtzke scales will continue to be used, if only by convention, to specify physical and subsystem impairment. Viable and meaningful alternatives are the new Minimal Record of Disability (IFMSS, 1985) and the numerical rating scale for neurologic involvement revised by Poser, Poser, and Paty (1984). Finally, the sex ratio of the sample must be attended to; there is empirical evidence that men, at least psychologically, may respond somewhat differently than do women to the disease process, and there may also be basic sex differences in neuropsychological test performance (Heaton, Grant, & Matthews, in press).

The choice of an appropriate control group can be a thorny problem in any research, with the final selection always dependent on the particular question being asked. MS presents a special dilemma, as it is difficult to think of another disease that is so protean in manifestation or unpredictable in progression. Rheumatoid arthritis is one physically incapacitating illness without CNS involvement that is prone to both remission and overall progression and in that sense may be a better control for certain psychological factors than are stable conditions, such as spinal cord injury. In other instances, normal groups, patients with CNS lesions, patients with progressive neurologic diseases without CNS involvement, and various psychiatric populations may be used either singly or in combination.

With regard to measures, investigators must be aware of the previously mentioned pitfalls in terms of motor and speech impairment. Visual disturbances, such as decreased acuity, diplopia, and decreased color discrimination, are also of concern in the choice of test instruments. In our experience, visual disturbances tend to be all-or-none phenomena. That is, patients can either see well enough to proceed or they cannot. On the other hand, motor impairment may interfere with but not preclude performance. Nevertheless, such factors must be taken into consideration.

With careful design and increased comparability of results, it is our hope and belief that continued neuropsychological research will further our understanding of the disease process in multiple sclerosis and play a valuable role in future therapeutic trials.

SUMMARY

There is an increasing body of knowledge concerning the neuropsychological aspects of multiple sclerosis. Cognitive deficits, mood disturbances, and psychoses may be present in persons with this CNS disease. Further delineation of the prevalence, severity, and nature of the neuropsychological sequelae of multiple sclerosis is required, with careful attention to research methodology.

ACKNOWLEDGMENTS

Preparation of this chapter was supported in part by the Medical Center Hospital of Vermont. The authors wish to thank Marion Croto, Erlene Preble, and Patricia Davis for their unflagging assistance in manuscript preparation.

REFERENCES

Adams, D. K., Sutherland, J. M., & Fletcher, W. B. (1950). Early clinical manifestations of disseminated sclerosis. *British Medical Journal, 2*, 431–436.

Adams, R. D., & Victor, M. (1977). *Principles of neurology*. New York: McGraw-Hill.

Alter, M. (1972). The distribution of multiple sclerosis and environmental sanitation. In U. Leibowitz (Ed.), *Progress in multiple sclerosis: Research and treatment* (pp. 99–114). New York: Academic Press.

Arbuse, D. I. (1983). Psychotic manifestations in disseminated sclerosis. *Journal of the Mount Sinai Hospital, 5*, 403–410.

Awad, A. G. (1983). Schizophrenia and multiple sclerosis. *Journal of Nervous and Mental Disease, 171*, 323–324.

Baldessarini, R. J. (1983). *Biomedical aspects of depression and its treatment*. Washington, DC: American Psychiatric Press.

Baldwin, M. V. (1952). A clinico-experimental investigation into the psychologic aspects of multiple sclerosis. *Journal of Nervous and Mental Disease, 115*, 299–342.

Baretz, R. M., & Stephenson, G. R. (1981). Emotional responses to multiple sclerosis. *Psychosomatics, 22*, 117–127.

Barnard, R. O., & Triggs, M. (1974). Corpus callosum in multiple sclerosis. *Journal of Neurology, Neurosurgery and Psychiatry, 37*, 1259–1264.

Bassoe, P. (1917). Report of a case of multiple sclerosis with a delusional state and terminal delerium: Necropsy. *Journal of Nervous and Mental Disease, 45*, 268–269.

Beatty, P. A., & Gange, J. J. (1977). Neuropsychological aspects of multiple sclerosis. *Journal of Nervous and Mental Disease, 164*, 42–50.

Bender, I. (1950). Die psychischen Varanderungen bei der multiplen sklerose. *Deutsche Zeitschrift Nervenkrankheiten, 163*–165, 483–526.

Berger (1906). In Raecke, J., Psychische Störingen bei der multiplen sklerose. *Archiv für Psychiatrie und Nervenkrankheiten, 41*, 482–518. (Original work published 1905)

Bergin, J. D. (1957). Rapidly progressing dementia in disseminated sclerosis. *Journal of Neurology, Neurosurgery and Psychiatry, 20*, 285–292.

Bertrando, P., Maffei, C., & Ghezzi, A. (1983). A study of neuropsychological alterations in multiple sclerosis. *Acta Psychiatrica Belgica, 83*, 12–21.

Birley, J. L., & Dudgeon, L. S. (1921). A clinical and experimental contribution to the pathogenesis of disseminated sclerosis. *Brain, 10*, 150–212.

Borberg, N. C., & Zahle, V. (1946). On the psychopathology of disseminated sclerosis. *Archives of Psychiatry and Neurology, 21*, 75–89.

Bourestom, N. C., & Howard, M. T. (1965). Personality characteristics of three disability groups. *Archives of Physical Medicine and Rehabilitation, 46*, 626–632.

Braceland, F. J., & Giffin, M. E. (1950). The mental changes associated with multiple sclerosis: An interim report. *Association for Research in Nervous and Mental Diseases, 28*, 450–455.

Brain, W. R. (1930). Critical review: Disseminated sclerosis. *Quarterly Journal of Medicine, 23*, 343–391.

Bramwell, B. (1905). The prognosis of disseminated sclerosis. *Review of Neurology and Psychiatry, 3*, 161–170.

Brody, J., Sever, J., & Hanson, T. (1971). Virus antibody titers in multiple sclerosis patients, siblings and controls. *Journal of the American Medical Association, 216*, 1441–1446.

Brown, J., Beebe, G., Kurtzke, J., Loewenson, R., Silberberg, D., & Tourtelotte, W. (1979). The design of clinical studies to assess therapeutic efficacy in multiple sclerosis. *Neurology, 29*, 3–23.

Brown, S., & Davis, T. K. (1921). The mental symptoms of multiple sclerosis. *Association for Research in Nervous and Mental Diseases, 2*, 76–82.

Brown, S., & Davis, T. K. (1922). The mental symptoms of multiple sclerosis. *Archives of Neurology and Psychiatry, 7*, 629–634.

Brownell, B., & Hughes, J. T. (1962). The distribution of plaques in the cerebrum in multiple sclerosis. *Journal of Neurology, Neurosurgery and Psychiatry, 25*, 315–320.

Burnfield, A., & Burnfield, P. (1978). Common psychological problems in multiple sclerosis. *British Medical Journal, 1*, 1193–1194.

Buzzard, T. (1897). Insular sclerosis and hysteria. *Lancet, 1*, 1–4.

Canter, A. H. (1951a). Direct and indirect measures of psychological deficit in multiple sclerosis. *Journal of General Psychology, 44*, 3–50.

Canter, A. H. (1951b). MMPI profiles in multiple sclerosis. *Journal of Consulting Psychology, 15*, 253–256.

Charcot, J. M. (1877). *Lectures on the diseases of the nervous system.* London: New Sydenham Society.

Chiappa, K. (1980). Pattern shift visual, brainstem auditory, and short-latency somatosensory evoked potentials in multiple sclerosis. *Neurology, 30*, 110–123.

Chiappa, K., & Ropper, A. (1982). Evoked potentials in clinical medicine. *New England Journal of Medicine, 306*, 1140–1150, 1205–1211.

Cottrell, S. S., & Wilson, S. A. K. (1926). The affective symptomatology of disseminated sclerosis. *Journal of Neurology and Psychopathology, 7*, 1–30.

Dalos, N. P., Rabins, P. V., Brooks, B. R., & O'Donnell, P. (1983). Disease activity and emotional state in multiple sclerosis. *Annals of Neurology, 13*, 573–577.

Dean, G., & Kurtzke, J. (1970). A critical age for the acquisition of multiple sclerosis. *Transactions of the American Neurological Association, 95*, 232–233.

Deltenre, P., Vercruysse, A., Van Nechel, C., Ketalaer, P., Capon, A., Colin, F., & Manil, J. (1979). Early diagnosis of multiple sclerosis by combined multimodal evoked potentials. *Journal of Biomedical Engineering, 1*, 17–21.

Desmedt, L., Severts, M., Geutjens, J., & Medaer, R. (1984). Intellectual impairment in multiple sclerosis. In R. F. Gonsette & P. Delmotte (Eds.), *Immunological and clinical aspects of multiple sclerosis* (pp. 342–345). Lancaster: MTP Press Limited.

Diers, W. C., & Brown, C. C. (1950). Psychosomatic patterns associated with multiple sclerosis: I. Wechsler-Bellevue patterns. *Archives of Neurology and Psychiatry, 63*, 760–765.

Duge (1929). In A. Ombredane, *Sur les troubles mentaux de la sclérose en plaques.* Paris: Thèse. (Original work published 1914)

Ebers, G., & Paty, D. (1980). CSF electrophoresis in 1000 patients. *Canadian Journal of Neurological Science, 7*, 275–280.

Ebers, G., Paty, D., Scheinberg, L., et al. (1984). *The diagnosis of multiple sclerosis.* New York: Thieme-Stratton.

Ebers, G., Paty, D., Stiller, C., Nelson, R., Seland, T., & Larsen, B. (1982). HLA-Typing in multiple sclerosis sibling pairs. *Lancet, 2*, 88–90.

Fink, S. L. & Houser, H. B. (1966). An investigation of physical and intellectual changes in multiple sclerosis. *Archives of Physical Medicine and Rehabilitation, 47*, 56–61.

Gallineck, A., & Kalinowsky, L. B. (1958). Psychiatric aspects of multiple sclerosis. *Diseases of the Nervous System, 2*, 77–80.

Geocaris, K. (1957). Psychotic episodes heralding the diagnosis of multiple sclerosis. *Bulletin of the Menninger Clinic, 21*, 107–116.

Gilberstadt, H., & Farkas, C. (1961). Another look at MMPI profile types in multiple sclerosis. *Journal of Consulting Psychology, 25*, 440–444.

Gilbert, J. J., & Sadler, M. (1983). Unsuspected multiple sclerosis. *Archives of Neurology, 40*, 533–536.

Goldstein, G., & Shelly, C. H. (1974). Neuropsychological diagnosis of multiple sclerosis in a neuropsychiatric setting. *Journal of Nervous and Mental Disease, 158*, 280–290.

Goodstein, R. K., & Ferrell, R. B. (1977). Multiple sclerosis presenting as depressive illness. *Diseases of the Nervous System, 38*, 127–131.

Gowers, W. R. (1898). *A manual of diseases of the nervous system* (Vol. 2, 2nd ed.). Philadelphia: P. Blakiston.

Grinker, R. R., Ham, G. C., & Robbins, F. P. (1950). Some psychodynamic factors in multiple sclerosis. *Association for Research in Nervous and Mental Diseases, 28*, 456–460.

Harrower, M. R. (1950). The results of psychosomatic and personality tests in multiple sclerosis. *Association for Research in Nervous and Mental Diseases, 28*, 461–465.

Harrower, M. R., & Kraus, J. (1951). Psychological studies on patients with multiple sclerosis. *Archives of Neurology, 66*, 44–51.

Heaton, R. K., Grant, I., & Matthews, C. G. (in press). Differences in neuropsychological test performance associated with age, education, and sex. In I. Grant & K. M. Adams (Eds.), *Neuropsychological assessment in neuropsychiatric disorders: Clinical methods and empirical findings*. New York: Oxford University Press.

Heaton, R. K., Nelson, L. M., Thompson, D. S., Burks, J. S. & Franklin, G. M. (1985). Neuropsychological findings in relapsing-remitting and chronic-progressive multiple sclerosis. *Journal of Consulting and Clinical Psychology, 53*, 103–110.

Herndon, R. A., & Rudick, R. A. (1983). Multiple sclerosis: The spectrum of severity. *Archives of Neurology, 40*, 531–532.

Hirschenfang, S., & Benton, J. G. (1966). Note on intellectual changes in multiple sclerosis. *Perceptual and Motor Skills, 22*, 786.

Hollender, M. H., & Steckler, P. P. (1972). Multiple sclerosis and schizophrenia: A case report. *Psychiatry in Medicine, 3*, 251–257.

Howes, S. F. H. (1927). Psychoses with multiple sclerosis. *Boston Medical and Surgical Journal, 196*, 310–315.

Ikuta, F., & Zimmerman, H. M. (1976). Distribution of plaques in seventy autopsy cases of multiple sclerosis in the United States. *Neurology, 6* (pt. 2), 26–28.

International Federation of Multiple Sclerosis Societies (1985). *Minimal record of disability for multiple sclerosis*. New York: National Multiple Sclerosis Society.

Ivnik, R. J. (1978a). Neuropsychological test performance as a function of the duration of MS-related symptomatology. *Journal of Clinical Psychiatry, 39*, 304–312.

Ivnik, R. J. (1978b). Neuropsychological stability in multiple sclerosis. *Journal of Consulting and Clinical Psychology, 8*, 913–923.

Jambor, K. L. (1969). Cognitive functioning in multiple sclerosis. *British Journal of Psychiatry, 115*, 765–775.

Jelliffe, S. E. (1921). Emotional and psychological factors in multiple sclerosis. *Association for Research in Nervous and Mental Diseases, 2*, 82–95.

Kahana, E., Leibowitz, U., & Alter, M. (1971). Cerebral multiple sclerosis. *Neurology, 21*, 1179–1185.

Kalb, R. C., & LaRocca, N. G. (1985). *Magnetic resonance imaging and psychological testing in assessment of cognitive function of multiple sclerosis patients*. Paper presented at the symposium on neuropsychology of multiple sclerosis of the meeting of the International Neuropsychological Society, San Diego.

Kellner, C. H., Davenport, Y., Post, R. M., & Ross, R. J. (1984). Rapidly cycling bipolar disorder and multiple sclerosis. *American Journal of Psychiatry, 141*, 112–113.

Keschner, M. (1950). The effect of injuries and illness on the course of multiple sclerosis. *Association for Research in Nervous and Mental Diseases, 28*, 533–547.

Knehr, C. A. (1962). Differential impairment in multiple sclerosis. *Journal of Psychology, 54*, 443–451.

Koenig, H. (1968). Dementia associated with the benign form of multiple sclerosis. *Transactions of the American Neurological Association, 93*, 227–228.

Kurtzke, J. F. (1965). Further notes on disability evaluation in multiple sclerosis with scale modifications. *Neurology, 15*, 654–661.

Kurtzke, J. (1977). Geography of multiple sclerosis. *Journal of Neurology, 215*, 1–26.

Kurtzke, J., & Hyllested, K. (1979). Multiple sclerosis in the Faroe Islands. *Annals of Neurology, 5*, 6–21.

Langworthy, O. R. (1948). Relation of personality problems to onset and progress of multiple sclerosis. *Archives of Neurology and Psychiatry, 59*, 13–28.

Langworthy, O. R. (1950). A survey of the maladjustment problems in multiple sclerosis and the possibilities of psychotherapy. *Association for Research in Nervous and Mental Diseases, 28*, 598–609.

Langworthy, O. R., Kolb, L. C., & Androp, S. (1941). Disturbances of behavior in patients with disseminated sclerosis. *American Journal of Psychiatry, 98*, 243–249.

Langworthy, O. R., & LeGrand, D. (1952). Personality structure and psychotherapy in multiple sclerosis. *American Journal of Medicine, 13*, 586–592.

Leibowitz, V., Kahana, E., & Alter, M. (1969). The changing frequency of multiple sclerosis in Israel. *Archives of Neurology, 29*, 107–110.

Lemere, F. (1966). Psychiatric disorders in multiple sclerosis. *American Journal of Psychiatry, 122* (Supple.), 55–58.

Likosky, W., & Elmore, R. S. (1982). Exacerbation detection in multiple sclerosis by clinical and evoked potential techniques: A preliminary report. In J. Courgon, F. Maugiere, & M. Revol, (Eds.), *Clinical applications of evoked potentials in neurology* (pp. 535–540). New York: Raven Press.

Lincoln, N. B. (1981). Discrepancies between capabilities and performance of activities of daily living in multiple sclerosis patients. *International Rehabilitation Medicine, 3*, 84–88.

Lumsden, C. E. (1970). The neuropathology of multiple sclerosis. In P. J. Vinken & G. W. Bruyn (eds.), *Handbook of clinical neurology: Vol. 9. Multiple sclerosis and other demyelinating diseases* (pp. 217–309). New York: American Elsevier.

Mackay, R. P., & Hirano, A. (1967). Forms of benign multiple sclerosis. *Archives of Neurology, 17*, 588–600.

Malhotra, A., & Goren, H. (1981). The hot bath test in the diagnosis of multiple sclerosis. *Journal of the American Medical Association, 246*, 1113–1114.

Malone, W. H. (1937). Psychosis with multiple sclerosis. *Medical Bulletin of the Veterans Administration, 14*, 113–117.

Marsh, G. G. (1980). Disability and intellectual function in multiple sclerosis patients. *Journal of Nervous and Mental Diseases, 12*, 758–762.

Matthews, C. G., Cleeland, C. S., & Hopper, C. L. (1970). Neuropsychological patterns in multiple sclerosis. *Diseases of the Nervous System, 31*, 161–170.

Matthews, W. B. (1979). Multiple sclerosis presenting with acute remitting psychiatric symptoms. *Journal of Neurology, Neurosurgery and Psychiatry, 42*, 859–863.

McLardy, T., & Sinclair, A. (1964). A case of presenile fulminating multiple sclerosis (with pathogenic considerations). *Confinia Neurologica, 24*, 417–424.

Mei-tal, V., Meyerowitz, S., & Engel, G. L. (1970). The role of psychological process in a somatic disorder: Multiple sclerosis. *Psychosomatic Medicine, 32*, 67–85.

Miller, H. (1964). Trauma and multiple sclerosis. *Lancet, 1*, 848–850.

Moxon, W. (1875). Insular sclerosis of the brain and spinal cord. *Guy's Hospital Reports, 3rd Series, 20*, 437–481.

Müller, 1906. In J. Raecke (Ed.), Psychische Störingen bei der multiplen sklerose. *Archiv für Psychiatrie und Nervenkrankheiten, 41*, 482–518. (Original work published 1904)

Mur, J., Kumpel, G., & Dostal, S. (1966). An anergic phase of disseminated sclerosis with psychotic course. *Confinia Neurologica, 28*, 37–49.

Namerow, N. S., & Thompson, L. R. (1969). Plaques, symptoms, and the remitting course of multiple sclerosis. *Neurology, 19*, 765–774.

Olmos-Lau, N., Ginsberg, M. D., & Geller, J. B. (1977). Aphasia in multiple sclerosis. *Neurology, 27*, 623–626.

O'Malley, P. P. (1966). Severe mental symptoms in disseminated sclerosis: A neuro-pathological study. *Journal of the Irish Medical Association, 58*, 115–127.

Ombredane, A. (1929). *Sur les troubles mentaux de la sclérose en plaques.* Paris: Thèse.

Parker, N. (1956). Disseminated sclerosis presenting as schizophrenia. *Medical Journal of Australia, 1*, 405–407.

Parsons, O. A., Stewart, K. D., & Arenberg, D. (1957). Impairment of abstracting ability in multiple sclerosis. *Journal of Nervous and Mental Diseases, 125*, 221–225.

Paulley, J. W., (1977). The psychological management of multiple sclerosis. *Practitioner, 218*, 100–105.

Peyser, J. M. (1983) *Experience in cognitive assessment in MS relevant to developing a simple rating system.* Invited address presented at the International Federation of Multiple Sclerosis Societies Conference on Multiple Sclerosis, Vancouver, British Columbia, Canada.

Peyser, J. M., & Becker, B. (1984). Neuropsychological evaluation in patients with MS. In C. Poser, D. Paty, L. Scheinberg, W. McDonald, & G. Evers (Eds.), *The diagnosis of multiple sclerosis* (pp. 143–158). New York: Thieme-Stratton.

Peyser, J. M., Edwards, K. R., Poser, C. M., & Filskov, S. B. (1980). Cognitive function in patients with multiple sclerosis. *Archives of Neurology, 37*, 577–579.

Philippopoulos, G. S., Wittkower, E. D., & Cousineau, A. (1958). The etiologic significance of emotional factors in onset and exacerbation of multiple sclerosis: A preliminary report. *Psychosomatic Medicine, 20*, 458–472.

Phillipe & Cestan (1929). In A. Ombredane, *Sur les troubles mentaux de la sclérose en plaques.* Paris: Thèse. (Original work published 1903)

Pirozzolo, F. J., Hansch, E. C., Mortimer, J. A., Webster, D. D., & Kuskowski, M. A. (1982). Dementia in Parkinson Disease: A neuropsychological analysis. *Brain and Cognition, 1*, 71–83.

Poser, C. (1972). Recent advances in multiple sclerosis. *Medical Clinics of North America, 56*, 1343–1362.

Poser, C. (1978). Diseases of the myelin sheath. In A. B. Baker & L. H. Baker (Eds.), *Clinical neurology* (Vol. 2). New York: Harper & Row.

Poser, C. Multiple sclerosis: A critical update. *Medical Clinics of North America, 63*, 729–743.

Poser, C. (1979b). Trauma, stress and multiple sclerosis. *Bulletin of the American Academy of Psychiatry and the Law, 7*, 208–218.

Poser, C. (1980). Exacerbations, activity and progression in multiple sclerosis. *Archives of Neurology, 37*, 471–474.

Poser, C. M., Alter, M., Sibley, W. A., & Scheinberg, L. C. (1984). Multiple sclerosis. In H. H. Merritt (Ed.), *Merritt's textbook of neurology* (7th ed., pp. 593–611). Philadelphia: Lea & Febiger.

Poser, C., Paty, D., Scheinberg, L., et al. (1983). New diagnostic criteria for multiple sclerosis. *Annals of Neurology, 13*, 227–231.

Poser, C., Paty, D., Scheinberg, L., McDonald, W., & Ebers, G. (Eds.). (1984). *The diagnosis of multiple sclerosis.* New York: Thieme-Stratton.

Poser, C., Poser, S., & Paty, D. (1984). A revised numerical scoring system for multiple sclerosis. In C. Poser, D. Paty, L. Scheinberg, W. McDonald, & G. Ebers (Eds.). *The diagnosis of multiple sclerosis* (pp. 234–241). New York: Thieme-Stratton.

Poser, C., Presthus, J., & Horsdal, O. (1966). Clinical characteristics of autopsy proved multiple sclerosis. *Neurology, 16*, 791–798.

Pratt, R. T. C. (1951). An investigation of the psychiatric aspects of disseminated sclerosis. *Journal of Neurology, Neurosurgery and Psychiatry, 14*, 326–336.

Prineas, J., & Connell, F. (1978). The fine structure of chronically active multiple sclerosis plaques. *Neurology, 28*, 68–75.

Raecke, J. (1906). Psychische Störungen bei der multiplen sklerose. *Archiv für Psychiatrie und Nervenkrankheiten, 41*, 482–518.

Rao, S. M., Glatt, S., Hammeke, T. A., Rhodes, A. M., & Pollard, S. (1984). *Ventricular size and memory impairment in chronic progressive multiple sclerosis.* Paper presented at the meeting of the International Neuropsychological Society, Houston.

Rao, S. M., & Hammeke, T. A. (1983). Hypothesis testing in patients with chronic progressive multiple sclerosis. *Brain and Cognition, 3*, 94–104.

Rao, S. M., Hammeke, T. A., McQuillen, M. P., Khatri, B. O., & Lloyd, D. (1984). Memory disturbance in chronic progressive multiple sclerosis. *Archives of Neurology, 41*, 625–631.

Reitan, R. M., Reed, J. C., & Dyken, M. L. (1971). Cognitive, psychomotor, and motor correlates of multiple sclerosis. *Journal of Nervous and Mental Disease, 153*, 218–224.

Robinson, R. G., & Szetela, B. (1981). Mood change following left hemisphere brain injury. *Annals of Neurology, 9*, 447–453.

Ross, A. T., & Reitan, R. M. (1955). Intellectual and affective functions in multiple sclerosis. *Archives of Neurology and Psychiatry, 73*, 663–677.

Ross, D. M. (1915). The mental symptoms in disseminated sclerosis. *Review of Neurology and Psychiatry, 13*, 361–373.

Russell, D. (1964). Trauma and multiple sclerosis. *Lancet, 1*, 978.

Sacks, B., & Friedman, E. D. (1922). General symptomatology and differential diagnosis of disseminated sclerosis. *Archives of Neurology and Psychiatry, 7*, 551–560.

Sai-Halász, A. (1956). Psychic alternations in disseminated sclerosis: A general, statistical and Rorschach-Test study on 200 patients. *Monaschrift für Psychiatry und Neurologie, 132*, 129–154.

Scheinberg, P., Blackburn, L. I., Kaim, S. C., & Stenger, C. A. (1953). Cerebral circulation and metabolism in multiple sclerosis: Correlative observations by electroencephalography and psychodiagonistic testing. *Archives of Neurology and Psychiatry, 70*, 260–267

Schiffer, R. B., & Babigan, H. M. (1984). Behavioral disorders in multiple sclerosis, temporal lobe epilepsy, and amyotrophic lateral sclerosis: An epidemiologic study. *Archives of Neurology, 41*, 1067–1069.

Schiffer, R. B., Caine, E. G., Bamford, K. S., & Levy, S. (1983). Depressive episodes in patients with multiple sclerosis. *American Journal of Psychiatry, 140*, 1498–1500.

Schiffer, R. B., Rudick, R. A., & Herndon, R. M. (1983). Psychologic aspects of multiple sclerosis. *New York State Journal of Medicine, 83*, 312–316.

Schmalzbach, O. (1954). Disseminated sclerosis in schizophrenia. *Medical Journal of Australia, 1*, 451–452.

Schumacher, G. (1971). *The evolution of management of multiple sclerosis—wading through fads*. Paper presented at the Twenty-fifth Anniversary Conference of the National Multiple Sclerosis Society, Los Angeles.

Schumacher, G., Beebe, G., Kibler, R., Kurland, L., Kurtzke, J., McDowell, F., Nagler, B., Sibley, W., Tourtelotte, W., & Willmon, T. (1965). Problems of experimental trials of therapy in multiple sclerosis. *Annals of the New York Academy of Sciences, 122*, 552–568.

Schwartz, M. L., & Pierron, M. (1972). Suicide and fatal accidents in multiple sclerosis. *Omega, 3*, 291–293.

Seiffer (1929). In A. Ombredane, *Sur les troubles mentaux de la sclérose en plaques*. Paris: Thèse. (Original work published 1905)

Sevush, S., & Sheremata, W. A. (1983). Multiple sclerosis: A neurobehavioral study. *Neurology, 33*(Suppl. 2), 65.

Sheremata, W. (1985). *Decreased cortical activation with random word recall in multiple sclerosis*. Paper presented at the symposium on multiple sclerosis of the meeting of the International Neuropsychological Society, San Diego.

Shontz, F. (1955). MMPI responses in patients with multiple sclerosis. *Journal of Consulting Psychology, 19*, 74.

Spiegel (1929). In A. Ombredane, *Sur les troubles mentaux de la Sclérose en plaques*. Paris: Thèse. (Original work published 1891)

Staples, D., & Lincoln, N. B. (1979). Intellectual impairment in multiple sclerosis and its relation to functional abilities. *Rheumatology and Rehabilitation, 18*, 153–160.

Strumpell (1929). In A. Ombredane, *Sur les troubles mentaux de la sclérose en plaques*. Paris: Thèse. (Original work published 1891)

Sugar, C., & Nadell, R. (1943). Mental symptoms in multiple sclerosis. *Journal of Consulting Psychology, 98*, 267–280.

Surridge, D. (1969). An investigation into some psychiatric aspects of multiple sclerosis. *British Journal of Psychiatry, 115*, 749–764.

Thygesen, P. (1953). *The course of disseminated sclerosis: A close-up of 105 attacks*. Copenhagen: Rosenkilde and Bagger.

Vowels, L. M., & Gates, G. R. (1984). Neuropsychological findings. In A. F. Simons (Ed.), *Multiple sclerosis: Psychological and social aspects* (pp. 82–90). London: William Heinemann.

Vulpian, A. (1894). *Maladies de système nerveux* (Vol. 2). Paris: Doin.

Warren, S., Greenhill, S., & Warren, K. G. (1982). Emotional stress and the development of multiple sclerosis: Case-control evidence of a relationship. *Journal of Chronic Disease, 35*, 821–831.

Whitlock, F. A., & Siskind, M. M. (1980). Depression as a major symptom of multiple sclerosis. *Journal of Neurology, Neurosurgery and Psychiatry, 43*, 861–865.

Wilson, H., Olson, W. H., Gascon, G. G., & Brumback, R. A. (1982). Personality characteristics and multiple sclerosis. *Psychological Reports, 51*, 791–806.

Wisniewski, H., & Keith, A. (1977). Chronic relapsing experimental allergic encephalomyelitis: An experimental model for multiple sclerosis. *Annals of Neurology, 1*, 144–148.

Young, A. C., Saunders, J., & Ponsford, J. R. (1976). Mental change as an early feature of multiple sclerosis. *Journal of Neurology, Neurosurgery and Psychiatry, 39*, 1008–1013.

Young, I., Pallis, C., Budder, G., Legg, N., & Steiner, R. (1981). Nuclear magnetic resonance imaging of the brain in multiple sclerosis. *Lancet, 2*, 1063–1066.

Ziehen (1929). In A. Ombredane, *Sur les troubles mentaux de la sclérose en plaques*. Paris: Thèse. (Original work published 1902).

CHAPTER 15

Dementia: Implications for Clinical Practice and Research

Jeffrey T. Barth and Stephen N. Macciocchi

Dementia is a generic term most often used to describe disease-related cognitive decline (Joynt & Shoulson, 1979; Valenstein, 1981) that usually involves widespread deterioration of the cerebral cortex (*Dorland's,* 1968; Pryse-Phillips & Murray, 1978). Cortical deterioration and subsequent cognitive disorganization may be caused by any one of several recognized neurological disorders, such as Alzheimer's disease, multi-infarct dementia (MID), Huntington's chorea, normal-pressure hydrocephalus (NPH), Creutzfeldt-Jakob disease, progressive multifocal leukoencephalopathy, subacute sclerosing panencephalitis, Wernicke-Korsakoff syndrome, Parkinson's disease, Parkinson's-dementia complex, amyotrophic lateral sclerosis (ALS), Pick's disease, Wilson's disease, or progressive supranuclear palsy (Armbrustmacher, 1979; Joynt & Shoulson, 1979; Merritt, 1973; Pryse-Phillips & Murray, 1978; Valenstein, 1980). These disorders are not mutually exclusive, and, in fact, patients may simultaneously experience effects of several diseases. Other conditions, such as head trauma, infections, toxicity, endocrine disorders, and renal disease, may also have cognitive consequences similar to the dementing disorders mentioned above even though they are not directly related to primary, progressive neuronal degeneration. Because Alzheimer's disease is by far the most prevalent dementing condition (Valenstein, 1981), it is the predominant focus of this chapter; however, before elaborating on the biological and neuropsychological aspects of Alzheimer's disease, several other well-recognized disease processes deserve brief description, and a short introduction to normal aging is necessary.

Other dementing disorders include multi-infarct dementia, Huntington's chorea, Creutzfeldt-Jakob disease, Wernicke-Korsakoff syndrome, and normal-pressure hydrocephalus. These processes differ with respect to etiology, age of onset, symptom pattern, and disease course, but in all cases severe cognitive disorganization is apparent, especially in later disease stages. Treatment effects are quite limited in all these disorders, and prognosis is extremely poor.

MULTI-INFARCT DEMENTIA

With the exception of Alzheimer's disease, multiple infarction is the most common cause of dementia in old age (Valenstein, 1980). Multi-infarct dementia is characterized by a relatively rapid, stepwise decline in cognitive abilities secondary to a series of cerebrovascular occlusions or hemorrhages, usually with lateralized neurological consequences (Armbrustmacher, 1979; Joynt & Shoulson, 1979). MID is distinguishable from generalized arteriosclerotic disease, which often produces dementia in a more gradual and global fashion. Nevertheless, disease onset may be rapid or more insidious, and affective changes and emotional symptoms are often evident before cognitive decline becomes apparent (Lishman, 1978). In some cases, multi-infarct dementia is treated with chemotherapeutic regulation of blood pressure, anticoagulants, and/or surgery to improve blood flow (Armbrustmacher, 1979; Joynt & Shoulson, 1979; Merritt, 1973), but usually treatment is ineffective, and MID results in death approximately four to five years after onset.

HUNTINGTON'S CHOREA

Huntington's chorea is an autosomal dominant disorder characterized by choreiform or irregular, uncontrollable body movements and progressive dementia secondary to degeneration of the cerebral cortex, caudate and lenticular nuclei, thalamus, and brain stem. Onset is usually in early to middle adulthood, and there is no accurate diagnostic test for the disorder before onset of the strikingly abnormal involuntary movements. The first symptom of this disease is mental deterioration, with choreiform movements usually developing sometime later in the course of the disorder. Typical mental changes include general cognitive decline, memory and concentrational deficits, impulsive behavior (often sexual), personality alterations or exacerbations, irritability, anxiety, depression, and apathy (Merritt, 1973). No effective treatment for Huntington's chorea is available, other than tranquilizing drugs, which are used to reduce the severity of choreiform movements. Death from chronic infections or suicide usually occurs within 15–20 years following the onset of symptoms (Merritt, 1973).

CREUTZFELDT-JAKOB DISEASE

Creutzfeldt-Jakob disease is a rare infectious condition that affects the "cerebral cortex, striate body, thalamus, globus pallidus... nuclei of the cerebellum, midbrain, pons, and medulla, [as well as] the gray matter of the spinal cord" (Armbrustmacher, 1979, p. 167). Changes in brain tissue are most readily seen histologically and often include neuronal loss and an increased number of vacuoles. Other disorders, such as progressive multifocal leukoencephalopathy and subacute sclerosing panencephalitis, are also considered slow, infectious, degenerative diseases of the central nervous system, though the infectious agents and mechanisms are different from those of Creutzfeldt-Jakob disease. In the latter, the infection appears to enter the system through breaks in the skin. The infectious agent does not provoke an immune system reaction, and neither radiation nor other intervention strategies have been successful in treating this disorder. The clinical features of the disease include progressive dementia, pyramidal and extrapyramidal (motor) deficits, and visuoperceptual disturbance. Onset usually occurs after age 40, and few patients survive more than a few years (Armbrustmacher, 1979; Merritt, 1973).

WERNICKE-KORSAKOFF SYNDROME

Wernicke-Korsakoff syndrome is believed to occur as a result of thiamine (B complex) vitamin deficiency, which is most often associated with alcohol abuse. Neuropathological changes associated with chronic, severe alcohol abuse and Wernicke-Korsakoff syndrome are peripheral neuropathy, general cerebral atrophy, ventricular dilatation, and cerebellar (vermis) and thalamic (dorsal nucleus) atrophy (Pryse-Phillips & Murray, 1978). Clinical features include severe memory deficits for immediate, delayed, and remote verbal and nonverbal information, ataxia, diplopia, and in some cases intellectual decline characterized by excessive confabulation. Treatment involves group or individual therapy to gain and maintain alcohol abstinence, megavitamin therapy (thiamine), and dietary controls. Motor, tactile, and visual functions often improve with treatment, but memory and general cognitive abilities remain refractory to intervention strategies, particularly in the later stages of the disorder (Pryse-Phillips & Murray, 1978).

NORMAL-PRESSURE HYDROCEPHALUS

Clinical symptoms usually associated with hydrocephalus sometimes occur in persons with essentially normal cerebrospinal fluid pressure (Hakin & Adams, 1965). This phenomenon, now referred to as normal-pressure hydrocephalus, has a pathological mechanism that is not fully understood but is believed to be either a blockage of cerebrospinal fluid movement from the ventricles to the subarachnoid space or a reduction of cerebrospinal fluid uptake in the venous sinuses. In either case, other neuropathological conditions, such as neoplasms, subarachnoid hemorrhages, and meningitis, may cause such symptoms (Merritt, 1973). Discrimination between normal-pressure hydrocephalus and primary degenerative disease, such as Alzheimer's disease, is aided by a noticeable lack of cortical atrophy in normal-pressure hydrocephalus (Merritt, 1973). Clinical symptoms include progressive dementia and confusion, gait disturbances, and urinary incontinence. Ventriculoperitoneal or ventriculoatrial shunts are reported to reduce symptoms in some cases, but the effectiveness of this treatment for NPH has been questioned (Armbrustmacher, 1979; Merritt, 1973; Pryse-Phillips & Murray, 1978).

NORMAL AGING

There is a paucity of literature on normal aging, but Valenstein (1980) and Terry (1980) outline the most salient morphological changes associated with the aging process. As humans age, central nervous system changes occur that are similar to the pathological processes observed in Alzheimer's disease. Although minimal changes in cerebral size and weight are observed between ages 25 and 85 years (Tomlinson, Blessed, & Roth, 1968), ventricular dilatation is increasingly evident as one ages (Hughes & Gado, 1981), and there is considerable debate as to whether this increase is more pronounced in demented populations (Jacobs, Kinkel, Painter, Murawski, & Heffner, 1978; Roberts & Caird, 1976). Mild cortical atrophy is also quite compatible with normal aging. However, atrophy may not correlate with ventricular enlargement or intellectual decline (Brunkman, Sarwar, Levin, & Morris, 1981; Ford & Winter, 1981; Kaszniak,

Garron, Fox, Bergen, & Huckman, 1979; Naeser, Gebhardt, & Levine, 1980; Roberts & Caird, 1976). Atrophy may be related to cell loss, since significant loss of neurons in the cerebral cortex is associated with normal aging (Ball, 1977; Brody, 1955; Colon, 1972; Shefer, 1973). Cell loss does not appear to be confined to the cortex and may include the cerebellum (Hall, Miller, & Corsellis, 1975) and certain brain stem nuclei (Brody, 1978), with the exception of the ventral cochlear nucleus and inferior olive (Konigsmark & Murphy, 1972; Monagle & Brody, 1974). Contradictory results have been reported on the loss of dendritic spines and synapses in the elderly, with some studies indicating cortical deterioration of these processes (Scheibel, Lindsay, Tomujasu, & Scheibel, 1975; Scheibel, Lindsay, Tomujasu, & Scheibel, 1976; Scheibel & Scheibel, 1975) and others finding no difference between normal young and aged adults (Cragg, 1975).

Histological abnormalities, as well as morphological changes, are related to aging. Neurofibrillary tangles (Ball, 1977; Dayan, 1970; Matsuyama & Nakamura, 1978; Tomlinson, Blessed, & Roth, 1968), granulovacuolar degeneration (Ball & Lo, 1977; Tomlinson, Blessed, & Roth, 1968), senile or neuritic plaques (Ball, 1977; Dayan, 1970), and increased aluminum levels (Perl & Brody, 1980) are all observable in elderly adults, though to a lesser degree than those found in patients with dementing conditions. Finally, changes in neurotransmitter production and activity are associated with the normal aging process. General neurotransmitter activity appears affected by aging, but changes in cholinergic systems appear most salient, including decreases in acetylcholine (ACL) and choline acetyltransferase (CAT) production, as well as loss of cholinergic receptor sites (White et al., 1977).

Overall, normal aging results in several morphological, physiological, and biochemical changes, all of which are also observed in Alzheimer's disease. Cell loss and dendritic spine reduction, neurofibrillary tangles, neuritic plaque formation, and cholinergic system abnormalities all occur in normal aging and, to a greater extent, in Alzheimer's disease. Even though normal aging and Alzheimer's disease appear similar, the cognitive decline of Alzheimer's disease does not appear to be simply accelerated aging (Roth, 1978). Additional information regarding Alzheimer's disease is presented below.

SENILE DEMENTIA, ALZHEIMER'S TYPE

For our purposes, presenile dementia, senile dementia, and Alzheimer's disease (DSM III classification, primary degenerative dementia, senile or presenile onset) collectively are referred to as senile dementia, Alzheimer's type (SDAT). SDAT is the most common cause of dementia and is estimated to affect more than 5% of the population over 65 years of age (Joynt & Shoulson, 1979). Women appear to develop SDAT more often than men (2.5 to 1) (Constantinidis, 1978; Merritt, 1973; Roth, 1978; Tomlinson, Blessed, & Roth, 1970). Disease onset is variable, particularly in presenile form, but the disorder is usually diagnosed after age 50. SDAT is characterized by progressive general cognitive decline, with memory deficits as the first symptom. Impairment of conceptual learning and abstraction ability begins relatively early in the disorder, and mental flexibility and insight also appear affected. Aphasic symptoms, dyspraxia, visuospatial-perceptual disturbances, and behavioral symptoms, such as apathy, loss of sense of humor, distractability, and depression, are often observed as the disorder progresses (Armbrustmacher, 1979; Coblentz et al., 1973; Joynt & Shoulson, 1979; Pryse-Phillips & Murray, 1978; Schneck, Reisberg, & Ferris, 1982; Valenstein, 1981). SDAT usually is a slowly progressive disorder that significantly affects qualify of life, eventually leads to total deterioration of higher cognitive functions (Armbrustmacher, 1979; Merritt, 1973), and reduces life expectancy by more than four years (Wang & Whanger, 1971). Cognitive disorganization appears directly related to morphological, physiological, and biochemical changes in patients with SDAT.

Cortical atrophy and ventricular dilatation may be pronounced in Alzheimer's patients. These structural changes seem related to neuronal loss (Ball, 1977; Herzog & Kemper, 1980; Hubbard & Anderson, 1981; Shefer, 1973; Terry, Peck, DeTeresa, Schechter, & Horoupian, 1981; Tomlinson, Blessed, & Roth, 1968; Tomlinson, Irving, & Blessed, 1981), yet Terry, Fitzgerald, and Peck (1977) and Wilkinson and Davies (1978) actually found no differences in neural cell counts between normal subjects and Alzheimer's disease patients. Nevertheless, Schneck, Reisberg, and Ferris (1982) speculate that deterioration occurs in dendritic spines rather than the cell bodies, which could explain the divergent findings. Additional systemic changes are also apparent in SDAT and can be documented by electroencephalography (EEG), evoked potential recording, and regional cerebral blood flow measurement. In SDAT, EEG changes are characterized by decreased alpha frequency and generalized slowing across the cerebral hemispheres (Gibbs, 1964; Kooi, 1971). Auditory and visual evoked potentials also indicate increased wave transmission latencies in demented subjects (Celesia & Daly, 1977; Goodin, Squires, Henderson, & Starr, 1978; Goodin, Squires, & Starr, 1978), and frontal, temporal, and parietal cerebral blood flow is compromised (Ingvar, Brun, Hagberg, & Gustafson, 1978; Lavy, Melamed, Bentin, Cooper, & Pinot, 1978; Melamed, Lavy, Siew, Bentin, & Cooper, 1978; Obrist, Chivian, Cronqvist, & Ingvar, 1979; Simard, Olesen, Paulson, Lassen, & Skinkj, 1971; Yamaguchi, Meyer, Yamamoto, Sakai, & Shaw, 1980).

In addition to suspected dendritic spine degeneration, SDAT patients develop neurofibrillary tangles, neuritic or senile plaques, and granulovacuolar bodies. Neurofibrillary tangles are dense, irregular fibers that develop primarily in the cytoplasm of cortical neurons, and the tangles are often highly concentrated in the hippocampus. Crapper, Kirshnan, and Dalton (1973) and Perl and Brody (1980) have made the observation that tangles are associated with unusually high levels of aluminum in the neurons of Alzheimer's disease patients, but no direct causal effect has been observed in related human or animal research (Alfrey, LeGendre, & Kaehny, 1976; Brun & Dictor, 1981; Crapper & Dalton, 1973; Klatzo, Wisniewski, & Streicher, 1965; Parsons & Prigatano, 1977). Neurofibrillary tangles also develop, to a lesser degree, in normal aging (Iqbal, Grundke-Iqbal, Wisniewski, & Terry, 1978; Yen, Gaskin, & Terry, 1981) as well as in pathological entities, such as Down's syndrome, subacute sclerosing panencephalitis, and progressive supranuclear palsy (Armbrustmacher, 1979; Ball & Nuttall, 1980; Ball & Nuttall, 1981; Mandybur, Nagpaul, Pappas, & Niklowitz, 1977; Schneck, Reisberg, & Ferris, 1982; Terry, 1980; Wisniewski, Jervis, Moretz, & Wisniewski, 1979; Valenstein, 1980).

Neuritic plaques are made up of amyloid, ostensibly a lipoprotein substance, surrounded by abnormal or degenerating neuronal processes consisting of axons, mitochondria, lysosomes, and helical filaments (Armbrustmacher, 1979; Terry, Gonatas, & Weiss, 1964). Abnormal neurites are generally found in the cerebral cortex, although they may develop in the brain stem, cerebellum, basal ganglia, and white matter. Not surprisingly, plaques are also observed in normal aging and Creutzfeldt-Jakob disease (Armbrustmacher, 1979; Schneck, Reisberg, & Ferris, 1982; Valenstein, 1980).

A residual microscopic pathological process in SDAT is the formation of granulo-vacuolar bodies, primarily in the hippocampus. These structures are small, clear, spherical vacuoles that surround irregular granules within cell cytoplasm (Valenstein, 1980). Ball and Lo (1977) determined that granulovacuolar bodies increase in number during normal aging, yet these vacuoles are many times more prevalent in patients who demonstrate Alzheimer's disease.

Neurochemical changes associated with SDAT include a reduction in cholineace-tyltransferase, acetylcholinesterase, norepinephrinc (NE), gamma-aminobutyric acid (GABA), and ACL receptor sites (Bowen, Smith, White, & Davison, 1976; Davies, 1978; Davies & Maloney, 1976; Perry, Blessed, Perry, & Tomlinson, 1980; Perry et al., 1977; Perry, Perry, Blessed, & Tomlinson, 1977; Pope, Hess, & Levin, 1964; Reisine, Yamamura, Bird, Spokas, & Enna, 1978; Soeninen, Halonen, & Reekkinen, 1981; White et al., 1977). Reduction in neurotransmitter activity, enzyme levels, and receptor sites is highly correlated with cellular changes, such as neuritic plaque and neurofibrillary tangle formation, as well as with the severity of dementia (Perry, 1980; Perry et al., 1978). Reduction in CAT is the most consistently observed biochemical alteration (Davies & Maloney, 1976; Perry, Perry, Blessed, Tomlinson, & Roth, 1979; Wilson et al., 1982). Cholinergic abnormalities appear related to relatively greater degeneration in the nucleus basalis of Meynert (NBM), a cholinergic nucleus in the substantia innominata. Cholinergic neurons in the NBM project directly to the cortex and hippocampus. Selective degeneration of cholinergic neurons in the NBM are thought to account for reduced CAT activity and impaired cognitive function in SDAT patients, but further research is needed to substantiate the relationship between NBM degeneration, cholinergic abnormalities, and cognitive dysfunction (White, et al., 1977).

Mental status changes in SDAT seem related to such morphological abnormalities as cell loss and dendritic spine degeneration. Abnormal histological developments, such as neurofibrillary tangles, neuritic plaques, and granulovacuolar body formation, also appear correlated with SDAT, but the precise cause of these abberations is unknown. Several theories that propose to account for these observations deserve mention.

Alzheimer's disease is hypothesized to be caused by a viral infection, since Creutzfeldt-Jakob disease, subacute sclerosing panencephalitis, and a rare progressive degenerative disease called kuru have symptoms similar to those of SDAT and all are classified as slow viruses. A major link to viral etiology was provided by Crapper and DeBoni (1979), who used material from SDAT patients' brains to culture structures similar to neurofibrillary tangles.

Another theory relates high concentrations of aluminum in the brains of SDAT patients to the development of neurofibrillary tangles (Crapper & Dalton, 1973; Perl & Brody, 1980). Similar but structurally different tangles have been experimentally created in animals by injecting aluminum (Klatzo, Wisniewski, & Streicher, 1965), but increased aluminum levels in human brain cells have not always been linked to neurofibrillary tangles (Crapper, Karlik, & DeBoni, 1978).

Hereditary factors also appear involved in the development of SDAT. Both auto-somal dominant and polygenetic models of inheritance are suggested (Schneck, Reis-berg, & Ferris, 1982), but family and twin case studies do not always support this genetic supposition (Cook, Schneck, & Clark, 1981; Nee et al., 1983; Sharman, Watt, Janota & Carrasco, 1979), and most researchers agree that genetics seems indirectly related to Alzheimer's and other similar degenerative conditions.

Two other theories regarding the etiology of SDAT include a proposed deficit in cerebral immune systems and overactive cerebral reactive antibodies, which appear to increase with age and may be involved in loss of neurons in both normal aging and SDAT (Schneck, Reisberg, & Ferris, 1982; Tkach & Hokama, 1970). Theories focusing on biochemical abnormalities, slow viruses, aluminum levels, genetics, and immune system disturbances have been proposed, but no single theory or combination of theories has received unequivocal support.

With the preceding foundation regarding the clinical features, biological aberrations, and theoretical approaches to dementia, a methodological review of neuropsychological dementia research is presented.

METHODOLOGY

A thorough literature review of any substantative research area is a challenging task, and the goal of this review is to provide a method of evaluating the neuropsychological strategies in dementia research. However, adequate strategy or method does not ensure a sound scientific approach, and, in fact, rigid methodology may preclude true scientific study (Kuhn, 1970). What follows is a systematic review of experimental design issues and factors that threaten internal-external validity and, consequently, the interpretability of neuropsychological observations in Alzheimer's disease. Neuropsychological research has been the focus of several general methodological critiques over the past several years (Parsons & Prigatano, 1978; Shallice, 1981; Smith, 1975), and much of the review presented here is a recapitulation of well-known experimental considerations that are particularly applicable to dementia research. Empirical findings regarding SDAT are presented, and then clinical and research data are integrated and recommendations proposed.

Experimental versus Quasi-experimental Designs

Even though many neuropsychological researchers describe their designs as experimental, in actuality, all studies of dementia are necessarily quasiexperimental. A quasiexperimental approach does not relegate studies to quasivalid status. Invalidity follows, not from the lack of true randomization, but from weak design that does not allow for efficient, unbiased interpretation of results or reduction in rival, plausible hypotheses (Campbell & Stanley, 1963). Neuropsychological researchers appear to have a penchant for several quasiexperimental designs that are particularly susceptible to threats to internal and external validity. In dementia research, four basic designs appear to predominate: the single-group descriptive study, the multiple-group discriminative approach, the single- or multiple-group cross-sectional design, and the single-case experimental study. In single-group descriptive research, Alzheimer's patients are most often compared with a control group through the use of several dependent measures. Inferences are made regarding these patients' neuropsychological functioning relative to that of the control subjects. Multiple-group discriminative studies also use control groups for selected comparisons between subjects, but an attempt is frequently made to discriminate SDAT from other neuropathological states, such as multi-infarct dementia and affective disorder, based on neuropsychological test scores. Cross-sectional studies usually involve studying dementia in the early, middle, and late stages, making the disease process the focus of study. In some cases, control groups are added to enhance cross-sectional comparisons. Finally, single-case experimental designs use selected cases to document neuropsychological patterns in dementia.

As a group, these methods present several idiosyncratic and shared potential threats to validity, but common to all is selection bias, which, depending on the circumstances, may threaten either internal or external validity. Selection factors are important in any quasi-experimental control group design and are especially relevant when experimental subjects are nonrandomly selected for study. Many of the suggestions that follow are related specifically to quasi-experimental research and especially to the issue of selection bias. In nonequivalent neuropsychological control group designs, certain subject variables, such as age, education and occupation, intelligence, illness onset and duration, and associated illnesses must be viewed as potential threats to validity. Each of these variables is considered below.

Age, Education, and Occupation

The subject's age is an obvious consideration for several reasons. First, age has been shown to have a significant effect on neuropsychological test performance (Goldstein & Shelly, 1981; Price, Fein, & Feinberg, 1980). The relationship between age and test performance is somewhat variable and dependent on many factors, but in general, as a person ages, neuropsychological test performance shows a mild decline (Benton, Eslinger, & Damasio, 1981). Age-related performance patterns are weakly understood, and valid age norms for intellectual and neuropsychological tests are needed (Price, Fein, & Feinberg, 1980). Nevertheless, in most cases, if control patients are younger than their demented cohorts, control subjects may be expected to evidence greater cognitive skill simply because of their age. As such, performance-level comparisons between subjects can be misleading. Age also figures prominently in neuropsychological studies because, even though presenile and senile dementia are now viewed as a single disease entity (SDAT), evidence suggests that the disease may progress more rapidly when onset is in the presenium (Constantinidis, 1978). Consequently, aging effects must be studied both independently and in concert with dementia, but until more research is completed, the total direct or indirect effects of aging on neuropsychological functions in dementia cannot be fully understood.

In most dementia research, subjects are matched with controls to establish comparisons on neuropsychological test performance, but if matching is to be successful, the aging process in its entirety must be considered. Because the matching process is difficult and frequently inadequate, control subjects are often younger than their demented cohorts; thus, a more conservative approach would be to select older control subjects. Also, occupational, medical, and family histories sometimes reveal dramatic differences between similarly aged and educated subjects. Patients with different personal histories and life-styles may not age similarly, and if this is the case, we must control for the aging process, as opposed to age itself. Precise recording of age and, more important, quantifying the aging process, may reduce competition from age-related explanations for differences between SDAT patients and control subjects.

Education, like age, may or may not be the controlling factor it is assumed to be. Thus far, dementia studies have most often equated subjects on educational level with little or no attention to occupation. Yet, many individuals of differing abilities obtain similar educational status, and once a generally average level of intellectual functioning is reached, educational achievement may reflect motivation as much as intelligence. Therefore, education must be explored beyond the simple, quantitative level. One approach to this problem is to consider the educational-occupational matrix, which seems to hold more promise for accurate representation of premorbid abilities than does simple educational level (Leli & Filskov, 1979). In addition, formal training, work history, and employment duties all contribute to a more accurate and appropriate estimate of premorbid functioning (Albert, 1981).

Intelligence

Neuropsychological test performance is directly related to intellectual ability (Chelune, 1982; Seidenburg, Giordani, Berent, & Boll, 1983). Brighter subjects perform better than less bright subjects on a wide range of neuropsychological measures, especially on complex concept formation and memory tests, and, parenthetically, the most difficult clinical discrimination is the question of declining cognitive efficiency in an elderly, premorbidly low intellectually functioning patient. Impaired scores mean little if the patient never demonstrated adequate cognitive ability. A better test of cognitive decline would be a rigorous assessment stressing adaptive capacities, such as self-care behavior, communication skills, and other behaviors that reflect important living skills but are not as heavily influenced by intellectual ability.

In many dementia studies, selection bias related to intellectual skill appears to be a viable alternative explanation for many of the differences observed between groups, especially when performance level is the major investigative focus. Subjects matched on age and education do not necessarily have similar premorbid intellectual abilities, and matched controls frequently demonstrate significantly better scores on intellectual assessment measures (Bigler, Steinman, & Newton, 1980; Davies, Hamilton, Hendrickson, Levy, & Post, 1978; Levy & Post, 1978; Storrie & Doerr, 1979; Weingartner, et al., 1981). Whether these scores indicate a premorbid advantage is unknown, but both premorbid and present intellectual functioning should be considered when test performance is used as a behavioral measure. It would be interesting to see how SDAT patients perform compared to normal subjects with similar intellectual skill as opposed to control subjects with significantly greater intellectual capacity. In any case, various methods of estimating premorbid intelligence have been proposed (Nelson & O'Connell, 1978; Wilson, Rosenbaum, Brown, & Roarke, 1979), but cognitive disorganization probably develops differently for individual patients, depending on the disease process, age, associated illnesses, intellectual ability, and other factors (Rosen & Mohs, 1982), which makes estimates of previous functioning difficult. Thus, control groups should reflect conservative matching procedures.

Illness Onset Duration

Symptoms typically have progressed for some time before patients seek diagnosis or treatment (Lishman, 1978). Although precise onset and duration of symptoms may be difficult to determine, the level and pattern of neuropsychological deterioration is highly dependent on the stage of the disorder. Some cross-sectional studies have compared and contrasted patients in various disease stages, but such studies do not specifically discuss illness duration, except in terms of time since diagnosis. Even then, it is often unclear exactly when dementing disorders had their initial effects, and thorough evaluation of cognitive-behavioral changes do not always elucidate the disease course. When duration of illness is unknown, understanding of the dementing process is obscured, and discrimination among various dementing disorders is also complicated if middle-stage SDAT patients are being compared with early-stage multi-infarct dementia patients, particularly when such ambiguous labels as early-, middle-, or late-stage disease are used. The time span from disease onset to incapacitating cognitive deterioration certainly varies from individual to individual, but more precise investigation of this parameter may prove helpful, not only in terms of improving our understanding of dementia from a diagnostic or etiological point of view, but from a treatment planning perspective as well.

Associated Disorders

Many medical and psychological disorders directly or indirectly produce cognitive impairment. Patients with chronic, psychiatric, or systemic disease pose a particular problem for the study of dementia. Illnesses that complicate or exacerbate cognitive impairment or decline should be considered in any study of dementia. For example, patients who have suffered repeated head trauma pose a threat to interpretation. In addition, a variety of systemic illnesses can decrease cognitive functioning and further obscure results (Albert, 1981). Even though the incidence of physical disorder increases with age, it is important that primary dementing illness not be confounded with the effects of psychiatric or physical disease. While it may be difficult to exclude all elderly patients with simple or complicated physical illnesses, thorough evaluation and documentation of associated illnesses makes assessment of disease interaction possible. Much of the research to date has excluded patients who demonstrated such significant complicating disorders as psychosis and chronic or acute neurological disease, but other considerations are important. For example, it may be inappropriate to exclude Alzheimer's disease patients with certain associated physical disorders, because external validity suffers if physical disorders have direct or indirect effects on Alzheimer's pathology (Albert, 1981).

Age, education and occupation, intellectual functioning, illness onset and duration, and associated disorders all present problems for nonequivalent control group designs. Experimental and control subject matching must be executed with care and sensitivity to potential selection bias especially, but not exclusively, when performance level is the primary experimental focus. Next, several important method variables, such as diagnostic criteria, test selection, and subject selection, are discussed.

Diagnostic Criteria

The basis for establishing a diagnosis is of obvious importance for neuropsychological studies of dementia. Diagnosis certainly varies depending on many factors, including subject characteristics, severity of the dementing process, sensitivity and specificity of the tests used, and the skill of the diagnostician. Clinical diagnosis via neurological procedures appears to be the minimal requirement for dementia research, but neurological examination, EEG, computerized tomography (CT) scan, and other procedures do not necessarily ensure an accurate diagnosis. Considering the wide range of dementing disorders, precise determination of etiology is quite difficult, and some professionals believe accurate diagnosis is confirmed only upon autopsy. This fact obviously complicates and prolongs experimental involvement. Certainly, any study using neuropsychological findings should include only subjects who have had a thorough neurological evaluation, preferably with highly reliable, multiple-rater diagnoses. Research, however, has varied from quite rigorous diagnostic inclusion by neurological methods (Weingartner, et al., 1981; Wilson, Kaszniak, & Fox, 1981) to simple assignment of nursing home subjects who were suspected of being demented (Diesfeldt, 1978). Suspicion of dementia is not sufficient for neuropsychological studies, and thorough documentation of the procedures and criteria used to arrive at diagnoses should be listed in the research report. Finally, if neuropsychological measures are used to identify potential subjects, these measures should be mentioned, because it would be redundant to classify patients based on neuropsychological test scores and then compare subjects on similar cognitive measures.

Subject Selection

Subject selection processes are often neglected in studies of dementia. Weak documentation of patients' representativeness significantly limits interpretability and generalizability of experimental findings. Often, patients are severely demented and untestable when presenting for hospitalization; however, several studies have identified dementias early in the disease process, when deficits are significant but relatively mild (Martin & Fedio, 1983; Storrie & Doerr, 1979; Weingartner, et al., 1981, 1982). As with other aspects of dementia research, subject selection is difficult to control, and several factors, such as age, education, and disease onset and duration, may systematically bias representativeness of samples such that most empirical findings are simply inaccurate for a significant percentage of dementia patients. In fact, few research reports actually state the process of subject selection or indicate reasons for subject exclusion. Thus, a better frame of reference must be developed for interpreting experimental results by fully elaborating on the means by which subjects are selected and to what degree they represent the population they are inferred to represent.

Test Selection

Test selection is an obviously complex theoretical and practical matter that should be related to the nature of the hypotheses being posed. However, in dementia research, test selection has been extremely variable. Most studies have used different procedures for studying similar theoretical constructs. For example, Bayles (1982) and Appell, Kertesz, and Fisman (1982) studied similar language functions using conceptually and methodologically different instruments. Of course, the following criticism could be directed at the entire body of psychological or neuropsychological research, but some attempt to provide consistency from one study to another regarding dependent measures should be undertaken, especially when similar theoretical constructs are being studied. In many ways, problems arise from quite diverse theoretical thinking and the competitive aspects of contemporary science. Nevertheless, given the sheer number of existing measures, some benefit may be gained by evaluating those already in use (Heaton &

Pendleton, 1981). Until theoretical developments occur, pragmatic considerations such as diagnostic utility and treatment planning may take precedence in the utilization of tests.

Summary of Methodology

The relative importance of subject and method variables to internal and external validity should not be underestimated. Overall, methodology used in dementia research must be more rigorous, and clinical studies must rely on quasi-experimentation. Full documentation of subject and method characteristics can significantly improve research strategies. While quasi-experimental approaches invite serious questions regarding validity, traditional factorial designs can be made more interpretable with proper planning and care. Alternative methods, such as causal models, path analysis, and structural equation models (Duncan, 1975), may ultimately allow more comprehensive evaluation of complex neuropsychological processes in dementing disorders. Many design and method problems are related to the special characteristics of Alzheimer's pathology and the quasi-experimental nature of neuropsychological research, but researchers should begin to overcome some inherent design problems with ingenuity, perseverance, and more adequate funding.

RESEARCH ON INTELLECTUAL, LANGUAGE, AND MEMORY FUNCTIONING IN SENILE DEMENTIA, ALZHEIMER'S TYPE

Several design considerations presented in the previous discussion are relevant to any neuropsychological study, but for our purposes, design issues were discussed first so that a common understanding of several threats to validity in quasiexperimental research could be established. We now proceed to analyze empirical findings, keeping these criticisms in mind. It is necessary to point out that the research we review neither exhausts the work completed on dementia, nor is it in every case characterized by exemplary methodology. In selecting studies for review, we attempted to include those with clinical relevancy and methodological sophistication. In some cases, we have succeeded; however, in others, considerable method and design problems complicate interpretation of results.

Intellectual Ability

Intellectual ability in SDAT has been studied using both descriptive and discriminative approaches. In descriptive studies, patients' performances are compared to control subjects' test scores. Not surprisingly, Alzheimer's disease patients perform less adequately than do controls on such intellectual measures as the Wechsler Adult Intelligence Scale (WAIS; Bigler, Steinman, & Newton, 1980; Butler, Dickinson, Katholi, & Halsey, 1983; Martin & Fedio, 1983; Storrie & Doerr, 1979; Weingartner, et al., 1982; Weingartner, et al., 1981), and WAIS Full Scale test score differences between controls and SDAT patients are usually quite dramatic, often approaching 20 points (Bigler, Steinman, & Newton, 1980). The magnitude of differences depends on many factors, such as disease onset and duration, premorbid cognitive ability, and associated disorders. The effect these factors have on patients' performance has been relatively uncontrolled in most Alzheimer's disease research. An exception is the work by Weingartner and colleagues (1981), which detailed WAIS test performance in a small sample of early-onset idiopathic dementia patients. Increased intertest variability and significantly decreased WAIS Performance IQ scores were apparent, while Verbal IQ scores remained statistically equivalent to control subjects' test performance. Longitudinal assessment was not completed, and test variability was not elaborated on, except to mention its occurrence. Nevertheless, contrary to most studies, Weingartner and colleagues (1981) studied premorbidly high-functioning patients in the early stages of progressive idiopathic dementia. Unfortunately, in this study, repeated measures were not obtained. Regardless, it was clear that patients who had recently become unemployed due to their symptoms evidenced impaired intellectual test scores on the WAIS, particularly on the Performance Scales.

Discriminative research has used intellectual test scores to differentiate Alzheimer's disease from other dementing conditions and affective disorders. In general, SDAT patients' WAIS test scores are significantly lower than those of normal subjects and patients with multi-infarct dementia, affective disorder, or vertebrobasilar insufficiency (Butler, Dickinson, Katholi, & Halsey, 1983; Perez et al., 1975; Perez, Stump, Gaye, & Hart, 1976). Other intellectual measures have been used in discriminative research, such as the Luria intellectual processes scale (Sulkava & Amberla, 1982), the Mill-Hill Vocabulary Test (Davies, Hamilton, Hendrickson, Levy, & Post, 1978), the Mental Status Questionnaire (Eastwood, Lautenschlaeger, & Corbin, 1983), and the Dementia Rating Scale (Eastwood, Lautenschlaeger, & Corbin, 1983; Gardner, Oliver-Munoz, Fisher, & Empting, 1981). Compared with various control populations, Alzheimer's disease patients also perform less adequately on these tests. The Extended Scale for Dementia (Hersch, 1979) and the Dementia Rating Scale are abbreviated, relatively broad-based assessment measures that evaluate orientation, simple reasoning skills, naming, and other functions. Such brief cognitive measures are often used to facilitate assessment of intellectual and neuropsychological functioning in moderately demented patients. These techniques may have less clinical utility in early-stage idiopathic dementia and at present seem more suited for performance level determination than for diagnostic or discriminative determination (Hersch, 1979), even though reliability seems adequate (Gardner, Oliver-Munoz, Fisher, & Empting, 1981; Hersch, 1979).

On the Halstead-Reitan Battery, Alzheimer's disease patients typically perform less adequately than do age- and education-matched control subjects, especially on the Category and Trail-Making Tests (Bigler, Steinman, & Newton, 1980; Storrie & Doerr, 1979), but demented patients appear to perform less adequately on all Halstead-Reitan measures except fine motor speed and strength tasks. Sulkava and Amberla (1982) attempted to discriminate between presenile and senile demented patients using the Luria Nebraska Battery and found that presenile patients performed more adequately but not statistically better than did senile patients and that test patterns in presenile and senile patients were remarkably similar. Dramatic deficits were observed on the Luria intellectual and memory subtests, while receptive and expressive speech skills remained relatively less impaired.

Few conclusions can be drawn regarding SDAT patients' intellectual test performance. Patients with early-stage Alzheimer's disease do demonstrate impaired test performance, and decline seems most apparent on Wechsler visuospatial-analytic tasks as opposed to verbal measures; however, verbal decline is apparent as well. As the disease progresses, patients typically show decline on both Wechsler Performance and

Verbal Intelligence scales, yet there is essentially no information available regarding rate or pattern of decline on the WAIS or Wechsler Adult Intelligence Scale-Revised (WAIS-R). Some evidence indicates that Luria Nebraska test patterns are consistent across senile and presenile patients and in moderately and severely demented patients, but small sample sizes and selection factors raise questions regarding these results. Halstead-Reitan testing indicates extremely weak concept formation and rapid information processing in early stage idiopathic dementia, but in general, much work is needed to elucidate the relationship between age, illness onset and duration, intellectual test level, and performance pattern. Since single-measurement descriptive and discriminative studies do not increase our understanding of these complexities, longitudinal studies would be quite helpful, as would cross-sectional studies with longitudinal measurement. Patterns of intellectual decline are important not only in studying neuropsychological processes but also in relating test behavior to biochemical and anatomical changes in Alzheimer's disease. For example, cerebral blood flow (Hagberg, 1978; Hagberg & Ingvar, 1976); structural changes (Merskey, et al., 1980); electroencephalographic abnormalities (Johannesson, Hagberg, Gustafson, & Ingvar, 1979); and certain enzyme activity, especially that of cholineacetyltransferase (Perry, et al., 1978), have been correlated with mental test scores. Research should begin as early as possible in the disease process and continue until the natural course can be documented.

Language Skills

Language functioning in Alzheimer's disease has been studied with both descriptive and discriminative methods. For the most part, research investigating language functions has been sparse, but recent investigations have focused on verbal fluency (Rosen, 1980), confrontation naming (Bayles & Tomeda, 1983; Martin & Fedio, 1983) and more broad-based language performance (Appell, Kertesz, & Fisman, 1982; Bayles, 1982). Research has implicated weak speech initiation (Stengel, 1964), impoverished vocabulary (Allison, 1962), and decreased semantic field differentiation in demented patients' language dysfunction (Obler, 1981). Regarding speech initiative, Alzheimer's disease patients evidenced reduced verbal fluency when compared to age-matched control subjects. Decreased verbal fluency was increasingly apparent as the disease worsened (Rosen, 1981); however, severe Alzheimer's disease patients were less educated than were their cohorts, a fact that complicates interpretation of these results. Naming skills also showed a decreasing linear relationship to disease severity. In general, animal naming performance was superior to controlled word associative retrieval, and Rosen concluded that in the early stages of Alzheimer's disease, patients do not seem to access category structures, since only the "clearest cases" in any category were recalled. Category access was severely impaired in advanced Alzheimer's disease, but patients were assigned to groups based on cognitive impairment, which again limits interpretation.

Bayles (1982) compared senile patients, (presumably with SDAT) and elderly normal subjects on several tasks, but again, selection bias was evident with weak matching on age and education. Diagnostic criteria were also weakly delineated, but demented patients performed significantly worse than did control subjects on all tests, including verbal expression, story retelling, verbal learning, and naming tasks. Patients did not recognize or correct semantic errors, and they often produced semantically inappropriate sentences. In contrast, a low frequency of phonology errors and relatively intact syntax were observed in mild to moderately involved patients (Bayles, 1982).

Several discriminative studies using confrontation naming have investigated language functioning in Alzheimer's disease patients (Appell, Kertesz, & Fisman, 1982; Bayles & Tomeda, 1982), and more general language assessment has also been carried out by Appell, Kertesz, and Fisman (1982) and by Martin and Fedio (1983). The Bayles and Tomeda study compared Alzheimer's disease, Huntington's chorea, Parkinson's disease, multi-infarct dementia, and normal patients with similar intellectual and educational skills. A response taxonomy for naming was used, and moderate Alzheimer's disease patients were found to be the most impaired in error frequency, although when mild and moderate Alzheimer's disease groups were considered together, there were no intergroup differences. Appell, Kertesz, and Fisman studied language functioning in Alzheimer's disease patients and compared their performance to that of aphasics and normal controls. Subjects were administered the Western Aphasia Battery (Kertesz, 1980) and a modified Boston Diagnostic Aphasia Battery (Goodglass & Kaplan, 1972). Speech disturbance was evident in about one-half the SDAT patients assessed, but only hospitalized patients who cooperated with testing were examined. Fluency was least impaired and repetition seemed well intact, though semantic jargon was very frequent. Alzheimer's disease patients performed worse than did normal control subjects on all measures except naming tasks. Compared to stroke patients, Alzheimer's disease patients demonstrated weaker comprehension and stronger fluency. Martin and Fedio (1983) found similarly disrupted semantic operations in early stage Alzheimer's disease patients. Access to attributes that determine word meaning was quite limited, while word definition skills remained generally intact.

Overall, language deterioration in SDAT seems related to substantially decreased cognitive performance and semantic processing, while, by contrast, there is relative sparing of speech initiation, articulation, repetition, and syntax, at least until the later stages of the disease. Reduced access to category structures and attributes is apparent in many Alzheimer's disease patients (Appell, Kertesz, & Fisman, 1982; Bayles & Tomeda, 1982; Martin & Fedio, 1983; Obler, 1983; Schwartz, Marin, & Saffran, 1979; Warrington, 1975). Decline in abstract reasoning and conceptual learning skills may parallel linguistic abnormalities, but further research is needed to investigate the interaction of cognitive disorganization and language dysfunction. Some observers (Martin & Fedio, 1983; Obler, 1981) believe that cognitive-linguistic deterioration in dementia is the antithesis of normal development, but such notions are probably simplistic and are certainly unsubstantiated (Obler, 1983). Longitudinal studies that focus on semantic processing, retrieval operations, and linguistic competence need to be initiated very early in the disease course.

Memory Functioning

Even though many cognitive functions are eventually affected by Alzheimer's disease, inefficient memory is cited as one of the first clinical signs (Sulkava & Amberla, 1982). Whether one can distinguish between learning and memory at this point is debatable, and only extremely intensive and sensitive research could hope to establish patterns of cognitive disorganization and to implicate learning, memory, or both processes in cognitive decline. In any case, new learning is dramatically affected by SDAT, and memory function is certainly essential to any learning process. In this regard, several aspects of memory functioning in Alzheimer's disease have been investigated, including immediate recall (Crookes & McDonald, 1972; Garron & Fox, 1979; Gibson, 1981; Hagberg, 1978), delayed recall (Dreisfeldt, 1978; Weingartner, et al., 1981, 1982), and remote recall (Wilson, Kaszniak, & Fox, 1981). Both descriptive and discriminative investigations have been pursued, and various dimensions of memory performance have been studied, such as free recall and recognition recall (Wilson, et al., 1983).

Focusing on immediate recall, Kaszniak, Garron, and Fox (1979) used the Wechsler Memory Scale to determine the effects of age and cerebral atrophy on memory. Not surprisingly, older subjects with more advanced atrophy evidenced the most memory impairment. Age itself did not appear to affect digit span performance, but paired associate learning scores did decrease as age increased. Atrophy correlated with impaired digit span, especially digit span backward performance, but digit span forward was relatively unimpaired compared to paired associate learning. Similar results were obtained by Weingartner and colleagues (1981, 1982), who found digit span forward essentially unimpaired in early-stage Alzheimer's disease, while other Wechsler Memory Scale scores were quite deficient. Unlike immediate numerical recall, immediate visuospatial memory seems significantly disturbed in demented patients (Crookes & McDonald, 1972; Weingartner, et al., 1981, 1982). Crookes and McDonald (1972) found that performance on the Benton Visual Retention Test was impaired in a sample of demented patients and depressives. The results indicated mostly size, lateral misplacement, and omission errors, but visuospatial recall was not adequately differentiated from perceptual and constructional skills.

Verbal and visual learning tasks have been found to differentiate demented patients from depressives and normal control subjects (Gibson, 1981). Demented patients' diagnoses were not made explicit, but these patients did evidence both quantitative and qualitative memory impairment. Demented subjects recalled significantly fewer words and did not evidence typical learning curves with serial position effects. Depressed patients demonstrated decreased learning capacity, but processing was quite similar to that in normal subjects, with serial position effects apparent. Serial position effects, verbal and visual learning, and free recall appear more disturbed than does forced choice recognition recall in SDAT patients (Whitehead, 1975). Demented patients perform better on recognition tasks, but, of course, these tasks are easier. Nevertheless, better forced choice performance may point to deficient retrieval, as opposed to an information encoding problem. Miller (1975) also found recognition recall superior to free recall in demented patients. Information was retrieved most efficiently when recognition tasks were simple and few alternative responses were available, but even under these conditions, recall was quite limited. Compared to normal subjects, recognition recall for rare words is quite impaired in demented patients, and this failure to retrieve rare words from memory was thought to reflect inattention and weak semantic processing (Wilson, et al., 1983).

Immediate and delayed memory performance patterns are apparent in the study by Weingartner and colleagues (1981). Early-stage SDAT patients were administered both clinical and laboratory memory tasks. Clinical data indicated generally average intellectual ability, while Wechsler Memory Scale performance was quite impaired. Memory deficiency was investigated further, and it was discovered that demented patients learned fewer words than did control subjects on tasks assessing learning and paired associate prompted recall. Unreliable recall of previously "learned" words was also observed, but, quite significantly, Alzheimer's disease patients learned unrelated words at the same rate as semantically related stimuli. Dementia seems to reduce patients' capacity to semantically encode information; consequently, both organizational and relational stimuli dimensions were underutilized by patients. Contrary to Miller (1975, 1978), Weingartner and colleagues (1981, 1982) argue that encoding, as opposed to retrieval, is disturbed in early-stage Alzheimer's disease patients. Alzheimer's disease patients' learning and recall are not enhanced by "repeating information, repeating forgotten information, providing sequential organization, or by increasing semantic relatedness" (Weingartner, et al., 1981, p. 194). These conclusions suggest that demented patients seem less able to use or impose organization on stimuli to be learned even though they may recognize the organization or structure when it is provided. These observations are consistent with language research, which points to a breakdown in semantic processing.

Remote memory hypothetically is the most refractory to dementing disorders, at least until the middle-stage disease. Wilson, Kaszniak, and Fox (1981) used the Famous Faces Test (Albert, Butters, & Levin, 1979) to assess remote memory capacity in demented patients. Patients did perform weakly on remote memory tests, but no temporal gradient in remote memory was found. A distinct decline in memory for the most recent two decades was noted, and it would be extremely interesting to know if disease duration is linearly or otherwise related to remote memory loss. Unfortunately, patients with varying onset and duration were not studied.

In summary, memory functions are dramatically affected in patients with Alzheimer's disease. These disturbances seem related to information processing problems that affect such normal learning phenomena as serial position effects and rare word advantage. Immediate, delayed, and remote retrieval processes are affected. In the initial disease stage, simple, immediate information retrieval, such as digit span, is not deficient, but other memory and verbal skills learning are significantly affected, primarily by defective semantic operations. Declining conceptual processing appears related to cognitive and linguistic dysfunction, and memory lapses seem to indicate a highly pathological process.

Summary of Research on Intellectual, Language, and Memory Functioning

Due to methodological limitations, research investigating intellectual, language, and memory functioning in SDAT must be cautiously interpreted, but methodological limitations aside, several findings emerge. SDAT patients do evidence cognitive decline that appears to affect intellectual, language, and memory skills in a consistent manner. SDAT seems to disturb conceptual learning and semantic association in many intellectual spheres. Information encoding and retrieval are both affected. In early stage dementia, verbal ability is less impaired than are visuospatial-motor skills and immediate and delayed memory functioning, but unfortunately, virtually no information regarding rate and pattern of cognitive decline is available. Overall, considerably more attention must be paid to methodology, since SDAT presents a particularly difficult research problem. Longitudinal research that focuses on clinical and etiological issues is needed.

CLINICAL ASSESSMENT

Neuropsychological assessment is often used to assist in the diagnosis and treatment of dementias, however, neuropsychological consultation is usually obtained after extensive neurological procedures have been completed. Following a thorough examination by a neurologist, several laboratory tests may be performed to determine if a patient's presenting problems are related to a dementing process. Depending on the circumstances, these procedures include a CT scan to evaluate cerebral atrophy and ventricular dilatation, serological tests, metabolic screening, hepatic and renal analysis, and tests for endocrine dysfunction, drug or heavy metal exposure, and vitamin deficiencies (Joynt & Shoulson, 1979). When normal-pressure hydrocephalus is considered, cister-nograms and pneumoencephalograms are often obtained to determine cerebral spinal fluid flow and uptake as well as to better visualize the subarachnoid space and cortical gyri. Angiography and blood flow studies are often required when multi-infarct dementia is suspected, and in extreme cases, brain biopsies are sometimes obtained (Sim, Turner, & Smith, 1966; Smith, Turner, & Sim, 1966). Once these tests have been completed, neuropsychological functioning is assessed.

Neuropsychological referral questions vary, but in most cases either descriptive or discriminative questions are proposed. Descriptive referral questions do not require a diagnostic formulation, principally because diagnosis has already been established. When descriptive referrals are made, neuropsychologists are interested in assessing present cognitive-behavioral efficiency in relation to self-care capacity or legal competency. As such, minimal attention is devoted to establishing or verifying diagnosis, but, of course, data suggesting misdiagnosis would not be ignored. Rather, such data would be integrated with original referral interrogatives. Test performance is also used to establish baseline functioning in order to assess the efficacy of medical interventions. Whether adaptive capacity or baseline assessment is the referral focus, diagnosis is usually not an issue when descriptive questions are posed. Alternatively, discriminative questions require neuropsychological diagnostic formulation, which may be used to assist in neurological diagnosis and treatment. If dementia is suspected, patients may be referred for assessment to determine whether cognitive decline has occurred and is consistent with SDAT. In such dichotomous classification situations, clinical sensitivity to cognitive decline related to aging and associated physical or psychiatric disorders is important, especially when formulations are based on a single evaluation. When repeated neuropsychological measurement is obtained, the magnitude and pattern of cognitive decline may be more easily established, but the assessment of demented patients is frequently complicated, and diagnostic accuracy in such instances is unknown. Diagnostic accuracy is dependent on at least the base rate of SDAT, test hit rate, and false positive-negative error rates (Meehl & Rosen, 1955). Unfortunately, test hit rate and false positive-negative rates probably change as SDAT progresses, which makes classification accuracy difficult to determine. Nevertheless, neuropsychological testing does provide an explicit method of documenting cognitive decline, especially if repeated measures are obtained.

Discrimination or multiple classification problems are most apparent when clinicians are asked to distinguish among normal aging, SDAT, affective disorder, and/or acute confusional states. For example, Albert (1981) elegantly discusses methods used to differentiate dementia from delirium, and the tests recommended include handwriting analysis, attentional assessment, and historical data, such as disease onset and duration. Even though extensive evaluation is usually not necessary (Albert, 1981), considerable clinical experience is necessary to establish diagnoses based primarily on a brief, principally qualitative evaluation such as that discussed by Albert. In any case, assessment considerations in such instances include the patient's age, education and occupation, any previous assessments, illness duration, associated disorders, mental status, and, of course, potential diagnoses. Since most tests used in neuropsychological assessment are not reliably normed for older patients, as patients' ages increase, many problems in estimating normative performance arise, with the result that impaired test scores do not always indicate functional disturbance (Benton, et al., 1981; Price, et al., 1980). Also, patients without significant educational and occupational achievement may perform weakly on tests, whether or not dementia or acute confusion is present. Such associated disorders as cardiovascular disease and head trauma may further complicate diagnostic decisions, and in most cases cognitive decline is multidetermined. If available, previous assessment data often help to estimate extent and pattern of decline; hence, diagnostic clarity may be gained. However, most patients have not had previous testing and are quite impaired, confused, and disoriented when assessed, especially when referred by primary medical care neurology services. Finally, illness duration is extremely important to either descriptive or discriminative referral questions. Patients in early-stage dementia may be thoroughly evaluated using fairly traditional measures, even extended neuropsychological batteries, but as the disease process progresses, data gathering and diagnosis become much more difficult. Most often, elderly patients' tolerance for assessment is limited, and historical data must be obtained from other sources, since many patients are incapable of relating accurate information. In addition, patients may evidence acute confusion related to toxicity, nutritional-metabolic inbalance, or infection, as well as to SDAT. Presenting problems are rarely mutually exclusive, and diagnosis is usually a conditional proposition, as opposed to a definitive statement. Hypotheses derived from assessment data may occasionally be validated or invalidated with such medical intervention as medication withdrawal, vitamin administration, and other treatments.

Assessment Model

Many assessment considerations must be weighed, but in general, intellectual functioning, abstract reasoning ability, visuospatial analysis, attention-concentration, language functioning, and memory capacity are appropriate areas on which to focus neuropsychological assessment (Albert, 1981; Wells & Buchanan, 1977), and a variety of tests are available to assess these cognitive functions. General intellectual ability may be measured using the entire WAIS-R or some combination of Verbal and Performance subtests (Ryan, Larsen, & Prifitera, 1983; Satz & Mogel, 1962). Several tasks, such as the Wisconsin Card Sorting Test (Berg, 1948) or the Category Test (Halstead, 1948), are recommended for assessing mental flexibility and discrimination learning capacity. Adequate auditory and visual attention are important for test performance, and both may be assessed using several tasks, such as digit span, tone discrimination, letter cancellation, and visual matching tests. Language assessment should evaluate naming and language repetition-comprehension, as well as reading and writing skills. Comprehensive aphasia batteries may be used, but several tests measuring individual skills may be assembled and adequately applied. Immediate, delayed, and remote memory functions also require assessment. Unfortunately, clinical memory assessment is complicated by the paucity of appropriate reliable and valid measures (Erickson & Scott, 1977); nevertheless, recent test development (Osborne, Brown, & Randt, 1982; Rabbitt, 1982) and validation (Baddeley, Sunderland, & Harris, 1982) may shortly provide alternatives to such traditional assessment techniques as the Wechsler Memory Scale. Finally, perceptual and constructional abilities can be assessed using many instruments, such as the Bender-Gestalt Test, portions of the Benton Visual Retention Test, Wechsler Memory Scale, and Halstead-Wepman Aphasia Screening test. As previously mentioned, in many cases, assessment of intellect, abstract reasoning, attention, language, and memory skills is precluded by patients' extremely disturbed mental status, principally disorientation and confusion. Nevertheless, brief neuropsychological evaluation can help to establish a baseline for medical intervention or behavioral treatment planning, and, in some cases, simple demonstration of the capacity to take a test can be an encouraging sign, even when performance is severely impaired. Also, instruments such as the Dementia Rating Scale (DRS), which is a relatively brief but broadly focused assessment measure, are sometimes of value. Even moderately demented patients are usually able to tolerate the DRS.

Research indicates that early-stage SDAT is characterized by impaired visuospatial analysis, conceptual learning, and memory functions, in contrast to a somewhat preserved verbal ability. Semantic processing deficits appear to affect intellectual, language, and memory skills, but these patterns may be observed in other primary degenerative disorders. In advanced SDAT, cognitive disorganization is so pronounced that discriminations among SDAT, MID, and acute confusional states are difficult to resolve based on test scores. Accurate diagnosis is frequently more difficult than one might expect or is led to believe. In contrast, affective disorders do appear somewhat less difficult to discriminate from SDAT than are confusional states and other dementing conditions (Weingartner, et al., 1982).

SUMMARY

In most discussions of neuropsychological assessment of dementia, accurate neuropsychological diagnosis is a major concern. However, in many cases, neuropsychological contributions to clinical practice involve documenting cognitive decline and assisting in treatment planning. A variety of neuropsychological procedures may be used to accomplish these tasks. Assessment must consider such patient characteristics as age, education, occupation, premorbid functioning, disease onset and duration, and proposed diagnoses, as well as such test characteristics as the skills measured, difficulty level, and information yield. When possible, broad-based assessment of intellect, reasoning, attention, language, and memory skills is recommended, but often patients are unable to tolerate extended neuropsychological assessment, with the result that brief cognitive-behavioral procedures must be used. Neuropsychological assessment is also appropriately and frequently used to delineate cognitive change resulting from medical intervention, such as vitamin administration or surgical procedures, however, only a small percentage of patients with dementia are offered such medical treatment. Nevertheless, information may be provided regarding the course of the disease, and environmental planning may be facilitated in many cases, since patients' families often are not fully aware of the effects of severe mental and physical decline, even though informative publications detailing behavioral changes in SDAT are available (Mace & Rabins, 1981).

Predictions that dementias are increasing in frequency are disturbing because of the tremendous physical, emotional, and economic cost to patients and families of SDAT patients. Neuropsychology's contribution to understanding and treating SDAT can be significant if, in the future, advancements in basic clinical research and neuropsychological assessment continue.

ACKNOWLEDGMENTS

We wish to express our sincere thanks and appreciation to Ms. Teresa Vaughn and Ms. Dawn King for their valuable assistance in the preparation of this manuscript.

REFERENCES

Adams, R. (1966). Further observation on normal pressure hydrocephalus. *Proceedings of the Royal Society of Medicine, 59,* 1135.

Albert, M.S. (1981). Geriatric neuropsychology. *Journal of Consulting and Clinical Psychology, 6,* 835–850.

Albert, M.S., Butters, N., & Levin, J. (1979). Temporal gradients in the retrograde amnesia of patients with alcoholic Korsakoff's disease. *Archives of Neurology, 36,* 211–216.

Alfrey, A.C., LeGendre, G.R., & Kaehny, W.D. (1976). The dialysis encephalopathy syndrome: Possible aluminum intoxication. *New England Journal of Medicine, 294,* 184–188.

Allison, R.S. (1962). *The senile brain.* London: Edward Arnold.

Appell, J., Kertesz, A., & Fisman, M. (1982). A study of language functioning in Alzheimer's patients. *Brain and Language, 17,* 73–91.

Armbrustmacher, V.W. (1979). Pathology of dementia. In S.C. Sommers & P.P. Rosen (Eds.), *Pathology annual: Part I* (Vol. 14, pp. 145–173). New York: Appleton-Century-Crofts.

Baddeley, A., Sunderland, A., & Harris, J. (1982). How well do laboratory-based psychological tests predict patients' performance outside the laboratory: In S. Corkin, K. Davis, J. Growdon, E. Usdin, & R. Wurtman (Eds.), *Alzheimer's disease: Progress in research* (Vol. 19, pp. 141–148). New York: Raven Press.

Ball, M.J. (1977). Neuronal loss, neurofibrillary tangles and granulovacuolar degeneration in the hippocampus with aging and dementia: A quantitative study. *Acta Neuropathologica (Berlin), 37,* 111–118.

Ball, M.J., & Lo, P. (1977). Granulovacuolar degeneration in the aging brain and in dementia. *Journal of Neuropathology and Experimental Neurology, 36,* 474–487.

Ball, M.J., & Nuttall, K. (1979). Neurofibrillary tangles, granulovacuolar degeneration, and neuron loss in Down's syndrome: Quantitative comparison with Alzheimer's dementia. *Annals of Neurology, 7,* 462–465.

Ball, M.J., & Nuttall, K. (1981). Topography of neurofibrillary tangles and granulovacuoles in hippocampi of patients with Down's syndrome: Quantitative comparison with normal aging and Alzheimer's disease. *Neuropathology and Applied Neurobiology, 7,* 13–20.

Bayles, K. (1982). Language function in senile dementia. *Brain and Language, 16,* 265–280.

Bayles, K.A., & Tomeda, C.K. (1983). Confrontation naming impairment in dementia. *Brain and Language, 19,* 98–114.

Benton, A.L., Eslinger, P.J., & Damasio, A.R. (1981). Normative observations on test performance in old age. *Journal of Clinical Neuropsychology, 1,* 33–42.

Bigler, E.D., Steinman, D.R., & Newton, J.S. (1980). Clinical assessment of cognitive deficit in neurologic disorder: I. Effects of age and degenerative disease. *Clinical Neuropsychology, 3,* 5–13.

Bowen, D.M., Smith, C.B., White, P., & Davison, A.N. (1976). Neurotransmitter-related enzymes and indices of hypoxia in senile dementia and other abiotrophies. *Brain, 99,* 459–496.

Brinkman, S.D., Sarwar, M.A.M., Levin, H.S., & Morris, H.H., III. (1981). Quantitative indexes of computed tomography in dementia and normal aging. *Radiology, 138,* 89–92.

Brody, H. (1955). Organization of the cerebral cortex: III. A study of aging in the human cerebral cortex. *Journal of Comparative Neurology, 102,* 511–556.

Brody, H. (1978). Cell counts in cerebral cortex and brainstem in Alzheimer's disease: Senile dementia and related disorders. In R. Katzman, R.D. Terry, & K.L. Bick (Eds.), *Alzheimer's disease: Senile dementia and related disorders* (Vol. 7, pp. 345–352). New York: Raven Press.

Brun, A., & Dictor, M. (1981). Senile plaques and tangles in dialysis dementia. *Acta Pathologica et Microbiologica Scandinavica. Section A, Pathology, 89,* 193–198.

Butler, R.W., Dickinson, W.A., Katholi, C., & Halsey, J.H. (1983). The comparative effects of organic brain disease on cerebral blood flow and measured intelligence. *Annals of Neurology, 13,* 155–159.

Campbell, D., & Stanley, J.C. (1963). *Experimental and quasi experimental designs for research.* Chicago: Rand McNally.

Celesia, G.G., & Daly, R.F. (1977). Effects of aging on visual evoked responses. *Archives of Neurology, 34,* 403–407.

Chelune, G. (1982). A reexamination of the relationship between the Luria-Nebraska and Halstead batteries: Overlap with the WAIS. *Journal of Consulting and Clinical Psychology, 4,* 578–580.

Coblentz, J.M., Mattis, S., Zingesser, L.H., Kasoff, S.S., Wisniewski, H.M., & Katzman, R. (1973). Presenile dementia: Clinical aspects and evaluation of cerebrospinal fluid dynamics. *Archives of Neurology, 29,* 299–308.

Colon, E.J. (1972). The elderly brain: A quantitative analysis in the cerebral cortex in two cases. *Psychiatria, Neurologia and Neurochirurgia (Amsterdam), 75,* 261–270.

Constantinidis, J. (1978). Is Alzheimer's disease a major form of senile dementia? Clinical, anatomical, and genetic data. In R. Katzman, R.D. Terry, & K.L. Bick (Eds.), *Alzheimer's disease: Senile dementia and related disorders.* New York: Raven Press.

Cook, R.H., Schneck, S.A., & Clark, D.B. (1981). Twins with Alzheimer's disease. *Archives of Neurology, 38,* 300–301.

Cragg, B.G. (1975). The density of synapses and neurons in normal, mentally defective, and aging human brains. *Brain, 98,* 81–90.

Crapper, D.R., & Dalton, A.J. (1973). Alteration in short-term retention, conditioned avoidance, acquisition, and motivation following aluminum-induced neurofibrillary degeneration. *Physiology and Behavior, 10,* 925–933.

Crapper, D.R., & DeBoni, U. (1979). Etiological factors in dementia. In *Abstracts: Satellite meeting on aging of the brain and dementia,* International Society for Neurochemistry. Abano Terme, Italy: FIDIA Research labs.

Crapper, D.R., Karlik, S., & DeBoni, U. (1978). Aluminum and other metals in senile (Alzheimer) dementia. In R. Katzman, R.D. Terry, & K.L. Bick (Eds.), *Alzheimer's disease: Senile dementia and related disorders* (Vol. 7, pp. 471–486). New York: Raven Press.

Crapper, D., Kirshnan, S.S., & Dalton, A.J. (1973). Brain aluminum distribution in Alzheimer's disease and experimental neurofibrillary degeneration. *Science, 180,* 511–513.

Crookes, T.G., & McDonald, K.G. (1972). Benton Visual Retention Test in the differentiation of depression and early dementia. *British Journal of Social and Clinical Psychology, 2,* 66–69.

Davies, G., Hamilton, S., Hendrickson, D.E., Levy, R., & Post, F. (1978). Psychological test performance and sedation thresholds of elderly patients, depressives and depressives with incipient brain change. *Psychological Medicine, 8,* 103–109.

Davies, P. (1978). Studies on the neurochemistry of central cholinergic systems in Alzheimer's disease. In R. Katzman, R.D. Terry, & K.L. Bick (Eds.), *Alzheimer's disease: Senile dementia and related disorders* (Vol. 7, pp. 453–460). New York: Raven Press.

Davies, P., & Maloney, A.J.F. (1976). Selective loss of central cholinergic neurons in Alzheimer's disease [Letter to Editor]. *Lancet, 2,* 1403.

Dayan, A.D. (1970). Quantitative histological studies on the aged human brain: II. Senile plaques and neurofibrillary tangles in "normal" patients. *Acta Neuropathologica (Berlin), 16,* 85–94.

Diesfeldt, H.F.A. (1978). The distinction between long-term and short-term memory in senile dementia: An analysis of free recall and delayed recognition. *Neuropsychologica,* 115–119.

Dorland's Pocket Medical Dictionary (21st ed.). (1968). Philadelphia: W.B. Saunders.

Eastwood, M.R., Lautenschlaeger, E., & Corbin, S. (1983). A comparison of clinical methods for assessing dementia. *Journal of the American Geriatrics Society, 6,* 342–347.

Erickson, R.C., & Scott, M.L. (1977). Clinical memory testing: A review. *Psychological Bulletin, 84,* 1130–1149.

Ford, C.V., & Winter, J. (1981). Computerized axial tomograms and dementia in elderly patients. *Journal of Gerontology, 2,* 164–169.

Gardner, R., Oliver-Munoz, S., Fisher, L., & Empting, L. (1981). Mattis Dementia Rating Scale: Internal reliability study using a diffusely impaired population. *Journal of Clinical Neuropsychology, 3,* 271–275.

Gibbs, C.J., Jr., & Gajdusek, D.C. (1978). Subacute spongiform virus encephalopathies: The transmissible virus dementias. In R. Katzman, R.D. Terry, & K.L. Bick (Eds.), *Alzheimer's disease: Senile dementia and related disorders* (Vol. 7, pp. 559–575). New York: Raven Press.

Gibbs, F.A., & Gibbs, E.L. (1964). *Atlas of electroencephalography: Neurological and psychiatric disorder* (Vol. 3). Reading, MA: Addison-Wesley.

Gibson, A.J. (1981). A further analysis of memory loss in dementia and depression in the elderly. *British Journal of Clinical Psychology, 20,* 179–185.

Goldstein, G., & Shelly, C. (1981). Does the right hemisphere age more rapidly than the left? *Journal of Clinical Neuropsychology, 1,* 65–78.

Goodglass, H., & Kaplan, E. (1972). *Assessment of aphasia and related disorders.* Philadelphia: Lea & Febiger.

Goodin, D.C., Squires, K.C., Henderson, B., & Starr, A. (1978). Age-related variations in evoked potentials to auditory stimuli in normal human subjects. *Electroencephalographic and Clinical Neurophysiology, 44,* 447–458.

Goodin, D.S., Squires, K.C., & Starr, A. (1978). Long latency event-related components of the auditory evoked potential in dementia. *Brain, 101,* 635–648.

Hagberg, B. (1978). Defects of immediate memory related to cerebral blood flow distribution. *Brain and Language, 5,* 366–377.

Hakin, S., & Adams, R.D. (1965). The special clinical problem of symptomatic hydrocephalus with normal cerebrospinal fluid pressure: Observations on cerebrospinal fluid hemodynamics. *Journal of Neurological Surgery, 2,* 307.

Hall, T.C., Miller, A.K.H., & Corsellis, J.A.N. (1975). Variations in the human Purkinje cell population according to age and sex. *Neuropathology and Applied Neurobiology, 1,* 267–292.

Heaton, R.K., & Pendleton, M.G. (1981). Use of neuropsychological tests to predict adult patients' everyday functioning. *Journal of Consulting and Clinical Psychology, 6,* 807–821.

Hersch, E.L. (1979). Development and application of the extended scale for dementia. *Journal of the American Geriatrics Society, 8,* 348–354.

Herzog, A.G., & Kemper, T.L. (1980). Amygdaloid changes in aging and dementia. *Archives of Neurology, 37,* 625–629.

Hubbard, B.M., & Anderson, J.M. (1981). A quantitative study of cerebral atrophy in old age and senile dementia. *Journal of the Neurological Sciences, 50*, 135–145.

Hughes, C.P., & Gado, M. (1981). Computed tomography and aging of the brain. *Radiology, 139*, 391–396.

Ingvar, D.H., Brun, A., Hagberg, B., & Gustafson, L. (1978). Regional cerebral blood flow in the dominant hemisphere in confirmed cases of Alzheimer's disease, Pick's disease, and multi-infarct dementia: Relationship to clinical symptomatology and neuropathological findings. In R. Katzman, R.D. Terry, & K.L. Bick (Eds.), *Alzheimer's disease: Senile dementia and related disorders* (Vol. 7, pp. 203–212). New York: Raven Press.

Iqbal, K., Grundke-Iqbal, I., Wisniewski, H.M., & Terry, R.D. (1978). Chemical relationship of the paired helical filaments of Alzheimer's dementia to normal human neurofilaments and neurotubules. *Brain Research, 142*, 321–332.

Jacobs, L., Kinkel, W.R., Painter, F., Murawski, J., & Heffner, R.R., Jr. (1978). Computerized tomography in dementia with special reference to changes in size of normal ventricles during aging and normal pressure hydrocephalus. In R. Katzman, R.D. Terry, & K.L. Bick (Eds.), *Alzheimer's disease: Senile dementia and related disorders* (Vol. 7, pp. 241–260). New York: Raven Press.

Johannesson, G., Hagberg, B., Gustafson, L., & Ingvar, D.H. (1979). EEG and cognitive impairment in presenile dementia. *Acta Neurologica Scandinavica, 59*, 225–240.

Joynt, R.J., & Shoulson, I. (1979). Dementia. In K.M. Heilman & E. Valenstein (Eds.), *Clinical neuropsychology* (pp. 475–502). Oxford, England: Oxford University Press.

Kazniak, A.W., Garron, D.C., & Fox, J. (1979). Differential effects of age and cerebral atrophy upon span of immediate recall and paired associate learning in older patients suspected of dementia. *Cortex, 15*, 285–295.

Kaszniak, A.W., Garron, D.C., Fox, J.H., Bergen, D., & Huckman, M. (1979). Cerebral atrophy, EEG slowing, age, education, and cognitive functioning in suspected dementia. *Neurology, 29*, 1273–1279.

Kertesz (1980). *Western aphasia battery.* London, Ontario, Canada: University of Western Ontario.

Klatzo, I., Wisniewski, H., & Streicker, E. (1965). Experimental production of neurofibrillary degeneration. *Journal of Neuropathology and Experimental Neurology, 24*, 187–199.

Konigsmark, B.W., & Murphy, E.A. (1972). Volume of the ventral cochlear nucleus in man: Its relationship to neuronal population with age. *Journal of Neuropathology and Experimental Neurology, 31*, 304–316.

Kooi, K.A. (1971). *Fundamentals of electroencephalography.* New York: Harper & Row.

Kuhn, T.S. (1970). *The structure of scientific revolutions.* Chicago: University of Chicago Press.

Lavy, S., Melamed, E., Bentin, S., Cooper, G., & Rinot, Y. (1978). Bihemispheric decreases of regional cerebral blood flow in dementia: Correlation with age-matched normal controls. *Annals of Neurology, 4*, 445–450.

Leli, D.A., & Filskov, S.B. (1979). Relationship of intelligence to education and occupation as signs of intellectual deterioration. *Journal of Consulting and Clinical Psychology, 4*, 702–707.

Levin, H.S., O'Donnell, V.M., & Grossman, R.G. (1979). The Galveston Orientation and Amnesia Test: A practical scale to assess cognition after head injury. *Journal of Nervous and Mental Disorders, 167*, 675–684.

Lezak, M.D. (1978). Living with the characterologically altered brain-injured patient. *Journal of Clinical Psychiatry, 39*, 592–598.

Lishman, W.A. (1978). *Organic psychiatry.* Oxford, England: Blackwell Scientific.

Mace, N.L., & Rabins, P.V. (1981). *The 36-hour day.* Baltimore: Johns Hopkins University Press.

Mandybur, T.I., Nagpaul, A.S., Pappas, Z., & Niklowitz, W.J. (1977). Alzheimer neurofibrillary change in subacute sclerosing panencephalitis. *Annals of Neurology, 1,* 103–107.

Martin, A., & Fedio, P. (1983). Word production and comprehension in Alzheimer's disease: The breakdown of semantic knowledge. *Brain and Language, 19,* 124–141.

Matsuyama, H., & Nakamura, S. (1978). Senile changes in the brain in the Japanese: Incidence of Alzheimer's neurofibrillary change in senile plaques. In R. Katzman, R.D. Terry, & K.L. Bick (Eds.), *Alzheimer's disease: Senile dementia and related disorders* (Vol. 7, pp. 287–297). New York: Raven Press.

Meehl, P.E., & Rosen, A. (1955). Antecedent probability and the efficiency of psychometric signs, patterns or cutting scores. *Psychological Bulletin, 52,* 194–216.

Mehraein, P., Yamada, M., & Tarnowska-Dzidusko, E. (1975). Quantitative study of dendrites and dendritic spines in Alzheimer's disease and senile dementia. In G.W. Kreutzberg (Ed.), *Advances in neurology* (Vol. 12, pp. 453–458). New York: Raven Press.

Melamed, E., Lavy, S., Siew, F., Bentin, S., & Cooper, G. (1978). Correlation between regional cerebral blood flow and brain atrophy in dementia. *Journal of Neurology, Neurosurgery and Psychiatry, 41,* 894–899.

Merritt, H.H. (1973). *A textbook of neurology* (5th ed.). Philadelphia: Lea & Febiger.

Merskey, H., Ball, M.J., Blume, W.T., Fox, A.J., Fox, H., Hersch, E.L., Kral, V.A., & Palmer, R.B. (1980). Relationships between psychological measurements and cerebral organic changes in Alzheimer's disease. *Canadian Journal of Neurological Sciences, 1,* 45–49.

Miller, E. (1975). Impaired recall and the memory disturbance in presenile dementia. *British Journal of Social and Clinical Psychology, 14,* 73–79.

Miller, E. (1978). Retrieval from long term memory in presenile dementia: Two tests of an hypothesis. *British Journal of Social and Clinical Psychology, 17,* 143–148.

Monagle, R.D., & Brody, H. (1974). The effects of age upon the main nucleus of the inferior olive in the human. *Journal of Comparative Neurology, 155,* 61–66.

Naeser, M.A., Gebhardt, C., Levine, H.L. (1980). Decreased computerized tomography numbers in patients with presenile dementia. *Archives of Neurology, 37,* 401–409.

Nee, L.E., Polinsky, R.J., Eldridge, R., Weingartner, H., Smallberg, S., & Ebert, M. (1983). A family with histologically confirmed Alzheimer's disease. *Archives of Neurology, 40,* 203–208.

Nelson, H.E., & O'Connell, A. (1978). Dementia: The estimation of premorbid intelligence levels using the new adult reading test. *Cortex, 14,* 234–244.

Obler, L. (1981). Review of *le langage des déments. Brain and Language, 12,* 375–386.

Obler, L. (1983). Language and brain dysfunction in dementia. In S. Segalowitz (Ed.), *Language function and brain organization.* New York: Academic Press.

Obrist, W.D. (1978). Noninvasive studies of cerebral blood flow in aging and dementia. In R. Katzman, R.D. Terry, & K.L. Bick (Eds.), *Alzheimer's disease: Senile dementia and related disorders* (Vol. 7, pp. 213–218). New York: Raven Press.

Obrist, W.D., Chivian, E., Cronqvist, S., & Ingvar, D.H. (1970). Regional cerebral blood flow in senile and presenile dementia. *Neurology, 20,* 315–322.

Osborne, D.P., Brown, E.R., & Randt, C.T. (1982). Qualitative changes in memory function: Aging and dementia in Alzheimer's disease. In S. Corkin, K. Davis, J. Growdon, E. Usdin, & R. Wurtman (Eds.), *Alzheimer's disease: A report of progress* (Vol. 19, pp. 165–170). New York: Raven Press.

Parsons, O.A. (1977). Neuropsychological deficits in alcoholics: Facts and fancies. *Alcoholism, 1,* 51–56.

Parsons, O.A., & Prigatano, G.P. (1978). Methodological considerations in clinical neuropsychological research. *Journal of Consulting and Clinical Psychology, 46,* 608–619.

Paula-Barbosa, M.M., Moto Cardoso, R., Guimaraes, M.L., & Cruz, C. (1980). Dendritic degeneration and regrowth in the cerebral cortex of patients with Alzheimer's disease. *Journal of the Neurological Sciences, 45,* 129–134.

Perez, F.I., Rivera, V.M., Meyer, J.S., Gay, J.R.A., Taylor, R.L., & Matthew, N.T. (1975). Analysis of intellectual and cognitive performance in patients with multi-infarct dementia, vertebrobasilar insufficiency with dementia and Alzheimer's disease. *Journal of Neurology, Neurosurgery and Psychiatry, 38,* 533–540.

Perez, F., Stump, D., Gay, J.R.A., & Hart, V.R. (1976). Intellectual performance in multi-infarct dementia and Alzheimer's disease: A replication study. *Canadian Journal of Neurological Sciences, 3,* 181–187.

Perl, D.P., & Brody, A.R. (1980). Alzheimer's disease: X-ray spectrometric evidence of aluminum accumulation in neurofibrillary tangle-bearing neurons. *Science, 208,* 297–299.

Perry, E.K. (1980). The cholinergic system in old age and Alzheimer's disease. *Age and Ageing, 9,* 1–8.

Perry, E.K., Perry, R.H., Blessed, G., & Tomlinson, B.E. (1977). Necropsy evidence of central cholinergic deficits in senile dementia. *Lancet, i,* 189.

Perry. E.K., Tomlinson, B.E., Blessed, G., Bergmann, K., Gibson, P.H., & Perry. R.H. (1978). Correlation of cholinergic abnormalities with senile plaques and mental test scores in senile dementia. *British Medical Journal, 2,* 1457–1459.

Perry, R.H., Blessed, G., Perry, E.K., & Tomlinson, B.E. (1980). Histochemical observations on cholinesterase activities in the brains of elderly normal and demented (Alzheimer-type) patients. *Age and Ageing, 9,* 9–16.

Pope, A., Hess, H.H., & Lewin, E. (1964). Microchemical pathology of the cerebral cortex in presenile dementias. *Transactions of the American Neurological Association, 89,* 15–16.

Price, L.J., Fein, G., & Feinberg, I. (1980). Neuropsychological assessment of cognitive function in the elderly. In L.W. Poon (Ed.), *Aging in the 1980's.* Washington, DC: American Psychological Association.

Pryse-Phillips, W., & Murray, T.J. (1978). *Essential Neurology.* Garden City, NY: Medical Examination Publishing.

Rabbitt, P. (1982). Development of methods to measure changes in activities of daily living in the elderly. In S. Corkin, K. Davis, J. Growdon, E. Usdin, & R. Wurtman (Eds.), *Alzheimer's disease: A report of progress* (Vol. 19, pp. 127–132). New York: Raven Press.

Reisine, T.D., Yamamura, H.I., Bird, E.D., Spokes, E., & Enna, S.J. (1978). Pre-and postsynaptic neurochemical alterations in Alzheimer's disease. *Brain Research, 159,* 477–481.

Roberts, M.A., & Caird, F.L. (1976). Computerized tomography and intellectual impairment in the elderly. *Journal of Neurology, Neurosurgery and Psychiatry, 39,* 986–989.

Rosen, W.G., & Mohs, R.C. (1982). Evolution of cognitive decline in dementia. In S. Corkin, K. Davis, J. Growdon, E. Usdin, & R. Wurtman (Eds.), *Alzheimer's disease: A report of progress* (Vol. 19, pp. 183–188). New York: Raven Press.

Roth, M. (1978). Epidemiological studies. In R. Katzman, R.D. Terry, & K.L. Bick (Eds.), *Alzheimer's disease: Senile dementia and related disorders* (Vol. 7, pp. 337–339). New York: Raven Press.

Ryan, J.J., Larsen, J., & Prifitera, A. (1983). Validity of two and four subtest short forms of the WAIS-R in a psychiatric sample. *Journal of Consulting and Clinical Psychology, 3,* 460.

Satz, P., & Mogel, S. (1962). An abbreviation of the WAIS for clinical use. *Journal of Clinical Psychology, 18,* 77–79.

Scheibel, M.E., Lindsay, R.D., Tomiyasu, U., & Scheibel, A.B. (1975). Progressive dendritic changes in aging human cortex. *Experimental Neurology, 47,* 392–403.

Scheibel, M.E., Lindsay, R.D., Tomiyasu, U., & Scheibel, A.B. (1975). Progressive dendritic changes in the aging human limbic system. *Experimental Neurology, 47,* 420–430.

Scheibel, M.E., & Scheibel, A.B. (1975). Structural changes in the aging brain. In H. Brody, D. Harman, & J.M. Ordy (Eds.), *Clinical, morphologic, and neurochemical aspects in the aging central nervous system* (Vol. 1, pp. 11–37). New York: Raven Press.

Schneck, M.K., Reisberg, B., & Ferris, S.H. (1982). An overview of current concepts in Alzheimer's disease. *American Journal of Psychiatry, 139,* 165–173.

Schwartz, M.F., Marin, O.S.M., & Saffran, E.M. (1979). Dissociation of language functions in dementia: A case study. *Brain and Language, 7,* 277–306.

Seidenberg, M., Giordani, B., Berent, S., & Boll, T.J. (1983). IQ level and performance on the Halstead-Reitan Neuropsychological Test Battery for Older Children. *Journal of Consulting and Clinical Psychology, 3,* 406–413.

Shallice, T. (1979). Case study approach in neuropsychological research. *Journal of Clinical Neuropsychology, 3,* 183–211.

Sharman, M.G., Watt, D.C., Janota, I., & Carrasco, L.H. (1979). Alzheimer's disease in a mother and identical twin sons. *Psychological Medicine, 9,* 771–774.

Shefer, V.F. (1973). Absolute number of neurons and thickness of the cerebral cortex during aging, senile and vascular dementia, and Pick's and Alzheimer's disease. *Neuroscience and Behavioral Psychology, 6,* 319–324.

Sim, M., Turner, E., & Smith, W.T. (1966). Cerebral biopsy in the investigation of presenile dementia. *British Journal of Psychiatry, 112,* 119–125.

Simard, D., Olesen, J., Paulson, O., Lassen, N.Q., & Skinhj, E. (1971). Regional cerebral blood flow in senile and presenile dementia. *Neurology, 20,* 315–322.

Smith, A. (1975). Neuropsychological testing in neurological disorders. In W.J. Friedlander (Ed.), *Advances in neurology* (Vol. 7, pp. 49–110). New York: Raven Press.

Smith, W.T., Turner, E., & Sim, M. (1966). Cerebral biopsy in the investigation of presenile dementia. *British Journal of Psychiatry, 112,* 127–133.

Soininen, H., Halonen, T., & Riekkinen, P.J. (1981). Acetylcholinesterase activities in cerebrospinal fluid of patients with senile dementia of Alzheimer type. *Acta Neurologica Scandinavica, 64,* 217–224.

Stengel, E. (1968). Psychopathology of dementia. *Proceedings of the Royal Society of Medicine, 57,* 911–914.

Storrie, M., & Doerr, H.O. (1979). Characterization of Alzheimer type dementia utilizing an abbreviated Halstead-Reitan Battery. *Clinical Neuropsychology, 2,* 78–81.

Sulkava, R., & Amberla, K. (1982). Alzheimer's disease and senile dementia of Alzheimer's type: A neuropsychological study. *Acta Neurologica Scandinavica, 65,* 651–660.

Terry, R.D. (1980). Some biological aspects of the aging brain. *Mechanisms of Ageing and Development, 14,* 191–201.

Terry, R.D., Fitzgerald, C., Peck, A., Millner, J., & Farmer, P. (1977). Cortical cell counts in senile dementia. *Journal of Neuropathology and Experimental Neurology, 36,* 633. (Abstract)

Terry, R.D., Gonatas, N.K., & Weiss, M. (1964). Ultrastructural studies in Alzheimer's presenile dementia. *American Journal of Pathology, 44,* 269–297.

Terry, R.D., Peck, A., DeTeresa, R., Schechter, R., & Horoupian, D.S. (1981). Some morphometric aspects of the brain in senile dementia of the Alzheimer type. *Annals of Neurology, 10,* 184–192.

Tkach, J.R., & Hokama, Y. (1970). Autoimmunity in chronic brain syndrome: A preliminary report. *Archives of General Psychiatry, 23,* 61–64.

Tomlinson, B.E., Blessed, G., & Roth, M. (1968). Observations on the brains of nondemented old people. *Journal of Neurological Sciences, 7,* 331–356.

Tomlinson, B.E., Blessed, G., & Roth, M. (1970). Observations on the brains of demented old people. *Journal of Neurological Sciences, 11,* 205–242.

Tomlinson, B.E., Irving, D., & Blessed, G. (1981). Cell loss in the locus coeruleus in senile dementia of Alzheimer's type. *Journal of Neurological Sciences, 49,* 419–428.

Valenstein, E. (1980). Age-related changes in the human central nervous system. In D.S. Basley & G.A. Davis (Eds.), *Aging: Communication processes and disorders* (pp. 87–106). New York: Grune & Stratton.

Valenstein, E. (1981). Dementia. In A.G. Reeves, *Disorders of the nervous system: A primer* (pp. 127–136). (J.D. Myers & D.E. Rogers, Eds.). Chicago: Year Book Medical.

Wang, J.A., & Whanger, A. (1971). Brain impairment and longevity. In E. Palmore and F.C. Jeffers (Eds.), *Predictions of life span* (pp. 95–106). Lexington, MA: D.C. Heath.

Warrington, E.K. (1975). Selective impairment of semantic memory. *Quarterly Journal of Experimental Psychology, 27,* 635–657.

Weingartner, H., Kaye, W., Smallberg, S., Cohen, R., Ebert, M.H., Gillin, J.C., & Gold, P. (1982). Determinants of memory failures in dementia. In S. Corkin, K. Davis, J. Growdon E. Usdin, & R. Wurtman (Eds.), *Alzheimer's disease: A report of progress* (Vol. 19, pp. 171–176). New York: Raven Press.

Weingartner, H., Kaye, W., Smallberg, S., Ebert, M., Gillin, J., & Sitaram, N. (1981). Memory failures in progressive idiopathic dementia. *Journal of Abnormal Psychology, 40,* 187–196.

Wells, C.E. (1977). Diagnostic evaluation and treatment in dementia. In C.E. Wells (Ed.), *Dementia* (pp. 247–276). Philadelphia: Davis.

White, P., Hiley, C.R., Goodhardt, M.J., Carrasco, L.H., Keet, J.P., Williams, I.E.I., & Brown, D.M. (1977). Neocortical cholineric neurons in elderly people. *Lancet, 1,* 668–671.

Whitehead, A. (1975). Recognition memory in dementia. *British Journal of Social and Clinical Psychiatry, 14,* 191–194.

Wilkinson, A., & Davies, I. (1978). The influence of age and dementia on the neurone population of the mamillary bodies. *Age and Ageing, 7,* 151–160.

Wilson, R.S., Bacon, L.D., Kramer, R.L., Fox, J.H., & Kaszniak, A.W. (1983). Word frequency effect and recognition memory in dementia of Alzheimer type. *Journal of Clinical Neuropsychology, 2,* 97–104.

Wilson, R.S., Kaszniak, A.W., & Fox, J.H. (1981). Remote memory in senile dementia. *Cortex, 17,* 41–48.

Wilson, R., Rosenbaum, G., & Brown, G. (1979). The problem of premorbid intelligence in neuropsychological assessment. *Journal of Clinical Neuropsychology, 1,* 49–53.

Wisniewski, K., Jervis, G.A., Moretz, R.C., & Wisniewski, H.M. (1979). Alzheimer neurofibrillary diseases other than senile and presenile dementia. *Annals of Neurology, 5,* 288–294.

Yamaguchi, F., Meyer, J.S., Yamamoto, M., Sakai, F., & Shaw, T. (1980). Noninvasive regional cerebral blood flow measurements in dementia. *Archives of Neurology, 37,* 410–418.

Yen, S-H.C., Gaskin, F., & Terry, R.D. (1981). Immunocytochemical studies of neurofibrillary tangles. *American Journal of Pathology, 104,* 77–89.

CHAPTER 16

Neuropsychology and the Field of Sleep and Sleep Disorders

G. Vernon Pegram, Bryan E. Connell,
James Gnadt, and Debra Weiler

Only a few research studies have been conducted in the area of the clinical neuropsychological aspects of sleep and its disorders. An expansion and explication of this area has led us to some new distillations and condensations of data that we feel are of interest. We have also taken this opportunity to expound on our personal ideas as to what the future of this new field could and should be.

The study of sleep has a very short-lived history. Not having dealt adequately with the awake portion of human circadian rhythm cycles, science left the area of sleep basically untouched until the mid-1950s. The neuropsychological study of sleep disorders began only in the 1980s. While sleep researchers have amassed a large body of knowledge in a relatively short period of time, our understanding of sleep and its disorders is still in its infancy. Thus, it is still not uncommon to see smirks appear on the faces of serious scientists and clinicians when the subject of sleep disorders is mentioned. However, to those afflicted, it is no laughing matter. For example, consider the living nightmares of individuals suffering from excessive daytime sleepiness: childhoods spent disappearing into closets to avoid being caught sleeping for fear of reprisal; clinical diagnoses of mental retardation and depression; and the labels of lazy, bum, loafer, shy, malingerer, and underachiever ascribed by laypersons.

While sleep deprivation (SD) studies point to the conclusion that we need sleep to function adequately, the precise nature of the function of sleep continues to elude sleep researchers. Interestingly, the amount of sleep necessary for adequate functioning shows a normal distribution, as demonstrated in a series of experiments conducted by Webb (1978). Too much sleep is nearly as detrimental to optimal human functioning as is too little. It is interesting that both extremes in the amount of sleep—too much or too little—leave a person feeling the same way: drowsy, unalert, uncoordinated, and weak. Thus, such complaints are often seen in patients who have difficulty with either side of this continuum.

While commonalities exist, specific sleep disorders also have unique effects on a person's functioning. This chapter includes discussions of these specific sleep disorders. For example, narcolepsy, with its uncontrollable sleep attacks and cataplexy, is both embarrassing and potentially life threatening (e.g., falling asleep while driving a car). It may severely incapacitate a person in carrying out work responsibilities, conducting a normal social life (with the necessary learning of interpersonal and social skills), and maintaining a sense of psychological well-being. Much of our sense of self-confidence depends on our being somewhat sure of our ability to function adequately in various roles and situations. The inability to foresee a narcoleptic and/or cataplectic attack obliterates the possibility of the afflicted individual's developing a sense of being in control.

Sleep apnea, another sleep disorder, can create very low life-threatening levels of oxygen saturation in the blood. In some cases, this extends over the majority of the time during which sleep is attempted. In our laboratory, this disorder has been compared to a slightly altered model of the effects of chronic obstructive pulmonary disease (COPD). Data currently being analyzed may serve to substantiate the possibility of decreased cognitive abilities in the areas of memory and information processing with both disorders. The chronic drowsiness often encountered in insomnia and nocturnal myoclonus may also prove to have substantial cognitive effects. Not only are the persons often not fully alert for much of the daytime, but sustained periods of uninterrupted rapid eye movement (REM) and nonrapid eye movement (NREM) sleep, which may serve cognitive functions, are disallowed.

Phasic sleep-wake disorders constitute one of the areas in which data have been reported, largely because this has been an area of interest to business. Work by Preston (1978) on airline pilots and jet lag, and by Dahlgren (1981) with shift workers has shown performance deficits associated with sleep periods phase-shifted out of their normally occurring position in the circadian rhythm.

Finally, and in no sense of little significance, the problems associated with both self- and physician-prescribed medications for sleep disorders are explored. Millions of units of over-the-counter products are sold annually for the sole use of putting Americans to sleep. The overuse of such medicines as diazepam (Valium) and other benzodiazepines for sleep disturbance has been documented both in the professional literature and in the lay communications media. Studies have determined that in many cases, morning "hangover" effects produce documentable decreases in both cognitive and performance abilities. An additional problem is the tolerance to such medications that can develop with repeated use. Larger doses may be required to achieve the same effect over time.

The problem in finding neuropsychological tests sensitive to sleep-wake disorders is twofold. First there is the ever-present problem of localization. Sleep and sleep deprivation probably do not affect any one cerebral lobe or hemisphere more than another. While many neuropsychological tests do not claim to be necessarily sensitive to one area of the brain, the overall results of test batteries are often used to imply the localization of the lesion or disorder that caused the impairment on the tests. Neuropsychological testing with sleep disorders should probably not be used in this manner. However, the testing can be very useful for describing the type of deficits that people suffering from these disorders commonly have, their degree of impairment (if any), and how these difficulties recover (if they do) with treatment of the disorder. The testing can also be used for assessing the relative efficacy of new or old means of diagnosing the disorders. It has been demonstrated (Broughton, 1982a) that a person's subjective report of degree of arousal may bear no resemblance to the person's ability to fall asleep or stay awake under controlled circumstances. The ability to perform given tasks should provide a better, more reliable (and, one hopes, more valid) measure in these instances.

The second problem regarding sleep-wake disorders and arousal concerns a drowsy person's ability to perform adequately in much of the testing, which has been done in normal populations, with various amounts and stages of sleep deprivation. It becomes readily apparent that in situations in which there is no real incentive to perform, the person is very drowsy. When pushed, however, the person can perform the required task. Is the person's mental functioning unimpaired? Of course not. There is simply not a test sensitive enough to detect the impairment. Of course, in the administration of neuropsychological tests, a person's optimal performance tends to be elicited. It has been posited that a person's performance in traditional neuropsychological testing, in which he or she is cheered on by the tester one on one, may not accurately reflect the person's abilities in day-to-day living. At some point, tests must be developed that are sensitive enough to reflect the specific kinds of disabilities that persons with sleep disorders suffer under both optimal conditions and day-to-day conditions as well.

This chapter deals with several aspects of sleep and its disorders that we feel are essential for understanding what might be encountered by neuropsychologists when assessing a person with either a primary or a secondary sleep disorder. First, a description of sleep and its disorders is presented. A brief section on some common treatments for the disorders is included. Next, sleep disorders or abnormalities that are secondary to other pathological conditions are discussed. This section includes the topics of head injury, epilepsy, and mental retardation (MR). Third, the neuropsychological assessment of sleep disorders, including the topics of sleep in the elderly and benzodiazepine effects, is discussed. Finally, directions for research are examined.

SLEEP AND ITS DISORDERS: AN OVERVIEW

Sleep is a behavior that occurs as a component of one's natural cycling pattern of sleep and wakefulness. A more detailed consideration of the sleep-wakefulness cycle, utilizing an electroencephalographic (EEG) analysis, reveals that mammalian behavior involves three distinct, readily identifiable behavioral states: wakefulness (W), NREM sleep, and REM sleep. If the fragile balance among these three behavioral states is altered by environmental change, psychological disturbance, pharmacological agents, or physical disease, a person begins to report the result of the fluctuations in terms that we call symptoms of sleep disorders. These complaints range from too much wakefulness (insomnia) to too much sleepiness (hypersomnia), representing the extremes of the imbalance of the sensitive sleep-wakefulness cycle.

The prevalence of sleep disorders in the general population is largely unknown. Adequate epidemiological information in this area is lacking (Smirne, Franceschi, Zamproni, Crippa, & Fernini-Strambi, 1983). However, a review of several studies that have measured the prevalence of sleep complaints suggests that as much as one-third of the adult population suffers from insomnia-related sleep disturbances to some degree (e.g., Bixler, Kales, Scharf, Kales, & Leo, 1976; Institute of Medicine, 1979; Kales, Kales, & Bixler, 1974; Karacan, et al., 1976; Thornby, et al., 1977). If we consider persons who experience excessive daytime sleepiness as well as those who suffer from parasomnias (e.g., sleep talking, sleepwalking, bruxism, enuresis, nocturnal myoclonus or restless legs, and nightmares), then we are probably safe in concluding that sleep disorders are rather common. The fact that approximately 10 million Americans visit their physicians each year complaining of sleep-related problems

(Hauri, 1982b) further substantiates this conclusion. The widespread prevalence of sleep problems calls for a systematic approach to their proper diagnosis and management.

Normal Sleep-Wakefulness Mechanisms

Most of the knowledge of the sleep-wakefulness cycle comes from recent research in sleep laboratories, even though the first report of extensive electroencephalograms of the brain's electrical activity came from Hans Berger in 1929. In the mid-1940s, Loomis and associates demonstrated that the human EEG can be subdivided into a series of discontinuous stages dependent on frequency and voltage criterion, thus laying the groundwork for sleep research. For further information on the development of sleep research, the reader is referred to historial reviews written by some of the people intimately involved in its evolution (Bremer, 1974; Dement & Mitler, 1974; Kleitman, 1963; Mendelson, Gillin, & Wyatt, 1977).

Sleep consists of two distinct states: REM sleep and NREM sleep. REM sleep is characterized on a psychological level by dreaming and on a physiological level by cortical activation (a mixed frequency, low-voltage EEG pattern), bursts of extraocular and middle-ear muscle activity, variability of heart and respiratory rates, actively induced atonia of major antigravity and locomotor muscles, and increased cerebral blood flow. In a normal adult, 20%–25% of each sleep period is spent in REM sleep. REM sleep may be described as consisting of a highly active brain in an immobilized body. Due to this paradoxical phenomenon, REM is often referred to as paradoxical sleep.

NREM sleep is usually subdivided into four stages on the basis of relatively distinguishable EEG brain wave patterns. Stage 1 is a brief transitional stage between wakefulness and sleep. It has a low-voltage, mixed frequency EEG pattern and accounts for approximately 5% of the total sleep period. Stage 2, defined on the basis of sleep spindles and K-complexes, usually constitutes 40%–55% of total sleep in the young adult. Stages 3 and 4 are often referred to as delta sleep because they are characterized by moderate and large numbers of delta-frequency slow waves, respectively. Most of stage 3 and 4 sleep occurs during the first one to three hours of sleep and usually constitutes 10%–20% of total sleep in healthy young adults.

One can conceive of NREM sleep as being organized according to depth. Specifically, stage 1 is the lightest sleep, and stage 4 is the deepest state, as determined by both arousal and threshold mechanisms and the appearance of the EEG. However, REM sleep does not fit into this organizational design. The arousal threshold is higher in REM sleep than in NREM sleep, and resting muscle potential is lower during REM sleep. Therefore, REM sleep is neither light sleep nor deep sleep but a different kind of sleep (Hartmann, 1979).

Normal nocturnal sleep is cyclic, with four or five cycles per sleep period. As healthy adults fall asleep, they enter stage 1, then stage 2, and finally stages 3 and 4. After a person sleeps for approximately 90–100 minutes, the first REM sleep occurs. This internal may be longer in some normal sleepers and older adults, but it is significantly shorter only under a few abnormal clinical and experimental conditions. After a brief (5–15 minute) REM period, the NREM-REM cycle begins again and is repeated throughout the sleep period. The first REM periods tend to be shorter, whereas later

REM periods may last 20–40 minutes; thus, most REM sleep occurs in the last third of the sleep period.

Sleep stages and sleep cycles are markedly altered by various changes affecting the individual (e.g., stress, a wide spectrum of drugs), including that one common, inevitable change—the aging process. Even though most human sleep data have come from young adults, increasing numbers of studies reveal that the EEG wave forms and sleep architecture change significantly with age. In newborns, for example, total sleep time averages about 14–18 hours per 24 hours, half of which may be spent in REM sleep. Young adults spend 16–17 hours awake and 7–8 hours asleep, only 1.5–2 hours of which are REM sleep. As adults enter middle age and old age, stages 3 and 4 often decrease markedly, and sleep tends to become progressively more fragmented, with brief arousals and longer periods of wakefulness. REM sleep percentages remain relatively constant after the first two to three years of life.

Individual differences in total sleep time are highly variable, and the acceptable range seems to be surprisingly wide. Average healthy adults require nearly 7.5 hours of sleep per 24 hours. However, some healthy adults require only 4 hours or less per 24 hours, while others require 10–12 hours in order to feel sufficiently rested. Individual variability is also found in the amount of time spent in each stage, but this pattern in each individual tends to be stable from night to night. In summary, a key concept is that sleep and the regulation of sleep is a complex, cyclic, and active process. Further, while there may be great variability in individualized sleep requirements, there exists a fragile balance of the three behavioral states within each person.

Classification and Diagnosis of Sleep Disorders

The classification of sleep disorders has changed as a result of the increasing accumulation of both basic and applied knowledge about sleep. The Association for the Psychophysiological Study of Sleep (APSS) has facilitated the sleep research carried out at university-based sleep disorder centers. A group of these centers joined to form the Association of Sleep Disorders (ASDC) in October 1975. One of the many specific aims of the ASDC was to develop standards and procedures for polysomnography, defined as the multidimensional evaluation of a patient during sleep. Another goal was the systematic classification of sleep disorders in a manner closely related to the chief complaints heard by primary-care physicians. Work toward this goal resulted in the development of such a classification scheme in 1979 (Association of Sleep Disorders Center, 1979). Currently, there are four recognized classes of sleep disorders: (1) insomnias have been grouped as disorders of initiating and maintaining sleep (DIMS); (2) disorders of excessive daytime sleepiness have been categorized as disorders of excessive somnolence (DOES); (3) disorders of the sleep-wakefulness cycle (e.g., those due to shift work, jet lag, etc.) are termed dyssomnias; (4) parasomnias are dysfunctions associated with sleep, sleep stages, or partial arousals, including sleepwalking, night terrors, and enuresis.

Preliminary Diagnosis of Insomnia

The first step in the differential diagnosis of sleep disorders is to separate sleep disorders on the basis of patient complaint, usually in two broad categories: insomnias and excessive somnolence. The more common category is insomnia. The complaint of insomnia may reflect any of a number of underlying physical and/or psychiatric conditions. For example, insomnia may be associated with medical or neurological problems, such as hyperthyroidism, epilepsy, or chronic pain. Alternatively, insomnia may reflect a primary sleep disorder, such as nocturnal myoclonus or sleep apnea. Insonmia is also commonly associated with the use of drugs and alcohol, such as tolerance to or withdrawal from central nervous system (CNS) depressants or stimulants. Finally, insomnia may be symptomatic of a psychophysiological disturbance; that is, a life crisis, or of a more persistent psychiatric disorder, such as anxiety or depression.

Differentiating the conditions involving the complaint of insomnia should always focus on possible *medical* etiology. The medical history should also focus on possible *psychiatric* etiology as well as on the interaction of both the medical and psychiatric aspects. A thorough workup for a chronic complaint of insomnia frequently includes information obtained from sleep diaries, questionnaires, interviews with the patient and the patient's bed partner, a psychiatric evaluation, and a physical examination. If the insomnia is (1) chronic and seriously interferes with normal functioning, (2) not secondary to medical or psychiatric problems, and (3) unresponsive to treatment (e.g., with hypnotics, revised sleep hygiene habits, or relaxation training) for at least six months, then referral to a sleep disorder center is probably indicated (Hauri, 1982a).

Preliminary Diagnosis of Excessive Daytime Sleepiness

If a patient reports feeling sleepy all day or falling asleep inappropriately and does not complain of sleeping poorly at night, there are several possible principal diagnoses. Excessive daytime sleepiness may reflect a transient psychophysiological disturbance or a more persistent psychiatric disturbance, such as depression. EDS may be symptomatic of such primary sleep disorders as narcolepsy-cataplexy or upper airway sleep apnea. It may also be seen in connection with drug abuse and/or dependence on central nervous system stimulants or depressants. Finally, EDS may be due to one of a group of intermittent or periodic hypersomnias, such as the Kleine-Levin syndrome and idiopathic hypersomnia.

In the workup of EDS, there are three key questions to ask. First, has the patient experienced muscular weakness or collapse during excitement, anger, laughter, or sexual arousal? If the answer is positive, narcolepsy should be strongly suspected. Second, does the patient snore loudly, or does the patient's bed partner complain of loud snoring? If so, sleep apnea should be suspected. Finally, is there a history of chronic stimulant or hypnotic use in the past few months or years? Or is the patient currently taking some other drug that may produce daytime sleepiness?

Primary Sleep Disorders

Despite the considerable growth of information related to sleep and sleep disorders, historically there has been little systematic or practical instruction in the diagnosis and treatment of sleep disorders. Therefore, we include the following brief review of a group of clinically distinct, primary sleep disorders that have received considerable attention in recent literature. These disorders include narcolepsy, the sleep apneas, nocturnal myoclonus, and restless legs syndrome. See Table 16.1 for the percentage of referrals to our sleep laboratory for these and other disorders.

Table 16.1.   Sleep Center Patient Population by Primary Diagnosis

Primary Diagnosis	Number of Patients 1/72–12/79	% Total Patients	Number of Patients 1/80–7/84	% Total Patients	Number of Patients 1/72–7/84	% Total Patients
Apnea	17	11.33	318	46.37	335	39.85
Bruxism	1	0.67	1	0.15	2	0.24
Enuresis	1	0.67	0	0.00	1	0.12
GER	0	0.00	5	0.73	5	0.59
Hypersomnolence	18	12.00	53	7.7	71	8.47
Impotence	0	0.00	17	2.47	17	2.03
Infant apnea	0	0.00	11	1.6	11	1.31
Insomnia	73	48.67	72	10.46	145	17.30
Narcolepsy	30	20.00	93	13.52	123	14.67
Night terror	2	1.33	11	1.60	13	1.55
Nocturnal myoclonus	2	1.33	62	9.01	64	7.64
Nocturnal seizures	3	2.0	2	0.30	5	0.59
Nonrestorative Sleep syndrome	2	1.33	0	0.00	2	0.24
Restless leg syndrome	2	1.33	2	0.30	4	0.48
Somnambulism	1	0.67	6	0.90	7	0.83
Other	0	0.00	13	1.89	13	1.55
No diagnosis	0	0.00	19	2.76	19	2.27
Number of Males	72	48.00	440	63.95	512	61.09
Number of Females	78	52.00	248	36.04	326	38.90
Total	150	100.00	688	100.00	838	100.00

Narcolepsy

Approximately 20%–25% of the patients presenting with EDS have narcolepsy (Coleman, 1983). However, the incidence of narcolepsy is rather low; approximately .04% of the United States population is afflicted (Hauri, 1982b; Kessler, Guilleminault, & Dement, 1974). There is ample evidence indicating that narcolepsy has a genetic component (e.g., Honda, Asaka, Tanimura, & Furusho, 1983). The participants in the First International Symposium on Narcolepsy defined narcolepsy as a syndrome characterized by abnormal sleep tendencies, including EDS, disturbed nocturnal sleep, and pathological manifestations of REM sleep. The most typical REM sleep manifestations are cataplexy (described later) and sleep onset REM periods (SOREMP), but sleep paralysis (the inability to move any muscles when falling asleep but especially upon awakening) and hypnagogic hallucinations (dreamlike experiences difficult to distinguish from reality that occur when falling asleep) may also be present. A relatively low percentage of patients experience all four manifestations of the disorder, known as narcoleptic tetrad.

The manifestations of excessive daytime sleepiness include inappropriate and irresistible sleep episodes, amnesic periods, and often severe drowsiness. Narcoleptics do not necessarily sleep more than normal individuals. Their problem is principally the uncontrollable nature of their sleepiness. Excessive daytime sleepiness is usually the earliest manifestation of narcolepsy. The onset of symptoms occurs between the teen years to the third decade of life. The majority of narcoleptic patients appear to experience EDS before the age of 20 (Gulleminault, Wilson, & Dement, 1974; Kales, et al., 1982), although one recent study found the median age of onset to be 22 years of age

(Billiard, Besset, & Cadilhac, 1983). EDS tends to worsen over time, often resulting in social embarrassment and employment difficulties.

Cataplexy appears to be a more prevalent symptom in narcolepsy than is either sleep paralysis or hypnagogic hallucinations. Cataplexy occurs in about two-thirds of all narcoleptic patients (Gulleminault, 1976; Zarcone, 1973), while hypnagogic hallucinations have been estimated to occur in 20%–50% of these patients and sleep paralysis is thought to occur in 14%–27% of these patients (Karacan, Moore, & Williams, 1979). Cataplexy is a sudden and reversible loss of skeletal-muscle tonus lasting for a few seconds to 30 minutes. It is usually triggered by an emotional stimulus such as anger or excitement. The most frequently affected muscles are those of the jaw, neck, and knees, but the attack may range in severity from a slight feeling of weakness to involvement of the entire voluntary musculature. Extraocular muscles are usually uninvolved, and the patient usually continues to breathe. The patients are apparently awake during the episodes and are aware of their surroundings. The frequency of the cataplectic attack in patients with narcolepsy-cataplexy is usually one and four episodes daily but may vary widely. Thus, the patients may learn to self-impose restrictions on their activities and/or emotions and present clinically as somewhat depressed or apathetic.

A patient presenting with the chief complaint of EDS who also has a history of cataplexy is strongly suspected of having narcolepsy. A definitive diagnosis can be made with a multiple sleep latency (MSL) determination done in a sleep laboratory. The MSL determination has become routine in the diagnosis of narcolepsy on the basis of the suggestion that sleep latency measured repeatedly in controlled nap situations might prove a useful tool in evaluating pathological sleepiness. Sleep latency can be defined as the time between the point at which an individual tries to sleep and the point at which electroencephalographic patterns of sleep first develop. This multiple nap procedure reveals that narcoleptics consistently fall asleep more readily than do control subjects and are more likely to exhibit SOREMPs (A REM episode occurring within the first 15 minutes after sleep onset) than are control subjects (Mitler, 1982; Zarcone, 1973). The MSL study must be conducted after the patient has been free of stimulant medication, hypnotics, alcohol, and psychotropic medication for at least two weeks.

The Sleep Apnea Syndromes

Sleep apnea, whether it produces the complaint of EDS or insomnia, is a serious and sometimes life-threatening disorder. It appears to be more common than narcolepsy (Coleman, 1983), occurring in approximately 1% of the population (Lavie, 1981). Some of the clinical features of sleep apnea syndromes are excessive daytime sleepiness, nocturnal insomnia, morning headaches, noisy snoring, abnormal motor activity during sleep, intellectual and personality changes, sexual impotence, systemic hypertension, pulmonary hypertension, cor pulmonale, heart failure, and polycythemia.

Sleep apnea has been recognized and studied since the mid-1970s. These studies have been well described by Gulleminault and Dement (1978a). Apnea is operationally defined as the cessation of air flow lasting at least 10 seconds. There are a number of important clinical subtypes of the sleep apnea syndromes, including upper airway obstructive sleep apnea, central sleep apnea, mixed apnea, pickwickian syndrome, and sudden infant death syndrome. Sleep apnea can appear from infancy to old age, but it is usually seen in modestly obese men over 40 years of age. The prevalence of sleep apnea in the general population is unknown at the present time (Smirne, 1983).

Clinically, patients report a variety of symptoms that may attract attention when all are present but may lead to diagnostic errors when only one or two symptoms are seen. Snoring is an important clue. The characteristic loud, pharyngeal snoring, interspersed with snorting, appears as the first clinical symptom in most patients, sometimes as early as six or seven years of age. The continuous snoring pattern can be interrupted by as many as several hundred apneic periods a night. These apneic episodes usually last 10–180 seconds. Accompanying the apneic episodes are abnormal movements ranging from small movements of the hands or feet to large flailing movements involving the entire upper and lower limbs. If the patient is awakened suddenly, he or she may appear confused and disoriented.

Most often, the presenting complaint is excessive daytime sleepiness. Daytime drowsiness may be so severe that patients fall asleep while eating, but they are especially susceptible during monotonous situations, such as driving, attending meetings, reading, or watching television. Personality changes resulting in reactive depression, abnormal outbursts of emotion, episodes of jealousy and suspicion, irrational behavior, and sudden impotence are also symptoms that may develop secondary to the sleep apnea syndrome. Morning headaches are also frequently observed in association with sleep apnea.

Ninety-four percent of the sleep apneic patients seen at Stanford Sleep Disorders Clinic were male. Such a significantly different incidence between men and women indicates that the sleep apnea is essentially a male syndrome (Guilleminault, 1979). Similarly, Hauri (1982b) reports that men outnumber women by a ratio of 30 to 1 in cases of obstructive apneas.

The definitive diagnostic test for sleep apnea syndrome is the all-night polysomno-gram. Polysomnography is a complex evaluation of a patient during sleep that involves assessment of the central nervous system. In the case of sleep apnea, polysom-nography also includes assessment of respiratory and cardiac function with the use of an ear oximeter, nasal and/or oral respiratory thermistors, electrocardiogram (ECG), and blood gas analysis in addition to the standard EEG measurements. It is essential to determine which subtype of sleep apnea the patient has, since the treatment varies accordingly.

Nocturnal Myoclonus

Patients with nocturnal myoclonus usually have pronounced jerks in both legs simul-taneously, but unilateral myoclonus has also been observed. These jerks, or twitches, may be accompanied by flexion at the ankle, knee, and hip. If the jerking is pronounced enough, it will arouse the patient. The leg movements are confined to sleep and are generally not seen in arousal. The myoclonic jerks generally occur every 20–40 seconds and last approximately 1.5–4 seconds. Several hundred leg movement episodes may occur during the night, with most occurring in NREM rather than in REM sleep.

Complaints of frequent arousals during sleep and aching leg muscles are common. Because myoclonus may "lighten" sleep and interfere with deep restorative sleep, patients are often chronically fatigued and may have symptoms of depression. Thus, nocturnal myoclonus is associated with both insomnia and hypersomnia. It is estimated that 12%–17% of serious insomniacs and 3%–11% of EDS patients suffer from nocturnal myoclonus (Coleman, et al., 1982; Coleman, Pollack, & Weitzman, 1978). However, at this point it is not possible to conclude that nocturnal myoclonus actually causes insomnia or hypersomnia (Coleman, et al., 1983). There is an increasing tendency in the sleep literature to refer to this disorder as periodic movements in sleep (PMS) to distinguish it from myoclonus associated with epilepsy (Coleman, et al., 1983).

Restless Legs Syndrome

The syndrome of nocturnal myoclonus frequently coexists with restless legs syndrome (Lugaresi, Cirignotta, Montagna, & Coccagna, 1983), although the latter may occur independently. This syndrome is so bizarre that patients often have difficulty describing the problem. Usually they say they feel as if there is something crawling inside their legs. This sensation occurs perhaps every hour or two during wakefulness as well as during sleep. Patients report that moving about alleviates the symptom. During sleep periods, patients must get out of bed and walk around before they can go back to sleep. The effects of this problem, as with the sleep apneas, result in a sleep pattern with a marked reduction of delta (or deep) sleep and in feeling chronically tired and sleepy during the day.

The physician can establish whether the restless legs syndrome or nocturnal myoclonus is related to complaints of insomnia by directly inquiring about the twitching in the patient's legs while the patient is asleep or falling asleep. Nocturnal and daytime recording from the right and left anterior tibialis muscles can firmly establish the diagnosis of restless legs syndrome (and/or nocturnal myoclonus). Patients suffering from the restless legs syndrome exhibit twitching in the waking and sleeping hours, while those suffering from nocturnal myoclonus exhibit twitching exclusively during sleep. Particular emphasis should be placed on whether the patient is awakened by the twitching.

Recent evidence suggests that the restless legs syndrome may be genetically transmitted in approximately one-third of all cases (Boghen & Peyronnard, 1976). The disorder seems to be transmitted as an autosomal dominant trait (Boghen & Peyronnard, 1976; Montagna, Coccagna, Cirignotta, & Lugaresi, 1983).

Insomnia

Most health care professionals have assumed that patients who complain of insomnia accurately describe their nighttime sleep. In treating a patient who complains, for example, that it requires one hour to fall asleep, the physician must remember that (1) it is likely that the patient falls asleep considerably more quickly (Bixler, Kales, Leo, & Slye, 1973; Kales, Kales, & Bixler, 1974; Weiss, McParland, & Kupfer, 1973); (2) under the best of circumstances, a hypnotic will probably shorten the objective sleep latency by only 10–20 minutes (Institute of Medicine, 1979); and (3) although the patient's estimate of the difficulty may be exaggerated, the subjective distress is real.

The following is a brief description of many of the various specific diagnoses of insomnia. These descriptions are presented in a modified version of the ASDC nosology in order to make the material useful to the practicing professional.

TRANSIENT AND SITUATIONAL INSOMNIA.   Acute insomnia may arise from a number of sudden changes in life. These may encompass medical, surgical, or traumatic conditions; sleeping in any new environment; personal stress and anxiety (as in bereavement); or disturbances of biological rhythms such as jet lag or shift work. Acute forms of insomnia usually respond to the passage of time, patient education, or the judicious use of hypnotics.

INSOMNIA ASSOCIATED WITH PSYCHOLOGICAL DISORDERS.   Varying degrees of depression, anxiety, and concern about physical well-being are common in insomniac patients. Hauri (1982a) noted that emotional and psychiatric problems appear to be the source of many insomnialike sleep disturbances. Coleman (1983), in a comprehensive study of over 7,000 sleep-disorder patients, observed that insomnia associated with psychiatric disorders was the most prevalent disorder in the DIMS category.

Insomniacs evidence more psychopathologic disorders than do good sleepers (Hauri, 1979; Kales, et al., 1978), especially when measured on a psychometric test such as the Minnesota Multiphasic Personality Inventory (MMPI). Insomniacs studies by Kales and colleagues (1978), when compared with controls, showed a significantly higher mean value on all eight major MMPI scales except hypomania (MA). Further, Beutler, Karacan, Thornby, and Salis (1977) found that the absolute amount of sleep latency is positively related to the development of hysterical characteristics, while the frequency of nocturnal awakenings is positively related to elevation in the MMPI   F scale and the schizophrenic scale. They suggested that sleep maintenance appeared to be more closely associated with more severe psychopathologic states (e.g., schizophrenia), whereas sleep latency appeared to be more closely related to anxiety and neurotic conditions.

INSOMNIA ASSOCIATED WITH DRUGS AND ALCOHOL.   Pharmocologic factors must always be evaluated in patients with insomnia. Dependence on, tolerance to, and withdrawal from hypnotic agents themselves may be major factors in the complaints of some insomniac patients. Alcohol is a particular issue in insomnia because it is the most commonly used self-medication for insomnia. Generally, alcohol may produce prompt sleep, but it also disrupts and fragments sleep if used in excess or on a chronic basis.

INSOMNIA ASSOCIATED WITH MEDICAL DISORDERS.   A thorough medical history, physical examination, and appropriate laboratory examinations must be included in the evaluation of chronic insomniac patients. Insomnia is rarely the presenting chief complaint of a medical disorder. Coexisting medical conditions and treatments must be considered while planning treatment for other types of insomnia. Hepatic or renal insufficiency, for example, may predispose certain patients to toxic reactions when taking hypnotics.

INSOMNIA ASSOCIATED WITH SLEEP-INDUCED VENTILATORY IMPAIRMENT.   As discussed with sleep apnea syndromes, unsatisfactory nocturnal sleep can be a complaint of a person with sleep apnea. The routine administration of hypnotic drugs to patients presenting with sleep apnea may be life threatening (Hartmann, 1978). Many hypnotics have been shown to produce obvious central nervous system depression, thus placing sleep apnea patients at greater risk.

INSOMNIA ASSOCIATED WITH NOCTURNAL MYOCLONUS OR RESTLESS LEGS SYNDROME. The closely associated nocturnal myoclonus and restless legs syndromes, previously discussed, present clinically in a person who cannot maintain sleep and suffers from brief arousals throughout the sleep period.

NO DIMS ABNORMALITY.   As mentioned earlier, some patients may exaggerate their sleep difficulties. The extreme case is that of the patient who complains of insomnia but exhibits no objectively documentable sleep problem in the sleep laboratory. This category also includes the "short sleeper," who apparently requires less sleep than the norm (e.g., 3–5 hours) to feel rested and to function effectively. In the case of the former individual, placebos may cure the perceived insomnia quite effectively. However, the genuine possibility exists that some of these patients may be suffering from yet undiscovered (and thus undiagnosable) sleep disorders (Hauri, 1982b). In the case of the latter individual, simply making the patient aware of individual differences in sleep requirements may ease the patient's concern over the apparent problem.

In conclusion, many persistent insomnias seem to be essentially learned habits of poor sleep, with conditioning and internal arousal playing important roles. In conditioned insomnia, the stimuli and rituals surrounding sleep have preceded poor sleep so many times that they themselves can trigger frustration and insomnia. In internal arousal insomnia, the patient's desperation to sleep causes increased arousal and inability to relax, thus leading to insomnia.

Current Therapeutic Regimes

Narcolepsy

In the narcoleptic patient, treatment depends on the patient's symptoms and previous history of therapy. Although current pharmacological interventions are not yet the ideal solution to narcolepsy, there are some cases in which the use of stimulant medication, such as dextroamphetamine, methylphenidate, or pemoline, are indicated for the EDS. Some narcoleptics may not respond well to stimulant treatment, chiefly because of side effects and the development of tolerance. In such cases, we have had success in alternating stimulants every few weeks to prevent tolerance or in suggesting that patients come off all medication on weekends. In addition, some patients have responded well to low doses of stimulants and scheduled brief naps during the day, while others have responded positively to scheduled naps alone. Cataplectic attacks usually respond well to divided doses of imipramine (75–100 mg/day). This dosage also effectively controls sleep paralysis and hypnagogic hallucinations (Dement, 1979). Some success in treating cataplexy has also been achieved with protriptyline (Schmidt, Clark, & Hyman, 1977). More recently, Kales, Cadieux, Soldatos, and Tjiauw-Ling (1979) have had success in the treatment of narcolepsy-cataplexy with propranolol, as have Broughton and Mamelak (1979), and Broughton and Mamelak (1979) with gammahydroxybutyrate.

One area of therapeutic need that is often neglected pertains to the psychological effect of narcolepsy. There is no evidence that narcolepsy is psychogenic, yet it can seriously affect the patient's ability to cope with stress and is often harmful to personal relationships. By clearly explaining the sleep disorder to family members, some of the stress and anxiety that is elicited by the nature of the illness can be reduced. In recent years, a group of narcoleptics organized an association whose goals are to provide a support and information system for patients and families alike. Local chapters of the American Narcolepsy Association are becoming increasingly widespread.

The Sleep Apnea Syndromes

Although sleep apnea can be diagnosed on the basis of a careful history and physical examination, myriad associated symptoms can result in diagnostic confusion. It is advisable to confirm the diagnosis of sleep apnea with an all-night polysomnogram because therapeutic indications depend on (1) the predominant type of sleep apnea, (2) the degree of disability, and (3) the severity of sleep-related cardiovascular symptoms. The existence of other clinical problems is significant as well.

For predominantly central sleep apnea, no truly effective therapeutic approach has been found. Fortunately, exclusively central apneas occur infrequently. However, some medications have been used to increase central respiratory drive, including medroxyprogesterone and chlorimipramine.

When a patient presents a predominantly obstructive sleep apnea, surgical correction of an anatomic defect, when present, is the treatment of choice. In some cases, significant weight loss can decrease the incidence and severity of apneic periods. However, when the patient is severely apneic, the most immediate and effective treatment is a tracheostomy to bypass the upper airway obstruction during sleep. The results of this procedure are often dramatic, with marked improvement in the patient's symptoms within the first few days of surgery.

The diagnosis and treatment of sleep apnea is attracting a lot of attention from a variety of medical disciplines. Thus, a variety of other treatments are being tested and may prove beneficial for certain types of apnea. Examples of recent advances in this field include mandibular osteotomy in patients with retrognathism (Kuo, West, Bloomquist, & McNeil, 1979), uvulo-palato pharyngoplasty for patients with large soft palates, (Silvestri, Guilleminault, & Simmons, 1983), the use of protriptyline for certain patients with upper airway obstruction (Clark, Schmidt, Schaal & Schaal, 1979), and the use of a nocturnal tongue-retaining device for patients with obstructive sleep apnea (Cartwright, et al., 1980).

Nocturnal Myoclonus

Currently there is no effective treatment for nocturnal myoclonus. Patients with this disorder do not generally benefit from routine sedative hypnotics and do, in fact, become habituated. However, diazepam and especially clonazopam have helped in some cases. Drug holidays are periodically necessary to restore effectiveness (Hauri, 1982a). There is evidence that a derivative of gammaaminobutyric acid (GABA), baclofen, may help to improve sleep continuity indexes as well as REM and delta indexes, while not reducing the occurrence of myoclonic activity per se.

Restless Legs Syndrome

As with nocturnal myoclonus, there is no effective treatment for restless legs syndrome. A variety of treatments have been used, including anticonvulsants, antianxiety agents, 5-hydroxytryptophan, antidepressants, CNS stimulants, sedative hypnotics, and muscle relaxation and exercise programs. To date, clonazepam appears to offer the best results generally (e.g., Coleman, et al., 1983). We have also found vitamin E (approximately 600 units/day) to be helpful. However, since the etiology of the syndrome is unknown and may in fact be varied (e.g., it hs been linked to caffeinism, iron and vitamin deficiencies, and a variety of diseases), treatment with clonazepam is not necessarily the method of choice. Much research is needed in this area before effective treatments become available.

Insomnia

Insomnia is a symptom resulting from multiple, simultaneous causes. The first step in treating insomnia is a careful medical and psychiatric evaluation. When the differential diagnosis of insomnia is not clear on the basis of a clinical evaluation, several nights' sleep in a sleep laboratory may be recommended.

Whenever possible, treatment of insomnia should focus on a specific illness or underlying causes. Thus, the treatment plan, varying from person to person, sometimes includes simply psychological support, a change in life patterns, or a change in environment; at other times, it involves psychotherapy or behavioral therapy. Sometimes treatment is aimed at a specific medical condition that causes pain or discomfort. Overall, in a great majority of instances, insomnia is best treated without hypnotic medication.

When medication is required, it is frequently an antidepressant, antipsychotic, or other medication intended to treat specific underlying conditions rather than a hypnotic aimed at the symptom of inability to sleep. There are times, however, when a benzodiazepine is appropriate. Such situations include transient situational insomnia, in which it is understood by both patient and physician that medication is being used for a brief period of time and will be gradually withdrawn. Fortunately, there are a number of short-acting benzodiazepines from which to choose (but see the later section on benzodiazepines in general for a discussion of drawbacks to their use). Periods of sleep difficulty associated with hospitalization and surgery or other clearly defined medical conditions are also good reasons for short-term use of hypnotics. Although the studies relating to hypnotic efficacy often are contradictory, the general belief is that most sedative-hypnotic drugs do not retain their sleep-inducing effectiveness for more than a few nights.

Pharmacological factors must always be evaluated in the patient with insomnia. Dependence on, tolerance to, and withdrawal from hypnotic agents themselves may be major factors in the complaint of some insomniac patients. Some of these patients apper to improve once they have ended their dependence on hypnotics. When multiple doses have been taken, these drugs should be withdrawn slowly under careful supervision in view of the dangers of major withdrawal symptoms, including convulsions.

On the market today are probably 100 nonprescription products that are claimed to be of benefit for insomnia and anxiety. It is estimated that 30 million packages of over-the-counter hypnotics are purchased annually by Americans. Findings from clinical studies regarding the relative efficacy of these drugs are often contradictory. Alternative approaches have also been used with 1-tryptophan (Hartmann, & Spinweber, 1979) and nicotinamide (Robinson, Pegram, Hyde, Benton, & Smythies, 1977). The results of these trials have been promising and offer some patients an opportunity to sleep better without the use of addictive medications.

In terms of recommendations that may be offered in office counseling, it is often useful for some patients to (1) establish rigid times of going to bed and, especially, of arising; (2) eliminate daytime naps; (3) recognize that bed is a place for sleep (and sexual activity) but not for wakefulness, reading, eating, watching television, worrying, letter writing, or any other activity; (4) get out of bed and occupy oneself until ready to return to sleep if one cannot go to sleep or cannot return to sleep upon awakening; (5) establish a program of daytime exercise, which tends to promote nocturnal sleep; and (6) engage in evening activities conducive to relaxation, including hobbies, rest, hot baths, drinking warm milk, and so forth.

As an alternative, various behavioral therapy techniques have recently been studied and have been found to be successful in treating insomnia (Knapp, Downs, & Alperson, 1976; Ribordy & Denney, 1977; Shealy, 1979). These methods should be most effective when insomnia is suspected to be the result of maladaptive learning and conditioning. Such methods include progressive relaxation, electromyographic biofeedback, autogenic training, systematic desensitization, and stimulus control therapy. Because of the time commitment involved in these therapies, the health care team approach is usually more practical. Exploration should be made of greater use of social workers, counselors, nurses, and physician's assistants, along with the clinical psychologist, in the formation of health care teams.

Sleep Disturbances in the Elderly

During recent years, there has been a growing interest in the aging process and the particular health needs of the elderly. The complaint of insomnia in the elderly is perceived as one of the more common problems. Sleep researchers have found that many changes in the sleep-wakefulness cycle do occur with age. There is a need to determine clearly which changes in sleep patterns are natural, immutable, and inevitable with age and might be best endured rather than intensively combatted (these changes are described later, under "Neuropsychological Assessment of Sleep in the Elderly"). Some investigators feel many sleep problems may even stem from elderly individuals' expectations that they will experience difficulty in sleeping.

It is interesting to note that 39% of the hypnotics prescribed in 1977 were for persons over the age of 60 years and that persons in that age group constitute only 15% of the population and account for approximately 11% of all visits to physicians' offices (Institute of Medicine, 1979). Not only do elderly persons receive a disproportionate amount of hypnotics, but they are also more vulnerable to the hazards of hypnotic use because they are more likely already to have disorders aggravated by hypnotics, such as impaired respiratory, hepatic, or renal function. The elderly are also more likely to be taking other medication, leaving them at increased risk for toxic interactions from the consumption of several different drugs at the same time.

Schwartz, Wang, Leitz, and Gross (1962) found that socioeconomic factors play an important role in the drug-taking behavior of the elderly. Difficulty in living on fixed incomes motivates them to turn to over-the-counter preparations and home remedies to avoid the cost of a doctor's visit. Fear, ignorance, or lack of transportation often contribute to potential overuse or misuse of drugs by the elderly. Several examples of drug misuse are taking medications irregularly because of lack of motivation, forgetfulness, expense, or self-determination of need; borrowing and lending medicine; mixing different drugs in one container; and overdosage by the ingestion of duplicate medications prescribed by different physicians. Complicating the problem is a lack of specified geriatric drug doses. Existing experimental data on drug metabolism are usually obtained from adults in their mid-twenties (Gorrod, 1974).

The few studies available show no particular hypnotic agent to be more effective than another for elderly persons. Prudent choice of a hypnotic for an elderly patient might be from among those drugs that are converted to inactive metabolites or have relatively short half-lives, so as to minimize the chance of accumulation and adverse effects. Recent pharmakinetic studies of the shorter-acting benzodiazepine anxiolytics, oxazepam (Serax) and lorazepam (Ativan), indicate that there is no impairment of the disposition and elimination in aged subjects when compared to younger adults (Hoyumpa, 1978). The effectiveness of these two drugs as hypnotics is still being evaluated.

Sleep disturbances represent a difficult problem for elderly persons, their families, and their physicians. The physician must recognize that hypnotics cease to be the most effective solution to the problem but are often the treatment choice because of the lack of reasonable alternatives. Before prescribing a hypnotic for an elderly person, it is often productive to suggest nonpharmocological measures, such as establishing a ritual for retiring to bed, avoiding daytime naps, and increasing the daily amount of physical activity. Nonpharmacological techniques for the management of insomnia in the elderly are discussed at length by Butler and Lewis (1977).

It is especially important to be aware of the tendency of the elderly to find their daytime hours unusually conducive to sleep. This pattern of daytime sleep must be changed rather than treating the nighttime insomnia that results from it. Most important in devising new daytime schedules with set times for rising and exercise is the assistance of those persons found in the elderly person's natural association of people—family, friends, and neighborhood social networks. There is a body of research to suggest that social supports have a direct effect on health by mediating the impact of stress and by strengthening the individual's coping efforts (Hamburg, Adams, & Brodie, 1976).

SLEEP AND SLEEP DISORDERS IN SOME AREAS OF NEUROPSYCHOLOGICAL INTEREST

Sleep Disorders in Preexisting Medical Conditions

Neuropsychologists may seldom be called on at this point in the field's history to evaluate a patient who comes in presenting with a sleep disorder per se. On the neurological ward, however, sleep disorders may be not uncommon in many patients, a situation that neuropsychologists are already seeing. The accompanying excessive daytime somnolence, possible memory deficits, impaired orientation, and confusion that may result from any of a variety of sleep disorders could very easily be mistaken as being symptoms solely related to the presenting neurological problem of the patient. For example, a patient who is already suspected of having a memory deficit concomitant with a tumor or closed head injury (CHI) may also have an unevaluated sleep disorder that could in some cases be fatal.

Sleep disorders are frequently observed in many areas familiar to neuropsychologists. It is important that neuropsychologists consider the many possible causes of sleep disorders when evaluating a given patient. The neurological affliction for which the patient is hosptialized may be affecting an area that also controls or effects sleep and/or the sleep cycle. Many organic processes also change significantly during sleep and during each sleep stage. Thus, a patient whose respiration is somewhat compromised while awake may have significant difficulties while asleep. The neuropsychologically documentable effects of sleep apnea are being assessed currently; the clinical lore of their cognitive and performance effects exist now.

Sleep apnea has frequently been reported in patients with documentable medical disorders. Apnea may also either appear as the result of or be exacerbated by medical procedures. Chung and Crago (1982) reported on the potential danger of the administration of anesthetics to patients with sleep apnea. The administration of some form of anesthesia for a wide variety of medical procedures is common. Patients with undiagnosed sleep apnea are reported to be at high risk for respiratory arrest under such conditions. Krieger and Rosomoff (1974a) observed the occurrence of sleep apnea in 10 patients (lasting from 3–32 days) after cordotomy. Each of these patients is reported to have complained of lethargy and asthenia, and to have appeared confused during this period of observed apnea. Krieger and Rosomoff (1974b) also reported the occurrence of sleep apnea after anterior spinal surgery. Rees, Clark, Cochrane, and Prior (1981) found significant sleep apnea in 3 of 8 patients with significant autonomic neuropathy accompanying diabetes. Coccagna, Mantovani, Parchi, Mironi, and Lugaresi (1975) observed alveolar hypoventilation and hypersomnia associated with myotonic dystrophy. In 1982, Power, Mosko, and Sassin found evidence of sleep-stage–dependent Cheyne-Stokes respiration after a cerebral infarct involving the right hemisphere parietal, temporal, and frontal lobes. A left hemisphere cerebellar defect was also noted. Kelly, Kirshnamoorthy, and Shannon (1980) reported an astrocytoma accompanied by sleep apnea in an infant. The apnea largely *subsided* after removal of the tumor. Westerman and Ferguson (1978) reported obstructive sleep apnea due to bilateral recurrent larngeal nerve palsies afflicting a patient. The patient, who refused tracheostomy, died four months after his evaluation. His death was reported to have occurred immediately following "an episode of loud stridor" (p. 825). This description is consistent with the associated features of sleep apnea.

The EEG has been a very reliable indicator of pathological conditions during both wakefulness and sleep. Orr (1976) published a good review of the literature on the uses of the sleep EEG in neurological diagnosis. Gross, Spehlmann, and Daniels (1978), and Hynd, Pisozzolo, and Maletta (1982) have reported on the characteristic sleep disturbances associated with progressive supranuclear palsy. The sleep EEG has been reported to have been influenced by fibrositis syndrome (Moldofsky, Scarisbrick, England, & Smythe, 1975), spinocerebellar degeneration (Osorio & Daroff, 1979), cerebellar pathology (Bergonzi, et al., 1981), olivopontocerebellar degeneration (Neil, Holzer, Spiker, Coble, & Kupfer, 1980), and high cervical lesions (Adey, Bors, & Porter, 1968).

Other types of sleep disorders have also been reported in patients with neurological disorders. Tamura, Karacan, Williams, and Meyer (1983) reported on sleep-wake cycle disturbances associated with vascular brain stem lesions. A gangliocytoma of the third ventricle that was responsible for EDS and dementia (among other symptoms) was reported by Beal, Kleinman, Ojemann, and Hochberg (1981). In another instance, a patient claimed to have dreamed that he could not command a word to appear on his CRT screen and then awakened to find himself aphasic, having suffered a stroke (Harrison, 1981).

It is recognized that in the cases described above, the patient's sleep disorder was clearly not the crux of the patient's problems or the focus of any neuropsychological evaluation that might have been done. It is emphasized, though, that had the accompanying sleep disorders not been recognized in these cases, the results of the patient's evaluation might not have been interpreted properly (as all of the necessary and appropriate determinants of the patient's symptoms would not have been taken into account).

The dementias have often been associated with changes in the sleep EEG (Serby, 1982). Perhaps therapeutic interventions might be aimed at improving the sleep patterns of these patients, with a concomitant improvement in the psychological state of such individuals. Many authors have reported increased REM time; decreased beta and theta bands; decreased delta sleep (stages 3 and 4); fragmentation of sleep with frequent awakenings; and broken, irregular sleep cycles associated with senile dementia of the Alzheimer's type (Allen, Stäheline, Seiler, & Spiegel, 1982; Coben, Danziger, & Berg, 1983; Kelly & Feigenbaum, 1982; Prinz, et al., 1982).

Parkinson's disease has also been found to have associated sleep EEG changes. Friedman (1980) and Myslobodsky, Mintz, Ben-Mayor, and Radwan (1982) have reported decreased delta sleep, disturbances in sleep phasing, and associated increases in stages 1 and 2 sleep in patients witih the disease.

Gilles de la Tourettes syndrome has also been found to have associated sleep EEG changes (Mendelson, Caine, Goyer, Ebert, & Gillin, 1979). Untreated patients were found to have 30% less delta sleep, which returned to normal after treatment with haloperidol.

Sleep and Head Injury

Recently, some research has appeared in the literature examining the sleep of patients with head injuries and the relationship between sleep disruptions and cognitive functioning in these individuals (Epstein & Simmons, 1983; Parsons & Ver Beek, 1982; Prigatano, Stahl, Orr, & Zeiner, 1982; Ron, Algom, Hary, & Cohen, 1980). To date, there is a lack of consistency in the findings. However, this is not surprising, as the few studies that have been conducted in this area differ on a number of important variables: degree of damage, anatomical location of the head injury, chronic versus acute nature of the injury, length of consciousness disruption, All Night Sleep Polysomnography (ANSP) studies versus self-report sleep measures, and self-terminated sleep versus awakening by the researcher after a predetermined sleep time.

Early reports of sleep in brain-injured, comatose patients revealed that the onset of a normal-appearing sleep pattern might be a reliable prognostic indicator of clinical improvement (Ron, Algom, Hary, & Cohen, 1980). Improvement in the patient's sleep architecture, as revealed by polysomnographic recording, was almost always concomitant with clinical indications of improvement of the comatose state. While many sleep abnormalities have been observed in brain-injured, noncomatose patients (e.g., a decrease in specific sleep rhythm, decreased spindles and K-complexes, low-level REM activity), these abnormalities have generally not been useful for individual or group prognosis (Ron, Algom, Hary, & Cohen, 1980).

How do the sleep patterns of head-injured patients compare with their sleep patterns before head injury? Parson and Ver Beek (1982) attempted to answer this question by comparing self-report sleep information from 75 subjects who had experienced minor head injury with a disturbance in consciousness. First, it is important to note that no ANSPs were conducted in this study, so objective verification of the self-report information was not possible. Further, it is essential to note that both pre- and post-trauma sleep measures were obtained post-injury. Thus, all information may be distorted due to memory impairment, a symptom often associated with minor head injury or cerebral concussion. It is well known that patients' subjective estimates of sleep are often inaccurate when compared with the polysomnographic record (Broughton, 1982a). The validity of such estimates in head-injured patients is likely to be even more questionable, considering the memory impairments that often accompany such injuries. Despite these serious shortcomings, we will proceed to describe this study in some detail because it constitutes an important source of information in an area desperately in need of further exploration.

The majority of the 75 subjects were males, ages ranging from 16–30 years, who had suffered a motor vehicle accident. All patients were tested with the Glascow Coma Scale (GCS) upon admission, with 85% receiving a score of 12 or greater (indicating a minimal disruption of consciousness) and only 8% receiving a score of less than 10. Fifty-three percent experienced consciousness disruption of less than one hour.

The sleep data were obtained from 50 self-report questions taken from the General Sleep Habits Questionnaire developed by Monroe (1967). Some of these items consisted of open-ended questions, while others consisted of a Likert-type rating scale. Assistance from family members, significant others, and staff was permitted in responding to the questionnaire. The possibility of self-report and injury-related inaccuracies in the obtained responses was acknowledged by the researchers.

The major findings of the study included statistically significant changes in the following sleep parameters when post–head-injury responses were compared to pre–head-injury responses: increased number of sleep interruptions per week and per night ($P < .004$, $P < .001$); increased number of times per month of early-morning awakenings associated with difficulty in returning to sleep ($P < .04$) and inability to return to sleep ($P < .02$); increased time needed to function at peak efficiency upon awakening ($P < .001$); decreased sleep quality ($P < .02$); and increased complaints about sleep ($P < .001$). This information was gathered approximately three months following injury.

As might be expected, the anatomical location of the injury did not significantly predict the postinjury sleep patterns. It is indeed difficult to say, without a computed tomography (CT) scan, that the surface site of the injury was even where the internal damage occurred. The gross division of patients into two groups (frontal head injury and other sites of head injury) may account for the lack of any observed relationship here.

Other findings of interest include (1) the majority of patients had no sleep difficulties at all in the first 24 hours after injury; (2) increased length of time of consciousness disruption was significantly correlated with earlier retirement (to bed) times, later awakening times, and decreased number and vividness of dreams recalled; (3) lower GCS ratings upon hospital admission were significantly correlated with an increased number of changes in sleep patterns.

While electrophysiological sleep changes were not used in this study, Parsons and Ver Beek suggested that these reported sleep changes probably indicated an increase in stage 2 and decrements in deep sleep and REM sleep. Interestingly, Ron and colleagues (1980) observed similar electrophysiological sleep changes in nine severely brain-injured patients. Early sleep recordings (i.e., two to six months postinjury) revealed an abundance of stages 1 and 2 with little REM and deep sleep. Increases in REM and deep sleep were noted over an average period of nine and one-half months, but these stages remained substantially reduced compared to those in normal control subjects. The observed REM decrement is consistent with observations of patients suffering from different kinds of brain damage (e.g., Appenzellar & Fisher, 1968; Bricolo, 1975; Feinberg, Koresko, & Heller, 1967; Harada, et al., 1976; Markand & Dyken, 1976).

Ron and colleagues (1980) also studied the relationship between sleep patterns and cognitive functioning in severely brain-injured patients. The patient sample and general procedures described here were also employed in their examination of sleep patterns in brain-injured patients described above.

Ron and associates (1980) studied a small sample ($N = 9$) of brain-injured patients with either penetrating injuries (caused by shrapnel from war) or blunt injuries (from either war or road accidents). All patients were drug free at the time of the study. The patients ranged from 1.0–6.0 months from the time of injury to first examination ($\bar{X} = 2.55$) and were comatose from 0.5–16 weeks ($\bar{X} = 5.17$). Each patient participated in 4–7 recording nights over a period ranging from 5–8 weeks. Average follow-up was 38 weeks (range, 22–52 weeks). All patients were rated on scales measuring independence, locomotion (voluntary movements only), and cognition. In the cognitive rating, patients were assessed on 11 variables: orientation in space and time, sensory recognition of stimuli, short-term memory, verbal recognition of concepts, recognition of association between objects, logical thinking, visual recognition of more complex stimuli, copy of simple shapes, reconstruction, drawing, and long-term memory.

The major finding of the study was a positive correlation between REM sleep and cognition in seven of the nine patients ($r = .89$). This is interesting becasue REM sleep has been posited by many (Feinberg, Braum, & Schulman, 1969; Dewan, 1970; Castaldo & Krynicki, 1973) as playing a major role in cognitive function integrity. Thus, this study demonstrated that the cognition-REM relationship exists not only in normal populations but also in brain-injured patients during the process of rehabilitation. In seven of the nine patients, the rates of improvement in REM and cognitive variables were similar throughout the study period (one year), while the improvements in independence and locomotion were both unrelated and uncorrelated with either REM sleep or cognition. As Castaldo and Krynichi (1973) have suggested, this correlation probably reflects the return in cognitive processing of information: the low cognitive capacity of a newly injured patient may be reflected in decreased REM sleep time. It is also as likely that the electrical summation responsible for the REM sleep pattern is mediated by the same mechanism responsible for some aspects of cognitive activity.

While a causal relationship here must be at once labeled as highly tentative, the recovery of normal sleep staging and especially the normalization of REM sleep may well be correlated with the return of cognitive abilities. While other studies have found no relationship between REM sleep and normal cognitive functioning, literature in the area of populations with decreased or limited cognitive capacity (mental retardation studies) lends some credibility to the possibility of such a relationship.

A study by Prigatano and colleagues (1982) yielded data inconsistent with that of Ron and colleagues (1980). Prigatano and associates did not find any relationship between REM sleep and cognitive functioning in 10 closed-head–injured patients 6–59 months postinjury. REM sleep percentages for these patients were not significantly different from those of 10 age-matched, healthy control subjects, yet the closed-head–injured patients frequently complained of reduced dreaming. The reason for the discrepancy in findings is unclear, although several possibilities exist. First, the samples were different in type of injury (Prigatano and colleagues studied 3 severely impaired, 4 moderately impaired, and 3 mildly impaired subjects, while patients with severe traumatic brain injury were the subjects in the study of Ron and associates), and the amount of time since injury (Prigatano and associates studied patients 6–59 months postinjury, while Ron and colleagues studied patients 1–6 months postinjury). Second, the sleep recording procedures were different (in the Prigatano study, subjects were awakened after 6–7 hours of sleep, while patients awakened spontaneously in the Ron study). The Prigatano procedure may have introduced restriction in range of sleep measures, especially with regard to REM sleep, as it tends to occur for longer periods of time toward morning. This may account for the statistically insignificant correlations between REM sleep and cognitive functioning measures (i.e., Wechsler Full Scale, Wechsler Memory Quotient, and Trails B). Prigatano and associates (1982) suggested that in the acute phase of injury (e.g., 6 months or less), dreaming may be impaired and REM sleep may be reduced, but as the patient recovers, REM sleep appears to approach normal limits. Thus, it would not be surprising to find different relationships between REM sleep and cognition in acutely injured versus less recently injured patients.

The study by Prigatano and colleagues (1982) also revealed other interesting sleep findings. Compared to controls, patients exhibited an increased number of awakenings and less stage 1. No other sleep stages were observed to be statistically different for the two groups.

In summary, acutely brain-injured patients seem to suffer from REM and deep sleep deficits. The sleep of such patients appears to be characterized by a high percentage of light sleep, frequent arousals, and difficulty in returning to sleep once awakened. Eventually, brain-injured patients may reestablish normal REM sleep percentages but still be troubled by frequent awakenings. Longitudinal research is needed before such conclusions can be fully justified. There is some evidence indicating that REM sleep and cognitive functioning may be positively correlated in acutely injured patients but unrelated in patients with longer recovery periods since injury. Closed-head injury represents a broad class of injuries from many types of accidents nad affects a vast range of structures. It should not be surprising if variable cognitive and sleep abnormalities are observed in such patients.

In a clinical review paper, Epstein and Simmons (1983) interviewed seven patients suffering from acute vascular accidents, each suffering from variable degrees of aphasia. Four of the patients were diagnosed with Broca's aphasia the others with varying symptoms of dysnomia, dysgraphia, dyslexia, and some comprehension difficulties. The interview question was "Tell me about your dreaming," as opposed to "Do you dream?" All answered that they had not dreamed since their strokes. Only one of the seven had visual modality function affected by the injury. The authors concluded that the visual modality need not be affected to preclude dreaming.

Although the aforementioned report has many methodological weaknesses and is not a study in the true sense of the word, it does speak to the fact that many patients have trouble in the area of dreaming and dream recall. The only way to truly study their complaints is through the use of an ANSP.

Sleep and Epilepsy

Sleep polysomnography has been used as a research method for documenting epileptic activity since Bennet (1963) observed seizures in normal subjects after considerable sleep deprivation (SD) (Degen, 1980). Although replication of the ability to induce seizure activity in normal subjects through sleep deprivation has had little success, SD has shown clinical applicability. The procedure is especially useful in documenting abnormal activity in the EEGs of known epileptics. The difficulty of obtaining documentation of such activity in the waking EEG has been demonstrated (Degen, 1980;

Rowan, Veldhuisen, & Negelkerke, 1982; Veldhuizen, Binnie, & Beintema, 1983). The ability to record epileptiform discharges in sleep records after sleep deprivation has been rather successful. For example, 54% of epileptic subjects on anticonvulsant medication in one study and 63% in another showed such discharges during sleep (Degen, 1977, 1980).

The question has arisen as to whether sleep induced by SD is better than sleep induced by medication. The data have been inconclusive (Rowan, Veldhuizen, & Negelkerke, 1982). Rowan and associates (1982) focused on this question with 43 epileptics, all of whom had normal waking EEGs. Sedation was achieved through the admission of 200 mg of secobarbitol (an additional 100 mg if sleep was not achieved in 30 minutes) or from 24 hours of sleep deprivation. Approximately 30 minutes of sleep were recorded in each case. Forty-one of the 43 patients had waking, sedated, and sleep-deprived EEGs recorded. Two patients had no waking EEG performed. The study revealed that new or additional information over and above that obtained from the waking EEG's was obtained in the records of 19 sleep deprivation recordings (44%), as compared to new information in only 14% of the pharmacologically sedated EEGs. This difference in information obtained was statistically significant.

Veldhuizen, Binnie, and Beintema (1983) made some interesting points about the use of the SD procedure. They noted that sleep researchers often mistakenly assume that a normal initial recording (post SD) will be followed by subsequent normal EEGs. However, Veldhuizen and associates point out that the routine EEGs of epileptic persons are extremely variable. The chance of finding epileptiform activity in a second, albeit SD, recording is greater simply due to regression to the mean. However, only one study reviewed by this group (Pratt, Mattson, Welkers, & Williams, 1968) noted this phenomenon. Pratt and colleagues (1968) concluded that after repeating the routine EEG after the SD EEG, approximately 18% of their 41% seizure gain was attributable to the regression phenomenon. In summary, Veldhuizen and colleagues (1983) concluded that, in order to establish a supremacy of the sleep EEG's effect, randomly occurring routine and sleep-deprived EEGs need to be performed.

In just such a study, Veldhuizen and associates reported that, although the effect of sleep on the EEG was confirmed (with mean discharge rates over the entire record after SD being significantly higher compared to those for barbiturate-induced sleep or normal recording), the effect was totally explained by the increased amount of recording time spent in sleep after SD. The study was performed on 72 difficult-to-diagnose epileptic patients, 60 of whom were taking antiepileptic medications. Medications were not changed for the study. It was concluded that sleep deprivation, being disagreeable to both patients, patients' families, and the nursing staff, should be stopped in favor of barbiturate-induced sleep. The sleep recording itself was still considered a valid means of evaluating epileptic activity.

Having seen drug artifact in the sleep record, and with the abundance of data on barbiturate effects (Williams & Karacan, 1976), Veldhuizen's preference seems to be based on shaky grounds. Regardless, the effectiveness of a properly run EEG in the diagnosis of epilepsy is confirmed.

A brief look at two other clinical syndromes will conclude our discussion of sleep in epilepsy. The first of these is the concept of nocturnal epilepsy, a clinical syndrome that appeared in the literature in the early 1950s (Davies, 1982). The other syndrome involves epilepsy in combination with sleep apnea. Multiple pathologic conditions are not uncommon, but a linkage between such diverse disorders as epilepsy and sleep apnea might seem a bit unusual. As will be seen, the treatment of one disorder may also greatly alleviate another.

Nocturnal epilepsy has been reported most often in the European literature and has received minimal attention in American medical journals (Davies, 1982). The disorder "may recur as a truly nocturnal neurological disturbance, which may have minimal, overt manifestations of the epileptic state during the awake hours" (Davies, 1982, p.267). In two cases reported by Davies (1982), the diagnoses went undetected for periods of 18 months and 2 years, respectively. The diagnoses were finally achieved from abnormal findings detected from a sleep EEG.

The symptoms of each case were similar in many respects. Each occurred in a child. The symptoms consisted of headache in the morning and difficulty in arousal. In each case, the child was considered to be irritable and uncooperative and also had trouble remaining awake. These behaviors occurred two to three times per month in the older, school-aged child and two to three times per week in the younger, preschool child. The consequences of the disorders were severe for each child: the school-aged child was in danger of failing a grade; the younger child had been placed in a foster home, being seen as uncontrollable. Both were seen having difficulties attributable to stress reactions. In both cases, past personal and familial histories were noncontributory, as were the physical examinations. Following sleep EEGs, phenytoin therapy caused radical and immediate cessation of the behavioral problems noted. The study revealed that, despite the resolution of behavioral problems, the conditions showed partial, but never complete remission (Davies, 1982).

Of course, many different psychological and/or medical disorders could have been found culpable for the behavioral disorders seen in these two cases. However, the possibility of nocturnal epilepsy should be considered. This is a good example of when a neuropsychologist might be consulted to make an evaluation. The data obtained from such an occasion should prove to be very informative. Cognitive-motor impairment should be examined, along with the child's behavior pertaining to drowsiness, irritability, and so on.

The second clinical study presented here is one of epilepsy complicated by sleep apnea (Wyler & Weymuller, 1980). Interestingly, some neuropsychological testing was done in this case. The patient was a 26½-year-old man with a diagnosis of intractable seizure disorder since the age of 1½ years. Special education classes were necessitated during school years. Since the age of 18 years, the patient had complained that he felt as if he were being strangled, and he would awaken during the night. These complaints were felt to possibly be due to his tendency to have auditory or visual hallucinations at the onset of his seizure activity. Epileptiform activity was documented on both sleep and routine EEGs. The CT scan was unremarkable. Neuropsychological testing of the man, with a history of lifelong mental retardation, revealed a WAIS Verbal IQ of 60, Performance IQ of 61, and Full Scale IQ of 58. ANSP revealed *central* sleep apnea episodes of approximately 20 seconds in length, not accompanied by behavioral arousal or signaled by epileptiform activity. The patient was placed on phenytoin and carbamazine and was subsequently followed up as an outpatient for 12 months. Seizure activity was continued at the rate of three to four per week. The patient was readmitted, and a permanent tracheostomy was inserted. After some immediate postoperative seizures, the patient was documented to be free from secondary generalized seizures, with the exception of two episodes resulting from blockage of his tracheostomy. No periods of apnea or frequent awakenings from sleep were subsequently reported.

Although the literature on SD EEG studies is mentioned, the authors failed to speculate further upon a possible mechanism for the reduction in his nongeneralized seizures. Unfortunately, no further neuropsychological testing was mentioned. It seems possible that through many prospective mechanisms (decreased drowsiness, increased sleep stage consolidation, decreased seizure activity), that the patient's neuropsychological measures might have improved. (See the section on the neuropsychological evaluation of apneics later in this chapter.)

Sleep and Mental Retardation

Sleep has been reported to be different in children with mental retardation than it is in normal children (Borrow, et al., 1980; Castaldo, 1969; Castaldo & Krynicki, 1973; Clark, Schmidt, & Schuller, 1980; Clausen, Sersen, & Lidsky, 1977; Feinberg, Braun, & Schulman, 1969; Loughlin, Wynne, & Victoria, 1981; Petre-Quadens & Jouvet, 1966; Shibagaki, Kiyono, & Watanabe, 1980, 1982). Sleep spindles are observed as being absent in MR children much more frequently than in normal children (Clausen, Sersen, & Lidsky, 1977; Shibagaki, Kiyono, & Watanabe, 1980, 1982). Reports of decreased REM time in MR subjects are also common (Borrow, et al., 1980; Castaldo, 1969; Castaldo & Krynicki, 1973; Clausen, Sersen, & Lidsky, 1977; Feinberg, Braun, & Schulman, 1969; Petre-Quadens & Jouvet, 1966; Shibagaki, Kiyono, & Watanabe, 1980, 1982). Extreme spindles (spindles comparable to those observed in normal children with exception of their diffuseness and higher voltages, of 200 and 400 microvolts) are also seen in MR children. Such spindles are rare in adult MR subjects and are considered abnormal in all nonretarded persons. (Shibagaki, Kiyono, & Watanabe, 1980, 1982).

ANSP studies have also revealed differences both within and between different etiologies of MR (Borrow, et al., 1980; Feinberg, Braun, & Schulman, 1969; Shibagaki, Kiyono, & Watanabe, 1980, 1982). Castaldo reported on Down's syndrome subjects divided into moderate and severe subgroups. Moderate group subjects spent significantly greater time in REM sleep than did severe group subjects. The amount of REM sleep in the moderate group was considered within normal limits (WNL). Castaldo concluded that variation in IQ above a minimal level (i.e., moderate group) was not reflected in REM sleep time. Severe group subjects also had a longer REM sleep latency. No other differences in sleep staging were seen. Feinberg and colleagues (1969) raised the possibility of using sleep EEG as a diagnostic tool in some MR syndromes. With the continuation of studies designed to reveal the basic sleep patterns of subgroups of retardates, the use of ANSPs in this manner seems plausible. Feinberg and colleagues also found differences between subjects with mongoloidism, phenylketonuria (PKU), or undifferentiated MR and subjects with chronic brain syndrome (CBS) or young normal subjects. Differences were found in total sleep time (TST), stage 1, eye movement, the number of REM sleep periods, spindling, stages 3 and 4, and sleep cycles. Petre-Quadens and Jouvet (1966) found that subjects with MR from metabolically definable causes and those with MR from undefined causes showed similar REM sleep abnormalities.

Various authors have raised the question of the functional significance of these ANSP differences. Shibagaki, Kiyono, and Watanabe (1982) reported that a tendency toward a lower developmental quotient (DQ) was seen among infants without spindles than among subjects of all age groups with spindles. They also reported findings that focused on four hypothyroid children without spindles who were given hormone therapy. Those children who displayed spindles at follow-up evaluation had normal DQs, while those who did not develop normal spindles had low DQs. A lower DQ was also reported by Shibagaki and associates (1980) in children with abnormal ANSPs throughout sleep than among children with abnormal ANSPs only in stages 1 and 2.

Feinberg, Braun, and Schulman (1969) studied the correlation between sleep parameters and the WPPSI Verbal, Performance, and Full Scale scores in an MR population. They reported a significant positive correlation between verbal scores and eye movement ($P < .01$). Performance scores were also significantly correlated with sleep latency, TST, and absolute value of stage 1 ($P < .01$). It was concluded that the level of intellectual function was positively correlated with estimates of REM sleep time in the MR subjects tested ($r = .73$). Phasic eye movement (EM) activity reflects the intensity of the REM sleep process. It was noted that mongoloid subjects have often been found to have a high incidence of visual disturbance on neural examination, suggesting that EM might be more highly correlated with visual disturbance than with IQ. However, the correlation between EM and WPPSI total score when mongoloid subjects were omitted was still significant ($r = .53$; $P < .02$). It was also revealed that Stanford-Binet scores taken from the hospital records of the patients had a rank order correlation of .77 with percent of eye movement. These correlations were somewhat variable among the various subgroups of MR subjects tested. The association between EM and WPPSI total scores was most evident for the undifferentiated group (largest N), with a moderate relationship seen for mongoloids and CBS groups, and no relationship seen with PKU subjects. The CBS group, which was distinguished from the other retardates by low stage 4 EEG, was the only group to show a positive correlation between stage 4 EEG and WPPSI score.

Similarly, Castaldo and Krynicki found a positive correlation between REM sleep and IQ as measured by the WAIS, but no correlation between REM sleep and Social Quotient (SQ) as measured by the Vineland Social Maturity Scale. Clausen, Sersen, and Lidsky (1977) reported that intelligence was significantly correlated with EM density ($r = .56$).

A study by Borrow and colleagues (1980) brings these findings into perspective. In looking at normal-intelligence schoolchildren, no correlation approached significance between various subscores and the composite score of the AH4 test of IQ and REM sleep. REM sleep also was not correlated with the children's academic assessments made by their teachers for the school year. Thus, REM sleep seems to have little, if any, correlation with normal intelligence. On the other hand, ANSPs may be able to tell us much about the diagnosis, type, severity, and prognosis of some MR disorders.

Down's syndrome patients have been noted to have an unexplained tendency toward pulmonary hypertension (Clark, Schmidt, & Schuller, 1980; Loughlin, Wynne, & Victoria, 1981). Clark and colleagues (1980) and Loughlin and colleagues (1981) suggest that nocturnal hypoxemia secondary to sleep-induced airway obstruction may contribute in part or totally to this condition. In other words, sleep apnea may be a common finding in this population. Of the three patients seen by Clark and associates (1980) and the five patients seen by Loughlin and associates (1981), all were noted to have experienced a considerable increase in alertness and level of intellectual function upon receiving treatment for their sleep apnea. The authors suggest that the general stygma of Down's syndrome may account for the tendency of Down's syndrome patients to have sleep apnea. In neither of these studies were the patients subsequently assessed to determine if their observable increases in alertness and intellectual functioning were documentable. This area appears ripe for research.

SLEEP, SLEEP DISORDERS, AND NEUROPSYCHOLOGICAL ASSESSMENT

The Role of Sleep in Learning and Attention-Concentration

The study of sleep in relationship to learning and memory has a long history, as research into psychological phenomena go. Hermann Ebbinghaus postulated in 1885 that sleep reduced the amount of forgetting in the retention interval (Crowder, 1976). Evidence indicated that when sleep occurred, 24-hour retention test performances were better than a constant forgetting function over the period would have predicted. The classic study of Jenkins and Dallenbach (1924) provided the first true experiment on the role of sleep in memory. Here, two subjects lived in the laboratory, learning nonsense syllable lists for later testing over various intervals of time. Retention periods were filled either with sleep or wakefulness. The results indicated that sleep had a beneficial effect on the retention of learned materials. Although this was a methodologically poor study by current standards, Ekstrand (1967) replicated the finding with only minimal necessary changes in the original procedures.

Myriad studies have since been conducted in this area. Seemingly, every possible kind of manipulation has been attempted in order to examine the relationships found by these early studies and to test new hypotheses. These have included learning with various amounts of sleep intervening between trials; learning with various amounts of time elapsing before the onset of sleep after the presentation of materials; learning per stage of sleep; learning in REM versus NREM sleep; learning with variable awakenings disturbing the continuity of sleep; learning with different types of stimuli; and so on. The list seems endless. Unfortunately, various types of methodological weaknesses have plagued much of this research. Further, the procedural inconsistencies among studies makes it difficult to generalize results across studies.

Several different cognitive theories have also been posited in an attempt to explain the influence of sleep, or a component of sleep, on learning and memory processes. Four of these theories are briefly presented here. The basic points taken into consideration in the development of these theories are addressed, along with their respective strengths and weaknesses. Each of the theories attempted to account for the data pertaining to the topic known at the time. New theories were developed when the old could not satisfactorily account of data obtained. A basic conceptual understanding of these theories is useful in evaluating the types of research done in the past as well as that performed in the present. As will be seen, the testing of these theories has often yielded results that were inconsistent or conflicting, depending on a variety of factors. Some of these issues will be addressed later.

The interference theory of forgetting has repeatedly come in and out of favor since its inception with McGeoch's theory of forgetting (Crowder, 1976). Sleep was theorized to have a seemingly obvious facilitative role in memory for stimuli by simply ensuring that nothing would interfere with the material learned before sleep. The basis and maintenance of the theory relied on the effects of both proactive inhibition (PI) and retroactive inhibition (RI). These items referred to the known ability of material learned either before other material (PI) or after other material (RI) to affect its retention. Sleep was postulated to be an inactive mental state. It was therefore proposed that sleep facilitated memory through disallowing the interference of any material that would have been present had the subject been in an active mental state, that is, awake. The idea was that nothing occurred during sleep that could retroactively inhibit the learning of material before sleep. Subjects were given material to learn with a period of either sleep or nonsleep intervening between the demonstration of learning and recall. Such studies replicated Jenkins and Dallenbach's (1924) original findings. Subjects who had an intertrial interval of sleep were found to have better recall than did those with wakefulness in the interval. This result was proffered as evidence for sleep as facilitating RI (McGeoch, 1942), or as reducing (releasing from) PI (Ekstrand, 1967).

The idea of the interference of the presentation of stimuli with memory for either past or future stimuli was instrumental in another cognitive theory, that of consolidation (Crowder, 1976). This theory posited that stimuli needed a given amount of time in which to become fixated in memory. Either practice (successive repetitions of the stimuli) or lack of interference from competing stimuli was reported as necessary during this period. These conditions were seen as facilitating the consolidative process of encoding the material to be learned in a form that maximized later retrieval potential. Any task that occurred during this time period competed, and therefore interfered with, the consolidation of nonfixated memories. Consolidation theory was in this sense consistent with Hebb's 1949 theory of neurobiotaxis. In that theory, time was considered necessary for the biologic fixation of memory through neural growth. The symptoms of retrograde amnesia victims, who after head trauma lose retention of the events occurring just before the trauma, have been cited as clinical evidence for this theory (Crowder, 1976). Sleep was postulated as a period for the general consolidation of the events of the day.

Goodenough, Sapan, Cohen, Portnoff, & Shapiro (1970) compiled a series of studies designed to determine the role of sleep in the consolidation of memory traces. In each case, words were shown to subjects shortly after each of several nightly awakenings (not stage-determined). Subjects were either permitted to return to sleep immediately after pronouncing the word or saying the word at a slight delay, or were kept awake performing psychomotor tasks (testlike and gamelike conditions) for five minutes. Memories for the words were then tested the following morning. The results indicated that retention was positively related to the amount of time taken to return to sleep following word presentation. Retention was found to be better when subjects remained awake after the acknowledgment of the words than with immediate return to sleep. The quality of retention depended on which of the two psychomotor tasks the subject performed during the awake interval, and the immediate versus the delayed articulation of the words.

Goodenough and colleagues (1970) proposed that the data were overall inconsistent with consolidation theory. Consolidation theory could not account for the fact that recall was better when a period of wakefulness occurred after stimulus presentation than when subjects were allowed to return to sleep immediately. In fact, it would predict the opposite effect: those permitted to return to sleep immediately following stimulus presentation should experience less potentially interfering stimuli and have more time in sleep to consolidate the material for morning recall.

An additional finding of this study has stimulated much current research. This finding also argued against consolidation theory. Merely keeping the subject awake following stimulus presentation was not facilitative to morning recall. Rather, mental activity during the awake interval was related to the demonstration of learning. This data touched on the role of arousal, attention, and concentration in learning and memory processes. Yet the facilitative role of sleep demonstrated in the earlier studies remained unexplained.

Early basic sleep researchers were somewhat perplexed by what came to be known as REM sleep. The EEG during this sleep stage looked more like an awake record. The eyes moved around quickly and erratically. Arousal from this stage was achieved more easily than from deeper sleep. From such observations, REM sleep was studied in an effort to determine if a specific portion of sleep was more beneficial to memory processes than were the others. Dewan (1968) proposed the REM consolidation theory of memory. REM sleep was proposed as that stage most responsible for the facilitative effects of sleep on learning and memory.

A vast array of studies in the animal literature have yielded findings very consistent with this theory. Retention over periods of REM-deprived (REMD) sleep versus that over periods of normal sleep has been shown to be lower for a variety of animal species. A good review of the REM sleep literature, of both a human and animal nature, is provided by McGrath and Cohen (1978). Unfortunately, the results with human subjects have not been so clear-cut. The animal literature also has recently received some critiques that damage the stability of its findings (McGrath & Cohen, 1978). The methodological difficulties involved in separating REM from NREM sleep are not minor in either animal or human studies. Researchers have used this factor, however, in arguing both for and against the results of studies in this area.

Other sleep stages have also been implicated as consistent with consolidation theory. Yaroush, Sullivan, and Ekstrand (1971) and later Fowler, Sullivan, and Ekstrand (1973) reported that stage 4, rather than REM sleep, was actually the stage of sleep most influential in memory processes. Retention over a period of stage 4 sleep was demonstrated to be better than that in subjects having REM sleep in the intertrial interval. The separation of sleep stages was accomplished in these studies by contrasting recall of those subjects presented material before stage onset and then awakened after four hours to those presented material after four hours of sleep and asked to recall in the morning. This separation of time of task preparation is based on the fact that the majority of stage 4 sleep occurs in the first half of the sleep period, while REM sleep is more plentiful in the second half. Obviously, there are many confounding variables in such research, including time of material presentation, level of arousal at the time of material presentation, and amount of sleep obtained in the previous 24-hour period. Additionally, stages 1 and 3 are also more prominent in the first half of the sleep period. Finally, all stages of sleep may occur in both halves of the sleep period in the normal sleeper.

Other theories of cognitive processing have focused more on the ideas of arousal, attention, and concentration. Tilley (1981) proposed that arousal is the most pertinent factor involved in recall. Categorizable lists of words presented in the middle of the sleep period showed differential recall across sleep stages. Higher recall levels were associated with the occurrence of REM sleep, as opposed to NREM sleep, during the retention interval. He states that sleep merely represents a place on a continuum of arousal. Therefore, that stage of sleep when the subject is most arousable should play the greatest part in learning. Tilley preferred that either the high arousal associated with REM sleep helped to maintain the memory trace, or that REM sleep consolidated the material toward improved retrieval. Arousal level was also assessed in this study by criticial flicker fusion (CFF) level out of arousal from different sleep stages. CFF rates increased between tests in the REM condition and decreased in the NREM, while no main effect of sleep was seen. Tilley states that the benefit if REM sleep on recall might be seen as due to the raising of arousal level out of NREM sleep—in essence, as a side effect.

Stones (1977) looked at retention of chunks and items per chunk of material across different types of stimuli. These were assessed over periods of no-previous-sleep and largely REM or NREM sleep. Significant differences were seen in both immediate and subsequent recall, with the NREM-sleep group demonstrating lower recall than both the no-previous-sleep and the REM-sleep groups. These included significant differences in the number of items per category recalled in the subsequent, but not immediate, recall by similar sleep staging. From these data, it does appear that recall is affected in some way by level of arousal, as reflected by sleep stage.

Several methodological problems arise when the role of sleep in cognitive function is addressed. Many of these problems are the same kinds of difficulties that plague other basic research. In other areas, however, spurious effects may be more easily distinguished from real effects. Scrima (1982) and Broughton (1982b) have discussed the fact that these difficulties are not so easily dealt with in the area of sleep research.

The first of these problems is associated with the continuity of sleep. Sleep must be looked at in terms of its role in bodily circadian rhythms. Sleep occurs naturally in a cyclic manner, that is, it recurs regularly. Sleep itself has stages that normally also cycle regularly. Most likely, any effects of sleep on cognitive function (and hence the demise of cognitive abilities when it is disturbed) are manifested when sleep is allowed to occur in a synchronized manner with all of the many other cyclic events that go on in the human body (see reviews of circadian rhythms and sleep by Webb, 1978; Weitzman, 1981; Weitzman, Czeisler, Zimmerman, Ronda, & Knauer, 1982 for more in-depth reviews of this area). With this very brief introduction in mind, let us review some difficulties with basic sleep and mental function studies.

Nocturnal learning is commonly used in examining the effects of sleep on learning. Subjects are often asked to learn materials in the middle of the night and are compared with subjects learning in the middle of the day. Recall is then assessed some time later. Often the only variable believed to be manipulated in these studies is whether sleep occurred in the intertrial interval. Obviously, factors include time of day, waking from sleep to learn (i.e., partial sleep deprivation), noncontinuous sleep, and the amount of time alert before being allowed to return to sleep. In short, there are a number of confounding variables present in such studies.

A second problem is unique to REM sleep deprivation studies. Researchers have often attempted to eliminate REM sleep for a variety of theoretical reasons. REMD paradigms, however, have been reported to be only 50%–85% effective in eliminating REM sleep (Scrima, 1982). To anthropomorphize, the more REM sleep deprived a subject is, the more the body "wishes" to be in REM sleep. This process is known as REM pressure. Accomplishing the task of REM depriving a subject over any lengthened period of time becomes a process of continually awakening the subject, because REM pressure continually builds, and REM sleep may eventually occur at sleep onset. The use of drugs to eliminate REM sleep (Castaldo, Goldstein, & Krynicki, 1974) brings with it unwanted drug-related side effects. Thus, it is practically impossible to fully deprive a subject of REM sleep. In addition, REM deprivation is confounded with sleep deprivation, noncontinuous sleep, and possibly the stress of the procedure.

A third major difficulty in this research area is that of the stimuli used. Scrima (1982) and Cartwright and colleagues (1975) point out the possibility that differences in learning across many studies may well stem from the different types of materials involved, such as paired associate words versus lists, words versus numbers, consonant trigrams (nonaffective) versus highly affective material, non–imagery-related versus imagery-related stimuli, and nouns versus adjectives or symbols. It is indeed difficult to make comparisons across such studies. It appears ambitious to conclude that each of these stimuli affect or are measures of the same cognitive processes.

A fourth factor, which for practical reasons is fairly impossible to study, is chronicity. Sleep deprivation or any of the other sleep research paradigms used have seldom been continued longer than a few days. A few Zeitgeber (environmental time cues) -lacking studies have been continued for a month or longer. At this point in the history of modern sleep disorder diagnosis, however, patients often have severe symptoms for years before seeking help or realizing that it is available. It is very difficult to generate working models of these disorders and their long-term effects.

As is evident from this review, the study of sleep and its relationship to cognitive processing is a very complicated area. One of the most consistent findings to arise from the research seems to be that material learned before a period of sleep is recalled better if that period of sleep is associated with a higher arousal level; that is, if the period of sleep is more similar to an awake state. Thus, the original question of concern since the study of Jenkins and Dallenbach (1924) remains unanswered. Why is recall better if a period of sleep, rather than wakefulness, occurs in the intertrial interval? The research that has been conducted has never successfully addressed this question. While both interference and consolidation theories speak to the issue, neither has given consistent results when tested, nor have models been presented as to how or why the results occurred.

The major conclusion that might be reached is that the nature of the effects of sleep on cognitive functioning is not known. The research methodologies used at this point have been inadequate largely due to confounding variables. The fact that sleep is an aspect of bodily circadian rhythms makes it difficult to evaluate the effect of many experimental manipulations.

In light of this conclusion, neuropsychological testing can be observed to play two possible roles in the area of sleep disorders. One role is to more effectively describe the nature of the dysfunction that the presenting patient knows is occurring. The other role is of a more basic nature. Patients with sleep disorders are naturally occurring populations with some of the kinds of sleep disturbances researchers have attempted to produce. Some sleep most comfortably during the day. Many have interruptions in their sleep at night. Narcoleptics may have REM sleep onset initiation of their sleep, which effectively isolates this stage from other stages. In other words, the types of cognitive *dysfunctions* that may eventually be found to be representative (if there are such patterns) of individual sleep disorders may represent the kinds of cognitive *operations* affected by the given sleep disruption.

Bizarre alterations in the circadian rhythms of otherwise normal subjects cannot approach the experience of a sleep-disorder–afflicted patient. Neuropsychological testing in sleep-disorder populations should provide much information on how the brain naturally functions in a chronically drowsy state. This information could prove to be worth the equivalent of years of studies in the areas of attention, concentration, and levels of alertness. It is common clinical lore that level of alertness (i.e., hyperactivity or drowsiness) affects test performance. How do these variables affect test performance? What factors or area of cognitive ability are most influenced by drowsiness? To what extent do these factors modify test performance? The quantitative aspects of this lore have never been explored. It is simply assumed that they exist. This is probably a proper assumption, but not a very scientific one. We need to test sleep-disorder populations in order to discern some of these answers empirically.

After years of scientists' running SD experiments, an area of specific interest has developed with regard to the type of test that would be a sensitive index of sleep loss. Research in this area has focused on identifying the parameters necessary to detect sleep loss (Wilkinson 1965, 1969, 1970, 1975). In a review of the literature, Wilkinson (1965) reported that the sensitivity of a test of sleep loss seemed to be determined by the following characteristics: duration of the test, level of complexity, interest value, and the degree to which feedback of test results was immediately available. The proper task to show the effects of SD would therefore be long, complex, and uninteresting and provide the subject with no feedback. Glenville, Broughton, Wing, and Wilkinson (1978) have since reported that lack of immediate feedback, and possibly task duration, may not be such critical factors.

Kjellberg (1977b) reports that factors that lead to earlier habituation of the subject of the stimuli should be the ones most sensitive to sleep loss. His major point is that dearousal occurs only within the limitations of the available stimuli. Hence, SD is not in itself the mediating factor between good and bad test performance. An interaction must exist between SD and the subject's habituation to the stimuli in the environment. Factors that might decrease the necessary time for habituation should therefore potentiate dearousal. A causal relationship is postulated between habituation and dearousal. Unfortunately, he does not expound on what these factors might be. It appears as though the factors identified by Wilkinson (1965) should be compatible with Kjellberg's (1977b) theory.

Wilkinson (1970) developed the Wilkinson Auditory Vigilance (WAV) test to evaluate subjects in SD experiments. It has become a standard instrument in such studies. The test is a one-hour auditory vigilance task. Subjects are required to listen to regularly spaced tones of 500 milliseconds in duration that occur at two-second intervals. During the hour, forty tones are randomly presented that are slightly shorter (400 milliseconds) than the others. A background of high-intensity (85-decibel) white noise accompanies the task. The task has been found to be quite sensitive to SD, usually in one-night SD studies (Broughton, 1982a; Herscovitch & Broughton, 1981; Wilkinson, 1965, 1970, 1975).

The simple reaction time task, based on a 10-minute auditory reaction time task used by Lisper & Kjellberg (1972), has been shown to produce similar results to the WAV (Glenville, Broughton, Wing, & Wilkinson, 1978). The test involves use of a portable cassette-recording apparatus. Stimulus onset corresponds with the onset of a digital millisecond clock, while the response is a key press that stops the clock and marks reaction time. The next stimulus onset then occurs randomly within a range of 1–10 seconds.

Another instrument that has been found to be sensitive to the effects of sleep loss is a four-choice portable cassette-recording apparatus (Wilkinson & Houghton, 1975; Glenville, Broughton, Wing, & Wilkinson, 1978). This task is a self-paced serial choice reaction time task involving four lights arranged in a square. Four corresponding keys are displayed beneath the lights. The light appears, and the subject presses a button corresponding to that light. Following this, the light extinguishes regardless of the correctness of the subject's response. In 120 milliseconds, either the same or another light is illuminated in a random order, with the cycle of light-response repeated over a 10-minute session.

The relevant information obtained from these tests has come to be known as gaps or lapses in responding (Williams, Lubin, & Goodnow, 1959; Guilleminault & Dement, 1977). A gap is a nonresponse period of over one second. These gaps have been interpreted as failures to discriminate the stimulus. Other useful data obtained include mean reaction time variability over task duration and split half differences in measures over the course of the task (i.e., performance often decreases significantly shortly into the task).

One clinically relevant conclusion from the use of these tests comes from a study by Glenville and associates (1978). In that study, the two shorter 10-minute tests gave information virtually equivalent to that obtained from the one-hour WAV test. Since the WAV necessitates one hour for completion, it has generally been considered clinically impractical.

Neuropsychological Assessment of Narcolepsy

One of the most often heard complaint of patients with diagnosed or suspected sleep disorders is that of excessive daytime somnolence. It occurs as a prominent symptom in such disorders as narcolepsy, ideopathic hypersomnia, symptomatic hypersomnia, sleep apnea syndromes, posttraumatic syndromes following head injury (discussed earlier), physician- and patient-originated drug intake, and various other metabolic and neurologic conditions (Broughton, 1982b). In narcolepsy, EDS is the most prominent and difficult symptom to eradicate. Broughton (1982b) posited three causes of reduced alertness: impaired waking arousal mechanisms, impaired pressure for NREM sleep, and impaired pressure for REM sleep. He stated: "This potential multiplicity of mechanisms is emphasized, because the effects of EDS on everyday activities or on formal objective measures might reasonably be expected to be qualitatively different for these three pathological processes"(p. S136). Various circadian-rhythm dysphasiac problems and psychological difficulties are also suspected as playing roles in narcolepsy.

Valley and Broughton (1981, 1983) have reported the results of two studies dealing with neuropsychological testing of narcoleptic populations. The testing did not consist of entire neuropsychological batteries with hours of testing involved. A few specific tests were done that were felt to be specifically sensitive to the symptoms of narcolepsy.

In the 1981 study, Valley and Broughton gave 10 narcoleptics (7 female, 3 male) aged 19–65 years ($\bar{X} = 42.0$) a battery of four tests. Sleep-deprived, normal control subjects were matched for sex, age, and occupation. All narcoleptics were taken off all CNS-active medications for at least 15 days before testing, with the exception of 2 patients, who were off medications for only 9 days. The four tests consisted of the WAV task (Wilkinson, 1970), and four-choice serial reaction time tasks (Wilkinson & Houghton, 1975), the paced auditory serial addition task (PASAT), and digit span from the Wechsler Adult Intelligence Scale (WAIS). In addition, the Stanford Sleepiness Scale (SSS; Hoddes, Dement, & Zarcone, 1972) was administered. This scale is a seven-point Lickert-type scale on which a subjective rating of level of sleepiness is written. While being polygraphically recorded, the tests were given, with the SSS filled out after each test. Interscorer reliability for the sleep recording was established ($r =$ 94.6).

The results revealed that the narcoleptics performed significantly worse on the vigilance and choice serial reaction times but not on the PASAT or digit span. Compared to reports of control subjects, narcoleptics reported that the PASAT required more effort, but as stated above, both groups performed similarly. The narcoleptics reported significantly more subjective sleepiness at all time than did the control subjects, but Pearson r correlations between SSS ratings and performance were at no time significant for either group. The ability of both sleep-deprived normal subjects and narcoleptics to perform normally under constant stimulation, even when subjectively very sleepy, remains a problem in their neuropsychological evaluation.

Physiologically speaking, overall differences in the EEG indexes of arousal were many. Control subjects were electroencephalographically awake 99% of the time, while the narcoleptics spent only 44% of the testing time physiologically awake. All narcoleptics showed stage 1 sleep, while two subjects even entered stage 2 sleep. Only five controls showed any stage 1 sleep. Lability of stage shifting was also greater in the narcoleptics than in the control subjects. When the testing EEG was measured in number of stage shifts per hour, there were 36 ± 10.2 (mean $\pm$ standard deviation) stage shifts per hour in the narcoleptic group, while there were only 3.6 ± 1.3 in the control group. This emphasizes the inability of the narcoleptics to sustain wakefulness.

The inability of the narcoleptic group to stay alert on the vigilance and serial reaction time test is consistent with the theory of Wilkinson (1965) dealing with aspects of tests sensitive to SD (i.e., low stimulation and lapses in intermittent responses). As pointed out earlier, the ability of narcoleptics to show normal performance on other types of tasks was also demonstrated in the study.

All the tests were taken in the morning, a factor held constant over narcoleptic and control groups. There needs to be further verification of the data obtained through testing done at other times of the day. It has not been established whether narcoleptics might show equal, attenuated, or greater impairment than normal subjects in other time periods, such as the "post-lunch dip" (Blake, 1967), the afternoon, or the evening.

The second study conducted by Valley and Broughton (1983) served a more theoretical purpose. Using the same data as in their 1981 study, they attempted to demonstrate the insufficiency of the lapse-microsleep hypothesis (Williams, Lubin, & Goodnow, 1959). In affirmation of Kjellberg's (1977b) theory (described briefly above), both lapses and false positives were shown to occur well before the ability to respond was abolished (microsleeps). Such results are explained in a quotation in Valley and Broughton (1981): "'Lapses represent only more extreme ends of a recurrent downward sliding of cerebral vigilance. General disorganization and inappropriateness of response are also consistent with decline'" (p. 248; in Oswald, 1962, p. 184). The results here also point to the fact that true sleep does not occur until stage 2 (Johnson, 1973). Also, only when the narcoleptics were able to sustain cortical wakefulness over time was performance comparable to that of the control group. This is consistent with Bonnet's (1983) findings, in which significant memory loss for events occurred during brief awakenings from sleep but was not as pronounced with longer awakenings.

Scrima (1982) looked to a narcoleptic population for help in furthering the study of a cognitive psychology question that has been around for a long time: Which stage of sleep (usually REM or NREM) accounts for the fact that memory for events after a period of sleep is inevitably better than after a period of wakefulness? Many of the problems described before in the basic research literature apply here. Does waking a person at the onset of the first REM sleep period allow one to say that no REM sleep occurred? The difficulty occurs when the researcher tries to isolate REM sleep from other stages, as REM sleep is invariably (in a normal population) preceded by other sleep stages. Having the subject learn the material immediately before REM sleep is problematic because of circadian rhythm disruption and the effect of waking the subject from sleep to learn (e.g., arousal level and possible proactive effect of sleep on learning). It is also very difficult to determine precisely the point at which REM sleep onset occurs. This means that one must usually awaken the subject when any signs of REM activity are present, which may be sometime before the actual REM episode would have occurred. One can either leave part of stage 2 on the record when one awakens the subject or let the subject proceed into REM sleep before awakening. Either way, one compromises what one wishes to do: to isolate REM from NREM sleep.

It is helpful to study narcoleptics, who are known to have REM sleep onset at times, when investigating this problem. The researcher may be able to isolate fairly precisely a REM period from a NREM period and have virtually no other stage preceding the REM stage. Scrima (1982) used 10 narcoleptics, 8 of whom were off all CNS-active medications, to look at this problem. The average age of the subjects was 41 years (range, 29–54 years). The subjects were instructed to say and spell out each solution to an anagram task (10 lists of 10 words each) that they could determine in the 60 seconds allowed. The subjects were also asked to picture the solution words and make some association with each word. A second task involved the self-paced serial learning of 6–8 consonant trigrams (e.g., CCC). The subjects needed to spell out each trigram and correctly anticipate the next trigram on the list. The task was repeated until mastered. The simple card game War was played between 6–8 testing sessions to prevent rehearsal for a 20-minute period after each trial. The results indicated that recall of the anagrams was significantly better after REM sleep, compared to after NREM and wakefulness, in that order. No significant findings occurred with the trigram task, as a ceiling effect was observed.

The role of sleep disorder populations in basic research has been the topic of the previous discussion. The study of pathologic populations to obtain information about a normal population is not new. It has not, however, been applied to the sleep-disorder population. This is a potentially fruitful area. Much can probably be learned from the systematic study of such disorders.

The Neuropsychological Assessment of Apnea

Describing the published articles on the neuropsychological evaluation of apnea would take no time whatsoever. To our knowledge, they do not exist. The descriptions of the disorder and of patients who have the disorder, however, contain many references to what should be neuropsychologically documentable impairment.

Guilleminault (1982) proposed that apneics should show various types of cognitive impairment based on clinical evidence. The greatest degree of this impairment is seen in the morning:

> Persistent sleepiness, tiredness, and fatigue are the leitmotiv of the ... sleep apnea syndrome. In addition, the patient often complains of deterioration of memory and judgement (particularly occurring in the morning), early morning confusion (which may be so pronounced that

toxic status or brain tumor has been suspected in some cases), automatic behavior and personality changes.... The degree of incapacity ranges from drastic impairment of daytime activities because of irresistible urges to sleep (often leading to occupational and/or driving accidents) to only moderate daytime sleepiness resulting in drowsiness or falling asleep during quiet situations, such as watching television or reading. (p. 161)

These differences are reported generally to improve over the course of the day, although culminating in an increased urge to fall asleep in the evening.

Each of the three forms of apnea has mechanisms by which Guilleminault's proposal might be confirmed. Three potential effectors are evident (see Guilleminault & Dement, 1978). First, sleep apnea is a disorder entailing the cessation of air flow, which causes a decrease in blood oxygen saturation and an increase in carbon dioxide levels. Second, the occurrence of sleep apnea disrupts the progress and continuity of sleep. The patient is thus deprived of a normal number of hours of continuous sleep. Finally, the usual complaint of patients presenting with sleep apnea is of excessive daytime somnolence. EDS itself has been studied as to its effects on daytime functioning (Valley & Broughton, 1981, 1983).

Mechanisms must also be proposed to account for the gradual improvement in daytime functioning. Improved functioning may be due to two factors. The first proposed factor that may play a part in this described functional increase is body circadian rhythmnicity (Broughton, 1982b). Circadian rhythms have been shown to be correlated with increased performance in both normal (Blake, 1967; Broughton, 1982a; Kleitman, 1939, 1963) and sleep-deprived subjects (Webb, 1978; Wilkinson, 1969). One other potential mechanism is hypothesized to account for this phenomenon. Apneic periods may be seen as brief periods of air flow cessation that deplete the blood of its oxygen content. This resulting blood oxygen saturation must therefore be momentarily rationed in its use over the body. As these episodes accrue over a night, the functional efficiency of the CNS in processing incoming stimuli may lessen. This level of efficiency may then be gradually raised with the renewed continuous air flow established during the waking hours. The ability of this impairment to be reversed over the course of a day might be less apparent in more chronic apneics. No study has been undertaken to explore these issues.

The Chronic Obstructive Pulmonary Disease Model

The effects of chronic low blood oxygen saturation (hypoxemia) and increased carbon dioxide (hypercapnea) levels have been studied in patients with chronic obstructive pulmonary disease (Adams, Sawyer, & Kvale, 1980; Grant, Heaton, McSweeney, Adams, & Timms, 1980; Krop, Block, Cohen, Croucher, & Schuster, 1977; Prigitano, Parsons, Levin, Wright, & Hawryluk, 1983). COPD patients have chronic hypoxemia as a result of their diseased lungs' impaired ability to exchange oxygen (Fleetham, et al., 1982; Shiffman, Trontell, Mazar, & Edelman, 1983). Excess carbon dioxide builds up because of the poor rate of oxygen exchange. Patients with COPD have frequently been noted to complain of difficulty in sleeping (Adams, Sawyer, & Kvale, 1980). Fleetham and colleagues (1982) and Shiffman and colleagues (1983) present evidence that the frequent arousals of patients with COPD are actually caused by their hyper-capnea, not their hypoxemia, by studying patients on continuous oxygen therapy. Apneics have been proposed to incur both hypoxemia and hypercapnea during apneic periods (Guilleminault, Cummisky, & Dement, 1980). COPD patients may therefore be considered an appropriate model from which to assess the role of hypoxemia-hypercapnea on cognitive functioning.

Prigitano and colleagues (1983) studied a group of 100 nonsevere (resting PaO_2, 55 mmHg) COPD patients who were matched with 25 normal control subjects on the factors of age, education, social class, percentage of males and females, and percentage of right- and left-handers. Significant differences ($P < .05$) were seen between the two groups of 8 and 17 neuropsychological tests (taken from the Halstead-Reitan Neuropsychological Test Battery, and Digit Symbol from the Wechsler Adult Intelligence Scale—Revised). Differences were seen on the Categories Test, Tactual Performance Test (TPT) (total time, dominant hand time, nondominant hand time, both hand times, and memory, but not localization), an aphasia screening examination, and the Digit Symbol test. Results of COPD subjects on the Trail-making Test were also found to be impaired, compared with the available norms for the test. This degree of impairment was not, however, significant in matched comparison analysis. Further, Grant and colleagues (1980) found evidence of impairment on the Halstead Reitan Battery in 93 of 121 COPD patients using the available test norms. Sustained attention-concentration ability is certainly among the capacities evaluated on those assessments and found to be impaired (Walsh, 1982).

Adams and colleagues (1980) cautioned against the possibility of mistaking practice effects for true recovery in the repeated testing of COPD patients. Krop and associates (1977), however, repeatedly administered a battery of neuropsychological tests to 19 elderly COPD men. Equivalent means for Wechsler Memory Scale (WMS) scores were established for two groups of these subjects. The groups were then placed on either continuous oxygen therapy, which effectively raises blood oxygen saturation (Jacobs, Alvis, & Small, 1972; Jacobs, Winter, Alvis, & Small, 1968) or a sham air mixture for one month. At the end of the month, the subjects were reevaluated by blind assessors. The oxygen and sham treatment groups then switched treatment procedures, with those formerly receiving oxygen using the sham air mixture and vice versa. After another month with the subjects in these opposite treatment groups, a final assessment took place. Significantly lower Wechsler Memory Quotients were found in those receiving the sham air mixture compared with those on oxygen therapy at each of the follow-up testings.

Thus, there appears to be evidence that chronic low blood oxygen saturation can affect the level of cognitive functioning. This has been demonstrated both on single and repeated evaluations. In addition, studies have been conducted using available norms for standard neuropsychological test batteries and using control or placebo test populations. Finally, at least in the Prigitano study (1983), adequate control on the extraneous measures of age, education, social class, sex, and handedness was achieved. The factor of hypoxemia-hypercapnea can therefore be reasonably considered a relevant element in the perceived apneic detriment in cognitive functioning ability.

The Sleep Deprivation Model

The second line of research focuses on the effects of the deprivation of sleep on the ability to function cognitively at an adequate level. Sleep deprivation has been the paradigm most often used the assess the effects of sleep on cognitive functioning (Broughton, 1982a). In such studies, subject sleep from some portion of the night, or not at all. A performance task is then initiated, and the results are compared to either those of a normal control group or those of the same subject after a normal night's sleep. The paradigm has been used in basically four forms. One often used SD paradigm is REM sleep deprivation (McGrath & Cohen, 1978). This is usually accomplished through EEG documentation of REM sleep onset. A less precise form of the paradigm considers the fact that substantially more REM sleep typically occurs during the second half of a given night relative to the first half of the night. Subjects in this form of the SD paradigm therefore sleep, for example, from 10:00 P.M. to 2:00 A.M. only. Their performances are then compared either to their performances after a normal night's sleep or to performances of subjects sleeping only from 2:00 A.M. to 6 A.M. (Fowler, Sullivan, & Ekstrand, 1973; Yaroush, Sullivan, & Ekstrand, 1971). A second form of the paradigm is that of partial sleep deprivation (Broughton, 1982a; Herscovitch & Broughton, 1981; Herscovitch, Stuss, & Broughton, 1980). In these studies, subjects are allowed to sleep some percentage of their usual amount. Often this is done over several days. Performance is measured either periodically throughout the paradigm or after the entire period of partial SD. Full SD has been used in many studies also (Fisher, 1980; Kjellberg, 1977a; Lubin, Moses, Johnson, & Naitoh, 1974; Sanders & Reitsma, 1982a, b; Tharp, 1978). With full SD, subjects are kept awake from 24 hours to several days. Performance is usually measured only at the end of a specified time period.

The final SD paradigm, which most closely approximates the experience of the patient with sleep apnea, is the paradigm of periodic arousal (Bonnet, 1983; Bonnet & Webb, 1979). In this paradigm, subjects are aroused after some specified short span of time periodically over the night. When awakened, they are asked either to perform a task or to remain awake for the length of time necessary to complete the task. Subjects then return to sleep, to be aroused after an equivalent period of time in a repetitious process. Stages of sleep are accounted for in awakening the patients. In this paradigm, the total amount of sleep time may not be truly decreased. Normal sleep continuity and stage pregression are, however, greatly disrupted.

Sleep deprivation has consistently been associated with decreases in the ability to sustain attention-concentration (Dement, 1974; Kjellberg, 1977a; Sanders & Reitsma, 1982a, b; Williams, Lubin, & Goodnow, 1959). Within the parameters noted, SD does seem to affect the ability of subjects to perform tasks requiring sustained attention-concentration. This is noted not only from paradigms involving total SD over many days but also from periodic arousals over the course of a single night. Because of their apnea, patients with sleep apnea are infrequently fully awakened for long periods of time. Periodic arousals from sleep apnea may, however, occur hundreds of times in a night. It therefore appears probable that SD plays a part in the clinical lore of performance deficits associated with sleep apnea.

The Excessive Daytime Somnolence Model

While briefest in terms of the number of articles in the literature, the final line of evidence is most comparable to the effects of sleep apnea. This line deals with the effects of non–sleep-deprived EDS on daytime functioning. The evidence stems from the work discussed earlier by Valley and Broughton (1981, 1983) with narcoleptics (see the section on neuropsychological assessment of narcoleptics). EDS has been shown to lower performance levels across a variety of tasks. Apneics incur EDS from the effects of multiple periods of oxygen desaturation and frequent arousals during the night, which lead to both a disruption in sleep continuity and an overall sleep-deprived state. Their performances should therefore be similar to those of narcoleptics.

The preceding three models pertained to possible mechanisms by which the sleep apnea syndrome might potentiate attention-concentration impairment. The discussion now turns to Guilleminault's (1982) proposal of a gradual return in function. As previously stated, adequate means for this functional increase must also be accounted for. Two bodies of evidence are proposed to account for this phenomenon: the circadian rhythm model and the resumption of air flow model.

The Circadian Rhythm Model

Circadian rhythms are defined as any group of biological rhythms approximating a daily, or 24-hour, schedule (Halberg, 1959). Circadian rhythms are evidenced in a variety of biological systems (Aschoff & Wever, 1976). Sleep itself has been discussed as a circadian rhythm (Webb, 1984). These rhythms have been assessed through a variety of manual and psychophysiological measures (Aschoff & Wever, 1976; Kokkoris, et al., 1978; Lowenstein & Lowenfeld, 1964, 1952; Mitler, 1982; Weitzman, 1981). One frequently used measure of circadian rhythms is core body temperature. This measure has been used since the discovery by Colin Pittendrigh in 1953 that the circadian rhythm period of oscillations was "temperature compensated" (Menaker, 1975). This relationship is not causal (Cairn, Knowles, & MacLean, 1982) but appears nonetheless to be consistent and accurate (Kokkoris, et al., 1978; Menaker, 1975; Weitzman, Czeisler, Knauer, Ronda, & Zimmerman, 1982).

Many aspects of human behavior have been researched for potential correlation between task performance and circadian rhythmnicity. Through simultaneous assessment of body core temperature and various performance measures, level of functioning has been shown to improve throughout the day as body temperature cycles from a nadir at approximately 0400–0500 hours to a peak at around 2000–2100 hours (Cairn, Knowles, & MacLean, 1982; Hockey & Colquhoun, 1972; Moses, Lubin, Naitoh, & Johnson, 1978; Rutenfranz, Aschoff, & Mann, 1972). The only exception to this data occurs as a transitory "post-lunch dip" (Blake, 1967) in performance level. Vigorous assessor-subject interaction (Boll, 1983, personal communication) has been proposed to have the potential to mediate this effect when optimal performance is necessary or desired. Such data have now accumulated across a variety of both cognitive and motor tasks (Cairn, Knowles, & MacLean, 1982). Kleitman (1939, 1963) found evidence of circadian rhythmnicity on tasks of card sorting, mirror drawing, code transcription, multiplication, hand steadiness, and body sway. Blake (1967) added the tasks of auditory vigilance and performance on a five-choice serial reaction time measure. Subjective assessments of arousal-sleepiness have also concurred with this data (Akerstedt, 1977; Akerstedt & Gillberg, 1981; Dahlgren, 1981; Hoddes, Dement, & Zarcone, 1972; Thayer, 1967). Disruptions of circadian rhythms through experimental manipulation (Taub & Berger, 1973, 1974, 1976), shift work (Dahlgren, 1981; Akerstedt, Torsvall, & Gillberg, 1982; Akerstedt & Gillberg, 1981), delayed sleep phase shifts from jet lag (Preston, 1978), and even adjustment to daylight savings time (Monk & Alpin, 1980) have been demonstrated to incur similar disruptions in performance accuracy and appropriateness.

No disruption of circadian rhythms is proposed to occur from the disorder of sleep apnea. It therefore appears plausible that apneic performance levels should be positively correlated with circadian cycling (as measured by core body temperature). This factor may be postulated to account to some degree for the rise in function over the course of a day hypothesized by Guilleminault (1982).

The Resumption of Air Flow Model

The final aspect of this discussion deals with the effect of a resumption of normal air flow and, hence, oxygen-carbon dioxide exchange, on level of performance in sleep apneics. Two possible models exist from which to assume a relationship between these two elements. The first stems from the work of Jacobs and colleagues (Jacobs, Winters, Alvis, & Small, 1969; Jacobs, Alvis, & Small, 1972) on the effects of cerebral oxygenation in COPD patients. In the first study, each subject received 99%–100% oxygen at 2.5 absolute atmospheres, for 90 minutes twice a day for 15 days. Thirteen male COPD patients were reported to show significant improvement in pre-post scores on the Wechsler Memory Scale, Bender-Gestalt, and an Organic Integrity Test. Five subjects serving as a sham (10% oxygen-air mixture) control showed no signs of improvement. In the second study, post-testing was delayed for various periods of time to assess the length of time such improvement might last with discontinuation of the oxygen treatment. Pretreatment scores of 23 of 32 COPD patients were scored as impaired. Records of 19 of those 23 patients in groups ranging from 24 hours to 10 days post–oxygen treatment were judged as improved at the post-treatment assessment. Edwards and Hart (1974) found a similar improvement in scores on the WMS and Wechsler Adult Intelligence Scale and some sensory assessments. Unfortunately, no placebo control group was used in this study. Goldfarb, Hochstadt, Jacobson, and Weinstein (1972) attempted to replicate those results. A high dropout rate (6 of 16 patients) complicated their experiment, and no differences were found in the 10 subjects completing the study.

One other line of evidence stems from an often-noted increase in daytime functioning in successfully treated sleep apneics. This clinical lore exists largely from patient and family reports. Many patients eagerly relate a return of driving ability, ease in morning arousal, job productivity, and a cessation of the urge to nap. All the factors discussed herein relate to these reports. Follow-up assessments of successful post-treatment apneics indeed reveal fewer apneic episodes and periods of oxygen desaturation (defined as $SaO_2 < 90\%$), and higher blood oxygen levels retained during any remaining desaturations. No direct evidence exists to indicate which effects of successful apneic treatment are responsible for these clinical reports. There is, however, no clinical doubt that the resumption of continuous air flow during sleep is at least partially responsible for the return in functioning seen in these patients. It therefore appears that the daily morning recurrence of normal breathing would have effects similar to those seen following successful treatment. Such treatment would of course reduce or eliminate the occurrence of apnea itself, thus also eliminating its other results and producing substantially more noticeable effects.

Two unsuccessful attempts to document impaired apneic performance have been made, although neither has been published. A variety of reasons are possible in explanation of their inability to document this clinically evident phenomenon. These studies are discussed below, along with a rationale for their respective failures. The two studies constitute the psychological assessments completed to date on this population and so are included here. Negative results in a study also serve as guidelines for future work and assessment methodology.

Kader (1983) presented neuropsychological assessment data on six patients with sleep apnea complaining of memory and attention-concentration deficits. These patients were assessed on the Wechsler Memory Scale, the Trail-making Test (forms A and B), and Digit Span from the Wechsler Adult Intelligence Scale—Revised (Wechsler, 1981). Patient performances all fell well within the normal range. These results were interpreted not as refuting or denying the patients' impairment complaints, but simply as reflecting the difficulties involved in documenting these phenomena. While not a true study, this report of clinical assessment was the first to be presented for the population of sleep apneics.

An experiment involving pre- and post-treatment assessment with sleep apneics was performed by Connell and colleagues (1984). In this study, 21 patients with sleep apnea were assessed on a variety of neuropsychological measures the evening before their ANSP. These measures included the Wechsler Memory Scale with Russell Scoring, the Trail-making Test (forms A and B), Digit Symbol from the WAIS-R, and a memory questionnaire (Broadbent, Cooper, Fitzgerald, & Parkes, 1982). The Satz-Mogel form of the WAIS-R was given in totality on the post-treatment measure to test for normality of the population. Significant subject dropout, unsuccessful treatment, and multiple sleep disorders were factors that precluded any meaningful information being obtained from the post-test data and pretreatment–post-treatment comparisons. The pretest data, however, again failed to document impaired scores in the subjects by the available test norms.

Two possibilities may be generated in explanation of this failure to find significant impairment in these two reports. The first problem is of adequate test sensitivity. The Wechsler Memory Scale is often used to document significant memory deficits, but only in those patients with much more severe impairment (Erickson & Scott, 1977). Prigitano (1978) comments on the lack of sensitivity of this measure to the more subtle degrees of memory impairment. The Trail-making Test is also often very sensitive to attention-concentration difficulties. Others, however, (Prigitano, Stahl, Orr, & Zeiner, 1983) have also found this measure to be insensitive to the cognitive impairment arising from hypoxemia-hypercapnea. The Digit Symbol and Digit Span subtest from the WAIS-R may also suffer from insensitivity to the impairment incurred in the sleep apnea syndrome.

The second explanation applies more easily to the data obtained before the subject's ANSP, in the early evening. Guilleminault (1982) proposes that sleep apneics would have shown a near total return in cognitive functioning by this time of day. This return may be accounted for by either the circadian rhythm model or the resumption of air flow model proposed in this report. Therefore, another possibility accounting for the failure to document significant impairment lies in the time of day at which the subjects were tested.

It appears necessary to assess patients with sleep apnea on multiple occasions in order to account for both their reported cognitive impairment and later functional return. Inherent in multiple testings is the problem raised by Adams, Sawyer, and Kvale (1980) of obtaining superious results due to practice effects. Use of vigilance tasks such as the Wilkinson Auditory Vigilance Task (WAVT) and the four-choice Serial Reaction Time Task (SRTT) circumvents this problem to a large extent. Other types of performance tasks (e.g., memory and information processing) may show large degrees of improvement simply from the subject's finding more efficient means of manipulating the test materials (Walsh, 1982). If no equivalent alternative forms of the tests exist, performance may be bettered simply by remembering the answers. These two vigilance tasks in question are of an entirely different nature. The only manipulation required by the subject is button pushing, as opposed to the page-scanning and arm-and-pencil coordination required by the Trail-making Tests. The stimuli presented occur at random intervals, thereby preventing any memorization of correct answers or interstimulus intervals. While it would be folly to insist that no practice effects occur in these tests (Wilkinson, 1965, 1970), the degree of its occurrence is minimized.

It is hoped that other sleep researchers will recognize this important, understudied phenomenon as a part of the clinical evaluation of the apneic patient. It also provides opportunity for continued study in naturally occurring models of cognitive impairment.

Neuropsychological Assessment of Insomnia

Insomnia occurs largely in two forms: difficulty in falling asleep and early awakening after relatively normal sleep onset time. These two aspects of sleep can be seen as having both similar and different properties. First, they each reduce the amount of total sleep time. Whether it takes one or two hours to fall asleep, or whether one awakens at 4:00 A.M., the total amount of time asleep is reduced. Second, in reducing sleep at either end of the night, the two forms of insomnia actually affect similar stages of sleep. Delta sleep (stages 3 and 4) is more likely to occur in the first half of the night, and REM sleep in the second half of the night. Therefore, by shortening sleep time in the later morning hours, REM sleep becomes disproportionally shortened. The same effect may occur if one takes longer to fall asleep, because in so doing one only displaces sleep onset; sleep architecture is not changed. So if wake-up time remains constant but sleep onset varies, REM sleep may also be shortened because the last half of the sleep period never gets completed. On the other hand, unlike the person who awakens in the middle of the night and cannot successfully return to sleep, the person who takes a while to fall asleep may subjectively feel that more continuous sleep was obtained once he or she did fall asleep.

Insomnia is also often strongly correlated with measures of depression (Hauri, 1982b). An EEG recording of an insomniac's sleep may appear very similar to that of a depressed patient. Depressed patients have difficulty in falling asleep, frequent shifts of sleep stage, increased time spent awake, early morning awakening, and a considerable decrease in stage 4 (Chen, 1979). The symptomatic similarities here are not the only factors that cause depression and insomnia to be well correlated. Insomniac patients often admit to feelings of depression, although they may be difficult for the patient to verbalize. As with any neuropsychological evaluation, good interview and background data should be helpful in this regard. Although other factors could possibly be involved in insomnia (e.g., medication control), a thorough assessment for depression should be done, involving the family and significant others.

A neuropsychological evaluation for an insomniac will probably indicate more than merely the effects of lack of sleep (e.g., depression). Although the findings of such an evaluation might be consistent with lack of sleep, the causal relationship may be turned around. In all probability, lack of sleep does not cause depression, although it may cause the patient some degree of worry. A good bet is that depression caused the initial insomnia, which in turn is causing the patient's current worry about falling asleep. Psychological concerns are probably the main contributing factor in causing insomnia (Pegram, Hyde, & Weiler, 1980).

The basic sleep deprivation paradigm is a possible model from which to proceed in evaluating the possible cognitive effects of insomnia. Although this paradigm has largely dealt with REM sleep deprivation (see McGrath & Cohen, 1978, for a good review), NREM and total sleep deprivation studies have also been done (Åkerstedt & Gillberg, 1979; Bonnet, 1983; Carskadon & Dement, 1979; Cartwright, 1972; Castaldo, Goldstein, & Krynicki, 1974; Crowder, 1976; Ekstrand, 1967; Goodenough, Sapan, Cohen, Portnoff, & Shapiro, 1971; Lubin, Moses, Johnson, & Naitoh, 1974; Stones, 1977; Tharp, 1978; Tilley, 1981; Williams, Geiseking, & Lubin, 1966; Yaroush, Sullivan, & Ekstrand, 1971). In reducing their total amount of time asleep, insomniacs may reduce both REM and NREM sleep (Hauri, 1982b). SD research has reported myriad cognitive deficits associated with the paradigm. Memory difficulties of both a short- and long-term nature have been reported. These studies have included the categories of verbal versus nonverbal; highly associative versus minimally associative; highly artificial versus common; and everyday affairs versus incidental, highly rehearsed material. Impairments on vigilance tasks, in motor skill performances, and in information processing have been reported after SD. Unfortunately for both the basic and clinical fields, the broad range of stimuli used, the circadian rhythm problems, the difficulties in assessing learning before and after differing amounts of sleep, and the difficulties in isolating specific sleep stages make it difficult to draw any clear, unambiguous inferences from this research. Of course, the most difficult aspect of insomnia to model is chronicity. The range and types of impairment seen from one to four nights of SD (the typical range studied) may bear little resemblance to that of the patient who presents having slept three to four hours per night for weeks, months, or years.

More research is needed in this area. The wide variety of people presenting with this problem need to be studied. Webb (1974) found that subjects sleeping for only five and one-half hours over an extended time period (60 days) showed minimal consistent effects on the WAV Task and Mood scales. Although these measures only minimally assessed the range of possible deficits the subjects could have shown, this type of paradigm probably comes closer to assessing the true length of sleep of most presenting insomniacs. Although this kind of research may have inherent difficulties in finding willing subject populations, data from such studies, short of using clinical populations, could yield relevant data from a somewhat controlled setting.

In evaluating a patient for insomnia, one is confronted with the difficult problem of the subjectiveness of the complaint. Patients have widely varying criteria for what amount of sleep is necessary for them to carry on daily functions. Minutes of lost sleep may seem like hours to a person with very rigid standards. Sleep logs or diaries have been found to be very informative both to the clinician and to the patient. Many patients realize, and subsequently feel better about, the actual amount of sleep they are getting after using a sleep log for one week. Of course, these may bring into clearer focus the true lack of sleep and the effects the patient experiences.

Another problem, too detailed to elaborate on at length, is that of addictive behaviors. Patients with insomnia often come into sleep clinics with a long history of drug-seeking behavior and/or a current addiction. Both the physical and psychological aspects of such a state need to be assessed. This assessment is important because any observed cognitive deficits may in fact be drug related. Also, the knowledge gained will affect the clinician-patient interaction. The clinician must be willing to confront the insomniac patient with the drug dependency-abuse issue. Further, a cure short of pharmacological intervention should be sought. This is no easy task, as such patients often find this information traumatic and ego threatening.

The neuropsychological evaluation of the insomniac often requires honed clinical skills. Often, extensive dealings will need to be made with the family, and significant personality and behavior problems may surface. True therapy sessions may be called for in order for the patient to work through feelings and emotions. If the neuropsychologist involved cannot provide these services, the patient should be referred (if the patient is willing) to an appropriate clinician. The data on relaxation and biofeedback with insomniac patients is inconsistent, but it is likely that some patients may respond to these interventions (Borkovec & Weirts, 1976). Working with the insomniac is regarded by many clinicians as difficult work with a low chance of success. Patients are often felt to have no motivation for change in the cessation of self-destructive behavior. The clinician who can generate a personal interest in such patients may find success possible.

Neuropsychological Assessment of Sleep Drunkenness

Sleep drunkenness refers to the patient complaint of arousing in the morning feeling disoriented or confused for a period of time (Roth, Nevsímalová, & Rechtschaffen, 1972). Patients may act irrationally or interpret the environment illogically. In addition to the cognitive clouding reported, bodily coordination may also be affected (Hauri, 1982b), resulting in symptoms characteristic of disorders of the cerebellum (Roth, Nevsímalová, Ságová, Parovbková, & Horáková, 1981). The disorder of sleep drunkenness has frequently been reported as being closely associated with disorders of excessive somnolence (Hauri, 1982b; Roth, Nevsímalová, & Rechtschaffen, 1972). Roth (1980), however, reports data indicating that sleep drunkenness often occurs without other DOES symptoms. This disorder, then, appears not merely to reflect the condition of the excessively sleepy individual, but may well represent a temporary condition of partial or incomplete arousal that need not be associated with the mechanisms involved in other DOES complaints. Such a disorder is therefore worthy of research pertaining to its neuropsychological aspects in and of itself.

A study of the neurological, psychological, and polygraphic findings in patients with sleep drunkenness was reported by Roth and colleagues (1981). In this study, eight patients who presented with a diagnosis of ideopathic hypersomnia and sleep drunkenness and eight normal control subjects were evaluated with a full sleep montage in the afternoon. Most of the diagnosed patients are reported to have fallen asleep during the recording. After 30–45 minutes, the patients were awakened and asked to perform five tests while the EEG recording continued. The test were memory for a short story, a test of attention involving performance on a set of standard corrections, a test of visuomotor coordination involving the reproduction of a set of geometrical figures, and tests of both fine (bead threading) and gross (performing 10 squats) motor coordination. An IQ test was also administered (the test employed was not mentioned).

All patients and control subjects were examined a total of three times after 4, 8 and 12 hours' sleep for the patients and after 4 and 8 hours' sleep for the control subjects. The control group was also assessed after 28–30 hours' sleep deprivation. The rationale for different time periods for control subjects and patients was not stated. Sleep drunkenness was observed in 78.2% of the patients and in 4.2% of the normal subjects. The duration of sleep had no effect on the occurrence of sleep drunkenness. The clinical neurological picture of sleep drunkenness was reported to have been reminiscent of alcohol-induced drunkenness. The positive signs included those of cerebellar hemispheric involvement (including ataxia and impaired motor coordination) and cerebellar vermis involvement (including staggering and marked orthostatic disequilibrium). Signs of proprioceptive hyporeflexia and even areflexia were prevalent, as was frequent vestibular disturbance. All signs were negative at a subsequent testing 20–30 minutes later.

Statistically significant improvements were seen between the first and second testings for memory, attention, and fine motor coordination for the patients with sleep drunkenness. Scores were also better over the two testings for normal subjects, but not at statistically significant levels. It seems strange that differences were not found in the abilities between the two groups in the evaluation of gross motor integrity. Of course, even with several raters, the quantification of such items is difficult and highly subjective.

Other authors have also demonstrated test effects in the confusional period of sleep drunkenness. These include the impairments of simple auditory reaction time (Scott & Snyder, 1968), visual choice reaction time (Feltin & Broughton, 1968), mental calculation (Fort & Mills, 1972), and perception of the spiral aftereffect (Lavie & Giora, 1973). Certainly a more precise definition of the occurrence and neuropsychological sequelae of this disorder can be obtained.

The disorder of sleep drunkenness is apparently always transient and inconsistent in its occurrence following sleep. There also appears to be no other associated or subsequent impairments involved. Spontaneous remission of the effects of this disorder occurs within a few minutes. Sleep drunkenness has not been reported to progress either in severity or duration over time, but by and large, the disorder and its concomitant effects have not been thoroughly described. With the limited information currently available, the possibility of long-term effects associated with the disorder cannot be ruled out. Sleep drunkenness appears to be another disorder of interest from both a clinical and a basic research standpoint. Through its evaluation, the behavioral and cognitive effects of partial arousal may be studied.

Neuropsychological Assessment of Circadian Rhythm Disturbance

There is disagreement among sleep researchers as to whether moderate changes in a regular pattern of sleeping and waking is harmful. In an interesting study, discussed earlier, by Webb and Agnew (1974), 15 male subjects slept for only 5½ hours per night for 60 days. Their previous nightly sleep average was 7-1/2–8 hours. Appropriate control subjects were matched on MMPI profiles, age, and sex. The performance measures of the WAV Task, the Wilkinson Addition Test, a word memory test, and grip strength were taken. Only the WAV Task showed a decline over the time period of chronically limited sleep time. Mood scales taken over the course of the study (Zung Depression Scale, Gough Adjective Check List) showed no changes associated with the procedure. Their conclusion was that sleep restricted by 2½ hours a night is not likely to bring about major behavioral difficulties.

Bonnet and Alter (1982) came to similar conclusions in their study of 12 males between the ages of 19 and 28. No control population was indicated in this study. As opposed to the Webb and Agnew (1974) study, the students were on the honor system, sleeping at home for much of the study. These college students, who normally had highly irregular sleep schedules, were placed on highly structured and personalized (irregular) schedules in an A (irregular)-B (regular)-A (irregular) design. Sleep logs, oral temperature monitoring, and several performance measures were carried out during the 38-day study. Time of day of testing was held constant relative to each person's schedule. This fact confounded the study in that 4 subjects were always tested in the morning, while 8 were always tested in the afternoon. The WAV task was given with a 30-minute practice tape, and a 75% hit rate was established before the test was given. Hit rates and false alarms were computed for split halves of the test. The Wilkinson Addition Task (Wilkinson, 1970) was also given, with subjects completing as many additions as possible in 2 hours. An adjective checklist was also given which measured "deactivation" (Thayer, 1967). The results showed that mean sleep length remained the same throughout the regular and irregular periods (7.5 versus 7.4 hours). Only the wake-up time was significantly different across these periods. No difference was found in subjects' sleep latency, but mean number of reported awakenings increased from the irreguiar to the regular sleep condition. No differences were found in the Thayer Deactivation-Activation Adjective Check List. Body temperature was found to be significantly higher during the day in the initial irregular sleep condition, as opposed to in the regular or final irregular sleep condition.

Taub (1978) reported that his group of irregular sleepers had higher daily body temperature than did his regular group. Irregular sleep schedules have been previously reported to flatten temperature cycling (Webb, 1978; Kokkoris, et al., 1978), which would predict both higher peaks and lower valleys in groups with regular sleep. Taub's (1978) data appear difficult to explain, except for the fact that body temperature shifts may take as long as three weeks to adjust (Bonnet & Alter, 1982). Possibly the temperature cycling remained out of phase with the irregular-regular-irregular sleep schedules of the subjects. The small amount of change seen in the Bonnet and Alter study (1982) may be explained by the fact that the subjects in the study were not sleeping on regular schedules originally. As the subjects reportedly were suffering no ill effects from their irregular schedules, little gain or improvement in their functioning might have been seen when they were placed on a regular schedule. Also, as any change in schedule may be disruptive to sleep, a certain degree of impairment (or lack of improvement) in the subjects' test performance might be anticipated on these grounds alone. Research in this area needs to continue, as the number of people on irregular sleep schedules is enormous. The advantages (or lack of them) associated with making sleep schedules more regular need to be explored.

In 1973, 1974, and 1976, Taub and Berger reported than on an experimenter-paced addition task (Williams & Lubin, 1967), an earlier version of the WAV (Wilkinson, 1968), and the Thayer Activation-Deactivation Adjective Check List (Thayer, 1967), significant differences were seen in subjects whose sleep was phase advanced over different time periods of the day. Ten subjects who regularly slept from 2400–0800 hours worked on the tasks following sleep. Sleep periods ranged from 2100–0800 hours (extended condition), 2100–0500 hours (advanced-shift condition), 2400–0800 hours (habitual condition), 0300–0800 hours (deprivation condition), and 0300–1100 hours (delayed-shift condition). During the shifted and altered (both shorter and longer) sleep duration conditions, both accuracy and speed of response on the vigilance task were significantly poorer. Negative affect, as determined by the adjective checklist, was also greater after these conditions than after the habitual (1200–0800 hours) condition. These measures were not correlated with sleep length or alterations in the subjects' sleep EEG.

Taub (1980) also assessed regular and ad lib sleep schedules. In this study, 16 males who regularly slept 7–8 hours were recorded over a 1200–0800-hour night and an ad lib session, when the subjects picked their own times to retire and arise. Assessments were made 30 minutes after awakening from each session. Indexes of short-term memory (consonant-vowel-consonant trigrams), visual choice reaction time, auditory vigilance, and the Stanford Sleepiness Scale were taken. The overall duration of sleep was significantly increased in the ad lib session ($\bar{X} = 7.5$ hours), due largely to later awakening times. A decline in performance was seen on all measures after the ad lib session, and subjective reports of sleepiness were higher up to 90 minutes after awakening.

These types of experimental manipulations closely approximate the type of impairment seen with sleep disorders involving displaced or out-of-phase circadian rhythms, though good models of other sleep disorders cannot usually be achieved in this manner. Phase-advance and phase-delay problems are usually caused by outside environmental influences. Therefore, the manipulations done in the laboratory are not unlike the environmental influences that cause the disorders to come about in the real world. This type of sleep disorder is usually experienced by workers with very irregular sleep schedules (e.g., those who change shifts often, night-shift workers who sleep at night on weekends, crew members and passengers who travel across time zones via airplane). Few reports in the literature (Kokkoris et al., 1978; Miles, Raynal, & Wilson, 1977) deal with spontaneous or "organic" hypernycthermal circadian rhythms.

The possible consequences of this disorder necessitate that a good model be developed soon. The disorder has been proposed to account for decreased productivity and efficiency in work situations, in addition to being dangerous (as in the case of pilots who experience jet lag almost constantly). Preston (1978) studied the flight records of pilots flying in Great Britain and the United States. He found that older crew members (statistics were not provided), who had a more difficult time adjusting to new time schedules than did younger crew members, could lose between 26 and 28 hours' sleep on a 15-day tour away from London. This problem was exacerbated by the frequent need for pilots to fly into a different time zone and remain there for up to three-fourths of a day, which inevitably meant that they would try to lock into the local time. After feeling that perhaps the airlines were pushing the pilots too hard, Preston then examined United States flight records. He found that United States pilots often logged the same amount of flight miles in as few as eight days as British pilots did in 15 days. Logging more miles over a shorter time would mean that the pilots would not have time to become accustomed to local time upon arrival. However, the resulting fatigue could affect safety in the precise performance of the detailed operations necessary in flying a jet.

Dahlgren (1981) took measures of physiological circadian rhythms (body temperature, sleep phases, and hormone release) in permanent night workers and rotating shift workers. He found that synchronous circadian rhythms were not synchronized in night workers even after 10 years of working the shift. These workers normally reverted to being night sleepers on weekends, which would actually qualify them as swing shift workers of a sort. However, swing shift workers showed sleep phase cycling and distributions that were more unsynchronized than those of the night shift workers. Swing shift workers also exhibited a steady tendency toward regaining synchronicity over the week on a shift. This appears to indicate the presence of a homeostatic mechanism. Of course, the next week began a new shift, effectively stifling any such mechanism.

Although no neuropsychological testing was done with this group of shift workers, the lack of synchronicity of sleep rhythms should correlate well with decreased performance on job-related skills and efficiency, and even with decreased ability to hold the job. Various authors (Dahlgren, 1981; Miles, Raynal, & Wilson, 1977; Weitzman & Pollack, 1979; Weitzman, 1981) have written about the psychological and financial manifestations of disorders of circadian rhythm. An inability to fall asleep and awaken when necessary not only precludes having a good night's sleep to feel refreshed in the morning but in some cases totally disables a person from maintaining alertness at all during the period when work is to be done (Miles, Raynal, & Wilson, 1977).

Adequately assessing a person's ability to maintain good cognitive functioning in the face of changing shifts or hours may be the key to making rehabilitative recommendations for patients afflicted with these disorders. Predicting who might not handle changing shifts well, what functional abilities are most likely to be effected by shifts in circadian rhythms, the extent of these impairments, and how fast they can be overcome (by invoking a period of no shift change) are all research areas of social importance. People perform efficiently in work settings and situations in large part due to their ability to maintain alertness, concentration, and attention. If it can be determined who cannot perform well under stressors that are shown to impair these abilities, then such people can possibly be directed into other areas of work. If it is found that human beings in general are strongly susceptible to such influences, then production and efficiency could be increased by the cessation of practices that eventually impair functioning. The lives of many people could be spared the stresses of trying to maintain functioning during these circadian rhythm shift manipulations.

Neuropsychological Assessment of the Effects of Common "Sleeping Pills": The Benzodiazepines

Sleep disorders are commonly treated pharmacologically, be it through the use of over-the-counter "sleeping pills" or drugs prescribed by physicians. Unfortunately, many drugs that are both recommended and frequently used as treatments for sleep disorders have unwanted side effects. First, a dosage sufficient to cause sleep may also cause moderate to severe morning hangover. The search for drugs that have a short enough half-life (in order to reduce morning hangover) and that are effective for a long enough period of time to facilitate a full night's sleep continues for drug companies. Second, negative effects on memory for events occurring during the time of their ingestion and on performance of some psychomotor tasks have been empirically demonstrated.

Benzodiazepines are probably the most frequently prescribed class of drugs for the sleep disorder of insomnia. Millions of units of these drugs are taken every day just for the purpose of falling asleep. In many individuals, the use of these drugs may become chronic. Many studies have been conducted recently in an attempt to discover if their use entails potentially dangerous side effects on a short-term and/or chronic basis.

Bixler, Scharf, Soldatos, Mitsky, and Kales (1979) report that some benzodiazepines, specifically lorazepam, bromazepam, diazepam (Valium), and flunitrazepam, are known to cause anterograde amnesia. For example, subjects have been found to routinely experience decreased recall for tasks completed during a period in the middle of the night after having been awakened. This appears related to both dose and route of administration. The effects are much less frequent with a lower dosage or with oral or intramuscular, as opposed to intravenous, administration. These effects have been reported by other authors as well (Hindmarch & Clyde, 1980; Hindmarch & Gudgeon, 1980; Lader, Melhuish, & Harris, 1982; Roth, Hartse, Saab, Piccione, & Kramer, 1980; Scharf & Jacoby, 1982).

Bixler and colleagues (1979) found no differences in the abilities of groups of secobarbitol (100 mg), flunitrazepam (2 mg) and placebo condition subjects to perform each of several tasks after being awakened three hours after sleep onset. Although dose equivalencies had not been established for the two drugs at the time of the study, the dosage of each was equivalent to that normally recommended for treatment of insomnia. The flunitrazepam subjects were, however, reported to be significantly less alert than the placebo subjects. Upon awakening the following morning, one flunitrazepam subject did not even remember being awakened during the night. Compared to placebo condition patients, subjects on both drug nights also showed significant decreases in detailed recall of the tasks completed. In the secobarbitol condition, patients' memories were deficient after the first drug night only.

Roth, Hartse, Saab, Piccione, & Kramer (1980) studied the effects of flurazepam, lorazepam, and triazolam on sleep and memory. Patients also were awakened three hours after sleep onset after taking clinically appropriate dosages (flurazepam, 30 mg; lorazepam, 4 mg; triazolam, .5 mg) or placebo for two days during each of four weeks in a repeated-measures, double-blind, Latin-square design. Both immediate (15 minutes after task completion) and morning memory were assessed. Immediate recall of the tasks completed during the night was significantly decreased with lorazepam and triazolam. All drugs decreased morning recall for all of the tasks. Overall, recall with flurazepam was better than with either lorazepam or triazolam. The authors concluded that, since pentobarbital has not been shown to produce anterograde amnesia, the effects seen were due not to sleep-inducing drugs per se, but to specific drugs, including the ones tested.

Hindmarch and Clyde (1980) examined the effects of triazolam and nitrazepam on a prolonged reaction time task, critical flicker fusion (CFF), mental arithmetic ability, and serial subtraction of numbers. Impaired reaction time, as well as reported hangover, was found with nitrazepam but not with triazolam. Both were found to affect the serial subtraction effort to some extent. Hindmarch and Gudgeon (1980) tested mental arithmetic, letter cancellation, and car handling ability after administration of clobazam and lorazepam. Both compounds were found to affect mental arithmetic and letter cancellation tasks, but not in a widespread or consistent manner. Lorazepam was found to produce a significant impairment of car driving tasks and on analogue scales of subject alertness (both measures were obtained via self-report). The low alertness level was documented on the Leeds Sleep Evaluation Questionnaire. Clobazam was not found to produce these detrimental effects.

Lader, Melhuish, and Harris (1982) tested flunitrazepam and placebo over 8 nights, with assessments made 10 and 13 hours after administration on days 1, 4, and 8. Testing included sleep, mood, and bodily self-ratings; finger tapping; visual reaction time; symbol copying and substitution; CFF; digit span; and cancellation. Dosages of 0.5 mg and 1 mg were administered. At the 0.5-mg dosage, subjective reports of increased alertness, contentment, and calmness were reported. Symbol substitution was marginally impaired, while symbol copying was reported to show improvement. At the 1-mg dosage, a subjective report of decreased alertness and contentment was revealed. Performances were impaired on finger tapping, symbol copying and substitution, and CFF.

Scharf and Jacoby (1982) conducted a clinically more appropriate study by administering 4 mg of lorazepam to insomniac, rather than normal, patients. It is not uncommon for medications to affect their appropriate populations quite differently than they affect a normal population. Thus, the study is a more appropriate test for drug effectiveness. Surprisingly, while strong effects were apparently seen, their documentation was limited to only a postsleep questionnaire and pre- and postsleep, mood, and anxiety state questionnaires. No testing of alertness or performance was done. All subjects reported experiencing a severe hangover and varying degrees of impaired functioning the first three days of drug use. Three subjects also reported experiencing anterograde amnesia during the day following their first drug night. All side effects eventually diminished over the course of the study.

This brief review of several studies of benzodiazepine treatments for sleep disorders leaves some questions unanswered. First, it is generally acknowledged that dose equivalencies have not been worked out for these drugs: the dosages given are those suggested based on clinical use or by the manufacturers as being effective for the disorder. Second, all of these studies, with the exception of that by Scharf and Jacoby (1982), were performed on normal subjects. If insomniacs are in fact hyperalert in some manner, might they not have different reactions to the drugs? That is, might the drug be lowering their arousal level from a higher tonic level and thus not produce so drastic an effect? Are the tasks that the subjects are being asked to perform valid and reliable across subjects; why not use previously developed standardized tests to measure such items as memory, mental arithmetic, or confusion in the morning? In fact, some of the studies did use tasks taken from test batteries previously determined to have sufficient reliability and validity.

In summary, an overview of the studies reveals that deficits were seen in memory (sometimes minutes after task completion and often in the morning) with a majority of the drugs tested. Subjects often complained of a morning hangover and a subjective decrease in mood. Performance on a variety of psychomotor tasks was also impaired. Millions of people are on the road in the morning with clinically documentable deficits in memory, mental efficacy, and impairments in driving ability. Sleep disorders have some known neuropsychologically documentable effects on mental efficiency, alertness, and psychomotor performance. The treatments for these disorders are not effective if they not only do not address these accompanying problems but actually help to exacerbate them! Research in this area has only just begun. In all probability, many more drug-related deficits exist that as yet are merely undocumented neuropsychologically. The evaluation of pharmacological treatments in this area must also consider the possible side effects they might produce. It is to be hoped that their side effects will not simply replace or exacerbate those of the disorder itself.

Neuropsychological Assessment of Sleep in the Elderly

It has been known for some time that sleep patterns change as age advances in human beings. Feinberg, Koresko, and Heller (1967) demonstrated greater fragmentation in sleep stagin and more frequent awakening during all-night studies. These observations have been repeatedly documented by other researchers. The amount of time spent in each stage also shows alterations with advancing age. REM sleep has been demonstrated to show a reduction in both amount and in latency (Feinberg, Koresko, & Heller, 1967;

Prinz, 1977). However, these findings are inconsistent. A marked reduction in REM sleep is probably confined to extreme old age (Miles & Dement, 1980). Stage 1 sleep increases from 5% in children to 15% or more in the elderly (Reynolds, Spiker, Hanin, & Kupfer, 1983). Slow-wave (delta) sleep also appears to show a reduction in amount (Feinberg, Koresko, & Heller, 1967; Prinz, 1977). Webb and Dreblow (1982), however, argue that slow-wave sleep may actually increase in amount if one dispenses with amplitude, using only frequency as the criterion. In effect, Webb and Dreblow (1982) proposed that a change in the representative wave form of slow-wave sleep takes place with advanced age. Williams, Karacan, and Hirsch (1974) argue that sex-related changes occur in the sleep of the elderly. They reported the finding that aged men slept less efficiently (a ratio of time asleep to time attempting to fall asleep) than did aged women and had less REM and slow-wave sleep. Webb's (1982b) results concurred with these findings.

With advancing age also comes an increased sensitivity to sleep deprivation. Webb and Levy (1982) found differences in sensitivity to sleep deprivation even in middle-aged men (40–47 years old) compared with younger men (18–22). After eliminating subjects who indicated significant sleep difficulties, 6 younger and 10 older men were given practice and test trials on a battery of 12 measures after both sleep and SD. The battery consisted of the Stanford Sleepiness Scale, a mood scale rating between 1 (very depressed) and 10 (elated), the Wilkinson Addition Test (Wilkinson, 1970), a visual search task (finding a target letter in a matrix), a word memory task (order-free recall of 5-letter, high-frequency, monosyllabic words), and word detection tasks (presence or absence of a word in a group presented at 10 items per second), a reasoning task (sentences that related pictorial scenes), a numerical estimation task, an object-use task, a remote association task, the WAV task (Wilkinson, 1970), a line judgment task, and an unobtrusive measure (compliance with instruction to enter a number into the computer when coming and going).

The results revealed that those items found by others (Kjellberg, 1977b; Wilkinson, 1970) to be sensitive to SD remained sensitive. Sleepiness, mood, auditory vigilance, and addition showed significant effects. Further, the older group revealed effects of the more cognitively demanding tests of object uses (number given), visual search, and reasoning (reasoning significant in this study at $P < .08$). It is interesting to note that object uses and reasoning were among a group of tests that revealed superior performance by the older group in the normal sleep condition. That the groups did not show overall equal performances in the normal condition might be problematic here. Webb and Levy stated that this effect "could reflect higher initial motivation in the older subjects which could not be sustained across the deprivation period." Alternatively, higher performance levels may be more susceptible to sleep deprivation and continuous performance. For whatever proposed reason, two points clearly emerge from this study. One, is that older subjects (really middle aged) revealed substantially greater deficits than did younger subjects when subjected to SD. The second, and perhaps more important, point is that the older subjects exhibited deficits of a higher cognitive nature, specifically in concept association (object used) and verbal processing (reasoning task).

With the finding of increased sensitivity to sleep deprivation, differential sensitivity to overall sleep schedule manipulations might be expected across age groups. A study by Webb, Agnew, and Dreblow (unpublished), however, failed to find this. Eight females aged 40–50 years (mean age, 46.6 years) were exposed to shifted sleep schedules of 2300–0700 hours (4 baseline nights), 0800–1600 hours (8 nights), and 2300–0700 hours (4 recovery nights). A 25-hour awake period followed the fourth baseline night, and a 7-hour awake period followed the eighth shifted night. Data from the nights following these periods were not evaluated. During the awake periods, subjects worked on the WAV task and the WAT (Wilkinson, 1970) or did anything else other than sleep. In short, the typical shift change effects (i.e., a sharp reduction in sleep latency in the shifted condition and in time to sleep onset during the recovery condition) were seen. No changes were revealed in overall sleep length or in REM sleep percent. However, REM sleep distribution was changed, in that an increased amount of REM sleep occurred in the first quarter of sleep, while less than normal REM sleep occurred in the final quarter of the sleep episode. A quasicontrol group consisting of 5 young males was available from a 1971 study (Webb, Agnew, & Williams) using a similar paradigm. The interesting finding here was that few significant differences were found in the sleep of the populations. The older group did have sharper reductions in sleep latencies and an increased amount of slow-wave sleep, compared to the younger population. All of these findings are, however, normally found in a comparison of the sleep of younger and older populations,[1] making it difficult to argue that these effects are attributable to the actual paradigm. A well-controlled replication of the study is needed, but this finding appears likely to hold.

Other basic research has been directed more at the known differences in the sleep of older populations. Webb and Campbell (1980) looked at the frequent problem of increased number of arousals in the elderly. In a study of 36 older women (mean age, 53.9 years; range, 50–60 years), the results indicated that the problem was twofold. Not only were an increased number of spontaneous arousals found, but the amount of time necessary to fall back to sleep was also significantly increased relative to a group of young (range, 21–23 years) men in an earlier study (Bonnet & Webb, 1979). In a longitudinal study, Webb (1982c) restudied the sleep of 6 of 15 males (mean age, 67.0 years; range 64–70 years) who had been recorded 15 years earlier (mean age, 52.6 years; range, 50–56 years). The findings indicated an increased number of within-sleep awakenings and shorter sleep stages above and beyond those found in the subjects' first recording. Webb cautions about making broad interpretations in time-extended studies, since much can happen to the subjects during the intervening time. Still, it does seem plausible that a trend such as the one identified in younger populations in their mid-forties (Webb, 1982b) would continue into later life.

Many theories have been postulated as to the effect of sleep on cognition; the role of REM sleep has been frequently explored (Crowder, 1976; Dewan, 1968; Lewin & Gombosh, 1973; Lewin & Glaubman, 1975; McGrath & Cohen, 1978; Scrima, 1982; Tilley & Empson, 1978; Valley & Broughton, 1981). The purpose here is not to go into a detailed discussion of these theories. However, the intense interest in the area of cognition and REM sleep has drawn researchers to any population that shows changes in REM sleep. The elderly are such a population, as the narcoleptics were shown to be.

Scores on many standard intelligence tests have been shown to decline with advancing age, especially after the sixth decade. While these results are largely confined to cross-sectional studies as opposed to longitudinal studies, decline has been noted in longitudinal studies using some especially sensitive subtests (Botwinick, 1977). Some

---

[1] Webb and Dreblow (1982) find increased amounts of slow-wave sleep in older populations when adapting their amplitude-free scoring criterion.

researchers have noticed a correlation between decreased amounts of REM sleep and the decreases in these measures (Prinz, 1977; Reynolds, Spiker, Hanin, & Kupfer, 1983). Fortunately, the speculations on the causes for this correlation have been kept plausible (each related to biochemical changes occurring as a function of either aging or some pathological process) in the studies presented here.

The initial study in this area was carefully planned and executed. It remains a standard citation in the area to this day. Feinberg, Koresko, and Heller (1967) looked at groups of young normal (YN) subjects, adult normal (AN) subjects, and chronic brain syndrome patients. They compared sleep and psychological assessments among these groups. The data on the CBS subjects will not be presented here. AN (and CBS) subjects were tested within two weeks of the study with the WAIS, the Wechsler Memory Scale, and the Progressive Matrices (PM) test. Age was found to be negatively correlated with eye movements, amount of stage 1 sleep, WAIS Performance scores, and WMS measures. Feinberg and associates stated that the finding "suggests that physiological functions underlying performance on these tasks in normal-aged subjects are estimated at least as well by these REM sleep measures as by age itself" (p. 123). WAIS Verbal scores were not correlated with either age or sleep. Correlations between stage 1 sleep and PM scores were not significant in the AN group. A significant positive correlation was observed, however, between PM and total sleep time, while a significant negative correlation was revealed between PM and percent of time awake. A significant negative correlation was also seen between stage 3 sleep and PM scores. This was the first study to reveal a correlation between intelligence test scores and sleep in normal populations. No correlations have been generally seen between WAIS scores and the sleep of young normal subjects. Unfortunately, as this study compared the AN subjects to a standardized normal control group and not to earlier scores of the same subjects, the actual decline of the subjects' scores over time could not be seen (such declines are rarely noted in longitudinal studies!).

In a study attempting to look at changing intelligence scores over time and sleep parameters, Prinz (1977) selected 12 subjects (3 men, 9 women) from a population of 50 subjects who had been routinely evaluated for the previous 18 years as a part of the Duke University Center for the Study of Aging and Human Development. Complete physical examinations of the subjects determined that they were free of cardiovascular and pulmonary disease and normotensive for their age range. The sleep evaluation criteria were a combination of Webb and Dreblow's (1982) amplitude-free delta sleep criterion and the normal criterion (Rechtschaffen & Kales, 1968), with the amplitude criterion reduced from 75 to 50 microvolts. This is the first non-Webb study (known by these authors) to have used this nonstandard criterion. The WAIS and WMS had been administered to these subjects 8 times over this 18-year period. Verbal and Performance scales scores were analyzed as to slope over time. The hard paired-associate scores from the WMS were averaged across the first and last 9-year periods, and a difference score was derived. The amount of REM and stage 4 sleep time of the subjects was positively correlated with both change and single scores of the intellectual test measure. WAIS performance scores were lower for this population compared to age norms (Wechsler, 1955). Both the WAIS Performance and WMS scores had showed a steady decline for most of the subjects since the first administration. The Performance scores of young normal subjects are usually remarkably stable (Wechsler, 1955). However, the Verbal score on the WAIS remained relatively stable over the 18 years of assessment.

The nightly amount of REM sleep was found to be correlated with both individual and change-over-time WAIS scores. A similar trend was seen with stage 4 sleep. A significant correlation was also reported between the time-changed, but not single, scores of the hard paired associates of the WMS. WAIS Verbal scores were again not found to be correlated. In a division of the subjects into high- and low-REM sleep groups, those with higher amounts of REM sleep (mean, 89 minutes) were found to have a more stable pattern of assessment scores than were those with an overall lower amount of REM sleep (mean, 64.6 minutes). No causal element should be assumed. It is again pointed out that no relationship has been found in young normal subjects between IQ scores and REM sleep (Borrow, et al., 1980; Feinberg, Koresko, & Heller, 1967; Feinberg, Braun, & Shulman, 1969). Overall, these results concur with those of Feinberg and colleagues (1967) that the amount of REM sleep "may be a sensitive indicator of a preexisting condition of moderately declining mental function" (Prinz, 1977, p. 183).

Comparisons of sleep in the elderly have pressed beyond studies of adult normal subjects to studies of persons with ongoing pathological processes. A study mentioned earlier regarding demented populations (Prinz, et al., 1982) may also be seen as a comparison between two older populations. In that study, 11 adult normal (AN) subjects (age range, 56–85 years) were compared to 10 inpatients with a diagnosis of senile dementia of Alzheimer's type (SDAT; age range, 56–88 years). All AN subjects were given the WAIS; no SDAT subject could perform the WAIS. Both AN and SDAT subjects were given the Dementia Rating Scale (Blessed, Tomlinson, & Roth, 1968) and the Mini-Mental State Examination (Folstein, Folstein, & McHugh, 1975). All AN subjects had perfect scores on the Dementia Rating Scale and the Mini-Mental State Exam. Patients with SDAT were found to have changes in sleep stages above and beyond those seen in the AN population. Specifically, significantly lower amounts of stage 3, stage 4 [not using the Webb and Dreblow (1982) criteria], and REM sleep, and increased fragmentation and frequent awakenings were seen in the sleep of the SDAT subjects. Examination of sleep-wake patterns also revealed a greater amount of circadian rhythm sleep disturbance in the SDAT group. Within both groups, WAIS Performance and Verbal scales and Dementia Rating Scale scores were correlated with percentages of REM sleep. A finding by Ishii (1966) suggests that neuronal degeneration may underlie the changes related to SDAT and those seen in sleep architecture.

Depression, as mentioned in the section dealing with insomnia, has long been known also to effect REM sleep in the elderly (Chen, 1979; Pflüg, 1978, 1976; Vogel, 1981; Vogel, et al., 1975). Depression is also a common complaint in patients with dementia (Spitzer, Endicott, & Robbins, 1978). Reynolds, Spiker, Hanin, and Kupfer (1983) studied the sleep of 9 elderly patients who met the DSM III criteria for dementia without having other ongoing concomitant or dementia-causing processes. These patients were compared to 9 patients diagnosed with major depression. Matching was identical or close on gender, outpatient-inpatient status, and age. Both unipolar and bipolar depressives were used in the study. The results indicated that patient populations could be correctly classified by sleep parameters. Using a cutoff score of 30 minutes for REM sleep latency. 14 of 18 patients, or 78%, were correctly classified. Six of 9 (67%) depressives had an REM sleep latency of less than 30 minutes, and 8 of 9 (87%) of the patients with dementia had REM sleep latencies of 30 minutes or greater. According to Vecchio (1966), this finding yielded a diagnostic confidence of 85.7% and was highly significant ($P = .008$). The parameter of REM sleep density (amount of REM sleep activity/total REM sleep time) was also of significant diagnostic value. Using a cutoff of 1.60, 13 of 18 patients (diagnostic confidence = 75.0%) were correctly identified; 6 of 9 depressive (67%) and 7 of 9 (78%) dementia patients were accurately labeled ($P = .03$). The parameter of scaled sleep maintenance (a normalized measure) yielded equivalent results, as did REM sleep density using a cutoff score of 5.00. The combination of these three factors was found in a discriminant analysis to be better than any one factor in the number of correctly classified patients (true positives = 87%), but yielded a lower percentage of true negatives (67%). The overall significance of the analysis remained high ($P = .008$; Reynolds, Spiker, Hanin, & Kupfer, 1983).

Although this type of diagnostic analysis obviously needs to be replicated with a larger and more specifically defined subject population, its clinical significance is intriguing. This measure may be a future addition to those sleep EEG measures already considered to be useful in clinical diagnostic practice (Orr, 1976).

DIRECTIONS FOR RESEARCH

It is somewhat difficult to point out areas that should be most fruitful for research in the field of the neuropsychological evaluation of sleep and sleep disorders, largely due to the fact that so little has been done. Not only have the disorders at this time been described largely by medical parameters, but the function of sleep is hard to pinpoint in the first place. Finding a test that will be affected by lack of sleep may eventually be found to be similar to finding a test for organicity. Organically impaired patients do everything worse than so-called normal populations. If the sleep disorder is severe enough, the patient may also show impaired performance on all measures. However, as was stated earlier, the very sleepy are known often to perform well on tests that do not last very long. Therefore, the researcher can go one of three ways: administer extensive neuropsychological test batteries and see who appears impaired, get good accompanying behavioral data, or do both. The authors know of no one who has attempted to do one, two, or especially, three.

What do we know? Sleep disorder populations can show impaired scores on such tests as the WAV task, the WAT, the four-choice Reaction Times task, and other tests of a similar nature. How do test results such as these correlate with patient and clinician reports of (1) decreased ability to remain alert or to sustain attention, (2) episodes of automatic behavior, (3) difficulty in complex problem solving, and (4) difficulty in simultaneously processing different kinds of stimuli or information? We do not know; the data simply are not in.

Sleep apnea may have a model in the COPD patient. This is currently being researched in our laboratory. It is impossible to tell at this point whether this is a reasonable model. We are pursuing it. COPD patients have shown deficits on most items of the Halstead Reitan Neuropsychological Test Battery, except Tactual Performance Test Location, Speech-Sounds Perception, Seashore Rhythm, Tapping, Trails A, Spatial relations, and perceptual score (Prigitano, Stahl, Orr, & Zeiner, 1982). Apneics complain frequently of memory and concentration problems. Digit span from the WAIS or WAIS-R is not a reasonable test of these by itself. Probably no single test will be sufficient to measure such impairment. How do Wechsler Memory Scale scores reflect memory and concentration problems? How about the Selective Reminding Test? Apneics might reasonably be assumed to show deficits on these as well as on the Tactual Performance Test. Also, lowered scores might be seen on Seashore Rhythm and Speech-Sounds Perception of the Halstead Neuropsychological

Test Battery because of their attentional components. A frequently heard complaint is the morning fogginess and headaches apneics experience. Perhaps the decreased oxygenation and interrupted sleep are somehow overcome by midday, and a time-of-day effect will be seen in testing them. Headache itself might be presumed to lower concentration. The presence and severity of headache could be assessed. Myoclonic patients also have severely disrupted sleep but do not have the low O_2 levels seen in apneics. How might these patients differ in the neurocognitive impairments? No one knows.

Truly, this is a wide-open field for research of both basic and applied nature. Research on the types of cognitive deficits occurring (if any!) in these populations will be extremely useful in describing the functions that sleep either enhances, protects, or allows to continue. Recent work by Crick and Mitchison (1983) suggests that dreaming (greater than 50% of which occurs during REM sleep) may serve to eliminate inappropriate or random cognitive associations. That is, dreaming allows cognitive "junk" to be eliminated from the system. Such a theory might also explain the differences in memory seen over periods of REM sleep and the differences in REM sleep seen in the elderly, MR patients, and other populations.

Neuropsychological research should be helpful in these basic areas. Applied neuropsychological research on sleep should also serve a much more immediate (though not necessarily better) cause: that of describing to patients, to their families, and especially to the largely medical group that has begun in the last several years to treat them, what the neurocognitive effects of sleep and the sleep disorders are. This task should not only prove to be helpful in evaluating and contributing to the treatment of these patients, it should also allow us to give many patients a rationale for their uncomfortable, disruptive, and sometimes bizarre symptoms. Peace of mind can be a very restful, relaxing experience.

REFERENCES

Adams, K.M., Sawyer, T.D., & Kvale, P.A. (1980). Cerebral oxygen and neuropsychological adaption. *Journal of Clinical Neuropsychology, 2,* 189–208.

Adey, W.R., Bors, E., & Porter, R.W. (1968). EEG sleep patterns after high cervical lesions in man. *Archives of Neurology, 19,* 377–383.

Åkerstedt, T. (1977). Inversion of the sleep wakefulness pattern: Effects on circadian variations in psychophysiological activation. *Ergonomics, 20,* 459–474.

Åkerstedt, T., & Gillberg, M. (1979). Effects of sleep deprivation on memory and sleep latencies in connection with repeated awakenings from sleep. *Psychophysiology, 16,* 49–52.

Åkerstedt, T., & Gillberg, M. (1981). The circadian variation of experimentally displaced sleep. *Sleep, 4,* 159–169.

Åkerstedt, T., Torsvall, L., & Gillberg, M. (1982). Sleepiness and shift work: Field studies. *Sleep, 5,* S95–S106.

Allen, S.R., Stähelin, H.B., Seiler, W.O., & Spiegel, R. (1983). EEG and sleep in aged hospitalized patients with senile dementia: 24-h recordings. *Experimentia, 39,* 249–255.

Appenzeller, O., & Fisher, A.P., Jr. (1968). Disturbances of rapid eye movements during sleep in patients with lesions of the nervous system. *Electroencephalography and Clinical Neurophysiology, 25,* 29–35.

Aschoff, J., & Wever, R. (1976). Human circadian rhythms: A multioscillatory system. *Federation Proceedings, 35,* 2326–2332.

Association of Sleep Disorder Centers. (1979). Diagnostic classification of sleep and arousal disorders. *Sleep, 2,* 1–137.

Beal, M.F., Kleinman, G.M., Ojemann, R.G., & Hochberg, F.H. (1981). Gangliocytoma of third ventricle: Hyperphagia, somnolence, and dementia. *Neurology, 31,* 1224–1228.

Bennett, D.R. (1963). Sleep deprivation and major motor convulsions. *Neurology, 13,* 953–958.

Berger, H. (1929). Über das elektroenkephalogramm des menschen. *Archives Psychiatrik Nervenkranken, 87,* 527–570.

Bergonzi, M., Gigli, G.L., Laudisio, A., Mazza, S., Mennoni, G., Morante, M.T., Neri, G., & Strusi, L. (1980). Sleep and human cerebellar pathology. *Journal of Neuroscience, 15,* 159–163.

Beutler, L., Karacan, I., Thornby, J., & Salis, P.J. (1978). Personality characteristics in four insomnia subtypes. *Sleep Research, 7,* 180 (Abstract).

Billiard, M., Besset, A., & Cadilhac, J. (1983). The clinical and polygraphic development of narcolepsy. In C. Guilleminault & E. Lugaresi (Eds.), *Sleep/wake disorders: Natural history, epidemiology and long-term evolution.* New York: Raven Press.

Bixler, E., Kales, A., Leo, L., & Slye, E. (1973). A comparison of subjective estimates and objective sleep laboratory findings in insomniac patients. *Sleep Research, 2,* 143 (Abstract).

Bixler, E.O., Kales, J.D., Scharf, M.B., Kales, A., & Leo, L.A. (1976). Incidence of sleep disorders in medical practice: A physician survey. In M.H. Chase, M.M. Mitler, & P.L. Walter (Eds.), *Sleep research* (Vol. 5). Los Angeles: UCLA Brain Information Service/Brain Research Institute, 160 (Abstract).

Bixler, E.O., Scharf, M.B., Soldatos, C.R., Mitsky, D.J., & Kales, A. (1979). Effects of hypnotic drugs on memory. *Life Sciences, 25,* 1379–1388.

Blake, M.J. (1967). Time of day effects on performance in a range of tasks. *Psychonomic Science, 9,* 349–350.

Blessed, G., Tomlinson, D.E., & Roth, M. (1968). The association between quantitative measures of dementia and senile change in the cerebral grey matter of elderly subjects. *British Journal of Psychiatry, 114,* 797–811.

Boghen, D., & Peyronnard, J.M. (1976). Myoclonus in familial restless legs syndrome. *Archives of Neurology, 33,* 368–370.

Bonnet, M.H. (1983). Memory for events occurring during arousal from sleep. *Psychophysiology, 20,* 81–87.

Bonnet, M.H., & Alter, J. (1982). Effects of irregular versus regular sleep schedules on performance, mood, and body temperature. *Biological Psychology, 14,* 287–296.

Bonnet, M.H., & Webb, W.B. (1979). The return of sleep. *Biological Psychology, 8,* 225–233.

Borrow, S.J., Adam, K., Chapman, K., Oswald, I., Hudson, L., & Idzikowski, C.J. (1980). REM sleep and normal intelligence. *Biological Psychiatry, 15,* 165–169.

Botwinick, J. (1977). Intellectual abilities. In J.E. Birren & E.W. Schaie (Eds.), *Handbook of the psychology of aging* (pp. 580–605). New York: Van Nostrand.

Bremer, F. (1974). Historical development in ideas on sleep. In O. Petre-Quadens & J.D. Schalg (Eds.), *Basic sleep mechanisms* (pp. 3–12). New York: Academic Press.

Bricolo, A. (1975). Neurosurgical exploration and neurological pathology as a means for investigating human sleep: Semiology and mechanisms. In G. Lairy & P. Salzarulo (Eds.), *The experimental study of human sleep: Methodological problems.* Amsterdam: Elsevier.

Broadbent, D.E., Cooper, P.F., Fitzgerald, P., & Parkes, K.R. The cognitive failures questionnaire (CFQ) and its correlates. *British Journal of Clinical Psychology, 21,* 1–16.

Broughton, R. (1982a). Human consciousness and sleep/waking rhythms: A review and some neuropsychological considerations. *Journal of Clinical Neuropsychology, 4,* 193–218.

Broughton, R. (1982b). Performance and evoked potential measures of various states of daytime sleepiness. *Sleep*, *5*, S135–S146.

Broughton, R., & Mamelak, M. (1979). The treatment of narcolepsy-cataplexy with nocturnal gamma-hydroxybutyrate. *Canadian Journal of Neurological Science*, *6*, 1–6.

Butler, R.N., & Lewis, M.I. (1977). *Aging and mental health: Positive psychosocial approaches* (2nd ed.). St. Louis: C.V. Mosby.

Cairn, J., Knowles, J.B., & MacLean, A.W. (1982). Effect of varying the time of sleep on sleep, vigilance, and self-rated activation. *Psychophysiology*, *19*, 623–628.

Carskadon, M.A., & Dement, W.C. (1979). Effects of sleep loss on sleep tendency. *Perceptual and Motor Skills*, *48*, 495–506.

Cartwright, R.D. (1972). Problem solving in REM, NREM, and waking. *Psychophysiology*, *9*, 108. (Abstract)

Cartwright, R.D., Lloyd, S., Butters, E., Weiner, L., McCarthy, L., & Hancock, J. (1975). Effects of REM time on what is recalled. *Psychophysiology*, *12*, 561–567.

Cartwright, R.D., Samelson, C.F., Weber, S., Gordon, L., Krasnow, R., Paul, L., & Stephenson, K. (1980). A mechanical treatment for obstructive sleep apnea: The tongue retaining device. *Sleep Research*, *9*, 188 (Abstract).

Castaldo, V. (1969). Down's syndrome: A study of sleep patterns related to level of mental retardation. *American Journal of Mental Deficiency*, *74*, 187–190.

Castaldo, V., Goldstein, T., & Krynicki, V. (1974). Sleep stage and verbal memory. *Perceptual and Motor Skills*, *35*, 1023–1030.

Castaldo, V., & Krynicki, V. (1973). Sleep pattern and intelligence in functional mental retardation. *Journal of Mental Deficiency*, *17*, 231–235.

Chen, C.C. (1979). Sleep, depression and antidepressants . *British Journal of Psychiatry*, *135*, 385–402.

Chung, F., & Crago, R.R. (1982). Sleep apnoea syndrome and anaesthesia. *Canadian Anaesthesia Society Journal*, *29*, 439–445.

Clark, R.W., Schmidt, H.S., Schaal, S.F., Boudoulas, H., & Schuller, D.E. (1979). Sleep apnea treatment with protriptyline. *Neurology*, *29*, 1287–1292.

Clark, R.W., Schmidt, H.S., & Schuller, D.E. (1980). Sleep-induced ventilatory dysfunction in Down's syndrome. *Archives of Internal Medicine*, *140*, 45–50.

Clausen, J., Sersen, E.A., & Lidsky, A. (1977). Sleep patterns in mental retardation: Down's syndrome. *Electroencephalography and Clinical Neurophysiology*, *43*, 183–191.

Coben, L.A., Danzinger, W.L., & Berg, L. (1983). Frequency analysis of the resting awake EEG in mild senile dementia of the Alzheimer type. *Electroencephalography and Clinical Neurophysiology*, *55*, 372–380.

Coccagna, G., Mantovani, M., Parchi, C., Mironi, F., & Lugaresi, E. (1975). Alveolar hypoventilation and hypersomnia in myotonic dystrophy. *Journal of Neurology, Neurosurgery and Psychiatry*, *38*, 977–984.

Coleman, R.M. (1983). Diagnosis, treatment, and follow-up of about 8,000 sleep/wake disorder patients. In C. Guilleminault & E. Lugaresi (Eds.), *Sleep/wake disorders: Natural history, epidemiology and long-term evolution* (pp. 87–98). New York: Raven Press.

Coleman, R.M., Blinise, D.L., Sajben, N., deBruyn, L., Boomkamp, A., Menn, M.E., & Dement, W.C. (1983). Epidemiology of periodic movements during sleep. In C. Guilleminault & E. Lugaresi (Eds.), *Sleep/wake disorders: Natural history, epidemiology and long-term evolution* (pp. 217–230). New York: Raven Press.

Coleman, R.M., Pollack, C.P., & Weitzman, E.D. (1978). Periodic nocturnal myoclonus occurs in a wide variety of sleep wake disorders. *Transmission of the American Neurological Association*, *103*, 230–235.

Coleman, R.M., Roffwarg, H.P., Kennedy, S.J., Guilleminault, C., Cinque, J., Cohn, M.A., Karacan, I., Kupfer, D.J., Lemmi, H., Miles, L.E., Orr, W.C., Phillips, E.R., Roth, T., Sassin, J.F., Schmidt, H.S., Weitzman, E.D., & Dement, W.C. (1982). Sleep-wake disorders based on a polysomnographic diagnosis, a national cooperative study. *Journal of the American Medical Association, 247*, 997–1003.

Connell, B.E., Spiers, M., Brown, L., Wolfe, S., & Pegram, G.V. (1984). *Neuropsychological assessment of sleep apnea patients.* Paper presented at the annual meeting of the Southern Sleep Society, Memphis, TN.

Crick, F., & Mitchison, G. (1983). The function of dream sleep. *Nature, 304*, 111–114.

Crowder, R.G. (1976). *Principles of learning and memory.* Hillsdale, NJ: Lawrence Earlbaum.

Dahlgren, K. (1981). Adjustment of circadian rhythms and EEG sleep functions to day and night sleep among permanent nightworkers and rotating shiftworkers. *Psychophysiology, 18*, 381–389.

Davies, S.M. (1982). Nocturnal epilepsy masquerading as a behavioral problem in childhood. *Journal of Family Practice, 15*, 267–269.

Degen, R. (1977). Die diagnostiches Bedeutung des Schlafs nach Schlafentzug unter antiepileptische Therapie. *Nervenarzt, 48*, 314–320.

Degen, R. (1980). A study of the diagnostic value of waking and sleep EEGs after sleep deprivation in epileptic patients on anticonvulsive therapy. *Electroencephalography and Clinical Neurophysiology, 49*, 577–584.

Dement, W.C. (1979). Narcolepsy—not as rare as we believed! *Medical Times, 107*, 51–55.

Dement, W.C., & Mitler, M.M. (1974). An introduction to sleep. In O. Petre-Quadens & J.D. Schlag (Eds.), *Basic sleep mechanisms* (pp. 271–298). New York: Academic Press.

Dewan, E.M. (1968). The P (programming) hypothesis for REMs. *Psychophysiology, 4*, 365–366. (Abstract)

Dewan, E. (1970). The programming (P) hypothesis for REM sleep. In E. Hartman (Ed.), *Sleep and dreaming.* Boston: Little, Brown.

Edwards, A.E., & Hart, G.M. (1974). Hyperbaric oxygenation and the cognitive functioning of the aged. *Journal of the American Geriatrics Society, 22*, 376–379.

Ekstrand, B.R. (1967). Effect of sleep on memory. *Journal of Experimental Psychology, 75*, 64–72.

Epstein, A.W., & Simmons, N.N. (1983). Aphasia with reported loss of dreaming. *American Journal of Psychiatry, 140*, 108–109.

Erickson, R.C., & Scott, M.L. (1977). Clinical memory testing: A review. *Psychological Bulletin, 84*, 1130–1149.

Feinberg, I., Braun, M., & Shulman, E. (1969). EEG sleep patterns in mental retardation. *Electroencephalography and Clinical Neurophysiology, 27*, 128–141.

Feinberg, I., Koresko, R.L., & Heller, N. (1967). Sleep: Electroencephalographic and eye movement patterns in patients with chronic brain syndrome. *Journal of Psychiatric Research, 5*, 107–144.

Feltin, M., & Broughton, R. (1968). Differential effects of arousal from slow wave versus REM sleep. *Psychophysiology, 5*, 231. (Abstract)

Fisher, S. (1980). The microstructure of dual-task attention: 4. Sleep deprivation and the control of attention. *Perception, 9*, 327–337.

Fleetham, J., West, P., Mezon, B., Conway, W., Roth, T., & Kryger, M. (1982). Sleep, arousals, and oxygen desaturation in chronic obstructive pulmonary disease. *American Revue of Respiratory Disorders, 126*, 429–433.

Folstein, M.F., Folstein, S.E., & McHugh, P.R. (1975). "Mini-mental state": A practical method for grading the cognitive state of patients for the clinician. *Journal of Psychiatric Research, 12*, 189–198.

Fort, A., & Mills, J.N. (1972). Influence of sleep, lack of sleep and circadian rhythm on short psychometric tests. In W.P. Colquhoun (Ed.), *Aspects of human efficiency: Diurnal rhythm and loss of sleep*. London: English University Press.

Fowler, M.J., Sullivan, M.J., & Ekstrand, B.R. (1973). Sleep and memory. *Science, 17*, 302–304.

Friedman, A. (1980). Sleep patterns in Parkinson's disease. *Acta Medica Polona, 21*, 193–199.

Fujita, S., Zorick, F., Conway, W., Roth, T., Hartse, K.M., & Piccione, P.M. (1980). Uvulo-palatopharyngoplasty: A new surgical treatment for upper airway sleep apnea. *Sleep Research, 9*, 197 (Abstract).

Glenville, M., Broughton, R., Wing, A.M., & Wilkinson, R.T. (1978). Effects of sleep deprivation on short duration performance measures compared to the Wilkinson Auditory Vigilance Task. *Sleep, 1*, 169–176.

Goldfarb, A.I., Hochstadt, N.J., Jacobson, J.H., & Weinstein, E.A. (1972). Hyperbaric oxygen treatment of organic mental syndrome in aged persons. *Journal of Gerontology, 27*, 212–217.

Goodenough, D.R., Sapan, T., Cohen, H., Portnoff, G., & Shapiro, A. (1971). Some experiments concerning the effects of sleep on memory. *Psychophysiology, 8*, 749–762.

Gorrod, J.W. (1974). Absorption, metabolism and excretion of drugs in geriatric subjects. *Gerontologia Clinica, 16*, 30–42.

Grant, I., Heaton, R.K., McSweeney, A.J., Adams, K.M., & Timms, R.M. (1980). Brain dysfunction in COPD. *Chest, 77* (Suppl. 2), 309–319.

Gronall, D.M. (1977). Paced auditory serial reaction task: A measure of recovery from concussion. *Perceptual and Motor Skills, 44*, 367–373.

Gross, R.A., Spehlmann, R., & Daniels, J.C. (1977). Sleep disturbances in progressive supranuclear palsy. *Electroencephalography and Clinical Neurophysiology, 45*, 16–25.

Guilleminault, C. (1976). Cataplexy. In C. Guilleminault, W.C. Dement, & P. Passovant (Eds.), *Narcolepsy: Advances in sleep research* (Vol. 3, pp. 125–144). New York: Spectrum.

Guilleminault, C. (1979). The sleep apnea syndrome. *Medical Times, 107*, 59–67.

Guilleminault, C. (1982). Sleep and breathing. In C. Guilleminault (Ed.), *Sleeping and waking disorders: Indications and techniques* (pp. 155–182). Menlo Park, CA: Addison-Wesley.

Guilleminault, C., Cummisky, J., & Dement, W.C. (1980). Sleep apnea syndrome: Recent advances. *Annual Review of Medicine , 81*, 347–372.

Guilleminault, C., & Dement, W.C. (1977). Amnesia and disorders of excessive sleepiness. In R.R. Drucken-Colin & T.L. McGaugh (Eds.), *Neurobiology of sleep and memory* (pp. 439–456). New York: Academic Press.

Guilleminault, C., & Dement, W.C. (1978a). *Sleep apnea syndromes*. New York: Alan R. Liss.

Guilleminault, C., & Dement, W.C. (1978b). Sleep apnea syndromes and related sleep disorders. In R.L. Williams & I. Karacan (Eds.), *Sleep disorders: Diagnosis and treatment*. New York: John Wiley & Sons.

Guilleminault, C., Wilson, R.A., & Dement, W.C. (1974). A study on cataplexy. *Archives of Neurology, 31*, 255–261.

Halberg, F. (1959). Physiologic 24-hour periodicity: General and procedural considerations with reference to the adrenal cycle. *Zeitschrift für Vitamin Hormon und Ferment Forschung, 10*, 225–296.

Hamburg, D.A., Adams, J.E., & Brodie, H.K. (1976). Coping behavior in stressful circumstances: Some implications for social psychiatry. In B.H. Kaplan, R.N. Wilson, & A.H. Leighton (Eds.), *Further explorations in social psychiatry* (pp. 158–177). New York: Basic Books.

Harada, M., Minani, R., Hattori, E., Nakamura, K., Kabashima, K., Shikai, I., & Sakai, Y. (1976). Sleep in brain damaged patients: An all night study of 105 cases. *Kumamoto Medical Journal, 29*, 110–127.

Harrison, M.J. (1981). Aphasia during sleep due to an abnormal vascular lesion [Letter to the editor]. *Journal of Neurology, Neurosurgery and Psychiatry, 44*, 739.

Hartmann, E. (1978). *The sleeping pill.* New Haven, CN: Yale University Press.

Hartmann, E. (1979). What we know about sleep. *Medical Times, 107*, 1d–19d.

Hartmann, E., & Spinweber, C.L. (1979). Sleep induced by L-tryptophan: Effect of dosages within the normal dietary intake. *Journal of Nervous and Mental Disease, 167*, 497–499.

Hauri, P. (1979). Behavioral treatment of insomnia. *Medical Times, 107*, 36–47.

Hauri, P. (1982a). *Current concepts: The sleep disorders.* Kalamazoo, MI: Upjohn.

Hauri, P.J. (1982b). Evaluating disorders of initiating and maintaining sleep (DIMS). In C. Guilleminault (Ed.), *Sleep and waking disorders: Indications and techniques* (pp. 225–244). Menlo Park, CA: Addison-Wesley.

Hebb, D.O. (1949). *The organization of behavior: A neuropsychological theory.* New York: John Wiley & Sons.

Herscovitch, J., & Broughton, R. (1981). Performance deficits following short partial sleep deprivation and subsequent recovery oversleeping. *Canadian Journal of Psychology, 35*, 308–322.

Herscovitch, J., Stuss, D., & Broughton, R. (1980). Changes in cognitive processing following short-term cumulative partial sleep deprivation and recovery oversleeping. *Journal of Clinical Neuropsychology, 2*, 301–319.

Hindmarch, I., & Clyde, C.A. (1980). The effects of triazolam and nitrazepam on sleep quality, morning vigilance and psychomotor performance. *Arzneimittel-Forschung, 30*, 1163–1166.

Hindmarch, J., & Gudeon, A.C. (1980). The effects of clobazam, and lorazepam on aspects of psychomotor performance and car handling ability. *British Journal of Clinical Pharmacology, 10*, 145–150.

Hoddes, E., Dement, W., & Zarcone, V. (1972). The development and use of the Stanford Sleepiness Scale (SSS). *Psychophysiology, 9*, 150. (Abstract)

Honda, Y., Asaka, A., Tanimura, M., & Furusho, T. (1983). A genetic study of narcolepsy and excessive daytime sleepiness in 308 families with a narcolepsy of hypersomnia proband. In C. Guilleminault & E. Lugaresi (Eds.), *Sleep/wake disorders: Natural history, epidemiology and long-term evolution* (pp. 187–200). New York: Raven Press.

Hoyumpa, A.M., Jr. (1978). Disposition and elimination of minor tranquilizers in the aged and in patients with liver disease. *Southern Medical Journal, 71*, 23–28.

Hynd, G.W., Pirozzolo, F.J., & Maletta, G.J. (1982). Progressive supranuclear palsy. *Journal of Neuroscience, 16*, 87–98.

Institute of Medicine: (1979). *Sleeping pills, insomnia and medical practice.* Washington, DC: National Academy of Science.

Ishii, T. (1966). Distribution of Alzheimer's neurofibrillary changes in the brainstem and hypothalamus of senile dementia. *Acta Neuropathologica, 6*, 181–187.

Jacobs, E.A., Alvis, H.J., & Small, S.M. (1972). Hyperoxygenation: A central nervous system activator. *Journal of Geriatric Psychiatry, 5*, 107–121.

Jacobs, E.A., Winter, P.M., Alvis, H.J., & Small, S.M. (1969). Hyperoxygenation effect on cognitive functioning in the aged. *New England Journal of Medicine, 281*, 753–757.

Jenkins, J.G., & Dallenbach, J.M. (1924). Oblivescence during sleep and waking. *American Journal of Psychology, 25*, 605–612.

Johnson, L.C. (1973). Are stages of sleep related to waking behavior? *American Scientist, 61*, 326–338.

Kader, G., & Danahy, S.A. (1982). *Psychometric evaluation in sleep apnea.* Paper presented at the Sixth Annual Southern Sleep Society Meeting, New Orleans.

Kales, A., Cadieux, R., Soldatos, C., & Tjiauw-Ling, T. (1979). Successful treatment of narcolepsy with propranolol: A case report. *Archives of Neurology*, *36*, 650–651.

Kales, A., Cadieux, R.J., Soldatos, C.R., Bixler, E.D., Schweitzer, P.K., Prey, W.T., & Veloa-Bueno, A. (1982). Narcolepsy-cataplexy: I. Clinical and electrophysiological characteristics. *Archives of Neurology*, *39*, 164–168.

Kales, A., Caldwell, A., Bixler, E.O., Healy, S., Kales, J., & Preston, T.A. (1978). Further evaluation of MMPI findings in insomnia: Comparison of insomniac patients and normal controls. *Sleep Research*, *7*, 189. (Abstract)

Kales, A., Kales, J., & Bixler, E. (1974). Insomnia: An approach to management and treatment. *Psychiatric Annals*, *4*, 28–44.

Karacan, I., Moore, C.A., & Williams, R.L. (1979). The narcoleptic syndrome. *Psychiatric Annals*, *9*, 69–76.

Karacan, I., Thornby, J.I., Anch, M., Holzer, L., Warheit, G.J., & Williams, R.L. (1976). Prevalence of sleep disturbances in a primarily urban Florida county. *Social Science Medicine*, *10*, 239–244.

Kelly, D.H., Krishnamoorthy, K.S., & Shannon, D.C. (1980). Astrocytoma in an infant with prolonged apnea. *Pediatrics*, *66*, 429–431.

Kelly, J., & Feigenbaum, L.F. (1982). Another cause of reversible dementia: sleep deprivation due to prostatism. *Journal of the American Geriatrics Society*, *30*, 645–646.

Kessler, S., Guilleminault, C., & Dement, W.C. (1974). A family study of 50 REM narcoleptics. *Acta Neurologica Scandinavica*, *50*, 503–512.

Kjellberg, A. (1977a). Sleep deprivation and some aspects of performance I. *Waking and Sleeping*, *1*, 139–143.

Kjellberg, A. (1977b). Sleep deprivation, arousal, and performance. In R.R. Mackie (Ed.), *Vigilance: Theory, operational performance, and physiological correlates* (pp. 529–536). New York: Plenum.

Kleitman, N. (1939). *Sleep and wakefulness as alternating phases in the cycle of existence.* Chicago: University of Chicago Press.

Kleitman, N. (1963). *Sleep and wakefulness.* Chicago: University of Chicago Press.

Knapp, T., Downs, D., & Alperson, J. (1976). Behavior therapy for insomnia: A review. *Behavior Therapy*, *7*, 614–625.

Kokkoris, C.P., Bradlow, H., Czeisler, C.A., Pollak, C.P., Spielman, A.J., & Weitzman, E.D. (1978). Long-term ambulatory temperature monitoring in a subject with hypernycthermal sleep-wake cycle disturbance. *Sleep*, *1*, 177–190.

Krieger, A.J., & Rosomoff, H.L. (1974a). Sleep-induced apnea: 1. A respiratory and autonomic dysfunction syndrome following bilateral percutaneous cervial cordotomy. *Journal of Neurology*, *39*, 168–180.

Krieger, A.J., & Rosomoff, H.L. (1974b). Sleep-induced apnea: 2. Respiratory failure after anterior spinal surgery. *Journal of Neurology*, *39*, 181–185.

Krop, H.D., Block, J., Cohen, E., Croucher, R., & Shuster, J. (1977). Neuropsychologic effects of continuous oxygen therapy in the aged. *Chest*, *2*, 737–743.

Kuo, P.C., West, R.A., Bloomquist, D.S., & McNeil, R.W. (1979). The effects of mandibular osteotomy in three patients with hypersomnia sleep apnea. *Oral Surgery*, *48*, 385–392.

Lader, M., Melhuish, A., & Harris, P. (1982). Residual effects of repeated doses of 0.5 and 1 mg. flunitrazepam. *European Journal of Clinical Pharmacology*, *23*, 135–140.

Lavie, P. (1981). Sleep habits and sleep disturbances in industrial workers in Israel: Main findings and some characteristics of workers complaining of excessive daytime somnolence. *Sleep*, *4*, 147–158.

Lavie, P., & Giora, A. (1973). Spiral after-effect durations following awakenings from REM and NREM sleep. *Psychophysiology, 14,* 19–20.

Lewin, I., & Glaubman, H. (1975). The effect of REM deprivation: Is it detrimental, beneficial, or neutral? *Psychophysiology, 12,* 349–353.

Lewin, I., & Gombosh, D. (1973). Increase in REM time is a function of the need for divergent thinking. In P. Koella & P. Levin (Eds.), *Sleep: Physiology, biochemistry, psychology, pharmacology, clinical implications* (pp. 399–402). Basel, Switzerland: Karger.

Lisper, H., & Kjellberg, A. (1972). Effects of 24-hour sleep deprivation on rate of decrement in a 10-minute auditory reaction time task. *Journal of Experimental Psychology, 96,* 287–290.

Loughlin, G.M., Wynne, J.W., & Victoria, B.E. (1981). Sleep apnea as a possible cause of pulmonary hypertension in Down's syndrome. *Journal of Pediatrics, 98,* 435–437.

Lowenstein, O., & Loewenfeld, I.E. (1952). Types of central autonomic regulation during fatigue and its reintegration by psychosensory controlling mechanisms. *Journal of Nervous and Mental Disease, 115,* 121–145.

Lowenstein, O., & Loewenfeld, I.E. (1964). The sleep-waking cycle and pupillary activity. *Annals of the New York Academy of Science, 17,* 142–156.

Lubin, A., Moses, J.M., Johnson, L.C., & Naitoh, P. (1974). The recuperations effects of REM sleep and stage 4 sleep on human performance after complete sleep loss: Experiment S. *Psychophysiology, 11,* 133–146.

Lugaresi, G., Cirignotta, F., Zucconi, M., Mondini, S., Lenzi, P.L., & Coccagna, G. (1983). Good and poor sleepers: An epidemiological survey of the San Marino population. In C. Guilleminault & E. Lugaresi (Eds.), *Sleep/wake disorders: Natural history, epidemiology and long-term evolution* (pp. 1–12). New York: Raven Press.

McGeoch, J.A. (1942). *The psychology of human learning.* New York: Longmans, Green.

McGrath, M.T., & Cohen, D.B. (1978). REM sleep facilitation of adaptive waking behavior: A review of the literature. *Psychological Bulletin, 85,* 24–57.

Menaker, M. (1976). Physiological and biochemical aspects of circadian rhythms: Introductory remarks. *Federation Proceedings, 35,* 2325.

Mendelson, W.B., Caine, E.D., Goyer, P., Ebert, M., & Gillin, J.C. (1980). Sleep in Gilles de la Tourettes syndrome. *Biological Psychiatry, 15,* 339–343.

Mendelson, W.B., Gillin, J.C., & Wyatt, R.J. (1977). *Human sleep and its disorders.* New York: Plenum.

Miles, L.E., Raynal, D.M., & Wilson, M.A. (1977). Blind man living in normal society has circadian rhythms of 24.9 hours. *Science, 198,* 421–423.

Mitler, M.M. (1982). The multiple sleep latency test as an evaluation for excessive somnolence. In C. Guilleminault (Ed.), *Sleeping and waking disorders: Indications and techniques* (pp. 145–154). Menlo Park, CA: Addison-Wesley.

Moldofsky, H., Scarisbrick, P., England, R., & Smythe, H. (1975). Musculoskeletal symptoms and non-REM sleep disturbance in patients with "fibrositis syndrome" and healthy subjects. *Psychosomatic Medicine, 37,* 341–351.

Monk, T.H., & Aplin, L.C. (1980). Spring and autumn daylight savings time changes: Studies of adjustment in sleep timings, mood, and efficiency. *Ergonomics, 23,* 167–178.

Monroe, L.J. (1967). Psychological and physiological differences between good and poor sleepers. *Journal of Abnormal Psychology, 72,* 255–260.

Montagna, P., Coccagna, G., Cirignotta, F., & Lugaresi, E. (1983). Familial restless legs syndrome: Long-term follow-up. In C. Guilleminault & E. Lugaresi (Eds.), *Sleep/wake disorders: Natural history, epidemiology and long-term evolution* (pp. 231–236). New York: Raven Press.

Moses, J., Lubin, A., Naitoh, P., & Johnson, L.C. (1970). Circadian variation in performance, subjective sleepiness, sleep, and oral temperature during an altered sleep-wake schedule. *Biological Psychology, 6,* 301–308.

Myslobodsky, M., Mintz, M., Ben-Mayor, V., & Radwan, H. (1982). Unilateral dopamine deficit and lateral EEG asymmetry: Sleep abnormalities in hemi-Parkinson's patients. *Electroencephalography and Clinical Neurophysiology, 54,* 227–231.

Neil, J.F., Holzer, B.C., Spiker, D.G., Coble, P.A., & Kupfer, D.J. (1980). EEG sleep alterations in olivopontocerebellar degeneration. *Neurology, 30,* 660–662.

Orr, W.C. (1976). The sleep EEG in neurological diagnosis. *American Journal of EEG Technology, 15,* 169–178.

Osorio, I., & Daroff, R.B. (1979). Absence of REM and altered NREM sleep in patients with spinocerebellar degeneration and slow saccades. *Annals of Neurology, 7,* 277–280.

Oswald, I. (1962). *Sleeping and waking.* Amsterdam: Elsevier.

Parsons, L.C., & Ver Beek, D. (1982). Sleep-awake patterns following cerebral concussion. *Nursing Research, 31,* 260–264.

Pegram, G.V., Hyde, P., & Weiler, D. (1980). Sleep and its disorders: An overview. *Alabama Journal of Medical Sciences, 17,* 147–155.

Petre-Quadens, O., & Jouvet, M. (1966). Paradoxical sleep and dreaming in the mentally retarded. *Journal of Neurological Science, 3,* 608–612.

Pflüg, B. (1976). The effect of sleep deprivation on depressed patients. *Acta Psychiatrica Scandinavica, 53,* 148–158.

Pflüg, B. (1978). The influence of sleep deprivation on the duration of endogenous depressive episodes. *Archiv für Psychiatric und Nervenkrankheiten, 225,* 173–177.

Power, W.R., Mosko, S.S., & Sassin, J.F. (1982). Sleep-stage-dependent Cheyne-Stokes respiration after cerebral infarct: A case study. *Neurology, 32,* 763–766.

Pratt, K.L., Mattson, R.H., Welkers, N.J., & Williams, R. (1968). EEG activation of epileptics following sleep deprivation: A prospective study of 114 cases. *Electroencephalography and Clinical Neurophysiology, 24,* 11–15.

Preston, F.S. (1978). Temporal discord. *Journal of Psychosomatic Research, 22,* 377–383.

Prigatano, G.P. (1978). Wechsler memory scale: A selective review of the literature. *Journal of Clinical Psychology, 34,* 816–832.

Prigatano, G.P., Stahl, M.L., Orr, W.C., & Zeiner, H.K. (1982). Sleep and dreaming disturbances in closed head injury patients. *Journal of Neurology, Neurosurgery and Psychiatry, 45,* 78–80.

Prinz, P.N. (1977). Sleep patterns in the healthy aged: Relationship with intellectual function. *Journal of Gerontology, 32,* 179–186.

Prinz, P.N., Peskind, E.R., Vitaliano, P.P., Raskind, M.A., Eisdorfer, C., Zemcuznikov, N., & Gerber, C.J. (1982). Changes in the sleep and waking EEGs of nondemented and demented elderly subjects. *Journal of the American Geriatric Society, 30,* 86–93.

Rechtschaffen, A., & Kales, A.A. (1968). *A manual of standardized terminology, techniques, and scoring system for sleep stages of human subjects.* Bethesda, MD: National Institute for Nervous Diseases and Blindness.

Rees, P.J., Clark, T.J., Cochrane, G.M., & Prior, J.G. (1981). Sleep apnea in diabetic patients with autonomic neuropathy. *Journal of the Royal Society of Medicine, 74,* 192–195.

Reynolds, C.F., Coble, P.A., Black, R.S., Holzer, B., Carroll, R., & Kupfer, D.J. (1980). Sleep disturbances in a series of elderly patients: Polysomnographic findings. *Journal of the American Geriatric Society, 28,* 164–170.

Reynolds, C.F., Spiker, D.G., Hanin, I., & Kupfer, D.J. (1983). Electroencephalographic sleep, aging and psychopathology: New data and state of the art. *Biological Psychiatry, 18,* 139–155.

Ribordy, S.C., & Denney, D.R. (1977). The behavioral treatment of insomnia: An alternative to drug therapy. *Behavior Research Therapy, 15,* 39–50.

Robinson, C., Pegram, G.V., Hyde, P.R., Beaton, J.M., & Smythies, J.R. (1977). The effects of nicotinamide upon sleep in humans. *Biological Psychiatry, 12*, 139–143.

Ron, S., Algom, D., Hary, D., & Cohen, M. (1980). Time-related changes in the distribution of sleep stages in brain injured patients. *Electroencephalography and Clinical Neurophysiology, 48*, 432–441.

Roth, B. (1978). Narcolepsy and hypersomnia. In R. Williams & I. Karacan (Eds.), *Sleep disorders: Diagnosis and treatment* (pp. 29–60). New York: John Wiley & Sons.

Roth, B. (1980). *Narcolepsy and hypersomnia.* Basel: S. Karger.

Roth, B., Hartse, K.M., Saab, P.G., Piccione, P., & Kramer, M. (1980). The effects of flurazepam, lorazepam, and triazolam on sleep and memory. *Psychopharmacology, 70*, 231–237.

Roth, B., Nevsímalová, S., & Rechtschaffen, A. (1972). Hypersomnia with "sleep drunkenness." *Archives of General Psychiatry, 26*, 456–462.

Roth, B., Nevsímalová, S., Ságová, V., Paroubková, D., & Horáková, A. (1981). Neurological, psychological, and polygraphic findings in sleep drunkenness. *Archives Suisses de Neurologic, Nirochirurgic, et de Psychiatric, 129*, 209–222.

Rowan, A.J., Veldhuizen, R.J., & Nagelkerke, N.J. (1982). Comparative evaluation of sleep deprivation and sedated sleep EEGs as diagnostic aids in epilepsy. *Electroencephalography and Clinical Neurophysiology, 54*, 357–364.

Rutenfranz, J., Aschoff, J., & Mann, H. (1972). The effects of cumulative sleep deficit, duration of preceding sleep period and body temperature on multiple choice reaction time. In W.P. Colquohoun (Ed.), *Aspects of human efficiency.* London: English Universities Press.

Sanders, A.F., & Reitsma, W.D. (1982a). Lack of sleep and covert orienting of attention. *Acta Psychologica, 52*, 137–145.

Sanders, A.F., & Reitsma, W.D. (1982b). The effect of sleep-loss on processing information in the functional visual field. *Acta Psychologica, 51*, 149–162.

Scharf, M.B. & Jacoby, J.A. (1982). Lorazepam: Efficacy, side effects, and rebound phenomenon. *Clinical Pharmacologic Therapy, 32*, 175–179.

Schmidt, H.S., Clark, R.W., & Hyman, P. (1977). Protriptyline: An effective agent in the treatment of the narcolepsy-cataplexy syndrome and hypersomnia. *American Journal of Psychiatry, 134*, 183–185.

Schwartz, D., Wang, M., Zeitz, L., & Goss, M.E. (1962). Medication errors made by elderly, chronically ill patients. *American Journal of Public Health, 52*, 2018–2029.

Scott, J., & Snyder, F. (1968). "Critical reactivity" (Pieron) after abrupt awakenings in relation to EEG stages of sleep. *Psychophysiology, 4*, 370. (Abstract)

Scrima, L. (1982). Isolated REM sleep facilities recall of complex associative information. *Psychophysiology, 19*, 252–259.

Serby, M. (1982). REM sleep and senile dementia [Letter to the editor]. *Journal of the American Geriatric Society, 31*, 422.

Shealy, R.C. (1979). The effectiveness of various treatment techniques on different degrees and durations of sleep-onset insomnia. *Behavior Research Therapy, 17*, 541–546.

Shibagaki, M., Kiyono, S., & Watanabe, K. (1980). Nocturnal sleep in severely mentally retarded children: Abnormal EEG patterns in sleep cycle. *Electroencephalography and Clinical Neurophysiology, 49*, 337–344.

Shibagaki, M., Kiyono, S., & Watanabe, K. (1982). Spindle evolution in normal and mentally retarded children: A review. *Sleep, 5*, 47–57.

Shiffman, R.L., Trontell, M.C., Mazar, M.F., & Edelman, N.H. (1983). Sleep deprivation decreases ventilatory response to CO_2 but not load compensation. *Chest, 84*, 695–698.

Silvestri, R., Guilleminault, C., & Simmons, F.B. (1983). Palatopharyngoplasty in the treatment of obstructive sleep apneic patients. In C. Guilleminault & E. Lugaresi (Eds.), *Sleep/wake disorders: Natural history, epidemiology and long-term evolution* (pp. 163–170). New York: Raven Press.

Smirne, S., Franceschi, M., Zamproni, P., Crippa, D., & Ferini-Strambi, L. (1983). Prevalence of sleep disorders in an unselected inpatient population. In C. Guilleminault & E. Lugaresi (Eds.), *Sleep/wake disorders: Natural history, epidemiology and long-term evolution* (pp. 61–72). New York: Raven Press.

Spitzer, R.L., Endicott, J., & Robbins, E. Research diagnostic criteria: Rationale and reliability. *Archives of General Psychiatry, 35,* 773–782.

Stones, M.J. (1977). Memory performance after arousal from different sleep stages. *British Journal of Psychology, 68,* 177–181.

Tamura, K., Karacan, I., Williams, R.L., & Meyer, J.S. (1983). Disturbances of the sleep wake cycle in patients with vascular brain stem lesions. *Clinical Electroencephalography, 14,* 25–46.

Taub, J.M. (1980). Effects of ad lib extended-delayed sleep on sensorimotor performance, memory, and sleepiness in the young adult. *Physiology and Behavior, 25,* 77–87.

Taub, J.M., & Berger, R.J. (1973). Performance and mood following variations in the length and timing of sleep. *Psychophysiology, 10,* 559–570.

Taub, J.M., & Berger, R.J. (1974). Acute shifts in the sleep-wakefulness cycle: Effects on performance and mood. *Psychosomatic Medicine, 36,* 164–173.

Taub, J.M., & Berger, R.J. (1976). The effects of changing the phase and duration of sleep. *Journal of Experimental Psychology, Human Perception and Performance, 2,* 30–41.

Tharp, V.K., Jr. (1978). Sleep loss and stages of information processing. *Waking and Sleeping, 2,* 29–33.

Thayer, R.E. (1967). Measurement of activation through self-report. *Psychological Reports, 20,* 663–678.

Thayer, R.E. (1978). Factor analytic and reliability studies on the Activation-Deactivation Adjective Check List. *Psychological Reports, 42,* 747–756.

Thornby, J.I., Karacan, I., Searle, R., Salis, P., Ware, C., & Williams, R. (1977). Subjective reports of sleep disturbance in a Houston metropolitan health survey. In M.H. Chase, M.M. Mitler, & P.L. Walter (Eds.), *Sleep Research* (Vol. 6). Los Angeles: UCLA Brain Information Service/Brain Research Institute, 180 (Abstract).

Tilley, A.J. (1981). Retention over a period of REM or non-REM sleep. *British Journal of Psychology, 72,* 241–248.

Tilley, A.J., & Empson, J.A. (1978). REM sleep and memory consolidation. *Biological Psychology, 6,* 293–300.

Valley, V., & Broughton, R. (1981). Daytime performance deficits and physiological vigilance in untreated patients with narcolepsy-cataplexy compared to controls. *Revue of EEG Neurophysiology, 11,* 133–139.

Valley, V., & Broughton, R. (1983). The physiological (EEG) nature of drowsiness and its relation to performance deficits in narcoleptics. *Electroencephalography and Clinical Neurophysiology, 55,* 243–251.

Vecchio, T.J. (1966). Predictive value of a single diagnostic test in unselected populations. *New England Journal of Medicine, 74,* 1171–1173.

Veldhuizen, R., Binnie, C.D., & Beintema, D.J. (1983). The effect of sleep deprivation on the EEG in epilepsy. *Electroencephalography and Clinical Neurophysiology, 55,* 505–512.

Vogel, G.W. (1981). The relationship between endogenous depression and REM sleep. *Psychiatric Annals, 11,* 423–428.

Vogel, G.W., Thormond, A., Gibbons, P., Sloan, K., Boyd, M., & Walker, M. (1975). REM sleep reduction effects on depression syndromes. *Archives of General Psychiatry, 32,* 765–777.

Walsh, J.K., & Katsantonis, G.P. (1984). *Somnofluoroscopy in predicting UPPP efficiency.* Paper presented at the annual meeting of the Southern Sleep Society, Memphis, TN.

Webb, W.B. (1978). The forty-eight hour day. *Sleep, 1,* 191–197.

Webb, W. (1982a). The sleep of older subjects 15 years later. *Psychological Reports, 50,* 11–14.

Webb, W.B. (1982b). *Biological rhythms, sleep, and performance.* New York: John Wiley & Sons.

Webb, W.B. (1982c). Sleep in older persons: Sleep structures of 50- to 60-year-old men and women. *Journal of Gerontology, 37,* 581–586.

Webb, W.B. (1984). *Sleep as a biological rhythm.* Paper presented at the annual meeting of the Southern Sleep Society, Memphis, TN.

Webb, W.B., & Agnew, H.W. (1974). The effects of a chronic limitation of sleep length. *Psychophysiology, 11,* 265–274.

Webb, W.B., Agnew, H.W., Jr., & Dreblow, L. *Sleep of older subjects on shift work.* Unpublished manuscript.

Webb, W.B., Agnew, H.W., & Williams, R.L. (1971). Effect of sleep on a sleep period time displacement. *Aerospace Medicine, 42,* 152–155.

Webb, W.B., & Campbell, S.S. (1980). Awakenings and the return to sleep in an older population. *Sleep, 3,* 41–46.

Webb, W.B., & Dreblow, L.M. (1982). A modified method for scoring slow wave sleep of older subjects. *Sleep, 5,* 195–199.

Webb, W.B., & Lery, C.M. (1982). Age, sleep deprivation, and performance. *Psychophysiology, 19,* 272–276.

Wechsler, D. (1955). *The Wechsler Adult Intelligence Scale.* New York: Harcourt Brace Jovanovich.

Weiss, B.L., McParland, R.J., Kupfer, D.J. (1973). Once more: The inaccuracy of non-EEG estimations of sleep. *American Journal of Psychiatry, 130,* 1282–1285.

Weitzman, E.D. (1981). Sleep and its disorders. *Annual Revue of Neuroscience, 4,* 381–417.

Weitzman, E.D., Czeisler, C.A., Zimmerman, J.C., Ronda, J.M., & Knauer, R.S. (1982). Chronobiological disorders: Analytic and therapeutic techniques. In C. Guilleminault (Ed.), *Sleeping and waking disorders: Indications and techniques* (pp. 297–330). Menlo Park, CA: Addison-Wesley.

Weitzman, E.D., & Pollack, C.P. (1979). Disorders of the circadian sleep-wake cycle. *Medical Times, 107,* 83–94.

Westerman, D.E., & Ferguson, A.D. (1978). Obstructive sleep-induced apnoea due to bilateral recurrent laryngeal nerve palsies. *South African Medical Journal, 54,* 825–827.

Wilkinson, R.T. (1965). Sleep deprivation. In O.E. Edholm & A.L. Bacharach (Eds.), *The physiology of human survival* (pp. 399–430). New York: Academic Press.

Wilkinson, R.T. (1969). Sleep deprivation: Performance tests for partial and selective sleep deprivation. In L.A. Abt & B.F. Reiss (Eds.), *Progress in clinical psychology* (Vol. 7, pp. 28–43). New York: Grune & Stratton.

Wilkinson, R.T. (1969). Sleep deprivation: Performance tests. In L.E. Abt & B.F. Riess (Eds.), *Progress in clinical psychology* (Vol. 7). New York: Grune & Stratton.

Wilkinson, R.T. (1970). Methods for research on sleep deprivation and sleep function. *International Psychiatry Clinica, 7,* 369–381.

Wilkinson, R.T., & Houghton, D. (1975). Portable four-choice reaction time test with magnetic tape memory. *Behavioral Research Methods and Instrumentation, 7,* 441–446.

Williams, H.L., Geiseking, C.F., & Lubin, A. (1966). Some effects of sleep loss on memory. *Perceptual and Motor Skills, 23,* 1287–1293.

Williams, H.L., & Karacan, I. (1976). *Pharmacology of sleep.* New York: John Wiley & Sons.

Williams, H.L., Karacan, I., & Hirsch, C.J. (1974). *Electroencephalography (EEG) of human sleep: Clinical applications.* New York: John Wiley & Sons.

Williams, H.L., & Lubin, A. (1967). Speeded addition and sleep loss. *Journal of Experimental Psychology, 73,* 313–317.

Williams, H.L., Lubin, A., & Goodnow, J. (1959). Impaired performance with acute sleep loss. *Psychological Monographs, 73,* 484–510.

Wyler, A.R., & Weymuller, E.A. (1981). Epilepsy complicated by sleep apnea. *Annals of Neurology, 9,* 403–404.

Yaroush, R., Sullivan, M.J., & Ekstrand, B.R. (1971). Effect of sleep on memory: 2. Differential effect of the first and second half of the night. *Journal of Experimental Psychology, 88,* 361–366.

Zarcone, V. (1973). Narcolepsy. *New England Journal of Medicine, 288,* 1156–1166.

PART FOUR

Current Issues and
Future Perspectives

CHAPTER 17

Psychological Rehabilitation in Traumatic Brain Injury

Bill H. Grimm and Joseph Bleiberg

"One fool can ask more questions in a minute than twelve wise men can answer in an hour."

—Attributed to Lenin, cited by Critchley, 1969

The need for psychological and neuropsychological interventions in the rehabilitation of traumatic brain injury is gaining increased recognition across service delivery systems. In this chapter, we review what presently is being accomplished in this area, emphasizing the multidimensionality of psychological interventions, and direct attention to what needs to be done in the future. As a preliminary step, an attempt is made to describe traumatic brain injury and its effects on the patient, family, and social system. A careful effort has been made to avoid presenting rehabilitation techniques in a simple how-to fashion, and, rather, to examine the topic from the perspective of the scientist-practitioner. As our review indicates, there tends to be more practitioner than scientist in the present service delivery systems. While we firmly believe that the clinical practices in existence today are valuable contributions to rehabilitation efforts, a scientific attitude will facilitate objective and realistic expectations and serve as a catalyst for scientifically based refinements in the field.

INCIDENCE AND DEMOGRAPHICS

Head injuries (craniocerebral trauma) have approached epidemic proportions in modern society. Recent advances in acute medical care have increased the likelihood that persons incurring severe head injuries will survive with varying degrees of physical, cognitive, and emotional impairments that frequently place tremendous burdens on personal, social, and health care systems (Jennett & Bond, 1975; Jennett et al., 1977; Levin, Grossman, Rose, & Teasdale, 1979; McKinlay, Brooks, Bond, Martinage, & Marshall, 1981). The magnitude of the problem is evident from recent surveys on the incidence of new head injuries, although it should be noted that estimates vary considerably according to the definition used for the criterion for inclusion. Kehlberg (1966) has estimated that 3 million persons suffer some form of head injury in

495

automobile accidents each year in the United States. In 1975, the Department of Health, Education and Welfare recorded 9,760,000 head injuries, of which 86% (or approximately 8,351,000) were considered mild, based on length of hospital stay (Caveness, 1977). Kraus (1980) estimates the occurrence of 1,275,000 cases of head injury in 1975 based on a survey of households and concludes that this may be an overestimate because superficial skull and facial injuries without central nervous system involvement were included. The National Head and Spinal Cord Injury Survey (HSCI) conducted by the National Institute of Neurological and Communicative Disorders and Stroke revealed 422,000 new cases of head injuries that were first treated as inpatients in the nation's hospitals in 1974 (Kalsbeek, McLaurin, Harris, & Miller, 1980). Because persons who were seen in consultation at the hospital but not admitted and persons who were dead on arrival at the hospital were not included, Anderson and Kalsbeek (1980) feel that the HSCI survey underestimated the occurrence of new cases by 15%. Nevertheless, the economic costs of direct health care and lost productivity are staggering, conservatively estimated to be $3.9 billion (Kalsbeek, McLaurin, Harris, & Miller, 1980). These data represent only the tip of the iceberg, since they refer only to new cases of head injury and do not account for the ever growing number of existing cases, estimated to be about 926,000 for the years 1970–1974 (Kalsbeek, McLaurin, Harris, & Miller, 1980).

While no one is immune to traumatic head injury, epidemiological studies indicate a greater incidence in children and young adults, with the most frequent cause being motor vehicle accidents (Jennett et al., 1977; Kalsbeek, McLaurin, Harris, & Miller, 1980; Kraus, 1980; Rimel & Jane, 1983). Other causes of injury generally include assaults, falls, industrial accidents, and sporting accidents. In an overwhelming proportion, alcohol and drug intoxication appear to be a contributing factor in the incidence rates (Jennett et al., 1977; Rimel & Jane, 1983). Finally, the rates for males tend to outnumber those for females by a factor of 2 to 1, presumably reflecting differences in activity patterns and life styles (Kalsbeek, McLaurin, Harris, & Miller, 1980).

Besides the accumulation of incidence rates, recent investigations have sought to examine the extent to which premorbid personality characteristics may play a role in the occurrence of severe head injuries. Symonds' (1937) often repeated observation that it is not only the kind of injury that counts but also the kind of head was originally a statement depicting the relationship between previous psychological endowment and postinjury adjustment, but the same declaration may hold some predictive value for the actual risk of incurring a brain injury. In central Virginia, Rimel and Jane (1983) found that 31% of the adult head-injured patients in their sample had previously been hospitalized for an earlier head injury. This finding suggests that having one head injury may predispose a person to have another, perhaps placing them at risk because of motor unsteadiness or faulty judgment. Furthermore, Rimel and Jane report that a substantial number had medical histories positive for previous alcohol abuse, drug abuse, and/or psychiatric disorders. Tobis, Puri, and Sheridan (1982) suggest that persons who are severely depressed and having significant difficulties coping with particularly stressful psychosocial situations also may be at risk for accidents leading to craniocerebral trauma. Psychopathic personality features also have been linked to an increased incidence of head injuries, especially in those persons prone to risk taking, carelessness, or the use of physical means in settling conflicts (Rosenoff, 1938).

It needs to be pointed out that these observations remain subject to interpretation based on the various samples studied. They may represent some interesting trends but should not be taken to suggest that all head-injured victims are maladjusted before their injury. Indeed, one needs only to read tomorrow's newspaper to learn of yet another young, industrious, well-adjusted person whose life has been irreparably and tragically altered by some senseless act of violence or by some irresponsible drunk driver.

NEUROPATHOLOGICAL PROCESSES

Interpreting his first neuropsychological protocol from a patient who incurred a severe closed head injury, one predoctoral intern was obsessed with what appeared to him to be highly specific and localized deficits, despite the overall depressed quality of the profile. Besides resembling phrenological thought and failure to take into account the underlying processes, this often encountered example cogently argues for the need for an adequate understanding of not only neuroanatomy and brain-behavior relationships but also the neuropathological processes related to craniocerebral trauma if one is to fully appreciate the neurobehavioral sequelae and the complexity of rehabilitation efforts. A comprehensive review of neuroanatomy is beyond the scope of this chapter, and the reader may wish to consult various textbooks in the area (e.g., Chusid, 1976; Snell, 1980) or briefer introductory reviews (e.g., Boll, 1978; Lezak, 1983). The general topic of functional brain-behavior relationships can be found elsewhere (Filskov, Grimm, & Lewis; 1981, Hecaen & Albert, 1978; Lezak, 1983; Luria, 1966, 1973; Walsh, 1978). The remainder of this section will focus on the neuropathological mechanisms set into motion by head trauma and the subsequent neurobehavioral syndromes.

Although there are many different ways to classify head trauma, it is usual to consider three separate groups: (1) open head injuries from penetrating objects, (2) closed head injuries (CHIs) from force applied to a stationary head, and (3) closed head injuries from rapid deceleration of a moving skull (Haymaker, 1969). The area of the head that receives the sudden application of physical force is also important, as are the structural and dynamic consequences of the immediate impact and the secondary delayed effects that may compound the damage (Adams & Victor, 1981; Jennett & Teasdale, 1981).

In civilian life, the most common cause of the penetrating open head injury is a high-velocity bullet fired from a handgun or rifle. This missile compresses air in front of it and produces an explosive effect on contacting tissue (Adams & Victor, 1981). Damage to the brain, therefore, entails not only the pathway bored by the missile but also the tissues surrounding the explosive shock waves (Haymaker, 1969; Adams & Victor, 1981). Further damage may be incurred from bone fragments driven into the brain as the missile shatters the skull. Intracerebral bleeding, edema, and secondary brain injuries subsequent to falling complicate and may potentiate the damage (Haymaker, 1969). The risk of infection, cerebrospinal fluid leakage, and recurrent seizures pose additional difficulties (Caviness, 1966).

Depending on the point of impact and the depth of penetration, virtually any combination of focal neurobehavioral deficits is to be expected; these will not be reviewed here. It is important to recognize that many persons after penetrating missile wounds also show signs of diffuse cerebral dysfunction, such as impaired attention and concentration, memory difficulties, reduced speed of mental functions, and deficits in higher-level reasoning and problem-solving abilities (Teuber, 1975). Newcombe (1969) notes that the diffuse impairments generally remit over time and that the more focal, highly selective deficits tend to persist even after 20 years.

When a stationary head is struck with sufficient force by a blunt object, a wedge-shaped contusion (bruise) with its base on the surface of the brain is formed at the point of impact. This area of damage, called the coup lesion, results from the suctionlike negative pressure effect that occurs when the skull rebounds from initial inbending (Haymaker, 1969). Contusions opposite the direct impact site (countrecoup lesion) may occur if sufficient force is applied and frequently result in more extensive tissue damage than that at the point of impact (Adams & Victor, 1981; Roberts, 1976). There also may occur scattered areas of focal tissue damage deep within the brain in line with force being translated through it (intermediate coup lesions) (Haymaker, 1969).

Similar mechanisms account for the seemingly focal deficits observed when a moving body and skull impact a stationary or more slowly moving object or when a blow to the head produces short but rapid acceleration of the brain, as is the case with a glancing punch to the jaw. However, two additional primary mechanisms related to these types of injuries have been identified and warrant special consideration. First, with rapid change in momentum, the brain, which is able to move somewhat within the skull, is subject to rotational forces, creating shear stresses that may rupture fragile blood vessels, stretch or tear white matter, and produce multifocal lesions throughout the brain (Adams, Mitchell, Graham, & Doyle, 1977; Oppenheimer, 1968; Strich, 1956, 1969). Because the brain is tethered by means of its extension to the spinal cord, the arclike rotation of the brain places considerable strain on the brain stem and midbrain reticular activating systems, resulting in varying degrees of altered consciousness (Denny-Brown & Russell, 1941; Ommaya & Genarelli, 1974). Plum and Posner (1980) also suggest that extensive or bilateral damage to the cerebral hemispheres may be responsible for comatose states.

Regardless of the site of impact in accelerational head injuries, common sites for contusions and lacerations are the orbital surface of the frontal lobe and the anterior temporal lobes (Courville, 1937; Jennett & Teasdale, 1981). These brain regions lie in close proximity to boney prominences on the floor of the cranial vault (i.e., the orbital ridges, sphenoid wings, and petrous bones) such that upon rapid deceleration, the brain literally is thrown against them.

In addition to these three primary mechanisms (direct impact coup, diffuse axonal and microscopic lesions caused by rotational stress, and frontotemporal contusions and lacerations), secondary delayed pathophysiological processes occur and may be more damaging than the original injury. The major focus of emergency room personnel is to prevent or minimize these delayed effects in order to increase the chances of survival. Furthermore, these interrelated secondary insults also may be central to determining the extent and severity of residual neurobehavioral difficulties.

Excellent recent reviews (Jennett & Teasdale, 1981; Levin, Benton, & Grossman, 1982; Merritt, 1979; Miller, 1983) describe in detail these interrelated processes. They include increased intracranial pressure related to edema, expanding mass lesions (epidural, subdural, or intracerebral hematomas), and obstructive posttraumatic hydrocephalus. Raised intracranial pressure is accompanied by a greater risk of brain shifts and herniation of the brain through various compartments within the cranial vault. Compression of cerebral blood vessels in the immediate area of contusional swelling or secondary to general edema may produce additional regions of infarction. Finally, co-occurrence of other severe internal injuries may have serious implications for the ultimate neurobehavioral outcome. For a more detailed discussion of these and other secondary lesions, the interested reader is referred to excellent recent reviews by Jennett and Teasdale (1981); Levin, Benton, & Grossman (1982) Merritt (1979); and Miller (1983).

NEUROBEHAVIORAL CONSEQUENCES

The neurobehavioral consequences of severe traumatic head injury span the gamut of symptoms and syndromes and pose extended adjustment issues that defy any unified global description. Much of this variability is associated with differences in the severity of the initial injury (e.g., Brooks & Aughton, 1979; Dikman, Reitan, & Temkin, 1983; Gronwell & Wrightson, 1981; Timming, Orrison, & Mikola, 1982), length of time since injury occurrence (e.g., Mandleberg, 1975; McLean, Temkin, Kikman, & Wyler, 1983), premorbid cognitive and personality factors (e.g., Lishman, 1973; Merskey & Woodforde, 1972), the extent of focal or multifocal lesions (e.g., Jennett & Teasdale, 1981; Lewin, 1968), environmental circumstances (e.g., Kelly, 1975; McKinlay, Brooks, & Bond, 1983), and age (e.g., Najenson et al., 1974), among other factors.

Deficits may be so subtle so as to only be noted by the most intimate of acquaintances or when the person is subjected to extreme and multiple environmental demands. On the other hand, deficits may be so obvious and profound as to severely tax the mental, emotional, and physical stamina of even the most dedicated staff and family. In this regard, Heaton and Pendleton (1981) accurately comment: "No two brain-damaged patients are alike in terms of their patterns of ability deficits and strengths, the requirements of their daily lives, or other factors (past experiences, social support system, financial resources, etc.) that may influence success in everyday functioning" (p. 815). It perhaps goes without saying that the foregoing comments provide the most cogent argument for a detailed, multifaceted, and individualized assessment of each individual (see Filskov & Boll, 1981; Lezak, 1983; and Boll, 1978, for further information on assessment issues).

We will not endeavor to list all of the psychological deficits associated with traumatic head injury, since the final product would be quite lengthy. Griffith (1983), for example, provides a list of 61 psychological and communicative disabilities resulting from head trauma. In constructing a standard problem list for brain-injury rehabilitation, Lynch and Mauss (1981) include approximately 34 specific difficulties of a psychological, cognitive, or sensory-motor nature. Unfortunately, nowhere in this compendium is mention made of the attention, concentration, or vigilance disorders that may be part of the more significant deficits underlying or at least contributing to all others.

Despite this seemingly endless array of reported deficits, certain prominent themes continue to arise in both the research literature and clinical practice, and these deficits warrant consideration as generalizations. Disorders of sustained attention, concentration, and memory have been extensively documented sequelae of head injuries in general (e.g., Brooks, 1983, 1976, 1974; Gronwall & Wrightson, 1981; Levin, Grossman, Rose, & Teasdale, 1979; Lezak, 1979; Luria, 1966; Richardson, 1978; Schacter &

Crovitz, 1977). Attributable to diffuse damage, frontolimbic shearing, and/or fronto-temporal contusions, these disorders render a person's capacity to learn, to simultaneously process multiple sources of information, and to formulate and execute plans severely compromised. In extreme cases, the injured person is forever bound to an extended present, with recollections of the past and anticipation of the future only fleetingly within awareness. In milder cases, where performance on experimental and psychometric memory tasks falls within premorbid expectations, attention and memory difficulties may show as periodic absent mindedness, especially when dealing with tasks that place a strain on these functions and that rarely can be simulated by conventional assessment procedures.

Diminished linguistic skills often are noted after head trauma, especially in cases involving focal left-hemisphere impairment (Luria, 1970). However, it is difficult to distinguish disorders of formal language from the more general communication deficits that accompany or represent byproducts of other cognitive deficits. Several investigators (Heilman, Safran, & Geschwind, 1971; Levin, Grossman, Rose, & Teasdale, 1979; Thomsen, 1975) have found dysnomic symptoms to be the most common form of aphasia associated with head trauma, but this deficit occurred within the context of other signs of diffuse cognitive disorganization. While recognizing that aphasic and dysprosodic disorders do occur in relation to head injury, we would agree with Halpern, Darley, and Brown (1973) that the most common disorder is confused language.

Cognitive and intellectual deficits have long been recognized clinically as the most frequent and troublesome consequences of severe head trauma, influencing ultimate adjustment to a greater extent than do physical or neurological residua (Panting & Merry, 1972). Earlier reports tended to rely on observational methods and subjective inferences as to the existence and extent of higher cognitive impairments, making it difficult to draw conclusions as to the nature or severity of these deficits and their potential implications (e.g., Oddy, Humphrey, & Uttley, 1978, 1980; Jennett, Snoek, Bond, & Brooks, 1981). Yet the qualitative descriptions contained throughout the literature, especially those concerning frontal lobe dysfunction, bear striking similarities to observations in clinical settings.

Higher cognitive processes related to the regulation of other processes are most adversely effected, resulting in compromised planning ability, foresight, and adaptability to changing circumstances (Boll, 1978; Luria, 1966, 1973; Halstead, 1947; Rimel et al., 1981). Goldstein (1942, 1943) notes that loss of abstract thought, referring to the ability to transcend the immediate and consider the demands of an entire situation, is a common observation. In many regards, this entails perhaps the most complex of all activities, since it implies a capacity to integrate past and present knowledge and perceptions, to make reasonably informed projections into the future regarding the multiple probabilistic consequences of an action plan, and to anticipate the semi-independent future state of the present situation. Frequently, head-injured persons demonstrate a curious dissociation between knowing how to solve some problem and the execution of a plan to solve it (Teuber, 1964; Luria, 1973). Regulation difficulties also show up as states of pathological inertia whereby the head-injured person fails to initiate a plan or to make the required strategic shifts when appropriate to do so. Such descriptors as decreased initiative, reduced spontaneity, perseveration, and rigidity may be linked to failures to appreciate and use ongoing feedback in the course of performing some behavioral sequence. Lezak (1983) observes that lack of awareness and loss of a critical attitude is often associated with seemingly self-satisfied and mildly euphoric affect. In addition, we might add that the self-centeredness often noted in head-injured persons may ultimately be an expression of concrete thought (in Goldstein's terms); lack of critical appraisal and analysis of one's own behavior; and faulty planning based on considering the most salient and primitive needs at the moment, namely, one's own.

Additional evidence for many of these clinical, qualitative observations has recently appeared in reports employing experimental, psychometric, and neuropsychological procedures. Studies comparing simple and choice reaction times between head-injured subjects and normal control subjects reveal that, as the complexity (i.e., number of choices) of a task increases, appreciably greater differences in reaction times are noted between groups, with brain-injured subjects performing significantly more slowly (Miller, 1970; Van Zomeren & Deelman, 1976). Results such as these are usually interpreted to reflect a reduction in information-processing capacity and decision-making efficiency in novel performance-oriented situations. Studies employing standard measures of intellectual functioning (i.e., the Wechsler Adult Intelligence Scales [WAIS]) indicate that overlearned verbal abilities tend to be more resilient than complex nonverbal skills during the posttraumatic amnestic period (Mandleberg, 1975; Levin, Grossman, Rose, & Teasdale, 1979) and that verbal abilities show a more rapid rate of improvement over time (Bond & Brooks, 1976). Relative to the performance of normal control subjects on a battery of neuropsychological measures, Dikman, Reitan, and Temkin (1983) found significant impairments related to closed head injury on tasks of complex reasoning and concept formation, mental flexibility, and psychomotor problem-solving efficiency, whereas few differences between groups were seen on measures of simple motor speed and strength. These problems also may be reflected in the behavioral rating studies of closed head injury survivors by Levin and colleagues (1979). Using the Brief Psychiatric Rating Scale (Overall & Gorham, 1962), staff ratings of patients' behavior subsequent to resolution of the acute confusional period revealed greater degrees of conceptual disorganization, disorientation, neurobehavioral slowing, and emotional dyscontrol with increasingly severe initial injuries (defined by length of coma and presence of specific neurological signs).

Auerbach (1983) convincingly argues that the cognitive and behavioral disorders subsequent to traumatic brain injury reflect two distinct classes of neurobehavioral problems: focal and diffuse syndromes. The core syndrome, associated with the more diffuse neurological damage, consists of disorders of mental control functions. Specifically, Auerbach describes three components of mental control: (1) the ability to initiate and maintain attention, (2) the ability to shift attention when appropriate, and (3) the ability to inhibit the inappropriate shifting of attention. The comatose patient is characterized by total failure to initiate attention. Confusional states reflect an inability to sustain attention, whereas perseveration may be seen as a deficit in the ability to shift attention when appropriate. Impaired ability to inhibit the shifting of attention is linked to impulsivity or distractibility. With seemingly optimal recovery, the difficulties with mental control functions may be elicited when the individual is faced with complex tasks demanding speed, simultaneous manipulation of several informational sources, divided attention, and/or fluid vigilance in an extremely distracting environment.

There appears to be an inextricably complex relationship among cognitive, behavioral, and emotional disturbances after traumatic head injury. Although the topic of personality change after brain injury has received considerable attention throughout the literature, this exceedingly nebulous domain has been operationalized differently across studies such that virtually every facet of human existence has been included under its rubric. Methodologically, evidence from clinical case material (e.g., Ford, 1976; Fowler & Fordyce, 1972; Lundholm, Jepsen, & Thornval, 1975; Lishman, 1973; Merskey & Woodforde, 1972; Najenson, Grosswasser, Mendelson, & Hackett, 1980; Weinstein & Wells, 1981); family interviews and checklists (e.g., Brooks & Aughton, 1979; McKinlay et al., 1979; McKinlay, Brooks, Bond, Martinage, & Marshall, 1981; Oddy, Humphrey, & Uttley, 1978; Weddell, Oddy, & Jenkins, 1980); self-report inventories (Dikman & Reitan, 1977; Fordyce, Rouesche, & Prigatano, 1983; Jellinek, Torkelson, & Harvey, 1982); and systematic behavioral ratings (Levin & Grossman, 1978; Levin, Grossman, Rose, & Teasdale, 1979) generally attest to significant emotional or personality disorders found in this group of subjects.

It is perhaps best to consider personality changes in the context of some preexisting reference groups, most commonly the family system. In this context, Lishman (1973) simply and eloquently comments that personality changes essentially refer to "a change from the type of person we knew before" (p. 311). Besides encompassing observable changes in mental endowment, the changes in how a person typically interacts with the environment include virtually every conceivable type of psychopathologic state to varying degrees. Exaggerated emotional reactions, reflecting poor control mechanisms and perhaps acquired disregard for the consequences of one's behavior, are often seen in minimally provoked temper outbursts, lability, sexual exhibitionism, or childish euphoria. On the other hand, apathy, indifference, loss of interest in former activities, and self-centeredness are manifested by social withdrawal and may present formidable challenges to therapeutic efforts because of the difficulty of finding reinforcers effective in motivating the person to engage in prescribed tasks. Reduced tolerance to stress and information overload may lead to increased irritability and tension. As insight and awareness of the consequences of the injury grows, as is often the case with partial recovery, depression and heightened anxiety may emerge. Traumatic brain injuries frequently result in an exaggeration of preinjury personality characteristics. Consequently, severe and disabling obsessive-compulsive, paranoid, or hysterical patterns may be observed in those who showed milder forms of these features previously. Weddell, Oddy, and Jenkins (1980) draw attention to the fact that those persons who show personality alterations after head injury are less likely to return to their former line of work, less likely to maintain social involvement to the extent reportedly characteristic of their preinjury life styles, and more likely to experience greater family friction.

Most personality changes exert a detrimental effect on family functioning as the equilibrium of established patterns and expectations is capsized. A few individuals, however, demonstrate personality changes that, in fact, are viewed somewhat positively by family members, as the following illustrates:

L.B. was a 41-year-old, married, father of 2 young boys (aged 6 and 8) who held a Ph.D. in English literature and was employed by a large state university for many years prior to suffering a severe closed head injury with a left temporal-parietal contusion in a motor vehicle accident. He was rendered comatose for approximately 2 weeks and proceeded through an extended confusional period of approximately 4 additional weeks. The consequences of his injury included a moderate to severe dysnomia, a mild right hemiparesis, and moderately impaired short-term memory. His wife described his premorbid style as being one of a social isolate, very serious, somewhat eccentric, and seemingly content to minimize his involvement in family affairs in favor of pondering the meaning of life, death, and the universe in his den during off-work hours. Although the nature of his deficits precluded his return to the university in the same capacity, placing considerable financial stress on the family, his wife was pleasantly surprised by his "changed outlook" on life. She reported that her husband was significantly more relaxed in interpersonal situations, generally more outgoing although not excessively so, and more inclined to spend more time in quality interactions with her and the children. She unabashedly acknowledged that these changes were indeed welcomed and helped to offset the financial stresses accompanying her husband's altered employment status at the university.

There remains considerable controversy over the etiology of such posttraumatic personality changes, although most writers tend to agree that it represents a complex interplay among neuropathological factors, premorbid coping styles, subacute and long-range reactive emotional processes, situational variables, and the compensatory strategies employed by the individual to master his or her altered status (Goldstein, 1944; Jennett & Teasdale, 1981; Kozol, 1945; Leftoff, 1983; Lishman, 1973).

RECOVERY

Recovery from head injury is complex, and at least four major approaches to studying recovery have been attempted: (1) studies relating preinjury characteristics of the patient (e.g., age and intellectual endowment) to postinjury outcome; (2) studies relating the nature and severity of injury to quality of outcome; (3) morbidity studies, in which head-injured patients are assessed at some interval following injury and their outcomes described; and (4) studies of the natural history of recovery, in which patients are followed serially and longitudinally to identify stages of recovery and the time frames and sequences of such stages. These four approaches clearly are complementary, and more recent studies reflect an attempt to combine two or more approaches.

Premorbid Factors

Increased age at time of injury consistently has been shown to be a negative prognostic factor. Najenson and colleagues (1974), reviewing a series of 169 patients who had undergone comprehensive rehabilitation following head injury, found that, at one year follow-up, 51% of patients 45 years of age or older were deceased or totally dependent, compared to 12% of younger patients. Timming, Orrison, and Mikula (1982) found 69% of patients aged 16–20 years to achieve functional independence, compared to 43% of patients aged 21–40 years and 33% of patients aged 41–55 years, though the sample size of this study was small. Using a larger sample of 225 consecutive cases and a prospective design, Miller and colleagues (1981) found a similar increase in mortality and decrease in "good recovery" with increased age, though the incidence of vegetative outcome was not found to be related to age. Brooks (1974), in a study of recognition memory following head injury, found that severity of injury as measured by duration of posttraumatic amnesia had a stronger relationship to memory deficit in older (30 years or older) than in younger (16–30 years) patients. The relationship between memory deficits and increased age was identified as early as 1932 by Russell. Another early finding that has not received recent attention is Adler's (1945) finding that psychiatric sequelae of head injury increase with age at time of injury.

Premorbid personality has been implicated in relationship to outcome, particularly in patients with mild injury. As would be expected, patients with a history of psychiatric disturbance before head injury have an increased risk of persistent or chronic disability (Hillblom, 1960; Symonds & Russell, 1943), though, as Lishman (1978) notes "it has proved difficult to specify in detail what special vagaries of personality are important." Similarly, the literature regarding "compensation neurosis" or "accident neurosis" has yielded contradictory and inconclusive findings, and two recent reviews (Lishman, 1978; Strub & Black, 1981) conclude that outcome following head injury is related to a *combination* of medicolegal, psychosocial, and biological factors.

Finally, premorbid intellectual endowment has been shown to influence outcome following head injury. Although clinicians treat this association as though it were self-evident (and to a large extent it is), it is notoriously difficult to study because premorbid intelligence can only be approximated in most head-injured populations. Dresser and colleagues (1973), however, used Armed Forces Qualification Test scores in a sample of 864 head-injured Korean war veterans 15 years postinjury and found employment status strongly related to premorbid mental endowment.

Nature and Severity of Injury

Although head injury results in a relatively consistent syndrome of deficits (Alexander, 1982), variations in outcome have been related to such injury parameters as duration of loss of consciousness (LOC), duration of posttraumatic amnesia (PTA), presence of depressed skull fracture or dural penetration, and posttraumatic epilepsy. Injury parameters related to outcome have potential utility for permitting reliable early assessment of prognosis. Jennett and Teasdale (1981) provide a detailed analysis of the advantages of refining current knowledge in this area and of the practical and methodological issues to be faced in doing so.

Timming, Orrison, and Mikula (1982) used computed tomography (CT) scan data to predict rehabilitation outcome in a group of 30 "severe" head-injured patients and found the group with enlarged ventricles to have the poorest outcome, with the group with focal intracranial lesions having the next poorest outcome. The groups with normal scans and scans showing cerebral edema (small ventricles) had similar outcome, though even in these groups persisting neurobehavioral deficits were common, which is similar to the finding of Snoek, Jennett, Adam, Graham, and Doyle (1979) that normal CT scans following severe head injury are typical to over a third of patients and can occur in the context of severe behavioral impairment and poor prognosis. Timming and associates (1982) also found that increased duration of LOC and presence of seizures at any time during hospitalization related significantly to poorer outcome. Presence of skull fracture showed a significant *positive* relation to good outcome, though Timming and colleagues did not differentiate among types of skull fracture and other studies have shown depressed skull fracture to be a negative prognostic factor (Jennett, 1979). Levin and Grossman (1978) also found CT scan abnormalities to be related to poor outcome.

Duration of PTA has long been used as a measure of general severity of head injury (e.g., Russell, 1932), and numerous studies consistently have demonstrated its utility as a prognostic measure regarding mental, social, and vocational outcome (Jennett & Teasdale, 1981; Jennett, Snoek, Bond, & Brooks, 1981; Lishman, 1968). Duration of

LOC similarly frequently has been associated with poor outcome across all spheres (e.g., Gilchrist & Wilkinson, 1979; Najenson et al., 1974). Posttraumatic epilepsy also has been associated with increased morbidity and poorer outcome (Jennett & Teasdale, 1981), and temporal lobe epilepsy is a frequent type (Jennett, 1969). The behavioral syndrome associated with temporal lobe epilepsy complicates the behavioral deficits associated with head injury (Alexander, 1982).

Numerous studies have shown that focal neurologic symptoms, such as hemiparesis, aphasia, hemianopsia, and occulovestibular deficits, are related to severity of injury and outcome (e.g., Gilchrist & Wilkinson, 1979; Levin, Grossman, Rose, & Teasdale, 1979; Najenson et al., 1974). However, when physical *versus* mental impairments are compared in relation to overall outcome and disability, the mental factors are by far the more significant contributants (Jennett, Snoek, Bond, & Brooks, 1981). Moreover, what may appear to be a focal sign, for example aphasia, when examined more closely in a head-injured population, often turns out to be a linguistic manifestation of impaired cognition rather than a true language deficit (Alexander, 1982). In general, the widespread and diffuse lesions typical to all closed head injuries appear to be the primary cause of prolonged disability and poor outcome, and the effects of these diffuse lesions overshadow the effects of all but the most debilitating focal lesions.

Morbidity Studies

Morbidity studies are difficult to summarize as a group, since they are plagued by incompatibilities from one study to the next. The most common areas of incompatibility also are the factors most relevant to interpretation of the data: severity of injury, definition of outcome, and duration of follow-up. These studies have been reviewed in detail elsewhere (Levin, Benton, & Grossman, 1982; Lishman, 1978; Strub & Black, 1981). Despite the large variability in findings and methodology across studies, Strub and Black (1981) offer a general summary of the outcome literature: "In general, the overall outcome from severe head injury is as follows: death occurs in 50 to 52% of cases before leaving the hospital, another 19% die during the initial 5 years after the accident, 3% remain in a persistent vegetative state and usually die within 1 year, 10% are severely disabled, 20% are moderately disabled and 17% have a good recovery"(p. 285). At the other end of the spectrum, patients with "minor" head injury recently have been shown to have unexpectedly extensive morbidity not explainable on the basis of "accident neurosis" or other compensation issues (Rimel et al., 1981).

Natural History of Recovery

Perhaps the most significant dimension in recovery from head injury is time. Patients change dramatically over the course of time, and it is virtually axiomatic during the early stages of recovery that a patient's status will show change. Despite the importance of the time dimension, serial and longitudinal studies in which the same patient is assessed repeatedly at different times during recovery have been relatively rare. Dikman, Reitan, and Temkin (1983) discuss the importance of a longitudinal, serial methodology to understanding the recovery process and present data from such a study. Patients were a selected subset of consecutive acute head injuries aged 15–44 years, and there were clear exclusion and inclusion criteria for subject selection. Assessment consisted of a comprehensive neuropsychological test battery administered when subjects first were alert and oriented following injury and at 12 months and 18 months thereafter. Perhaps the most important finding of this study was the absence of evidence that recovery slowed after one year, which is consistent with clinical observations that some patients show improvement for years following injury. Other findings of interest were that recovery occurs in complex as well as simple functions and that the degree of initial deficit predicted both the magnitude of improvement and the amount of residual deficit.

Another approach to the natural history of recovery is provided by Alexander (1982). Alexander divides the recovery process into seven stages: coma, unresponsive vigilance, mute responsiveness, confusional state, independent for self-care and casual social interaction, intellectual independence, and complete social recovery. Alexander further provides a description of the neuropathology of each stage and the primary management concerns. Note that Alexander's description, although consistent with other clinical descriptions and extremely informative, is primarily a clinical description and is not derived from formal data.

REHABILITATION EFFORTS: A CONCEPTUAL FRAMEWORK

Rehabilitation generally refers to a set of therapeutic services designed to restore an individual to maximal level of functioning after illness or injury. In the case of severe traumatic brain injury, when individuals frequently suffer from multiple physical, cognitive, emotional, and medical disorders, it is customary to encounter the specialty services of many health care providers, including physical therapists, occupational therapists, psychologists, physicians, nursing personnel, vocational counselors, biomedical engineers, social workers, and recreational specialists.

The definition of rehabilitation is sufficiently nebulous to invoke different connotations and expectations for those involved in the complex process. For families and patients, the entire notion of rehabilitation frequently renews hope and optimism, and engenders expectations that the patient will be restored to normal or near-normal functioning. Unfortunately, such expectations often are slowly eroded later by the harsh reality of enduring disability. Professionals enter the process with serious commitments, diligent efforts, and idealized goals. However, the perception of diminishing returns on their efforts or the confrontation of a plateau in performance not only heralds the imminent discharge of the patient from further formal therapy but also leads to frequent frustration, dejection, or a sense of failure for therapists, especially if significant residual deficits have resisted their efforts.

Several features of the definition of rehabilitation require clarification. It is important for all concerned to recognize that this definition does not imply that services be solely directed to the patient but only that the patient should in some way benefit from them. Provisions for special equipment or alterations in the physical environment that would enhance a patient's functioning would, therefore, qualify as rehabilitation services in this regard. This example also points to the need for services to extend beyond the confines of a designated treatment center. The recipient of services traditionally has been defined as the possessor of the injury, in this case head injury. Yet, because the individual is an element in various mutually interacting systems, it is apparent that there are other victims as well. Head injury renders not only the possessor dysfunctional but also the various systems in which he or she is involved, for example the family. Such reasoning obviously expands the definition of who should receive treatment. With respect to the ideal of restoring the recipient to the "maximal level of functioning," it may be more accurate to add the term *realistic* to reflect the types of goals being pursued. Some patients may require constant supervision and care, a reality that does allow them to function maximally. Family members may never get over their emotional pain and loss or come to welcome the attendant burdens of care imposed on them when a member is injured, yet realistically they may be able to adapt with reasonable success as well as hardship. It must also be recognized that realistic goals tend to be adjusted over time in concert with the progress or regress of the individual's functional status. The dynamic interactive nature of recovery, adaptation, and rehabilitation goals is usually the most difficult aspect of treatment to conceptualize or predict and consequently is likely to place the participants on something of an emotional roller coaster. Finally, the goals and objectives of rehabilitation services generally tend to be hierarchically and interactively related, the attainment of basic goals providing the foundations for subsequent skill attainment and adaptation.

In order to conceptualize and link potential activities constituting comprehensive rehabilitation, we find it useful to think in terms of three broad dimensions: levels of intervention, objectives of intervention, and level of functioning. These dimensions are depicted in Figure 17.1. The specific activities defined by each dimension are discussed below and are somewhat arbitrarily classified in the figure. Each activity actually may fulfill more than one objective and have implications for more than one target level. As is noted later, the present conceptualization greatly broadens the scope and definition of problems associated with traumatic head injuries and therefore points to the need for an expansion of efforts to address long range social and ethical obligations.

The level of intervention dimension refers to the target of intervention efforts. Using the assumptions set forth historically by general systems theory (e.g., Miller, 1978; von Bertalanffy, 1968), each level actually defines a system. Systems tend to be hierarchically related to the extent that lower-level systems form the components of higher ones, which in turn become the environments in which lower-level systems operate. Implicit in this reasoning is the idea that the functioning of systems are mutually dependent such that a change in one component will effect a change in others in an effort to regain a state of equilibrium. Systems also are characterized by a tendency to change or evolve over time, using feedback to adapt to changing conditions. The concept of hierarchically related systems is not new to the field of neuropsychology, as evidenced in the writings of Hughlings Jackson (Taylor, 1932) and Alexander Luria (1966, 1973), both of whom espoused the hierarchical organization of brain-behavior relationships. Rehabilitation efforts traditionally have focused on the individual and biological systems, although, as noted earlier, brain injury produces negative repercussions for higher-level systems, which also may require intervention. Besides being adversely effected, higher-level systems often are recruited to play a crucial role in helping to improve or maintain the functioning of the individual, which would therefore require a different, educationally oriented type of intervention.

The second dimension in Figure 17.1, intervention objectives, can be defined by the general goals of specific intervention strategies. Although originally derived to depict the various approaches to psychiatric treatment associated with community mental health (Caplan, 1964), the notions of primary, secondary, and tertiary intervention

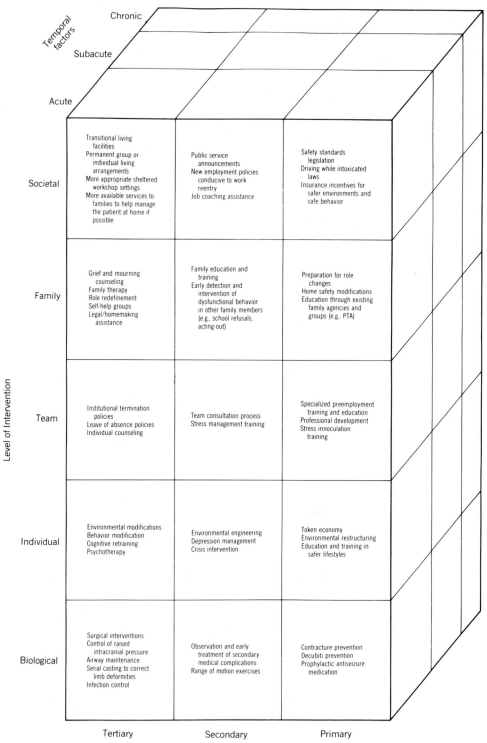

Figure 17.1. A conceptual framework for rehabilitation efforts and some possible examples.

objectives also appear to have significant conceptual relevance for describing the activities generally connected with rehabilitation.

For the most part, rehabilitation efforts address tertiary objectives, that is, the aim is to reduce or eliminate residual difficulties in an individual who has already incurred an injury. Secondary intervention objectives refer to efforts designed to lower the prevalence of emerging disorders by early detection and treatment. These aims are often less salient but are equally as important as the more obvious tertiary goals, and explicitly recognize the dynamic interplay between improvement on the one hand and emergent secondary problems on the other as recovery unfolds. Secondary objectives also play a crucial role behind the rationale for a multidisciplinary team approach to treatment, which emphasizes close communication among team constituents so as to quickly note evolving difficulties and make efforts to contain them. Examples of these objectives more readily are apparent when one considers the frequent assessment or surveillance activities of medical and nursing personnel, such as the habitual recording of temperature to detect early signs of infection and the periodic monitoring of serum anticonvulsant medication levels to quickly note subtherapeutic levels and institute dosing changes to prevent seizure activity. Since recovery often is accompanied by increased self-awareness, which may lead to an understandable depressive reaction of varying magnitude and may set the stage for learning all sorts of maladaptive behavior patterns, early detection, crisis intervention, and management of depression may reduce the chances of learning inappropriate behaviors that interfere with other activities. Emergent frustration on the part of the patient usually signals the need to institute a change, such as more frequent rest periods, a less stimulating environment, or a reduction in task difficulty until mastery of earlier steps has been assured.

Primary prevention objectives are designed to lower the overall rate of newly occurring problems. To do so, an understanding of the circumstances that produce disorders is necessary in order to alter them. Programs aimed at primary prevention usually entail concerted social action in order to either raise the public consciousness for various health and safety issues or introduce mandatory safety legislation and regulations. Examples include automobile seat belt laws, occupational safety standards, legislation governing the use of child restraint devices to reduce potential injury to young automobile passengers, and public service messages on the dangers of drinking and driving. On a less grand but equally vital level, as part of our group psychotherapy sessions for head trauma patients, we devote a series of sessions to a presentation and discussion of risk factors associated with having had a head injury. The preventive measure is fairly clear: to reduce the chances that a head trauma patient will have another injury. Although we are not certain of the impact such a program has had, it was indeed heartening to hear that one outpatient, who enjoyed and was fully capable of riding her bicycle, went out and purchased a safety helmet immediately after one such discussion. As this example makes clear, such efforts are intended to supply individuals with the necessary equipment, both literally and figuratively, that may ultimately reduce the overall incidence of head injury and other injuries. Although not traditionally identified with rehabilitation, greater participation of rehabiltation personnel in primary preventative efforts at virtually all systems levels is warranted.

The last component in our model is more difficult to define. It depicts the dimension of time spanning the period of acute treatment to a state of chronic adaptation. This factor was added in recognition of the fact that "things change" for reasons that are not always fully understood, with or without specific intervention, and for better or for worse. Time, as a dimension of this model, is perhaps a misnomer, since it subsumes changes in the individual with the passage of time (recovery or regression), changes in environmental circumstances, and modifications in family structure and functioning and even in the severity of the problem of head injuries at the societal level defined statistically by the ever-increasing roster of victims and survivors who plainly "just don't fit in" any longer. The basic question that this dimension seeks to address concerns the timing of various interventions and their associated objectives. For example, at what point in time and in consideration of a patient's level of functioning are cognitive remediation exercises appropriate treatment options? Are family needs different at various stages of adaptation, and do they require modifications in treatment approaches? There are no hard and fast rules that may be applied to answer these and other related questions. In the final analysis, the practitioner must rely on past experience and sound clinical judgment to guide this type of decision making.

REHABILITATION AT THE INDIVIDUAL LEVEL

The present section reviews methods of psychological rehabilitation of head-injured adults. The review is selective and is intended to illustrate the range of techniques, strategies, and programs that have been applied. As will be seen shortly, rehabilitation efforts have had multiple sources of origin in a variety of professional disciplines, and there is no single conceptual or theoretical framework for organizing the studies. A primary objective of the present section, therefore, is to categorize and identify the major theoretical models, and in some cases the absence thereof, in the existing literature. Implicit in doing so is clarification of the terminology that has been employed and in some cases invented, since fabricated terminology frequently obscures underlying conceptual commonalities among rehabilitation approaches and retards the systematic accumulation of information and experience regarding clinical intervention methods.

An increasingly asked and entirely justified question is: Do these techniques, methods, and programs work? A second objective of this section is to explore this question, using a simultaneously benign and critical attitude. The adoption of a critical attitude is based on obvious reasons of scientific rigor. The reasons for a benign attitude are equally important, though perhaps not as readily apparent. Efforts to rehabilitate head-injured persons only recently have become widespread and of sufficient magnitude to permit reasonable evaluation of effectiveness. Moreover, for a number of reasons that are discussed in detail later, there are great technical difficulties inherent in this area, and the types of studies that would be scientifically convincing simply have not yet been performed in adequate numbers. We fervently wish that our critical review of the outcome data be viewed as a call for more and better-designed outcome studies and for the concomitant increase in treatment programs to be evaluated, rather than as a suggestion that these programs have not demonstrated their effectiveness. The latter view is entirely premature and could have long-term damaging effects on the very pressing clinical issue of providing adequate and effective treatment to an increasingly large and societally taxing population of patients.

Most rehabilitation efforts have been directed toward the individual patient. Indeed, the foremost concern immediately after head injury is survival, with attention only later directed to the interactions between the individual and other systems. Because

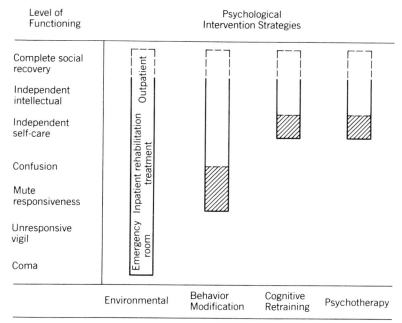

Figure 17.2.   Diagrammatic conceptualization of the clinical implementation of various general psychological intervention strategies in relationship to level of patient functioning. Diagonal lines refer to the general timing for when various interventions may begin, although their value may be quite limited if the patient remains at that level. Dashed lines conceptually depict the questionable need for special services if in fact the patient recovers fully and resumes a former life-style without alteration (adapted from Alexander, 1982).

change in the person's level of functioning is usual, intervention strategies used need to be constructed in the context of dynamic clinical processes and revised as appropriate. Figure 17.2 depicts the relationship between a patient's level of functioning and the types of psychological interventions employed to foster naturally occurring recovery, avoid complications, or actively ameliorate impaired functions. The categorization of methods is somewhat arbitrary and is based on various untested assumptions about an individual's level of functioning, ability to learn and self-direct, and capacity to tolerate and adapt to more complex environmental demands. It is clinically necessary to keep in mind that level of severity of impairment decreases a patient's ability to learn and benefit from various treatment approaches. Our intention, therefore, is to review a variety of clinical approaches with apparent applicability at different levels of functioning and not limit discussion to intervention strategies that may be appropriate only for the so-called "higher-level patient," who may well benefit from intensive cognitive rehabilitation.

Environmental Management Strategies

Environmental management generally refers to efforts directed toward developing and implementing a set of environmental conditions to facilitate and maximize the functioning of a patient, or conversely, avoid conditions that will detract from performance (Auerbach, 1983). Specifying precisely what those environmental conditions should be is extremely difficult, given the complexity of even the simplest setting, although most rehabilitation professionals endeavor to do so, albeit in rather vague terms. Jennett and Teasdale (1981), for example, argue that the creation of an environment that is stimulating, understanding, and well-structured is probably as important in CHI rehabilitation as are the contributions of specialty therapists. Similarly, Gilchrist and Wilkinson (1979) present data showing the positive influence of a supportive family environment on increasing the percentage of CHI patients who were able to return to work and home as opposed to undergoing extended hospital stays.

Several assumptions require special consideration. First, the concept of environmental engineering is not new or unique to CHI rehabilitation. It has been cited as a crucial concern in every conceivable arena of human functioning from business and industry to education, generally under the related heading of ergonomics. In the present context, environment will be defined to include both the physical and interpersonal aspects of any given setting.

Second, in its extreme form, environmental management of CHI may require little if any new learning on the part of the individual. The environment is essentially tailor-made to the functional needs of the individual, as opposed to the usual approach of trying to alter the individual's repertoire, so that the individual can cope better with environmental conditions that may be beyond any therapist's control. This type of adaptation is fittingly described by Lindsley's (1964) phrase "prothetic environment."

For the severely impaired or those in the early stages of recovery, a carefully structured environment becomes perhaps the treatment of choice for maintaining attention and reducing behavioral problems. Table 17.1 outlines only a few of potential problems exhibited by CHI patients and some of the commonly employed management strategies. Severe distractibility requires highly salient and visible task items and simplified instructions against a quiet background in order to ensure adequate attention (Alexander, 1982; Auerbach, 1983; Strub, 1982). In confusional states, analysis of the circumstances associated with agitation often reveals stimulus bombardment from a noisy and hectic hospital environment. Because inhibitory controls, judgment, and learning are substantially impaired, aggressive acting out on the part of confused patients does not readily respond to reasoning, which may only reinforce attention to the precipitating event. Capitalizing on the individual's distractibility by abruptly changing topics or introducing a new task may benignly keep things from escalating. Understandably, many, if not all, patients who emerge from coma and confusional states are disoriented. This can be extremely frightening. Providing the patient with simplified orienting information, reassurance, and familiar family members can be quite comforting. Visual aids, such as signs, calendars, clocks, and schedules, have been used widely in rehabilitation settings to improve orientation and compensate for memory difficulties. However, the value of such measures usually is limited by the extent to which an individual makes spontaneous use of them, as illustrated by the following:

D.A. is a 35-year-old male who suffered a severe CHI 2½ years earlier in a motor vehicle accident that rendered him comatose for 8 months and produced severe contractures in all four extremities. A recent CT scan showed moderately dilated ventricles consistent with cerebral atrophy. When admitted to a rehabilitation unit in a large midwestern city for further evaluation and activities of daily living (ADL) upgrading, the patient was fully alert, responsive, pleasant, and mildly euphoric. He was completely disoriented to place, time, and present situation. There were severe attention, memory, and control difficulties. He was able

Table 17.1.   Examples of Clinically Useful Techniques for the Environmental Management of Problematic Behaviors Attendant upon Head Injury

Clinical Problem	Management Strategy
Confusion	Creation of a repetitive, simplified, and reassuring environment
	Constant one-to-one attention by consistent care givers for safety, guidance, and security
	Avoidance, if possible, of unanticipated changes in basic routine activities
	Careful explanation of impending, unavoidable activities (e.g., laboratory workups)
	Modeling of calm, quiet, confident behavior
Disorientation	Repetition of correct time, date, place, and identity of others in the environment
	Signs and wall charts with correct information (including calendars and clock)
Distractibility	Use of high visibility approaches to capture attention
	Maintenance of a quiet, low-stimulus value background
	More frequent treatment sessions of shorter duration
	Starting with easily understood tasks first
	Use of treatment materials that may be of premorbid interest to the patient
	Redirection of attention
Memory difficulties	Providing patient with a daily schedule to follow
	Use of written memos in conjunction with verbal instructions
	Multimodal demonstrations of required tasks
	Central bulletin board, memory notebook, or other such reminders
	Ample use of cueing techniques
Agitation and shallow irritability	Providing ample rest periods after treatment sessions and appropriate preparatory instructions
	Quiet reassurance; not leaving the patient totally alone
	Distracting patient abruptly to a new, unrelated topic
	Environmental time-out; removal of the source of irritation or overstimulation
	Redirection of attention
	Avoidance of guilt-inducing behavior
Impaired judgment	Restructuring of immediate environment for maximum safety
	Judicious supervision of activities
	Considering restriction of environmental demands to those for which the patient has demonstrated clinical competence
	Cueing and step-by-step instructions related to a given task

to provide some accurate biographical information that required no ongoing updating, such as birth date, but was unable to correctly extrapolate from this in order to provide his present age. The difficulty with registering and integrating continuous information was accompanied by confabulations and extremely poor awareness that anything was wrong with him or had happened. When asked where he was, he would invariably state "I don't know" or give the name of his hometown and state on the east coast. Correct location information was given to him literally thousands of times with a corresponding number of rehearsals over a 3-month period. Signs in his room also declared his present location, although he did not spontaneously use them. He had the added benefit of ongoing informal orienting information by way of television and radio announcements. After all of these efforts, he could only retain correct location information for approximately 5–10 minutes, and without further cueing would thereafter fall back to his established response. He was subsequently discharged to a nursing home facility in his hometown. As expected, this move could easily be seen as a radical form of environmental management, which upon mental status examination earned this patient a few extra points on orientation questions despite the fact that no change in "real" information-processing capabilities had occurred.

The example presented above illustrates that some environmental changes can create the impression of better functioning. Sometimes the cost of some measures, (i.e., relocation) far outweighs any practical utility. In other cases, with individuals who continue to improve and demonstrate varying degress of learning, memory, and reasoning skills, environmental concerns take on new and more practical meaning. Therapeutic tasks need to be carefully graded to ensure an optimal balance between the probability of successful performance and the impression of challenge. The creation of credible, meaningful, and appealing tasks may elicit greater compliance and may forestall the inevitable complaints that activities are too childish, boring, and simple to be taken seriously. Along similar lines, energetic encouragement even to the point of emotional inspirationalism (Ben-Yishay & Diller, 1983) has been seen as a crucial ingredient in maintaining motivation and persistence.

As can be seen in Figure 17.2, the potential impact of various environmental conditions should be of therapeutic concern throughout the recovery continuum. For individuals who seemingly make excellent progress and appear capable of some type of gainful employment, environmental changes may be essential to help them circumvent specific residual deficits. The "forgetful" individual may benefit from prosthetic memory aids, such as having work assignments written down for continued concrete reference instead of relying on the less visible and more easily forgotten audioverbal mechanisms. While attention and concentration difficulties may result in less than satisfactory accuracy and speed of performance in jobs requiring meticulous detail, frequently, provisions to work in a quiet, shielded setting without distracting interruptions can allow an individual to continue working satisfactorily. It is interesting to know that many individuals who attain a good recovery status actually learn to restructure their environments to permit optimal functioning.

The area of environmental management has undergone no systematic evaluation to date, with evidence of its effectiveness coming strictly from clinical experience and anecdotal reports. Part of the problem stems from the fact that at some point it is difficult to distinguish between the spurious effects of environmental changes and deliberate attempts to alter the behavioral repetoire of an individual based on learning principles. Obviously, environmental factors not only support new learning but also challenge further adaptation. As a therapeutic consideration, analysis and use of environmental factors in rehabilitation requires ingenuity, patience, and above all highly educated trial and error practice.

Behavioral Approaches

With increasing frequency, one finds reference to the use of behavior modification in rehabilitation programs for CHI. Unfortunately, most references equate behavior modification with a specific set of standard procedures, without a clear understanding of the underlying processes and principles and the circumstances when such procedures might be useful (Kazdin, 1978; Melamed & Siegel, 1980). In the present context, behavior modification is defined according to the criteria of Mahoney, Kazdin, and Lesswing (1974) as (1) the clinical use of a heterogeneous set of procedures that frequently have been derived from experimental psychological research and (2) emphasis on an experimental and functionally analytic approach to clinical problems, utilizing objective and measurable outcomes. A detailed review of the numerous behavior modification techniques and principles is beyond the scope of this chapter and can be found elsewhere (e.g., Craighead, Kazdin, & Mahoney, 1976; Ince, 1976; Melamed & Siegel, 1980; Minke, 1980).

Historically, behavioral approaches to practical problems generally have been associated with the principles of learning or conditioning (Minke, 1980). The concept of learning occupies a pivotal position in providing a framework from which to view most, if not all, active treatment efforts. There is little doubt that application of behavioral principles ideally should form an integral part of all rehabilitation efforts, yet unfortunately behavioral programs are frequently seen as an adjunct to "specialized" therapies. As mentioned earlier, one difficulty in this regard has been in distinguishing between efforts that call for the strict modification of environmental contingencies or conditions designed to control behavior and those expressly developed for repertoire enhancement, the latter of which may have broader implications for generalization of achieved gains.

As indicated in Figure 17.2, we believe that application of behavioral designs in the rehabilitation of CHI usually is more meaningful in a practical sense with individuals who recover some degree of learning and memory capabilities. We are the first to admit, however, that this premise is based on a loose extrapolation from experimental human and animal studies on the biochemical and structural mechanisms underlying learning failures and mostly on clinical experience. Interestingly, Bayle and Greer (1983), using operant procedures with three patients in chronic vegetative states, found variable responsiveness to contingent music following emission of targeted behaviors (eye squeeze, finger movements, and mouth movements). Although this study is indeed encouraging and suggests that operant procedures may be valuable contributions in the assessment and treatment of comatose patients, we generally find that the use of behavioral principles for more socially meaningful problems is more effacious with patients no longer in confusional states.

Since the early 1960s, there has been an increasing number of reports on the application of behavioral principles to the rehabilitation needs of patients experiencing a wide range of congenital, physical, medical, and neurological disorders. Excellent reviews of this literature can be found in Ince (1976, 1980) and Melamed and Siegel (1980). Despite this growing recognition, relatively few reports have appeared that specifically address the behavioral difficulties of the CHI population. Those investigations that have appeared can be arbitrarily grouped into three overlapping categories according to the major class of behaviors targeted for intervention: disruptive and aggressive behaviors, excess disability related to deficient motivation and persistence, and skill attainment.

Hollon (1973) reports on the successful use of a differential reinforcement strategy to reduce or eliminate aggressive, belligerent, and complaining behaviors in two traumatically brain-injured adults. These undesirable behaviors were exactly the ones that received the greatest amount of staff attention. The basic approach taken was to identify more socially acceptable behaviors (i.e., asking appropriate questions or talking about one's family in a calm way) that were not being strongly reinforced and to explicitly reinforce them with additional staff attention and approval while systematically not responding to incompatible disruptive behavior.

Crewe (1980) describes a similar program for a young man who suffered a severe closed head injury and exhibited obscene language and a tendency to grab the breasts and hips of any woman within reach. The behavior modification program combined extra social attention with repeated statements of the contingencies in effect. The patient was essentially told that staff would leave immediately if he misbehaved by touching or using foul language. If he behaved, the staff member (female, in this case) would reward him by spending extra time with him. The frequency of the problem reportedly decreased significantly within one week.

Sand, Trieschmann, Fordyce, and Fowler (1970) describe a behavioral program to reduce tantrum behaviors in a seven-year-old boy who had suffered a traumatic brain injury after being thrown from a horse two and one-half years earlier. The tantrums usually occurred when he was asked to do something and significantly interfered with ambulation training and other ADL tasks. A time-out procedure was made contingent upon tantrum behavior. In addition, extrinsic reinforcers in the form of tokens that could be exchanged for tangible rewards were used contingently to increase proper behavior. This differential reinforcement program produced dramatic improvements in compliance and a substantial reduction in disruptive behaviors.

The reinforcement contingencies maintaining disruptive or negativistic behavior are not always obvious or intuitively logical. Kushner and Knox (1973) report on a 25-year-old man with diffuse brain damage resulting from an automobile accident who persisted in tilting his head back, staring at the ceiling, and claiming to be unable to see testing materials in an obvious display of uncooperative behavior. A paradoxical procedure, referred to as the utilization technique, was used to encourage the patient to engage in the undesired behavior he already was exhibiting. Each time he was directed in this manner, he would state his dislike at being ordered around and resist the directions by engaging in the evaluation tasks. An explanation as to why the procedure was effective in this case is not immediately apparent but may have to do with the idea that control over one's environment, in whatever way possible, may be extremely reinforcing.

Behavior modification techniques appear to hold much promise in reducing excess disability, which may be defined as functional incapacities in excess of those expected on the basis of a given physical or neurological state (Miller, 1977). Clinically, excess disability has usually been explained in terms of poor patient motivation or persistence. From a behavioral standpoint, motivation becomes synonymous with reinforcement (Ince, 1976; Fordyce, 1982). Instead of conceptualizing poor motivation as an independent, personal attribute of the patient, poor motivation behaviorally is operationalized as an inadequate response rate that in turn is sensitive to consequences. In rehabilitation programs for severe head injuries, the use of positive reinforcement contingencies, then, can be seen as an attempt to maintain adequate motivation. Token economy systems on either a program-wide basis (Rosenbaum, Lipsitz, Abraham, & Najenson, 1978) or individually tailored (Goldstein & Ruthvan, 1983) would appear to serve this purpose well. Application of the Premack principle (Premack, 1959), which basically calls for the use of more probable responses or activities to reinforce less frequently occurring target behaviors, has been effective in improving therapy attendance and persistence with other physically and neurologically impaired groups (see Ince, 1976) and may prove to be of benefit with head-injured patients.

One of the more difficult and challenging aspects of employing these methods is to locate appropriate reinforcers that effectively "motivate" the patient manifesting the profound and relatively unyielding apathy characteristic of severe frontal lobe damage.

In this type of individual, one often observes a surprisingly impressive level and array of potentially intact behavioral patterns that unfortunately are seldomly executed. In summary, the distinction between the ability to do something and the probability that it will be done is crucial in any functional analysis of behavior (Fordyce, 1982).

Learning new skills and relearning old ones pose special problems for head-injured patients. The head trauma victim may, in this context, be at a triple-barreled disadvantage. Not only is the "hard-wiring" diagram for learning altered for the worse, but residual physical, cognitive, and behavioral deficits frequently demand mastery of alternative and compensatory ways of adaptation when the organism is in a less than optimal learning state to do so. Furthermore, subsequent to injury, environmental contingencies change and often unintentionally contribute to the maintenance of the very behaviors deemed undesirable.

A major task of rehabilitation is to teach what Fordyce (1982) calls "disability-appropriate behaviors." This generally refers to behaviors that are congruent with one's abilities after injury. Examples of such behavioral classes might include learning new ways of communicating, getting around town without driving, asking for assistance when needed, and compensating for memory failures. Unfortunately, little is actually known about the learning characteristics of brain-injured subjects. Correspondingly, there have been few studies in the literature describing attempts to teach new skills to such persons.

Helffenstein and Wechsler (1982) compared the effectiveness of 20 hours of Interpersonal Process Recall Training to an equal amount of nontherapeutic nonspecific attention in remediating the interpersonal and communication skills deficits in young adult brain-injured patients. Training involved 10–15 minute, structured and unstructured videotaped interactions with a staff member. After this, the remainder of the hour was spent reviewing the tape, providing feedback, identifying deficient skill areas, developing alternative means of interacting that then were modeled by staff, and, finally, rehearsal by the subject. Relative to control subjects, experimental subjects showed significant improvement in interpersonal and communication skills as rated by other staff who were unaware of group placement, significant reduction in trait anxiety, and significant secondary increase in self-concept. One month follow-up data showed maintenance of achieved gains.

In contrast to the studies reviewed earlier that sought to reduce aggressive behavior by modifying environmental contingencies, Lira, Carne, and Masri (1983) applied stress innoculation training to reduce impulsivity and aggressive outbursts in a traumatically brain-injured individual. Their patient was a 22-year-old man who suffered a severe head injury six years earlier as the result of a motorcycle accident. Two months after his injury, he began to exhibit poor impulse control; low frustration tolerance; and destructive, angry outbursts that impaired virtually all aspects of his social and vocational functioning. Various medication regimens had no effect on his violent behavior. He was subsequently admitted to a multidisciplinary psychiatric treatment program, in which baseline data on the frequency of his outbursts were recorded over a four-week period. For the next four weeks, he participated in 12 30-minute sessions of stress innoculation training. The procedure consisted of three phases. The cognitive preparation component involved explanations of the function of anger, explorations and rationale for developing alternatives, and identification of problematic situations. Phase 2 involved skill development, including cognitive and behavioral techniques used to maintain a relaxed attitude, reevaluate situations, and increase the use of positive self-verbalization incompatible with acting out. The final component consisted of covert role playing and rehearsal in response to a hierarchy of real-life anger situations and opportunities to practice these skills on the inpatient unit with therapist support. Data on the frequency of outbursts showed a dramatic decline, from an average of 2.75 per week during baseline, to zero during the two-week posttreatment period. Five-month follow-up revealed effective generalization of treatment gains and significant positive adjustment in other socially relevant areas. Following treatment, this patient was able to obtain a part-time clerical job and master independent living. No severe outbursts were reported by family, the vocational counselor, or his employment supervisor.

The value of self-instructional training may extend beyond behavioral control to more cognitively oriented tasks for a select group of patients. Webster and Scott (1983) investigated the effects of self-regulation training on remediating attentional and memory deficits in a highly motivated 24-year-old construction worker who had suffered a closed head injury two years earlier. Neuropsychological assessment indicated cognitive skills adequate to benefit from the planned treatment approach. The training program involved teaching the patient two basic strategies. One consisted of a set of self-statements designed to prepare him to listen and ask for repetition if his attention wandered. The second strategy essentially involved learning a rehearsal technique to subvocally repeat each word spoken to him. Substantial improvements in self-regulation and concentration were shown and maintained over an 18-month follow-up period.

The last two studies reviewed provide preliminary support for the efficacy of cognitive-behavioral techniques in compensating for various neurobehavioral consequences of CHI. However, it becomes essential to delineate more fully the nature of the behavioral difficulties being remediated. Theoretically, it must be remembered that the distinction between primary deficits associated with head trauma and those maladaptive patterns learned secondarily in the reaction to the initial ones is not always clear, and that the two classes of behavior may present equivalently upon gross examination. From a practical standpoint, it may be that secondary learned patterns of maladaptive response patterns, contributing to "excess disability," are more amenable to intervention of the types just described than are primary deficits. The following vignette illustrates our point:

> A patient, two years post–head injury, presented with persistent complaints of memory impairment. Neuropsychological test results were unusual in that the patient performed poorly on overt tests of memory (e.g., Wechsler Memory Scale) but extremely well on more covert memory measures (e.g., Tactual Performance Tests, Memory, and Location). Similarly, over a span of several interviews, he spontaneously showed excellent recall of prior interviews and details of prior conversations, but during each interview did poorly on a mental status memory exam. We finally asked the patient to describe his thoughts while engaged in a memory exam. Upon presentation of three words which he was to remember, his first reported thought was "Oh [expletive], I'm going to forget," accompanied by feelings of anxiety, and this was followed by feelings of humiliation. These thoughts and feelings interfered with the basic process of attending, rehearsal, and learning. This patient had had a mild though significant head injury, with one hour loss of consciousness and clear confusion for several days. He returned to a very intellectually demanding job for a large corporation two weeks following his injury, made spectacular and disastrous business decisions, and was

fired several weeks later. He obtained an equally demanding new job three weeks later and lasted less than a week before being fired, and he attributed both job failures to "forgetfulness." It is more than likely that the memory impairment truly existed in the weeks following injury, but that the disastrous consequences led to the patient's developing thought patterns that would have interfered with intentional memory in even the healthiest of brains. These thought patterns became habitual (the patient had excellent memory of his memory impairment) and resulted in disability two years later, when in all likelihood the patient had largely recovered from the biologic components of his injury.

Although application of behavioral techniques to the rehabilitation of severe head trauma still is in its infancy, an obvious and intuitively logical trend appears to be emerging. Strict management of environmental contingencies to shape, reinforce, and maintain previously overlearned skills and therapy-conducive behaviors appears applicable throughout the continuum of severity. For those patients with better residual cognitive skills, behavioral approaches that emphasize more complex self-regulatory, interpersonal, and communicative skills required by conceptually more fluid environmental conditions may be effective. To be sure, behavioral techniques are by no means a panacea for the problems associated with closed head injuries. The few studies in the literature addressing applications to head-injured adults attests to the state of the art as being a technique-building phase of development and in need of further well-designed and controlled studies. Finally, the success of any behavior modification program is dependent on the skill and consistency of those in contact with the patient. Often, behavioral programming efforts need to extend to staff and family, with the intent of shaping and reinforcing appropriate behavior modification skills in their own right.

Cognitive Rehabilitation

Given that cognitive-mental impairments usually are considered the more severe and limiting sequelae of traumatic brain injuries, the next logical question becomes: What can be done to remediate these deficits? Questions such as this generally have reflected a shift in the field of clinical neuropsychology from merely describing deficits to efforts aimed at treating them (Diller, 1976). To borrow a phrase from Kanfer and Karoly's (1972) article on behavioral self-control, the entire area of cognitive rehabilitation may indeed represent yet another excursion into the "lion's den," fraught with challenge and intense controversy.

The term *cognitive rehabilitation* presents the same difficulties as discussed earlier for the term *behavior modification*. Contrary to its implied meaning, the term does not refer to a standard set of therapeutic activities prescribed to someone with a particular generic deficit, although certain intervention protocols reported in the literature seem to suggest just that. Ginautsos (1980), for example, defined cognitive rehabilitation as "a service designed to remediate disorders of perception, memory and language in brain-injured persons" (p. 37). Many rehabilitation programs adopt a similar slogan in their marketing efforts, despite the fact that interventions for cognitive deficits still are being developed and only recently have been subjected to the most elementary of scientific inquiry. The future very well may see the development of adequately validated cognitive retraining "packages," but we are a far cry from this at present.

Instead of a set of standard therapeutic procedures, cognitive rehabilitation begins as a complex clinical process, commencing with the detailed analysis of the neuropsychological structure of a particular skill defect (Luria, Naydin, Tsvetkova, & Vinarskaya, 1969). For example, a disturbance in writing ability may be related to impaired acoustic analysis of the phonetic composition of a word, failure to translate phonemes into appropriate graphemes, manipulospatial or visual-spatial deficits, impaired motor sequencing and kinesthetic feedback utilization, or loss of intention maintenance (goal directedness). According to Luria, the next task is to assess and take advantage of intact functional systems that may be able to express the skill, albeit in a qualitatively different fashion. The third principle entails the development and overlearning of the complete and expanded compensatory act. Finally, constant control of the function needs to be addressed via extended practice and feedback in an effort to introduce a positive change in the self-regulatory system.

An operational model for cognitive retraining activities in rehabilitation has been articulated by Diller (1976; Diller & Gordon, 1981). A neuropsychological skill defect is operationalized by the tasks used to adequately reflect it. Tasks, therefore, must be analyzed and can be varied in terms of their stimulus characteristics (e.g., speed of presentation, complexity, sensory modalities, level of abstractness, etc.) and their response demands (e.g., speed of response, duration, nature of errors, etc.). The skill and the task should have some bearing on activities of daily living or other meaningful activities in an individual's life. Furthermore, the skill defect should be considered in relation to neurological correlates that may suggest coexisting deficits and may confound interpretation of change associated with intervention. Intervention strategies should then be designed to make tasks initially easier by varying their stimulus and response characteristics. Finally, positive results need to be examined along several dimensions, including within-training sessions changes, changes in criterion tasks external to training tasks, impact on functional skills, and changes in psychometric instruments. These steps serve only as guidelines for treatment and are not rigid procedural recommendations.

The remainder of this section will be devoted to a recent history of applied cognitive retraining activities. The material is somewhat arbitrarily organized in terms of major trends and approaches, covering early clinical derivation, isolated techniques, multifaceted programs, and computer-assisted training. Although attempts to remediate aphasic and language-related difficulties certainly could be considered within this context, we have chosen to limit ourselves to content areas that may have more general implications for the problems associated with closed head injuries.

Clinical Foundations

The present interest in remediating cognitive functions in brain-damaged subjects can be traced to several separate but overlapping areas of research and development over the past two decades. Perhaps the most influential of these endeavors can be found in the work of Luria (1963, 1966, 1969), based on his theory of the functional organization of the brain. Remediation from this viewpoint entails three possible mechanisms: (1) restoration of function via deinhibition of temporarily impaired cerebral systems, (2) transfer of functional control of activity to intact systems, and (3) complete radical reorganization of activities using compensatory brain structures. Based on his intense and detailed analysis of an individual's deficits and strengths and the stimulus proprieties and psychological demands of various tasks, Luria (1963) has developed a wide variety of retraining strategies that have offered new hope for brain-damaged individuals. His methods, derived through intense work with individual patients, most of whom had suffered localized brain lesions, have not been subjected to any rigorous scientific scrutiny to test their effectiveness.

Busse and Lighthall (1966), using techniques similar to those described by Luria (1963), provide one of the earlier studies using an untreated patient control group to examine the effectiveness of conceptual retraining in a mixed group of patients, most of whom had suffered from right hemisphere cerebrovascular accidents. Adopting a developmental perspective, these investigators sought to teach patients how to form schemas or abstract common attributes of objects, progressing from simple concepts of color and shape to more complex ones, such as composition and use. Posttest measures showed no difference between groups in their ability to abstract shape or color. Interestingly, the experimental group was slightly superior in being able to form a new schema: height. There was no generalization to improved visual perception or abstract verbal concept formation.

Visual-Perceptual Rehabilitation

A second major trend in the literature has been the development of techniques to remediate visual-perceptual deficits in right brain-damaged patients subsequent to cerebrovascular accidents (CVAs). At the forefront of these efforts has been the work of Diller and his colleagues (Diller & Weinberg, 1977; Weinberg et al., 1977, 1979), whose studies and rationales have been comprehensively reviewed elsewhere (Diller & Gordon, 1981a, b). Expanding on the original methodology, more recent studies have demonstrated improved visual scanning, visual-spatial orientation, and time judgments in acute stroke patients and nonstroke elderly patients when compared to untreated control subjects (Carter, Caruso, Languirand, & Berard, 1980; Carter, Howard, & O'Neil, 1983). Young, Collins, and Hren (1983) attempted to delineate the cumulative effect of various visual-perceptual remediation techniques with groups of right CVA patients and found that the addition of systematic block-design training enhanced the effects of visual-scanning training on a set of criterion tasks similar to those used in actual training. Approaching the task of remediating left-hemispatial neglect from a totally different angle, Stanton, Flowers, Kuhl, Miller, and Smith (1979) attempted to teach patients to use verbal self-instructional skills to attend to their neglected side. Although showing significantly less neglect on the training tasks after treatment in comparison to control subjects, no generalization of training effects was observed. Instead of using stroke victims, Rao and Bieliauskas (1983) report the use of visual-perceptual training, self-instructional techniques, and traditional psychotherapeutic techniques with a 45-year-old radiologist 2½ years after a right temporal lobe resection for a malignant tumor. After retraining, improvements were noted on neuropsychological test data and visual scanning tasks. Generalized improvements, as reported by the patient's wife, included resumption of leisure reading, improved social skills, improved recall of movies, safer driving, and greater accuracy in the ability to read radionucleotide scans to the point of resuming his medical practice under supervision. Despite the promising results of the above-mentioned studies, a precautionary note is sounded in a recent report by Johnston and Diller (1983), who found an overriding tendency for right hemisphere CVA patients to underestimate their likelihood of making errors on a cancellation task and to recognize, post hoc, where or when mistakes had occurred. The significance of this report lies in the fact that the patients they studied had all received perceptual-cognitive retraining earlier!

Traumatically brain-injured patients also may have significant signs of left-hemispatial neglect, depending on the nature of their lesion and complications resulting from intracerebral, subdural, or epidural hemorrhages. Unfortunately, there is virtually no literature on the subject of retraining visual scanning behavior for these individuals. Furthermore, many CHI patients exhibit difficulties with manipulospatial functions, not necessarily due to impaired visual-spatial skills but, rather, related to deficient analytic reasoning, problem-solving, and goal directedness. Therapeutic activities addressing eye-hand coordination and analytic-constructional abilities, among others, have been described in the context of multifaceted programs and will be considered later.

Memory

There now exists a growing body of case reports and experimental studies on the effects of memory retraining in a variety of neurologically impaired patients, since, as Lewin (1968) notes, memory difficulties tend to form one of the greatest obstacles to successful rehabilitation. The efforts to date, relying heavily on controlled paired-associate learning tasks, have met with variable degrees of success and generally have not demonstrated any practical significance for their use.

The use of visual imagery, in which two verbal items are visualized in bizarre interaction with one another, has been a popular theme for improving encoding and recall of word lists and paired associates. Patten (1972) used this technique and a similar peg-word method successfully with four patients who suffered nontraumatic left hemisphere damage. Although the practical application of the methods taught were speculative, Patten reports a favorable by-product of this training in the form of improved patient self-esteem, confidence, and motivation. Three patients with global memory impairments, inability to form vivid images, poor awareness of their memory problems, and no associated interest in improving their memory could not benefit from training. In a more controlled study, using a mixed group of amnestic subjects, Kovner, Mattis, and Goldmier (1983) found that linking target words together in a highly ridiculous and bizarre story line was significantly superior for increasing the recall of words after a one-week delay than was a rote rehearsal strategy. Jones (1974) found that imagery could enhance the paired-associate recall of patients who had undergone left temporal lobe resection. Right temporal lobectomized patients generally performed as did normal subjects and therefore may simply have resorted to using their intact verbal encoding skills or rote memorization. Interestingly, two amnestic patients with bilateral temporal lobe removals did not benefit from imagery training. They had no difficulty generating visual images for the word pairs but generally forgot the images in addition to the words themselves.

Lewinsohn, Danaher, and Kikel (1977) taught a group of 19 patients, predominately CVA victims, to use bizarre interacting visual images to remember word lists and found significant improvements upon initial and 30-minute recall. However, no gains were noted after one week. A similar conclusion was reached by Cermak (1980) using a group of alcoholic Korsakoff's syndrome patients. Visual imagery tended to facilitate short-term storage and retrieval of paired associates, use of verbal labels, and short-term retention of nonverbal visual material. Semantic analysis of verbal material improved short-term performance on a verbal memory task. However, the effects of training were indeed transient, as patients required constant reminders of the specific mnemonic strategy they were supposed to be using or that one had been used at all. The author concludes that since these patients are likely to forget the mnemonic aid just as they are apt to forget the specific material for which the technique is being used, "attempts to improve their memory are not likely to produce long-term effects of critical therapeutic value" (p. 168).

Gasparrini and Satz (1979) report on two experiments designed to compare the effects of visual imagery training to those of rote memorization or semantic elaboration on paired-associate learning in a group of 30 left hemisphere–damaged males. The first experiment, comparing visualization to rote rehearsal, produced only one significant difference out of six dependent measures in favor of the imagery group: better performance on the paired-associate list used in training! In experiment 2, patients served as their own controls and were instructed in the use of visual imagery and semantic elaboration in a counterbalanced research design. The imagery condition was clearly superior in paired-associate learning.

Whereas most studies reported have provided subjects with extensive guidance in forming visual images and sentence construction, Binder and Schreiber (1980) merely gave subjects (recovering alcoholics) instructions to form their own mnemonic aid without being given the mediating link for pairs of words to be learned. The results suggested that for some subjects, simply telling them to form a sentence or imagine a picture of their own choosing can substantially improve performance on this type of task.

Using single-case methodology, Gianutsos and Gianutsos (1979) tested the effects of semantic elaboration training (teaching patients to embed words to be remembered in sentences and stories) with three patients suffering from right hemisphere cerebrovascular disorders and one congenitally brain-damaged, mildly retarded patient. Two features of this study make it unique. First was the incorporation of various interpolated reading tasks after the presentation of stimulus words to control for simple rehearsal. Second, initiation of treatment was staggered after initial baseline performance was obtained, in order to separate training and recovery effects. Although all individuals reportedly benefitted from training, outcome was quite variable, with better results associated with younger age, high motivation, more recent onset of disorder, better premorbid personal adjustment, and absence of aphasic symptoms.

Crovitz (1979) also used a semantic elaboration technique, his now well-known Airplane List, and reports generally favorable results in ensuring "deeper" encoding in two patients, one with alcoholic Korsakoff's syndrome and one with severe brain trauma. His impressionistic conclusions are subject to alternative interpretations, however. Both patients demonstrated total recall failure after a 30-minute delay. Extensive structural, phonetic and semantic cueing produced errorless performance for the Korsakoff's syndrome patient. The transcript of the closed head injured patient's cued performance was much less impressive, characterized by considerable perseveration and intrusion errors that basically resembled random guesswork. Placing his findings in perspective, Crovitz suggests that retraining not only should be directed at ensuring deep and elaborate encoding of material, but also should make external cueing available until the issue of training patients to cue themselves can be addressed.

Besides the Crovitz study, only a few other reported studies have attempted to address memory retraining in traumatic brain-injured persons specifically. Glasgow and his colleagues (1977) report on two such cases, both college students suffering mild neuropsychological deficits from head injuries sustained in automobile accidents. For one individual, retraining consisted of teaching her a study skill technique known as the PQRST approach. The acronym refers to a set of attending, self-probing, rehearsal, and organizational skills that can be applied to both written and auditorily presented information. Laboratory tasks clearly demonstrated the superior efficacy of this method compared to the patient's typical and unknown preintervention strategy. The other individual expressed difficulty in remembering the names of people whom he frequently encountered. Initially, a complex imagery procedure that included repetition, transformation of the name into a highly imaginable noun or nouns, selection of an outstanding feature of a person's face, and visually linking the transformed name to the facial feature was attempted but proved too complex and ineffective. A simplified strategy was then developed that involved having the patient write the names of people he had difficulty remembering on index cards and reading these cards three times a day while visualizing the person. This rehearsal method substantially reduced the number of names forgotten from average baseline levels of four names per day to less than one. Although the strategies used in both case studies required considerable amounts of time on the part of subjects, they nevertheless reveal considerable promise for remediating practical memory difficulties for certain types of clients.

Malec and Questad (1983) outline a memory retraining program built upon semantic elaboration, visual imagery, and self-generated questions used with a 27-year-old male with low-average full-scale IQ who sustained a traumatic head injury 12 weeks before training that lasted 6 weeks. Pre- and posttreatment neuropsychological test data revealed specific and significant improvements in memory areas but only minimal improvement on tests of other cognitive abilities. An important clinical observation was also reported: that the patient, toward the end of treatment, began to initiate spontaneous use of the techniques taught, a seemingly crucial element in the practical use of such techniques.

Finally, Laatsch (1983) provides a preliminary report on the effectiveness of a memory retraining program with a 16-year-old boy who suffered a traumatic brain injury 5 years earlier in a motor vehicle accident. Training activities are reported to have spanned the 1982–1983 school year. A unique feature of this program included attempts to teach the patient about his own memory, a sort of metamemory approach for increasing knowledge about one's memory. In addition, the patient was exposed to specific mnemonic strategies, including categorical clustering and organization, semantic elaboration, rehearsal, and visualization techniques. Although a significant and unexpected improvement was noted on a test of complex reasoning skills (Halstead Category Test), no significant changes occurred on posttraining measures of memory functions.

As the reader may have concluded, the literature on the effectiveness of memory rehabilitation is neither extensive nor conclusive. Variable and often limited gains are reported, in part stemming from the fact that many reports specifically address strengthening storage and virtually ignore the fact that memory is a fluid, dynamic process. For example, the Webster and Scott (1983) study reviewed earlier, found that memory deficits in their head-injured patient actually were related to a deficient prerequisite process, attention. Furthermore, variability of effectiveness may be related to characteristics of the trainee, since it appears that some minimal, as yet unspecified, level of functioning in the areas of memory, self-awareness, motivation, and goal directedness are prerequisites to successful employment of the techniques being taught. As an alternative to memory retraining, use of prosthetic memory aids, such as a central bulletin board, daily schedule, or memory notebook, may be helpful, although once again, spontaneous use of these aids may require the same prerequisites as stated above. We know many CHI patients with moderate frontal-lobe signs who carry their memory books, write in them daily, and rarely refer to them when appropriate to do so, having learned to use this aid on a relatively automatized level.

Yet for some head-injured patients, it may be possible to develop an artificial memory in the form of task algorithms that may relieve the patient from failure experiences and promote greater adaptation to changing circumstances (Gedye, 1968).

Obviously, further research is needed to answer more fully these and related questions. Specific attention needs to be directed at generalization issues and the practical memory demands of everyday living. Yet, it is encouraging to note the development of creative and innovative treatment programs that await validation.

Multifaceted Programs

The techniques reviewed above may find greater applicability in those individuals who exhibit exquisitely specific deficit areas. However, their isolated use with traumatic brain-injured patients may well be limited. Because of the interdependent constellation of cognitive, behavioral, and emotional problems (not to mention the physical and neurological disorders) associated with head injuries, it often is desirable to develop a comprehensive treatment program that incorporates to varying degrees all the therapeutic strategies listed in Figure 17.2. Such a treatment philosophy explicitly proposes that the synergistic effect of combined treatment efforts may far exceed the sum of its parts. This is not to say that every patient, irrespective of the extent of recovery, will benefit from the combined treatment efforts but, rather, that a multifaceted program ideally should be prepared to meet the changing needs of the individual as recovery unfolds (or arrests). For the moment, discussion of multifaceted programs will be limited to those aspects that emphasize cognitive skill rehabilitation. In a later section, we will discuss psychological issues pertinent to multidisciplinary teams.

Currently there is no sharp delineation as to what constitutes cognitive rehabilitation from the perspective of multifaceted programs. Auerbach (1983) notes that early in recovery from CHI, retraining activities basically are limited to eliciting and sustaining attention from the patient by using all sensory modalities, and establishing a system of communication by which to engage the patient. Such activities obviously rely heavily on appropriate environmental management. As improvements are noted, tasks may be developed to exercise the ability to appropriately shift attention. Matching and/or grouping tasks graded for difficulty may be appropriate. Even later in recovery, more complex tasks with greater demands for problem-solving abilities in an increasingly more distracting environment may be added. At this later stage, specific remedial techniques for learning new information, such as "chunking" and use of mnemonics, may be useful (Auerbach, 1983). However, even with seemingly advanced recovery, disordered attention and concentration may continue to constitute one of the major impediments to higher-level cognitive skill remediation (Ben-Yishay & Diller, 1983).

Perhaps the most innovative and certainly the most widely publicized work on multifaceted cognitive rehabilitation has been conducted in Israel and at the New York University Medical Center Institute of Rehabilitation Medicine (Ben-Yishay & Diller, 1983; Ben-Yishay, 1980, 1983; Ben-Yishay et al., 1978, 1979; Diller, 1976).

Espousing an extremely benevolent and supportive treatment philosophy, this program basically incorporates four types of interventions designed to treat the whole individual. These interventions include: (1) a series of generic cognitive remediation modules, (2) small group exercises in communication and interpersonal skills, (3) community activities, and (4) personal counseling. Training proceeds in a systematic, orchestrated fashion, first addressing generic skills and then extending to functional activities. Attempts are made to coordinate the various therapies to be mutually reinforcing, to provide maximum feedback to the patient, and to develop a therapeutic environment maximally conducive to improved functioning and adaptation.

The cognitive retraining modules have perhaps attracted the greatest attention from the rehabilitation community. Development and application of these techniques are based on the premise that traumatic brain injuries disturb basic generic skills that can be conceptualized along a continuum of complexity. These generic skills include orientation and arousal (attention, concentration, and vigilance), psychomotor skills (eye-hand coordination and dexterity), cognitive-perceptual integration (constructional skills), visual information processing skills, verbal-ideational skills, memory functions, and general interpersonal and communication skills. A hierarchy of specific tasks has been constructed for each of these areas. Since these tasks are too numerous to describe here in detail, only a few examples will be given. Attention, concentration, and vigilance tasks include having patients develop shorter response latencies in depressing a switch at the onset of a signal (i.e., reaction time) or attempt to anticipate and stop a moving target at a designated location by pressing a button. Eye-hand coordination tasks involve training on various adaptations of the Purdue Pegboard Test, nuts-and-bolts assembly tasks, or manual tool (pliers, scissors, screwdriver) usage. Cognitive-perceptual training may include block-design assembly using a saturation-cueing method, with extension to three-dimensional constructions. Training in visual scanning and paraphrasing written material may facilitate visual information processing skills. Verbal-ideational training activities include verbal concept formation along a continuum of more abstract categories, and learning to extract relevant information from complex situations and construct a telegram to summarize it. Memory retraining may proceed along lines described earlier.

Since human behavior and cognition obviously do not unfold within a vacuum, and given the importance of the personal, social, and vocational aspects of human existence, multifaceted programs recognize the need to extend the products of cognitive retraining into functionally relevant domains in which environmental influences become of paramount importance. Communication skills, for example, appear to rely heavily on the generic cognitive skills described above. To further enhance and develop these skills, small group activities in which role-playing and role-taking exercises, feedback, reinforcement, shaping, and therapist modeling are extensively utilized may be helpful (Ben-Yishay, 1980). Small cohesive groups also may exert beneficial peer pressure toward social conformity for the behaviorally disordered patient, a process referred to as "therapeutic leverage" (Ben-Yishay, 1980). A therapeutic milieu within the boundaries of the treatment setting may serve as a "proving ground" gradually approximating a more naturalistic uncontrolled environment for patients to refine and experiment with their developing skills, hopefully without the tragic and negative consequences characteristic of highly demanding everyday life. Prevocational explorations and training, emphasizing to a large extent effective interpersonal skills in addition to work habits and aptitudes may be included as well. Depending on progress made, actual trial occupational placement, on a gradual basis either within the host facility (when possible) or in cooperation with understanding and benevolent employers would appear to hold great promise for some. An extremely desirable feature of such programs, mandatory by some (e.g., Ben-Yishay et al., 1978, 1979), is a strong commitment on the part of family members to actively participate so that modifications in their behavior might increase the probability of developing a more supportive and mutually reinforcing environment. Finally, personal counselling or various other psychotherapeutic interventions (discussed more fully in a later section), may be called for to help manage the behavioral and emotional by-products of radically altered lifestyles.

Computer-Assisted Cognitive Rehabilitation

As it has in nearly all other areas of modern life, the microcomputer has entered the realm of rehabilitation, generating much enthusiasm among cognitive retrainers. A relatively new publication, *Cognitive Rehabilitation,* with its content advocating (often without restraint) the use of computer-based retraining methods, attests to this new wave of excitement. It is important to keep in perspective that the microcomputer is merely a tool for therapeutic activities that heretofore have been attempted using other, perhaps, less efficient methods. However, in the area of cognitive retraining, it has the potential to offer several distinct advantages not only to the patient but also to the therapist.

As a tool, the microcomputer has the capacity to offer greater accuracy, consistency, and flexibility in presentation of stimulus materials and in the recording of the trainee's responses. Commercially available educational and entertainment software, supplemented by a growing number of programs specially written for the neurologically impaired population, seems to require, challenge, or stimulate many of the cognitive functions that have been compromised as the result of traumatic brain injuries. Specifically, many programs appear to place a premium on attention, concentration, visual scanning, logical problem-solving skills, memory ability, and reasoning. Educational programs may be useful in upgrading impaired academic skill areas, provided that the format and presentation of material are not so obviously oriented to preschoolers so as to insult or demean the adult patient. For many patients, the novelty of working with a recent "invention," with all its intrigue and unusual displays, seems to heighten curiosity and attention, eliciting new motivation and interest to offset an otherwise monotonously repetitive therapy regimen.

The selection and development of appropriate software for use in cognitive retraining exercises requires considerable clinical judgment and intuition. Wilson (1983) has listed several important points to consider, including: (1) the difficulty and complexity of the task, (2) the degree to which it is possible to shift to different levels of complexity, (3) the flexibility in allowing the introduction of new items, (4) the ease and readability of instructions, (5) the consistency of the response format, (6) content appeal, (7) the amount of supervision required, (8) the type and informativeness of feedback given, (9) the degree of parameter control (e.g., speed of presentation, length of items, response latency intervals, display size), (10) how errors are handled (e.g., feedback, provisions for corrections or second chances), and (11) how data is kept and reported to the user.

Because it is a relatively new phenomenon on the treatment scene, only a few studies of computer-assisted training have appeared in print, although an appreciably larger number have been reported at various conferences and workshops. Those appearing in the literature usually report on case studies, show substantial variability in the extent to which subject variables and training regimens are adequately described, and generally have produced inconclusive results. Furthermore, since cognitive-based techniques usually are applied in the contexts of other treatment programs, it becomes difficult to ferret out the contributions, if any, of these treatment modalities.

Bracy (1983) reports on two cases, both receiving computer-based retraining, the details of which are not specified. One subject, a 12-year-old girl, following a severe head injury with a right-frontal impact focus and a 14-day barbiturate coma, began retraining 3.4 years after onset. Her major difficulties included severe visuoperceptual deficits; visuomotor incoordination; difficulties with math, spelling and memory; left hemispatial neglect; poor attention and concentration; and left side weaknesses. All other therapies except special education placement had terminated before the present one. Serial intelligence testing over the ensuing 1.25 years showed appreciable gains, especially in areas heavily dependent on academic experiences and visual discrimination.

The second case reported by Bracy (1983) involved a 32-year-old nurse who has suffered an embolic shower related to pericarditis, and a subsequent prolonged period of status epilepticus. Her major problems were listed as a right hemiparesis; visuoperceptual difficulties; right hemianopia; dyslexia; dyscalculia; conceptual problems; and difficulties with attention, initiation, and inhibition. A computer-based program emphasizing organizational skills for the treatment of memory disorders was initiated 3 years after onset, after all therapies except physical therapy had terminated. Serial psychometric tests of intelligence and memory showed major gains on tests of over-learned verbal skills, arithmetic reasoning, immediate auditory attention, and mental control. No pretraining data are reported for nonverbal manipulospatial tasks for reasons that are not described. Other tests from the WAIS-R and Wechsler Memory Scale did not show any appreciable change.

Parente and Anderson (1983) report on two subjects who were involved in a computer-based program emphasizing organizational skills for the treatment of memory disorders. Both subjects began training one year after onset and after being administered the Wechsler Memory Scale twice as baseline measures. Both showed significant gains on the posttraining testing, having raised their memory quotients 36 and 24 points, respectively, over baseline levels.

On the other hand, Laatsch (1983) found improved concept formation skills but no significant changes in measures of memory after a memory retraining program involving computer-based exercises and didactic instructions over an entire school year with a 16-year-old head trauma victim five years after onset.

While the value, contributions, and limitations of computerized retraining programs for the treatment of specific or generalized cognitive disorders have yet to be systematically and adequately explored, this general approach to treatment may be of considerable subjective emotional benefit for some patients. A sensitive testimonial written by Susan Graham (1983), herself a victim of a stroke at age 28, highlights the improved confidence, renewed optimism, and acceptance of one's situation related to progress observed on computer-training modules. For many patients unable to work after various cerebral injuries, a home-based computer rehabilitation program may provide something that is constructive, task-oriented, and emotionally therapeutic in an otherwise barren and idle existence.

In the course of computer-assisted cognitive retraining exercises, ample opportunities arise for the therapist to observe and intervene with the more psychological, in contrast to cognitive, issues that may emerge. Valuable insights into patients' attitudes and belief systems, expectations and frustrations, and coping patterns may be revealed during the course of retraining that may not be apparent in the consulting room. From a purely clinical standpoint, it is not uncommon during treatment to observe patients who expect too much or too little of themselves, who dislike being told what to do, or who otherwise attempt to use coping strategies that were relatively successful for them before injury but no longer are effective. Although seemingly strange bedfellows, computer training and psychotherapeutic intervention, which we conceptualize in aggregate as neuropsychological rehabilitation, may hold significant advantages clinically over either strategy alone in facilitating the monumental adjustment tasks faced by many patients.

Critique

Whether or not cognitive retraining programs will prove to have practical value in the treatment of closed head injuries (or other neurological disorders) requires further study. Although several reports suggest an affirmative answer to the question (e.g., Gianutsos & Gianutsos, 1979; Glasgow, Zeiss, Barrera, & Lewinsohn, 1977), others do not (e.g., Cermak, 1980; Lewinsohn, Danaher, & Kikel, 1977). Evaluation of the effectiveness of such procedures is very much a function of the criteria used to assess them. In this regard, Barth and Boll (1981) note that outcome measures of cognitive retraining methods often closely resemble the training tasks themselves, leaving unanswered the question of generalizability. This is simply not sufficient, and further research is needed to determine if one is actually restoring "cognition" or merely training a specific behavioral facsimile. In essence, greater attention needs to be directed toward the effects of retraining on meaningful classes of behavior.

Cognitive retraining as a therapeutic modality has yet to come of age, and, as noted with other interventions for brain-injured patients, remains at present in the technique-building phase of development. Besides questions of effectiveness and generalizability, other research questions bearing on its utility need to be raised and addressed in more carefully controlled studies. Since recovery from traumatic brain injuries must be conceptualized in terms of years and not months, future studies need to control for the potential confounding effect of spontaneous recovery, a problem common to literally all treatment outcome research. Phrased in a slightly different way, does cognitive retraining facilitate a more rapid recovery to some unspecified plateau of functioning that would otherwise come about over a longer period of time without retraining? Additionally, the extent to which specific retraining exercises potentiate or add something new and unique to existing programs that place various cognitive demands on the patient in a less systematic fashion remains to be addressed. Along similar lines, in the context of multifaceted programs, are reported gains related specifically to the cognitive retraining methods; to nonspecific components of the program, such as encouragement, reinforcement, suggestion, or alleviation of emotional interferences; or to some combination? It is our belief that the complementarity of the elements of a multifaceted program provides the most sound clinical approach to remediating cognitive deficits. Finally, it is important to recognize the limitations of examining any outcome in isolation. Outcome of retraining is more fully and appropriately understood in relation to the amount of intervention necessary to achieve that outcome. Hence, greater attention should be directed to examining not only outcome but also process variables, such as acquisition curves under massed or distributed training trials.

Based on the accumulated research to date, it appears that the characteristics of the trainee weigh heavily in contributing to the success of cognitive retraining. When information is reported about trainee characteristics, it is clear that, to benefit from training, most subjects function at a relatively advanced state of recovery or possess sufficiently intact functions. Subjects in the report of Glasgow, Zeiss, Barrera, and Lewinsohn (1977) on memory retraining were college students with average to bright-average psychometric intelligence and Halstead Impairment Ratings indicative of mild neuropsychological deficits. The mean IQ of amnestic subjects in the study of Kovner, Mattis, and Goldmeier (1983) was 110. Webster and Scott (1983) successfully taught self-instructional techniques to compensate for attentional deficits in a CHI patient who possessed sufficient verbal memory and linguistic skills to benefit from the strategy. Finally, criteria for participating in the program of Ben-Yishay and colleagues (1979, 1981, 1983) are quite rigorous, including a minimum IQ of 80 on either the WAIS Verbal or Performance Scale (having been raised from an earlier level of 75); no history of significant psychiatric problem, drug or alcohol abuse, or sociopathy; independent self-care living skills; stamina to participate five hours per day, four days a week; and no more than moderate aphasia or dysarthria. From these data and our own experiences, the most likely candidates for cognitive retraining are those well beyond the confused level of functioning, as depicted in Figure 17.2. While further research may determine other patient characteristics conducive to retraining exercises, persistent frontal lobe signs indicating impoverished ability to form stable intentions and plans necessary for control over subsequent behavior also seem to lessen the effectiveness of this mode of treatment. It would not be surprising if differences in the generalizability of the retraining efforts were related to differences in the severity of compromised frontal lobe functions, although such a statement awaits further validation.

At present, there are no agreed-upon standards as to who is qualified to plan, carry out, and evaluate the effectiveness of cognitive retraining. At a minimum, formal coursework in the neurosciences, neuropsychology, human information processing, memory, perception, and experimental methods seems to be required. Unfortunately, we are aware that there are many would-be retrainers who have few if any of these basic prerequisites and instead simply buy a computer and plug it in. The basic issues are related to quality assurance, professional integrity, and consumer protection. Vulnerable, uninformed families desperate for long-term help for a severely impaired member frequently have turned to the new "cognitive retraining centers" opening up throughout the country in hopes of finding additional assistance, only later to come away bitter and dejected over false promises alluded to in well-worded announcements. As one father of a severely impaired young man commented, "J. J. became quite good at shooting down Martians.... If only we could teach him to tie his shoes and ask for the urinal." The point is that if this mode of treatment is to remain viable and credible, practitioners of the art must exercise professional restraint as to whom they admit for training or at least avoid false claims of effectiveness by carefully delineating the limitations in our present knowledge and the need for further research. For over two decades of research on cognitive retraining methods, the resounding message has been a call for further research. Some apparently have become desensitized to it. Our intention here is not to dampen enthusiasm for this potentially powerful therapeutic modality but, rather, to stimulate further developments in the field by describing where we have been and where we must go.

PSYCHOTHERAPEUTIC INTERVENTIONS

After suffering a severe closed head injury six months earlier, resulting in a 12-day coma and mild residual cognitive deficits, one female patient in her mid-twenties commented that she would have rather broken every bone in her body than to have had a head injury. This comment was made despite the fact that this patient had made an excellent recovery and was preparing to resume her previous job, and seems to reflect in part the emotional distress that many brain trauma victims experience consequent to fuller appreciation of the importance of cerebral functions in adapting to environmental demands.

Any professional who has worked in a rehabilitation setting can attest to the emotional distress (anger, depression, anxiety, and loss in self-esteem and confidence) and the various strategies used by patients to cope with the fears and threats associated with significant acquired physical and mental disorders. As a preliminary step, however, it is necessary to distinguish between emotional reactions secondary to some awareness of altered function and emotional disorders that are the product of some central nervous system lesion (Valenstein & Heilman, 1979). In this section, we will not attempt to unravel this complicated diagnostic issue but, rather, will focus on those emotional consequences of brain injuries that become the target for psychotherapy of one form or another.

The need for psychotherapeutic interventions in rehabilitation settings in general recently has been explored in a number of studies. Gans (1980) found that 28% of 100 patients in consecutive psychiatric consultations in a rehabilitation hospital manifested some type of clinical depression, two-thirds of which were either wholly or partially reactive to the patients' disability. In eight other cases in which the consultation involved suspected depression, the patients' feelings were judged to be appropriate for the condition, situation, and stage of rehabilitation. In another six cases, psychiatric symptoms of depression did not appear to be psychologically meaningful reactions but were judged to be manifestations of mental changes secondary to the neurological condition (e.g., dementia, Parkinson's disease, stroke, frontal lobe syndrome) or medication reactions. Missel (1978) observed that over a one-year period, 15% of requests for psychiatric consultation in a rehabilitation facility were related to concerns over suicidal risks. Besides the rapid appearance of emotional crises during the acute and subacute phases of recovery, secondary emotional disorders may unfold in a delayed, more chronic fashion with emergent awareness and in the process of concrete reality testing outside the confines of a protective environment. Fordyce, Roueche, and Prigatano (1983) found that chronic head-injured patients (more than six months post onset) demonstrated greater emotional distress in the form of anxiety, depression, social isolation, and confusion than did patients less than six months post onset, independent of differences in neuropsychological abilities between the groups. Lezak (1978) also points out that subtle problems with fatigue, distractibility, and perplexity are perhaps the most common and troublesome consequences of brain injuries in adults, often leading to secondary emotional difficulties that may be prevented with adequate preparation and counselling.

As early as 1956, Muller and Naumann recommended the combination of early ambulation and psychotherapy (guidance, reassurance, suggestion, and short-term psychoanalytically oriented therapy) for the treatment of closed head injuries after the patient becomes lucid. They present some interesting data suggesting that such a program may significantly prevent the development of a prolonged postconcussional syndrome by reducing secondary nervousness and restlessness in patients for whom dizziness and headaches do not run the usual course. Despite the fact that the benefits of psychotherapy in the treatment of traumatic brain injuries have not been well documented, such interventions are increasingly being recognized as vital components of comprehensive rehabilitation services, especially in view of the significant adjustment issues faced by patients at different stages in their recovery.

Psychotherapy with brain-injured adults necessitates explicit recognition of several crucial issues that differentiates it from traditional psychotherapeutic work with the so-called functional disorders. First, Barth and Boll (1981) remind us that the behavior displayed by persons with central nervous system damage may not be seen as equivalent to the same behavior displayed by neurologically intact persons in the context of psychotherapy. In this context, Goldstein (1936, 1944) construes many of the psychological symptoms (e.g., fatigue, perseveration, denial) following brain injury as protective mechanisms serving to facilitate adaptation, avoid failures, and forestall catastrophic anxiety. In contrast, traditionally held defense mechanisms are viewed as means of coping with anxiety over conflicts that originate in the individual's life history. Small (1973) argues that the therapist must reconceptualize symptoms of psychopathology in brain-injured patients by taking into account deficits in higher cognitive function and should avoid overinterpretation. Impaired memory is not necessarily a symptom of repression. Compulsive behavior may not always arise from intrapsychic conflicts but may stem from an inability to shift and deal with an ever-changing environment, a form of compensatory stereotype. Regression to earlier forms of behavior may be the direct result of impaired higher-order cognitive and integrative functions, not necessarily a response to a psychologically traumatizing event. Leftoff (1983) also argues that the development of paranoid thinking following brain dysfunction can be viewed as the product of a cognitive-perceptual disorder, the compensatory attempts of the individual to make sense of deranged perceptions, and a way of reasserting a sense of importance to oneself when self-esteem is particularly threatened. Denial of disability can be conceptualized in a similar fashion, not only representing the product of impaired cognitive functions necessary to achieve detailed awareness but also serving to protect the psychological integrity of the individual by limiting the influx of potentially devastating information.

Second, the nature and severity of cognitive deficits associated with traumatic brain injuries have significant implications for who may be appropriate candidates for psychotherapy. Obviously, severe memory disorders, severe apathy, and confusion would preclude ability to benefit from traditional psychotherapy. At some point, defined either by level of severity or stage of recovery, psychotherapy may indeed be indicated, as illustrated in Figure 17.2. Behavioral approaches conceivably could be included under the rubric of psychotherapy, but we have chosen to deal with this mode of intervention separately.

A further consideration concerns the timing of intervention and the associated objectives of treatment. Generally speaking, psychotherapeutic strategies can be conceptualized as primary preventive, emphasizing education and preparation for changed life-styles; secondary strategies, including early detection and crisis intervention, to keep emotional reactions and maladaptive patterns from escalating; and tertiary care, addressing the substantial and chronic emotional pathology. In this regard, Nichols (1979) observes that it is frequently the case that a patient must demonstrate significant deterioration and show a rather obvious psychiatric disorder before intervention is initiated. Greater efforts directed at prevention and early detection may be more efficient and more humane for those who have to struggle with significant cognitive deficits and psychological losses related to brain injury.

It is a common clinical observation that many traumatic brain-injured patients, in the early stages of recovery, are seemingly oblivious to their situation and consequently show relatively little subjective distress beyond shallow irritability. If such patients begin to improve, becoming more acutely aware of the implications of their injuries, a curious recovery paradox is noted. These patients begin to look better functionally and cognitively but at the same time start to subjectively feel worse, experiencing more anxiety, depression, fear, and worry. Often these problems may not surface in full-blown fashion while a patient is in an inpatient setting where enthusiastic staff, with attendant hope and optimism, contagiously help to forestall emotional difficulties. As a result of and based on a relatively successful mastery of the benevolent and structured hospital routine, many patients receive some degree of reinforcement of their extended denial and come to overestimate their adaptive capabilities. However, secondary emotional distress may arise when such patients leave the hospital and find themselves unable to cope successfully with the more complex and ever changing demands of everyday life. The maladaptive effects of denial, leading a patient to ignore reality and engage in emotionally risky endeavors that carry only a small probability of success, are frequently reinforced by family and friends, who may overtly or covertly communicate to the patient that life will once again be as it was before the injury (Rosenthal, 1983). Although attempts usually are made to prepare the patient psychologically for the realities that lie ahead after discharge, many fail to heed this rather abstract information. Unfortunate as it may seem, some patients seem more likely to accept therapeutic interventions once they have had a chance to concretely test reality for themselves. As a result, psychotherapeutic interventions may take the form of preventive educational programs before development of distress, crisis interventions based on early detection, or more long-term involvement sometimes indicated in the chronic adaptation stages.

A comprehensive text on psychotherapy with brain-injured persons has yet to be written. Various techniques and general approaches have been described, all of which have as their general goals the alleviation of emotional pain and distress, the promotion of a more healthy and productive adaptation, and the acceptance of what Ben-Yishay (1980) calls the "existential dilemma": maintenance of a sense of self-worth in the face of significant cognitive, physical, personal, and vocational losses. Above all else, we explicitly recognize that the success of the approaches to be described below rests in large part on the interpersonal and clinical skills of the therapist, the ability to actively engage the patient, and the accurate conceptualization of the patient's difficulties.

In dealing with the partial death caused by traumatic brain injury, Muir (1979) makes explicit use of neuropsychological test data to help attenuate the insecurity and uncertainty patients frequently experience. Combining educational and supportive approaches, feedback to the patient as to which functions may be damaged and which are spared seems to decrease the confusion and sense of disorder, and may promote greater acceptance on the part of the patient. Furthermore, engaging the patient in cognitive retraining exercises often results in the devotion of a great deal of time to discussion of psychological and psychosocial issues.

A somewhat different approach was taken by Leftoff (1983) with a 39-year-old executive who suffered a left hemisphere cerebrovascular accident and later developed blatant paranoid constructions. Conceptualizing the paranoia as a product of misinterpreted reality secondary to cognitive-perceptual dysfunction and the ensuing compensatory strategies of the patient designed to protect his sense of importance and worth, a therapeutic strategy was devised based on a cognitive relearning-restructuring model. Treatment proceeded by helping the patient understand his difficulty in shifting mental perspective and to learn to adopt the framework of other people. Compensating for his deficit involved learning to formulate alternative hypotheses and explanations for the behavior of other persons and understanding the importance of consensual validation for one's interpretations. Activities generally included social learning techniques and role playing along a hierarchy of tasks beginning with neutral situations. Therapy continued for one year, with significant improvements noted in the patient's ability to accept alternative explanations and to evaluate his own interpretations, although when angry or stressed, he reverted to his self-referential stance.

Ben-Yishay (1983) tends to emphasize a general approach to psychotherapy with brain-injured patients that relies heavily on various tenets from social learning theories. Specifically, the primary focus of treatment is on changing overt behaviors, which leads to secondary changes in attitudes and beliefs. (An excellent review of this general orientation as contrasted with traditional psychotherapy can be found in Goldstein & Simonson, 1979.) Therapy takes on a very directive tone and usually takes place in small group settings. The objectives of treatment are to induce the patient: (1) to accept coaching in the presence of others, usually by persuasion and exhortation; (2) to follow examples set by the therapist and other patients; (3) to behave in prescribed ways and change various targeted behaviors; (4) to endorse and engage in the prescribed behaviors publicly; (5) to publicly state his or her sincerity; and (6) to make a public commitment to practice new behaviors until the act has become a new habit. While recognizing that higher-level patients may benefit from traditional "insight-oriented" therapy, Ben-Yishay notes that most brain-injured patients are poorly suited for the cognitive demands of such an approach and recommends this behavioral-focused method as an alternative.

The use of group psychotherapeutic modalities for brain-injured patients has gained wide acceptance in recent years, despite no systematic research showing its effectiveness. Yet, clinically, there appears to be considerable sentiment in the therapeutic community supporting its benefits. In general, group therapy usually embodies both an educational and a supportive objective. Educationally, topics for discussion may include presentations on what a head injury is, how the brain works and what various symptoms mean, managing depression, and general problem-solving schemes. The emotionally supportive aspects of group experiences need little elaboration but often include reassurance, a sense that one is not alone in one's plight, a sense of being able to help others through benevolent advice giving, and general cathartic experiences by which ventilation and understanding are achieved. The group also may provide patients with a common reference and resource, engendering a sort of new identity, given the drastic personal losses resulting from brain injuries. Peer pressure and reinforcement also can supply powerful incentive for constructive behavior changes. Finally, as Ben-Yishay (1980) notes, group settings provide the ideal medium for practicing, refining, and reacquiring basic interpersonal communication skills. However, a final word of caution is in order. Just as group psychotherapy may not be indicated and may actually be harmful for some functionally disordered patients (Bedmar & Lawlis, 1971), group involvement may be contraindicated for some brain-injured patients. Specifically, patients with severe acting-out tendencies may only be further alienated by a group experience if their behavior proves resistant to group pressures. Furthermore, group therapy may pose added risks to patients who are easily confused, extremely vulnerable to anxiety, or ultrasensitive to corrective feedback unless special precautions are taken to structure group interactions. The ultimate decision as to which patients are likely candidates for group experiences rests with the judgment and experience of the clinician.

It is obvious that further work needs to be done in the area of psychotherapeutic interventions with traumatic brain-injured patients. Longitudinal studies are needed to examine the ultimate adjustment patterns of chronic patients. One area that requires further development is related to crisis intervention techniques. We have observed on several occasions that a seemingly good adaptation is temporarily shattered as the result of some crisis that comes at a time that reawakens the original loss for the patient. Often this is connected with being fired from a job, discharge from extended treatment services, the anniversary date of one's accident, the death of a friend or relative, or some other failure that essentially recreates the despair and hopelessness experienced at an earlier stage of recovery. All too often, patients may be referred to local mental health facilities, where their problems are inaccurately conceptualized as a functional or neurotic manifestation instead of the product of impaired cognitive processes, fragile coping skills, and the residual emotional scars of the original trauma. Creation of a calm, deliberate, and reassuring environment, coupled with permission to ventilate one's fears and a future-oriented exploration of alternatives, appears helpful as an initial measure. If assessment suggests the risk of self-injurious behavior or suicidal intent, such as a wish to join a dead relative, appropriate safety precautions should be implemented without hesitation.

REHABILITATION AT THE TEAM LEVEL

Reports of neuropsychological rehabilitation programs usually implicitly (e.g., Horton & Howe, 1981) or explicitly (Muir et al., 1983) emphasize the importance of well-coordinated team approaches. We are aware of no literature critical of the team approach or suggesting that it is not the approach of choice. However, despite unanimous positive regard for the team approach, there appears to be little detailed analysis of exactly what constitutes an ideal team, how personnel become qualified for team membership, how team members divide and share responsibility, and who leads the team.

Goldstein and Ruthven (1983) provide a preliminary exploration of several of the issues cited above. They directly address the issue of team leadership by unequivocally advocating that the team leader be a "*clinical neuropsychologist* or *behavioral neurologist.*" Not surprisingly, they also suggest that the team leader be an "effective administrator" with egalitarian management style, good communication skills, and the acumen to run a financially sustainable program. Regarding staffing pattern, these authors state: "The staffing pattern of a rehabilitation program should include a neurobehavioral specialist, a physician, a group of rehabilitation specialists including a speech pathologist, occupational therapist and a line staff that is trained to perform more than the traditional nursing or educational duties. Such training may be in the area of behavior therapy, or more specifically in the application of specialized rehabilitation techniques and strategies to brain-damaged patients" (p. 97). These authors also outline a curriculum to be used for in-service training of team members. The curriculum emphasizes behavioral neuroscience and behavior therapy.

The team as described and conceptualized by Goldstein and Ruthven (1983) represents one of many possible model teams. This raises several difficult and as yet unresolved issues. The general belief that team treatment is the approach of choice rests almost exclusively on clinical judgment and at least to some extent is a reflection of institutional habits in matters of patient care. There is no body of research comparing one team configuration to another or comparing team treatment to specific single-discipline treatments. Moreover, reports of programs in which the team approach is emphasized and strongly advocated (e.g., Ben-Yishay, et al., 1978) tend to be detailed regarding treatment procedures but vague regarding team membership and team operation issues. An excellent example of this is the report of Crain (1982), in which a comprehensive, detailed, and admirably thoughtful treatment program is described, with all aspects of treatment decision making and specific procedures explicated in detail, but the personnel providing treatment are never described and are simply referred to as "we."

It perhaps is unreasonable to expect questions regarding team treatment to be answered during the present very early stages in the evolution of neuropsychological rehabilitation as a clinical service. At the same time, the questions are inescapable. Teams *are* providing treatment in many centers throughout the country and world. Various disciplines, such as speech pathology, occupational therapy, psychiatry, psychiatrics, neurology, special education, and psychology are entering the treatment arena and attempting to establish themselves as legitimate treatment providers. Attendant to the influx of these diverse disciplines are issues of defining roles, clinical prerogatives, and disciplinary domains. Currently operating teams also are experiencing dynamic issues in their relationships with patients and families, and it is not premature to address issues such as burnout or even hatred (Gans, 1983). Thus, while it is often difficult to know exactly what is meant when talking about the treatment team, such discussion is urgently needed.

Using the remarks above as a caveat regarding the current limitations of in-depth analysis of team treatment, there are several issues that can be explored in some detail.

Team Activities

The single most frequent staff activity in a rehabilitation setting is teaching (Bleiberg & Merbitz, 1983). Therapeutic services provided by speech, physical, occupational, and other therapists consist essentially of efforts to assist brain-injured persons to learn or relearn skills. Although numerous authors have conceptualized rehabilitation using a learning model, and Bleiberg and Merbitz (1983) have provided empirical demonstration, the learning model has not been an explicit core around which rehabilitation efforts have been organized. Rather, because rehabilitation programs historically have been under medical sponsorship and leadership, the medical model has predominated, and the learning model, though always implicitly present, has been obscured.

The confounding of conceptual models has caused particular problems for the development of team treatment. Most brain-injured patients are initially in clinical settings in which the medical model is mandatory. As the medical problems are resolved or stabilized, treatment issues focus on modifying the patient's behavioral repertoire, and the learning model becomes most appropriate. Confounding of models begins on admission to the rehabilitation hospital, where frequently the patient has continuing needs for medical management and treatment but at the same time has achieved sufficient medical progress that behavioral factors require and are amenable to intervention. The treatment team in the rehabilitation hospital or unit thus must proceed from the outset with both models interwoven.

Although both models are operating, frequently the medical model is explicit and the learning model implicit. Treatment personnel conceptualize and organize their efforts around the explicit model, even while pursuing activities subsumed by the implicit model. As the patient achieves greater medical stability, behavioral issues gradually become the primary focus of treatment, and the learning model would be the logical framework for organizing the therapeutic program. However, because the learning model rarely is made explicit, this does not happen, and teaching-learning interventions are pursued by a team lacking the conceptual framework and organizational structure for pursuing such interventions effectively. These remarks are in no way intended as a criticism of the medical model: it is without question the necessary first step in the treatment of brain-injured persons. Our point is that a learning model and a treatment team based on such a model constitute an equally necessary second step.

Thus, one method of organizing a treatment team is for the team members to view themselves as therapists with a common focus on teaching and learning. Several implications follow, some of which have been identified by Goldstein and Ruthven (1983). Team members are better able to transcend narrow disciplinary views of the patient: rather than seeing the patient as an ambulation problem, a dressing problem, a feeding problem, and a floor management problem, they focus on treatment of the underlying cognitive and behavioral deficits. Explicit adoption of a learning model also permits team members more readily to view their therapies as teaching and behavior change endeavors and thereby more readily to utilize the substantial existing body of knowledge and technique in the areas of effective teaching methods, human learning (and learning deficits associated with brain damage), behavior modification, and milieu treatment. Improved access to the learning model is not a trivial accomplishment, since many therapeutic disciplines, such as physical and occupational therapy and nursing, do not routinely emphasize teaching and learning in their academic and professional training programs.

Another advantage of explicit adoption of the learning model is that it provides the members of diverse disciplines on the rehabilitation team with a common data language. As detailed elsewhere in this chapter, outcome research for brain injury rehabilitation efforts has not been compelling, and our impression is that one reason for the scarcity of good research in this area is that the clinical work often is done by a heterogeneous group of professionals lacking a common conceptual framework and therefore a common data language.

The learning model also clarifies the role of the psychologist or, optimally, the neuropsychologist. First, the psychologist should assist the team in identifying those aspects of a patient's program in which the learning model is relevant or, as sometimes happens, to clarify that what the team already is doing fits a learning model. The psychologist then can serve as a resource in the areas of behavior modification, human learning and cognition, neuropsychology, and research and evaluation design. Having the team members conceptualize their efforts around a learning model helps them to understand the ways in which the psychologist can assist them and facilitates the psychologist's service as a useful consultant, in addition to the direct patient-care provided by the psychologist.

We have not addressed the issues of team leadership and qualifications for team membership. When the patient's clinical condition requires treatment within the medical model, these issues have well-defined answers: the physician is the leader, and the team members have various forms of accreditation or licensing for their respective disciplines. Once treatment enters the learning model, however, standards and precedents evaporate, and it would not be an overstatement to describe the situation as a clinical free-for-all. Currently, one becomes a "cognitive therapist" or "cognitive retrainer" by self-proclamation.

Various arguments can be mounted for why one discipline or another should be included on the team or have leadership. The danger in promulgating such arguments is that they risk becoming self-serving and territorial. A second danger is that, even when the arguments are sound at a general level, they may be misleading at the individual practitioner level. For example, a convincing case can be made that psychologists should lead the team. However, at the individual practitioner level, the choice may be between a psychologist trained primarily to perform long-term dynamic psychotherapy and a speech pathologist with extensive training in neuroscience and years of direct clinical experience with brain-injured patients.

Given the current absence of standards and accepted practices, and the enormous individual variation in training and experience among personnel of different disciplines, it is premature to draw conclusions regarding team membership and leadership. This is not to say that such conclusions are not possible and will not be made in the future. The field of education has been able to establish standards and criteria for personnel training and competence, and to define roles and responsibilities. Viewing rehabilitation of brain-injured patients using a learning model would likely facilitate similar developments.

Staff-Patient Interactions

Despite the many remaining unresolved issues regarding treatment teams, the fact of the matter is that such teams exist and provide care to patients. These teams have evolved organizational structures and role assignments, and, although they may vary widely one from the other, they have in common a commitment to improving the behavioral outcome for brain-injured persons. These teams also share exposure to common stresses associated with their work.

Learned helplessness (Seligman, 1975) is a concept often used to explain depression in patients. It is an equally appropriate concept for understanding distress experienced by treatment teams. Treatment teams are vulnerable to experiencing helplessness in all aspects of their work. They may deliver their services with consummate skill, dedication, and compassion, yet the patient may show no benefit whatsoever, be entirely unappreciative of their efforts, and sometimes not even remember the efforts or the personnel making them. Families undergoing massive disruption from having a head-injured member look to the team for a "cure" that the team knows may not be forthcoming to the degree or extent hoped for by the family, or sometimes the team is aware that the patient has subtle but very significant deficits not likely to be noticed by the family until after discharge and anticipates the family's distress upon eventually perceiving such deficits and their implications. Some team members are highly aware of the great expense incurred by families and wonder if the results of treatment justify the high costs. Such self-doubts are amplified by segments of the medical community and insurance carriers who question the efficacy of treatment or simply reject it as having no proven value. These are but a few of the factors stimulating feelings of helplessness in the team.

In many areas of medical treatment, the probable efficacy or benefit of a therapeutic procedure is known beforehand. In rehabilitation of brain-injured patients, however, the methods are recently developed, and convincing studies of efficacy are scarce. Team members employ these methods and in many cases devise entirely novel and untested methods in a sincere and ethical attempt to provide patients with the best treatment possible. However, the methods remain sufficiently experimental, and our basic knowledge of brain function and recovery from brain damage remains sufficiently incomplete that team members are highly vulnerable to feelings of self-doubt, incompetence, and dejection that their efforts, which sometimes border on the heroic, "do not make a difference."

Psychologists, psychiatrists, and other behavioral scientists on the team can be very useful in helping the team to manage feelings of helplessness and particularly in promoting adaptive, rather than maladaptive, responses to helplessness. Competence in neuropsychology is essential, and the psychologist must have credibility and the team's confidence in this regard. Such credibility permits the psychologist to reassure the team that treatment procedures reflect the state of the art and at least are conceptually and theoretically sound, even if unproven. Neuropsychological evaluation further reassures the team that deficits have been identified and that treatment is focused on the patient's areas of need. Neuropsychological evaluation and other empirical methods of the psychologist also assist the team with objective measures of a patient's progress. Moreover, in a broader context, the psychologist can assist the team in developing an empirical attitude and in incorporating evaluation and experimental design with the overall treatment effort. Besides having obvious scientific impact, this can assist the team emotionally by counterbalancing feelings of helplessness with feelings of optimism that additional and new knowledge is being generated and that team members are working instrumentally to address the root causes of their helplessness.

A second broad front on which the psychologist can assist the team is in promoting adaptive, rather than maladaptive, responses to helplessness. Gans (1983, 1979) and Gunther (1979, 1977) have analyzed this issue extensively and provide recommendations useful to the psychologist or other behavioral scientist on the team. To implement these recommendations effectively, the psychologist, in addition to having the neuropsychological skills noted above, also must be competent in clinical psychology. Note that the description that is evolving of the characteristics of the psychologist is consistent with the competencies emphasized by Meier (1981).

Gans (1983) explores in detail a number of maladaptive responses to helplessness, of which the primary response is graphically summarized in the title of his paper, "Hate in the Rehabilitation Setting." Gans views the team's helplessness as an assault to their self-image and self-esteem: "They feel guilty over what they assume is a personal deficiency in their healing ability." Feelings of guilt, ineffectiveness, and outright incompetence are painful for staff to tolerate, and the patient may in overt or disguised ways come to be hated. Generally, overt hatred is rarely seen because it is not a socially acceptable public response in the rehabilitation setting and because the conscious experience of hatred of a patient is inconsistent with the self-image of most team members and, when experienced, only intensifies their feelings of failure and guilt.

Disguised feelings of hatred are far more prevalent, and Gans (1983) describes several mechanisms. Projection is a common mechanism and fits readily into the rehabilitation setting because brain-injured patients frequently *do* express hatred of the team, and sometimes do so quite freely and with great verbal and physical vigor. The team thus has an already prepared setting in which to focus on how much the patient hates *them* and to translate this into concerns about the patient's poor motivation or poor cooperation with treatment. Displacement is another mechanism, and the team may become angry at one of its members, at the treating physician or team leader, at a member of the patient's family who may be meddlesome or indifferent, or at the hospital administration. Alternatively, the team may react by redoubling its efforts and pursuing unrealistically ambitious or heroic treatment efforts as a reaction formation.

Another reaction to helplessness is a simple withdrawal. Team members may withdraw their investment, energy, and enthusiasm. They may experience fatigue, lower their criteria for when they are sick enough to stay home from work, and generally show signs of depression. Depending on the psychological makeup of individual team members, this burnout will progress in the direction of increased personal distress for the team member or increased psychological abandonment of the distressing situation. Either direction leads ultimately to increased staff turnover and lowered moral.

The stresses and pressures to which the team is subject indicate the need for the psychologist to provide appropriate consultation to the team in addition to providing clinical services to patients. Lipowski (1977) and Gunther (1979) have described the consultation process, with emphasis on promoting the team's insight regarding the way patients make them feel and the way team members react and respond to these feelings. Countertransference issues may appear to be remote in the context of rehabilitating motor, sensory, and cognitive disturbances, but Gunther (1977) and Gans (1983) provide a compelling demonstration to the contrary.

Helping the team to cope adaptively with helplessness requires, as a necessary first step, that the psychologist be able to identify and tolerate his or her own feelings of helplessness and be able to conceptualize the factors and processes involved in helplessness, whether such conceptualization be behavioral (Seligman, 1975) or psychodynamic (Gunther, 1977). For example, it is our observation that a frequent defense mechanism of psychologists working with brain-injured patients is intellectualization, usually derived from mature scientific curiosity regarding brain functioning but frequently placed in the service of emotional protection from the terrifying empathic identification with the patient. Intellectualization may serve as a useful and entirely appropriate mechanism for the research neuropsychologist who has no additional role obligations that conflict with viewing the patient as a human experimental preparation. Psychologists with clinical responsibilities to treatment teams, however, have the additional obligation and burden of self-awareness regarding their reactions to the life-altering events experienced by patients. Such self-awareness forms the basis for modeling adaptive responses to helplessness for the rest of the team and for understanding the specific dynamics of a given team's reaction to a specific patient.

Note that insight into the team's defense mechanisms does not imply that the psychologist must work to have the team abandon those mechanisms. Rather, insight permits the psychologist to monitor adaptive, protective, and ultimately productive uses of defenses, as opposed to maladaptive and ultimately painful and nonproductive uses. For example, intellectualization can lead the team to become better informed regarding neuroscience, human learning, rehabilitation techniques, and research methods, and thereby *productively* address the team's feelings of helplessness. However, if the team, for example, is confronting a situation in which, despite their best efforts, the patient and family are experiencing a tragic outcome that the team is helpless to alter, their excessive intellectualization may obstruct the team's effective functioning. This might take the form of the team's focusing intently on the "interesting" nature of the patient's lesion and consequent behavioral deficits, and not focusing enough on the more clinically compelling issues of the family's emotional needs for support and empathy. The team later may be puzzled because, although they are giving the patient the benefit of the most sophisticated neuroscience knowledge available, the family is in great distress and feels that the team has been cold and callous. Moreover, the team at some level is aware that they have failed in their clinical mission, and the resulting feelings of helplessness cannot be delayed indefinitely.

A more adaptive response in the example described above would be for the psychologist to assist the team in acknowledging their feeling of helplessness. This might be unpleasant, but the unpleasantness would be mitigated by group support and consensual validation. Further, because the feelings have become a topic for "public" discussion, the realistic basis for those feelings can be reviewed, and the sense of helplessness can be divested of the personal distortions given it by individual team members (e.g., "I'm incompetent," "If only I knew more about neuroanatomy, I'd be a better therapist," "I wish families would get more realistic and stop making unreasonable demands," etc.). Reduction in such distortions would permit improved empathic understanding of the family, which in turn might lead to effective clinical interventions directed toward the family. Should such interventions prove effective (frequently they are the most effective of the various interventions in the case of severely brain-injured patients with poor outcome), then the team will have reduced its sense of helplessness *realistically* by virtue of having identified a sphere for potentially successful intervention. Note that the identification of such a sphere first involved a painful component of empathy.

We hope that the foregoing discussion has provided a glimpse of the complexities of the psychologist's role, as well as its importance, and has demonstrated the importance of the psychologist's being a competent clinical psychologist as well as a neuropsychologist. We have treated the dual roles of the psychologist as residing within one person, which is consistent with the training and competency model proposed by Meier (1981). In settings where this model is not possible, the roles may be divided among personnel according to area of competency. The subtleties of consultation to treatment teams were merely hinted at, and the reader is referred to Gunther (1977, 1979) and Gans (1979, 1983) for a more detailed discussion of the issues.

FAMILY TREATMENT

Head injury affects not only the patient but the entire family and social system. The effects are quite negative and disruptive, although there are data to document the rare case in which the family perceives the head injury to have produced a beneficial outcome (e.g., Blyth, 1981). In this regard, we are reminded of one of our patients, who had asked his wife for a divorce one evening, went riding on his moped later that evening, fell off, sustained a closed head injury, and much to his wife's satisfaction, had retrograde amnesia for both the request for and the intent of divorce. The retrograde amnesia was a welcome event for this wife with five young children, as was the contrast between the patient's now mildly blunted and slightly euphoric affect and his former volatile and abusive character. Needless to say, our efforts to explain these changes as neurobehavioral deficits were treated as irrelevant by the wife.

In the present section, we review studies of the effects of head injury on families. Because this is a small though emerging area of study, we also selectively review the literature regarding the effects of other types of brain dysfunction on families. Finally, we examine treatment approaches that have been suggested or found useful, and attempt to conceptualize treatment approaches along the dimensions of severity of the patient's deficits, premorbid family structure, and the time frame of the recovery process.

Effect on Families

Studies of the effects on the family of having a brain-injured member have differed widely in methodology and in the part of the world in which they have been conducted, but the findings are highly consistent across studies in showing that not only the patient but the entire family and social system are altered. Moreover, some deficits secondary to brain injury appear to be more potent disruptors of family functioning than are others.

Rosenbaum and Najenson (1976) compared wives of brain-injured Israeli soldiers with wives of paraplegic soldiers and wives of uninjured soldiers one year after the October 1973 war, using a comprehensive set of questionnaires and mood inventories. This methodology permitted separating the general effects of major handicap (paraplegia) from the specific effects of brain injury. Wives of brain-injured patients showed substantial and distressing changes in virtually all areas of family, social, and personal life compared to wives of the other two groups and also showed greater objective evidence of depression. Wives of the brain-injured saw their husbands as self-centered and childishly demanding and unable to share or take responsibility for family needs, which is similar to Lezak's (1978) observations of patients in the United States. Interestingly, wives in the paraplegic group reported greater "sexual difficulty" but less "dislike of physical contact with husband," while the reverse was reported in the brain-injured group: that is, brain-injured patients had greater sexual capabilities, but their wives found physical contact with them unpleasant as compared to the paraplegic group. Negative changes extended to relationships with in-laws. Wives in both the brain-injured and the paraplegic group reported increased frequency of contact with their in-laws as compared to the normal group. However, wives in the brain-injured group reported less "closeness" with in-laws, while wives in the paraplegic group reported the reverse. Wives in the brain-injured group reported the greatest increase in closeness with their own parents. The larger social context also was disrupted. Wives of the brain-injured patients reported the greatest disruption in amount and enjoyability of leisure time, the worst social life, and the highest rate of desertion by old friends of the family.

These findings suggest that the behavioral handicaps associated with brain injury cause significantly greater disruption in family and social life than do purely sensory and motor handicaps, which is similar to the conclusions of others in several countries (Lezak, 1978; Rosenthal & Muir, 1983; Brooks, 1979; Thomsen, 1974; Bond, 1975;

Panting & Merry, 1972; Oddy, Humphrey, & Uttley, 1978; McKinlay, Brooks, Bond, Martinage, & Marshall, 1981). These studies uniformly implicate changes in personality, loss of motivation and initiative, and memory impairment as sources of family distress, while physical disabilities and language disturbance (McKinlay, Brooks, Bond, Martinage, & Marshall, 1981) are relatively less disruptive to the family.

Consequences to the family depend also on the premorbid circumstances of the patient. In this regard, Alexander (1982) and Bond (1983) note that the greatest prevalence of head injury is in persons "on the threshold of adult life." This group actually contains two quite diverse subgroups: those currently living with their parents or in the process of separating from them, and those who already have separated and are recently married or otherwise in the early stages of establishing independent households and families. The two groups can be thought of as having different definitions of family, with the former group having parents as the primary family and the latter group having spouses and sometimes young children as the primary family. Relationships with parents, though frequently stormy during adolescence and early adulthood, when separation is occurring, are durable in the sense that parents have previous experiences with the patient as a dependent member, contain long-standing emotional and financial commitments, and typically do not have role-responsibility expectations, such as that the patient be the head of the household. Relationships with spouses, on the other hand, usually have a shorter history, with more recently evolved emotional commitments, and have a narrower range of acceptable role responsibilities. Thus, although a high proportion of head-injured patients are within a narrow age range, the implications to the family may vary widely. The few studies that have compared parent-child with spouse-spouse relationships have found the former to be less disrupted following head injury (Thomsen, 1974; Panting & Merry, 1972).

Stresses to the family go beyond the social and emotional disruptions described above. We are not aware of studies of the financial effects on families, but our experience is that dramatic financial changes can be experienced and that the nature of such changes is highly variable, ranging from severe depletion of family financial resources to substantial increase when compensable injuries are involved. Other stresses to the family include increased risk of medical illness. Livesy (1972), reviewing the effects of chronic illness and disability on families, emphasizes the increased risk of physical illness in other family members. Oddy, Humphrey, and Uttley (1978), using a population of head-injured patients and their families, found an increase particularly in stress-related illnesses.

The emphasis to this point has been on how families are affected by having a head-injured member. It is equally important to understand how head-injured patients are influenced by the behavior and attitudes of their families. Unfortunately, we have found no studies addressing this facet of the problem. The influence of families, however, has been studied in other rehabilitation populations. Adler, Adler, Magora, Shanan, and Tal (1969), in a comprehensive study of over 5000 stroke patients, selected a stratified subsample of 120 patients and their families for a more detailed examination of the relationship between family attitudes and the status of patients' activities of daily living. Family attitudes found to be related to better ADL status included family desire for the patient to be active and independent, family perception that the patient was not a burden, and family desire to avoid rehospitalization. The results of this study are not directly applicable to head-injured patients because stroke patients are different from head-injured patients along many significant dimensions (Alexander, 1982). However, the study of Adler and associates is useful in highlighting the importance of studying how family attitudes and behavior can affect a patient's outcome.

Treatment of Families

The previously described studies show substantial and multiple forms of distress in relatives of brain-injured patients and provide a compelling argument for the need for family treatment and support. Clinical programs for brain-injured patients typically emphasize family involvement and have components of family treatment integrated within the overall rehabilitation program (Diehl, 1983; Rosenthal & Muir, 1983). Research in the area of head-injury rehabilitation has reached the stage of documenting family morbidity and the need for family treatment but, unfortunately, has not yet reached the stage of systematic studies of treatment outcome or effectiveness. Family interventions thus must be fashioned on the basis of knowledge derived from other patient populations and, to a large extent, on the basis of clinical judgment and experience.

Note that the absence of "hard" data on the efficacy of family treatment in cases of head injury hardly serves as adequate justification for not providing such services. Such data are and probably will continue to be notoriously difficult to obtain. As noted previously, the definition of family can vary greatly even within a homogeneous age range of patients, and the premorbid characteristics of families are also likely to show wide variation. Combined with other sources of variation, such as severity of injury and premorbid adjustment of the patient, controlled studies will be difficult and complex undertakings. Further, given the large number of different treatment services typically delivered to a head-injured patient and the patient's family, sorting the effects of any single treatment from the effects of all other treatments may be an unrealistic expectation unless large-scale multicenter coordinated studies are attempted.

A more realistic first step in developing an empirical basis for the treatment of the families of brain-injured patients would be studies to identify family factors related to positive patient outcomes. Such studies would form the basis for establishing goals and targets of family treatment. At present, the goals of family treatment in cases of brain injury can be stated only in a very general and crude fashion: there are data to show that families experience distress, and the goal of family treatment is to reduce this distress. Family treatment can include far more than reduction of distress and, in particular, can include counseling and training to promote family skills and attitudes to facilitate optimal patient and family adaptation to head injury. Studies to identify relevant family skills, attitudes, and behaviors are methodologically feasible, and the data would have direct translation to clinical practice. In this regard, Newcombe, Brooks, and Baddeley (1980) and Ron, Najenson, and Mendelson (1977) emphasize that such studies also would have to be longitudinal because of the long-term and changing nature of sequelae of head injuries.

For example, one of the most commonly advocated family interventions is reassurance (Lishman, 1978; Newcombe, Brooks, & Baddeley, 1980). In actuality, very little is known about the effects of this seemingly simple and straightforward intervention, particularly its potentially different effects at different stages of the recovery process and for patients with different degrees of severity of injury and prognosis. Further, *reassurance* is a vague term as it is currently used and probably has different operational meanings to different clinicians.

Several conceptual frameworks for family intervention have been proposed. Bray (1977), using a sequential stage model, identified three stages of family adjustment: the anxiety stage, the acceptance stage, and the assimilation stage. In the anxiety stage, family members progress from fear that the patient will die to relief that the patient has not died and finally to painful confrontation with the permanence of the patient's handicaps. This stage is characterized by widely and rapidly fluctuating family mood and expectation and powerful ambivalence toward clinical staff. Bray followed 180 families and noted this stage to last an average of nine months. The acceptance stage, which in Bray's sample occupied the second year of recovery, is characterized by the family's yielding their defensive posture and actively seeking to accommodate the change in the patient and the family system and to reestablish homeostasis. During this stage, the information that was presented by staff to the family during the anxiety stage, which the family often rejected, ignored or denied, now is sought out by the family and has a reassuring and motivating effect. Indeed, our clinical experience is that, not infrequently, families criticize us for not providing information sooner, when in fact we did provide the information but could not penetrate the dense denial typical of the anxiety state. The acceptance stage also signals family members' increased access to their deeper, subjective responses to the patient's illness and its effects on their lives: "It is not unusual for family members to express hidden and often guilt-ridden feelings…anger and hostility can be expressed openly toward the severely injured person. These feelings need to be expressed, discussed and resolved" (Bray, 1977, p. 238). The last stage, the assimilation stage, is not described in detail by Bray, though the implication is that it is lengthy, if not chronic, and involves a process of adjustment of family roles to accommodate the changed capacities of the impaired member.

Rosenthal and Muir (1983) conceptualize family intervention by proposing three categories of intervention: patient-family education, family counseling, and family therapy. The distinctions among categories are not made clear by the authors, and our clinical experience suggests that in practice these categories are virtually entirely interwoven. A comprehensive description of the patient-family education program is provided by Diehl (1983), and Muir (1979) offers a detailed and intriguing conceptualization of family therapy based on "mobile mourning" and "partial death." Muir (1979) also notes that both family education and family therapy are facilitated by competent neuropsychological evaluation. This facilitation occurs through the use of neuropsychological evaluation to identify areas of intact and impaired brain function and then to communicate the information to families in understandable language. The resulting family education is therapeutic by virtue of reducing family bewilderment and confusion, and permitting the family to understand and participate in the patient's treatment program, thereby reducing the family's sense of helplessness.

The information typically most urgently desired by families is a clear and accurate statement of the patient's long-term prognosis (Oddy, Humphrey, & Uttley, 1978). Unfortunately, as Rosenthal and Muir (1983) and Newcombe, Brooks, and Baddeley (1980), among others, have noted, substantial progress has been made in the ability to predict outcome, but it still is difficult to forecast with accuracy the particular outcome of a specific patient. Moreover, even when clinical staff have formed an opinion regarding prognosis, clinical judgment and sensitivity must be used in presenting the information to the family in such a fashion that they can assimilate it and use it constructively. Families can differ in the way they utilize information in the service of coping and adaptation—including, for example, the "minimization" and "vigilant focusing" dimension described by Lipowski (1970) and elaborated by Kiely (1972)—and the clinician must achieve a balance between what the family needs to know and the process by which the family will best learn it. Since much of what the clinician communicates to the family falls into the category of "bad news," it would be useful to study the effects on the clinician of delivering bad news and the effects on the families of receiving it, something that Gans (personal communication) is undertaking.

RAMIFICATIONS AT THE SOCIETAL LEVEL: WHERE DO WE GO FROM HERE?

Very few studies have adequately examined the long-term implications of surviving severe closed-head injury. The major importance of such work would be to determine what becomes of these individuals in the long run, to what extent they become reintegrated into society, and whether the extended needs of this growing segment of society are being adequately addressed. Society in general has much at stake. For one thing, as discussed earlier, those who survive place tremendous financial, emotional, and behavioral stresses on the systems within which they operate.

Resumption of gainful employment is generally considered an important criterion in western societies, distinguishing those individuals who have become productive and contributing members from those who require further expenditure of resources. Table 17.2 provides a selective sample of studies examining this criterion in the traumatically head-injured population over varying time intervals. Although direct comparisons across studies are not possible because of differences along a number of dimensions, including selection ratios, patient variables, severity of injury, etiologies, criterion measures, time intervals, and economic conditions, there appears to be a general trend of increasing employment rates with longer time intervals and with penetrating head injuries. However, many of the reemployed must settle for lower-status and less-demanding jobs (Najenson et al., 1974), a reality necessitated by the nature of their residual cognitive and physical limitations.

Special arrangements with employers who remain supportive and understanding of the problems faced by brain-injured persons may allow some once again to become productive, or seemingly so (Rosenbaum, Lipsitz, Abraham, & Najenson, 1978; Jennett, Smoek, Bond, & Brooks, 1981). Carefully coordinated trial job placements within the hospital setting itself may be of benefit to some. Some severely impaired persons may be suited only for sheltered workshop training, although, as Ford (1976) notes, the brain-injured person does not fit easily into workshops designed for the elderly or the developmentally disabled. Many brain-injured patients retain memories of their former competencies and do not identify with these other populations. Also, workshops frequently cannot deal with many of the behavioral disorders presented by brain-injured victims. Those with profound cognitive and physical deficits may be placed in long-term nursing homes or extended care medical facilities (Ford, 1976; Gilchrist & Wilkinson, 1979). In some cases, involved family members may be able to care for the disabled member at home and, once having learned aspects of therapy that they competently can carry out, may even provide more intensive and continuous treatment than would be practical or economically feasible within a hospital setting (Jennett & Teasdale, 1981).

But what becomes of persons with good physical functions and independent ADL skills who are cosmetically unremarkable, yet possess significant residual behavioral and cognitive difficulties that make their chances of holding a job relatively remote? Romano (1974) observes that communities, threatened by these peculiar behaviors, tend to demand the exclusion of the brain-injured person from the mainstream of the usual community life. Some find their way into psychiatric facilities (Ford, 1976; Gjone, Kristiansen, & Sponheim, 1972; Gilchrist & Wilkinson, 1979) and/or end up in the criminal justice system (Weinstein & Wells, 1981). Many can be managed with constant supervision at home, often at great emotional expense to the family (Lezak, 1978).

For those who remain under the protective care of the family, long-range planning needs to take into consideration the fact that even severely impaired persons have only a five-year reduction in life expectancy over the next 20 years in comparison with the general population (Roberts, 1979). Consequently, many impaired individuals may be expected to live 20–40 years after their original injury, placing even more strenuous burdens on aging parents, who in turn may be expected to suffer medical difficulties of their own and therefore may be unable to meet the obligations undertaken earlier. Also, given these figures, brain-injured young adults may be expected frequently to outlive their parents. We then may ask what becomes of those who do not resume some degree of self-management competencies and fail to develop the necessary prerequisites for gainful employment without the aid of benefactors.

Three general interlocking societal and community trends have emerged in response to this state of affairs. Although only incompletely developed, these trends may provide the thrust behind future efforts to meet the burgeoning needs of all concerned—the patient, the patient's family, and society.

As has occurred in conjunction with other chronic diseases and disabilities, growing recognition of the stresses placed on the family and care givers of head-injured persons has led to the development of the National Head Injury Foundation, an organization formed in 1980 by the parents of head-injured persons. The purposes of this organization are to serve as a centralized clearinghouse for the collection and dissemination of information concerning head injury to all interested parties, to provide an emotional support resource for families and other care givers, and to stimulate the formation of local family and parent support groups. With its growing number of members and professional affiliates, the National Head Injury Foundation will undoubtedly serve an important role in stimulating legislative efforts to meet more adequately the needs of head-injured persons at all levels. On the local front, parent and family support groups fulfill the vital functions of locating and developing community resources designed to improve the quality of life for impaired persons and to assist in the difficult tasks of adjustment. One cannot underestimate the value of such self-help organizations. According to Riesman (1965), the act of helping may be of as much benefit to the helper as to the helpee.

Table 17.2. Summary of Studies on the Vocational Status of Brain-Injured Patients at Follow-up

Investigator	N	Etiology of Head Injury	Follow-up Time Interval	Work or Social Status at Follow-up	Negative Prognostic Factors
Ford (1976)	30	Mostly closed head injuries due to traffic accidents	3–6 months	43% returned to some type of work or education	Prolonged unconsciousness (a few days to 2 weeks) The longer the hospital stay, the poorer the prognosis
Gjone, Kristiansen, & Sponheim (1972)	92	50% traffic accidents	After 3 months of hospital treatment	30% returned to former jobs	History of Alcoholism
Najenson et al. (1974)	149	66% traffic accidents 34% gunshot wounds	1–6 years	23% dead or vegetative state 12% ADL independent only 36% employed at professional, simple, or sheltered workshop 46% capable of work but not placed	Prolonged unconsciousness Age over 45 years Severe motor deficits or aphasia History of seizures Hemianopia
Gilchrist & Wilkinson (1979)	84	Traffic accidents	9 months to 15 years	30% working	Moderate to severe mental changes Unconsciousness over 1 week Extensive neurological damage Cerebral hypoxia Inadequate family support

Study	N	Cause of injury	Follow-up period	Employment outcome	Factors associated with poor outcome
Jellinek, Torkelson, & Harvey (1982)	22		Average, 4 years; Range, 1–11 years	41% in work or educational activities	Age over 40 years; Secondary medical complications
Lewin (1968)	64	"Concussion" Traffic accidents	6–24 years	40% gainfully employed	Lack of adequate follow-up treatment and advice; Dependent in ADL functions
Rusk, Block, & Lowman (1969)	157	Mostly traffic accidents	5–15 years	46% in some type of gainful employment	Unconsciousness over 4 weeks; Severe mental impairments; Older patients
Lundholm, Jepsen, & Thornval (1975)	30	Traffic accidents	8–14 years	27% "economically independent"; 73% partially or totally dependent economically	Lower premorbid level of intelligence; Persisting speech, motor, or visual impairments; Seizures; Evidence of diffuse damage
Dresser et al. (1973)	864	Mostly penetrating head injuries (Korean Conflict veterans)	15 years	75% able to return to work	Prolonged unconsciousness; Moderate to severe motor deficits; Moderate to severe aphasia; Moderate to severe cognitive deficits; Lower premorbid education; Frontal lobe syndrome
Najenson, Groswasser, Mendelson, & Hackett (1980)	147	Mostly blunt head injuries	6 months or more after hospital discharge	18% skilled work; 25% unskilled work; 18% sheltered workshop; 39% unemployed	

A second emergent trend at the societal level is the development of alternative extended treatment facilities, including transitional living facilities. Muir and colleagues (1983) provide an excellent brief synopsis of the few existing programs geared toward retraining in those basic social and problem-solving competencies necessary for independent or semi-independent living. Along similar lines, there have been numerous appeals for the development of more extended sheltered-workshop training facilities to accommodate the special existential needs of head-injured persons (Caveness, Walker, & Critchley, 1969; Ford, 1976). Based on their experience with brain-injured patients treated within a therapeutic community in Israel, Rosenbaum, Lipsitz, Abraham, and Najenson (1978) suggest the consideration of permanent placements within these sheltered and structured environments as an alternative for those who cannot be rehabilitated to function more effectively in other settings. Whatever form extended treatment or placement may take, continuity of care with qualified professionals is likely to help patients sustain the progress achieved. In this regard, Rusk, Block, and Loman (1969) observe that patients who are left to their own devices tend to lose the functions they have gained.

Finally, renewed interest in the old adage "an ounce of prevention is worth a pound of cure" appears to be forming at all levels of society. Recent legislation on automobile safety equipment, speed limit regulations, and industrial and sporting safety standards all point to the growing recognition of the benefits of accident prevention for the individual and society. Any legislation intended to reduce accidents in general is likely to have positive impact on the incidence of head injuries as well. Educational programs and mass media announcements also attempt to persuade the general public to prevent accidents in the home, to settle disputes without resorting to violence, to avoid driving while intoxicated, and to help deter crime. In addition to attempts to convince society to create a safer environment for people, effort needs to be directed at helping people modify their behavior in relation to known but unalterable hazards (Jennett & Teasdale, 1981). For example, seat belts are useful only for the person who is willing to wear them. Since many seem incapable of altering their own behavior, safety engineers have introduced, with some success, passive restraint systems that require no special added behaviors on the part of "slow learners." More stringent penalties for intoxicated drivers may help some to alter their behavior. Many but not all states have mandatory laws on the use of protective headgear by motorcyclists, some of whom argue that such laws are unconstitutional by depriving them of their freedom of choice. If a head injury to a solitary motorcyclist affected only that rider, the argument might have some merit. However, as pointed out repeatedly throughout this chapter, the repercussions of such an injury extend well beyond the individual, and, in sufficient numbers, such injuries cost all of us dearly in more ways than one.

Preventive programs at the societal level require the cooperative efforts of legislators, community leaders, health care professionals, and the general public. Despite the tremendous expenditure of resources geared toward accident prevention and the progress made to date, there remains much that can be accomplished in the future. For behavioral scientists, more active participation in prevention efforts is desperately needed. Their general role is likely to be fourfold: (1) compiling the often gruesome statistics attesting to the need for social action, (2) identifying the segments of society at high risk for various accidents, (3) designing and implementing more compelling educational programs, and (4) more intense study of those who find it difficult to modify their own behavior.

REFERENCES

Adams, J.H., Mitchell, D.E., Graham, D.I., & Doyle, D. (1977). Diffuse brain damage of immediate impact type. *Brain, 100,* 489–502.

Adams, R.D., & Victor, M. (1981). *Principles of neurology* (2nd ed.). New York: McGraw-Hill.

Adler, E., Adler, C., Magora, A., Shanan, J., & Tal, E. (1969). *Stroke in Israel, 1957–1961: Epidemiological, clinical, rehabilitation, and psychosocial aspects.* Jerusalem: Polypress.

Alexander, M.P. (1982). Traumatic brain injury. In P.F. Benson & D. Blumer (Eds.), *Psychiatric aspects of neurologic disease* (Vol. 2, pp. 219–248). New York: Grune & Stratton.

Anderson, D.W., & Kalsbeek, W.D. (1980). The National Head and Spinal Cord Injury Survey: Assessment of some uncertainties affecting the findings. *Journal of Neurosurgery, 53* (Suppl.), S32–S34.

Auerbach, S.H. (1983). Cognitive rehabilitation in the head injured: A neurobehavioral approach. *Seminars in Neurology, 3,* 152–162.

Barth, J.T., & Boll, T.J. (1981). Rehabilitation and treatment of central nervous system dysfunction: A behavioral medicine perspective. In C.K. Prokop & L.A. Bradley (Eds.), *Medical psychology: Contributions to behavioral medicine* (pp. 241–266). New York: Academic Press.

Bayle, M.E., & Greer, R.D. (1983). Operant procedures and the comatose patient. *Journal of Applied Behavioral Analysis, 16,* 3–12.

Bednar, R.L., & Lawlis, G.F. (1971). Empirical research in group psychotherapy. In A.E. Bergin & S.L. Garfield (Eds.), *Handbook of psychotherapy and behavior change: An empirical analysis* (pp. 812–838). New York: John Wiley & Sons.

Benton, A.L. (1968). Differential behavioral effects of frontal lobe diseases. *Neuropsychologia, 6,* 53–60.

Ben-Yishay, Y. (Ed.). (May 1980). *Working approaches to remediation of cognitive deficits in brain-damaged.* Supplement to the Eighth Annual Workshop for Rehabilitation Professionals, New York.

Ben-Yishay, Y. (Ed.). (May 1983). *Working approaches to remediation of cognitive deficits in brain-damaged.* Supplement to the Eleventh Annual Workshop for Rehabilitation Professionals, New York.

Ben-Yishay, Y., Ben-Nachum, Z., Cohen, A., Gerstman, L., Gordon, W., Gross, Y., Hofien, D., Piasetsky, E., & Ratlok, J. (June 1978). *Working approaches to remediation of cognitive deficits in brain-damaged.* Supplement to the Sixth Annual Workshop for Rehabilitation Professionals, New York.

Ben-Yishay, Y., & Diller, L. (1983). Cognitive remediation. In M. Rosenthal, E.R. Griffith, M.R. Bond, & J.P. Miller (Eds.), *Rehabilitation of the head injured adult* (pp. 367–380). Philadelphia: F.A. Davis.

Ben-Yishay, Y., Diller, L., Ratlok, J., Ross, B., Schaier, A., & Scherger, P. (May 1979). *Working approaches to remediation of cognitive deficits in brain-damaged.* Supplement to the Seventh Annual Workshop for Rehabilitation Professionals, New York.

Binder, L.M., & Schreiber, V. (1980). Visual imagery and verbal mediation as memory aids in recovering alcoholics. *Journal of Clinical Neuropsychology, 2,* 71–74.

Bleiberg, J., & Merbit, C. (1984). Learning goals during initial rehabilitation hospitalization. *Archives of Physical Medicine and Rehabilitation, 64,* 448–451.

Blyth, B. (1981). The outcome of severe head injuries. *New Zealand Medical Journal, 93,* 267–269.

Boll, T.J. (1978). Diagnosing brain impairment. In B. Wolman (Ed.), *Diagnosis of mental disorders: A handbook* (pp. 601–675). New York: Plenum.

Bond, M.R. (1979). Assessment of psychosocial outcome after severe head injury. In R. Porter & D.W. Fitzsimons (Eds.), *Outcome of severe damage to the central nervous system* (Ciba Foundation Symposium 34). Amsterdam: Elsevier.

Bond, M.R., & Brooks, D.N. (1976). Understanding the process of recovery as a basis for the investigation of rehabilitation for the brain injured. *Scandinavian Journal of Rehabilitation Medicine, 8,* 127–133.

Bracey, O.L. (1983). Computer-based cognitive rehabilitation. *Cognitive Rehabilitation, 1,* 7–8, 18.

Bray, G.D. (1977). Reactive patterns in families of the severely disabled. *Rehabilitation Counseling Bulletin,* March, 236–239.

Brooks, D.N. (1974). Recognition memory, and head injury. *Journal of Neurology, Neurosurgery and Psychiatry, 37,* 794–801.

Brooks, D.N. (1976). Wechsler Memory Scale performance and its relationship to brain damage after severe closed head injury. *Journal of Neurology, Neurosurgery, and Psychiatry, 39,* 593–601.

Brooks, D.N. (1979). Cognitive recovery during the first year after severe blunt head injury. *International Journal of Rehabilitation Medicine, 1,* 166–172.

Brooks, D.N. (1983). Disorders of memory. In M. Rosenthal, E.R. Griffith, M.R. Bond, & J.D. Miller (Eds.), *Rehabilitation of the head injured adult* (pp. 185–196). Philadelphia: F.A. Davis Company.

Brooks, D.N., & Aughton, M.E. (1979). Psychological consequences of blunt head injury. *International Rehabilitation Medicine, 1,* 160–165.

Busse, T.V., & Lighthall, F.F. (1966). Conceptual retraining of brain-damaged adults. *Perceptual and Motor Skills, 22,* 899–906.

Caplan, G. (1964). *Principles of Preventive Psychiatry.* New York: Basic Books.

Carter, L.T., Caruso, J.L., Languirand, M.A., & Bernard, M.A. (1980). Cognitive skill remediation in stroke and non-stroke elderly. *Clinical Neuropsychology, 2,* 109–113.

Carter, L.T., Howard, B.E., & O'Neil, W.A. (1983). Effectiveness of cognitive skill remediation in acute stroke patients. *American Journal of Occupational Therapy, 37,* 320–326.

Caveness, W.F. (1977). Incidence of craniocerebral trauma in the United States, 1970–1975. *Annals of Neurology, 1,* 507.

Caveness, W.F., Walker, A.E., & Critchley, M. (1969). Prospectus for the future. In A.E. Walker, W.F. Caveness, & M. Critchley (Eds.), *The late effects of head injury* (pp. 529–538). Springfield, IL: Charles C Thomas.

Caviness, V.S. (1966). Epilepsy and craniocerebral injury of warfare. In W.F. Caveness & A.W. Walker (Eds.), *Head injury: Conference proceedings.* Philadelphia: J.B. Lippincott.

Cermak, L.S. (1980). Improving retention in alcoholic Korsakoff patients. *Journal of Studies on Alcohol, 41,* 159–169.

Chusid, J.G. (1976). *Corrective neuroanatomy and functional neurology.* Los Altos, CA: Lange.

Courville, C.B. (1937). *Pathology of the central nervous system* (Part 4). Mountain View, CA: Pacific.

Craine, C.J. (1982). Principles of cognitive rehabilitation. In L.E. Trexler (Ed.), *Cognitive rehabilitation.* New York: Plenum.

Crewe, N.M. (1980). Sexually inappropriate behavior. In D.S. Bishop (Ed.), *Behavioral problems and the disabled: Assessment and management* (pp. 120–141). Baltimore: Williams & Wilkins.

Critchley, M. (1969). Introduction. In A.E. Walker, W.F. Caveness, & E.M. Critchley (Eds.), *The late effects of head injury* (pp. 3–9). Springfield, IL: Charles C Thomas.

Crovitz, H.F. (1979). Memory retraining in brain-damaged patients: The Airplane List. *Cortex,* *15,* 131–134.

Denny-Brown, D., & Russell, W.R. (1941). Experimental cerebral concussion. *Brain, 64,* 7–164.

Diehl, L.N. (1983). Patient-family education. In M. Rosenthal, E.R. Griffith, M.R. Bond, & J.D. Miller (Eds.), *Rehabilitation of the head injured adult* (pp. 395–401). Philadelphia: F.A. Davis.

Dikmen, S., & Reitan, R.M. (1977). Emotional sequelae of head injury. *Annals of Neurology, 2,* 492–494.

Dikmen, S., Reitan, R.M., & Temkin, N.R. (1983). Neuropsychological recovery in head injury. *Archives of Neurology, 40,* 333–338.

Diller, L. (1976). A model for cognitive retraining in rehabilitation. *Clinical Psychologist, 29,* 13–15.

Diller, L., & Gordon, W.A. (1981a). Interventions for cognitive deficits in brain-injured adults. *Journal of Consulting and Clinical Psychology, 49,* 822–834.

Diller, L., & Gordon, W.A. (1981b). Rehabilitation and clinical neuropsychology. In S.B. Filskov & T.J. Boll (Eds.), *Handbook of clinical neuropsychology* (Vol. 1, pp. 702–733). New York: John Wiley & Sons.

Diller, L., & Weinberg, J. (1977). Hemi-inattention in rehabilitation and the evolution of a rational remediation program. In E.A. Weinstein & R.P. Freidland (Eds.), *Advances in neurology.* New York: Raven Press.

Dresser, A.C., Meirowsky, A.M., Weiss, G.H., McNeel, M.L., Simon, G.A., & Caveness, W.F. (1973). Gainful employment following injury. *Archives of Neurology, 29,* 111–116.

Filskov, S.B., Grimm, B.H., & Lewis, J.A. (1981). Brain-behavior relationships. In S.B. Filskov & T.J. Boll (Eds.), *Handbook of clinical neuropsychology* (Vol. 1, pp. 39–73). New York: John Wiley & Sons.

Ford, B. (1976). Head injuries: What happens to survivors. *Medical Journal of Australia, 1,* 603–605.

Fordyce, W.E. (1982). Psychological assessment and management. In F.J. Kottke, G.K. Stillwell, & J.F. Lehmann (Eds.), *Krusen's handbook of physical medicine and rehabilitation* (3rd ed., pp. 124–150). Philadelphia: W.B. Saunders.

Fordyce, D.J., Roueche, J.R., & Prigatano, G.P. (1983). Enhanced emotional reactions in chronic head trauma patients. *Journal of Neurology, Neurosurgery and Psychiatry, 46,* 620–624.

Fowler, R.S., & Fordyce, W. (1972). Adapting care for the brain-damaged patient. *American Journal of Nursing, 72,* 2056–2059.

Gans, J.S. (1979). Consulted-attended interview: Approach to liaison psychiatry. *General Hospital Psychiatry, 1,* 24–30.

Gans, J.S. (1981). Depression diagnosis in a rehabilitation hospital. *Archives of Physical Medicine and Rehabilitation, 62,* 386–389.

Gans, J.S. (1983). Hate in the rehabilitation setting. *Archives of Physical Medicine and Rehabilitation, 64,* 176–179.

Gasparrini, B., & Satz, P. (1979). A treatment for memory problems in left hemisphere CVA patients. *Journal of Clinical Neuropsychology, 1,* 137–150.

Gedye, J.L. (1968). Automated instructional techniques in the rehabilitation of patients with head injury. *Proceedings of the Royal Society of Medicine, 61,* 858–860.

Gianutsos, R. (1980). What is cognitive rehabilitation? *Journal of Rehabilitation, 46,* 36–40.

Gianutsos, R., & Gianutsos, J. (1979). Rehabilitating the verbal recall of brain-injured patients by mnemonic training: An experimental demonstration using single-case methodology. *Journal of Clinical Neuropsychology, 1,* 117–135.

Gilchrist, E., & Wilkinson, M. (1979). Some factors determining prognosis in young people with severe head injuries. *Archives of Neurology, 36,* 355–359.

Gjone, R., Kristiansen, K., & Sponheim, N. (1972). Rehabilitation in severe head injuries. *Scandinavian Journal of Rehabilitation Medicine, 4,* 2–4.

Glasgow, R.E., Zeiss, R.A., Barrera, M., & Lewinsohn, P.M. (1977). Case studies on remediating memory deficits in brain-damaged individuals. *Journal of Clinical Psychology, 33,* 1049–1054.

Goldstein, A.P., & Simonson, N.R. (1971). Social psychological approaches to psychotherapy research. In A.E. Bergin & S.L. Garfield (Eds.), *Handbook of psychotherapy and behavior change: An empirical analysis* (pp. 154–195). New York: John Wiley & Sons.

Goldstein, K. (1942). *After effects of brain injuries in war.* New York: Grune & Stratton.

Goldstein, K. (1943). Brain concussion: Evaluation of the after-effects by special tests. *Diseases of the Nervous System, 4,* 3–12.

Graham, S. (1983). From the patients point of view. *Cognitive Rehabilitation, 1,* 11–12.

Griffith, E.R. (1983). Types of disability. In M. Rosenthal, E.R. Griffith, M.R. Bond, & J.D. Miller (Eds.), *Rehabilitation of the head injured adult* (pp. 23–32). Philadelphia: F.A. Davis.

Gronwall, D., & Wrightson, P. (1981). Memory and information processing capacity after closed head injury. *Journal of Neurology, Neurosurgery and Psychiatry, 44,* 889–895.

Gunther, M. (1977). The threatened staff: A psychoanalytic contribution to medical psychology. *Comprehensive Psychiatry, 18,* 385–397.

Gunther, M. (1979). The psychopathology of psychiatric consultation: A different view. *Comprehensive Psychiatry, 20,* 187–198.

Halpern, H., Parley, F.L., & Brown, J.R. (1973). Differential language and neurologic characteristics in cerebral involvement. *Journal of Speech and Hearing Disorders, 38,* 162–173.

Halstead, W.C. (1947). *Brain and intelligence.* Chicago: University of Chicago Press.

Haymaker, W. (1969). *Bing's local diagnosis in neurological disease* (15th ed.). St. Louis: C.V. Mosby.

Hécaen, H., & Albert, M.L. (1978). *Human neuropsychology.* New York: John Wiley & Sons. ,

Heilman, K.M., Safran, A., & Geschwind, N. (1971). Closed head trauma and aphasia. *Journal of Neurology, Neurosurgery and Psychiatry, 34,* 265–269.

Hillborn, E. (1960). After-effects of brain injuries. *Acta Psychiatrica et Neurologica Scandinavica, 142* (Suppl.), 1–195.

Holbourn, A.H.S. (1943). Mechanics of head injury. *Lancet, 2,* 438–441.

Hollon, T.H. (1973). Behavior modification in a community hospital rehabilitation unit. *Archives of Physical Medicine and Rehabilitation, 54,* 65–68.

Horton, A.M., Jr., E. Howe, N.R. (1981). Behavioral treatment of the traumatically brain-injured: A case study. *Perceptual and Motor Skills, 53,* 349–350.

Ince, L.P. (1976). *Behavior modification in rehabilitation medicine.* Springfield, IL: Charles C Thomas.

Ince, L.P. (Ed.). (1980). *Behavioral psychology in rehabilitation medicine: Clinical applications.* Baltimore: Williams & Wilkins.

Jackson, J.H. (1932). *Selected writings* (Vol. 2), J. Taylor (Ed.). London: Hodder & Stoughton.

Jellinek, H.M., Torkelson, R.M., & Harvey, R.F. (1982). Functional abilities and distress levels in brain injured patients at long-term follow-up. *Archives of Physical Medicine and Rehabilitation, 63,* 160–162.

Jennett, B., & Bond, M. (1975). Assessment of outcome after severe brain damage. *Lancet, 1,* 480–484.

Jennett, B., Snoek, J., Bond, M.R., & Brooks, N. (1981). Disability after severe head injury: Observations on the use of the Glasgow Outcome Scale. *Journal of Neurology, Neurosurgery and Psychiatry, 44*, 285–293.

Jennett, B., & Teasdale, G. (1981). *Management of head injuries.* Philadelphia: F.A. Davis.

Jennett, B., Teasdale, G., Galbraith, S., Pickard, J., Grant, H., Braakman, R., Avezaat, C., Maas, A., Minderhoud, J., Vecht, C.J., Heiden, J., Small, R., Caton, W., & Kurze, T. (1977). Severe head injuries in three countries. *Journal of Neurology, Neurosurgery and Psychiatry, 40*, 291–298.

Johnston, C.W., & Diller, L. (1983). Error evaluation ability of right-hemisphere brain-lesioned patients who have had perceptual-cognitive retraining. *Journal of Clinical Neuropsychology, 5*, 401–402.

Jones, M.K. (1974). Imagery as a mnemonic aid after left temporal lobectomy: Contrast between material-specific and generalized memory disorders. *Neuropsychologia, 12*, 21–30.

Kalsbeek, W.D., McLaurin, R.L., Harris, B.S.H., & Miller, J.D. (1980). The National Head and Spinal Cord Injury Survey: Major findings. *Journal of Neurosurgery, 53* (Suppl.), S19–S31.

Kanfer, F.H., & Karoly, P. (1972). Self-control: A behavioristic excursion into the lion's den. *Behavior Therapy, 3*, 398–416.

Kazdin, A.E. (1978). The application of operant techniques in treatment rehabilitation and education. In S.L. Garfield & A.E. Bergin (Eds.), *Handbook of psychotherapy and behavior change* (2nd ed., pp. 549–589). New York: John Wiley & Sons.

Kehlberg, J.K. (1966). Head injuries in automobile accidents. In W.F. Caveness & A.E. Walker (Eds.), *Head injury: Conference proceedings.* Philadelphia: J.B. Lippincott.

Kelly, R. (1975). The post-traumatic syndrome: A ratiogenic disease. *Forensic Science, 6*, 17–24.

Kiely, W.F. (1972). Coping with severe illness. *Advances in Psychosomatic Medicine, 8*, 105–118.

Kovner, R., Mattis, S., & Goldmeier, E. (1983). A technique for promoting robust free recall in chronic organic amnesia. *Journal of Clinical Neuropsychology, 5*, 65–71.

Kozol, H.L. (1945). Pretraumatic personality and psychiatric sequelae of head injury. *Archives of Neurology and Psychiatry, 53*, 358–364.

Kraus, J.F. (1980). Injury to the head and spinal cord: The epidemiological relevance of medical literature published from 1960 to 1978. *Journal of Neurosurgery, 53* (Suppl.), S3–S10.

Kuschner, H., Knox, A.W. (1973). Application of the utilization technique to the behavior of a brain-injured patient. *Journal of Communicative Disorders, 6*, 151.

Laatsch, L. (1983). Development of a memory training program. *Cognitive Rehabilitation, 1*, 15–18.

Leftoff, S. (1983). Psychopathology in the light of brain injury: A case study. *Journal of Clinical Neuropsychology, 5*, 51–63.

Levin, H.S., Benton, A.L., & Grossman, R.G. (1982). *Neurobehavioral consequences of close head injury.* New York: Oxford University Press.

Levin, H.S., & Grossman, R.G. (1978). Behavioral sequelae of closed head injury: A quantitative study. *Archives of Neurology, 35*, 720–727.

Levin, H.S., Grossman, R.G., Rose, J.E., & Teasdale, G. (1979). Long-term neuropsychological outcome of closed head injuries. *Journal of Neurosurgery, 50*, 412–422.

Lewin, W. (1968). Rehabilitation after head injury. *British Medical Journal, 1*, 465–470.

Lewinsohn, P.M., Danaher, B.G., & Kile, S. (1977). Visual imagery as a mnemonic aid for brain-injured patients. *Journal of Consulting and Clinical Psychology, 45*, 717–723.

Lezak, M.D. (1978). Subtle sequelae of brain damage: Perplexity, distractibility, and fatigue. *American Journal of Physical Medicine, 57*, 9–15.

Lezak, M.D. (1979). Recovery of memory and learning functions following traumatic brain damage. *Cortex, 15,* 63–70.

Lezak, M.D. (1983). *Neuropsychological assessment* (2nd ed.). New York: Oxford University Press.

Lipowski, Z.J. (1977). Psychiatric consultation: Concepts and controversies. *American Journal of Psychiatry, 134,* 523–528.

Lira, F.T., Carne, W., & Masri, A.M. (1983). Treatment of anger and impulsivity in a brain damaged patient: A case study applying stress innoculation. *Clinical Neuropsychology, 5,* 159–160.

Lishman, W.A. (1968). Brain damage in relation to psychiatric disability after head injury. *British Journal of Psychiatry, 114,* 373–410.

Lishman, W.A. (1973). The psychiatric sequelae of head injury: A review. *Psychological Medicine, 3,* 304–318.

Lishman, W.A. (1978). *Organic psychiatry: The psychological consequences of cerebral disorder.* London: Blackwell Scientific.

Livsey, C.G. (1972). Physical illness and family dynamics. *Advances in Psychosomatic Medicine, 8,* 237–251.

Lundholm, J., Jepsen, B.N., & Thornval, G. (1975). The late neurological, psychological, and social aspects of severe traumatic coma. *Scandinavian Journal of Rehabilitation Medicine, 7,* 97–100.

Luria, A.R. (1966). *Higher cortical functions in man.* New York: Basic Books.

Luria, A.R. (1970). *Traumatic aphasia: Its syndrome, psychology and treatment.* The Hague, Netherlands: Mouton, 1970.

Luria, A.R. (1973). *The working brain: An introduction to neuropsychology.* New York: Basic Books.

Luria, A.R., Naydin, F.L., Tsvetkova, L.S., & Vinarskaya, E.N. (1969). Restoration of higher cortical function following local brain damage. In P.J. Vinken & G.W. Bruyn (Eds.), *Handbook of clinical neurology* (Vol. 3, pp. 368–433), Amsterdam: North Holland Public.

Lynch, W.J., & Mauso, N.K. (1981). Brain injury rehabilitation: Standard problem lists. *Archives of Physical Medicine and Rehabilitation, 62,* 223–227.

Mahoney, M.J., Kazdin, A.E., & Lesswing, W.J. (1984). Behavior modification: Delusion or deliverances? In C.M. Franks & G.T. Wilson (Eds.), *Annual review of behavior therapy: Theory and practice* (Vol. 2, pp. 11–40). New York: Brunner/Mazel.

Malec, J., & Questad, K. (1983). Rehabilitation of memory after craniocerebral trauma: Case report. *Archives of Physical Medicine and Rehabilitation, 64,* 436–438.

Mandleberg, I.A. (1975). Cognitive recovery after severe head injury: 2. Wechsler Adult Intelligence Scale during post-traumatic amnesia. *Journal of Neurology, Neurosurgery and Psychiatry, 38,* 1127–1132.

McKinlay, W.W., Brooks, D.N., & Bond, M.R. (1983). Post-concussional symptoms, financial compensation, and outcome of severe blunt head injury. *Journal of Neurology, Neurosurgery and Psychiatry, 46,* 1084–1091.

McKinlay, W.W., Brooks, D.N., Bond, M.R., Martinage, D.P., & Marshall, M.M. (1981). The short-term outcome of severe blunt head injury as reported by relatives of the injured persons. *Journal of Neurology, Neurosurgery and Psychiatry, 44,* 527–533.

McLean, A., Temkin, N.R., Kikman, S., & Wyler, A.R. (1983). The behavioral sequelae of head injury. *Journal of Clinical Neuropsychology, 5,* 361–376.

Meier, M.J. (1981). Education for competency assurance in human neuropsychology: Antecedents, models, and directions. In S.B. Filskov & T.J. Boll (Eds.), *Handbook of clinical neuropsychology* (Vol. 1, pp. 754–781). New York: John Wiley & Sons.

Melamed, B.G., & Siegel, L.J. (1980). *Behavioral medicine: Practical applications in health care.* New York: Springer.

Merritt, H.H. (1979). *A textbook of neurology* (6th ed.). Philadelphia: Lea & Febiger.

Mersky, H., & Woodeforde, J.M. (1972). Psychiatric sequelae of minor head injury. *Brain, 95,* 521–528.

Miller, E. (1970). Simple and choice reaction time following severe head injury. *Cortex, 6,* 121–127.

Miller, E. (1977). The management of dementia: A review of some possibilities. *British Journal of Social and Clinical Psychology, 16,* 77–83.

Miller, J.D. (1983). Early evaluation and management. In M. Rosenthal, E.R. Griffith, M.R. Bond, & J. D. Miller (Eds.), *Rehabilitation of the head injured adult* (pp. 37–58). Philadelphia: F.A. Davis.

Miller, J.D., Butterworth, J.F., Gudemana, S.K., Faulkner, J.E., Choi, S.C., Selhorst, J.B., Harbison, J.W., Lutz, H.A., Young, H.F., & Becker, D.P. (1981). Further experiences in the management of severe head inury. *Journal of Neurosurgery, 54,* 289–299.

Miller, J.G. (1978). *The living systems.* New York: McGraw-Hill.

Missel, J.L. (1978). Suicide risk in the medical rehabilitation setting. *Archives of Physical Medicine and Rehabilitation, 59,* 371–376.

Muir, C.A. (1979). *Brain injury: Use of neuropsychological data to facilitate the mobile mourning process.* Paper presented at the Forty-first Annual Meeting of the American Academy of Physical Medicine and Rehabilitation.

Muir, C.A., Haffey, W.J., Ott, K.J., Karaica, D., Muir, J.H., & Sutko, M. (1983). Treatment of behavioral deficits. In M. Rosenthal, E.R. Griffith, M.R. Bond, & J.D. Miller (Eds.), *Rehabilitation of the head injured adult* (pp. 381–393). Philadelphia: F.A. Davis.

Müller, R., & Naumann, B. (1956). Early ambulation and psychotherapy for treatment of closed head injury. *Archives of Neurology and Psychiatry, 76,* 597–607.

Najenson, T., Groswasser, Z., Mendelson, L., & Hackett, P. (1980). Rehabilitation outcome of brain damaged patients after severe head injury. *International Rehabilitation Medicine, 2,* 17–22.

Najenson, T., Mendelson, L., Schechter, I., David, C., Mintz, N., & Groswasser, Z. (1974). Rehabilitation after severe head injury. *Scandinavian Journal of Rehabilitation Medicine, 6,* 5–14.

Newcombe, F., Brooks, N., & Baddeley, A. (1980). Rehabilitation after brain damage: An overview. *International Journal of Rehabilitation Medicine, 2,* 133–137.

Nichols, K.A. (1979). Psychological care for the ill and injured. In D.J. Osborne, M.M. Gruneberg, & J.R. Eiser (Eds.), *Research in psychology and medicine* (Vol. 2, pp. 361–369). New York: Academic Press.

Oddy, M., Humphrey, M., & Uttley, D. (1978). Subjective impairment and social recovery after closed head injury. *Journal of Neurology, Neurosurgery and Psychiatry, 41,* 611–616.

Ommaya, A.K., & Gennarelli, T.A. (1974). Cerebral concussion and traumatic unconsciousness: Correlation of experimental and clinical observations on blunt head injuries. *Brain, 97,* 633–654.

Oppenheimer, D.R. (1968). Microscopic lesions in the brain following head injury. *Journal of Neurology, Neurosurgery and Psychiatry, 31,* 299–306.

Overall, J.E., & Gorham, D.R. (1962). The brief psychiatric rating scale. *Psychological Reports, 10,* 799–812.

Panting, A., & Merry, P.H. (1972). The long-term rehabilitation of severe head injuries with particular reference to the need for social and medical support for the patient's family. *Rehabilitation, 38,* 33–37.

Parente, F., & Anderson, J. (1983). Techniques for improving cognitive rehabilitation: Teaching organization and encoding skills. *Cognitive Rehabilitation, 1,* 20–22.

Patten, B.M. (1972). The ancient art of memory: Usefulness in treatment. *Archives of Neurology, 26,* 25–31.

Plum, F., & Posner, J. (1980). *The diagnosis of stupor and coma.* Philadelphia: F.A. Davis.

Premack, D. (1959). Toward empirical behavior laws: 1. Positive reinforcement. *Psychological Review, 66,* 219–233.

Rao, S.M., & Bieliauskas, L.A. (1983). Cognitive rehabilitation two and one-half years post right temporal lobectomy. *Journal of Clinical Neuropsychology, 5,* 313–320.

Richardson, J.T.E. (1979). Mental imagery, human memory and the effects of closed head injuries. *British Journal of Social and Clinical Psychology, 18,* 319–327.

Riessman, F. (1965). The "helper therapy" principle. *Social Work, 10,* 27–32.

Rimel, R.W., Giordani, B., Barth, J.T., Boll, T.J., & Jane, J.A. (1981). Disability caused by minor head injury. *Neurosurgery, 9,* 221–228.

Rimel, R.W., & Jane, J.A. (1983). Characteristics of the head-injured patient. In M. Rosenthal, E.R. Griffith, M.R. Bond, & J.D. Miller (Eds.), *Rehabilitation of the head injured adult* (pp. 9–21). Philadelphia: F.A. Davis.

Roberts, A.H. (1976). Long-term prognosis of severe accidental head injury. *Proceedings of the Royal Society of Medicine, 69,* 137–140.

Roberts, A.H. (1979). *Severe accidental head injury: An assessment of long-term prognosis.* London: McMillan.

Romano, M.D. (1974). Family response to traumatic head injury. *Scandinavian Journal of Rehabilitation Medicine, 6,* 1–4.

Ron, A., Najenson, T., & Mendelson, L. (1977). Development of comparative methods of evaluating rehabilitation after cerebrocranial injury. *Scandinavian Journal of Rehabilitation Medicine, 9,* 141–146.

Rosanoff, A.J. (1983). *Manual of psychiatry and mental hygiene.* New York: John Wiley & Sons.

Rosenbaum, M., Lipsitz, N., Abraham, J., & Najenson, T. (1978). A description of an intensive treatment project for the rehabilitation of severely brain-injured soldiers. *Scandinavian Journal of Rehabilitation Medicine, 10,* 1–6.

Rosenbaum, M., & Najenson, T. (1976). Changes in life patterns and symptoms of low as reported by wives of severely brain-injured soldiers. *Journal of Consulting and Clinical Psychology, 44,* 881–888.

Rosenthal, M. (1983). Behavioral sequelae. In M. Rosenthal, E.R. Griffith, M.R. Bond, & J.D. Miller (Eds.), *Rehabilitation of the head-injured adult* (pp. 197–208). Philadelphia: F.A. Davis.

Rusk, H.A., Block, J.M., & Lowman, E.W. (1969). Rehabilitation of the brain-injured patient: A report of 157 cases with long-term follow-up of 118. In A.E. Walker, W.F. Caveness, E.M. Critchley (Eds.), *The late effects of head injury* (pp. 327–332). Springfield, IL: Charles C Thomas.

Russell, W.R. (1932). Cerebral involvement in head injury. *Brain, 55,* 549–603.

Sand, P.L., Trieschmann, R.B., Fordyce, W.E., & Fowler, R.S. (1970). Behavior modification in the medical rehabilitation setting: Rationale and some applications. *Rehabilitation Research and Practice Review, 1,* 11–24.

Schachter, D.L., & Crovitz, H.F. (1977). Memory function after closed head injury: A review of the quantitative research. *Cortex, 13,* 150–176.

Seligman, M.E. (1975). *Helplessness: On depression, development, and death.* San Francisco: W.H. Freeman.

Small, L. (1973). *Neuropsychodiagnosis in Psychotherapy.* New York: Brunner/Mazel.

Snell, R.S. (1980). *Clinical neuroanatomy for medical students.* Boston: Little, Brown.

Snoek, J., Jennett, B., Adam, J.H., Graham, D.I., & Doyle, D. (1979). Computerized tomography after recent severe head injury in patients without intracranial hematoma. *Journal of Neurology, Neurosurgery and Psychiatry, 42,* 215–225.

Stanton, K.M., Flowers, C.R., Kuhl, P.K., Miller, R.M., & Smith, C.H. (1979). Language oriented training program to teach compensation of left side neglect. *Archives of Physical Medicine and Rehabilitation, 60,* 540. (Abstract)

Strich, S.J. (1956). Diffuse degeneration of the cerebral white matter in severe dementia following head injury. *Journal of Neurology, Neurosurgery and Psychiatry, 19,* 163–185.

Strich, S.J. (1969). The pathology of brain damage due to blunt head injuries. In A.E. Walker, W.F. Caveness, & E.M. Critchley (Eds.), *The late effects of head injury* (pp. 501–524). Springfield, IL: Charles C Thomas.

Strub, R.L., & Black, F.W. (1981). *Organic brain syndromes: An introduction to neurobehavioral disorders.* Philadelphia: F.A. Davis.

Strub, R.L. (1982). Acute confusional state. In D.F. Benson & D. Blumer (Eds.), *Psychiatric aspects of neurologic diseases* (Vol. 2, pp. 1–23). New York: Grune & Stratton.

Symonds, C.P. (1937). Mental disorder following head injury. *Proceedings of the Royal Society of Medicine, 30,* 1081–1092.

Thomsen, I.V. (1974). The patient with severe head injury and his family: A follow-up study of 50 patients. *Scandinavian Journal of Rehabilitation Medicine, 6,* 180–183.

Thomsen, I.V. (1975). Evaluation and outcome of aphasia in patients with severe closed head trauma. *Journal of Neurology, Neurosurgery and Psychiatry, 38,* 713–718.

Timming, R., Orrison, W.W., & Mikula, J.A. (1982). Computerized tomography and rehabilitation outcome after severe head trauma. *Archives of Physical Medicine and Rehabilitation, 63,* 154–159.

Tobis, J.S., Puri, K.B., & Sheridan, J. (1982). Rehabilitation of the severely brain-injured patients. *Scandinavian Journal of Rehabilitation Medicine, 14,* 83–88.

Valenstein, E., & Heilman, K.M. (1979). Emotional disorders resulting from lesions of the central nervous system. In K.M. Heilman & E. Valenstein (Eds.), *Clinical neuropsychology,* (pp. 413–438). New York: Oxford University Press.

Van Zomeren, A.H., & Deelman, B.G. (1976). Differential effects of simple and choice reaction after closed head injury. *Clinical Neurology and Neurosurgery, 79,* 81–90.

von Bertalanffy, L. (1968). *General systems theory.* New York: Braziller.

Walsh, K.W. (1978). *Neuropsychology: A clinical approach.* New York: Churchill Livingstone.

Webster, J.S., & Scott, R.R. (1983). The effects of self-instructional training on attentional deficits following head injury. *Clinical Neuropsychology, 5,* 69–74.

Weddell, R., Oddy, M., & Jenkins, D. (1980). Social adjustment after rehabilitation: A two year follow-up of patients with severe head injury. *Psychological Medicine, 10,* 257–263.

Weinberg, J., Diller, L, Gordon, W.A., Gerstman, L.J., Lieberman, A., Lakin, P., Hodges, G., & Ezrachi, O. (1977). Visual scanning training effect on reading-related tasks in acquired right brain damage. *Archives of Physical Medicine & Rehabilitation, 58,* 479–486.

Weinberg, J., Diller, L., Gordon, W.A., Gerstman, L.J., Lieberman, A., Lakin, P., Hodges, G., & Ezrachi, O. (1979). Training sensory awareness and spatial organization in people with right brain damage. *Archives of Physical Medicine and Rehabilitation, 60,* 491–496.

Weinstein, G.S., & Wells, C.E. (1981). Case studies in neuropsychiatry: Post-traumatic psychiatric dysfunction—diagnosis and treatment. *Journal of Clinical Psychiatry, 42,* 12–122.

Wilson, P. (1983). Software selection and use in language and cognitive retraining. *Cognitive Rehabilitation, 1,* 9–10.

Young, G.C., Collins, D., & Hren, M. (1983). Effect of pairing scanning training with block design training in the remediation of perceptual problems in left hemiplegics. *Journal of Clinical Neuropsychology, 5,* 201–212.

CHAPTER 18

Concepts and Methods in the Design of Automata for Neuropsychological Test Interpretation

Kenneth M. Adams

Under what circumstances will the computer be helpful in the interpretation of neuropsychological test results? This chapter presents information that will answer this question in at least one respect.

Computing machinery or equipment has been in use in many neuropsychology laboratories for years, principally as an adjunctive aid to persons examining patients. Halstead (1940) produced one of the first perceptual research consoles, as well as a later variety of devices designed to present stimuli, signal feedback to the subject, and measure responses. This equipment was primarily electromechanical and relied heavily on the relay and servomechanisms so prominent in the electrical engineering technology of that time.

More recent advances in electronics have produced devices for testing that are several orders of magnitude smaller, lighter, and more efficient than their predecessors. Nearly every facet of behavior in the laboratory can be passively measured or actively influenced through monitoring by or interaction with microdevices of some type.

This progress is both exciting and gratifying to neuropsychologists hard at work in creating better assessment devices. However, comparable progress has not been achieved in the development of computer programs for the analysis and interpretation of neuropsychological test data. We turn now to the examination of the necessity for neuropsychological interactive *automata,* or sequential machines, and some barriers to their realization.

A NEED FOR PUBLIC SPECIFICATION

Clinical assessment and judgment is a rational, sequential process. As such, it would seem to be possible to apply the theory of automata (Bavel, 1983) to this enterprise. Regardless of the observations or test tools used, a process must exist that combines measurement and appraisal of the patient's behavior and results in predictions. Such predictions are probabilistic estimates concerning cerebral dysfunction, current psychological abilities, and future adaptive functioning.

Some would be quick to object to the simplicity of this conceptualization of clinical judgment. It is important to reaffirm that many variables can and do come to bear on the process of clinical interpretation. Problems or conditions specific to particular patients (e.g., limited sensory functioning and peripheral injuries) may require consideration.

However, a main process or plan must be available that spells out the procedures and strategy of the interpretation of observations and data. These "rules and interpretation" need to be codified, public, and subject to verification. The existence of such rules and constant scrutiny for their improvement represent the critical differences between private belief and scientific knowledge. No amount of explanation concerning the complexity of clinical interpretation can substitute for its specification. Without such rules, no scientific standard for judgment or improvement can exist.

THE PROSPECTS FOR NEUROPSYCHOLOGICAL RULES

Given the demand for public specification of interpretative rules, how can neuropsychologists respond?

Two types of rules can be drafted to satisfy the specification requirement. General rules can be written that direct a *mode* of evaluation of neuropsychological data. That is, one can write rules by which to examine parameters of data common to all such variables. For example, a *general* rule can be written to examine the level of performance, latency, or frequency characteristics of groups of variables regardless of their particular content. In contrast, *specific* rules can be written so that individual tests or observations are treated in a unique way so as to facilitate prediction. That is, particular data points may be subjected to sequential analysis on the basis of previous research or information in predicting specific behaviors.

As simple as this process may sound, few attempts have been made in neuropsychology to formulate such rules, especially general rules. Most methodologists in neuropsychology prefer to attribute this dearth of rules to the relative newness of the clinical neuropsychological enterprise and its rapidly evolving knowledge base. These explanations appear to be losing their appeal as clinical neuropsychology begins to show signs of stability and acceptance as a very highly developed area of medical psychology. Thus, the time to specify interpretative procedures and examine critically their accuracy has surely arrived.

ENTER THE COMPUTER

To use interpretative rules in clinical neuropsychology, a computer may not be necessary. A flowchart that has the potential to produce excellent results can be created and used manually. However, as the computational requirements of rules increase, computers provide a significant savings of time with increased capability and precision. The use of a computer also reduces the likelihood of tampering with the flowchart and the attendant risk of reduced reliability. Moreover, the computer may be deployed in interpretation so that its rules may be improved by the addition of data entered from each case.

AVAILABLE RULES AND EARLIER PROGRAMS

The designs of previous programs for automated interpretation have employed various conceptual schemes. These programs can be described as (1) taxonomic systems; (2) geometric, or geographical, systems; (3) ability-based systems; or (4) systems modeled after neuropsychological inference strategies used by clinicians.

Taxonomic Systems

The taxonomic approach (e.g., Russell, Neuringer, & Goldstein, 1970) is adapted from biological protocols used to classify samples of plant and animal life in appropriate categories. In these applications, impaired subjects are characterized according to comparisons against fixed standards and between various test scores. Rules are established that systematically sift the available test scores according to a decision tree. In these models, all subjects are classified.

The advantages of such an approach are similar to those enjoyed by numerical taxonomic methods (Sneath & Sokol, 1973). There is a degree of objectivity based on the operational definitions of psychological measurement. At the same time, such systems may or may not capture important information concerning qualitative psychological differences. In research practice, overreliance on numerical taxonomic methods can actually produce misleading or erroneous results (Adams, 1985).

In clinical interpretation, the numerical taxonomy method can conceivably work if (1) the "characters" of each key are reliable, (2) the data points used are valid, and (3) the particular objects or types defined for each endpoint of a key are sufficiently homogenous to allow consistent and sensible outcomes upon its application.

In many interpretative tasks, this final criterion is difficult to achieve. For example, in psychiatric populations, neuropsychological evaluation and interpretation is extremely difficult due to the large number of influences on test performance (Heaton, Baade, & Johnson, 1978). Moreover, diagnostic definitions of subgroups in psychiatric practice have much less reliability and consensus clarity in their use than do comparable definitions in neurology and neurosurgery.

This difficulty in criterion specification for some tasks might suggest that a more definite focus—the brain itself—might be more suitable. We turn next to such a conception.

Geometric, or Geographical, Systems

The general class of geometric, or geographical, procedures is adapted from mathematics (e.g., Swiercinsky, 1978a). Test scores and profiles are "fitted" to the patient's brain such that greater or lesser degrees of correlation with a numerical, geometric criterion "moves" the site of suspected dysfunction along a Cartesian set of axes (x, y, z) utilizing a Euclidean geometric approach. There is high dependence on the strengths and

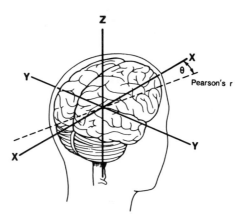

Figure 18.1. Illustration of the relationship between a test correlation coefficient (θ) and a Cartesian coordinate system in the brain.

weaknesses of the geometric model in any system of this type. Not all subjects can be classified with such systems.

Figure 18.1 illustrates how the correlation coefficient can be used as a geographical reference point in such a multiaxial system. In this case, the angle represented by theta (θ) is a geometric translation of a test correlation coefficient. The possibilities of multiplanar transposition are considerable in this "general case."

Swiercinsky's (1978a) SAINT (System for Analysis and Interpretation of Neuropsychological Tests) protocol relies on a varient of this general model. The program is a flexible one, allowing use of various tests and providing for revised rules as needed. Fundamentally, the various rules contribute points on a scale from −3 to +3 in a three-dimensional Cartesian space of the kind described above. The three planes to which the rules are related are labeled sagittal, frontal, and transverse in this system.

When used in concert with more general and traditional summary rules concerning the existence and severity of impairment, Swiercinsky's model has great potential value in the objective evaluation of localization rules presumed to be of value in clinical neuropsychology.

In the original documentation (Swiercinsky, 1978a), a plan for narrative interpretative statements was described. We now turn to a different approach, which depends greatly on interpretation rules to select appropriate narrative statements regarding neuropsychological status from amongst a library of possibilities generated by expert clinicians.

Ability-Based Systems

Ability-based systems (e.g., Adams, 1975) are based on the orderly comparison of scores on various combinations of tests thought to be related to particular brain-sensitive abilities. These ability structures are defined on an a priori basis. The results in each case are compared with previous cases, and probabilistic statements are made concerning the existence and locus of brain dysfunction from the abilities. Not all subjects are classified with respect to localization.

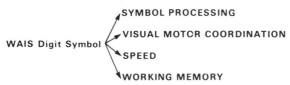

Figure 18.2. Example of how an individual test may be broken down on the basis of presumed ability content.

Figure 18.2 provides an illustration of the conceptual progress involved in such ability "decomposition." The Digit Symbol Test from the Wechsler Adult Intelligence Scale can be viewed as encompassing the four component abilities involved. Evidence for such specification of abilities can come from a variety of factor analytic and theoretical sources. Such ability-based models of brain-behavior relationships have shown considerable overlap and can be objectively tested (Newby, Hallenbeck, & Embretson, 1983; Swiercinsky, 1978b).

Figure 18.3 illustrates the second step in an ability-based interpretation. Results from tests involving the same abilities or components are sifted for relative quality of performances, and a conclusion is made concerning the etiology of an impaired performance. Computer programs using such approaches must search systematically through data according to a specified conceptual scheme.

The ultimate step in the Adams' ability-based program is the making of a series of inferences concerning the integrity of brain processes from the profile of abilities in individual patients. Tests are grouped according to common abilities and considered by virtue of their scores to be more or less well performed. This step is illustrated in Figure 18.4.

Based on the specific configural pattern of scores, one of a variety of preprogrammed interpretative statements is selected from among a library prepared by expert clinicians concerning the particular ability profile in question. Finally, a numerical ability rating is assigned to the ability in question. This rating is based on a prepared rating of the paragraph by experts. In turn, the numerical rating serves as a basis for a profile of brain-behavior abilities.

While this approach does have a certain common-sense appeal, it may not correspond to the ways in which some clinicians conduct their clinical interpretations. For this type of program, we turn next to another exemplar.

Systems Modeled after Neuropsychological Inference Strategies Used by Clinicians

The final approach attempts to copy the ways in which expert clinicians actually study their neuropsychological protocols (e.g., Finkelstein, 1977). In effect, the computer program is an attempt to recreate different ways in which the level of scores, scatter, special patterns, and other phenomena are handled in practice.

Finkelstein's (1977) program is similar to the protocol of Russell, Neuringer, and Goldstein (1970) in that absolute levels of test scores and relational rules are used to

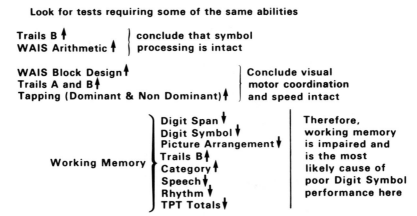

Figure 18.3.   Example of how an individual test finding can be reconciled with those of other tests requiring the same abilities.

calculate the probability, severity, and type of impairment for each case. Hom (1979) has written a hand-scoring version of Finkelstein's (1977) program.

The organization of these rules is guided by a general model of clinical interpretation for neuropsychological case data that is available without the computer (Reitan, 1974) and has a well-defined set of principles and objectives available in published form.

The output from this particular program is brief, most often consisting of one to four declarative statements concerning the likelihood of cerebral dysfunction, the locus of the dysfunction, the acuity of the dysfunction, and the etiology of the dysfunction.

The development of this type of program presupposes that expert clinicians can make their process of interpretation objective and public. This requirement may seem obvious, but careful consideration will suggest to the reader that few published guidelines for the comprehensive analysis and interpretation of assessment results exist.

Many individual findings and results from research can be brought to bear by the trained neuropsychologist; but a number of the major approaches to neuropsychological assessment in North America do not have codified systems for the interpretation of individual clinical records of patients. This lack of a specified interpretative protocol impedes any plan for automation. More important, the absence of these essential rules places these approaches beyond evaluation—and conceivably outside the realm of science.

It is important, too, to note the distinction between public specification of knowledge and the automation of *all* the clinician's activity. The professional neuropsychologist performs a wide variety of tasks beyond the capability of any computer. In suggesting that objective principles of clinical interpretation be put forth, there is *no* conflict created between this objective and the wider clinical, educational, and research activities of the clinician. Rather, it remains essential for any discipline pretending to scientific status to spell out in general form the relationship between knowledge and its application.

Given the foregoing descriptions of the philosophical approaches to neuropsychological interpretative automata to date, we now turn to a synopsis of results reported in their use.

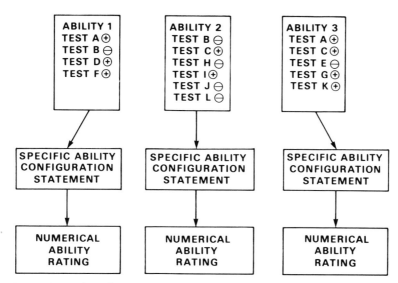

Figure 18.4.   Illustration of how particular configuration of ability findings in a patient may result in specified clinical interpretations.

RESULTS TO DATE USING EXISTING APPROACHES

It is important to emphasize that each of the computer programs described above was written as an experimental or demonstration tool for research. None of the above types of programs has been held out by the developers to be definitive or generalizable to clinical settings.

In general, clinical tests of these types of programs have produced mixed results. With respect to the Key program of Russell, Neuringer, and Goldstein (1970), Swiercinsky and Warnock (1977) found that this computer algorithm was more accurate (86.8%) than a linear discriminant analysis method (68.2%) in the identification of patients having cerebral damage. However, this advantage was offset by a far greater rate of false positive diagnostic errors in non–brain-damaged patients by the program (51.3%) in comparison to the discriminant equation (28.2%). These investigators concluded that neither of the two approaches to classification could be considered as being more accurate than the other. More generally, the results would not seem to support the use of either method in clinical practice.

Goldstein and Shelly (1982) found that the Key approach produced satisfactory results in their cross-validation study. However, Anthony and associates (Anthony, Heaton, & Lehman, 1980) did not find either the Key approach or the approach of Finkelstein (1977) to be adequate.

In a more recent study (Adams, Kvale, & Keegan, 1984), we compared three of the above systems (the Key system, Adams' ability-based system, and Finkelstein's clinical inference program). Two separate samples of patients were used in the study and carefully screened. Individual case results were entered into each of the programs, and the computer predictions were compared to the known criterion information concerning the brain.

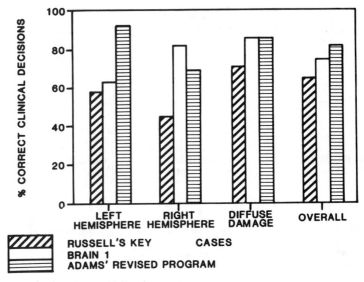

Figure 18.5.   Results of a study comparing the accuracy of three automated interpretation programs in identifying the presence of cerebral dysfunction.

The results of the second of the two studies by Adams and colleagues (1984) studies are illustrative. Some 30 well-screened patients (mean age, 60.7 years, and standard deviation, 7.0 years; mean education, 11.6 years, and standard deviation, 3.2 years) were evaluated and found to have precise and truly uncomplicated neurological dysfunction etiologies involving cerebrovascular disease. All the patients received comprehensive and equivalent neuropsychological examinations at the same point in clinical course.

When the individual cases were subjected to evaluation by the three methods described above, the accuracy of the methods in identifying the existence of neuropsychologists proved to be roughly equivalent. The results of this study are shown in Figure 18.5.

When the programs were again compared with respect to their capability to predict the brain locus or diffuse nature of cerebral dysfunction, the results were again equal in accuracy over the three programs. Figure 18.6 presents these data for the various programs and subjects.

While some marginal advantages in the accuracy of prediction could be gleaned from the results, the overall outcome indicated that none of the programs were successful in predicting the existence and localization of cerebral dysfunction, given the very high base rates for impairment in the sample and the well-specified nature of the patients' disease.

These initial findings should not be discouraging, but should instead foster research concerning how programs could be improved and made to perform more adequately in clinical trials. There is ample evidence from clinical psychological research demonstrating the superiority of actuarial interpretative systems over clinical judgment in individual cases. Given that neuropsychological interpretation programs developed to date are neither well-developed nor actuarial, it may be the case that future algorithms will be able to produce equal or better results than expert clinicians on a routine basis.

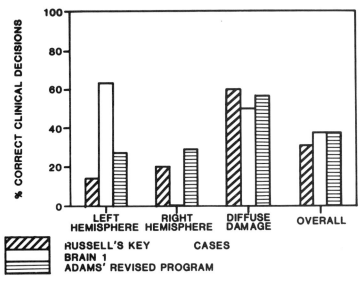

Figure 18.6.   Results of a study comparing the accuracy of three automated interpretation programs in identifying the locus of cerebral dysfunction.

The only direct comparison between the diagnostic accuracy of a currently available computer program and expert clinicians was reported in a study by Heaton and associates (Heaton, Grant, Anthony, & Lehman, 1981). Briefly, they compared expert neuropsychologists' ratings of impairment in patients against similar judgments produced by the Key program of Russell and associates (1970). The results of this study indicated that experienced clinicians can make more accurate predictions concerning the existence, locus, and nature of neuropsychological deficit than can the Key program.

This outcome should not be construed to mean that expert judges are inherently better than comparable automata. Were this to be the case, clinical neuropsychological interpretation would be the first diagnostic enterprise in medical history to fail to profit via specification and automation of its decision process.

HOW TO DEVELOP BETTER COMPUTER PROGRAMS FOR AUTOMATED NEUROPSYCHOLOGICAL INTERPRETATION

This brings us to the current state of research on neuropsychological interpretative automata. In this portion of the chapter, we turn to some ideas that may serve to improve automata by taking better advantage of the computer's strengths.

Improvements in programs may be realized by pursuing one or both of two strategies: (1) the improvement of automata via complete or careful correspondence to theories of brain behavior relationships and (2) the improvement of automata via more complete or careful correspondence to existing methods of clinical interpretation.

While the concordance is not complete, these two strategies may be seen as roughly equivalent to improving (1) Swiercinsky's (1978a) geographic or Adams' (1975) ability-based approach and (2) Russell's taxonomic Key or Finkelstein's (1977) Brain I. None of these programs has shown a clear superiority over the others, or acceptable predictive accuracy in the absolute sense (Adams, Kvale, & Keegan, 1984). Thus, it may be most useful to first attempt development of the interpretative model with the greatest degree of construct validity in relation to the task at hand: clinical neuropsychological interpretation.

A MODEL FOR IMPROVEMENT

By any standard, the most fully specified method of clinical neuropsychological interpretation is that offered by Reitan (1974). We will not review here the details of his method, except to note the four major modes of clinical interpretation: (1) level of performance, (2) left-right comparisons, (3) differential patterns, and (4) pathognomonic signs.

These four approaches to neuropsychological case interpretation are generalizable to any set of tests possessing public, objective, and acceptable technical characteristics (American Psychological Association, 1974).

For purposes of this discussion, we have set for comparison four levels of analysis that we have described as desirable in neuropsychological interpretative schemes (Adams & Brown, 1984). The intersection of these modes and levels can be seen in Figure 18.7.

A comprehensive and evolving model of neuropsychological interpretation will, in general, be able to address the need for information used by each of the cells in Figure 18.1. For purposes of this chapter, we will describe how each of the modes of analysis might be more fully represented in future neuropsychological automata.

LEVEL OF PERFORMANCE

Neuropsychological interpretation has depended more on level of performance judgments than any other mode. Advances have been made from earlier days in which level of performance judgments were made in terms of various rough indices for "brain damage" (Hewson, 1949; Wechsler, 1958) or in terms of "cut points" that might simply identify impaired patients. In more recent times, sophisticated regression formulae (Wilson, Rosenbaum, & Brown, 1979) and Bayesian probability equations (Gordon, 1977) for calculating predictive information have brought neuropsychological inference to a more adequate conceptual state.

The power of the computer has special appeal for this mode of analysis, and some of the possible aids to interpretation can be listed: (1) calculation of scores and ratios, (2) calculation of special scales and indexes, (3) calculation of actuarially based cutoff scores, (4) calculation of Bayesian probabilities of performance, and (5) calculation of binomial probabilities of performance based on actuarial tables.

In well-developed programs, algorithms can be developed to conduct comparisons of each case against (1) norms available from the development of tests (e.g., manual), (2) norms available from previously published studies, and (3) norms available from local laboratory experience with similar cases. In addition, level of performance analysis can be conducted on a multivariate mathematical level to compute (1) indexes of scatter and shape (e.g., Cattell, Coulter, & Tsujioka, 1966), (2) goodness of fit with

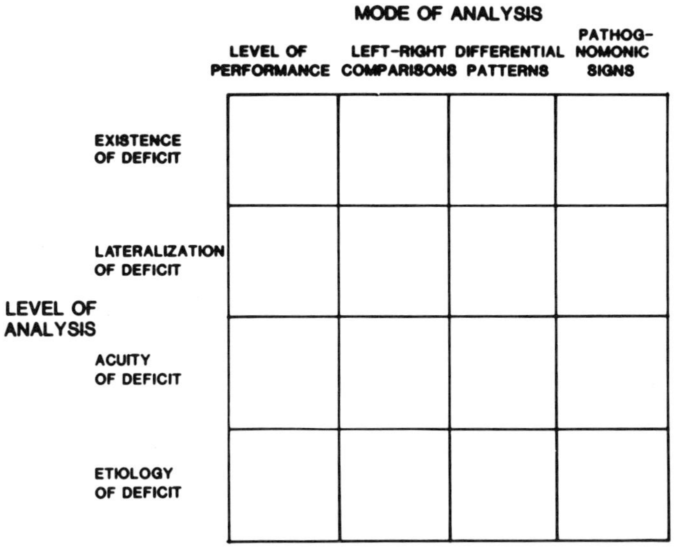

MODE OF ANALYSIS

Figure 18.7.   Clinical issues and some modes of interpretation.

previous case profiles (e.g., Knights, 1973), and (3) indexes of agreement with ideal cases or published standards (e.g., Rourke & Adams, 1984). Finally, any of these level of performance calculations requires careful programming development if the resultant predictors are to be useful. In general, some provisions must be included to (1) consider the effect of any missing data, (2) include data concerning patient status (inpatient, outpatient), (3) include variables that may influence interpretation (e.g., drug status, peripheral injury), (4) integrate a rating of reliability of the patient's performance, and (5) assign a rating of confidence concerning criterion information about the patient's brain and enter the case into the appropriate position in the computer's memory.

If the tasks enumerated above were to be accomplished by a computer program, a good deal of the potential of level of performance data could be realized. It should be obvious that most clinicians do not have the time to do all the calculations described above for each of their cases. While most knowledgeable clinical neuropsychologists would agree that such calculations would be desirable, the automation of such lengthy and complex comparisons would make them possible on a routine basis.

LEFT-RIGHT COMPARISONS

A situation similar to that for performance level exists with respect to left-right comparisons. Most neuropsychologists include in their assessment some form of measurement of sensory and motor performances with both sides of the body. Yet rarely is this information treated in a rigorous manner with respect to (1) age, sex, body weight, drug states, occupational status, psychophysical thresholds, and risk conditions (e.g., peripheral neuropathy, retinopathy, etc.); (2) a hierarchical analysis of sensory-motor performance with respect to task complexity; (3) an analysis of consistency and probability with respect to motor performance over trials and time (e.g., finger tapping); (4) the likelihood of various sensory and motor performances, given cognitive skills and abilities (e.g., IQ); and (5) the relationships of hand, foot, and eye preference to performance or inferred lateralization. Predictions concerning cerebral lateralization and function represent the second most frequent type of inference made by neuropsychologists in their clinical interpretations.

To date, few objective rules have been developed or reported concerning this process. To be sure, some standards have been declared, such as Reitan's rule of thumb that motor performance should be 10% more efficient with the preferred hand (Reitan, 1974). No known rules have been published concerning the ways in which demographic and behavioral variables can be combined to make left-right comparisons most useful in various levels of analysis, although new studies of high quality are emerging (Bornstein, 1985, 1986; Heaton, Grant, & Matthews, 1986).

Finally, we should note that the use of the computer as a transducer or data acquisition device has its most clear promise with respect to sensory-motor variables. That is, sensory-motor functions can be more completely measured and analyzed by using microprocessor devices to time and record stimulus and response patterns. Recent developments with microcomputer devices make measurement and monitoring possible without disrupting the interpersonal nature of the examination.

Sensory-motor measures constitute the most valid indexes of the lateralization of impairment. Therefore, special efforts need to be made to capture more finely grained qualitative measurements of rates, latencies, forces, and errors in the laboratory situation.

DIFFERENTIAL PATTERNS

In interpreting neuropsychological protocols, most clinicians conduct a reconnaisance of various tests to look at scores and patterns of scores that characteristically are influenced by an underlying construct (e.g., left-hemisphere mediated, visual content, short-term memory demand, etc.). These various ways and means of looking at data constitute *differential patterns* in the broadest sense.

It should be possible for clinicians to specify the ways and means of comparing various portions of a data set—both between and within tests. These agendas can be executed far more rapidly and reliably by a computer. A computer can also qualify these comparisons on the basis of stored actuarial information concerning the performance of the demographic subgroups to which the subject belongs.

In addition, a computer can conduct analyses of data to provide information on (1) ability groupings; (2) the comparison of subject performances against known factor analytic structures (e.g., Newby, Hallenbeck, & Embretson, 1983); (3) the comparison of various features of patient performances against profiles of subjects having certain syndromes; and (4) the likelihood of the existence acute or chronic impairment, based on disciplined inspection of individual performances (e.g., Smith, 1981). These tasks could be amended or replaced in a variety of ways, depending on evaluation research outcomes. To date, differential patterns have had the greatest unrealized potential of any of the evaluation modes and could provide far more information to the clinicians concerning acuity and etiology of neuropsychological impairment.

To do this, it is necessary to pursue the developmental process of rule creation and testing. The application of differential pattern rules is a time-consuming job not systematically completed by many neuropsychologists doing "routine" evaluations. It is the consistent completion of this scrutiny that will result in improved interpretation.

PATHOGNOMONIC SIGNS

This last mode of clinical analysis, the use of pathognomonic signs, is perhaps the most difficult to subject to computer analysis. Styles of performance, irregularities in visual-motor performance, and flaws in problem solving are difficult to capture in objective form.

Nevertheless, such specification is necessary and possible. For example, drawings and other subject reproductions can be made on devices that will instantly digitize and record the behavior for playback and analysis. Positional recording devices for such objects as Koh's blocks are easily created and can keep flawless records of each subject movements. Finally, similar voice recording digitizers can capture and encode subject vocalizations for playback and analysis.

Some of the practical problems involved in capturing pathognomonic signs in a reliable way will require ingenuity and considerable developmental work. However, the nature of pathognomonic signs of neuropsychological impairment make this work necessary. The high degree of predictive accuracy and behavioral specificity of these low–base-rate phenomena would seem to justify such efforts. At present, no objective or systematic way of evaluating such signs exists, although some preliminary attempts at rating some pathognomonic signs have been described (e.g., Russell, Neuringer, & Goldstein, 1970). The balance of such signs reset either in the realm of clinical lore and are highly dependent on the subjective judgment and objective skill of the interpreter.

THE FINAL PRODUCT

The four modes of analysis described above can be incomparably assisted by the use of neuropsychological interpretative automata. While some excellent models for individual tests have been advanced (Delis, Kramer, Ober, & Kaplan, 1983), no general systems for the analysis of neuropsychological results can accomplish the ambitious set of tasks described above. Adams and Heaton (1985) have reviewed the performance of general systems and suggested the ways in which an "ideal" program could be conceptualized.

Even if all the tasks described above could be accomplished, the resultant computer product would likely be a technical report requiring the expert clinician's inspection. Even if the computer were to produce interpretative statements (Adams, 1975), no responsible psychologist could advocate the use of such output information without human scrutiny. Fortunately, the specter of assessment and diagnosis by machine (Lezak, 1983) is not a realistic problem for ethical professionals.

There is no shortage of dilemmas for the clinical researcher in the development and use of computers in neuropsychology (McSweeny, 1984). The recent creation of task force study groups by the International Neuropsychological Society (INS) and the Division of Clinical Neuropsychology of the American Psychological Association would seem to indicate a significant level of concern among clinicians and researchers.

Be that as it may, the use of automata in clinical neuropsychological assessment is likely to increase. This may be seen soonest in terms of test administration, but the introduction of interpretative schemes such as the one described here may hasten the day when the rules of clinical interpretation are more clearly set forth for study and improvement.

SUMMARY

The use of the computer to interpret neuropsychological test results requires program architects to specify the procedures to be used. This need for objective specification is absolute and can only advance understanding of neuropsychological practice in the long term. Existing programs have been developed from taxonomic, geometric, and clinical inference conceptions. These programs have not produced acceptable results to date, and no responsible practitioner would utilize the available systems to supplant clinician-mediated neuropsychological interpretation. Some directions for further development of algorithms are suggested, with emphasis on the main modes of clinical interpretation in use by human clinicians. These improvements will need to proceed in compliance with the very highest standards of scientific rigor, quality, assurance, and ethical restraint.

REFERENCES

Adams, K.M. (1975). Automated clinical interpretation of the neuropsychological test battery: An ability based approach. *Dissertation Abstracts International, 35*, 6085B. (University Microfilms No. 75-13, 289)

Adams, K.M. (1985). Theoretical, methodological, and statistical issues. In B.P. Rourke (Ed.), *Neuropsychology of learning disabilities: Essentials of subtype analysis* (pp. 17–39). New York: Guilford Press.

Adams, K.M., & Brown, G.G. (1984). Automating the expertise of the neuropsychologist. *Henry Ford Hospital Medical Journal, 32*, 182–187.

Adams, K.M., & Heaton, R.K. (1985). Automated interpretation of neuropsychological tests. *Journal of Consulting and Clinical Psychology, 53*, 790–802.

Adams, K.M., Kvale, V.I., & Keegan, J.F. (1984). Performance of three automated systems for neuropsychological interpretation based on two representative tasks. *Journal of Clinical Neuropsychology, 6*, 413–431.

American Psychological Association. (1974). Standards for education and psychological tests. Washington, DC: American Psychological Association.

Anthony, W.Z., Heaton, R.K., & Lehman, R.A.W. (1980). An attempt to cross-validate two actuarial systems for neuropsychological test interpretation. *Journal of Consulting and Clinical Psychology, 48*, 317–326.

Bavel, Z. (1983). *Introduction to the theory of automata.* Reston, VA: Reston.

Bornstein, R. (1985). Normative data on selected neuropsychological measures in a nonclinical sample. *Journal of Clinical Psychology, 41*, 651–659.

Bornstein, R. (in press). Normative data on intermanual differences on three tests of motor performance. *Journal of Clinical and Experimental Neuropsychology, 8.*

Cattell, R.B., Coulter, M.A., & Tsujioka, B. (1966). The taxonomic recognitions of types and functional emergents. In R.B. Cattell (Ed.), *Handbook of multivariate experimental psychology* (pp. 288–329). Chicago: Rand McNally.

Delis, D.C., Kramer, J., Ober, B.A., & Kaplan, E. (1983). *The California verbal learning test: Administration and interpretation.* Martinez, CA. (Available from D.C. Delis, V.A. Medical Center, San Diego, Ca., 92161)

Finkelstein, J.N. (1977). BRAIN: A computer program for interpretation of the Halstead-Reitan Neuropsychological Test Battery. *Dissertation Abstracts International, 37,* 5349B. (University Microfilms No. 77-8, 8864)

Goldstein, G., & Shelly, C. (1982). A further attempt to cross validate the Russell, Neuringer and Goldstein neuropsychological keys. *Journal of Consulting and Clinical Psychology, 50,* 721–728.

Gordon, N. (1977). Base rates and the decision-making model in clinical neuropsychology. *Cortex, 13,* 3–10.

Halstead, W.C., Walker, A.E., & Bucy, P.C. (1940). Sparing and nonsparing of "macular" vision associated with occipital lobectomy in man. *Archives of Ophthalmology, 24,* 948–962.

Heaton, R.K., Grant, I., Anthony, W.Z., & Lehman, R.A.W. (1981). A comparison of clinical and automated interpretation of the Halstead-Reitan Battery. *Journal of Clinical Neuropsychology, 3,* 121–141.

Heaton, R.K., Grant, I., & Matthews, C.G. (1986). Differences in neuropsychological test performance associated with age, education, and sex. In I. Grant & K.M. Adams (Eds.), *Neuropsychological assessment of neuropsychiatric disorders* (pp. 100–120). New York: Oxford University Press.

Heaton, R.K., Baade, L.E., & Johnson, K.L. (1978). Neuropsychological test results associated with psychiatric disorders in adults. *Psychological Bulletin, 85,* 141–162.

Hewson, L. (1949). The Wechsler-Bellevue Scale and the Substitution test as aids in neuropsychiatric diagnosis. *Journal of Nervous and Mental Disease, 109,* 158–183, 246–266.

Hom, J. (1979). *A hand-scoring procedure for the evaluation of individual patients using Halstead-Reitan neuropsychological test data.* Unpublished manuscript, Ralph M. Reitan and associates, Tucson, AZ.

Knights, R.M. (1973). Problems of criteria: A profile similarity approach. *Annals of the New York Academy of Sciences, 205,* 124–131.

Lezak, M. (1983). *Neuropsychological assessment* (2nd ed.). New York: Oxford University Press.

McSweeny, J. (1984, February). *Professional and ethical issues in the use of computers in neuropsychological assessment.* Paper presented at the Twelfth Annual Meeting of the International Neuropsychological Society, Houston.

Newby, R.F., Hallenbeck, C.E., & Embretson, S. (1983). Confirmatory factor analysis of four general neuropsychological models with a modified Halstead-Reitan battery. *Journal of Clinical Neuropsychology, 5,* 115–134.

Reitan, R.M. (1974). Methodological problems in clinical neuropsychology. In R.M. Reitan & L.A. Davison (Eds.), *Clinical neuropsychology: Current status and applications* (pp. 19–46). Washington, DC: V.H. Winston & Sons.

Rourke, B.P., & Adams, K.M. (in press). Quantitative approaches to the neuropsychological assessment of children. In R. Tarter & G. Goldstein (Eds.), *The neuropsychology of childhood* (Vol. 2, pp. 79–108). New York: Plenum.

Russell, E.W., Neuringer, C., & Goldstein, G. (1970). *Assessment of brain damage: Neuropsychological key approach.* New York: John Wiley & Sons.

Smith, A. (1981). Principles underlying human brain functions in neuropsychological sequelae of different neuropathological processes. In S.B. Filskov & T.J. Boll (Eds.), *Handbook of clinical neuropsychology* (Vol. 1, pp. 175–226). New York: John Wiley & Sons.

Sneath, P.H.E., & Sokal, R.R. (1973). *Numerical taxonomy.* San Francisco: W.H. Freeman.

Swiercinsky, D.P. (August 1978a). *Computerized SAINT: System for analysis and interpretation of neuropsychological tests.* Paper presented at the Eighty-sixth annual convention of the American Psychological Association, Toronto, Ontario, Canada.

Swiercinsky, D.P. (1978b). *Manual for the adult neuropsychological evaluation.* Springfield, IL: Charles C Thomas.

Swiercinsky, D.P., & Warnock, J.K. (1977). Comparison of the neuropsychological key and discriminant analysis approaches in predicting cerebral damage and localization. *Journal of Consulting and Clinical Psychology, 45,* 808–814.

Wechsler, D. (1958). *The measurement and appraisal of adult intelligence* (4th ed.). Baltimore: Williams & Wilkins.

Wilson, R.S., Rosenbaum, G., & Brown, G.G. (1979). The problem of premorbid intelligence in neuropsychological assessment. *Journal of Clinical Neuropsychology, 1,* 49–54.

CHAPTER 19

Statistical Models and Their Application in Clinical Neuropsychological Research and Practice

Campbell M. Clark

The primary purpose of the current chapter is to suggest that many neuropsychological research questions are better examined by the psychometric analytic model (i.e., individual differences or correlational methods) than by the experimental or treatment model. Moreover, it is suggested that the results from psychometrically based research studies can be applied directly to the clinical setting. Within this context, it is argued that by overapplying the experimental model of Fisher (1925),[1] weak and perhaps incorrect theories of brain-behavior relationships may have evolved in neuropsychology. In order to place these arguments in a historical and methodological context of psychology, Cronbach's differentiation between correlational (i.e., individual differences) and experimental models of human behavior are reviewed in terms of the assumptions concerning the determinants of behavior (Cronbach, 1957). In addition, the resulting methodological paradox are discussed in terms of statistical partitioning of variance and experimental methods. To illustrate these points in studies examining neuropsychological functions in normal subjects, a commonly used neuropsychological test, the dichotic listening task, is considered with reference to the experimental and individual differences models. In particular, it is argued that the question of interest is an individual differences problem, not an experimental one, and that the individual differences approach may yield stronger and more encompassing theory for elucidating brain-behavior relationships in normal subjects.

Then the logic and empirical efficacy of studies comparing normal and abnormal samples by means of null hypothesis testing or experimental statistics are examined. First, it is argued that because the three design assumptions of the experimental model are violated, the expected outcome of these clinical differentiation studies should be to reject the null hypothesis (Meehl, 1978). Second, the empirical efficacy of these studies is considered in terms of hit rate. Here, it is argued that because the design assumptions of the experimental model are violated, the efficacy of these studies is slightly better than chance (Meehl, 1973). The third issue to be considered is the actual information

---

[1] Although the experimental approach was developed by many statisticians and methodologists, these aspects will be subsumed, for brevity, under the general term *Fisher's experimental or treatment model.*

validated or provided by these studies (Payne, 1958). Specifically, it is suggested that the obtained information is of limited value for developing behavioral theories and classification models for brain dysfunction.

The final portion of the current chapter illustrates how the results of individual differences studies of normal subjects can be employed in single-subject studies in either the clinical or the experimental setting. Specifically, by using the statistical model for the single case study proposed by Payne and Jones (1957), probabilistic statements can be made concerning a subject's performance relative to the normal population. Clinical issues to be considered are (1) a clinically relevant definition of statistically abnormal behavior; (2) the determination of an abnormal difference score between, for example, right and left motor behavior; and (3) the assessment of clinically significant changes over time or treatment. Essentially, the outlined approach is consistent with the classic single-case study method employed by, for example, Broca (1865), except that probabilistic statements concerning behavioral deficits can be made. Therefore, in the experimental setting, replication over subjects allows for the further development of a taxonomic structure of cognitive-behavioral abnormalities resulting from brain disorders. Subsequently, these categories can be related to such neuroanatomical variables as site of lesion. Although, the issues and arguments to be presented here have been well-elucidated elsewhere in the psychological literature, this chapter attempts to integrate these issues and present them within the framework of neuropsychology.

THE TWO DISCIPLINES OF SCIENTIFIC PSYCHOLOGY

Cronbach (1957) averred that there are two distinct approaches in psychology for examining or attempting to understand human behavior. The first approach is based on the tenet that individuals differ in terms of abilities, traits, or attributes. Moreover, individual differences on pertinent attributes are predictive of behavior. The second approach examines the effect of specific situations or stimulus-reinforcement conditions on behavior. The underlying assumption of the second approach is that individuals respond to environmental manipulations or conditions in a systematic or consistent manner. Cronbach (1957) and others (e.g., Bindra & Schier, 1954) argue convincingly that a representative theory of psychology must encompass both individual differences and environmental effects. However, because the methods of the two approaches are designed to maximize the respective assumptions concerning human behavior, the two approaches are, in a sense, antithetical in terms of sampling, experimental design, and statistical partitioning of variance. In order to show the differences between these two approaches, the next two sections describe briefly the goals, methods, and analytic procedures of each method.

The Individual Difference Model

The foundation of the individual differences approach is based on the conceptual approach and statistical work of Spearman (1904, 1910, 1913). Spearman believed that individuals differ in basic cognitive ability (G). Therefore, he developed a statistical model for demonstrating that these differences could be measured reliably across individuals and that these differences could be related to subsequent behavior. The first objective in the approach is to define an attribute of interest and empirically show that it can be measured reliably. Reliability may be estimated over a set of items (i.e., internal consistency), over time (i.e., test-retest), or over forms (i.e., parallel forms) (Thorndike, 1967). Regardless of the type of reliability estimated, the test or measure of reliability is the stability of subject ranking within the distribution of scores. Therefore, because the statistic of interest is usually a type of correlation, the approach is often labeled correlational psychology.[2] To maximize the reliability coefficients, the operational measure of the attribute should be given to a heterogenous sample, thus ensuring large individual differences on the attribute. In addition, the operational measure of the attribute should consist of many items, representative of the hypothesized interest area (e.g., arithmetic ability) because the magnitude of a coefficient is dependent, in part, on the number of items or estimates. Similarly, intervening, or nuisance, variables should be minimized in order to prevent shifts in ranking within the distribution due to nonspecific environmental or experimental factors. In other words, the environmental and experimental factors should be minimized, while intersubject differences should be maximized. These procedures will minimize errors of measurement, and thereby the estimate of reliability will be maximized (Stanley, 1971).

After a reliable measure of an attribute has been developed, the second empirical phase of the individual differences approach is to demonstrate the validity of the attribute. Although there are many types of validity (Nunnally, 1967; Cronbach, 1971), validity, at its simplest level, can be considered as illustrating the scientific relevance or utility of the measure. For example, intelligence as operationally measured by the Wechsler series (Wechsler, 1949, 1955, 1974, 1981) has been shown to be related to academic achievement (Matarazzo, 1973; Zimmerman & Woo-Sam, 1973). By establishing the validity of a construct, the scientific merit is demonstrated. Moreover, theoretical models can be developed for explaining the observed interrelations or correlations among attributes. The validity component may be considered the scientific or knowledge-increasing aspect of the individual differences model, whereas the reliability component defines the stability and hence potential scientific merit of the attribute.

The interplay between reliability and validity at the statistical level is of primary import. Specifically, an attribute may be very reliable but not valid. Similarly, if an attribute cannot be measured reliably, then the validity of the attribute can never be experimentally demonstrated. For example, the measurement of head size in adults may be very reliable but have no relationship to cognitive abilities or other variables of interest. Therefore, although establishing that an attribute can be measured reliably is the first step of the approach, demonstrating only reliability is not of direct scientific interest. In contrast, if an attribute cannot be measured reliably, then validity cannot be established because the upper limit of a correlation between two measures is the lower reliability of the two measures (Guttman, 1945). Although the researcher may use formulae to correct for the lack of reliability in the measures, a problem arises because the lower the reliability, the greater the correction. Hence, the corrected interattribute correlation may be spuriously inflated because the attribute cannot be measured reliably (Guttman, 1945).

[2] The author acknowledges that reliability can be estimated by using analysis of variance techniques (e.g., Hoyt, 1941; Cronbach, 1951) and that, mathematically, correlational or analysis of variance techniques are essentially the same. However, for the sake of exposition and historical development, the correlational and analysis of variance techniques will be treated as different.

Because the individual differences approach is based on the assumption that conceptual meaningful attributes can be measured reliably, testing the null hypothesis in order to determine if a test is significantly reliable is not a defensible position. For example, if an hypothesized attribute has a reported test-retest reliability of .40 for a heterogenous sample of 100, one would conclude that there was considerable shifting among subjects in terms of ranking. Therefore, the test would probably not be termed reliable even though the obtained reliability coefficient is significantly different from zero. Defensible values for reliability estimates are based, first, on deviation from perfect reliability (i.e., $r = 1.0$) and, second, on situation demands. In contrast, for validity studies, it may be of equal scientific interest to demonstrate that two reliable attributes are uncorrelated, or independent, as to demonstrate interattribute dependency. For example, the technique of factor analysis is designed to partition measures of different attributes into homogeneous subsets and estimate the shared variance between subsets (Harman, 1967).

The preceding discussion has been confined to the classic, or historical, development of the individual differences model. Moreover, the discussion has been limited to the basic tenets of the individual differences approach and subsequent experimental ramifications. However, there have been remarkable advances in analytic methods for examining individual differences issues. For example, Cronbach, Gleser, Nanda, and Rajaratman (1972) have applied their generalizability theory for scores and profiles to the Porch Index of Communication Ability. Discussion of such methods and their direct application to neuropsychological issues is beyond the scope of this chapter. The primary purpose of the preceding discussion of the individual differences model is to provide a basis of contrast with the experimental model.

The Experimental Model

The experimental, or treatment, approach was designed to estimate the effect of specific environmental manipulations on an interest variable. Fisher (1925) originally proposed the basic statistical models to test whether a treatment-related increase in crop yield had occurred that was greater than could be expected by chance alone. To ensure that the null hypothesis is the expected outcome of the experiment, specific design conditions or assumptions should be met. First, the subjects (or experimental units) should be randomly sampled from the population of interest to ensure that the subjects are representative of the interest population. Second, the subjects should be randomly assigned to the treatment and control groups. These procedures of random selection and assignment ensures that the experimental groups have been equated by chance. If these procedures are not done, there is no basis for assuming that the null hypothesis is the expected outcome. The final design condition is that the treatment within a group is the same for all subjects. These design conditions have to be met before a researcher can infer that a found difference is caused by the experimental treatment and not by selection-biased or treatment variations. Moreover, these conditions can only be considered minimum criteria for inference and/or generalization. For a more extensive consideration of these design conditions and the general topic of experimental validity in psychological research, the reader is referred to Campbell and Stanley (1963) and Mahoney (1978).

If the three basic design assumptions have been met, then the null hypothesis can be tested by the appropriate statistical test (i.e., nonparametric or parametric). The basis of the statistical test, in the parametric case, is whether the variance attributable to treatment is greater than the variance found in individuals and whether this difference in variance is more than one would expect by chance alone. If the variance attributed to treatment is significantly larger than the subject variance, then the researcher may reject the null hypothesis and infer that the treatment did have an effect at the predetermined level of confidence.

It should be apparent from the preceding description that the statistical model is designed to measure consistent change across subjects due to the application of a controlled and defined treatment. Moreover, intersubject variations constitute the error term. Therefore, at the simplest experimental level, statistical power (i.e., the probability of rejecting the null hypothesis) is a function of the magnitude of treatment effects and the magnitude of intersubject variability. Thus, to increase statistical power, the researcher attempts to both maximize treatment effects and minimize intersubject variability by selective sampling.

Because in the experimental approach, the error term is intersubject variability, and the interest area is change due to treatment and conversely, in the individual difference approach, the interest area is intersubject variability, and the error term is change among subjects, Cronbach (1957) suggested that one psychologist's interest area is another psychologist's error term. Therefore, depending on the question of interest (i.e., subject attributes or treatment effects), the goals of the sampling procedures are opposite (i.e., to maximize or to minimize intersubject differences). Similarly, in the individual differences approach, one attempts to eliminate all environmental influences, whereas in the experimental approach, one attempts to maximize a specific environmental or treatment influence. Moreover, in the experimental approach, one attempts to randomize systematic nuisance variables, whereas in the individual differences approach, one attempts to hold the effect of these variables constant.

NEUROPSYCHOLOGICAL RESEARCH

The foregoing discussion of the individual differences and experimental approaches for understanding human behavior attempted to demonstrate the different theoretical assumptions underlying each approach. In particular, it should be apparent that the question or problem of interest dictates the experimental and statistical methods. In addition, because each approach attempts to maximize the systematic variance accounted for by the area of interest, good methods in one approach constitute poor methods in the other. The next two sections of this chapter examine these issues first for studies of normal neuropsychological function and then for studies of neuropsychological function in abnormal samples.

Neuropsychological Studies of Normal Subjects

Neuropsychological research on normal subjects usually involves the examination of such subject attribute variables as language functions, visual-spatial abilities, and lateral preference or advantage. However, it is relatively common to find studies examining these attributes using experimental and statistical methods traditionally associated with the treatment approach to human behavior. In these studies, it is often not possible to delineate a controlled and well-defined environmental treatment.

Similarly, subject sampling is selective, and nuisance variables are randomized. However, the purpose of these studies appears to be the examination of the distributions and interactions of particular attributes. Therefore, it is suggested here that such questions are better examined, and hence understood, by the application of individual differences methodologies. To illustrate this argument, one well-known neuropsychological technique, the dichotic listening task, will be considered with respect to specific assertions based on research findings and the individual differences model.

Kimura (1961a, b) first applied the dichotic listening technique of Broadbent (1954) within a neuropsychological setting. Her basic research hypothesis was that the digit recall score for the ear contralateral to the speech-dominant hemisphere would be greater than the digit recall score for the ear ipsilateral to the speech-dominant hemisphere. In other words, if an individual is left-hemisphere dominant for speech, then the digit recall score for the right ear would be higher than the digit recall score for the left ear. Kimura validated the hypothesis by examining digit recall scores of epileptic patients whose speech dominance had been determined by the Wada Amytal test and by testing the difference between right- and left-ear digit recall scores in normal subjects. The statistical test between right- and left-ear recall scores was a t-test, even though there was no treatment manipulation in the study. Moreover, the mean accuracy rates for the right- and left-ear scores for the normal subjects were 92.25 and 90.25 of 96 possible correct responses. Therefore, on the majority of the 32 items, the subjects must have performed equally well for the right and left ears. Hypothetically, the difference could arise from a right-ear advantage on two items and equal-ear performance on the remaining 30 items. However, because the difference between the average left- and right-ear recall scores was significantly different from zero, Kimura suggested that the data supported her hypothesis.

Because the dichotic listening task appeared to be a noninvasive and safe means of determining speech dominance, it rapidly gained popularity as a neuropsychological research technique. However, subsequent research has shown that the magnitude, presence, and direction of the ear advantage can be environmentally manipulated. Bryden (1964) and Satz (1967) have shown that the magnitude of the ear advantage is dependent on stimulus load (e.g., number of dichotic pairs) and stimulus type (e.g., words versus digits). In addition, Cullen, Thompson, Hughes, Berlin, and Samson (1974) have shown that degrading the right-ear stimulus relative to the left-ear stimulus reduces or eliminates the advantage. Similarly, Spreen and Boucher (1970) have shown that filtering high-frequency sounds (i.e., consonants) from the words eliminates the ear advantage.

Besides these and other studies of stimulus manipulation, there have been studies examining the effects of more general environmental manipulations. Morais and Bertelson (1973) found that if speakers were used rather than headphones, a right-ear advantage was found when the speakers were aligned with the ears. However, when one speaker was placed in front of the subject, the recall for the center speaker was better than for the right or left speaker. Similarly, Goldstein and Lackner (1974) found that if subjects wore prism glasses, the magnitude of ear advantage was related to the degree and direction of visual field displacement.

Because these studies are essentially treatment studies, they should, and typically do, employ the experimental and statistical methods of Fisher. Specifically, to increase the probability of finding a right-ear advantage and to reduce intersubject variations, the subjects are typically right-handed. In addition, headphone configuration is usually alternated to randomize any constant bias in the tapes or stimulus list. These techniques are acceptable because the basic goal of these studies is to demonstrate that the group mean for an ear advantage score can be shifted by means of an environmental manipulation.

However, the results of these studies have led to different theoretical interpretations. For example, Studdert-Kennedy and Shankweiler (1975) suggest that variations in ear advantage scores reflect cerebral asymmetries of cognitive function and that a continuum of stimulus-laterality effects could be developed. Kinsbourne (1974) argues that because the magnitude of ear advantage can be shifted, laterality is not a hard-wired phenomena but, rather, is affected by environmental priming. The difficulty with these interpretations is that the attribute is assumed to exist, although the existence has not been experimentally demonstrated.

In contrast, some researchers argue that the measurement of ear advantage is not reliable and therefore question whether the task can be used to make inferences about individuals or inferences concerning cerebral specialization for groups (Teng, 1981). However, the majority of reliability studies of ear advantage use the experimental procedures of the treatment model (e.g., selective sampling and randomization of nuisance variables), not the experimental procedures of the individual differences model (Pizzamiglio, De Pascallis, & Vignati, 1974; Hines & Satz, 1974; Hines, Fennel, Bowers, & Satz, 1980; Teng, 1981). By using these procedures, the reliability coefficient, whether internal consistency, test-retest, or parallel form, is reduced because intersubject differences are reduced.

What is ironic about this debate is that one group (e.g., Studdert-Kennedy & Shankweiler, 1975) makes inferences about attributes (e.g., cerebral specialization) based on environmental manipulation studies, whereas the other group (e.g., Teng, 1981) makes inferences about attributes based on studies using treatment methodologies and individual differences statistics. Because the individual differences and experimental approaches have been confounded in terms of the question of interest, experimental methods, and statistical analyses, it is difficult, if not impossible, to make reasoned statements concerning the constructs of laterality, speech dominance, and cerebral specialization. Specifically, if a reliability study uses selective sampling procedures and randomizes nuisance variables, the resulting estimate of reliability is suspect. Therefore, when a low reliability coefficient is found, the value can be a function either of employing improper experimental methods or of the fact that the attribute cannot be measured reliably. Conversely, when an experimental study reports changes in the magnitude of ear advantage due to a manipulation, no statements can be made concerning individual performance because relative ranking of subjects has not been examined. For example, the mean value for advantage may change, but the relative ranking of subjects may or may not change across conditions. If the ranking does not change, then one can conclude that the experimental conditions are measuring the same attribute and that this attribute is affected by stimulus conditions. However, if the rankings do change, one may be measuring different phenomena in the experimental conditions.

Thus far, it has been argued that environmental manipulations can change the degree and direction of ear advantage. Therefore, with respect to Kimura's original hypothesis, it is apparent that the absolute obtained score for ear advantage cannot be used to determine the hemisphere of speech dominance because the distribution of scores can be shifted by environmental manipulations. Repp (1977) recognized this fact and, at one point, argues that validity and reliability are the real issues of concern. However, Repp (1977) also argues that dichotic stimuli and paradigms should be developed that yield large ear advantages. Repp is not alone in this contention; rather, it appears to be the accepted criterion for a good laterality test. For example, Wexler, Halwes, and Heninger (1981) have followed this argument in their work. They suggest that by using statistical criteria for defining a significant ear advantage score for a subject, the frequency of classified subjects is consistent with neurological expectancy. However, one can establish a large right-ear advantage by simply presenting no stimuli to the left ear. Moreover, if one expects 90% of the normal population to be left-hemisphere dominant for speech (Wada & Rasmussen, 1960), the average incorrect classification rate will be only 10%, (i.e., the subjects who are not left-hemisphere dominant for speech). This example should illustrate that the magnitude of ear advantage is a poor criterion for evaluating the efficacy or sensitivity of a particular dichotic listening paradigm for speech dominance or, more generally, for cerebral specialization. Conversely, although a particular paradigm does not yield a significant ear advantage for a group of subjects, the paradigm may still be an excellent measure of hemispheric specialization because the paradigm may yield a large range of scores and high reliability coefficients. Moreover, if there are large intersubject differences in the score (i.e., the error term in the environmental treatment model), the probability of finding a significant right-ear advantage is reduced.

Another but similar issue is the actual measurement of ear advantage or laterality. A variety of laterality coefficients have been suggested, including difference score, difference score divided by total score, percentage of correct or error, and phi-coefficient (Kuhn, 1973; Marshall, Caplan, & Holmes, 1975). Discussion of these coefficients has been centered on two issues. The first is the relationship between the laterality score and overall accuracy. Many coefficients are related in complex ways to overall accuracy (Repp, 1977; Stone, 1980), and such a property is obviously undesirable. When possible, I suggest scoring each item as a right, left, or no preference based on Colbourn's arguments (Colbourn, 1978). The second issue of concern is that a laterality coefficient may yield different estimates of preference over different dichotic tasks. This concern is fallacious because a score on any measure has meaning only when it is considered relative to the standard deviation of the sample. For example, a subject may score −.5 and .5 on a particular laterality coefficient for two different tasks. However, for both of these scores, the subject may be one standard deviation above the group mean laterality scores on the respective tasks. Therefore, the subject's laterality has not changed; rather, the nature of the tasks has shifted the distribution of subject scores.

Given that the magnitude of advantage is not good criterion for evaluating the efficacy of specific laterality tasks or the validity of the construct, the remainder of this section will attempt to develop a statistical model for evaluating cerebral specialization based on the individual differences approach and a modification of Kimura's original hypothesis. From clinical data on speech dominance, one may posit two shapes for the distribution of scores obtained from a test purported to measure cerebral specialization or speech dominance. One distribution would be bimodal with one mode being considerably larger than the other. This shape of the distribution would be based on the theory that speech is unilaterally represented in either the right or the left hemisphere. The larger mode would represent the fact that the majority of individuals appear to be left-hemisphere dominant for language. The second possible shape of the distribution of scores would be a skewed (probably negatively) normal distribution. This distribution would reflect a theory suggesting that, besides unilateral speech representation, bilateral speech representation is also possible (Subirana, 1958; Branch, Milner, & Rasmussen, 1964). These two theoretical distributions are illustrated in Figure 19.1. It is imperative to understand that where these distributions sit on a range of laterality scores is of no theoretical consequence. The individual differences model requires only that there are intersubject differences on the measure of interest and that these differences are stable over items, time, and forms. With respect to Kimura's original hypothesis, the critical aspect is where a particular subject score falls in the distribution relative to other subject scores, not whether an individual exhibits a right- or left-ear advantage. In other words, the scale of measurement is relative, not absolute.

Because laterality is posited to be an attribute of individuals, it is incumbent upon the researcher to first demonstrate that the attribute can be measured reliably. Therefore, the experimental procedures must maximize individual differences and minimize errors of measurement. Individual differences may be maximized by heterogeneous, rather than homogeneous, sampling and by increasing the number of dichotic items. Errors of measurement may be reduced by not randomizing systematic sources of variance. For example, a 5-decibel difference in channel volume may be present on a specific tape. If the headphone configuration is not altered, then this 5-decibel difference will have a constant effect of pulling the distribution in one direction. It should not, however, affect the relative ranking of the subjects in the distribution of the range of scores. In contrast, if the headphone configuration is altered, the distribution is pulled one way on half of the items and the other way on the other half of the items. This procedure obviously reduces the range of individual differences and thereby decreases the obtained reliability coefficient.

Because criteria such as the magnitude of ear advantage have been used to evaluate dichotic listening tasks, Kimura's original free recall task has come under criticism as

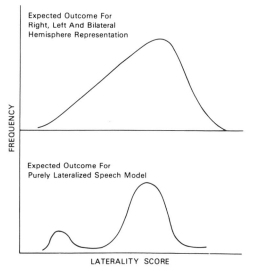

Figure 19.1.   Expected distribution of laterality scores for two theoretical models of hemispheric speech dominance.

not being a good laterality paradigm. However, Clark and Spreen (1983) did a true reliability study of this format and found it to be very reliable with a limited number of items (18). They examined all three aspects of reliability—internal consistency, test-retest, and parallel forms—by using two different 18-item dichotic tapes of word pairs, given twice, one week apart. Cronbach's alpha for composite reliability over forms and time was .93, whereas Hoyt's ANOVA over the total of 72 items was .95 (Hoyt, 1941; Cronbach, 1951). These reliability coefficients are easily comparable to the best standardized psychological test, for example, the Wechsler Adult Intelligence Scale (WAIS) (Wechsler, 1955). With respect to the theoretical distribution of ear advantage (Fig. 19.1), Clark and Spreen found that the distribution of ear advantage over 60 subjects was not significantly different from normal. Given that the distributions approximated normal, it is apparent that the test cannot be used to accurately classify individuals in a dichotomous manner, that is, as either left- or right-hemisphere speech dominant. One can, however, assign laterality scores in terms of z-scores or percentile rankings with a high degree of confidence.

At present, there are many excellent experimental studies in the dichotic listening literature demonstrating that the distribution of laterality can be environmentally manipulated. However, there is a paucity of true individual differences studies examining the reliability of the construct of laterality. As mentioned earlier, the majority of supposed reliability studies have used experimental methods that are not consistent with the individual differences model. Therefore, their reported reliability coefficients must be suspect. The Clark and Spreen study demonstrate that (1) ear advantage can be measured reliably and (2) the free recall paradigm is an excellent measure of ear advantage. What is yet to be determined is whether ear advantage is a valid measure of speech dominance, hemisphere specialization, or laterality. The preceding discussion should also illustrate what constitutes an acceptable reliability study and why it is theoretically important to use the appropriate experimental methods.

Given that true reliability studies are done on other reputed measures of laterality (e.g., dichotic and visual half-field techniques), then the more interesting question of validity can be examined. For example, do different stimuli only pull the distribution to the right or left, or are different functions lateralized differently across individuals? Do visual half-field studies measure the same construct as dichotic studies? Are there relations between the attribute of laterality and other attribute measures, for example, handedness, gender, or reasoning abilities? The first question in all these studies should be: How well do the distributions map onto each other? Once that question has been answered, one can test for mean differences. Some such studies have been attempted, but they usually employ selective sampling techniques and other experimental methods of the treatment model. By not using individual differences methodology, the resulting correlations may be attenuated because individual differences have been minimized. Therefore, it is not possible to determine if two attributes are unrelated because of methodological flaws in experimental design or whether the two attributes are truly unrelated.

Besides the fact that the individual differences model is designed to address the research question of interest, the individual differences model also has advantages in terms of generalization of findings. Because in the individual differences approach, the samples should be heterogeneous or broad, results may be generalized with more confidence than in an experimental study. This property alone should justify a greater application of the approach.

In this section, it has been argued that because neuropsychological studies of normal subjects are predominantly concerned with attributes of individuals, the appropriate approach is the individual differences methodology, not the treatment model of Fisher. The primary question of interest is how well distributions of scores map onto one another, not whether the distributions can be moved up or down a scale of measurement by environmental manipulation. Moreover, the fact that a distribution of scores can be moved along a continuum by means of stimulus or environmental manipulation provides minimal information concerning the validity of the hypothesized attribute. However, if the ranking within a distribution can be manipulated or disrupted in a usually reliable measure, then the validity of the attribute must be reexamined. For example, if one assumes that a measure with demonstrated reliability does reflect cerebral specialization, the implications of disrupting the ranking of the distribution by means of an environmental manipulation are profound with respect to either the assumed validity of the measure or our understanding of brain function. Although the dichotic listening technique of Kimura was used for illustrative purposes, the presented arguments are valid for any hypothesized neuropsychological functions. Moreover, an interactive model of cognitive function could be developed such that one can determine if an attribute is related to cerebral specialization or other cognitive behaviors of interest. Thus far, the methodological reasons and theoretical advantages for employing the individual differences approach have been discussed. Although these issues justify the application of the classic individual differences methodology, it will be shown later in this chapter how the results of individual differences studies also can be applied directly in the clinical setting.

Neuropsychological Studies in the Clinical Setting

The majority of clinical studies in neuropsychological research employ the statistical model of Fisher to determine if differences exist between groups. This assertion is well illustrated by a methods paper on clinical neuropsychological research by Parsons and Prigatano (1978). In this article, the basic assumption is that the statistical methods of choice are multivariate analysis of variance and its degenerate cases (e.g., linear discriminate function analysis, analysis of variance, or t-tests). In addition, they suggest that there are three major, or prevalent, types of clinical neuropsychological research questions. The first type is concerned with differential diagnosis either between patient groups or between normal subjects and patients. The second type is concerned with elucidating changes in brain-behavior relationships due to changes in brain states. The third type examines the effect of specific noxious agents on brain states. For the purposes of the subsequent discussion, this second and third type will be considered equivalent. In addition, they suggest a fourth type of study, examining the effects of specific rehabilitation techniques on recovery.

I contend that, except for the fourth type of study, the studies mentioned above do not conform to the design assumptions of the treatment model. Specifically, subjects are not randomly selected from the same population and are not randomly assigned to controlled treatment conditions. Instead, the clinical groups are defined by an uncontrolled and differential treatment (e.g., stroke, head injury, epilepsy). Moreover, whether systematic selection factors predetermine group membership is rarely considered. In other words, most clinical neuropsychological studies examine experiments of nature, not carefully controlled manipulations by the experimenter. Although the design assumptions of the experimental model are violated, the majority of clinical studies do employ the statistical methods of Fisher. Therefore, this section will review the arguments put forward by Meehl (1973, 1978) and Payne (1958) concerning the validity of this approach. Meehl (1973, 1978) argues that the empirical efficacy of the procedures is too weak and not consistent with true scientific theory testing. Payne suggests that the procedures do not contribute to our understanding of patient behavior per se but, rather, they are designed to predict how another criteria (e.g., a physician) would classify a group of patients. By using statistical relationships, he shows that a test can have very high agreement with another classification system (e.g., medical diagnosis) and yet have no relationship to the patient behavior of interest. Because these two arguments have direct bearing on the scientific merit of specific clinical neuropsychological research studies, they will be reviewed.

Meehl has questioned the use of the null hypothesis testing in clinical research on two grounds: logic (Meehl, 1978) and empirical efficacy (Meehl, 1973). The primary purpose of the later paper was to integrate clinical psychological research into the mainstream of scientific thought and philosophy. Therefore, the majority of his arguments and discussion are beyond the scope of this chapter. However, he does argue that if one starts with two different groups, one should not be surprised to find that they do differ on a carefully selected variable. Rather, if one did not find differences, one should be surprised. In other words, the expected outcome of a study examining two different populations should be to find differences. In contrast, in the true treatment study, the groups have been equated by chance through random selection and treatment assignment. Therefore, the expected outcome in the true experimental model is that the groups will not differ (i.e., the null hypothesis); hence, when a difference is found, it can be attributed to treatment.

Even though the expected outcome of a clinical differentiation study is to find differences, one may still argue that these differences do discriminate between groups and hence have scientific validity. Currently, the accepted alpha rate for statistical and, by implication, theoretical significance is .05. Meehl (1973) proposed a method of determining the clinical efficacy of this criterion. If two different groups (e.g., normal subjects and abnormal subjects) are given a test and a significant t-value at .05 is found between the scores of each group, then the clinically relevant question is how well the test classifies individuals into their respective groups: normal and abnormal. The efficacy of a test in differentiating groups should be the criteria of differential diagnosis study. Consider the two-group example in which each of two groups has 20 subjects and the respective group scores are distributed normally with a standard deviation of 5. The critical t-value at .05 for this study would be 2.02 for a two-tailed test. By substituting the above values and rearranging the standard formula for a t-value, it is possible to calculate the required difference between means for significance. For the values given here, the required difference is 3.19 units. Therefore, if one group had mean of 25.0, then the other group must have a mean of either 21.81 or 28.19. For this example, the value of 28.19 will be used. In Figure 19.2, these hypothetical data and their distributions are illustrated. Meehl (1973) points out that the maximal, or best, cutting score for group differentiation is where the two distributions intersect or meet mathematically midway between the means. In this case, the best cutting score would be 26.6 units. However, as shown in Figure 19.2, there is considerable overlap between the two distributions. To calculate the actual correct and incorrect classification rates,

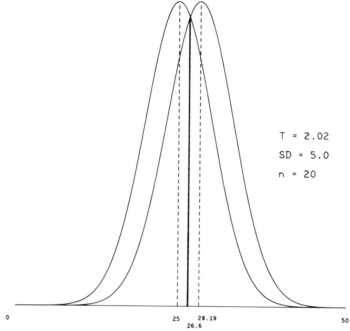

Figure 19.2.   Overlap of sample distributions at $P = .05$.

the maximal cutting score (i.e., 26.6) can be converted to a z-score for the respective distributions. For example, for the distribution with a mean of 25.0, a score of 26.6 represents a z-score of .32 (i.e., 1.6/5.0). Any member of this group who scores above 26.6 or .32 standard z-scores would be misclassified as member of the other distribution. By consulting a table of cumulative normal probabilities (e.g., Hayes, 1973), it is apparent that 62.6% of the subjects would score below 26.6 and therefore be correctly classified. Hence, the misclassification rate is 37.4%. Obviously, the reverse argument holds for the other distribution, and therefore the misclassification rate is the same, 37.4%.

Meehl argues that because of the high misclassification rate, a significant difference between groups at $P \leqslant .05$ is not an acceptable or meaningful criteria for clinical research. It should also be noted that as the number of subjects in each group increases, the misclassification rate also increases if the alpha level is kept constant. In addition, if the number of subjects is not varied, the misclassification rate is constant because a t-value is a ratio of between groups and within group variability. The correct classification rates for different probability levels of the t-test with N of 20 subjects per group are given in Table 19.1. This table shows that the correct classification rate does not increase dramatically relative to the decreases in the alpha.

The weakness of the statistical criteria discussed above is accented further when they are applied within clinical reality. For example, a clinician may decide to employ the test outlined above in a clinical setting. Ideally, the test would differentiate a particular disorder from other disorders and normal subjects. Assuming that the incidence rate of the disorder of interest is 10% within this particular clinical setting, the actual incidence of correct prediction of group membership is given in Table 19.2

Table 19.1.   Classification Rates of Varying Probability Levels in the Two-Group Case
($N = 20$ Subjects per Group, Standard Deviation $= 5.0$)

Critical t-Value (df, 38)[a]	Probability Level	$\bar{X}_a - \bar{X}_b$	Correct Classification Rate (%)
2.70	.01	4.27	66
2.94	.005	4.65	68
3.50	.001	5.53	71

[a]df = degrees of freedom.

for a sample of 100 clinical referrals (i.e., 10 patients with the disorder of interest and 90 other referrals). As above, the test would correctly identify 6 of the 10 patients with the disorder and 54 of the persons without the disorder, yielding an overall correct classification rate of 60%. However, if the clinician just classified all cases as not having the disorder, the correct classification rate would be 90%. Therefore, by using the test, the clinician's overall accuracy in diagnosis is decreased by 30%.

Meehl's arguments illustrate that (1) in terms of correct classification rates, the criterion of a significant difference at the .05 level is slightly better than chance; and (2) because the classification rate is based on a model of only two and equally represented groups in the general population, when the test is applied in a clinical setting, the accuracy rate can be substantially worse than when just employing base rate statistics. Moreover, the hypothetical examples presented were "best case" circumstances. For example, the problem of multiple tests and inflated type 1 error rates were not considered, distributions were assumed to be normal, and the selection criteria for group membership were assumed to be perfect. Therefore, even when the best case is considered, one must conclude that a significant difference at a .05- or even a .001-level (see Table 19.1) is not sufficient or strong enough evidence to argue that a test has diagnostic validity.

The second type of clinical neuropsychological research question suggested by Parsons and Prigatano (1978) is the examination of specific types of brain dysfunction on behavior. Although these studies typically employ the same experimental and statistical methods as the clinical differentiation study, the goal is to develop a better understanding of brain-behavior relationships. Therefore, one may argue that, even though the difference between two groups (e.g., right- versus left-hemisphere–damaged patients) is small, the presence of a statistically significant difference implies differences in hemispheric or area function. In other words, the dependent variable may not have strong group discrimination, but the found significant difference does suggest that a disruption in function or processing is related to the site or side of lesion. The problem with this assertion is that the validity of the inference can only be as good as the criteria for group classification. Moreover, although the test may have high agreement with the classification system, it may have little or no relationship to patient behavior. Payne (1958) developed these points in terms of the clinical psychologist working in the psychiatric setting. This section will review some of Payne's argument within a neuropsychological context.

A neuropsychologist may wish to examine language function in brain-damaged adults. A typical experimental design would be to sample patients who have been diagnosed as either brain-damaged with aphasia (BDA) or brain-damaged without

Table 19.2.   Experiment and Clinical Classification by Test and Base Rate ($N = 100$)

	Experimental (Test Validation)			

Assumptions

1. Only two groups (1, 2 exist in population).
2. Groups are equally represented.

	Predicted state			
	Group	1	2	
True	1	30	20	Correct classifications: 60%
state	2	20	30	

	Clinical (Test Application)			

Assumptions

1. 10% of referrals are members of group 2.
2. 90% of referrals are not members of group 2.
   Therefore, the test should classify them in group 1.

Using Test Scores

	Predicted state			
	Group	1	2	
True	1	54	36	Correct classifications: 60%
state	2	4	6	

Using Base Rates

	Predicted state			
	Group	1	2	
True	1	90	0	Correct classifications: 90%
state	2	10	0	

aphasia (BDNA). The classification of patients (i.e., BDA or BDNA) would obviously be done independently, for example, by a neurologist. Once the designations of BDA and BDNA have been made, a test or a set of tests of language function are administered to each subject. Subsequently, the data are analyzed by means of a t-test if there is only one variable or a linear discriminate function analysis in the multivariate case. For variables, when differences are found, inferences are drawn concerning differences in language function between the groups.

However, there are certain logical and empirical flaws with this method. First is the fact that the neurologist may use myriad symptoms to classify patients. For example, site of lesion, presence or absence of other cognitive impairments, and the actual degree of language involvement all may have weightings in the diagnosis. Payne (1958) points out that because the classification is categorical (in this case, dichotomous) there may be no relationship between test scores and the number or severity of symptoms a particular subject exhibits. For example, a particular patient, in the neurologist's opinion, may be the best example of a patient with solely language deficits resulting from brain insult (i.e., BDA). However, this patient may or may not have the lowest scores on the test battery. By using the outlined design strategy, it cannot be determined whether the scores of this "best case" patient reflect the patient's performance. However, from a logical point of view, this patient is the target case. Other patients, in the neurologists' opinion, may be poorer examples of BDA, but in terms of test performance, these patients may score lower than the best case. Payne

(1958) argues that the outlined design will provide accurate estimates of the diagnostic decision but not of the severity or gradations within the classification. Specifically, the test may be unrelated to these gradations.

The second point Payne (1958) raises is the problem of the reliability of the classification system. As mentioned earlier, a neurologist may weigh a variety of symptoms in order to derive a diagnosis. However, different neurologists may differentially weigh the presenting symptoms to arrive at a diagnosis. For example, one neurologist may be more behaviorally oriented than another. Or the presence of a left-hemisphere lesion may increase the sensitivity to language dysfunction in one neurologist more than another. Such differences among neurologists, coupled with the difficulty of the differential diagnosis problem, causes the criterion to be less than perfect. Therefore, before any statements concerning the presence of differences between groups can be made, one should have some estimate of the classification system's reliability.

In Figure 19.3, this hypothetical study is illustrated with the relevant statistics. Specifically, the interneurologist reliability study found a correlation of .7 between two raters, or a 75% agreement rate, in classification. Similarly, for the test of interest, a between-group t-value of 4.16 was found. The correct classification rate for this t-value is 75%, and a correlation between test score and group membership of .7 is statistically equivalent to this t-value. The study may be described as a neurologist observes a set of patient behaviors and classifies patients into groups based on these behaviors. Interneurologist agreement in classification is 75%. Subsequently, a test is administered to the patients and validated against the classification system. Again, a correct classification rate of 75% is found. For the data provided, the actual correlation between patient behavior and the test (dotted line in Figure 19.3) may be as low as 0.0 or as high as 0.7 because each of the tested relationships accounts for only 49% of the variance. In other words, the test results may bear no relationship to the patient behavior of interest; rather, it may be sensitive to some other aspect of the classification system. In this example, the test may be sensitive only to the aspects of language function that a neurologist in fact observes in a completely different dimension of the patient's behavior. Payne (1958) suggests that the pertinent question of interest for a clinical psychologist concerns the relationship between patient behavior and the test (dotted line in Figure 19.3), not the relationship between the test and an alternative classification system.

It is apparent that Payne's criticisms can be applied to any clinical neuropsychological study that examines differences between groups based on an alternative classification system (e.g., Broca's versus Wernicke's aphasia, right- versus left-hemisphere damage). However, the hypothetical groups of BDA and BDNA were chosen because there are two studies (Lawriw, 1976; Crockett, Clark, Spreen, & Klonoff, 1981) in the literature that illustrate Payne's arguments in terms of these two groups. Both studies used the same patient population, 142 neurologically diagnosed BDA patients and 64 neurologically diagnosed BDNA patients, and the same aphasia battery, the Neurosensory Centre Comprehensive Examination for Aphasia (NCCEA) (Spreen & Benton, 1977). The Lawriw study (1976, as quoted in Spreen & Risser, 1981) validated the aphasia battery with the neurological diagnosis. Lawriw found that linear discriminant analysis yielded a 76%–90% correct classification, and discriminate weights were successfully cross-validated. These findings suggest that specific subsets have predictive validity in terms of a neurological classification model.

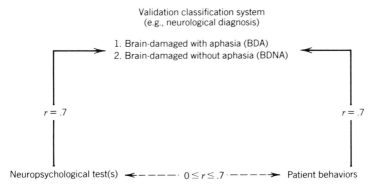

Figure 19.3. Design of a typical validation paradigm. Hypothetical statistics for the validation paradigm are $r = .7$, t-value $= 4.17$, classification rates $= 75\%$, and probability (P) $= .001$. These are equivalent statistics.

In contrast, Crockett, Clark, Spreen, and Klonoff (1981) employed factor analytic technique on the NCCEA subtests and then used cluster analytic techniques on the resulting factor scores to determine naturally occurring or homogenous clusters of language impairment. The purpose of this study was to examine many aspects of the patients' language function independent of neurological diagnosis. The cluster analytic techniques suggested a five-group solution was best. A discriminate function analysis using the factor scores as predictors of group membership yielded a 94.1% correct classification rate, suggesting that the five groups were well separated in space and internally very homogenous. The three groups with the most impaired language functions were composed solely of BDA patients. However, the composition of the other two groups was made up of both BDA and BDNA patients. In the least language-impaired group, 45 of 79 (57%) members were diagnosed BDNA, whereas in the more impaired group, 19 of 68 (28%) members were diagnosed as BDNA. Similarly, only 59 of the 142 (42%) BDA patients were clearly separated from the 64 BDNA patients in terms of group membership. At first glance, these data seem contrary to the Lawriw study. However, from these data, it is apparent that the NCCEA clearly measures aspects of language function that are independent of those aspects used in neurological diagnosis of BDA and BDNA. The Lawriw study determined which aspects of language function weigh heavily in forming a neurological diagnosis of BDA or BDNA, whereas the study of Crockett and associates suggests that there are aspects of impaired language function in patients diagnosed as BDNA and that these aspects do not weigh heavily in neurological diagnosis.

The question arises concerning the goals of clinical neuropsychological research studies. By using an external classification system (e.g., medical diagnosis) and then predicting group membership based on a set of test scores, one is essentially demonstrating the efficacy of the tests in predicting these predetermined classifications. However, no statements can be confidently made concerning patient behavior, because the study was not designed to examine patient behavior. In other words, this validation paradigm is not designed to develop meaningful taxonomies of behavioral deficit or impairment resulting from brain insult. More important, the validation paradigm may yield impressive statistics in terms of classification rates and t- or f-values, and yet the tests may have no relationship to the patient behavior of interest. Specifically, the relationship between test performance and patient behavior can only be as good as the reliability of the classification model, and, in fact, this relationship can be considerably worse even though the results indicate a good fit between the tests and the classification system. Therefore, one can argue that the use of this validation paradigm and the associated statistical techniques should not be used to elucidate brain-behavior relationships, because the results may have no relationship to actual patient behavior and hence may be misleading.

The final criticism of this experimental design and null hypothesis testing procedure is that when groups of patients with different lesion sites are compared, only one theory of brain function is tested. For example, a function or process is hypothesized to be mediated by a specific brain structure or area. Therefore, subjects with a lesion in that structure or area are compared to subjects with lesion in other structures or areas on a test measuring the function or process of interest. If the null hypothesis is rejected, then the conclusion is that the structure of interest mediates (is involved with) the process or function of interest. By solely employing this approach, only a brain model of functional-structural invariance can be validated. Furthermore, this validation process is extremely weak because of the criteria for rejection of the null hypothesis. Specifically, to reject the null hypothesis, the groups need not be truly disparate in terms of levels of performance (see Figure 19.2). Rather, a small difference in performance levels is taken as support for the theory. In addition, subjects or patients who might contradict the specific functional invariance hypothesis being tested are typically excluded (e.g., left-handers), thus increasing the probability of rejecting the null hypothesis at the expense of generalization and development of alternative theories. Because this null hypothesis testing procedure ensures that only one model of brain function can be validated (i.e., functional invariance) and because the criteria for accepting the theory is very weak, the scientific validity of the procedure is extremely limited. Finally, reported data on speech dominance, for example, suggest that functional invariance is not always the rule. Instead, one or both hemispheres may be involved in speech production (Branch, Milner, & Rasmussen, 1963). Such findings suggest that a simple theory such as functional invariance cannot fully account for the known facts.

To illustrate these arguments, consider a case in which two patients have identical and abnormal profiles on a battery of tests but at the same time have lesion sites in very different regions of the brain. Such a finding has direct ramifications for brain-behavior relationships and for the test battery. However, if the subjects' performance is compared only in terms of lesion site, then the fact that their profiles are identical even though their lesion sites are different will never be known. In order to generate a comprehensive understanding of brain-behavior relationships, the analysis models must allow alternative facts or theories to be evaluated. An approach that tests only one theory is by definition limited.

SINGLE-CASE METHODOLOGY IN THE CLINICAL AND RESEARCH DOMAINS

Thus far, this chapter has been critical of on-going research paradigms in neuropsychology and has offered few if any constructive alternative approaches to the problems. I and others have argued that the first step in developing a comprehensive theory of neuropsychology is to construct a reliable behavioral taxonomy of brain dysfunction (Kertesz & Phipps, 1977, 1980; Doehring, Hosko, & Bryans, 1979; Petrauskas & Rourke, 1979; Morris, Blashfield, & Satz, 1981; Clark, Crockett, Klonoff, & Macdonald, 1983). Specifically, before relating behavior to brain function, one must develop an internally reliable classification model of abnormal cognitive behavior.

Currently, a variety of multivariate techniques, such as cluster analysis and Q-factor analysis, have been suggested as first approximations for building such a taxonomy. A problem with these statistical methods is that they capitalize on the variance classically ascribed to errors of measurements. In cluster analysis, the resulting clusters can only be as reliable as the scales used for clustering, whereas Q-factor analysis is based solely on intrasubject differences, the most unreliable aspect of the obtained scores (Cronbach, 1971). Therefore, some authors suggest using composite scores (e.g., z-scores or factor scores) to increase the reliability of a particular cognitive dimension. Specifically, test scores on a dimension of cognitive function are averaged, and then a set of relatively independent dimensions are analyzed. These cognitive dimensions are based on studies of normal subjects. From a neuropsychological and statistical point of view, these procedures have two drawbacks. First, if two cognitive dimensions are independent, then by definition, subject performance on one dimension has no relationship to subject performance on the other. Therefore, a finding of a large discrepancy between two dimensions (e.g., verbal versus visual-spatial) within a group is not unexpected, because the dimensions are unrelated. Second, by averaging over a set of tests that have been found to be highly correlated in normal subjects, those subjects with a precise, salient deficit in that dimension will not be identified, due to averaging. For example, I once assessed a patient whose WAIS verbal scores were all within normal limits. However, the word fluency score was extremely low (i.e., an average of four words per letter). If these verbal tests are highly correlated in normal subjects, the procedure of averaging over verbal scores (i.e., including word fluency) would obscure this type of salient feature in a patient.

A second major problem of these two statistical techniques is that the resulting clusters or profiles may not reflect truly abnormal clinical states. The clusters or profiles found may be common in normal populations or at least may not reflect pathological behavioral anomalies. Therefore, although these statistical procedures attempt to find taxonomies or clusters within a set of subjects and variables, the procedures have specific limitations or drawbacks. An ideal procedure would (1) allow the researcher to be confident that a found difference, cluster, or profile was not just a function of measurement errors but that, rather, the difference, cluster, or profile was truly abnormal relative to the normal population; and (2) ensure that small salient feature groups would not be lost through averaging. A contaminant problem in clinical neuropsychological research is premorbid intellectual-cognitive status. Therefore, a third property of an ideal procedure would be to identify individuals whose overall function may be in the normal range but whose pattern of scores is abnormal. The presence of this abnormal pattern may be indicative of a decrement in cognitive function due to brain insult.

Historically, the taxonomies of behavioral deficit in neuropsychology have been based on a case study approach with replication. For example, as described in Benton (1981), Broca (1865) based his conclusion that we speak with the left hemisphere on a series of clinical patients and subsequent autopsy findings. Similarly, Geschwind has primarily employed the case study approach in his development of disconnection syndromes (Geschwind, 1965). Two powerful aspects of the case study are (1) the observed behavior deficit can be replicated for the subject and (2) that the lesion site and size usually remain constant for the experimental period. In contrast, when groups of patients are examined, there is obviously going to be intersubject, and hence intragroup, variations in lesion site and size. Similarly, the subject scores over a test or tests also will vary, reflecting measurement errors and true differences. These variations in lesions and test scores can cause an increase in the error component if grouping procedures (e.g., right versus left parietal damage) are employed. Moreover, the error introduced by actual variations in the lesions is in fact treatment variation, not true error. For example, two patients may have lesions in the frontal lobes due to the same causes. However, subtler differences in these lesions may cause behavioral differences between the two patients. By combining patients in a group composed of frontal lobe lesions, these potential systematic differences are treated as error. Therefore, an ideal model for the understanding of brain-behavior relationships must also provide a means of examining these variations in lesion site and size across patients with respect to their behavioral variations.

In 1957, Payne and Jones suggested statistical methods for examining the performance of a single subject in the clinical setting (Payne & Jones, 1957). Although their position was confined to the clinical case, the model can be applied to clinical research in general. The following section first reviews the clinical application of the model and then argues for its implementation into a general research framework. In order to apply the model, it is necessary to know the psychometric properties of the administered tests. As mentioned earlier, this fact is another reason why good psychometric studies of normal performance on neuropsychological tests are necessary, first for clinical practice and second for clinical research. Due to the paucity of such studies, the presented examines will be confined to the Wechsler Adult Intelligence Scale or hypothetical data. Although the WAIS was not designed as a neuropsychological test and hence has many limitations in terms of clinical neuropsychology, it is an excellent example of a well-standardized and reliable measurement instrument. For brevity, the discussion will be limited to tests with normal distributions of scores in the standardization sample.

Clinical Neuropsychological Problems

It has been argued elsewhere in this chapter that statistical significance as defined by null hypothesis testing is not a valid criterion in clinical research. Some authors (e.g., Garfield, 1978) differentiate clinical from statistical significance. However, the real issue is to define a clinically relevant statistical criterion for significance. Specifically, the statistical model should be consistent with the problem area. The criterion of significance should be internally valid and thus by definition have conceptual significance. In the examples presented here, a clinically significant difference is defined in terms of deviations from normal. The actual criterion, in terms of the number of standard deviations and hence the level of confidence, is left to the clinician's discretion. In the examples cited here, the criterion varies depending on the question of interest. Similarly, it is left to the clinician's discretion whether to employ one- or two-tailed tests of significance. There has been a historical and ongoing debate concerning these issues, and in the clinical setting, many nonstatistical issues come into play in the decision-making process. The purpose of this section is, not to enter the debate, but rather to describe the procedures of Payne and Jones. It should be noted that the underlying premise of Payne and Jones' procedures is to employ the standardization sample as the control group. Therefore, the obtained results for a single case are only as valid as the standardization study. For example, if the standardization sample is college students, it would be inappropriate to compare a 60-year-old to this sample.

With respect to the clinical case, a clinician may be presented with two basic questions: (1) whether a particular patient exhibits any behavior that would be considered abnormal relative to the normal population, and (2) whether there is any measurable and unexpected change in a patient's state due to, for example, treatment or recovery. Payne and Jones (1957) developed statistical models for examining these questions.

The question of the presence of abnormal behavior in a patient's test performance is twofold. The first question is whether, on a set of tests, a patient performs on any particular test at a level consistent with the label of deficit. This deficit can be defined as 1.67 standard deviations below the mean of the normal population or below the 5 percentile. For example, a Full Scale Intelligence Quotient of 75 or lower [i.e., $100 - (1.67)(15)$] or subtest scaled score of 5 or lower [(i.e., $10 - (1.67)(3)$)][3] would be consistent with the label of deficit. Moreover, if the clinician is concerned about type 1 error due to the number of tests given, fatigue, and so on, a similar test both statistically (i.e., highly correlated) and in task demands (e.g., the Benton Visual Retention Test and the Wechsler Visual Memory Test) may be given, or the original test may be readministered at a later time.

However, if on all tests the patient's performance is above this defined floor of the normal range (i.e., 1.67 standard deviations below the mean), the second question is whether the patterning or profile of scores may still be abnormal. Specifically, the range of test scores may be extreme. This large range may suggest that a patient is performing on some tasks below his or her optimal or premorbid status. These variations cannot, however, be assessed visually because the magnitude of the variations is dependent on the underlying psychometric properties of the tests. For example, if two tests are perfectly correlated, then any difference between standardized test scores is significant. In contrast, if two tests are uncorrelated, then by definition performance on one test has no relationship or predictive function with regard to performance on another. Moreover, the theoretical upper limit of an intertest correlation is the reliability of the less reliable test. Therefore, two standardized test scores may have a large discrepancy between them, but this discrepancy may be common in the normal population and hence not clinically significant.

Payne and Jones (1957) proposed a statistical test for determining the probability of occurrence for a found difference between two test scores as follows:

$$z_D = \frac{z_1 - z_2}{(S_{1z}^2 + S_{2z}^2 - 2rS_{1z}S_{2z})^{1/2}} \tag{1}$$

where z_D = z-score for difference score
    z_1, z_2 = respective z-scores obtained for two tests by the subject
    S_{1z}, S_{2z} = standard deviation of z-scores, which by definition equals 1
    r = correlation between the two tests in the normal population

---

[3] It should be noted that the subtest scaled scores on the WAIS are not corrected for age. Therefore, the mean standardized scores by age group should be employed in the single-case study.

Because the standard deviation of z-score is 1, the above equation reduces to

$$z_D = \frac{z_1 - z_2}{(2 - 2r)^{\frac{1}{2}}} \tag{2}$$

For example, if a 19-year-old person obtains a verbal intelligence quotient (VIQ) of 115 (i.e., $z_1 = 1$) and a performance intelligence quotient (PIQ) of 100 (i.e., $z_2 = 0$), the probability of finding such a discrepancy in the normal population can be determined from equation 2. From the WAIS-R manual (Wechsler, 1981, p. 38), the correlation between VIQ and PIQ for the 18–19-year-old standardization sample is .7. Therefore, equation 2 becomes

$$z_D = \frac{1 - 0}{[2 - 2(.7)]^{\frac{1}{2}}}$$

$$z_D = 1.29$$

By consulting a table of the cumulative normal distribution (e.g., Hayes, 1973), a z-score of 1.29 or higher occurs in approximately 10% of the standardization sample. Therefore, in 10% of the standardization, the VIQ was 15 or more points higher than PIQ. Conversely, in 10% of the standardization sample, the PIQ was 15 or more points lower than the VIQ. Therefore, a difference of 15 points or more between PIQ and VIQ was found in 20% of the standardization sample.

This example also illustrates two clinical issues. First, from a clinical standpoint, the question of interest is whether a found difference between two test scores is abnormal relative to the standardization sample. This question is different from that concerning whether two tests are measureably different. Some authors (e.g., Wechsler, 1981; Lezak, 1977) argue or suggest that a measurable difference may have clinical import. However, the fact that two test scores are measureably different provides no data concerning whether such difference should be expected (i.e., normal) or unexpected (i.e., abnormal). Payne and Jones' test is designed to estimate the probability of finding such a difference in the standardization sample. Second, the example should illustrate the danger of employing rules of thumb in clinical practice. If the cited data were obtained for a 40-year-old person, equation 2 would yield a z-difference score of 1.58 because in this age group the correlation between VIQ and PIQ is .80. Therefore, a 15-point discrepancy is found only in 12% of this portion of the standardization sample.

One limitation of Payne and Jones' procedure is the fact that there is a paucity of standardization data for the majority of neuropsychological tests. For example, a patient's finger-tapping speed may be within normal limits for both hands. In order to determine if there is an abnormal discrepancy in right versus left performance, the clinician must know the correlation between right and left finger tapping. Hypothetical data for a standardization sample and a patient are presented in Table 19.3. The raw patient data have been converted to z-scores based on the standardization data. By substituting the appropriate values in equation 2, the z-score for difference between right and left finger tapping is as follows:

$$z_D = \frac{1.0 - (-0.5)}{(2 - 2(.85)^{\frac{1}{2}}}$$

$$= 2.74$$

Table 19.3   Hypothetical Finger-Tapping Data

| Data | Standardization Sample | | Patient Data | |
	$\bar{X}$	Standard Deviation	Raw Scores	z-Scores
Right	50.0	5.0	55.0	1.0
Left	45.0	6.0	42.0	−0.5
$R_{R \cdot L}$		0.85		

From a table of z-scores, it is apparent that such a discrepancy occurs in less than 1% of the standardization sample. Therefore, even though the patients' actual right and left scores were well within the normal range, the clinician now has evidence to suspect unilateral damage to either the peripheral or central nervous system.

The second limitation of this method is statistical. Given that the number of possible contrasts between tests is a quadratic function of the number tests (i.e., number of contrasts = [(number of tests)^2 − (number of tests)] / 2), the type 1 error rate can rapidly inflate. Moreover, the contrasts are not independent; rather, they are dependent. To gain better control of the type 1 error rate, the clinician must know (1) base rate expectancies for the standardization sample in terms of the number of significant contrasts usually found over a set of tests and (2) whether there are types of patterns that are typically associated with brain dysfunction. The first problem can be solved by examination of the standardization data (e.g., on average, how many significant differences would we expect by chance done from a normal profile?). The second problem can be resolved in the research domain by relating obtained patterns to other pathological models. These limitations are not a function of the method per se; rather, they are a function of the limited availability of pertinent data.

The second clinical question that Payne and Jones (1957) suggested as a statistical model for resolving is change over time. For example, a patient may be examined subsequent to trauma and present with specific abnormalities. A year later, the patient is referred again to determine if any recovery of function has occurred. Hypothetically and for simplicity, assume that on the initial assessment the patient obtained a VIQ of 95 and PIQ of 70. Moreover, there was no significant scatter on the Verbal or Performance subtests on the initial testing. Because the PIQ was 2 standard deviations below the mean, the clinical psychologist reported that, for these cognitive domains, the individual performance was abnormally low. Moreover, because the Verbal-Performance discrepancy was significant at $P < .01$, the clinician also suggested that the performance deficit was probably a function of trauma. Because no premorbid data were available to the clinician and the patient exhibited no obvious language deficits, the clinician also reported that it could not be determined if the patient's language function had been impaired by the trauma. However, on retest, the patient obtained a PIQ of 85 and a VIQ of 110.

Payne and Jones (1957) argue that the appropriate statistical model for addressing the question of change over time is regression. Specifically, if the test-retest correlation, means, and standard deviations for a test are known, one can predict what score should be obtained by an individual on retest and bound this score by a set number of standard errors of prediction. If the actual obtained scores fall outside this boundary, one can conclude that a significant change has occurred at the specified level of confidence. Specifically, the prediction equation for z-scores is as follows:

$$z_{\text{pred}} = (z_1)r \tag{3}$$

where z_{pred} = predicted z-score based on the initial performance
　　　　z_1 = z-score obtained on the test the first administration
　　　　r = test-retest correlation

The equation for standard error of prediction for z-scores ($\text{SD}_{z\text{pred}}$) is as follows:

$$SD_{z\text{pred}} = (1 - r^2)^{\frac{1}{2}} \tag{4}$$

In Table 19.4, these equations are applied to the hypothetical clinical case using the standardization data in the WAIS-R manual (Wechsler, 1981). For this particular example, a two-tailed 95% confidence interval was used. From the data, one may conclude that the patient exhibited a significant increase in VIQ, whereas the 15-point increase in PIQ was not significant. The actual PIQ increase of 15 points is relatively close to the expected change due to regression alone (i.e., $z_{\text{pred}} = -1.88$, $z_2 = -1.56$). From these data, a clinician could conclude, retrospectively, that the trauma did cause impairment in verbal functions and that this impairment is decreasing. However, there has been no significant improvement in performance skills, even though the PIQ increased by 15 points.

These examples of Payne and Jones' procedures should illustrate why good standardization data are required in clinical practice and, when available, how these data should be employed in a probabilistic model for the single clinical case. These data can only be generated within a psychometric model. In contrast to the data originating from many experimental studies, the psychometric data allow for identification of truly abnormal patterns and for statistical confidence in clinical statements. Within the

Table 19.4.　Calculation of a Significant Change in VIQ and PIQ

	VIQ	PIQ	Reason/Source
Standardization data:			
Time 1	Mean, 102.0　SD, 14.0	Mean, 103.0　SD, 15.6	WAIS-R Manual (pg. 32): age, 25–34
Time 2	Mean, 105.3　SD, 14.3	Mean, 111.9　SD, 17.2	
Retest reliability	0.94	0.89	
Subject data:			
Time 1	90	70	Hypothetical
z Time 1	$\dfrac{90 - 102}{14.0} = -.86$	$\dfrac{70 - 103}{15.6} = -2.12$	z-score transformation
z Predicted	$(-.86)(.94) = -.81$	$(-2.12)(.89) = -1.88$	Equation 3
SD z_{pred}	$[-1 - (.94)^2]^{\frac{1}{2}} = .34$	$[1 - (.89)^2]^{\frac{1}{2}} = .46$	Equation 4
1.96(SD)	$1.96(.34) = .67$	$1.96(.46) = .89$	Two-tailed at .05
Confidence bounds	$-1.47 < z_{\text{pred}} < -.14$	$-2.77 < z_{\text{pred}} < -.99$	$z_{\text{pred}} \pm 1.96(\text{SD})$
Actual performance:			
Time 2	105	85	Hypothetical
z Obtained	$\dfrac{105 - 105.3}{14.3} = -.02$	$\dfrac{85 - 111.9}{17.3} = -1.56$	z-score transformation
Conclusions	Significant improvement	No change	

NOTE: SD, standard deviation.

classic diagnostic model, one of the four properties is met: description. For the remaining three goals—etiology, treatment, and prognosis—to be met, the relationship between abnormal behavior states and these three components have first to be examined in the research domain.

A Clinical Research Paradigm

Earlier in this chapter, the properties of an ideal neuropsychological research paradigm were outlined. These properties may be summarized as follows: (1) more than one theory of brain-behavior relationships is tested, (2) the inherent variability in tests and lesion sites may be statistically related, (3) criteria for differences are represented by a significant deviation from normal, (4) salient feature groups may be identified, and (5) premorbid status may in part be controlled. Further, it was suggested that in order to achieve these properties, the single-case methodology with replication was scientifically the most powerful. The Payne and Jones' procedures (1) are designed for the single case and (2) allow for probabilistic statements concerning behavioral abnormality to be made. By applying the test for an abnormal difference to individual patients in a research study, it would be possible first to generate reliable behavioral taxonomies of deficit or impairment and then to relate these taxonomies to other clinical data (e.g., lesion site and size, etiology, and treatment responsiveness). In addition, the five outlined properties of an ideal research paradigm would be met.

For example, if 20 well-standardized neuropsychological tests are given to 50 persons with confirmed brain lesions (e.g., by computed tomographic scan), the data for each subject over the 20 tests may be analyzed by applying the test for a clinically abnormal difference to all possible intertest differences (i.e., number of differences = $(20^2 - 20)/2 = 190$). Subsequently, subjects with similar abnormalities in their profiles may be grouped, and subjects with no abnormalities in their profiles can also be identified. For the subjects with no abnormal differences in their profiles, the question of interest is whether they perform significantly below the normal sample on the majority of tests (i.e., 1.67 standard deviations). For subjects who meet this criterion, a label, such as globally impaired, can be applied. For subjects with abnormal profiles, the first question of interest is whether identical or at least very similar profiles can be identified. Within the single-case methodology, the existence of more than one identical profile can be considered replication. Although, within this framework, the probability of finding significant differences between tests is high due to the number of possible contrasts, the probability of finding identical profiles is very low due to the number of potential permutations of profiles. Therefore, if similar profile types are found, one may conclude that a systematic phenomenon does exist. From a scientific point of view, the attempt to find similar profiles may be viewed as establishing internal consistency within the domain of interest (e.g., cognitive behavior).

If similar profile types are found, then these profiles, including the globally impaired group, can be related to, for example, the lesion site. If specific profile types are related to specific lesion sites, then the theory of functional invariance between the specific lesion site and profile is validated. If, however, some profile types are related, not to specific lesion sites but to many, one may have gained insight into specific aspects of brain circuitry or test demands. It should be also noted that this process of matching profiles to lesion site should not be considered a validation procedure. Specifically, when a profile type does not match with a lesion site, one can gain greater insight into brain function. In addition, if common profile types are found, then one can also reexamine unique profiles (i.e., only one case) with respect to either lesion site or profile types. For example, if a particular profile type is associated with a specific lesion area, are there cases with similar lesions but with different or unique profiles? If such cases are found, then the obvious question is why. Conversely, there may be a unique profile that is similar in some respects to a certain profile type but different in other respects. Can this difference be explained by differences in lesion size or site?

This outlined paradigm is considerably more challenging, statistically and conceptually, than the null hypothesis testing technique. In order to analyze the data, "canned" computer programs cannot be used directly; rather, computer packages have to be manipulated. Similarly, each case has to be analyzed separately. Because the procedure also has stricter criteria for scientific significance, the probability of finding significant results is lower. However, if common profile types are found, they will provide a stronger theoretical basis and better understanding of brain-behavior relationships. Specifically, from a scientific point of view, multiple theories are tested, and the criterion for testing is appropriate for the research question. Finally, if behavioral subtypes can be identified, the clinician will have target behavioral profiles of brain dysfunction. Therefore, obtained clinical profiles can be assessed relative to expected patterns of brain dysfunction.

REFERENCES

Benton, A. (1981). Aphasia: Historical perspectives. In M. Sarno (Ed.), *Acquired aphasia* (pp. 1–25). New York: Academic Press.

Bindra, D., & Scheir, I. (1954). The relationship between psychometric and experimental research in psychology. *American Psychologist, 9,* 69–71.

Branch, C., Milner, B., & Rasmussen, T. (1964). Intracarotid sodium amytal for lateralization of cerebral speech dominance. *Journal of Neurosurgery, 21,* 339–405.

Broadbent, D. (1954). The role of auditory localization in attention and immediate memory. *Journal of Experimental Psychology, 47,* 191–196.

Broca, P. (1865). Du siège de la faculté du langage articulé. *Bulletin de la Societé d'Anthropologie, 6,* 337–393.

Bryden, M. (1964). Order of report in dichotic listening. *Canadian Journal of Psychology, 6,* 291–299.

Campbell, D., & Stanley, J. (1963). *Experimental and quasi-experimental designs for research.* Chicago: Rand McNally.

Clark, C., Crockett, D., Klonoff, H., & MacDonald, J. (1983). Cluster analysis of the WAIS on brain-damaged patients. *Journal of Clinical Neuropsychology, 5,* 149–158.

Clark, C., & Spreen, O. (1983). Psychometric properties of dichotic words tests. *Journal of Clinical Neuropsychology, 5,* 169–179.

Colbourn, C. (1978). Can laterality be measured? *Neuropsychologia, 16,* 283–289.

Crockett, D., Clark, C., Spreen, O., & Klonoff, H. (1981). Severity of impairment on specific types of aphasia. *Cortex, 17,* 83–96.

Cronbach, L. (1951). Coefficient alpha and the internal structure of tests. *Psychometrika, 16,* 297–334.

Cronbach, L. (1957). The two disciplines of scientific psychology. *American Psychologist, 12*, 671–684.

Cronbach, L. (1970). *Essentials of psychological testing* (3rd ed.). New York: Harper & Row.

Cronbach, L., Gleser, G., Nanda, H., & Rajaratman, N. (1972). *The dependability of behavioral measurement: Theory of generalizability for scores and profiles.* New York: John Wiley & Sons.

Cullen, J., Thompson, C., Hughes, L., Berlin, C., & Samson, D. (1974). The effects of varied acoustic parameters on performance in dichotic speech perception tests. *Brain and Language, 1*, 307–322.

Doehring, D., Hosko, M., & Bryans, B. (1979). Statistical classification of children with reading problems. *Journal of Clinical Neuropsychology, 1*, 4–16.

Fisher, R. (1925). *Statistical methods for research workers.* Edinburgh, Scotland: Oliver & Boyd.

Garfield, S. (1978). Research problems in clinical diagnosis. *Journal of Consulting and Clinical Psychology, 46*, 596–607.

Geschwind, N. (1965). Disconnection syndromes in animals and man. *Brain, 88*, 237–294.

Goldstein, L., & Lackner, J. (1974). A sideways look at dichotic listening. *Journal of Acoustical Society of America, 55*, (Suppl.) 51, 510A.

Guttman, L. (1945). A basis for analysing test/retest reliability. *Psychometrika, 10*, 255–282.

Harmon, H. (1967). *Modern factor analysis.* Chicago: University of Chicago Press.

Hays, W. (1973). *Statistics for the social sciences.* New York: Holt, Rinehart & Winston.

Hines, D., Fennel, E., Bowers, D., & Satz, P. (1980). Left-handers show greater test/retest variability in auditory and visual asymmetry. *Brain and Language, 10*, 208–211.

Hines, D., & Satz, P. (1974). Cross-model asymmetries in perception related to asymmetry in cerebral function. *Neuropsychologia, 12*, 239–247.

Hoyt, C. (1941). Test reliability obtained by analysis of variance. *Psychometrika, 6*, 153–160.

Kertesz, A., & Phipps, J. (1977). Numerical taxonomy of aphasia. *Brain and Language, 4*, 1–10.

Kertesz, A., & Phipps, J. (1980). The numerical taxonomy of acute and chronic aphasia syndromes. *Psychological Research, 41*, 179–198.

Kimura, D. (1961a). Cerebral dominance and the perception of verbal stimuli. *Canadian Journal of Psychology, 15*, 166–171.

Kimura, D. (1961b). Some effects of temporal-lobe damage on auditory perception. *Canadian Journal of Psychology, 15*, 156–165.

Kinsbourne, M. (1974). Mechanisms of hemispheric interaction in man. In M. Kinsbourne & L. Smith (Eds.), *Hemispheric disconnection and cerebral function* (pp. 260–285). Springfield, IL: Charles C Thomas.

Kuhn, G. (1973). The phi-coefficient as an index of ear differences in dichotic listening. *Cortex, 9*, 447–457.

Lawriw, I. (1976). *A test of the predictive validity and a cross-validation of the Neurosensory Centre Comprehensive Examination for Aphasia.* Unpublished master's thesis, University of Victoria, British Columbia, Canada.

Lezak, M. (1976). *Neuropsychological assessment.* New York: Oxford University Press.

Mahoney, M. (1978). Experimental methods and outcome evaluation. *Journal of Consulting and Clinical Psychology, 46*, 660–662.

Marshall, J., Caplan, D., & Holmes, J. (1975). The measure of laterality. *Neuropsychologia, 13*, 315–321.

Matarazzo, J. (1972). *Wechsler's measurement and appraisal of adult intelligence* (5th ed.). Baltimore: Williams & Wilkins.

Meehl, P. (1973). Why I do not attend case conferences. In *Psychodiagnosis: Selected papers* (pp. 225–302). Toronto, Canada: G.J. McLeod.

Meehl, P. (1978). Theoretical risks and tabular asterisks: Sir Karl, Sir Ronald and the slow progress of soft psychology. *Journal of Consulting and Clinical Psychology, 46,* 806–834.

Morais, J., & Bertelson, P. (1973). Laterality effects in dichotic listening. *Perception, 2,* 107–111.

Morris, R., Blashfield, R., & Satz, P. (1981). Neuropsychology and cluster analysis: Potential problems. *Journal of Clinical Neuropsychology, 3,* 79–99.

Nunnally, J. (1967). *Psychometric theory.* New York: McGraw-Hill.

Parsons, O., & Prigatano, G. (1978). Methodological considerations in clinical neuropsychology. *Journal of Consulting and Clinical Psychology, 46,* 608–619.

Payne, R. (1958). Diagnostic and personality testing in clinical psychology. *American Journal of Psychiatry, 115,* 25–29.

Payne, R., & Jones, H. (1957). Statistics for the investigation of individual cases. *Journal of Clinical Psychology, 13,* 115–121.

Petrauskas, R., & Rourke, B. (1979). Identification of subtypes of retarded readers: A neuropsychological, multivariate approach. *Journal of Clinical Neuropsychology, 1,* 17–37.

Pizzamiglio, L., DePascalis, C., & Vignati, A. (1974). Stability of dichotic listening test. *Cortex, 10,* 203–205.

Repp, B. (1977). Measuring laterality effects in dichotic listening. *Journal of the Acoustical Society, 62,* 720–737.

Satz, P. (1968). Laterality effects in dichotic listening. *Nature, 218,* 277–278.

Spearman, C. (1904). The proof and measurement of association between two things. *American Journal of Psychology, 15,* 72–101.

Spearman, C. (1910). Correlation calculate from faulty data. *British Journal of Psychology, 3,* 271–295.

Spearman, C. (1913). Correlation of sums and differences. *British Journal of Psychology, 5,* 417–426.

Spreen, O., & Benton, A. (1977). *Neurosensory Centre Comprehensive Examination of Aphasia.* Victoria, British Columbia, Canada: University of Victoria, Neuropsychology Laboratory.

Spreen, O., & Boucher, A. (1970). Effects of low pass filtering on ear asymmetry in dichotic listening and some uncontrolled error sources. *Journal of Auditory Research, 10,* 45–51.

Spreen, O., & Reisser, A. (1981). Assessment of aphasia. In M. Sarno (Ed.), *Acquired aphasia* (pp. 67–128). New York: Academic Press.

Stanley, J. (1971). Reliability. In R. Thorndike (Ed.), *Educational measurement* (pp. 356–442). Washington, DC: American Council on Education.

Stone, M. (1980). Measures of laterality and spurious correlation. *Neuropsychologia, 18,* 339–345.

Studdert-Kennedy, M., & Shankweiler, D. (1975). A continuum of lateralization for speech perception. *Brain and Language, 2,* 212–225.

Suberana, A. (1958). The prognosis in aphasia in relation to cerebral dominance and handedness. *Brain, 81,* 889–923.

Teng, E. (1981). Dichotic ear difference is a poor index of functional asymmetry between cerebral hemispheres. *Neuropsychologia, 19,* 235–240.

Wechsler, D. (1949). *Manual for the Wechsler Intelligence Scale for Children.* New York: Psychological Corporation.

Wechsler, D. (1955). *Manual for the Wechsler Adult Intelligence Scale.* New York: Psychological Corporation.

Wechsler, D. (1974). *Manual for the Wechsler Intelligence Scale for Children—Revised.* New York: Psychological Corporation.

Wechsler, D. (1981). *Manual for the Wechsler Adult Intelligence Scale—Revised.* New York: Psychological Corporation.

Zimmerman, I., & Woo-Sam, J. (1973). *Clinical interpretation of the Wechsler Adult Intelligence Scale.* New York: Grune & Stratton.

CHAPTER 20

Nonlocality and Localization in the Primate Forebrain

Karl H. Pribram

The fact that items in memory (engrams) become to some extent distributed in brain systems (e.g., Lashley, 1950), has led to a search for mechanisms that mediate distribution. Among such mechanisms, the holographic hypothesis of brain function (Pribram, 1966, 1969a, 1971; Pribram, Nuwer, & Baron, 1974) in memory and perception has stirred a considerable amount of controversy (e.g., Arbib, 1972) that has sometimes become manifest in overweaning interest (*Psychology Today*, February 1979; *Re-vision*, Summer/Fall, 1978; *Omni*, October 1982) and at others in simply being ignored (Edelman & Mountcastle, 1978). In the brain-behavioral sciences, the tendency is to latch on to a concept and try to make it do more than the evidence warrants: the thalamic theories of emotion and the all encompassing and often unspecified role of the reticular formation in emotion, motivation, thought, learning, decision making, consciousness, and attention come to mind as historically interesting examples. There is good reason, therefore, to review once again what the holographic hypothesis is about, its basis, and its claims and limitations and to juxtapose this review with one that deals with the formation of localized neural programs that operate on the nonlocal input store. A clear statement concerning what the holographic hypothesis is *not* about can also be helpful.

Let us begin with the last item: what the holographic hypothesis is not. It is not a theory or model addressed to how the brain works in general. It does not aim to account for all brain physiology or all of the problems of psychology. For example, the holographic hypothesis has little to say about the orderly sequencing of behavior, which is explained much more readily by recourse to models based on computer programming (e.g., Miller, Galanter, & Pribram, 1960). Evidence for localized storage of programs is reviewed in Part 2 of this chapter.

Nor does the holographic hypothesis of brain function take as its primary model the optical hologram. Both the optical hologram and aspects of brain function are considered to be instantiations of Gabor's mathematical proposition that encoding the Fourier or related transforms of a display allows image reconstruction of greater resolution than that provided by encoding the image per se. An additional instantiation of this mathematics is performed when digital computers perform (by way of the Fast Fourier Transform, or FFT) image reconstructions as in computed tomography (CT) scans.

Furthermore, the holographic hypothesis of brain function does not claim to contradict the localization of neural processes within systems of the brain. As we shall see, both local and nonlocal neural functions depend on precisely arranged connections between brain and peripheral structures, and among brain systems. Such connections determine what is encoded in the several brain systems, a topic reviewed in Part 2 of this chapter. By contrast, the holographic hypothesis addresses the intrinsic connectivity within each system that determines how events become encoded. The strongest form of the holographic hypothesis is based on the Fourier transform, but weaker forms admit of cascades of convolutions (e.g., Gabor, 1969), of averaging over Laplacians of a Gaussian distribution, and similar linear transforms.

What, then, does the hypothesis claim? The hypothesis claims to provide a model at the neurological level that accounts for the apparent distribution of memory storage, the vast capacity of that storage, the imaging capability of human sensory systems, and some of the properties of associative recall. The hypothesis does not claim exclusivity (i.e., that other models cannot account for these phenomena), but since it can be manipulated independently of brain, it can provide insights into the necessary constraints such models must embody. Such in vitro procedures are successfully applied in other sciences, for example, biochemistry, in which reactions can be examined in test tubes apart from the biological context in which they occur.

Finally, although the mathematical expressions (forms of orthogonal polynomials) that describe the theory are known as spread functions and their optical realization in photography can result in a boundariless distribution of information on film, these global transforms are not the only form of holography. In radioastronomy (e.g., Bracewell, 1965) and radar applications, as well as in constructing multiplex optical holograms, strips or patches of holographically transformed information are spliced to provide not only a three-dimensional image, as in ordinary holography, but also a moving image. As we shall see, such patch, strip, or muiltiplex holograms, represented mathematically by Gabor and not Fourier transforms, provide models more consonant with the brain facts than does any globally distributed system. Most of the objections that have been formulated (e.g., Julesz & Caelli, 1979) have addressed the limitations of global Fourier transforms to deal with psychophysical data.

These don'ts and do's have characterized the model from its inception. Over the 20 years that have intervened, however, these characteristics have become articulated in more precise terms, and data have accumulated in support of the model.

The first part of this paper concerns, for the most part, these accumulations of data. Most of the data were not gathered with the model in mind. And the model itself did not originate in brain-behavior studies but from the problems posed by morphogenesis during embryological development; structural theories based on the principle of chemical gradients and resonances that "tune" specific locations in cytoplasm as inductors for organelles have been influential in embryology since before the turn of the century (e.g., Loeb, 1907; Weiss, 1939). In 1906, Goldscheider suggested that the structures of perception and memory might be similarly constructed by resonances among wave fronts created by sensory inputs in brain, especially cortical, tissue. In 1942, Lashley adopted this view as an alternative both to Köhler's field (as stated in final form in 1958) and to a localizationist view in which one percept, or engram, one feature of experience, is matched to one neuron or neuron assembly. Lashley was never satisfied with this adoption because he could not envision the specific mechanisms that would give rise to resonant (and interfering) wave fronts in brain tissue and, equally important, how these in turn might be responsible for the structures that make up perception and engram. He nonetheless held to the view that neither field nor localization (as, e.g., in the sophisticated development by Hebb, 1949) could account for the complex relationship between brain anatomy and phenomenal experience or deal adequately with the encoding of memory.

The holographic hypothesis provides specific mechanisms that can give rise to resonant (and interfering) wave fronts (which can as well be viewed in statistical terms as composed of vectors in matrices or latices of neural events in brain tissue) and demonstrates how these in turn might be responsible for the images that constitute perception and the distributed engrams that make up the memory store. In order to fully display the utility of the model, it will be contrasted with two other major classes of proposals, field theory and feature correspondence theory, which until very recently provided the only major alternative classes of models. Field theory is shown wanting with respect to perception, although it plays an important role in learning. The chapter then proceeds to apply the results of research on feature correspondence and holographic encoding to object perception, which is found to depend on the interaction of the sensory with the motor mechanisms of the brain. Part 2 details the operations of further stages of motorlike programming to constitute the cognitive operations embedded in various techniques of learning and memory encoding.

PART 1: FIELDS, FEATURES, AND NEURAL HOLOGRAPHY

We have already noted that until the present, there really have been only three classes of neural mechanisms proposed to explain the properties of perception. The three may, for convenience, be labeled field theoretic, feature correspondent, and holographic.

Wolfgang Köhler proposed that direct current (DC) fields were set up in the brain cortex by sensory stimulation and that these fields were isomorphic with, that is, had the same shape as, the phenomenally perceived stimulus. Köhler and Wegener (1955) showed that in fact sensory stimulation did result in DC shifts, and in our laboratory we showed that such shifts were accompanied by desynchronization of the electrocorticogram (Gumnit, 1960).

However, several experiments that throw doubt on the relationship between such shifts and perceptual performance were performed by Lashley, by Sperry, and by Pribram. In these experiments, gold foil was placed over the surface of the cortex (Lashley, Chow & Semmes, 1951); mica strips were implanted in crosshatched cortex (Sperry, Miner, & Myers, 1955); and aluminum hydroxide cream was injected in minute amounts into the cortex to produce gross abnormalities (Figures 20.1, 20.2) (Pribram, 1951; Kraft, Obrist, & Pribram, 1960; Stamm & Knight, 1963).

In none of these experiments did the animals show any change in their ability to discriminate among cues; gross alteration of the cortical DC field was not accompanied by any gross change in perceptual performance. These findings take additional meaning from the facts that the aluminum hydroxide cream implantation produced a fivefold retardation of learning and that imposing direct currents across cortex impairs (when cathodal) and enhances (when anodal from surface to depth) learning (Stamm & Rosen, 1972). Direct current fields are thus shown capable of biasing learning rate; and at the same time, such fields seem to be unrelated to the structuring of percepts. We turn, therefore, to the evidence for feature correspondence and holographic encoding for explanations of the neural mechanisms responsible for perceptual phenomena.

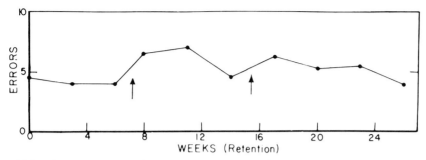

Figure 20.1. Average number of errors made by a group of four monkeys whose primary visual cortex had been implanted with an epileptogenic agent (aluminum hydroxide cream). The first arrow indicates when implantations were made, the second when electrical seizure patterns began. Such electrical seizures (spike and dome) were recorded sporadically while the monkeys' visual discrimination performance remained above the 90% level.

FEATURE CORRESPONDENCE THEORY

Definition

Field theory and feature correspondence concepts either explicitly or implicity imply a brain-perceptual isomorphism. In the case of feature correspondence, isomorphism is thought to be established when a particular cell or cell assembly responds uniquely to a feature of the phenomenally experienced image, that is, a feature of the imaged object is detected. It is then assumed that the organism's response to the total object is

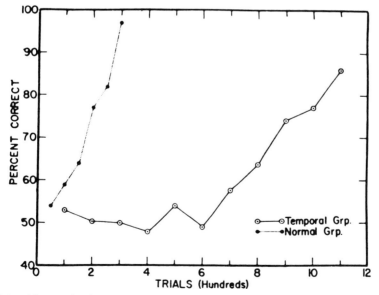

Figure 20.2. Visual discrimination learning curves of monkeys in which electrical seizure patterns were induced by aluminum hydroxide implantations before the beginning of behavioral testing. Note the elongation of the period of stationarity and the similarity between slopes of the curves once learning has become manifest. This similarity is even more striking when backwards learning curves for individual subjects are compared.

composed by convergence of the outputs from a set of feature selective elements onto a higher level neuroperceptual unit: a "pontifical" cell or cell assembly composed of like elements ("cardinal" cells).

In the late 1950s and early 1960s, Hubel and Wiesel (e.g., 1959) discovered that the center-surround organization of the dendritic microstructure of cells (their receptive fields) in the peripheral visual system became elongated. Further, they presented indirect evidence that this elongation might be due to convergence onto the cortical cells of fibers from cells with center-surround receptive fields. Their demonstration emphasized that cells in the visual cortex responded best to bars of light presented in specific orientations. It was easy to generalize these findings into a Euclidian geometry of brain function; points to oriented lines, to curves and planes, to complex figures of all sorts. The search for feature detectors was on.

The results of the search were by no means meager. For instance, one cell in monkey cortex was found to respond maximally to a monkey's hand (Gross, Bender, & Rocha-Miranda, 1969); another cell was shown to respond best when a stimulus was repeated six times (Groves & Thompson, 1970); still others appeared to be activated largely by vocalizations of their own species (Maurus & Ploog, 1971).

Features Extracted from Noise

There is a considerable body of evidence that supports the conception that at least some of the feature properties are inborn (e.g., Wiesel & Hubel, 1965a, b; Chow, 1961, 1970; Ganz, 1971). True, these properties must be exercised in an ordinarily rich environment lest they deteriorate and/or develop abnormally (Wiesel & Hubel, 1965a, b; Pettigrew, 1974). And there is some additional tuning that can occur as a result of specialized environmental inputs (Hirsch & Spinelli, 1970; Blakemore, 1974). In the context of phenomenal perception, these data can be taken to indicate that a feature matrix is a relatively stable property of the organism's sensory (receptor to cortical) system. Tuning of elements in that matrix by sensory input from the environment is feasible, but the elements to be tuned are characteristic of the organism.

An additional experimental result bears on this issue: Sutter (1976), in my laboratory, identified a cortical unit with simple receptive field properties and then stimulated it with visual white noise created by a random presentation of spots on a TV monitor. The experiment was undertaken to determine whether the response of the cell was linear (i.e., whether all of the variance could be accounted for by the first kernel of a Wiener polynomial). Much to our surprise, within the first 30 milliseconds, the cell responded only to those spots within its receptive field, exactly as it does to the conventional mapping procedure using a lines in particular orientations. Ten milliseconds later, an inhibitory flank appeared, as would be predicted for simple receptive field properties from intracellular recordings (Creutzfeldt, Kuhnt, & Benevento, 1974). In effect, the cell extracted the features elongation and orientation from noise on the basis of its own propensities. Similar results were obtained for frequency selection in the auditory system (Hosford, 1977). Clearly, the cells are selecting from the multiform sensory input only those properties to which they are sensitive (Figures 20.3 and 20.4).

The Conjoining of Features by Single Neurons

The specific selectivities of neurones can be misleading, however, if they are interpreted as showing that the cells in question function as feature detectors. To serve as a

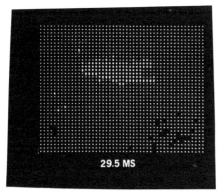

Figure 20.3.   An elongated receptive field of a single cell in the visual cortex of a cat. This field was demonstrated despite the fact that the visual system was stimulated with visual white noise, that is, with a spatiotemporally pseudorandom appearance of spots on an oscilloscope face. When the appearance of a spot in a certain location was correlated for approximately 30 milliseconds with an increase (bright dot), decrease (no dot), or no change (avg dot) in the forming of the neuron, the receptive field pattern emerged.

detector, the output of the cell must uniquely reflect the input feature, and this is only occasionally the case. More often, a cell responds to a variety of feature triggers. In the visual system, for example, a cell that responds selectively to lines in a specific orientation will modify that response with a change in luminance, with the direction of movement of those lines and the velocity of such movement (Spinelli, Pribram, & Bridgeman, 1970; Pribram, Lassonde, & Ptito, 1981). Furthermore, that very same cell may show a different response to color and even be tuned to a specific auditory frequency (Spinelli, Starr, & Barrett, 1968). Finally, the number of lines, their widths and spacings, also influence the response of the cell, which suggests that "stripes," rather than "lines," form the critical stimulus dimension for their orientation selectivity (DeValois, Albrecht, & Thorell, 1979; Glezer, Ivanoff, & Tscherbach, 1973; Movshon, Thompson, & Tolhurst, 1978a, b, c; Pollen & Taylor, 1974; Schiller, Finlay, & Volman, 1976). More of this in a moment.

Findings such as these—and they are equally true of other systems (e.g., Evans, 1966—for cells in the auditory cortex) make untenable the view that these cortical cells

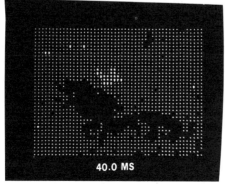

Figure 20.4.   An inhibitory flank appears when the correlations performed as for those in Figure 20.3 are carried out for approximately 40 milliseconds. 10-millisecond delay agrees with the results of intracellular recordings by Creutzfeld and colleagues (1974), who showed that the effect is due to lateral inhibition.

are simple detectors of features. Nonetheless, each cell is selectively responsive to variety of highly specific stimulus dimensions, the "feature triggers." Some of these dimensions appear to be mapped into recognizable patterns in adjacent cells; for example, orientation selectivity has been related to the columnar structure of cortex (Hubel & Wiesel, 1977) and selectivity to line width, and spacing has been reported to be a function of cortical layers (Maffei & Fiorentini, 1973). Other stimulus dimensions, such as the tuning of cells in the visual cortex to auditory frequencies, are distributed without any apparent regularity over much wider expanses of cortex. These distributed forms of organization become especially evident when recordings are made from groups of neurons when problem solving is being investigated (John, Bartlett, Shimokochi, & Kleinman, 1973; Gross, Bender, & Gerstein, 1979; Pribram, Spinelli, & Kamback, 1967).

The view obtained from the results of these studies is that, rather than feature detection by single neurons, some sort of feature selection is effected by neuron networks. For example, at the time Hubel and Wiesel discovered the orientation selectivity of receptive fields of cells in the visual cortex (1959), they also described additional properties, called simple, complex, and hypercomplex, by which various receptive fields could be distinguished. (The simple property is characterized by an elongated excitatory band flanked by one or more inhibitory sidebands, the complex property by a more homogenous excitatory field, and the hypercomplex property by end-stopping of the excitatory band by inhibition.) These discoveries have led to the almost universal interpretation that the *neurons* of the visual cortex can be classified according to their receptive field properties.

Based on this seminal work of Hubel and Wiesel in the late 1950s, which assigned cells to categories such as concentric, simple, complex, and hypercomplex (1959, 1962), a series of studies was begun in our laboratory during the mid 1960s (Spinelli & Barrett, 1969; Spinelli, Pribram, & Bridgeman, 1970; Phelps, 1973, 1974). We attempted to make a quantitative assessment of the nature of the properties, defining these categories by using a computer-controlled experimental situation in which single, double, and multiple spots and lines were drifted across the visual field of cats and monkeys. In this way, the receptive field of a cell could be accurately mapped because the computer "knew" where the spots or lines were located and could assign the response of the unit to that location in a set of bins that represented the possible locations in which the spots or lines might appear. In addition, elementary sensitivities of the cells to such stimuli as color, and the direction and velocity of movement were assessed.

The most striking result of these and subsequent experiments (Pribram, Lassonde, & Ptito, 1981) was the fact that each cell in the primary visual projection cortex has *multiple* selectivities and that the cells differed in the combinations of these selectivities. Thus, it became impossible to classify the cells; only the properties of a network of receptive fields were amenable to specification and classification. These properties were to a large extent, though not exclusively, characterized by the elementary stimuli that were used to study the receptive field network. In short, each neuron in the primary visual cortex has already conjoined elementary sensory properties in some characteristic combination.

Following are some examples. Henry (1977) has noted, in several thousand explorations, that hypercomplex properties (i.e., an inhibition when elongation of the structure extends beyond certain limits) were found only rarely and that, when they were present, the receptive field also showed either complex (i.e., responsive to such a stimulus anywhere in its receptive field) or simple (i.e., showing excitatory and inhibitory regions within its receptive field) properties. Schiller, Finlay, and Volman (1976) found so many properties for each neuron they examined that they attempted classification via a multidimensional statistical analysis. Though not undertaken by them, Henry and Schiller's approach, drawn to its logical conclusion, results in a classification of receptive field (i.e., network) properties not a classification of single neurons (Pribram, Lassonde, & Ptito, 1981).

Thus any conceptualization based on the idea that sensory feature elements are kept isolated in the primary visual projection systems is wrong. Whatever the nature of feature analysis and of channel separation, it is not due to a limited line, neuron-to-neuron mechanism.

This point bears repeating, for it is critical to any understanding of the issue of whether perception is constructed by conjoining features separately represented in a single cell. Some of these same cells in the visual cortex are, as well selectively tuned to acoustic frequencies (Spinelli, Starr, & Barrett, 1968), and groups of neurons and even single cells show late responses (300–400 milliseconds after a stimulus is presented) only to a rewarded cue in a problem-solving situation (Pribram, Spinelli, & Kamback, 1967; Bridgeman, 1982).

This conjoining of properties in a receptive field of a neuron does not mean, however, that each neuron represents those conjunctions that characterize any particular object. No pontifical "grandfather" or "grandmother" cell has been found whose output is *uniquely* specified by an object. It remains possible that such specificity becomes encoded in the pattern of the output of a neuron—a pattern that can be specified by an interresponse interval histogram or burst profile. But to date, this has not been accomplished.

How, then, can we account for the perception of objects and events? Most likely, the perception of objects and events must be constructed by addressing a population of neurons whose response forms a spatial pattern unique to that feature. According to this formulation, the population of neurons responds to a feature much as does an audience when asked: All those who are blond, please raise your hand. Now, all those wearing red sweaters raise your hand. And now, those who are female raise yours. Each query elicits a distinct pattern that simultaneously selects a unique pattern from a pool of properties in which these properties are already to some extent haphazardly conjoined. The next stage of processing thus involves the recognition of spatial pattern that is dependent on the precise anatomical connectivity between the primary sensory receiving cortex (the striate, for vision) and its perisensory (the prestriate) surround.

Feature selection by neural networks can be considered a form of feature correspondence. As noted above, however, the nature of the features responded to by a neural network response pattern is considerably different from their perceived phenomenal nature. The spatial pattern made by neurons that respond to a feature, though unique to that feature, do not resemble the feature in any way. Feature correspondence must be viewed, therefore, as nonisomorphic; that is, there is no geometric correspondence between phenomenal experience and the neural patterns to which that experience corresponds. Given this caveat, the evidence for feature correspondence is substantial. Unique neural response patterns can be abstracted from the multiple conjoined selectivities of neurons and neuron assemblies. The question remains as to how this abstraction is accomplished.

Object Perception and the Motor Systems of the Brain

It is the importance of movement to perception that provides the key to an answer to the second question posed earlier: How does the selection-conjunction process proceed to emphasize some features to the exclusion of others? Try the following demonstration. Have someone touch you with a pencil or other object. You feel the touching, rubbing, pressure, and so on. These are elementary qualities of tactile sensibility. Now grasp and rotate the same object in your palm by active manipulation. Suddenly an object (a pencil) has materialized!

There is an intermediate perception that can be achieved when the passive touching is performed in a reasonably regular fashion. Thus an X or a T may be identified as a pattern—somewhat intermediate between a passive sensation and an object. Auditory perceptions are based on the relative frequencies of vibratory stimuli; movement in time is involved. It is likely that a similar mechanism operates in vision. Here, the mechanism is based on relationships among spatial frequencies, one of the feature properties of the receptive field matrix of the visual cortex (Campbell, Cooper, & Enroth-Cugell, 1969; Campbell & Robson, 1968; DeValois, Albrecht, & Tharell, 1979; Glezer, Ivanoff, & Tscherbach, 1973: Maffei & Fiorentini, 1973; Movshon, Thompson, & Tolhurst, 1978a, b, c; Pollen & Taylor, 1974; Pribram, Lassonde, & Ptito, 1981; Schiller, Finlay, & Volman, 1976). Movement is provided by the constant tremorlike displacements of the eyeball. When an image is artificially stabilized on the retina, pattern vision ceases within seconds (Ditchborn & Ginsborg, 1952; Riggs, Ratliff, Cornsweet, & Cornsweet, 1953; Heckenmueller, 1968).

How are such stable spatial patterns generated in the cortex? Recall that direction of movement and orientation as well as frequency characterize the spatial properties of the receptive field network. These properties can combine into geometric (Fourier) descriptors that designate contours of patterns. Schwartz, Desimone, Albright, and Gross (1983) have analyzed the spatial frequency spectra at many orientations of a stimulus (Fourier descriptors are derived from the response of neurons to spatial frequency at each orientation of a stimulus) of receptive fields in the inferotemporal cortex and decoded them in terms of Fourier descriptors: a variety of stick figure contours emerge. The inferotemporal cortex does more than develop contours, as we shall see below, but contours are a prerequisite to its function in object identification and choice. Where contours are developed is at present unknown, although some preliminary evidence suggests that the prestriate cortex is critically involved.

Pattern perception based on contours is not identical with object perception, however. The characteristic that identifies the perception of objects is constancy across changes in the sensory patterns they elicit. Constancy is achieved by a connectivity that allows the variety of images and their contours to be correlated so that only invariances remain. The averaging procedure used in analyzing event-related brain electrical potentials is an example that extracts constancies from noise. Edelman and Mountcastle (1978) have detailed a model of connectivities that achieve constancies by eliminating irrelevant information. Mathematically, such "degenerative" procedures are nonlinear and irreversible.

An important question for research is whether such nonlinearities are introduced at the object level of processing. Constancies can be developed when the functions of motor programs are initiated in systems interwoven with and adjacent to the sensory projections in the brain. One of the characteristics of the development of the mammalian brain is the progressive separation of motor from sensory cortex, which may allow a substitution of the Edelman type of degenerative connectivity for the more locally symmetrical connectivities (Burgess, Wagner, Jennings, & Barlow, 1981; Pribram, 1960) of the projection cortex per se. This is especially true in the somatic modality. But to some extent, it is also true of the other senses (see Pribram, 1974a).

For instance, electrical excitation of the peristriate cortex (which surrounds the visual projection area) of monkeys produces eye movements, which raises the possibility that object constancy in the visual mode is a function of this visuomotor system. This possibility is enhanced by the finding that, in one experiment (Ungerleider, Ganz, & Pribram, 1977), size constancy was shown to depend on this system. After extensive damage, monkeys respond exclusively to the retinal image size of an object, ignoring the contextual environmental and organismic factors responsible for constancy.

Sperry (1947), Held (1968), and Festinger, Burnham, Ono, and Bamber (1967) each have suggested that all of perception is essentially a motor process. In part, this suggestion stems from the fact that neurons are sensitive to transients, and movement produces transients. However, their analysis has failed to account for our inability to basically alter images of scenes, despite occasional illusory conjunctions of features. As developed here, the motor systems are assigned a more restricted role: that of developing object constancies. Objects are perceived as invariant when the organism actively moves about the environment—whether with eyes, hands, or whole body.

As noted, Schwartz, Desimone, Albrecht, and Gross (1983) have devised precise mathematical models that can extract geometric (e.g., Fourier) descriptors of shape (invariances) from such figure-ground perimetry. Richards and Kaufman (1969) have pointed out the relevance of this type of model to "center of gravity" tendencies that occur for spontaneous optic fixations onto figures in the presence of flow patterns of visual background noise (ground). They suggest that each pattern boundary

> sets up a wave [in the cortical receptive field matrix] which is propagated at a constant velocity. The point at which all waves converge together will be the apparent position of the whirlpool [the fixation point]. For simple figures with no imagination, this position will be the center of gravity of the figure. The positions of the whirlpool for more complex figures can be calculated as outlined by Blum (1967).

They conclude by stating that they would like to consider the possibility that a "center of gravity" analysis "which regulates oculomotor activity may be occurring at the same time that the form of the pattern is analyzed. Thus, it is the flow pattern and not the form of the pattern which is the principal correlate of the fixation behavior." And, I will add, the flow pattern in a natural setting is, of course, largely determined by movement. It is movement-produced flow patterns that initiate the emphases and deemphases (conceptualized as wave fronts and vectors) that constitute selection within the feature matrix of the cortex. Note here that the direction of control is from the peristriate to the striate cortex. Control can be effected via corticofugal efferents to subcortical loci, which in turn influence the geniculo-striate system, or control may be exercised directly via peristriate to striate corticocortical connections.

As in the Richards and Kaufman experiment, flow patterns can originate in the environment or, as often occurs naturally, they are initiated by movement of the organism. Movement can consist of directional displacement, or it can be oscillatory, as in the spontaneously occurring eye movements that prevent the fade-out that occurs when retinal images are experimentally made stationary. In either case, the peristriate cortex becomes involved in fixating the "whirlpool" of the flow patterns.

In the olfactory mode, such oscillatory movements are produced by respiration. In this regard, Freeman (1981) has elegantly demonstrated that oscillatory movements create the formation of wave packets that interact in terms of their spatial frequency. Both Freeman (1981) and Grossberg (1981) have presented mathematical models of the development of perceptual constancies based on such interactions.

NONLOCALITY AND HOLONOMIC THEORY

Definition

A likely mechanism by which the abstraction necessary to object perception is achieved lies in the powerful correlational facility of holonomic transformations, the transformations that make holography possible. The idea that the neural network performs holonomic transformations on sensory input must be clearly distinguished from both field theories and feature correspondence theories. In a holonomic transformation, the various stimulus dimensions become enfolded into every part of the transform domain, a set of neural signals is transformed, and transfer functions, readily dealt with either by wave form or statistical mathematics, describe the transformation. This duality makes holonomic theory akin to quantum mechanics, in which the dual nature of quanta of electromagnetic phenomena are described. Thus, a combination of wave form and statistical approaches has been found to be most powerful (see, e.g., Julesz, 1971, for the visual system and Flanagan, 1972, for the auditory system). Transformation of a set of signals into an enfolded order is very different from simply generating a DC field in cortex by the arrival of neural signals. Holonomic theory, a quantum theory, is therefore not a field theory, although it is related to field theory in that wave mechanical descriptions are relevant and holistic, rather than point-to-point, analysis is emphasized.

Holonomic theory thus resembles feature correspondence theory to some extent, although, once again, the two can be sharply distinguished. The similarity comes from the fact that performing a transform a second time will reinstate the image (with all its features) from the transform domain. The difference between holonomic transformation and feature correspondence is that the transform domain is recognized in the strongest form of the theory as the domain in which neural networks operate. The finding of multiple feature selectives of most brain cells and cell assemblies is compatible with such a view. As we shall see, however, this strongest form of the theory does not account for all the available data, thus necessitating some specifiable modifications. In either the strongest or modified version, *features are generated, constructed, when the encoded transform domain is addressed* through additional sensory input or by "reference" from other neural processes, such as sensitivities to internally produced stimulation.

There is thus no brain-perceptual isomorphism in the holonomic theory, as there is in the field theories. Rather, phenomenal experience is generated when sensory or internally derived inputs activate a holographic process or store. There is therefore no necessary geometrical identity between neural response patterns and phenomenal experience, just as in an optical hologram there is no identity between the patterns of silver grains on the photographic film and the image produced when that film is properly illuminated. Even a functional identity between phenomenal experience and brain processes becomes suspect if this means ignoring the input to senses from the world outside the organism and the input to other receptors from within the body.

The Neural Microstructure

A fundamental observation concerning the structure and function of the nervous system is the fact that the relationship between locations that characterize peripheral receptors and effectors is reflected in the organization of the input to and output from the brain cortex. The peripheral relationship may become distorted through convergence in the pathways to synaptic way stations that are intercalated between periphery and cortex and by divergence from those way stations, but enough of the relationship is maintained to be recognizable as a mapping of periphery onto cortex. In order for such cortical mapping to be possible, signals must be transmitted from and to specific locations in the periphery by way of pathways of nerve axon systems in which impulses are generated and propagated.

A second fundamental fact about the organization of the nervous system is that these peripheral-cortical axonal pathways are interlaced at every station, that is, in the periphery (as at the retina) and at the cortex (for example, in the striate cortex), with cells that possess either very short, fine-fibered axons or no axons at all. Such cells, called local circuit neurons (Rakic, 1976) are incapable of maintaining and transmitting action potentials, the nerve impulses, which convey signals over distances. Instead, these local circuit neurons are characterized by profusely branching dendrites that intersect with others from adjacent neurons. The electrical potential changes in such dendritic structures tend to be graded rather than impulsive, and when impulses are generated, they are small in amplitude, decay rapidly, and thus are not conducted over any considerable distance (Rall, 1970; Shepherd, 1974). In sum, the potential changes in these dendritic arborizations are most often hyperpolarizing and thus inhibitory (e.g., Benevento, Creutzfeldt, & Kuhnt, 1972).

The interaction between vertical (i.e., periphery-to-cortex) axonal transmission pathways and the interlaced horizontal dendritic networks has been worked out in several sensory systems by extracellular recordings made from the separate neurons composing the axonal transmission pathways. In essence, the interaction leads to a center-surround organization when a discrete stimulus excites the neuron. A center-surround organization is one in which the spatial extent of the signals transmitted becomes enveloped in a penumbra of signals of opposite sign. This center-surround organization often displays the characteristics of a wave form in that several excitatory and inhibitory bands surround the center, much as ripples are formed in a pond when the surface is excited by a pebble. Precise mathematical descriptions of such center-surround organizations have been given by Bekesy for the auditory and somatosensory systems (1959) and by Hartline (1940) and by Rodieck and Stone (1965) for the visual system (see also the review of early formulations by Ratliff, 1961). The data obtained from the olfactory system appear somewhat more complicated (Shepherd, 1974), but mathematical treatment has been successfully achieved by Freeman (1975).

The results of these studies have in common the finding that whatever the nature of the inciting stimulus to receptor excitation, such excitation and its subsequent processing can be readily formulated in terms of a calculus describing the microstructure of a network of hyper- and depolarizations. This formulation shows that the principle of superposition applies to the local spatial interactions between excitation (depolarizations) and inhibition (hyperpolarizations). Superposition indicates that the system is linear within the ranges examined and that a wave form interpretation of the data is useful. This does not necessarily mean that the dendritic potentials actually make up discernible wave fronts; what it does mean, at the minimum, is that the center-surround data describe transfer functions by which a matrix of discrete polarizations is related to an exciting input, functions that can readily be treated by linear wave equations.

Holography

These mathematical treatments of the data obtained from recordings of potentials of single neurons in the nervous system are akin to those that spawned holography. In 1946, Dennis Gabor devised a mathematics which showed that image reconstruction might attain greater resolution if, instead of intensity, the pattern of wave fronts generated on a photographic film by an exciting electron or photon were recorded. Gabor addressed his mathematics to electron microscopy, but in the early 1960s optical holography succeeded in implementing this image-processing technique in such a way that the properties of holograms became readily demonstrated (Leith & Upatnicks, 1965). The essential properties are (1) the holographic store is distributed; (2) vast amounts of storage can be concentrated in a small holographic space; (3) image reconstruction is three-dimensional, displaying constancies and parallax, and is highly textured; (4) images do not appear coextensive with the holographic store but are projected away from the film surface; and (5) the hologram has associative properties, meaning that when it is made by the reflected light of two objects, subsequent illumination of the stored hologram by light reflected from only one object will reconstruct a "ghost" image of the missing object.

These properties of holograms are so similar to the elusive properties that neuroscientists and psychologists (e.g., Boring, 1942) sought in brain tissue to explain perceptual imaging and engram encodings that the holographic process must be seriously considered as an explanatory device. In doing this, the caution must, however, constantly be exercised that it is the mathematics of holography and brain function that needs to be compared and tested, not the optical holograms or computer instantiations of holography.

The essentials of this mathematics can best be summarized by reference to a particular form of holography: the construction of a Fourier hologram. The Fourier theorem states that any pattern, no matter how complex, can be decomposed into a set of component, completely regular, "sine" waves. The Fourier transform of an image is formed by encoding these component wave forms. Thus, in the transformed record, each point indicates the presence of a particular component wave form rather than the corresponding local intensity, as in an ordinary record. Take, for comparison, an ordinary photograph and a Fourier-transformed record. The ordinary photograph is made up of a mosaic of points of varying intensities, the intensity of each point corresponding to the intensity of a point of light reflected from a specific location on the object being photographed. In the Fourier-transformed record, by contrast, each point represents the amount of energy present in a wave form component of the entire array of light reflected from the object. The band width of that component may vary; the resolving power of the transform is in part dependent on this band width.

To make a (Fourier) hologram, two such Fourier-tramsformed records must be linearly superposed. Mathematically, this is performed by the transfer function in which one record is convolved with the other and the resultant complex conjugate is stored. In essence, convolving consists of "multiplying" the wave forms together. Now each point in the record contains this "multiplication," that is, the resultant of superposing the energy contained in two wave form components derived from the entire array of reflected light. A holographic record can be made by superposing the Fourier transform of the light reflected from two (or more) objects or by using the transform of a nonreflected reference. When two or more objects are used, the light reflected from each serves as a reference for the other or others. This accounts for the property of associative recall noted above. In addition, since parts of objects as well as whole objects serve as sources of reflection and thus as references for other parts, constancies are generated when images are constructed or reconstructed. Constancies are therefore the result of the fact that the transformed "view" of any part of the objects acts as a reference for every other part.

It is these enfolding properties of holograms that make them so counterintuitive. Within the holographic domain, geometry, as we sense it, disappears and is replaced by an order in which the whole becomes enfolded and distributed into every part, thus the term *hologram*. But from each part, the whole can be reconstituted. This is due to another property of the Fourier theorem: applying the identical transform inverts the wave form domain back into the image! The process (the Fourier transform function) that converts images into wave forms can therefore also accomplish the inverse and convert wave forms into the images.

This parsimony in processing raises the question of utility. If image and wave form domain are so readily transformed into each other, why bother? The answer to this question is that correlations are much simpler to accomplish in the wave form domain—they essentially entail superposition, multiplication. That is why the Fast Fourier Transform (FFT) has proved so useful in computer programming, as, for instance, when image reconstruction by CT scan in x-ray tomography is desired. It is this power of the Fourier domain that the brain can exploit.

The Transform Domain

What, then, are the transfer functions that describe the transformations of sensory and bodily imputs into a brain holographic process? And what are the limits of explanatory power of such transfer functions with respect to the data at hand? The first suggestion that brain processing might involve a Fourier analysis was made a century ago for the auditory system by Ohm, who also formulated Ohm's law of electricity. This suggestion was adopted by Hermann von Helmholtz, who performed a series of experiments that led to the place theory of hearing, essentially a view of the cochlea as a piano keyboard whose keys, when struck by acoustic waves, would initiate nerve impulses to the brain, where resonant neurons were activated. This view was modified in this century by George von Bekesy (1959), whose experiments showed the cochlea and peripheral neurosensory mechanism to operate more as does a stringed instrument sensitive to superposition of acoustic wave forms. Good evidence has accrued to the effect that a major effect of initial auditory processing can be described in terms of a time-limited Fourier transform (i.e., a Gabor-like transform) of the acoustic input (Evans, 1974).

Bekesy then went on to make a large-scale model of the cochlea composed of a set of five vibrators set in a row (1959). The model could be placed on the forearm and the phase of the vibrators adjusted. At particular adjustments, the phenomenal perception produced by the model was that of a point source of stimulation. When two such model cochleas were properly adjusted and applied, one to each forearm, the point source appeared at first to jump alternately from one forearm to the other and then suddenly to stabilize in the space just forward and between the two arms. In short, the stimulus was projected away from the stimulating source and receptive surface into the external world.

Both macro- and microelectrode studies have shown that multiple vibratory stimulations of the skin also evoke unitary responses in cortex (Dewson, 1964; Lynch, 1971). The electrical potentials do not reflect the actual physical dimensions of the stimulus. Instead, they indicate that the sensory process has transformed the physical stimulus according to some transfer functions. Bekesy noted that sensory inhibition, effected by lateral inhibitory dendritic networks of neurons, is the responsible agent in the transformations.

Evidence is therefore at hand to indicate that the input to the ear and skin becomes transformed into neural patterns that can be described by sets of convolutional integrals of the type that Gabor (1969) has suggested as stages in achieving a fully developed holographic process. In the visual system as well, such transformations have been described by Rodieck (1965) as convolving input with retinal receptive field properties as recorded from units in the optic nerve (Figure 20.5).

The manner in which such a stepwise process occurs is best worked out for the visual system. A second step in the process occurs at the lateral geniculate nucleus, where each geniculate cell acts as a peephole "viewing" a part of the retinal mosaic. This is due to the fact that each geniculate cell has converging upon it some 10,000 optic nerve fibers originating in the ganglion cells of the retina. The receptive field of the geniculate neuron is composed of a center surrounded by concentric rings, each consecutive ring of sharply diminishing intensity and of sign opposite to that of its neighbors (Hammond, 1972). This type of organization is characteristic of units composing a near-field Fresnel hologram (Figures 20.6, 20.7) (Pribram, Nuwar, & Baron, 1974).

At the cortex, the transformation into a Fourier-like domain becomes complete. As noted in the section on feature analysis, Campbell and Robson (1968); Pollen, Lee, and Taylor (1971); Maffei and Fiorentini (1973); and Glezer, Ivanoff, & Tscherbach (1973) began to use gratings as stimuli (e.g., Schiller, Finlay, & Volman, 1976; Pribram, Lassonde, & Ptito, 1981). These studies have repeatedly confirmed that the cells in visual cortex are selectively tuned to a limited band width of spatial frequency of approximately an octave (½ to 1½ octaves). The spatial frequency (or wave number) of a grating reflects the width and spacings of the bars making up the grating. When such widths and spacings are narrow, the spatial frequency is high; when widths and spacings are broad, the spatial frequency is low. Ordinarily the term *frequency* implies a temporal dimension; in the case of spatial frequency, this temporal dimension can be evoked by sequentially scanning across the grating. (The temporal effect is most dramatic if an object is moved across the light path of a projected grating.) Conversion to a temporal dimension is, however, not necessary. The grating is a filter whose

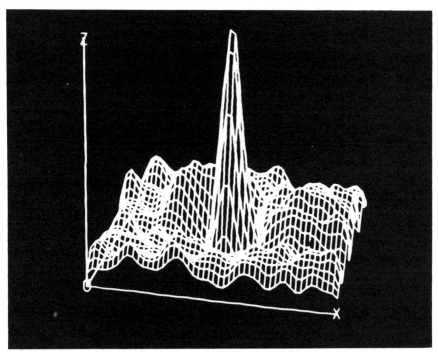

Figure 20.5. A "Mexican hat" three-dimensional configuration of a receptive field of a single neuron in the lateral geniculate nucleus of a cat. The procedure by which such receptive fields are plotted is detailed in the legend of Figure 20.6.

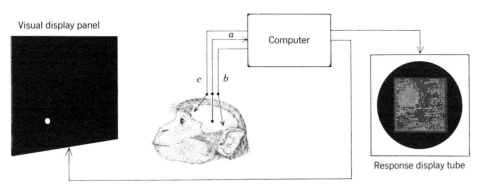

Visual display panel

Computer

Response display tube

Figure 20.6. The method by which a receptive field is plotted. A computer controls the location of a spot and correlates the number of impulses (recorded by a) emitted by the neuron while the spot is in that location. The "Mexican hat" configuration shown in Figure 20.5 results when the plane on which the spot is displayed is represented by the x and y axes and the number of impulses by the z axis. When the crown of the hat is sectioned parallel to the brim, two standard deviations above background activity, the ordinarily shown two-dimensional circular-surround (excitatory-inhibitory) receptive field results. This concentric receptive field arrangement is seen at the right.

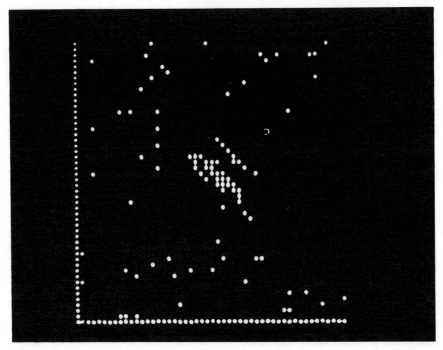

Figure 20.7.   When the procedure detailed in Figure 20.6 is performed with recordings from a cortical cell in the visual system, the elongated receptive field with inhibitory flank or flanks similar to those in Figures 20.3 and 20.4 is obtained. The elongation of the receptive field accounts for the fact that lines are the preferred stimulus to activate the cortical cells.

characteristics can be expressed either as spatial or temporal or both (Figures 20.8, 20.9).

The difference between a feature correspondence and a holographic transform approach has recently been brought into sharp focus by tests of hypotheses devised to contrast the two. In the visual cortex, the center-surround organization of visual receptive fields that obtains in the geniculate nucleus gives way to an elongated receptive field with side bands of the opposite sign. Hubel and Wiesel, in their original discovery of this change (1959), emphasized that lines presented at specific orientations were most effective stimuli to activate units with such receptive fields. They also presented evidence that elongated fields might be composed by convergence from geniculate cells with spotlike concentric fields. The feature-hierarchy Euclidian view of feature correspondence grew naturally from these early results and their interpretation. More recently it has been shown, as noted above, that these cells with orientation-selective, elongated receptive fields also vary their output with changes in luminance, movement of lines across the receptive field, the direction of that movement, its velocity, and the number and spacings of such lines (gratings of various spatial frequencies). In addition, it has been shown that changes in the width of single lines have little effect on the responses of these cells (Henry & Bishop, 1971; DeValois & DeValois, 1980).

Finally, in direct confrontation of feature correspondence theory, DeValois, Albrecht, and Thorell (1979) showed that a complex stimulus, such as a plaid or checkerboard,

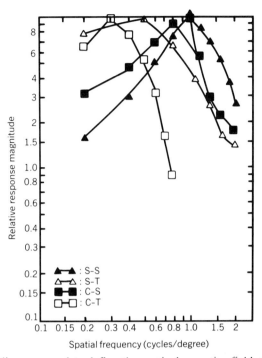

Figure 20.8. When lines are used to define the cortical receptive field, the lines may vary in width and spacing. Such variations are designated as changes in spatial frequency in cycles per degree. Tuning curves for cortical cells are obtained by stimulating the visual system with gratings (multiple lines) of varying spatial frequency. The tuning curves obtained in the study presented in this figure were obtained with above-threshold stimulation and remained unchanged by electrical stimulation of frontal and posterior brain systems.

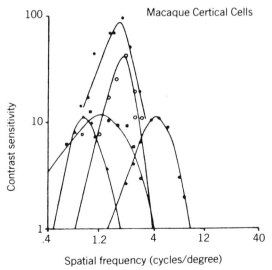

Figure 20.9. Tuning curves obtained in the manner described in the legend of Figure 20.8 but at contrast threshold (from DeValois & DeValois, 1980).

had to be rotated in such a way that the axes of the Fourier transform, rather than the edges per se of the stimulus pattern, would engage the orientation selectivity of the cell. Every cell examined responded maximally when the plaid or checkerboard pattern was rotated to the degree and minute of visual angle predicted by Fourier (and no other) transform of the pattern as determined by computer (using the Fast Fourier Transform). The cortical cells were thus shown to respond holistically (i.e., to the Fourier transform of the entire pattern) rather than feature by feature. Movshon, Thompson, and Tolhurst (1978), in another elegant experiment, detailed the complementarity between the spatial profile of the receptive fields of these cells and the Fourier transform of the stimulus giving rise to that profile. That cells in the visual cortex encode in a Fourier-like domain is thus an established fact (Figure 20.10).

These findings do not, however, mean that the visual system performs a global Fourier transform on the input to the retina (see also Julesz & Caelli, 1979). The moving retina decomposes the image produced by the lens of the eye into a "Mexican hat" receptive field organization that can be described as convolving retinal organization with sensory input (Rodieck, 1965). But the *spread function*, as such convolutions are called, does not encompass the entire retina: rather, it *is limited to the receptive field of a retinal ganglion cell*. Similarly, at the cortex, full-fledged encoding in the Fourier domain is restricted to the receptive field of the cortical neuron. There the effect of lateral inhibition produces a Gaussian envelope, which limits the otherwise boundaryless Fourier transform (Marjella, 1980; Burgess, Wagner, Jennings, & Barlow, 1981). The resulting transformation is called a Gabor function. This patchy organization of the transform domain (Robson, 1975) does not impair its holographic characteristics.

The technique of patching or stripping together Gabor, Fourier-like transformed images has been utilized in radioastronomy by Bracewell (1965) to cover expanses that cannot be viewed with any single telescopic exposure. The technique has been further developed by Ross (see Leith, 1976) into a multiplex hologram to produce three dimensional moving images when the inverse transform is effected. Movement is produced when the encoded strips capture slightly different images, as, for instance,

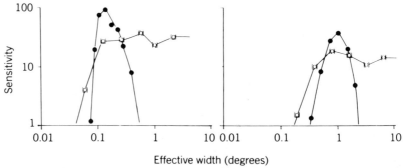

Figure 20.10. Comparison of tuning curves (for a cat, at left, and a monkey, at right) obtained in Figures 20.8 and 20.9 with those obtained when a single line of varying width is used to stimulate the visual system. Note that the line can be considerably broadened without any change in its output. This indicates that the cell is better tuned to spatial frequency than to lines per se. See the text for additional experiments that support this finding.

when adjacent frames of a motion picture are used as the image base for the transformation.

In the multiplex hologram, spatial relationships among the Gabor-transformed patches or strips become important. Thus, this form of hologram is a hybrid from which movement can be derived. A simple hologram is characterized by translational invariance; that is, the image that results from applying the transformation is essentially stationary and appears the same from different vantages except for changes in perspective (object constancy). By contrast, the hybrid multiplex form has encoded the spatiotemporal domain as well as the transform domain, and this has considerable advantage for moving organisms.

Suggestions have been made that the orientation selective elongated receptive fields that compose the visual cortex are arranged in Fibonacci spirals along the axes of cortical columns (Schwartz, 1977). Such an arrangement of the spatial relationships among the Gabor-transformed patches of receptive field would enhance still further the power of the transform domain in that three-dimensional movement (and therefore the resultant space-time relationship) would be readily explained.

Counterpoint

As noted, the multiplex hybrid nature of cortical holographic organization serves as a warning that any simply conceived "global-Fourier-transform-of-input-into-cortical-organization" is untenable. Furthermore, the multiple selectives of cortical cells in the visual (Spinelli, Pribram, & Bridgeman, 1970; Spinelli, Starr, & Barrett, 1968; Morrell, 1972), auditory (e.g., Evans, 1974) and somatosensorimotor (e.g., Bach-y-Rita, 1972) projection areas clearly indicate that such cells serve as nodes in neural networks in which the Gabor transform is only one, albeit an important, process. Several attempts have been made, therefore, to characterize more fully such cortical networks in terms of their essential properties. Thus, Longuet-Higgins (Willshaw, Buneman, & Longuet-Higgins, 1969) proposed an associative-net model and Leon Cooper (1973) has developed this model into a self-organizing distributed net whose mathematical description contains as a special case the Fourier transform hologram. Julesz (1971), Uttal (1978), Borsellino and Poggio (1973), Poggio and Torre (1980), and, in our laboratories, Sutter (1976) have taken a more statistical stance. Thus, Uttal emphasizes spatial autocorrelation functions, while Poggio and Sutter rely on Wiener polynomial expansions. In addition, Poggio treats the dendritic potential microstructure in terms of the Volterra solution of cable equations. His carefully worked-out proposal includes a stage of Fourier analysis and another in which the Laplace transform occurs.

Marr, Poggio, and Richards (Marr, 1976a, b; Marr & Poggio, 1977; Richards, 1977; Richards & Polit, 1974) have developed a model based on repetitive convolving of Laplacians of a Gaussian distribution. E. Roy John speaks of "hyperneurons" constituted by a distributed system of graded potentials recorded from the brains of problem-solving animals. Such organizations have been described in terms of Lie groups by Hoffman (1947); vector matrices by Stuart, Takahashi, and Umezawa (1978); and tensor matrices by Finkelstein (1976), in which the tensors represent multidimensional Fourier transforms. Finally, Edelman and Mountcastle (1978) have proposed a degenerative group model, also based on an essentially random connectivity.

The commonalities and distinctions in these proposals can be summarized as problem areas that need further inquiry:

1. To what extent is the idealization warranted that the brain cortical connectivity is essentially random? This issue has been discussed earlier in this chapter. In addition, the models proposed by Hoffman and by Poggio clearly opt for nonrandomness, while others are neither explicitly or implicitly based on an assumption that an ideal system may consist of random connectivities.

2. To what extent can brain systems be treated with linear (and reversible) equations, and to what extent must nonlinearities be introduced to explain the available data? Good evidence is at hand that the primary input and output systems (e.g., Granit, 1970) are essentially linear in most of their overall operations, despite many local nonlinearities. More of this in the next section.

PART 2: LOCALIZATION OF NEURAL PROGRAMS

Overall, nonlinearities may be introduced into the system when decisions have to be made—decisions involving discrimination between inputs, the performance of this rather than that action. On the other hand, decisions may be reached by virtue of correlation functions, essentially by cascades of linear filters. In either case, decisional operations have been shown to be local functions of the intrinsic (association) systems of the brain (Pribram, 1954, 1958a, 1958b, 1972a, 1972b, 1974a, 1977). Decisional operators can enter the system in two ways: the decisions can be attained by serial hierarchical abstraction of the relevant variables (e.g., Gross, 1973; Mishkin, 1973; Weiskrantz, 1974), or they can be imposed by a parallel corticofugal process upon the sensory-motor systems (Pribram, Spinelli, & Reitz, 1969; Ungerleider & Pribram, 1977; Christensen & Pribram, 1979; Pribram, 1971, 1974b). It is, of course, also possible that the hierarchical serial process operates during learning (as, e.g., suggested by Hebb, 1949), while parallel corticofugal operators determine momentary perceptions and performances. These operators are localized to one or another brain system. In any case, two major classes of such decisional operators can be distinguished: (1) a set of sensory-specific processes that involve the posterior cerebral convexity (inferotemporal cortex for vision, superior temporal for audition, anterior temporal for taste, and posterior parietal for somesthesis) and (2) a set of higher-order executive (i.e., context-sensitive) processes that involve the frontolimbic portions of the forebrain (e.g., reviews by Pribram, 1954, 1969c, 1973).

THE AGNOSIAS AND THE POSTERIOR CORTICAL CONVEXITY

Sensory Specificity

Between the sensory projection areas of the primate cerebral mantle lies a vast expanse of parietotemporopreoccipital cortex. Clinical observation has assigned disturbance of many cognitive and language functions to lesions of this expanse. Experimental psychosurgical analysis in subhuman primates of course is limited to nonverbal behavior; within this limitation, however, a set of sensory-specific agnosias (losses in the capacity to identify and categorize cues) have been produced. Distinct regions of primate cortex have been shown to be involved in each of the modality-specific cognitive functions: anterior temporal in gustation (Bagshaw & Pribram, 1953), inferior temporal in vision (Mishkin & Pribram, 1954), midtemporal in audition (Weiskrantz & Mishkin, 1958; Dewson, Pribram, & Lynch, 1969), and occipitoparietal in somesthesis (Pribram & Barry, 1956; Wilson, 1975). In each instance, categories learned before surgical interference are lost to the subject postoperatively, and great difficulty (using a "savings" criterion) in reacquisition is experienced, if task solution is possible at all.

The behavioral analysis of these sensory-specific agnosias has shown that they involve a restriction in sampling of alternatives, a true information processing deficit, a deficit in reference learning. Perhaps the easiest way to communicate this is to review the observations, thinking, and experiments that led to the present view of the function of the inferior temporal cortex in vision.

Search and Sampling Procedures

All sorts of differences in the physical dimensions of the stimulus, for example, size, are processed less well after inferiortemporal lesions (Mishkin & Pribram 1954), but the disability is more complex than it at first appears, as illustrated in the following story.

One day, when testing my lesioned monkeys at the Yerkes Laboratories at Orange Park, Florida, I sat down to rest from the chore of carrying a monkey a considerable distance between home cage and laboratory. The monkeys, including this one, were failing miserably at such visual tasks as choosing a square rather than a circle. It was a hot, muggy, typical Florida summer afternoon, and the air was swarming with gnats. My monkey reached out and caught a gnat. Without thinking, I also reached for a gnat—and missed. The monkey reached out again, caught a gnat, and put it in his mouth. I reached out—missed! Finally, the paradox of the situation forced itself on me. I took the beast back to the testing room. He was still deficient in making visual choices. However, as indicated by his ability to catch gnats, when no choice was involved, his visually guided behavior appeared to be intact. On the basis of this observation, the hypothesis was developed that *choice* was the crucial variable responsible for the deficient discrimination following inferotemporal lesions. As long as a monkey does not have to make a choice, his visual performance should remain intact.

To test this hypothesis, monkeys were trained in a Ganzfeld made of a translucent light fixture large enough so the animal could be physically inserted into it (Ettlinger, 1957). The animal could press a lever throughout the procedure but was rewarded only during the period when illumination was markedly increased for several seconds at a time. Soon, response frequency became maximal during this "bright" period. Under such conditions, no differences in performance were obtained between inferotemporally lesioned and control animals. The result tended to support the view that if an infero-temporally lesioned monkey did not have to make a choice, he would show no deficit in behavior, since in another experiment (Mishkin & Hall, 1955), the monkeys failed to choose between differences in brightness.

In another instance (Pribram & Mishkin, 1955), we trained the monkeys on a task in which they had to choose between easily discriminable objects: an ashtray and a

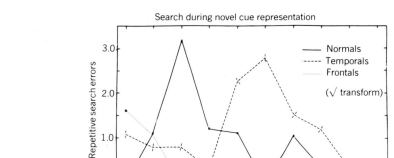
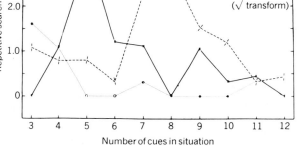

Figure 20.11.   Average number of repetitive errors made by three groups of monkeys (normal control monkeys, monkeys with inferotemporal resections, and monkeys with far frontal resections) while searching for a peanut hidden under one of several (2–12) junk objects. Note the changes in the curves of the control and inferotemporal-resected monkeys. Note also that for the lower number of cues that the control monkeys are performing better than the monkeys with inferotemporal resections. For an explanation of this result, see Figure 20.12. Note also that the monkeys with far frontal resections were immediately attracted to the novel cue, which covered the peanut in each situation, thus making few repetitive search errors. See also Figure 20.19.

tobacco tin. These animals had been trained for two or three years before surgery and were sophisticated problem solvers. This, plus ease of task, produced only a minimal deficit in the simultaneous choice task. When given the same cues successively, the monkeys showed a deficit when compared with their controls, despite their ability to differentiate the cues in the simultaneous situation.

This result gave further support to the idea that the problem for the operated monkeys was not so much in "seeing" but in being able to *refer* in a useful or meaningful way to what had been reinforced previously. Not only the stimulus conditions but an entire range of response determinants appeared to be involved in specifying the deficit. To test this more quantitatively, I next asked whether the deficit would vary as a function of the *number of alternatives* in the situation (Pribram, 1959). It was expected that an informational measure of the deficit could be obtained, but something very different appeared when I plotted the number of errors against the number of alternatives (Figure 20.11).

If one plots repetitive errors made before the subject finds a peanut—that is, the number of times a monkey searches the same cue—versus the number of alternatives, at this stage the monkeys with inferotemporal lesions were doing better than the controls! This seemed a paradox. However, as the test continued, the controls no longer made so many errors, whereas the lesioned subjects began to accumulate errors at a greater rate than shown earlier by the controls.

When a stimulus sampling model was applied to the analysis of the data, a difference in sampling was found. The monkeys with inferotemporal lesions showed a lowered sampling ratio; they sampled fewer cues during the first half of the experiment. Their defect can be characterized as a restriction on the number of alternatives searched and

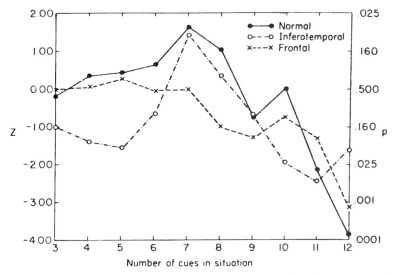

Figure 20.12. The explanation for the results obtained in Figure 20.11 is that the monkeys with resections of the inferotemporal cortex restricted their sampling to a limited range of cues, thus gaining a temporary advantage over the normal control subjects.

sampled. Their sampling competence, their competence to process information, had become impaired. The limited sampling restricted the ability to construct an extensive memory store and to reference that memory during retrieval (Figure 20.12).

Element Learning

The multiple object task was administered in a Yerkes testing apparatus operated manually. Because administration was tedious and time consuming, and because inadvertent cueing was difficult to control, an automated testing device was developed (Pribram, Gardner, Pressman, & Bagshaw, 1962; Pribram, 1969b). The resulting computer controlled Discrimination Apparatus for Discrete Trial Analysis (DADTA) proved useful in a large number of studies, ranging from testing one-element models of learning (Blehert, 1966) to plotting Response Operator Characteristic (ROC) curves to determine whether bias was influenced toward risk or toward caution by selected brain resections (Spevack & Pribram, 1973; Pribram, Spevack, Blower, & McGuinness, 1980).

To investigate whether learning proceeds by sampling one element at a time, eight monkeys were trained on a two-choice and a five-choice sample of which only one cue was rewarded. The choices of individual monkeys were plotted for each of the cues sampled. As can be seen from the accompanying figure (Figure 20.13), sampling of cues is initially random, producing prolonged periods of stationarity. Then, at some point, behavior becomes concentrated on the rewarded cue in steps, each of which is preceded by another period of stationarity, and the elimination (i.e., choice drops to zero) of one of the unrewarded cues.

The study was undertaken in order to determine whether crosshatching (with a cataract knife) of the inferior temporal cortex would produce subtle effects that would

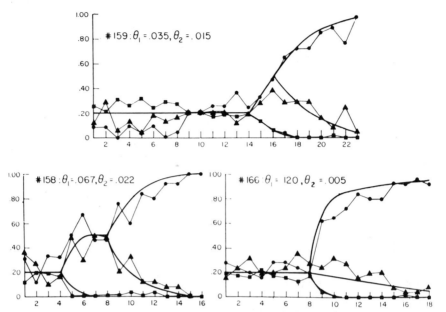

Figure 20.13. Graphs of the actual learning curves of three monkeys mastering a discrimination that involved three separable features. Note how performance is enhanced as each nonrewarded feature is discriminated and eliminated from the response repertoire.

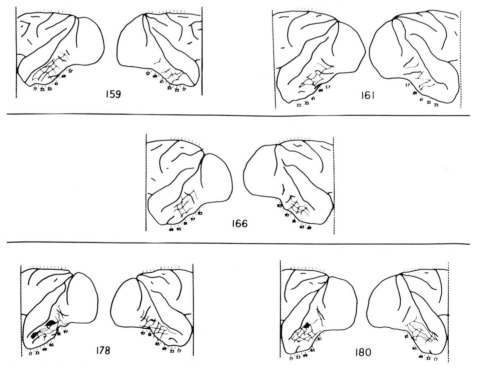

Figure 20.14. Reconstructions of the brains of monkeys whose inferotemporal cortex has been crosshatched. For the results on behavioral testing, see Figure 20.16.

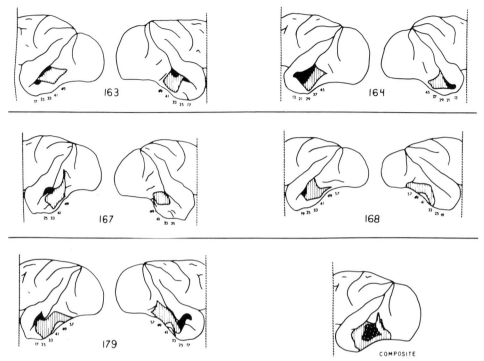

Figure 20.15. Reconstructions of the brains of monkeys whose inferotemporal cortex has been undercut. The composit figure shows both the area common to all cuts (black) and the sum of all the undercut areas. For the effects on behavioral testing, see Figure 20.16.

otherwise be missed. No such effects were observed. By contrast, restricted undercutting of the inferior temporal region, which severed its major input and output connections, produced the same severe effects as did extensive subpial resection of the cortex per se. Sampling was severely restricted as in the multiple object experiment (Pribram, Blehert, & Spinelli, 1966).

Subtle effects are obtained, however, when abnormal electrical foci are induced by implanting epileptogenic chemicals in the cortex. In such preparations the period of stationarity in a two choice task is increased fivefold. Despite this, the slope of acquisition, once it begins, remains unaffected. Obviously, during the period of stationarity, something is going on in the nervous system, something that becomes disrupted by the process that produces the electrical abnormality. Perhaps that something devolves on distributing the effects of trial and error over a sufficient reach of the neural net until an adequate associative structure is attained.

Cognitions

How do the search and sampling systems interact with the perceptual and motor systems to produce skilled performance? Recovery functions in the primary visual and auditory systems are influenced by electrical stimulations of the sensory-specific intrinsic and the frontolimbic (see the next section) systems (Spinelli & Pribram, 1966). This influence is a function of the attentive state of the monkey (Gerbrandt, Spinelli, & Pribram, 1970). Visual receptive fields have also been shown to become altered by such

	Animal	3 vs. 8	R vs. G	3 vs. 8
Crosshatch	158	380	82	0
	159	180	100	0
	161	580	50	0
	166	130	0	0
Undercut	163	[1014]	100	300
	164	[1030]	200	[500]
	167	704	50	0
	168	[1030]	150	[500]
Normal	160	280	100	0
	162	180	100	0
	165	280	100	0
	170	350	100	0

Figure 20.16. The behavioral results of crosshatching and undercutting the inferotemporal cortex. Note the absence of the effects of crosshatching and the severe deficits resulting from undercutting.

stimulation (Spinelli & Pribram, 1967). Finally, the pathways from the sensory-specific intrinsic and from frontolimbic formations (see the next section) to the primary input systems have been in great part delineated (Reitz & Pribram, 1969). Perhaps the most surprising finding of these studies is that input control is to a large measure effected through the basal ganglia, structures that had hitherto been thought of as regulating motor function (Figures 20.14, 20.15, 20.16).

Thus, the functions of the brain in cognition as we know it now are considerably different from the ones that early learning theorists thought they were working with. Most formulations of learning depended heavily on the concept of associative strength based on contiguity and number. Configural variables were relegated to perception, and perceptual learning was, until the past two decades, denied or ignored. Further, the configural and sampling aspects of perceptual learning had not been teased apart.

An even more pervasive difficulty with classical learning theory was its dependence on the reflex-arc, stimulus-organism-response model of brain function. We now know that the brain is organized along servomechanism principles: the discovery of the function of the gamma efferent fibers of motor nerves made it necessary to modify conceptions of the organization of the reflex and therefore of the control of behavior. The data on input control cited above indicate that even the "highest" (the cognitive) systems of the brain exert their influence via the input to the brain rather than via its output. In fact, the control over input is exercised via the same motor structures (the basal ganglia) that, when they influence motor behavior, do so by "setting" the muscle spindle receptors by means of the loop.

Feedback and feedforward loops, not unidirectional input-output arcs, are ubiquitous in central nervous system organization. Sensory functions are controlled by motor systems; behavior is regulated, not by a piano keyboard type of control over muscle contraction, but by servocontrol of the setting of muscle receptors (Pribram, Sharafat, & Beekman, 1983). Programs are constructed that organize perceptions and compose a behavioral repertoire. And these programs operate by virtue of tests, matches, and mismatches between configurations of neural patterns in memory and those produced by sensory input.

AMNESIAS AND THE FRONTOLIMBIC FOREBRAIN

The second major division of the cerebral mantle to which memory functions have been assigned by clinical observation lies on the medial and basal surface of the brain and extends forward to include the poles of the frontal and temporal lobes. This frontolimbic portion of the hemisphere is cytoarchitecturally diverse.

The expectation that different parts might be shown to subserve radically different functions was therefore even greater than that entertained for the more uniform posterior cortex. To some extent, this expectation was not fulfilled: lesions of the frontolimbic region, irrespective of location (dorsolateral frontal, caudate, cingulate-medial frontal, orbitofrontal, temporal polar-amygdala, and hippocampal) disrupted "delayed alternation" behavior. The alternation task demands that the subject alternate responses between two cues (for example, between two places or between two objects) on successive trials. On any trial, the correct response is dependent on the outcome of the previous response. This suggests that the critical variable that characterizes the task is its temporal organization. In turn, this leads to the supposition that the disruption of alternation behavior produced by frontolimbic lesions results from an impairment of the process by which the brain achieves its temporal organization. This supposition is only in part confirmed by further analysis: it has been necessary to impose severe restrictions on what is meant by *temporal organization*, and important aspects of spatial organization are also severely impaired. For instance, skills are not affected by frontolimbic lesions, nor are discriminations of melodies.

What is affected is the dimension "familiarity/novelty." A large range of memory processes are involved. These clearly include tasks that demand matching from memory the spatial location of cues (as in the delayed response problem) (Anderson, Hunt, Vander Stoep, & Pribram, 1976) as well as their temporal order of appearance (as in the alternation task) (Pribram, Plotkin, Anderson, & Leong, 1977). A similar deficit is produced when, in choice tasks, shifts in which cue is rewarded are made over successive trials (Mishkin & Delacour, 1975). The deficit appears whenever the organism must fit the present event into a "context" of previous familiar occurrences and there are no cues that address this context is the situation at hand at the moment of response.

The Registration of Events as Familiar Episodes

As noted, different parts of the frontolimbic complex would, on the basis of their anatomical structure, be expected to function somewhat differently within the category of contextual memory processes. Indeed, different forms of contextual amnesia are produced by different lesions. In order to be experienced as familiar events must be fitted to context. A series of experiments on the orienting reaction to novelty and its registration have pointed to the amygdala as an important locus in the "context-fitting" mechanism. The experiments were inspired by the results from Sokolov's laboratory (Sokolov, 1960).

Sokolov presented human subjects with a tone beep of a certain intensity and frequency, repeated at irregular intervals. Galvanic skin response (GSR), heart rate, finger and forehead plethysmograms, and electroencephalograms were recorded. Initially, these records showed perturbations that were classified as the orienting response. After several repetitions of the tone, these perturbations diminish and finally vanish. They habituate. Originally it had been thought that habituation reflected a lowered sensitivity of the central nervous system to inputs. But when Sokolov decreased the intensity of the tone beep, leaving the other parameters unchanged, a full-blown orienting response was reestablished. Sokolov reasoned that the central nervous system could not be desensitized but that it was less responsive to sameness: when any difference occurred in the stimulus the central nervous system became more sensitive. He tested this idea by rehabituating his subjects and then occasionally omitting the tone beep or reducing its duration without changing any other parameter. As predicted, his subjects now oriented to the unexpected silence.

The orienting reaction and habituation are thus sensitive measures of the process by which context is organized. We therefore initiated a series of experiments to analyze in detail the neural mechanisms involved in orientating and its habituation. This proved more difficult than we imagined. The dependent variables—behavior, GSR, plethys-mogram, and electroencephalogram—are apt to dissociate (Koepke & Pribram, 1971). Forehead plethysmography turned out to be especially tricky, and we eventually settled on behavior, the skin conductance, heart and respiratory responses, and the electrical brain manifestations as most reliable.

The results of the first of these experiments (Schwartzbaum, Wilson, & Morrissette, 1961) indicated that, under certain conditions, removal of the amygdaloid complex can enhance the persistence of locomotor activity in monkeys who would normally decrement their responses. The lesion thus produces a disturbance in the habituation of motor activity (Figure 20.7).

The results of the experiments on the habituation of the GSR component of the orienting reaction (Bagshaw, Kimble, & Pribram, 1965) also indicated clearly that amygdalectomy has an effect (Figure 20.8). The lesion profoundly reduces GSR amplitude in situations in which the GSR is a robust indicator of the orienting reaction. Concomitantly, deceleration of heartbeat, change in respiratory rhythm, and some aspects of the EEG indices of orienting also are found to be absent (Bagshaw & Benzies, 1968). As habituation of motor activity and also habituation of earflicks (Bateson, 1969) had been severely altered by these same lesions, we concluded that the autonomic indicators of orienting are in some way crucial to subsequent behavioral habituation. We identified the process indicated by the autonomic components of the orienting reaction as "registering" the novel event.

However, the registration mechanism is not limited to novelty. Extending the analysis to a classical conditioning situation (Bagshaw & Coppock, 1968; Pribram, Reitz, McNeil, & Spevack, 1979) using the GSR as a measure of conditioning, we found that normal monkeys not only condition well but produce earlier and more frequent anticipatory GSRs as time goes by. Amygdalectomized subjects fail to make such anticipatory responses. As classical conditioning of a striped muscle proceeded normally, it is not the conditioning per se which is impaired. Rather, it appears that registration entails some active process akin to rehearsal, some central mechanism aided by viscero-autonomic processes that maintains and distributes excitation over time.

Behavioral experiments support this suggestion. Amygdalectomized monkeys placed in the two-cue task described in the previous section fail to take proper account of reinforced events. This deficiency is dramatically displayed whenever punishment is used. For instance, an early observation showed that baboons with such lesions will repeatedly (day after day and week after week) put lighted matches in their mouths despite showing obvious signs of being burned (Fulton, Pribram, Stevenson, & Wall, 1949). These observations were further quantified in tasks measuring avoidance of shock (Pribram & Weiskrantz, 1957). The results of these two experiments have been confirmed in other laboratories and with other species so often that the hypothesis needed to be tested that amygdalectomy produces an altered sensitivity to pain. Bagshaw and Pribram (1968) put this hypothesis to test and showed that the amplitude of GSR to shock is not elevated, as it would be were there an elevation of the pain threshold. Rather, the threshold is, if anything, reduced by the ablation.

These experimental results can be related to other observations and experiments which involve retrograde amnesia. The duration of such retrograde amnesia varies as a function of the severity of the injury. This suggests that the process of registering an experience in memory takes some time and that the injured brain cannot carry out this process. McGaugh took this observation into the laboratory using electroconvulsive shock to produce retrograde amnesia. He then modified the severity of the amnesia by injecting chemical substances prior to and after the administration of shock. The times of injection were varied in order to chart the course of the registration process. Once McGaugh had accomplished this, he set out to locate the brain systems involved in the process. The amygdala seemed a good choice as a starting point in the search. Consolidation, his term for registration, was now successfully manipulated by electrical and chemical stimulations of the amygdala, much as had previously been done by peripheral chemical injections. In any such series of experiments, however, the possibility remained that all one is accomplishing by the brain stimulation is the boosting of a peripheral chemical secretion, so that in essence one is doing no more than repeating the original experiments in which peripheral stimulation had been used. To control for this, Martinez, working with McGaugh, removed various peripheral structures such as the adrenal gland. They found that, indeed, when the adrenal medulla, which secretes epinephrine and norepinephrine, was absent, the amygdala stimulations had no effect (Martinez et al., 1981).

McGaugh's experiments indicate, as had ours, that the amygdala influences the learning process via visceral and glandular peripheral processes largely regulated by the autonomic nervous system. Electrical excitation of the amygdala—as well as of the entire anterior portion of the limbic cortex: anterior cingulate, medial and orbital frontal, anterior insula, and temporal pole—in anesthetized monkeys and humans produces profound changes in such visceroautonomic processes as blood pressure and respiratory rate (Kaada, Pribram, & Epstein, 1949). The amygdala thus serves as a

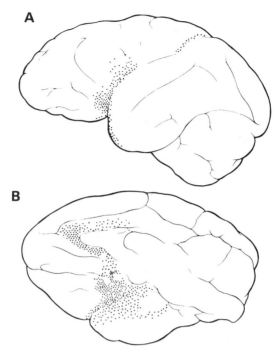

Figure 20.17.   Representation of the mediobasal motorcortex showing the cortical points on the mediobasal surface of the monkey brain from which changes in blood pressure, heart, and respiratory rate are obtained on electrical stimulations (top, lateral view; bottom, mediobasal view).

focus for a mediobasal motor cortex, which regulates visceroautonomic and other activities (such as head turning, which is also produced by the stimulations) related to orienting (Figure 20.17).

It appears from all this research that such peripheral activities, when they occur, can boost the consolidation process and thus facilitate the registration of experience in memory. Vinogradova (1975) has suggested that the boost given by this visceroautonomic system stands in lieu of repetition of the experience. As noted above, the experiments on conditioning suggest that visceroautonomic arousal acts somewhat like internal rehearsal. One can take visceroautonomic arousal as an indication that interest and emotions have been engaged: thus the mechanism has been tapped, which accounts for the well known fact that emotional involvement can dramatically influence learning.

Processing Novelty

Context is not composed solely of the registration of reinforcing and reinforced events. As important are the errors, the nonreinforced aspects of a situation, especially if on previous occasions they had been reinforced. It is resection of the primate hippocampal formation (Douglas & Pribram, 1966) that produces relative insensitivity to errors, frustrative nonreward (Gray, 1975), and, more generally, to nonreinforced aspects of the environment (the SΔ of operant conditioning, the negative instances of mathematical psychology).

In their first experience with a discrimination learning situation, subjects with hippocampal resections show a peculiar retardation, provided there are many nonrewarded alternatives in that situation. For example, in an experiment using the computer-controlled automated testing apparatus (DADTA), the subject faced 16 panels, discriminable cues were displayed on only two of these panels, and only one cue was rewarded. The cues were displayed in various locations in a random fashion from trial to trial. Hippocampectomized monkeys were found to press the unlighted and unrewarded panels for thousands of trials, long after their unoperated controls ceased responding to these "irrelevant" items.

It is as if, in the normal subject, a "ground" is established by enhancing "inattention" to all the negative instances of those patterns that do not provide a relevant "figure." This inattention is an active process, as indicated by the behavior shown during shaping in a discrimination reversal task, when the demand is to respond to the previously nonreinforced cue: unsophisticated subjects often begin by pressing on various parts of their cage and the testing apparatus before they hit upon a chance response to the nonrewarded cue.

These and many similar results indicate that the hippocampal formation is part of a mechanism that helps to establish the "ground," which determines what is novel and what is familiar.

The Spatiotemporal Structure of Context

In some respects, the far frontal resection produces memory disturbances characteristic of both hippocampectomy and amygdalectomy, though not so severe. Whereas medial temporal lobe ablations impair context formation by way of habituation of novel and familiar events, far frontal lesions wreak havoc on yet another contextual dimension, that of organizing the spatial and temporal structure of the context (Pribram, 1961; Anderson, Hunt, Vander Stoep, & Pribram, 1976; Pribram, Plotkin, Anderson, & Leong, 1977).

The effect is best demonstrated by an experiment in which the normal scallop produced by a fixed interval schedule of reinforcement fails to develop and another in which the parameters of the classical alternation task were altered. Instead of interposing equal intervals between trials (go right, go left every 5 seconds) in the usual way, couplets of right (R) and left (L) were formed by extending the intertrial interval to 15 seconds before each R trial (R 5 seconds, L 15 seconds; R 5 seconds, L 15 seconds; R 5 seconds, L 15 seconds; and so on). When this was done, the performance of the far frontally lesioned monkeys improved immediately and was indistinguishable from that of the controls (Figure 20.18) (Pribram & Tubbs, 1967; Pribram, Plotkin, Anderson, & Leong, 1977).

This result suggests that, for the subject with a bilateral far frontal ablation, the alternation task is experienced similarly to reading this page without any spaces between the words. The spaces, like the holes in doughnuts, provide the contextual

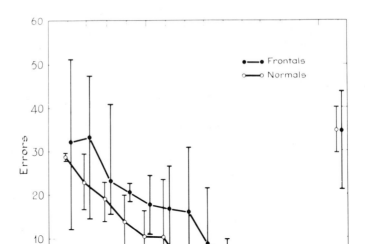

Figure 20.18. The learning curves of monkeys with reactions of the far frontal cortex and of unoperated normal control monkeys on a delayed alternation task in which the delay period was made asymmetrical (5 seconds and 15 seconds). Note the excellent performances of the subjects with the resection and that they failed the symmetrical delay (5 seconds and 5 seconds) task despite having been given much experience (1000 trials) on this task.

structure, the parcelation or parsing of events by which the outside world can be coded and deciphered.

Transfer and Context as a Function of Reinforcing Contingencies

Classically, disturbance of "working" short-term memory has been ascribed to lesions of the frontal pole. Anterior and medial resections of the far frontal cortex were the first to be shown to produce impairment on delayed response and delayed alternation problems. In other tests of context-formation and fitting, frontal lesions also take their toll. Here, also, impairment of conditioned avoidance behavior, of classical conditioning, and of the orienting GSR is found. Furthermore, as shown in Figure 20.9, error sensitivity is reduced in an operant conditioning situation. After several years of training on mixed and multiple schedules, the animals were extinguished over four hours. The frontally lesioned animals failed to extinguish in the four-hour period, whereas the control monkeys did (Pribram, 1961). This failure in extinction accounts in part for poor performance in the alternation already described: the frontally lesioned animals again make many more repetitive errors. Even though they do not find a peanut, they go right back and keep looking (Pribram, 1959).

This result was confirmed and amplified in studies by Wilson (1962) and by Pribram, Plotkin, Anderson, and Leong (1977) in which we asked whether errors followed alternation or nonreinforcement. A situation was devised in which both lids over two food wells opened simultaneously, but the monkey could obtain the peanut only if he had opened the baited well. Thus, the monkey was given "complete"

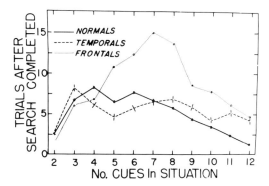

Figure 20.19. Graph showing the number of trials taken to come to criterion after finding the peanut in the multiple task by monkeys with far frontal and inferotemporal cortex resections and by a normal control group. Note that only the far frontal group repeatedly examined objects that covered no peanut despite their having found the object that did cover a peanut. See also Figures 20.11 and 20.12.

information on every trial, and the usual correction technique could be circumvented. There were four procedural variations: correction-contingent, correction-noncontingent, noncorrection-contingent, and noncorrection-noncontingent. The contingency referred to whether the position of the peanut was altered on the basis of the monkey's responses (correct or incorrect) or whether its position was changed independently of the monkey's behavior. The relationship between each error was then analyzed. Figure 20.19 shows that, for the normal monkey, the condition of reinforcement and nonreinforcement of the previous trial makes a difference. For the frontally lesioned monkey, this is not the case. Change in location, however, affects both normal and frontal subjects about equally. In this situation, as well as in an automated computer-controlled version of the alternatives problem, frontal subjects are simply uninfluenced by rewarding or nonrewarding consequences of their behavior.

In a multiple-choice task (Pribram, 1959) (see Figure 20.19), the procedure calls for a strategy of returning to the same object for five consecutive times, that is, to criterion, and then a shift to a novel item. The frontally lesioned animals are markedly deficient in doing this. Again, the conditions of reinforcement are relatively ineffective in shaping behavior in animals with frontal lesions, and the monkeys' behavior becomes nearly random when compared to that of normal subjects (Pribram, Ahumada, Hartog, & Roos, 1964). Behavior of the frontally lesioned monkeys thus appears to be minimally controlled by the expected outcome.

These effects on expected outcome are dramatically demonstrated when transfer learning is tested. When we take a monkey who has learned to choose between circles of different sizes and ask him to transfer his experience to a situation in which he must choose among ellipses of different sizes (Bagshaw & Pribram, 1965), he will quickly master the new task unless he has a lesion of the limbic forebrain. This is not due to faulty generalization (Hearst & Pribram, 1964a, b)—generalization is impaired by lesions of the posterior cortical convexity. Rather, the difficulty stems from an inability to transfer what has been learned in one situation to another that is more or less similar.

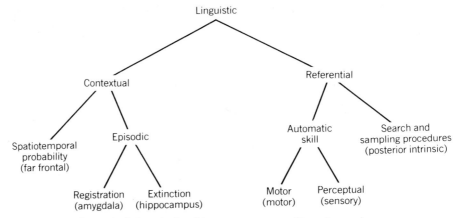

Figure 20.20.   Diagram of the relationships among types of learning and memory processes. Note that the functions of the neural systems described in this chapter make up the end points of each of the branches of the tree. The term *contextual* is used in preference to such terms as *working memory* (based on the alternation paradigm), *declarative memory* (based on computer programming paradigms), or *pragmatic memory* (based on linguistic paradigms) because it is more general in meaning. The term *referential* is used, whereas in linguistics and cognitive psychology the term *semantic* would apply.

Summary of Localization Studies

Most approaches to the organization of learning and memory have relied on the elucidation of differences in terms of dichotomies, such as episodic versus semantic, procedural versus declarative, and working versus referential. The temptation is to identify these dichotomies despite the fact that they stem from disparate data bases. The research results reported here suggest another approach, that is, a hierarchical arrangement of processes in a treelike structure akin to computer programming. Figure 20.20 presents such an arrangement. The specifics must necessarily remain tentative, but certain features of such a scheme are worth noting. At the base of each branch is a neural system whose operation has been identified in some considerable detail. What remains unclear is the anatomical and physiological nature of the process that brings together the branches of the tree in the behaviorally determined higher-order nodes. Nor is it at present known how the various basic system programs address the distributed memory store, although suggestions (see "Conclusion") have been tendered.

CONCLUSION

When the decisional processes involving the posterior cortical convexity operate on the distributed memory store they re-member an input that had on earlier occasions become dismembered. The sensory-specific operators deal with identifying and processing of referentially meaningful information. The frontolimbic operators deal with recall and with the pragmatics of processing context sensitive, episode related familiarities and novelties (for review see, e.g., Pribram, 1971, 1977).

Both neuroscientists and cognitive psychologists currently frame their models in information-processing terms. The data showing that decisional operators influence receptive field properties (Spinelli & Pribram, 1966; Pribram, Lassonde, & Ptito, 1981), though incomplete on this point, are consonant with a proposal made by Gabor (1946) and extended by Brillouin (1962) and MacKay (1969) that the Fourier domain may become segmented into informational units called Logons by the operation of a "window" that limits band width. The interesting aspect of Gabor's proposal is that the window can be so adjusted that on some occasions processing occurs primarily in the holographic domain (leading to such nonlocal operations as translational invariance, object and size constancy, etc.), while on other occasions, processing occurs in the space-time domain (leading to locating objects in time and space). Models such as Spinelli's (1970) content-addressable and Pribram's Zoomar proposals (1971) are consonant with a Logon information-processing approach, but more precise data are needed to establish the viability of this form of the information-processing approach.

The persistent puzzle that brain functions appear to be both localized and distributed is thus resolved. Memory storage is shown to be distributed; decisional operators involved in coding and retrieval are localized. These operators can be conceived as separate brain systems, genetically inherent in their function but dependent on sensory input from the environment to trigger and shape their development (see, e.g, Chomsky, 1980; Pribram, 1971). In short, there are "boxes in the brain," each box corresponding to a faculty of mind. But these boxes operate on a distributed matrix that is nonlocal and therefore available to all.

Perhaps the easiest way to conceptualize these problems is in terms of states and operators on those states. At present, it appears reasonable to continue to search for linearities in the state descriptions of sensory perception, highly practiced skilled action, and memory storage processes. These momentary states come under the control of localized nonlinear operators whenever discriminative (e.g., recognition) or selective (planned) actions are involved. Whether these nonlinearities are abstracted serially and hierarchically from the states, or whether they are imposed corticofugally by a parallel process, or both, continues to be an active area of investigation.

There is a considerable intellectual distance between Lashley's despair in finding a localized engram in the 1950s and the richness of data and theory on cerebral localization and distribution in the 1980s (Pribram, 1982). To his credit, Lashley recognized the problem and specified it in sufficient detail so that the generation of investigators standing on his shoulders could deal effectively with it. That so much progress has been made reflects the support given by society to the brain and behavioral sciences during this 30-year period. Should this support continue, the issue of localization-distribution, which has mobilized such differing views over the past two centuries, may yet be resolved to everyone's satisfaction before the ending of the twentieth century.

REFERENCES

Anderson, R. M., Hunt, S. C., Vander Stoep, A., & Pribram, K. H. (1976). Object permanency and delayed response as spatial context with monkeys with frontal lesions. *Neuropsychologia,* *14*, 480–490.

Arbib, M. A. (1972). *The metaphorical brain*. New York: John Wiley & Sons.

Bach-y-Rita, P. (1972). *Brain mechanisms in sensory substitution*. New York: Academic Press.

Bagshaw, M. H., & Benzies, S. (1968). Multiple measures of the orienting reaction to a simple non-reinforced stimulus after amygdalectomy. *Experimental Neurology, 20*, 175–187.

Bagshaw, M. H., & Coppock, H. W. (1968). GSR conditioning deficit in amygdalectomized monkeys. *Experimental Neurology, 20*, 188–196.

Bagshaw, M. H., Kimble, D. P., & Pribram, K. H., (1965). The GSR of monkeys during orienting and habituation and after ablation of the amygdala, hippocampus and infero-temporal cortex. *Neuropsychologia, 3*, 111–119.

Bagshaw, M. H., & Pribram, K. H. (1953). Cortical organization in gustation (macaca mulatta). *Journal of Neurophysiology, 16*, 499–508.

Bagshaw, M. H., & Pribram, K. H. (1965). Effect of amygdalectomy on transfer of training in monkeys. *Journal of Comparative Physiology and Psychology, 59*, 118–121.

Bagshaw, M. H., & Pribram, K. H. (1968). The effect of amygdalectomy on shock threshold of the monkey. *Experimental Neurology*, 197–202.

Bateson, P. P. G. (1969). *Ear movements of normal and amygdalectomized monkeys*. [Private communication, 1969]

Bekesey, G. von. (1959). Synchronism of neural discharges and their demultiplication in pitch perception in the skin and in hearing. *Journal of the Acoustical Society of America, 31*, 338–349.

Benevento, L. A., Creutzfeldt, O. D., & Kuhnt, U. (1972). Significance of intracortical inhibition in the visual cortex: Data and model. *Nature and Biology, 238*, 124–126.

Blakemore, C. (1974). Developmental factors in the formation of feature extracting neurons. In F. O. Schmitt & F. G. Worden (Eds.), *The neurosciences: Third study program* (pp. 105–113). Cambridge, MA: MIT Press.

Blehert, S. R. (1966). Pattern discrimination learning with rhesus monkeys. *Psychological Reports, 19*, 311–324.

Blum, H. (1967). A new model of global brain function. *Perspectives in Biology and Medicine, 190*, 381–496.

Boring, E. (1942). *Sensation and perception in the history of experimental psychology*. New York: Appleton-Century Crofts.

Borsellino, A., & Poggio, T. (1973). Convolution and correlation algebras. *Kybernetik, 13*, 113–122.

Bracewell, R. (1965). *The Fourier transform and its application*. New York: McGraw-Hill.

Bridgeman, B. (1982). Multiplexing in single cells of the alert monkey's visual cortex during brightness discrimination. *Neuropsychologia, 20*, 33–42.

Brillouin, L. (1962). *Science and information theory*. New York: Academic Press.

Burgess, A. E., Wagner, R. F., Jennings, R. J., & Barlow, H. B. (1981). Efficiency of human visual signal discrimination. *Science, 214*, 93–94.

Campbell, F. W., Cooper, G. F., & Enroth-Cugell, C. (1969). The spatial selectivity of the visual cells of the cat. *Journal of Physiology, 203*, 223–235.

Campbell, F. W. & Robson, J. G. (1968). Application of Fourier analysis to the visibility of gratings. *Journal of Physiology, 197*, 551–566.

Chomsky, N. *Rules and representations*. New York: Columbia University Press, 1980.

Chow, K. L. (1961). Anatomical and electrographical analysis of temporal neocortex in relation to visual discrimination learning in monkeys. In J. F. Delafresyne, A. Fessard, & J. Konorski (Eds.), *Brain mechanisms and learning* (pp. 375–392). Oxford: Blackwell Scientific.

Chow, K. L. (1970). Integrative functions of the thalamocortical visual system of cat. In K. H. Pribram & D. Broadbent (Eds.), *Biology of memory* (pp. 273–292). New York: Academic Press.

Christensen, C. A., & Pribram, K. H. (1979). The effect of inferotemporal or foveal prestriate ablation on serial reversal learning in monkeys. *Neuropsychologica, 17*, 1–10.

Cooper, L. N. (1973). A possible organization of animal memory and learning. In F. Lindquist & S. Lindquist (Eds.), *Proceedings of the Nobel Symposium on Collective Properties of Physical Systems* (pp. 252–264). New York: Academic Press.

Cruetzfeldt, O. D., Kuhnt, U., & Benevento, L. A. (1974). An intracellular analysis of visual cortical neurones to moving stimuli: Responses in a cooperative neuronal network. *Experimental Brain Research, 21*, 251–272.

DeValois, R. L., Albrecht, D. G., & Thorell, L. G. (1979). Cortical cells: Line and edge detectors, or spatial frequency filters? In S. Cool (Ed.), *Frontiers of visual science* (pp. 544–556). New York: Springer-Verlag.

DeValois, R. L., & DeValois, K. K. (1980). Spatial vision. *Annual Review of Psychology, 31*, 309.

Dewson, J. H., III. (1964). Cortical responses to patterns of two-point cutaneous stimulation. *Journal of Comparative Physiology and Psychology 58*, 387–389.

Dewson, J. H., III, Pribram, K. H., & Lynch, J. (1969). Ablations of temporal cortex in the monkey and their effects upon speech sound discriminations. *Experimental Neurology, 24*, 579–591.

Ditchborn, R. W., & Ginsborg, B. L. (1952). Vision with a stabilized retinal image. *Nature, 170*, 36.

Douglas, R. J., Barrett, T. W., Pribram, K. H., & Cerny, M. C. (1969). Limbic lesions and error reduction. *Journal of Comparative Physiology and Psychology, 68*, 437–441.

Douglas, R. J., & Pribram, K. H. (1966). Learning and limbic lesions. *Neuropsychologia, 4*, 197–220.

Edelman, G. M., & Mountcastle, V. B. (Eds.). (1978). *The mindful brain*. Cambridge, MA: MIT Press.

Ettlinger, G. (1957). Visual discrimination following successive unilateral temporal excisions in monkeys. *Journal of Physiology (London), 140*, 38–39.

Evans, D. C. (1966). Computer logic and memory. *Scientific American, 215*, 74–85.

Evans, E. F. (1974). Neural processes for the detection of acoustic patterns and for sound localization. In F. O. Schmitt & F. G. Worden (Eds.), *The neurosciences: Third study program* (pp. 131–145). Cambridge, MA: MIT Press.

Festinger, L., Burnham, C. A., Ono, H., & Bamber, D. (1967). Efference and the conscious experience of perception. *Journal of Experimental Psychology, 74*, 1–36.

Finkelstein, D. (1976). Classical and quantum probability and set theory. In W.L. Harper, & C.A. Hooker, (Eds.), *Foundations of probability theory, statistical inference, and statistical theories of science* (Vol. 3, pp. 111–119). Dordrecht, Holland: D. Reidel.

Flanagan, J. L. (1972). *Speech analysis synthesis and perception*. Berlin: Springer-Verlag.

Freeman, W. (1975). *Mass action in the nervous system*. New York: Academic Press.

Freeman, W. J. (1981). A physiological hypothesis of perception. *Perspectives in Biology and Medicine*, Summer, 561–592.

Fulton, J. F., Pribram, K. H., Stevenson, J. A. F., & Wall, P. D. (1949). Interrelations between orbital gyrus, insula, temporal tip and anterior cingulate. *Transactions of the American Neurological Association, 74*, 175.

Gabor, D. (1946). Theory of communication. *Journal of the Institute of Electrical Engineers, 93*, 429.

Gabor, D. (1969). Information processing with coherent light. *Optica Acta, 16*, 519–533.

Ganz, L. (1971). Sensory deprivation and visual descrimination. In H. L. Teuber (Ed.), *Handbook of sensory physiology* (Vol. 8, pp. 7–16). New York: Springer-Verlag.

Gerbrandt, L. K., Spinelli, D. N., & Pribram, K. H. (1970). The interaction of visual attention and temporal cortex stimulation on electrical recording in the striate cortex. *Electroencephalography and Clinical Neurophysiology, 29*, 146–155.

Glezer, V. D., Ivanoff, V. A., & Tscherbach, T. A. (1973). Investigation of complex and hypercomplex receptive fields of visual cortex of the cat as spatial frequency filters. *Vision Research, 13*, 1875–1904.

Goldscheider, A. (1906). Uber die materiellen veranderungen bei der associationsbildung. *Neurological Zentralblatt, 25*, 146.

Granit, R. (1970). *The basis of motor control*. New York: Academic Press.

Gray, J. A. (1975). *Elements of a two-process theory of learning*. London: Academic Press.

Gross, C. G. (1973). Inferotemporal cortex and vision. In E. Stellas & J. M. Sprague (Eds.), *Progress in physiological psychology* (pp. 77–124). New York: Academic Press.

Gross, C. G., Bender, D. B., & Gerstein, G. L. (1979). Activity of inferior temporal neurons in behaving monkeys. *Neuropsychologia, 17*, 215–229.

Gross, C. G., Bender, D. B., & Rocha-Miranda, C. E. (1969). Visual receptive fields of neurons in inferotemporal cortex of the monkey. *Science, 166*, 1303–1305.

Grossberg, S. (1981). Adaptive resonance in development, perception and cognition. *SIAM-AMS Proceedings, 13*, 107–156.

Groves, P. M., & Thompson, R. F. (1970). Habituation: A dual-process theory. *Psychological Review, 77*, 419–450.

Gumnit, R. J. (1960). DC potential changes from auditory cortex of cat. *Journal of Neurophysiology, 6*, 667–675.

Hammond, P. (1972). Spatial organization of receptive fields of LGN neurons. *Journal of Physiology, 222*, 53–54.

Hartline, H. K. (1940). The nerve messages in the fibres of the visual pathway. *Journal of the Optical Society of America, 30*, 239–247.

Hearst, E., & Pribram, K. H. (1964a). Facilitation of avoidance behavior in unavoidable shocks in normal and amygdalectomized monkeys. *Psychological Reports, 14*, 39–42.

Hearst, E., & Pribram, K. H. (1964b). Appetitive and aversive generalization gradients in normal and amygdalectomized monkeys. *Journal of Comparative Physiology and Psychology, 58*, 296–298.

Hebb, D. O. (1949). *The organization of behavior: A neuropsychological theory*. New York: John Wiley & Sons.

Heckenmueller, E. G. (1968). Stabilization of the retinal image: A revision of method, effects and theory. In R. N. Habor (Ed.), *Contemporary theory and research in visual perception* (pp. 280–294). New York: Holt, Rinehart & Winston.

Held, R. (1968). Action contingent development of vision in neonatal animals. In D. P. Kimble (Ed.). *Experience and capacity: Fourth conference on learning, remembering and forgetting* (pp. 31–111). New York: Academy of Sciences.

Henry, G. H. (1977). Receptive field classes of cells in the striate cortex of the cat. *Brain Research, 133*, 1–28.

Henry, G. H., & Bishop, P. O. (1977). Simple cells of the striate cortex. In W. D. Neff (Ed.), *Contributions to sensory physiology*. New York: Academic Press.

Hirsch, H., & Spinelli, D. N. (1970). Visual experience modifies distribution of horizontally and vertically oriented receptive fields in cats. *Science, 168*, 869–871.

Hoffman, B. (1947). *The strange story of the quantum* (p. 285). New York: Dover.

Hosford, H. L. (1977). *Binaural waveform coding in the inferior colliculus of the cat: Single unit responses to simple and complex stimuli*. Unpublished doctoral dissertation, Stanford University, Stanford, CA.

Hubel, D. H., & Wiesel, T. N. (1959). Receptive fields of single neurons in the cat's striate cortex. *Journal of Physiology, 148*, 574–591.

Hubel, D. H., & Wiesel, T. N. (1962). Receptive fields, binocular interaction and functional architecture in the cat's visual cortex. *Journal of Physiology, 160*, 106–154.

Hubel, D. H., & Wiesel, T. N. (1977). Functional architecture of macaque monkey cortex. *Proceedings of the Royal Society (London), B198*, 1–59.

John, E. R., Bartlett, F., Shimokochi, M., & Kleinman, D. (1973). Neural readout from memory. *Journal of Neurophysiology, 36*, 893–924.

Julesz, B. (1971). *Foundations of cyclopean perception*. Chicago: University of Chicago Press.

Julesz, B., & Caelli, T. (1979). On the limits of Fourier decompositions in visual texture perception. *Perception, 8*, 69–73.

Kaada, B. R., Pribram, K. H., & Epstein, J. A. (1949). Respiratory and vascular responses in monkeys from temporal pole, insula, orbital surface and cingulate gyrus. *Journal of Neurophysiology 12*, 347–356.

Koepke, J. E., & Pribram, K. H. (1971). Effect of milk on the maintenance of sucking in kittens from birth to six months. *Journal Comparative Physiology and Psychology, 75*, 363–377.

Köhler, W. (1958). The present situation in brain physiology. *American Psychologist, 13*, 150.

Köhler, W., & Held, R. (1949). The cortical correlate of pattern vision. *Science, 10*, 414–419.

Köhler, W., Neff, W. D., & Wegner, J. (1955). Currents of the auditory cortex in the cat. *Journal of Cellular Comparative Physiology, 45*, 1–24.

Köhler, W., & Wegener, J. (1955). Currents of the human auditory complex. *Journal of Cellular Comparative Physiology, 45*, 25–54.

Kraft, M., Obrist, W. D., & Pribram, K. H. (1960). The effect of irritative lesions of the striate cortex on learning of visual discrimination in monkeys. *Journal of Comparative Physiology and Psychology, 53*, 17–22.

Lashley, K. S. (1942). The problem of cerebral organization in vision. In *Visual mechanisms* (Biological Symposia, Vol. 7, pp. 301–322). Lancaster: J. Cattell Press.

Lashley, K. S. (1950). In search of the engram. In Society for Experimental Biology (Great Britain), *Physiological mechanisms in animal behavior* (pp. 454–482). New York: Academic Press.

Lashley, K. S., Chow, K. L., & Semmes, J. (1951). An examination of the electrical field theory of cerebral integration. *Psychology Review, 58*, 123–136.

Leith, E. N. (1976). White-light holograms. *Scientific American, 235*, 80.

Leith, E. N., & Upatnicks, J. (1965). Photography by laser. *Scientific American, 212*, 24–35.

Loeb, J. (1907). *Comparative physiology of the brain and comparative psychology*. New York: Putnam.

Lynch, J. C. (1971). *A single unit analysis of contour enhancement in the somesthetic system of the cat*. Unpublished doctoral dissertation, Stanford University, Stanford, CA.

MacKay, D. M. (1969). *Information mechanism and meaning*. Cambridge, MA: MIT Press.

Maffei, L., & Fiorentini, A. (1973). the visual cortex as a spatial frequency analyzer. *Vision Research 13*, 1255–1267.

Marcelja, S. (1980). Mathematical description of the responses of simple cortical cells. *Journal of the Optical Society of America, 70*, 1297–1300.

Marr, D. (1976a). Early processing of visual information. *Philosophical Transactions of the Royal Society B., 275*, 483–524.

Marr, D. (1976b). Analyzing natural images: A computational theory of texture vision. *Cold Spring Harbor Symposium on Quantitative Biology, 40*, 647–662.

Marr, D., & Poggio, T. (1977). From understanding computation to understanding neural circuitry. *Neuroscience Research Progress Bulletin, 15*, 470–488.

Maurus, M., & Ploog, D. (1971). Social signals in squirrel monkeys: Analysis by cerebral radio stimulation. *Brain Research, 12*, 171–183.

McGaugh, J. L., & Hertz, M. J. (1972). *Memory consolidation.* San Francisco: Albion.

Miller, G. A., Galanter, E., & Pribram, K. H. (1960). *Plans and the structure of behavior.* New York: Holt.

Mishkin, M. (1973). Cortical visual areas and their interaction. In A. G. Karczmar & J. C. Eccles (Eds.), *The brain and human behavior* (pp. 187–208). Berlin: Springer-Verlag.

Mishkin, M., & Delacour, J. (1975). An analysis of short-term visual memory in the monkey. *Journal of Experimental Psychology: Animal Behavior Processes, 1*, 326–334.

Mishkin, M., & Hall, M. (1955). Discrimination along a size continuum following ablation of the inferior temporal convexity in monkeys. *Journal of Comparative Physiology and Psychology, 48*, 97–101.

Mishkin, M., & Pribram, K. H. (1954). Visual discrimination performance following partial ablations of the temporal lobe: 1. Ventral vs. lateral. *Journal of Comparative Physiology and Psychology, 47*, 14–20.

Morrell, F. (1972). Visual system's view of acoustic space. *Nature (London), 238*, 44–46.

Movshon, J. A., Thompson, I. D., & Tolhurst, D. J. (1978a). Spatial summation in the receptive fields of simple cells in the cat's striate cortex. *Journal of Physiology, 283*, 53–77.

Movshon, J. A., Thompson, I. D., & Tolhurst, D. J. (1978b). Receptive field organization of complex cells in the cat's striate cortex. *Journal of Physiology, 283*, 79–99.

Movshon, J. A., Thompson, I. D., & Tolhurst, D. J. (1978c). Spatial and temporal contrast sensitivity of neurons in areas 17 and 18 of the cat's visual cortex. *Journal of Physiology, 283*, 101–120.

Pettigrew, J. D. (1974). The effect of visual experience on the development of stimulus specificity by kitten cortical neurones. *Journal of Physiology, 237*, 49–74.

Phelps, R. W. (1973). The effect of spatial and temporal interactions on the responses of single units in the cat's visual cortex. *International Journal of Neurosciences, 6*, 97–107.

Phelps, R. W. (1974). Effects of interactions of two moving lines on single unit responses in the cat's visual cortex. *Vision Research 14*, 1371–1375.

Poggio, T., & Torre, V. (1980). New approach to synaptic interactions. In H. Palm (Ed.), *Approaches in complex systems.* Berlin: Springer-Verlag.

Pollen, D. A., & Feldon, S. E. (1979). Spatial periodicities of periodic complex cells in the visual cortex cluster at one-half octave intervals. *Investigation in Ophthalmology and Visual Science, 18*, 429–434.

Pollen, D. A., Lee, J. R., & Taylor, J. H. (1971). How does the striate cortex begin the reconstruction of the visual world? *Science, 173*, 74–77.

Pollen, D. A., & Ronner, S. F. (1981). Phase relationships between adjacent simple cells in the visual cortex. *Science, 212*, 1409–1410.

Pollen, D. A., & Taylor, J. H. (1974). The striate cortex and the spatial analysis of visual space. In F. O. Schmitt & F. G. Worden (Eds.), *The neurosciences: Third study program* (pp. 239–247). Cambridge, MA: MIT Press.

Pribram, K. H. (May 1981). *On feature, space, object perception, and categorizing.* Invited address presented at Canadian Psychological Association.

Pribram, K. H. (1954). Toward a science of neuropsychology: Method and data. In R. A. Patton (Ed.), *Current trends in psychology and the behavioral sciences* (pp. 115–142). Pittsburg: University of Pittsburg Press.

Pribram, K. H. (1958a). Comparative neurology and the evolution of behavior. In A. Roe & G. G. Simpson (Eds.), *Behavior and evolution.* New Haven, CN: Yale University Press.

Pribram, K. H. (1958b). Neocortical function in behavior. In H. H. Harlow & C. N. Woolsey (Eds.), *Biological and biochemical bases of behavior.* Madison: University of Wisconsin Press.

Pribram, K. H. (1959). On the neurology of thinking. *Behavioral Sciences, 4*, 265–287.

Pribram, K. H. (1960). The intrinsic systems of the forebrain. In J. Field & H. W. Magoun (Eds.), *Handbook of physiology: Neuropsychology* (Vol. 2, pp. 1323–1344). Washington, DC: American Physiological Society.

Pribram, K. H. (1961). A further experimental analysis of the behavioral deficit that follows injury to the primate frontal cortex. *Experimental Neurology, 3*, 432–466.

Pribram, K. H. (1961). A further experimental analysis of the behavioral deficit that follows injury to the primate frontal cortex. *Experimental Neurology, 3*, 432–466.

Pribram, K. H. (1966). Some dimensions of remembering: Steps toward a neuropsychological model of memory. In J. Gaito (Ed.), *Macromolecules and behavior* (pp. 165–187). New York: Academic Press.

Pribram, K. H. (1969a). The neurobehavioral analysis of limbic forebrain mechanisms: Revision and progress report. In D.S. Lehrman, R.A. Hinde, & E. Shaw (Eds.) *Advances in the study of behavior* (Vol. 2, pp. 297–332). New York: Academic Press.

Pribram, K. H. (1969b). DADTA III: An on-line computerized system for the experimental analysis of behavior. *Perceptual and Motor skills, 29*, 599–608.

Pribram, K. H. (1969c). The neurophysiology of remembering. *Scientific American, 220*, 73–86.

Pribram, K. H. (1972a). Neurological notes on knowing. In J. R. Royce & W. W. Rozeboom (Eds.), *The second Banff Conference on Theoretical Psychology* (pp. 449–480). New York: Gordon & Breach.

Pribram, K. H. (1972b). Association: Cortico-cortical and/or cortico-subcortical. In T. Frigyesi, E. Rinvik, & M. D. Yahr (Eds.), *Corticothalamic projections and sensorimotor activities* (pp. 525–549). New York: Raven Press.

Pribram, K. H. (1973). The primate frontal cortex-executive of the brain. In A. R. Luria & K. H. Pribram (Eds.), *Psychophysiology of the frontal lobe* (pp. 293–314). New York: Academic Press.

Pribram, K. H. (1974a). The isocortex. In D. A. Hamburg & H. K. H. Brodie (Eds.), *American handbook of psychiatry* (Vol. 6, pp. 10–54). New York: Basic Books.

Pribram, K. H. (1974b). How is it that sensing so much we can do so little? In F. O. Schmitt & F. G. Worden (Eds.), *The neurosciences: Third study program* (pp. 249–261). Cambridge, MA: MIT Press.

Pribram, K. H. (1977). Modes of central processing in human learning and remembering. In T. J. Teyler (Ed.), *Brain and learning* (pp. 147–163). Stamford, CN: Greylock Press.

Pribram, K. H. (1982). Localization and distribution of function in the brain. In J. Orbach (Ed.), *Neuropsychology after Lashley* (pp. 273–296). New York: Erlbaum.

Pribram, K. H. (1982). *Languages of the brain: Experimental paradoxes and principles in neuropsychology.* New York: Brandon House.

Pribram, K. H. (1983). Proceedings of the 11th Conference on the Unity of the Sciences, Philadelphia (pp. 1373–1401). New York: ICF Press.

Pribram, K. H., Ahumada, A., Hartog, J., & Roos, L. (1964). A progressive report on the neurological processes distributed by frontal lesions in primates. In J. M. Warren & K. Akert (Eds.), *The frontal granular cortex and behavior* (pp. 28–55). New York: McGraw-Hill.

Pribram, K. H., & Barry, J. (1956). Further behavioral analysis of the parieto-temporo-preoccipital cortex. *Journal of Neurophysiology, 19*, 99–106.

Pribram, K. H., Blehert, S., & Spinelli, D. N. (1966). The effects on visual discrimination of crosshatching and undercutting the inferotemporal cortex of monkeys. *Journal of Comparative Physiology and Psychology, 62*, 358–364.

Pribram, K. H., Douglas, R., & Pribram, B. J. (1969). the nature of non-limbic learning. *Journal of Comparative Physiology and Psychology, 69*, 765–772.

Pribram, K. H., Gardner, K. W., Pressman, G. L., & Bagshaw, M. H. (1962). An automated discrimination apparatus for discrete trial analysis (DADTA). *Psychological Reports, 11*, 247–250.

Pribram, K. H., Lassonde, M., & Ptito, M. (1981). Classification of receptive field properties. *Experimental Brain Research, 43*, 119–130.

Pribram, K. H., & Mishkin, M. (1955). Simultaneous and successive visual discrimination by monkeys with inferotemporal lesions. *Journal of Comparative Physiology and Psychology, 48*, 198–202.

Pribram, K. H., Nuwer, M., & Baron, R. (1974). The holographic hypothesis of memory structure in brain function and perception. In R. C. Atkinson, D. H. Krantz, R. C. Luce, & P. Suppes (Eds.), *Contemporary developments in mathematical psychology* (pp. 416–467). San Francisco: W. H. Freeman.

Pribram, K. H., Plotkin, H. C., Anderson, R. M., & Leong, D. (1977). Information sources in the delayed alternation task for normal and "frontal" monkeys. *Neuropsychologia, 15*, 329–340.

Pribram, K. H., Reitz, S., McNeil, M., & Spevack, A. A. (1979). The effect of amygdalectomy on orienting and classical conditioning. *Pavlovian Journal 14*, 203–217.

Pribram, K. H., Sharafat, A., & Beekman, G. J. (1984). Frequency coding in motor systems. In H. T. A. Whiting (Ed.), *Human motor actions.* New York: JB Lipincott Co.

Pribram, K. H., Spevack, A., Blower, D., & McGuinness, D. (1980). A decisional analysis of the effects of inferotemporal lesions in the rhesus monkey. *Journal of Comparative Physiology and Psychology, 94*, 675–690.

Pribram, K. H., Spinelli, D. N., & Kamback, M. C. (1967). Electrocortical correlates of stimulus response and reinforcement. *Science, 3784*, 94–96.

Pribram, K. H., Spinelli, D. N., & Reitz, S. L. (1969). Effects of radical disconnection of occipital and temporal cortex on visual behavior of monkeys. *Brain, 92*, 301–312.

Pribram, K. H., & Tubbs, W. E. (1967). Short-term memory, parsing and the primate frontal cortex. *Science, 156*, 1765.

Pribram, K. H., & Weiskrantz, L. (1957). A comparison of the effects of medial and lateral cerebral resections on conditioned avoidance behavior in monkeys. *Journal of Comparative Physiology and Psychology, 50*, 74–80.

Rakic, P. (1976). *Local circuit neurons.* Cambridge, MA: MIT Press.

Rall, W. (1970). Dendritic neuron theory and dendro-dendritic synapses in a simple cortical system. In F. O. Schmitt (Ed.), *The neurosciences: Second study program* (pp. 552–565). New York: Rockefeller Institute.

Ratliff, F. (1961). Inhibitory interaction and the detection and enhancement of contours. In W. A. Rosenblith (Ed.), *Sensory communication (pp. 183–204).* New York: John Wiley & Sons.

Reitz, S. L., & Pribram, K. H. (1969). Some subcortical connections of the inferotemporal gyrus of monkeys. *Experimental Neurology, 25*, 632–645.

Richards, W. (1977). Stereopsis with and without monocular cues. *Vision Research, 17*, 967–969.

Richards, W., & Kaufman, L. (1969). "Center-of-gravity" tendencies for fixations and flow patterns. *Perception and Psychophysics, 5*, 81–84.

Richards, W., & Polit, A. (1974). Texture matching. *Kybernetick, 16*, 155–162.

Riggs, L. A., Ratliff, F., Cornsweet, J. C., & Cornsweet, T. N. (1953). The disappearance of steadily fixated test objects. *Journal of the Optical Society of America, 43*, 495–501.

Robson, J. G. (1975). Receptive fields, neural representation of the spatial and intensive attributes of the visual image. In E. C. Carterette (Ed.), *Handbook of perception: Vol. 5. Seeing.* New York: Academic Press.

Rodieck, R. W. (1965). Quantitative analysis of cat retinal ganglion cell response to visual stimuli. *Vision Research, 5*, 583–601.

Rodieck, R. W., & Stone, J. (1965). Response of cat retinal ganglion cells to moving visual patterns. *Journal of Neurophysiology, 28*, 833–850.

Schiller, P. H., Finlay, B. L., & Volman, S. F. (1976). Quantitative studies of single-cell properties in monkey striate cortex. *Journal of Neurophysiology, 39*, 1288–1374.

Schwartz, E. L. (1977). Spatial mapping in the primate sensory projection: Analytic structure and relevance to perception. *Biological Cybernetics, 25*, 181–194.

Schwartz, E. L., Desimone, R., Albright, T. D., & Gross, C. G. (1983). Shape recognition and inferior temporal neurons. *Proceedings of the National Academy of Science, U.S., 80*, 5776–5778.

Schwartzbaum, J. S., Wilson, W. A., Jr., & Morrissette, J. R. (1961). The effects of amygdalectomy on locomotor activity in monkeys. *Journal of Comparative Physiology and Psychology, 54*, 334–336.

Shepherd, G. (1974). *The synaptic organization of the brain: An introduction.* New York: Oxford University Press.

Sokolov, E. N. (1960). Neuronal models and the orienting flux. In M. A. Brazier (Ed.), *The central nervous system and behavior* (pp. 187–196). New York: Josiah Macy, Jr., Foundation.

Sperry, R. W. (1947). Cerebral regulation of motor coordination in monkeys following multiple transection of sensorimotor cortex. *Journal of Neurophysiology, 10*, 275–294.

Sperry, R. W., Miner, N., & Myers, R. E. (1955). Visual pattern perception following subpial slicing and tantalum wire implantations in the visual cortex. *Journal of Comparative Physiology and Psychology, 48*, 50–58.

Spevack, A. A., & Pribram, K. H. (1973). A decisional analysis of the effects of limbic lesions on learning in monkeys. *Journal of Comparative Physiology and Psychology, 82*, 211–226.

Spinelli, D. N. (1970). OCCAM: A content addressable memory model for the brain. In K. H. Pribram, & D. Broadbent, (Eds.), *The biology of memory* (pp. 273–306). New York: Academic Press.

Spinelli, D. N., & Barrett, T. W. (1969). Visual receptive field organization of single units in the cat's visual cortex. *Experimental Neurology, 24*, 76–98.

Spinelli, D. N., & Pribram, K. H. (1966). Changes in visual recovery functions produced by temporal lobe stimulation in monkeys. *Electroencephalography and Clinical Neurophysiology, 20*, 44–49.

Spinelli, D. N., & Pribram, K. H. (1967). Changes in visual recovery function and unit activity produced by frontal cortex stimulation. *Electroencephalography and Clinical Neurophysiology, 22*, 143–149.

Spinelli, D. N., Pribram, K. H., & Bridgeman, B. (1970). Visual receptive field organization of single units in the visual cortex of monkeys. *International Journal of Neuroscience, 1*, 67–74.

Spinelli, D. N., Starr, A., & Barrett, T. W. (1968). Auditory specificity in unit recordings from cat's visual cortex. *Experimental Neurology, 22*, 75–84.

Stamm, J. S., & Knight, M. (1963). Learning of visual tasks by monkeys with epileptogenic implants in temporal cortex. *Journal of Comparative Physiology and Psychology, 56*, 254–260.

Stamm, J. S., & Rosen, S. C. (1972). Cortical steady potential shifts and anodal polarization during delayed response performance. *Acta Neurobiologiae Experimentalis, 32*, 193–209.

Stuart, C. I., Takahashi, Y., & Umezawa, H. (1978). On the stability and non-local properties of memory. *Journal of Theoretical Biology, 71*, 605–618.

Sutter, E. (1976). A revised conception of visual receptive fields based on pseudo-random spatio-temporal pattern stimuli. In P. Z. Marmarelis & G. D. McCann (Eds.), *Proceedings of the First Symposium on Testing and Identification of Nonlinear Systems* (pp. 353–365). Pasadena, CA: California Institute of Technology.

Ungerleider, L., Ganz, L., & Pribram, K. H. (1977). Size constancy in rhesus monkeys: Effects of pulvinar, prestriate and inferotemporal lesions. *Experimental Brain Research, 27*, 251–269.

Ungerleider, L., & Pribram, K. H. (1977). Inferotemporal versus combined pulvinar-prestriate lesions in the rhesus monkey: Effects on color, object and pattern discrimination. *Neuropsychologia, 15*, 481–498.

Uttal, W. R. (1978). *The psychobiology of the mind*. Hillsdale, NJ: Lawrence Erlbaum.

Vinogradova, O. S. (1975). Functional organization of the limbic system in the process of registration of information: Facts and hypotheses. In R. L. Isaacson & K. H. Pribram (Eds.), *The hippocampus: Vol. 2. Neurophysiology and behavior* (pp. 3–64). New York: Plenum.

Weiskrantz, L. (1974). The interaction between occipital and temporal cortex in vision: An overview. In F. O. Schmitt & F. G. Worden (Eds.), *The neurosciences: Third study program* (pp. 189–204). Cambridge, MA: MIT Press.

Weiskrantz, L., & Mishkin, M. (1958). Effects of temporal and frontal cortical lesions on auditory discrimination in monkeys. *Brain, 1*, 406–414.

Weiss, P. (1939). *Principles of development: A text in experimental embryology*. New York: Holt.

Wiesel, T. N., & Hubel, D. H. (1965a). Comparison of the effects of unlateral and bilateral eye closure on cortical unit responses in kittens. *Journal of Neurophysiology, 28*, 1029–1040.

Wiesel, T. N., & Hubel, D. H. (1965b). Extent of recovery from the effects of visual deprivation in kittens. *Journal of Neurophysiology, 28*, 1060–1072.

Willshaw, D. J., Buneman, O. P., & Longuet-Higgins, H. C. (1969). Nonholographic associative memory. *Nature, 222*, 960–962.

Wilson, M. (1975). Effects of circumscribed cortical lesions upon somesthetic and visual discrimination in the monkey. *Journal of Comparative Physiology and Psychology 50*, 630–635.

CHAPTER 21

Issues in Graduate and Postgraduate Training in Clinical Neuropsychology

Louis D. Costa, Joseph D. Matarazzo, and Robert A. Bornstein

The general model for graduate education and training has been a topic of continuing discussion and formal debate at the national level for many years (see Matarazzo, 1983, 1986a for a review). The general consensus of the five national conferences held since 1949 has been that, at the graduate level, one is educating and training psychologists first and specialists second. These national conferences have confronted several difficult issues, including what common core, if any, should be a required part of doctoral education in psychology (regardless of the area of ultimate professional specialization); the role of nondoctoral level training in professional psychology; and the role of specialized training experiences. While the initial development of these training models occurred in relationship to clinical psychology, the emergence of specialty or subspecialty disciplines (e.g., neuropsychology) once again raises the questions of the format and content of training programs in applied psychology.

A CORE CURRICULUM FOR GRADUATE EDUCATION IN PSYCHOLOGY

As noted above, the conferees at each of the five national conferences have pondered the wisdom of a mandated core of generic coursework for graduate students in psychology. As discussed by Matarazzo (1983, 1986a), several of the national conferences on training in psychology have recognized or recommended that there is or should be such a core but were simultaneously reluctant to mandate what that core should contain. Nevertheless, there has been consistent opinion that there is a need to emphasize a generic psychological core of knowledge for *all* graduate students in psychology. In spite of the reluctance by psychology to stipulate the specific nature of the core curriculum, there have been external pressures from licensing constituencies as well as the health insurance industry for psychology to define itself.

 The rapid growth of psychology since the 1950s has presented problems for the state licensing boards in psychology. Specifically, under the auspices of the laws that a psychologist is a person who has earned a doctoral degree in psychology *or its equivalent*, many individuals with degrees in associated areas (e.g., guidance and counseling, education, child development, etc.) began to seek licensure as professional psychologists. Thus, in the absence of objective criteria and guidelines for what represented a degree in psychology, the state boards were faced with having to make subjective decisions as to whether the coursework represented on a transcript was in psychology or essentially similar to such a program. In addition to this problem confronting the licensing boards, pressure was exerted on psychology by the various private and state insurance agencies and other third-party payers of health care costs. Specifically, these groups, which pay for mental health services provided by psychologists, began to insist that the profession distinguish which of its generically licensed psychologists were qualified, by virtue of training and experience, to provide mental health services that were reimbursable under the policies of those components of the health insurance industry.

These pressures, as well as others, led to the formation of a National Task Force on Education and Credentialing, which began to search for a definition of the curricular qualifications to be met by educational institutions wishing to be recognized as offering doctoral training in psychology.

The Task Force included representatives of the American Psychological Association (APA) (including various committees and the relevant divisions), the American Association of State Psychology Boards, the Council of Graduate Departments of Psychology, the National Register of Health Service Providers in Psychology, and other interested constitutents. After several years of deliberation, the Task Force has put forth the recommendation that, henceforth, doctoral programs in psychology must have a minimum core content if their graduates are to be recognized by legal (state licensing boards) or quasilegal (the National Register) bodies as having completed a doctorate in psychology. If this report is formally accepted, all doctoral-level graduates of psychology programs, regardless of intended career specialization, will have completed this core training in psychology in order to be licensed or otherwise credentialed as psychologists. As recommended by the National Task Force, the irreducible minimum core that a doctoral program in psychology must contain will require *every* student, regardless of eventual special interest, to demonstrate knowledge and use of *scientific and professional ethics and standards, research design and methodology, statistics, psychological measurement, and history and systems of psychology.* Furthermore, such programs will require each student to demonstrate knowledge in each of the following substantive areas of psychology:

1. Biological bases of behavior (e.g., physiological psychology, comparative psychology, neuropsychology, psychopharmacology);
2. cognitive-affective bases of behavior (e.g., learning, memory, perception, cognition, thinking, motivation, emotion);
3. social bases of behavior (e.g., social psychology, cultural ethnic and group processes, sex roles, organizational and systems theory);
4. individual differences (e.g., personality theory, human development, individual differences, abnormal psychology, psychology of women, psychology of the handicapped).

In addition to the above, the recommendations included an advanced sequence of studies (not necessarily limited to coursework in psychology) appropriate to each graduate's later career track.

A CORE NEUROPSYCHOLOGICAL CURRICULUM

Within the context of clinical neuropsychology, a separate task force has issued its recommendations for the requisite coursework and experience needed for competence in neuropsychology. This task force was preceded by numerous symposia dealing with the question of training in neuropsychology that had been held at the meetings of the APA (1975, 1978, and 1982) and of the interdisciplinary International Neuropsychological Society (INS) in 1979 and 1981. The Task Force on Education, Accreditation, and Credentialing was created in 1978 by the psychologist members of the INS following their request to the American Board of Professional Psychology (ABPP) for recognition as one of the specialities within applied psychology (Meier, 1978). This task force became a joint venture with the establishment of Division 40 of the American Psychological Association in 1980 (Meier, 1981a, b). Meier's report included several models for the training of neuropsychologists as well as recommendations for the requisite experiences for the later professional credentialing and licensure of the doctoral graduates of these proposed training programs. These recommendations for the types of formal educational and experiential backgrounds that constitute necessary training for neuropsychologists have largely been incorporated as requirements for credentialing by the American Board of Clinical Neuropsychology (ABCN), which was created in 1982 and sanctioned by the American Board of Professional Psychology (ABPP) in 1983.

In view of the expected major impact that this credentialing process will have for the future of clinical neuropsychology, it seems appropriate to describe briefly a set of criteria toward which future doctoral training programs should be developed. The development of competency-based curricula for training is by definition intimately related to the formulation of identifiable areas of clinical and research skill. The areas of predoctoral and postdoctoral training and experience required by ABCN include basic neurosciences, neuroanatomy, neuropathology, clinical neurology, psychological assessment, clinical neuropsychological assessment, psychopathology, and psychological intervention. In addition to these areas of training, the ABCN eligibility criteria also require five years of postdoctoral experience, which must include at least three years of experience in clinical neuropsychology for those individuals without supervised training and two years of experience (at least one year postdoctoral) in neuropsychology for those individuals with the equivalent of one full-time year of supervised training. The areas of training listed above reflect both the neuroscience and clinical psychology heritage of clinical neuropsychology.

The results of these two task forces, therefore, have produced what may be regarded as a model for the generic and specialty components of training in neuropsychology. Although working independently, the two task forces have identified interrelated sets of the psychological knowledge base that are required for the education of individuals who pursue careers in clinical neuropsychology. The recommendations of the INS-APA joint task force may be seen as a subdiscipline-specific set of educational and training experiences that satisfy the previously noted curricular recommendations of the National Task Force for an "advanced sequence of studies appropriate to each student's career track." The feasibility of the integration of these two sets of educational criteria is amply demonstrated by the models for training in neuropsychology proposed by Meier (1981b). It is important to note that each of the approaches presented (in particular, models 3 and 4, which are primarily focused on neuropsychological content) includes an extensive generic psychological core. Review of the generic components of those programs indicates that the recommendations of the National Task Force would be satisfied by such programs. This confirms that these models for the development of competencies in the various components of neuropsychological endeavor are committed to the principle of a core of psychological knowledge that is generic to *all* graduate-level psychological training.

With the identification of a generic knowledge base and set of specialty-specific competencies, the issue is raised of how and when specialty specific training is to be instituted. Related to this general issue of specialty training are a number of questions of (1) the existence and identity of psychological specialties, (2) the level of training required for "journeyperson" provision of neuropsychological services, and (3) various models for implementation of specialty training. Differing positions have been adopted with respect to these as well as other questions.

NEUROPSYCHOLOGY AS A DISTINCT SPECIALTY

As indicated, there is less than complete agreement as to whether neuropsychology is a distinct psychological specialty. To be precise, according to APA as of 1986, there are *no* specialty areas within psychology. However, as discussed below, this situation may change in the future, and Division 40 (among other constituencies within psychology) is in the process of preparing an application for specialty status to be submitted when APA is in a position to consider such applications. Although APA does not separately credential specialities, the ABPP does identify, through its diplomas, several distinct "areas of practice" within psychology. In the context of the present discussion, and as noted above, it is of some interest that clinical neuropsychology has recently gained this status. Nevertheless, Matarazzo (1983, 1986a, 1986b) has discussed a number of intradisciplinary and societal issues related to the sociology of professions and the means by which specialties evolve. He identified eight stages through which a field must pass in order to be discernibly unique relative to the rest of psychology. These stages include (1) the existence of national and international organizations; (2) specialty-oriented scientific journals; (3) acknowledgment from peers in psychology via the mechanisms of designation, accreditation, and licensure that the subject matter, methodologies, and applications of the discipline differ from those of other psychological disciplines; (4) the development of postdoctoral training sites and a group of specialty-specific skills and procedures distinct from those of other areas of psychology; (5) the acknowledgment of the existence of the field by the allocation of discipline-specific funds for research and training by the National Institutes of Health and other federal agencies; (6) the establishment of discipline-specific departments in medical schools, other university units, and hospitals; (7) acceptance by peers inside and outside of psychology and by the courts that there are individuals who are experts in the field; and (8) designation as a specialty area by the American Board of Professional Psychology.

In the context of these criteria, which Matarazzo views as a minimum necessary for the establishment of a specialty, he argues that today there is *not even one* bona fide, universally acknowledged specialty in psychology. Matarazzo argues that, in spite of the accreditation of clinical psychology programs and graduates by the APA and ABPP since 1949 and 1947, respectively, the discipline of clinical psychology has almost achieved the above stages and may soon be acknowledged by significant others as a specialty in psychology. Matarazzo's basic position may be summarized by saying that, as of 1986, psychology is still for the most part a generic discipline in which evolving proficiencies developed by different subsets of psychology are applied in a variety of settings or problem areas. Thus, such terms as *neuropsychology, clinical psychology, industrial psychology, physiological psychology*, and the like, merely describe the client population and professional services context in which the generic discipline of psychology is applied.

It is clear, however, that the establishment of a specialty area begins with the parent discipline. The eight stages described by Matarazzo (1983, 1986) support this view, in that the majority of those stages refer to developments largely within the profession of psychology. Within the specific context of neuropsychology, it would appear that most, it not all, of the criteria described above have been or soon will be met. For example, the International Neuropsychological Society was formed in the late 1960s, and more recently the Division of Clinical Neuropsychology has been established within the APA. Numerous journals deal primarily or exclusively with neuropsychological investigations, including *Journal of Clinical and Experimental Neuropsychology, Cortex, Brain and Language, Brain and Cognition,* and *Neuropsychologia.* There is acknowledgment from our peers that clinical neuropsychology does represent a unique set of methods and application. This is reflected in practice by the fact that patients with symptoms related to the nervous system are referred specifically for neuropsychological examination and that, in some instances, referrals for such problems, while not specifically requesting a neuropsychological assessment, are nevertheless channeled (however informally) by a chief (clinical) psychologist to the attending staff neuropsychologist. Intraprofessional recognition of a distinct area of expertise also is reflected in the fact that clinical psychologists often consult their neuropsychological colleagues on cases in which there is some question of the potential relevance of a particular set of clinical observations. The professional recognition of neuropsychology is also reflected by the fact that some legal constituencies are beginning to consider and implement specialty licensing or specialty registers in neuropsychology. In the academic arena, an increasing number of graduate psychology programs designate in the description of their programs the existence of and opportunity for students to pursue a track in neuropsychology. This indicates that academic departments of psychology do identify a discernable area of endeavor in neuropsychology. It is clear that there is a group of assessment procedures that have been developed in the context of, and used exclusively for, neuropsychological assessment. These include the measures developed by Halstead, Reitan, Benton, Spreen and Hamsher, and Goodglass and Kaplan. In addition, there is a growing number of formally established divisions and department of neuropsychology in the hospitals and medical centers of North America. A review of recent issues of the *APA Monitor* and *INS Bulletin* reveals that these departments are not restricted to major cities and hospitals. Many clinical neuropsychologists have had the experience of testifying in medical-legal proceedings and in this context have been accepted by the courts to present expert testimony in neuropsychology. The eighth stage identified by Matarazzo involves formal designation by the ABPP as a distinct area of practice. In that context, it is particularly noteworthy that the ABPP has recently concluded an agreement with ABCN to grant its fifth diploma in the practice area of clinical neuropsychology. This agreement represents clear evidence that, within professional psychology, clinical neuropsychology is a discriminable and legitimate area of professional practice. Thus, in the context of Matarazzo's suggestions for the stages necessary for intradisciplinary and societal establishment of a discipline, it would appear that if clinical neuropsychology has not yet reached this stage of evolution, it will do so in the near future.

PROFICIENCIES AND DE FACTO AND DE JURE SPECIALTIES

Having identified a difference of opinion within psychology as to whether clinical neuropsychology (or clinical psychology or health psychology, etc.) has today achieved the status of a specialty, it also is important to add that such a difference may be more semantic than substantive. Matarazzo (1983, 1986a, b) bases his opinion that no such specialties in psychology are yet well established and generally accepted by significant others in society on such realities as that only in 1983 did the American Psychological Association Subcommittee on Specialization for the first time propose the steps by which a division of the APA or another subset of psychologists might apply for designation as a specialty within psychology (Sales, Bricklin, & Hall, 1983). Sales and associates (1983) report that for a number of years, the APA has received requests from a number of constituencies of psychologists (i.e., forensic psychology, psychoanalysis, and several divisions of the APA) wishing to have their subfield officially declared a bona fide specialty of psychology. Acknowledging that it had no criteria by which to honor or support such requests, the APA, acting through the Committee on Standards of Providers of Psychological Services (COSPOPS) of its Board of Professional Affairs (BPA), established in 1978 a Task Force on Specialty Criteria (TFSC) to fill this void. After five years of work (in August 1983), TFSC produced a draft *Manual for the Identification and Continued Recognition of Proficiencies and New Specialties in Psychology* (Sales, Bricklin, & Hall, 1983), which for the first time helped American psychology chart its course on the path toward officially recognizing the first bona fide specialties, per se, in psychology. Thus, although beginning with the establishment of the American Board of Professional Psychology in 1947, the profession of psychology has recognized special areas for the professional practice of psychology (i.e., clinical, counseling, industrial and school, and, in 1983, clinical neuropsychology), no one of these five areas has ever been officially acknowledged by APA as a specialty inasmuch as no criteria for such designation or credentialing has ever been ratified and thus been officially approved by the organization that represents most of the country's psychologists.

   That fact notwithstanding, these "special areas" of psychology were accorded special status by the ABPP and since 1947 have been evolving into bona fide specialties despite this lack of a nationally ratified set of criteria that a subset of psychology would need to meet in order to be declared a specialty. As a much-needed step to clarify what has been an ambiguous situation for all parties involved, one of the major contributions of the 1983 manual published by TFSC may well be that Sales and colleagues (1983) make a distinction between a proficiency and a specialty, a distinction that should do much to help clear up the differences of opinion among psychologists, and between the APA and some of its divisions that represent professional psychologists, which were identified earlier in this chapter. Thus, according to Sales and associates, recognition of a proficiency such as competent neuropsychological assessment or expertise in relaxation training minimally requires the identification of substantial knowledge and skills in one of the following relatively unique areas: (1) the client population, (2) services rendered, (3) problems addressed, and (4) settings and services that form the foundation of the specialty. On the other hand, recognition as a bona fide specialty of psychology (clinical, neuropsychology, health, etc.) minimally requires the identification of substantial knowledge and skills in each of these same four areas (Sales, Bricklin, & Hall, 1981). Thus, if the Sales report is formally adopted, the four steps required for an area of psychology to be officially designated a specialty of psychology will finally be clearly defined, which should make it much easier for special areas, such as clinical neuropsychology, to do a self-study and apply for specialty designation, and, if the application is approved, better continue its evolution with this newly won, public endorsement.

Sales and colleagues do not deny the reality that some psychologists already believe that their area has achieved specialty status. Specifically, they add to the psychologist's understanding of the complex issues surrounding this process by their insightful distinction between two generic categories of specialization: de facto and de jure. De facto specialization is the result of the informal process of self-selection (or being pressured to select) a more limited sphere of professional practice that involves a special client area, set of skills and services, problems addressed, and settings for professional services. De jure specialization, on the other hand, involves a more formal, quasilegal process of certification or recognition indicating that a practitioner is a specialist. Psychology clearly has been moving toward de jure recognition of specialists through the establishment of such bodies as the ABPP and the National Register. However, with few exceptions, state licensing boards and state and federal laws have yet to define a specialist in psychology. Such laws quite likely will be passed as soon as the APA begins to formally accredit specialties, a process that should occur in the next several years if APA distributes a manual that contains the steps and the criteria to be followed by subsets of psychologists wishing to have their area declared a specialty of psychology (Sales, Bricklin, & Hall, 1983).

Although these new terms are presented here only in capsule form, it appears that much of the recent debate over whether clinical neuropsychology, health psychology, and clinical psychology are or are not specialties revolves around the different frames of reference of each of the protagonists. Now that the distinctions between *proficiency* and *specialty* and between *de facto* and *de jure* specialties have been clarified, it is quite likely that the proponents of the position that there are today no bona fide specialties and those arguing that there are will find, to their relief, that they are and have been in agreement. Specifically, the history of clinical psychology, health psychology, and neuropsychology leaves little question that each subdiscipline has evolved unique proficiencies and also that by now each quite likely has achieved de facto recognition as a specialty. If this is true, then the earlier argument thus may have been replaced by an argument over a narrower and possibly less difficult aspect of the debate: which of these three areas is today also a de jure specialty by the criteria described in general terms for all professions by Matarazzo (1986) and by Sales and associates (1983) specifically for psychology? Continuing experience and debate will no doubt make it easier for the protagonists to reach a consensus on the answer to this better-defined question.

LEVEL OF TRAINING FOR JOURNEYPERSON PROVISION OF NEUROPSYCHOLOGICAL SERVICE

Assuming that, within the discipline of psychology, there is a subdiscipline or specialty area called neuropsychology, the question arises as to the point in the educational process at which an individual becomes a specialist in that area. Matarazzo (1986a, b) strongly espouses the position that, to the extent that it exists at all, specialization in psychology occurs only at the postdoctoral level. Consistent with his arguments, cited above, Matarazzo (1983, 1986a, b) maintains that graduates of psychology doctoral programs are at that point no more than generic psychologists, regardless of the number and scope of specific career-oriented courses, internship, and research experiences. He argues that graduates receiving the doctorate possess the bare minimum of core knowledge in generic psychology and a rudimentary foundation in an area of specialized skill (e.g., neuropsychology). In this regard, programs such as those described by Meier (1981b) are in Matarazzo's view to be regarded more as prespecialty programs that require further development via formal postdoctoral training. Matarazzo (1986b) describes in great detail the demands that the discipline of psychology and related societal institutions must meet in order to develop and implement widely available, quality postdoctoral training in psychology. It may be pointed out that some groups within professional psychology may be moving toward *requiring* such formal postdoctoral training. In particular, the Division of Health Psychology may move to require a formal two-year postdoctoral "residency" for persons desiring to be certified as specialists in health psychology. Some details regarding what might be included in such formal residency type postdoctoral training programs are discussed by Matarazzo (1986b).

Postdoctoral training has a long history in clinical neuropsychology as well. Many currently practicing neuropsychologists obtained their neuropsychological training after completing doctoral degrees in other areas of psychology (e.g., clinical, experimental). Upon completion of doctoral training, these persons sought additional, formal, supervised training through programs offered under the direction of some of this country's foremost neuropsychologists. Some of these postdoctoral training programs have been available for many years (Matthews, 1976, 1981) and have produced a number of today's leaders in the field of neuropsychology. This continues to be a viable format for obtaining the necessary competencies for the practice of clinical neuropsychology and in fact is included as an alternative by Meier (1981a, b). In addition, the role of this format for training in neuropsychology may be expanding, given the numerous opportunities for such placements reflected in issues of the *APA Monitor*.

Nevertheless, the models presented by Meier (1981b) also demonstrate the feasibility of presenting adequate training within doctoral programs to provide individuals with the competencies for practice of neuropsychology at the journeyperson level. Although such training would be designed to establish an adequate level of training upon receipt of the doctorate to begin to provide neuropsychological services, it is clear that such predoctoral programs are insufficient to provide the full level of training for full independent practice of neuropsychology (or any other subdiscipline). The necessity of postdoctoral experience in conjunction with formal predoctoral training in neuropsychology is further demonstrated by the ABCN (and ABPP) criteria for credentialing cited earlier, which, to reiterate, require a period of formal postdoctoral experience.

The importance of postdoctoral experience for the full development of clinical neuropsychological expertise is further demonstrated by the growth of the knowledge base in neuropsychology. As this base continues to broaden, it will become increasingly difficult for training programs to incorporate all areas of potential neuropsychological expertise in the context of two years of predoctoral specialty training. Thus, it is possible that in the future, training programs will focus on "generic neuropsychology," which will stress core areas of knowledge and skill that will be applicable in all the potential employment settings of neuropsychologists. In this respect, predoctoral generic specialty training will complement the predoctoral generic core training in the initial years of the training program. As Matarazzo has suggested, refinement of professional skills (regardless of specialty) beyond the predoctoral specialty track always occurs in the postdoctoral years. Certainly, training programs in any of the new specialties, no matter how comprehensive, cannot hope to produce clinicians who will be thoroughly prepared for all possible employment settings. For example, in respect to neuropsychology, it is unrealistic that trainees would be equally well equipped, on completion of their training, with the specific job skills required for the various areas of pediatric, geriatric, and rehabilitation psychology as well as general neuropsychology. The development of an individual's specific professional competencies would undoubtedly require further on-the-job refinement based on the particular employment setting. This model of generic predoctoral specialty training after a generic general psychology background in the overall context of a Boulder model program would seem to offer an optimal balance of scientific and professional training that will be needed in the further development of the field of neuropsychology as well as in other areas (e.g., health psychology).

There does appear to be general agreement that postdoctoral refinement of professional skills is required for an individual to attain the level of skill necessary for certification or designation as a specialist. The issue, therefore, is in relation to the point at which journeyperson level proficiency in neuropsychology is attained. Matarazzo and others would argue that this level of ability is reached only after a minimum of two years of postdoctoral training in addition to whatever predoctoral internship or "apprenticeship" experiences may have been completed.

Another view, espoused by Costa and others, is that, upon completion of a doctoral program containing the elements suggested by the ABCN criteria and including a supervised clinical neuropsychology internship ("apprenticeship"), an individual has attained the necessary competencies to provide neuropsychological service at the journeyperson level. This view clearly acknowledges the importance of further postdoctoral supervision and refinement of clinical skill as reflected in the ABCN criteria, but simultaneously maintains that a graduate of such a program possesses adequate skill to practice neuropsychology in an institutional setting. This view, then considers the postdoctoral refinement of skill to the level of ABPP criteria as being comparable (by analogy) to the difference between a journeyperson and a master craftsman. In support of this view, the historical precedent since 1949 has been that the Ph.D. is the entry-level (journeyperson) degree for professional practice. While this position has developed in the context of clinical psychology and from the outset has stressed the importance of further postdoctoral enhancement of skills, the Ph.D. (in clinical psychology) has nevertheless been a "union card" for entry into general mental health service delivery. As psychology and its various subdisciplines and specialty areas begin to experiment with new training models (e.g., postdoctoral residencies), the question of when journeyperson-level professional skill is attained will be further debated.

ROLE OF WORKSHOPS IN NEUROPSYCHOLOGICAL TRAINING

In the context of the foregoing discussion of whether competence in neuropsychology is attained at the doctoral or postdoctoral level, some discussion of the workshop phenomena as a vehicle for training in neuropsychology is required. Postdoctoral and continuing education workshops have a well-respected role, not only in psychology, but in virtually all professions. The importance of remaining up to date on developments in one's chosen field is strongly emphasized by the requirement of many professional organizations, as well as of licensing laws, that individuals complete a number of continuing education experiences in order to maintain their licensure or professional standing. Even when used as a means to learn some specific new technique to be incorporated into a previously established set of competencies, the continuing education workshop maintains a valued role. However, it is clear from this discussion and the report by the joint INS-APA task force that workshop training as the sole means of establishing any level of competence in neuropsychology (or any other field, for that matter) is completely inadequate. As an analogy, it is easily conceivable that a graduate of an APA-approved program in clinical psychology could (and should) further develop his or her level of skill by attending a continuing education workshop in which the graduate learned some new therapeutic technique to incorporate into his or her armamentarium of clinical skills. On the contrary, it is completely inconceivable that a "nonclinical" Ph.D. could learn the field of clinical psychology in the context of a weekend or even a one-week workshop.

In spite of the great complexities of the field of clinical neuropsychology, there is a disturbingly large number of individuals engaged in neuropsychological activities with no more training in the neurosciences and related biomedical fields than one or several workshop experiences. Even individuals who are well meaning and otherwise qualified in such areas as clinical psychology may be engaged in such practice with the notion that their training is adequate. While some Ph.D. clinical students may in fact pursue elective coursework during their training that would satisfy the ABCN criteria, most do not; and it is the latter individuals about whom the present concerns are being expressed. These concerns also apply to those individuals with experimental or physiological psychology backgrounds who may possess somewhat greater understanding of brain function but completely lack any foundation in clinical training.

These concerns over the workshop phenomenon in neuropsychology have been expressed in many other forums. Matthews (1976), in a discussion of sources of disenchantment for applicants to the University of Wisconsin postdoctoral training program, described what he refers to as "workshopitis." This condition essentially represents the problem that, after exposure to "the promised land" via a brief workshop experience, the postdoctoral program itself was unable to maintain the learning curve established in the first glimpse into the work of neuropsychology. Matthews (1981) subsequently noted the fact that, although the workshop issue had been discussed in the context of attendees' seeking formal postdoctoral training, this was the exception rather than the rule. In this regard, many in the field of neuropsychology have observed that there is a rapid proliferation of these "weekend wonders" who purport to offer neuropsychological services. The oversimplifications, misinterpretations, overinterpretations, and other forms of patent nonsense generated by such individuals are encountered all too frequently and have been commented on by others (Reed, 1976; Boll, 1978; Rourke, 1976). Although the literature that accompanies and announces the availability of such "beginning" and so-called "advanced" workshops often contains the disclaimer that such workshops are insufficient for establishing adequate competence in neuropsychology and should be supplemented with further study and supervision, little is done to enforce this suggestion. The "graduates" of these workshops are at least implicitly filled with the confidence that a reading list, combined with an introductory (and in some instances "advanced") workshop, is sufficient preparation for neuropsychological practice.

Matthews (1981) points out that judgments regarding the value of neuropsychological expertise are based on the quality of the product provided. In settings where the only individual claiming to offer neuropsychological services bases his or her credentials on workshop experiences, the field of neuropsychology is "at risk." Therefore, particularly in the context of new medical referral sources, a few reports containing dramatic overinterpretations of doom and gloom or presenting neurologically incompatible statements will be sufficient to prevent any further referrals from that source. In addition to the general societal cost arising from the discrediting of neuropsychology in certain settings, equally important human costs arise from the activities of these individuals. Patients may be unfortunate enough to have the difficulties that caused their referral to a "neuropsychologist" in the first place compounded by professional misinterpretation and incompetence bordering on charlatanism. One of the many possible examples that might be cited is that of the child with "learning disabilities" who, after examination by the "neuropsychologist," is pronounced to have brain damage. This label then follows the child for the rest of his or her life and may have dramatic impact on major areas of the child's life. That is, given the low level of sophistication regarding neuropsychology that exists in many school systems, a child labeled brain damaged is likely to be channeled in certain directions that may not be consistent with his or her potential level of ability. Thus, the misapplied label may cause the child to be directed toward a vocational stream, when, with some prudent neuropsychological wisdom, competent test interpretation, and communication with referral sources, the child may otherwise have been assessed to be capable of completing a university program. The life-long vocational pathway that thus can influence a child's life through the educational system then can be linked directly to the misapplication of a label by a "professional" who was unqualified to make such judgments.

One refrain often heard from the graduates of such workshops relates to the fact that they have received their training through "the school of hard knocks." That is, after completing these basic and advanced workshops, they have engaged in several years of neuropsychological activity and now *feel* like specialists. While the ABCN criteria recognizes that many neuropsychologists (particularly older ones) in practice today obtained their training through ad hoc programs and did not have access to formal training programs, it is abundantly clear that today, workshop experience alone is inadequate. Spending the first week of a neuropsychology "career" learning improper test administration and misinterpretation and spending the next five years perfecting those same mistakes is not a satisfactory venue for achieving or demonstrating competence in clinical neuropsychology.

What, then, is the role (if any) of the workshop in neuropsychology? Certainly, as discussed previously, adequately trained individuals with established competence in neuropsychology will continue to develop and amplify their skills via continuing education workshops. Although these workshops may have filled a role in the history of neuropsychology by stimulating promising students to seek additional training, in the context of current developments of core competency training in neuropsychology, these workshops have no role to play. In addition to the above-noted role in continuing education of individuals with established competencies, workshops may assume other functions for those individuals wishing to pursue this aspect of health service delivery. In particular, one function may be in regard to consumer education. There appears to be an untapped reservoir of medical, psychological, and educational practitioners who might be interested in attending a workshop to discover what clinical neuropsychology is (and is not), when and how to refer a patient, what to expect and what not to expect in neuropsychological consultation, and how to implement the results of such a consultation. While many of us teach these principles in an informal fashion in the context of our daily endeavor, this referral oriented, educational application of the workshop approach would serve both the interests of society as well as the profession of neuropsychology.

IMPLEMENTATION OF SPECIALTY TRAINING IN NEUROPSYCHOLOGY

Given the divergent views discussed in previous sections of this chapter, the final issue to be addressed relates to the strengths and weaknesses of various models of providing training in neuropsychology. One approach would be to restrict specialty training to the postdoctoral level. This would permit extensive development of expertise in basic psychological science and would provide a strong foundation for the development of specialty competencies. The basic background would then be supplemented by post-doctoral training experience of varied duration that would be specialty specific. That is, distinct specialized "residency" programs could be offered to different subsets of doctorate holding psychologists aiming for careers in health psychology, behavioral medicine, clinical psychology, industrial psychology, or neuropsychology. This approach would be very similar to the medical and dental models of basic training followed by specialty residency (and fellowship) programs. One problem with this analogy with medical training is that training in medicine and dentistry is geared primarily to produce clinicians. Physicians wishing to gain some competence in research skills typically tend to do so in some institutions outside the realm of their primary medical training by pursuing M.Sc. or Ph.D. degrees in their chosen fields. In addition, most medical school curricula include two years of basic science followed by two years of clinical hospital experience. This approach produces physicians who, following the successful completion of the state licensing examination and some period of internship, are licensed by the state to practice as physicians.

A major problem, then, with similarly limiting specialty psychology training (including clinical) to the postdoctoral years is that this would delay individual entry to the general service delivery field, thus reducing the availability of psychological services. While having a documented specialty might enhance our role in the eyes of our physician specialist colleagues, there is some question of the willingness or capability of society at large to pay for a profession (psychology) comprised entirely of specialists. Another argument against completely generic predoctoral training in psychology is that such a background would likely not present an adequate background for the execution of detailed doctoral calibre research in the areas of special interest. For example, such a general background would not provide the in-depth training in the basic and clinical neurosciences that an emerging neuropsychologist would need to do research in the areas of particular neurological conditions (e.g., epilepsy or cerebro-vascular disease). Even the inclusion of some survey or introductory courses in the various specialties as part of the core predoctoral curriculum would be insufficient for the development of sufficient levels of sophistication for specialty research topics.

At the opposite end of the continuum are the professional psychology (Psy.D.) programs that focus primarily if not exclusively on applied (as opposed to research) training. These programs have been in existence for several years in relation to clinical psychology, but as Meier (1981b) points out, they are untested in the context of training for clinical neuropsychology. The validity of this approach to training in clinical psychology is underscored by the fact that several Psy.D. programs have been accredited by the American Psychological Association. Since this does appear to be a viable format for training clinicians, the question arises as to whether the Psy.D. type of program is appropriate for training in clinical neuropsychology.

The viability of training programs oriented toward the development of applied expertise would seem to be predicated to a large extent on the existence of a sufficiently large body of accumulated basic knowledge to form the basis for training of practitioners. This is not dissimilar to training in medicine, where the large data base from biology, physiology, anatomy, etc. forms the foundation for clinical training. The rather recent appearance of Psy.D. programs in clinical (or professional) psychology implies that such a "critical mass" of knowledge may have been developed to allow the movement toward practitioner oriented training. However, in the relatively new and still emerging fields such as neuropsychology, accumulation of this "critical mass" would at the present time appear not yet accomplished. Many (if not most) aspects of brain-behavior relationships are poorly understood, and in spite of the rapidly increasing knowledge base, there is still a long way to go. In this context, the viability of a Psy.D. type program for training in neuropsychology, would seem not yet firmly established. At some point in the future, there is no doubt that there will be room for neuropsychologists trained primarily to be practitioners, but for the near future there appears to be a predominant need for training neuropsychologists capable of creating and expanding the data base upon which the profession will be practiced.

These observations would seem to indicate the need for continuation of training scientist-practitioners who can continue to build and refine their chosen specialties. This would seem best accomplished in the context of the existing Boulder model programs which provide a common core of psychological knowledge for all trainees regardless of eventual subspecialty. This core curriculum is then supplemented, at the predoctoral level with training in a given individual's specific career interests, be they industrial, clinical, neuropsychology, or health psychology. Although the specific implementation of the core curriculum will obviously be varied (depending on the characteristics of the institutions mediating this approach), it would appear to have a number of distinct advantages. First, it allows trainees, regardless of eventual specialization, to have a common knowledge base, and also to benefit from interaction with other students whose view of, and integration of, the same basic core information may be very different. This early interaction between potential specialists in widely diverse areas of psychology may reap dividends in the future in that areas which now may seem to have little in common may eventually find common ground (e.g., social psychology and health psychology) (Eiser, 1982; De Matteo & Friedman, 1982). This scientist-practitioner model with a generic foundation followed by specialty training has demonstrated its value in regard to clinical psychology and will likely prove equally effective in structuring training in the newer specialties.

While assimilating a common core students will increasingly emphasize their own specialties in the later years of their program. While in most current programs this specialization is in clinical, there could also be parallel specialty tracks for neuropsychology, health psychology, and so on. In neuropsychology, specialty tracks would, like the generic aspects of the program, be largely independent on the activities and interests of the faculty of the department members of other affiliated neuropsychology units. Thus, although there would likely tend to be some overlap in content and format, there would also be considerable variability in the specifics of neuropsychological training provided by various universities.

The idea of parallel predoctoral specialty tracks based on a generic core has additional merits in terms of encouraging interaction among trainees from various specialty tracks while they are in their respective training programs. Because of the interrelated nature of the specialty fields (e.g., neuropsychology, health psychology and clinical psychology) it is likely that some "specialty" predoctoral coursework will be applicable to all trainees (e.g., interviewing skills and assessment approaches). Thus, as the students begin to develop their specific professional skills and expertise, there will be opportunities for these trainees to learn of the concepts, approaches and skills of their colleagues in related areas of psychology. It is clear, however, that a neuropsychology trainee who takes an introductory health psychology course is not competently trained to practice in the general area of health psychology; nor is a health psychology student who takes an introductory neuropsychology course competently trained to practice neuropsychology. Nevertheless, this approach will likely pay dividends in their professional practice in that these professionals, while not having particular skills in all areas, will at least have an appreciation for what the other specialties have to offer. On the basis of this informal interaction, health psychologists or clinical psychologists could begin to assimilate some understanding of neuropsychological practice while concurrently the neuropsychologist could develop a comparable understanding of the nature of potential for treatments provided by specialists in health psychology or behavioral medicine. For example a predoctoral introductory course in neuropsychology would be a requirement for students in the neuropsychology track but might be an optional course for students in the clinical or health psychology tracks. Similarly a course on biofeedback might be required for students in health psychology, and be an option for those in the clinical or neuropsychology tracks. These initial learning experiences could then be further enhanced and developed as the trainees entered their internships and has an opportunity to witness the professional interactions among various psychologist specialties. In addition to early fostering of communication among psychologists, this approach would be economical in terms of program development. Thus, a particular department would not be faced with having to generate separate (overlapping) courses on particular topics for inclusion in distinct specialty tracks. Rather, the existing faculty resources could be employed to generate coursework relevant to a variety of specialty oriented students.

FUTURE DIRECTIONS IN TRAINING IN CLINICAL NEUROPSYCHOLOGY

The foregoing discussions have primarily considered possibilities for the implementation of neuropsychological training within the context of established educational and service delivery facilities. However, developments in the future may lead to alternative vehicles for the establishment or further development of various specific proficiencies. One such vehicle is that of the "assessment center" approach. There are a number of preliminary steps which must be achieved before this approach can begin to be considered for actual implementation. However, many recent developments in competency-based education may be viewed as initial steps which could be integrated into an assessment center approach.

In particular, an assessment center would be a setting in which individuals may engage in focused study of particular areas of knowledge or skill. The center could present various self-contained instructional modules to be studied by each individual. These modules would have been developed in relation to specific core competencies or proficiencies required for credentialing in a particular field (e.g., neuropsychology). The assessment center approach might be best suited (but clearly not restricted) to the individual with an established career who wishes to either change careers or to enhance his or her skills in a particular content area. Conceived in this manner the goals of an assessment center would be directly related to the previous discussion of proficiencies and specialties. Thus an individual could participate in an assessment center with the goal of establishing a set of specific neuropsychological proficiencies, or could pursue a more comprehensive approach in terms of the development of a broader base of skill and knowledge with the eventual goal of credentialing as a specialist in neuropsychology.

One example of how the assessment center could be utilized is the case of a clinical psychologist, who because of the nature of his or her practice or by virtue of continuing professional development, decides to obtain greater sophistication of skills in neuropsychological assessment. It likely would be impractical for such an individual to discontinue his practice for a year or two in order to enroll in a formal postdoctoral training program. The assessment center, however, would provide an option in that the individual could, over the course of several years, spend months of concentrated study in the center, which could be supplemented by home study during the remainder of those years. The person could maximize the use of the time spent in the "assessment center" in terms of the acquisition and demonstration of specific proficiencies. A similar approach could also be employed by psychologists in "nonclinical" fields who desire retraining in the area of neuropsychology. It is clear that different sets of proficiency-oriented modules would have to be completed by individuals depending on the nature of their background or experience.

In addition to the initial establishment of proficiencies in various neuropsychological activities, the assessment center would also have a role for the individual with previously established competencies. Thus, an individual who seeks to shift the focus on his or her neuropsychological practice (e.g., from psychiatry to pediatrics) might wish to avail him- or herself of the services of the assessment center as a time-efficient way of becoming reacquainted with the specific issues related to a specific practice area within clinical neuropsychology.

Obviously, the feasibility of the assessment center approach is directly linked to the identification of specific professional competencies that can be incorporated into an objective outline of the particular group of skills and knowledge required for professional competence in neuropsychology. The establishment of the ABCN (and ABPP) criteria, combined with the recent report of the Task Force of Specialty Criteria are the first general steps in this direction. Long-term goals for the implementation of the assessment center approach would require identification of very precise and specific competency oriented educational goals. Related to this would be the extensive investigation of how best to communicate these skills, and the massive job of the actual development of the specific proficiency-oriented educational modules. In the current state of development of the profession of neuropsychology, there clearly must be a reliance on more traditional approaches to training and education. However, the long-term future of neuropsychology may be able to incorporate innovative approaches to training and education, of which the assessment center may be only one example.

SUMMARY

We maintain that the area of clinical neuropsychology is one of the rapidly growing specialty areas in psychology. In the field of psychology, there appears to be general (if not unanimous) agreement regarding the necessity of a generic core of knowledge in psychology upon which is based intensive training in neuropsychology. Although there is substantial agreement on these issues, there is some divergence of views regarding the identity of neuropsychology as a unique and distinct specialty area and, also related to this, the question of the point in graduate education at which an individual attains a level of competence for journeyperson-level practice of neuropsychological skills. The increasing need for postdoctoral refinement of professional skills as a prerequisite for competent practice in neuropsychology is acknowledged. Workshop training in isolation is completely inadequate as a vehicle for attaining full service delivery competence in neuropsychology. Several possible models for implementation of graduate neuropsychological training have been discussed, and it is concluded that, for the foreseeable future, there will be a continued need for training psychologists (in all specialty areas) in the scientist-practitioner model to continue building the critical mass of data necessary for practice of the profession of clinical neuropsychology.

REFERENCES

Boll, T.J. (1978). Diagnosing brain impairment. In. B.B. Wolman (Ed.), *Diagnosing of mental disorders: A handbook*. New York: Plenum.

DiMatteo, M.R., & Friedman, H.S. (1982). A model course in social psychology and health. *Health Psychology, 1,* 181–193.

Eiser, J.R. (Ed.). (1982). *Social psychology and behavioral medicine*. New York: John Wiley & Sons.

Matarazzo, J.D. (1983). Education and training in health psychology: Boulder or bolder. *Health Psychology, 2,* 73–113.

Matarazzo, J.D. (1986a). Relationships of health psychology to other segments of psychology. In G.C. Stone, S.M. Weiss, J.D. Matarazzo, N.E. Miller, J. Rodin, C.D. Belan, M.J. Follick, & J.E. Singer (Eds.), *Health psychology: A discipline and profession*. Chicago: University of Chicago Press (In press).

Matarazzo, J. D. (1986b). Postdoctoral education and training for service providers in health psychology. In G. C. Stone, S. M. Weiss, J. D. Matarazzo, N. E. Miller, J. Rodin, C. D. Belan, M. J. Follick, & J. E. Singer (Eds.), *Health psychology: A discipline and a profession*. Chicago: University of Chicago Press (In press).

Matthews, C.G. (1976). Problems in training of neuropsychologists. *Clinical Psychologist, 29,* 11–13.

Matthews, C.G. (1981). Neuropsychology practice in a hospital setting. In S.B. Filskov & T.J. Boll (Eds.), *Handbook of clinical neuropsychology* (Vol. 1, pp.645–685). New York: John Wiley & Sons.

Meier, M.S. (1978). *Current status of professional development in human neuropsychology*. Invited address presented at the American Board of Professional Psychology, Toronto.

Meier, M.J. (1981a). *Report of the Task Force on Education, Accreditation and Credentialing of the International Neuropsychological Society*. International Neuropsychological Society Bulletin.

Meier, M.J. (1981b). Education for competency assurance in human neuropsychology: Antecedents, models, and directions. In S.B. Filskov & T.J. Boll (Eds.), *Handbook of clinical neuropsychology* (Vol. 1, pp. 754–781). New York: John Wiley & Sons.

Reed, H.B.C. (1976). Pediatric neuropsychology. *Journal of Pediatric Psychology, 1*, 5–7.

Rourke, B.P. (1976). Issues in the neuropsychological assessment of children with learning disabilities. *Canadian Psychological Review, 17*, 89–102.

Sales, B., Bricklin, P., & Hall, J. (1983). *Manual for the identification and continued recognition of proficiencies and new specialties in psychology*. Washington, DC: American Psychological Association.

Author Index

Numbers in *italics* refer to pages on which full references appear.

Abraham, J., 516, 546, 550, *558*
Achenbach, K., 205, 206, *212*
Ack, M., 112, *118*
Acker, W., 260, *275*
Adam, J. H., 504, *559*
Adam, K., *483*
Adams, C. B. T., 66, *79*
Adams, D. K., 384–385, *393*
Adams, J. E., 443, *486*
Adams, J. H., 498, *551*
Adams, K. M., 11, 13, *16, 17,* 28, 31, 34, *36, 38, 39,* 235, *251,* 451–452, 462, 463, 467, 480, *482, 486,* 563, 564, 567, 569, 570, 571, 573, *574, 575*
Adams, R. D., 261, *278,* 374, *393,* 402, *420, 422,* 497–498, *551*
Ader, R., 273, *275*
Adey, W. R., 83, *101,* 444, *482*
Adler, C., 543, *551*
Adler, E., 543, *551*
Adler, N. E., 22–23, *36*
Agnew, H. W., 471, 477–478, *493*
Agnew, H. W., Jr., *493*
Agras, W. S., 22–23, *36*
Ahumada, A., 639, *648*
Aita, J. A., 262, *275*
Ajmone-Marsan, C., 90, *101, 338, 365*
Akerstedt, T., 465, 469, *482*
Albert, M., 32, *38,* 308, *332*
Albert, M. L., 45–46, *78,* 497, *554*
Albert, M. S., 75, *76,* 408, 409, 416, 417–418, *420*
Albrecht, D. G., 611, 614, *643*
Albright, T. D., 614–615, *649*
Alexander, D., 200, *208*
Alexander, M. P., 504–505, 511, 543, 544, *551*
Alfrey, A. C., 268, *275,* 404, *420*
Algom, D., 445–447, *491*
Allan, A. N., 264, *276*
Allen, D. A., 127, *160*
Allen, D. V., 127, *160*

Allen, S. R., 445, *482*
Allison, R. S., 413, *420*
Allport, F. H., 292, *301*
Alperson, J., 33, *39,* 441, *488*
Alpin, L. C., 465
Alter, J., 471–472, *483*
Alter, M., 368, 382, 383, 389, *393, 395, 396, 397*
Alterman, A., 253
Alvis, H. J., 463, 466, *487*
Amberla, K., 412, 414, *426*
American Psychological Association, 273–274, 570, *574*
American Rheumatism Association Committee, 275
Aminoff, M., 100, *102*
Aminoff, M. J., *250*
Anastasi, A., 55, 60, *76*
Anch, M., 430, *488*
Andersen, A. L., 310, *332*
Anderson, D. C., 22, *41*
Anderson, D. W., 496, *551*
Anderson, H. R., Jr., *278*
Anderson, J., 528, *558*
Anderson, J. M., 404, *423*
Anderson, L., 308, *332*
Anderson, R. A., 356, *359*
Anderson, R. M., 633, 637–638, *641, 648*
Andrews, J., 347, *360*
Androp, S., 383, 389–390, *396*
Annett, M., *208*
Anter-Ozer, N. S., 202, 206, *208*
Anthony, W. Z., 71, *76,* 567, 569, *574, 575*
Aplin, L. C., *489*
Appell, J., 410, 413–414, *420*
Appenzellar, O., 446, *482*
Aps, E. J., 260, *275*
Apstein, M. D., 109, *118*
Apter, N. S., *36*
Aram, D. M., 122, 127, 159, *160, 162*
Arana, G., 311, 314–316, *333*
Arbib, M. A., 606, *642*

Subject Index

Benton Visual Retention Test, Alzheimer's
disease and, 415, 419
Benzodiazepines, neuropsychological assessment
of effects of, 474–476
Block Design Test, 51, 53
distribution type in, 54
Blood pH, brain function and, 265
Blood pressure, changes in, brain function and,
263
Blood system, neuropsychology and, 258–259
Boston Aphasia Test, 74
Boston Diagnostic Aphasia Battery, Alzheimer's
disease and, 414
Boston Diagnostic Aphasia Examination, 190–
191
Boston Naming Test, 184
Boxing, professional, neurocognitive deficits and,
115
Brain:
abscess in, 96, 97
cardiovascular system and, 262–265
Cartesian coordinate system of, 566
and computerized tomography, 93–100
connective tissue system and, 273–274
digestive system and, 259–262
edema in, 96, 97
and EEG, 82–91
electrical activity of, see Electrical activity,
of brain
endocrine system and, 269–272
hematoma in, 95, 96
hemolytic system and, 258–259
and holographic hypothesis, 608–610
imaging techniques of, 91–93
and immune-neuroendocrine interactions,
272–273
immune system and, 272
model of functional-structural invariance for,
596–597
motor systems of, object perception and,
616–618
and nonneurological diseases, 257
and nuclear magnetic resonance, 100
posterior cortical convexity of, 629–635
relationship of function to area of, 55–61
respiratory system and, 265–267
taxonomy of dysfunction of, need for,
595–597
tumor in, see Neoplasm; Tumor, in brain
urinary system and, 267–269
see also Frontolimbic forebrain
Brain damage:
affect communication following, see Affect
communication
classification of, 215–216
techniques for, 594–596
cognitive and perceptual impairments in, 305
and compound function testing, 59

and differential sensitivity of tests, 61–68
diffuse, 62
and differential test sensitivity, 67–68
emotional reaction following, see Emotional
reaction
forms of, 67
general effect and, 60
language assessment following, 172–191
neuropsychological performance and, 213–214
and testing range required, 55
traumatic, see Traumatic brain injury
WAIS and HRB limitations and, 214–215
and WAIS patterns, 63–64
Brain perfusion, brain function and, 263–264
Brain scan, see Isotope brain scan
Brevity, in diagnostic assessment, 9–11
Brief tests, advantages and disadvantages of,
52–53
Broca's aphasia, 192
Burn victims, neurocognitive deficits in,
114–115
B vitamins, brain function and, 261

CADL, see Communicative Activities of Daily
Living
CAPD, see Continuous ambulatory peritoneal
dialysis
Carbon dioxide, brain function and, 265
Carbon monoxide poisoning, neurocognitive
deficits and, 117
Cardiac disease, brain function and, 263
Cardiology, behavioral, 25
Cardiovascular system, neuropsychology and,
262–265
Carriers, of disease, neurocognitive deficits in,
112
Cartesian coordinate system, 563
Case study approach, to brain dysfunction
taxonomy, 594
CAT, see Computerized axial tomography
Cataplexy, 428–429, 435
Catastrophic reaction, brain damage and,
305–308, 325
evaluation criteria for, 309, 310
Category Test, Alzheimer's disease and, 418
Cells:
categories of, 614
pontifical, 612, 615
see also Neurons
"Center of gravity" analysis, oculometer
activity and, 615
Central nervous system, 257
disruption to, neurocognitive deficits and, 115
and multiple sclerosis, 366
neural microstructure in, 619–620
Cerebral arteriosclerosis, 67
Cerebral dysfunction, and accuracy of automated
interpretation, 567–569